**STOGDILL'S
HANDBOOK OF
LEADERSHIP**

RALPH M. STOGDILL (1905–1978) was Professor Emeritus of Management Science and Psychology at Ohio State University, where he had served earlier for many years as Associate Director of the Ohio State Leadership Studies. Included among his numerous publications were *Individual Behavior and Group Achievement* (1959) and *Managers, Employees, Organizations* (1965). He was recognized by *American Men and Women of Science, Leaders in American Science, Who's Who in Science,* and *Who's Who in American Education* and was a former Management History Director of the Academy of Management. A biannual prize for the best contribution to the study of leadership has been named in his honor.

BERNARD M. BASS is Professor of Organizational Behavior at the State University of New York, Binghamton, and was former director of the Management Research Center at the University of Pittsburgh (1965–1968) and the University of Rochester (1969–1972). His earlier books on leadership and organizations include *Leadership, Psychology and Organizational Behavior* (1960), *Organizational Psychology* (1965, 1979), *Assessment of Managers: An International Comparison* (1979), and *People, Work and Organizations* (1972, 1981). He is listed in *Who's Who in America, Who's Who in the World,* and in *American Men and Women of Science.* He served as President of the Division of Organizational Psychology of the International Association of Applied Psychology (1978–1982).

# STOGDILL'S HANDBOOK OF LEADERSHIP

*A Survey of Theory and Research*

**Revised and Expanded Edition**

**BY**

# BERNARD M. BASS

**THE FREE PRESS**
*A Division of Macmillan Publishing Co., Inc.*
NEW YORK

**Collier Macmillan Publishers**
LONDON

04-887

The Free Press
A Division of Macmillan Publishing Co., Inc.
866 Third Avenue, New York, N.Y. 10022

Collier Macmillan Canada, Ltd.

Library of Congress Catalog Card Number: 80–70210

Printed in the United States of America

printing number

5  6  7  8  9  10


**Library of Congress Cataloging in Publication Data**

Stogdill, Ralph Melvin, 1904–1978
    Stogdill's handbook of leadership.

Previously published as: Handbook of leadership.
    Includes index.
    1. Leadership—Abstracts.   2. Leadership—Bibliog-
raphy.   I. Bass, Bernard M.   II. Title.   III. Title:
Handbook of leadership.
HM141.S83   1981        016.3023′4        80-70210
ISBN  0-02-901820-X                    AACR2

*To my mentors at Ohio State University,*
*Ralph Stogdill* and *Cal Shartle,*
who introduced me to the study of leadership.

# CONTENTS

# PREFACE TO THE REVISED AND EXPANDED EDITION

Shortly before he died in 1978, Ralph Stogdill asked me to collaborate with him on a new edition of his Handbook of Leadership, which first appeared in 1974. I accepted the assignment willingly, but I have had to carry on alone taking full responsibility for this revised edition.

After Stogdill's three decades of dedication and contributions to leadership research, the Handbook was a fitting final extension of his seminal publication in 1948, "Personal Factors Associated with Leadership" (*Journal of Psychology,* 25: 35–71), which did so much to redirect efforts in leadership research away from trait to situational analyses, although Stogdill himself clearly showed that both were important. The point of view advanced in *Leadership, Psychology and Organizational Behavior* (Bass, 1960) fits with his position and still seems relevant: some of the variance in leadership is due to the situation, some is due to the person, and some is due to the interaction of person and situation. Sometimes, personal traits are paramount. For example, assertiveness and initiative are dominant in effect in most situations. Sometimes, the situation is the prime determinant. Any person at the center of a communications network is likely to exert more leadership than any person at the periphery. Sometimes, it is a combination effect: the right person, in the right place, at the right time.

I have attempted to maintain some of the essence of the first edition. Nevertheless, in addition to a considerable amount of new material from the industrial management and political science literature, the *Handbook* has been updated by extensive incorporation of relevant publications that appeared between 1974 and 1981. I have tried to use the same criteria for inclusion of material that Stogdill employed in the first edition. However, I accept full responsibility for whatever shortcomings remain in this edition. On occasion I have put more weight on generalizations that are emerging from the body of softer literature dealing with organizational and management development than on some of the seemingly harder, antiseptic, laboratory studies of dragooned college students in brief encounters with an experimenter. Also, topics that were given no special attention in the first edition of the Handbook, such as leadership among women, blacks, and other cultures now form separate chapters.

A multiplicity of themes is likely to appear in any one leadership study. Leadership itself may be the independent, dependent, or intervening variable. In organizing the studies and seeking to extract generalizations from the organization, I hoped to avoid the structure of a Wagnerian opera in which different themes continually appear, disappear, and reappear. As much as possible I have attempted to compile finding in tight thematic bundles.

A handbook should promote both understanding and application. One cannot understand leadership in a vacuum. Thus, an appreciation of effective leadership in modern West Germany requires understanding of what kinds of participatory practices have been legislated since World War II as well as what firmly entrenched traditions accepted by both leaders and subordinates about the "leadership principle" have been carried forward from the Second Reich of a century ago. On matters of routine, the subordinate's job is spelled out in detail. When delegated by superiors to carry out such routines, subordinates are obligated to give unquestioning obedience but are left alone to complete the task. For unprogrammed activities, however, superiors are supposed to consult with their subordinates. When the superior finally decides, it is the subordinate's duty to accept the decision. A similar mix of tradition and modern improvements emerges as the Japanese Ringi method for circularizing ideas among subordinates and gaining their inputs before a seemingly "unanimous" decision is announced by their leader. While the German and Japanese post-1945 economic miracles are due to much more than effective leadership, such leadership did play an important part.

A search of the computerized files of abstracts of ERIC (The Educational Resources Information Center), the Psychological Abstracts, and the Sociological Abstracts uncovered 525 titles of consequence published between 1974 and 1978. Journals such as the *Journal of Applied Psychology,* the *Administrative Science Quarterly,* the *Academy of Management Journal, Personal Psychology,* and *Organizational Behavior and Human Performance* were searched for the 1960–1979 period. A comparable number of preprints which crossed my desk also figured in the final literature which was surveyed along with many earlier items not included in the original handbook. The original 3,000 references have increased to 5,000.

The following reviews and books have been useful for locating materials on special topics:

*Leadership theory and research:* Argyris, 1976; Barrow, 1977; Bass, 1960; Bell, Hill, and Wright, 1961; Bennis, 1976; Biddle and Thomas, 1966; Campbell, Dunnette, Lawler, and Weick, 1970; Cartwright, 1965; Fiedler and Chemers, 1974; Fox, Walton, Kirchner, and Mahoney, 1954; Gardner, 1974; Gibb, 1954; Goode, 1951; de Grazia, 1949; Harlow, 1957; Harrell, 1961; Jenkins, 1947; Jacobs, 1971; Jennings, 1960; Lerner, 1952; Lloyd, 1964; Mann, 1959; Matthews, 1951; Mesics, 1960; Miller, 1960; Miller and Coghill, 1961; Narain, 1955; Psychological Services, 1953; Pigors, 1935; Ross and Hendry, 1957; Ruch, 1953; Rushlau and Jorgensen, 1966; Shartle, 1956; Smith and Krueger, 1933; Stogdill, 1948; Vroom and Yetton, 1975; and Wasserman and Silander, 1958.

*Readings on leadership:* Brown and Cohn, 1958; Gibb, 1969; Gouldner, 1950; Herman and Milburn, 1977; Higham, 1978; Hunt and Larson, 1974, 1975, 1977; King and Fiedler, 1978; McCall and Lombardo, 1978; Metcalf, 1931; Petrullo and Bass, 1961; Sherif, 1962; and Stone, 1976.

*Reviews of small-group theory and research:* Altman, Pendleton, and Terauds, 1960; Blum, 1953; Bonner, 1959; Borgatta, 1960; Hare, 1962; Hare, Borgatta, and Bales, 1955; Lindzey, 1954; Lindzey and Aronson, 1969; McGrath and Altman, 1966; March, 1965; March and Simon, 1963; Raven, 1959, 1965; Roseborough, 1953; Stogdill, 1959; Strodtbeck and Hare, 1954; and Wasserman, 1959.

*Readings on the small group:* Cartwright and Zander, 1968; Gibbard, Hartman, and Mann, 1974; Hyman and Singer, 1968; and Indik and Berrien, 1968.

*Works on special leadership topics:* Aral, 1974; Burns, 1978; Olmstead, 1974; T. Gordon, 1977; Gordon and Rosen (undated); Gorton, 1976; Johnson and Johnson, 1975; Lassey and Fernandez, 1976; Loye, 1977; Maccoby, 1978; Magid, 1976; McMurray, 1974; Paige, 1977; Price, 1976; Richman and Farmer, 1974; Schul, 1975; Schutz, 1977; Schultz, 1975; Stewart, 1978; Turner, 1977; West, 1978; Yura, 1976; and Zaleznik and DeVries, 1975.

I wish to thank Jerry Hunt, Peter Weissenberg, Tom Harrell, Fred Fiedler, Marvin E. Shaw, and David D. Van Fleet and his students for their many useful suggestions on ways to improve the *Handbook.* Others who have been most helpful include Rensis Likert, Jack Miner, Richard Franke, Frank Heller, Chet Schreisheim, Jerri Frantzve, and Michael Manning. I am particularly indebted to Caroline Simmonds for her effective assistance in the original computer search, to Jenny Kage and especially to Lorraine Warren for competent secretarial assistance in helping with the manuscript, and to Elaine Demore, Kevin Geoghan, and Robert Vasina for taking on the heavy burden of completing an accurate list of references. I also wish to express my appreciation to the Center for Creative Leadership for support in preparing the manuscript.

B.M.B.

# PREFACE TO
# THE FIRST EDITION

In 1966 the Smith Richardson Foundation suggested that the author undertake a systematic analysis and review of the literature on leadership. At that time, it was estimated that the work could be completed in two or three years. The undertaking proved much larger than anticipated.

The author defined his task as that of assembling all the published evidence on a given topic and summarizing the findings. The result is a sourcebook of experimental products. A book of this nature is obviously not intended to entertain, inspire, or offer simple recipes for solution of leadership problems. It is intended for the serious reader who wants to know what results have been obtained, who did the research, and what conclusions can be drawn from the accumulated evidence.

Four decades of research on leadership have produced a bewildering mass of findings. Numerous surveys of special problems have been published, but they seldom include all the studies available on a topic. It is difficult to know what, if anything, has been convincingly demonstrated by replicated research. The endless accumulation of empirical data has not produced an integrated understanding of leadership. There is a need for a stocktaking—for an inventory of results. Leadership practice should be based on valid experimental findings. Future research should be designed to explore new problems rather than repeat what has been done in the past. Indeed, the desire to know is in itself sufficient justification for undertaking a comprehensive analysis of the literature on leadership.

The task of reviewing and abstracting the literature on leadership was begun in 1946, under a grant from the Office of Naval Research. One result of the navy-sponsored survey was "Personal Factors Associated with Leadership: A Survey of the Literature," 1948. This, the most widely quoted reference on leadership, is reprinted here with the kind permission of the Journal Press. Systematic abstracting has continued with support from the College of Administrative Science, The Ohio State University. In 1966, a two-year grant from the Smith Richardson Foundation permitted a full-time attack on the task. The Ohio State University has supported the project since 1969.

It is the author's aim in this book to bring to bear on a given problem all the competent research directly relevant to it. No doubt, a few stray publications have been overlooked. But it can be stated with confidence that such omissions are too few to alter the conclusions reached on any given topic. More than five thousand abstracts were prepared. Only those with a direct bearing on leadership were included in the survey. The criterion for including a given study was the author's conclusion that an experimental or theoretical undertaking had been competently executed. A large body of inspirational and advisory literature was ignored. Small-group studies only indirectly related to leadership were excluded. The well-informed reader will note omission of a chapter on the charismatic leader. This important variant of the leadership role has not been a willing or frequent subject of research that involves measurement or experimentation. Numerous biographical studies of charismatic leaders are available, but they provide comparatively little information that adds to an understanding of leadership.

The method employed for the analysis involved the following stages: (1) preparation of a comprehensive abstract of a book or journal article, (2) sorting and resorting of the abstracts into relevant categories, (3) tabulation of all findings bearing on a topic, and (4) analysis, summarization, and interpretation of results.

The purpose of the analysis was to determine what is known about leadership. The author used a dual criterion for determining this. First, results on a given topic were regarded as validated when several investigators, using different research designs and methodologies, obtained similar results. Second, an unusually competent piece of research was given greater credence than a poorly designed experiment. The second criterion was used infrequently. Critical evaluation of individual experiments and points of view has been kept to a minimum. The replication of findings, when it occurs, can usually be depended upon to overcome the inequalities inherent in different research designs.

The author was assisted in the demanding task of abstracting by Katheleen Koehler Haas, William G. Nickels, and Adele Zimmer. Special thanks are due Carroll L. Shartle and the late Edwin R. Henry for their encouragement to undertake the project. The support of the Smith Richardson Foundation is greatly appreciated. This support was the crucial factor in transforming the project from a hope into a reality.

R.M.S.

**STOGDILL'S
HANDBOOK OF
LEADERSHIP**

part

# INTRODUCTION TO LEADERSHIP THEORY AND RESEARCH

# 1 CONCEPTS OF LEADERSHIP

## THE BEGINNINGS

The study of leadership is an ancient art. Discussions of the subject will be found in Plato, Caesar, and Plutarch, just to mention a few from the classical era. The Chinese classics are filled with hortatory advice to the country's leaders. The ancient Egyptians attributed three qualities of divinity to their king. They said of him, "Authoritative utterness is in thy mouth, perception is in thy heart, and thy tongue is the shrine of justice." The Egyptians demanded of their leader the qualities of authority, discrimination, and just behavior (Frankfort et al., 1949). An analysis of Greek concepts of leadership, as exemplified by different leaders in Homer's *Iliad* identified: (1) justice and judgment—Agamemnon; (2) wisdom and counsel—Nestor; (3) shrewdness and cunning—Odysseus; and (4) valor and action—Achilles. All these qualities were admired by the Greeks (Sarachek, 1968). Shrewdness and cunning are not regarded as highly in our contemporary society as they once were. Thus, the patterns of behavior regarded as acceptable in leaders differ from time to time and from one culture to another. A scholarly highlight of the Renaissance was Machiavelli's *The Prince,* still widely quoted as a guide to effective leadership of sorts; it formed the basis for a modern line of investigation by Christie and Geis (1970) and their Mach scale.

### Universality

Leadership is a universal human phenomenon. Citing various anthropological reports on primitive groups in Australia, Fiji, New Guinea, the Congo, and elsewhere, H. L. Smith and Krueger (1933) concluded that leadership occurs universally among all people regardless of culture, whether they are isolated Indian villagers, Eurasian steppe nomads, or Polynesian fisherfolk. Parenthood makes for ready-made patterns of leadership. Nevertheless, for J. M. Burns (1978), "leadership is one of the most observed and least understood phenomena on earth."

### Theory versus Problem Orientation

The earliest literature on leadership was concerned almost entirely with theoretical issues. Theorists sought to identify different types of leadership and to relate them to the functional demands of society. In addition, they sought to account for the emergence of

5

leadership either by examining the qualities of the leader or the elements of the situation.

Earlier theorists can be differentiated from more recent ones primarily by virtue of the fact that (1) they failed to consider the interaction between individual and situational variables; and (2) they tended to develop more comprehensive theories than do their more recent counterparts. Until about 1960, students of leadership devoted more of their efforts to empirical research, appearing to distrust the theoretical approach. As a consequence, various issues regarded as important by the theorists were largely ignored by the researchers. The most popular current theories tend to focus on a few phenomena. They are less ambitious than those of the past.

Leadership in various segments of the population (students, military personnel, and business managers) has been heavily researched, whereas others (politicians, labor leaders, and criminal leaders) have been relatively neglected. With the increase of people employed in the health, social science, and protection fields, an upsurge in leadership studies of nurses, case workers, and police has occurred. In the same way, the increase and upgrading of minorities in the U.S. labor force has resulted in examining leadership with and by women and blacks. Finally, cross-cultural leadership studies have burgeoned.

The failure of recent researchers to investigate certain areas of the leadership problem can be attributed in part to their empirical as opposed to their theoretical orientation. Whereas theorists may attempt to comprehend a problem in its entirety, empiricists tends to concern themselves with those aspects of the problem that are perceived as researchable in terms of availability of samples and measurability of variables. Another factor that appears to operate is a value orientation in recent schools of social and behavioral scientists which dismisses certain problems in the study of leadership as unimportant. But theory and research combine to yield insight into a problem.

In general, an effort has been made in the next few chapters to discuss problems as they appeared in the literature in historical sequence. But closely related studies are grouped together regardless of publication date. As a result of this treatment, it becomes evident that several different schools of thought have prevailed simultaneously since the very beginnings of leadership study. The early sociological theorists tended to explain leadership in terms of either the person or the environment. Researchers during the past decades have tended to view leadership as an aspect of role differentiation or as an outgrowth of social interaction processes. They illustrate B. M. Bass's (1974) argument that theory and empirical research should flow forward together, each stimulating, supporting, and modifying the other. Neither can stand alone. An elegant theory without prospects of elegant data to test it is just as wasteful as elegant data gathering for a sketchy theory. Early in a line of investigation, crude data and theory may be useful. Later, as understanding develops and practice improves, more stringent standards are required.

The research discussed in the following chapters is based on a wide variety of theoretical assumptions. Despite differences in guiding philosophy and research methodology, there is remarkable convergence of findings on many problems. This convergence, when it occurs, can be regarded as a source of strong evidence of the validity of the findings.

An almost insurmountable problem is the question of the extent to which, in new theorizing, we pour old wine into new bottles. Julius Caesar's descriptions of his own leadership style are clear, succinct endorsements of the need for what Blake and Mouton (1964) would see as "9–9" style, a style that Fleishman (1953a) would describe in terms of high initiation and consideration, and that in the year 2000 some young theorist will have given new names. When does a field advance? Are we beyond Caesar's understanding of how to lead infantry shock troops?

Our hope in this book is to catalog what we know about leadership and to suggest some of the things that we don't know that we should try to find out.

## THE MEANING OF LEADERSHIP

Leadership appears to be a rather sophisticated concept. Words meaning head of state, military commander, princeps, proconsul, chief, or king are the only ones found in many languages to differentiate the ruler from other members of society. A preoccupation with leadership as opposed to headship based on inheritance, usurpation, or appointment occurs predominantly in countries with an Anglo-Saxon heritage. The *Oxford English Dictionary* (1933) notes the appearance of the word "leader" in the English language as early as the year 1300. However, the word "leadership" did not appear until the first half of the nineteenth century in writings about political influence and control of British Parliament.

There are almost as many different definitions of leadership as there are persons who have attempted to define the concept. Nevertheless, there is sufficient similarity between definitions to permit a rough scheme of classification.

Different definitions and conceptions of leadership have been reviewed briefly by Morris and Seeman (1950), Shartle (1951a,b, 1956), L. F. Carter (1953), C. A. Gibb (1954, 1969a), and B. M. Bass (1960).

### Leadership as a Focus of Group Processes

Early on, definitions of the leader tended to view the leader as a focus of group change, activity, and process. Cooley (1902) maintained that "the leader is always the nucleus of a tendency, and, on the other hand, all social movements, closely examined, will be found to consist of tendencies having such nuclei." Mumford (1906–1907) observed that "leadership is the preeminence of one or a few individuals in a group in the process of control of societal phenomena." Blackmar (1911) saw leadership as the "centralization of effort in one person as an expression of the power of all." Chapin (1924b) viewed leadership as "a point of polarization for group cooperation." According to L. L. Bernard (1927), leaders are influenced by the needs and wishes of the group members. In turn, they focus the attention and release the energies of group members in a desired direction. M. Smith (1934) commented in regard to personality dominance of the leader that "the social group that expresses its unity in connected activity is always composed of but two essential portions: the center of focal activity, and the individuals who act with regard to the center." For Redl (1942), the leader is a central or focal person who integrates the group.

J. F. Brown (1936) maintained that "the leader may not be separated from the group, but may be treated as a position of high potential in the field." Following in the same tradition, Krech and Crutchfield (1948) observed that "by virtue of his special position in the group he serves as a primary agent for the determination of group structure, group atmosphere, group goals, group ideology, and group activities." Knicker-bocker (1948) followed a line of thought that seems to place him in the group centrality school of theorists, maintaining that "when conceived in terms of the dynamics of human social behavior, leadership is a function of needs existing within a given situation, and consists of a relationship between an individual and a group."

The trend of thought represented by the above definitions has been influential in directing attention to the importance of group structure and group processes in the study of leadership. It is interesting to note that two of the earliest theorists (Cooley and Mumford) exhibited a high degree of sophistication in their perceptions of the leadership problem. On the other hand, several of the definitions seem to place the leader in a particularly fortuitous, if not helpless, position in the inexorable progress of the group. They remind one of the folk definition of leaders as persons who are one pace ahead of the group so that they, the leaders, will not be run over.

Currently, centrality of location in the group is seen and known to be of consequence to control of communications and hence is likely to place a person in a position of leadership, but centrality is not leadership.

### Leadership as Personality and Its Effects

The concept *personality* appealed to several early theorists who sought to explain why some persons are better able than others to exercise leadership. A. O. Bowden (1926) equated leadership with strength of personality. He stated, "Indeed, the amount of personality attributed to an individual may not be unfairly estimated by the degree of influence he can exert upon others." Bingham (1927) defined a leader as a person who possesses the greatest number of desirable traits of personality and character. Kilbourne (1935) suggested a similar definition. According to L. L. Bernard (1926), "Any person who is more than ordinarily efficient in carrying psychosocial stimuli to others and is thus effective in conditioning collective responses may be called a leader." The leader must possess prestige and "must know what stimuli will condition adequate responses for his purposes and develop a technique for presenting these stimuli." Tead (1929) regarded leadership as a combination of traits that enables an individual to induce others to accomplish a given task. Bogardus (1934) defined it as "personality in action under group conditions . . . not only is leadership both a personality and a group phenomenon; it is also a social process involving a number of persons in mental contact in which one person assumes dominance over the others." Previously, Bogardus (1928) described leadership as the creating and setting forth of exceptional behavior patterns in such a way that other persons respond to them.

The personality theorists tended to regard leadership as a one-way influence effect. Although recognizing that leaders may possess qualities differentiating them from followers, such theorists generally failed to acknowledge the reciprocal and interactive characteristics of the leadership situation. What we now see is that the personal qualities of a would-be leader determine his or her esteem in the eyes of potential followers. Some personality traits such as ascendancy or social boldness more often than not go hand-in-hand with being esteemed and attaining leadership, but social boldness is not leadership. At the extreme, in times of crisis, a highly dominant figure, empathic to the critical needs is endowed by followers with *charisma*. The hero's personality makes possible enormous feats of leadership (S. Stark, 1977).

### Leadership as the Art of Inducing Compliance

Munson (1921) defined leadership as "the ability to handle men so as to achieve the most with the least friction and the greatest cooperation. . . . Leadership is the creative and directive force of morale." According to F. H. Allport (1924), "leadership means direct, face-to-face contact between leader and followers; it is personal social control." B. V. Moore (1927) reported the results of a conference at which leadership was defined as "the ability to impress the will of the leader on those led and induce obedience, respect, loyalty, and cooperation." Similarly, Bundel (1930) regarded leadership as "the art of inducing others to do what one wants them to do." According to T. R. Phillips (1939), "leadership is the imposition, maintenance, and direction of moral unity to our ends." Again, L. A. Allen (1958) regarded a leader as "one who guides and directs other people." For Bennis (1959), "leadership can be defined as the process by which an agent induces a subordinate to behave in a desired manner."

The compliance induction theorists, perhaps even more than the personality theorists, tended to regard leadership as a unidirectional exertion of influence and as an instrumentality for molding the group to the leader's will. They expressed little recognition of the rights, desires, and necessities of the group members or of the group's traditions and norms. This disregard for the followers and the group was rejected by various theorists who sought to remove by definition any possibility of legitimizing an authoritarian conception of leadership. Yet, regardless of the sentiments of some behavioral scientists, we cannot ignore the fact that much leadership is authoritarian, directive, and even coercive. Its effects are seen in public compliance but not necessarily in private acceptance.

### Leadership as the Exercise of Influence

Use of the concept *influence* marked a step in the direction of generality and abstraction in defining leadership. J. B. Nash (1929) suggested that "leadership implies influencing change in the conduct of people." Tead (1935) defined it as "the activity of influencing people to cooperate toward some goal which they come to find desirable." Stogdill (1950) termed it "the process (act) of influencing the activities of an organized group in its efforts toward goal setting and goal achievement."

Shartle (1951a,b) proposed several definitions based on the influence process. Thus, the leader may be considered an individual "who exercises positive influence acts upon others" or "who exercises more important influence acts than any other members of the group or organization." Similarly, Tannenbaum, Weschler, and Massarik (1961) defined leadership as "interpersonal influence, exercised in a situation and directed, through the communication process, toward the attainment of a specified goal or goals."

Haiman (1951) suggested that "direct leadership is an interaction process in which an individual, usually through the medium of speech, influences the behavior of others toward a particular end." For Cartwright (1965), leadership was equated with the "domain of influence.'' Katz and Kahn (1966) considered ''the essence of organizational leadership to be the influential increment over and above mechanical compliance with routine directions of the organization.'' They observed that, although all supervisors at the same level of organization possess equal power, they do not use it with equal effectiveness to influence individuals and the organization. In the same way, Hollander and Julian (1969) suggested that ''leadership in the broadest sense implies the presence of a particular influence relationship between two or more persons.''

According to Bass (1960), an individual's ''effort to change the behavior of others is *attempted* leadership. When the other members actually change, this creation of change in others is successful leadership. If the others are reinforced or rewarded for changing their behavior, this evoked achievement is *effective* leadership.'' The distinctions are important because the dynamics of each are quite different.

The influence concept recognizes the fact that individuals differ in the extent to which their behaviors affect activities of a group. It implies a reciprocal relationship between leader and followers, but one not necessarily characterized by domination, control, or induction of compliance on the part of the leader. It merely states that leadership exercises a determining effect on the behaviors of group members and on activities of the group.

Defining effective leadership as successful influence by the leader that results in goal attainment by the influenced followers, that is, defining leadership in terms of goal attainment is particularly useful, for it permits the transfer of reinforcement theory to understanding leader–follower behavior.

### Leadership as Act or Behavior

One school of theorists prefers to define leadership in terms of acts or behaviors. For L. F. Carter (1953), ''leadership behaviors are any behaviors the experimenter wishes to so designate or, more generally, any behaviors which experts in this area wish to consider as leadership behaviors.'' Shartle (1956) defined a leadership act as ''one which results in others acting or responding in a shared direction.''

Hemphill (1949a) suggested that ''leadership may be defined as the behavior of an individual while he is involved in directing group activities.'' Fiedler (1967a) proposed a somewhat similar definition, as follows: ''By leadership behavior we generally mean the particular acts in which a leader engages in the course of directing and coordinating the work of his group members. This may involve such acts as structuring the work relations, praising or criticizing group members, and showing consideration for their welfare and feelings.''

### Leadership as a Form of Persuasion

Several early theorists attempted to remove any implications of coercion from their definitions of leadership, while at the same time retaining the concept of the leader as a determining factor in the relationship with followers. The use of persuasion seemed to meet this specification. Schenk (1928) suggested that ''leadership is the management of men by persuasion and inspiration rather than by the direct or implied threat of coercion. It involves immediate concrete problems by applying knowledge of, and sympathy with, human factors.'' According to Cleeton and Mason (1934), ''leadership indicates the ability to influence men and secure results through emotional appeals rather than through the exercise of authority.'' Copeland (1942) maintained that ''leadership is the art of dealing with human nature. . . . It is the art of influencing a body of people by persuasion or example to follow a line of action. It must never be confused with drivership . . . which is the art of compelling a body of people by intimidation or force to follow a line of action.'' Odier (1948) differentiated between the value and the valence of a leader. *Valence* is the power of a person to act upon the feeling or value of another person or group of persons; of modifying (strengthening or weakening) it in one fashion or another. Thus, valence is defined not by the value of the leader's personality but by the sound quality of the influences he or she exerts upon the members of a group. Koontz and O'Donnell (1955) regarded leadership as ''the activity of persuading people to cooperate in the achievement of a common objective.''

Persuasion is a powerful instrument for shaping expectation and belief—particularly in political, social, and religious affairs. The definition of leadership as a form of persuasion tended to be favored by students of politics and social movements, and by military and industrial theorists opposed to authoritarian concepts. It was also the province of rhetoricians and communications theorists. Research on persuasion and persuasibility has paralleled leadership research (W. Weiss, 1958). Currently, persuasion is seen as one form of leadership (Bass & Barrett, 1981). Much of what has been learned from studies of persuasion can be incorporated into understanding leadership.

### Leadership as a Power Relation

J. R. P. French (1956) and Raven and French (1958a,b) defined leadership in terms of differential power relationships among members of a group. Interpersonal power is conceived ''as a resultant of the maximum force which A can induce on B minus the maximum resisting force which B can mobilize in the opposite direction.'' Five bases of power were postulated. These are referent power (liking), expert power, reward power, coercive power, and legitimate power. And Janda (1960) defined ''leadership as a particular type of power relationship characterized by a group member's perception that another group member has the right to prescribe behavior patterns for the former regarding his activity as a member of a particular group.'' The operation of power seems implied in Warriner's (1955) suggestion that ''leadership as a form of relationship between persons requires that one or several persons act in conformance with the request of another.'' According to Gerth and Mills (1953), ''leadership, most broadly conceived, is a relation between leader and led in which the leader influences more than he is influenced: because of the leader, those who are led act or feel differently than they otherwise would. As a power relation, leadership may be known to both leader and led, or unknown to either or both.'' M. Smith (1948) equated leadership with control of the interaction process. Thus, ''the initiator of an interaction, A, in giving a stimulus to the second participant, B, would be asserting his control by interfering with B's original course of action.'' Bass (1960) defined leadership in somewhat similar terms: ''When the goal of one member, A, is that of changing another, B, or when B's change in behavior will reward A or reinforce A's behavior, A's effort to obtain the goal is leadership.''

Power is regarded as a form of influence relationship. It can be observed that some leaders more than others tend to transform any leadership opportunity into an overt power relationship. In fact, the very frequency of this observation, combined with the often undesirable consequences for individuals and societies, has induced many theorists to reject the notion of authoritarian leadership. Nevertheless, many of those most committed at one time to trust building, openness, and participatory approaches, like Bennis (1970), when faced with the world as it is, not as they would like it to be, have come to acknowledge the importance of power relations in understanding leadership.

### Leadership as an Instrument of Goal Achievement

Numerous theorists have included the idea of goal achievement in their definitions. Several have defined leadership in terms of its instrumental value for accomplishment of group goals and satisfaction of needs. According to Cowley (1928), "a leader is a person who has a program and is moving toward an objective with his group in a definite manner." Bellows (1959) defined leadership as "the process of arranging a situation so that various members of a group, including the leader, can achieve common goals with maximum economy and a minimum of time and work." For Knickerbocker (1948), "the functional relation which is leadership exists when a leader is perceived by a group as controlling means for the satisfaction of their needs." R. B. Cattell (1951) defined the leader as "a person who produces group syntality different from that which would have existed had he not been present in the group." By *syntality* is meant the various performances exhibited by the group in its effort to achieve a goal. Thus, leadership may be measured in terms of its effects on group performances.

The classical organizational theorists defined leadership in terms of reaching group objectives. R. C. Davis (1942) referred to leadership as "the principal dynamic force that stimulates, motivates, and coordinates the organization in the accomplishment of its objectives." Similarly, Urwick (1953) stated that the leader is "the personal representation of the personification of common purpose not only to all who work on the undertaking, but to everyone outside it." K. Davis (1962) defined leadership as "the human factor which binds a group together and motivates it toward goals."

### Leadership as an Emerging Effect of Interaction

Several theorists have viewed leadership not as a cause or control of group action but as an effect of it. Bogardus (1929) stated that "as a social process, leadership is that social interstimulation which causes a number of people to set out toward an old goal with new zest or a new goal with hopeful courage—with different persons keeping different places." For Pigors (1935), "leadership is a process of mutual stimulation which, by the successful interplay of individual differences, controls human energy in the pursuit of a common cause."

For H. H. Anderson (1940), "a true leader in the psychological sense is one who can make the most of individual differences, who can bring out the most differences in the group and therefore reveal to the group a sounder base for defining common purposes." Merton (1969) regarded leadership as "an interpersonal relation in which others comply because they want to, not because they have to."

This group of theorists was important in calling attention to the fact that emergent leadership grows out of the interaction process itself. It can be observed that leadership truly exists only when acknowledged and conferred by other members of the group. Although the authors probably did not mean to imply it, their definitions suggest that this quality amounts to little more than passive acceptance of the importance of one's status. In fact, for leadership to emerge, as in initially leaderless group discussions, the group must begin with everyone equal in status. We see that an individual emerges as leader as a consequence of interactions within the group that arouse expectations that he or she rather than someone else could serve the group more usefully in attaining its objectives.

### Leadership as a Differentiated Role

One of the outstanding achievements of modern sociology is the development of role theory. Each member of society occupies a status position in the community as well as in various institutions and organizations. In each position, the individual is expected to play a more or less well-defined role. Leadership may be regarded as an aspect of role differentiation. H. H. Jennings (1944) observed that "leadership thus appears as a manner of interaction involving behavior by and toward the individual 'lifted' to a leader role by other individuals." Similarly, C. A. Gibb (1954) regarded group leadership as a position emerging from the interaction process itself. For T. Gordon (1955), leadership can be conceptualized as an interaction between a person and a group or, more accurately, between a person and the group members. Each participant in this interaction may be said to play a role, and in some way these roles must be differentiated from each other. The basis for this differentiation seems a matter of influence—that is, one person, the leader, influences, and the other persons respond.

Sherif and Sherif (1956) suggest that leadership is a role within the scheme of relations and is defined by reciprocal expectations between the leader and other members. The leadership role is defined, as are other roles, by stabilized expectations (norms) that, in most matters and situations of consequence to the group, are more exacting and require greater obligations from the leader than those for other members of the group.

Newcomb, Turner, and Converse (1965) observed that members of a group make different contributions to goal achievement. Insofar as any members' contributions are particularly indispensable, they may be regarded as leaderlike; and insofar as any member is recognized by others as a dependable source of such contributions, he or she is leaderlike. To be so recognized is equivalent to having a role relationship to other members.

Much of the research on emergence and differentiation of roles pertains equally well to leadership. As indicated by Sherif and Sherif (1956), roles are defined in terms of the expectations that group members develop in regard to themselves and other members. Thus, the theory and research pertaining to reinforcement, confirmation, and structuring of expectations applies also to the leadership problem. Of all available definitions, the role conception of leadership is most firmly buttressed by research findings.

The recognition of leadership as an instrument of goal attainment, as a product of interaction processes, and as a differentiated role adds to the development of a coherent theory that fits much of the facts available to date. Leadership as a differentiated role is required as a means of integrating the various other roles of the group and of maintaining unity of action in the group effort toward goal achievement.

### Leadership as the Initiation of Structure

Several commentators viewed leadership not as the passive occupancy of a position or acquisition of a role but as a process of originating and maintaining role structure. M. Smith (1935a) equated leadership with management of social differentials through the process of giving stimuli that are responded to integratively by other people. LaPiere and Farnsworth (1936) observed that situations may be distinguished one from the other by the extent to which they are organized by one member of the group. Such organization is usually spoken of as leadership, whose nature and degree vary in different social situations.

Gouldner (1950) suggested that there is a difference in effect between a stimulus of a follower and one from a leader. The difference is in the probability that the stimulus will structure group behavior. A leader's stimulus has a higher probability of structuring a group's behavior because of a group-endowed belief that he or she has a legitimate source of stimuli. Gouldner disagreed with C. A. Gibb (1947) on the notion that, once group activity has become dominated by an established and accepted organization, leadership tends to disappear. Thus Bavelas (1960) defined organizational leadership as the function of "maintaining the operational effectiveness of decision-making systems which comprise the management of the organization."

Homans (1950) identified the leader of a group as a member who "originates interaction." For Hemphill (1954), "to lead is to engage in an act that initiates a structure in the interaction as part of the process of solving a mutual problem." And Stogdill (1959) defined leadership as "the initiation and maintenance of structure in expectation and interaction."

This group of theorists attempted to define leadership in terms of the variables giving rise to the differentiation and maintenance of role structures in groups. For this reason, the definitions appear to have greater theoretical utility than those that are more concrete and descriptive: they lead to a consideration of the basic processes involved in the emergence of the leadership role.

Again, what must be kept in mind is that leadership is more than just the initiation of structure. As Gouldner (1950) noted, we need room for acts of leadership in the completely structured group. Stogdill's (1959) inclusion of maintenance of structure is important. Further, if structure is the consistent pattern of differentiated role relationships within a group, we must be sure also to include appreciation of the persons, resources, and tasks within the differentiated roles.

## LEADERSHIP AND HEADSHIP

*Leadership* can be conceived to include *headship* or the two concepts can be completely differentiated. Leadership can be defined broadly, as Bass (1960) did, to include the many ways it is exerted by leaders and heads and the various sources of power that make it work. Or it can be defined more narrowly, as for instance C. A. Gibb (1969a) did, distinguishing leadership from headship as follows:

1. Headship is maintained through an organized system and not by the spontaneous recognition, by fellow group members, of the individual's contribution to group progress.
2. The group goal is chosen by head persons in line with their interests and is not internally determined by the group itself.
3. In headship, there is little or no sense of shared feeling or joint action in pursuit of the given goal.
4. In headship, there is a wide social gap between the group members and the head, who strives to maintain this social distance as an aid in the coercion of the group.
5. The leader's authority is spontaneously accorded by fellow group members and particularly by followers. The authority of the head derives from some extra-group power which he or she has over the members of the group, who cannot meaningfully be called followers. They accept domination, on pain of punishment, rather than follow (in anticipation of rewards) (p. 213).

Kochan, Schmidt, and de Cotiis (1975) agreed with Gibb because they saw that managers, executives, agency officers, and so on do much more than just lead. Also, one cannot ordinarily attribute all leadership that occurs in a group to just one of its members. Yet, with the broader definition, for Bass (1960) heads lead as a consequence of their status—the power of the position they occupy. Without such status, leaders can still gain commitment to goals and can pursue arbitrary coercive paths with their power if their esteem—their accorded value to the group—is high. Both status and esteem are not all-or-none quantities. In any group, members will vary in both. Therefore, leadership will be distributed among them in similar fashion. Until, an "academy of leadership" establishes a standard definition, we must continue to live with both broad and narrow definitions, making sure to understand which kind is being used in any particular analysis.

## AN EVOLVING CONCEPTUALIZATION

### Changing Purposes

Definitions can be used to serve a variety of purposes. Various investigators, either by explicit statement or by implication, have developed definitions to serve the following purposes: (1) identify the object to be observed; (2) identify a form of practice; (3) satisfy a particular value orientation; (4) avoid a particular orientation or implication for practice; and (5) provide a basis for theory development. (The hope is that the definitions will provide critical new insight into the nature of leadership.)

A progression of thought is indicated in the definitions. The earliest ones cited tended to identify leadership as a focus of group process and movement. The next type of definition considered it as the art of inducing compliance. The most recent definitions tend to conceive of this factor in terms of power differentials, role differentiation, and initiation of structure. However, a parallel tabulation of dates for the different types of definitions indicates that various trends of thought were taking place simultaneously.

### Concepts

A variety of concepts was brought into play for the definition of leadership. Among these were the following: nucleus of tendency, personality in action, induction of compliance, influence relation, power differential, persuasion, influence act, influence on goal achievement, effect of interaction, status position, role differentiation, reinforcement, and initiation of structure. Leadership may involve all of these things. But it is doubtful that all the concepts are equally pertinent to a theory of leadership.

*Applicability*

We face a dilemma. A definition that identifies a thing for the factory manager or agency head is not necessarily the most useful one for development of broad theory. Thus, a definition enabling us to identify a group leader—the person whose behavior exercises a determining effect on the behavior of other group members—may not give us much insight into the processes and structures involved in the emergence and maintenance of leadership. But if we wish our research results to be applied by the factory manager or agency head, then we must couch our concepts as close as possible to their ways of "wording the world" (Van de Vall & Bolas, 1980).

A definition should do more than identify leaders and indicate the means by which they acquire their positions. It should account also for the maintenance and continuation of leadership. Thus, few groups engage in interaction merely for the purpose of creating leaders and dropping them as soon as they emerge. For the purposes of this Handbook, leadership must be defined broadly. Leadership is an interaction between members of a group. Leaders are agents of change, persons whose acts affect other people more than other people's acts affect them (Gurnee, 1936; LaPiere & Farnsworth, 1936). Leadership occurs when one group member modifies the motivation or competencies of others in the group. Research in the 1970s often expressed this as the directing of attention of other members to goals and the paths to achieve them. It should be clear that with this definition, any member of the group can exhibit some amount of leadership. Members will vary in the extent they do so.

The introduction of the concepts goal attainment and problem solution in certain definitions gives recognition to the fact that leadership serves a continuing function in a group. But these concepts do not account for its continuation. The concepts role, position, reinforcement of behavior, and structuring expectation serve better to account for the persistence of leadership. For purposes of theory development, it would seem reasonable to also include in the definition of leadership variables that account for the differentiation and maintenance of group roles. Although Hemphill, Pepinsky, Shevitz, et al. (1954) found it useful to limit leadership to acts involving the initiation and alteration of group structure—consistent patterns of interaction within the group, in studying leaders, all the preceding conceptualizations must be implicit, at least, in the definition of leadership that will provide sufficient breadth for the development of useful theory and practice.

# TYPES AND FUNCTIONS OF LEADERSHIP

After defining leadership to suit one's purposes, one usually developed a handy classification as the next step. Thus, in the *Republic,* Plato offered three types of leaders: (1) the philosopher–statesman to rule the republic with reason and justice; (2) the military commander to defend the state and enforce its will; and (3) the businessman to provide for citizens' material needs and satisfy their lower appetites. This typology was the first in a long series of attempts. New ones are probably being formulated right at this moment for presentation in the popular press·and professional journals.

## EXAMPLES OF CLASSIFICATIONS

### Crowd Leaders

Opening the twentieth century, LeBon (1897) described the crowd leader as a persuasive person of action whose intense faith and earnestness resists all reasoning and impels the mob to follow. Influenced by LeBon, Conway (1915) observed three types of crowd leader: (1) the crowd-compeller inflames the followers with his or her point of view; (2) the crowd-exponent senses what the crowd desires and gives expression to it; and (3) the crowd-representative merely voices the already formed opinions of the crowd.

### Organizational and Institutional Leaders

Bogardus (1918) suggested four types of leaders: (1) the autocratic type who rises to office in a powerful organization; (2) the democratic type who represents the interests of a group; (3) the executive type who is granted leadership because he is able to get things done; and (4) the reflective-intellectual type who may find it difficult to recruit a large following. J. H. Burns (1934) proposed the following types: the intellectual, the business type, the adroit diplomat, the leader of small groups, the mass leader, and the administrator.

Cowley (1931) differentiated between leadership and headship. This particularly important and useful distinction was articulated by Gibb (1969) as already noted in Chapter 1. Leadership emerges as a characteristic of the individual; headship, as a characteristic of office and position.

Influenced by Leopold's (1913) analysis of prestige, Chapin (1924a) differentiated political-military leaders who imbue the crowd with their own personality from socialized leaders who seek to lead their followers to identify themselves with the common program or movement. Bartlett (1926) presented a somewhat different classification. Institutional leaders become established by virtue of the prestige of their position. Dominative types gain and maintain their position through use of power and influence. Persuasive types exercise influence through their ability to sway the sentiments of followers and to induce them to action.

Sanderson and Nafe (1929) proposed four types of leaders. The static leader is a professional or scientific person of distinction whose work influences the thought of others. The executive leader exercises control through the authority and power of position. The professional leader has the function of stimulating followers to develop and use their own abilities. The group leader represents the interests of group members.

In seminal German publications in 1921–1922, Weber (1947) proposed three types of legitimate authority, each associated with a specific type of leadership. The bureaucratic leader operates with a staff of deputized officials and is supported by legal authority, based on rational grounds and resting on belief in the legality of normative rules and the right of those elevated to authority under such rules to issue commands. The patrimonial leader operates with a staff of relatives rather than officials. The leader is supported by traditional authority resting on the sanctity of immemorial traditions and the legitimacy of status of those exercising authority under them. The charismatic leader operates with a staff of disciples, enthusiasts, and perhaps bodyguards. Such a leader tends to sponsor causes and revolutions and is supported by charismatic authority resting on devotion to the sanctity, heroism, or inspirational character of the leader and on the normative patterns revealed or ordained by the leader.

Jennings (1960) subdivided these charismatic and strong patrimonial leaders somewhat differently. The great men and women who are rule breakers and value creators are supermen and -women; those who are dedicated to great and noble causes are heroes; and those who are motivated principally to dominate others are called princes. The princes may maximize the use of their raw power or they may be great manipulators. Heroes come in many varieties also: heroes of labor, consumption, and production, risk-taking heroes, and so on. Supermen may or may not seek the power to dominate others.

Golembiewski (1967) proposed two types of leadership in formal organizations. The colleague model implies a functional type which allows leadership to pass from individual to individual at the same level in the organization. The traditional model implies a functional type which retains leadership within the positions established by a hierarchy of authority relationships.

### Educational Leaders

Harding (1949) proposed twenty-one types of educational leaders, as follows: autocrat, cooperator, elder statesman, eager beaver, pontifical type, muddled person, loyal staff man, prophet, scientist, mystic, dogmatist, open-minded person, philosopher, business expert, benevolent despot, child protector, laissez-faire type, community-minded person, cynic, optimist, and democrat.

*Student Leaders*

As a result of observations and interviews, Spaulding (1934) classified elected student leaders into the following five types: the social climber, the intellectual success, the good fellow, the big athlete, and the leader in student activities.

*Public Leaders*

With respect to public leadership, Bell, Hill, and Wright (1961) identified formal leaders (who hold official positions, either appointed or elected), reputational leaders (who are believed influential in community or national affairs), social leaders (who are active participants in voluntary organizations, and influential leaders (who influence others in their daily contacts).

Haiman (1951) suggested that five types of leaders are needed in a democracy. These are the executive, the judge, the advocate, the expert, and the discussion leader.

Kincheloe (1928) distinguished prophets from nonprophets. Prophets are leaders without offices. Prophets may arise in time of crisis, but they create their own situation. Their real ability is shown in arousing their followers' interest so that they, the followers, will accept prophetic goals and support them enthusiastically. Prophets become a symbol of the movement they have initiated, and their authoritative words tend to release inhibited impulses within their supporters. Leadership patterns in African independent churches were seen to cluster into two types by Kiernan (1975): preachers and prophets, a modification of Sunkler's three religious types: chiefs, prophets, and messiahs.

Pursuing a purely empirical approach, Bass and Farrow (1977) generated six types of political leaders. After reading considerable amounts of biographical literature written mainly by the immediate subordinates of the leaders, pairs of judges independently completed a 135-item questionnaire to describe the leaders on thirty-one factors. The fifteen leaders were intercorrelated according to their scores on the thirty-one factors through use of the Bass and Valenzi systems model (Bass, 1976). An inverse factor analysis generated six clusters around leader–subordinate behavior with highest loadings for clustered figures as follows:

> autocratic-submissive—Hitler, Stalin, Nicholas II, Louis XIV
> trustworthy subordinates—Hirohito, Alexander the Great, F. D. Roosevelt
> clear, orderly, relationships—Winston Churchill, Andrew Carnegie
> structured, sensitivity to outside pressures—La Guardia, J. F. Kennedy, F. D. Roosevelt
> satisfying differential power—Lenin, Nicholas II
> equalitarian, analytic—Thomas Jefferson.

*Legislative Leader Types.* J. M. Burns (1978) classified legislative leaders into ideologues, tribunes, careerists, parliamentarians, and brokers. Ideologues speak for doctrines (economic, religious, xenophobic) that may be supported widely throughout their district but more typically are held by a small but highly articulate minority. Tribunes are the discoverers or connoisseurs of popular needs, the defenders of popular interests or the advocates of popular demands, aspirations, and governmental action. Careerists see their legislative careers as a steppingstone to higher offices by doing a job that impresses constituents and observers. Parliamentarians, as political technicians, either expedite or obstruct legislation. They bolster the parliament as an institution of tradition, courtesy, and mutual forbearance and protection of fellow members. Brokers mediate among antagonistic legislators, balancing interests to create legislative unity and action.

*Transactional versus Transformational Leaders.* In democracies, W. F. Buckley (1979) sees the successful, political leader as one who "crystallizes" what it is that people desire, "illuminates" the rightness of that desire, and coordinates its achievement. A most valuable distinction has been presented by J. M. Burns (1978) between transactional and transformational leaders. Transactional political leaders are those who "approach followers with an eye to exchanging one thing for another: jobs for votes, or subsidies for campaign contributions. Such transactions comprise the bulk of the relationships among leaders and followers, especially in groups, legislatures, and parties." The transformational leader also recognizes an existing need for a potential follower, but he or she goes further, seeking to satisfy higher needs, in terms of Maslow's (1954) need hierarchy, to engage the full person of the follower. Transforming leadership results in mutual stimulation and elevation "that converts followers into leaders and may convert leaders into moral agents." If the follower's higher-level needs are authentic, we see moral leadership occurring.

Transactional political leaders can be classified as opinion leaders, bargainers or bureaucrats, party leaders, legislative leaders, and executive leaders. Transformational leaders can be categorized as intellectual leaders, leaders of reform or revolution, and heroes or ideologues (J. M. Burns, 1978).

Most experimental research, unfortunately, has focused on transactional leadership (for example, see Hollander, 1978), whereas the real movers and shakers of the world are transformational leaders. Although both involve sensing followers' felt needs, it is the transformational leader who raises consciousness about higher considerations through articulation and role modeling. Aspiration levels are raised, legitimatized, and turned into political demands.

### Types of Opinion Leaders

Saunders, Davis, and Monsees (1974) found it useful to classify 587 women attending a family planning clinic in Lima, Peru, into early or late adopters and as pre-or-post acceptors in determining their opinion leadership in their community.

### Experimental and Small Group Leaders

The needs of experimental social science and the study of small group behavior and processes began to call for different sorts of typologies. Thus, Pigors (1936) observed that leaders in group work tend to act either as master or as educator. Cattell and Stice (1954) identified four types of leaders in experimental groups. These are (1) persistent, momentary problem solvers, high in interaction rate; (2) salient leaders, picked by observers as exerting the most powerful influence on the group; (3) sociometric leaders, nominated by their peers; and (4) elected leaders, attaining office by election.

Also mainly directing his attention to the small group setting, S. Levine (1949) named four types of leaders: (1) the charismatic leader helps the group rally around a common aim, but tends to become dogmatically rigid; (2) the organizational leader, emphasizing effective action, tends to drive people; (3) the intellectual leader usually lacks skill in attracting people; and (4) the informal leader tends to adapt his or her style of performance to group needs.

Clarke (1951) proposed three types of leaders: (1) popular leaders wield influence because of their unique combination of personality traits or ability; (2) group leaders, through their understanding of personality, enable group members to achieve satisfying experiences; and (3) indigenous leaders arise in a specific situation when group members seek support and guidance.

Getzels and Guba (1957) offered three types of leadership, two associated with separate dimensions of group activity: (1) nomothetic leadership is involved with the roles and expectations that define the normative dimensions of activity in social systems; (2) ideographic leadership is associated with the individual needs and dispositions of members that define the personal dimensions of group activity; and (3) synthetic leadership reconciles the conflicting demands arising from the two contrasting systems within a group.

Using factor analysis of behavioral ratings, Oliverson (1976) identified four types of leaders in studying twenty-four encounter groups: technical, charismatic, caring-interpersonal, and peer-oriented. The technical type emphasized a cognitive approach; the charismatic, the leader's own impressive attributes; and the last two types emphasized facilitating interpersonal relations with caring and friendship. Similarly, after observing sixteen group therapeutic leaders of varying theoretical persuasions, Lieberman, Yalom, and Miles (1973) formulated three types of group leaders: (1) charismatic energizers, who emphasized stimulation; (2) providers, who exhibited high levels of cognitive behavior and caring; and (3) social engineers, who stressed management of the group as a social system for finding intellectual meanings. Three other styles—impersonals, laissez-faire types, and managers—were variants of the initial three. Change in participants was highest with providers and lowest with managers. Casualties were highest with energizers and impersonals, lowest with providers.

### Sociopsychological Classifications

*Dynamic.* The classification of leaders according to some model of leader–subordinate social or psychological dynamics was pioneered by Nafe (1930), who presented a perceptive analysis of the dynamic–infusive leader who directs and redirects followers' attention to perceptual and ideational aspects of an issue until thought has been transferred into emotion and emotion into action: "The attitude of the leader toward the led and toward the project is found to be a problem in name only. The leader needs only to have the appearance of possessing the attitude desired by the following." The real problem is the attitude of the led toward the leader. The attributes of leadership exist only in the minds of the led: "The leader may be this to one and that to another, but it is only by virtue of having a following that he or she is a leader."

In contrast to the infusive type was its opposite: adhesive. Nafe proposed the following additional categories for describing leaders: static versus dynamic; impressors versus expressors, volunteer versus drafted, general versus specialized, temporary versus permanent, conscious versus unconscious, professional versus amateur, and personal versus impersonal.

*Psychoanalytic.* Pursuing a psychoanalytical orientation, Redl (1942) suggested that instinctual and emotional group processes take place around a member whose role may be that of patriarch, leader, tyrant, love object, object of aggression, organizer, seducer, hero, bad example, or good example. Continuing in the same vein, Zaleznik (1974) contrasted charismatic leaders with consensus leaders. Charismatic leaders are inner-directed and identify with objects, symbols, and ideals connected with introjection. Consensus leadership "presents" the leader as brother or peer rather than as father. Charismatics may fall victim to megalomania, paranoia, and other psychoses.

*Genetic.* Showing the influence of genetic conceptualizations, Krout (1942) identified the social variant arising out of the group's need to bring its goals and the lagging behavior form into some type of agreement. Hybrid leaders seek to change social structure through discontinuous rather than continuous methods to achieve group goals. Mutants are innovators who redefine the culture patterns of their group and may set new goals in order to achieve their objectives for the group.

### Communalities in Typologies

What we see in common among many of the typologists is reference to the following types of leaders:

| | |
|---|---|
| authoritative | considerate |
| dominative | intellectual |
| directive | eminent |
| autocratic | expert |
| persuasive | executive |
| arousing | bureaucrat |
| charismatic | administrator |
| seductive | head |
| convincing | representative |
| democratic | spokesperson |
| participative | advocate |
| group developing | |

It is interesting to note that most recent researchers have devoted comparatively little attention to three of these types: persuasive, intellectual, and representative. The armchair theorizing of the older generation has been rejected as unrealistic and misleading. Yet, their insights do not appear to be without validity. Recent theorists have been concerned primarily with two of the types—authoritative and democratic. Both have been elaborated and refined. The authoritative type correlates with the directive type in the list; the democratic type correlates with the participative or considerate type. The executive is not regarded as a separate type, but is classified as either task-oriented (authoritative) or relations-oriented (democratic). The persuasive pattern of behavior is a subclass of task-oriented or initiating behavior. However, in many situations the representative (spokesperson) pattern of behavior is independent of task orientation and relations orientation. The intellectual type, the expert, is seldom regarded as a leader under many recent definitions, although we shall see that any systems theory with emphasis on the processing of information must take individual expertise into account. Nevertheless, as a whole, leadership typologies have not been highly influential in stimulating and directing empirical research of any kind. Paradoxically, typologies continue to be most popular in leadership practice.

### Typolopy Applied

Since it is easier for managers to grasp typologies rather than theories, Reddin (1977), for example, has developed a popular management diagnosis and training program built around eight types which are a synthesis of approaches to leader behavior descriptions such as will be seen in many of the following chapters, especially Chapters 18–22. Each type is a consequence of being low or high in three well-known dimensions of leadership (to be discussed in Chapter 20). Managers come in various combinations of this three-dimensional typology.

| Leadership Type | Relationships Orientation | Task Orientation | Effectiveness |
|---|---|---|---|
| Deserter | Low | Low | Low |
| Autocrat | Low | High | Low |
| Missionary | High | Low | Low |
| Compromiser | High | High | Low |
| Bureaucrat | Low | Low | High |
| Benevolent Autocrat | Low | High | High |
| Developer | High | Low | High |
| Executive | High | High | High |

Types of leaders will be transliterated into leaders' styles with more sophisticated definition and measurement in Chapters 18–22.

## FUNCTIONAL TYPOLOGIES

Several authors have classified leaders according to the kinds of functions they perform. Mooney and Reiley (1931) identified three scalar processes in an organization. These are leadership, delegation, and functional definition. The functional effect of leadership is determinative (legislative); the effect of delegation is applicative (executive); and the effect of functional definition is interpretive (judicial). Coffin (1944) suggested that the three functions of leadership are formulation (planning) execution (organizing), and supervision (persuading). Barnard (1946b) identified the functions of leadership as (1) the determination of objectives, (2) the manipulation of means, (3) the instrumentation of action, and (4) the stimulation of coordinated effort. Krech and Crutchfield (1948) proposed a number of leadership functions. These are executive, planner, policy maker, expert, external group representative, controller of internal relationships, purveyor of rewards and punishments, arbitrator and mediator, exemplar, symbol of the group, surrogate for individual responsibility, ideologist, father figure, and scapegoat. K. Davis (1951) is in agreement with several theorists in suggesting that the functions of the business leader are to plan, organize, and control an organization's activities. Kessing and Kessing (1956), in a study of leadership in Samoa, identified the following functions: consultation, deliberation, negotiation, public opinion formation, and decision making. E. Gross (1961) proposed several functions of leadership. These are to define goals, clarify and administer them, choose appropriate means, assign and coordinate tasks, motivate, create loyalty, represent the group, and spark the membership into action.

Selznick (1957) suggested that the functions of organizational leadership are: (1) definition of institutional mission and goals; (2) creation of a structure for accomplishment of purpose; (3) defense of institutional integrity; and (4) reevaluation of internal conflict.

Katz and Kahn (1966) proposed three functions of leadership. These are: (1) the introduction of structural change (policy formation); (2) the interpretation of structure (piecing out incompleteness of existing formal structure); and (3) the use of structure formally provided to keep the organization in motion and effective operation (administration). Wofford (1967) suggested setting objectives, organizing, leading, and controlling as functions of management.

Bowers and Seashore (1967) maintained that the functions of leadership are support of members, interaction facilitation, goal emphasis, and work facilitation. Cattell (1957) observed that the leader performs the following functions: services in maintaining the group, upholding role and status satisfactions, maintaining task satisfactions, keeping ethical (norm) satisfactions, selecting and clarifying goals, and finding and clarifying means of attaining goals.

The leader may play the role of final arbitrator, the superordinate whose judgment settles disputes among followers. This function was often believed critical for the avoidance of anarchy in many political states. The maintenance and security of the state depended on the existence of a legitimate position at the top to which all followers would acquiesce to avoid the continuation of conflict amongst themselves.

### Idealized versus Empirically Determined Functions of Management

The classical theories of management suggested that the primary functions of the executive are planning, organizing, and controlling. Various theorists have added coordinating, supervising, motivating, and the like to the list. But the most critical theorists have maintained that the added functions are merely varieties of organizational and control functions.

On the other hand, leadership functions identified by the behavioral theorists and researchers included:

defining objectives and maintaining goal direction
providing means for goal attainment
providing and maintaining group structure
facilitating group action and interaction
maintaining group cohesiveness and member satisfaction
facilitating group task performance.

The list of functions identified by the behavioralists grew out of research on basic group processes and emergence of the leadership role. Behavioralists focus attention on the performances, interactions, and satisfactions of members engaged in the group task. The functions proposed by the classical theorists, on the other hand, are concerned with the rationalized processes of formal organizations. Although highly generalized and abstract, the processes are by no means lacking in reality; however, they ignore the human nature of members constituting the organization. Yet, organizations strive for rationality. Understanding the purposes of the manager requires consideration of the planning, directing, and controlling functions of the manager for whom supervision and leadership is the most important but not the only aspect of his or her assignment. Further discussion of management functions will be presented in Chapter 17.

### Experimental and Small Group Leaders

Research on experimental groups suggests a somewhat different set of functions. Bales and Slater (1955) observed that the leader performs two essential functions. The first is associated with productivity. The second is concerned with socioemotional support of the group members. Benne and Sheats (1948) suggested that group members play three types of functional roles: (1) group task roles; (2) group building and maintenance roles; and (3) individual roles. Similarly, Bales (1958a) observed two major functions of the leadership role in experimental groups. These are task functions and group maintenance and support functions.

From another point of view, Roby (1961) developed a mathematical model of leadership functions based on response units and information load. The following leadership functions were identified: (1) to bring about congruence of goals between the members; (2) to balance group resources and capabilities with environmental demands; (3) to provide group structure that will focus information effectively upon problem solution; and (4) to make certain that all needed information is available at a decision center when required. Consistent with this view, Stogdill (1959) suggested that it is the function of the leader to maintain group structure and goal direction, and to reconcile conflicting demands arising within and outside the group.

According to Schutz (1961b), the leader has the functions of (1) establishing and recognizing a hierarchy of group goals and values; (2) recognizing and integrating the various cognitive styles existing within the group; (3) maximizing the use of group members' abilities; and (4) helping members resolve problems involved in adapting to external realities as well as those involving interpersonal needs.

For Hollander (1978), goal setting is also seen as a particularly important function for the leader. And P. J. Burke (1966a,b) showed that antagonism, tension, and absenteeism occur when the leader fails in this function. According to Hollander, the leader also provides direction and defines reality, necessary to the group's effectiveness. If successful, such leader direction is a valued resource. As a definer of reality, the leader communicates relevant information about progress and provides needed redirection to followers.

### Place of Typologies

Typologies have their uses. Early on, they make for easy conceptualization. They are also easy to communicate and understand. But with continued research they give way to more sophistocated conceptualizations.

# AN INTRODUCTION TO THEORIES AND MODELS OF LEADERSHIP

Nothing is supposed to be as practical as a good theory; nothing seems more impractical than a bad one. A theory may be good for one purpose and bad for another. For theory is supposed to be a way of trying to understand fact. Sometimes, leadership theory becomes a way of obscuring fact. Much effort is expended on coping with the obscurity (Bass, 1974). Again, we are facing a dilemma. If a theory of leadership is to be used for diagnosis, training, and development, it must be grounded theory—grounded in the concepts and assumptions acceptable and used by managers, officials, and emergent leaders (Glaser & Strauss, 1967). But such a theory is less likely to achieve relevance or to agree with basic theory in psychology, sociology, or other social sciences. Moreover, in grounding theory we may suffer the loss of generality and the opportunity for employing standardized measurements. Theories of leadership attempt to explain either the factors involved in emergence of leadership or the nature of leadership and its consequences. Models are replicas or reconstructions of the realities, using selected variables conceived to be involved. Both can be useful in defining research problems for the social scientist and in improving prediction and control in the development and application of leadership.

Here we will survey the variety of theories and models posed at one time or another, reserving more detail about them for later chapters.

## A REVIEW BY KINDS OF THEORY

### Great-Man Theories

For many, history was shaped by the leadership of great men. Without Moses, the Jews would have remained in Egypt. Without Churchill, the British would have given up in 1940. The eighteenth-century rationalists felt that luck had to be added to the personal attributes of great men to determine the course of history. The Russian Revolution would have taken a different course if Lenin had been hanged by the Old Regime instead of exiled. For the romantic philosophers, such as Nietzsche, a sudden decision by a great man could redetermine history (Jefferson's decision to purchase Louisiana). To William James (1880), the mutations of society were due to great men. They initiated movement and prevented others from leading society in another direction.

Influenced by Galton's (1869) study of the hereditary background of great men,

26

several early theorists attempted to explain leadership on the basis of inheritance. Woods (1913) studied fourteen nations over periods of five to ten centuries. The conditions of each reign were found to approximate the ruler's capabilities. The brothers of kings (as a result of natural endowment, of course) also tended to become men of power and influence! Woods concluded that the man makes the nation and shapes it in accordance with his abilities. Wiggam (1931) advanced the proposition that the survival of the fittest and intermarriage among them produces an aristocratic class differing biologically from the lower classes. Thus, an adequate supply of superior leaders depends upon a proportionately high birth rate among the abler classes.

Carlyle's (1841) essay on heroes tended to reinforce the concept of the leader as a person endowed with unique qualities that capture the imagination of the masses. The hero would contribute somehow, no matter where he was found. (Despite Joan of Arc, Elizabeth I, and Catherine the Great, great women were ignored.) Dowd (1936) maintained that "there is no such thing as leadership by the masses. The individuals in every society possess different degrees of intelligence, energy, and moral force, and in whatever direction the masses may be influenced to go, they are always led by the superior few." Jennings (1960) presented a comprehensive survey and analysis of the great-man theory of leadership.

### Trait Theories

If the leader is endowed with superior qualities that differentiate him from his followers, it should be possible to identify these qualities. This assumption gave rise to the trait theories of leadership. L. L. Bernard (1926), Bingham (1927), Tead (1929), and Kilbourne (1935) explained leadership in terms of traits of personality and character. Bird (1940) compiled a list of seventy-nine such traits from twenty psychologically oriented studies. A similar review was completed by Smith and Kruger (1933) for educators and by W. O. Jenkins (1947) for understanding military leadership.

### Environmental Theories

Many early theorists advanced the view that the emergence of a great leader is a result of time, place, and circumstance. For Hegel, the great man was an expression of the needs of his times. What the great man did was automatically right to do because he fulfilled what was needed. He actually couldn't help what he did, since he was directed and controlled by his historical environment. The needs for civil peace made it mandatory for Octavian to form the Roman Principate and destroy republicanism. For Herbert Spencer, societies evolved in a uniform, gradual, progressive manner. No great man could change the course of this development. The American Civil War was an inevitable clash as the conflicting economic interests of North and South evolved. For Engels, Marx, and their successors, economic necessity made history. Obstacles to expanding production must be cleared. The greater the obstacles, the greater the need and the more capable must be the leader. But who he or she turns out to be is irrelevant (Hook, 1943).

Mumford (1909) maintained that the leaders that emerge depend on the abilities and skills required at the time to solve the social problems existing in times of stress, change, and adaptation. Leadership is an innate as well as acquired modal societary tendency of force. As such, it is related to the organized and organizing phases of the social process or to the habitual tensional-adaptive phases of association. Bogardus (1918) presented the view that the type of leadership a group will develop or accept will be determined by the nature of the group and the problems it must solve. Hocking (1924) went even further in suggesting that leadership resides in the group and is given to leaders only when they advance a program that the group is willing to follow. Person (1928) advanced two hypotheses to account for leadership: (1) any particular situation plays a large part in determining leadership qualities and the leader for that situation; and (2) the qualities in an individual which a particular situation may determine as leadership qualities are themselves the product of a succession of prior leadership situations which have developed and molded that individual. J. Schneider (1937) found that the number of great military leaders in England was proportional to the number of conflicts in which the nation engaged. Thus, the societal situation was related to the achievement of leadership. According to A. J. Murphy (1941), leadership does not reside in a person but is a function of the occasion. The situation calls for certain types of action; the leader does not inject leadership but is the instrumental factor through which a solution is achieved. Spiller (1929) concluded that a sweeping survey of the field of human progress would show that 95 percent of the advance was unconnected with great men. The great man, like Mahatma Gandhi or Martin Luther King, appears at a critically important advancement of a socially valued cause, devotes himself to it, and profits greatly from the work of many others.

Although wars and other crisis situations present opportunities for acquisition of leadership by persons who would remain submerged in the daily round of routine activities, various theorists have maintained that the situation is not in itself sufficient to account for leadership. How many crisis situations arise that do not produce a person equal to the occasion?

### Personal-Situational Theories

Both the great-man theorists and the situational theorists attempted to explain leadership as an effect of a single set of forces. The interactive effects of individual and situational factors were overlooked. Westburgh (1931) suggested that the study of leadership must include the affective, intellectual, and action traits of the individual as well as the specific conditions under which the individual operates. Case (1933) maintained that leadership is produced by the conjunction of three factors: (1) the personality traits of the leader; (2) the nature of the group and of its members; and (3) the event (change or problem) confronting the group. J. F. Brown (1936) proposed five field-dynamic laws of leadership. Leaders must: (1) have membership character in the group they are attempting to lead; (2) represents a region of high potential in the social field; (3) adapt themselves to the existing field structure; (4) realize the long-term trends in the field structure; and (5) recognize that leadership increases in potency at the cost of a reduction in the freedom of leadership.

Hook (1943) noted that there is some restriction in the range of traits permitted the emergent leader by a given situation. Heroic action is decisive only where alternative courses of action are possible. Napoleon on Elba had alternatives; on St. Helena he had none.

Bass (1960) argued that the great-man versus environment controversy was a pseudo-problem. For any given case, some of the variance in what happens is due to the situation, some is due to the individual, and some to the interaction of individual and situation. Thus, Mao Zedung played a critical role in the Chinese Revolution, but without the chaotic state of Chinese affairs under Kuomontang leadership his rise to power would not have been possible.

Theories of leadership cannot be constructed for behavior in a vacuum. They must contain elements about persons as well as elements about situations. Any theory of leadership must take account of the interaction between situation and individual. Barnard (1938) and many others (LaPiere, 1938; Jenkins, 1947; Murphy, 1941; C. A. Gibb, 1947) echoed this view, declaring that the conditions in which organizational management is demanded determine to some extent the leadership qualities needed. Rainio (1955) attempted to resolve the "situation–personality" controversy by suggesting that leadership behavior is a less consistent attribute of individuals than such traits as non-suggestibility, energy, and maturity, which empirically and theoretically tend to be associated with overt leadership behavior. Some consistency exists in individual leader behavior transcending situations although situational variation of significance to leader behavior is multidimensional.

' Stogdill (1948) concluded that the leaders' traits must bear some relevant relationship to the characteristics of the followers. An adequate analysis of leadership involves not only a study of leaders, but also of the situation. Stogdill's position strongly influenced the theorization that followed. According to Gerth and Mills (1952), "to understand leadership, attention must be paid to (1) the traits and motives of the leader as a man, (2) images that selected publics hold of him and their motives for following him, (3) the features of the role that he plays as a leader, and (4) the institutional context in which he and his followers may be involved." C. A. Gibb (1954) suggested that "leadership is an interactional phenomenon arising when group formation takes place. The emergence of a group structure, whereby each of its members is assigned a relative position within the group depending upon the nature of his [or her] interactional relations with the other members, is a general phenomenon and a function of the interrelation of individuals engaged in the pursuit of a common goal." Stogdill and Shartle (1955) proposed to

> study leadership in terms of the status, interactions, perceptions, and behavior of individuals in relation to other members of the organized group. Thus leadership is regarded as a relationship between persons rather than as a characteristic of the isolated individual. When data for all the members of a group . . . are combined and interrelated, they provide a means for studying leadership in terms of the structural and functional dimensions of organization.

Bennis (1961) suggested a revision of leadership theory to include the following sets of considerations: (1) impersonal bureaucracy and rationality of measures; (2) informal organization and interpersonal relations; (3) benevolent autocracy that gets results because it structures the relationship between superiors and subordinates; (4) job enlargement and employee-centered supervision that permits individual self-actualization; and (5) participative management and joint consultation that allow integration of individual and organizational goals.

Cattell (1951) maintained that the two primary functions of leadership are helping the group to find the means to a goal already agreed upon and helping the group to decide upon a goal. The first deals with the syntality (measure of performance) and the second with synergy (drive and goal direction) of the group. Leadership represents a dynamic interaction between the goals of the leader and the goals and needs of the followers. It serves the function of facilitating selection and achievement of group goals.

Hollander (1958, 1964) suggested that the leader of a group, as a result of initial compliance with the norms and expectations of the group, acquires idiosyncrasy credit. After acquiring such credit, the leader is later permitted by group members to depart from group norms without jeopardizing his or her status in the group. The leader may need considerable freedom for innovation in order to act in the best interests of the group. Experimental studies based on Hollander's theory will be detailed in Chapter 19.

### Psychoanalytic Theories

Freud himself (1922) as well as many other psychoanalytically oriented writers such as Frank (1939), Fromm (1941), Erikson (1964), and H. Levinson (1970) addressed the leadership issue at length. Favorite interpretations see the leader as father figure, as source of love or fear, as embodiment of the superego, as the emotional outlet for followers' frustrations and destructive aggression, as in need to distribute love and affection fairly among followers, and so on (Wolman, 1971). Psychoanalysis has had a marked influence on psychohistorians trying to understand adult political leaders in terms of their childhood deprivations, cultural, milieu, and relationships with parental authority, and the psychodynamic needs they fulfill among their followers. Illustrative is the variety of psychoanalytic treatises available on Adolf Hitler alone, such as those of Langer (1972), Gatzke (1973), and Waite (1977).

Using the methods of psychohistory to delve deeper into questions concerning social insight, G. Davis (1975) showed how the psychodynamics of Theodore Roosevelt's childhood found expression in his "affective" insights as an adult leader. Personal recollections, published accounts, journalism, and biographies about Roosevelt as a child are meshed with an analysis of the relevant cultural developments which occurred in the United States at the same time. Roosevelt's psyche resolved the childhood experience of his generation.

Psychoanalytical theory was also used by M. F. DeVries (1977) and by Hummel (1975) to show how the interaction of leader personalities and situations is dramatized in times of crisis. For DeVries, the question whether or not charismatic leaders who arise in crises—out of a sense of their own grandiosity and the group's sense of helpless dependency—serve the group well depends on whether the leaders can transform their "paranoid potential" and sense of omnipotence into reality testing. Such charisma in fragmented societies may give rise to an integration of institutions and loyalties or it may spawn opposition movements (G. T. Stewart, 1974). For Hummel, Freudian projection by the followers is at the root of the intense love for the charismatic leader. The leader is seen as a superhuman hero because the followers cannot become consciously aware of their unconscious projections.

More detail on the charismatic leader will be found in Chapter 10 and later.

*Interaction-Expectation Theories*

*Leader Role Theory.* Homans (1950) developed a theory of the leadership role using three basic variables: action, interaction, and sentiments. It is assumed that an increase in the frequency of interaction and participation in common activities is associated with an increase in sentiments of mutual liking and in clarity of group norms. The higher the rank of persons within the group, the more nearly their activities conform to the group norms, the wider their range of interactions, and the larger the number of group members for whom they originate interactions. Leadership is defined in terms of the origination of interaction.

In Hemphill's (1954) theory, leadership arises in situations in which component parts of group tasks are dependently related to one another and to the solution of a common problem among group members. His theory emerges from the differentiation of structure-in-interaction which permits prediction of future interaction activity with an accuracy exceeding chance. The role structure of the group and the office of the leader are defined by institutionalized expectations with respect to initiation of structure-in-interaction. The probability of success of an attempted leadership act is a function of the members' perceptions of their freedom to accept or reject the suggested structure-in-interaction. When such structure leads to the solution of mutual problems, it acquires value and strengthens the expectation that all group members will conform to the structure. Thus, leadership acts initiate structure-in-interaction, and leadership is the act of initiating such structure.

*Role Attainment Theory.* Stogdill (1959) developed an expectancy-reinforcement theory of role attainment. As group members interact and engage in mutual task performance, they reinforce the expectation that each will continue to act and interact in accord with his previous performance. Thus, the individual's role is defined by mutually confirmed expectations relative to the performances and interactions he will be permitted to contribute to the group. The leadership potential of any given member is defined by the extent to which he initiates and maintains structure in interaction and expectation.

*Reinforced Change Theory.* In a theory proposed by Bass (1960), leadership is the observed effort of one member to change the motivation and understanding of other members or to change their behavior. If a member is successful, a change is observed in other members accepting leadership. Motivation is changed by changing the expectations of reward or punishment. A group is a collection of individuals whose existence is rewarding to members or enables them to avoid punishment. Changes occur in the behavior of group members in order to increase the rewards for performance. Leaders acquire their position by virtue of their perceived ability to reinforce the behavior of group members by granting or denying rewards or punishments. Since group effectiveness is evaluated in terms of the group's ability to reward its members, leaders are valued when they can enable a group to provide expected rewards. The congruence of a leader's status, esteem, and ability can account for the leader's success and effectiveness. Incongruence generates conflict and failure. This emphasis on congruence is found also in Halal's (1974) general theory. A particular style of leadership is congruent with specific task technologies and specific subordinate motivation. There is an adjustment toward congruence.

Bass argued that the emergence of leadership and what would promote effectiveness depended on the interaction potential in the situation—the physical, psychological, and social distance among individuals. The likelihood that two individuals will interact depends on group size, geographical proximity, social proximity, contact opportunity, intimacy and familiarity, mutuality of esteem and attraction, and homogeneity of abilities and attitudes. Monge and Kirste (1975) extended the examination of proximity as a time-and-space opportunity, again showing its positive association with the potential to interact and satisfaction with the interaction.

*Path-Goal Theory.* Georgopoulos, Mahoney, and Jones (1957) and again M. G. Evans (1970a) suggested that the leader can determine the follower's perception of the abundance of rewards available to him or her. The leader also can determine the follower's perception of the paths (behaviors) through which rewards may be attained. As popularized by House (1971), the path-goal theory of leadership states that leaders enhance the psychological states, that is, arouse subordinates to perform and achieve satisfaction from the job to be done. The leaders clarify the goals of their subordinates as well as the paths to those goals. They enhance satisfaction with work itself and provide valued extrinsic rewards contingent on the subordinates' performance. The leader controls what subordinates value (Bass, 1960). The situation determines what leader behavior will accomplish these leadership purposes. Two situational aspects of consequence are attributes of the subordinates and environmental forces such as the structure of the task to be done (House & Dessler, 1974). Path-goal theory is in agreement with what was detailed earlier by Bass (1960) but has updated the definitions of work such as autonomy and job scope. Fortunately, the facts do not change, so that, if one looks carefully, one can see a great deal of agreement among earlier and more recent theoretical efforts. We will discuss empirical studies dealing with path-goal propositions in Chapter 25. In order to reconcile the theory with experimental results, House (1972) proposed that the effects of a leader's behavior are contingent on three kinds of moderator variables: task variables such as role clarity, routine, and externally imposed controls; environmental variables; and individual differences such as preferences, expectations, and personality. This is very similar to the position reached by Bass and Valenzi (1974) in empirical studies of leaders and subordinates as a system.

*A Two-Stage Model.* Yukl (1971) postulated that whereas leader initiation increases subordinate task skill, leader consideration and decision centralization increase subordinate motivation. In turn, subordinate skill and motivation improve the subordinates' effectiveness.

*Contingency Theory.* Along with path-goal experiments. Fiedler's theory has dominated much of the research activity during the 1970s. For Fiedler (1967a), the effectiveness of a given pattern of leader behavior is contingent upon the demands imposed by the situation. The task-oriented leader is most likely to be effective in situations that are most favorable or most unfavorable to him or her. The relations-oriented leader is most likely to be effective in situations between the two extremes. A situation is favorable to the leader if the leader is esteemed by the group to be led, if the task to be done is structured, clear, simple, and easy to solve, and if the leader has legitimacy and power due to position.

If person and situation are to be matched, most other person-situation theorists focus on how the person needs to be developed to best adapt to the needs of the situation. But Fiedler's research and theory tended to emphasize the need to place the person in the situation for which he or she was best suited, that is, for task-oriented people to lead very favorable or unfavorable situations and for relations-oriented people to lead situations neither high nor low in favorability. However, more recently he and his associates have evolved "leader match" training (Fiedler, Chemers & Mahar, 1976), that is, how to help the leader of designated orientation to change the situation or better adjust to the favorability or unfavorability of the situation. The Fiedler, Chemers, and Maher (1976) leadership training program consists of first identifying the trainee's particular style—task- or relations-oriented; teaching the trainee how to analyze and classify leadership situations for their favorableness or what is now called situational control. Next are considered the best fit of situation and style and how to change one's style to suit the occasion or how to change the situation to better fit one's style. Fiedler's lifelong work illustrates the movement from empirical discoveries to theory formation (not vice versa) to more empirical testing and theory revision, still more testing, then finally to practical application and validation of the application. We will devote a section of Chapter 20 to a review of research based on Fiedler's theory and a section of Chapter 33 to discussion of its applications.

*A Multiple Screen Model.* More recently, Fiedler has developed and tested the Multiple Screen Model to explain the relationship between leader intelligence and task performance. Fiedler and Leister (1977a,b) suggest and provide empirical support for the proposal that various interpersonal and personal factors block or screen the relation between leader intelligence and group performance. This relationship is strong when leaders are highly motivated and have experienced good leader–boss relations, and good leader–group relations.

### Humanistic Theories

The theories of Argyris, Blake and Mouton, Likert, and McGregor are concerned with development of effective and cohesive organizations. The human being is by nature a motivated organism. The organization is by nature structured and controlled. It is the function of leadership to modify the organization in order to provide freedom for individuals to realize their own motivational potential for fulfillment of their own needs and at the same time contribute toward the accomplishment of organizational goals.

McGregor (1960, 1966) postulated two types of organizational leadership—Theory X and Theory Y. The former, based on the assumption that people are passive and resistant to organizational needs, attempts to direct and motivate people to fit these needs. Theory Y, based on the assumption that people already possess motivation and desire for responsibility, attempts to arrange organizational conditions in such a manner as to make possible fulfillment of their needs while directing their efforts toward achieving organizational objectives.

Argyris (1957, 1962, 1964a) perceived a fundamental conflict between the organization and the individual. It is the very nature of organizations to structure member roles and to control performance in the interest of achieving specified objectives. It is the individual's nature to be self-directive and to seek fulfillment through exercising initiative and responsibility. An organization will be most effective when its leadership provides the means whereby followers may make a creative contribution to it as a natural outgrowth of their own needs for growth, self-expression, and maturity.

Likert (1961a,b, 1967) suggests that leadership is a relative process in that leaders must take into account the expectations, values, and interpersonal skills of those with whom they are interacting. Leaders must present behaviors and organizational processes perceived by followers as supportive of their efforts and of their sense of personal worth. Leaders will involve followers in making decisions that affect their welfare and work. Leaders will use their influence in order to further the task performance and personal welfare of followers. Leaders build group cohesiveness and motivation for productivity by providing freedom for responsible decision making and exercise of initiative.

Blake and Mouton (1964, 1965) conceptualize leadership in terms of a managerial grid on which concern for people represents one axis and concern for production represents the other axis. Leaders may be high or low on both axes, or they may be high on one and low on the other. The individual who rates high on both develops followers committed to accomplishment of work, and his sense of interdependence through a common stake in the organizational purpose leads to relationships of trust and respect.

Hersey and Blanchard's (1969, 1972) *Life Cycle Theory of Leadership* is a theory of leadership effectiveness synthesizing Blake and Mouton's (1964) managerial grid postulations, Reddin's (1977) 3-D Effectiveness typology, and Argyris' (1964a) Maturity-Immaturity theory. Leader behavior is related to the maturity of subordinates. As subordinates' maturity increases, leader behavior should be characterized by a decreasing emphasis on task structuring and an increasing emphasis on consideration. As maturity continues to increase, there should be an eventual decrease in consideration. Maturity is defined in terms of subordinates' experience, achievement motivation, and willingness and ability to accept responsibility.

A full discussion of experimental and field studies based on these humanistic theories will form the basis of Chapters 18 and 20.

### Exchange Theories

One set of theories (Homans, 1958; March and Simon, 1958; Thibaut and Kelley, 1959; and Gergen, 1969) is based on the assumption that social interaction represents a form of exchange in which group members make contributions at a cost to themselves and receive returns at a cost to the group or other members. Interaction continues because members find social exchange mutually rewarding. Blau (1964) begins with the fact that for most people being elevated to a position of high status is rewarding; it is also rewarding for members to associate with their high-status leaders. But leaders tend to deplete their power when members have discharged their obligations to the leaders, who in turn then replenish their power by rendering valuable services to the group. "Since the leader benefits as much as the rest do from their following his good suggestions, rather than somebody else's poorer ones, the compliance his contributions earn him constitutes a surplus profit of leadership."

T. O. Jacobs (1971) formulated a social exchange theory and buttressed it with a wide range of research findings. The group provides status and esteem satisfactions to leaders in exchange for their unique contributions to goal attainment. Authority relationships in formal organizations define role expectations that enable group members to perform their tasks and to interact without the use of power. Leadership implies an equitable exchange relationship between leader and followers. When role obligations are mutually acknowledged, each party can satisfy the expectations of the other on an equitable basis. Chapter 23, among several, will deal with research based on exchange theories.

### Behavioral Theories

As early as 1929, Aaronovich and Khotin (1929) reported using differential cued reinforcement to alter the leadership behavior of monkeys in uncovering boxes of food. Mawhinney and Ford (1977) reinterpreted path-goal theory in terms of operant conditioning. W. E. Scott (1977) saw the need to replace conceiving of leadership as due to influence or persuasion with an analysis of the observable leader behaviors that change the behavior of subordinates. Emphasized were reinforcement and making rewards contingent on the subordinate behaving as desired. Sims (1977) demonstrated that a leader's positive reward behavior will increase a subordinate's performance.

Davis and Luthans (1979) conceived the leader's behavior as a cue

> to evoke the subordinate's task behavior. The subordinate's task behavior in turn can act as a consequence for the leader which, in turn, reinforces, punishes, or extinguishes the leader's subsequent behavior. Similarly, the subordinate's behavior has its own consequences . . . which serve to reinforce, punish, or extinguish this behavior. The consequences for the subordinate's behavior may be related to the leader's subsequent behavior, the work itself, and its outcomes, or other organization members. (p. 239)

Supervisors do not directly cause subordinate behavior; they merely set the occasion or provide a discriminative stimulus for the evocation of the subordinate behavior. Subordinate behavior depends on its consequences. Environmental cues, discriminative stimuli, behaviors, and consequences form a behavioral contingency for analysis.

But Davis and Luthans leave room for cognitive processes to enter the scenario "to assign concepts to behavior and to infer relationships between events." Their functional analysis of the leader–subordinate dynamic uses the Luthans (1977) S-O-B-C model where $S$ is the antecedent stimulus, $O$ is the organism's covert processes, $B$ is the behavior, and $C$ is the consequence.

Particular attention will be paid to the interactive effects of leader and follower on each other in Chapter 16.

### Perceptual and Cognitive Theories

These perceptual and cognitive theories include attribution theory, systems analyses, and rational-deductive approaches.

*Attribution Theory.* Each member is seen to have his or her own theory of leadership. If we want to understand a leader's behavior, we must begin by going inside the leader's head to find out what he or she is thinking about the situation in which they would be leaders (Pfeffer, 1977). And whether or not they are seen to act like leaders depends on others' implicit theories about leadership (Eden & Leviathan, 1975; Calder, 1977). We observe the behavior of leaders and infer the causes of these behaviors to be various personal traits or external constraints. If these causes match the observer's naïve assumptions about what leaders should do, then "leadership" is used to describe the person observed. For Calder (1977), leadership changes from a scientific concept to a study of the social reality of members and observers. Leadership is seen as a study in how the term is used, when it is used, and assumptions about the development and nature of leadership. Ratings by observers and subordinates are biased by their own individual social realities (Mitchell, Larson & Green, 1977; H. M. Weiss, 1977), which accounts for the low correlations often found between supervisor, peer, and subordinate ratings of the same leaders (Ilgen & Fujii, 1976; T. R. Mitchell, 1970a; Bernardin & Alvares, 1975) as well as for the confounding of evaluations of subordinate performance and leader's behavior (Rush, Thomas & Lord, 1977).

To understand a leader's behavior from what he or she perceives is the cause of the follower's behavior, Green and Mitchell (1979) formulated a model to study such attributional processes in leaders. For example, if presented with an incident of poor subordinate performance such as low productivity, lateness, a missed deadline, or disruptive behavior, leaders form an implicit theory about the subordinate and the situation, judging that the cause was due to the subordinate's personality, ability, or effort, or that it was due to an externality such as lack of support, a difficult task, or insufficient information. Causality is attributed more to the subordinate than to the situation if the subordinate has had a poor history of performance and if the effects of the poor performance have severe outcomes (Mitchell & Wood, 1979). The leader will focus remedial action on the subordinate rather than on the situation in such circumstances even if in reality it was the situation that was the cause of the problem.

*Leadership as Human Problem Solving.* Following Newell and Simon's (1972) theory that focused attention on the problem solver's subjective "problem space"— containing the encodings of goals, initial situations, intermediate states, rules, constraints, and other relevant aspects of the task environment—Lord (1976) saw the utility of studying leaders and followers in terms of their shared problem spaces when tackling a common task, for example, by hypothesizing and demonstrating that a leader devoted more effort to developing an orientation and definition of the problem for the group when the actual task lacked structure.

*Systems Analysis.* Sensitivity to the larger environment and organization in which the leaders and their subordinate groups are embedded is dictated by a systems point of view. Osborn and Hunt (1975a,b) formulated an adaptive-reactive model of leadership to incorporate macro-variables such as environmental constraints or organizational demands as antecedents of leader behavior. Likewise, Bass and Valenzi (1974) used systems theory to construct a model of leader–follower relationships. Leaders and their followers can be conceived as open social systems. The systems are open to the outside environment and they are sensitive to the constraints imposed on them by the outside. The system imports energy (power) and information from the outside, transforms it, and exports goods and services.

To transform inputs into outputs, two cyclical flows occur within the system, one of power, the other of information. Feedback to the system from the effect of the outputs on the environment completes the cycle. The relations within the system grow and become more intricate with repeated cycles (Katz & Kahn, 1966).

How can the transformation process be increased in rate and intensity? Leaders and/or followers can import and introduce more information. Directive leaders do it alone. If followers are included, the process is participative. Energy levels can be increased by selecting as leaders and followers more highly motivated individuals or by increasing reinforcements accruing from outputs and transformations.

The Bass-Valenzi model (Bass, 1976) proposes that whether leaders are directive, negotiative, consultative, participative, or delegative depends on their perceptions of the system's inputs and within-systems relations. The leader and his or her immediate work group form an open system of inputs (organizational, task, and work group variables); within-system relations (power and information differentials) and outputs (productivity and satisfaction).

Consistent with Bass (1960), the Bass-Valenzi model thus posits that leaders will be more directive if they perceive that they have more power and information than their subordinates. They will consult if they perceive that they have the power, but their subordinates have the necessary information to solve the group's problems. They will delegate where subordinates are seen to have both power and information, and they will negotiate when they, the leaders, perceive they have the information, but not the power. A small-space analysis of empirical data by Shapira (1976) supported these propositions.

Lieberman (1976a) offered a proposal for examining change-induction groups such as psychotherapy groups, encounter groups, self-help groups, and consciousness-raising groups in terms of systems analysis. Five structural characteristics of the system were seen to affect the change-induction process: (1) level of psychological distance between participant and leader; (2) felt causes, sources, and cures of psychological misery; (3) the extent to which the group is seen as a social microcosm; (4) the degree to which members stress differentiation rather than similarity; and (5) the relationship between the cognitive and expressive behavior of the leader.

Bryson and Kelley (1978) offered a systems model for understanding the emergence, stability, and change in legislative leadership and organizations where members select their formal leaders, such as universities, cooperatives, professional associations, and political groups. Building on earlier formulations by Peabody (1976) and Van de Ven (1976), they list (the simplest of models) clusters of individual, processual, structural, and environmental variables likely to be of consequence.

*Rational-Deductive Approach.* Some of the accepted facts about leadership were joined rationally into prescribing what is most likely to succeed—direction or participation—by Vroom and Yetton (1974). They posed ten questions which leaders should ask themselves in deciding whether to be directive or participative in decision making with their subordinates and whether to do so one at a time with individual subordinates or with the whole group all at once. Essentially, they argued that supervisors ought to be directive when they are confident that they know what needs to be done and when their subordinates do not have this knowledge. Furthermore, Vroom and Yetton suggested that in this situation a decision made by the supervisor will be accepted by subordinates. On the other hand, if the subordinates have more of the information than the supervisors, if their acceptance and commitment are of paramount importance, and if subordinates can be trusted to concern themselves with the organization's interests, the supervisor should be participative.

Empirical research deriving from the Bass-Valenzi and Vroom-Yetton models will be presented in Chapter 19.

## IMPLICATIONS

Theorists no longer explain leadership solely in terms of the individual or the group. Rather, it is believed that characteristics of the individual and demands of the situation interact in such a manner as to permit one, or perhaps a few, persons to rise to leadership status. Groups become structured in terms of positions and roles during the course of member interaction. A group is organized to the extent that it acquires differentiated positions and roles. Leadership represents one or more of the differentiated positions in a group. The occupant of a leadership position is expected to play a role that differs from the roles of other group members. The expectancy reinforcement models seem best designed to explain the emergence and persistence of leadership in initially unstructured groups. They attempt to explain what leadership is and how it comes into existence. They do not explain who will emerge as a leader in any particular kind of situation.

In this respect, cognitive theories seem more promising. Whereas behavioral theories of leadership have been seen to be most useful in research, generalizations about the emergence of leadership—cognitive approaches such as those of Green and Mitchell, Bass and Valenzi, and Vroom and Yetton—appear more immediately applicable and relevant to diagnosis and training.

### An Applied Model

Winter (1978, 1979) described a model of leader and management behavior based on a skills test battery and behavioral competency measures for over one thousand naval personnel. Figure 3.1 shows the emergent model, based on empirical cluster analyses and subsequent regression analyses, to link different skills with particular performances. Linkages differed empirically for leaders at different levels. For example, for differences among petty officers, positive expectations as revealed in a series of tests and questionnaires signaled their differential optimization behavior (assigning tasks to those subordinates most likely to do them well and making tradeoffs between task requirements and individual needs). More optimization and goal setting both contributed to more delegation. Increased monitoring resulted in more positive expectations, disciplining, and giving advice and counsel. For commanding and executive officers, more negative expectations also contributed to more optimization. Differential optimization and conceptualization were associated with more monitoring of results. More such monitoring contributed to more feedback, which in turn led to more disciplining and giving advice and counsel.

### Some Problems in Model Evaluation

Research on the traits of leaders tends to rely heavily upon the use of tests, questionnaires, and scales for the collection of data. With the development of the small-group experiment, it became important to know what was happening in the group. Expert or trained observers were used to keep a running record of the behavior of group members, and members themselves also might report their feelings and observations. In some cases, observers merely reported what they saw. In others, they were provided with

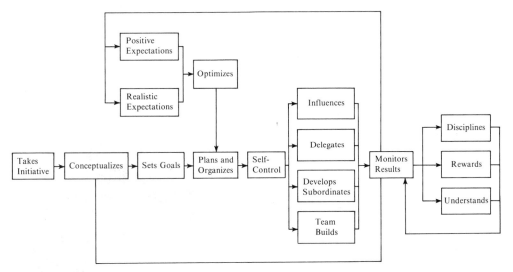

**FIGURE 3.1. Flow Chart of the Navy Leadership and Management Processes in Terms of the Cross-Validated Competencies**

SOURCE: *Adapted from Winter (1978).*

check lists of behaviors or processes to be reported. The most widely used is the set of behavioral categories developed by Bales (1950). Carter and associates (1951), Mann (1961), Bales and Cohen (1980), and others have also developed observational categories.

Observational studies have identified a number of behaviors not anticipated by the trait theorists. Whereas the trait theorists were interested in the subjective aspects of personality dynamics, the group experimenters were concerned with observable behaviors. Perhaps it is not surprising that the two approaches produced somewhat different results.

By now, it is fair to say that every procedure known to social science in general has been applied specifically to the study of leadership. Included have been autobiographical analysis, biographical analysis, case studies, news records, analysis of speeches, biodata analysis, studies of communication patterns, autologs and observer logs of leaders' activities, ratings by observers, superiors, peers, subordinates, and clients, judgments of verbal protocols, and individual interviews.

Particularly promising have been Heller's (1969a) group interviews with managers following questionnaire data analysis to obtain their interpretation of the results. Jacoby (1974) has reported substantial construct validity based on agreement among three methods of assessing opinion leadership: self-designating, sociometric, and key informant.

Research that relates various leader characteristics to different measures of group performance will be discussed in later chapters. In this connection, it may be noted that research on role differentiation and the emergence of leadership in initially unstructured groups has produced a list of characteristics differing somewhat from those investigated by researchers who use tests and questionnaires.

part

# THE LEADER
# AS A PERSON

# LEADERSHIP TRAITS: 1904–1947

Smith and Krueger (100) have surveyed the literature on leadership to 1933. Recent developments in leadership methodology, as related especially to military situations, were reviewed in 1947 by Jenkins (54). The present survey is concerned only with those studies in which some attempt has been made to determine the traits and characteristics of leaders. In many of the studies surveyed leadership was not defined. In others the methods used in the investigation appeared to have little relationship to the problem as stated. An attempt has been made to include all studies bearing on the problem of traits and personal factors associated with leadership. In all except four cases the original book or article has been read and abstracted in detail. The data from one American and three German publications have been derived from competent abstracts.

The present survey lists only those factors which were studied by three or more investigators. Evidence reported by fewer investigators has not been regarded as providing a satisfactory basis for evaluation. It is realized that the number of investigations in which a factor was studied is not necessarily indicative of the importance of the factor. However, the frequency with which a factor was found to be significant appears to be the most satisfactory single criterion for evaluating the data accumulated in this survey, but other criteria, such as the competency of the experimental methods employed and the adequacy of the statistical treatment of data have also been regarded in evaluating the results of a particular study.

In analyzing data obtained from various groups and by various methods the question arises as to the extent to which results may be influenced by differences in social composition of the groups, differences in methodology, and differences in leadership

This chapter is a reprint of "Personal Factors associated with leadership: A survey of the literature," by Ralph M. Stogdill, which appeared in the *Journal of Psychology*, 1948, *25*, 35–71. It is reprinted by permission of The Journal Press, Provincetown, Massachusetts. [This classic is included as it stands in this revised *Handbook of Leadership* since its publication marked the turning point in the study of leadership. Before this date, universal traits of leadership were emphasized. After the publication of this paper, specific situational analyses took over, in fact dominated the field, much more than argued for by Stogdill. As we will see, both individual traits and situational assessments as well as the interaction between them are important, and that was Stogdill's main thesis.

In keeping with the original, citations in Chapter 4 are numbered to make possible easier listings of studies. Year of publication is used in the other chapters. The numbered references will be found at the end of Chapter 4 and also in combined set of references at the back of the book. —BMB]

Research for the paper was supported by a grant from the Office of Naval Research (N6ori-17 T.O III NR171123).

criteria. There is no assurance, for example, that the investigator who analyzes the biographies of great men is studying the same kind of leadership behavior that is revealed through observation of children's leadership activities in group situations. It is of interest, however, that some of the studies employing the two different methods yield remarkably similar results. On the other hand, there are some factors that appear only in certain age and social groups or only when certain methods are employed.

## METHODS

The primary methods which have been employed for the identification and study of the personal characteristics of leaders have been the following: (a) observation of behavior in group situations, (b) choice of associates (voting), (c) nomination of rating by qualified observers, (d) selection (and rating or testing) of persons occupying positions of leadership, and (e) analysis of biographical and case history data. The various studies employing these methods are listed, and the salient details of the methods are briefly described below.

### Observation and Time Sampling of Behavior in Group Situations (21, 22, 40, 47, 49, 50, 55, 63, 73, 78, 81, 89, 112, 115, 118)

In these studies the behavior of two or more individuals is observed in situations which permit the emergence of leadership activities. The situation may be highly structured in advance, as in the studies of children's groups by Henning (49), Luithlen (63), Miller and Dollard (73), and Terman (112); or the situation may be natural and uncontrolled, as in some of the boys' gangs studied by Thrasher (115). The periods of observation may range from five-second periods at definitely spaced intervals to an hour or more of continuous observation. The relative merits of the various time sampling methods have been evaluated by Arrington (2). Chapple and Donald (21) have devised a method for recording the frequency and duration of observed social contacts by executives on a polygraph.

The observational studies which have yielded the most relevant data on leadership are those of Chevaleva-Ianovskaia (22) and the pioneering investigation of Terman (112). Henning (49) has devised a number of ingenious experimental situations for the study of leadership in pairs of children, but the investigations in which these methods are employed have proved disappointingly unproductive.

### Choice of Associates (Voting, Naming, Ranking, Sociometrics) (4, 7, 10, 15, 16, 31, 32, 33, 34, 35, 39, 52, 53, 55, 60, 66, 68, 74, 77, 78, 79, 82, 86, 101, 106, 108, 117, 124)

The usual procedure in these studies, most of which use children or students as subjects, is to ask the members of a group to name the persons whom they would prefer as leaders, and, in some cases, to describe the characteristics of each nominee which make him desirable as a leader. Sociometrics is an extension of this method which involves the construction of a "sociogram" or chart showing graphically the preference relationship of each member to every other member of the group. The outstanding

investigation of this group is that of Jennings (55), who has combined observational with sociometric methods to produce a study of unusual human insight. Another study which is characterized by insight into human behavior is that of Buttgereit (15). Other studies which are outstanding as to methodology and statistical treatment of data are those of Dunkerley (33), Partridge (82), and Tryon (117).

### Nomination by Qualified Observer (3, 14, 23, 25, 26, 57, 80, 88, 95, 96, 102)

In these studies, leaders are named by teachers, club leaders, or other adult observers who are regarded as being in a position to identify the leaders in the groups selected for study. The leaders are compared with the members of control groups. None of the studies employing this method are in any way outstanding.

### Selection of Persons Occupying Positions of Leadership (5, 8, 11, 12, 17, 18, 20, 24, 37, 38, 41, 42, 44, 45, 46, 51, 61, 67, 72, 75, 76, 85, 90, 91, 92, 93, 94, 99, 109, 111, 116, 120, 121)

Leadership in these studies is regarded as synonymous with holding office or some position of responsibility. The majority of the studies use high school or college subjects, and define leadership as holding some office such as president of student body, president of a fraternity or sorority, captain of athletic or debating team, chairman of a club, and the like. However, a number of the studies deal with adults in rural communities and small cities. The study of Carlson and Harrell (18) is concerned with congressmen. Thurstone (116) studied government administrators. The most competent of the studies from the point of view of methodology and treatment of data are those of Bellingrath (5), Caldwell and Wellman (17), Flemming (38), Sward (109) and Thurstone (116).

### Analysis of Biographical and Case History Data (1, 6, 13, 27, 30, 58, 59, 69, 70, 71, 83, 104, 105, 114, 122, 123)

Ackerson (1) and Brown (13) base their studies on the analysis of case histories of delinquent children. The remaining studies are based on the analysis of biographical data. The works of Merriam (69, 70) and Michels (71) might be classified with this group. Outstanding contributions based on these methods are those of Ackerson (1) and Cox (27).

### The Listing of Traits Considered Essential to Leadership (29, 41, 48, 56, 107, 110)

In all of these studies except that of Jones (56) the authors have asked different groups of persons, usually business executives and members of the professions, to list the traits which they believe to be essential to leadership. Little uniformity is found among the items contained in such lists. Only intelligence, initiative, and responsibility are mentioned twice each among the top five items in the lists reported by Gowin (41), Heath and Gregory (48), Jones (56), and Starch (107).

*Supplementary Aspects of Methodology*

Various supplementary measures have been employed in an effort to determine the traits associated with leadership. The most frequently used are tests of intelligence and personality; but questionnaires, rating scales, and interviews have been utilized in some cases. For purposes of reference, the various studies employing these methods are listed below.

  *a.* Standardized tests.
  1. Intelligence tests (1, 8, 12, 28, 37, 50, 66, 67, 68, 78, 82, 88, 90, 91, 118).
  2. Personality tests (7, 14, 25, 26, 45, 46, 62, 75, 92, 93, 94).
  3. Intelligence and personality tests (9, 17, 33, 34, 52, 53, 65, 98, 109, 116).
  *b.* Questionnaires (5, 11, 23, 24, 29, 41, 42, 48, 60, 102, 111).
  *c.* Rating scales (3, 4, 27, 32, 34, 35, 36, 38, 40, 42, 57, 72, 80, 82, 91, 95, 97, 113, 117, 119, 120, 124).
  *d.* Interviews (11, 13, 20, 51, 76, 78, 88, 96, 106, 109).
  *e.* Factor analysis (9, 18, 26, 33, 38, 43, 116, 117).

*Age Groups Studied*

For purposes of reference and evaluation the various investigations are classified below according to age groups studied.

  *a.* Preschool age (40, 47, 81).
  *b.* Elementary school age (1, 7, 15, 50, 61, 64, 66, 68, 73, 78, 79, 82, 85, 89, 112, 117, 118).
  *c.* High school age (1, 3, 5, 11, 12, 13, 15, 16, 17, 23, 24, 34, 35, 37, 38, 39, 55, 61, 64, 78, 82, 85, 86, 88, 90, 91, 94, 95, 96, 101, 102, 108, 117, 120).
  *d.* College students (4, 8, 14, 32, 33, 36, 44, 45, 48, 52, 53, 57, 65, 67, 72, 74, 75, 77, 80, 92, 97, 98, 106, 109, 119, 124).
  *e.* Adults (6, 18, 20, 21, 25, 26, 29, 30, 41, 42, 46, 51, 52, 58, 59, 69, 70, 71, 76, 83, 93, 99, 103, 104, 105, 107, 110, 111, 114, 116, 122, 123).

RESULTS

The results of this survey are presented in the form of discussions of the evidence accumulated on those factors which were studied by three or more investigators. When contradictory evidence is presented, the bibliographic references are listed to show separately those studies presenting positive, negative, and neutral data respectively.

*Chronological Age*

  *a.* Leaders found to be younger (3, 5, 37, 39, 53, 90).
  *b.* Leaders found to be older (5, 15, 40, 41, 75, 78, 79, 81, 82, 124).
  *c.* No differences found (1, 11).
  *d.* Differs with situation (17).

The evidence as to the relation of age to leadership is quite contradictory. Pigors (84) observes that leadership does not appear in children before the age of two or three years, and even then usually takes the form of overt domination. Active leadership of a group seldom appears before the age of nine or ten, at which age the formation of groups and gangs may become a noticeable feature in the social development of children. According to Pigors the four following stages are necessary for the appearance of leadership in children: (1) development of determination and self-control; (2) grasp of abstractions and social ideals; (3) awareness of personalities; and (4) sufficient memory span to pursue remote goals rather than immediate objectives. Arrington (2), however, finds no evidence from a survey of time sampling experiments to support the proposition that leadership increases with age in preschool children.

Baldwin (3), Finch and Carroll (37), Garrison (39), Hunter and Jordan (53), and Remmelin (90) find leaders to be younger than their followers. In the latter two studies these differences are statistically reliable. Bellingrath (5) finds girl leaders to be younger than nonleaders, but boy leaders to be older. Leaders are found to be older than followers by Buttgereit (15), Goodenough (40), Gowin (41), Moore (75), Newstetter (78), Nutting (79), Parten (81), Partridge (82), and Zeleny (124). Gowin found outstanding executives to be 12.2 years older on the average than the average of lesser executives. Ackerson (1) and Brown (11) do not find leaders and followers to be differentiated on the basis of age. The correlation coefficients reported by a number of these authors are shown in Table 4.1. These correlation coefficients range from −.32 to .71, with the average coefficient being approximately .21.

**TABLE 4.1**
**Correlation of Variables with Leadership**

| Author | IQ | Grades | Age | Height | Weight |
|---|---|---|---|---|---|
| Ackerson (boys) | .18 | | −.01 | | |
| (girls) | .32 | | −.11 | | |
| Bellingrath (boys) | −.14* | .05* | .27 | .17 | .25 |
| (girls) | | | −.32 | .44 | .42 |
| Drake | .47 | | | | |
| Eichler | .06 | .12 | .21 | | |
| Flemming | .44 | | | | |
| Garrison (School 1) | | .30 | −.12 | −.02 | −.02 |
| (School 2) | | .36 | −.25 | −.13 | −.04 |
| Goodenough | .10 | | .71 | .71 | .52 |
| Howell | .08 | .39 | | | |
| Levi (Elem.) | .26 | −.27 | | | |
| (Jr. H.S.) | .25 | −.00 | | | |
| Newstetter | .17 | | .45 | | |
| Nutting | .90 | .11 | .20 | | |
| Parten | .34 | | .67 | .67 | |
| Partridge | .54 | | .55 | .43 | .46 |
| Reynolds | .22 | .27 | | | |
| Sheldon | .06 | .19 | | .05 | .02 |
| Zeleny | .44 | | .49 | .35 | .20 |

*Total scores of boys and girls combined.

According to Caldwell and Wellman (17), the relationship of age to leadership differs in various situations. Leaders in athletics are found to be close to the class average in age, while boy editors and student council members are younger than average, as are girl club leaders and student council and citizenship representatives. In view of these various findings, chronological age cannot be regarded as a factor which is correlated with leadership in any uniform direction or degree.

### Height

a. Leaders found to be taller (5, 34, 40, 41, 75, 81, 82, 97, 124).
b. Leaders found to be shorter (39, 53).
c. No differences found (3, 91).
d. Depends upon situation (17).

Inspection of Table 4.1 reveals correlations between height and leadership ranging from − .13 to .71. The general trend of these studies is to indicate a low positive relationship between height and leadership, the average correlation being about .30. Hunter and Jordan (53) and Garrison (39) find student leaders to be somewhat shorter than nonleaders, and Baldwin (3) and Reynolds (91) find no relation between height and leadership in students.

### Weight

a. Leaders found to be heavier (3, 5, 40, 41, 82, 97, 124).
b. Leaders found to be lighter (53, 75).
c. No differences found (39, 97).

The correlation coefficients shown in Table 4.1 suggest a low positive relationship between weight and leadership. The average correlation coefficient is about .23. Hunter and Jordan (53) find leaders to be significantly lighter than nonleaders. Garrison (39) and Moore (75) also report leaders to be somewhat lighter than followers, although the differences are not significant.

### Physique, Energy, Health

a. Physique (6, 57, 79, 97, 119).
b. Athletic ability, physical prowess (15, 38, 82, 87, 106, 115, 119).
c. Energy (5, 13, 27, 108, 120).
d. Health (3, 5, 88, 108).
e. Health and physical condition not a factor (1, 3, 8, 53).

Bernard (6), Kohs and Irle (57), Nutting (79), Sheldon (97), and Webb (119) report that superior physique is a characteristic of leaders. However, the correlation coefficients of .28, .18, .114, and .23 reported by Kohs and Irle (57), Nutting (79), Sheldon (97), and Webb (119) respectively suggest that this relationship is very slight. Bowden (8) concludes from the results of his study of college students that leadership is not the result of a dominating physique. Baldwin (3) finds that high school leaders do not differ from followers in freedom from physical defects.

Leaders, according to Baldwin (3), Bellingrath (5), Reals (88), and Stray (108) appear to have some advantage over nonleaders in possessing better health, although Ackerson (1) and Hunter and Jordan (53) do not find health to be a differentiating factor.

Athletic ability and physical prowess do appear to be associated with leadership status in boys' gangs and groups. Evidence to this effect is presented by Buttgereit (15), Flemming (38), Partridge (82), Puffer (87), Spaulding (106), Thrasher (115), and Webb (119). Coefficients of correlation of .38, .62, and .40 between athletic ability and leadership are reported by Flemming, Partridge, and Webb respectively.

According to Bellingrath (5), Brown (13), Cox (27), Stray (108), and Wetzel (120), leaders are also characterized by a high rate of energy output. Cox (27) finds various groups of great leaders to differ markedly in physique, energy output, and athletic prowess, with only the military leaders being outstanding in these traits.

### Appearance

a. Leaders present a better appearance (3, 4, 6, 11, 33, 38, 80, 82, 88, 112, 117).
b. Leaders are better dressed (33, 112).
c. No relationship found (124).
d. Appearance negatively correlated with leadership (1, 40).

The evidence presented in these studies suggests a possible relationship between appearance and leadership. Dunkerley (33) found that students chosen as leaders in social activities differed significantly from nonleaders in appearance and dress, but students chosen as leaders in intellectual and religious activities did not differ markedly from nonleaders in these respects. Partridge (82) found a correlation of .81 between appearance ratings and leadership status. A correlation of .21 between attractive appearance and leadership is reported by Flemming (38), but the correlation between beautiful and leadership is .05. Tryon's (117) study suggests that appearance is more closely associated with leadership in boys than in girls. She reports correlation coefficients of .49 and .06 respectively for 15-year-old boys and girls, while the correlation coefficients for 12-year-old boys and girls are .31 and .08 respectively. In Goodenough's (40) study, beauty was found to be negatively correlated with leadership in preschool children, the correlation coefficient being −.20. Ackerson (1) reports correlation coefficients of .12 and −.06 between slovenly and leadership for boys and girls respectively, while slovenly and leading others into misconduct are correlated .32 and .31 for delinquent boys and girls.

### Fluency of Speech (6, 14, 22, 40, 45, 60, 65, 70, 98, 112, 116, 117, 124)

Baldwin (3) reports a definite trend for leaders to be rated by their teachers as confident in tone of voice, while nonleaders tend to be rated as lacking in confidence as to tone of voice. A factor analysis (38) of teachers' ratings of high school leaders reveals "pleasant voice" as one of the four factors found to be associated with leadership. Flemming (38) reports a correlation of .28 between "pleasing voice" and leadership in high school students. Partridge (82) reports that boy leaders can be reliably distinguished from nonleaders when taken into the presence of strange boys hidden from view so that judgments must be made on speech alone. However, Fay and Middleton (36), in repeating this experiment under somewhat similar conditions, found a correlation of only .08 between leadership ratings and degree of leadership as estimated by voice alone. Eichler (34) also reports a correlation of −.112 between voice and leadership.

Talkativeness and leadership are reported by Tryon (117) to be correlated to the extent of .41 and .31 for 12-year-old boys and girls respectively, while the correlation coefficients for 15-year-old boys and girls are .15 and .44 respectively. In Goodenough's (40) study a correlation of .61 between talkativeness and leadership is found. Thurstone (116) did not find highly paid administrators to surpass their lesser well-paid associates in word fluency test scores but he did find a significant difference in linguistic ability test scores. Simpson (98) also reports verbal ability to be correlated with capacity to influence others. The correlation coefficient is .45.

Chevaleva-Ianovskaia (22) finds that child leaders are characterized by longer duration of verbal excitation. Terman (112) reports that leaders are more fluent of speech, and Leib (60) finds leaders to excel in speaking ability. The same skills are reported in adult leaders by Bernard (6) and Merriam (70). Zeleny (124) reports a correlation of .59 between leadership ratings and total remarks made in class. Interesting conversation and leadership are correlated .28 in Flemming's (38) study. Further evidence is found in the studies of Burks (14) and Malloy (65), who report that vividness and originality of expression and facility of conversation are associated with successful social relationships. Considering the size of the erxperimental groups, the competence of the experimental methods employed, and the positive nature of the evidence presented, it would appear that fluency of speech, if not tone of voice, is a factor to be considered in the study of leadership. It has long been recognized that effective leadership cannot be maintained in an organization without an adequate system of intercommunication. Thus, it does not seem surprising that some of the most searching studies of leadership should reveal the capacity for ready communication as one of the skills associated with leadership status.

### Intelligence

*a.* Leaders brighter (1, 11, 12, 27, 33, 38, 40, 50, 53, 57, 67, 78, 79, 81, 82, 91, 97, 101, 109, 112, 113, 119, 124).
*b.* No difference (5, 11, 34, 52, 98).
*c.* Too great differences militate against leadership (37, 50, 64, 67, 118).

All except four of these studies present evidence which indicates that the average child or student leader surpasses the average member of his group in intelligence. Statistically reliable differences are reported by Hunter and Jordan (53), Remmelin (90), and Sward (109). In most of these studies there is considerable overlapping of intelligence test scores, indicating that superior intelligence is not an absolute requirement for leadership. Nevertheless, the general trend of the findings indicate that leadership status is more often than not associated with superiority in intelligence. The correlation coefficients shown in Table 4.1 reveal a consistently positive relationship. The average of these coefficients is approximately .28.

Recent factorial studies reveal a number of points which may be of considerable significance for the future study of leadership. Cattell (19), for example, reports that the intelligence factor is heavily weighted with such character elements as wise, emotionally mature, persevering, mentally alert, vigorous, conscientious, etcetera. These items correspond fairly closely to the factors which are found in the present survey to be supported by an excess of positive over negative evidence. Thorndike (114) reports a correlation of .60 between intellectual ability and estimability of character in 305 male members of European royal families. Thus, it appears that high intelligence may be associated with other characteristics which contribute toward a person's value as a leader.

One of the most significant findings concerning the relation of intelligence to leadership is that extreme discrepancies between the intelligence of potential leaders and their followers militate against the exercise of leadership. Hollingworth (50) found that "among children with a mean IQ of 100, the IQ of the leader is likely to fall between 115 and 130 IQ. That is, the leader is likely to be more intelligent, but *not too much more* intelligent than the average of the group led." Observation further showed that a child of 160 IQ has very little chance of being a popular leader in a group of children of average intelligence but may become a leader in a group of children with a mean IQ of 130. One of the difficulties in this connection seems to be communication. The average child cannot comprehend a large part of the vocabulary employed by a child of unusually superior intelligence to express exact meanings in relation to his more mature and complicated interests. Differences in interests, goals, and activity patterns also act as barriers to joint participation, which is a necessary condition for group leadership. Hollingworth's findings are confirmed by a number of investigations. Finch and Carroll (37), studying groups of sixty-six gifted, sixty-six superior, and sixty-six average children, arrive at the conclusion that "given a superior group of children to lead, the leading will tend to be done by the gifted children," even though the leaders as a group tend to be younger than the group led. In an early study of the formation of boys' gangs, Warner (118) found that leaders and followers differ much more in chronological age than in mental age. She observed that older boys with mentalities below normal tend to group with younger boys who have a mental age near their own and slightly higher, and that when groups of retarded delinquent boys contact groups of brighter delinquents the contacts are "so short and non-social that no noticeable event takes place." Maller (64), studying cooperation and competition among children, found that homogeneity of intelligence rather than level of intelligence is important in cooperative behavior. McCuen (67) studied leadership in fifty-eight college student organizations. He found that "there is a tendency to select leaders with scores slightly above the average of their respective groups." He concludes that "the crowd seems to desire to be led by the average person. Evidently in a democratic society the leader must not be too far detached from the group."

Two studies by Lehman (58, 59) are of interest in this connection. In the earlier study he determined the age intervals at which outstanding men in various professions made their best contributions. In the second study he determined the optimal age intervals for eminent leadership. Chemists, for example, were found to make their best contributions during the age intervals 28–32 years, while the optimal ages for eminent leadership in chemistry are 45–49 years. Thus it appears that even in science, a man's contributions and communications must be understood by, and in accord with the thinking of, his contemporaries in order for him to rise to a position of leadership in his profession.

*Scholarship*

a. Leaders make better scholastic records (1, 3, 5, 15, 17, 28, 33, 39, 52, 53, 75, 80, 90, 91, 97, 98, 109, 112, 119, 120, 121, 123).
b. Leaders make poorer scholastic records (79).
c. No differences found (5, 24, 34, 57).

Leaders are found, with a high degree of uniformity, to make better average scholastic grades than do nonleaders. These results are not surprising in light of the fact that leaders are found to be more intelligent on the average than their followers. The findings by such investigators as Buttgereit (15), Caldwell (17) and others suggest that superior scholarship may not be a mere byproduct of superior intelligence, but may possess direct value for leadership status when it comprises one aspect of a general ability to get things done. There is also a suggestion that superior accomplishment along lines that are valued by the group carries prestige value which may also contribute toward leadership status. But there is an abundance of evidence which indicates that a position of leadership is ordinarily not founded upon superior intelligence and accomplishment alone since these two factors may be present to a high degree in many persons who do not occupy positions of leadership. The magnitude of the correlation coefficients shown in Table 4.1 suggests that intelligence and scholarship account for only a fraction of the total complex of factors associated with leadership status.

*Knowledge (10, 14, 15, 16, 31, 38, 71, 79, 89, 108, 124)*

The results of these studies suggest that persons chosen as leaders tend to be those who know how to get things done. Of particular interest is Caldwell's (16) experiment in which he asked 282 high school pupils to nominate boy and girl leaders for three different situations: (1) a trip to the wharf; (2) the production and presentation of a program before a neighboring school and; (3) the reorganization of a program for administering athletics in the school. There was revealed ''a clear judgment on the part of these pupils as to the members of the group best fitted to lead them.'' The most important abilities ascribed to these leaders were intelligence and practical knowledge relative to the situations for which they were chosen as leaders. In this connection it seems worthwhile to consider the findings of Baldwin (3) and Burks (14) relative to the association between leadership and the ability to make constructive and creative suggestions. Burks, for example, finds that ability to present constructive ideas relative to difficult situations is closely associated with successful social relationships. Also in this connection should be considered the studies of Cox (27), Drake (32), Flemming (38), Stray (108), and Thrasher (115), who find that originality and constructive imagination are characteristics of leaders. Additional evidence relative to the ability to get things done is presented by Bellingrath (5) and Dunkerley (33). Cox (27) and Peck (83) report that great leaders are characterized and differentiated from the average by greater intensity of application and industry. In summarizing the results of these various studies, it appears that specialized knowledge and ability to get things done are factors which contribute toward leadership status.

*Judgment and Decision*

*a.* Soundness and finality of judgment (5, 32, 33, 38, 119).
*b.* Speed and accuracy of thought and decision (26, 33, 45, 119).

In view of the positive correlations found between intelligence and leadership, it is not surprising to find a similar relationship between judgment and leadership. Bellingrath (5), Drake (32), and Webb (119) report correlations ranging from .34 to .69 between common sense and leadership, while Bellingrath (5), Drake (32), Flemming (38), and Webb (119) report correlations of .60, .34, .28, and .69 respectively between judgment and leadership. Farsightedness and leadership are found to be correlated to the extent of .55, .25, and .33 in the studies of Bellingrath, Drake, and Webb. Two of the factor analysis studies, those of Cowley (26) and Dunkerley (33), reveal soundness and finality of judgment as a factor common to leaders. In addition to the judgment factor, Cowley (26) also found three factors which appeared to represent speed of decision. In spite of the small number of studies bearing on judgment and decision, the general competence of the methods employed lends confidence to the results obtained. Hanawalt, Richardson, and Hamilton (45) find that leaders use the "?" or "undecided" response on the Bernreuter test significantly less frequently than nonleaders, and this tendency is especially noticeable on the most differentiating items.

*Insight*

*a.* Keenly alive to environment, alert (13, 15, 17, 27, 33, 35).
*b.* Ability to evaluate situations (8, 15, 22, 70, 116).
*c.* Social insight (8, 47, 55, 84, 124).
*d.* Self-insight (27, 77).
*e.* Sympathetic understanding (10, 14, 38, 47, 55, 74, 119).

Traditionally, insight has been regarded as one aspect of general intelligence. However, the discussion of Jennings (55) and others suggests that insight may be socially conditioned to a high degree. Some of the most competent investigators of the leadership problem have contributed evidence which suggests that insight and awareness are factors associated with leadership ability. Brown (13), Buttgereit (15), Caldwell and Wellman (17), Cox (27), Dunkerley (33), and Fauquier and Gilchrist (35) find that leaders are characterized by alertness and keen awareness of environment. Ability to evaluate situations is found to be a factor in the studies of Bowden (8), Buttgereit (15), Chevaleva-Ianovskaia (22), Merriam and Gosnell (70), and Thurstone (116). Less clearly defined is social insight, reported to be a factor associated with leadership in the studies of Bowden (8), Hanfmann (47), Jennings (55), Pigors (84), and Zeleny (124). "Studies the motives of others" is an item found by Brogden (9) and Guilford (43) to measure Guilford's *T* factor, which is described as intellectual leadership or thinking introversion. The results of these various studies suggest that alertness to the surrounding environment and understanding of situations are intimately associated with leadership ability, yet very little is understood regarding the nature of these processes. No worker who is responsible for improving the social effectiveness of individuals can fail to be impressed by the persistent blindness of maladapted individuals to the social situations in which they are attempting to adjust. From the point of view of understanding personal qualifications for leadership, it would appear that one question which is in need of thorough investigation is that concerning the fundamental nature of awareness and social insight.

### Originality (5, 14, 27, 32, 38, 108, 119)

Although the number of studies containing data on this trait is rather small, the magnitude of the correlations found suggests that the relationship between originality and leadership is worthy of further investigation. The correlation coefficients reported by Bellingrath (5), Drake (32), Flemming (38), and Webb (119) range from .38 to .70, and are higher on the average than those for any other trait except popularity. Cox (27) finds great leaders to rate unusually high in originality.

### Adaptability (8, 14, 17, 21, 22, 34, 38, 47, 70, 85)

These studies suggest that ready adaptability to changing situations is a factor which may be associated with leadership capacity, although the correlation coefficients of .13 and .21 reported by Eichler (34) and Flemming (38) are not impressive. Ability to adjust to situations has also been regarded traditionally as an aspect of general intelligence but, as described in the references considered here, this factor appears to contain a large social component. This fact has long been recognized by clinical observers, who have repeatedly pointed out that persons of high intelligence may be rendered ineffectual in their vocational, social, and other adjustments through extreme self-preoccupation and inhibition to action, the latter of which is found to be negatively correlated with leadership.

### Introversion-Extroversion

*a*. Leaders found to be more extroverted (17, 40, 75, 92, 109).
*b*. Leaders found to be more introverted (27, 72).
*c*. No differences found (5, 32, 53, 90).

The only studies which report a marked relationship between extroversion and leadership are those of Goodenough (40) and Sward (104). Goodenough reports a correlation of .46 between extroversion and leadership in children. Sward finds that leaders rate reliably higher than nonleaders in extroversion as rated on the Heidbreder scale. Richardson and Hanawalt (92) find that college leaders rate reliably lower in introversion that the Bernreuter norms and also lower than nonleaders, although the difference between leaders and nonleaders is not significant. Hunter and Jordan (53) and Remmelin (90) also report that Bernreuter introversion scores do not differentiate leaders from nonleaders. Middleton (72) finds leaders rating low in extroversion, while Bellingrath (5) and Drake (32) find no significant correlations between introversion-extroversion scores and leadership.

All the groups of great leaders except soldier-statesmen in Cox's (27) study are rated as introverted, with soldier-fighters rating very high in introversion. Thurstone's (116) study of Washington administrators revealed successful administrators as rating higher than less successful administrators in Guilford's (43) *T* factor, which is measured by such items as "introspective, analyzes himself," "often in a meditative state," "analyzes the motives of others," and "not more interested in athletics than in intellectual pursuits." Brogden and Thomas (9) add to this last such items as "he does not want anyone to be with him when he receives bad news," "he does not try to find someone to cheer him up when in low spirits," "prefers to make hurried decisions alone." These items are of interest when considered in relation to the findings on mood control. In view of the diversity of findings it appears very doubtful that leaders can be described with any degree of uniformity in terms of introversion-extroversion.

Much the same situation exists in regard to self-sufficiency. Hunter and Jordan (53) and Richardson and Hanawalt (93) find that leaders make high self-sufficiency scores on the Bernreuter test, but Dunkerley (33), Remmelin (90), and Richardson and Hanawalt (92) find no significant differences.

### Dominance

*a.* Leaders found to be more dominant, ascendant (1, 8, 21, 27, 32, 53, 75, 90, 92, 93, 117).
*b.* Bossy, domineering persons rejected as leaders (10, 16, 47, 55).
*c.* No differences found (34, 119).

The evidence concerning the relationship of dominance to leadership is contradictory. Cox (27) and Drake (32) find "desire to impose will" to be associated with leadership, but Webb (119) reports a zero-order correlation between those two factors. Ackerson (1) reports a correlation of approximately .20 between bossiness and leadership in problem children. Leadership and bossiness are related to some extent in the children studied by Tryon (117), who reports correlations of .28 and .29 between these two factors for 15-year-old boys and girls respectively. Chapple and Donald (21), Richardson and Hanawalt (92, 93), and Hunter and Jordan (53) find leaders to be significantly more dominant than nonleaders. Small but positive differences in ascendance are reported by Bowden (8) and Moore (75). Eichler (34), however, finds that leaders and nonleaders do not differ in dominance. Still stronger contradictory evidence is presented by Broich (10), Jennings (55), and Hanfmann (47) who find that bossy, domineering persons are rejected as leaders. Caldwell (16) reports that high school pupils express preference for leaders who can keep order without being bossy. These findings indicate that leadership cannot be defined in terms of personal dominance.

### Initiative, Persistence, Ambition

*a.* Initiative and willingness to assume responsibility (1, 5, 14, 15, 18, 32, 33, 45, 74, 97, 108, 120).
*b.* Persistence in the fact of obstacles (5, 15, 27, 32, 71, 72, 74, 84, 85, 97, 119, 124).
*c.* Ambition, desire to excel (3, 5, 6, 27, 32, 44, 119).
*d.* Application and industry (5, 18, 27, 33, 38, 83).

All except one of the studies in which initiative was found to be a trait ascribed to leaders were investigations in which student leaders were nominated by their associates and the traits which were thought to make them desirable as leaders were described. The study of Carlson and Harrell (18) represents some departure from this method, in that fifty-three Washington correspondents were asked to name the ten ablest senators and ten ablest representatives in rank order, and to rate them from 1 to 10 on integrity, intelligence, industry, and influence. A factor analysis of these ratings revealed Factor I to be heavily loaded with industry and influence, and might be called push or aggressiveness. Industry and leadership are correlated .55 and .16 in the studies of Bellingrath (5) and Flemming (38). Dunkerley's (33) factor analysis also reveals a trait cluster identified as initiative which is descriptive of intellectual and social leaders, but not religious leaders. Drake (32) and Sheldon (97) report correlations of .56 and .52 between aggressiveness and leadership.

Cox (27) finds that great face-to-face leaders are characterized to an outstanding degree by "persistence in the face of obstacles," "capacity to work with distant objects in view," "degree of strength of will or perseverance," and "tendency not to abandon tasks from mere changeability." Pigors (84) finds that the development of determination and sufficient memory span to pursue remote goals rather than immediate objectives are necessary conditions for the appearance of leadership in children. The remainder of the studies which present evidence on this point represent a variety of points of view. Pinard (85), in an experimental study of perseveration in 194 "difficult" children, ages 8 to 15, found that of twenty-four leaders, seventeen belonging to the moderate nonperseverator group were rated as more reliable, self-controlled and persistent, and as the most constructive leaders. Drake (32) and Webb (119) find correlations of .23 and .59 between leadership and strength of will. Webb (119) reports a correlation of .70 between leadership and "persistence in overcoming obstacles," and of .53 between leadership and persistence. In Bellingrath's (5) study of high school students, persistence is found to be correlated with leadership to the extent of .68, while Eichler (34) and Sheldon (97) report correlations of .23 and .339 between leadership and persistence. An interesting sidelight is presented in Ackerson's (1) study of problem children, among whom stubbornness was correlated with leadership to the extent of .15 for boys and .12 for girls.

Cox (27) also presents evidence which indicates that great face-to-face leaders, such as soldiers, religious leaders, and statesmen, are characterized to an outstanding degree by "desire to excel at performances." Hanawalt and Hamilton (44), in a study of twenty college leaders and twenty nonleaders, found that level of aspiration of leaders is significantly higher than that of nonleaders. Coefficients of correlation of .47, .29, and .64 between leadership and desire to excel are reported by Webb (119), Drake (32), and Bellingrath (5) respectively.

That leadership is related to work, rather than to passive status or position, is suggested by the fact that a number of investigators have found leaders to rate high in application and industry. Cox (27) finds great leaders to rank unusually high in this respect. The correlation coefficients reported by Bellingrath (5), Flemming (38), and Webb (119) range from .16 to .55.

*Responsibility (1, 3, 5, 14, 16, 27, 32, 33, 38, 55, 74, 79, 82, 85, 108, 119, 120)*

Student leaders are found to rate somewhat higher than followers in dependability, trustworthiness, and reliability in carrying out responsibilities in the studies of Baldwin

(3), Bellingrath (5), Burks (14), Caldwell (16), Dunkerley (33), Moore (74), Nutting (79), Pinard (85), and Wetzel (120). Trustworthiness and leadership are correlated .64 in Webb's (119) study, .37 in Drake's (32) study, and .10 in Flemming's (38) study. Correlations of .42, .21, and .53 between conscientiousness and leadership are reported by Webb (119), Drake (32), and Bellingrath (5) respectively. Partridge (82) reports a correlation of .87 between dependability and leadership. Jennings (55) finds that the girls chosen as leaders tend to be those who inspire confidence. Cox (27) finds all groups of great face-to-face leaders rating high in trustworthiness and conscientiousness, with religious leaders rating outstandingly high in these traits.

*Integrity and Conviction*

a. Integrity, fortitude (6, 18, 27, 70, 72, 83).
b. Strength of convictions (17, 20, 27, 71, 74, 98, 119).

Intellectual fortitude and integrity of character represent traits which are apparently associated with eminent leadership in maturity. All the studies which contribute evidence on this point are concerned with outstanding adult leaders, except that of Middleton (72), who found that "character" is one of the traits associated with leadership in college students.

Michels (71) reports that strength of convictions is also a characteristic of successful political leaders. Cox (27) finds that the great face-to-face leader is characterized to an outstanding degree by "absence of readiness to accept the sentiments of his associates." This trait is especially conspicuous in revolutionary statesmen. Webb (119) reports a correlation of $-.32$ between leadership and acceptance of sentiments of others. Caldwell and Wellman (17) find that one of the characteristics of high school leaders is insistence upon acceptance of their ideas and plans.

Adult leaders, in a community studied by Chapin (20), appeared to hold opinions similar in general to those of the group but they "expressed the trends of opinion of the rank and file more sharply, more decisively, and more consistently." Simpson (98), in a study of those who influence and those who are influenced in discussion, found that influence score correlated $-.41$ with influenceability score. It appears that persons in various types of groups may be valued as leaders because they know what they want to accomplish and are not likely to be swayed from their convictions.

The evidence on liberalism-conservatism suggests that the attitudes which will be regarded as acceptable in leaders are largely determined by the nature of the situation. Hunter and Jordan (53) found college student leaders to be somewhat more liberal than nonleaders in attitudes toward social questions. Newcomb (77) reports that in a college where liberalism is a tradition and ideal those women students having the most prestige are regarded as most liberal. Middleton (72), on the other hand, reports campus leaders to be rated low in radicalism. In Thurstone's (116) study of Washington administrators the Allport-Vernon Social Values scale was found to be the most effective of a battery of seventy-five tests in differentiating higher salaried from lower salaried administrators. Successful administrators rated significantly higher in social and theoretically values and significantly lower in economic and religious values. Drake (32) and Webb (119) have found low positive correlations between leadership and interest in religion.

*Self-Confidence*

a. Self-assurance (5, 15, 26, 27, 32, 74, 92, 93, 117, 119, 124).
b. Absence of modesty (1, 27, 38, 72, 117, 119).

The authors reporting data on the relationship of self-confidence to leadership are uniform in the positive direction of their findings. The following correlation coefficients are reported: .58 by Bellingrath (5), .59 by Drake (32), and .12 by Webb (119). Cowley (26) found self-confidence to be one of six factors possessed in common by three widely different types of leaders. Cox (27) finds great leaders to be characterized to an unusual degree by such traits as self-confidence, esteem of own special talents, and tendency to rate them correctly. Buttgereit (15), Moore (74), and Zeleny (124) also report leaders to rate high in self-confidence. Richardson and Hanawalt (92, 93) find college and adult leaders to make higher self-confidence scores on the Bernreuter test than nonleaders. Hunter and Jordan (53) and Remmelin (90) do not find Bernreuter self-confidence scores to differentiate between leaders and nonleaders. Tryon (117) describes leaders as assured in class and as assured with adults.

Sward (109) finds that inferiority scores on the Heidbreder rating scale do not differentiate leaders from nonleaders, although women leaders rate themselves higher in inferiority attitudes than do their associates. Ackerson (1) reports correlations of − .02 and .08 between inferiority feelings and leadership in boys and girls.

The following findings suggest that leaders tend to be persons who are not handicapped by an excessive degree of modesty. Cox (27) reports that great military leaders and statesmen are characterized to a greater than average degree by eagerness for the admiration of the crowd, and desire for the limelight, although they exhibit offensive manifestations of self-esteem to a lesser degree than average. Middleton (72) also finds leaders to rate low in modesty. A correlation of − .09 between leadership and modesty is reported by Flemming (38). Eagerness for admiration is correlated − .16 with leadership in Webb's (119) study, while Drake (32) reports a correlation of − .11 between conceit and leadership. Both Ackerson (1) and Tryon (117) report positive correlations between leadership and attention-getting or show-off tendencies. These correlation coefficients range from .15 to .30. The general trend of these findings suggests that leaders rate higher than their followers in self-confidence and self-esteem.

*Mood Control, Mood Optimism*

a. Controlled in mood, seldom gloomy (17, 55, 65, 119).
b. Moods not controlled (1, 27).
c. Happy, cheerful disposition (32, 40, 117, 119).
d. Happiness not a factor (1, 3).
e. Sense of humor (14, 32, 38, 108, 117, 119).

Jennings (55) states that one of the characteristics of girl leaders in an institution is the ability to control their own moods so as not to impose their negative feelings, depressions, and anxieties on others. Caldwell and Wellman (17) and Malloy (65) also find leaders to be characterized by constancy of mood. Webb (119) reports a correlation of − .45 between depression and leadership. Ackerson (1) and Cox (27), however, report some association between leadership and moods of depression, although not to a significant degree, and the extent differs with different groups.

Drake (32), Tryon (117), and Webb (119) find that a cheerful, happy disposition is associated with leadership. These authors report correlation coefficients ranging from .29 to .60 between leadership and cheerfulness. Ackerson (1) and Baldwin (3) do not find cheerfulness to be a distinguishing factor in leadership. Ackerson (1) finds that "unhappy" and "leadership" are correlated − .03 for boys and .06 for girls. Drake (32), Flemming (38), Tryon (117), and Webb (119) report correlation coefficients ranging from .34 to .64 between leadership and sense of humor. Stray (108) also finds leaders to be characterized by a sense of humor. Goodenough's (40) finding of a correlation of .53 between leadership and laughter is also relevant to this subject.

The scarcity of evidence concerning the relation of mood control to leadership cannot be regarded as confirmation of its unimportance. The evidence available suggests that mood control may be significantly related to leadership effectiveness. The question appears to warrant thorough investigation.

*Emotional Control*

a. Leaders found to be more stable and emotionally controlled (3, 5, 8, 17, 32, 34, 72, 84, 112, 119, 120).
b. Leaders found to be less well controlled (1, 27, 35, 97, 117).
c. No differences found (32, 38, 124).

A number of manuals which outline the practical techniques for gaining friends and becoming a leader regard self-control as a very important prerequisite for attaining these goals. The evidence relating to this contention is divided. Eichler (34) reports a correlation of .18 between leadership and self-control. Baldwin (3), Pigors (84), and Wetzel (120) also find self-control to be a factor related to leadership. Bellingrath (5) and Drake (32) report correlation coefficients of .70 and .38 respectively between leadership and stability. Leaders are found by Middleton (72) and Terman (112) to rate low in emotionality, while Bowden (8) and Caldwell and Wellman (17) find leaders to be well balanced and self-composed in comparison with their followers. Webb (119) reports correlations of − .25 between irritability and leadership, and − .36 between readiness for anger and leadership.

Cox (27), however, finds great face-to-face leaders to rate high in degree of excitability. This trait is present to an unusual degree in revolutionary statesmen. Ackerson (1) reports correlation coefficients of .12 for boys and .36 for girls between irritability and leadership in problem children. A correlation of .16 between leadership and excitability was found by Sheldon (97). Fauquier and Gilchrist (35) also report leaders to be more excitable than nonleaders. Zeleny (124) finds no difference between leaders and nonleaders in degree of emotional control. Drake (32) and Flemming (38) report zero-order coefficients of correlation between leadership and excitability.

The data relating to anger and fighting throw further light on this subject. Cox (27) finds great face-to-face leaders, except statesmen, to be characterized by a tendency toward liability to anger, and "a tendency to flare up on slight provocation." Ackerson (1) reports that "temper tantrums" and "leader" are positively correlated, while "temper tantrums" and "follower" are negatively correlated. Webb (119), however, finds a correlation of $-.12$ between leadership and occasional extreme anger. Tryon (117) reports correlation coefficients of .59, .48, .25, and .40 between fighting and leadership for 12-year-old boys, 15-year-old boys, 12-year-old girls, and 15-year-old girls respectively. Ackerson (1) finds fighting and leadership to be correlated .13 for boys and $-.17$ for girls, but fighting and leading others into bad conduct are correlated .20 for boys and .36 for girls. Incorrigibility and defiance are also positively correlated with leadership and to a still higher degree with leadership in misconduct, while these traits are correlated negatively with "followers."

These studies do not lend convincing support to the view that leaders are necessarily persons who are characterized by a high degree of self-control or by lack of capacity for emotional expression.

### Social and Economic Status

*a.* Leaders come from higher socioeconomic background (5, 11, 12, 20, 30, 39, 51, 53, 88, 90, 99, 104, 109, 111, 123).

*b.* No difference (3, 40).

Evidence presented in studies representing a wide variety of leadership situations indicates that leaders tend to come from a socioeconomic background superior to that of the average of their followers. Only two investigators, Baldwin (3) and Goodenough (40), report negligible differences. On the other hand, the differences in social and economic status between leaders and nonleaders are usually not extreme. Only Remmelin (90) finds differences which are statistically reliable.

### Social Activity and Mobility

*a.* Leaders participate in more group activities (1, 3, 5, 11, 12, 20, 24, 45, 53, 62, 70, 77, 88, 90, 91, 92, 94, 102, 103, 124).

*b.* Leaders exhibit a higher rate of social mobility (104, 105, 115, 118, 123).

Baldwin (3), Brown (11), Chapin (20), Courtenay (24), Richardson and Hanawalt (92), Roslow (94), Link (62), Merriam (70), Reals (88), Smith and Nystrom (102), Sorokin (103), and Zeleny (124) find that leaders surpass followers in the number, extent, and variety of group activities in which they participate. Zeleny (124) reports correlations ranging from .17 to .682 between leadership and participation in extracurricular activities. Leadership has been defined by a number of authors as "occupying one or more positions of responsibility in group activities."

Physical and social mobility is found by Sorokin (103), Sorokin and Zimmerman (105), and Winston (122) to be a factor associated with adult leadership. Sorokin and Zimmerman report that farmer leaders are characterized to a high degree by a tendency to shift from place to place, and from one occupational or economic position to another. The same tendency in inventors is observed by Winston (123). Social mobility, or perhaps more properly, social detachment, appears to be a factor in the formation of boys' gangs studied by Thrasher (115) and Warner (118).

### Biosocial Activity

a. Active in games (10, 13, 15, 31, 89, 117).
b. Lively, active, restless (1, 13, 21, 22, 38, 60, 65, 74, 117).
c. Daring, adventurous (112, 115, 117).

This list of traits is difficult to classify, since in few cases is the behavior clearly defined. The majority of investigators appear to emphasize the social aspects of these behaviors, although in some cases emphasis seems to be placed on an underlying physical component of energy or vitality. This is merely one example of the difficulty, and perhaps futility, mentioned by a number of investigators, of attempting to analyze human behavior into distinct and separate traits.

Broich (10), Brown (13), Buttgereit (15), and Reininger (89) find that child leaders are more active in games than nonleaders. In Tryon's (117) study leadership and "active in games" are correlated .52 to .74 for groups of 12- and 15-year-old boys and girls. Terman (112), Thrasher (115), and Tryon (117) find leaders to be more daring and adventurous than followers. Correlations of .57 to .78 between daring and leadership are reported by Tryon (117). Cowley (26) finds motor impulsion to be a factor common to different types of leaders. According to Chevaleva-Ianovskaia (22), leaders are characterized by a predominance of excitation over inhibition. Liveliness is reported by Leib (60) and Brown (13) to characterize leaders. Flemming (38) finds a correlation of .47 between leadership and liveliness, while Goodenough (40) reports a correlation of .29 between physical activity and leadership. Ackerson (1) and Tryon (117) report correlation coefficients of the order of approximately .20 between "restlessness" and leadership. These findings suggest that physical activity and mobility are factors associated with leadership.

### Social Skills

a. Sociability (1, 7, 14, 34, 38, 40, 55, 65, 72, 74, 77, 86, 97, 117).
b. Diplomacy, tact (6, 32, 38, 47, 81, 108, 119, 120).

Fairly high positive correlations between sociability and leadership are reported by Bonney (7), Drake (32), Flemming (38), Eichler (34), Goodenough (40), Sheldon (97), Tryon (117), and Webb (119). These correlation coefficients are shown in Table 4.2.

Burks (14), Malloy (65), Middleton (72), and Prosh (86) also find student leaders to rate higher than nonleaders in sociability. Ackerson (1) finds that belonging to a gang is correlated .26 with leader and .21 with follower. Leader and intimate circle are correlated .39 in Webb's (119) study. Moore (74) and Newcomb (77) report friendliness and social skills respectively as factors which distinguish leaders from followers. Cox (27) also finds great leaders to rate above average, but not to an outstanding degree in fondness for companionship and social gatherings.

Courtesy, tact, and diplomacy are found by Bernard (6), Wetzel (120), Drake (32), Flemming (38), Hanfmann (47), Parten (81), Stray (108), and Webb (119) to be

**TABLE 4.2**
**Correlation between Traits and Leadership**

| Investigator | Variable | Correlation with Leadership |
|---|---|---|
| Bonney | Social skills | .53 |
| Drake | Sociability | .52 |
| Flemming | Sociability | .33 |
| Eichler | Social intelligence | .10 |
| Goodenough | Sociability | .98 |
| Sheldon | Sociability | .47 |
| Tryon | Friendly | .44 to .74 |
| Webb | Sociability | .39 |

traits which distinguish leaders from nonleaders. Drake, Flemming, and Webb report correlations of .08, .27, and .73 respectively between tact and leadership. Flemming (38), however, finds a correlation of − .03 between courtesy and leadership. Ackerson (1) reports correlations of .10 and .07 between rudeness and leadership for boys and girls respectively, while the correlations between rudeness and leading others into bad conduct are .24 and .40 for boys and girls respectively. Ackerson also finds that both bashfulness and seclusiveness are negatively correlated with leadership.

Ackerson (1), Goodenough (40), and Webb (119) find correlations ranging from − .29 to .21 between offensive manifestations and leadership. Ackerson's (1) findings suggest that misconduct is not necessarily a bar to leadership. Stealing, for example, is correlated .12 and .21 with leadership, while stealing and leading others into misconduct are correlated .46 and .16 for boys and girls respectively.

*Popularity, Prestige (1, 5, 18, 27, 39, 71, 73, 79, 117, 124)*

Evidence from a diversity of studies indicates that leaders are persons who tend to rate higher than average in popularity. The correlation coefficients shown in Table 4.3 reveal a fairly high relationship between popularity and leadership. Nutting (79) points out, however, that popularity cannot be regarded as synonymous with leadership. The evidence presented by Ackerson (1), Bellingrath (5), Carlson and Harrell (18), Cox (27), Garrison (39), Michels (71), Miller and Dollard (73), Nutting (79), Tryon (117), and Zeleny (124) indicate that popularity and prestige are rather closely associated with leadership status.

*Cooperation*

a. Cooperativeness (3, 10, 16, 32, 33, 35, 47, 65, 77, 119, 120).
b. Work for the group, corporate responsibility (10, 15, 27, 55, 60, 79, 84, 119).
c. Ability to enlist cooperation (3, 16, 47, 55, 69, 70, 79).

Leaders are found by Baldwin (3), Dunkerley (33), Fauquier and Gilchrist (35), Newcomb (77), and Wetzel (120) to rate higher in cooperativeness than followers. Drake (32) and Webb (119) report correlations of .44 and .69 between cooperativeness and leadership. Ability to enlist cooperation and to control others in a group enterprise are found by Baldwin, (3), Caldwell (16), Hanfmann (47), Merriam (69, 70), and Nutting (79) to be characteristics associated with leadership ability. Broich (10), Jennings (55), Leib (60), Nutting (79), and Pigors (84) find that leaders tend to be persons who are able to work for the group welfare. A sense of social responsibility is found by Buttgereit (15) to be a characteristic of leaders. Webb (119) reports a correlation of .69 between leadership and corporate spirit. Cox (27) also reports that great leaders rate outstandingly high in sense of corporate spirit.

### Patterns of Leadership Traits Differ with the Situation (1, 5, 17, 23, 25, 27, 29, 33, 45, 46, 55, 76, 77, 82, 95, 96, 109, 112, 116)

There is a preponderance of evidence from a wide variety of studies which indicates that patterns of leadership traits differ with the situation. Ackerson's (1) study reveals marked differences in the conduct and personality patterns of children who are regarded as leaders in general and children who are regarded as leaders in misconduct. Boys and girls in these two groups also differ somewhat. Bellingrath (5) finds marked differences in the extent to which leaders in athletics, student government, publications, and clubs participate in extracurricular activities and are chosen as leaders under varying circumstances. The investigation of Caldwell and Wellman (17) reveals athletic leaders to be tallest among the leaders and to excel in physical achievements, while editors are younger, and shorter than average, but rank higher in scholarship than other groups of leaders studied. Cowley's (25) studies reveal marked differences in the traits of criminal leaders, army leaders, and student leaders. The profiles of average trait ratings of groups of great leaders studied by Cox (27) differ markedly from one group to another, especially in physical and emotional traits, but much less so in traits which might be classified as intellectual, self-regard, and persistence. Dunkerley's (33) factor analysis of the intercorrelations of fifteen variables representing trait ratings of 167 women college students reveals a factor identified as social leadership and two factors identified as religious leadership.

Hanfmann (47) observes three types of leadership among preschool children: (1)

**TABLE 4.3**
**Correlation between Popularity and Leadership**

| Investigator | Variable | Correlation with Leadership |
|---|---|---|
| Ackerson (boys) | Popularity | .32 |
| (girls) | | .40 |
| Bellingrath | Popularity | .80 |
| Garrison (School 1) | Admiration | .82 |
| (School 2) | | .58 |
| Nutting | Popularity | .60 |
| Tryon (boys, age 12) | Popularity | .47 |
| (boys, age 15) | | .64 |
| (girls, age 12) | | .23 |
| (girls, age 15) | | .68 |

the objective leader who engages in constructive play and gets what he wants by saying why he needs it; (2) the social leader whose goal is play with another rather than play in itself; and (3) the gangster who gets his way by force and complete disregard for others. Schuler (95) concludes that as age increases, dominant-submissive behavior in adolescent boys may be ascertained with increasing reliability by teachers in one situation, such as the school, but at the same time it becomes less possible to predict those tendencies in another environment, such as the home.

Superior socioeconomic status as well as higher intelligence and scholastic attainment are found by Sward (109) to differentiate 125 campus leaders from 125 followers. However a classification of the leaders into subgroups reveals the following distinguishing differences: (1) bright, relatively unmotivated, unsocial, self-confident campus editors; (2) rather insecure, intellectualistic and very intelligent debaters; (3) strongly socialized and intellectually mediocre campus politicians; and (4) extroverted women leaders.

Terman (112) finds that children who are leaders in one experimental situation may not be leaders when matched against different children in other situations. Children who are "automatons," or nonleaders, in most situations may achieve leadership in some situations. Those children who are leaders in most situations are said by their teachers to be characterized by intelligence, congeniality, liveliness, and goodness.

In Tryon's (117) study, the trait clusters found to characterize boys and girls at 12 years of age differ from those found at 15 years of age. This is especially true for girls, who appear to mature somewhat more rapidly in social interests than do boys. The leadership cluster for 12-year-old boys is composed of the items: daring, leader, active in games, friendly; while that for 15-year-old boys contains the items: daring, leader, active in games, fights. The leadership trait cluster for 12-year-old girls contains the items: daring, leader, humor about jokes; while for 15-year-old girls the following items appear: popular, friendly, enthusiastic, happy, humor about jokes, daring, leader.

The total weight of evidence presented in this group of studies suggests that if there are general traits which characterize leaders, the patterns of such traits are likely to vary with the leadership requirements of different situations.

*Transferability and Persistence of Leadership (23, 24, 57, 61, 80, 96)*

Followup studies, although yielding somewhat variable results, suggest a certain degree of persistence or transferability of leadership. Levi (61) studied 230 leaders in elementary and junior high school, 206 of whom were studied again in senior high school. The correlation between leadership in elementary school and leadership in senior high school is .19, while the correlation between junior high school leadership and leadership in senior high school is .52. There is a low negative correlation between athletic leadership in elementary school and in high school, but a correlation of .44 was found between athletic leadership in the junior and senior high school situations.

Kohs and Irle (57) made a followup study of the military careers of 116 college students. Three faculty members rated these students on various traits. Correlations between army rank and various ratings ranged from .11 to .39. The best criteria for predicting military success were found to be judges' estimates of potential value to the service and judges' estimates of intelligence. Judges' estimates of leadership were correlated .11 with army rank. Scholarship was not predictive of army rank. Page (80), studying cadets at West Point, found first-year leadership rank to be correlated .67 with fourth-year leadership rank. Rank in bearing and appearance was most highly correlated with rank in leadership; while rank in athletic activities, tactics, and academic standing were correlated with leadership rank in progressively lesser degrees.

Clem and Dodge (23) made a comparative study of the postschool success of twenty-seven leaders, thirty-six high-ranking scholars, and thirty-eight random pupils from six successive high school graduating classes. Leaders rank highest in outstanding achievements, number of honors received, and quantity of publications. The random group ranks highest in community leadership and amount of money accumulated. In general, the leaders tended to be more successful than scholars and the random group, although the differences are not impressive. Courtenay (24) studied 100 women leaders and 100 nonleaders from thirteen successive high school graduating classes. The two groups were matched as to socioeconomic background, ethnic heritage, scholarship, and age at graduation. It was found that seventy-two leaders went to college, while only twenty-nine nonleaders went to college. Twice as many leaders as nonleaders were engaged in professional work. The average salary of leaders exceeded that of nonleaders. The leaders were more active in community work. Shannon (96) compared leaders, scholars (honor roll members), and a random group from five high school graduating classes. It was found that graduates who were on the honor roll were but little more successful than the random group. It was concluded that "whatever is required to excel in the extracurricular life of the high school, seems to be the same thing that contributes most to success later."

These findings suggest rather strongly that high scholarship alone may not be predictive of success after graduation from high school. Leadership in school activities is somewhat more predictive of later success, but the extent to which leadership persists and transfers is not clearly determined.

## SUMMARY

1. The following conclusions are supported by uniformly positive evidence from fifteen or more of the studies surveyed:

   *a.* The average person who occupies a position of leadership exceeds the average member of his group in the following respects: (1) intelligence; (2) scholarship; (3) dependability in exercising responsibilities; (4) activity and social participation; and (5) socioeconomic status.

   *b.* The qualities, characteristics, and skills required in a leader are determined to a large extent by the demands of the situation in which he is to function as a leader.

2. The following conclusions are supported by uniformly positive evidence from ten or more of the studies surveyed:

   *a.* The average person who occupies a position of leadership exceeds the average member of his group to some degree in the following respects: (1) sociability; (2) initiative; (3) persistence; (4) knowing how to get things done; (5) self-confidence; (6) alertness to, and insight into, situations; (7) cooperativeness; (8) popularity; (9) adaptability; and (10) verbal facility.

3. In addition to the above, a number of factors have been found which are

specific to well-defined groups. For example, athletic ability and physical prowess have been found to be characteristics of leaders in boys' gangs and play groups. Intellectual fortitude and integrity are traits found to be associated with eminent leadership in maturity.

4. The items with the highest overall correlation with leadership are originality, popularity, sociability, judgment, aggressiveness, desire to excel, humor, cooperativeness, liveliness, and athletic ability, in approximate order of magnitude of average correlation coefficient.

5. In spite of considerable negative evidence, the general trend of results suggests a low positive correlation between leadership and such variables as chronological age, height, weight, physique, energy, appearance, dominance, and mood control. The evidence is about evenly divided concerning the relation to leadership of such traits as introversion-extroversion, self-sufficiency, and emotional control.

6. The evidence available suggests that leadership exhibited in various school situations may persist into college and into later vocational and community life. However, knowledge of the facts relating to the transferability of leadership is very meager and obscure.

7. The most fruitful studies, from the point of view of understanding leadership, have been those in which leadership behavior was described and analyzed on the basis of direct observation or analysis of biographical and case history data.

## DISCUSSION

The factors which have been found to be associated with leadership could probably all be classified under the general headings of *capacity, achievement, responsibility, participation,* and *status:*

1. *Capacity* (intelligence, alertness, verbal facility, originality, judgment).
2. *Achievement* (scholarship, knowledge, athletic accomplishments).
3. *Responsibility* (dependability, initiative, persistence, aggressiveness, self-confidence, desire to excel).
4. *Participation* (activity, sociability, cooperation, adaptability, humor).
5. *Status* (socioeconomic position, popularity).
6. *Situation* (mental level, status, skills, needs and interests of followers, objectives to be achieved, etcetera).

These findings are not surprising. It is primarily by virtue of participating in group activities and demonstrating his capacity for expediting the work of the group that a person becomes endowed with leadership status. A number of investigators have been careful to distinguish between the leader and the figurehead, and to point out that leadership is always associated with the attainment of group objectives. Leadership implies activity, movement, getting work done. The leader is a person who occupies a position of responsibility in coordinating the activities of the members of the group in their task of attaining a common goal. This leads to consideration of another significant factor.

A person does not become a leader by virtue of the possession of some combination of traits, but the pattern of personal characteristics of the leader must bear some relevant relationship to the characteristics, activities, and goals of the followers. Thus, leadership must be conceived in terms of the interaction of variables which are in constant flux and change. The factor of change is especially characteristic of the situation, which may be radically altered by the addition or loss of members, changes in interpersonal relationships, changes in goals, competition of extragroup influences, and the like. The personal characteristics of the leader and of the followers are, in comparison, highly stable. The persistence of individual patterns of human behavior in the face of constant situational change appears to be a primary obstacle encountered not only in the practice of leadership, but in the selection and placement of leaders. It is not especially difficult to find persons who are leaders. It is quite another matter to place these persons in different situations where they will be able to function as leaders. It becomes clear that an adequate analysis of leadership involves not only a study of leaders, but also of situations.

The evidence suggests that leadership is a relation that exists between persons in a social situation, and that persons who are leaders in one situation may not necessarily be leaders in other situations. Must it then be assumed that leadership is entirely incidental, haphazard, and unpredictable? Not at all. The very studies which provide the strongest arguments for the situational nature of leadership also supply the strongest evidence indicating that leadership patterns as well as nonleadership patterns of behavior are persistent and relatively stable. Jennings (55) observes that "the individual's choice behavior, in contrast to his social expansiveness, appears as an expression of needs which are, so to speak, so 'central' to his personality that he must strive to fulfill them whether or not the possibility of fulfilling them is at hand." A somewhat similar observation is made by Newstetter, Feldstein, and Newcomb (78), who report that:

> Being accepted or rejected is not determined by the cordiality or antagonism of the individual's treatment of his fellows, nor evidently, is the individual's treatment of his fellows much affected by the degree to which he is already being accepted or rejected by them. Their treatment of him is related to their acceptance or rejection of him. Their treatment of him is, of course, a reaction to some or all of his behaviors, but we have been completely unsuccessful in attempting to measure what these behaviors are.

The authors conclude that these findings provide "devastating evidence" against the concept of the operation of measurable traits in determining social interactions. The findings of Newstetter and his associates do not appear to provide direct evidence either for or against a theory of traits, but they do indicate that the complex of factors that determines an individual's status in a group is most difficult to isolate and evaluate.

The findings of Jennings and Newstetter suggest that the problem of selecting leaders should be much less difficult than that of training nonleaders to become leaders. The clinician or group worker who has observed the fruitless efforts of socially isolated individuals to gain group acceptance or leadership status is aware of the real nature of the phenomena described by Jennings and Newstetter. Some individuals are isolates in almost any group in which they find themselves, while others are readily accepted in most of their social contacts.

A most pertinent observation on this point is made by Ackerson (1), who reports that "the correlations for 'leader' and 'follower' are not of opposite sign and similar magnitude as would be expected of traits supposed to be antithetical." These may not be the opposite poles of a single underlying trait. "It may be that the true antithesis of 'leader' is not 'follower,' but 'indifference,' i.e., the incapacity or unwillingness either to lead or follow. Thus it may be that some individuals who under one situation are leaders may under other conditions take the role of follower, while the true 'opposite' is represented by the child who neither leads nor follows.''

The findings suggest that leadership is not a matter of passive status nor of the mere possession of some combination of traits. It appears rather to be a working relationship among members of a group, in which the leader acquires status through active participation and demonstration of his capacity for carrying cooperative tasks through to completion. Significant aspects of this capacity for organizing and expediting cooperative effort appear to be intelligence, alertness to the needs and motives of others, and insight into situations, further reinforced by such habits as responsibility, initiative, persistence, and self-confidence. The studies surveyed offer little information as to the basic nature of these personal qualifications. Cattell's (19) studies suggest that they may be founded to some degree on basic intelligence, but Cattell and others also suggest that they are socially conditioned to a high degree. Problems which appear to be in need of thorough investigation are those relating to factors which condition social participation, insight into situations, mood control, responsibility, and transferability of leadership from one situation to another. Answers to these questions seem basic not only to any adequate understanding of the personal qualifications of leaders, but also to any effective training for leadership.

## REFERENCES TO CHAPTER 4

1. ACKERSON, L. *Children's behavior problems: relative importance and intercorrelation among traits.* Chicago: University of Chicago Press, 1942.

2. ARRINGTON, R. E. Time sampling in studies of social behavior: a critical review of techniques and results with research suggestions. *Psychol. Bull., 1943, 40,* 81–124.

3. BALDWIN, L. E. A study of factors usually associated with high school male leadership. Columbus: Ohio State University. Unpublished Master's thesis, 1932.

4. BARKER, R. G. The social interrelations of strangers and acquaintances. *Sociometry,* 1942, *5,* 169–179.

5. BELLINGRATH, G. C. Qualities associated with leadership in extra-curricular activities of the high school. *Teach. Coll. Contr. Educ.,* 1930, No. 399.

6. BERNARD, J. Political leadership among North American Indians. *Amer. J. Sociol.,* 1928, *34,* 296–315.

7. BONNEY, M. E. The constancy of sociometric scores and their relationship to teacher judgments of social success and to personality self-ratings. *Sociometry,* 1943, *6,* 409–424.

8. BOWDEN, A. O. A study of the personality of student leaders in colleges in the United States. *J. abnorm. soc. Psychol.,* 1926, *21,* 149–160.

9. BROGDEN, H. E., & THOMAS, W. F. The primary traits in personality items purporting to measure sociability. *J. Psychol.,* 1943, *16,* 85–97.

10. BRIOCH, K. Führeranforderungen in der Kindergruppe. *Z. angew. Psychol.,* 1929, *32,* 164–212.

11. BROWN, M. Leadership among high school pupils. *Teach. Coll. Contr. Educ.,* 1933, No. 559.

12. BROWN, M. Leadership among high school pupils. *Teach. Coll. Rec.,* 1934, *35,* 324–326.

13. BROWN, S. C. Some case studies of delinquent girls described as leaders. *Brit. J. educ. Psychol.*, 1931, *1*, 162–179.

14. BURKS, F. W. Some factors related to social success in college. *J. soc. Psychol.*, 1938, *9*, 125–140.

15. BUTTGEREIT, H. Führergestalten in der Schulklasse. *Z. angew. Psychol.*, 1932, *43*, 369–413.

16. CALDWELL, O. W. Some factors in training for leadership. *Natl. Assn. Secondary School Principals, Fourth Yearbook*, 1920, 2–13.

17. CALDWELL, O. W., & WELLMAN, B. Characteristics of school leaders, *J. educ. Res.*, 1926, *14*, 1–15.

18. CARLSON, H. B., & HARRELL, W. An analysis of *Life's* "Ablest Congressman" poll. *J. soc. Psychol.*, 1942, *15*, 153–158.

19. CATTELL, R. B. *Description and measurement of personality*. New York: World Book, 1946.

20. CHAPIN, F. S. *Community leadership and opinion in Red Wing*. Minneapolis: University of Minnesota Press, 1945.

21. CHAPPLE, E. D., & DONALD, G. Jr. A method of evaluating supervisory personnel. *Harvard bus. Rev.*, 1946, *24*, 197–214.

22. CHEVALEVA-IANOVSKAIA, E. & SYLLA, D. Essai d'une étude sur les enfants meneurs. *J. Psychol.*, 1929, *26*, 604–612.

23. CLEM, O. M. & DODGE, S. B. The relation of high school leadership and scholarship to post-school success. *Peabody J. Educ.*, 1933, *10*, 321–329.

24. COURTENAY, M. E. Persistence of leadership. *School Rev.*, 1938, *46*, 97–107.

25. COWLEY, W. H. Three distinctions in the study of leaders. *J. abnorm. soc. Psychol.*, 1928, *23*, 144–157.

26. COWLEY, W. H. Traits of face-to-face leaders. *J. abnorm. soc. Psychol.*, 1931, *26*, 304–313.

27. COX, C. M. *The early mental traits of three hundred geniuses*. Stanford, Calif.: Stanford University Press, 1926.

28. CRAWFORD, A. B. Extra-curriculum activities and academic work. *Personnel J.*, 1928, *7*, 121–129.

29. DASHIELL, J. F. Personality traits and the different professions. *J. appl. Psychol.*, 1930, *14*, 197–201.

30. DAVIS, J. A study of one hundred sixty-three outstanding communist leaders. *Publ. Amer. Sociol. Soc.*, 1930, *24*, 42–55.

31. DETROIT TEACHERS COLLEGE. *How children choose friends*. Detroit: Detroit Teachers College, 1929.

32. DRAKE, R. M. A study of leadership. *Charac. & Pers.*, 1944, *12*, 285–289.

33. DUNKERLEY, M. D. A statistical study of leadership among college women. *Stud. Psychol. & Psychiatr.*, 1940, *4*, 1–65.

34. EICHLER, G. A. Studies in student leadership. *Penn. St. Coll. Stud. Educ.*, 1934, No. 10.

35. FAUQUIER, W., & GILCHRIST, T. Some aspects of leadership in an institution. *Child Develop.*, 1942, *13*, 55–64.

36. FAY, P. J., & MIDDLETON, W. C. Judgment of leadership from the transmitted voice. *J. soc. Psychol.*, 1943, *17*, 99–102.

37. FINCH, F. H., & CARROLL, H. A. Gifted children as high school leaders. *J. genet. Psychol.*, 1932, *41*, 476–481.

38. FLEMMING, E. G. A factor analysis of the personality of high school leaders, *J. appl. Psychol.*, 1935, *19*, 596–605.

39. GARRISON, K. C. A study of some factors related to leadership in high school. *Peabody J.*

*Educ.*, 1935, *11*, 11–17.

**40.** GOODENOUGH, F. L. Interrelationships in the behavior of young children. *Child Develop.*, 1930, *1*, 29–48.

**41.** GOWIN, E. B. *The executive and his control of men*. New York: Macmillan, 1915.

**42.** GOWIN, E. B. *The selection and training of the business executive*. New York: Macmillan, 1918.

**43.** GUILFORD, J. P., & GUILFORD, R. B. Personality factors, *D, R, T,* and *A. J. abnorm. soc. Psychol.*, 1939, *34*, 21–36.

**44.** HANAWALT, N. G., HAMILTON, C. E., & MORRIS, M. L. Level of aspiration in college leaders and non-leaders. *J. abnorm. soc. Psychol.*, 1934, *38*, 545–548.

**45.** HANAWALT, N. G., RICHARDSON, H. M., & HAMILTON, R. J. Leadership as related to Bernreuter personality measures. II. An item analysis of responses of college leaders and non-leaders. *J. soc. Psychol.*, 1943, *17*, 251–267.

**46.** HANAWALT, N. G., & RICHARDSON, H. M. Leadership as related to the Bernreuter personality measures. IV. An item analysis of responses of adult leaders and non-leaders. *J. appl. Psychol.*, 1944, *28*, 397–411.

**47.** HANFMANN, E. Social structure of a group of kindergarten children. *Amer. J. Orthopsychiat.*, 1935, *5*, 407–410.

**48.** HEATH, C. W., & GREGORY, L. W. What it takes to be an officer. *Infantry J.*, 1946, *58*, 44–45.

**49.** HENNING, H. Ziele und Möglichkeiten der experimentellen Charakterprüfung. *Jahrbuch d. Charakterol.*, 1929, *6*, 213–273.

**50.** HOLLINGWORTH, L. S. *Gifted children*. New York: Macmillan, 1926.

**51.** HOOKER, E. R. Leaders in village communities. *Soc. Forces*, 1928, *6*, 605–614.

**52.** HOWELL, C. E. Measurement of leadership. *Sociometry*, 1942, *5*, 163–168.

**53.** HUNTER, E. C., & JORDAN, A. M. An analysis of qualities associated with leadership among college students. *J. educ. Psychol.*, 1939, *30*, 497–509.

**54.** JENKINS, W. O. A review of leadership studies with particular reference to military problems. *Psychol. Bull.*, 1947, *44*, 54–79.

**55.** JENNINGS, H. H. *Leadership and isolation*. New York: Longmans, Green, 1943.

**56.** JONES, A. J. *The education of youth for leadership*. New York: McGraw-Hill, 1938.

**57.** KOHS, S. C., & IRLE, K. W. Prophesying army promotion. *J. appl. Psychol.*, 1920, *4*, 73–87.

**58.** LEHMAN, H. C. The creative years in science and literature. *Sci. Mon.*, 1937, *45*, 65–75.

**59.** LEHMAN, H. C. Optimum ages for eminent leadership. *Sci. Mon.*, 1942, *54*, 162–175.

**60.** LEIB, A. Vorstellungen und Urteile von Schülern über Führer in der Schulklasse. *Z. angew. Psychol.*, 1928, *30*, 241–346.

**61.** LEVI, I. J. Student leadership in elementary and junior high school, and its transfer into senior high school. *J. educ. Res.*, 1930, *22*, 135–139.

**62.** LINK, H. C. The definition of social effectiveness and leadership through measurement. *Educ. psychol. Measmt.*, 1944, *4*, 57–67.

**63.** LUITHLEN, W. F. Zur Psychologie der Initiative und der Führereigenschaften. *Z. angew. Psychol.*, 1931, *39*, 56–122.

**64.** MALLER, J. B. Cooperation and competition: an experimental study in motivation. *Teach. Coll. Contr. Educ.*, 1925, No. 384.

**65.** MALLOY, H. Study of some of the factors underlying the establishment of successful social contacts at the college level. *J. soc. Psychol.*, 1936, *7*, 205–228.

**66.** McCANDLESS, B. R. Changing relationships between dominance and social acceptability during group democratization. *Amer. J. Orthopsychiat.*, 1942, *12*, 529–535.

**67.** McCUEN, T. L. Leadership and intelligence. *Education*, 1929, *50*, 89–95.

68. McGahan, F. E. Factors associated with leadership ability. *Texas Outlook*, 1941, *25*, 37–38.

69. Merriam, C. E. *Four American party leaders*. New York: Macmillan, 1926.

70. Merriam, C. E., & Gosnell, H. E. *The American party system*. New York: Macmillan, 1929.

71. Michels, R. *Political parties*. New York: Macmillan, 1915.

72. Middleton, W. C. Personality qualities predominant in campus leaders. *J. soc. Psychol.*, 1941, *13*, 199–201.

73. Miller, N. E., & Dollard, J. *Social learning and imitation*. New Haven, Conn.: Yale University Press, 1941.

74. Moore, L. H. Leadership traits of college women. *Sociol. soc. Res.*, 1932, *17*, 44–54.

75. Moore, L. H. Leadership traits of college women. *Sociol. soc. Res.*, 1935, *20*, 136–139.

76. Nafe, R. W. A psychological description of leadership. *J. soc. Psychol.*, 1930, *1*, 248–266.

77. Newcomb, T. M. *Personality and social change*. New York: Dryden Press, 1943.

78. Newstetter, W. I., Feldstein, M. J., & Newcomb, T. M. *Group adjustment: a study in experimental sociology*. Cleveland: Western Reserve University, 1938.

79. Nutting, R. L. Some characteristics of leadership. *School Soc.*, 1923, *18*, 387–390.

80. Page, D. P. Measurement and prediction of leadership. *Amer. J. Sociol.*, 1935, *41*, 31–43.

81. Parten, M. B. Leadership among preschool children. *J. abnorm. soc. Psychol.*, 1933, *27*, 430–440.

82. Partridge, E. D. Leadership among adolescent boys. *Teach. Coll. Contr. Educ.*, 1934, No. 608.

83. Peck, E. M. A study of the personalities of five eminent men. *J. abnorm. soc. Psychol.*, 1931, *26*, 37–57.

84. Pigors, P. Leadership and domination among children. *Sociologus*, 1933, *9*, 140–157.

85. Pinard, J. W. Tests of perseveration. *Brit. J. Psychol.*, 1932, *32*, 5–19.

86. Prosh, F. The basis on which students choose their leaders. *Amer. phys. educ. Rev.*, 1928, *33*, 265–267.

87. Puffer, J. A. Boys gangs. *Ped. Sem.*, 1905, *12*, 175–213.

88. Reals, W. H. Leadership in the high school. *School Rev.*, 1938, *46*, 523–531.

89. Reininger, K. Das soziale Verhalten von Schulneulingen. *Wien Arb. pädag. Psychol.*, 1927, *7*, 14.

90. Remmelin, M. K. Analysis of leaders among high school seniors, *J. exp. Educ.*, 1938, *6*, 413–422.

91. Reynolds, F. J. Factors of leadership among seniors of Central High School, Tulsa, Oklahoma. *J. educ. Res.*, 1944, *37*, 356–361.

92. Richardson, H. M., & Hanawalt, N. G. Leadership as related to Bernreuter personality measures. I. College leadership in extra curricular activities. *J. soc. Psychol.*, 1943, *17*, 237–249.

93. Richardson, H. M., & Hanawalt, N. G. Leadership as related to Bernreuter personality measures. III. Leadership among adult men in vocational and social activities. *J. appl. Psychol.*, 1944, *28*, 308–317.

94. Roslow, S. Nation-wide and local validation of the *PQ* or Personality Quotient test. *J. appl. Psychol.*, 1940, *24*, 529–539.

95. Schuler, E. A. A study of the consistency of dominant and submissive behavior in adolescent boys. *J. genet. Psychol.*, 1935, *46*, 403–432.

96. Shannon, J. R. The post-school careers of high school leaders and high school scholars. *School Rev.*, 1929, *37*, 656–665.

97. SHELDON, W. H. Social traits and morphologic type. *Person. J.*, 1927, *6*, 47–55.

98. SIMPSON, R. H. A study of those who influence and of those who are influenced in discussion. *Teach. Coll. Contr. Educ.*, 1938, No. 748.

99. SMITH, C. Social selection in community leadership. *Soc. Forces*, 1937, *15*, 530–545.

100. SMITH, H. L., & KRUEGER, L. M. A brief summary of literature on leadership. *Bull. School Educ., Indiana Univ.*, 1933, *9*, No. 4.

101. SMITH, M. Comparative study of Indian student leaders and followers. *Soc. Forces*, 1935, *13*, 418–426.

102. SMITH, M., & NYSTROM, W. C. A study of social participation and of leisure time of leaders and non-leaders. *J. appl. Psychol.*, 1937, *21*, 251–259.

103. SOROKIN, P. A. *Social mobility.* New York: Harper, 1927.

104. SOROKIN, P. A. Leaders of labor and radical movements in the United States and foreign countries. *Amer. J. Sociol.*, 1927, *33*, 382–411.

105. SOROKIN, P. A., & ZIMMERMAN, C. C. Farmer leaders in the United States. *Soc. Forces*, 1928, *7*, 33–46.

106. SPAULDING, C. B. Types of junior college leaders. *Sociol. soc. Res.*, 1934, *18*, 164–168.

107. STARCH, D. *How to develop your executive ability.* New York: Harper, 1943.

108. STRAY, H. F. Leadership traits of girls in girls' camps. *Sociol. soc. Res.*, 1934, *18*, 241–250.

109. SWARD, K. Temperament and direction of achievement. *J. soc. Psychol.*, 1933, *4*, 406–429.

110. SWIGART, J. S. A study of the qualities of leadership and administrative qualifications of thirty-eight women executives. Columbus: Ohio State University, Master's thesis, 1936.

111. TAUSSIG, F. W., & JOSLYN, C. S. *American business leaders.* New York: Macmillan, 1932.

112. TERMAN, L. M. A preliminary study in the psychology and pedagogy of leadership. *Ped. Sem.*, 1904, *11*, 413–451.

113. TERMAN, L. M., et al. *Genetic studies of genius. I. Mental and physical traits of a thousand gifted children.* Stanford, Calif.: Stanford University Press, 1925.

114. THORNDIKE, E. L. The relation between intellect and morality in rulers. *Amer. J. Sociol.*, 1936, *42*, 321–334.

115. THRASHER, F. *The gang: a study of 1,313 gangs in Chicago.* Chicago: University of Chicago Press, 1927.

116. THURSTONE, L. L. *A factorial study of perception.* Chicago: University of Chicago Press, 1944.

117. TRYON, C. M. Evaluations of adolescent personality by adolescents. *Monogr. soc. res. Child Develop.*, 1939, *4*, No. 4.

118. WARNER, M. L. Influence of mental level in the formation of boys' gangs. *J. appl. Psychol.*, 1923, *7*, 224–236.

119. WEBB, U. Character and intelligence. *Brit. J. Psychol. Monogr.*, 1915, No. 20.

120. WETZEL, W. A. Characteristics of pupil leaders. *School Rev.*, 1932, *40*, 532–534.

121. WILKINS, E. H. On the distribution of extra-curricular activities. *School Soc.*, 1940, *51*, 651–656.

122. WINSTON, S. Studies in negro leadership: age and occupational distribution of 1,608 negro leaders. *Amer. J. Sociol.*, 1932, *37*, 595–602.

123. WINSTON, S. Bio-social characteristics of American inventors. *Amer. soc. Rev.*, 1937, *2*, 837–849.

124. ZELENY, L. Characteristics of group leaders. *Sociol. soc. Res.*, 1939, *24*, 140–149.

# 5

## TRAITS OF LEADERSHIP:
## A FOLLOWUP TO 1970

At the beginning of the present century, leaders were generally regarded as superior individuals who, as a result of fortunate inheritance or social adventure, became possessed of qualities and abilities that differentiated them from people in general. The search for the specific qualities occupied the next two generations of communicators and researchers. But in the 1940s, three reviews—by Bird (1940), by W. O. Jenkins (1947), and particularly by Stogdill (1948)—sounded the seeming deathknell of a purely traits approach to the study of leadership. Bird (1940) analyzed twenty studies which considered seventy-nine traits. Of these, 65 percent were mentioned in only a single study. Only four of the traits (extroverted, humor, intelligent, and initiative) appeared in five or more studies. W. O. Jenkins (1947) reviewed seventy-four military studies and found that, although military leaders tend to show some superiority over followers in at least one of a wide variety of abilities, there was little agreement as to the abilities characterizing the leaders. Jenkins concluded that leadership is specific to the military situation under investigation. And Stogdill's (1948) review of 124 trait studies, reprinted as Chapter 4, found leaders characterized by several clusters of items that could be classified as capacity, achievement, responsibility, participation, and status. He also noted that the traits of leaders tend to differ with the situation.

The reviews by Bird, Jenkins, and Stogdill have been cited frequently as evidence in support of the view that leadership is entirely situational in origin and that no personal characteristics are predictive of leadership. This view seems to overemphasize the situational and underemphasize the personal nature of leadership. Strong evidence indicates that different leadership skills and traits are required in different situations. The behaviors and traits enabling a mobster to gain and maintain control over a criminal gang are not the same as those enabling a religious leader to gain and maintain a large following. Yet certain general qualities—such as courage, fortitude, and conviction—appear to characterize both. In most situations, to be successful, a leader needs to be somewhat more competent than those who follow. A review by R. D. Mann (1959) of leadership in small groups supports this conclusion. In a survey of research on the relation of personality to small-group performance, Mann found positive relationships in 71 percent to 80 percent of the studies for intelligence, adjustment, extroversion, dominance, masculinity, and sensitivity.

## TRENDS IN METHODOLOGY

Between 1948 and this followup into the 1970s, much change was recorded in methods and measurement. The one-variable-at-a-time experiment gave way to the factorial and multivariate experiment. The effects of various contributions of treatments could be analyzed in the same experiments. Theory was now guiding much of the data collection. Questionnaire methodologists introduced a variety of techniques to reduce errors of halo, leniency, and social desirability and to increase the relevance and reliability of results although their efforts often met with limited success. The critical incidents technique, forced-choice check lists, behaviorally anchored rating scales, and semantic differentials were just a few of the specific new methods introduced. Factor analysis became the basic tool in the search and verification of the existence of traits of consequence. Other multivariate regression procedures also became commonplace in efforts to establish the relative importance of different traits to successful leadership. Internationalization of efforts also became common. Whether or not the same traits of leadership were relevant to rural agricultural leaders in Chile and Mali, whether the same traits of leadership led to promotion to higher management in Norway, Italy, and Japan, were subjects examined in the third quarter of the century. And in the United States, particularly in the 1960s and 1970s, whether different traits would emerge of importance for black leaders and women leaders became a topic of considerable interest (see Chapters 30, 31, and 32).

## TRENDS IN EXPERIMENTATION

The human potential movement sparked awareness of the needs to sense group process and leadership within the context of the encounter group at a level of socioemotional feeling deeper than surface intellectual perception. Trait descriptions dealing with empathy, psychic energy, intuition, and interpersonal competence blossomed.

The whole field of small-group experimentation exploded. At the same time, much more vigor was introduced into the study of small-group interaction processes ranging from standardized coding such as the Bales technique to videotape analyses. Open-ended sessions to check back with the groups of participants what they had meant in the questionnaire responses were introduced. And most important of all, experimenters became aware of the many threats to the validity of their findings and the paradox that the more precise their experiments and measurements, the less generalizable could be their conclusions.

We will now present a comparative enumeration of results for a 1970 survey. Then, fifty-two factor analytic studies will be reviewed.

## COMPARISON OF 1948 AND 1970

The followup survey completed in 1970 by Stogdill is based on 163 studies of leader characteristics. The numbered references are listed at the end of the first section. Table 5.1 shows a comparison of findings from the 1948 survey with those of the 1970 survey. Positive findings of the 1948 survey are listed in column 1; zero and negative findings are listed in column 2. Results of studies conducted since 1948 are shown in column 3. Because the more recent survey involved several abstracters, it cannot be safely assumed that all negative findings were recorded on the abstracts. Moreover, it is probable that many of the negative results remain unpublished. For these reasons, only positive findings are reported in column 3. Caution is urged in interpreting conclusions based on these *published* positive and negative findings. David Bakin has pointed to the existence of a farcical but not necessarily fanciful prospect about positive and negative findings in social science. Suppose, he argues, the true difference between A and B is really zero. Thus, in 95 percent of all studies of A and B, we will expect to reach a negative conclusion finding no statistically significant difference between A and B at the 5 percent level of confidence. But, in 5 percent of all studies, our research will reach a positive but erroneous conclusion that there is a difference between A and B. Who publishes? Only those with positive findings! So, if we depend on a count of publications of positive and negative findings, we will draw the wrong inference about the true difference between A and B. Unfortunately, there is some truth to Bakin's burlesque: there is a reluctance among researchers and even more so among journal editors to publish negative findings. There is little question that positive findings are more likely to be published than negative ones. Let the reader beware.

In the surveys, a positive, or significant, relationship means that either (1) a given trait was significantly correlated with some measure of leader effectiveness; (2) a sample of leaders was found to differ significantly from a sample of followers on the trait; (3) a sample of effective leaders was found to differ significantly from a sample of ineffective leaders on the trait; or (4) a sample of high-status leaders was found to differ significantly from a sample of lower-status leaders on the trait, for example, top managers were shown to be different than first-line supervisors.

The discussion of Table 5.1 will be by clusters of individual traits: physical characteristics, social background, intelligence and ability, personality, task-related characteristics, and social characteristics.

**TABLE 5.1**
**Characteristics of Leaders (Number of Findings)**

|  | 1948 | | 1970 |
|---|---|---|---|
|  | *Positive* | *Zero or Neg* | *Positive Only* |
|  | *1* | *2* | *3* |
| Physical Characteristics |  |  |  |
| Activity, energy | 5 |  | 24 |
| Age | 10 | 8 | 6 |
| Appearance, grooming | 13 | 3 | 4 |
| Height | 9 | 4 |  |
| Weight | 7 | 4 |  |

**TABLE 5.1**
**Characteristics of Leaders (Number of Findings)**
*(Continued)*

|  | 1948 | | 1970 |
|---|---|---|---|
|  | *Positive*<br>*1* | *Zero or Neg*<br>*2* | *Positive Only*<br>*3* |
| Social Background |  |  |  |
| Education | 22 | 5 | 14 |
| Social status | 15 | 2 | 19 |
| Mobility | 5 |  | 6 |
| Intelligence and Ability |  |  |  |
| Intelligence | 23 | 10 | 25 |
| Judgment, decisiveness | 9 |  | 6 |
| Knowledge | 11 |  | 12 |
| Fluency of speech | 13 |  | 15 |
| Personality |  |  |  |
| Adaptability | 10 |  |  |
| Adjustment, normality |  |  | 11 |
| Aggressiveness, assertiveness |  |  | 12 |
| Alertness | 6 |  | 4 |
| Ascendance, dominance | 11 | 6 | 31 |
| Emotional balance, control | 11 | 8 | 14 |
| Enthusiasm |  |  | 3 |
| Extroversion | 5 | 6 | 1 |
| Independence, nonconformity |  |  | 13 |
| Objectivity, tough-mindedness |  |  | 7 |
| Originality, creativity | 7 |  | 13 |
| Personal integrity, ethical conduct | 6 |  | 9 |
| Resourcefulness |  |  | 7 |
| Self-confidence | 17 |  | 28 |
| Strength of conviction | 7 |  |  |
| Tolerance of stress |  |  | 9 |
| Task-Related Characteristics |  |  |  |
| Achievement drive, desire to excel | 7 |  | 21 |
| Drive for responsibility | 12 |  | 17 |
| Enterprise, initiative |  |  | 10 |
| Persistence against obstacles | 12 |  |  |
| Responsible in pursuit of objectives | 17 |  | 6 |
| Task orientation | 6 |  | 13 |
| Social Characteristics |  |  |  |
| Ability to enlist cooperation | 7 |  | 3 |
| Administrative ability |  |  | 16 |
| Attractiveness |  |  | 4 |
| Cooperativeness | 11 |  | 5 |
| Nurturance |  |  | 4 |
| Popularity, prestige | 10 |  | 1 |
| Sociability, interpersonal skills | 14 |  | 35 |
| Social participation | 20 |  | 9 |
| Tact, diplomacy | 8 |  | 4 |

*Physical Characteristics*

Measures of physical characteristics such as age, height, weight, and appearance showed both positive and negative findings in the 1948 survey. However, between 1948 and 1970, there was little concern with such leaders' physical characteristics. Yet height and weight above the average of the peer group is certainly not a disadvantage in achieving leadership status. Many organizations like to be represented by impressive physical specimens. Frederick the Great required that all his soldiers be tall; on the other hand, Napoleon is often cited as an example of the fact that a man of small stature can rise to a position of great power. Thus, physical stature may complement a leader, or a leader may compensate for lack of physical stature. Yet, there is a rational element involved. Robert Peel, who introduced the "bobbies" to London, made a highly effective police force without firearms by choosing only large men who could dominate the scene of social conflicts. Conversely, it has been noted that smaller-sized policemen are more likely to suffer attack and injury.

*Activity, Energy, Stamina (7, 9, 12, 14, 21, 22, 24, 44, 49, 53, 55, 57, 60, 61, 66, 70, 78, 80, 119, 125, 127, 130, 131, 158, 163\*).* Results of the 1970 survey, much more so than the 1948 survey, suggest that the leader tends to be endowed with an abundant reserve of energy, stamina, and ability to maintain a high rate of physical activity. Even when handicapped by physical disability or poor health, the highly successful leader tends to exhibit a high rate of energy output.

*Age (5, 77, 89, 92, 114, 151\*).* Age appears related to leadership in a complicated fashion. Surveys by Lehman (1953) and C. M. Cox (1926) on the relation of age to achievement in science, art, politics, and other fields found that great men tend to exhibit signs of outstanding accomplishment at a relatively early age. Many, but not all, had the advantage of special education or training because of early recognition of their talents. However, it takes time to rise to the top in a corporate structure. Standard and Poors (1967) reported that 74 percent of 66,336 American executives in the 1967 Register of Corporations, Directors, and Executives were over 50 years of age. Only 168 executives were under 30 years of age, while 8,085 were in the 71–80 age group. The two sets of findings indicate that the creative individual is likely to exhibit evidences of his or her ability at an early age; however, large organizations are not designed to use such creative gifts in administrative capacities. Rather, organizations tend to rely upon administrative knowledge and demonstration of success that comes with experience and age. It would appear that young persons desiring quick recognition of their talents might be advised to consider a profession in which prestige is based on individual accomplishment rather than an administrative career involving a long climb up the status structure of an organization. Recent federal legislation barring mandatory retirement for all but college professors will slow up the hierarchial promotion process even more as top executives in the 65-to-70-year age group remain with the firm or agency, preventing movement upwards of all below them.

As we will note in Chapter 32 dealing with cross-cultural issues, the age-grade lockstep seems to vary considerably from one country to another.

---

\*These numbers identify the references listed at the end of the section.

*Social Background*

*Social Status (40, 47, 71, 79, 89, 94, 98, 103, 108, 114, 115, 120, 126, 127, 134, 140, 143, 150, 159).* Studies of the socioeconomic background of leaders continued to proliferate between 1948 and 1970. D. R. Matthews (1954) found that 58 percent of presidents, vice presidents, and cabinet members during the years 1789 and 1934 had fathers in the professional, proprietor, or official occupations. Only 4 percent had fathers who were wage earners, but 38 percent were farmers. It is apparent that high social status has provided an advantage in rising to high levels of political leadership.

Newcomer (1955) and *Scientific American* (1965) reported that in 1965 more top executives came from the poorer and middle-income groups rather than the wealthy strata of society than in 1900. Those with college degrees increased from 28.3 percent in 1900 to 74.3 percent in 1964. The percentage of entrepreneurs and capitalists has greatly decreased, whereas the percentage of engineers, scientists, and managers has increased. G. F. Lewis (1960) reviewed several studies indicating that small businessmen have less education and more often start their careers as unskilled or semiskilled workers than do top executives in large firms. A. Porter (1965) found that father's background during the executive's childhood was significantly related to the latter's adult level in organization and authority for making policy—but not to pay, organization size, status in the business world, or career progress satisfaction. Miller and Dirksen (1965) reported that highly visible community leaders are differentiated from their less visible peers by the following characteristics: business oriented, Republican, member of Chamber of Commerce, and name in mass media. Hidden leaders were characterized as follows: administrative or professional job, not owner of large businesses, not native of city, family background in city not prominent. Finally, R. M. Powell's (1969) large-scale survey of the executive promotion process indicated that religious and ethnic background were also important factors.

*Mobility (22, 66, 67, 126, 134, 159).* Jennings (1967a) presented an insightful analysis of the problems, stresses, and adaptations involved in rapid upward mobility in the large corporation. Cussler (1958) found that women executives, once they reach middle management, find it difficult to rise higher in the industrial organization (see Chapter 30).

*Education (31, 37, 59, 71, 77, 89, 94, 99, 114, 115, 126, 143, 150, 159).* In regard to first-line foremen, Johnson, Peterson, and Kahler (1968) studied 496 foremen in a company over the years 1940 to 1961. Average age increased from 31.2 years in 1940–1944 to 41.2 years in 1955–1959. Years of schooling increased from 10.8 to 11.2 during the same period.

Studies of the social background of student leaders by Martin, Gross, and Darley (1952), Weinberg (1965), Krumboltz (1959), and Kumar (1966) reveal few consistent relationships across samples. Williamson (1948) found that fraternity members occupied a disproportionately large share of leadership positions on the college campus.

The most significant conclusions to be drawn from surveys of social background factors are that (1) high socioeconomic status is an advantage in attaining leadership status; (2) leaders who rise to high-level positions in industry at present tend to come from lower socioeconomic strata of society than they did a half century ago; and (3) they tend to be better educated now than formerly. The rise in the general education level of the population is common knowledge. Requirements for managerial and administrative positions increasingly demand a graduate degree such as the MBA. The trend toward reduced emphasis on social status and more emphasis on education is expected to accelerate as the effects of affirmative action manifest themselves. As firms and agencies aggressively make possible the promotion of women, blacks, and other minorities, we expect to see considerable increase in their upward mobility. In 1960, women and blacks were hardly observed in MBA programs. In 1980, women formed 30 to 40 percent of MBA classes, and business schools were actively engaged in trying to achieve substantial increases in black and minority students in their programs (more on this in Chapters 30 and 31).

### Intelligence and Ability

*Intelligence (1, 7, 14, 16, 37, 39, 40, 41, 42, 43, 46, 47, 72, 83, 86, 98, 119, 124, 125, 131, 132, 133, 137, 139, 157).* In 1970, twenty-five reports of positive relations between leadership, intelligence, and ability were found. In the 1948 survey, Stogdill listed seventeen studies correlating intelligence test score with leadership status. The average correlation was .28. Five competent studies suggested, however, that "one of the most significant findings concerning the relation of intelligence to leadership is that extreme discrepancies between the intelligence of potential leaders and that of their followers militate against the exercise of leadership. . . ." Ghiselli (1963b) reported supporting evidence. In a study of three groups of managers he found that "the relationship between intelligence and managerial success is curvilinear with those individuals earning both low and very high scores being less likely to achieve success in management positions than those with scores at intermediate levels."

*Other Abilities.* Table 5.1 presents uniformly positive findings for studies completed between 1948 and 1970 which indicate that leaders are characterized by superior judgment and/or decisiveness (37, 39, 107, 133, 154), knowledge (24, 62, 68, 74, 107, 111, 127, 133, 141, 149, 152, 157), and fluency of speech (6, 17, 19, 53, 56, 60, 63, 82, 85, 96, 106, 127, 137, 154, 163). Nevertheless, as noted above, leaders can also be too able for those they lead. Persons with higher abilities may suffer from extreme self-preoccupation. A large discrepancy in capability between leader and led may make communications difficult. The leader's ideas may be too far in advance of the followers, so they are rejected. (Pioneers are seldom outstanding leaders.) The discrepancy in abilities is likely to be paralleled by discrepancies in interests and goals. Also, we need to keep in mind Korman's (1968) extensive review on prediction of managerial performance. Korman reported that "intelligence, as measured by verbal ability tests, is a fair predictor of first-line supervisory performance, but not of higher-level managerial performance." But one must also reckon that only those who already possess above-average intelligence are likely to have achieved top management positions in the organization. So there is a restriction in range, making it impossible for intelligence tests to discriminate the good from the bad performers at the top of the organization. Nevertheless, it should be clear that a high-level intelligence test which discriminates verbal intelligence among those at the upper end of the population's intelligence such as the Miller Analogies (used for predicting success in graduate and professional schools) is also likely to be a valid predictor of potential to rise in firms, agencies, and institutions.

*Personality*

Several differences may be noted in the 1948 and 1970 lists of personality characteristics. These differences might well be attributed to change in theories regarding the
structure of personality. Characteristics with uniformly positive findings in the 1948 list
only are adaptability and strength of conviction. Those that appear in the 1970 list only
are adjustment (20, 34, 39, 43, 55, 69, 87, 100, 102, 155, 156), aggressiveness or
assertiveness (9, 12, 17, 22, 45, 66, 68, 107, 109, 112, 133, 139), independence (9, 11,
14, 20, 51, 70, 121, 123, 127, 128, 133, 145), objectivity (1, 7, 23, 44, 55, 66, 87),
resourcefulness (3, 12, 65, 67, 122, 124, 141), enthusiasm (46, 93, 129), and tolerance
of stress (3, 20, 53, 55, 73, 91, 106, 145, 146). Characteristics that appear with positive
findings in both the 1948 and 1970 lists are alertness (22, 38, 112, 122), originality (3,
17, 44, 49, 51, 62, 69, 107, 119, 121, 123, 132, 133), personal integrity (24, 38, 52,
54, 125, 135, 141, 152, 154), and self-confidence (3, 4, 7, 8, 9, 15, 20, 29, 40, 42, 45,
47, 52, 54, 55, 57, 66, 68, 70, 74, 80, 83, 84, 97, 110, 112, 142, 163).

Ascendance (8, 9, 12, 14, 20, 21, 26, 53, 54, 55, 56, 57, 65, 66, 78, 95, 97, 98,
106, 109, 110, 118, 119, 121, 123, 131, 139, 140, 146, 158, 163), emotional balance
(3, 7, 12, 15, 20, 23, 44, 63, 66, 69, 74, 83, 102, 154), and extroversion (58) showed
almost as many negative as positive findings in the 1948 survey. These results suggest
that dominance, self-control, and outgoing personality may characterize some leaders
but not others.

The differences between 1948 and 1970 may be due primarily to the larger percentage of studies of the 1970 survey from the world of work rather than children's and
social groups. Also, Stogdill suspected that some of the absence of positive findings for
the 1970 survey might not have been reported because of his abstracters. We also must
be cautious about the volume of results obtained for some traits and not for others.
Researchers tend to pursue fads. In this decade, it is need achievement; in the next
decade, it may be assertiveness.

It seems more reasonable to conclude that personality traits have been found to
differentiate leaders from followers, successful from unsuccessful leaders, and high-
level from lower-level leaders. One practical application of this is the assessment center
for determining leadership potential among candidates for managerial positions (Bray &
Grant, 1966, Bray, Campbell & Grant, 1974). By the mid-1970s, over one thousand
such assessment centers were in operation. For two to three days, candidates are observed in interviews, leaderless group discussions, and other situational tests. They are
also tested individually with personality and aptitude tests. The In-Basket, a sampling of
managerial action requirements, is also often used. Observers meet to try to pool results
based on inferences from test results and what they observed to yield a picture of the total
personality of the candidate and his or her leadership potential in positions familiar to the
observers.

*Task-Related Characteristics*

Both surveys produced uniformly positive results which indicate that leaders are
characterized by high need for achievement (2, 7, 22, 26, 30, 45, 51, 52, 54, 56, 66, 69,
70, 95, 104, 109, 132, 140, 145, 149) and responsibility (3, 11, 13, 17, 22, 44, 48, 50,

52, 59, 81, 107, 121, 125, 132, 135, 155). They tend to exhibit a high degree of task orientation (29, 53, 60, 61, 66, 74, 104, 112, 127, 130, 138, 139, 149) and are responsible and dependable in pursuit of objectives (8, 52, 74, 104, 127, 135). They exhibit enterprise and initiative (40, 42, 44, 58, 64, 80, 107, 121, 124, 132) and are persistent in overcoming obstacles. All these items suggest that leaders are individuals with strong motivation, drive, and persistence.

### Social Characteristics

The positive findings on social characteristics suggest that leaders are active participants in various activities. They interact easily with a wide range of personalities (31, 58, 60, 61, 70, 88, 108, 110, 136), and this interaction is valued by others. They are not only cooperative with others (3, 9, 55, 150, 154) but also are able to enlist cooperation (9, 129, 152) and to execute (administer) projects (22, 24, 40, 42, 54, 66, 79, 81, 90, 106, 109, 118, 127, 132, 152, 163). Interpersonal skills (9, 15, 17, 18, 22, 28, 29, 43, 45, 46, 53, 55, 56, 57, 58, 63, 65, 67, 68, 69, 78, 90, 99, 106, 110, 111, 119, 124, 136, 144, 145, 152, 154, 157), including tactfulness (65, 69, 81, 155), make them attractive to followers (40, 53, 58, 129). They are valued by group members because they possess characteristics such as nurturance (24, 53, 92, 135) and popularity (61) that foster loyalty and group cohesiveness.

### IMPLICATIONS

The leader is characterized by a strong drive for responsibility and task completion, vigor and persistence in pursuit of goals, venturesomeness and originality in problem solving, drive to exercise initiative in social situations, self-confidence and sense of personal identity, willingness to accept consequences of decision and action, readiness to absorb interpersonal stress, willingness to tolerate frustration and delay, ability to influence other persons' behavior, and capacity to structure social interaction systems to the purpose at hand.

It can be concluded that the clusters of characteristics listed above differentiate leaders from followers, effective from ineffective leaders, and higher-echelon from lower-echelon leaders. In other words, different strata of leaders and followers can be described in terms of the extent to which they exhibit some of the characteristics. Research by Bass (1953), Moore and Smith (1953), and Tarnopol (1958), however, suggests that isolates—and, to some extent, followers—are described more accurately by the antonyms of trait names describing leaders. The characteristics generate personality dynamics advantageous to the person seeking the responsibilities of leadership. The conclusion that personality is a factor in leadership differentiation does not represent a return to the trait approach. It does represent a sensible modification of the extreme situationist point of view. The trait approach tended to treat personality variables in an atomistic fashion, suggesting that each trait acted singly to determine leadership effects. The situationist approach, on the other hand, denied the influences of individual differences, attributing all variance between persons to fortuitous demands of the environment.

Again, we state that some of the variance in who emerges as leader and who is successful and effective is due to traits of consequence in the situation; some of the variance is due to situational effects and some of the variance is due to the interaction of traits and situation. For example, suppose we test candidates for management positions in three situations: social service agencies, industrial firms, and military organizations. We are likely to find that individual interpersonal competence is in the aggregate predictive of successful performance. But it is also most predictive in social service agencies and least predictive in military organizations. Considering the importance of task competence and interpersonal competence at two stages in the careers of public accountants, engineers, and other kinds of technical specialists, both are important to performance. During the early years with a firm, technical competence is most strongly indicative of successful performance, but after two to five years, interpersonal competence becomes more important.

The element of chance would appear to play a part in the rise of individual leaders. A given leader may be able to rise to the top of the hierarchy in competition with one group of peers, whereas he or she might be unable to do so in another group of peers. An individual's upward mobility would seem to depend to a considerable degree upon being at the right place at the right time. Finally, it should be noted that to a very large extent our conceptions of characteristics of leadership are culturally determined, as will be elucidated in Chapter 32. Situational contingencies will be examined fully in Chapters 23 through 29.

## REFERENCES TO THE PRECEDING NUMBERING USED IN THIS CHAPTER

1. ALBRECHT, P. A., GLASER, E. M., & MARKS, J. Validation of a multiple-assessment procedure for managerial personnel. *J. appl. Psychol.*, 1964, *48*, 351–360.

2. ANDREWS, J. D. W. The achievement motive and advancement in two types of organizations. *J. pers. soc. Psychol.*, 1967, *6*, 163–168.

3. ARGYRIS, C. Some characteristics of successful executives. *Personnel J.*, 1953, *32*, 50–63.

4. BAKER, R. A., WARE, J. R., SPIRES, G. H., & OSBORN, W. C. The effects of supervisory threat on decision making and risk taking in a simulated combat game. *Behav. Sci.*, 1966, *11*, 167–176.

5. BASS, A. R. Some determinants of supervisory and peer ratings. *Dissertation Abstr.*, 1964, *24*, 5526.

6. BASS, B. M. Interrelations among measurements of leadership and associated behavior. Baton Rouge: Louisiana State University, unpublished report, 1955.

7. BASS, B. M., McGEHEE, C. R., HAWKINS, W. C., YOUNG, P. C. & GEBEL, A. S. Personality variables related to leaderless group discussion behavior. *J. abnorm. soc. Psychol.*, 1953, *48*, 120–128.

8. BEER, M., BUCKHOUT, R., ROROWITZ, M. W., & LEVY, S. Some perceived properties of the differences between leaders and nonleaders. *J. Psychol.*, 1959, *47*, 49–56.

9. BENTZ, V. J. The Sears experience in the investigation, description and prediction of executive behavior. Chicago: Sears, Roebuck, unpublished report, 1964.

10. BIRD, C. *Social psychology.* New York: Appleton-Century, 1940.

11. BLAKE, R. R., & MOUTON, JANE S. Perceived characteristics of elected representatives. *J. abnorm. soc. Psychol.*, 1961, *62*, 693–695.

12. BORG, W. R., & TUPES, E. C. Personality characteristics related to leadership behavior in two types of small group situational problems. *J. appl. Psychol.*, 1958, *42*, 252–256.

13. BORGATTA, E. F., FORD, R. N., & BOHRNSTEDT, G. W. The work components study (WCS): a revised set of measures for work motivation. *Multivariate behav. Res.*, 1968, *3*, 403–413.

14. BRAY, D. W., & GRANT, D. L. The assessment center in the measurement of potential for business management. *Psychol. Monogr.*, 1966, *80*(17), No. 625.

15. BROWN, D. S. Subordinates' views of ineffective executive behavior. *Acad. Mgmt. J.*, 1964, *7*, 288–299.

16. BRUCE, M. M. The prediction of effectiveness as a factory foreman. *Psychol. Monogr.*, 1953, *67*, No. 12, 1–17.

17. BURNETT, C. W. Leadership on the college campus. *Educ. res. Bull.*, 1951, *30*(2), 34–41.

18. CARP, FRANCES M., VITOLA, B. M., & McLANATHAN, F. L. Human relations knowledge and social distance set in supervisors. *J. appl. Psychol.*, 1963, *47*, 78–80.

19. CARTER, L., & NIXON, M. Ability, perceptual, Personality, and interest factors associated with different criteria of leadership. *J. Psychol.*, 1949, *27*, 377–388.

20. CATTELL, R. B., & STICE, G. F. Four formulae for selection of leaders on the basis of personality. *Hum. Relat.*, 1954, *7*, 493–507.

21. CHAPPLE, E. D., & DONALD, G., Jr. A method of evaluating supervisory personnel. *Harvard bus. Rev.*, 1946, *24*, 197–214.

22. COATES, C. H., & PELLEGRIN, R. J. Executives and supervisors: contrasting self-perceptions and conceptions of each other. *Amer. soc. Rev.*, 1957, *22*, 217–220.

23. COBB, K. Measuring leadership in college women by free association. *J. abnorm. soc. Psychol.*, 1952, *47*, 126–128.

24. COLYER, D. M. The good foreman—as his men see him. *Personnel*, 1951, *28*, 140–147.

25. COX, C. M. *The early mental traits of three hundred geniuses.* Stanford, Calif.: Stanford University Press, 1926.

26. CUMMINGS, L. L., & SCOTT, W. E. Academic and leadership performance of graduate business students. *Business Perspectives*, 1965, *1*, 11–20.

27. CUSSLER, MARGARET. *The woman executive.* New York: Harcourt, Brace & World, 1958.

28. DUBRIN, A. J. Trait and interpersonal self descriptions of leaders and nonleaders in an industrial setting. *J. indus. Psychol.*, 1964, *2*, 51–55.

29. DUNTEMAN, G., & BASS, B. M. Supervisory and engineering success associated with self, interaction, and task orientation scores. *Personnel Psychol.*, 1963, *16*, 13–22.

30. EDEL, E. C. Need for success as a predictor of managerial performance. *Personnel Psychol.*, 1968, *21*, 231–240.

31. FEIL, MADELEINE H. A study of leadership and scholastic achievement in their relation to prediction factors. Columbus: Ohio State University, Doctoral Dissertation, 1950.

32. FERGUSON, L. W. The L.O.M.A. merit rating scales. *Personnel Psychol.*, 1950, *3*, 193–216.

33. FIEDLER, F. E. Leadership experience and leader performance—another hypothesis shot to hell. *Org. behav. hum. Perform.*, 1970, *5*, 1–14.

34. FITZSIMMONS, S. J., & MARCUSE, F. L. Adjustment in leaders and nonleaders as measured by the sentence completion projective technique. *J. clin. Psychol.*, 1961, *17*, 380–381.

35. FLANAGAN, J. C. Critical requirements: a new approach to employee evaluation. *Personnel Psychol.*, 1949, *2*, 419–425.

36. FOREHAND, G. A., & GUETZKOW, H. The administrative judgment test as related to descriptions of executive judgment behaviors. *J. appl. Psychol.*, 1961, *45*, 257–261.

37. Fox, V. A study of the promotion of enlisted men in the army. *J. appl. Psychol.*, 1947, *31*, 298–305.

38. Frankfort, H., Frankfort, H. A., Wilson, J. A., & Jacobsen, T. *Before philosophy*. Baltimore: Penguin Books, 1949.

39. George, E. I., & Abraham, P. A. A comparative study of leaders and non-leaders among pupils in secondary schools. *J. psychol. Researches*, 1966, *10*, 116–120.

40. Ghiselli, E. E. Traits differentiating management personnel. *Personnel Psychol.*, 1959, *12*, 535–544.

41. Ghiselli, E. E. Intelligence and managerial success. *Psychol. Rep.*, 1963, *121*, 898.

42. Ghiselli, E. E. The validity of management traits in relation to occupational level. *Personnel Psychol.*, 1963, *16*, 109–113.

43. Ghiselli, E. E. Maturity of self-perception in relation to managerial success. *Personnel Psychol.*, 1964, *17*, 41–48.

44. Ghiselli, E. E., & Barthol, R. P. Role perceptions of successful and unsuccessful supervisors. *J. abnorm. soc. Psychol.*, 1956, *40*, 241–244.

45. Gibb, C. A. The principles and traits of leadership. *J. abnorm. soc. Psychol.*, 1947, *42*, 267–284.

46. Gibb, C. A. Some tentative comments concerning group Rorschach pointers to the personality traits of leaders. *J. soc. Psychol.*, 1949, *30*, 251–263.

47. Goldberg, Miriam L. Leadership and self-attitudes. *Dissertation Abstr.*, 1955, *15*, 1457–1458.

48. Gordon, L. V. Personal factors in leadership. *J. soc. Psychol.*, 1952, *36*, 245–248.

49. Gordon, L. V. *Gordon Personal Inventory Manual*. New York: Harcourt, Brace & World, 1963.

50. Gordon, L. V., & Medland, F. F. Leadership aspiration and leadership ability. *Psychol. Rep.*, 1965, *17*, 388–390.

51. Gordon, L. V. Work environment preference schedule—WEPS: preliminary manual, 1966 (mimeo).

52. Gough, H. G., McClosky, H., & Meehl, P. A personality scale for social responsibility. *J. abnorm. soc. Psychol.*, 1952, *47*, 73–80.

53. Grant, D. L., & Bray, D. W. Contributions of the interview to assessment of management potential. *J. appl. Psychol.*, 1969, *53*, 24–34.

54. Gruenfeld, L. W., & Weissenberg, P. Supervisory characteristics and attitudes toward performance appraisals. *Personnel Psychol.*, 1966, *19*, 143–151.

55. Guilford, Joan S. Temperament traits of executives and supervisors measured by the Guilford Personality Inventories. *J. appl. Psychol.*, 1952, *36*, 228–233.

56. Hardesty, D. L., & Jones, W. S. Characteristics of judged high potential management personnel—the operations of an industrial assessment center. *Personnel Psychol.*, 1968, *21*, 85–98.

57. Harrell, T. W. The personality of high earning MBA's in big business. *Personnel Psychol.*, 1969, *22*, 457–463.

58. Harrell, T. W. *Personality differences between extreme performers during a fourth discussion session*. Stanford, Calif.: Stanford University, Graduate School of Business, Technical Report No. 12, 1966.

59. Harrell, T. W., Burnham, Lucy E., & Lee, H. E. *Correlations between seven leadership criteria*. Stanford, Calif.: Stanford University, Graduate School of Business, Technical Report No. 4, 1963.

60. Harrell, T. W., Burnham, Lucy E., Hunt, Ruth S., & Lee, H. E. *Reliability and intercorrelations for thirteen leadership criteria*. Stanford, Calif.: Stanford University, Graduate School of Business, Technical Report No. 8, 1964.

**61.** HARRELL, T. W., & LEE, H. E. *An investigation of the product moment intercorrelations among small group leadership criteria.* Stanford, Calif.: Stanford University, Graduate School of Business, Technical Report No. 6, 1964.

**62.** HARRIS, B. M. Leadership prediction as related to measures of personal characteristics. *Personnel Admin.*, 1964, *27*, 31–35.

**63.** HARVILLE, D. L. Early identification of potential leaders. *J. coll. student Personnel,* 1969, *10*, 333–335.

**64.** HELFRICH, MARGARET L., & SCHWIRIAN, K. P. The American businesswoman—entrepreneur or bureaucrat? *Bull. bus. Res.*, Ohio State University, 1968, *43*(11), 1, 6–9.

**65.** HEMPHILL, J. K., GRIFFITHS, D. E., & FREDERIKSEN, N. *Administrative performance and personality: a study of the principal in a simulated elementary school.* New York: Teachers College, Columbia University, 1962.

**65a.** HENRY, E. R. *Social science research reports,* vol. 1, 2, 3. New York: Standard Oil Company (New Jersey), 1963, 1964.

**66.** HENRY, W. E. Executive personality and job success. *Amer. Mgmt. Assn., Personnel Series No. 120,* 1948, pp. 3–13.

**67.** HICKS, J. A., & STONE, J. B. The identification of traits related to managerial success. *J. appl. Psychol.*, 1962, *46*, 428–432.

**68.** HOBERT, R., & DUNNETTE, M. D. Development of moderator variables to enhance the prediction of managerial effectiveness. *J. appl. Psychol.*, 1967, *51*, 50–64.

**69.** HOLTZMAN, W. H. Adjustment and leadership: a study of the Rorschach test. *J. soc. Psychol.*, 1952, *36*, 179–189.

**70.** HORNADAY, J. A., & BUNKER, C. S. The nature of the entrepreneur. *Personnel Psychol.*, 1970, *23*, 47–54.

**71.** HULIN, C. L. The measurement of executive success. *J. appl. Psychol.*, 1962, *46*, 303–306.

**72.** IZARD, C. E. Personality correlates of sociometric status. *J. appl. Psychol.*, 1959, *43*, 89–93.

**73.** JAQUES, E. *Measurement of responsibility.* Cambridge, Mass.: Harvard University Press, 1956.

**74.** JENKINS, D. H., & BLACKMAN, C. A. *Antecedents and effects of administrator behavior.* Columbus: Ohio State University, College of Education, 1956.

**75.** JENKINS, W. O. A review of leadership studies with particular reference to military problems. *Psychol. Bull.*, 1947, *44*, 54–79.

**76.** JENNINGS, E. E. *The mobile manager: a study of the new generation of top executives.* Ann Arbor: University of Michigan, Bureau of Industrial Relations, 1967.

**77.** JOHNSON, A. C., PETERSON, R. B., & KAHLER, G. E. Historical changes in characteristics of formen. *Personnel J.*, 1968, *47*, 475–481, 499.

**78.** KAESS, W. A., WITRYOL, S. L., & NOLAN, R. E. Reliability, sex differences, and validity in the leadership discussion group. *J. appl. Psychol.*, 1961, *45*, 345–350.

**79.** KATZELL, R. A., BARRETT, R. S., VANN, D. H., & HOGAN, J. M. Organizational correlates of executive roles. *J. appl. Psychol.*, 1968, *52*, 22–28.

**80.** KAUFMAN, R. A., HAKMILLER, K. L., & PORTER, L. W. The effects of top and middle management sets on the Ghiselli Self-Description Inventory. *J. appl. Psychol.*, 1959, *43*, 149–153.

**81.** KAY, B. R. Key factors in effective foremen behavior. *Personnel*, 1959, *36*, 25–31.

**82.** KAY, E., & MEYER, H. H. The development of a job activity questionnaire for production foremen. *Personnel Psychol.*, 1962, *15*, 411–418.

**83.** KIESSLING, R. J., & KALISH, R. A. Correlates of success in leaderless group discussion. *J. soc. Psychol.*, 1961, *54*, 359–365.

**84.** Kipnis, D., & Lane, W. P. Self-confidence and leadership. *J. appl. Psychol.*, 1962, *46*, 291–295.

**85.** Kirscht, J. P., Lodahl, T. M., & Haire, M. Some factors in the selection of leaders by members of small groups. *J. abnorm. soc. Psychol.*, 1959, *58*, 406–408.

**86.** Korman, A. K. The prediction of managerial performance: a review. *Personnel Psychol.*, 1968, *21*, 295–322.

**87.** Krishnan, B. The leadership qualities among the college students as assessed by the "L" scale of the Mysore Personality Inventory. *Psychol. Studies*, 1965, *10*, 23–36.

**88.** Krumboltz, J. D., Christal, R. E., & Ward, J. H. Predicting leadership ratings from high school activities. *J. educ. Psychol.*, 1959, *50*, 105–110.

**89.** Kumar, P. Certain personal factors in student leadership. *J. psychol. Researches*, 1966, *10*, 37–42.

**90.** Lange, C. J., Campbell, V., Katter, R. V., & Shanley, F. J. *A study of leadership in army infantry platoons.* Washington, D.C.: Human Resources Office, George Washington University, 1958.

**91.** Lange, C. J., & Jacobs, T. O. *Leadership in army infantry platoons: study II.* Washington, D.C.: George Washington University, Human Resources Research Office, 1960.

**92.** Lehman, H. C. *Age and achievement.* Princeton, N.J.: Princeton University Press, 1953.

**93.** Lemann, T. B., & Soloman, R. L. Group characteristics as revealed in sociometric patterns and personality ratings. *Sociometry*, 1952, *15*, 7–90.

**94.** Lewis, G. F. A comparison of some aspects of the backgrounds and careers of small businessmen and American business leaders. *Amer. J. Sociol.*, 1960, *65*, 348–355.

**95.** Lindsey, G., & Urdan, J. A. Personality and social choice. *Sociometry*, 1955, *18*, 47–63.

**95a.** MacKinney, A. C. The longitudinal study of manager performance: phase I variables. Unpublished report, 1968.

**96.** MacNaughton, J. D. A study of foremen's communication. *Personnel pract. Bull.*, 1963, *19*, 10–17.

**97.** Mahoney, T. A., Jerdee, T. H., & Nash, A. N. *The identification of management potential.* Dubuque, Iowa: Brown, 1961.

**98.** Mahoney, T. A., Sorenson, W. W., Jerdee, T. H., & Nash, A. N. Identification and prediction of managerial effectiveness. *Personnel Admin.*, 1963, *26*, 12–22.

**99.** Mandell, M. M. Supervisors' attitudes and job performance. *Personnel*, 1949, *26*, 182–183.

**100.** Mann, J. H. The relation between role playing ability and interpersonal adjustment. *J. gen. Psychol.*, 1960, *62*, 177–183.

**101.** Mann, R. D. A review of the relationships between personality and performance in small groups. *Psychol. Bull.*, 1959, *56*, 241–270.

**102.** Martin, W. E., Gross, N., & Darley, J. G. Studies of group behavior: leaders, followers, and isolates in small organized groups. *J. abnorm. soc. Psychol.*, 1952, *47*, 838–842.

**103.** Matthews, D. R. *The social background of political decision-makers.* New York: Random House, 1954.

**104.** Medow, H., & Zander, A. Aspirations for the group chosen by central and peripheral members. *J. pers. soc. Psychol.*, 1965, *1*, 224–228.

**105.** Meyer, H. D., & Fredian, A. J. Personality test scores in the management hierarchy: revisited. *J. appl. Psychol.*, 1959, *43*, 212–220.

**106.** Meyer, H. H. Factors related to success in the human relations aspect of work-group leadership. *Psychol. Monogr.*, 1951, *65*(3), No. 320.

107. MILES, R. E. Conflicting elements in managerial ideologies. *Indus. Relat.*, 1964, *4*, 77–91.

108. MILLER, D. C., & DIRKSEN, J. L. The identification of visible, concealed, and symbolic leaders in a small Indiana city: a replication of the Bonjean-Noland study of Burlington, North Carolina. *Soc. Forces*, 1965, *43*, 548–555.

109. MINER, J. B. The early identification of managerial talent. *Personnel guid. J.*, 1968, *46*, 586–591.

110. MOMENT, D., & ZALEZNIK, A. *Role development and interpersonal competence.* Boston: Harvard University, Graduate School of Business Administration, 1963.

111. MOORE, J. V., & SMITH, R. G. Some aspects of noncommissioned officer leadership. *Personnel Psychol.*, 1953, *6*, 427–443.

112. NELSON, P. D. An evaluation of a popular leader. *USN MNPRU Rep. No. 63–9.*

113. NELSON, P. D. Similarities and differences among leaders and followers. *J. soc. Psychol.*, 1964, *63*, 161–167.

114. NEWCOMER, MABEL. *The big business executive: the factors that made him, 1900–1950.* New York: Columbia University Press, 1955.

115. O'DONOVAN, T. R. Differential extent of opportunity among executives and lower managers. *Acad. Mgmt. J.*, 1962, *5*, 139–149.

116. PALMER, G. J. Task ability and effective leadership. *Psychol. Rep.*, 1962, *10*, 863–866.

117. PALMER, G. J. Task ability and successful and effective leadership. *Psychol. Rep.*, 1962, *11*, 813–816.

118. PETERSEN, P. B., & LIPPITT, G. L. Comparison of behavioral styles between entering and graduating students in officer candidate school. *J. appl. Psychol.*, 1968, *52*, 66–70.

119. PICKLE, H., & FRIEDLANDER, F. Seven societal criteria of organizational success. *Personnel Psychol.*, 1967, *20*, 165–178.

120. PORTER, A. Validity of socioeconomic origin as a predictor of executive success. *J. appl. Psychol.*, 1965, *49*, 11–13.

121. PORTER, L. W. Differential self-perceptions of management personnel and line workers. *J. appl. Psychol.*, 1958, *42*, 105–108.

122. PORTER, L. W. Self-perceptions of first-level supervisors compared with upper management personnel and with operative line workers. *J. appl. Psychol.*, 1959, *43*, 183–186.

123. PORTER, L. W. Perceived trait requirements in bottom and middle management jobs. *J. appl. Psychol.*, 1961, *45*, 232–236.

124. PORTER, L. W., & GHISELLI, E. E. The self perceptions of top and middle management personnel. *Personnel Psychol.*, 1957, *10*, 397–406.

125. POWELL, R. M. Sociometric analyses of informal groups—their structure and function in two contrasting communities. *Sociometry*, 1952, *15*, 367–399.

126. POWELL, R. M. *Race, religion, and the promotion of the American executive.* Columbus: Ohio State University, College of Administrative Science, 1969.

127. POWELL, R. M., & NELSON, D. H. The business executive's self-image versus his image of the politician. *Personnel J.*, 1969, *48*, 677–682.

128. PRESTHUS, R. *Behavioral approaches to public administration.* Montgomery; University of Alabama Press, 1965.

129. PRICE, MARY A. *A study of motivational factors associated with leadership behavior of young women in a private school.* Columbus: Ohio State University, Doctoral Dissertation, 1948.

130. PRIEN, E. P., & CULLER, A. R. Leaderless group discussion participation and interobserver agreements. *J. soc. Psychol.*, 1964, *62*, 321–328.

**131.** RAINIO, K. *Leadership qualities: a theoretical inquiry and an experimental study of foremen*. Helsinki: Submalaisen Tiedeakatemian Toimituksia Annales Academie Scientiarum Fennicae, 1955.

**132.** RANDLE, C. W. How to identify promotable executives. *Harvard bus. Rev.*, 1956, *34* (3), 122–134.

**133.** ROADMAN, H. E. The industrial use of peer ratings. *J. appl. Psychol.*, 1964, *48*, 211–214.

**134.** ROE, ANNE. *The psychology of occupations*. New York: Wiley, 1956.

**135.** ROFF, M. A. A study of combat leadership in the air force by means of a rating scale: group differences. *J. Psychol.*, 1950, *30*, 229–239.

**136.** ROSE, A. M. Alienation and participation: a comparison of group leaders and the "Mass." *Amer. sociol. Rev.*, 1962, *27*, 834–838.

**137.** ROWLAND, K. M., & SCOTT, W. E., Jr. Psychological attributes of effective leadership in a formal organization. *Personnel Psychol.*, 1968, *21*, 365–377.

**138.** RUBENOWITZ, S. Job oriented and person oriented leadership. *Personnel Psychol.*, 1962, *15*, 387–396.

**139.** RYCHLAK, J. F. Personality correlates of leadership among first level managers. *Psychol. Rep.*, 1963, *12*, 43–52.

**140.** SANDERS, E. P. Evolutionary performance, managerial abilities, and change: an exploratory investigation of organizations. *J. appl. Psychol.*, 1968, *52*, 362–365.

**141.** SARACHEK, B. Greek concepts of leadership. *Acad. Mgmt. J.*, 1968, *11*, 39–48.

**142.** SCHILLER, M. A new approach to leadership assessment. *Personnel Psychol.*, 1961, *14*, 75–86.

**143.** SCIENTIFIC AMERICAN. The big business executive: 1964. *Scientific American*, 1965.

**144.** SHARTLE, C. L. *Some psychological factors in foremanship*. Columbus: Ohio State University, Doctoral Dissertation, 1933.

**145.** SHARTLE, C. L. A clinical approach to foremanship. *Personnel J.*, 1934, *13*, 135–139.

**146.** SINHA, D., & KUMAR, P. A Study of certain personality variables in student leadership. *Psychol. Studies*, 1966, *11*, 1–8.

**147.** SISSON, E. D. Forced choice—the new army rating. *Personnel Psychol.*, 1948, *1*, 365–381.

**148.** SMITH, G. A., & MATTHEWS, J. B. *Business, society, and the individual; problems in responsible leadership of private enterprise organizations operating in a free society*. Homewood, Ill.: Irwin, 1967.

**149.** SPRINGER, DORIS. Ratings of candidates for promotion by co-workers and supervisors. *J. appl. Psychol.*, 1953, *37*, 347–351.

**150.** STANLEY, D. T., MANN, D. E., & DOIG, J. W. *Men who govern: a biographical profile of federal political executives*. Washington, D.C.: Brookings, 1967.

**151.** STANTON & POORS. *Register of corporations, directors, and executives*. New York: Stanton & Poors, 1967.

**152.** STEPHENSON, T. E. The leader-follower relationship. *Sociol. Rev.*, 1959, *7*, 179–195.

**153.** STOGDILL, R. M. Personal factors associated with leadership: a survey of the literature. *J. Psychol.*, 1948, *25*, 35–71.

**154.** STRYKER, P. *The character of the executive*. New York: Harper & Row, 1960.

**155.** TARNOPOL, L. Personality differences between leaders and non-leaders. *Personnel J.*, 1958, *37*, 57–60.

**156.** TERRELL, G., & SHREFFLER, JOY. A developmental study of leadership. *J. educ. Res.*, 1958, *52*, 69–72.

**157.** THORNTON, G. C. The relationship between supervisory-and-self-appraisals of executive performance. *Personnel Psychol.*, 1968, *21*, 441–455.

**158.** TUPES, E. C., CARP, A., & BORG, W. R. Performance in role-playing situations as related to leadership and personality measures. *Sociometry, 1958, 21,* 165–179.

**159.** WARNER, W. L., & ABEGGLEN, J. C. *Occupational mobility in American business and industry, 1928–1952.* Minneapolis: University of Minnesota Press, 1955.

**160.** WEINBERG, C. Institutional differences in factors associated with student leadership. *Sociol. soc. Res.,* 1965, *49,* 425–436.

**161.** WILLIAMSON, E. G. The group origins of student leaders. *Educ. psychol. Measmt.,* 1948, *8,* 603–612.

**162.** WILSON, R. C., BEEM, HELEN P., & COMREY, A. L. Factors influencing organizational effectiveness. III. A survey of skilled tradesmen. *Personnel Psychol.,* 1953, *6,* 313–325.

**163.** WOLLOWICK, H. B., & McNAMARA, W. J. Relationship of the components of an assessment center to management success. *J. appl. Psychol.,* 1969, *5,* 348–352.

## FACTOR ANALYTIC SUMMARIES OF TRAITS OF LEADERSHIP (1945–1970)

Stogdill completed a survey of factorial studies published since 1945 to determine whether they had identified many factors in common. The analysis was based on fifty-two factorial studies. They included surveys of large numbers of military and industrial personnel, studies of leadership in military and industrial groups, and reports on experimental groups.

Factors identified by three or more researchers are listed in Table 5.2. Factors found by only one or two authors are not listed. Table 5.3 shows the authors who found each of the factors. The references are listed at the end of the chapter.

It may be observed in Table 5.2 that the most frequently occurring factors are descriptive of various skills of the leader. They include the following: social and interpersonal skills, technical skills, administrative skills, intellectual skills, leadership effectiveness and achievement, social nearness, friendliness, group task supportiveness, and task motivation and application.

These factors describe leaders differing from each other consistently in making effective use of interpersonal, administrative, technical, and intellectual skills. Some can be described as highly task-motivated, others are most capable of maintaining close, friendly, personal relationships. Chapter 6 will concentrate on these competencies.

The next most frequent set of factors is concerned with how leaders relate to their groups. Behaviors include: maintaining group cohesiveness, coordination, task motivation, task performance, and high quality of output. Concern for group performance is softened by nurturant behavior and the use of informal controls. These factors are as follows: maintaining cohesive work group, maintaining coordination and teamwork, maintaining standards of performance, informal group control (group freedom), and nurturant behavior.

Next in frequency are factors concerned strictly with personal characteristics of leaders. They may be described in terms of how much they are emotionally well-balanced, willing to assume responsibility, ethical in conduct, able to communicate readily, dominant, energetic, experienced, courageous, and mature. These factors are as follows: willingness to assume responsibility, emotional balance and control, ethical conduct, personal integrity, communicative, verbality, ascendance, dominance, per-

**TABLE 5.2**
**Factors Appearing in Three or More Studies**

| Factor No. | Factor Name | Frequency |
|---|---|---|
| 1 | Social and interpersonal skills | 16 |
| 2 | Technical skills | 18 |
| 3 | Administrative skills | 12 |
| 4 | Leadership effectiveness and achievement | 15 |
| 5 | Social nearness, friendliness | 18 |
| 6 | Intellectual skills | 11 |
| 7 | Maintaining cohesive work group | 9 |
| 8 | Maintaining coordination and teamwork | 7 |
| 9 | Task motivation and application | 17 |
| 10 | General impression (halo) | 12 |
| 11 | Group task supportiveness | 17 |
| 12 | Maintaining standards of performance | 5 |
| 13 | Willingness to assume responsibility | 10 |
| 14 | Emotional balance and control | 15 |
| 15 | Informal group control | 4 |
| 16 | Nurturant behavior | 4 |
| 17 | Ethical conduct, personal integrity | 10 |
| 18 | Communication, verbality | 6 |
| 19 | Ascendance, dominance, decisiveness | 11 |
| 20 | Physical energy | 6 |
| 21 | Experience and activity | 4 |
| 22 | Mature, cultured | 3 |
| 23 | Courage, daring | 4 |
| 24 | Aloof, distant | 3 |
| 25 | Creative, independent | 5 |
| 26 | Conforming | 5 |

sonal soundness, good character, physical energy, experience and activity, mature, cultured, courage, daring, aloof, distant, creative, independent, and conforming.

If the order of frequency of factors is significant, it would appear that successful leadership involves certain skills and capabilities—interpersonal, technical, administrative, and intellectual—enabling leaders to be of value to their group or organization. These skills allow them to maintain satisfactory levels of group cohesiveness, drive, and productivity. They are further assisted in execution of the above functions if they possess a high degree of task motivation, personal integrity, communicative ability, and the like. In sum, the factorial studies seem to provide a rather well-balanced picture of the skills, functions, and personal characteristics of the leader.

**TABLE 5.3**
**Authors (Identified by Reference Number) Who Found a Given Factor**

| Factor | \multicolumn{26}{c}{Author Number} | | | | | | | | | | | | | | | | | | | | | | | | |
|---|---|---|---|---|---|---|---|---|---|---|---|---|---|---|---|---|---|---|---|---|---|---|---|---|---|---|
| | 1 | 2 | 3 | 4 | 5 | 6 | 7 | 8 | 9 | 10 | 11 | 12 | 13 | 14 | 15 | 16 | 17 | 18 | 19 | 20 | 21 | 22 | 23 | 24 | 25 | 26 |
| 1 | × | × | | | | | | × | | | | × | | | × | × | | × | × | | × | × | × | × | | |
| 2 | × | × | | | | | | | | | | | | | × | × | × | | | | × | × | × | × | | |
| 3 | | | × | | × | | | | | | | | | | | × | × | | | | | | | | | |
| 4 | | | | × | × | | | × | | | | × | | × | | | | × | × | × | | × | | | | × |
| 5 | | × | | | × | | | | × | × | | | × | × | | | | × | | | | | | | | × |
| 6 | | | | × | × | × | × | | | | | | | | | | | | | | | | | | | |
| 7 | | | × | | | | × | | | × | | | × | | | | | | | | | | | | × | × |
| 8 | | | | | | | | × | | | | | | | | | | | | | | | | | × | |
| 9 | | | × | | | | | | × | | | | × | | | | | | | | | × | × | × | | |
| 10 | × | × | | | | | | | | | | | | | | × | | | | | × | × | × | | | |
| 11 | | | | | × | | × | | | | × | | | × | × | | × | × | × | × | × | × | | × | × | |
| 12 | | | | | | | | × | | | | × | | | × | | | × | | × | | | | | | |
| 13 | | | | | × | | | | × | | | × | | | × | | × | × | | | | | | | | |
| 14 | | | | | | | | × | | | × | | | | × | | | | | | | | | | | |
| 15 | | | | | | | | | | | | | | | | | | | | | | × | | | | |
| 16 | | | | | | | | × | | | | | | | × | × | | × | | | | × | | | | × |
| 17 | | | | | | | | | | | × | | | | | | | | | | | | | | | |
| 18 | | | × | | | | | | | | | | | | × | | | | | | | | | | | |
| 19 | | | × | × | × | | | × | | | | | | | | | | | | | | | | | | |
| 20 | | | | | × | | | | | | | | | | | | | | | | | | | | | |
| 21 | | | × | | | | | | | | × | | | | | | | | | | | | | | | |
| 22 | | | | | | | | | × | | × | | | | | | | | | | | | | | | |
| 23 | | | | × | | | | | | | | | | | × | | | | | | | | | | | |
| 24 | | | × | | | | | | | | | | | | | | | | | | | | | | | |
| 25 | | | | × | | | | | | | | | | | | | | | × | | | | | | | |
| 26 | | | | | | | | | | | | | | | | | | | | | | | | | | |

**TABLE 5.3**
**Authors (Identified by Reference Number) Who Found a Given Factor**
*(Continued)*

| Factor | | | | | | | | | | | | | | | | Author Number | | | | | | | | | | |
|---|---|---|---|---|---|---|---|---|---|---|---|---|---|---|---|---|---|---|---|---|---|---|---|---|---|---|
| | 27 | 28 | 29 | 30 | 31 | 32 | 33 | 34 | 35 | 36 | 37 | 38 | 39 | 40 | 41 | 42 | 43 | 44 | 45 | 46 | 47 | 48 | 49 | 50 | 51 | 52 |
| 1 | | × | × | | | | | | | | | | | | × | | | | | | | | × | | | |
| 2 | | | | × | | × | | | × | × | | | × | × | × | | | × | × | | × | × | × | | × | × |
| 3 | × | | | × | | | × | | × | × | × | | × | × | | | | × | | | × | × | | | | × |
| 4 | | | × | × | | × | | | × | × | × | | | × | | | | | | | | × | × | | | |
| 5 | × | | | | × | | | | | | | | × | × | | × | × | | | | | | | × | | × |
| 6 | | × | | × | | | | | | | | × | | | × | | | | | | | × | | × | | |
| 7 | | | | × | | | | | | | × | | × | | × | | | | | | × | | | | × | |
| 8 | | | | × | | | | | | | | × | × | | | | | | | | × | | | | × | × |
| 9 | × | | × | | × | | | | | | | | × | | × | | × | | | | | | | | | × |
| 10 | | × | | | | | × | | | × | | | × | | × | | × | × | | × | | | | | | |
| 11 | | × | | | × | | | | | × | × | | × | | | | × | | | × | | | | | × | |
| 12 | × | | | | | | | | | | | | × | | | | | | × | × | | | | | | × |
| 13 | | | | | | | × | × | | | | | | | | | | | | | | | | | | |
| 14 | | | × | × | | | | × | | | | | × | × | × | × | | × | | | × | | × | | | |
| 15 | × × | | × | | | | | | | × | | | × | | | × | | | × | | | | | | | |
| 16 | × × | | | | | | | | | × | | | × | | | | | | | | | | | | | |
| 17 | × | | × | × | × | | × | × | | × | | | × | × | | | | | | × | × | | | × | | |
| 18 | | | × | | | | × | × | × | × | × | | | × | × | | × | | × | × | × | × | × | | | |
| 19 | | | × | | | | | | × | | | | × | | × | | × | × | | | × | × | × | | | |
| 20 | | | | × | | × | | × | × | × | | | × | | | | | × | | | × | | × | | | |
| 21 | | | × | | | | | | | | | | | | | | | | | | | | | | | |
| 22 | | | × | × | | | | | | × | | | | | × | | | | | | | | | | | |
| 23 | | | × | | | | | | | | | | | | × | | | | | | | | | | | |
| 24 | | × | × | | | | | | | | | | | × | | | | | | | | | | | | |
| 25 | | × | | | | | | | | | | | | | | | × | × | | | | | | | | |
| 26 | | | | | | | | | | | | × | | | | × | × | × | | × | | | | | | |

*Caveats*

The factors that emerged from the analysis of intercorrelations of items describing leaders depended to a large degree on (1) the kinds of items on which descriptions were obtained (item mix); (2) the numbers of items in different descriptive categories; and (3) the nature of the population described. Few factorial studies of leadership were comparable when matched against these three criteria. As a result, few studies produced identical factors; however, certain factors with the same or similar names appeared with considerable frequency.

If factors with the same name appear in two different studies, they did not necessarily contain loadings on identical items. In other words, it could not be assumed that the factors described identical behaviors. A factor was identified or named on the basis of the nature of items with the highest loadings on the factor. If several similar items have high loadings, the element of item similarity is usually given heavy consideration in naming the factor.

The frequency with which a given factor appeared in the published literature did not necessarily represent the frequency of its occurrence among leaders in general. An item could not appear in a study unless measures were obtained on characteristics represented by the factor. Researchers, of course, differed in their ideas about what is important in the study of leadership. As a result, they tended to use different sets of variables in their efforts to measure leadership. Furthermore, it cannot be assumed that the listed factors constituted a complete catalog of the leader's qualities and abilities. One of the values of factor analysis is that it brings together on the same factor all items acting alike in describing the individuals in the samples. The resulting factor describes a generalized form of behavior rather than the minute details of behavior. Finally, it should be kept in mind that factors can emerge only from leaders behaving differently on different orthogonal dimensions. Thus, for initiation and consideration factors to emerge, the correlation must be low between them. The same leaders who are high in initiation should vary in consideration from high to low. Those who are low in initiation should likewise vary from high to low in consideration. Conceptually, most leaders could be high in both and the factor could fail to appear although the different behaviors could still be seen.

If the correlation is high between them, only a single factor generally will appear containing items of both kinds. Nevertheless, the same leaders who are high in consultative behavior are also likely to share in decision making (be participative) and delegate. Only one factor, consideration, will appear. Consultation where the leader decides, participation where decisions are consensual, and delegation where subordinates decide are conceptually distinct despite the fact that the same leaders who tend to use one of the approaches a great deal, also use the other two approaches a great deal. And the distinctions are important both to theory and to practice. It may be particularly important for a leader to consult rather than delegate in one circumstance. In another, it will be best if he or she delegates. More will be said about this in Chapters 19 and 21. Nevertheless, the generalized behaviors described by the twenty-six factors produce a more meaningful, logical picture of the leader than would be provided by a list of 100 haphazardly selected items, all correlated with leadership status and effectiveness. The results of the factorial studies indicate that there is no need for an infinitely large number of variables in order to obtain a well-balanced description of the leader.

## REFERENCES TO THE FACTOR ANALYTIC STUDIES

1. BARE, R. A factor analytic description of the performance of enlisted personnel. *USN Bur. naval pers. tech. Bull.*, 1956, No. 56–1, 1–37.

2. BARTLETT, C. J. Dimensions of leadership behavior in classroom discussion groups. *J. educ. Psychol.*, 1959, *50*, 280–284.

3. BASS, B. M., WURSTER, C. R., DOLL, P. A., & CLAIR, D. J. Situational and personality factors in leadership among sorority women. *Psychol. Monogr.*, 1953, *67* (16), 1–23.

4. BORG, W. R. Prediction of small group role behavior from personality variables. *J. abnorm. soc. Psychol.*, 1960, *60*, 112–116.

5. BORGATTA, E. F. Analysis of social interaction: actual, role playing, and projective. *J. abnorm. soc. Psychol.*, 1955, *51*, 394–405.

6. BORGATTA, E. F. A systematic study of interaction process scores, peer and self-assessments, personality and other variables. *Genet. psychol. Monogr.*, 1962, *65*, 219–291.

7. BORGATTA, E. F., COTTRELL, L. S., & MANN, J. H. The spectrum of individual interaction characteristics: an interdimensional analysis. *Psychol. Rep.*, 1958, *4*, 279–319.

8. BORGATTA, E. F., & ESCHENBACH, A. E. Factor analysis of Rorschach variables and behavior observation. *Psychol. Rep.*, 1955, *1*, 129–136.

9. BORGATTA, E. F., & EVANS, R. R. Behavioral and personality expectations associated with status positions. *Multivariate behav. Res.*, 1967, *2*, 153–173.

10. CARTER, L. F., HAYTHORN, W., & HOWELL, MARGARET. A further investigation of the criteria of leadership. *J. abnorm. soc. Psychol.*, 1950, *45*, 350–358.

11. CASSENS, F. P. *Cross cultural dimensions of executive life history antecedents (biographical information)*. Greensboro, N.C.: Creativity Research Institute, Richardson Foundation, 1966.

12. CATTELL, R. B., & STICE, G. F. The psychodynamics of small groups. Urbana: University of Illinois, Laboratory Personality Assessment & Group Behavior, 1953 (mimeo).

13. CLARK, R. A. Analyzing the group structure of combat rifle squads. *Amer. Psychologist*, 1953, *8*, 333.

14. COUCH, A., & CARTER, L. F. A factorial study of the rated behavior of group members. *Amer. Psychologist*, 1953, *8*, 333.

15. CRANNELL, C. W., & MOLLENKOPF, W. G. Combat leadership. In F. Wickert (ed.). *Psychological research on problems of redistribution.* Army Air Forces Aviation Psychology Program Research Reports No. 14 (1946 mimeo), 37–77.

16. CREAGER, J. A., & HARDING, F. D. A hierarchical factor analysis of foremen behavior. *J. appl. Psychol.*, 1958, *42*, 197–203.

17. FLANAGAN, J. C. Defining the requirements of the executive's job. *Personnel*, 1951, *28*, 28–35.

18. FLANAGAN, J. C. Leadership skills: their identification, development, and evaluation. In L. Petrullo & B. M. Bass. *Leadership and interpersonal behavior.* New York: Holt, Rinehart & Winston, 1961.

19. FRUTCHER, B., & SKINNER, J. A. Dimensions of leadership in a student cooperative. *Multivariate behav. Res.*, 1966, *1*, 437–445.

20. GHISELLI, E. E. Individuality as a factor in the success of management personnel. *Personnel Psychol.*, 1960, *13*, 1–10.

21. GRANT, D. L. A factor analysis of managers' ratings. *J. appl. Psychol.*, 1955, *39*, 283–286.

22. GRANT, D. L., KATKOVSKY, W., & BRAY, D. W. Contributions of projective techniques to assessment of management potential. *J. appl. Psychol.*, 1967, *51*, 226–232.

23. HAUSMAN, H. J., & STRUPP, H. H. Non-technical factors in supervisors' ratings of job performance. *Personnel Psychol.*, 1955, *8*, 201–217.

24. HAYTHORN, W. The influence of individual members on the characteristics of small groups. *J. abnorm. soc. Psychol.*, 1953, *48*, 276–284.

25. HEMPHILL, J. K., & COONS, A. E. Development of the leader behavior description questionnaire. In R. M. Stogdill & A. E. Coons. *Leader behavior: its description and measurement*. Columbus: Ohio State University, Bureau of Business Research, monogr., 1957.

26. HIGH, W. S., GOLDBERG, L., & COMREY, A. L. Factored dimensions of organizational behavior. II. Aircraft workers. *Educ. psychol. Measmt.*, 1955, *15*, 371–382.

27. HIGH, W. S., GOLDBERG, L., & COMREY, A. L. Factored dimensions of organizational behavior. III. Aircraft supervisors. *Educ. psychol. Measmt.*, 1956, *16*, 38–53.

28. HOGUE, J. P., OTIS, J. L., & PRIEN, E. P. Assessments of higher-level personnel. VI—Validity of predictions based on projective techniques. *Personnel Psychol.*, 1962, *15*, 335–344.

29. HUSSEIN, A. L. Factors emerging from favorableness judgments of basic interview data in six occupational fields. Columbus: Ohio State University, Doctoral Dissertation, 1969.

30. JENKINS, J. G., et al. *The combat criteria in naval aviation*. Washington, D.C.: U.S. Navy, Division of Aviation Medicine, Bureau of Medicine & Surgery, 1950.

31. KLEIN, S. M., & RITTI, R. R. Work pressure, supervisory behavior, and employee attitudes: a factor analysis. *Personnel Psychol.*, 1970, *23*, 153–167.

32. MANDELL, M. M. Supervisory characteristics and ratings: a summary of recent research. *Personnel*, 1956, *32*, 435–440.

33. MOORE, J. V. A factor analysis of subordinate evaluations of non-commissioned officer supervisors. *USAF Hum. Resour. Res. Cent. res. Bull.*, 1953, No. 53–6.

34. NORMAN, W. T. Toward an adequate taxonomy of personality attributes: replicated factor structure in peer nomination personality ratings. *J. abnorm. soc. Psychol.*, 1963, *66*, 574–583.

35. PALMER, G. J., & McCORMICK, E. J. A factor analysis of job activities. *J. appl. Psychol.*, 1961, *45*, 289–294.

36. PERES, S. H. Performance dimensions of supervisory positions. *Personnel Psychol.*, 1962, *15*, 405–410.

37. PRIEN, E. P. Development of a supervisor position description questionaire. *J. appl. Psychol.*, 1963, *47*, 10–14.

38. RAINIO, K. *Leadership qualities: a theoretical inquiry and an experimental study on foremen*. Helsinki: Academiae Scientiarum Fennicae, 1955.

39. ROACH, D. E. Factor analysis of rated supervisory behavior. *Personnel Psychol.*, 1956, *9*, 487–498.

40. ROFF, M. A study of combat leadership in the air force by means of a rating scale: group differences. *J. Psychol.*, 1950, *30*, 229–239.

41. SAKODA, J. M. Factor analysis of OSS situational tests. *J. abnorm. soc. Psychol.*, 1952, *47*, 843–852.

42. STAGNER, R. Personality variables in union-management relations. *J. appl. Psychol.*, 1962, *46*, 350–357.

43. STOLTZ, R. E. Factors in supervisors' perceptions of physical science research personnel. *J. appl. Psychol.*, 1959, *43*, 256–258.

44. TRIANDIS, H. C. A comparative factorial analysis of job semantic structures of managers and workers. *J. appl. Psychol.*, 1960, *44*, 297–302.

45. TURNER, W. W. Dimensions of foreman performance: a factor analysis of criterion measures. *J. appl. Psychol.*, 1960, *44*, 216–223.

46. URRY, V. W., & NICEWANDER, W. A. Factor analysis of the commander's evaluation report. *U.S. Army Enlisted Evaluation Center tech. res. Study*, 1966, No. 40, 28 pp.

47. VAN DUSEN, A. C. Measuring leadership ability. *Personnel Psychol.*, 1948, *1*, 67–79.

48. WHERRY, R. J., & FRYER, D. H. Buddy ratings: popularity contest or leadership criteria? *Personnel Psychol.*, 1949, *2*, 147–159.

49. WILLMORTH, N. E., TAYLOR, E. L., LINDELIEN, W. B., & RUCH, F. L. A factor analysis of rating scale variables used as criteria of military leadership. *USAF Personnel Train. Res. Cent. Res. Rep.*, 1957, No. 57–154, 52 pp.

50. WILSON, R. C., HIGH, W. S., & COMREY, A. L. An iterative analysis of supervisory and group dimensions. *J. appl. Psychol.*, 1955, *39*, 85–91.

51. WILSON, R. C., HIGH, W. S., BEEM, H. P., & COMREY, A. L. A factor-analytic study of supervisory and group behavior. *J. appl. Psychol.*, 1954, *38*, 89–92.

52. WOFFORD, J. C. Factor analysis of managerial behavior variables. *J. appl. Psychol.*, 1970, *54*, 169–173.

# 6

# ACTIVITY LEVEL,
# COMPETENCE,
# AND EMERGENCE
# AS A LEADER

The many traits and factors found associated with leadership in Chapters 4 and 5 all tend to contain the seeds of two propositions: to emerge as a leader, one must participate; to remain acceptable to others as a leader, one must exhibit competence. This chapter will review theory and research about these two propositions indicating how each must be qualified.

## ACTIVITY LEVEL AND LEADERSHIP

### Attempts to Lead

Gray, Richardson, and Mayhew (1968) found that the amount of influence exercised by a group member tended to increase with increases in attempted influence.

Also, Hemphill, Pepinsky, Shevitz, et al. (1954) demonstrated that attempts to lead depend on earlier success as a leader. In sixteen groups, participants whose relevant knowledge helped to solve the group's problems, were the members who exhibited initiative and attempted leadership of the group on subsequent trials. Conversely, participants whose knowledge hindered the group reduced their attempts to lead on subsequent trials.

Leadership must be attempted before it can be judged successful or unsuccessful in influencing others' ways of handling the problems the group faces. Also, the attempts to lead must be followed for the leader's performance to be deemed effective or ineffective in coping with the group's problems and meeting its needs (Jones, 1938). It also follows that one who expects to be successful in influencing others will be more likely to attempt leadership. And members will be inclined to follow a particular leader whom they expect will achieve desired results (Bass, 1960).

According to Good and Good (1974), in a study of forty-eight undergraduates, one will be more inclined to want to lead in a group perceived to be closer in attitudes to oneself where it should be easier to function as an effective leader. Hemphill, Pepinsky, Kaufman, and Lipetz (1957) studied groups varying in motivation to achieve group goals and the expectancy of success in doing so. They found that group members attempt to lead more frequently when the rewards for mutual problem solution are relatively high and when there is a reasonable expectation that attempts to lead will result in contributions to task accomplishment. At the same time, Banta and Nelson (1964) obtained results which indicate that member agreement about who should lead increases the attempts to lead.

*Participation and Attempted Leadership*

It is not surprising to find strong associations between attempted leadership and overall participation in the group's activities; members participate to a considerable degree if earlier they had been successful in influencing others to cope effectively with the group's problems (Hemphill & Pepinsky, 1955). The silent member usually has little influence on others in a group except as a possible threat to force the group to reconsider its deliberations if the silent member finally speaks out.

## RATE OF TALKING, PARTICIPATION, AND LEADERSHIP

Hollander (1978) noted that effective leadership depends upon receiving, processing, retaining, and transmitting information, much of it through talking with others. Talking calls attention to the speaker. The sheer quantity one emits increases the likelihood of emerging as a leader. But quality may also make a difference.

*Quantity of Talking*

A convincing body of research indicates that the member who participates most actively in group activities where no one has been appointed or elected to lead is most likely to emerge as a leader. Research by Bass (1949, 1954a, 1955b,c) on the leaderless group discussion indicated that the group member who talked most tended to emerge as a leader. Time spent talking in discussions correlated between .65 and .96 with rated success as a leader. When the measures of successful leadership were completely objective, conference leadership success likewise was found to be strongly related to participation (Conference Research, 1950). Tryon (1939) reported correlations of .41, .31, .15, and .44 between talkativeness and leadership among adolescents. Goodenough (1930) and Chevaleva-Ianovskaia and Sylla (1929) found similar results in children. Confirming results were reported by Bales (1953), J. R. P. French (1950), Hurwitz, Zander and Hymovitch (1953), Riecken (1958), Kirscht, Lodahl and Haire (1959), Regula (1967), Burroughs and Jaffee (1969), Jaffee and Lucas (1969), Regula and Julian (1973), and Gintner and Lindskold (1975).

Chapple and Donald (1946) developed the interaction chronograph as a method of recording subject behavior. By pressing a button, the observer recorded on a moving tape the duration of talking and the time interval between periods of talking under different experimental conditions. Executives were found to differ significantly from individuals in nonsupervisory positions in activity rate, quickness of response, speed of response when interrupted, and ability to speed up rate of interaction in interruption periods.

Hemphill (1954) defined leadership as "the initiation of structure in interaction." Bates (1952), Bass (1954a), Borgatta (1954), Berkowitz (1956b), and Riecken (1958) reported results which indicated that the group member who emerges as a leader tends to exhibit a high rate of activity in initiation of structure and in directing the activities of others (see Chapter 11). Bales, Strodtbeck, Mills, and Roseborough (1951) reported that if participants of a group are ranked by the total number of acts they initiate they will also be ranked by (1) the number of acts received; (2) acts they address to specific individuals; and (3) acts they address to the group as a whole. That is, the four variables were positively correlated.

*Regulation of Talk Rates.* The motivation to attempt to influence others is not the only factor affecting a member's rate of talking. A member may talk merely in response to questions from others, for example. Furthermore, as Olmsted (1954) and Talland (1957) found, groups tend to develop norms regulating the length of time that is appropriate for members to talk. Talland suggested that the norm tends to reduce irrelevant loquacity. Olmsted observed that task-oriented groups differ from process-oriented groups in developing norms that permit longer speeches by members.

How much one can participate is a relative matter. Borgatta and Bales (1953a) studied groups of nine men divided into subgroups, each with three members. The members of subgroups rotated in different sessions until each of the nine men had worked with each of the others. It was hypothesized that in groups composed of all high or all low interactors, the members would inhibit each other's interactions. The hypothesis was confirmed, particularly for high participators. Regardless of the members' characteristic performance, their rates of interaction were an inverse function of the average rate of interaction of other members. "There appears to be associated with each individual's characteristic interaction rate an upper bound which for him appears to operate no matter how much opportunity he has to participate."

In a field study, Bonjean (1966) observed similarly that when a group of young, highly educated managers entered to staff a new firm in a predominantly rural community, established businessmen of the community tended to withdraw from certain community activities as the younger managers became increasingly active and influential.

*A Multiplicity of Antecedents.* Many different elements contribute to one's efforts to participate and to attempt to lead. Hemphill (1961) summarized the results of four different experiments concerned with conditions under which group members will attempt to initiate leadership acts. It was found that the following conditions facilitate attempts to lead: (1) large rather than small rewards promised for task success; (2) reasonable expectations of successful task completion; (3) acceptance by others of the individual's leadership attempts; (4) tasks requiring a high rate of group decision; (5) possession of superior task-relevant information; and (6) previously acquired status as group leader. This last consideration was consistent with findings by Rock and Hay (1953) and Jackson (1953b) who observed in industrial field studies that members of a work group increase their participation when placed in the role of leader.

### Quality of Talk

The substance of one's talk does make a difference in one's success in emerging as a leader. When Alpander (1974) surveyed 217 corporations to determine their highest priority training needs for managers currently employed, oral communication abilities rated highest as a needed supervisory skill. Further, Mold (1952) reported that 490 industrial supervisors expressed as most important a need for more development on "how to sell ideas to my superior." Consistent with this, Comrey, High, and Wilson (1955b) found that "high-producing" supervisors in the aircraft industry communicate effectively. Again, satisfaction with the effectiveness of officers and noncoms among over 30,000 U.S. army personnel was strongly associated with their ability to communicate effectively with their subordinates according to both superior and subordinate ratings. But technical competence was also important (Penner, Malone, Coughlin & Herz, 1973).

Skill in oral communication is measured routinely in assessment centers (Bray, Campbell, and Grant, 1974) although skill as a receiver has not been examined fully. Extensive work has been reported by Klauss and Bass (1981) on the extent to which supervisors have been seen by their colleagues as both careful transmitters and careful listeners.

*Quality versus Quantity.* The comparative importance to leadership of the quantity and quality of one's participation was examined by Sorrentino and Boutillier (1975). They planted trained confederates of the experimenters in problem-solving groups who varied their quantity and quality of verbal interaction. The confederates' quantity of verbal participation predicted their ability to lead and created a favorable impression about their motivation, perhaps because quantity was a clearer indication of a group member's intentions than quality. But the quality of the confederates' verbal interaction predicted perceived differences on such variables as competence, influence, and contribution to the group's goals. Furthermore, according to McClintock (1963), a high rate of activity did not result in emergence as a group leader if the individual exhibited a large amount of negative affect and behavior detrimental to group movement. Gintner and Lindskold (1975) placed seventy-two female undergraduates in four-person problem-solving groups to judge the quality of paintings. A confederate in each group was identified as either expert or inexpert, made expert or inexpert contributions, and either talked a lot or relatively little. Talking a lot increased the choice of the confederate as leader in the inexpert condition but sheer talkativeness was not as important in emerging as a leader in the expert condition.

*Consistency.* Inconsistency of contributions may not be as deleterious as we might expect. Contrary to hypothesis, Goldberg and Iverson (1965) found that members of high status perceived that their status rather than the consistency of their statements was related to their influence on the group. They did not lose influence if they changed their opinions several times during a discussion.

*Timing.* The timing of participation makes a difference in its influence on other members. M. Smith (1935a) noted the importance of opportunity. He or she who succeeds as leader may be but one of several who might have been just as successful had he or she not been present to attempt leadership first. Hollander (1978) concluded that to emerge as a leader one needs to participate early. But M. E. Shaw (1961) found that the group members who stated their opinions either early or late were better able to have their opinion accepted than those who stated their opinion in the middle of a discussion. Bass (1967a) studied groups of male managers in which the group head revealed his opinion at the beginning or end of the session, or not at all. The group members were able to influence each other the most when the head remained silent, but they exhibited greater coalescence around him when he revealed his opinion. Silent heads were most influenced by the other members and were most dissatisfied with their own final judgments.

## LEADERSHIP AND INTERACTION TENDENCIES

Individuals differ in preference and ability to initiate and sustain interactions with other persons. Some individuals are more comfortable in a face-to-face situation, others in the small informal group, and still others in the large formal organization. There are individuals who find almost all interactions stressful and unpleasant. On the other hand, skilled public speakers seem to enjoy their encounters with large audiences. According to Hall and Donnell (1979) who compared 1,884 managers who were either fast, medium, or slow in their career advancement, more rapid promotion was directly related to self-rated interpersonal competence. Again, Wolberg (1977) noted that the ability to relate as a peer in role-playing and to avoid immature "acting out" behavior during training is critical in identifying potential as a group leader.

H. H. Jennings (1943) observed that individuals differ not only in the number of persons they characteristically choose as interaction partners (emotional expansiveness), but in the numbers they contact as interaction partners (social expansiveness). There is a low but significant relationship between emotional expansiveness (many choices) and social expansiveness (many interactions). The degree to which an individual's choices of others are reciprocated by them is highly related to the degree of expansiveness shown by others toward him or her. Although the rate of interaction tends to increase with increased length of membership in the group, emotional expansiveness (choice) does not increase with time. The individual's capacity to maintain choice relationships appears to be a highly stable characteristic that in some degree determines interaction competence as well as esteem in the eyes of other members and leadership (see Chapter 10). Geier (1963) studied the emergence and acceptance of leaders in successive stages of problem solving. Those members perceived as uninformed, unparticipative, and rigid tended to be eliminated as potential leaders in the early sessions. An intensive struggle for leadership was observed in the second stage. Contenders in this stage who were perceived as authoritarian or offensive in verbalization tended to be rejected.

### Dominance and Assertiveness

Interaction capacity may be strongly associated with the need to be dominant and assertive. And group members scoring high on tests of dominance tend to emerge as leaders. Rohde (1951) reported that discussion groups composed of different combinations of dominant and submissive members tended to prefer dominant members as leaders. Although dominant members exhibited more controlling behaviors, they also tended to agree more than submissive members and were better able to adapt themselves to the situational demands imposed by other members.

Berkowitz and Haythorn (1955) studied groups composed of dominant and submissive members. Submissive members tended to choose dominant members and reject submissive members as leaders. But dominant members chose dominant and submissive members about equally. Megargee, Bogart, and Anderson (1966) studied pairs of participants, one scoring high and the other low on a test of dominance. When instructions emphasized the task, dominant participants did not assume the leadership role significantly more often than those lacking in dominance. However, when leadership was emphasized, dominant participants emerged as leaders in 90 percent of the pairs.

In another research domain, historical analyses disclosed that activism, forcefulness, and militant behavior characterized the great American presidents (Wendt & Light, 1976).

### Time Expenditures

The sheer quantity or percentage of time spent in interaction and working with others seems to contribute to one's success as a leader. Thus, P. Miller (1953) found that of 250 high school principals, those spending more time in supervision and less in research and pupil affairs were rated as more adequate leaders. Studies of naval leadership revealed a correlation of .53 between nominations for success as leader and the number of times a naval officer was mentioned as one with whom others spent the most time getting work done (Shartle, Stogdill & Campbell, 1949). Smith and Nystrom (1937) found that high school leaders devoted more time to extracurricular and leadership activities than did nonleaders. City political bosses were observed by Salter (1935) to be joiners, highly active in community groups. Similarly, Olmsted (1954) concluded that the more people participated in community activities, the more likely they were to be regarded as community leaders. Katz and Lazarsfeld (1955) noted that opinion leaders—women most likely to influence personally the buying practices of others—were gregarious "joiners" with many friends. Again, in laboratory analyses of communication nets (see Chapter 28), Shaw and Gilchrist (1956) found a positive relation between the tendency to initiate letters to others and one's subsequent rank as a leader.

Thus, the data support the contention that participation and leadership are coincidental, both arising out of interpersonal interchanges directed toward achieving coordination and consensus. Yet, above and beyond the amount of participation, Burke (1974) suggests that leaders must maintain interpersonal control over participation.

### Observed Behavior Patterns

Participation that contributes to leadership in both experimental and established groups includes such observed behavior patterns as initiation of spontaneity in groups, stimulation of a wider range of group actions, and the tendency to make others feel included in the group. Thus, H. H. Jennings (1943) studied leadership in a training school for girls. A leader, compared with average girls and isolates, was characterized as follows: protects and encourages the weak, exhibits personal integrity and dependability, shows tactful consideration of others, inspires confidence and encouragement, widens the field of participation for others, initiates spontaneity in others, controls own moods rather than inflicting depressions and anxieties on others, and establishes rapport quickly with a wide range of personalities. Some of these behaviors differed markedly from those identified by the trait theorists.

Other researchers have identified similar behaviors. Some of the patterns for which the most evidence is available are initiation of spontaneity, widening boundaries, and acceptance of others.

*Initiation of Spontaneity.* H. H. Jennings (1943) observed that girl leaders, by virtue of their spontaneity, were valued because they stimulated spontaneity in others. However, Newstetter, Feldstein, and Newcomb (1938) found that individual leadership attributed to a member in the group was determined more by the cordiality received from others than by cordial behavior toward others. Subsequently, Grosser, Polansky, and Lippitt (1951) and Bandura and Huston (1961) observed that group members act more spontaneously under a friendly than under an unfriendly or detached leader.

In a study of boys in a summer camp, Polansky, Lippitt, and Redl (1950) found that members in high-prestige positions were more likely than others to act spontaneously in their groups and made more direct attempts to influence others. Their readiness to act spontaneously also resulted in their being more susceptible to behavioral contagion (being influenced without intention or awareness) than those of low prestige. Individuals who felt themselves lacking in prestige were more subject to contagion from others. Similar results were obtained by Lippitt, Polansky, Redl, and Rosen (1952) and by Lefkowitz, Blake, and Mouton (1955).

*Widening Boundaries.* Some but not all leaders reveal the competence to widen the range of actions in the group by other members. H. H. Jennings (1943) observed that the emergent leader tended to widen the field of participation for others. But Lippitt (1940) found that only democratic leaders tended to provide group members with freedom for decision and action. J. R. P. French (1941) noted that group freedom was greater in organized than in unorganized groups. Further, Cattell and Stice (1953) found that emergent leadership was associated with group unity, freedom to participate, influence, and interdependence. Results obtained by Gebel (1954) indicated that leaders differ from followers in greater tolerance for ''exposing the phenomenal field'' thus providing for greater scope of action. Heslin and Dunphy (1964) and Reid (1970) suggested that members are better satisfied with a leader who provides freedom for participation, action, and expression of feeling.

*Acceptance of Other Group Members.* Again, some but not all leaders tend to make others feel included. Leaders identified by sociometric choice are characterized by ready acceptance of other group members and by protection of the weak and underchosen (H. H. Jennings, 1943). Ziller (1963, 1965a) found that leaders of effective groups differed from those of ineffective groups in being less severe in evaluating members lacking in achievement potential and in encouraging the development of those whose performance was marginal.

Bass (1967b) revealed that task-oriented leaders, in comparison with self-oriented and interaction-oriented leaders, exhibited a relatively high tolerance for deviant opinion and conflicting ideas. Furthermore, several studies of norm conformity suggested that leaders tend to be more tolerant of the deviate than are other group members. Similarly, A. R. Cohen (1958) found that high-status members who have consolidated their positions communicate more with low-status members than do leaders in unstable positions.

*Other Observed Behavior.* Peer ratings of performance of everyone else in one's group in five problem-solving sessions resulted after $Q$ factor analysis in identifying the following characteristics of leaders compared to nonleaders: giving directions, formulating goals, and being self-assured. Leaders were also rated lower than nonleaders on being more quarrelsome and less sensible. These characteristics of emergent leaders were assigned to them early, remained relatively consistent, and seemed independent of personality characteristics (B. Schultz, 1974).

Gitter, Black, and Fishman (1975) studied the effects of nonverbal and verbal communications, along with race and sex, among 151 college students on their perceived leadership. The investigators concluded that nonverbal communications were even more important than verbal ones.

## COMPETENCE AND LEADERSHIP

Quantity of participation forecasts emergence as a leader because it is correlated with quality. Continued ignorant talk will be nonreinforced or rejected by others. As we have already seen in the Sorrentino and Boutillier (1975) and Gintner and Lindskold (1975) experiments, the "windbag" or compulsive talker lacking in interpersonal or task competence ultimately will fail in attempting to lead. Again, Hollander (1960) found that when groups are given tasks leaders are usually evaluated with respect to their comptence. This acknowledged competence builds up their credit so that they can subsequently depart from the group norms, move the group in novel ways, yet still be accepted by their group.

### Task and Socioemotional Competence

As we have noted in Chapter 5, the most frequently obtained leader skill factors tended to involve task or socioemotional performance. Thus, Hollander (1978) noted that leadership competence included being a good facilitator, enabling others to make an effective contribution, having skill in handling the inner workings of the group, maintaining activities on a relatively smooth course, giving direction to activity, acquainting followers with their role in the main effort. The leader gives competent guidance to other group members concerning their job. The leader must be able to discriminate between good and bad work and to evaluate such work.

Limerick (1976) offered a method and two-factor theory to sort leadership in small groups into performance influencing content and performance influencing process. In the same way, in a study of adolescent peer groups in suburban areas, Dunphy (1963) identified two mutually supportive roles—leader and sociocenter. The leader was influential in group activities, while the sociocenter relieved group tensions. Again, using Bales's method of observational ratings of actual leader behaviors, Bales and Slater (1955) and Slater (1955) proposed that leadership behaviors include two types: socioemotional and task-oriented.

### Technical Competence

Many surveys document the importance of technical competence to effectiveness as a leader (for instance, Penner, Malone, Coughlin & Herz, 1973). Thus, Farris and Swain (1971) showed that among 117 NASA professionals, including twenty supervisors, those identified as the informal leaders in the informal organization were technically more competent as well as in more active contact with their colleagues. They were also more motivated by the technical aspects of their work, better rewarded, and more influential regarding their own work.

*Multiple Competencies*

Many specific competencies of consequence to leadership can be more fully detailed, given the multiple functions which may be involved in specific situations such as serving as a naval officer or as a member of Congress. To determine what distinguished the activity patterns of superior and average naval officers, Spencer (n.d.) and Winter (1978) identified officers' activities according to what motivation, skills, and activities were required to carry them out. The information gathered could be applied to selection and training. Analysis of approximately 800 incidents of leadership and management performance among a cross-section of commissioned and noncommissioned naval officers identified twenty-seven leadership and management competencies. (Competency was defined as a knowledge, skill, motivation, or behavior variable that can be shown empirically to predict successful on-the-job performance.) The twenty-seven competencies subsequently were grouped by factor analyses into five factors. Four of those five factors significantly predicted superior leadership and management performance in a new sample.

The four competency factors which differentiated between superior and average leadership and management performance in both fleets were: task achievement, skillful use of influence, management control, and advising and counseling. The fifth factor, coercion, did not distinguish superior from average performers. Those individuals rated superior engaged in a wider range or repertoire of behaviors reflecting a broader array of skills and abilities.

Similarly, congressional leadership was seen in Bryson and Kelley's (1978) review of studies to depend upon a variety of competencies. Personability, style, and skill were deemed crucial in determining who becomes a leader and who stays a leader, but these include trait and behavioral considerations along with political "savvy."

*Contingencies Affecting Whether Competence Results*
*in Success as a Leader*

Hollander and Julian (1970) conducted a set of four experiments concerned with competence and leadership. Six-hundred college students served as participants in various group discussion tasks. In the first experiment, perceived competence of the leaders was more important than the manner of gaining office in members' evaluations of them. Strong interest in the group task tended to raise somewhat the status of the incompetent leaders. In the second experiment, neither being elected or appointed nor being group-oriented or self-oriented was significantly related to the leaders' influence on the group. Only the leaders' competence was highly related to influence. There was a slight tendency for members to be more willing to admit having been influenced by elected rather than by appointed leaders. In the third experiment, leaders were either elected or appointed to act as spokesmen for their groups. If elected, incompetent leaders were rejected regardless of their success at the group task, whereas success increased the endorsement of the competent leaders. If appointed, the competent leaders were immune to the effects of success or failure, but incompetence resulted in rejection. Justis (1975) found that leader competence has a lower impact on performance when members are less dependent on the leader.

Leaders of guidance groups made up of members with different kinds of problems must include among their competencies a great deal of flexibility (Hollander, 1978).

The differences in ability to solve the group's problems may be due to particular aptitudes, such as verbal facility, or to more specific proficiencies, such as knowledge of parliamentary procedures. Thus, in field studies with army combat squads performing a variety of field problems, Goodacre (1951), Greer, Galanter, and Nordlie (1954), and Havron and McGrath (1961) reported that the characteristics of the squad leaders most highly associated with their unit's effectiveness were overall ability, job knowledge, knowledge of their men, emotional stability, and willingness to act.

Experiments demonstrated the same thing. Hollander (1964) assigned an ambiguous task to groups. After a first trial, they were required to predict what would occur on the next trial. A planted confederate of the experimenter played the role of deviate from the group norms, but was provided with the correct answers. Influence as a leader was measured by the number of trials on which the confederate's suggestion was accepted as the group's choice. Such influence increased as the trials progressed despite the confederate's violation of group norms. Perceived ability influenced emergence as a leader. Similarly, Goldman and Fraas (1965) assembled thirty-two student groups of four members each to solve discussion problems. The groups worked under four types of leadership, as follows: (1) leader appointed because of ability; (2) leader arbitrarily appointed; (3) leader elected by group members; and (4) no leader present. Groups worked best in the situations with the leader whom they perceived had been correct in previous situations.

Bugental (1964) obtained a significantly positive correlation between attempted and successful influence. But participants trained in task-related skills emerged as leaders more often than did untrained participants. The influence attempts made by task-trained participants were more successful than those made by socially sensitive participants, and the latter were more successful than insensitive participants in the social condition, but not in the task condition. G. J. Palmer (1962a,b) studied groups in which the members differed in task ability. Task ability was related to successful leadership—successfully influencing others' performance—and still more strongly to effective leadership—obtaining the task goals. Followership was better accounted for by lower ability than leadership was by higher ability. Hollander (1966) varied three characteristics of group leaders: self-oriented versus group-oriented, task-competent or -incompetent, and elected or appointed. Leaders perceived by members as task-competent exerted significantly more influence than those perceived as incompetent. Elected and appointed leaders did not differ in influence. Although self-oriented leaders were regarded as unfair in how they distributed rewards, they did not differ from group-oriented leaders in influence over the group. Finally, Hollander and Julian (1970) found that a less competent leader would continue to be tolerated if the leader was seen to be highly task-motivated.

### Impact on Group Effectiveness

Bass (1960) proposed that groups will be more effective if the hierarchy of influence in the group matches the members' abilities. A demonstration was provided by Rohde (1954a,b,c), who studied experimental groups in which members differed in ability to perform the task. Rohde found that if the leader is qualified to do this the group performs more effectively than if the leader is unqualified regardless of followers' ability. The qualified more often than the unqualified leader played the role of initiating ideas and coordinating group activities, whether the followers were similar or dissimilar in ability. It was more difficult for an unqualified than for a qualified leader to retain group control. Further, it was more difficult to retain control when the followers were similar than when they were widely dissimilar in ability.

The linkage of leader competence and group effectiveness was also seen by T. G. Walker (1976) who examined the leadership in state supreme courts. Walker found that where leaders were selected on the basis of their merit instead of their seniority, the courts generated lower levels of dissent with their rulings. Additional results reported by Jackson (1953b) and by Rock and Hay (1953) suggest that the emergence of leaders is not a matter of mere chance, unjust discrimination, or keeping the good person down. Both leader and group members appear to recognize their comparative potentialities for advancing the group purpose, and the group is more effective if each plays the role for which he or she is perceived to be best fitted.

## RELEVANCE OF TASK COMPETENCE

Rudraswamy (1964) reported that participants possessing task-relevant information exhibited a significantly higher rate of leadership attempts than uninformed subjects. Interobserver correlations of .73 and .83 were obtained.

But competencies must be relevant to the task demands. Thus, Dubno (1963) obtained results which indicate that groups with slow decision leaders under quality task conditions were more effective than groups with fast decision leaders under pressure for speed. However, Dubno (1965) found fast decision leaders less compulsive than slow decision leaders. Fast decision leaders managed more effective groups than slow decision leaders.

Fundamental to situational analyses of leadership is to realize that ability to solve the group's problems is a relative matter. An ability relevant to solving the problems of a group of Iowa farmers may be irrelevant to solving the problems of a submarine crew, except to the extent that general intelligence may be important in both situations. A mathematician may be vastly superior to stevedores in the arithmetics of space, yet communication difficulties alone are likely to make it impossible for the math expert to supervise effectively the stevedores' loading of the hold of a ship. Similarly, the mathematician may successfully serve as head of a mathematics department but remain inadequate to solve the problems of a department of agricultural statistics. Ability of a member to help a group must be considered in light of the group's problems (Bass, 1960). As J. F. Brown noted (1936), the leader must be superior to other members in one or more characteristics relevant to the problems facing the group. The choice of leader is dictated by the needs of the group (Murphy, 1941).

Following a review of military leadership, W. O. Jenkins (1947) observed that leaders in a given field were superior to other members in skills pertinent to that field. To lead and earn esteem from skilled followers, one must be a master of the craft. Thus, in one of the early experiments on the relation of task ability to leadership, Carter and

Nixon (1949a,b) found that one's scores on mechanical tests were related to one's leadership in groups performing mechanical tasks. On the other hand, word fluency and clerical aptitude were related to emergence as leaders in clerical tasks. No test of ability was uniquely related to leadership on intellectual tasks.

Carter, Haythorn, Shriver, and Lanzetta (1951) compared the behavior of appointed and emergent leaders. All leaders in all situations differed from followers in diagnosing situations and giving information on carrying out action. But in addition, the behavior of leaders differed with the task. In the reasoning task, they asked for information or facts, but in the mechanical assembly task they asked that things be done. In the discussion task they asked for expression of feelings or opinion. Emergent leaders tended to show more total activity than appointed leaders and to take over the situation, presumably as a consequence of having to struggle for status, which was not necessary if one had already been appointed as leader (see Chapter 13).

### Exclusive Possession of Information

Possession of information of consequence to leadership is a relative matter. Alford and Scoble (1968) found that less educated, active leaders were better informed about community affairs than highly educated nonleaders.

To further detail the impact of the relevance of task ability, Hemphill, Pepinsky, Shevitz, Jaynes, and Christner (1956) studied groups in which one member was given information which would provide an advantage in the solution of the group problem. Those given such special information scored significantly higher in attempts to lead in assembly and construction tasks, but not in discussion tasks. Shevitz (1955), using construction and mathematical tasks, found that the exclusive possession of information by a group member resulted in the member's making a greater number of attempts to lead, in differentiation of the member's position from that of the other members, and in consolidation of the member as leader. (That reliable observation of attempted leadership acts can be made was evidenced by an interobserver correlation of .96.)

Shaw and Penrod (1962) varied the amount of information provided the members of different groups. They found that moderate amounts of information improved group performance, whereas large amounts did not. With large amounts of information, the informed member was unable to validate suggestions, thus making them appear implausible and unacceptable to the group. M. E. Shaw (1963a) compared groups in which one member was provided with either two units or six units of information. The informed member entered the discussion earlier and initiated more task-oriented communication than uninformed members in the two-unit condition, but this difference was reversed in the six-unit condition. The informed member's suggestions were accepted more frequently. The member was named more often as leader in the two-unit, but not in the six-unit condition.

Results of the foregoing studies indicate that the possession of task-relevant information provides an advantage in attempting and gaining leadership in a group. However, an informational excess tends to operate as a disadvantage if it places a strain on the credulity of group members or makes the member too much superior to the other members. More follows on such limitations.

*Contingencies Modifying the Impact on Group Effectiveness
    of Relevant Task Competence*

*Too Much Ability.*    General competence is not enough to account for effective
leadership, even if it is relevant to the group's task demands. The studies cited in Chapters 4 and 5 revealed correlations generally below .30 between tested intelligence and
leadership performance. Experience yielded a median correlation of − .12 with leadership performance in analyses of thirteen studies completed by Fiedler (1970a). As noted
in Chapters 4 and 5, the leader cannot be too superior in ability to those to be led. The
leader must be more able to solve the problems of the group, but not too much more
able. Thus, Hollingworth (1926) found that among children with a mean IQ of 100, the
IQ of the leader was between 115 and 130. A child of 160 IQ had very little chance to
emerge as leader of the group, although the same child might have been successful if the
average IQ in the group had been 140 instead of 100. Finch and Carroll (1932), comparing sixty-six gifted, sixty-six superior, and sixty-six average children, Warner (1923),
studying boys' gangs leaders of college student organizations, and McCuen (1929),
examining leaders of college student organizations, reached the same conclusions. Leadership potential goes with being "smart, but not too smart" (Riley & Flowerman, 1951).

A number of factors may militate against the "too superior" member as a leader in
addition to communication difficulties. If vastly superior in ability, the would-be leader
may no longer appreciate the group's problems or be interested or concerned with helping solve them. Rather than lead the group, he or she may withdraw from it. The ideas of
the overly capable individual may call for too great a change in behavior by the group
(Bass, 1960).

*A Multiple Screen Model.*    Fiedler and Leister (1977a,b) developed a model to
explain the only modest association between the leader's intelligence and the task performance of the group led. The model posits a series of screens of variable permeability
which the leader's intellectual output must traverse before task performance can be affected. The screens are displayed in Figure 6.1. Leaders with greater intelligence will
produce more task-effective groups if the leader is motivated (sees being leader as valuable), experienced, if there is little stress between leader and superior, and if relations are
good between the leader and subordinates. A field study of 158 army infantry squad
leaders provided empirical support. Thus, leader intelligence and task performance correlated .36 with experienced squad leaders and .15 with inexperienced ones, .30 with
motivated leaders and .14 with unmotivated ones, .40 with leaders unstressed by their

**FIGURE 6.1.   Schematic Representation of Multiple Screen Model**

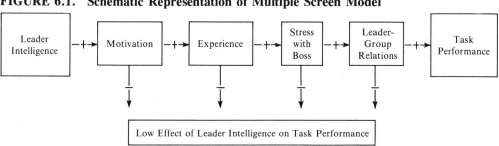

SOURCE: *Fiedler and Leister (1977a).*

boss and .07 with stressed leaders, .30 with good subordinate relations as seen by the leader and .15 with poor relations. However, when leader–subordinate relations were evaluated by the subordinates, a reversal occurred. Good relations generated a correlation of .07 between leader intelligence and group performance but .34 when relations were seen as poor by subordinates.

There is other evidence that intelligence and competence must be combined with other contingent variables to produce successful and effective leadership. Thus, Moment and Zaleznik (1963) used sociometric ratings to identify four sets of group members: (1) stars (receiving many choices) scored high in ideas and congeniality; (2) technical specialists were high in ideas and low in congeniality; (3) social specialists were high in congeniality but low in ideas; (4) the underchosen were low in both ideas and congeniality. Stars were able to fuse the different leadership, task, and social demands made upon them. They were most participative, involved, interdependent, and varied in behavior. The technical specialists were most independent and achievement-oriented but participated least. The social specialists were highest in interaction and task orientation and were most dependent. The underchosen were most competitive and counterdependent but least interested. These results suggest that the perceived personality of a leader is highly related to the kind of role that he or she plays in a group.

Similarly, Borgatta, Couch, and Bales (1954) studied groups led by "great men." Identified in the first session on the basis of peer nominations for leadership, sociometric choice on "enjoyed participation with," intelligence test score, and number of influence acts initiated, great men tended to retain their leadership throughout the sessions. Groups led by great men showed less inhibited response to the task situation, less tension, less withdrawing from active participation, and more solidarity than groups in which no great man was present.

Julian and Hollander (1966) reported that the willingness of group members to accept a leader's influence attempts depended upon the leader's competence, source of authority, concern for group members, and perceived commitment to participation in group activities. Finally, Perlmutter (1954) found that the greater were leaders' abilities to influence other group members, the larger were the number of traits applied to the leaders and the more desirable the traits attributed to them.

One trait, in particular, which has captured the imagination of many a leadership theorist, but confounded the best intentions of empiricists, is empathy. How important is it to effective leadership? This is the subject of Chapter 7, which follows.

# 7

# SOCIAL INSIGHT, EMPATHY, AND LEADERSHIP

In this chapter, we will focus on the extent to which leadership of a group depends on the leader's ability and motivation to estimate accurately the group's attitudes, motives, and current level of effectiveness. For as Bass (1960) noted:

> It is not enough for a leader to know how to get what followers want, or to tell them how to get what they want. The leader must be able to know what followers want, when they want it, and what prevents them from getting what they want. . . .
>
> Empathic success should increase with increased motivation to attend to clues. It should also increase with information available about others' behavior. Two persons may display the same success in guessing the motives of some other members. One estimator may be more apt; the other estimator may be more interested in the question because of momentary situational demands or acquired motives. . . . An alert teacher "senses" from facial expressions, questions or lack of them, restlessness, and lack of response whether he (or she) is continuing to meet the needs of the student audience. An effective orator or actor requires similar skills [pp. 167, 168].

Many others have offered similar propositions. Wittenberg (1951) emphasized the need-estimating aspect of leadership. The leader must know what the individual members need and then employ the group process so that the members will satisfy these needs. Coyle (1948) suggested that to work with youth, group leaders must understand the various motives that draw the group together in order to "find the appropriate form to clothe their collective needs." For political and organizational leadership, Titus (1950) and J. M. Burns (1978) noted that the leader must be able to choose the group's objectives wisely, forecast the cost of obtaining the objectives, the likelihood of doing so, and the degree to which goal attainment will be satisfying to the members.

People generally expect that leaders will be more insightful. Thus, Shartle, Stogdill, and Campbell (1949) found that nominations for "Popular Leader" were correlated .47 with predictions of "who will be most accurate in estimating group opinion." Alertness to changing circumstances and shifts in needs is seen as of much importance as well (Hollander, 1978). Finally, in a study of 153 supervisors in seven organizations, E. J. Frank (1973) observed that leaders who perceived their roles to require sensitivity to others, also perceived themselves as being sensitive. Along with this felt sensitivity, there appeared to be feelings that the leaders were openly accepted by the group and that the working environment was a pleasant one.

In traditional Japan, ostensibly the head of a group made its decisions for it, and once the leader made the decision, it was regarded as the "will of the group" and accepted without challenge. But if one looked more carefully, one saw that the leader had the responsibility to sense the will of the group to understand what was wanted, both intellectually and emotionally, as a consequence of extensive consultation. He had to *hara de wakaru* or "understand with his belly" (Kerlinger, 1951). It appears that this is still common Japanese practice (see Chapter 32). In all, early on, it was thought that insight and empathy gave the individual the competence to gain, hold, and maintain the leadership position.

### GENERALIZED SOCIAL INSIGHT AND EMPATHY

In their most general sense, *empathy* refers to the awareness or appreciation and *insight* refers to the understanding of what others are thinking and feeling about a matter. But their linkages to leadership are complicated by the varying definitions and ways of measuring empathy and insight.

Empathy and insight can refer to awareness and understanding of social phenomena at a general level, knowledge of cultural norms, social intelligence, or understanding of the most probable tendencies of generalized others.

Various researchers developed measures of social insight at this general level. These measures required participants to estimate the number of group members who will endorse the items on a test of personality, attitudes, or job satisfaction. Participant accuracy was measured by how well their estimates matched actual endorsement by others of a standardized test.

#### Mixed Findings

Chowdhry and Newcomb (1952), Bell and Hall (1954), Nagle (1954), Trapp (1955), and Fleishman and Salter (1963) found leaders more accurate than nonleaders in estimating such group responses or norms for a general population. Kerr and Speroff (1951) and Van Zelst (1952) reported notable success in forecasting salesmanship success, union leadership success, and foremanship success with a brief test at the general level purporting to measure individual differences in empathic ability. However, Sprunger (1949), Hites and Campbell (1950), Gage and Exline (1953), Talland (1954), Bugental and Lehner (1958), and Cohn, Fisher, and Brown (1961) did not find leaders significantly more accurate than nonleaders. Along the same lines, Marchetti (1953) found no relation between grocery managers' ability to predict employees' attitude test responses and the managers' rated efficiency by their superiors. Finally, Shartle, Stogdill, and Campbell (1949) reported a slight negative relation between naval officers' popularity as leaders and tested ability to estimate group opinion. Thus, decidedly mixed results have been found for the relations between generalized social insight, generalized empathy, and leadership.

Generalized empathy results must be understood in terms of the local conditions. In fact, it is questionable whether such generalized empathy exists. Although Cline and Richards (1960, 1961) found low but significant correlations between a variety of different measures of ability to judge the behavior of other persons, Ausubel and Schiff (1955), Bender and Hastorf (1950), and Crow and Hammond (1957) found no support for the hypothesis that there is a general ability to predict interpersonal responses. For one thing, education and general intelligence are likely to affect outcomes of measures of empathy and insight at the general level.

## LOCALIZED INSIGHT AND EMPATHY

At the other extreme from generalized insight and empathy are perceptual sensitivities at a very local level, in a designated group working with specific other members. This presents a multiple measurement problem. A model was first formulated by Cronbach and Glaser (1953). Bass, Burger, et al. (1979) employed the model to study managers' ability to judge the life goals of specific other managers with whom they had been working in small exercise groups for several days.

The procedure was as follows. Participants ranked each of eleven life goals in order of importance to themselves. Then they ranked the goals in order of importance to each of the other members of their exercise group.

Three correlational indexes were calculated of importance to our discussion here:

1. Empathy or accuracy in judging others—the correlation between a participant's judgments about other members' life goals and the other members' self-judgments. (This assumes that people generally had an accurate appreciation of their own goals).

2. Projection or assumed similarity to others—the correlation between the rankings participants assigned to themselves and what they assigned to everyone else in the group.

3. Actual similarity to others—this is the correlation of a participant's self-ratings with the self-ratings of each of the other members. For the group as a whole, this is an index of its homogeneity.

### Assessment Problems

*Effects of Assumed Similarity.*   In addition to scoring biases pointed out by D. T. Campbell (1955), studies of empathy at the local level are likely also to suffer from the generalized tendency of judges to assume themselves similar to others. Thus, for 1,026 managers in twelve countries, Bass, Burger, et al. (1979) found assumed similarity (the correlation of own ratings with judgments of others' ratings) to average .50. But true similarity or homogeneity evidenced by the average correlation of self-ratings among all participants was only .21. Consistent with this, following a review of eight studies, Lazar (1953) concluded that in judging the attitudes of groups, people err in the direction of their own beliefs or opinions.

### Effects of Homogeneity

The amount of actual similarity or homogeneity also affects what kinds of outcomes can be achieved. Thus, Notcutt and Silva (1951) found that the smaller the difference between actual self-descriptions and others' own self-descriptions, the smaller the error when pairs of persons predict each other's responses.

*Leader Accuracy about Group Opinion.*   By definition, the opinions of a group following interaction are more strongly influenced by the leaders of the group. It follows that the forecasts of group opinion made by leaders will be more accurate than estimates made by nonleaders, since the opinions are close to those held by the leaders. Thus, when leadership was defined in terms of influence on the group decision, Talland (1954) demonstrated that leaders are better estimators of final group opinion because it is closer to their own initial opinion. But leaders are not more accurate in estimating opinion prior to interaction.

### Positive Results

Despite the problems just enumerated, a considerable array of positive findings supports Stogdill's conclusion in Chapter 4 that "alertness to the surrounding environment and understanding of 'social' situations are intimately associated with leadership ability, yet very little is understood regarding the nature of these processes."

*Early Research.* Empirical studies abound. Some of the early researchers on leaders' characteristics determined that alertness to the environment and ability to size up situations differentiated leaders from followers. A. O. Bowden (1926), Buttgereit (1932), Chevaleva-Ianovskaia and Sylla (1929), Cowley (1931), Merriam and Gosnell (1929), Thurstone (1944), and Carter, Haythorn, Shriver, and Lanzetta (1951) found leaders characterized by the ability to evaluate situations. Insight into the motives, thoughts, feelings, and actions of others was found to characterize leaders by A. O. Bowden (1926), Brogden and Thomas (1943), Guilford and Guilford (1938), Hanfmann (1935), H. H. Jennings (1943), Pigors (1933), and Zeleny (1939).

*Evidence.* Reviews of the literature on localized social insight and empathy have been presented by D. T. Campbell (1955), Cronbach (1955), Crow (1957a,b), Hatch (1962), Kerr and Speroff (1951), R. D. Mann (1959), H. C. Smith (1966), Strunk (1957), Bronfenbrenner, Harding, and Gallwey (1958), Cline and Richards (1963), W. F. O'Conner (1963), and Shrauger and Altrocchi (1964). Generally, they have affirmed the empathy-leadership connection. Thus, for example, after surveying fifteen studies reporting 101 results concerning leadership and empathy, R. D. Mann (1959) noted that 74 percent of the results were positive and he concluded that although researchers generally have been unable to obtain positive results which are statistically significant, they have obtained positive results with impressive consistency. To illustrate, Williams and Leavitt (1947a,b), G. H. Green (1948), Greer, Galanter, and Nordlie (1954), and Lansing (1957) used sociometric nominations as a basis for studying insight. Group members were asked to nominate other members for leadership and to estimate the ranking that others would ascribe to them. Leaders were found more accurate than nonleaders in estimating their own sociometric rank or, in some studies, the rank of others. That is, leaders more accurately estimated their esteem or value to the group in the eyes of the other members. In the same way, Gallo and McClintock (1963) also found that leaders were more accurate than nonleaders in perceiving their esteem in the group. Consistent with this, it should be kept in mind that Fiedler's (1967a) theory of leadership (Chapter 20), in particular, hinges on the linkage of empathy and leadership. In his early formulations, ASo—assumed similarity to others—was the main measure of consequence in his analyses. In these early studies by Fiedler (1953a, 1953b, 1954a) of basketball teams and surveying teams, he found that the teams were more effective if their esteemed members, likely to be the team leaders, perceived preferred members to differ from rejected members. Fiedler (1954b, 1955, 1956) obtained similar findings for B-29 bomber crews, tank crews, and open-hearth steel shop groups. The groups were more effective if the crew leader or foreman discriminated more distinctly between behavior of members with whom he could work well and behavior of members with whom he had difficulty. But at the time this sort of discriminating ability was regarded by Fiedler as representing something of a social distance effect. It was not seen necessarily as an ''empathic'' characteristic. As will be detailed in Chapter 20, he subsequently changed his explanations.

Nagle (1954) reported high correlations between departmental productivity and the ability of department supervisors to estimate employee attitudes. Anderhalter, Wilkins, and Rigby (1952) noted that Marine OCS candidates showing the highest ability to predict other candidates' future effectiveness were likely to make effective company officers themselves. Infantry squad leaders were found by Greer, Galanter, and Nordlie (1954) to be more accurate than other squad members in their perceptions of the esteem of other members. Schrage (1965) reported that veridical perception and interpretation of their environment was more important than power motivation or need for achievement in differentiating successful from unsuccessful entrepreneurs. Finally, results obtained by Jennings (1952a) suggested that supervisors who do not understand the behavior of their subordinates tend to feel inadequate and insecure. As their frustration increases, they, the supervisors, become less able to obtain cooperation and satisfactory performance.

### Negative Results

Based on a survey of managers and their subordinates, Hatch (1962) concluded that the empathic accuracy of the managers might be ''described as characterized by statistical significance, but limited practical significance.'' He found no significant differences between the empathic accuracy of the managers described by their superiors as high in maintaining good human relations with subordinates and those described as low in human relations characteristics. Similarly, Jerdee (1964) reported that supervisors' predictions of subordinate morale were negatively related to employee morale scores. Again, Andrews and Farris (1967) noted that subordinates' innovation was correlated negatively with their supervisor's planning effectiveness if the supervisor was sensitive to individual differences, but the correlation was positive if the supervisor was insensitive to differences between people. Williams and Leavitt (1947) observed that more successful leaders were the ones who most underestimated the sociometric status accorded them by other group members. Finally, Shartle, Stogdill, and Campbell (1949) found that popular leader nominations were correlated $-.08$ with error in estimating group opinion. Error scores were correlated .03 with predictions of who would be most accurate. Popular leaders were not more accurate than unpopular leaders in estimating group opinion, although other group members expected them to be so.

### Contingencies

More often than not positive or negative results have to be qualified by conditions. Only under particular situational circumstances is one likely to find that the leader was more insightful or empathic than the nonleader.

*Cohesiveness.* Exline (1960) assigned members to high- or low-congeniality groups to discuss a task. Accuracy of knowledge of each other's opinion position (task-relevant) and sociometric preferences (person-relevant) were measured. The leader was a more accurate judge of popularity only in cohesive (person-relevant) groups. Lemann and Solomon (1952) also found that accuracy of interpersonal perception was higher in cohesive groups than in uncohesive groups. Since cohesive groups usually involve considerable mutuality of choice among the high-status members, the leadership clique should exhibit higher accuracy scores than the members of lower status.

*Ambiguous Situations.* D. S. Werner (1955) reported that estimates of psychological probability were not influenced by either leadership or event probability alone. Leadership and event probability interacted to influence psychological probability. However, leaders estimated probabilities more successfully in ambiguous than in highly structured situations.

*Relevance.* Chowdry and Newcomb (1952) found that leaders tended to judge group opinion better than nonleaders or isolates, but the superiority of leaders over nonleaders was restricted mainly to issues relevant to the specific groups in which they were leaders. When matters concerned groups in which they were not leaders, their superiority tended to disappear. Similarly, Northwood (1953) collected facts and opinions from a sample of residents in a housing project. Office holders were found to be significantly more accurate than informal (sociometrically nominated) leaders and followers as judges of fact and opinion (group norms); they were not superior judges of nonrelevant scores. Greer, Galanter, and Nordlie (1954) emphasized this type of contingent outcome, suggesting that they obtained positive results, whereas others such as Hites and Campbell (1950) did not because their leaders were asked to estimate matters more relevant to the members' goals.

*Familiarity.* Studies attempting to correlate a member of a newly formed group's first impressions of others with the member's initial success as a leader have been negative in outcome for the most part (G. B. Bell, 1951; H. E. Hall, 1953). Hatch (1962) found that only if managers felt that they were well-acquainted with a subordinate, were they able to predict the latter's attitudes beyond chance accuracy. When the measured discordance between the attitudes of two subordinates was small, managers were unable to predict the discrepancy with accuracy greater than would be expected by chance alone.

Member familiarity with others in the specific group was found directly related to accuracy by Filella (1971), who divided thirty-two Indian college students who were together in summer school for three weeks into four groups of eight. Members were asked first to rank themselves and then each of the other group members beginning with the person they felt they knew best, then the person they felt they knew second best, and so, down to the person they felt they knew least. The results are as follows:

| | Most Familiar | | | | | | Least Familiar |
|---|---|---|---|---|---|---|---|
| Order of familiarity of raters with ratee | 1 | 2 | 3 | 4 | 5 | 6 | 7 |
| Mean accuracy of raters about ratee | .54 | .48 | .43 | .27 | .21 | .19 | .12 |

Lupfer (1965) recorded group members' interactions in a business game. At the end of each session, each subject indicated on a questionnaire a prediction of, and prescription for, the behavior of every other member. As the sessions progressed, role behavior tended to conform to prescriptive norms, and the prediction of behavior increased in accuracy.

However, in a reversal of the above findings, Browne and Shore (1956) found that although department managers were less close to the workers than were the foremen, the managers were somewhat more accurate in predicting employee attitudes than were the foremen.

*Focusing Attention.* Lundy (1956) administered a scale of values to fifty-two students who met later in pairs to discuss a problem. Then each predicted the responses of the other, using the value scale both with attention focused on self and with attention focused on the partner. Lundy found that focusing attention on the partner increased accuracy of predicting the partner's responses.

*Substance of Judgments.* Foa (1960) found that workers' predictions of their foremen's responses to a projective (picture) test were more accurate when the foreman had described the action in the ambiguous picture as positive and focused on the job rather than upon interpersonal relations.

Holmes (1969) compared leaders' estimates of the interaction frequency and speech duration of group members with recordings of group performance. Leaders evaluated the duration of follower behavior more accurately than its frequency.

*Organizational Considerations.* E. L. Scott (1956) analyzed the organization charts drawn by 696 officers and men aboard ten submarines in which the status structure was thought to be well-defined. He found marked differences between ships and between departments within ships in accuracy of status perception. The most frequent type of error was to perceive superiors as peers, peers as subordinates, and persons outside own department as subordinates in own department. High-ranking personnel made fewer errors in perceptions of superiors and peers, but not in total errors. The more widely superiors interacted with other persons, the greater was the perceptual error of their subordinates, who perceived status relationships more accurately when superiors retained authority in their own hands and delegated less. The greater the disparity between an officer's rank and the level of his position aboard ship, the greater were the perceptual errors of his subordinates. Scott's study was exceptional in that it indicated some potent organizational factors operating to determine the accuracy with which leadership status is perceived in highly structured situations.

## METHODOLOGICAL CONCERNS ABOUT EMPATHY, INSIGHT, AND LEADERSHIP

### Other Plausible Explanations for Results

The conclusion that leaders excel in ability to diagnose situations and understand the motives and actions of other individuals appears to be based on the observation that leaders are able to respond adequately to situations as they change and develop. It was perhaps natural to assume that such adequate coping responses are the outgrowth of prior, conscious diagnosis and evaluation of situations. But there are other possible explanations. Adequate coping behavior may be based on cognitions and information-processing behaviors not subject to high degrees of conscious or rational control.

In trying to assess at the general level individual differences in empathy by asking a leader to guess how others will respond to a personality test calls for a highly rationalized procedure. Absent are all the cues that would enable him or her to respond adequately in face-to-face interaction. The guessing task would appear to measure calculation rather than response to interpersonal situations. In trying to resolve some of the differences in conclusions reached by different investigators, it should be kept in mind that leaders are not required to solve all problems or to be sensitive to all problems; rather they ought to be sensitive to those problems found in groups they lead.

*Assumed Similarity.* Both rationally and empirically it follows that we can be more accurate about others who happen to be like us because of the general tendency to assume that others are indeed like us. A leader's accuracy may be accounted for by the bias toward assumed similarity and the homogeneity of the leader and the group. In fact, in order to be a leader of a group, one must usually share many attitudes, values, and goals with the other members (Cartwright, 1951).

*Norm Conformity.* The findings on group cohesiveness and the influence of prescriptive behavior suggest that predictions become more accurate when groups develop norms to which the members comply. In this case, it would appear that predictive accuracy is a function of norm conformity rather than insight into situations.

*Factual Knowledge.* The findings indicate that leaders tend to exceed followers in factual knowledge about persons and events. But factual knowledge is not synonymous with insight and empathy. The hypothesis that leaders are better able than followers *to diagnose social situations* is not well-supported by research results nor is it convincingly rejected.

*Alternative Designs Needed.* There is a need for new research designs to provide definitive tests of the hypothesis linking leadership and empathy, because any theory of leadership of consequence includes the notion that the leader fulfills some of the needs of the group by helping it cope with its internal and external environment. Generalists like J. M. Burns (1978) see the needs including ways of dealing with any aspects of the group's performance. Structuralists like Hemphill (1954) and J. A. Miller (1974) limit leadership to fulfilling those needs dealing with the structuring of the interrelations among the members and their objectives. In either case, it would appear obvious that leaders are likely to be more able to meet such needs if they can sense better than other members what is needed. Sensitivity, awareness, and empathy, one would think, would be likely to appear to a greater degree among leaders than nonleaders and among more successful and effective leaders. Unfortunately, the evidence is decidedly mixed. Theories must be able to deal with the extent to which successful leaders may often be obtuse to the detriment of their followers. Great men in the tragedies of history characterize this phenomenon.

*Methodological Suggestions*

We may need to probe more deeply to test whether leaders are better able than nonleaders to diagnose social situations. For instance, if as we suspect empathy is often emotional, intuitive, and unconscious [Fiedler, Warrington, and Blaisdell (1952) noted the importance of unconscious attitudes in sociometric choice], then we must use fantasy and projective techniques more frequently in its study rather than objective assessments, even though objective techniques tend to have greater validity and reliability and are more suitable for measurement and experiment.

Stimulated recall represents another untapped possibility, using audio- or video-tape recordings to recreate for participants an event they have just experienced. During the recreation, participants can freely associate into a tape recorder what they had been thinking about during the original event.

Statistical controls should be employed more frequently to eliminate the extent to which the leadership-empathy relation is contaminated by the correlation of both with a third variable such as assumed similarity, calculation accuracy, or conformity to the group norms.

Finally, if diagnostic skill and empathy contribute to successful leadership, then, if we place people in an effective training program (see Chapter 33) to accomplish one or the other, the result should be reflected not only in improved diagnostic skill and empathy, but also in greater success as a leader.

# 8

# AUTHORITARIANISM AND LEADERSHIP

As will be detailed in Chapters 11 and 14, leadership can be based on power and authority. For this reason, it was thought reasonable to expect that those persons who strongly endorse the exercise of power and authority in dealing with subordinates and followers would be motivated to lead. But Christie and Cook (1958) pointed out that the authoritarian personality syndrome was not to be confused with the overt exercise of authority.

## THE AUTHORITARIAN PERSONALITY

An authoritarian type of personality was postulated by Adorno, Frenkel-Brunswik, Levinson, and Sanford (1950). This personality was characterized as politically and religiously conservative, emotionally cold, power-seeking, hostile toward minority groups, resistant to change, opposed to humanitarian values, and the like. A test, the $F$ Scale, was devised to measure authoritarianism. According to Bass and Valenzi (1974), authoritarianism was one of the four personality factors which emerged empirically in a search to understand the system of variables describing the relations among leaders and followers and their outputs. It appeared independently of assertiveness--shyness, sense of fairness, and introversion–extroversion. Campbell and McCormack (1957) found that air force cadets were more authoritarian than college students. But, contrary to expectations, authoritarianism scores decreased with increased time in the air force. R. Christie (1954) suggested that low scores (equalitarian) on the $F$ Scale could be explained on the basis of a well-ingrained tendency for liberals to reject the ideological clichés associated with right-wing politics. Shils (1954) found the context of the $F$ Scale items such as to justify Christie's interpretation.

### How Much Acquiescence?

Bass (1955a) and Chapman and Campbell (1957b) completed research analyses suggesting that, to a large degree, scores on the $F$ Scale could be explained by response set, a tendency to endorse attitude statements in general. However, a flurry of subsequent studies indicated that the percentage of variance due to this acquiescence tendency was less in amount than first suggested by Bass (based on an error in calculation). Acquiescence appeared to account for about one-quarter rather than three-quarters of the variance in $F$ scores.

**120**

*Relation to Competence*

Based on their reviews of the research literature, both Titus and Hollander (1957) and Christie and Cook (1958) concluded that scores on the *F* Scale are negatively correlated with intelligence. Equalitarians tend to be brighter than authoritarians. They are also better educated. Newcomb (1961) observed that equalitarians were better able than authoritarians to determine which group members agreed with them and let their sociometric choices be determined accordingly. Wilkins and deCharms (1962) reported that equalitarians were less influenced by external power cues in evaluating others. They used more behavioral cues in describing others. Authoritarians were more highly influenced by status and power cues in making evaluations.

Courtney, Greer, and Masling (1952) administered the *F* Scale to a representative sample of residents of Philadelphia. The residents scoring highest on authoritarianism were laborers and those with the least education. The lowest scores were made by managers, officials, and clerical and sales people. Professionals, semiprofessionals, and university students scored between these two groups. Haythorn, Couch, Haefner, Laugham, and Carter (1956a) formed two groups, one high on the *F* Scale and conservatism, the other low on the *F* Scale and liberal. The thirty-two participants viewed a film and met in their groups to compose dialog for the film. According to pairs of reliable observers, low *F* leaders were significantly more sensitive to others, contributed more toward moving the group closer to goals set by the group, showed greater effective intelligence, and were more submissive in attitudes toward other group members than were high *F* leaders. Using the same design, the same investigators (Haythorn, Couch, et al., 1956b) found again that high *F* leaders were less sensitive to others (a potential contributor to leadership as noted in Chapter 7).

*Preferences in Leadership*

Milton (1952) found that authoritarian college students as measured by the *F* Scale supported for president in 1952 the nomination of Douglas MacArthur, who symbolized and emphasized power and authority in leadership, whereas students with low *F* scores supported the nomination of Adlai Stevenson, who portrayed the leader as a more consultative problem solver. Sanford (1950) administered an authoritarian-equalitarian scale to 963 randomly selected adults in Philadelphia. Those who scored high on authoritarianism wanted a leader to be competent, educated, helpful to people, understanding, and stern. Those scoring low preferred leaders who were kind, guided by the people, one of the people, strong, and friendly. Both agreed that leaders should be competent, intelligent, able to handle people, and honest and fair. The strong leader and the one who tells people exactly what to do was accepted by authoritarians but rejected by equalitarians. Equalitarians wanted either to be told nothing or to be told what to do, but not how to do it. Authoritarians tended to choose a leader for his or her personal magnetism, high status, competence, and ability to do things. Equalitarians preferred a humanitarian leader who did things for people. Thus, authoritarians favored being led by an autocratic, directive, structuring, task-oriented leader; equalitarians favored being led by a democratic, participative, considerate, relations-oriented leader. (These styles will be discussed in Chapters 18 through 21.)

*Attitudes and Performance*

According to Masling, Greer, and Gilmore (1955), equalitarians among 1,900 military personnel tended to rate more group members favorably than did authoritarian personnel, but both rated leaders more favorably than nonleaders. Likewise, Medalia (1955) studied enlisted men in the air force. Authoritarians expressed greater acceptance of formal leaders than did equalitarians. Contrary to hypothesis, cohesiveness as measured by reenlistment rate was higher among equalitarians. For both authoritarians and equalitarians, leader acceptance was unrelated to group cohesiveness. But, for those medium in authoritarianism, leader acceptance was related to cohesiveness. Medalia concluded that extreme equalitarians may be as rigid in behavior as extreme authoritarians. Haythorn, Couch, et al. (1956b) found that high $F$ followers were more satisfied with appointed leaders and were less critical of their own group's performance.

Contrary to hypothesis, authoritarianism was not highly valued by air crew commanders studied by Rohde (1952).

## AUTHORITARIANISM AND LEADER BEHAVIOR

*Use of Reward and Punishment*

Dustin and Davis (1967) asked participants to indicate whether they would use monetary rewards and penalties or evaluative communications in order to stimulate maximum performance in hypothetical followers. Compared with equalitarians, authoritarians used negative sanctions (monetary penalty or negative evaluation) significantly more often. W. P. Smith (1967a) also found that authoritarians tend more than equalitarians to use punishment rather than reward as a method of inducing performance in others.

*Unstructured Situations*

Bass, McGehee, Hawkins, Young, and Gebel (1953) demonstrated that authoritarian personalities as measured by the $F$ Scale are least likely to attempt or exhibit successful leadership behavior in initially leaderless discussions—a socially ambiguous situation which calls for considerable flexibility if one wishes to attempt to emerge as a leader in the situation. Again, Bass and Coates (1952) found significant correlations of .32 and .33 between the tendency of ROTC cadets to display successful leadership in initially leaderless group discussions and their scores on two measures of perceptual flexibility. In the same way, Geier (1963) observed that overly rigid members tended to be eliminated as leaders in the early stages of group discussion.

Equalitarian leaders tend to promote more participation. Thus, when low $F$ leaders emerged or were appointed in the Haythorn, Couch, et al. (1956a,b) experiments, followers tended to be able to exert more influence and to express more differences in opinion. High-scoring (authoritarian) leaders were described as more autocratic, less democratic, and less concerned with group approval than low-scoring (equalitarian) leaders.

*Structured Situations*

Rohde (1952) administered the *F* Scale to 176 air crew members who were also rated by their crew commanders on three criteria. Authoritarianism was correlated − .33 with willingness of the commanders to take the men into combat, − .46 with desirability as a friend, and − .11 with confidence in the crew members. Hollander (1954) obtained nominations for student commander from 268 naval aviation cadets. Nominations for leadership were correlated − .23 with authoritarianism scores.

In an industrial study, Ley (1966) found an extremely high correlation of .76 between employee turnover rate and the authoritarian scores of their supervisors. Masling (1953) studied 2,139 naval recruits. Authoritarianism was negatively related to popularity. As expected, among chief petty officers, authoritarianism and the number of demerits they gave recruits were positively related. But contrary to hypothesis, leader's authoritarianism was not significantly related to several measures of group effectiveness and performance. Likewise, Hamblin, Miller, and Wiggins (1961) failed to find a significant correlation between leader's authoritarianism and measures of group morale and success.

*Community Leadership and Authoritarianism.* Community leaders were reported by Courtney, Greer, and Masling (1952) to be significantly more equalitarian than followers. Greer (1953) interviewed twenty-nine leaders in Philadelphia. Their scores on the authoritarian-equalitarian scale were significantly more equalitarian than those of nonleaders. Tarnapol (1958) obtained similar results.

## CONTINGENCIES MODIFYING THE EFFECTS OF A LEADER'S AUTHORITARIANISM

The effects of a leader's authoritarianism tend to depend to a considerable degree on his or her followers' authoritarianism or equalitarianism and various situational factors.

*Followers' Personality*

Researchers often focused on the impact of the followers' authoritarianism on the leadership process, for firmly entrenched in the authoritarian personality was submissiveness and obedience to higher authority. Contrary to hypothesis, Campbell and McCormack (1957) found that such authoritarianism and orientation toward superiors decrease with increasing military experience in varied samples of military personnel. This was due probably to one's increased ability to cope with the situation as one's experience is increased.

As expected, Vroom (1960a) obtained results indicating that authoritarian employees tended to be less well-satisfied and less highly motivated under participative leadership than equalitarians. Equalitarians were better satisfied and more highly motivated under participative leadership.

Haythorn, Couch, Haefner, Langham, and Carter (1956a), who had assembled different combinations of leaders and followers on the basis of high or low scores on the *F* Scale, found that compared to equalitarian followers, authoritarian followers generally were rated by observers as less democratic and less sensitive to others, were more satisfied with appointed leaders, and rated their groups higher in productivity and goal motivation. Unexpectedly, authoritarian followers were not more submissive to leadership than equalitarians, and they exercised more influence in their groups than did the latter. Observers rated equalitarian followers lower than authoritarian followers in productivity and goal orientation and higher in withdrawing from the field of activity.

Frey (1963) studied the disruptive behavior of groups under authoritarian and equalitarian leaders. Most disruption occurred in groups composed of both authoritarian leaders and followers; the least in groups composed of equalitarian leaders and followers. Group performance was highest in groups composed of both authoritarian leaders and followers; lowest in groups composed of equalitarian leaders and authoritarian followers.

*Impact on Leader.* Bass and Farrow (1977), using path analysis, showed how the authoritarianism of leaders and followers determined whether a leader would be directive, negotiative, consultative, participative, or delegative (see Chapter 19). A short form of the $F$ Scale was completed by seventy-seven managers and their 407 subordinates from industry and public agencies. The authoritarianism of managers or their subordinates did not affect the extent to which the managers were directive. However, authoritarian or equalitarian personality did determine how much the managers were negotiative (manipulative and opportunistic) as well as how much they tended to consult with their subordinates. Managers were seen by their subordinates to be more frequently negotiative if they had authoritarian subordinates, particularly if the managers had short-term objectives rather than long-term perspectives. In turn, the manager's short- or long-term perspectives were an intervening variable influenced by authoritarianism. Specifically, managers with authoritarian personalities were short-term maximizers, and managers who were short-term maximizers more frequently used a negotiative leader style. On the other hand, managers were more likely to be consultative when their subordinates were equalitarian and fairminded. As with directiveness, the other styles of leadership studied, participation and delegation, were unaffected by the authoritarianism of the managers or their subordinates.

*Congruence.* Tosi (1973) tested a congruency hypothesis. A personality match between the supervisor and subordinate was expected to result in greater satisfaction and morale and in less conflict than a mismatch. Data were collected from 488 managers of consumer loan offices. Four groups were formed, high $F$ and low $F$ groups who worked for bosses either high or low on tolerance for freedom on the Leadership Behavior Description Questionnaire, Form XII (see Chapter 21). The congruency hypothesis was partially supported. Job satisfaction and degree of participation were highest for the high $F$ subordinate working for the boss lacking in tolerance for freedom. But a low $F$ subordinate working with a high-tolerance-for-freedom boss unexpectedly reported the lowest level of participation and satisfaction. These results suggested that some degree of structure or direction had to be present, whether in the boss or in the subordinate, to define the situation in which work was done (Valenzi, Miller, et al., 1972).

*Reactions to Leadership and Authority.* In a seminal study in a package delivery firm, Vroom (1959, 1960a) found that the extent to which employees were satisfied and effective under participative supervision depended on their being equalitarian and high in need for independence. Campion (1969) replicated Vroom's results in an experimental study. But another replication of Vroom's study by Tosi (1970) using the same survey method as Vroom with a different organization and different jobs failed to corroborate Vroom's findings. Tosi noted that his respondents were also different from Vroom's in terms of values, interests, and other personality characterisitics as well as sex.

Thibaut and Riecken (1955a) studied the effects of influence attempts on authoritarians and equalitarians by persons differing in status (rank) in the organization. They found that authoritarians were more sensitive to the rank of a leader than were equalitarians. E. E. Jones (1954) found similar results. However, equalitarians saw the forceful stimulus person as more powerful and the passive leader as less powerful than did those who scored high on the $F$ Scale. The lows were more highly sensitized to personal power differences and behavioral cues, while the highs tended to differentiate in terms of institutional status. Thibaut and Riecken (1955b) also studied group reactions to the leader's attempts to instigate aggressive behavior. Neither the authoritarianism of the group members nor the status of the leaders influenced their initial acceptance. However, authoritarian participants facing a high-status instigator changed toward greater submission while low-status instigators received greater rejection. In overt communication, less intense rejection was directed toward the higher than toward the low-status instigators. Lipetz and Ossorio (1967) found equalitarians more hostile toward high-status than low-status target persons whether or not they attempted to instigate aggression. Roberts and Jessor (1958) used projective tests to study the attitudes of authoritarians toward frustrating persons. Compared with equalitarians, authoritarians tended to exhibit personal hostility toward low-status frustrators and to express indirect hostility toward frustrators of high status.

## Situational Contingencies

The size and structure of the group make a difference in the effects of the authoritarianism or equalitarianism of the leader. Authoritarian personalities appear to do better where interaction among members is constrained by group size, centralization of organization, or task structure (see Chapters 27 and 28 for more details about the effects of interaction potential).

*Large Size.* Vroom and Mann (1960) compared large and small work groups. Supervisors scoring high on the $F$ Scale were accepted better in large than in small groups. Equalitarians were better accepted in small groups. In large groups, authoritarian supervisors were described by employees as more participative, exerting less pressure on employees, and creating less tension between themselves and higher management than equalitarian supervisors. Authoritarian supervisors in small groups were seen as less participative and creating more tension with both supervisors and subordinates than low-authoritarian supervisors. Vroom and Mann (1960) also examined the relationship between authoritarianism of the supervisors and satisfaction of their subordinates. Subordinates whose jobs were characterized by a low degree of interaction between themselves and their supervisors, and by a low degree of interdependence possessed more positive attitudes about authoritarian supervisors.

*Centralized Communications.* M. E. Shaw (1955) studied the effects of authoritarian and equalitarian leadership in different communication nets. He found that groups under authoritarian leaders were highly productive but suffered in morale. M. E. Shaw

(1959a) further reported that, as expected, groups with leaders scoring high in authoritarianism performed better in centralized networks, whereas groups with equalitarian leaders performed better in less highly centralized networks.

*Task-Oriented.* In task-oriented groups, authoritarians tended to emerge as leaders; in socioemotional groups, equalitarians tended to emerge as leaders (Harrell, Burnham & Lee, 1963).

Equalitarianism is but one among many values of consequence to leadership. Now we turn to examining some of the more important of these in the next chapter.

# VALUES, NEEDS, AND SATISFACTIONS OF LEADERSHIP

Baltzell (1980) contrasted the values of upper class Protestant Boston and upper class Protestant Philadelphia. Puritan Boston saw man as inherently sinful, in need of authoritative institutions headed by righteous leaders of superior education. Quaker Philadelphia saw man as inherently good, individually perfectable, without need of mediation by state or church, erudition, or professionalism. For Boston's Brahmins, public service became obligatory; not so, for Philadelphia's. Boston's Adams, Cabot, and Lowell families produced a good many eminent political leaders; Philadelphia's Biddle, Cadwalader, and Wharton families did not. Baltzell attributed the difference to the original Puritan and Quaker values inculcated in succeeding generations of family members. The Bostonians, who pursued political leadership, and the Philadelphians, who did not, clearly differed in their attitudes and opinions about what was important to them and what interested them. In turn, these values and interests altered the strength of their motives to work in one direction or another, oriented them toward various goals and unfulfilled needs they claimed. Satisfaction accrued from perceived fulfillment of those needs.

Different leadership studies have focused on values, interests, motives, orientation, goals, needs, and satisfactions, terms which have often overlapped in meaning. For the purposes of this chapter, we will look at these various aspects of choice of work and reward mainly by their substantive content: self-actualization, task orientation, organizational loyalty, and so on. We will try to see whether leaders differ from nonleaders in such preference, and how this preference relates to their leadership performance. We will examine what leaders value and regard as important, how it affects their performance, and whether or not they are satisfied with the extent to which they achieve what they value. Then we will consider how these outcomes depend upon the situation in which the leadership is to occur.

The many studies of the attitudes of managerial personnel have been stimulated by an interest in managerial motivation and because manager's needs, interests, and values play an important role in their success. Thus, in a review of available research, Ghiselli (1968a) noted that managers' personal values correlated from .25 to .30 with criteria of their effectiveness. Research on management attitudes have also been reviewed by Herzberg, Mausner, Peterson, and Capwell (1957), Vroom (1965), Porter and Lawler (1965), and Cummings and ElSalmi (1968).

More specifically, Vroom (1962) found that persons who are ego-involved on their jobs are rated higher in job performance than those who are less involved. However, although expected to do so, the autonomy provided by the job failed to make a difference in the relationship. Ghiselli (1968a) also found that personality traits and motivational factors interacted to determine the job success of managers. Need for job security was the strongest and need for power was the weakest moderator in producing interaction between traits and success. Schock and Matthews (1974) demonstrated that to locate opinion leaders of sewing practices in a community, one had to search out early those interested in home practices.

England and Lee (1974) suggested six reasons for the influence of personal values on a leader's performance: (1) they influence a leader's perception of situations and problems faced; (2) they influence a leader's decisions and solutions to problems; (3) they influence the way in which a leader looks at other individuals and groups of individuals, thus, they influence interpersonal relationships; (4) they influence the perception of individual and organizational success as well as their achievement; (5) they set the limits for the determination of what is and what is not ethical behavior by a leader; and (6) they influence the extent to which a leader accepts or resists organizational pressures and goals.

It is obvious that what leaders value as an activity for its own sake obviously depends on the locale of the leadership. Among government leaders, strong political values are expected; in the military, one is likely to see among leaders strong interests in adventure; in business, one is likely to see strong interest in computational and clerical matters; in science, strong preference for theoretical activities—understanding the "whys" of things. Thus, E. K. Strong's (1943) research from the 1920s onward showed how distinct patterns of interests marked off different professions.

## INTERESTS, NEEDS, MOTIVES, AND GOALS

*Interests*

Tagiuri (1965) found that executives and research managers placed greater value on theoretical, economic, and political values than on social, religious, or esthetic values than would be expected from, say, artists, ministers, or social service personnel. Interests were related to attainment and effectiveness. Bedrosian (1964) found that higher-level managers exhibited a higher level of socioeconomic interest than did middle- or lower-level managers. From a review of the literature on managerial interests, A. N. Nash (1965) concluded that four interest patterns are consistently related to managerial effectiveness: (1) social service; (2) persuasion; (3) business and business contacts; and (4) rejection of scientific, technical, and skilled trade interests.

Interests were seen to differ as well in small-group and student leaders. Martin, Gross, and Darley (1952) determined that sociometrically selected leaders tended to identify with middle class values, while informal leaders tended to identify with lower class values. Brainard and Dollar (1971) studied ninety students divided into three samples according to the extent to which they emphasized vocational, academic, or collegiate social aims. Leaders who felt most concerned with academic or vocational aims scored high in applied interests and low in need for closeness and friendliness.

A rather arbitrary decision is involved in discussing motivation separately from interests. The two kinds of studies have much in common; their methodology is similar. The primary difference lies in the assumptions concerning the personality dynamics that account for motivation and interests.

### Economic Motivation

Strong interest in pay and profitability mark the successful entrepreneur and business manager.

*Pay.* In response to traditionalists' overemphasis on pay as a motivator, behavioral science overreacted in attempting to minimize its importance to managers and their subordinates. Nevertheless, according to reviews of research on pay and managerial motivation by Opsahl and Dunnette (1966), Dunnette et al. (1967), and Porter and Lawler (1968), pay remains a strong motivator for managerial personnel. Lawler and Porter (1967) found that presidents and vice presidents stressed the importance of pay slightly less than managers at lower levels, but pay was highly significant for all. Pay may satisfy not only lower-order needs such as for safety and security but also higher-order needs such as for autonomy and self-actualization. Porter and Lawler (1968) conducted research relevant to this issue. They found that those managers who perceive a high probability of pay depending upon job performance tended to perform better on their jobs when performance was rated by both themselves and by their superiors. The relation between probability estimates and effort was stronger for those who attached high reward value to pay. Effective performance was related to the extent to which it was seen as instrumental to higher pay.

*Use of Pay as a Motivator.* In simulations, awarding more or less pay to subordinates seems to be a matter of the recommenders' values. Bass (1968a) reported that students' value orientations are related to their generosity in recommending pay increases for fictitious engineers. Those students who were lower in intelligence and ability and those who scored high in social and service values, as opposed to theoretical and economic values, were more generous in recommending salary increases. In an international survey of 4,255 managers, Bass, Burger, et al. (1979) found that more successful managers recommended significantly greater salary increases for an average meritorious fictitious engineer, but they were no different than their slower-climbing counterparts in their salary recommendations for engineers on other grounds.

### Profitability versus Interpersonal Concerns

Numerous investigations of the goals and objectives of managers are available. Objectives are almost always a manifold mix of personal and organizational factors. For managers to restrict themselves to a single objective function—profit maximization—is a fictional convenience for classical economists and some operational research specialists. (Dent, 1959). Shartle (1956) conducted a program of studies on the elements that individuals value in varying degrees in several kinds of organizations. A factor analysis of item intercorrelations produced nine factors describing the value dimensions for business firms: (1) organizational magnitude, expansion, and structure; (2) internal consideration for welfare, health, and comfort; (3) degree of competition, strategy, and shrewdness; (4) degree of ethical and social responsibility; (5) quality of product or service;

(6) degree of change; (7) degree of organization control over member identifications; (8) degree of external political participation; and (9) degree of member equality and recognition.

Bass, Burger, et al. (1979) found that, given a limited budget, from 46 to 77 percent of 5,122 managers were willing to spend for safety, employee relations, product quality, and pollution control. Willingness to spend for such organizational needs was positively associated with social orientation to share and trust others and negatively correlated with political orientations to bluff and maintain psychosocial distance (Bass, 1968c). England (1967b) reported that managers of middle-sized companies rated organizational stability generally higher in importance than did managers of large and small companies. Managers of large companies rated organization stability as least crucial. Goals depended also on a manager's functions. Thus, Browne (1950a,b,c) and Dearborn and Simon (1958) found that top-ranking executives of a business firm tended to perceive organizational goals in terms of the functions of their own departments.

Perceived goals are associated with attitudes. Vroom (1960b) studied the attitudes and goal perceptions of executives in a large firm. Actual goals consisted of the average of the statements made by twenty-three top-ranking executives about the organization's goals. It was found that the more positive an individual's attitude toward the organization, the greater the correspondence between the organization's goals and his perception of these goals.

Nevertheless, given the choice, managers do tend to place a particular premium on profitability and performance. Thus, England (1967a,b) who studied managers in nine levels of hierarchy, found general agreement on the importance of organization effectiveness and productivity and a lack of perceived importance of social welfare as goals of organization. This was despite differences among the managers at the different levels.

In the same way, the results of several studies (Sequeira, 1962; Kelly, 1964; Mandell & Duckworth, 1955; Moore, Kennedy & Castore, 1946) indicate that first-line supervisors view the technical aspects of their jobs as more important than the human relations aspect. Managers tend to agree with these evaluations (Rubenowitz, 1962). Among midwestern community leaders of middle-sized cities, most of whom were in business or banking, economic development was seen as the paramount goal of university extension services (Moss, 1974). But a similar sample did not regard environmental concerns of much importance to their communities (Sofranko & Bridgeland, 1975). And rural Georgia community leaders saw less need for economic exchange compared to coordination than did rural heads of households with whom they were compared (Nix, Singh & Cheatham, 1974).

### Achievement Motivation

Managers appear to thrive when given opportunities to achieve. Both Berlew and Hall (1966) and Vicino and Bass (1978) found that the degree of first-year challenge sensed by managers predicted their subsequent success as much as six years later.

*Task Orientation.* As has already been seen in Chapter 5, task orientation was seen as a characteristic of persons who in social settings "will [try] hardest to help obtain the group's goals, solve its problems, overcome barriers preventing the successful completion of the group's tasks, and who persist at . . . assignments" (Bass, 1960a, p. 149).

This was distinguished from interaction orientation (to have fun, work cooperatively, be helpful) and from self-orientation (to be praised, recognized, respected, and have loyal associates). The Orientation Inventory (Bass, 1962) was developed to measure the three valued approaches to working with others. According to a review by Bass (1967b), those in higher-status positions in organizations uniformly were more task-oriented. Thus, top managers scored higher than middle managers, middle managers higher than supervisors, supervisors higher than nonsupervisory workers. College campus student leaders were found to be higher in self- and interaction orientation. The higher participants' task orientation in sensitivity training groups, the more they were rated positively by their peers on the following: help members express their ideas; help group stay on target; help get to meat of issues; give good suggestions on proceeding; give good summaries; encourage high productivity; take lead; work hard; and offer original ideas (Bass & Dunteman, 1963). Assessment center observers rated temporary supervisors under consideration for promotion who were high in task orientation as more promotable (Bass, 1967b).

Task orientation was higher among second-line supervisors rated "best" by their superiors rather than "less than best." Likewise, task orientation was higher among top- and middle-performing first-line supervisors than among those low in performance (Dunteman & Bass, 1963).

A variety of other overlapping indicators of task orientation generally has been positively linked to attitudes and performance in work settings and their effects. Thus, Rubenowitz (1962) found that superiors in an industrial situation tended to rate their subordinates higher in effectiveness when the latter were production-oriented rather than person-oriented. F. C. Mann (1965) noted that supervisors higher in technical than in human relations skills reported that they were dissatisfied with promotion and wages, worried about advancement, felt in the middle between workers and management, and tended to take risks.

*Need for Achievement.* Relying on a projective measure, the Thematic Apperception Test, McClelland (1961, 1965a,b, 1966a,b, 1969) and McClelland and Winter (1969) provided strong evidence to support the proposition that need for achievement is an important value for effective leaders, particularly successful entrepreneurs.

A number of studies both in the United States and abroad demonstrated that managerial success was predicted by need for achievement (Meyer & Walker, 1961; Meyer, Walker & Litwin, 1961). Cummin (1967) found that more successful executives were higher in need for achievement (as well as need for power). Similarly, Wainer and Rubin (1969) found that for fifty-one technical entrepreneurs who founded and operated their own firms, need for achievement of the entrepreneurs was related to the growth rate of their companies. The highest performing companies where those whose owner was high in need for achievement and moderate in need for power. Again, data from over one thousand managers gathered by Hall & Donnell (1979) found that their speed of career advancement was associated with their achievement orientation.

Other corroborative studies reached similar conclusions. Mussen and Porter (1959) found that leaders effective in group discussion scored significantly higher than ineffective leaders in need for achievement as well as on feelings of adequacy and need for affiliation.

England (1967a,b) found that managers rated high the personal goals of achievement, success, and creativity; security and leisure were rated low.

*LPC.* A most prominent line of investigation, to be detailed in Chapter 20, builds on a simple set of semantic differential scales yielding a score describing one's Least Preferred Coworker. Although the interpretation remains controversial, Fiedler (1967a) has presented a large body of evidence to justify using LPC scores to measure one's task orientation (least preferred coworker is judged unfavorably). LPC score alone cannot determine a leader's likely effectiveness. Rather, it all depends on how favorable the situation is to him or her.

*Internal–External Orientation.* Rotter's (1966) I–E scale discriminates among those controlled by internal forces and those controlled by outside influences. Anderson, Hellreigel, and Slocum (1977) found that internal managers were more task-oriented. However, after reviewing the literature, DeBolt, Liska, and Weng (1976) concluded that internal control, as measured by the I–E Scale, failed to relate consistently to leadership in small student groups. Anderson and Schneier (1978) disagreed, pointing particularly to results with managers. Thus, Goodstadt and Hjelle (1973) found that external managers were more likely to be coercive and threatening, whereas internal managers were more likely to rely on persuasion. Mitchell, Smyser, and Weed (1975) obtained similar results. They noted that external supervisors were more likely to use coercion and legitimate authority, whereas internal supervisors used rewards, respect, and expert power (see Chapter 11). Pryer and Distefano (1971) confirmed that internals are more considerate as nursing supervisors (Chapter 21), and Mitchell, Smyser, and Weed (1975) found that internal subordinates demonstrated greater satisfaction with participative supervisors, while externals were more satisfied with directive supervisors (Chapter 19). However, Durand and Nord (1976) found that the ideal supervisor may be external in orientation since externals were perceived as being more considerate and showing more initiative.

### Power Motivation

Research results point to power motivation as a highly important domain of values and attitudes for understanding leadership. Thus, Shaw and Harkey (1976) found that groups in which the leaders have ascendant tendencies did better than groups in which nonascendant people were leaders. Veroff (1957) found that individuals scoring high on projective measures of power motivation also score high on satisfaction with leadership status and are rated high in argumentation and attempts to convince others. Again, McClelland and Burnham (1976) observed that good managers have a strong power motivation, but one that is oriented toward serving the organization rather than personal aggrandizement. Those more in need for power than affiliation generate among their subordinates more of a sense of responsibility, organizational clarity, and team spirit. But need for power as measured by Stewart's social-maturity scale failed to predict emergence as a leader in initially leaderless discussions among male and female students (Frantzve, 1979). At the same time, Browning and Jacob (1964) observed that whether needs for achievement and power direct individuals toward the economic or political arena depends on which arena in the community is open and available to them. Similar conclusions were reached about leaders' effectiveness as a function of their desire to influence or to be influenced by others. O'Brien and Harary (1977) measured the difference between the strength of the desire for power and the opportunity to fulfill that desire. They observed in several studies that a leader's effectiveness was greater as this discrepancy became smaller.

### Self-Actualization and Autonomy

Self-actualization and autonomy are the least well-satisfied managerial needs (Haire, Ghiselli & Porter, 1963; Johnson & Marcrum, 1968; L. W. Porter, 1961a,b, 1962) and are rated the most important needs by managers. However, hourly workers, and to some extent first-line supervisors, are more interested than managers in job security (Centers, 1948, Centers & Bugental, 1966; Edel, 1966; Garbin & Bates, 1966; N. George, 1958; Herzberg et al., 1957; Haire, Ghiselli & Porter, 1963; Porter, 1961a,b, 1962; Raube, 1947; Raudsepp, 1962; Weiss, Dawis, England & Lofquist, 1964). These differences as a consequence of hierarchical level will be discussed in more detail later.

Among 3,082 mostly middle managers from twelve countries, Bass, Burger, et al. (1979) found a clear set of preferences when the managers were asked to rank eleven life goals. At the top were self-realization and independence. For the 3,082 managers as a whole, Bass, Burger, et al. reported the order of importance of the eleven goals as follows (with 1.00 = most important, and 11.00 = least important): self realization, 4.09; independence, 4.89; expertness, 5.17; affection, 5.21; leadership, 5.32; security, 5.50; service, 6.01; pleasure, 6.78; duty, 7.08; prestige, 7.65; and wealth to build a large estate, 8.27. But the standard deviations of 2.6 to 3.3 suggested that in the total group there were some managers who rated the same goal first in importance while others ranked it eleventh. Wide individual differences particularly across the 12 cultures studied (see Chapter 32) were the rule rather than the exception.

Among 65,000 IBM personnel who completed the rankings, two strong factors emerged, accounting for 54 percent of the variance. The first factor denoted attaching more importance to comfort (pleasure, security, and affection) rather than accomplishment (expertness, prestige, and duty). The second factor dealt with assertiveness (leadership, independence, and self-realization) rather than service (Hofstede, 1978).

*Relation to Success.* The 3,082 managers were sorted into those higher and those lower in rate of advancement—the speed with which they had moved up the executive ladder in their own organizations.

Overall, higher-level needs such as self-realization were judged of greater importance by managers than lower-level needs such as pleasure. But also in terms of Hofstede's factors, goals dealing with assertiveness and accomplishment were more often given emphasis by faster-climbing managers, whereas those associated with comfort tended to be favored by those lower in rate of advancement. In the same way, Hall and Donnell (1979) found that in comparing 190 slow, 442 average, and thirty-two fast career-advancing managers, the fast managers stressed self-actualization, belonging, and esteem needs in motivating their subordinates. They paid only average attention to safety and security needs. The slow managers emphasized mainly safety and security. The average managers were in between. This is consistent with Porter and Lawler's (1968) finding that performance differences were more highly related to self-actualization and autonomy needs than to security, social, and esteem needs.

It should be kept in mind that self-realization can come about through attainment of a variety of alternative goals in addition to personal growth. Executives may see it in their attainment of leadership; technologists in their attainment of expertise; and entrepreneurs, in attaining wealth. Similarly, Maslow's social need can be satisfied within the family and friends through affection, on the job through service, and in the organization or community through duty. Wainer and Rubin (1969) studied entrepreneurs who had founded their own companies. High need for achievement and moderate need for power were associated with company success. Ghiselli (1968b), analyzing middle managers and hourly workers, found that successful managers exhibited less desire for security and financial reward than unsuccessful ones. Managers did not differ from workers in desire for power.

Harrell and Alpert (1979) concluded that to maximize success and satisfaction, the need for autonomy should be strong among business entrepreneurs, moderate among tenured professors, and weak among bureaucrats. Appelbaum (1977) obtained data from seventy-five suburban government supervisors which strongly supported Harrell and Alpert's suggestion about bureaucrats. However, Henderson (1977) failed to find support for expectations about the effects of self-actualization on choice of leadership style.

### Valuing of Interpersonal Competence

Interpersonal competence was a global concept offered by Argyris (1962) to describe the differences between traditional approaches to interpersonal relations and those fostered by the group dynamics movement. The traditional view of good interpersonal relations emphasized acceptance of authority, avoidance of conflict, and "hiding behind polite facades." The group dynamics movement stressed awareness, openness to discussions about feelings as well as substantive issues, consensual solutions to conflict, and development of commitment to actions. Managers with interpersonal competence were seen as more willing to depend on trust, shared decision making, and group goal setting rather than power (Zaleznik, 1965). Sgro, Worchel, Pence, and Orban (1980) obtained significant positive correlations between a measure of interpersonal trust of forty-one cadet leaders and their subordinates' evaluations of them on various dimensions of the leader's behavior such as the leader's initiation and consideration (see Chapter 21) as well as how satisfied they were with the leader.

In international samples using self-appraisals and other self-reporting instruments, Bass, Burger, et al. (1979) concluded that compared with those lower in rate of advancement, those higher in rate of advancement judged themselves higher in actually understanding "why I do what I do"; they preferred to be slightly lower in concern for rules, less imitative, and less involved in group decision making. They were more task-oriented and possibly more willing to discuss feelings with others. They were not as extreme as those slower in rate of advancement in "we–they" bias. The overall pattern suggests that the faster-climbing manager sees less value in being interpersonally competent but in fact is more competent than those lower in rate of advancement on a variety of different assessments.

*Pragmatism versus Idealism*

Using a Personal Values Questionnaire, England and Weber (1972) contrasted the extent to which U.S. managers regarded various issues (England & Lee, 1974, p. 111) as "successful," as "right," and as "pleasant." From these judgments, managers were seen to emphasize either what is pragmatic, what is moral, or what is pleasurable. England and Lee (1974) then administered the Personal Values Questionnaire to almost two thousand U.S., Australian, Indian, and Japanese managers. The success of these managers was measured by their income adjusted for their age. In all four countries, successful managers were more likely to hold pragmatic values emphasizing productivity, profitability, and achievement.

Bass (1975a) developed Exercise Objectives in which participants' performance can be a gauge of their pragmatism or idealism. In Exercise Objectives, five budgeting decisions are required dealing with questions about whether or not to budget money to deal with problems of safety, labor relations, management morale, product quality, and environmental pollution.

An unpublished study of 113 MBA students revealed a significant correlation of .24 between economic value scores on the Allport-Vernon Study of Values and an unwillingness to spend on the five problems in Exercise Objectives. Unwillingness to spend was also significantly related in this sample with an economic Theory X rather than a humanistic Theory Y ($r = .20$) attitude as described by McGregor (1960).

For an international sample of 5,122 managers on all five budgeting problems, faster-climbing managers tended to exhibit more pragmatism than idealism in that they were less willing to spend money to handle the requests for safety, to settle a strike, to deal with morale, to improve product quality, or to halt a stream pollution problem. Although they did not want to risk wasting money, faster-climbing managers did value generosity and fairmindedness. The picture which emerged of the faster-climbing managers was that of persons who wanted productive value for their expenditures (Bass, Burger, et al., 1979).

*Risk Preference*

Attempts to lead and success in leading others is greater among those willing to take greater risks. Wallach, Kogan, and Bem (1962) found that high risk takers were more influential in discussion than low risk takers. Marquis (1962) and Collins and Guetzkow (1964) observed that high risk takers are more persuasive than more cautious members of a group. Clausen (1965) and Burnstein (1969) accounted for these results by suggesting that high risk takers tended to score high in self-confidence which in turn led them to attempt and to succeed in influencing the group to follow their lead.

So to lead one must be willing to take risks in the absence of complete information. Many of the failures among the great men of history were instances where they were immobilized when facing the need to decide in crises. Nevertheless, there is no guarantee that taking action will be effective and satisfying to the group. Lack of necessary caution and complete analysis has also been an important characteristic of mismanagement. Bass, Burger, et al. (1979) failed to find any association between the rate of advancement of 1,044 managers in an international sample and their self-rated actual and preferred risk taking under uncertainty.

*Trust.* Closely associated with the willingness to risk is the willingness to trust. According to Devine (1977), who completed a survey of opinion leadership in Bemidji, Moorhead, and St. Cloud (all in Minnesota), both opinion leaders and opinion followers showed willingness to trust others, but opinion isolates were less likely to do so.

## MATCHING OF REQUIRED ATTRIBUTES AND SITUATION

It has often been possible to develop an especially cross-validated key for the Strong-Campbell Vocational Interest Blank to discriminate among those who subsequently achieve more success as leaders in their organizations. The inventory is examined item-by-item (Laurent, 1968). This illustrates how what values and interests that are important to success as a leader vary from one locale to another. Consistent with this specificity of result, managers who identify themselves with and express interests similar to those of their particular superiors are more satisfied than those who do not identify with their superiors (Eran, 1966; Gruenfeld & Foltman, 1967; Mordechai, 1966; M. S. Myers, 1966).

### Judged Requisites for Success

What is judged by managers as important and valuable for success as a manager is related to their success. Managers who stress the importance of inner-directed behavior (imagination, self-confidence, and so on) are rated more effective in their jobs than those who see their roles as demanding high degrees of other-directed behavior (cooperativeness, tactfulness, etcetera), according to Lawler and Porter (1967a,b), Mitchell and Porter (1967), and Porter and Lawler (1968). Consistent with these results, Bass, Burger, et al. (1979) found generosity, fairmindedness, sharpwittedness, and steadiness judged more important for top management by those faster in rate of advancement as managers; tolerance and adaptability were judged more important for top managers among those slower in rate of advancement.

Attributes judged most important for middle management by those higher in rate of advancement were: generosity, sharpwittedness and reliability, but tolerance, adaptability, and self-control were judged most important for middle managers by those lower in rate of advancement.

For first-line supervisors, attributes judged most important by those faster in rate of advancement were generosity and reliability. However, fairmindedness, tolerance, and adaptability were judged most important for first-line supervisors according to those slower in rate of advancement.

Other attributes valued by faster-climbing managers—more than by those advancing more slowly—included objectivity and productivity. The accelerated manager emerged as valuing task orientation and results orientation. Compared with the slower-advancing manager, the faster-climbing manager valued being less dependent upon higher authority and higher decision making. In attributions they seemed to be more interpersonally competent than their slower-advancing colleagues, but they valued interpersonal competence less than the slower climbers. They valued a longer-range view of affairs and greater reliance on persuasiveness rather than on authority.

A kind of discounting seems to occur based on perceived abundance or scarcity of attributes. In a study of a hospital, Jensen and Morris (1960) found that supervisors valued more highly the abilities of leadership and executive ability least prevalent among themselves and valued least the qualities of social adjustment and personal charm that they possessed.

## ORGANIZATIONAL ISSUES

Leadership occurring within organizational settings is affected by individual differences such as how much one needs to identify with the organization, how one's location in the organization makes a difference in one's values, emergence of dual loyalties, and changes in lifestyles.

### Belonging, Identification, and Loyalty

One value of importance to many persons gained from membership in an organization is a feeling of belonging and identification (Mullen, 1954; Wald & Doty, 1954). Mullen (1954) made a survey of 140 foreman clubs in thirty-two states. He found that 88 percent of the foremen surveyed wanted to feel identified with the company, and 71 percent reported that they were treated as if they were a part of management. Again, D. D. Braun (1976) found that lack of alienation was even more strongly associated than participation in community activities with community leadership in Mankato, Minnesota.

*Affiliation to Success.* J. C. White (1964) found that identification with management related to success in attaining a management position. Lawler and Porter (1968) observed that managers tended to value interactions with superiors more highly than those with subordinates. They also attached more value to interactions initiated by themselves than to those initiated by others. Consistent with this, R. E. Miles (1964a) obtained results which indicated that top managers preferred and rated as more effective those subordinates whose attitudes and values were similar to their own. Yet, the managers did not regard lower-level supervisors highly promotable when they identified only with the company. Similarly, Mann and Dent (1954) found that supervisors and employees agreed that the promotable supervisor is one who will stand up for employees and their rights, train them for better jobs, and let them know where they stand on matters that concern them. Read (1962) found that the upward mobility of managers was related to the degree of their problem-oriented communication with superiors. Willingness to communicate with superiors was found associated with feelings of trust and perceptions of superiors' influence.

*Relation to Affective Leadership.* The extent to which supervisors enhance the sense of belonging to the organization of their subordinates tends to pay off in better subordinate performance. Habbe (1947) demonstrated that insurance agents who feel that they are fulfilling their managers' expectations sell more policies and experience fewer lapses than those who feel they are not meeting management expectations. Simultaneous upward and down orientation and sensitivity is required of the effective supervisor. Sarbin and Jones (1955) reported that a successful foreman is competent in the eyes of his superiors and at the same time fulfills the expectations of his subordinates. According to Wray (1949), this is not an easy task since superiors and subordinates present conflicting expectations that are difficult to reconcile. (For a review of research dealing with this conflict of the "man-in-the-middle" and how it is resolved, see Bass [1960, pp. 318–322].) For instance, in his study of an industrial plant, H. Rosen (1961a,b) found that managers tended to exhibit an upward orientation toward the demands of their superiors while at the same time remaining sensitive to the demands of subordinates.

Downward orientation itself has been seen to be of consequence. Maier, Hoffman, and Read (1963) compared managers who had previously held the jobs of their subordinates with peers who had not held these jobs. Having held the subordinate's job did not facilitate communicative effectiveness. Subordinate trust was positively related to mutual agreement about the subordinate's problems for "held" pairs, but not for "nonheld" pairs.

How much time a supervisor believes should be spent interacting with subordinates may make a considerable difference in the effectiveness of the relationship. Whereas Speroff (1955) reported a correlation of $-.76$ between worker satisfaction scores and frequency of interviews between worker and plant manager, Klauss and Bass (1981) showed that increased communication between managerial and professional supervisors and their superiors, peers, and subordinates in various large organizations had a direct impact on increasing the judged trustworthiness of the focal person and in turn resulted in increased satisfaction of colleagues with that person. Probably the most valid picture was provided by A. N. Turner (1955), who found that some personnel valued interaction because it signified a friendly relationship. Others preferred to be left alone and interpreted frequent interaction as interference and indication of criticism.

*Leader Behavior and Subordinate Identification to Organization.* Supervisors who value belonging do much to increase the sense of "ownership" in activities among their subordinates. Riegel (1955) found that employee interest in company success increased when their supervisor was seen to help them with their difficulties, to give necessary training and explanations, and to "take an interest in us and our ideas." Consistent with this, according to Anikeeff (1957), the greater the satisfaction of managers, the greater the similarity between the attitudes of managers and workers. Satisfied managers contribute least to attitude cleavage between workers and management. Again, Weiss (1977) demonstrated that subordinates tended to be more likely to share values with their supervisors if the supervisors displayed considerate behavior (see Chapter 21) toward their subordinates. Obrochta (1960) reported that worker attitudes toward the foreman were favorable only when the foreman held favorable attitudes toward the workers. Murray and Corenblum (1966) observed that although loyalty to superior did not alternate between levels in the organization's status structure, it was found to be significantly related to the superiors' perception of their group as a primary source of social support.

### Dual Loyalties: Management versus Union

People belonging to two different organizations tend to maintain loyalty to both even though certain aims of the organizations may be in conflict. Stagner (1954), for example, obtained a correlation of .33 between workers' attitudes toward the company and their attitudes toward the union. Purcell (1954) found that although more workers identified with the company than with the union, 73 percent of the men and women surveyed expressed loyalty to both. Foremen and steward groups each tended to identify with the organization that they represented officially but, generally, both foremen (57 percent) and stewards (88 percent) felt favorable toward the others' organization.

*Reciprocities.* Obrochta (1960) found that foremen and workers were most closely agreed on their attitudes toward the company and least well agreed on their attitudes toward union leaders. Foremen were more favorable toward union leaders and toward the company than were hourly workers. The latter tended to feel more favorably toward the union than foremen. Workers' attitudes were also somewhat more favorable toward their foreman than the foreman was toward them. Further evidence on reciprocity was gathered by Derber, Chalmers, Edelman, and Triandis (1965) in a study of thirty-seven industrial plants. They obtained results indicating that managers' attitudes toward the union and union leaders' attitudes toward management were positively and significantly correlated. Each group was moderately favorable in its attitude toward the other. But Stagner, Chalmers, and Derber (1958), using separate scales for measuring attitudes toward company and union, found no relation between attitudes of management toward the union and union attitudes toward management. Investigating managerial attitudes in a southern city, Alsikafi, Jokinen, Spray, and Tracy (1968) found that those managers with negative attitudes toward unions were also not highly committed to the company. Results obtained by Dent and de la Paz (1961) suggested that unfavorable managerial attitudes toward the union tended to be associated with the inclusion in labor contracts of union security clauses perceived to challenge management authority to manage.

*Perceived Conflict and Stress.* K. F. Walker (1962) found that managers and union leaders were quite accurate in predicting each other's attitudes, but both perceived more conflict than actually existed. Foremen and stewards who wanted company and union to coexist amicably experienced more stress than normal and tended to hold favorable attitudes toward each other (Purcell, 1954).

*Substantive Disagreements.* Results of the above studies indicate that members of two different organizations with conflicting goals tend to express loyalty to both. Managers and union officials tend to regard each other in generally favorable terms. Conflict between them is concerned with substantive issues, particularly those involving their respective powers.

However, the underlying basis for evaluating management and union differ. Stagner, Derber, and Chalmers (1959) studied the feelings of two labor leaders and two managers in each of forty-one establishments. A composite score for each establishment was computed for each of thirty-five attitude and satisfaction variables. A factor analysis produced ten factors. Management evaluation of the union emerged as a single general factor. Union evaluations were described by two factors, one involving union–management relations and the other concerned with union achievement.

Remmers and Remmers (1949) and Miller and Remmers (1950) examined the attitudes of managers and labor leaders toward human relations-oriented supervision (Chapter 20). Managers tended to overestimate labor leaders' scores whereas labor leaders underestimated managers' scores. In a comparative study of managers and union officials, Weaver (1958), as expected, found that union officials exhibited strong pro-labor attitudes. But not as obviously, managers were neutral about grievances, arbitration, the labor movement, and working during a strike. Again, Schwartz and Levine (1965) compared the interests of managers and union officials in the same companies. Managers scored higher in supervisory initiative and production interests. Union officials scored significantly higher on power seeking, propaganda, bargaining, arbitration, and disputation. Bogard (1960) compared the values of management trainees and labor leader trainees. He found that management trainees scored higher in aggressiveness and lower in altruistic values than union trainees.

*Attributions.* S. M. Peck (1966) found that union stewards justified the unfavorable behavior of top officials on the grounds that strong methods are required in order to cope with existing conditions and that corruption abounds everywhere. At the same time, Miles and Ritchie (1968) reported that high-ranking union officials "agreed" that shop stewards and rank-and-file members should be encouraged to participate more in decision making and that such participation would result in improved morale, better decisions, and willingness to accept bargaining goals. However, they were "uncertain" whether stewards and rank-and-file members would be likely to set reasonable goals for themselves given the opportunity.

### Hierarchial Differences in Values

As one rises on the organizational ladder, one usually finds shifts in values that cannot be attributed to age, education, or seniority. Status differences emerge. Generally, commitment to the organization is greater the higher one's level in the organization. Pfiffner and Wilson (1953) surveyed two levels of supervisors. Their results indicated that high-level supervisors felt at ease with superiors and were interested in duties involving management functions. Low-level supervisors identified with their work groups and were less critical of workers than high-level supervisors. Rosen and Weaver (1960) found four levels of management agreed on emphasizing the importance of factors affecting job effectiveness (authority, knowledge of plans, consultation) as opposed to the importance of a role in policy making and upward communication. But first-line supervisors differed in emphasizing the importance of consideration and fairness in management. Compared with workers, managers at all levels regarded themselves as upholders of group norms (Fruchter & Skinner, 1966). W. K. Graham (1969) factor-analyzed the intercorrelations between job attitude scores for three levels of organization in life insurance agencies. Higher-level managers differentiated managerial actions from organizational climate, while supervisors and agents did not. But we need to be more specific. As noted earlier, many studies have found that the importance of self-actualization and autonomy increases with one's status in an organization, whereas those of lower status attach more value to security and working conditions. For example, Porter (1963b) found that higher-level managers placed greater emphasis on autonomy and self-actualization needs than did lower-level managers. Furthermore, there is also considerable uniformity in finding that the higher the level of a manager's position, the greater drive and motivation for achievement is seen (Beer et al., 1959; Henry, 1949; McClelland, 1961; Meyer & Walker, 1961; Pellegrin & Coates, 1957; Veroff et al., 1960; Vroom, 1965). Similarly, higher-level managers exceed those in lower levels in desire for inner-directed as opposed to outer-directed motivations (Eran, 1966; Mordechai, 1966; Porter & Henry, 1964; Uris, 1958). But relatively temporary rank may not make much difference in a student population. Thus, F. J. Michaelson (1951), in a study of military cadets, found that those of high rank did not differ from those of low rank in desire for advancement, human relations orientation, or identification with high socioeconomic status.

*Job Meaning.*  Triandis (1960) factor-analyzed the meanings attached to job descriptions by managers and workers. Six factors were isolated, five of which were similar for managers and workers. However, in a study of meanings attached to words describing jobs and people, Triandis (1959) found that upper-level managers stressed the importance of status, polish, and education; lower-level managers stressed power and position; and workers stressed money and dependability. But when Schwartz, Jenusaitis, and Stark (1966) compared the values of foremen and workers, they found that the two groups agreed in placing higher value on job security, wages, and working conditions than on interpersonal relations. Similarly, Friedlander (1966a) found few differences between the values of civil service employees at different status levels. But Lennerlöf (1965b), comparing the attitudes of managers, superiors, and workers, discovered that workers value good personal relations to a greater extent than do supervisors, and supervisors value it more than do their superiors. Also, the supervisors and their workers felt more strongly than did their superiors that the supervisor should strive to attain an independent and influential position.

*Lifestyles and Level.*  We have already noted that managers who attain higher organizational levels when young value self-actualization and achievement (Bass, Burger, et al., 1979). A most comprehensive comparison of the assessed values of those who had advanced further in the Bell System with those who had not was reported by Bray, Campbell and Grant (1974). Over the eight years of the survey, systematic changes occurred in the lives of 400 Bell System managers who were followed up after assessment center evaluations. Two contrasting lifestyles were identified: the "enlarger" and the "enfolder." The enlarging lifestyle stressed innovation, change, self-development, and movement away from traditional ways of thinking and doing things; the enfolding lifestyle was oriented more toward tradition and maintaining the close family and friendship ties which the individual had gained through adolescence and college years. Enfolders were less likely to leave their hometown area and were much less likely to engage in any self-improvement activities. More successful managers were enlargers; less successful managers were enfolders. Enlargers sharply gained in occupational interests and sharply lost concern with parents and family; enfolders either suffered small losses or remained the same. Enlargers sharply reduced their concern for recreational and social activities; enfolders showed only a small loss in such interests.

*Cause or Effect?*  Which is cause, which effect? As managers rise faster and higher, they may have less time for family ties and recreation, at the same time gaining increasingly more satisfaction from their job. Less successful managers are likely to derive less satisfaction from the job and also have more time for family and recreation. However, we cannot ignore the evidence that most successful people were higher on some themes, such as the occupational theme, before they actually began to work, suggesting that individuals bring to their job at least some semblance of a lifestyle which will interact with their success in the organization to accent or decrease certain life themes. (This is congruent with our remarks concerning managerial motivation in Chapter 22.)

*Effects of Differences.*  These differences in needs, values, interests, and goals are a structural source of conflict between managers at different hierarchical levels as well as between leaders and followers in the community. Thus, Fiedler, Fiedler, and Campf (1971) showed that whereas leaders felt that poor government, neighborhood disunity, and failure of public services were the concerns of consequence, householders felt that crime, immorality, traffic, and unemployment were the issues that needed attention. Managers and union leaders generally overemphasize dissatisfaction of employees with their pay and underemphasize worker concerns for security and opportunity (Bass & Ryterband, 1979).

## SATISFACTION WITH THE LEADERSHIP ROLE

### Rank, Level, and Satisfaction

One of the most consistent findings in behavioral science is the positive correlation between one's status—importance of one's position—in an organization and one's satisfaction with one's status. Relying on early survey evidence, G. B. Watson (1942) was convinced that managers and supervisors tended to be more satisfied with their work than were rank-and-file employees. Furthermore, it became clear that top managers are generally more satisfied than managers at lower levels (Bass, 1960). T. R. Mitchell (1970a,b) studied line and staff officers of different rank and in different commands abroad. Satisfaction rose with rank. Furthermore, line officers of all ranks were found better satisfied than those in staff positions, but this feeling varied greatly from one situation to another (staff positions are usually of lower status than line positions).

In a review of the literature, Porter and Lawler (1965) concluded that each level of personnel from worker to top manager is more highly satisfied than the next lower level. Line managers tend to be somewhat more satisfied than staff members and perceive more fulfillment of needs for self-esteem and self-actualization (Porter, 1963b). But satisfaction is not related to span of managerial control.

In the laboratory, Guetzkow (1954) found that key persons in a communication network saw themselves as most important and were more satisfied than members with less important positions. Bass, Pryer, Gaier, and Flint (1958) found that satisfaction was greater in a member assigned more power compared with four others at a much lower level. Attractiveness of a group was significantly lower for the average member when members were assigned control differentially in contrast to groups where all members were equal. The results of studies (J. W. Campbell, 1948; DeLora, 1963; Edel, 1966; Eran, 1966; Johnson & Marcrum, 1968; Kolstad, 1944; E. L. Miller, 1966a,b; L. W. Porter, 1961a,b, 1962; Porter & Mitchell, 1967; Renck, 1955; Troxell, 1954; and Vroom, 1965) also support the contention that the higher the level of individuals' positions in the organization, the greater the degree of their job satisfaction. And the reasons are not hard to find. Compensation is greater. Needs for self-actualization and autonomy are better satisfied (L. W. Porter, 1963a). Nevertheless, there are alternative plausible explanations in some organizations where status is not related to power and influence (see Chapter 11). Thus, Ritchie and Miles (1970) studied 330 managers in five levels of organization. Satisfaction did not differ as a consequence of level of position, but to amount of participation in decision making.

*Clarity about Status and Role.* It should seem obvious that a leader's satisfaction is strongly associated with the clarity of the position held and agreement about its importance, power, and what is required for satisfactory performance on it. This was corroborated by Gross, Mason, and McEachern (1958) who conducted an extensive study of the perceptions of role interactions between school board members and superintendents. The results indicated that the greater the degree of consensus among board members, the higher they rated the superintendent, the higher he rated the board, and the greater the superintendent's job satisfaction. The board's rating of the superintendent was not related to his measured personality or to his consensus with the board. Within both samples, the degree of consensus in expectations of a position was related to the extent to which role demands of the position had been formally or legally codified.

### Organization Characteristics and Managerial Satisfaction

Size, structure, and type of organization have effects on managerial satisfaction.

*Size.* L. W. Porter (1963a) reported a curvilinear relation between managerial satisfaction and size of company, with somewhat greater satisfaction in larger rather than small companies. In addition, lower levels of management were better satisfied in small than in large companies, whereas higher levels of management were better satisfied in large than in small companies. But ElSalmi and Cummings (1968) found that, for top managers, small companies produce more need fulfillment than large companies. For middle and lower managers, the reverse was true. However, Cummings and ElSalmi (1970) reported that role diversity and level of position were more highly related to need satisfaction than size of department or company.

*Structure.* Flat organizations have few hierarchical levels with many units at each level; tall organizations have many more levels, with fewer units at each level. Porter and Lawler (1964) and Porter and Siegel (1965) found that flat organizations did not produce greater managerial satisfaction than tall organizations. However, in small organizations, managerial satisfaction was greater in flat than in tall organizations. The findings were reversed for large companies (with more than 5,000 employees). Tall organizations yielded greater satisfaction with security and social needs, while flat organizations gave greater satisfaction with self-actualization. But structure was not related to esteem and autonomy needs. In the same way, Esser and Strother (1962) found no relationship between rule orientation of managers and size or type of their organization. Ghiselli and Johnson (1970) showed that satisfaction of needs for esteem, autonomy, and self-actualization was higher in flat than in tall organizations. However, satisfaction of security and social needs did not differ in the two types of organizations. At the same time, ElSalmi and Cummings (1968) found that at top levels, tall structures produced less fulfillment than flat or intermediate structures. For lower levels, tall structures produced more fulfillment.

*Type.* Managers in business organizations were better satisfied than were those in military (Porter and Mitchell, 1967) or governmental organizations (Paine, Carroll and Leete, 1966; Rinehart et al., 1969). Rainey (1979) found that, compared to business managers, government managers: (1) express weaker performance-extrinsic reward "expectancies"; (2) are lower on satisfaction measures; (3) perceive personnel rules—civil service systems—as constraints on incentives; but (4) show no difference on role perceptions and motivation scales.

*Satisfaction with Compensation*

One obvious reason that those of higher status in the organization tend to be more satisfied than subordinates is that ordinarily they earn more pay. (But this is not always true. Deans may earn less than senior professors; supervisors may earn less than skilled subordinates.) However, satisfaction with earnings is relative. One feels relatively deprived depending on with whom one compares oneself. In a highly inflationary economy, dissatisfaction with pay is seen as primarily due to inflation, government policy, and OPEC, not necessarily to one's employer. In a depression, relatively modest compensation may be highly satisfying. Furthermore, the greater the congruence between the managers' feeling about how pay should be determined and their perception of how it is determined, the greater their satisfaction with their pay (Lawler, 1966c, 1967).

Penzer (1969) found that expectations regarding external opportunities were major determinants of managerial satisfaction with pay. Those who attended college bring with them different expectations than those who have not, and these expectations, when compared with external reference groups, partially determine satisfaction with pay. Among the internal factors, commendations, rapid advancement, salary increases, and the like tend to inflate expectations. Satisfaction of managers with their pay is obviously related to how much they earn in an absolute sense as well as the correspondence between expected pay and actual pay. Managers prefer pay based on performance and merit, but they tend to define merit in terms of traits that they perceive themselves to possess.

More effective managers tend to feel more satisfied with their pay (Lawler & Porter, 1966; Porter & Lawler, 1968). Managers who score high in risk preference, but not in achievement motivation prefer pay based on performance (Meyer & Walker, 1961). However, the higher managers rate themselves in comparison with their peers on variables such as education, experience, productivity, effort, and skill, the more importance they attach to these variables as determinants of pay.

Further support that managerial satisfaction is related to the extent to which level of pay corresponds with expectations for pay was obtained by Klein and Maher (1966). Middle managers overestimated the pay of subordinates and underestimated the pay of superiors. They felt the difference between their pay and that of the persons above and below them was too small. The smaller the perceived difference between own pay and that of subordinates, the less satisfied the managers were with their own pay (Lawler, 1965, 1967).

*Age, Education, and Satisfaction*

Although J. G. Mauer (1969) in a study of industrial supervisors found that their job satisfaction was not related to age, education, degree of work involvement, income, or size of plant, most other studies have found that satisfaction with leadership role depends on education and age. Andrews and Henry (1963) and Klein and Maher (1966, 1968) reported that with more education, managers felt less satisfied with their pay. But Stogdill (1965) and Lawler and Porter (1966) found no such relation between education and satisfaction with pay.

Stogdill (1965a) studied 422 managers and supervisors in six departments of an aircraft plant. He found that the better educated managers were least satisfied with the company and with their freedom on the job, but that education was not consistently related to attitude toward pay.

Esser and Strother (1962) found that managers with average amounts of education tended to be rule-oriented. Those with the least education were least rule-oriented, followed closely by those with the most education. According to Friedlander (1963), less well-educated supervisors tended to derive satisfaction from the social and technical rather than the self-actualizing aspects of their work. And England (1967a) found that managers with less education placed more value on organizational stability. Those with college majors in humanities, fine arts, and social sciences stressed the importance of productivity and efficiency as organizational goals.

With regard to age, Saleh and Otis (1964) asked eighty managers, aged 60 to 65, to think back over their careers and indicate the age at which they had derived the most satisfaction from their work. Satisfaction increased to age 59, then showed a sharp decrease. Another sample, aged 50 to 55, also showed an increase in satisfaction to age 59, then anticipated a decrease in satisfaction after age 60. The authors interpreted the reduced enjoyment after age 60 as due to a blockage of channels for further development and advancement.

Friedlander (1963) found that older supervisors tended to derive more satisfaction from the social and technical aspects of their work and less from self-actualization than did younger supervisors. Results reported by England (1967a) indicated that older managers placed higher value on social welfare and lower value on organizational growth and leadership in the industry as goals of organization. Gruenfeld (1962) found younger industrial supervisors more interested than older ones in high wages and fringe benefits. Older supervisors preferred regular hours, freedom from stress, and freedom from working with people.

Stogdill (1965a), in his study of an aircraft plant, found that managers tended to be more satisfied with the company but less satisfied with the recognition they received as age increased. Number of years in the same position tended to involve a negative relation to all aspects of satisfaction, but particularly to satisfaction with advancement. However, Hall, Schneider, and Nygren (1970) reported that tenure but not position was related to identification with the organization and need satisfaction in the U.S. Forest Service.

*Performance and Satisfaction*

Consistently, evidence is positive that more satisfied managers perform better.

Lawler and Porter (1967b) found that the degree of an individual's need satisfaction is related to his or her job performance as evaluated by peers and superiors and that this relationship is stronger for managers than for nonmanagers. Porter and Lawler (1968) reported that managers rated high in performance by self and superiors expressed higher degrees of such satisfaction than those rated low in performance. Managers rated higher in effort also reported more need fulfillment for all need areas. Finally, Slocum, Miller, and Misshauk (1970) also reported that high-producing foremen were better satisfied than low producers.

More successful performance as a leader is also associated with one's esteem and accorded status. This will be considered next.

# 10 STATUS, ESTEEM, CHARISMA, AND LEADERSHIP

## STATUS AND VALUED ROLES

Role theorists regard leadership as an aspect of role differentiation. Status is accorded members of a group differentially according to the importance of the roles they play and the positions they occupy. The leaders of a group play roles with high status and occupy positions of importance to the group.

### Status Differences among Animals

Status differences predate the emergence of humankind. Allee (1945, 1951) and Allee et al. (1949) maintained that all vertebrates living in groups exhibit social organization and leadership. Generally, high-ranking males feed more freely than other members of the group and tend to have more ready access to females. In some cases, high status involves guard duty and protection of the herd. In the past several decades, numerous long-term studies of mammals in the wild have been completed. They reveal consistent ways in which status hierarchies are established and maintained. These hierarchies, mainly male, but sometimes female (as in the case of the elephant), determine feeding arrangements, sexual practices, and survival strategies.

*Pecking Order.* Individual animals dominate or submit local spaces to others in the well-known pecking order. In one of the early experiments on animal social relations, Murchison (1935) placed roosters at opposite ends of a narrow runway and measured the distance that each advanced toward the other. As a result of successive pairings, he was able to determine a strict hierarchy of dominance. Rooster A invariably dominated all the remaining subjects. At the bottom of the hierarchy was the rooster who yielded to all the others.

Douglis (1948) removed hens from their home flocks and for short periods of time placed them in other flocks. The hen's pecking order in each flock was observed. It was found that a hen can become an assimilated member in at least five different flocks with a different status in each. She can recognize and react to the status of as many as twenty-seven individuals. Highly dominant individuals become assimilated within three days, but low-status hens required three to six weeks to become assimilated. Once established, a status hierarchy tended to exist.

*Status Effects in Primates.* Miller and Murphy (1956) and Warren and Maroney (1969) tested pairs of monkeys in competition for food in an area. A strict dominance

**146**

hierarchy was observed. Subordinate animals were more successful in obtaining low-preference rather than middle- or high-preference foods. I. S. Bernstein (1964) observed that when the dominant male was removed from a group of monkeys the activities of other males increased. After he returned, he resumed his dominant status and the activities of other males decreased.

C. R. Carpenter (1963) studied societies of monkeys and apes. His general findings suggested that the leader tends to control group movement in its search for food and shelter, regulate intragroup status, defend the group, and maintain its integrity in its contacts with other organized groupings. When the dominant male is removed from a group, the territory covered by the group is markedly reduced. The leader tends to enlarge the freedom of group movement. Carpenter and others observed that the dominant male tends to be avoided by low-ranking males. In some bands, the one or two males next in rank below the leader may stand by him in warding off intruders and may be permitted to groom him on occasion.

Again, W. A. Mason (1964) reported that leaders of groups of monkeys and apes appear to have the primary function of initiating progressions and determining the line of march. The dominant males quell intragroup fights, protect the females and young, are attractive to all members, are sought out by females, and influence the size of the group's territorial range. Zajonc (1969) interpreted the fact that fighting disappears almost entirely in primate groups after a dominance hierarchy has been established as evidence that groups develop norms. The norms are learned by group members, they are stable but can be changed, and they are complied with by the majority of members. Koford (1963) observed that the relative dominance of two bands of monkeys that meet at an eating place is usually determined by the relative dominance of the leaders of the bands. Once the dominance of a band has been established, it is observed by the other group even in the absence of the other leader. In primate groups, leaders obtain privileges that tend to bolster their dominance. Their presence is an advantage to the group in gaining possession of desired territory and in expanding the area of free group movement. However, whether or not these findings are relevant to understanding the human condition remains controversial.

### Primitive Bases for Status in Humans

Warner, Meeker, and Eells (1949) observed that all societies and social groups of any size or complexity possess status systems. Status stucture and the differentiation of function are necessary for coordination of effort. Even collectives designed to minimize functional specialization and differential distribution of rewards develop well-defined status structures (E. Rosenfeld, 1951).

The old man, regardless of who he was, was accorded particular status as the occupant of a position by the younger boy, regardless of who he was as a person. The details differed from one social organization to another concerning what was expected of the occupant of each position, what role they should play, but all societies still appear to recognize the following positions and the differences in value among them: infant, boy, girl, young man, young woman, old man, old woman (Linton, 1945). Cues are provided occupants of various positions making it easy to identify their status. Status differences in military organizations are clearly visible. In many societies, the adolescent often is easily discriminated by dress from the preadolescent; the married woman from the un-married. Until modern times, each profession had its own identifiable costume. As will be noted in Chapter 27, group members tend to maintain some degree of physical distance between themselves and other members who differ from them in status. To communicate to others working at a distance, organizational members send memos to those above or below them in status; the members telephone those who are at their same level in status (Klauss & Bass, 1981).

### Positions as Sources of Information and Power

Some positions provide occupants with direct control over what is rewarding to others. Such occupants of positions of greater importance to the reward of others in the group have greater status in the organization (Barnard, 1951). In turn, such status-derived power makes it possible for its possessors to exert leadership and influence over others (Chapter 11). Some roles make it possible for the role players to have access to the information and ability to solve the group's problems.

*Status and Competence.*   Sherif, White, and Harvey (1955) found that the higher a member's status, the greater his or her competence as judged by other members. It fits with the facts of everyday life. Studies of the occupational status hierarchy in social organizations show that positions give their occupants more status if all occupants of those positions either acquire more knowledge once they occupy the position or are selected for the position only if they have the knowledge. Those occupations with highest status (that is, value or importance to society), according to college students, include physician, lawyer, banker, engineer, and school administrator, all requiring a great deal of education and specialized knowledge. Low-status occupations include truck driver, coal miner, janitor, wood carver, and ditch digger, all with little or no educational demands. Status of occupations is remarkably stable. For twenty-five occupations, the correlations in status in 1925, 1946, and 1967 were all above .9 (Hakel, Hollman & Dunnette, 1968). Miners and laborers perceive an occupational status differentiation similar to that of the college students (Cattell, 1942). In primitive societies, the status of medicine man and the tribal elders was partly due to the knowledge held by anyone occupying such positions. Conversely, the lower status of women and children was often due to their lack of knowledge of magic, ritual, and tribal history.

According to Sherif and Sherif (1953) those in positions of control (high status) are endowed with superior personal traits. Perlmutter (1954) confirmed that the greater the perceived capacity of individuals to influence the perceiver, the greater the total number of traits will be assigned to them and the more desirable will be the traits assigned to them. In the same way, Courtney, Greer, et al. (1953) noted that military recruits given positions with the most responsibility and authority were most esteemed. Barnard (1951) agreed that abilities will be imputed to persons of higher status even when the abilities cannot be recognized. This, he suggested, is a way that low-status followers maintain their own self-esteem. They rationalize that they are being persuaded by the suggestions of the most capable members of the organization rather than being coerced through mere status differences.

## Value of a Position

A price tag can be set on one's status in firms and agencies. Job evaluation establishes the worth of each position to the organization. One's pay, then, depends on the position's established value regardless of who occupies the position. Status and value to one's family, clan, or social organization was clearly fixed in Anglo-Saxon law. The "man-price," or wergild, varied with a man's status in society. It was to be paid to a man's relatives as retribution if he were murdered or killed by accident. The various social strata were valued by their respective prices. The church placed its own members on the wergild scale. It equated a priest with a thane. The price of a king was from six to fifteen times that of a thane (Whitelock, 1950).

## Status and Acceptance by Others

How well one is liked is related to one's status (A. Pepitone, 1964). But similarity in status may increase or decrease attractiveness. Byrne, Clore, and Worchel (1966) and R. A. Ellis (1956) found that interpersonal attraction was significantly related to similarity in socioeconomic status. But Jackson and Fuller (1966) found that lower class school pupils rated middle class teachers as better liked and less authoritarian than lower class teachers.

Status will determine the continued acceptability of one's behavior. Sabath (1964) presented a new member as having either high or low status to groups performing discussion and construction tasks. During the construction task, the new member exhibited disruptive behavior followed by actions that enhanced or impeded group task performance. High-status members were seen in a generally favorable manner regardless of their behavior, while low-status members were favorably viewed only when their performance enhanced the group functioning.

A. Pepitone (1958) reviewed research which indicated that the higher the status position of group members, the greater the tendency to attribute good intentions to their positive and negative acts and to perceive their positive and negative actions as justified. Persons perceived to have high status were more acceptable as authority figures and their idiosyncratic behavior received greater acceptance (Hollander, 1961a). Group members expected more of their high-status members and tended to overestimate their performance (O. J. Harvey, 1953).

## Loss of Status

In a study of experimental groups with the possibility of losing status, Berkowitz and Macaulay (1961) found that highly accepted members whose status can change (1) tend to be more highly attracted to other members; (2) are favorably impressed with the quality of group discussion; and (3) admit a desire for high status. Burnstein and Zajonc (1965a) found that group members' performance tended to improve when their status was increased and tended to suffer when their status was decreased.

Since individuals tend to evaluate themselves in terms of opinions and reactions of fellow group members, they tend to feel sensitive toward changes in their own status, provided that this change is perceived to involve a change in evaluation by the group. But D. W. Olmsted (1957) showed that members can drop from leadership to participant status without reducing their activities or losing their liking for the group.

H. H. Kelley (1951) studied the written communications of group members in high-status and low-status positions, with and without the possibility of status mobility. Low status was associated with relative dislike for the group task. High-status members who could lose their status made fewer positive comments than those whose status was secure. Low-status members with the possibility of upward mobility made fewer negative comments than those who had no such opportunity. The lows and controls who chose another job communicated more conjecture about other members who made a similar choice and communicated more relevant messages, suggesting that communication may serve as a substitute for mobility. Low-status members, when dissatisfied, tended to communicate to those with high status, whereas the latter tend to communicate dissatisfaction to others on the same level. These results suggest that the attractiveness of a position depends not only on how it is evaluated by self and peers, but also by other status levels.

The loss of status is negatively valued, as suggested by the fact that downward mobility tends to be associated with decreasing satisfaction with self, task, and group. It may also be associated with hostility. Lindzey and Kalnins (1958) asked students to compare self and other persons with figures in a picture test of projective attitudes. The students tended to identify themselves with hero figures, while other persons were more often identified with nonhero figures. Changes in status after frustration showed increased aggression carried out by the hero against others or self, and by others against the hero. But there was no change in aggression of others against others. Worchel (1961) found that expressions of hostility were reduced by restoration of lost status.

*Upward Status Striving*

Bechtel and Rosenfeld (1966) gave students incorrect information about their status in their dormitory, then asked the students either to select new roommates from among ten status levels or to estimate their chances of acceptability at each level. The students tended to choose above their own status and their estimates of being accepted by other status levels decreased as the distance between their own status and other status levels increased.

Individuals not only like to occupy comfortably high status positions within groups but also enjoy, within limits, association with high-status groups. J. W. Mann (1961) found that members preferred to associate with groups of similar or higher status than their own group. Their expectations tended to focus on the group next in status above the membership group. The low-status members, more than the high-status members, tended to prefer membership in a group with higher status than their own.

Kipnis (1964) reported that mobility expectations are generally related to satisfaction with work. Vroom (1966) studied master's students in a business school before and after they accepted positions. Organizations were rated more attractive when perceived as instrumental to personal goal attainment. Accepting a position in a company increased its attractiveness and decreased the attractiveness of the unchosen. H. H. Kelley (1951) found that high-status members with no possibility of promotion were least attracted to a group. Conversely, in yet another laboratory study, Spector (1953) reported as most satisfied those participants placed in a pseudo-military hierarchy who were promoted. In the Air Force, Borgatta noted that personnel who saw adequate opportunities for advancement to officer positions also were less critical of the rewards and punishments possible in the Air Force. However, those actually striving for advancement in status were more critical than those who did not seek promotion.

This striving for status—usually positions of leadership—often involves motivation to achieve congruence in status among the various positions one holds. Dissatisfaction with one's status in one organization may be due to one's status in another. Benoit-Smullyan (1944) hypothesized that individuals with different status in different groups would attempt to equalize their stature in the various groups. Thus, a business leader may endow an art institute to gain status in cultural circles. Fenchel, Monderer, and Hartley (1951) found that subjects' strivings for status in five groups to which they belonged were higher in groups where their current status was low.

Persons in important positions will be concerned about avoiding their loss of status. E. L. Thorndike (1940) noted that for many, perhaps most persons, political power is a habit-forming psychological drug. Abdications are rare. It is one's general status that is involved, not the specific position. A president of the Teamsters' Union is tenacious about maintaining his union office because it is inconceivable for him to return to driving a truck after a term in such a higher-status position. On the other hand, a cabinet secretary or the president of the American Association of University Professors can return to high status in academia after serving a team in office and so usually is not as reluctant to relinquish office (Selznick, 1943).

Those with lower status in a group are more likely to be concerned about raising their status than those who already have attained leadership roles of importance. In three industrial plants, M. Dalton (1950) observed that the lower-status executives tried to get more personnel to supervise, tried to transfer from staff to line positions (but line executives did not seek staff jobs), were more concerned about entering the management "eating circle," and were more concerned about personal distinctions. Similarly, V. J. Bentz (n.d.) observed that college faculty members who accorded themselves higher status tended to report less concern within their department about rank and status.

*Rejection of Upward Mobility.* Sociologists have called attention to the fact that status mobilty in the open community may involve changes in habitat, associates, and pattern of living. Rapid upward mobility within an organization may be accompanied by change of status in the community. Upward mobility also involves a change in relationships with friends, associates, and former coworkers within the organization. In addition, a higher-status position involves change in responsibility and accountability for results. Not all members of an organization welcome upward mobility. Springer (1956) studied 10,533 workers recommended for promotion to leadman, assistant foreman, or foreman. Thirteen percent refused promotion. The reasons given for refusal were more often concerned with working conditions than with change in status.

Reider (1944) studied the emotional breakdown of medical officers in World War II. Promotion to a higher-level position of responsibility and status was a major factor. The young officer who depended upon a superior for support not only lost it when he became a status peer, but he was also expected to provide support for his subordinates.

## ESTEEM, PERSONAL ATTRACTIVENESS, AND CHARISMA

Esteem is the value to the group of members as persons. It is their perceived potential to help the group attain its goals, independent of the position they occupy. Recognition of differences in esteem among members is established in a natural group's history (Sherif, 1967) and increases in discrimination with the age of the group (Lippitt, Thelen & Leff, n.d.). Such evaluations of adequacy as a group member are found among children as early as 8 years old or younger (Campbell & Radke-Yarrow, 1956). Members with more personal ability regardless of their position will be more esteemed, since, through their personal ability to solve the group's problems, they can bring goal attainment to the group. In the same way, members with more personal power regardless of their position will be more esteemed, since they can directly give or deny love, friendship, security, and other rewards. Members with esteem primarily due to their personal ability will be more successful in persuading others whenever they attempt to do so (Mowday, 1979). Members with esteem primarily due to their personal power can be more successful in directing others. If their esteem depends on both, they may be more successful as a participative leader if they so choose (Bass, 1960).

### Charisma

Charisma (literally, endowment with divine grace) is seen in extremely highly esteemed persons (Weber, 1946). Such individuals tend to exude confidence, dominance, a sense of purpose, and the ability to articulate the goals and ideas for which followers are already prepared psychologically (Fromm, 1941; House, 1977). The response of followers is likewise extreme. It is both cognitive and emotional, as well as devoted and unquestioning. As J. M. Burns (1978) notes, such leaders have extraordinary influence over their followers, who become mobilized with moral inspiration and purpose. They become zealots and leaders in their own right.

Although most attention has been paid to charismatics in the political arena, they also appear in organizational and military settings (Handy, 1976). Charismatic leaders often emerge in times of crises as prospective saviors who by their magical endowments will fulfill the unmet emotional needs of their completely trusting, overly dependent and submissive followers. If sucessful, charismatic leaders bring about a radical transformation in society. J. M. Burns (1978) preferred to speak about heroic leadership believing that charisma has been overworked in usage. Again, the highly esteemed individual becomes a hero. There is:

> belief in leaders because of their personage alone, aside from their tested capacities, experience, or stand on issues; faith in the leaders' capacity to overcome obstacles and crises; readiness to grant to leaders the powers to handle crises; mass support for such leaders expressed directly—through votes, applause, letters, shaking hands—rather than through intermediaries or institutions. Heroic leadership is not simply a quality or entity possessed by someone; it is a type of relationship between leader and led. A crucial aspect of this relationship is the absence of conflict [p. 244].

The heroic, transcending leader excites and transforms previously dormant followers into active ones. For example, leaders of an exodus heighten motivation, purposes, and missionary zeal. Followers become proselytizers acting as leaders in turn as a consequence of their own raised awareness.

Hollander (1978) also noted that charisma could be a property of position as well as person. An American president has a lot of luster which is lost after he leaves office.

*Esteem and Competence*

M. A. Price (1948) studied esteem among 223 girls in a junior college. Significantly more-chosen-than-rejected girls were mentioned on a ''guess who'' test as being like the person who has good ideas, expresses joy and satisfaction, keeps the central idea in mind, appeals for group loyalty, and makes others feel they will benefit by following her suggestions. The rejected were more frequently mentioned as being like the person who expresses fear and worry and embarrasses others. Bass and Coates (1953) found positive correlations between intelligence test scores and ratings of esteem in ROTC by peers. Listed on a peer evaluation scale for assessing esteem among Marine OCS cadets were such ''ability'' items as: well-trained, experienced, performs well before group, sound judgment, thinks quickly, exhibits imagination, well-educated, and fine athlete (Hoffman & Rohrer, 1954). Again, among institutionalized girls, H. H. Jennings (1943) noted that the ''overchosen'' exhibited more ingenuity, planning, and organization. The more esteemed members of Whyte's (1943) street-corner society were known for their resourcefulness and the past success of their ideas. In the same way, Zeleny (1946–1947) found that cadets with exceptional ability in flying were more likely to be chosen as a flying partner. Likewise, Feinberg (1953) noted that, regardless of economic background, esteemed adolescent boys were higher in athletic and scholastic proficiency than those boys who were rejected by their peers. But choosing friends, as in the case of leadership and intelligence, Riley and Flowerman (1951) suggested, goes with being ''smart, but not too smart; pretty, but not too pretty.''

Demonstrated competence increases one's esteem. Gilchrist (1952) found that persons became more attractive to others if they consistently succeeded on assigned tasks. In the same way, Lippitt et al. (1952) reported that in a summer camp, boys with a history of success were most liked. Ability of an individual to help the group can be increased, of course. R. E. Andrews (1955) suggested providing supervisors with as much information about policies and decisions as possible to enhance their standing with their subordinates. Zander and Havelin (1960) showed that those who were highly competent in experimental groups were preferred over those lacking in competence. Again, Jackson (1953) found that when members of a formal organization judged other members of the work group, they tended to value most those perceived to contribute to group goals and conform to group standards.

*''Unearned'' Esteem.*   Yet, it must be clear that one can be esteemed for a variety of reasons that have little or nothing to do with ability to help the group. Persons may gain esteem merely because of similarity to stereotypes or popular conceptions of esteemed or popular figures. The youthful-looking, gray-haired, handsome face is a strong political asset in television campaigning. Family name may be equally important. Again, Whyte (1943) noted that leaders can increase or maintain their perceived value to their group by making sure the group engages in activities at which they, the leaders, are most proficient. Experimentally, it was possible to raise or lower the esteem of a neutral stranger merely by attaching some false cues to the stranger (Asch, 1946). The results

depend on attitudes toward those cues. H. H. Kelley (1950) introduced two persons to an audience, one as "warm," the other as "cold." Audience perceptions of the personality of the two was altered by the adjective used in introducing them.

### Esteem and Conformity

Before new individuals can be accepted by the other members of an established group and rise in esteem, they usually must demonstrate that they will abide by the rules of the group and share its ways of behaving and its goals (Whyte, 1943; Thrasher, 1927; Merei, 1949; N. Anderson, 1923). Thus, Bonney and Powell (1953) found that the highly esteemed children in sociometric analyses were more cooperative. Again, Christie (1952) found that if a new army recruit increased in acceptance of prevailing authoritarian attitudes he was more likely to be esteemed by his peers after six weeks in service. Similarly, Havighurst and Taba (1949) noted that adolescents who conform best to the middle class standards of the school are most likely to be esteemed by their middle class peers. Following a survey of the literature, Northway, Frankel, and Potashin (1947) concluded that esteem is highest in children who are not extremely shy or so aggressive as to interfere with activities of the group. We esteem those in a group whom we regard as most similar to us in attitudes, interests, and abilities. We tend to reject those whom we regard as different or unlike us.

*Perceived Similarity.* According to Bonney (1946a,b), individuals tend to choose as friends others close to themselves in socioeconomic status. H. M. Richardson (1940), Precker (1952), and Stotland, Zander, and Natsoulas (1961) found that experimental participants preferred others whose values were similar to their own. But perceived similarity was a function of group interaction only when the subjects did not know each other beforehand (Stotland, Cottrell & Laing, 1960).

Fiedler, Warrington, and Blaisdell (1952), Fensterheim and Tresselt (1953), Davitz (1955), A. J. Smith (1957), and Byrne and Clore (1966) demonstrated that attitude similarity is a significant factor in sociometric choice. In the same way, the acceptance of a stranger was related to attitude similarity (Byrne, 1965), prestige (Byrne, Griffitt & Golightly, 1966), and topic importance (Byrne & Nelson, 1965a; A. J. Smith, 1958). A stranger perceived to have attitudes similar to one's own was better liked than a stranger with dissimilar attitudes and was adjudged more intelligent, more moral, and better informed (Byrne, 1961).

Perceived similarity in personality characteristics is significantly related to interpersonal choice (Lindzey & Urdan, 1954; Hoffman, 1958; Izard, 1960; Lundy et al., 1955; Secord & Backman, 1964; and Steiner & Dodge, 1957). A review by Berscheid and Walster (1969) also suggests that similarity of attitude and personality is associated with interpersonal attraction—mutuality of esteem.

*Mutual Attractiveness.* Aronson and Worchel (1966) found that participants who were led to believe that they were either liked or disliked by their partners in interaction responded to liking above and beyond attitude similarity or dissimilarity. But Byrne and Nelson (1965b) and Byrne and Griffitt (1966b) suggested that perception of attitude similarity on a number of items also acts to reinforce interpersonal attractiveness. Byrne and Griffitt (1966a) repeated the experiment by Aronson and Worchel with an extended range of attitude similarity–dissimilarity and found that both liking and attitude similarity affect interpersonal attraction. The expectation of being liked by a participant in an experimental task was significantly related to interpersonal attraction in studies by Backman and Secord (1959) and Darley and Berscheid (1967). Newcomb (1956) also found that individuals in a group tended to like members who liked them. Agreement on interpersonal liking was more potent than mutual liking for inanimate objects in determining interpersonal attraction. Interpersonal attraction was predicted by frequency of interaction and perception of similarity in personality and attitudes.

Similarity in competence also makes a difference in personal attractiveness. Zander and Havelin (1960) obtained results that indicated that members of experimental groups tended to be most attracted to others whose competence was closest to their own. J. R. P. French (1956) assembled groups of three friends and a stranger in which only the stranger was permitted to succeed. Participants high in achievement orientation chose significantly more previously successful partners than those low in achievement orientation. Finally, Marwell (1966) assigned participants to different partners to perform three different kinds of tasks. In choosing partners for the second task, participants tended to select the person who had previously cooperated in a similar task, thus matching experience to task demands regardless of degree of liking for the partner.

### Need for Esteem

Maslow (1954) popularized attention to this important need. Just as we would like to occupy valued positions, most of us also desire to be valued as persons. Lippitt, Thelen and Leff (n.d.) hypothesized that we are more concerned about being criticized personally than about being criticized for the social role we play. This concern with one's value was implicit in Festinger's (1954) theory of social comparison processes.

We are more satisfied with situations and groups that provide us with esteem. Van Zelst (1951) obtained results indicating that highly esteemed workers were more satisfied with their job and with their firm. Similarly, Heyns (1950) found that conference participants who felt they were accepted, were more satisfied with the conference decisions. But Flint, Bass, and Pryer, (1957a) failed to obtain any relation between esteem and attraction to problem-solving groups.

## STATUS AND ESTEEM

### Interrelations

Although conceptually distinct, status—value due one's role or position—and esteem—value due to one as a person—empirically tend to be interrelated. This was found to be so by Flint, Bass, and Pryer (1957b) in two-thirds of thirty-four laboratory groups they examined.

Status is often gained through personal ability, competition, and effort. Persons likely to be esteemed because of their personal characteristics are also likely to obtain positions of greater worth in formal hierarchical organizations. Esteem often leads to status achievement (Pellegrin, 1952). Promotion to higher status in industrial and military organizations often depends on merit ratings by superiors of one's worth to the organization, although, of course, upward mobility in status can also be due to chance, tradition, or favoritism unrelated to one's esteem.

Conversely, one's status increases one's esteem. For example, esteem is higher for individuals with the status of owners and professionals in agricultural communities (Hooker, 1928). Similarly, prestige and popularity are higher for persons who are heads of organizations in their communities (J. E. White, 1950). D. T. Campbell (1953) noted that in seven out of ten submarines, the commanding officer was most esteemed, receiving the most nominations as the person others wanted to see in command. Merit ratings (esteem) of military officers tended to be higher, the higher their rank (status) (Robins, Willemin & Bruekel, 1954). A review of officer efficiency ratings from 1922 to 1945 revealed a positive correlation between the rank of officers and their merit ratings. Those of higher grades in service received more favorable combat performance ratings in Korea (USA, 1952). In the same way, in a study of 1,900 military personnel, Masling, Greer, and Gilmore (1955) found that the higher individuals ranked in the military organization, the greater the number of favorable sociometric mentions they tended to receive in regard to both military and personal matters. Again, according to D. T. Campbell (1956), the leader behavior descriptions and nominations for leadership of submarine officers were highly correlated with the officer's rank and level of their position. The interrelations are apparent from an analysis by Jencks et al. (1979) who looked at thirteen demographic variables comparing fathers and concluded that father's occupation, family background, education, and intelligence are the best predictors of son's occupational success.

### Approaches to Study

Sociometry (Moreno, 1934, 1953) and rated observation are the common ways of measuring the status and esteem of members.

*Sociometry.* Sociometry has been used primarily to assess the esteem and other attributes of members of groups as individuals. It has also been applied to assess accorded status. Each member may be asked, "Whom do you spend the most time with getting work done?" Stogdill and Koehler (1952) found that the extent to which persons in lower echelons mentioned an individual as one with whom they spend the most time correlated .82 with the mentioned person's level in the organization. However, this measure to some extent was confounded by the contacted occupant's esteem, for it correlated .31, .33 and .23 with ratings of the extent to which the frequently contacted job occupant was also preferred as a leader. Another sociometric measure, based on the tendency to be mentioned by persons in units other than one's own as a person with whom most time was spent, was completely independent of esteem (r = − .08), yet correlated highly with status (r = .69) indicated by formal level in the organization. Similarly, Browne (1949) found that an executive mentioned frequently as one with whom others spend time was also an office-holder who described himself as higher in authority and who was in a higher echelon in the organization.

### Observation

The studies of leadership and dominance in animal societies indicate that members of such groups quickly recognize the status structure of their group. The leader's dominance may go unchallenged; if challenged, a fight settles the issue; thereafter, the status structure exhibits considerable stability. Among humans, even in the complete absence of symbols and signs of office, formal authority, and other common attributes of status in formal organizations, potential role and status differences are rather quickly recognized by group members; and group members do as well as trained observers (Stein, 1971). Vielhaber and Gottheil (1965) studied 117 cadets who were rated by four judges after only twenty to thirty-five seconds of observation. The ratings correlated .45 with upper classmen's ratings after four weeks of observation and correlated .31 with composite aptitude for service evaluations made fourteen weeks later! Similarly, Gronlund (1955b) correlated an individual's rank in status in a group with the individual's ranking of group members. The median rank order correlations were about .40 for 104 graduate students. Gronlund (1955a) observed that members quickly perceive structure in a group and that the relationship between sociometric status and acquaintance span is not high. In other words, group members are about as well agreed on their relative status positions at the beginning of interaction as they are after extended acquaintanceship. In the same way, in experiments with the self-esteem of members of dyads, Levinger (1959) found that although later behavior influenced partner behavior more than first impression, there was a tendency for first impression to determine behavior throughout the experiment. Again, Barker (1942) demonstrated that a group of strangers, after a few moments of getting acquainted, exhibited a high degree of agreement in choosing members for seatmates. Expressions of choice were highly related to descriptions of behavior and appearance. The strangers preferred as seatmates were rated good-looking, popular, bold, and daring.

*Agreement and Stability of Ratings of Status and Esteem.* Blake, Mouton, and Fruchter (1954) studied ten groups, each with three members, in a discussion task. Changes between sessions 1 and 2 included varying the task, group membership, and identity of observers. Evaluations were made on a 12-item questionnaire. There was statistically significant agreement between self–observer, self–members, observer–member, and observer–group in each of the two sessions for esteem and accorded status as evidenced by leadership, contributions to group decision, and amount of clerical work performed.

Bass and White (1951), Bass and Coates (1952), and Bass and Wurster (1953a,b) reported that pairs of observers tend to reach agreement as to which member of an initially leaderless group emerges with highest accorded status. Correlations between observers ranged from .51 to .83. Prien and Culler (1964) found, however, that observers are better agreed on those who participated a little rather than on those who participate a lot. While sociometric ratings among very young children seem to lack consistency from one period to the next (Lazar, 1953), the age of campers increases the stability of their sociometric ratings (Newstetter, Feldstein & Newcomb, 1938). Northway (1946) reported rate-rerate correlations of .8 to .9 when summer campers rerated each other a week after a first rating, and Bjerstedt (1956) reported correlations of .82 between ratings and reratings four months apart among 867 Swedish school children 9 years and older. Even after thirteen months, the rate-rerate correlation was .73. McGuire, Lammon, and White (1953) found similar consistency among adolescents from one year to the next. Even when half the children, aged 6 to 12, in a group are replaced with new members, the remaining children's esteem ratings are consistent to some extent with earlier ratings (E. Campbell, n.d.). Likewise, peer ratings of esteem and accorded status among adults are highly consistent. For example, a Horst reliability of .68 was obtained as an index of agreement among ratings by two to seventeen ROTC cadets rating a total of 307 fellow cadets (Bass & Coates, 1953).

## LEADERSHIP, STATUS, AND ESTEEM

A summary of experimental evidence strongly supports the conclusion that attempted and successful leadership is greater among those accorded more status and esteem in the group (Bass, 1960).

### Status and Leadership

Doyle (1971) showed how the process analysis of the productivity of school teachers was linked systematically to their principals' achieved status. Bass (1963) found that attempts to lead were more likely to be successful when the members differed in accorded status and when they were highly motivated (Bass, 1963) than under the opposite conditions. Again, a correlation of .88 was found between echelon in the company of 131 oil refinery supervisors and their success in leading discussions for which no one was appointed chairman (Bass & Wurster, 1953b). If the problem concerned company matters, the correlation was even higher (Bass & Wurster, 1953a). Bass (1964) reported a correlation of .51 between rank among 264 ROTC cadets and their tendency to lead discussions among associates. When 180 cadets were retested in a new discussion among their associates a year after an initial discussion, those who during the year rose in rank from cadet noncommissioned officer to first lieutenant or higher gained significantly more in observed success as leaders on the retest compared to the original discussion than those who received promotions to cadet second lieutenant only.

Prior status differences between group members affect their patterns of leader behavior. J. C. Moore (1968) found that when dyads work on an ambiguous task, high-status partners show a greater number of "self" resolutions of perceived differences between themselves and their ostensibly lower-status partners. Lower-status partners in the same experimental condition tend to defer to the choices made by their high-status partners. Subsequently, J. C. Moore (1969) showed that agreement among partners tended to erode the differential self–other performance expectations activated by the status differences. An adequate description of the behavior of the low-status member, in contrast with the leader, has to include "face-saving."

Gerard (1957) found that high status produced control-oriented behavior, regardless of the clarity of role relationships. Low-status participants required a clearly defined set of role expectations in order to be effective. Without group goals, high-status participants assumed broader prerogatives, whereas low-status participants performed ineffectively. High-status participants worked more effectively when fewer restrictions were placed on their activities, whereas low-status participants seemed bewildered under the same conditions. High-status participants perceived themselves to have more freedom of action than did low-status participants.

More attention is paid to high-status persons. Pedestrians at a traffic signal committed significantly more violations when they witnessed violations committed by an experimenter dressed to represent a person of high social status than when he was dressed to represent a person of low social status (Lefkowitz, Blake & Mouton, 1955). Group members address more remarks to high-status than to low-status members (H. H. Kelley, 1951; Katz, Goldston & Benjamin, 1958).

### Effects of Socioeconomic Status

In Chapter 4, fifteen studies were noted suggesting that leaders come from a socioeconomic background according them higher status. However, some of this may be confounded with the tendency of higher socioeconomic status to be correlated with greater intelligence, education, and opportunities. Hollingshead's (1949) Elmstown's youth displayed leadership behavior as a function of the social class in Elmstown of their family. The leaders of a Connecticut industrial town tended to be from wealthy families with "connections" (M. Smith, 1937). The descendants of colonial merchants and statesmen, pioneering businessmen, and mining and railroad tycoons of Philadelphia all went to school with one another, lived in fashionable neighborhoods, were Episcopalian, joined the same clubs, intermarried, and eventually entered the elite class. They became community leaders (Baltzell, 1958).

J. A. Davis (1929) found that only 19 percent of 163 Russian communist leaders had peasant fathers, while only 21 percent had working class fathers. Taussig and Joslyn (1932) observed that 70 percent of the fathers of 7,371 American business executives were businessmen although businessmen comprised only 10 percent of the working force. Even labor leaders tend to be the sons of professionals and businessmen (Sorokin, 1927b).

An array of studies of opinion leaders attest to the strong linkage of socioeconomic status and leadership. Switzer (1975) showed that in a progressive, industrial-agrarian department in Colombia, peasant leaders were more educated and more economically secure with clearer land title than peasant leaders in a rural, conservative department. Farmers in Orissa, India, were more effective in motivating other farmers to improve their agricultural techniques if they were higher in socioeconomic status (Rath & Sahoo, 1974). Again, Roy, Jaiswal, and Shankar (1974) reported that sociometrically identified leaders in four villages in Bihar, India, tended to be higher in caste and size of land holding than followers. But Chesterfield and Ruddle (1976) warn that extension agents may pay little attention to the less visible opinion leaders in rural Venezuela such as relatives, symbolic kin, and older community members.

Systematic changes are occurring. Thus, the United States Air Force Command will pass in the 1980s to officers quite different from those who derived from engagement in World War II. According to Margiotta (1976), because of broader social recruitment in the 1950s and 1960s, air force leaders in the 1980s will be more representative of the U.S. population in terms of socioeconomic origin, regional affiliation, size of hometown, and religion. In the same way, after fifteen years of socialism, 96 percent of managers in Poland report they came from working or lower middle classes (see Chapter 32).

### Esteem and Leadership

Moreno (1934, 1953) observed that the higher the esteem of group members, the greater will be the volume of words expected and accepted from them by other members.

The esteemed member will be permitted more frequently to assume the initiative and to terminate activities. Likewise, Bird (1940) concluded that leadership must reflect the esteem to which the member is held. Similarly, Homans (1950) proposed that those of "higher social rank" in a group initiate the interaction. Lazarsfeld, Berelson, and Gaudet (1948) suggested that the influence on opinion of personal contact depended on trust in esteemed persons. A positive relation was found by Bass (1955b) between discussion members' esteem ratings of each other and an objective measure of the extent to which each successfully led the others in initially leaderless discussions. Garrison (1933) obtained a correlation of .82 between the tendency of high school seniors to be chosen as leader and their tendency to be admired. In the same way, H. H. Jennings (1947) found the sociometrically "overchosen" compared to the "average chosen" in a girls' institution to exhibit four times as much behavior "making new events happen" or "enlarging the extent of activities." When free to choose a leader, H. H. Jennings (1943) found that they tended to select someone who displayed spontaneity and enlarged the field of action for others. In seventy-two business and government conferences, Crockett (1955) noted that emergent leaders were rated as those members most needed by the group. In another industrial study, N. A. Rosen (1969) obtained ratings of worker preference for eight foremen. Foremen high and low in preference then changed places. The greater the worker consensus in weeks 1 to 10 that the new foreman "is our leader," the greater the increase in productivity and cohesiveness in weeks 11 to 16. The findings suggest that the new foremen were evaluated in terms of their ability to help the group.

In a report on seventy-two men in the Antarctic for a year, P. D. Nelson (1964b) concluded that what differentiated leaders from the men in maintaining their esteem as leaders was their stronger motivational commitment to the group. Rosen, Levinger, and Lippitt (1961) found that school children and college students rate helpfulness and fairness as the most important traits that enable individuals to influence others. Adults rated fairness first and helpfulness second in importance. Kelman (1970), Olsen (1968), and Sells (1968) placed particular importance on the confidence and trust which could be seen in leaders by their followers. Such confidence and trust in the leader are linked to the competence of the leaders. However, the feelings aroused by leaders are multidimensional. R. D. Mann, Gibbard, and Hartman (1967) obtained college students' expressions of feeling toward different leaders as well as descriptions of followers' responses. Student responses were intercorrelated and factor-analyzed. The six factors revealed a wide range of feeling toward the leader. These included feelings about the leader as an analyst, as an authority figure, as a manipulator, as a listener, as a source of status anxiety and as whether or not committed to the leader member relationship. The investigators found that leaders were valued for supporting member independence, identification, and social closeness. Group members played various roles, including those of hero, moralistic spokesman, scapegoat, independent enactor, and collapsing colleague. But such perceived esteem in leaders can be induced in subordinates by their own needs and desires for particular leader behaviors (M. G. Evans, 1973; Lawler & Hall, 1970). Such distortion becomes great in the charismatic leader who for some followers would be seen to be able to "walk on water."

Therapeutic group leaders were seen as more helpful if they were evaluated as higher in self-disclosure and mental health (May & Thompson, 1973). Bolman (1973) reported on the extent to which such leaders were favorably characterized by group members, member liking of leaders, and therapeutic improvement (self- and peer ratings). However, Bolman failed to replicate previous findings in which liking and member improvement had been positively related.

Charismatic qualities of fatherliness, capacity to inspire loyalty, high energy level, and optimism were seen as needed in 100 vacant medical school senior chairs in psychiatry in a three-year survey (GAP—Group for the Advancement of Psychiatry, 1974). Bryson and Kelley (1978) concluded in a review of biographical studies of successful national political leaders that the leaders had been members in good standing in their home political organizations, were ideologically in the mainstream, and were able to gain seniority and experience in their home organizations, all increasing their value in the eyes of their constituencies.

*Expert Opinion.* We accept readily the influence attempts of those whom we esteem as experts. H. T. Moore (1921) observed that students shifted their judgments (about linguistic, ethical, and musical matters) in the direction of what they were led to believe by the experimenter was the opinion of experts. In the same way, Mausner (1953) found that when students took the Meier Art Judgment test a second time, they shifted to wrong responses suggested to them by partners introduced as art experts. Brim (1954) discovered that mothers changed toward more permissive child-rearing practices the more they esteemed the physician who had suggested the change. But the prestigeful doctor was not enough to sustain the new behavior. It required their husbands' approval, support, and reinforcement of the suggested future satisfactions to be expected as a consequence of the change. Lanzetta and Haythorn (1954) observed that the more students esteemed their instructors, the more their opinions would coalesce with their instructors'.

### Hierarchy of Effects on Leadership

Influence is more strongly associated with one's sociometrically rated value or ability than one's sociometrically determined popularity or visibility. Table 10.1 shows the results of a sociometric study of 203 salesmen reported by Bass (1960). In each of their sales units, the salesmen nominated seven others as "liked as a coworker." They also rejected seven people. They repeated these nominations and rejections on "value to company," "ability to solve the company's problems," and "influence." Each salesman's "score" was the number of his nominations less the number of rejections by others on each criterion. His "visibility" was based on the percentage of all salesmen in his division who knew him. It can be seen that merely being liked was correlated more highly with influence (.68 and .74). Ability and popularity both correlated more with value than they did with each other. Thus, each contributed to value something independent of the other. Popularity differed from the other measures in its lack of relation with visibility. Riedesel (1974) has stressed that popularity distorts sociometric studies of leadership.

**TABLE 10.1**
**Median Intercorrelations among Five Sociometric**
**Ratings of 203 Salesmen by Their Associates**

|  | Visibility | Popularity | Value | Ability | Influence |
|---|---|---|---|---|---|
| Visibility |  | − .05 | .39 | .38 | .29 |
| Popularity | − .05 |  | .60 | .49 | .50 |
| Value | .39 | .60 |  | .73 | .68 |
| Ability | .38 | .49 | .73 |  | .74 |
| Influence | .29 | .50 | .68 | .74 |  |

SOURCE: Bass, 1960, p. 282.

*Types.*    To examine conditions when esteem, popularity, and leadership are or are not correlated, P. B. Smith (1963) classified group members in terms of their sociometric nominations of other members for competent ideas, leadership, and liking. Differentiation between leader and liking rankings were related to the ranker's attraction to the group. Differentiation in ranking was not related to status consensus in the group or lack of feedback to frequent speakers. The rankers were divided into four types:

Type I.    Leadership highly correlated with liking and ideas: this group was composed of active members attracted to the group. They were most active in discussing the usefulness of meetings and making rules for procedure.

Type II.    Leadership highly correlated with ideas but not with liking: the members of this group were low in activity and were unattracted to the group. They were seen as most active in attempting to draw people in, withdrawing from group, and submitting to others' wishes.

Type III.    Leadership highly correlated with liking but not with ideas: the members were perceived to be striving for individual recognition and to be unattracted to the group.

Type IV.    Leadership not highly correlated with ideas or liking. This group was low in both activity and attraction to the group.

*Competence and Value Are Most Important Elements.*    Whereas being liked, being visible, and being popular may still be of some importance to one's influence in play situations, competence and value are of most importance to influence in task situations.

Moreno (1934, 1953) and H. H. Jennings (1943) observed that group members exhibited higher degrees of emotional expansiveness in choice of friends than in choice of work partners. M. A. Price (1948) and Burnett (1951a,b) found that fewer members of a group were chosen for leader than for friend, but nominations received for leader and friend were positively related (C. A. Gibb, 1950; Borgatta, 1954; Hollander & Webb, 1955). However, nominations for leadership and followership ($r = .92$) were more highly correlated than nominations for leadership and friendship ($r = .47$). Leadership and participation were highly and positively correlated, but friendship and participation were not (Lana, Vaughn & McGinnies, 1960).

C. A. Gibb (1950) and Borgatta (1954) observed that ratings of leader effectiveness were highly related to choices received as work partner, but they were unrelated to choices received as friend. Nominations for "influence on the group" were more highly related to effectiveness ratings than nominations for work partner or friend (C. A. Gibb, 1954). Making many choices or being expected to make them was not related to leader effectiveness ratings. The member exhibiting a great deal of structuring and participation attracted a large portion of the positive affect behavior of group members. Activity in the positive affect area, however, was associated only with popularity. Yet, Newstetter, Feldstein, and Newcomb (1938) found that an individual's leadership in a group was determined largely by the cordiality received from others rather than by his or her cordiality toward them.

Durojaiye (1969) studied the effects of sex and race on sociometric choice among school children 8 to 11 years of age. These children preferred friends of their own sex and race. However, neither sex nor race influenced choice for leadership. Tagiuri and Kogan (1957) found that self-confidence enhanced an individual's visibility in a group. Mutuality of choice and self-confidence produced the highest degree of visibility.

### Limitations

We have already noted that to gain and maintain esteem and accorded status, which makes it possible for one to exert leadership, one must accept the group's norms. But, with esteem and accorded status, one still is limited in what influence can be exerted. Hollander (1961a) conducted an experiment in which his participants were given brief descriptions of persons who were to be ranked from high to low in accorded status. The participants were then given lists of behaviors that might be exhibited by the persons whom they had ranked. As perceived status increased of those ranked, progressively less disapproval was shown for "suggesting changes from group plans" and "discussing group concerns with outsiders." However, "interrupting others to make comments" was increasingly disapproved for persons with increasing status. The high-status member was permitted to innovate group changes but was not expected to interrupt low-status members.

## SELF-ACCORDED STATUS AND ESTEEM

### Discrepancies with Actual Status and Esteem

Self-esteem and self-accorded status can be quite different from the esteem and status accorded a person although ordinarily one would expect some correlation between them. Shapiro and Klein (1975) found such a correlation in encounter groups, but only after two days of meetings and only for a composite profile of the leaders by themselves and as seen by the nonleaders. Similarly, Willerman and Swanson (1953) demonstrated that members' evaluations of themselves are related to some extent to other members' evaluations of them.

According to sociometric analyses in a girls' school by H. H. Jennings (1943), a comparison of self-estimates with estimates by others showed that the most chosen group appraised itself most accurately on having good ideas and making others feel benefited, while the underchosen group estimated itself most accurately in expressing discouragement and being easily hurt. In addition, each girl was asked to describe the different members of her family and to name the member whom she most closely resembled. The leaders (in terms of sociometric choice and offices held) were found to identify themselves with the member of the family whom they described as sociable, encouraging independence, and reliable. Nonleaders tended to identify themselves with the member whom they described as expressing discouragement, anxiety, and worry.

### Relation to Group Cohesiveness

Festinger, Torrey, and Willerman (1954) assembled four-person groups made to vary in cohesiveness; members were induced either to succeed or to fail in a group task. The results indicated that the stronger the attachment of members to a group, the stronger were the feelings of inadequacy of those not performing as well as others and the stronger were the feelings of adequacy of those performing better than others in the group. In turn, Dittes (1959) found that persons made to feel accepted in a group found the group more attractive than those made to feel poorly accepted. But this difference was significantly greater among persons with low self-esteem than among persons with high self-esteem. Low self-esteem was seen to indicate a strong need for acceptance. Indirectly consistent with this, Thibaut (1950) studied groups that could gain or lose in status. He found that when group attempts toward upward mobility were frustrated over a period of time, central members tended to develop into a highly cohesive clique within the group.

### Leaders and Nonleaders' Accuracy

Leaders tend to be more accurate about their status and esteem than other members. But this is not surprising since everyone in the group can make more accurate judgments about the leader than about other members. The leader's behavior is more visible, more frequent, and more observable than the behavior of most other members (Bass, 1949).

## LEADERSHIP AND SELF-ACCORDED STATUS AND ESTEEM

Stogdill, in Chapter 4, reported that most of seventeen studies reviewed showed that leaders rate themselves higher in self-confidence and self-esteem. Twenty-eight additional positive findings were identified in Chapter 5.

### Self-Accorded Status

Self-accorded status—self-estimates of the importance of one's position—produces more attempts and to a lesser extent more successful leadership. Guetzkow (1954) showed that key persons' ratings of their own importance to communication networks correlated with their influence behavior in the networks. Gold (1951–1952) described how tenant–janitor interaction in a multiple dwelling changed when the janitor's concept of his own status changed as he adopted "professional standards" when he began earning a higher salary than some of his tenants.

*Self-Esteem and Leadership*

More evidence is available demonstrating the relationship between self-esteem and leadership. Thus, market research studies conclude that a majority of fashion opinion leaders and personal grooming opinion leaders are high in self-esteem. Hemphill and Pepinsky (1955) found attempted leadership higher among participants who felt personally accepted or esteemed. Wurster, Bass, and Alcock (1961) obtained results with ninety-five initially leaderless discussion participants indicating that they felt more responsive toward the suggestions and opinions of persons whom they esteemed than toward those of people in general. Thus, the highly esteemed person had an advantage in that followers tended to feel responsive toward his or her behavior. A correlation of .38 was found between self-esteem and attempted and successful leadership. But since esteem and self-esteem did not relate highly to each other, the correlations between self-esteem and objective success as a leader subsequently were only .17 and .18 for a total of ninety-five participants (Bass, 1955b).

J. M. Burns (1978) noted that the most potent sources of political leadership are unfulfilled needs for esteem and self-esteem. But Barber (1965) felt that deciding to become a candidate for political office is indicative of either very high or very low self-esteem.

In a study of sixty-five elementary school principals, Mowday (1979) showed that their leadership in four decisions was related to their self-confidence. They were more likely to be persuasive if they were self-confident. Similarly, Kipnis and Lane (1962) obtained results indicating that supervisors who lacked confidence in their leadership ability were significantly less willing than self-confident supervisors to hold face-to-face discussions with subordinates and more often attempted to solve supervisory and development problems by the use of administrative rules or by referring the subordinate to a superior for decision.

Status and esteem also generate power as we will detail next.

part

# POWER AND LEGITIMACY

# 11

Power has been of concern to priests, philosophers, and kings since the beginnings of civilization and to chiefs and medicine men before that. Who can influence whom clearly depends on who is more powerful and who is less so. Only with God on his side could Moses convince Pharoah to let his people go.

In this chapter, we will explore the current definitions of social power, the bases of such power, and how it contributes to leadership in communities, formal organizations, and small groups.

## DEFINITIONS OF SOCIAL POWER

Definitions of social power fall into two main classes: (1) power as potential social force; and (2) power as potential social exchange.

### Power as Force

Russell (1938) defined power as "the production of intended effects." For Bierstedt (1950) power was "the ability to employ force." Wrong (1968) limited power to the intended, successful control of others. Most behavioral theorists maintain, however, that power can be exerted without intention. For J. R. P. French (1956) as well as Cartwright (1959a,b) the power of A over B was "equal to the maximum force which A can induce on B minus the maximum resisting force which B can mobilize in the opposing direction." For Dahl (1957), "A has power over B to the extent that A can get B to do something that B would not otherwise do."

### Power as a Function of Social Exchange

Simon (1957) saw power as a manifestation of an asymmetry in the relationship between A and B. For Presthus (1960) it was a matter of their rapport. Cartwright (1965) conceived power in terms of control of information and personal affection, while Bierstedt (1950) focused on prestige. But Homans (1958) suggested that individuals tend to maintain a balance in the exchange of social values. Thibaut and Kelley (1959) regarded power as an exchange relation in which one member has either behavioral control or fate control over the behavior of another. Gouldner (1960) advanced the view

**169**

that the differentiation of social roles that results in organizations is based initially on such exchange relations.

Blau (1964) and Adams and Romney (1959) saw power as negative, as influence through the use of deprivation, aversive stimulation, or sanctions. Harsanyi (1962a,b) weighed social benefits against social costs in defining power relations. Bass (1960) defined power of A over B as A's control of what was needed and valued by B. If B was satiated or uninterested in what A controlled, A lost power over B. J. M. Burns (1978) agreed. In this view, Cartwright (1965) emphasized the importance of ecological control: power can be exercised by controlling resources or necessities, by occupying space, or by avoiding or boycotting a location.

French and Raven (1959) identified five kinds of power:

1. Reward power depends on ability of A to provide rewards for B.
2. Coercive power is based on B's perception that A can provide penalties for nonconformity.
3. Legitimate power is based on the internalization of common norms or values.
4. Referent power is based on B's identification with, or liking for, member A.
5. Expert power is based on B's perception of A's competence.

French and Raven's terminology has become widely used, although many problems remain with it. The five bases and their effects will be discussed in detail in the last half of this chapter.

The exchange calculus is not as simple as French (1956) or Dahl (1957) would have it, for leaders of more powerful followers are likely to be more powerful than leaders of less powerful followers. The leaders can mobilize the power of their followers. They can be granted or deprived power from their followers. In combination with their followers, they collectively can acquire more power (J. M. Burns, 1978). This mutuality in the power relation is seen when followers must complete their assignments if the leader is to be rewarded along with the subordinate. Subordinate slowdown or inattention can result in loss of benefits for the supervisor.

This social exchange is also seen in the exchange relation between the Roman patron and his freedmen clients and between the ward boss and his neighborhood constituents. The clients' and constituents' votes and obedience provided the bases of power for patron and ward boss in return for which the followers received protection, security, and material support. The ethnic political leader in the United States disperses tangible divisible rewards, favors, and services to his constituents. A study by Borowiec (1975) of eighty-three Polish-American leaders in Buffalo indicates that they provide constituents with special information and personal assistance in dealing with public agencies.

### Power Is Not Synonymous with Influence

Unfortunately, power often is used as synonymous with influence. Tautologies have been endemic. We observe that A leads B; therefore we conclude that A has more power than B. Inferences about power and its effects must begin with measures of power that are completely independent of observed relations between A and B. The observed relations are a product of the power differences between A and B, not the behavior observed.

Leadership and influence obviously are a function of power. Power is the potential to influence inferred from observed influence. It is the probable rate and amount of influence of a person or a position occupant. Thus, for instance, Barber (1966) inferred that the power relations among legislative committee members could be accounted for by the following factors: attributed leadership, rate of success in getting suggestions accepted, rate of agreement received, and group-related surplus. Although Lord (1977) found that among 144 undergraduates perceived leadership and social power were related, unexplained variance required maintaining their separate conceptual distinctions.

But power is not an absolute amount. As already noted, it depends on the power of those to be influenced both positively and negatively. The power of those influenced adds to the total power available in the situation and can be increased by the synergistic action of the leader and followers. The leader's power may be diminished to the extent that it can be offset by the power of individual followers.

We begin with examining the sources of power, independent of the effects of such power. But in doing so, we are unlikely to avoid overlapping empirically with antecedents and consequences of power. Further overlap occurs because power begets power. The individual whose power is based on control of rewards and punishments can acquire legitimate power through internalization processes. Although we may be able to sort out conceptually the different bases of power, in nature they are likely to be intertwined. Thus, group members tend to defer to the perceived expert. Perceived expertness tends to legitimize the leadership role (Goodstadt & Kipnis, 1970).

## POWER: PERSONAL AND POSITIONAL

Students who were asked to write essays by Falbo (1977) on "How I Get My Way" generated sixteen different approaches to social power. Nevertheless, two sources can be discerned: power due to one's person and power due to one's position.

### Personal Power

Power can derive from one's person or one's position (Bass, 1960). Those with personal power can grant to others affection, consideration, sympathy, recognition, and secure relationships and attachments. Rosen, Levinger, and Lippitt (1961) asked teachers and emotionally disturbed boys to rank six items of social power in order of importance. The two groups basically agreed on the relative importance of physical strength, sociability, expertness, fairness, fearlessness, and helpfulness as sources of social power. But those with personal power also can punish others by becoming more distant, formal, cold, and businesslike.

Bass and Wurster (1961) demonstrated that we want to be valued and esteemed mainly by those we value and esteem. We endow such persons with personal power. Hurwitz, Zander, and Hymovitch (1953) showed that we seek the affection and support of those we hold to be personally powerful. Professional personnel were continually reshuffled to form thirty-two sextets. The power to influence and the extent to which each member was liked after the first half-hour of interaction were assessed. Those of low esteem wanted most to be liked by those of high esteem.

*Identification and Power.* The "father figure" can serve as the focus of positive emotional feelings, as the ideal object for psychoanalytic transference and identification

(Kelman, 1958). Transference of coping with problems to father figures provides escape from responsibility and decisions by followers—let the leader do it (Fromm, 1941). Followers identify with their successful superiors. According to Henry (1949), business executives see successful superiors as symbols of achievement. In gangs of delinquents the leader becomes the superego of the members, according to Deutschberger (1947). By submitting to the leader, members are relieved of all personal responsibility for their antisocial activities.

*Charisma and Personal Power.* The ultimate in personal power is the charismatic leader, some of whose effects we have already discussed in Chapter 10. The charismatic is endowed by followers with infallibility, wisdom, and often a "touch of the supernatural" (Weber, 1947). Charisma resides in the miraculous transcending power of a religious savior, such as Christ, or of national leaders, such as Winston Churchill or Charles de Gaulle, who became the symbols of national pride, honor, and glory. Charisma has many aspects of personal power: emotional bonding between leaders and followers, father figure dependence, endowment of the leader by followers with omniscience and virtue, supernatural powers, and deep-seated love and affection for the leader by the followers. Charismatics such as the Rev. Jim Jones and the Ayatollah Khomeini have the power to induce the most extremes of behavior—mass suicide and martyrdom—in their followers. Understanding of such personal power requires examination of strong emotional fixations that go beyond ordinary considerations of social exchange, cognition, rewards, and punishments.

### Power of Role and Position

One of the most important powers is to be in a position to reward or punish others. Superiors can be the "purveyors of rewards and punishments" to their subordinates (Krech & Crutchfield, 1948). Such power can be wielded crudely and overtly or with subtlety. Overtly, a superior may have the power to recommend or deny pay increases to subordinates; less obviously, a first-line supervisor, for example, may have power because of influence with even more powerful leaders higher up in the organization (Pelz, 1951). This, in turn, may be due to attitudes of the higher-ups about the role of supervisors lower in the organization as well as to personal attributes and merit of specific supervisors. Pelz found that only those supervisors with influence with higher-ups exhibited behavior that made a difference in their subordinates' satisfactions. Supervisors without influence "upstairs"—although they tried—were much less likely to have effects on their subordinates. Supervisors with influence with higher-ups were much more likely to be able to obtain rewards for their employees. Their power was greater and therefore what they did in their own group made more of a difference to their men.

Hollander (1978) pointed out how a supervisor's position in a hierarchy provides him or her with various sources of power. Supervisors command resources not ordinarily available to subordinates. They have discretion in assigning dirty and boring or interesting and challenging tasks. They can open or close doors to opportunities for the subordinates' growth and advancement. They have power to reduce uncertainty and prolonged anxiety in subordinates by providing hard information. They can act as a buffer to keep their subordinates from becoming too vulnerable to an unstable external environment to sustain optimism and hope.

*Socialization Processes and Power.* Gouldner (1960) maintained that power is based on socializing norms, role differentiation, and organization that binds people together in the same social system. Janda (1960) characterized the power relationship as one where one member is seen to have the right to prescribe behavior patterns for the other.

In many cultures, business transactions are conducted without written contracts because norms of obligation are regarded as binding (Macauley, 1963). Similarly, politicians wield considerable power based on I.O.U.'s through which favors they granted to other politicians in the past can be expected to be reciprocated when the legislators call in their "chits" for past "services rendered." Gilman (1962) agreed that a power relationship is authoritative anywhere within the boundaries of a social system that gives it consensual support (Blau, 1964; Golembiewski, 1967).

### POWER EFFECTS

Research studies of the effects of power are recent in origin. Cartwright (1959), in his review of the literature, listed only thirty-three references, not all experimental. In a later review, Cartwright (1965) listed 180 references, mostly experimental. Nevertheless, in all humility, let us recognize that the ancients were well aware of its effects. For instance, consider what Epictetus said in his discourses on freedom about coercive power in the first century A.D.: no one is afraid of Caesar himself, but he is afraid of death, loss of property, prison, disenfranchisement. Nor does anyone love Caesar himself, unless in some way Caesar is a person of great merit; but we love wealth, a tribuneship, a praetorship, a consulship. When we love and hate and fear these things, it needs must be that those who control them are masters over us. . . . That is how at a meeting of the Senate a man does not say what he thinks, while within his breast his judgment shouts loudly [Starr, 1954, p. 144].

Epictetus was describing the coercive power of the princeps. The occupant of the imperial throne had control over the rewards and punishments to influence behavior overtly, but not necessarily covertly. His power obtained public acceptance but not private commitment.

### Power and Attempts to Lead

One's attempts to lead are increased with increases in one's power, even if the power accrues from a lottery. Bass, Gaier, and Flint (1956) studied male ROTC groups in which members varied in amount of control over each others' rewards for performance. Each member drew a card which determined that he would exercise one, two, three, or four units of control. Members with four units attempted twice as much leadership as those with one unit under high motivation, but the two did not differ under low motivation. Attempted leadership increased with amount of control one obtained in the lottery. But control ceased to have import when what was controlled was unimportant to members. Bass, Pryer, Gaier, and Flint (1958) found that a member attempts more leadership acts when control is high and when what is controlled is strongly desired. Thus, they have *power* to influence when they have *control* over what is desired (Bass, 1960).

Bass, Flint, and Pryer (1957b) and Bass (1963) studied groups varying in motivation and member status level. They found that for an individual to influence group decisions it was necessary to participate. But active participation did not necessarily influence group decision when members varied greatly in status or were highly motivated.

Bass (1961c) found that attempts to lead were more successful among able and esteemed leaders, especially when the congruence between the leader's esteem and self-esteem was great. Similarly, Levinger (1959) found that perceived relative power of a member in a group correlated .55 with number of influence attempts, .51 with range of assertiveness, and .48 with degree of assertiveness of the member. Change in influence attempts tended to change along with change in perceived power as the group continued with the problem.

### Power and Success as a Leader

Michener and Burt (1975) examined the components that determined the success of leaders in inducing compliance. They found that compliance was greater when leaders justified their demands as good for the group, had power to punish persons who did not do as the leaders had asked, and had a legitimate right to make demands of subordinates. Neither the success or failure of the groups nor the approval of the leaders by their subordinates affected the leaders' ability to influence. Gamson (1968) suggested that leaders would shift toward coercion of subordinates if they felt they lacked subordinate approval but did have the legitimate authority for asking for compliance.

*Effects of Leadership Functions.*   Lord (1977) identified twelve functions typically performed by a leader, such as developing plans, proposing solutions, and providing resources. He watched to see how often each leader in his sample displayed the twelve functions. In addition, he determined which motive basis the leaders employed in attempts to exert their power, using the five bases of French and Raven (1959) cited at the beginning of this chapter. Lord then correlated the occurrence of each leadership function with the basis of power the leader used. He found that task behavior to complete the work of the group correlated with the type of power used, but socioemotional relations efforts by the leader did not. For example, the extent to which leaders relied on themselves as experts correlated with the extent to which they proposed solutions, but the extent to which the leaders were liked did not correlate with their socioemotional efforts.

## POWER IN DIFFERENT SITUATIONS

We will now review what is known about the way power, the potential to lead, is distributed in communities, in formal organizations, and in smaller groups.

### Community Power Structures

*Monolithic or Pluralistic?*   The earliest research on power was concerned with the identification of individuals with the potential to influence in localized communities. Lynd and Lynd (1929) pointed the way in their study *Middletown*. F. Hunter (1953) used interviews in a large city to obtain a list of 175 persons mentioned as wielding influence in the community. Reasons were given for believing they had such potential to influence. A panel of experts reduced the list to forty persons regarded as constituting a "monolithic" power structure in the city. On the other hand, Dahl (1961) maintained that the nominating technique hid important details that could be uncovered by a study of community issues, and he traced them to individuals who had played key roles in promoting or blocking the issues. His analysis suggested a pluralistic power structure in the city. Using both the Hunter and Dahl methods, Freeman, Fararo, Bloomberg, and Sunshine (1963) and Presthus (1964) found that the two methods identified a common core of power figures. The Dahl method revealed additional subgroups of individuals who could influence different issues.

*Power and Status.* The status and power structures of various communities were studied by Blumberg (1955), Schulze (1958), Bonjean (1963, 1964), Form and Sauer (1963), Olmsted (1954), Fanelli (1956), Clelland and Form (1964), Wildavsky (1964), and Lowry (1968). Consistently, those identified as having power tended also to rate high in social and economic status. Educational level, as such, was less important (Alford & Scoble, 1968).

Differentiating status, power, and authority may not be as important in smaller communities. V. Williams (1965) studied leadership in small rural communities, finding that some communities were able to function effectively without the differentiation of roles that were specialized in power and authority.

*Interlocking Office Holding.* Perrucci and Pilisak (1970) compiled a list of 434 organizations in a community of 50,000 population. Of 1,677 executives in these organizations, 1,368 held a position in one organization; twenty-six executives occupied positions in four or more organizations; the latter were compared with twenty-six executives occupying only one position. The multi-organizational leaders were regarded by both groups as being more influential on actual and theoretical issues, as more powerful, and were named more often as social and business friends. The multi-organizational leaders were found to constitute a powerful network of influence relationships.

City bosses are a dying breed of community leaders. Mayor Richard Daley of Chicago epitomized the use of social exchange relationships with other bloc leaders and centers of community power to build the powerful political machine that claimed to "make Chicago work." The city boss as a special type of political power figure has been studied in detail by Moos and Koslin (1951), Zink (1930), and Banfield and Wilson (1963).

### Power in Formal Organizations

*Status and Power.* One of the most consistent findings in social science is the general tendency for those higher in status in an organization to wield more power to influence those lower in status. Thus, among many studies of the relationship, Blankenship and Miles (1968) found hierarchical position a more important determinant of managerial decision behavior than size of company or number of subordinates supervised. Nevertheless, interesting exceptions can be cited. General managers may be less influential than their subordinate staff experts. Thus, B. Walter (1966) traced the transmission of influence in two municipal organizations. Staff subordinates were found more influential than their superiors in novel decisions, and superiors were not more influential than subordinates in making decisions.

*Organizational Decentralization.* Legitimate power is usually disseminated outward when an organization decentralizes. The effects were seen by Baum (1961), who studied the U.S. Civil Service Commission and eight other agencies. The commission formulates and enforces policies which must be applied by the agencies in hiring and promoting personnel. Baum found that the decentralization of operational functions (hiring and promotion) were handled effectively only when the agencies accepted, and attempted to comply with, the policies of the controlling commission. Executives in successful agencies regarded delegation as authority, but the poorer agencies saw the delegated function as work.

M. W. Meyer (1968) surveyed 254 city, county, and state departments of finance. With size of organization held constant, Meyer found that with decentralization of decision making, the number of organizational subunits decreased, but the number of levels of supervision increased. Most important, decentralization was associated with an increased development of rules for evaluation of decisions.

*Effects of the Total Amount of an Organization's Power and Control.* A. S. Tannenbaum (1956a,b, 1968) suggested that the power, authority, and control of an organization is a variable rather than a fixed amount. It can be expanded by increasing authority—legitimate power—in one or two levels or in all levels of the organization. An organization tends to gain most in total control of its members when authority is expanded all the way down the line, particularly to its lowest levels. In studies of two industrial plants (1956a) and four labor unions (1956b), Tannenbaum found that organizations of the same type can differ in the amount of authority exercised by executives at different levels and in the total amount of organizational control.

Smith and Tannenbaum (1963) studied 200 units of large firms. They found that the total amount of organizational control was positively and significantly related to member loyalty, member morale, and judged effectiveness, but not to objective measures of effectiveness. Nevertheless, member–officer agreement on ideal amount of control and actual total amount of control over members was related to rated effectiveness. On the other hand, when Smith and Tannenbaum (1965) examined the effects of the total amount of control in women's organizations by their members, total amount of control failed to increase coordination leadership, although such leadership contributed to group effectiveness.

In a study of insurance agencies, Bowers (1964b) found that total organizational control was related to member satisfaction and cost performance, but not to volume of business, growth of business, or personnel turnover. Amount of power at different levels of organization was not associated with effectiveness. Smith and Ari (1964) found that consensus between work group members and between superiors and subordinates is related to total amount of organizational control but not to amount of control of individuals at the work level.

Ivancevich (1970) also studied the effects of the total amount of organization control and member satisfaction in an insurance agency. Agent satisfaction with status, autonomy, and growth was correlated about .30 with control over agency by manager, control over agency by agent, and total amount of organizational control. Agents were equally satisfied whether control was exercised by the manager or by themselves. Likewise, in another study of insurance agencies, Bachman, Smith, and Slesinger (1966) found agent satisfaction highly related to total amount of control, control by manager, and control by agents.

Results of the above studies suggest that organizations differ in the total amount of control exercised by members. The total amount of organizational control is higher when exercised by members in all echelons rather than in one or two levels of the hierarchy. The total amount of control, but not control in the various echelons, is related to productivity and member satisfaction. Members tend to feel more satisfied in some organizations when the top-level leader exercises strong control over organizational activities.

Although not examined, it may be that the key ingredient producing satisfaction and productivity with high total control is that goals and expectations are much clearer for members, and conflict is minimized, than when its opposite—organizational anarchy—exists.

### Power in Experimental and School Settings

*Pecking Orders Observed.* In an observational study of kindergarten children, Hanfmann (1935) found a power structure similar to a pecking order. On the other hand, H. H. Anderson (1937, 1939) studied the dominative and integrative behavior of pairs of children at play in nursery schools and found that dominative behavior on the part of one child tended to stimulate a like response in his or her companion. But dominative was unrelated to integrative behavior. Gellert (1961) observed pairs of preschool children during three play periods. In a significant proportion of the dyads, the same child maintained the same position of dominance or submission during the three play periods, again suggesting that pecking orders were at work.

*Dominance.* Rohde (1951) assembled small groups composed of five members who were high, low, or heterogeneous in dominance. Dominant members were chosen as leaders more often than submissive members, exhibiting significantly more controlling behavior, but they agreed and cooperated more often than submissive members.

*Congruence Necessary.* The importance of congruence of power in role assignment and personality was illustrated by Smelser (1961) who selected students scoring high or low on a personality test of dominance. The most productive groups were composed of pairs in which the dominant partner was assigned a dominant role and the submissive partner a submissive role. The least productive groups were those in which role assignments were reversed.

*Effects of Perceived Power.* Lippitt, Polansky, Redl, and Rosen (1952) studied children in a summer camp and found that self-perceptions of own power were highly correlated with power attributed by others. Those with more attributed powers were better liked, made more attempts to influence others, and scored higher in initiation of behavioral contagion. Consistent with these results, Levinger (1959) demonstrated that members of experimental groups, informed that they had more power than other members, tended to perceive themselves as having more power, became more assertive, and made more attempts to influence others.

*Effects of Actual Power.* As might be expected, Wolman (1956) found a high degree of relation between a leader's power and the leader's acceptability to members as seen by observers and by peer ratings. Again, Ziller (1955) showed that group opinion was influenced more strongly by a high-power than by a low-power figure. As noted earlier, Bass, Gaier, and Flint (1956) and Bass, Pryer, Gaier, and Flint (1958) varied the amount of control that could be exercised by various group members in an experimental task. Such control was obtained by lottery and was the weight assigned to evaluations by members upon which rewards depended. Attempted leadership was highly related to the amount of control a member could exercise.

*Satisfaction with Power.* Blake and Mouton (1961a) asked a supervisor and a subordinate to rank lists of items in order of importance. Each felt better satisfied and more responsible for the task when wielding more power than the other. The level of satisfaction and responsibility of both combined was higher when they alternated in exercising power.

Results of the above studies indicate that groups are better satisfied and more productive when high-power positions are occupied by individuals scoring high in personal dominance. Those members who perceive themselves to have more power tend more than other members to influence group activities. They are better liked than members low in power and their influence attempts are better accepted.

## POWER BASE EFFECTS

Since the French and Raven (1959) classification of the bases of power has become popular in controlled experimentation, we will conclude this chapter by using it to review research that focused on each of the bases' effects on influence and leadership (reward, coercive, legitimate, referent, and expert). The reader should keep in mind that expertise is valued so that personal power sources like expert and referent power are likely to be correlated empirically, that is, lodged in the same people. In the same way, the position holder with power to reward is also likely to have the power to punish. The position will give some degree of legitimacy as well. By definition, formal hierarchies are a structure of legitimate, reward, and coercive power relationships. The question is what happens when one rather than another of these sources of power is emphasized in attempts to influence those with less power. A supervisor can emphasize promises of reward or threats of punishment. Are the effects the same? As we shall see, the effects are quite different. In general, subordinates are more satisfied when their superiors exercise expert and referent power (due to their person) than when they exercise reward, coercive, or legitimate power (usually due to their position).

### Expert Power

It has already been noted (Hemphill, Pepinsky, Shevitz, Jaynes & Christner, 1954) that those members of a group who have the relevant information about a task will attempt leadership. What follows is that such attempts are likely to be successful if one is perceived to be expert and to be effective if one really has the expertise. Groups tend to defer to the actual and the perceived expert. They are likely to be persuaded by the perceived expert, to accept both publicly and privately the expert's opinion (Bass, 1960). Mausner (1953) introduced one student as an art student and another as an art authority. Group opinion was more strongly influenced by the expert than by the student. In another experiment, Mausner (1954b) demonstrated that subjects tend to agree more often with a partner observed to succeed than with one observed to fail. In the same way, Luchins and Luchins (1961) demonstrated that an expert's opinion was more influential than majority opinion of the group in determining group response to a judgmental task. Torrance (1952) and M. A. Levi (1954) both obtained greater improvement on survival problems when groups were fed back expert information after an initial training period. G. M. Mahoney (1953) found employees more satisfied with a wage incentive system when the supervisor was reported to be doing a good job of explaining reasons for changes in the system.

Evan and Zelditch (1961) studied experimental groups with supervisors who differed in knowledge of the task. Differences in supervisor knowledge did not affect group productivity; however, group members exhibited more covert disobedience and resistance to the least informed than to the moderately or well-informed supervisor. This effect was attributed to changes in follower attitude regarding the right of the poorly informed supervisor to occupy the leadership position. (Similar results were reported by G. M. Mahoney [1953] who found workers much more satisfied with a wage incentive system when the supervisor could ably explain reasons for changes in the system.) Collaros and Anderson (1969) studied groups with one expert, all experts, and no experts. Compared to control groups, groups in which all members were told that they were experts were more inhibited in their performance.

*Limitations.* Some qualifications are in order. The stronger status-leadership relation can override expert power. Torrance (1955a) found that high status, rather than knowing the correct answer, contributed more to influencing other members to accept the correct answer to a problem. Again, Torrance and Aliotti (1965) studied groups involved in information seeking with one or two randomly selected students in the role of expert. Groups with two experts obtained more accurate information than those with one expert but were less certain of their judgment. Finally, the impact of expert power has its limits as expressed in the earlier admonition (Chapter 6) that would-be leaders must be able but not too much more able than their followers.

### Referent Power

In Chapter 10, we reviewed the extent to which individuals who are generally esteemed as persons are more likely to be leaders. For instance, Bass (1960) examined seventeen studies of executives in various types of organizations. Esteem as estimated by merit ratings was rather highly related to criteria of "real life" success as a leader. Here we see more of the same result in controlled experimental settings, but with qualifications based on selected experimental manipulations of referent power—the degree to which followers like and respect the leader. Thus, for instance, French and Snyder (1959) found that more highly accepted leaders in experimental groups attempted more influence and had more effective groups than those who were less well accepted. Followers also attempted more influence when accepted by their leader.

*Acceptance, Popularity and Power.* Zander (1953) and Zander and Cohen (1955) introduced two strangers to groups of persons. The one introduced as a high-prestige person felt better accepted and more at ease than the one assigned a low-prestige role, as expressed by group responses. Hurwitz, Zander, and Hymovitch (1953) combined and recombined members of discussion groups of six members each. Each individual rated each other on degree of liking and perceived power and participation. Members with high degrees of power were better liked and participated more often than those low in power.

*Ingratiation.* As mentioned earlier, Bass, Wurster, and Alcock (1961) demonstrated that we want to be esteemed by those whom we esteem. We are more concerned with being liked and accepted by those whom we respect and accept, those who have referent power. This, in turn, may lead to ingratiation—a striving by followers to be valued and rewarded by those they esteem or see as more powerful in other ways as well. A line of investigation by Jones and Jones (1964) suggested that followers who want to be liked by high-power figures employ subtle ingratiation tactics in an effort to gain acceptance. Jones, Gergen, Gumpert, and Thibaut (1965) showed that participants facing the prospect of poor task performance attempted to ingratiate themselves with their experimental supervisor by presenting themselves as strong and competent, but only if the supervisor was open to influence. The use of flattery did not vary with experimental conditions. L. Wheeler (1964) showed that low-power subjects remembered more autobiographical statements made by the high-power figure. However, Wheeler failed to find that participants who are highly dependent on their task leader will use information seeking as a means of ingratiation or to increase their own power. Along similar directions, A. R. Cohen (1958) demonstrated that low-status members who could increase their status in the group tended to communicate in friendly, ingratiating ways, designed to protect and enhance their relations with those controlling the mobility process. But those members with little perceived opportunity for status increase made relatively few such attempts. There may be a rational payoff in ingratiating behavior. Kipnis and Vanderveer (1971) observed that leaders tend to reward their ingratiating followers.

A. R. Cohen (1953, 1959) found that in the face of high power followers experienced more threat in unstructured than in structured groups. Followers low in self-esteem also tended to experience threat in the presence of power, and such threat was intensified in unstructured situations.

### Reward Power

Reward power implies the ability of one individual to facilitate the attainment of desired outcomes by others. Marak (1964) studied groups some of which were rewarded for a correct decision whereas others were not rewarded. Results indicated that the ability to provide rewards was related to leadership as measured by sociometric, interaction, and influence scores. The more valuable the rewards a member could provide, the more closely this ability was related to leadership. Evidence for emergence of a leadership structure was suggested by finding that attempted leadership, actual influence, and rewards for initiating leadership increased as the sessions progressed. Similarly, Herold (1977) showed that subordinate behavior in thirty-two three-member groups depended on the manipulation of monetary rewards by group leaders.

Many of the critical behaviors separating successful from unsuccessful noncommissioned officers in situational tests were found by Flanagan, Levy, et al. (1952) due to the differential reinforcements provided by the noncoms. Successful noncoms more often encouraged their men to follow rules and regulations, gave pep talks when the men were tired, and constantly checked the behavior of their men. However, S. Kerr (1975) noted that leaders as well as organizations in the desire for one kind of behavior unintentionally reward another kind. Greene (1976a,b) completed the first longitudinal study of the effects of rewarding leader behavior and concluded that reward behavior was the cause of subordinate performance. Sims (1977), Sims and Szilagyi (1978), and Szilagyi (1979b) also found a causal relationship between reward behavior and performance in a series of longitudinal studies.

Justis (1975) examined effective leadership as a function of the extent to which followers' rewards depended on the leader's competence and performance. Leader effectiveness and influence were greater the more the leader was seen to be competent and the more followers' rewards depended on the leader's performance.

*Coalition Formation.* Experiments on the distribution of reward power are often designed as bargaining models. Mills (1953) assembled triads in which one member was given high reward power, one medium power, and one low power. A strong tendency was found for two of the members to form a coalition acting in opposition to the third member. Expectations of support from others were found by Lawler (1975) to be a most important cognitive determinant of coalition against inequitable and threatening leaders.

Vinacke and Arkoff (1957) confirmed hypotheses advanced by Caplow (1956) that: (1) when all members of a triad are equal in power all possible combinations will be formed; (2) when two equals are in combination stronger than the third member they will form a coalition in opposition to him or her; (3) when one member is weaker than two equals, he or she will form a coalition with one of them; and (4) when one member is stronger than the other two combined no coalition will ensue. Turk and Turk (1962) confirmed the fourth of the above hypotheses. But Kelley and Arrowood (1960) found that the results reported by Vinacke and Arkoff depend on the clarity of the game and on whether or not a player is assured of a certain return independent of joining a coalition. Caplow (1968) presented a detailed analysis of power relations in the triad.

*Interdependence Effects.* Berkowitz (1957b) studied pairs in which one or both members could earn a reward. The perception of interdependency increased motivation when both members were eligible for valued rewards. Participants were motivated to work toward their partner's reward even though they themselves were not eligible. In the same way, Berkowitz and Daniels (1963) demonstrated that participants work harder for a "supervisor" whose success is dependent upon their performance than when no such dependency relation exists. Berkowitz and Connor (1966) varied both success and dependency for pairs who could win rewards. Participants experiencing failure expressed stronger dislike for their partner the greater their feeling of responsibility toward the partner. Successful participants, however, worked harder for their dependent partner than did the control participants.

*Distributing Rewards.* A norm common to students and workers in the same small-group settings often is "to share and share alike." Thus, Morgan and Sawyer (1967) found that pairs of boys, when permitted to earn equal or unequal rewards, preferred equal rewards, whether their partners were friends or strangers. But perception of the other's expectation played an important part in determining preference. Even ingratiating subordinates who disparaged the competence of their student supervisors failed to modify the allocation of rewards by the supervisor (Fodor, 1974). And when Shriver (1952) gave leaders of discussion groups checks of varying amounts with which they were required to reward the contributions of other members, some leaders solved the problem by drawing lots. Others, after delay and emotional upset, passed out the checks quickly and departed. Shriver interpreted these results as indicating that there are limits to the reward power that an emergent leader can exercise with comfort. Nevertheless, W. P. Smith (1967b) found that participants with a highly valued outcome liked their partners less than those with less highly valued outcomes. Those with little power valued their outcome more highly and used their power more positively than did those with much power.

Yet, equity and loyalty considerations do have an impact on the situation. Thibaut and Faucheux (1965) varied equity and loyalty to group in bargaining to gain. Partners who were told that they had greater power tended to use it; other partners tended to acquiesce. Low-power members appealed for "a fair share" when the high-power members could manipulate rewards, but they appealed to "loyalty" when rewards were manipulated by an outsider. Again, Thibaut and Gruder (1969) found that participants tended to form contractual agreements when they discovered that an agreement restricted the power of each to prevent their joint attainment of maximum outcomes. P. Murdoch (1967) observed that members tended to develop contractual norms when the reward divider was presented as likely to withdraw from the relationship.

Butler and Miller (1965) and McMartin (1970) suggested that participants tend to distribute rewards in proportion to the difference in average rewards received from others. Swingle (1970a) demonstrated that cooperative participants were exploited more when they were powerful than when they were weak, even when such exploitation resulted in reduced reward for the exploiter.

*Effects of Promises to Cooperate for Mutual Benefit.* Tedeschi, Lindskold, Horai, and Gahagan (1969) studied reactions to participants who repeatedly promised to cooperate, but who varied in credibility (degree of cooperation following promises). Powerful teammates ignored the promises and failed to cooperate. Equal-power participants were most cooperative with the willing member. In turn, weak-power subjects became more exploitative as the credibility of promises increased. L. Solomon (1960) demonstrated that unconditional offers of cooperation by one member of an experimental pair is responded to by exploitative behavior and less liking when the two members are of equal power, but conditional offers of cooperation elicit greater cooperation and liking. These differences are reversed in the unequal power situation.

*Precise and Imprecise Power Effects.* W. P. Smith (1968) demonstrated that participants react to imprecise power as compared with precise power by becoming more passive, exhibiting higher satisfaction with outcomes, and maintaining the affiliation for a longer time despite poor outcomes. These results suggest that ambiguous power situations yield comparatively high degrees of control over behavior.

*Antecedents to Usage and Effects.* Hinton and Barrow (1976) showed that leader-reward behavior was most frequently used by leaders who were responsible, confident, and enthusiastic. Studies by Barrow (1976) and Herold (1977) found that leaders were rewarding toward good performers and more punitive toward poor performers. Hunt and Schuler (1976), Oldham (1976), and Sims (1980) found likewise. But, Greenberg and Leventhal (1976) reported that leaders will offer financial bonuses to poor performers to motivate them *when that is the only sanction they have available.*

Bennis, Berkowitz, Affinito, and Malone (1958) studied reward power in a hospital. When rewards given were congruent with those hoped for by subordinates, supervisors exercised more influence than supervisors in hospitals with less effective reward systems. The hospitals were more effective under reward congruency. But supervisors exhibited little awareness of reward preferences and showed still less ability to manipulate rewards for the benefit of the nurses supervised.

According to Hinton and Barrow (1976), who studied 126 male undergraduates in triads involved in a simulated production organization, the tendency to use one of three reinforcing styles was associated with the undergraduates assessed personality, anxiety, and sense of security.

### Coercive Power

Coercive power implies the ability to impose penalties for noncompliance. French and Raven (1959) demonstrated that conformity by followers (public acceptance with private rejection) is a direct function of earlier threats of punishment for noncompliance. French and Raven's emphasis was on punishment. Although coercion most commonly involves punishment and its threat, more subtle uses of power to coerce may involve promises of reward for compliance. One will comply publicly but perhaps not privately (illustrating being under coercion) as a consequence of such promises and one's concern about failing to obtain promised rewards in the absence of compliance. Bass (1960) argued that A has power over B if A can control whether B is rewarded or punished. Seeking reward and the avoidance of punishment, B will behave according to the demands of A (although privately B may reject A).

A clear demonstration of the coercion resulting from power was reported by J. R. P. French and associates (Institute for Social Research, 1954). In laboratory assignments where supervisors could assess monetary fines, subjects exhibited a much greater discrepancy between their public and private reactions than if no fines were established.

*Usage.* Simon (1947) argued that the use of coercive power is hard to avoid in any formal hierarchy for five reasons: (1) we develop expectations for obedience to symbols of higher status; (2) personality needs for security from ''substitute fathers or mothers'' may be in force—the superior can satisfy these needs; (3) the subordinate may share the same goals as the superior and perceive that blind obedience provides a means to the goals; (4) the subordinate is freed from taking responsibility for difficult decisions and the superior bears the burden for the subordinate; and (5) most simply, the superior may be able materially to reward or punish the subordinate.

Subordinates in the industrial organization are coerced by sources in addition to their immediate superiors. They, the subordinates, may have to accept publicly, yet reject privately, the dictates of buyers of the organization's products, contractual agreements with labor unions or industrial cartels, and demands of government, custom, and tradition (Bass, 1960).

Coercive powers dominated supervisory–subordinate relations, according to Goode and Fowler (1949), in a factory where workers had strong needs to remain in the work group: they were marginal, handicapped employees without skills, unable to get jobs elsewhere. Nevertheless, although coercive power figured strongly in their performance, other bases of power were also employed for formal leaders to maintain compliance. Katz, Maccoby, Gurin, and Floor (1951) found that the low-producing railroad section gangs were those led by punitive foremen. Kipnis and Cosentino (1969) studied the types of corrective actions used by military and industrial executives. Industrial supervisors tended to use transfer and leader reprimand. Military supervisors more often used instruction, reassignment, extra work, and reduced privileges as corrective measures.

Boise (1965) studied supervisors' attitudes in the city departments of Police, Street, and Water. Police supervisors tended to disagree with the concept of uniform penalty, while supervisors in the other departments agreed with the concept. Scores on the *F* Scale (authoritarian) were positively related to agreement with the uniform penalty concept. According to T. R. Mitchell (1979), supervisors' recourse to their coercive powers will depend on to what they attribute noncompliance and poor performance by their employees, and on factors within the employee such as ability and motivation or external to the employee such as policy and chance.

Coercive power is most likely to be used to deal with noncompliance. Greene (1976b)'s longitudinal study concluded that supervisors are punitive *in reaction to* poor performance by their subordinates. Goodstadt and Kipnis (1970) studied student work groups under different types of supervisory power. Student supervisors tended to use coercive power to solve disciplinary problems, but they used expert power to solve problems arising from ineptness. Sims (1980) concluded from a review that both longitudinal field and laboratory studies suggested that punishment tends to be more a result than a cause of employee behavior. More specifically, managers tend to increase punitive behavior in response to poor employee performance, but rewards have a much stronger effect on employee performance. Sims and Szilagyi (1975) and Sims (1977) found that use of rewards by leaders generally correlated positively with their subordinates' performance. Punitive leadership had no correlation with subordinate performance for professional and technical groups, but it had a significant inverse correlation with performance in administrative and service subordinates. Szilagyi (1979a) also found that higher levels of punishment tended to follow higher levels of employee absenteeism. Other studies demonstrating the tendency of supervisors to become coercive as a consequence of inadequate subordinate performance were completed by Bankart and Lanzetta (1970), Hinton and Barrow (1975), and Barrow (1976).

Again, illustrating the use of punishment in reaction to other events, including the loss of other bases of power, Greene and Podsakoff (1979) found that after a contingent (positive reinforcement) pay plan at two paper plants had been abandoned, supervisors began to use rewards less and punishment more. Fodor (1976) likewise found that leaders were more authoritarian and coercive with disparaging and disruptive subordinates: they rated such subordinates lower and gave them less pay than other subordinates. In this same study Fodor noted that supervisors subjected to group stress (see Chapter 26) also tended to become more coercive and less rewarding.

*Supports for Coercive Power.* Legitimacy coupled with coercion will increase the public and private acceptance of coercive demands. In a study of experimental groups, Levinger, Morrison, and French (1957) found that the threat of punishment induced conforming behavior on the part of group members before punishment, but not after punishment. Most to the point was the fact that the perceived legitimacy of punishment reduced resistance to conformity. Particularly important is the support of the status structure. Iverson (1964) presented taped speeches by persons identified as high or low in status. Listeners formed more favorable personality impressions of high-status than of low-status speakers who made punitive remarks. Another support for ready obedience are immature participants. Kipnis and Wagner (1967) found that immature participants performed better than mature participants under a leader whose decisions to administer punishment were backed up by superior authority. Brass and Oldham (1976) examined the reactions of first-line supervisors to an in-basket simulation. Overall, the supervisors punished more often than they rewarded. The leadership effectiveness of the foremen was rated by their respective superintendents. The more active supervisors (see Chapter 22), who used both more reward and more coercive power, were rated as more effective by their superintendents.

Based on available theory and research, Arvey and Ivancevich (1980) offered a set of propositions outlining the conditions under which punishment is likely to be effective in organizational settings. It should be delivered as close as possible to the time of the undesired subordinate behavior. It should be moderate in intensity. It should be delivered by an otherwise close and friendly supervisor. It should be consistent. It should be accompanied by explanation. Alternatives to the undesired behavior should be available.

*Resistance to Coercive Power.* Milgram (1965b) instructed students to activate a device which supposedly administered electric shock to subjects who made errors in a learning experiment. It was found that, upon command, students were willing to administer "dangerous" degrees of shock. These findings were interpreted as indicating that individuals exhibit strong tendencies to obey authority. But later, Milgram demonstrated that when students administering shock were permitted to observe two other individuals who refused to do this, the number of refusals was significantly increased. Stotland (1959) found that when participants were required to work with a domineering supervisor, they tended to identify with the supervisor. However, when able to interact with a peer from another group they would exert more independence from the power figure, show more hostility toward him, and exhibit greater motivation to reach the goal despite the supervisor's hindrance. French, Morrison, and Levinger (1960) observed that greater threat of punishment induces greater conformity after threat, but not after the threat has terminated. Resistance after threat reduces conformity. The strength of resistance varies inversely with attraction to the power figure. Strength of attraction decreases with threat and punishment. Resistance decreases as perceived legitimacy increases.

A form of "group compensation" may arise, according to Stotland (1959), as a reaction to attempts to coerce if the opportunity is made available to do so. Individuals subject to the veto power of a "supervisor" used models to design a city. Work was interrupted twice. Some of the participants were given the opportunity to meet privately in the absence of the "supervisor." Others were not. Those who met privately became much more aggressive and hostile toward the supervisor. Those not meeting continued to accept the supervisor publicly. Private assembly permitted formation of an informal organization to present a unified front against continued attempts to coerce the participants. In sum, threat of punishment tends to induce compliance. Leaders exercising coercive power are found less attractive than those using other methods of influence. Group members are better able to resist coercive power when they have an opportunity to interact with peers or to observe other members who disobey.

Resisting attempts by superiors to exercise their coercive power may be productive. Horwitz, Goldman, and Lee (1955) demonstrated that students frustrated by the arbitrary refusal of a teacher to repeat instructions were much more likely to shift to more favorable attitudes toward the teacher, be less annoyed, and regard the teacher as less coercive when the teacher read student opinions and agreed to repeat instructions than when the teacher was informed by "higher authority" that the instructions should be repeated. Problem-solving and learning were best when direct action could be taken by students to "reform" the coercive teacher, somewhat less efficient when they could only state their grievances, and poorest when they were led to perceive that all the other students accepted the coercive teacher's refusals to repeat instructions.

*Unintended Consequences of Coercion.* Well-known are the side effects of coercion. The costs of depending on coercive power in formal organizations are well-known. For instance, satisfaction with supervision is almost uniformly lower. Thus, whereas life insurance agents' satisfaction was related positively to referent and expert power exercised by the manager, it was related negatively to perceived degree of reward and coercive and legitimate powers exercised by the agency manager (Bachman, Smith & Slesinger, 1966). Weschler, Kahane, and Tannenbaum (1952) observed that a research laboratory headed by a coercive leader was more productive but less satisfying to its members than another laboratory under less coercive leadership. Zander and Curtis (1962) found that participants evaluated their performance and were less motivated to perform a coercive rather than referent relationship with other participants. In the coercive situation they found each other less attractive and less well accepted than in the referent situation. Weiss and Fine (n.d.) found that participants who had experienced insult and failure were receptive to arguments to be hostile and punitive, whereas comparable participants given satisfying experiences were more ready to accept communications to be lenient. Hostility toward power figures who can coerce other members was also found by Stotland (1959).

Participants may withdraw from the problems at hand to avoid being coerced. Withdrawal from the important problems was noted by Riecken (1952) as a reaction to the frustration of coercion. Oldham (1976) related personal punishment by leaders to evaluations of their subordinates' effectiveness. Generally, punishment was not consistently associated with subordinate performance, but leader punitiveness was negatively correlated with subordinate motivational effectiveness.

A line of investigation beginning with Janis and Feshbach (1953) generally supports the contention that a high degree of threat is less productive than moderate or mild threats. In the prototype experiment, conditions of strong, mild, and minimal fear were included in propaganda about dental hygiene, and resistance to counterpropaganda was measured by Janis and Feshbach. Minimum fear arousal appeared to provide the most persistent influence. Maximum fear arousal resulted in ignoring or avoiding the influence attempts (a form of withdrawal) or the development of conflicting tendencies to minimize the importance of the threatening propaganda. Based on similar findings, Kelman (1953) argued that when coercion is too great, interfering responses and hostility toward the coercer made participants less prone to accept influence attempts.

### Legitimate Power

Legitimate power is based on norms and expectations held by group members regarding behaviors appropriate in a given role or position. The legitimation of a role is derived from such norms and expectations. Power is but one aspect of role definition.

French and Raven (1959) suggested three bases of legitimate power: (1) cultural values endowing some members with the right to exercise power; (2) occupancy of a position organized to confer authority; and (3) appointment or designation by a legitimizing agent. According to Michener and Burt (1975a, 1975b), studies of college students indicated that endorsement of the leader's rights to exercise power were not as important in their compliance as recognition of the authority of the leader's office.

The importance of legitimate power was illustrated in an experiment by Mulder et al. (1966) who varied the power distance between leaders and followers by permitting leaders to distribute rewards of different amounts. The legitimate leader was elected by the group. The illegitimate leader forced himself into the experimental control booth and took over the leadership function. Under conditions of large power distance, followers resisted the illegitimate leader more than the legitimate leader. Likewise, P. B. Read (1974) demonstrated the importance of perceived legitimacy in a study of mock trial juries.

Hollander and Julian (1969) demonstrated that leaders are in the best possible condition to get things done if they have emerged in the group and then been elected by the members. Election gives followers a greater sense of responsibility for the leadership. They share heightened expectations for the leader's performance (Hollander, 1978). If the leaders are also confident in themselves, they are likely to use their legitimate power as well as persuasion instead of punishment to correct poor performance (Goodstadt & Kipnis, 1970).

*Sources.* Bleda, Gitter, and d'Agostino (1977) observed that enlisted personnel's satisfaction with army life was related more to the leadership of those who were seen as the originators rather than the relayers of daily orders to them.

*Subordinates' Status.* Vecchio (1979) showed that legitimate power was particularly important in the performance of those subordinates who were not part of the leader's "inner circle" of confidants and trusted assistants. These inner circle subordinates did best when their superiors did not possess power due to their formal positions. The inner circle was most optimistic about its leader when the out-group treated their leader in a friendly rather than in a hostile manner (Koulack, 1977).

*Sources of Enhancement in Legitimate Power.* In addition to such familiar augmentations of legitimacy as symbols of office and inheritance, experiments have shown that legitimacy is enhanced through permanency rather than temporariness of office, election rather than emergence as a leader, and appointment by higher authority rather than election. Torrance (1954) studied decision making in established and newly formed groups. The members' influence on decision making was found to depend on their position in the power structure of the group and to be stronger in permanent than in transitory groups. Further, Raven and French (1958a) examined groups with elected and emergent leaders, although the authors concluded that "the very occupation of a key position in a structure lends legitimacy to the occupant." Elected leaders were better liked and their influence was better accepted than that of emergent leaders. Anderson, Karuza, and Blanchard (1977) found that individuals elected to an undesirable rather than a desirable leadership position had greater social power. Appointment made no difference.

Julian, Hollander, and Regula (1969) found that the appointed leaders in experimental groups had a source of authority perceived to give them stability in their positions. But election, rather than making the leaders more secure, made them more vulnerable to censure if they later proved inadequate. Members were most willing for the leaders to continue in their positions when they were competent in the task, interested in group members, and involved in group activities.

*Sources of Reduction in Legitimate Power.*  Countervailing power can reduce legitimacy; failure can offset it. Caplow (1968) observed that a majority coalition formed in opposition to the leader may not only undermine the legitimacy of his or her position but may in fact assume the leadership function.

Worthy, Wright, and Shaw (1964) created groups in which a confederate of the investigators accused a naïve teammate of losing the game. Other group team members were less willing to interact with the accused than with others when the accusation was legitimate. They were less willing to interact with either the accused or the accuser in the nonlegitimate situation. Thus, we see that members tend to accept the position of the leader and his or her influence as legitimate when the leader holds attitudes in conformity with norms of the group or organization. Appointment or election to a position tends to legitimize the leadership role to a greater extent than emergence through interaction or capture by force.

## MORE ON BASES OF POWER

### Comparisons in Usages and Effects

Willingness to use one power rather than another was seen by Rosenberg and Pearlin (1962), who studied the attitudes of 1,138 hospital nurses toward power. Among these, 54 percent stated that they would use persuasion; 38 percent, benevolent manipulation; 5 percent, legitimate authority; 1 percent, contractual power; and 2 percent, coercive power.

Ivancevich (1970) reported that life insurance agent satisfaction correlated .35 with use of referent power, expert power, and reward power by the agency manager. But satisfaction correlated − .28 with use of coercive power and .14 with use of legitimate power by the manager. Again, Bachman (1968) found that college faculty members are better satisfied under deans with high power (control over college affairs) whose influence was based on expert and referent power rather than under deans who rely on reward, legitimate, or coercive power. However, in a study of salesmen's perceptions of branch managers' power, Ivancevich and Donnelly (1970) found that coercive and legitimate powers were not related to productivity. Only expert and referent powers were positively related to productivity.

### Proposed Improvements in the Power Model

Filley and Grimes (1967) studied forty-four full-time professional employees in a nonprofit organization who reported to a single director and an associate director. Members were interviewed about hypothetical incidents which might require them to seek a decision from the director or associate director. Respondents were asked about whom to go to for a decision, to whom they would like to go, and to whom they would in fact go, and why. Answers to the "why" questions were classified according to the bases of power to which the organization members responded.

**TABLE 11.1**
**A Framework for Analyzing Social Influence, with Some Examples**

| Person exerting influence | | | Target(s) of influence | | | |
|---|---|---|---|---|---|---|
| *Characteristics* | *Resources* | *Decision role with respect to target* | *Characteristics* | *Needs* | *Decision role with respect to influencer* | *Effect of influencer on target* |
| Expertise; special training, special experience, etc. | Knowledge about how to reach certain goals | Investigates, makes tests, gives information to others | Unexpert | Wants to find best ways to reach goals | Reviews information presented by experts | Sees new options; sees new favorable or unfavorable consequences following various actions |
| Occupies important position in hierarchy | Control over material rewards (money, promotion, etc.) | Makes request, coupled with promise of reward for compliance | Occupies less important position in hierarchy | Wants rewards controlled by influencer | Decides whether to accede to request of others | Compliance seen as means to reward |
| Occupies important position in hierarchy | Control over material penalties (fines, demotions, etc.) | Gives orders, coupled with threats of punishment for noncompliance | Occupies less important position in hierarchy | Wants to avoid punishment but maintain self-esteem | Decides whether to accede to order | Compliance seen as way of avoiding penalty but may be seen as blow to self-esteem |

SOURCE: Patchen, 1974.

**TABLE 11.1**
**A Framework for Analyzing Social Influence, with Some Examples**
*(Continued)*

| Person exerting influence | | | Target(s) of influence | | | |
| --- | --- | --- | --- | --- | --- | --- |
| *Characteristics* | *Resources* | *Decision role with respect to target* | *Characteristics* | *Needs* | *Decision role with repsect to influencer* | *Effect of influencer on target* |
| Strong; successful; has attractive qualities | Approval | States own opinions, preferences | Less strong, less successful | Wishes to be similar to, approved by, influencer | Hears opinions, preferences of influencer | Seeks compliance as way of being similar to, approved by, influencer |
| Occupies legitimate position of authority; secured position by legitimate methods | Symbols of legitimacy; label of others' action as right or wrong | Announces decision; asks for support | Occupies position of subordination; accepts legitimacy of others' position | Wishes to fulfill moral obligations | Gets request from authority | Sees conformity to requested action as morally correct |
| Is affected by certain decisions (by virtue of work needs, responsibilities, etc.) | Own cooperation (may also have some resources listed in other rows) | Vigorously makes preference known to others | Peers or final decision-making authority | Want high level of cooperation from influencer | Decides whether to accept recommendation | Sees accepting recommendation as leading to future cooperation by influencer |

SOURCE: Patchen, 1974.

Twelve different bases were detected. For example, instead of one category for legitimate power, several emerged, including power based on formal authority, responsibility, control of resources, bureaucratic rules, and traditional rules.

Patchen (1974) suggested that the French and Raven classification was limited. It was inadequate because the various bases of power were not defined in a conceptually parallel way. Thus, reward power and coercive power are defined in terms of resources available to the influencer. Referent and legitimate power are described in terms of the characteristics and motives of the target person. Finally, "expert power" depends on characteristics of the influencer and resources he or she possesses.

Patchen created a scheme, shown in Table 11.1, which looks at power in terms of the characteristics and roles of the person exerting the influence as well as the characteristics of the target person, the resources available to the person with power and the needs to be fulfilled, and the effects on the targeted person. Student (1968) also had problems with the French and Raven classification. He regarded referent power and expert power as sources of "incremental influence" that characterize the individual, whereas reward power, legitimate power, and coercive power are organizationally derived. He found that supervisory scores on incremental influence, referent power, and expert power were positively and significantly related to quality of group performance and to costs. But average earnings declined with reward power of the supervisor, and maintenance costs of the group rose with coercion.

We now turn to a basic key to understanding groups, organizations, and societies—the distribution of power.

# 12 POWER DISTRIBUTION AND LEADERSHIP

## DISTRIBUTION OF POWER

The distribution of power has been a main theme in both political history and the history of management–worker relations. Although leadership resulting from power—particularly coercive power and to a lesser extent personal, reward, and legitimate power—may guarantee public success and acceptance, resistance, privately at least, yields unintended consequences such as mentioned in Chapter 11. Power sharing, leveling, and equalization are seen by many behavioral science theorists (Lippitt, 1942; R. Likert, 1961a; McGregor, 1960; and Argyris, 1957) as approaches to developing among followers full commitment and acceptance, both public and private.

### Power Distribution and Group Power

In some groups, most of the power resides in the leader; in others, it may be widely shared, equalized among members and leader.

With such power equalization, the members become as influential as the leader and their effects on each other become important to the interpersonal influence process. Thelen (1954) noted the power and control of the group over its members. Group agreements ''have teeth in them.'' The determination of what is possible, at what cost or with what reward, is under the control of the group. Leadership occurs in changing the agreements and working out new ones to fit the continual diagnosis of realities in the group-problem situation.

According to Tannenbaum and Massarik (1950), sharing in decision making increases the likelihood that workers will accept goals desired by management, resulting in greater worker satisfaction and increased efforts to move toward the selected goals. Likewise, McGregor (1944) argued that worker effectiveness will be increased with opportunities to participate in solutions of problems and discussions of actions affecting themselves and with opportunities to assume responsibilities when ready for them. For if members of a group participate to some extent in setting goals, they will be more motivated to achieve the goals. If they have the capabilities, they can be delegated more responsibility or freedom to act without review by higher authority (Learned, Ulrich & Booz, 1951).

*Variance Effects.* Bovard (1951a) observed that in groups of little status differentiation where all have similar power to influence each other, verbal interaction is higher and more influencing is attempted than when a single person of higher status alone

**192**

directs activities. More persistence in the face of rejection is likely to be required of the would-be leader of the group where all members are equal in status and power.

Status and power differentiation in a group results in inhibition of the ventilation of feelings by the members lower in the status and power hierarchy. Thus, Thibaut and Coules (1952) demonstrated that the communication of hostility toward instigators will reduce the residual hostility toward them. Furthermore, when all members are equal in status and power, more communication of feelings will occur (Bovard, 1952). However, in groups with members varying in status and power, the low-status members will be less likely to communicate their feelings upward.

This does not mean that all communications are easier when members are equal in status and power. Shepherd and Weschler (1955) studied work groups that differed in status stratification. Although groups with little status differentiation exhibited higher rates of mutual sociometric choice and fewer expressed communication difficulties, they did experience more inferred communication difficulties.

### Power Distribution and Organizational Structure

Power equalization is a basic tenet of modern organizational development (Bennis, 1965) and the human potential movement (Maslow, 1965). It has its roots in those aspects of democratic and equalitarian values which stress the importance of dependence on informal trusting relationships rather than on a formal structure where relations depend upon authority of position and role requirements. Practical applications have included unstructured leadership, job enlargement, leadership sharing, participative management, consultative supervision, joint consultation, workers' councils, and other forms of industrial democracy. Thus, Patchen (1970), who administered questionnaires to ninety employees in plants operated by the TVA, found that degree of workers' control over their jobs was significantly correlated with their general job interest, concern with work innovation, and pride in work.

*Structuralism versus Behaviorism.* Bass and Ryterband (1979) have summarized the differences between the power equalization as espoused by behaviorists and structural approaches. Structuralism—as enunciated by classical management theorists such as Taylor, Urwick, and Davis—depends on external constraints to yield compliance and commitment of followers. Power equalization is expected to gain even more commitment as well as compliance through individual awareness and insight into effective interpersonal relations and trust.

Structuralism calls for someone to be responsible for supervising all essential activities. The industrial pyramid of supervisor–subordinate relationships is mandated. Power sharing proposes that any group member take on leadership responsibilities as the member sees the need to do so. The autonomous team with no formally appointed leader is the extreme example.

Structuralism avoids duplication or overlapping of responsibilities. However, overlapping, cross-training, rotation, and other forms of sharing responsibilities to increase system reliability are encouraged by behaviorists when informal relationships are developed between workers committed to see that their group prospers.

Job simplification is fundamental to a structuralist approach. No individual should be responsible for a wide assortment of unrelated acts. In opposition are behaviorists calling for job enlargement and job enrichment. Subordinates become closer in power to superiors because they receive bigger jobs to do with greater responsibilities.

The extreme structural position calls for subordinates to receive clear, written job specifications and role assignments on how they must complete their tasks. The extreme behavioral position calls for making goals clear and allowing subordinates, commensurate with their training and experience, to decide how to reach the goals.

Both structuralists and behaviorists agree that authority should be delegated so that decisions take place as close as possible to the action. For structuralists, the decision maker is the superior in the situation; for behaviorists, as much as possible, the decision is shared or delegated to the subordinates.

Structuralists emphasize the chain of command. Behaviorists argue that organizations require much communicating, reporting, proposing, influencing, complying, and deciding with complex diagonal and horizontal paths not shown on the formal organizational charts. Again, participants need some sense of power equalization for this flow to occur effectively.

Allee (1945), Whyte (1953), and Simon (1957) argued for structure, power, and status differentiation; they felt that hierarchical organization is the natural, biological, and sociological solution for ensuring group survival. Thus, R. B. Cattell (1953) hypothesized that status differentiation promotes decision speed and faster goal attainment. Communication-net studies (Chapter 28) such as by McCurdy and Eber (1953) support this contention. On the other hand, Argyris (1957) and McGregor (1960) were equally convinced that individuals, motivated by basic desires for autonomy and self-actualization, are frustrated by organizational structure, specialization of work, and philosophies of management that assume that workers will remain complacent and unproductive unless subjected to controls frustrating worker initiative.

Neither extreme has a monopoly on the truth. Situational elements and individual preferences, as we shall see later, strongly affect which approach pays off. Some pupils thrive in schools with a great deal of freedom in choosing what and how to learn. Other pupils do best in a highly structured environment. Juvenile delinquents who adjust most readily to institutionalization, once back on the streets may have more difficulty in avoiding antisocial, criminal behavior. Young professional knowledge workers are likely to demand more power equalization than older, unskilled employees. The optimum power differentiation is likely to lie between the extreme structuralist and extreme behaviorist positions depending on the situation. In the 1980s, in our pluralistic society, the only thing we can safely say is that wide differences in performance, attitudes, and response to hierarchy are likely to depend on task, time, place, immediate needs, and the like.

*Legitimacy of Hierarchy.* Legitimate differences in power are manifested in an organization in how much members' roles in the organization are structured; that is, prescribed, bound by rules and regulations or the dictates and policies of higher authority. An infantry squad is highly structured; an initially leaderless group discussion is not. There is a clear legitimate hierarchy of power from the squad leader down to the new private. Initially, there is no hierarchy in the leaderless group discussion.

*Power and Status Differentiation.* The move toward power dispersion in rural communities was described from 189 interviews and from the reconstructed history of a county in the southeastern United States since 1900 by Nix, Dressel, and Bates (1977).

Stages included bossism, informal cliques, organized pluralism, bifactionalism, multi-factionalism, and amorphous leadership. Accompanying the dispersion of power were increasing community complexity and division of labor.

Equality in status and power are more commonly found when familiarity, homogeneity, and the potential to interact among members is high. Caplow and Forman (1950) observed that when neighborhoods contained families homogeneous in length of residence, interests, and type of dwelling, no status differentiation occurred. Form (1945) reported similar findings for Greenbelt, Maryland, when it was newly established as a community for federal white-collar employees of similar occupations, age, nativity, and housing. In the same way, Munch (1945) found that the homogeneous inhabitants of isolated Tristan da Cunha in the South Atlantic can maintain their community without status differentiation and institutionalized government.

Bass (1960) argued that by creating greater differences in power and status between leader and followers, one can increase the proportion of success of the leader's leadership acts. This was observed by Hemphill, Seigel, and Westie (1951) in a study of 100 groups varying in status differentiation. Such leadership was also likely to be more dominating, directive, and coercive, and more likely to define and structure the work for the membership. Again, as expected, a related study of 212 air crews by Rush (n.d.) found air crew commanders much less considerate of their subordinates when the crews were highly stratified.

Situational factors contribute to power equalization or differentiation. Nix, Dressel, and Bates (1977) reported that power is more likely to be dispersed in rural communities. Historically, it moves from initial bossism to informal cliques.

*Measurement of Power Distribution.* Power distribution is ordinarily inferred from observing the variance among members of a group in the success of their efforts to influence each other. This leads to a pure tautology. Observed differences in influence indicates the distribution of power; differential power begets differential influence. Power equalization is seen in shared leadership. Power differences are also inferred from status differences. The general has more power than the colonel.

Measuring the responsibility, authority, and delegation associated with a position is a more direct way to tap an incumbent's power. These will be discussed in Chapter 14. Another direct measure of power differentiation independent of observed influence and status was originated by Bass and Valenzi (1974). Subordinates and managers were asked to describe the power—mainly legitimate—the manager had over the system, which included the manager and his or her subordinates, and the power the subordinates had over the same system. Questionnaire items dealing with the manager's power over the system included the extent to which the manager had the power to override or veto any decision subordinates made, grant or deny promotion or salary increases to subordinates, reverse the priorities of subordinates, control the size of subordinate budgets, and get higher authority's support for what the manager wanted to do.

Although not ordinarily and formally recognized, the subordinate may have various amounts of power over the system including the power to bring outside pressure to support what the subordinate wants; do the opposite of what the manager wants done; maintain final control over his or her own plans, assignments, and targets regardless of what the manager thinks about them; submit his or her own requests to higher authority ignoring the manager; and nominate or vote for who will be the manager.

Bass and Valenzi obtained alpha coefficients of .60 for the reliability of both management's and subordinates' power based on simple summation of responses to scales of extent. On scores ranging from 1 to 9, superiors' power is typically above 6 while subordinates score below 4. Shapira (1976), using small-space analysis, showed that the differences between managerial and subordinate power when combined with the information each had could predict, according to theoretical expectations, which style of leadership would be most often displayed by the manager. Managers with more power and information relative to their subordinates were most directive; managers with more power but less information than their subordinates were most consultative; managers with more information but less power were most negotiative; and managers with less power and information relative to their subordinates were most delegative. (Chapter 19 will discuss these leader styles.)

Kotter (1978) plied a different route to studying power differences in organization. His interviews focused on whom the incumbent in a particular management position felt dependent and on the incumbent's efforts to obtain cooperation, compliance, and deference from others in the system. Integrating these concerns about power and dependence with concern for the organization's goals is seen as the key to effective performance and is consistent with McClelland and Burnham's (1976) demonstration that effective managers have strong needs for power (Chapter 9) but are oriented toward organizational goals rather than self-aggrandizement.

## THE POWER OF THE GROUP

Power sharing with all members of a group does not necessarily mean increased member initiative and freedom. On the contrary, powerful groups can more strongly constrain and influence their individual members than any individual leader with power might be able to do. Mere membership in a group makes a difference. Deutsch and Gerard (1954) found that individuals formed in a group were more influenced by observed standards than those not in a group. Katz and Lazarsfeld (1955) observed that people are more likely to change their opinions if their small group of family or friends are undergoing a similar change. The changes are also more likely to persist if supported by such group affiliations. In the same way, individuals are more influenced by mass media when listening in groups than when alone.

Socialization processes in organizations are a familiar observation. After liberal students enter the world of work, they tend to adopt more conservative attitudes involving the norms of the firms they join. S. Lieberman (1954) found that workers promoted to foremen tended to shift attitudes toward favoring management as they became members of management. Workers with the same attitudes of those who became foremen, but who subsequently were elected as union shop stewards, shifted attitudes in the union direction after twelve months in office as stewards.

### The Tendency to Conform

Conradi (1905), H. T. Moore (1921), Bechterew and Lange (1931), Wheeler and Jordan (1929), Marple (1933), Thorndike (1938), and Hilgard, Sait, and Magaret (1940) demonstrated the tendency of members of a group to shift in attitudes and behavior of the group.

Bass (1957b), Hare (1953), and McKeachie (1954) found in various experiments that members increase more in agreement with each other, both publicly and privately, after holding a group discussion than by reading or listening to arguments. Generally, such group discussion leads to improvement in members' understanding, commitment, and decision-making. But the reverse is also true. "Groupthink" was seen by Janis (1972) as the reason why highly competent members made extremely poor collective decisions such as occurred in the Bay of Pigs fiasco. Highly cohesive, they assumed a unanimous view when it did not exist. Conformity occurred out of a sense of mutual loyalties to the group.

*Behavioral Change.* In accordance with K. Lewin's (1943) prototype experiment in influencing housewives' meat choice behavior, group discussion will produce more member change than individual argumentation. Group discussion has been found superior to lecture techniques in modifying food habits, merit-rating tendencies of supervisors, prejudice, hostile attitudes, solutions to community problems, alcoholism, and emotional disturbances in children (Lichtenberg & Deutsch, 1954). In addition, Radke and Klisurich (1947) observed that mothers of newborn infants, who engaged in discussion among themselves under the leadership of a dietician and eventually reached group decisions coinciding with the usual recommended procedures, adopted the desired behavioral patterns much more effectively than a control group receiving individual instruction. Similarly, Levine and Butler (1952) significantly reduced the halo effect in merit ratings by foremen by permitting them to discuss and make decisions regarding more realistic evaluations. Torrance and staff (1955) found that B-29 crews were more likely to reach a state of efficiency enabling them to go into combat if earlier in survival school the crews had been observed to participate in decision making.

Coch and French (1948), J. R. P. French (1950), and French and Zander (1949) reported the results of an experiment in a clothing manufacturing plant. The factory had experienced considerable labor turnover after each change in operating methods. The experimenters studied four groups of employees. For the control group, a change was merely announced. For three experimental groups, the workers were given an opportunity to discuss the change, to offer suggestions, and to agree on the necessity for the change. Productivity increased and personnel turnover decreased in the experimental groups but not in the control group.

The same plant studied by Coch and French and a second plant acquired by merger were studied in 1962, 1964, and 1969 by Seashore and Bowers (1963, 1970) and by Marrow, Bowers, and Seashore (1968). Both managers and workers were given group training in joint problem solving. Employee satisfaction did not change to a marked degree; however, employee task commitment improved and productivity norms were raised. Productivity also increased.

Ronken and Lawrence (1952) studied a firm experiencing difficulties in communication. Small groups and committees were formed to discuss and analyze the problem and to suggest solutions. Communications were freed and operations were conducted more smoothly. Lawrence and Smith (1955) compared groups of workers setting their own production goals with other groups that merely discussed production problems. Groups setting their own goals showed significantly greater increases in productivity.

Lawler and Hackman (1969) reported experimental results using group power to develop a pay incentive plan for maintenance crews. Three groups developed their own pay incentive plans to reward good attendance on the job. The plans were then imposed on other groups. One type of control group was given a lecture about job attendance; another received no experimental treatment. Only the groups developing their own plans increased in attendance.

*Attitude Change.* Sharma (1955) surveyed 568 teachers in twenty school systems. Teacher satisfaction was related to the extent to which they reported that they were involved in decision making as individuals or as groups. Zander and Gyr (1955) examined employees' attitudes toward a merit rating system. Significant attitude change required monthly feedback. Consultation and discussion were somewhat more effective than mere explanations of the system. In addition, under both conditions it was found that attitude change occurred only when the supervisor was described by subordinates as sincere, when he or she knew the plan and the issues, when supervisors and subordinates agreed in opinions, and when the supervisor skilled as chairman.

*Subtle Influences.* In a series of well-known experiments, Asch (1952) showed that conformity to a simulated group opinion can be induced even when the group decision defies the senses. A fair proportion of participants will agree that the clearly shorter of two lines is longer if they see all the other persons (all confederates) in the same situation stating that the shorter line is the longer one.

More subtle influences of group power were measured by M. L. Hoffman (1956) and Horwitz (1954). Hoffman confronted participants with group norms alternately agreeing and disagreeing with the participant's own responses. Psychogalvanic skin responses of participants suggested that tension was reduced when they believed themselves to have conformed to the group rather than when they saw themselves in disagreement with others. Horwitz (1954) found that members were under greatest tension, according to their greater recall of interrupted tasks (Zeigarnik effect), when they personally voted not to continue when the group voted to continue the task.

*Persistence.* Conformity effects persist even after the group disbands. When partners are separated after experiencing a judging situation together, they continue to exert mutual influence on each other's judgments when asked to judge alone (E. Cohen, 1956). The tendency to be affected in this way was found by Bovard (1948) to persist for at least twenty-eight days.

*Output Restriction.* Well-known are the signs of conformity of worker performance as a consequence of the work group's power over its members. Fear of "rate-busting" and of management lowering the price per piece paid to workers results in distributions of outputs of workers which peak at an arbitrary limit set by the group. The variance in output is not normal; the distribution is truncated at the upper end (Rothe, 1946, 1947, 1949, 1960, 1961; Rothe & Nye, 1958, 1959).

### Effects of Increased Group Power

The more power the work group has over its members, the less difference will be seen in the output of its members. Thus, Seashore (1954) found less variance in productivity among different members of the more cohesive of 228 factory groups.

The more members expect to be rewarded and to avoid punishment through membership in the group, the more they value the group, and the more the group will have the power to produce conformity in the Asch line-judging experiment (Deutsch & Gerard,

1954). Gerard (1954) noted that the greater the attraction of the members to a group, the more they coalesced in opinion. Gorden (1952) observed more conformity by members who were identified most with the group. Similarly, Newcomb (1943) observed that the extent to which Bennington College students wanted to "belong" on campus determined the extent to which they shifted their social attitudes in the direction of the modal prevailing, liberal attitudes on campus. Again, Rasmussen and Zander (1954) found that teachers' level of aspiration conformed more to the ideal of their group, the more they were attracted to the group, that is, saw the group as potentially rewarding.

*Visibility and Salience of the Group.*  Groups will exert more power over their members when their members' behavior is visible rather than unobservable (Deutsch & Gerard, 1954). The conformity effects can be increased by giving the group more power by making it more important to its members. For example, Dickinson (1937) observed that the effectiveness of group wage incentives depend on mutual policing. Members working for group rewards are more likely to keep up with each other in groups sufficiently small to permit effective mutual observation. Again, members of such groups, rewarded as groups, were found by Grossack (1954) to demand more uniformity from each other than did individuals competing with others for rewards.

Significant to a group's power over its members is whether the members are clear concerning the modal or majority opinion of the other members. The clearer the members are as to what they must conform, the more they are likely to conform. In judging intelligence from photos, participants tended to shift their judgments toward the group decision if they obtained knowledge of the decision (S. C. Goldberg, 1954). Gorden (1952) observed that when expressing their public opinion, members of a cooperative living project tended to be influenced by what they perceived to be group opinion. Bennett (1955) found more compliance with a request for volunteers among those who perceived most others doing the same. Pennington, Haravey, and Bass (1958) obtained the greatest objective increase in agreement among members in groups where members made public their initial opinions in discussion or when a group decision was announced. Coalescence of opinion was less when either decision or discussion was absent and it was least when both were absent. Similarly, in studies of autokinetic judgment, N. Walter (n.d.) found that agreement among participants decreased when information concerning the judgments of typical students in an esteemed school was no longer given to them.

## POWER, LEADERSHIP, AND STRUCTURE

As noted earlier, power differences are established in formal organizational structures. Some positions and roles are assigned in power over others. Power decreases as we move from the top to the bottom of the organization. Management–worker hierarchies and political bureaucracies replaced traditional structures based on family, class, community, tribe, wealth, strength, and age. Even in a country with three hundred years of democratic tradition, preferences for formal structure vary. Some pupils prefer highly structured, cognitive educational settings; other prefer highly unstructured ones.

### Preferences for More or Less Structure

There are situations under which everyone wants total structuring. Automobile drivers on through streets want assurance that drivers coming from side streets stop at stop signs and red lights and that oncoming drivers stay on their side of the white dividing lines. Conversely, at a social gathering, the hostess may be faulted for trying to structure interactions. But in working and educational settings, much divergence of opinion occurs. Thus, Heron (1942) observed that if employees must learn by trial and error when they do not have access to information about rules and procedures, they are dissatisfied and fear to take initiative because of possible infractions and penalties. Seeman (1950) found that a majority of school teachers preferred a group-oriented style of leadership. However, they exhibited a substantial demand for a type of leadership calling for power differentiation.

Bradshaw (1970) obtained ratings of ideal leader behavior as well as actual leader behavior in a professional organization. The rank order of the means for both observed and desired leader behavior was as follows: (1) structuring expectations; (2) tolerance of freedom; (3) consideration; and (4) production emphasis. Observed tolerance of freedom was close to the ideal, but more structure was desired than was provided by supervisors. More autonomy and self-actualization were desired than realized. Bradshaw concluded that deficiencies in structure were associated with deficiencies in satisfaction of higher-order needs. In other words, structure is needed for satisfaction of these needs.

Wispé and Lloyd (1955) found that low producers preferred a structured group, whereas high producers favored a permissive group and perceived their superiors as less threatening than did low producers. Lowin and Craig (1968) studied supervisors in experimental groups. Results indicated that supervisors advocated more structure and closer supervision of subordinates lacking in competence, which is consistent with what we have already noted in Chapter 11 about the impact of subordinate incompetence on supervisor punitiveness.

### Structure and Effectiveness

If any sizable group is to reach a common objective, some degree of structure in the role relations within the group is required. Individuals need to be able to predict each others' behavior. Unless informal means are possible, reliability of individual performance will be obtained only by distributing authority, power, and responsibility to holders of the various positions in the group through a structure, without which the group is likely to remain highly ineffective. Thus, Lucas (1965) who studied the effects of feedback on problem solving in groups found that group effectiveness was related to degree of group structure. Gerard (1957) observed that leaders tend to perform more effectively when they have wider scopes of freedom but that followers are more effective in a somewhat more highly structured situation. Gross, Martin, and Darley (1953) found that groups with strong formal leaders were more productive and more cohesive than those with weak informal leaders. Again, Sexton (1967) studied 170 line workers in jobs varying widely in structure as rated by supervisors and the workers themselves. Degree of job structure was positively and significantly related to employee need satisfaction. Hickson, Pugh, and Pheysey (1969) studied a variety of organizations in England. The structuring of activities, role specialization, and functional specialization were positively and significantly related to group size and productivity. Similarly, in a study of manufacturing firms, Pheysey, Payne, and Puch (1971) found that formality and rules orientation were related to employee satisfaction with promotion and with fellow workers and to generation of greater involvement of managers with group. Bass and Valenzi (1974) found a positive association between the perceived effectiveness of work groups and the extent to which relations between manager and subordinates in such groups were structured.

Hobhouse, Wheeler, and Ginsberg (1930) rated some 200 primitive cultures as to level and complexity of development. They found that efficient government resulting from a strong and stable leadership position or council of leaders was positively correlated with high cultural achievement. Two opposite factors were found to reduce the power of the chief. In the less well-developed societies, the frequent absence of permanent government deprived the chiefs of any effective structure for exercising power except for sporadic undertakings. In the more highly developed societies, the presence of a stable governing council limited the powers of the primary chief.

Fox, Lorge, et al. (1953) compared the effectiveness of six- to eight-man discussions of air force officers with groups of twelve to thirteen. The larger groups yielded higher quality decisions. The large groups overcame their disadvantage by organizing themselves to solve the problem to make maximum use of the larger number of participants. In the same way, F. L. Bates (1953) observed that the performance of four medium bomber wings was better when there was a greater use of authority, and a greater frequency of production plans, orders, and instructions sanctioned by authority.

*Bureaucracy and the Distribution of Power.* The theory of bureaucracy is concerned with problems involved in the structure of power relations in formal organizations. Weber (1947) observed that bureaucracy is characterized by continuous organization of official functions bound by rules, specified spheres of competence, hierarchical ordering of authority relations, and impersonality in that responsibility and authority reside in the office rather than in the person. Bureaucratic structure does not necessarily limit all autonomy for the organization's managers, although as expected Engel (1970) found that manager autonomy was greater in organizations with moderate than in those with extreme bureaucratic structures. Case studies by Peabody and Rourke (1965); Merton, Gray, Hockey, and Selvin (1952); and Bennis (1970) suggested that when organizations become overly concerned with rules and formalities there is a tendency for them to lose touch with the external demands made upon them and to become insensitive to the internal problems that they generate. (These defects are not confined only to bureaucracies.) Dissatisfaction and ineffectiveness are unintended effects. Although it is the rational purpose of bureaucracy to use specialized talent effectively, bureaucratic organizations and institutions often emphasize formalisms and legalisms to such a degree that perpetuation of the system takes precedence over the function it was intended to perform. In agreement, J. M. Burns (1978) declared:

> Bureaucracy is the world of explicitly formulated goals, rules, procedures . . . specialization and expertise, with the roles of individuals minutely specified and differentiated . . . organized by purpose, process, clientele, or place. [It] prizes consistency, predictability, stability, and efficiency . . . more than creativity and principle. Roles and duties are prescribed less by superiors . . . than by tradition, formal examinations, and technical qualifications. Careers and job security are protected by tenure, pensions, union rules, professional standards, and appeal procedures. The structure . . . approaches the . . . elimination of personalized relationships and . . . reciprocity, response to wants, needs, and values—that is, transactional leadership. . . .

Through its methodical allotment of tasks, its mediating and harmonizing and "adjustment" procedures, its stress on organizational ethos, goals, and authority, bureaucracy assumes consensus and discounts and discredits clash and controversy, which are seen as threats to organizational stability. Bureaucracy discourages the kind of power that is generated by the tapping of motivational bases among employees and the marshaling of personal—as opposed to organizational—resources. Bureaucracy pursues goals that may as easily become separated from a hierarchy of original purposes and values as from human needs. And bureaucracy, far from directing social change or serving as a factor in historical causation, consciously or not helps buttress the status quo [pp. 295–296].

Thus, the status and power differentiation of bureaucracy, initially organized to meet objectives expeditiously and efficiently, often experiences "hardening of the arteries" when it fails to adapt to changes in outside conditions and its own personnel. But complete lack of structure may be worse.

*Lack of Structure and Ineffectiveness.* L. M. Smith (1967) observed an experimental elementary school over a period of one year. Administration, scheduling, curriculum, teaching, and discipline were highly unstructured. Authority resided in the pupils. The teachers engaged in a continual struggle for power. There was continuous confusion, delay, noise, and frustration. All but two of the teachers decided to leave at the end of the year. In the same way, Kingsley (1967) studied a group of therapists which disbanded after the demise of structure due to the departure of their discussion leader. Members were unable to maintain interactive relationships in the absence of the structure provided by a leader.

### Moderators

A variety of moderator variables systematically alter the structure-effectiveness relationship. According to Maas (1950), leaders tending to project blame on others exhibit a desirable behavior change when they lead relatively informal, unstructured groups, whereas leaders tending to absorb blame show desirable change when they lead formal, structured groups. When placed in reversed situations, the leaders exhibit anxiety and signs of stress.

Sirota (1959) found that medium amounts of information about management philosophy, goals, and operations procedures were more highly associated with employee satisfaction and advancement than large or small amounts of information.

Dalton, Barnes, and Zaleznik (1968) shifted power downward in selected departments of a research and development organization. The managers of various levels experienced a reduction of hierarchical power and favored slowing the process as a consequence. But the scientists at the different levels gained in functional power and favored an accelerated rate of change.

When anti-aircraft crews of three men each performing all functions were contrasted with arranging them in a hierarchical structure, performance improved with such structure, but was unnecessary under lower loads (Lanzetta & Roby, 1955). Naylor and Dickinson (1969) observed that task structure (complexity and organization of the task), but not work structure (distribution of work components among group members) was positively related to group effectiveness.

*Clarity.* Perceived clarity of structure and roles seems particularly important.

E. E. Smith (1957) studied experimental groups in which both productivity and satisfaction were found related to the degree of role clarity. Similarly, Lenski (1956) noted that group members with low degrees of status crystallization tended to experience difficulty in establishing effective, satisfying patterns of interaction with others. Again, Dyer and Lambert (1953) observed that bomber wings were more efficient when members had a clear recognition of the status structure. In a study conducted by the Life Insurance Agency Management Association (LIAMA, 1964a), it was found that agents who reported that the job was accurately described before they were hired were less likely to terminate than those less clearly informed. Similarly, Wanous (1973) showed that newly recruited telephone operators who were told both the good and the bad about the job were less likely to quit than those who were told about the good aspects only. Trieb and Marion (1969) studied two companies, finding that the extent to which new employees had been oriented to the job is highly related to job satisfaction and loyalty to company.

*Timing and Need.* Kinder and Kolmann (1976) found that self-actualization from sensitivity training groups (see Chapter 33) were greatest when leaders' and members' roles were highly structured at first and less structured later on. Similarly, Bridges, Doyle, and Mahan (1968) found that hierarchically undifferentiated groups were more effective than differentiated groups in analysis of problems, but not in the synthetic phases of problem solving.

## INDUSTRIAL DEMOCRACY

Power may formally be redistributed by assigning worker representatives to management boards and committees. The redistribution may be voluntary on the part of management, as in the United States, or mandated by legislation, as in West Germany. This industrial representative democracy is in contradistinction to power sharing at the workplace. In the latter, workers participate directly with their immediate supervisor in decisions of consequence to their own work and working situation. As Heller and Clark (1976) wisely noted, it is important to distinguish between real power sharing, in which employees actually participate in decision-making processes of consequence, and the semblance of participation which may not yield the same degree of commitment, motivation, and productivity (March and Simon, 1958). Workers may sit on the boards of directors in Yugoslavia, but in fact party members, financial experts, and technocrats exhibit most of the power, initiative, and influence (Obradovic, 1975). Moreover, as we have already seen and as Heller and Clark observed, both individual preferences and situational considerations affect the optimum balance of self-direction and preset structure.

### Voluntary Programs

Selekman (1924) reported the results of a management sharing plan in a chemical firm. In order for management to gain a better understanding of the workers' point of view, two boards were created. The Board of Operatives was composed of elected workers and was responsible for working conditions, grievances, recreation, training, company housing, and the like. The Board of Management, which was composed of executives and stockholders, was responsible for production, wages, farm equipment, hours, and financial policies. Although the Board of Operatives was slow to accept responsibilities, gradually it participated in planning and decision making. Effects attributed to the experiment were a reduction in personnel turnover and greater cooperation in improvement of production.

McCormick (1938, 1949) described a scheme called "multiple management." Appointed were a Junior Board of Executives (consisting of the most promising younger executives) and a Factory Board of Executives (consisting of foremen and departmental heads). Each board was responsible for formulating and recommending plans for improvement of all aspects of management and organization. They were judged to have played a crucial role in the vitality and growth of the firm.

Given (1949), a company president, experimented with a "bottom-up management" plan, in which he delegated authority down the line to employees and encouraged the use of employee initiative and responsibility. Another company president decided to work directly with employees in order to stimulate responsibility and initiative at the work place. He found that his activities placed foremen under great conflict and stress, but he worked with them until they accepted his philosophy of participation. He concluded that his organization became more informal, and his workers more responsible and involved (Richard, 1959).

*Joint Consultation.* Wyndham and White (1952) found that workers in an Australian refinery tended to regard the elected representative to worker–management committees as an alternative to their foremen. The latter regarded their positions as threatened, even though they were members of the joint consultation committees. H. Campbell (1953) concluded that, in order for joint consultation to be effective, the foreman must be involved in the process as an active participant.

Jaques (1952) presented a detailed case study of a British firm which introduced works councils and work committees to participate in management. Workers tended to feel dissatisfied with the performance of their elected representatives. The representatives were under heavy stress due to different conflicting demands, little authority for making decisions, and increasing separation from the workers.

A study by W. H. Scott (1952) of joint consultation in three British industrial firms also indicated that the procedure is subject to strains in different segments and levels of the organization. Although workers' representatives were generally well accepted in their discussions with management, both workers and their representatives reported that little was accomplished because only trivial issues were discussed. Workers felt they were neither consulted nor kept informed by representatives. Foremen reported they were bypassed in communications between management and workers' representatives. Workers and their representatives complained that foremen failed to take action on many matters which could have been handled more effectively on the spot rather than being referred to joint consultation. Although the majority of workers' representatives were also union stewards, union members complained that they were not adequately represented. Scott concluded that joint consultation resulted in few advantages that could not be produced as well by responsible leadership.

An intensive study by Jaques (1952) of a single factory revealed similar problems, but it throws greater light on details of the consultative procedure. His findings suggest that the difficulties encountered may result not so much from the unwillingness of either management or employees to make the system work as from confusion relative to their respective responsibilities. Management tended to feel that it should not trespass upon the responsibilities of workers' representatives in the works council, particularly on matters involving social relationships; hence, managers tended to take passive roles. Workers' representatives tended to regard operative problems and policies as responsibilities of management, adopting passive attitudes in relation to these matters. As the general manager of the factory was enabled to accept the idea that he was responsible for all aspects of organizational life and activity and that giving orders is not necessarily autocratic or unethical, he was able to "assume more fully his leadership mantle and his subordinates in turn accepted theirs. With their duties more sharply in focus, they were able to take the lead in building a Works Council more broadly representative of the factory." Jaques's study suggested that members cannot act effectively either in their own interests or in behalf of the group unless the leader exercises the functions of his/her role and takes the initiative in providing clarity of role definition throughout the system.

*Scanlon Plan.* The Scanlon Plan is a means for sharing reductions in unit costs that are under the control of labor. Such reductions are determined first by establishing a normal labor cost for the factory. The labor cost may be arrived at by a joint worker–management agreement. Whenever labor costs fall below the norm, the workers receive anywhere from 50 to 100 percent of the amount. A second element of the Scanlon Plan is a suggestion system where benefits accruing from reduction in the labor costs are shared with all workers in the plant. Reports indicate that as many as 80 percent of the suggestions submitted in a Scanlon Plan plant are accepted, while plants with individual suggestion plans commonly accept 25 percent. Further, with the Scanlon Plan there is no reason for the worker to withhold suggestions that will increase productivity; the only result is lower labor costs and consequently a bonus for everyone (Lesieur, 1958).

A survey was made of nine firms with eleven plants producing many different products which had introduced the Scanlon Plan. The workers' skills ranged from manual labor to highly technical. In the eleven plants surveyed over a two-year period, the gain in productivity varied from 11 percent to 49 percent with mean gain of 23 percent. Bonuses averaged 17 percent of gross pay based on splitting the labor cost savings, with 75 percent to the workers and 25 percent to the company. Beside the direct benefits from increased production and higher profits, there was also better service to the customer, higher quality products, improved competitive position, and no decline in employment (Puckett, 1958).

### Mandated Programs

While such legislative action has never succeeded in the United States, it was the American military government in postwar Germany in 1950 that required formal worker representation on management governing boards. This was seen as a way to prevent the reemergence of industrial support for political fascism in Germany. To illustrate, W. M. Blumenthal (1956) studied the management of steel plants in Germany. Each plant was managed by a board of three men, one a union representative. The general trend of development was for the two management representatives to assume responsibility for production, while the union representative assumed responsibility for personnel, wages, and grievances.

Evaluations of the operations and effectiveness of workers councils have been reported for West Germany (Hartmann, 1970; Wilpert, 1975), Norway (Thorsrud & Emery, 1970), Britain (K. Walker, 1974), Yugoslavia (Rus, 1970; Obradovic, 1970, 1975), Sweden (Link, 1971), and in socialist countries (Sturmthal, 1961, 1964). The conclusions arrived at by Derber (1970) apply to some other studies as well. He observed that (1) as managers become more professional, their professionalism imposes a barrier against involving employees in decision making; (2) the mass of employees is not strongly motivated to assume managerial responsibilities as long as their financial and other personal needs are satisfied; (3) when union officials and employee representatives become involved in management decision making, they stir up political and fractional conflicts that weaken their influence with workers; and (4) joint decision making involves too much management time for efficient operations. Bass and Shackleton (1979) called attention to the exclusion of the lower and middle management levels from the participatory process when worker representatives meet with top management. These lower-level managers, often ignored and eliminated from the mechanisms of industrial democracy, disassociate themselves from the participatory process and undermine its potential effectiveness.

Obradovic (1975), offer a carefully planned observational study of Yugoslav worker–management council meetings, concluded that initiatives came mainly from the engineers, financial experts, and communist party members. Their attempts to lead were also more likely to be successful in contrast to attempts by ordinary workers. Nevertheless, a massive twelve-country longitudinal survey still in progress at the time of this writing has revealed extensive behavioral changes in organizational relationships derived from mandatory programs of industrial democracy (IDE, 1979).

Bass and Rosenstein (1977) and Bass and Shackleton (1979) argue that a complex problem calls for complex solutions. They argue that industrial democracy is most likely to work well for some issues, such as dealing with pay and benefits, career development, working conditions, and job security, but not for others, such as job dissatisfaction, financial planning, or marketing strategies. The twelve-country consortium study (IDE, 1979) is likely to reveal in detail the extent to which these arguments are valid.

## SHARING RESTRUCTURING EFFORTS
## AT THE IMMEDIATE WORK GROUP LEVEL

Roethlisberger (1941) observed that any technological change on the part of management may affect not only the physical but also the social location of an individual in the organization. The possibility of social dislocation within the organization constitutes a severe threat to many members.

Individuals in leadership positions tend to feel more tolerant of change and stress than those in follower positions. In addition to being more receptive, members in leadership positions usually have access to information enabling them to predict some consequences of change. The member in a follower position seldom has access to such information unless it is provided by the management. Rumor, imagination, and speculation often lead to grossly inaccurate evaluations of the effects of an announced change. Participation in planning change provides at least a minimum base of information in terms of which a member may evaluate some possible effects of a given change on his work, status, and relationship to the organization. Considerations such as those discussed above have suggested the hypothesis that workers will feel more receptive to change if they are involved in planning it.

Reducing the power differences between superior and subordinate at the shopfloor level, within the work group, is a main theme of behavioral theorists and practictioners' interventions. "Every employee a manager" sums up M. S. Myers's (1968) changeover of supervisor–subordinate power relations. Formerly, the powerful supervisor fully planned for and controlled the performance of the electronic assembly operator whose only responsibilities were to carry out orders. Now, as much as possible the operator becomes self-planning, self-directing, and self controlling.

*Sharing the Power to Plan Change.* Shifting the power distribution results in a sharing of planning and control with positive effects on operator commitment, understanding, satisfaction, and productivity. Structure still remains, but it is based not on power differences but rather on structural design to which the operator has contributed. The utility of such self-planning was reaffirmed in a series of experiments by Bass and Leavitt (1963), Bass (1970), and Bass (1977).

Jn a first simulation, Bass and Leavitt (1963) demonstrated the importance of self-planning both to productivity and to satisfaction. Several simple exercises were devised. In each, trios of managers in training developed a plan for themselves and then exchanged plans with another trio. A counterbalanced order was used so that half of the teams executed their own plan first and half executed the other team's plan first. Then they executed both plans. Managers were more productive and satisfied when operating their own plan.

In a similar simulation, 1,416 managers completed "Exercise Organization" (Bass, 1975h). As expected, objective output and efficiency were significantly greater when executing own plans. Moreover, self-planning resulted in greater felt responsibility, job satisfaction, and satisfaction with the plan. However, payoff was much greater from self-planning by participants with practice (that is, more experience and knowledge) than without practice.

*Importance of Leadership.* The importance of maintaining some special elements which the supervisor can bring to the planning process, such as more experience and knowledge, was illustrated by Schlacter (1969), who studied six highway maintenance crews over a period of twenty-five weeks. In two crews, the foremen assisted their supervisor in planning and reported results back to their crews. In two others, the crews assisted their superiors in planning. In the third pair of crews, the crews assumed full responsibility for planning. The first two crews maintained stable job satisfaction scores and production records throughout the twenty-five weeks. The third crew gained significantly in job satisfaction, but lost significantly in productivity.

Similarly, Latham and Saari (1979) showed experimentally that supportive leadership resulted in higher goals being set by student participants than did nonsupport.

*Rationale.* Reasons given by participants in Bass (1970) for the utility of reducing power differences for the purposes of planning included: (1) the sense of accomplishment when carrying out the plan may be heightened; (2) it generates more efforts to confirm the validity of the plan by executing it successfully and more confidence to see that it can be done; (3) there may be more commitment to see that the plan works well; (4) there may be more flexibility, more room for modification, and more initiative to make improvements; (5) understanding of the plan is likely to be greater; (6) human resources may be better used; (7) there may be fewer communication problems and consequent errors and distortions in following instructions; and (8) competitive feelings aroused between planners and those who must execute the plans are avoided.

*Reviews.* For more on pursuing power sharing and redistribution to effect planned change, the reader may wish to examine Bennis, Benne, and Chin (1962), Zollschan and Hirsch (1964), and French, Bell, and Zawacki (1978), all edited collections of readings on the theory and techniques of planned change. Theoretical and technical reviews have been published by McMurray (1947), Bavelas (1948), Low (1948), Zander (1949, 1950), Tannenbaum and Massarik (1950), Cartwright (1951), Spicer (1952), Sofer (1955), Ginzberg and Reilley (1957), Lippitt, Watson, and Westley (1958), Burns and Stalker (1961), Patchen (1964), Schein and Bennis (1965), Bennis (1963, 1965, 1966), and Winn (1966).

# 13 CONFLICT AND LEGITIMACY IN THE LEADERSHIP ROLE

## ROLE CONFLICTS

Lyndon Johnson wanted every American to love him, but Harry Truman opined that "if you can't stand the heat, stay out of the kitchen!" National leaders must settle for less than universal affection. They must be willing to be unloved. They must deal with conflict (J. M. Burns, 1978). And so must most other leaders, for conflict often attends the leadership role. No leader can be successful if not prepared to be rejected (T. O. Jacobs, 1970).

Sources of role conflict for the leader—resulting in anxiety or other stress-induced responses—include role ambiguity, various incongruities, personal inadequacy to meet role demands, incompatibility among several roles the leader must play, conflicting demands upon the leader, mixed costs and benefits associated with playing the role, and discrepancies between actual and self-accorded status.

Role ambiguity occurs when the leaders' roles are not clearly defined. Leaders cannot determine what they are expected to do (R. L. Kahn et al., 1964). An incongruence occurs when, for instance, old, experienced workers are assigned to young, inexperienced supervisors. The workers are likely to perceive a discrepancy between their seniority and their rank in the status hierarchy (S. Adams, 1953). The leader may not be able to meet the task as well as the interpersonal demands made upon the role (D. J. Levinson, 1959).

There may be interrole incompatibility. An individual may play two or more roles in a group. The demands made upon the several roles may be incompatible; for example, the role of group representative may be incompatible with the role of enforcer of discipline (Stouffer, 1949). Or there may be within-role conflict. Different followers or subgroups may make conflicting demands upon a given leadership role. The role occupant will find it difficult to exhibit any course of action that will satisfy the various sets of differing expectations (Merton, 1940).

Conflicts and disagreements may arise in the legitimation process, in the right to function as a leader. On the other hand, if members can agree on the leadership structure, they are more likely to be satisfied with the group, according to results obtained by Shelley (1960b). Similarly, Bass and Flint (1958) found that early agreement on the leader increases group effectiveness. Finally, Heslin and Dunphy (1964) obtained results indicating that member satisfaction was high when the degree of status consensus among members was also high.

*Organizational Locus*

More role ambiguity occurs for lower-level managers. The responsibilities and authority of first-line supervisors and middle managers are less clearly defined than those of top management. Uncertain about what they are allowed and expected to do, they experience more tension than top managers and less job satisfaction. Thus, D. C. Miller and Schull (1962) reported that middle managers register more role stress than top managers, more frequently stating that they are unclear as to the scope of their responsibilities and what their colleagues expect of them. In the same way, Brinker (1955) reported that first-line supervisors in industry work under more or less constant frustration because they are not given enough authority to feel that they are part of management or to solve the problems presented by their subordinates. Supervisors surveyed in 140 management clubs wanted more identification with higher management, most feeling that they did not know the company policy on many important matters with which they were concerned and that as a result they had to work in the dark (Mullen, 1954). Again, Moore and Smith (1953) found that it was military noncommissioned officers rather than higher-ups who felt constant pressure due to inadequate authority, a lack of distinction between supervisors and technicians, and conflicts between the leadership philosophies of different levels of organization. Consistent with all the above, in a study of insurance agencies, Wispé and Thayer (1957) found more consensus about the functions of the manager than those of the assistant manager. The assistant manager's role was found ambiguous in that both manager and assistant manager did not know whether certain functions were obligatory or optional. Strain and tension were highest in the most ambiguous role, that of the assistant manager.

*Relation to Leader Behavior and Satisfaction*

As expected, both role ambiguity and role conflict are deleterious to leadership performance and satisfaction. Rizzo, House, and Lirtzman (1970) found in two industrial firms that with more perceived role ambiguity and sensed conflict, less overall leadership behavior was reported on the Leader Behavior Description Questionnaire, Form XII (see Chapter 21) as well as less job satisfaction. Compared to role conflict, role ambiguity showed a higher negative relation with job satisfaction. Tosi (1971) also found role conflict negatively related to job satisfaction, but not to group effectiveness.

*A Moderator Effect*

Supervisors seem to be able to tolerate role conflict better if they do not have to interact much with their own immediate supervisors. In a study of seven companies, supplemented by a national survey, R. L. Kahn et al. (1964) found that the experience of role conflict increased as the ambiguity of the situation increased with high but not with low rates of communication. Likewise, job satisfaction decreased as role conflict increased only under conditions of high communication. It was inferred that most role conflict had its source in interactions with one's immediate superiors.

## STATUS AND ESTEEM INCONGRUITIES

### Status–Status Incongruence

Ordinarily, we have multiple roles and positions. For each we are accorded status. These statuses may be matched in value or they may be incongruent. Conflict results if they are incongruent. For example, military enlisted personnel high in civilian status positions were more dissatisfied with their officers than enlisted personnel who came from civilian jobs lower in status (Stouffer, Suchman, et al., 1949). Among those for whom the status structure was regarded as lacking in legitimacy, there was a tendency to evaluate one's situation in comparison with a wider range of statuses (Merton & Kitt, 1950). Jaques (1952) observed much anxiety and confusion when a British worker (low status) was assigned to chair (high status) a conference with management. Relief and satisfaction came only after the managing director assumed the chair. Conversely, in a study of fifty workers in one department of a firm, Zaleznik, Christensen, and Roethlisberger (1958) found that members with high status congruence were most likely to meet the productivity standards of management. Likewise, S. Adams (1953) demonstrated that group members are better satisfied when high-level positions are occupied by persons ranking high in age, education, experience, prestige, and the like. But group productivity was highest under medium degrees of status congruence. Shepherd and Weschler (1955) presented confirming evidence. Susman (1970) asked work group members to assign tasks to fellow members and found that workers and their helpers did not view age and seniority alike. Highly valued tasks were assigned to high-status (older and more experienced) members in some groups, but not in others. In the same way, S. Adams (1953) showed that group members tended to be dissatisfied when status incongruity existed in the leadership positions. Group productivity also tended to suffer when the high-status positions were occupied by persons ranking low in other aspects of status (age, education, experience, social position, and the like). Yet Singer (1966) found that although status incongruence in groups was associated with tension, organization, and hostile communications, it was not necessarily related to group productivity or member satisfaction.

The dissatisfaction with status incongruence was illustrated by Trow and Herschdorfer (1965) who demonstrated that groups with congruent status structures that were free to change did not do so, whereas those with incongruent structures tended to change. Furthermore, groups with high degrees of status incongruency were rated low in task performance and member satisfaction.

### Formal–Informal Incongruence

The incongruence of the formal and informal structures in any organization was seen as a threat to organizational stability by Selznick (1948). Moreno (1953) noted that formal groupings superimposed by higher authority upon informal, spontaneous groupings are a chronic source of conflict. In the same way, Roethlisberger and Dickson (1947) associated the relation of worker dissatisfaction with the existence in an industrial plant of discrepancies between the formal and informal organizations of the workers. Stouffer, Suchman, et al. (1949) observed that discussions were more satisfying to the participants when the informal leaders were given higher status by being placed in the position of discussion leader.

Cause and effect may be reversed. Inadequacy and dissatisfaction with the formal organization may give rise to an informal organization at variance with the formal one. An informal organization, unrelated to the formal one, may arise as a means of resisting the coercive demands of high-status members (Shartle, 1949b). It may arise if the formal organization cannot provide the membership with rewards such as recognition or opportunity (Pfiffner, 1951). It may develop by by-passing incompetent, high-status members to achieve the goals of the formal organization (Lichtenberg & Deutsch, 1954). (Such usurpation will be discussed later in this chapter.)

On the other hand, conflict is least and group performance best when the formal and informal structures are merged. Haythorn (1954a) reported that bomber crew performance and cohesiveness were highly related to the extent to which the aircraft commander (the formal leader) performed the informal leadership roles usually expected of the formal group leader.

### Role–Role Incongruence

Playing a variety of roles is not necessarily stressful. The average individual learns to play the role of child, sibling, parent, subordinate, peer, and superior without apparent effort. Some individuals play only dependent roles well. Others are content only when they play the role of superior. Individuals in the professions tend to assume the role of authoritative, independent agent as a characteristic pattern of behavior. Professional actors appear to enjoy the enactment of a great variety of roles, but can run into personal conflict separating their real selves from the parts they play, separating their private life from their public image. Although we may not be accomplished actors, we can play a variety of roles without apparent stress. Nevertheless, we may find different roles incompatible with each other and therefore a source of conflict for us. Thus, Getzels (1963) found that school teachers were expected to maintain a socioeconomic role at a higher level than their salaries would sustain. In their role as citizens, they were often expected to be more active in church affairs and less active in political affairs than the average citizen. In their professional roles, they were expected to be certified as experts in various fields of knowledge, but they could be challenged by any parent or taxpayer. Thus, teachers were subject to several sources of strain in each of several incompatible roles. Getzels and Guba (1954) also studied individuals with two or more roles with contradictory or mutually executive expectations. They found that such role conflict tended to increase when the individual's role was not also perceived as a legitimate role.

### Status–Esteem Incongruence

Conflict ensues and group performance is adversely affected when the member of high status in a group—in a position of importance—is low in esteem—value as a person (Bass, 1960). A naval air squadron of high morale was contrasted by J. G. Jenkins (1948) with one of low morale. In the high-morale group, the squadron commander and executive officer, high in status, were also esteemed; that is, they were most often nominated as individuals with whom others would want to fly. On the other hand, in the low-morale squadron, nominations were unrelated to occupying positions as commander or executive officer. Conversely, Palmer and Myers (1955) found a correlation of .38 between the effectiveness with which forty anti-aircraft radar crews maintained their equipment and the extent to which they esteemed their key noncommissioned officer. Similarly, Bass, Flint, and Pryer (1957b) obtained a correlation of .25 between the extent to which status was correlated with esteem in an experimental group and its subsequent effectiveness. According to interview studies, Shils and Janowitz (1948) concluded that the German enlisted World War II soldiers' motivation to resist surrender and their high morale seemed primarily due to their esteem for their officers.

Firestone, Lichtman, and Colamosca (1975) had college students elect their own group leader after participating in an initially leaderless group discussion. Groups subsequently were most effective in an emergency when led by the elected member with the highest ratings for performance in the leaderless group discussion. Groups were worst in the emergency if they were led by the person they believed had the lowest ratings for performance in the preceding leaderless group discussion.

Essentially negative results were obtained by Nelson (1964). He found that agreement between supervisors in evaluations of personnel was unrelated to their degree of mutual esteem. Nor was esteem held for supervisors by their subordinates related to supervisor–subordinate agreement in evaluating personnel. However, agreement between supervisors was related to the esteem held for them by their subordinates. Gottheil and Vielhaber (1966) also observed that groups performed more effectively when leaders were esteemed and when members were esteemed by each other.

If one would lose power, esteem, autonomy, or self-determination by joining or forming another group, conflict results. Members may reject the opportunity to join suggested coalitions with others in three-way bargaining situations, even if it would be rewarding otherwise, because joining would cause a loss of esteem relative to the other members (Hoffman, Festinger & Lawrence, 1954). Similarly, analyses of French cabinets and college interfraternity councils led Holt (1952a,b) to infer that otherwise mutually rewarding coalitions were rejected because loss of autonomy or self-determination was involved.

Conflict due to the failure to match status and esteem can be reduced by incorporating the results of subordinates' evaluations into promotion policies or building up the esteem of those of high status (Bass, 1960). Conflict due to the rise of status of one member at the expense of the others can be avoided by bringing in an outsider to lead the group.

To avoid internal dissention, when kingdoms were reconstituted in countries such as Bulgaria, Greece, and Sweden, outsiders were brought in from Germany, France, and elsewhere. Daum (1975) looked at the impact of internal promotion versus bringing in an outsider to lead the group. Results were as expected. The selection of a member from within a group to become a leader tended to cause the remaining members to express lower overall satisfaction and to reduce their voluntary participation following the change.

## COMPETENCE TO MEET ROLE DEMANDS

It seems obvious that if those of high status also are competent for their role assignments, the group will be more productive and satisfied. Conversely, incompetence at high levels should produce conflict, dissatisfaction, and group failure. Yet, as we have noted in Chapters 4, 5 and 6, some curvilinearity in outcomes may be expected, for leaders sometimes may be too able for the groups they lead. Nevertheless, strong positive congruence-effectiveness associations have been found in surveys and experiments. Back in 1913, Woods (1913) published the correlation between the judged ability (strong, mediocre, or weak) of 386 European sovereigns from the eleventh century to 1789. A correlation of .60 was found between judged ability and ratings of the political, material, and economic progress (progress, no progress, decline) of the realm governed by the sovereign. In the same way, Rohde (1954) reported correlations of .29, .63, and .63 between the success of groups in maze learning and the adequacy of the pretest performance of the person in charge of each of the groups. Again, in a comparison of nine orientation discussion groups Stouffer, Suchman, et al. (1949) observed that members were much more likely to say they "got a lot out of the discussion" when the member of the group chosen to lead the discussion was better educated. Bass (1961c) found that successful leadership was more highly related to ability and esteem in effective than in ineffective groups, and that discrepancies between group esteem and self-esteem were associated with unsuccessful leadership.

The choice of a competent leader was a major determinant of team effectiveness and seemed to stimulate effective mutual influence among other group members (Borg, 1956). Thus, after analyzing a large number of small group studies, Heslin and Dunphy (1964) concluded that group members are most likely to achieve consensus regarding status structure of the group when (1) the leader is perceived as highly competent; (2) a leader emerges to play a role high in both group task and group maintenance functions; or (3) two mutually supportive leaders emerge, one specializing in task functions and the other in group maintenance functions. (But two leaders often present problems, as we will note later on.)

The importance of matching competence and status was seen by Goldman and Fraas (1965), who compared groups whose leaders were elected, appointed for competence, or appointed randomly. Groups with leaders appointed for competence did best, groups with elected leaders did next best. The poorest performance was found in groups without leaders or where leaders had been appointed randomly. Finally, mismatching of status and competence in a group is likely to produce downgrading of the group leader. Thus, Ghiselli and Lodahl (1958a) found that a supervisor was likely to be poorly regarded by higher management if he was assigned to a group containing a line worker superior to him in supervisory ability.

*Personality*

Competence may be a matter of expectations. Violated expectations generate conflict. Lipham (1960) tested the hypothesis that personality traits compatible with the expectations about a leadership role would be related to the leader's effectiveness. In a study of principals, those scoring high in expected characteristics such as drive, emotional control, and sociability were rated more effective than those scoring high in unexpected characteristics such as submissiveness and abasement.

In a study of insurance agencies, Wispé (1955, 1957) found that successful agents were characterized by a high drive for success. But the same success attitude, when exhibited by the agency manager, was at variance with the agents' expectations of a more humane, considerate orientation toward their problems. Thus, the characteristic that contributed to successful selling did not necessarily contribute to effective management.

Conflict can be avoided (at a price) if those of lower status hide their abilities from those of higher status. College girls used to "play dumb" on dates just as blacks used to display "feeblemindedness" in dealing with white superiors. Ordinarily, a better way to avoid conflict and enhance satisfaction and performance is by suitable promotion policies matching competence with status (Bass, 1960).

### Other Incongruities

Exline and Ziller (1959) assembled groups in which members held positions that were congruent as to both competence and power. In other groups, competence and power were incongruent. While interpersonal conflict did not occur, as expected, in the incongruent groups, congruent groups were rated by subjects as significantly more congenial, as exhibiting stronger intermember agreement, and as involving less overlap of activities.

Evan and Simmons (1969) studied students hired to work as proofreaders. In one experiment their pay (supposedly an indicator of the worth and importance of their position) was inconsistent with their acknowledged level of competence. In a second situation, their pay was inconsistent with their level of authority. Incongruity, particularly that consisting of underpayment in relation to authority, resulted in reduced quality of work and reduced conformity to organizational rules.

## WITHIN-ROLE CONFLICT

Brandon (1965) observed that the negative affect associated with status incongruence in groups is largely attributable to discrepancies between role performance and expectation. Such stress is experienced by an individual when different individuals or groups make contradictory demands that cannot be satisfied by any compatible course of action. While this source of stress and its effects will be considered here, an examination of leadership under stressful conditions, in general, will be completed in Chapter 26.

### Discordant Expectations

Discrepancies between a role player's own role expectations and the expectations about the role of his or her subordinates, peers, superiors, and clients have been studied extensively as fundamental sources of conflict. Similar attention has been paid to the discrepancies between what is done and what ought to be done. Thus, Colmen, Fiedler, and Boulger (1954) reported little agreement among forty-five USAF leaders in evaluating their own duties. Further confusion resulted from the discrepancy between what potential leaders thought they ought to do and what they actually did do. Halpin (1957b) found little relationship between how aircraft commanders and school superintendents said they might behave and how they actually behaved according to their subordinates.

Stogdill, Scott, and Jaynes (1956) asked members of a large naval organization to describe what they do and what they ought to do. In addition, subordinates were asked to describe what their immediate superiors do and ought to do. Self-descriptions and self-expectations were rather highly related. The average correlation for forty-five items was above .70. Members of organizations perceived themselves as behaving very much as they think they should behave. Subordinates also described their superiors as behaving very much as subordinates expected them to behave. The average correlation between subordinates' descriptions and expectations of superiors was above .50.

Subordinates' self-expectations were much more highly related to their expectations for superiors than their self-descriptions were related to their descriptions of superiors; that is, subordinates appeared to entertain similar expectations for themselves and for their superiors. Except for handling paperwork and other forms of individual effort, however, they did not perceive their own behavior as resembling that of their superiors. In the leader behavior variables only, subordinates' self-descriptions were closer than their self-expectations to their descriptions of seniors' behavior. In general, subordinates expected to behave as they perceived their superiors to behave. In interpersonal performances, subordinates' self-expectations were closer than their self-descriptions to their expectations for superiors. In most respects subordinates perceived themselves to behave as they expected their superiors to behave.

Discrepancy scores were computed by subtracting the "does" score from the "ought to do" scores. The discrepancy score for each item for both superiors and subordinates was correlated with a number of criterion scores. The discrepancy scores were also correlated with descriptions and expectations. Discrepancies between superiors' self-descriptions and their self-expectations were highly related to their level in the organization, the number of members interacting with them, and their level of responsibility as described by subordinates. Superiors obtaining high scores on level, interaction, and responsibility tended to perceive themselves as having too much responsibility, as engaging in integrative behavior, and as acting as representatives of their followers more extensively than they should. They also reported spending too little time in inspection of the organization and too much time in paperwork. Superiors rated high in responsibility by subordinates described themselves as engaging in all forms of leader behavior more extensively than they should. Superiors conscious of their active leadership were perceived by subordinates as highly responsible (see Chapter 14).

Discrepancies between subordinates' self-descriptions and self-expectations were related to their superiors' level in the organization, rate of interaction, delegation, integrative behavior, and relationships with subordinates. When superiors occupied high-level positions and were recipients of frequent interactions, their followers perceived themselves as doing more than they ought to in representing their subordinates, attending conferences, interviewing personnel, and handling paperwork. When superiors were described as high in delegation, integrative behavior, and other forms of leader behavior, their subordinates described themselves as having too much responsibility and as spending less time than they ought to in coordination and professional consultation. Superiors high in integrative behavior had subordinates who perceived themselves as highly active in all aspects of leader behavior. In all, discrepancies in expectations of superiors and subordinates about each other indicating dissatisfaction and tension among the subordinates were most frequently related to the level and rank of their superiors. Discrepancies bearing on control of technical operations were most frequently related to the leader behavior of their superiors. These findings suggested that interpersonal tensions tended to be associated with status structure, whereas leadership was concerned with the group task and operations.

Along similar lines, Triandis (1959a) found that the smaller the discrepancy between ideal and actual descriptions of supervisor behavior, the better liked the supervisor was by his workers. Results obtained by Holden (1954) indicated that the greater the extent to which the leader's behavior conformed to member expectations, the greater was the productivity of the group. Again, Havron and McGrath (1961) suggested that the leaders of highly effective groups either behave as expected or are successful in inducing group members to form ideals similar to their behavior. Thus Foa (1956) studied foremen and workers in Israeli factories and found that foremen and workers agreed on ideal behavior for a foreman, but that they did not agree on the foremen's actual behavior. The smaller the difference between ideal and perceived behavior of foremen, the better satisfied the workers were with their foremen. Workers identifying with their foreman tended to attribute to him the ideals that they held. Ambivalent workers attempted to conform to the ideal attributed to their foreman while being aware of the foreman's deviation from the ideal. Indifferent workers felt less inclined to accept the ideal of the foreman in their own behavior and were also less likely to notice discrepancies between ideal and real behavior. But F. J. Davis (1954) obtained data which failed to support the hypothesis that agreement between leader and follower as to the leader's role would be associated with successful follower adjustment.

For whatever the reason, uncertainty about one's performance was a source of ineffectiveness. Pepinsky, Pepinsky, Minor, and Robin (1959) studied experimental groups working on a construction problem. For half the groups, the leader was required to work with a superior officer whose approval or disapproval of transactions could be predicted. The other half consisted of groups in which the leader was required to deal with a superior whose behavior could not be predicted. Team productivity was higher under conditions of high predictability than under conditions of low predictability.

Jambor's (1954) results suggest that when supervisors' perceptions of their role differ from their superior's perception of it, they will experience more anxiety than when their role perception differs from their subordinates' perceptions of their role. This raises the more general issue of conflict of men and women "in the middle."

### The Man or Woman in the Middle

The most common example of persons facing conflicting role demands from two sources are supervisors at various levels in an organization hierarchy. Smith (1948), C. A. Gibb (n.d.), Gardner and Whyte (1945), among others, pointed out that most supervisors within an organization are confronted by conflicting demands from superiors and subordinates. Superiors and subordinates differ in their expectations relative to the role performance of supervisors. In business firms, superiors expect results, initiative, planning, firmness, and structure. Subordinates expect recognition, opportunity, consideration, approachability, encouragement, and representation (Brooks, 1955). L. W. Porter (1959) reported that first-line supervisors saw themselves as careful and controlled in their approach to the job and to other people. Managers, in contrast, described themselves in terms of enterprise, originality, and boldness. First-line supervisors differed from line workers as much as they differed from managers. They perceived themselves as significantly more careful and controlled than workers saw themselves. The supervisory role imposed demands for behavior patterns differing from those of superiors and subordinates. However, Graen, Dansereau, and Minami (1972b) failed to find the expected discrepancy in the role expectations about executives as perceived by their subordinates and superiors. In military organizations, officers above and enlisted air personnel below disagree on what characterizes the good noncommissioned officer in between (USAF, 1952). Factor-analytic studies by J. V. Moore (1953) showed, for example, that subordinates of officers focused on the value of their being less strict, whereas superiors emphasized military bearing and ability. Halpin (1957b) found that air crew commanders emphasizing consideration were most highly rated by their subordinates, whereas aircrew commanders who initiated structure were more likely to be rated effective leaders by their superiors. Similarly, Zentner (1951) noted that 87 percent of officers thought that a good noncom was one who follows orders, but only 44 percent of enlisted men accepted this. At the same time, 49 percent of enlisted men felt a good noncom had to gain popularity, whereas only 7 percent of officers agreed with them.

That more conflict is experienced by supervisors ''in the middle'' than operatives ''at the bottom'' was found by Snoek (1966). Both because they have a wider diversity of interactions than operating personnel and because of conflicting demands on them, supervisors experience more role strain, according to Snoek's study of interactions. But, as we already noted from Jambor's (1954) results, downward sources of contradictory demands are likely to generate more strain than upward sources.

### Other Sources of Within-Role Conflict

Contradictory demands may stem from discrepancies between one's immediate work group and one's reference group. Professors may be caught between the demands of their cosmopolitan, professional reference groups and the role demands of their local campus for quality research, quality teaching, and student relations. Industrial scientists may be caught between demands of their professional reference groups for publications and their business firms' demands for secrecy. That these conflicts are a source of dissatisfaction are illustrated in an industrial study by Browne and Neitzel (1952), who found that workers' satisfaction declined as the disagreement between what their leaders demanded of them and what was wanted by their reference groups increased. Similarly, Jacobson (1951) and Jacobson, Charters, and Lieberman (1951) studied foremen, union stewards, and workers. Foremen expected the stewards to play a passive role in the organization, whereas stewards expected to play an active role on behalf of employees and the union. Workers also expected stewards to play an active role. Foremen and stewards whose expectations deviated from their reference group norm got along more easily with each other.

Supervisors in training are often caught in a conflict when their superiors are opposed to what the supervisor is being taught by the trainer. The success or failure of the trainer depends on the trainee's supervisor. The trainer is much more likely to succeed in modifying the behavior of the supervisor if the supervisor's superior shows interest in the program, participates in its development, and takes the course first (W. Mahler, 1952). (More on this in Chapter 33).

To some extent, role conflict and its effects is in the eye of the beholder. Maier and Hoffman (1965) studied role-playing groups. They found that when the discussion leader perceived interpersonal conflict in terms of problem subordinates, the group reached a lower quality of decision than if the leader saw disagreement as a source of innovation and new ideas.

### Resolving Conflicting Demands

Halpin and Winer (1957) suggested several ways for the airplane commander to resolve the conflicts with superiors and subordinates: (1) identify completely with superiors and the formal organization and disparage the need to be considerate of the welfare of subordinates; (2) reduce intimacy with subordinates to minimize guilt feelings about being inconsiderate of them; (3) be inconsiderate on the job but considerate of subordinates and "pal around with them" off the job; and/or (4) identify completely with subordinates. That some of the alternatives are commonly practiced was evidenced in a factor analysis by Hites (1953), who noted that leaders vary in their loyalty and deference to superiors. Independent of this, they also vary in loyalty to their subordinates. A followup study of eighty-nine B-29 aircraft commanders by Halpin (1953) found that aircrew commanders were likely to·be highly rated both by their superiors and their subordinates if they exhibited consideration, friendliness, and warmth toward their subordinates and at the same time initiated clear patterns of organization and ways of accomplishing missions.

Pelz (1952) and Likert (1961a,b) observed that the leader, as well as each group member, is a member of overlapping subgroups. The effective leader identifies with both superiors and subordinates. They have sufficient influence with superiors to represent effectively their subordinates' interests. They are well enough identified with their subordinates to be supported by them. They are both good leaders and good followers, able to satisfy the expectations of both subordinates and superiors. Summarizing the results of the organizational surveys, Kahn and Katz (1960) inferred that effective leaders differ from ineffective ones in making clear the differentiation of their role from subordinates by not performing the subordinates' function, by spending time on supervision but not closely supervising subordinates, and by concerning themselves with their subordinates' needs rather than with rules.

A chain effect was illustrated by Bowers (1963, 1964a) who studied foremen–management–worker relations in an industrial firm. The following hypotheses were tested and supported. The less supportively the foreman's superior behaves toward him the lower will be his self-esteem. The lower the foreman's self-esteem, the more often he will discuss his problems with subordinates and the poorer he will perceive to be their attitude toward him. The poorer the attitude which the foreman perceives his superior and subordinates to share regarding him, the more he will alienate himself from subordinates. The more alienated he feels, the less supportively he will behave toward subordinates. It was concluded that "the foreman's self esteem is a process that translates for him the behavior of his superior into a mandate for his own action."

Further indirect evidence of this linkage was seen by Kamano, Power, and Martin (1966) in a study of nursing supervisors. They reported that those evaluated as superior rather than inferior by high-level administrators likewise tended to rate their subordinates more highly.

*"Machiavellian" Solutions.* The above research assures that the contradictory demands somehow can be compromised by the person-in-the-middle. Often, such is not the case, and more subtle behaviors are seen. Information may be withheld from superiors or subordinates and feelings may be masked. Thus, W. H. Read (1962) found that managers who communicated to their superiors with less complete accuracy were more upward mobile. The relationship was conditioned by the extent to which managers trusted their superiors and perceived them to have influence with higher management. Walker, Guest, and Turner (1956) studied the problems of supervisors on an assembly line where the workers were under constant pressure because of inability to control their speed of work. The most effective supervisors were found to absorb the pressures and criticisms from higher management without communicating their frustrations and tensions to workers.

Consistent with Jambor (1954), persons in the middle may acquiesce to one party (usually their more powerful superiors) and rationalize their position with their conflicting party (usually their less powerful subordinates). Thus, Roff (1950) reported that subordinates rated their immediate combat officers as less sincere, less impartial, and more concerned about personal advantage than did the superiors of these officers. Yet, according to a study reported by Wickert (1947), an officer must appear sincere and consistent to be rated a successful combat crew leader.

Political leaders are caught in a cauldron of conflicting demands from their various constituencies. Followers have difficulty checking on the authenticity of their leaders who often can maintain office indefinitely without such sincerity and consistency. According to Titus (1950), "hypocrisy may be necessary when working with followers but it should be held to the barest minimums." (One person's hypocrisy is another's tactfulness.) For Jameson (1945), leaders need to "wear masks," disguising their own feelings to live up to expectations despite conflicting demands upon them. Barnard's (1938) "fine art of executive decision" noted that superiors' demands for conflict-laden decisions by the executive must be met. However, responsibility for them can be delegated. Subordinates' demands for such decisions need only be met when important. They cannot be delegated. The tactful executive can avoid conflict-laden decisions on questions not now pertinent as well as premature decisions, impossible solutions, and decisions others should make.

*Openness, Trust, and Confrontation.* Behavioral scientists argue otherwise. Shartle (1956) pointed to the efficacy of substitution. Leaders should have a balanced, flexible set of identifications with various organizational projects and plans. If they find themselves blocked in one line of activity, they can shift to another, thus avoiding a strong feeling of frustration and defeat. J. M. Burns (1978) saw conflict as an opportunity to display leadership. The leader (in contrast to the status quo administrator) converts the demands, values, and goals of conflicting constituencies into workable programs: "Leaders, whatever their professions of harmony, do not shun conflict; they confront it, exploit it, ultimately embody it. Standing at the points of contact among latent conflict groups, they can take various roles, sometimes acting directly for their followers, sometimes bargaining with others, sometimes overriding certain motives of followers and summoning others into play."

What is required here is the belief that discussion of conflict can be constructive and that conflicting parties can be trusted to work toward effective outcomes if communications between them are open. Evidence is mixed in support of this contention. Friedlander and Margulies (1969) found that the task motivation and involvement of research personnel were maximized by high management trust and by freedom from burdensome routine duties. Wilcox and Burke (1969) concluded that openness between workers and supervisors resulted in greater job satisfaction for both. However, Rubin and Goldman (1968) found no difference between effective and ineffective managers in openness of communication. Willits (1967) studied twenty small manufacturing firms. Although, as expected, measures of company success were positively related to the president's openness in communicating ideas, they were negatively related to his open communication of feelings. Furthermore, open communication by the other executives did not coincide with company success. But Culbert and McDonough (1980) still feel that essential to organizational and individual effectiveness is the awareness of self-interests and the need to deal with them.

*Converting Conflict into Problem Solving.* Walton and McKersie (1965, 1966) and Likert and Likert (1978) think that conflict resolution is possible if it can be converted from win–lose negotiations to a problem solving situation from which both parties can emerge as winners. Furthermore, Likert and Likert think it is particularly important that conflicting parties avoid having to debate solutions to the conflict before they have reached agreement on what they deem as essential in the outcomes and what they regard as desirable. This position is consistent with Bass's (1966b) finding that negotiators who begin with committed solutions were much more likely to deadlock than those who entered negotiations without firm solutions in mind. They also fit with Maier's (1967, 1970) results indicating that an early focus on solutions causes groups to neglect trying to find more creative ways of meeting their problems. Solution-minded groups cling to those solutions that they favored prior to negotiations.

An increase in the status and esteem congruence and an awareness of the discrepancies between the formal and informal hierarchies in groups are likely to reduce potential conflict. According to Whyte and Gardner (1945), supervisors of the formal organization need to make themselves aware of the informal organization, discover the informal leader, and obtain his or her cooperation and agreement to work toward common goals. Supervisors can use the informal organization constructively to convey attitudes, locate grievances, and maintain social stability (K. Davis, 1951). They need to identify the differences and values that buttress the informal compared to the formal organization. Such differences were seen within air force technical units. On the one hand, there was agreement between the formal and informal organizations that cooperation and pride in the formal organization were desirable and that the most competent personnel were most valuable. But there was conflict in attitudes of the formal and informal organization about punishment for laxity and the need for high standards of performance (Anonymous, 1945–1946).

Others who have advocated and reviewed behavioral approaches to conflict resolution include Janis and Mann (1977) and Levi and Benjamin (1977).

## ROLE SANCTION, LEGITIMATION, AND CONFLICT

Role legitimation refers to others' perception of an individual's right to function in a given position. Appointment of an individual to a given position legitimizes his or her role performance, at least for those who do the appointing. Election to an office legitimizes the role of the elected individual, at least in the eyes of those who voted for the candidate. But these forms of legitimation may be lost if the individual fails to perform as expected.

The discrepancies between what others expect and one's own expectations will be a source of role conflict. Failure of one group to achieve consensus in expectations about their own or others' requirements likewise causes conflict. Conversely, agreement about role requirements and conformity to normative expectations generally are found to contribute to effectiveness in organizational life.

Many research analyses point to the dissatisfaction and ineffectiveness that result from such divergencies in political, educational, military, and industrial settings. Schein and Ott (1962) studied the attitudes of managers, union leaders, and college students toward the legitimacy of influencing various kinds of behavior. The three groups were agreed on the legitimacy of influencing job-related behaviors, but they differed on other categories of behavior. F. J. Davis (1954) repeated the Schein and Ott study with students in the air force. Contrary to hypothesis, air force personnel did not endorse the legitimacy of actions considered illegitimate by managers, union leaders, and students. All groups consider it legitimate for a supervisor to influence job performance and work environment.

Substantive conflicts in legitimation of the leader's rights can best be catalogued in the context of their social settings.

### Public and Community Settings

J. M. Burns (1978) has noted that conflict may be sharper in public bureaucracies because of their legal obligations to respond to clients who can exert pressure on them. Conflict within public bureaucracies is exacerbated when the external political climate restricts objective goal setting and even-handed decision making. Those located at the outer boundaries of the bureaucracy are much more likely to face such politically based conflict than those located far inside the organization (Katz & Kahn, 1966).

Eisenstadt (1954) studied resettlement communities in Israel. Each had developed specific norms although incorporating the norms of the surrounding culture. Norms were perceived as prescribing proper types of behavior for given roles and role situations. To some extent, reference group norms served as general standards in terms of which various patterns of behavior were evaluated. Leaders, because of their wider range of reference groups, served as a medium for consolidating the subgroups and integrating them into an effective larger group. Leadership was found ineffective when followers were apathetic toward an issue requiring integrative action, when the leaders' broader orientation did not correspond with the practical issues faced by followers, when the leaders had no authority on broader issues, and when they were in conflict with other leaders.

Although, as will be seen later in this chapter, in experimental settings, election or appointment makes a difference in legitimization and success as a leader, Vengroff (1974) failed to observe that community participation in the development of thirty-one villages in Botswana was influenced by whether leaders were elected councillors or traditional tribal chiefs.

*Business and Industry*

In a study of managers' attitudes, Schein and Lippitt (1966) found that those in roles involving close supervision and high centralization of responsibility regarded it as legitimate to influence subordinates in more areas than other management groups. Contrary to hypothesis, managers whose subordinates had more visible roles and interacted more frequently with outsiders did not exercise more influence than those whose subordinates had less visible roles.

Both superiors and subordinates expected communication, development, delegation, understanding, know-how, and teamwork from supervisors, according to Brooks (1955). Autonomy rather than legitimacy was critical to the supervisors themselves. In a study of first-line supervisors, Klein and Maher (1970) found that lack of autonomy was related to role conflict. But neither the perceived legitimacy of autonomy nor the discrepancy between legitimate and actual autonomy was related to role conflict for the supervisors. However, Ulrich, Booz, and Lawrence (1950) observed that superiors may make conflicting demands on the supervisory role. Conflict was latent in Freeman and Taylor's (1950) survey in which 100 top executives said they looked for aggressive, energetic applicants for management positions in the company, even though they personally wanted "tactful subordinates." They attributed their own success to "brains and character," but they preferred "emotionally controlled and balanced" subordinates rather than overly bright or highly ethical ones. The conflict was illustrated most clearly in these self-perceptions of top management when compared with those in middle management. Whereas the top managers emphasized their self-determination, enterprise, and dignity, 170 middle managers emphasized their own discreetness, modesty, practicality, patience, deliberateness, and planfulness. Whereas the top executives disavowed stinginess, shyness, and lack of ambition, the middle managers avoided describing themselves as reckless, disorderly, aggressive, and outspoken (Porter & Ghiselli, 1957).

Wernimont (1971) found that workers also tended to make contradictory demands on their supervisors. On the one hand, they expressed a desire for clear instructions and goal setting. On the other hand, they wanted considerable freedom to do work their own way. In the same way, Foa (1956) compared ideal and actual behavior descriptions of foremen and workers in Israeli factories. He found that workers complained most frequently about foremen's ineffective social relations. However, workers were more critical of their own conduct than of their foremen's conduct. But foremen complained little about work behavior. The smaller the discrepancy between their ideal for the foreman and their descriptions of his actual behavior, the better satisfied were workers with him. When the workers identified with their foreman, they attributed to him the same ideals that they held for themselves.

There seems to be a fundamental difference in the ideals of managers' roles and how they actually are required to enact them. Hortatory admonitions, managerial ideals, the popular literature, and normative expectations all counsel the need for system and deliberation at all levels. As McCall (1977) has noted, these assume that managers are likely to be engaged in a small number of events with enough time to ponder about how they should behave in response to the events. Nevertheless, the demands on a typical manager make such deliberation impossible. Thus, Guest (1956) found that foremen in one investigation were involved in 583 activities in a single day; 200 and 270, in another. S. Carlson (1951) reported that Swedish top executives in his study remained undisturbed for only an average of twenty-three minutes during a day. Mintzberg (1973) found that half the activities of five top executives lasted nine minutes or less, concluding that executives' activities were fragmented, brief, and varied with little control over it. Ninety-three percent of their contacts were arranged on an ad hoc basis. They initiated only 32 percent of them.

### Educational Settings

Torrance (1959) studied groups under different degrees of instructor pressure to accept a new food. He found that group members expected instructors to exercise influence and that such influence was not perceived as high pressure.

Lee, Horwitz, and Goldman (1954) completed an experiment in which each of three instructors of ROTC cadet classes were given more or less authority to decide whether certain instructions should be repeated. Most students voted to repeat, but in each class, the instructor arbitrarily decided to not repeat the assignment. The instructor met the greatest resentment and hostility when the students believed that he had little authority to make a decision. Thus, the "planted" instructor who acted as if he had a great deal of authority but did not in the eyes of the students, met with the greatest rejection. An instructor believed to have the authority could act in this manner and be less resented for doing so.

M. V. Campbell (1958) reported that when teachers' needs and role behavior were close to the principal's expectations for them, teachers tended to feel better satisfied, were more confident of the principal's leadership, and were rated as more effective by the principal. Seeman (1953, 1960) studied principals and teachers in twenty-six communities. Although teachers expected the principal to attend to matters within the school, the principal's success in improving the school situation depended on devoting time to public relations matters outside the school. When principal and teachers disagreed about the principal's role, the principal reported less indecision than did teachers, for the principal was required to take actions more often than were the teachers.

Gross, Mason, and McEachern (1958) and Gross, McEachern, and Mason (1966) studied role conflict in school superintendents who differed in their perceptions of the legitimacy of various expectations held for them and of the severity of sanctions that might be applied in case of noncompliance with expectations. Those with a moralistic orientation tended to conform to legitimate expectations and reject illegitimate ones regardless of the sanctions involved. Those with an expedient orientation (who gave priority to sanctions) tended to conform to those expectations attended by the strongest sanctions for noncompliance or to compromise in order to minimize sanctions. A third type of superintendents gave equal weight to legitimacy and sanctions.

Gross, Mason, and McEachern (1958) also studied reference group identifications and consensus among school board members and superintendents. The latter were more strongly identified than board members with external professional reference groups. In division of responsibilities, groups assigned more tasks to their own position than to the other. They expressed greater approval of by-passing the other group than their own position. Superintendents rated boards more highly and were better satisfied when there was consensus on the board. The greater the consensus on the board, the higher was its rating of the superintendent, but the board's rating of the superintendent was not related to agreement with the board.

### Situations with Two Leaders

Osborn, Hunt, and Skaret (1977) looked at the potential conflicts between the two leaders in thirty-three local chapters of a national business fraternity—the chapter adviser and the elected president, whose duties overlapped. The authors concluded that organizational effectiveness would be enhanced if only one leader played an active role in influencing subordinates and exchanges with other units. Whyte (1943) noted that a conflict in his street corner gang was most likely due to a quarrel between two highly influential members, the gang leader and his lieutenant.

Borg (1957) also showed that teams in which two leaders emerged scored significantly lower on effectiveness than where one or even where no leader emerged. Furthermore, Borg (1956) showed that the effectiveness of an emergent leader was significantly lower if an appointed leader was also present. Choosing an ineffective leader served to suppress the emergence of a more capable one. Hunt, Osborn, and Larson (1973) examined these two-leader configurations in mental institutions, and reviews were completed by Hunt, Hill, and Reaser (1973), Kerr, Schriesheim, Murphy, and Stogdill (1974), and Nealy and Fiedler (1968).

### Military Settings

Levy (1954) contrasted aircrews led in periodic discussion by their own aircrew commanders with aircrews whose discussions were led by clinical psychologists. In the groups led by their own commander, members had more favorable attitudes toward their own group and greater improvement in sense of well-being than in groups led by the clinical psychologist.

Many other military studies were completed dealing with the effects of role sanctions, legitimation, and conflict. Greer (1954) observed that among the more effective of twenty-six infantry rifle squads in six hours of simulated combat, appointed leaders were seen to act more closely to what was desired and expected of them by the rest of the squad. Failure to live up to subordinates' expectations was likely to result in conflict.

World War II officers and enlisted personnel were found by Stouffer, Suchman, et al. (1949) to disagree markedly on whether officers should maintain social distance from enlisted personnel. While 82 percent of enlisted personnel agreed that "an officer will have the respect of his men if he pals around with them off duty," only 27 percent of captains, 39 percent of first lieutenants, and 54 percent of second lieutenants agreed. Similarly, E. L. Scott (1956) found that enlisted personnel on small ships perceived the organization's status structure more accurately when superiors interacted less extensively throughout the organization, retained authority in their own hands, and delegated less freely.

Merton and Kitt (1950) found that enlisted personnel who expressed attitudes in conformity with the army norm were promoted more rapidly. If they accepted the status structure of the army as legitimate, they were more readily identified with others at their own or next higher status level.

### Experimental Settings

Knapp and Knapp (1966) studied elected officers and nonofficers as group leaders in a verbal conditioning experiment. Officer-led groups exhibited a higher rate of response and conditioned more readily than groups led by nonofficers. Thus, official status facilitated group learning.

*Election versus Appointment.* Experimentation offered the opportunity to study legitimation of the leadership role by election in contrast to legitimation by appointment. Experimental groups were permitted by Raven and French (1957) to elect one of their members as supervisor. In half of the groups, the elected supervisor was replaced by an appointed leader. In contrast to appointed leaders, election established the leaders' right to their position, increased their personal attractiveness, and resulted in acceptance of their suggestions by members.

Hollander and Julian (1970) found in an experiment with problem-solving groups that members were more willing to accept selfish action by an elected leader than by an appointed one. In another experiment by Hollander and Julian (1970), team members ranked several items as to relative importance. The leader could accept the team ranking or reverse it. Elected leaders deviated from their groups more than appointed leaders. Both types of leaders deviated more with strong than with weak support from group members. The authors concluded that more is expected of the elected than of the appointed leader, and the former is given greater latitude to deviate and act on behalf of group goals. But the leader must be aware of this advantage in order to profit from it.

When persons to speak for the group were elected rather than appointed, again legitimacy was greater, but the elected speaker was more likely to be rejected than the appointed one if he or she was seen to be incompetent or unable to produce results. The appointed person satisfied group members only if he or she was competent or successful (Julian, Hollander & Regula, 1969). According to Hollander (1978), election created higher demands by group members for the leader's performance. Such elected speakers for the group showed greater firmness than appointed persons. Only if they could consult their members, were persons appointed to speak for the group as firm (Hollander, Fallon & Edwards, 1977). Elected speakers also felt freer to yield than appointed ones (Boyd, 1972) and to accept or reject the decisions of the group they were representing (Hollander & Julian, 1970).

### The Struggle for Status and Legitimacy

When all members in the community, the work unit, or the experimental setting are initially equal in status—the value of their initial positions in their groups—a struggle for status will result.

The "right to lead," the office of leader, may not exist in an informal discussion. Gaining the right to lead and obtaining the status of leader will depend on individual initiative, assertiveness, competence, and esteem. To the degree that individuals strive for status, a struggle for such status is likely to be seen where no leader has been elected or appointed in advance. Many factors will affect this struggle including each combatant's self-estimates and credibility as well as situational contingencies. Leaders seem more concerned than followers about maintaining their status. Gallo and McClintock

(1962) studied leaders and nonleaders in the presence of three accomplices who supported the participant in the first session but withdrew their support in the second session. Leaders initiated more task-oriented behaviors than followers, especially when their positions were threatened in the second session. They also exhibited more hostility and antagonism when their status was threatened. Gartner and Iverson (1967) informed experimental groups that one member would be selected for a superior position in another group. The chance for upward mobility in status interfered with task performance in well-established groups, but it reduced member morale rather than productivity in newly formed groups.

*Overestimated Status.* The struggle for status is augmented by the tendency for members of organizations and groups to overestimate their own status and power (Bass & Flint, 1958a). There is a general tendency to believe oneself to hold a more important position than the importance others ascribe to the position. Self-accorded status is higher than accorded status (Bass, 1960). Role conflict is obvious. Those at a designated organizational level see all below them having "smaller" jobs than the job holders themselves see they occupy. All those above see the job holder at the designated level as holding a "smaller" job than perceived by the job holder himself or herself (Haas, Porat & Vaughan, 1969). In the same way, J. D. Campbell (1952) found that 250 Boston residents tended to rate their own jobs higher in value than jobs very similar to their own.

Conflict results when people interacting or working together each overestimate the importance of their own positions and underestimate the importance of others with whom they interact. A janitor of an apartment house may adopt "professional standards," according himself more status than his tenants grant that he has. Resentment and conflict are likely (Gold, 1951/1952). A foreman may accord himself more status and authority than his unionized subordinates grant to him. His attempts to lead his subordinates will meet with rebuff (Wray, 1949).

*Visibility and Clarity.* The struggle is most likely among a group of strangers. But if the abilities and past performance records of members are made clear to all, if their esteem is made more visible, the conflict about who shall lead is reduced. Bradford and French (1948) emphasized that the productivity of group thinking depended on the ability of group members to perceive clearly each other's roles. Drucker (1946) observed that despite the informality of relations among executives in the different divisions of General Motors, they worked together with relatively little conflict. The absence of conflict was attributed to objective measures of division performance which made the effectiveness of the executives visible to each other.

Legitimation also depends on clear and accepted group norms. B. R. Clark (1956) found that high status members of a group could not be fully legitimized as such if the group norms were not clearly defined and not well accepted by the members.

*Credibility.* Legitimation involves gaining credibility as being trustworthy and informative. Strong positive correlations have been found by Klauss and Bass (1981) in social service agencies, military organizations, and industrial firms between such credibility and success of managers as leaders as seen by their subordinates. Trustworthiness develops from gaining "membership character," by being seen as loyal to the group, conforming to the prevailing norms, and establishing that one is motivated to belong and identify with the group (Hollander, 1958).

*Stability of Legitimacy.* The stability of legitimate power tends to depend on the existence of validators. Hollander (1978) pointed out that leaders have validators of their positions who can support the leader's legitimacy or withdraw it. The validators uphold the leader's right to office even where such a leader's performance is inadequate. Unable to admit their errors, with investment in the leader and sense of responsibility for the leader, they continue to support the failing leader, particularly when the leader's term of office is fixed (Hollander, Fallon & Edwards, 1977).

Another force for stability legitimacy was demonstrated by A. R. Cohen (1958), who found that leaders under threat of status reduction may also redefine the group boundaries in such a manner as to isolate themselves from the very members whose support they need. Cohen found that high-status members in unstable positions communicate less with low-status members than high-status members in stable positions.

A third reason for stability was suggested by Caro (1974). The incumbent leader amasses knowledge of rules and regulations, development of the required organization contacts and contracts, and the trappings of power.

Higher authority may provide the fourth reason for stability. Katz, Blau, Brown, and Strodtbeck (1957) studied groups of four members engaged in discussion in time 1. In time 2, each member ranked three tasks as to desirability and chose a task for the next session. In time 3, half the groups performed the chosen task and others were required to perform unchosen tasks. The chances of remaining a leader in time 3 was significantly related to whether the task of the leader's choice was chosen by the group or imposed by the experimenter. If the group's choice of task was guided by the leader, the imposition of a different task threatened his leadership, but his position was strengthened if he did not enforce the imposed task rejected by the group. The greater the degree of disagreement he stimulated in time 1, the less his chance of remaining a leader in time 3, suggesting that the leader may "sow the seeds of his own downfall." When the leader experienced little initial opposition, his choice of a task was supported by the group. He was more likely to retain his leadership when a task was imposed upon the group than when its chosen task was performed. These results suggest that when a group that challenges its leader is overruled by a superior authority, this fact reinforces the leader's position.

A fifth reason may lie in high-status members blocking restructure of the situation if such a restructure would involve loss of their status (Burnstein & Zajonc, 1965b).

*Changes in Leader Behavior.* Heinicke and Bales (1953) and Whyte (1953) noted that only after the struggle for status has ended and a stable hierarchy has been organized, can those who had been characterized by a great deal of overt interaction (Chapter 6) reduce their activity level. Once a person is fully recognized by the other members as the leader, once he or she has won the struggle for status, he or she needs to attempt less leadership to exhibit the same amount of successful leadership. Thus, Bass, Gaier, and Flint (1956) found that when all the members of a group of ROTC cadets were equal in control over each other, in order for a member to exhibit more than an average amount of public leadership, he had to attempt more than the average amount of leadership. But in groups in which members differed initially in control over each other, successful leadership was less dependent on a great deal of attempts to lead. However, this did not apply to private success as a leader. Moreover, Bass, Pryer, Gaier, and Flint (1958) failed to find that groups where members were equal in control of each other exhibited a greater total amount of attempted leadership to solve problems than groups where some members had more control than others. It may be that as much conflict and rejection of leadership attempts occurred when members differed initially in control as when they were equal, but for different reasons. In these fifty-one groups of ROTC cadets, a subsequent analysis made by Bass and Flint (1958a) showed that although members of greater power attempted more leadership and were seen by others to have exhibited more success, they actually were no more successful. Moreover, high-control members significantly overestimated their esteem compared to members of low control. The control and power differences arbitrarily assigned to some of these participants may have aroused hostility and resentment among those without control. Although members of low control saw themselves as submitting to the powerful members, they actually rejected in greater proportions the attempts by the more powerful to lead.

*Usurpation.* As noted earlier in the chapter, when the legitimate leader continues to be inadequate in meeting the needs of the group, usurpation may occur. According to Crockett (1955) who studied conference leadership, emergent leaders tended to take control when the designated chairman performed few acts in the area of goal setting, information seeking, solution proposing, and problem proposing—and when cliques with divergent goals were present in the conference. Similarly, Lowin and Craig (1968) found that members initiated more structure in work groups when the superiors were incompetent. Others who found that members initiate if the leader fails to do so include Mulder and Stemerding (1963), Hamblin (1958), Helmreich and Collins (1967), Polis (1964), and Carlson (1960). Again, in groups of men engaged in railroad maintenance work, Katz, Macoby, Gurin, and Floor (1951) found that when the supervisor failed to exercise his leadership functions, one of the workers in the group exercised them in his stead. Heyns (1948) also found that when the appointed leader of a group fails to perform his duties satisfactorily, the leadership attempts of other group members are more readily accepted than when the leader is adequate. In the same way, P. J. Burke (1966a,b) noted that disruptive behavior in experimental groups was significantly related to the leader's failures to establish an authority structure for the group.

Stogdill (1965a) studied twenty-seven organizations of six types. In metal shops involving high degrees of precision in which a piece of work could be ruined by interference and adjacent horseplay, the workers applied pressure on deviant group members when the supervisor failed to provide structure. In textile mills, women operators of high-speed sewing machines paid on an output basis, applied pressure on deviant members if their supervisors were inexperienced or failed to keep order.

J. R. P. French and J. Gyr (Institute for Social Research, 1954) contrasted the performance of an elected supervisor with one who usurped the status. Under the usurper's occupancy of the leadership position there was greater private rejection of leadership efforts compared with those of the legitimately elected supervisor and more discrepancy between public and private compliance of the membership.

## Leadership Replacement

In addition to usurpation, more legitimate forms of replacement of the leader are strongly associated with their failure to serve the group adequately. They are disposed and replaced when their validators or higher authority completely lose confidence in their competence to serve the needs of the organization or group (Hollander, 1978). Such loss of confidence, usually associated with deterioration in the group's performance, results in change of leadership. Furthermore, Ziller (1965b) obtained results suggesting that rapid replacement of group leaders provides a means of creating new ideas leading to continued group success.

In addition to lack of follower acceptance, leader turnover also may be attributed to lack of role orientation (Graen & Ginsburgh, 1977). Although the cause-effect relations remain controversial, Grusky (1963) found a negative relationship between baseball win–loss records and a relatively high frequency of replacing team managers. But Lieberson and O'Connor's results (1972) implied that changes in corporate sales, profit, and profit margins of industrial organizations over a twenty-year period (1946 to 1965) could be explained by factors other than changes in the corporate president or chairman of the board. Durbrow (1971) analyzed the biographical sketches of some 5,300 executives in 429 organizations classified in ten major industries. Mobility was positively correlated with education, but negatively correlated with age and number of years with firm. Mobility rates were highest in the aerospace, electronics, and office equipment industries; lowest in gas utility, electric utility, and chemical industries. Burbrow found that firms with low rates of executive turnover made the highest profits in high-mobility industries. Firms with high rates of executive turnover made the highest profits in low-mobility industries.

Trow (1961) reported no consistent effect of the average rate of succession on company performance. Hamblin (1958b) found that lower-performing experimental groups of college students were most likely to want to replace their leader. Eitzen and Yetman (1972) and Trow (1961) felt that the results best supported a curvilinear relationship. There is an optimum leadership turnover rate. Nevertheless, Schendel et al. (1976) found 80 percent of turnaround strategies associated with replacement of top managers. Similar results were reported by Graham and Richards (1979) for the railroad industry. But a study of fifty-four petrochemical firms by Helmich (1978) found that presidential turnover was linked mostly to merger activities. More will be said about leadership succession in Chapter 29.

We now turn to three concepts central to the legitimacy of formal leadership: authority, responsibility, and delegation.

# 14

## AUTHORITY, RESPONSIBILITY, AND DELEGATION

### AUTHORITY

A key issue in management is the meshing of responsibility, authority, and delegation. Subordinates queried by Bass and Valenzi (1974) commonly reported that their superiors tended to delegate a great deal of responsibility to them without the necessary authority to go along with it.

#### *Meaning of Authority*

Traditionalists defined authority as the right to command and to induce compliance. Behaviorists following the influence of Barnard (1938) maintained that leaders have authority only to the extent that followers are willing to accept their commands (Petersen, Plowman & Trickett, 1962). Both traditional and behavioral definitions are phrased in terms of value judgments in support of two conflicting moralities or ideologies (Wells, 1963). Stogdill (1957b, 1959) and Petersen, Plowman, and Trickett (1962) defined authority operationally in terms of the areas of freedom available to members of an organization in carrying out their responsibilities.

Peabody (1962) found that executives in a city welfare agency emphasized legitimacy and position as bases of authority, whereas policemen stressed competence as the basis. In a later study, Peabody (1964) studied authority relations in a police department, a welfare agency, and a public school. Supervisors tended to think of authority in terms of internal (superior–subordinate) relations, whereas the people supervised tended to think of it in terms of external (worker–client) relations. More frequently, police accepted conflict-producing instructions without question. Unacceptable use of authority was more common in the welfare agency than in the police department or public school.

Authority specifies a member's perceived area of freedom of action and interaction, the delegated or recognized right to initiate action. Members act in accordance with their perception of (1) the degree of freedom allowed them and (2) of the initiative that they feel they can safely exercise. Their own perception may or may not coincide with the expectations of their supervisors, peers, and subordinates.

*Authority and Leadership.* In general, group leaders perceive themselves to have a higher degree of authority than do the leaders of subgroups, and these in turn perceive their authority as higher than the perceived authority of individual members responsible for individual task performance. Authority gives legitimate power which depends on the norms and expectations held by a group appropriate to a given role—the accorded rights, duties, and privileges that go along with appointment or election to a position.

*Authority and Delegation.* Authority is an interactional relationship. Leaders can restrict the authority of subordinates by withholding the right to act and decide. They can increase the authority of followers by delegating the right to act. Followers can reduce leader authority by failure or refusal to accept their decisions. They can increase leader authority by referring matters to the leaders for decision. The area of freedom of members depends not only on the behavior of their superiors and subordinates but also on perceptions of the behavior and expectations of their superiors and subordinates. As already noted in Chapter 12, Filley and Grimes (1967) found that 864 responses of forty-four professional employees under a single department head could be classified into many different sources of authority such as formal authority, responsibility and function, manipulation, expertise, control of resources, and so on. Conflict results if the leader exceeds the limits of his or her authority as seen by colleagues (Pondy, 1967). U.S. workers would find it unacceptable if their supervisors gave them orders about where they should live. According to Haas, Porat, and Vaughan (1969), an almost universal source of conflict is the tendency for individuals at any designated level to see themselves as having more authority and responsibility than their superiors believe they have. Lennerlöf (1965a) also reported a tendency for supervisors to rate themselves as having more authority than their superiors reported delegating to them.

As Hollander (1978) notes, legitimacy may be awarded by higher officials, but it still depends on the acceptance of subordinates. Followers give a form of consent to legitimacy. They can grant or withhold it, sometimes at considerable cost.

*Authority and Power.* Authority is not power. "No amount of legal authority over the grizzly bears of British Columbia would enable you to get yourself obeyed by them out in the woods" (National Research Council, 1943). In supervisor–subordinate relationships, coercive and reward power as well as legitimate power are expected in the supervisor's position along with authority, but subordinates have learned to associate reward and punishment with the supervisory position and its symbols of status and authority. An analysis of authority and power requires examining attitudes and expectations about authority figures and symbols as well as the rules and regulations describing what we should expect of holders of positions of authority (Bass, 1960).

As J. M. Burns (1978) notes, authority is power legitimated by tradition, religion, and rights of succession and is distinguished from force and coercion. In traditional societies, authority was the legal support for the father, the priest, and the noble. It came from God, the Will of Heaven, or Nature. In modern societies, formal authority derives from man-made constitutions, compacts, charters, judges' rulings, and due process. The state has the authority to charter the board. The board has the authority to appoint the organization president. The president has the authority to hire a staff, and so on. At the same time, decisions can be reversed in the same way. Those who appoint a leader to a given position usually have the authority to revoke functions previously assigned, to remove units of organization from the leader's jurisdiction, and to dismiss him or her from office. Even when supported by his superiors, an appointed leader may find himself frustrated and powerless when subordinates (like grizzly bears) refuse to obey his commands. A once powerful elected leader is likely to find that he no longer has influence after his followers withdraw their support from him or give it to an opponent. Thus, the concept of role legitimation (Chapters 12 and 13) calls attention to the fact that the power and influence of a leader are dependent upon acknowledgment of his authority by followers and in some circumstances by superiors or peers.

### Strength and Ubiquity of Authority

As noted earlier, in Milgram's (1965) experiment, participants accepted a much higher than expected amount of experimenter authority in their willingness to deliver supposedly "dangerous" shocks to other students. In a study of more than 1700 individuals in formal organizations, Stogdill (1957a) found that only about 1 in 500 checked the statement "I have no authority whatsoever." Even unskilled mechanics rated themselves as having more than zero responsibility and authority. Authority is not confined to the leadership structure. All members of an organization possess some degree of freedom (authority) for the performance of their job. Furthermore, Zander, Cohen, and Stotland (1957) observed that the possession of authority and the exercise of authority tended to be highly correlated.

*Status Effects on Acceptance of Authority.*   Contrary to hypothesis, Scheffler and Winslow (1950) found that persons in low-status positions did not reject authority more than did high-status members. W. E. Scott (1965) studied the attitudes of workers in a professional organization that allowed very little autonomy on the job. Workers tended to accept the system of restrictive supervision. However, those who were professionally (externally) oriented, were more critical of the authority structure than those who identified themselves internally.

*Motivational Effects on Acceptance of Authority.*   Chapter 11 suggested that control over what others want is what provides power over them (Bass, 1960). Such power for leaders, rather than empty formal authority, depends on the extent to which they can activate the needs and motives of their subordinates (J. M. Burns, 1978). The stronger the motivational base the leader can tap, the more authority, power, and control can be exercised. Thus, Hollander and Bair (1954) reported that highly motivated members of a group tended to identify more strongly with authority figures than members low in motivation. Berkowitz and Lundy (1957) observed that individuals low in interpersonal confidence tended to be influenced more readily by peers than by authority figures, whereas the reverse was true for persons high in interpersonal confidence.

### Scope of Authority and Its Effects

D. E. Tannenbaum (1959) found in five agencies that the board of directors can enlarge or restrict the chief executive's role by its willingness or refusal to delegate authority to act and decide. S. Epstein (1956) studied the effects of this enlargement or restriction on supervisors in experimental groups who were given different degrees of freedom of action. Severe restriction induced the supervisors to (1) restrict the behavior of their subordinates; (2) supervise them more closely; and (3) supervise in a management-oriented manner. But absence of restriction on the supervisors induced them to give their subordinates more freedom and to supervise them less closely. Dalton, Barnes, and Zaleznik (1968) studied the changed authority structure of some departments of a research organization. Other departments were left unchanged. In those departments where authority was removed from department heads and given to scientists and engineers, the latter favored the change, but department heads did not. Heightened expectations in the control departments triggered by the changes in the experimental department resulted in dissatisfaction with superiors in the control department and in a greater tendency of those whose authority remained unchanged to seek positions elsewhere.

*Discretionary and Nondiscretionary Leadership.* Hunt, Osborn and Schuler (1978) conceptualized leadership to consist of a discretionary and a nondiscretionary component. Discretionary leadership was that under control of the leader. Nondiscretionary leadership was that invoked by the organizational setting in which the leader operated. For approving and sanctioning leader behavior in a large engineering division of a public utility, the leader's nondiscretionary score was that portion of the original score predicted by organizational practices. The discretionary score was equal to the difference between predicted and original scores.

Table 14.1 shows the relative extent to which each of four original leader behaviors toward subordinates (approval, consideration, disapproval, ego deflation) was accounted for as discretionary and nondiscretionary. It can be seen that the rewarding leader behavior had more of a nondiscretionary component.

Subordinates may also display discretionary leader behavior. Goodacre (1953) studied good and poor combat units on performance problems. There was a greater tendency in good units for the men without authority to take initiative for giving orders during the problem and to be better satisfied with their leaders' management of the problem than was the case in poor-performing units.

## RESPONSIBILITY

### Meaning of Responsibility

Authority in organizations is meant to be used to fulfill assigned responsibilities (Hollander, 1978). Responsibility is a member's perception of the expectations placed upon him or her to perform on behalf of the group. Generally, leaders perceive their responsibilities to be broader and more far-reaching than other group members perceive their own responsibilities. Leaders see their responsibilities as concerned with making policies and initiating action for the group as a whole, whereas subordinate levels of

**Table 14.1**
**Percent of Variance Accounting for Discretionary
and Nondiscretionary Components of a Manager's Behavior**

|  | Leader Behavior | | | |
| --- | --- | --- | --- | --- |
|  | *Approval* | *Consideration* | *Disapproval* | *Ego Deflation* |
| Discretionary | 77 | 77 | 90 | 81 |
| Nondiscretionary | 20 | 22 | 9 | 1 |
| Error | 3 | 1 | 1 | 18 |

SOURCE: Hunt, Osborn, and Schuler (1978).

leadership and other members perceive theirs as concerned with initiating action for specified subgroups or executing individual assignments.

*Interdependence.*   Like authority, responsibility also depends on leader–follower relations. The leader can reduce the responsibility of other group members by failure or refusal to relinquish duties that others could perform, by overly close supervision, and by requiring consultation before performance. Other group members can reduce the leader's responsibility by performing tasks that he or she would be expected to perform. They can increase the leader's responsibility by failing to carry out assigned and expected duties. Even when they are rather closely defined, the actions of superiors tend to condition the responsibilities of subordinates and the performance of subordinates tends to condition the duties of the leader.

### Distribution

H. H. Meyer (1959) found that foremen and general foremen did not differ significantly in their evaluations of how much responsibility the foreman had on seventy-seven items. However, more effective foremen rated themselves significantly higher in responsibility than did ineffective foremen. In a later study of twenty-one plants, Meyer (1970b) found that the most effective foremen assumed that they had full responsibility when there was any ambiguity about who was in charge. Ziller (1959) studied group leaders in a difficult decision problem that risked the safety of their group. The leaders could base their actions on a throw of dice or by making a rational decision. Leaders who accepted responsibility for group action tended to be nonconformists and to possess personal resources which enabled them to take risks without undue stress and strain.

### Accountability

Hollander (1978) pointed out that leaders more than others are likely to be held accountable, despite circumstances. A leader cannot evade the consequence of more influence over others, more control over events, greater visibility and recognition, and greater responsibility for failures, misplaced efforts, or inaction in the face of an evident threat to the group's well-being. However, leaders may try to avoid accountability or displace blame by resorting to collective responsibility vested in a committee or board or shared authority.

### DELEGATION

Delegation implies that one has been empowered by one's superior to take responsibility for certain activities. The degree of delegation is associated with the trust the superior has for the subordinate to whom responsibilities have been delegated. The relation of a leader's trust in subordinates and the tendency to delegate will be discussed in Chapter 19. When a group is the repository of authority and power, it likewise may delegate responsibilities to individual members.

Delegation should not be confused with laissez-faire leadership (Chapter 22) or abdication. A leader who delegates still remains responsible for followup as to whether the delegation has been accepted and the requisite activities have been carried out.

Delegation of decision making implies that the decision making is lowered to a lower hierarchical level closer to where the decisions will be implemented. Such delegation is consistent with what was presented in Chapter 12 on encouraging self-planning.

## ORGANIZATIONAL STUDIES OF AUTHORITY, RESPONSIBILITY, AND DELEGATION

### *Measurement: The RAD Scales*

Stogdill and Shartle (1948) developed the RAD scales measuring organizational responsibility (R), authority (A), and delegation (D). The self-rated responses by individual job occupants formed scales which exhibited high reliabilities (Stogdill, 1957a; Stogdill & Shartle, 1955). Correlational results were obtained in ten organizations engaged in manufacture of metal products, chemicals, and governmental work.

*Relations of R, A, and D.* As expected, responsibility and authority of job occupants were uniformly positive in correlation in all ten organizations ranging from .13 to .63 with a mean of .45. But relations to delegation were not as consistently high. Responsibility averaged .17 in correlation with delegation for the ten organizations, ranging from − .27 to .38. Authority averaged in correlation only .23 with delegation, ranging more widely in correlation from organization to organization, from − .42 to .49.

A critical complaint of managers is that often they are delegated a great deal of responsibility by their superiors without the associated authority. Satisfaction and productivity, it would seem, are likely to be greater where R, A, and D are highly interrelated, rather than low or negative in correlation (Bass, 1976). Thus, in the most highly aberrant organization of the ten studied by Stogdill and Shartle in which the correlation was − .42 between a manager's self-rated delegation and actual authority, one would expect dissatisfaction and ineffectiveness. In the eight organizations where delegation matched authority, to some extent satisfaction and effectiveness should have been higher.

Similar arguments could be voiced about the wide range of correlations (from .13 to .63) obtained between responsibility and authority. In the organization in which they correlated .63 one would have expected to see a smoother working system than in the organization in which the correlation found was only .13.

*Other RAD Results.* Some other patterns of interest emerged in the Stogdill and Shartle data. Age and seniority varied in their relation to R, A, and D. In one organization, authority, for example, was invested in older members; in another, in younger ones. (Such organizations were more likely to differ in technology, growth patterns, and so on, ranging as they did from metal products, chemicals, textiles, to government.) But more often than not education correlated positively with responsibility (.27) and with authority (.17). A leader's own perceived R, A, and D was unrelated to his or her subordinates' job satisfaction but a mean correlation of .19 for the 10 organizations was found between a leader's perceived authority and the extent to which his or her superior tended to be seen as considerate in leadership behavior (that is, the higher one rises in an organization, the higher one's authority is perceived and the more one is treated with consideration). More will be said about this in Chapters 18 through 21. If we assume that, generally, followers in formal organizations want autonomy, we should expect leaders who say they delegated freely to be described as considerate. Employee satisfaction should also have been highly related to delegation. But the effects obtained by Stogdill and Shartle were marginal. Subordinates often feel that their superiors do not really delegate to them the authority to accompany the responsibilities delegated. Also, superiors may believe they are delegating; their subordinates may see the same behavior as abdication, a most unsatisfying state of affairs for subordinates (Chapter 22).

The reported range of results across organization points to the moderating effects of organization on RAD relationships. In fact, H. J. Bowman (1964) found that school principals describing their superiors high in consideration on the Leader Behavior Description Questionnaire tended to rate themselves high in responsibility, authority, and delegation.

Some organizational differences were apparent and overriding. For example, the correlation between age and authority ranged from − .26 to .45. It does not take much imagination to contrast the organization in which self-estimated authority correlated .45 with age to the one in which the correlation as − .26. The former, with the negative correlation, is likely to have been a rapidly expanding high technology firm; the latter, with the high positive correlation, a stable agency with a strong age-promotion lockstep. The RAD scales thus are a useful way of describing important variations among organizations.

### Status, Salary, and RAD

Using RAD scales to study large governmental organizations, Kenan (1948) found, as expected, that executives in higher-level positions described themselves higher in responsibility, authority, and delegation than those in lower-level positions. Correspondingly, Browne (1949) noted that executive salary related positively to self-estimates of responsibility, authority, and delegation. D. T. Campbell (1956) reported that authority and delegation but not responsibility were positively and significantly related to one's level in various organizations, military rank, time in position, and receiving nominations for leadership.

### RAD and Leader–Subordinate Relations

In four large naval organizations, Stogdill and Scott (1957) found that the responsibility and authority of subordinates were related to the responsibility of their superiors, but not to the authority of their superiors. When superiors rated themselves high in level of responsibility, their subordinates rated themselves high in both responsibility and authority, but no such relationship was found with the authority of superiors. The higher the responsibility and authority of superiors, the less their subordinates tended to delegate. However, those superiors who delegated the most had subordinates who rated themselves highest in responsibility, authority, and delegation. Thus, the responsibility, authority, and delegation of superiors exerted different effects upon the behavior of their subordinates.

Stogdill and Scott (1957) correlated the responsibility, authority, and delegation scores of commanding officers and executive officers with the average RAD scores of junior officers on submarines and landing ships. Executive officers tended to delegate more freely on both types of ships when commanding officers exercised wider scopes of responsibility and authority and delegated more freely. Executive officers reported more responsibility and authority when commanding officers were high in responsibility, authority, and delegation on submarines, but the reverse was true on landing ships. The extent to which junior officers delegated was more highly related to the R, A, and D of executive officers than those of commanding officers. Juniors delegated less freely as superiors increased in R, A, and D. As the authority of the executive officer increased, the R, A, and D of junior officers tended to decrease. When the commanding officer delegated more freely, junior officers reported an increase in responsibility on landing ships, but a decrease on submarines. These findings suggested that commanding officers could increase or decrease the workload and freedom of action of their executive officers. Subordinates tended to tighten their controls as superiors increased their own responsibility and freedom of action. However, responsibility and authority did not flow without interruption down the chain of command. The responsibility, authority, and delegation of subordinates were more highly influenced by immediate supervisors than by higher-level officers.

*Expectations and Performance.* Stogdill, Scott, and Jaynes (1956) found that the performance and expectations of subordinates were related to the responsibility, authority, and delegation of their supervisors. When followers described their leader as having a large amount of responsibility, they described their own responsibility as large and described themselves as devoting considerable time to planning and computations. These same subordinates reported that they spent little time in teaching and observation, and a great deal of time attending meetings. They felt that they spent more time than they ought to in interpretation, consulting subordinates, and observation, and less time than they ought to in coordination and consulting outsiders.

The authority of superiors as perceived by subordinates was more highly related to subordinates' expectations than to their performance. When leaders were perceived to have a high degree of authority, their followers rated themselves high in responsibility and in spending comparatively large amounts of time in planning and interpretation. They spent less than average amounts of time in supervision. These subordinates felt that they ought to have more authority and that they ought to spend much time in planning, attending meetings, and consulting with outsiders, but that they should spend little time in supervision and personal contacts. The higher the authority of superiors, the greater was the tendency of their subordinates to feel that they had too much responsibility and that they had to spend more time than they ought to in research, preparing procedures, negotiations, and training. They felt that they ought to spend more time than they did in coordination and professional consultation.

When superiors were perceived to delegate freely, their subordinates not only rated themselves high in responsibility and authority, but they also felt that they should have a high degree of responsibility and authority. But they felt they had more responsibility than they ought to have and that they spent too much time in inspections, preparing procedures, training, and consulting peers—and not enough time in coordination and interpretation.

The responsibility of subordinates appeared more highly related than their authority or delegation to the responsibility, authority, and delegation of superiors. An increase in any one of these variables had the effect of increasing the responsibility of subordinates, but it did not necessarily increase their authority—which, as we said before, was a latent cause of dissatisfaction. Nor did it affect the extent to which they delegated to their own subordinates. The responsibility, authority, and delegation of superiors exerted different effects upon the performance and expectations of subordinates. An increase in any one of these variables, however, appeared to impose a demand upon subordinates for an increase in coordination.

*Discrepancies and Conflict.* Browne and Neitzel (1952) found that the greater the difference between superiors and subordinates in estimating the superiors' responsibility, the lower was the subordinates' job satisfaction. Disparities in perceptions of the superiors' authority and delegation were not related to subordinate satisfaction.

### Smaller versus Larger Organizations

The results for small ships differed rather markedly from those obtained in larger organizations (Stogdill & Scott, 1957). This was particularly true for delegation, the effects of which continued unbroken down the chain of command in large organizations. On small ships, the delegation process was broken or reversed in the third echelon down from the top. Characterized by a high rate of face-to-face interaction, the small ships were subject to greater interpersonal stresses and strains than the large organizations. The formalized interactions in highly stratified larger organizations appeared to reduce some of the tensions found in smaller organizations where personal interaction is conducted on a less formal basis. A formalized interaction structure had the effect of enlarging members' area of freedom of action, whereas the contest inherent in face-to-face interaction tended to restrict freedom of action for some group members. These findings are in accord with those reported by Cattell, Saunders, and Stice (1953), Shepherd and Weschler (1955), and others.

The linkage of superior-subordinate RAD's will now be considered in the larger framework of superior-subordinate interdependence.

part

# LEADER–FOLLOWER INTERACTION

# 15

## REINFORCEMENT AND THE PROPENSITY TO INTERACT

It takes at least two for leadership to occur. Someone has to act; someone else has to react. Whether the actions and reactions will take place will depend on who the "some-ones" are, their needs, competencies, and goals. If one can be instrumental in the goal attainment of the other, or is perceived as such, the stage is set for an interaction and mutual influence to occur.

As we have concluded from the immediately preceding chapters, if the "some-ones" begin equal in power, status, and esteem, someone will emerge as leader, some-one as follower. If someone has been appointed as leader or accorded more status and esteem, he or she will attempt to act as leader; the other person will serve as follower. What moves each to interact? What are the structures or consistent patterns of interaction of consequences to leadership within an organization or small group? What lies behind them and what are their effects? Answers to these questions form the subject of this chapter.

### SOCIOMETRY

In Chapter 10, we introduced sociometry as the first and most prominent method for gauging the status and esteem of members of a group. But Moreno (1953) by 1934 had invented this approach actually to investigate the patterns of "who interacts with whom." He constructed sociograms from the responses obtained when he asked each member of a group to list the others on some criterion, such as whom he or she liked best. Usually, a few members gathered the large share of choices. Figure 15.1 shows a sociometric diagram for a group of eight members. Only the first and second choices are shown. Member A, who received five choices, is the most highly preferred member of the group. Members B and E, who did not receive any choices, are isolates.

#### Sociometrics of Leadership

Illustrative of the different uses made of sociometry in the study of leadership are works by H. H. Jennings (1950), R. L. French (1951), Roby (1953), Levi, Torrance, and Pletts (1954), and Massarik, Tannenbaum, et al. (1953). H. H. Jennings (1950) used sociometry to distinguish the choice of leaders from other choices. She found that group members are much more selective in choosing leaders than they are in choosing friends

**FIGURE 15.1.  Sociometric Diagram**

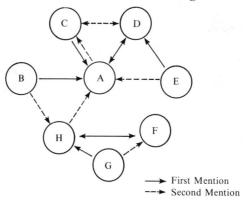

or roommates. R. L. French (1951) studied the choice structure of companies of naval recruits, finding that frequency of sick bay attendance was negatively related to sociometric score. Leadership ratings were positively related to sociometric choice by peers. But in a study of bomber crews, Roby (1953) found that the sociometric scores of members were unrelated to ratings of crew effectiveness. However, Levi, Torrance, and Pletts (1954) observed that the effectiveness of aircrews was enhanced when the officially designated leader was also the sociometrically chosen leader of the crew. (The formal and informal structures were congruent—see Chapter 13.)

Massarik, Tannenbaum, Kahane, and Weschler (1953) used five sociometric indices in a study of an organization. The indices were (1) relations prescribed by the organization chart; (2) perceived relations; (3) reported interactions; (4) preferred interactions; and (5) rejected interactions. Preferred interactions were more highly related to member satisfaction than prescribed or reported interactions. The members related more freely and were better satisfied under participative than under more directive leadership (see Chapter 19).

*Peer Ratings.*   As already noted in Chapter 10, sociometric ratings (peer ratings) forecast success as a leader. Sociometric choice as to value to the organization as a person and sociometric choice as to competence were more strongly related to subsequent success in the organization than were sociometric popularity (being liked) or visibility (being mentioned as known by the chooser). Since first introduced three decades ago to forecast subsequent success as a leader, military officer, manager, salesperson, or professional, peer ratings have continued to demonstrate strong predictive validities (Bass & Barrett, 1981).

*Propensity to Initiate and Receive Contacts*

One's esteem, competence, and status affect one's tendencies to make and receive contacts with others in a group.

*Effects of Esteem and Competence.*   Blau (1954a) found that those members of an organization rated most competent by their superiors tended to be recipients of contacts from others but did not initiate more interactions than less competent members. Blau (1955) observed that the most highly esteemed members of organizations were more accurate in recalling contacts with other members and received more contacts than less highly esteemed members. Less competent members found it easier to consult peers than superiors, but found that peers cease to be peers if consulted too frequently.

*Effects of Status.* T. Burns (1954) reported that middle managers spent more time with superiors than with subordinates, while the reverse was true for first-line supervisors. Likewise, Guest (1956) and Piersol (1958) also reported that first-line supervisors spent more time with subordinates than with superiors. The initiation of interactions with superiors may serve the function of reducing anxiety and increasing feelings of security rather than communicating about business matters (A. Kadushin, 1968; Schwartzbaum & Gruenfeld, 1969). But Zajonc and Wolfe (1966) found that managers in high-level positions and those performing staff functions maintained the widest range of formal contacts within the organization. However, informal contacts did not seem to follow any distinct pattern associated with hierarchical level or function.

Stogdill (1949) asked members of organizations to estimate the amount of time spent with other members on a working basis. Sociometric charts of working relationships were superimposed upon the informal organization chart to determine the correspondence between formally specified and actual working relationships and to diagnose communication problems within the organization. Such a chart is shown in Figure 15.2. It will be noted that the vice president, rather than the president, is the focus of working interactions. Department heads A and B also tend to be foci of interactions. Department head C is by-passed by his own subordinates, who do not interact much with each other, suggesting that the department head is not an effective leader of his group. With such a pattern of interactions, it is apparent that coordination is effected either by the vice president or by the cross-departmental contacts between section heads. The dominant trend of contact is upward rather than downward.

Stogdill (1951a) analyzed the total number of mentions given and total number of mentions received as a work partner in a small naval organization of twenty-two officers.

**FIGURE 15.2. Sociometric Diagram Superimposed on Organization Chart**

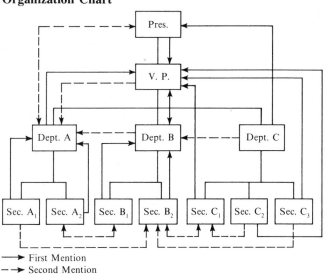

Those officers occupying high-level positions tended to mention subordinates and outsiders more frequently, and superiors less frequently, than did officers in lower-level positions. The same trend was observed in scores for mentions received. High levels of responsibility were related to more total mentions given and received and to more mentions received from members inside one's own unit and from superiors. Scope of authority was not significantly related to any sociometric scores. Those who delegated most freely tended to be mentioned most frequently as work partners by members inside their own units of organization.

## INTERACTION POTENTIAL

### Familiarity, Intimacy, and the Propensity to Interact

As we will note in Chapter 24, the potential to interact with another particular member increases as the group becomes smaller. Physical proximity and network connection between members will also increase the likelihood of interaction (Chapters 27 and 28). In addition, familiarity breeds interaction. Likewise, interaction breeds familiarity. The more intimate or familiar we are with one another, the more likely we are to interact. The more we interact, the more intimate we become (Bass, 1960). Thelen (1954) noted that subgroups composed of friends rather than strangers are likely to have more energy to spend in participating.

Intimacy and familiarity are not identical. Caplow and Forman (1950) found that length of residence in a college community merely increased the number of one's acquaintances rather than the intensity of relationships with one's neighbor. We can be familiar without being intimate. According to Klauss and Bass (1981), data from a large government agency indicated that familiarity of a colleague with a focal person was associated directly with frequency of their contact during any given week as well as the length of their acquaintanceship. Likewise, intimacy among seventy-five college students was a function of the frequency and amount of hours of contact among the students (Fisher, 1953). In studying a rumor's origin and spread, Festinger, Cartwright, et al. (1947) observed that people are less restrained in talking to close friends than to mere acquaintances. Again, Hare and Hare (1948) noted a positive correlation between amount of social activity and number of family friends among seventy families in a veterans' housing project. Increased congeniality of members was noted by Curtis and Gibbard (1955) with increased experience in both voluntary and compulsory college groups. Likewise, Seashore (1954) found that attraction for each other was greater in factory groups where members were friends for longer periods of time. Finally, Faunce and Beegle (1948) found that cliques at a teen-age farmers' camp gradually developed on the basis of newly emerged familiarities although they were initially formed around homogeneity of age, sex, and country of origin. Bass (1960) advanced two reasons for interaction to increase as a function of the familiarity and intimacy of members of groups and organizations: (1) members feel more secure in interacting with each other than with strangers; and (2) they can predict each other's actions, hence can interact with less difficulty.

*Impact on Effectiveness.* Effectiveness in the form of goal attainment tends to be associated with increased interaction. If so, effectiveness should be associated with increased familiarity and/or intimacy. Husband (1940) found that pairs of close friends took less time than pairs of strangers to solve problems in code, puzzles, and arithmetic. Similarly, Goodacre (1953) reported that among the more effective of twenty-six infantry squads in handling field problems, there was a greater tendency of squad members to socialize together after hours. However, Horsfall and Arensberg (1949), in a study of a shoe factory, failed to find any relationship between productivity and the interaction rate of supervisors.

Klauss and Bass (1981) reported that among 577 government professionals, greater trust, informativeness, and dynamism was seen by their colleagues in more familiar focal persons. Colleagues also felt more satisfied in their relations with more familiar focal persons. A correlation of .27 emerged between familiarity and perceived effectiveness of relations. But length of acquaintanceship between colleagues and focal persons was unrelated to these measures of communication effectiveness. However, a higher frequency of interaction between colleagues and focal persons correlated with satisfaction and effectiveness but not with the colleagues' judgments of the trustworthiness and informativeness of the focal persons.

### Mutual Esteem and the Propensity to Interact

Individuals are more likely to interact, the more they value each other and the more they value the interaction between them (Bass, 1960). Thus, Blau (1954a) found that the more esteemed members of a law enforcement agency were contacted by the rest of the group more frequently. Conversely, Festinger and Hutte (1954) reported that people tended to talk least to those toward whom they felt indifferent. Some interaction between individuals is usually necessary before they can increase or decrease their evaluation of each other. If the interaction or its effects are unrewarding, mutual esteem between the individuals is likely to fall.

Mutual esteem, familiarity, and contact are interdependent. When sorority women chose the seven most and seven least valued members, correlations of .48 to .58 emerged between tendency to be mentioned at all and selection as competent leader (Bass, Wurster, et al., 1953). As noted in Chapter 10, similar results were obtained with salesmen. The tendency to be mentioned (visibility) correlated positively with sociometrically rated value, ability, and influence as a salesman (Bass, 1960). Moreno (1953) also observed that esteem is related to frequency of contact. Contact can depend on propinquity. He found that members of a group who lived together valued each other more highly than those who did not live together. Bovard (1951b) reported that more pleasant interactions yielded greater attraction among members. But Festinger and Kelley (1951) found that unpleasant interactions resulted in no change in mutual attraction. However, according to Seashore (1954), longer duration of shared group friendship yielded greater cohesiveness among 228 factory groups. Similarly, a mean increase in "likability" among dramatics participants over an eleven-week rehearsal period was found by Timmons (1944). If, like familiarity, mutual esteem increases interaction, it should also increase effectiveness; and such was found by Van Zelst (1952). Carpenters and bricklayers who were paired with work partners they chose sociometrically, showed higher productivity than similar pairs when partners were assembled arbitrarily.

*Rewards, Motives, and the Propensity to Interact*

If individuals are rewarded or avoid punishment through group activity and membership, they will increase their attempts to influence each other through interaction (Gerard, 1954). Grossack (1954) contrasted the written communications of experimental participants rewarded as a group with participants in groups but rewarded as individuals. Those rewarded as a group were more likely to send messages attempting to influence others. Again, as we have noted in Chapter 6, Hemphill, Pepinsky, et al. (1956) found that individuals were more likely to attempt interaction, the greater the rewards they received for task success.

*Values, Goals, and the Propensity to Interact.* The most active members in voluntary organizations are the small percentage who strongly subscribe to the organizations' purposes and activities. Thus, Seidman, London, and Karsh (1951) observed that it was the most active union members who were most convinced of the value of union aims and operations. (The majority of members in most voluntary groups are both inactive and less interested in the means and ends of their groups than the highly active members.)

### Interaction and Homogeneity

Individuals interact more with those like themselves than those unlike themselves (Bass, 1960). Thus, Pfiffner (1951) observed that employees of the same age and seniority and doing the same work tend to associate together. Those similar in age, physical attractiveness, marital status, education, and race tend to group. Strangers first associate on the basis of their homogeneity of sex, age, and place of origin, according to Faunce and Beegle's (1948) study of campers. Again, Caplow and Forman (1953) found that interaction among neighbors in a university community was greater if families were homogeneous in occupation, number of children in the family, length of residence, and type of housing.

Homogeneity of the leader and the led is seen as particularly important to effective interaction in therapy groups (MacLennan, 1975).

### Lateral Orientation

Duffy (1973) demonstrated that supervisory and nonsupervisory personnel in two state mental hospitals tended to increase or decrease their sideward interactions and leadership if they were oriented toward peer rather than vertical relations, if they were required to do so, and if they preferred secrecy.

### Other Situational Variables Affecting the Propensity to Interact

Alcohol and drugs obviously can raise or lower interaction tendency among members of a group. Boredom has its effects also. If two persons have nothing else to do in each other's presence, they are more likely to interact than if they are otherwise occupied (Bass, 1960). Thus, when music was introduced into a factory, worker productivity on repetitive, boring jobs was increased the most where opportunities for conversation formerly had been greatest (H. C. Smith, 1947).

*Third Parties.* Third parties may influence the rate of interaction between two group members. An extension from Heider's (1958) propositions suggests that if B and C are hostile toward each other and if A and B are hostile, A will more likely interact with C than with some completely neutral member, such as D. If B and A are hostile and B and C are interacting to attain some goal, A will be less likely to interact with C than with D. If B and A are interacting to obtain a goal, and B and C are likewise cooperating, A will more likely interact with C than with D.

*Primacy.* The primacy of an interaction is important. For example, Hemphill, Pepinsky, et al. (1954) found that an individual who had more relevant information on the first task of a sequence of tasks was more likely to interact throughout the sequence than an individual who had more relevant information only on a later task in the sequence.

Other situational factors that influence the propensity to interact among individuals, according to Dodd (1955), include message potency, amount of stimulation to act in the environment, and the amount of time available for interaction.

### Individual Differences

Obviously, maturation from infancy through adolescence increases the propensity to interact (Gesell & Thompson, 1934). Intelligence also makes a difference. R. D. Mann (1959) found that intelligence was positively associated with total activity rate in all thirty-six analyses reported in six studies.

*Mental Health.* As noted by Whiteman (1954), withdrawal tendencies by schizophrenics associated with their changed social perception again will obviously lead to a lower rate of interaction with others. Institutionalized neurotics, as well, according to Levine, Laffal, et al. (1954) tend to be less influenced by group standards, and as a consequence exhibit lower interaction rates. Consistent with this, R. D. Mann (1959) found psychological adjustment correlated positively with rate of total activity in 74 percent of forty-two reported analyses.

S. Rosen (1954) studied the behavior of boys in new groups. In new groups, the overaggressive (according to previous case studies) interacted more, while the overinhibited interacted less. R. D. Mann (1959) noted that extroversion was associated positively with total activity rate in 79 percent of fourteen analyses.

## REINFORCEMENT, LEADERSHIP, AND FOLLOWERSHIP

Much of the differentiation in who attempts and continues to lead and who attempts and continues to follow can be explained by differential reinforcement. As already observed in some detail in Chapter 6, to be successful in influencing others, one must attempt to lead. Such attempts to lead, highly related usually to one's participation, verbal output, and responsivity, all have been shown to be systematically increased by positive reinforcement and decreased by negative reinforcement. The inhibition of one person by negative reinforcement can by itself augment the participation rate of the latter. The positive reinforcement of one partner can result in "crowding out" the other partner.

*Differential Reinforcement*

Mausner (1954a) gave participants either positive, negative, or no reinforcement when working alone on a judgmental task. When combined in pairs, there was a significant tendency for nonreinforced partners to shift their judgments to comply with those of their reinforced partners, while the reinforced participants did not change. Those participants who had received positive reinforcement were significantly less influenced by their partners than those who had received negative reinforcement. Thus, Mausner demonstrated that perception of the success of partners gave them prestige and reinforced the expectation of future success. Partners working with previously successful partners were significantly more influenced by them than by unsuccessful partners in a judgmental task. Banta and Nelson (1964) showed that the probability of positively reinforced participants having their suggestions adopted increased over sixty trials, while the probability for negatively reinforced participants decreased.

Along similar lines, Bandura, Ross, and Ross (1963) demonstrated that when children observed pairs of adults, one of whom had power to reward the other, with the other merely a recipient of rewards, the children tended to imitate the model who possessed rewarding power rather than the recipient of rewards. Kanareff and Lanzetta (1960) also demonstrated that imitation is responsive to rate of reinforcement.

Bavelas, Hastorf, Gross, and Kite (1965) studied active and less active participants in a discussion session. In a second session, one discussant was reinforced for participation by the flashing of a green light. In some groups, the remaining members were additionally inhibited by the flashing of a red light. The reinforced discussants significantly increased their talking and were ranked higher in sociometric choice after reinforcement than before. It was necessary not only to reinforce the initially least active talker, but to inhibit the initially most active talker, for the least active one to gain in talking and sociometric status. The least active discussant's gain was mostly at the expense of the most active talker and highest status member.

*Rates.* Jaffee (1968) and Jaffee and Skaja (1968) reinforced the leadership acts of one member of a pair of experimental partners. Those reinforced by the appearance of a light significantly exceeded nonreinforced and control participants in number of leadership attempts. The effects lasted over a test period of one week and were found to generalize to a different experimental situation. In the same way, Binder, Wolin, and Terebinski (1965, 1966) and Wolin and Terebinski (1965) controlled the proportion with which each member of a group was reinforced for decisions as a leader. The results fit a Markov model. Behavior was found responsive to changes in rates of reinforcement.

Zdep and Oakes (1967) likewise demonstrated that reinforcement of a group member's leadership acts resulted in an increase in talking and leadership. The same results were apparent in groups in which individuals had previously ranked each other as to sociometric status and in groups in which no such rankings had been made. Zdep (1969) assembled groups of four members in which one member scored either high or low on the Leadership Scale of the California Psychological Inventory. Participation rate increased under reinforcement for high scorers but not for low scorers. As participation rose, subsequent leadership ratings increased for high scorers. But reinforcement of one member builds up expectations about that member among the others, as discussed in the immediately preceding sections on influence and choice. Low scorers who failed to respond under reinforcement were rated as poorer leaders than low scorers who were not reinforced.

*Support.* McClintock (1966) used paid accomplices who either supported, shifted support, or did not support the leader of discussion groups. Leaders evidenced more tension release, more positive affect, and more task-oriented responses under support than nonsupport.

Cohen and Lindsley (1964) gave pairs of subjects a monetary reward for social responses and punishment (blackout of the room) for individual responses. Leadership acts were rewarded by opening a panel that permitted subjects to see each other briefly. Differential leadership responses were established by the human reinforcement.

*Reward versus Punishment.* Aiken (1965a) rewarded in a second session that group member who had talked the least in a previous session. The other three members were punished for speaking in the second session. Reward significantly increased verbal output in comparison with a control group, but punishment did not significantly decrease it. After the second session other members rated the rewarded member higher than control group members in leadership, participation, and self-confidence. Aiken (1965b) also demonstrated that the operant conditioning of specific behaviors, such as giving suggestions and asking for contributions, resulted in marked changes in leadership style and produced a tense, anxious leader. This suggested that simple reinforcement technology, by itself, may be inadequate for leadership training. The shaping of one member's responses must take into consideration the larger context of the interaction with other active participants.

*Choice as Leader and Teammate.* James and Lott (1964) rewarded some members of an experimental task group with six nickels, others with three, and others with none. Those rewarded with six nickels chose each other significantly more often than those with the three or zero reward condition. G. Gardner (1956) studied groups of boys who were assigned fictitious scores for success in operating switches that activated various combinations of lights. Scores correlated .93 with nominations for team captain. Observed success appeared to reinforce the perception of a group member's suitability for the leadership role. Katz, Blau, Brown, and Strodbeck (1957) found that the greater the extent to which the leader's suggestions were accepted and supported by the followers in the first session of a discussion task, the greater the extent to which the leadership was retained in later sessions. Likewise, York (1969) and Hastorf (1965) demonstrated that reinforcement of members' behavior in the group significantly increased their leadership. Gilchrist (1952) studied groups of four members in which two succeeded and two failed. These facts were communicated to group members, who then chose partners for the next problem. In the third session, the successes were made to fail and the failures were made to succeed. Both success (S) and failure (F) participants tended to choose other successes for further activity. Participants who succeeded twice (SS) chose other SS participants while those who failed twice (FF) distributed their choices between SS and FF participants. When the mutually chosen successes (SS) were again combined and made to fail, while the failures (FF) succeeded, in the third session the FFS participants tended to choose other FFS participants. The experience of success after failure enabled the previously failing participants to choose each other. The eventual experience of success operated to reinforce the expectation of success among those who had initially failed.

Lott and Lott (1960) studied children's groups in which some members were rewarded and others were not. On a subsequent sociometric test, rewarded children chose significantly more of their peer group members than did those who were not rewarded. These results suggested that reinforcement increased subgroup cohesiveness (Lott, 1961).

Results are the same when participants can directly reinforce each other. Griffitt (1968) found that participants are more attractive if others expect positive rather than negative reinforcement from them. Again, Berkowitz (1960) demonstrated that participants tend to dislike others from whom they receive experimental letters if the tone of the letter (friendly or unfriendly) does not meet previously established expectations.

*Group Reinforcement.* Although less clearly related to each individual member's performance, positive reinforcement for group success also tends to enhance performance of the members. R. L. Hall (1957) required two participants to perform a simple task while hidden from each other. They were given confounded feedback, consisting of the average of their two scores. Despite this, with practice, scores increased in team accuracy and role differentiation in who contributed most to group output.

Cook (1968) studied managers who participated in a business simulation game. Improvement in both attitude and performance was found directly related to the frequency of performance reports (feedback).

### Variables Interacting with Reinforcement

Hamblin, Miller, and Wiggins (1961) studied the effects of leader competence, leader reinforcement, and conflicting suggestions by group members on group morale. Reinforcement rate, perceived leader competence, leader success manipulation, and group morale were all highly and significantly intercorrelated. Opposition by members to the leaders' suggestions, and their failures to gain acceptance of their suggestions, were negatively related to leader reinforcement, success, competence, and group morale.

Mausner and Bloch (1957) found that reinforcement and partner prestige interacted in a judgmental task. Partner prestige and prior reinforcement were additive in the success, but not in the failure, condition. Reinforcement did not overcome the effect of a partner's failure to make correct judgments in a prior situation.

We next turn to an examination of mutual reinforcement—a key process in the relation between leaders and followers.

# 16

## INTERDEPENDENCE OF LEADERS AND FOLLOWERS

INTRODUCTION

The differential reinforcement we discussed at length in Chapter 15 derives most frequently from interpersonal reinforcement of the leader by the followers and the followers by the leader. Much of the differentiation of member roles and the emergence of leadership in a group comes about as a result of mutual reinforcement of intermember expectations. Because of their initiative, interaction, and contributions to the group task, some members reinforce the expectations that they will be more likely than other members to establish conditions which will promote task movement, member freedom and acceptance, and group cohesiveness. Other members, by compliance, reinforce the expectation that whoever has started and succeeded with it should continue in the leadership role. Similarly, members build up expectations regarding the contribution that they are to make. The reactions of other members confirm the expectation that they are (or are not) to continue in the same role. The role system and the status structure of a group are determined by a set of mutually reinforced intermember expectations. Thus, in a verbal learning experiment, Bachrach, Candland, and Gibson (1961) observed that the members of a group differentially reinforce the behavior of other members. Such differential reinforcement accounts, in large part, for individual differences in role specialization and norm conformity.

Leader–follower interaction and mutual support is seen in the case of political leaders and their followings. The leaders activate and mobilize support for their objectives, control the communication media, and make use of intermediary opinion leaders. Followers may be actively interested to varying degrees or ready to be motivated into political activity. Multilayered networks are formed of leaders and followers. Those below yield an aggregate of public opinion to support the aims of those at the top. The importance of such follower support for leaders was seen by Pepinsky, Hemphill, and Shevitz (1958) who studied experimental groups working on construction problems. When leaders were made to believe that they were accepted by the members, the groups were more productive and exhibited high degrees of satisfaction and participation. When leaders were made to feel that they were rejected, the groups made fewer poor decisions and also exhibited less participation and satisfaction.

## A RECIPROCAL RELATIONSHIP

Both J. M. Burns (1978) and Hollander (1958) felt that the study of leadership and the study of followership were divorced for too long. Actually, the leader and the follower depend on each other, for whoever leads and whoever follows stimulates and reinforces the other's behavior. The leader initiates, questions, or proposes; the follower complies, resists, or ignores.

### Transactional Social Exchange

Leadership and followership are mutual activities of influence and counter-influence. Leaders and followers both give and both receive benefits. The relationship is maintained by this social exchange and this mutual influence (Hollander, 1978). As Hollander and Julian (1969) noted, when leaders are effective, they give something and get something in return. This transactional approach to leadership involves a trading of benefits. The leader provides a benefit by directing the group toward desirable results. In return, the followers provide the leader with status, the privileges of authority, influence, and prestige. However, the leader may demand what followers regard as excessive energy expenditure. Follower compliance to reach the group goal and desired outcomes may not match the perceived effort to attain them. As members become less involved in the group's success, they complain less about obstacles to such success but more about demands for expending their time and energy (Willerman, 1954). Bass, Gaier, and Flint (1956) observed that ROTC cadets strongly motivated to enter advanced training complained about the difficulty of a test screening applicants, whereas those low in such motivation complained about having to take the test.

### Idiosyncracy Credit

The interplay that fashions who will lead and who will follow has been explained by Hollander (1958). The interplay builds up idiosyncracy credit for the leader relative to the follower.

Both competence with the group's task and conformity to the group norms earn idiosyncracy credit for a member and aids in his or her emergence as leader, or success as appointed leader, as well as in the compliance of the followers (Hollander, 1958). A buildup of such credit makes subsequent initiatives even more likely to be accepted. Status as a leader is strengthened. Idiosyncracy credit also allows the leader nonconforming deviations not permitted those, such as newcomers, without the necessary credit. Derivative credit may be brought from another group, based on reputation.

*Maintaining Credit.*   Michener and Lawler (1975) measured six elements to see which of them had the greatest effect on the tendency of members to endorse continuing leaders in their position. They found that members were more likely to endorse their leaders when the group was successful, members got more rewards than the leader, or the leader was not permanently fixed in the office. But they were less enthusiastic about endorsing leaders if the support received from members was inconsistent or if the leaders were inconsistent in their competence or fairness. Polansky, Lippitt, and Redl (1950) and Grosser, Polansky, and Lippitt (1951) showed that those group members who attempted more influence and those whose influence attempts were more successful also felt more secure in their positions and were more susceptible to contagious influence. They were more likely than those attempting to exert influence unsuccessfully to act in reference to the demands of the group situation than in terms of their own needs. Although able to react spontaneously to others and to initiate spontaneity in others, they also felt secure enough to resist direct attempts to influence them. They could maintain conformance to the steady state as well as enlarge the freedom of actions of members.

There is a complex interplay between the requisite competence and the requisite conformity in maintaining credit. Alvarez (1968) demonstrated that greater leader deviance from norms was tolerated when accompanied by group success. In a study of a simulated organization, Alvarez found that the leader lost esteem at a slower rate than followers, but only in successful organizations. The leader lost esteem at a faster rate than followers in unsuccessful organizations.

Not all kinds of deviance are permitted to the holders of idiosyncrasy credit. For example, they have less latitude to deviate from particular role obligations (Hollander, 1961a,b). However, members with credit may deviate with less cost from norms applied to members in general. In effect, the leader's freedom to deviate from general norms is exchanged for conforming more closely to the expectations others have about the requirements of the leader role.

Furthering the maintenance of the satisfactory interchange between leader and followers are mutual trust (Deutsch, 1973), sense of fairness and equity, mutual support, involvement, and wider latitudes of acceptance (Graen, 1976; Dansereau & Dumas, 1977).

### Negotiation for Equity

In the social exchange, the followers may assert influence and make demands on the leader. Negotiation may be required on what will be done and by whom. The negotiation may consider the distribution of effort and rewards between leader and followers. Considerations of equity and fairness are of consequence. Mention has already been made in Chapter 11 about the distribution of rewards. Dyer, Lambert, and Tracy (1953) observed that in the more effective of two bomber wings (where more successful leadership was likely), more favorable attitudes existed toward the method of "allocating rewards and punishments." But the interdependence of the followers may make a difference. According to Miller and Hamblin (1963), differential rewarding for relative achievement decreased group productivity when the members were highly interdependent, but not when they were less interdependent.

Equity is relative. Members judge the equity of their costs and benefits in comparison to the costs and benefits of others whom they regard as similar to themselves (J. S. Adams, 1963).

Negotiations may be between leader and group or leader and individual members. Graen and Cashman (1975) suggest that such individualized exchanges will be closer. Such closeness will increase acceptance of more responsible tasks by followers and greater assistance by the leader to them. There will also be more support, sensitivity, and trust in a close relationship.

Commonplace is the formation of an inner clique with whom the leader has closer relations than the rest of the group. The inner clique gets more attention and more approval and possibly more status at the cost of being expected to be more loyal, of arousing the envy of outer circle members, and of sharing greater responsibility and blame for the leader's failures.

*Distortions in Follower Compliance.* Members may suffer from pluralistic ignorance, each follower not knowing every other member's views (Schanck, 1932). Followers may try to avoid confrontation as too costly or withdraw into anomie, apathy, or alienation. Followers may rationalize away the leader's excess demands or incompetence. Ansbacher's (1948) interviews of German prisoners of war provided extensive evidence that although many continued to esteem Hitler and maintain confidence in him, they personally disagreed with him on many significant issues and developed interpretations of his directions to suit their own needs. Hitler demanded that Germany should never capitulate. But a majority of those who had confidence in him believed he did not want unnecessary bloodshed. Therefore, they felt he would consider it his duty to end a lost war. Hitler issued explicit orders that soldiers were to fight to the end, but his supporters rationalized that it was all right to surrender.

Followers also may continue to accept the leader's direction but displace their aggression against less powerful targets. Purcell (1953) found packinghouse employees more ready to blame their lower-status supervisors than their top management for difficulties.

### Leadership That Transcends Social Exchange

Not all leadership can be explained as a social exchange—a short-term transaction between leader and follower. The leadership of Shackleton in the Antarctic whose men overcame superhuman obstacles; the leadership of Joan of Arc, Martin Luther King, Mahatma Ghandi, Winston Churchill—the charismatic leader—can only be conceived as leadership which transforms the follower from needs at lower levels to higher-level concerns for achievement, glory, humanity, fortune, country, faith, or family which demand excessive costs relative to tangible benefits (J. M. Burns, 1978). It is difficult to conceive of the emotional response of the Iranian masses to the Ayatollah Khomeini merely as social exchange between leader and follower.

## MUTUAL INFLUENCE OF LEADERS AND FOLLOWERS

### Dyadic versus Group Analysis

Relatively few studies have investigated the complete two-way influence process; most of those available are limited to showing how leaders condition the responses of followers and to a lesser extent how followers condition the responses of leaders. Graen (1976), in concentrating on the dyadic relation between the leader and a designated member of the group, has noted that they form a behavioral interdependence between their respective roles. These are seen to vary in "quality." At one extreme is the "partnership" involving reciprocal influence, extracontractual behavioral exchange, role-defined relations, and loosely coupled fates (Dansereau, Graen & Haga, 1975). Graen and Schiemann (1978) observed that agreement about the relationship was higher between manager and subordinate if the "quality" of their behavioral interdependencies were high. But Fujii (1977) found that analyses of leader–subordinate relations in an experimental setting based on dyads did not differ greatly from analyses based on mean group results.

*Range of Relationships.* With reference to role relations with their subordinates as a whole, leaders range from "all to none" in their effects. At the one extreme can be found the rule-governed, fully programmed administrator, the paper-pushing absentee supervisor, the symbolic office holder without power. They are glorified doormen whose behavior is almost fully determined by others. At the other extreme are the highly involved supervisors, the rule makers, the role changers, and the charismatic politicians who make a great difference in what happens to others. The inflated view of the leader's effects is declaring as Napoleon did that he would rather have an army of rabbits led by a lion, than an army of lions led by a rabbit. The deflated view reduces the effects of leadership to the eyes of its beholder, to the "theories of leadership" held by the followers, or to a useless concept for understanding social influence (Calder, 1977; Pandey, 1976). Needless to say, neither extreme is supportable.

### Two-Way Evidence

Conviction about the two-way nature of leadership and followership can be strengthened by a review of the few investigations that directly and simultaneously examined the two-way effects. A laboratory experiment, a simulation, and a survey are illustrative.

*Experiment.* Herold (1974) carried out a double-substitution laboratory experiment in which both leaders' and subordinates' actual behaviors were intercepted and substituted with fully programmed supervisory and subordinate behaviors. Thirty-two groups of three persons each, consisting of one leader and two subordinates, were balanced in treatment so that in half the groups the subordinates were powerful and the other half the leader was powerful. Within each group one subordinate received a punitive comunication following performance while the other received a supportive communication. The leader of each group received a "good product" from one of the subordinates and a "bad product" from the other. The experimental task consisted of proofreading manuscripts and finding errors. Herold found strong mutual effects on attitudes of leaders and followers toward each other and toward the situation. Whether or not the leader received a good or bad product from a subordinate strongly affected what the leader did, but whether or not the subordinate received a punitive communication from the leader had somewhat less of an impact on the subordinate. The leader's power was important in its effects on subordinates; but subordinate power was not significant in affecting the leader's behavior. This lack of symmetry was also seen by G. J. Palmer (1962a,b), who studied leaders and followers in a difficult task situation. He concluded that followership in such a situation is explained largely by lack of ability. Leadership, on the other hand, required a more complex explanation involving both individual and situational variables.

*Simulation.* In Exercise Supervise (Bass, 1975c), over 3,400 managers in training workshops played one of three supervisory roles: authoritarian, persuasive, or participative, or one of three subordinate roles: highly involved, moderately involved, or uninvolved. Meetings took place between dyads composed of one supervisor and one subordinate. The three tasks were to decide on the five among twenty-five traits which are most and least characteristic of lower, middle and top management. A Latin-Square design was completed so that data about all nine possibilities emerged.

Although the uninvolved, apathetic subordinate was least preferred by supervisors as a whole, and the participative supervisor was most preferred by the subordinates as a whole, as might be expected, the fastest and easiest-to-complete interactions tended to take place between the authoritarian supervisor and the uninvolved, apathetic subordinate. Subordinate and supervisor dissatisfaction tended to be greatest for the highly involved subordinate meeting with the authoritarian supervisor; satisfaction tended to be greatest for the highly involved subordinate meeting with the participative supervisor. The interaction effects of persuasive supervision and subordinates at the three different levels of involvement fell between satisfaction and speed of decision (Thiagarajan & Deep, 1970; Bass, Burger, et al., 1979).

*Survey.* An exhaustive survey examination of the mutual effects of leaders and subordinates was completed by Greene (1979). He queried sixty subordinates from five manufacturing organizations who had joined the management of their firms within the past three months and who had never worked before for their immediate superior. Greene assumed that because of the newness of their appointments, the subordinates' expectations were unclear and their full compliance was undeveloped. Subordinates completed House and Dessler's (1974) adaptation of the Leader Behavior Description Questionnaire (see Chapter 21) to measure leaders' consideration and initiation of structure. Subordinate expectations, compliance, performance, and satisfaction were assessed as well. The data were gathered three times in three-month intervals to permit path analyses. Consistent with path-goal theory (Chapter 25), early role clarifying initiation of structure by a leader directly resulted in greater subordinate satisfaction and compliance three and six months later. Role clarification by the leader also was seen to enhance subordinate expectations that greater effort by them would produce better performance. But only early performance-contingent reinforcement by the leader subsequently resulted in better subordinate performance along with more compliance and satisfaction. Satisfaction accompanied the leader's rewarding of subordinates for their good performance, and dissatisfaction emerged from punishment by the leader for poor subordinate performance.

Early subordinate behavior exerted considerable influence on the supervisor as well. If subordinates were more compliant and performed better early on, their supervisor in the following quarter was seen to display more considerate, supportive, and participative leadership. On the other hand, poor subordinate performance early on produced more initiation of structure and role clarification later on by the supervisor. Poor performance and particularly lack of compliance by subordinates generated the leader's greater use of punishment three or six months later.

### Further Evidence of Mutual or Joint Effects

Friedlander (1966b) asked members of a research and development organization to describe various aspects of member interaction and group performance. Group effectiveness was associated with open discussion and with the leader's suggestions of new approaches to problems. At the same time, member influence with other members was associated with member influence with the leader. Members accepted the leader's influence when policies were clear-cut and group tensions were low. The members tended to play their expected roles and discuss divergent ideas when the leader was oriented toward productivity and efficiency.

Back (1948) studied interactions of leaders and followers in two types of discussion groups—work-centered and emotionally toned. When leaders emphasized work performance more than followers in period 1, followers increased their work responses in period 2. When leaders emphasized friendliness more than followers in period 1, followers exhibited more friendly responses in period 2. The emotionally toned group devoted more time in period 1 to establishing stable intermember relations and group structures. The work-oriented group spent more time in strengthening goal-directed activities. In period 2, the emotionally toned group spent more time in maintenance of participation between members and with leaders. In the work-oriented group the leader tended to lose importance, whereas interactions between members were strengthened. Thus, it appeared that leader behavior influenced group response and group response influenced leader status.

*Joint Competence.*　Rohde (1958) observed different combinations of qualified and unqualified leaders and followers under four conditions of reward and punishment. Leader task ability was found more highly related to group performance than motivation. Poorest performance was exhibited by groups with both unqualified leaders and followers. Almost equally poor were groups with qualified leaders and two unqualified followers.

Blades (1976) studied the joint effects of leader and subordinate intelligence, task ability, and motivation on their group's performance in army mess halls. Ratings of group performance by inspectors were correlated with ratings of intelligence, ability, and leadership behavior by 102 mess hall personnel. Blades found that subordinate intelligence, task ability, and motivation correlated positively with performance only under participative management and highly motivated subordinates. But leader intelligence correlated positively with performance only under directive management with highly motivated leaders and subordinates. Leader task ability correlated positively with group performance only with directive supervision of highly motivated subordinates. Leader motivation correlated positively with group performance only with directive supervision of highly motivated subordinates. Blades concluded that competent, motivated subordinates can be led best if allowed to participate in the decision process while competent, motivated leaders do best with a directive style if their subordinates are limited in competence.

*Compatibility.*　Fujii (1977) concluded from a review of the literature that compatibility between the leader and his or her followers was one of the most important interpersonal factors in the leadership setting. As a consequence, he conducted an experiment in which the independent variables were manipulated by simulating a division of a greeting card company. Eighty paid male volunteers participated as work group leaders or workers in the bogus organization. Follower performance based on leader merit ratings by the leader, but not on objective performance, was positively related to greater interpersonal compatibility between leader and members. Extrinsic satisfaction increased with leader–member compatibility. The relationship between leader–member compatibility and intrinsic and overall satisfaction was moderated by the amount of cooperation required by the task and the amount of experience with the task. Leader–member compatibility was positively related to relations-oriented leader behavior and less so to task-oriented leader behavior. McLachlan (1974) reported a study of group therapy with ninety-four alcoholic inpatients in which patients and therapists were matched for conceptual compatibility based on Hunt's Paragraph Completion Test. Matched therapist/patient pairs were positively associated with outcomes as evaluated by staff ratings twelve to sixteen months later. Beutler, Jobe, and Elkins (1974) also investigated the effects of patient-therapist matching on attitudes. Matched attitude was associated with self-rated improvement (although some attitude dissimilarity did result in more attitude change in patients). Again, Greer (1961) reported that authoritarian infantrymen and airmen worked better under authoritarian leaders while equalitarian men did better when led by equalitarians. Group performance was positively related to followers' perceptions of the leaders as problem solvers and the extent to which they met followers' expectations. W. W. Burke (1965) studied student leaders in twenty-four groups participating in an interfraternity contest. Each group performed a clerical and organizational task as well as a decision-making task. Followers high in need achievement scores working with relations-oriented leaders reported more tension regardless of task than did high-need achievement followers working with task-oriented leaders. Low-need achievement followers working with task-oriented leaders reported more tension than those working with relations-oriented leaders. The more relaxed situation occurred when the leader's personality was such as to meet the needs of the follower group.

Selvin (1960) examined older and young military trainees under three types of leadership—persuasive, weak, and arbitrary. The arbitrary leadership generated the most tension and escape activities; persuasive leadership, the least. But older and younger trainees reacted differently to the leadership styles. Under persuasive leadership, the younger trainees tended to exhibit aggressive behavior—fighting, drunkenness, and "blowing up." Under arbitrary leadership, the younger trainees exhibited relatively personal forms of behavior, such as attending mass, entertainment, sports events, and hobbies. Older trainees under the arbitrary leader tended to "blow their tops."

*Self-, Interaction, and Task Orientation.* Bass, Dunteman, Frye, Vidulich, and Wambach (1963) studied self-, interaction-, and task-oriented individuals. They reported that high self-oriented scores were obtained by dominant, aggressive individuals searching for recognition. Interaction orientation was associated with needs for affiliation and dependency. Task orientation tended to be associated with strong personality integration and desire for task challenge. Task-oriented participants in discussion groups, in general, were evaluated most favorably and interaction-oriented participants least favorably as leaders and followers by other group members and by outside observers. Bass and Dunteman (1963) studied sensitivity training groups (see Chapter 34) composed of participants homogeneous in each of the orientations. The leaders who emerged in task-oriented groups tended to be even more highly task-oriented than the average member. However, the leaders of the self-oriented participants were relatively low in self-orientation. Interaction-oriented groups tended to be most satisfied with their highly interaction-oriented leaders. Stimpson and Bass (1964) found that interaction-oriented participants in problem solving groups, when compared with task-oriented and self-oriented participants, allowed their work partners to be less successful as leaders, allowed less coalescence, and caused partners to participate less, feel less responsibility, and experience more conflict.

Bass (1967b) observed task-oriented and interaction-oriented followers under coercive and persuasive styles of leadership. Task-oriented followers were found to produce greater quantities of work under persuasive leadership. Interaction-oriented followers produced both high quantities and quality of work under coercive leadership. Task satisfaction of followers was significantly higher under a directive interaction-oriented leader than under a participative interaction-oriented leader. Conversely, satisfaction was lower under a directive than under a persuasive task-oriented leader.

## FALLING DOMINOES PHENOMENON

Another interaction effect that has been well-documented occurs in the chain of command between a leader's superior, the leader, and the subordinate of the leader. Linkages have also been found between the horizontal peer and client relations of leaders and how the leaders interact with their subordinates. The relations are not necessarily cumulative in the sense that if A kicks B, B will kick C. B may become solicitous of C after being kicked by A. For example, D. T. Campbell (1956), in a study of shipboard organizations found that although the leadership scores and sociometric interaction scores of the commanding officer were positively correlated with measures of shipboard efficiency and morale, the leadership and interaction scores of the executive officer, the commander's immediate subordinate, were negatively related to the ship's efficiency and morale.

### Functional Activities

As evidence of the systematic connections between A, B, and C, Stogdill and Goode (1957) found that when leaders interacted frequently with their superiors, their subordinates felt that the leaders should spend more time than they did in interviewing personnel and in coordination. However, when leaders interacted a lot with their subordinates, subordinates felt their leaders spent too much time in technical performance, too little time in inspection and preparation, and that they, the subordinates, ought to have more responsibility. Leaders who interacted frequently with peers had subordinates who felt that their leaders had too little responsibility, were less active than they ought to be in representing their subordinates, but spent too much time in planning. When leaders interacted extensively with persons outside their own units, their subordinates reported having to delegate and represent their groups too much. These followers also felt they ought to spend more time than they did in inspection, planning, and preparation.

In a study of a large naval organization, Stogdill and Haase (1957) found that the more time superiors actually spent in highly personal interactions with others, such as interviewing personnel, the less their own subordinates actually interacted with their peers and initiated interaction with members of other subgroups where their interactions were reciprocated. However, a more impersonal performance, such as inspection, by superiors kept subordinates within their own subgroups. When superiors spent little time in preparing procedures and much time in technical performances, their subordinates tended to interact with peers but superiors who spent more than average amounts of time in supervision had subordinates who tended to interact with their own subordinates. A high rate of communicating and integrating behavior by superiors enlarged the total number of interactions initiated by their subordinates as well as received by them, increased reciprocated interactions within the subgroups, and decreased interactions with members outside the subgroups.

*Interaction Patterns.* Stogdill (1955) studied the effects of interactions among superiors upon their subordinates' interactions. Subordinates tended to interact with their own followers and subgroup members when their superiors interacted with subordinates and their own subgroup members. The interactions of their subordinates with members outside the subgroup were affected by whether or not superiors were the initiators or recipients of interaction within their own subgroups. If superiors were initiators of interaction with subgroup members, their subordinates tended to interact less frequently with members outside the subgroup. However, subordinates tended to interact more frequently with members outside the subgroup when their superiors were recipients of interaction within the subgroup. When superiors interacted frequently with members outside their subgroups, subordinates also interacted with members outside this unit, but the subordinates interacted less often with their own superiors.

When superiors interacted with their subordinates' peers, the subordinates tended to initiate more interactions with the superiors, but tended to receive fewer interactions in return. In general, superiors' interactions with subordinates and members within the subgroup induced similar patterns of relating among subordinates. Superiors' interactions with their own superiors exerted the strongest effects in restricting the area of interaction of subordinates.

### Influence and Identification

Pelz (1949, 1951, 1952) noted that when supervisors who had influence with their superiors took the side of their subordinate employees, the employees tended to feel satisfied. But when a supervisor without influence identified with their subordinates' interests, the subordinates tended to be dissatisfied. Closeness to employees and taking their side increased job satisfaction only when the supervisors had enough influence with superiors to provide conditions that fulfilled employee expectations. Likewise, Nahabetian (1969) found that group members were better satisfied under leaders with influence with superiors than those without such influence. Influential leaders were seen to facilitate the group task whereas those without infuence higher up were seen to hinder task accomplishment. Ronken and Lawrence (1952) reported similar findings.

The falling dominoes phenomenon is seen also in the effects of charismatic leaders on their immediate disciples. The disciples are converted into effective leaders in their own right. The dedication, caring, and participation obtained by the charismatics is multiplied outward from themselves through their disciples, followers of their disciples, and so on (J. M. Burns, 1978). They become the models to be imitated by successive expanding layers of followers.

Bowers and Seashore (1966) found that the pattern of leader behavior exhibited by top managers in insurance agencies was reflected in similar behavior in subordinate supervisors. The extent to which followers emphasized goals was related to the extent to which supervisors emphasized goals and interaction facilitation with their subordinates.

Hill and Hunt (1970) observed that, although the leader behavior of supervisors one level removed from employees was not related to employee satisfaction, the combined behavior of first- and second-level supervisors affected their satisfaction. Much initiative by both first- and second-level supervisors was significantly related to employee satisfaction with esteem and autonomy.

### Contingent Effect of Organization Change

The falling dominoes phenomenon was qualified by Smith, Moscow, Berger, and Cooper (1969) who found weak support for the hypothesis that under conditions of slow organization change, good interpersonal relations between managers and superiors were associated with good relations between managers and subordinates. But strong support was found for the hypothesis that under rapid organizational change, good relations between managers and their superiors polarized into poor relations between the managers and their subordinates. No doubt, the greater need for rapid change put pressure on the manager to push subordinates for performance and rapid response. Superiors encouraged the managers; subordinates were disturbed.

## LEADERS' IMPACT ON FOLLOWERS

It goes without saying that, by definition, successful leaders influence their followers, that is, they bring about changes in their followers' attitudes and behavior. What specifically occurs does so in considerable variety and amount. Modeling takes place. Followers' interests are enlarged. Followers become better and more fully informed. Followers' expectations are developed. Risk preferences are altered. Followers' satisfaction with their own roles are strongly influenced by their leadership. But followers and their performance may or may not benefit from the leadership exerted. The successful influence on the followers may or may not be effective in achieving goals of consequence to the followers.

### Effective Leadership

Performance of the individual worker or work group depends on their energy and direction. Another way of saying it is that performance depends on their competence and motivation to perform what is required to reach the objectives of their positions in the system. The leader may contribute to the adequacy of their performance by (1) clarifying what is expected of followers, particularly the purposes and objectives of their performance; (2) explaining how to meet such expectations; (3) spelling out the criteria for the evaluation of effective performance; (4) providing feedback as to whether the individual or work group is meeting the objectives; and (5) allocating rewards contingent on meeting objectives. Effective leadership develops understanding and agreement about the leader's and subordinate's roles in the above process. For instance, as in Management-by-Objectives, it may take the form of periodic discussion in which a review of past performance and obstacles to effectiveness are the basis for setting mutually acceptable objectives for the next period. Legitimacy for both roles is provided by organizational policies that declare and support it.

*Leaders as Models for Their Subordinates*

R. Cooper (1966) showed that workers tended to pattern their own behavior after that of their supervisor. Task-oriented leaders supervised groups in which workers made fewer errors in their work and exhibited lower rates of absenteeism and tardiness than was true for groups with leaders lacking in such task orientation. In the same way, according to a study by Kern and Bahr (1974) of approximately 100 staff personnel in the Washington State Division of Parole, those parole officers who interacted a lot with their superiors used their superiors as models for the way they, the parole officers, supervised their parolees. But such modeling did not occur when the parole officers interacted less frequently with their supervisors. H. M. Weiss (1977) studied 141 superior–subordinate dyads, obtaining from each member of the dyad a self-description of their own supervisory behavior along with the subordinate's evaluation of the superior's competence and success. These were then correlated with the degree of similarity found in the self-descriptions of the superior–subordinate dyads. There was a tendency for subordinates to choose for role models those superiors they saw as more competent and successful.

Behavioral contagion is less obvious modeling. A cigar-smoking boss can spawn a batch of cigar-smoking subordinates. Sometimes, the subordinates pick up the boss's expressions of speech, intonations, and peculiarly nonverbal mannerisms.

*Leaders as Cues.* Beyond modeling by followers of their leader's behavior, Graen and Cashman (1975) noted that followers also enlarged their interests to match closer with those of their leader. In other words, the followers attempted to increase their esteem in the eyes of their leader and to ingratiate themselves with the leader (E. E. Jones, 1964).

Daniels and Berkowitz (1963) experimentally varied supervisor–worker dependence for goal attainment, degree of liking, and time required for supervisor to learn of worker's performance. They found that participants worked hardest under independent conditions when they believed that the superior would learn about their performance quickly. They also worked hardest when they had to depend on a supervisor whom they liked. Followers may come to depend on their leader's view of reality as their prime source of information and expectations.

*Leaders as Molders of Expectations.* According to M. T. Edwards (1973), the most effective supervisors are those who can create high performance expectations for subordinates to fulfill. Less effective managers fail to develop such expectations. And the more ambiguous the criteria for evaluating the group's performance, the greater is the leader's influence in defining expectations of the situation. Arvey and Neel (1974) showed that the performance level of 130 engineers was a function of their expectations that their effective job performance would be rewarded and that their supervisor was concerned about them. Summarizing research outcomes, Livingstone (1969) noted that what managers expect of their subordinates strongly influences the subordinates' performance and progress. Subordinates tend to do what they believe is expected of them. This Pygmalian effect has become a popular subject of study.

*Leaders as Communicators*

Much of leader behavior is communicating with others. An intensive study of nine senior executives by S. Carlson (1951) over a four-week period noted that they spent approximately 80 percent of their time talking with others. Again, another detailed study of four departmental-level managers found that more than 80 percent of their time was spent in conversation. Zelko and Dance (1965) noted that when managers were asked how much of the work day was spent in communicating, the replies ranged from about 88 percent to 99 percent with most saying that it was above 90 percent. Similar results were reported by P. A. Stewart (1967), Lawler, Porter, and Tannenbaum (1968), and Mintzberg (1973).

*Consequences on Effectiveness.* Strong positive linkages were found by Klauss and Bass (1981) between such communication tendencies of superiors as careful transmission, many two-way communications, attentive listening, trustworthiness, and informativeness and their subordinates' role clarity, satisfaction with their supervision, and the effectiveness of their work groups.

Hain (1972) reported that productivity and profitability showed the greatest increase in a General Motors plant that also showed the greatest improvements in communications among four plants surveyed. Similar parallel improvements in other GM plants were reported by Widgery and Tubbs (1975) and Tubbs and Widgery (1978). Hain and Tubbs (1974) found increased efficiency, reduced grievances, and absenteeism associated with employees' ratings of the communication effectiveness of their supervisors. Communication effectiveness of supervisors was the best predictor of low grievance activity in still another GM automotive assembly plant (Tubbs & Porter, 1978). Such communication effectiveness included agreement that supervisors were friendly and easy to talk to, were interested and paid attention to what one was saying, were willing to listen to one's problems, and were receptive to ideas and suggestions and showed one how to improve performance. (These behaviors are usually included on measures of leadership. Thus Klauss and Bass (1981) found correlations as high as .65 between various communication styles of supervisors and their leadership styles as described by their subordinates. More will be presented about this in Chapter 19.)

### Leaders as Sources of Satisfaction

Early job satisfaction surveys conducted by Houser (1927), Kornhauser and Sharp (1932), Bergen (1939), and McG. Smith (1942) indicated that employee satisfaction was positively related to favorable attitudes toward supervisors. Viteles's (1953) survey of research on job satisfaction produced similar conclusions. Lawshe and Nagle (1953) found that attitude toward supervisor was also related to work group productivity. Since then, as subordinates' satisfaction is one of the criteria usually measured when studying leader behavior, countless survey studies can be cited to support the contention that the leader makes a difference in subordinates' satisfaction (see Chapters 19 through 22). Less frequent are data supporting the argument that the leaders' satisfaction depends on their subordinates' performance. More will be said about this as we look at how followers affect their leaders' behavior.

## FOLLOWER EFFECTS ON LEADERS

Follower compliance is the mirror image of successful leadership. Just as successful leadership may be seen as influence on task completion and socioemotional relations, so compliance can be seen as instrumental to task completion and both public and private socioemotional acceptance of the leadership effort. In the same way, just as the leader can influence subordinates by initiatives and information, so the subordinates can complete the process and influence their leaders by giving feedback to them. Thus, Hegarty (n.d.) demonstrated that feedback of subordinates' ratings to supervisors resulted in positive changes in the supervisors' behavior. The employee of the fifty-eight supervisors in the experimental and control groups completed an information-opinion survey. The survey results were used to prepare feedback reports to the experimental but not the control supervisors. A second survey was conducted ten weeks later to measure change. After adjustment for initial scores, all seventeen measures of change were found to have shifted more in the expected direction in the experimental than the control supervisors, six significantly so. Such feedback has become common in many organizations as a means for improving effectiveness of leaders and their operations (Likert, 1967; Cammann & Nadler, 1976; Bowers & Franklin, 1975; Bass, 1976).

### Followership and Leadership

The follower as a source of influence on the leader also means that contrary to popular notions, rather than followership being the obverse of leadership, followership and leadership are highly similar as are followers and leaders. Hollander and Webb (1955) showed that the same peers who are nominated as most desired as leaders are also nominated as most desired as followers. Again, Nelson (1964) found that among seventy-two men on a U.S. Antarctic expedition, the characteristics which made the men liked were about the same for the leaders as for the followers. This may be due to the fact, as J. M. Burns (1978) noted, that there are no sharp boundaries between the roles of leader and follower. There always must be both roles played in any group. Leaders cannot exist without followers, nor followers without leaders. Moreover, leaders and followers exchange roles over time and in different settings. Many persons are leaders and followers at the same time.

*Opposites.* If not the followers, then who are the opposites to the leader? They are those who are barred from the process (for instance, the underaged denied the vote). There are also those who exclude themselves from participation. They are the apathetic, the alienated, and the anomic. The apathetic may be too busy with other affairs. The apathetic poor are too busy just surviving. The alienated may reject and resist participation; they see the control in the hands of others for the benefit of others. The anomic feel powerless, normless, aimless; the leaders are indifferent to their needs (J. M. Burns, 1978). Sociometrically, these form a large proportion of the isolates and rejectees.

### Follower Readiness

Followers strongly affect the likelihood of a leader's success as a consequence of whether or not they are ready for the leader. J. M. Burns (1978) suggested that followers could be ripe for mobilization or imprisoned by fixed beliefs that make it impossible to lead them. Nie, Powell, and Prewitt (1969) found five attitude sets of consequence to such readiness among political followers in Germany, Italy, Mexico, the United States, and Britain: (1) sense of duty; (2) information about politics; (3) stake in political outcomes; (4) sense of political efficiency; and (5) attentiveness to politics.

*Follower Maturity.* According to L. I. Moore (1976), effective leadership entails mature followership. Moore developed a maturity index based on observations of verbal and nonverbal behavior of followers in task groups. Dimensions of maturity are achievement motivation, ability and willingness to take responsibility, task-relevant education or experience, activity level, dependency, behavior variety, interest, perspective, position, and awareness. Knowledge of follower maturity can facilitate and modify follower and leader behavior.

*Preceding Preparation and Experience.* Readiness to accept leadership suggestions will depend on immediately preceding experiences. For instance, negative arguments introduced before an attempt to persuade students to volunteer for civil defense work were found more likely to reduce the success of the positive arguments than if the negative arguments came later (Feierabend & Janis, 1954).

Another antecedent determining the success of a subsequent attempt to lead is the extent to which the attempted leadership fits with previous experiences. Weiss and Fine (n.d.) found that groups first subjected to failure and insult were more influenced by suggestions to be punitive; groups first subjected to rewarding experiences were more likely to respond to suggestions to be lenient.

### Follower Agreement on Approaches

Heller (1969a) noted that some level of agreement about procedures, interest, and norms among followers is necessary before effective participatory leadership can occur. Also important are the followers' competence and past success.

*Follower Competence.* If the time required by participation of subordinates in decision making is more expensive than the value of their contribution, effective supervisors will be more directive with them (Tannenbaum & Massarik, 1950). On the other hand, if the supervisors value their subordinates, they will be more participative (Likert, 1959). Thus, Hsu and Newton (1974) found that supervisors of unskilled employees in a manufacturing plant were more directive than supervisors of skilled employees in the same plant. Similar results were obtained experimentally by Lowin and Craig (1968). Ashour and England (1971) found in experimental teams of supervisors and secretaries that perceived follower competence was the major determinant in assigning of discretionary tasks. Supervisors allowed competent secretaries more discretion than was permitted incompetent secretaries.

As we shall continue to find, leaders' punitiveness results as a reaction to incompetent followers. Studies by Barrow (1976) and Herold (1977) found that leaders behaved more punitively toward poor performers and rewarded good performers. So did Farris and Lim (1969), who divided 200 graduate students into twenty groups of four members each to play a business discussion game. Some leaders, appointed at random, were told that they had high-producing groups. Other leaders were told they had low-producing groups. Leaders who were told that their groups were high producers were significantly more likely than leaders of low-producing groups to be described by their groups as sensitive, nonpunitive, maintaining high standards, exerting less pressure for producing, allowing freedom, and emphasizing teamwork. In turn, subordinates in the "high-performance" condition were better satisfied, felt they had more influence, and described their groups as more cohesive. Again, Curtis, Smith, and Smoll (1979), in studies of the behavior of eighty-two coaches of boys' baseball teams, observed that when compared to the behavior of winning coaches, proportionately more of the observed behaviors of coaches on losing teams were reactions to player mistakes and misbehaviors. (Of course, players on losing teams usually make more mistakes.) But more important, players perceived coaches of losing teams as more punitive and less supportive than winning coaches. With older-age teams, team attitudes became more significant to their performance. Kessler (1968) hypothesized that highly rated subordinates in a governmental agency would be highly motivated to act in accord with their superiors' expectations. Instead, Kessler found that the most highly rated subordinates were most independent. Simmons (1968) observed that in a business game students rated as very low, low, or average complied more closely to management expectations than those rated high in performance. Evidently, the competent, highly valued subordinate felt greater freedom than the less highly valued subordinate to deviate from management expectations in a conflict situation.

Lowin (1968) used students who thought themselves to be on part-time jobs. When the students thought they lacked competence for the tasks to be done, they were more appreciative of close, directive supervision than when they considered themselves competent. Likewise, Heller (1969a) reported that whenever managers saw a big difference in technical ability, decisiveness, and intelligence between themselves and their subordinates, they were more likely to use autocratic decision methods. On the other hand, when subordinates were valued for their expertise, they were more likely to be invited to share in the decision process with their supervisors.

C. D. Fisher (1979) completed an experiment with 168 college students indicating that supervisors gave feedback sooner when subordinate performance was poor than when it was good, contrary to hypothesis. Fisher felt that results would be reversed in any long-term field study.

Follower competence may produce resistance. Thus, Mausner (1954a) showed that participants with a past history of positive reinforcement in a given type of judgment are less influenced by their partners in a group judgment situation than participants with a history of negative reinforcement. Nevertheless, effective followers are those who despite their own competence can avoid being overly resistant to influence from others because of their capacity and willingness to learn from others, to listen, to discriminate, and to be guided by others without feeling loss of status or threat (J. M. Burns, 1978).

*Follower Interpersonal Behavior*

According to Kirchner (1961) and Kirchner and Reisberg (1962), better supervisors tended to look for and reward independent action in subordinates, whereas less effective supervisors tended to reward conformity and group action. The better supervisors were also less lenient.

Fodor (1974) found that leaders became more authoritarian when faced with a disparaging and disruptive subordinate. Naturally, they rated that subordinate lower and gave the subordinate less pay than subordinates who did not engage in such behavior. In an experiment by Crowe, Bochner, and Clark (1972), male management students were asked to play the role of a leader. Each was confronted with accomplices of the experimenters serving as subordinates and acting either democratically or submissively. Democratic subordinates showed initiative by putting forth ideas and trying to set their own goals. Submissive subordinates avoided taking any initiative and asked for detailed instructions which they followed without question. The leaders' behavior was affected accordingly. For example, they were more autocratic with the submissive subordinates and more democratic with the democratic ones.

### Task Objectives of Followers

What subordinates seek in their jobs affects what their supervisor can and will do, according to Maier (1965). Jones, James, and Bruni (1975) showed that whether or not the degree to which the trust and confidence of 112 engineering employees correlated with the behavior of their supervisors was affected by whether or not the employees were involved in their work. If the subordinates preferred to avoid risk, if they did not wish to become involved in the task, if they were uninterested in the task, and if such interest was of no relevance to getting the job done, leaders became directive. But if subordinates wanted to be involved and were more interested in what happened, more supervisory leadership occurred to engage them. Thus, among British managers surveyed by Heller (1969a), when a decision was seen as important to subordinates but not the company, a high degree of power sharing was used. Conversely, when a decision was a matter of concern to the company but not to subordinates, power centralization was preferred. More will be said about this as we now turn to examining managers' performance and their leadership styles.

part

# MANAGEMENT AND STYLES OF LEADERSHIP: ANTECEDENTS AND CONSEQUENCES

# 17

# LEADERSHIP AND MANAGEMENT IN THE WORKING SITUATION

## INTRODUCTION

Leaders must manage and managers must lead but the two are not synonymous. F. C. Mann (1965) suggested that leaders may facilitate interpersonal interaction and positive working relations; they may promote structuring of the task and work accomplishment; and they may plan, organize, and evaluate the work done. The main recognized functions of management include planning, investigating, investigating, coordinating, evaluating, supervising, staffing, negotiating, and representing (Mahoney, Jerdee & Carroll, 1965). All of these functions can be seen to be potentially influential activities of leaders on their subordinates and associates.

### Interpersonal Skills Needed at All Levels

Skill as a leader and in relating to others is a most important requirement at all levels of management. For instance, interviews with seventy-one corporate executives (by Glickman, Hahn, et al., 1969) noted that at the top of the corporation, the group of consequence is relatively small. Its members have highly personal relationships. They interact with each other as in a small firm. A high proportion of group involvement is usual. Informal procedures supplant formal ones. When queried by Richards and Inskeep (1974) about what kind of continuing education was most needed by middle managers, eighty-seven business school deans, fifty-eight business executives, and forty executives in trade associations gave top priority to improving human relations skills. Improving quantitative and technical skills were seen to be of secondary importance. At the same time, Mahoney, Jerdee, and Carroll (1965) found that the single most important function of first-line managers was that of supervising others. Although eight important functions were recognized by Mahoney, Jerdee, and Carroll (1965)—planning, investigating, coordinating, evaluating, supervising, staffing, negotiating, and representing—their questionnaire survey of 452 managers from thirteen companies in a variety of industries varying in size from 100 to over 400 employees revealed that more time was spent on supervision than on any other function (28.4 percent). Supervising, along with the four other functions of planning, investigating, coordinating, and evaluating, accounted for almost 90 percent of all the time spent at work by the sample of managers.

Consistent with these results, Solem, Onachilla, and Heller (1961) asked 211 such supervisors to post and select problems for discussion in twenty-six discussion groups.

In all, 58.8 percent of first-line supervision and 35.3 percent of middle management wanted to talk about the motivation of subordinates to follow instructions, to meet deadlines, or to maintain quality and quantity of production. Over 40 percent of staff supervisors were concerned about dealing with resistance to change as were 36.4 percent of middle managers and 22.7 percent of first-line supervisors. Most important for the first-line supervisor were disciplinary problems and problems of promoting, rating, and classifying employees, while middle managers felt most ready to talk about problems of selecting, orienting, and training employees.

## CONCEPTUALIZATIONS OF MANAGEMENT FUNCTIONS

Traditional commentators on management and administration (for example, F. W. Taylor, Urwick, Fayol, and R. C. Davis) maintained that the primary functions of leadership were planning, organizing, and controlling. Others added that coordination should be regarded as a major function. Research demonstrated that leaders do in fact perform these functions. Nevertheless, an analysis of administration in terms of such general functions inhibited a more searching type of inquiry into the nature of executive performance which would provide a more detailed picture of what administrators, managers, and executives do. Not all of what they do is leadership, of course. But leadership remains an important component to the degree that management means getting work done with and through others.

### Varied Activities

MacKenzie (1969) illustrated the great variety of activities that may be performed by a typical manager. Figure 17.1 shows the different elements, tasks, functions, and activities that may be part of the manager's job. At the center are people, ideas, and things, for these are the basic components of every organization with which the manager must work. According to MacKenzie, ideas create the need for conceptual thinking; things, for administration; people, for leadership.

Three functions—problem analysis, decision making, and communication—are important at all times and in all aspects of the jobs held by managers; therefore, these three functions are shown to permeate the entire work process. However, other functions usually occur in a predictable sequence; thus, planning, organizing, staffing, directing, and controlling are shown in that order on one of the bands. How much managers are involved in these sequential functions depends on their position and the stage of completion of the projects with which they are most concerned. The relevant activities and their definitions are shown on the outermost bands of the diagram. Managers must, at all times, sense the pulse of their organization.

We may quarrel with limiting leadership to the people element. More often, administration and conceptual thinking required are so interlocked with the influence processes that the distinction is academic rather than of practical consequence. However, the important aspect of the diagram is the sheer diversity of activities and their linkages to the functions and tasks of management pointing to the inadequacies of any simple approaches to capture what is involved in the managerial process.

**FIGURE 17.1. Leadership and Management Elements, Tasks, Functions, and Activities**

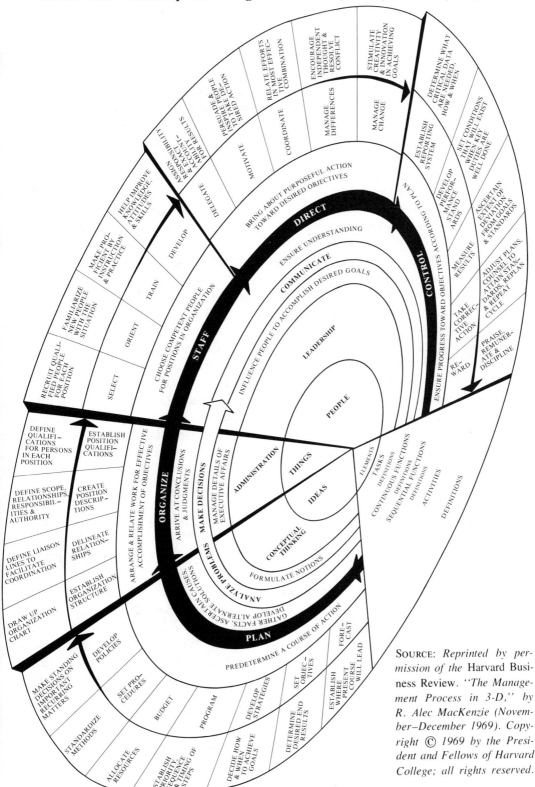

SOURCE: *Reprinted by permission of the* Harvard Business Review. *"The Management Process in 3-D," by R. Alec MacKenzie (November–December 1969). Copyright © 1969 by the President and Fellows of Harvard College; all rights reserved.*

## MANAGERIAL POSITION ANALYSES

*Reliability and Validity*

Empirical analyses have been completed of how managers say they actually spend their time, what work they do, and what functions they perform. Carlson and James (1971) reviewed research on the reliability and validity of various methods employed to measure executive work performance. Among these are the studies by Anderson and Nilsson (1964), T. Burns (1954), Carroll and Taylor (1968), Flanagan (1951, 1954), Haas, Porat, and Vaughan (1969), Hemphill (1959), Kay and Meyer (1962), O'Neill and Kubany (1957), Shartle (1956), and P. A. Stewart (1967).

*Reliability.* Illustrative of reliabilities which can be obtained, Carlson and James (1971) asked 88 insurance agency managers and 252 supervisors to record their work activities over five week periods, and again six months later. Correlations between first and second measures ranged from .78 to .96, indicating a rather high degree of stability in reported work performance over time.

*Validity.* Illustrative of validation attempts, Kelly (1964) used activity sampling in a study of manufacturing executives. His results showed that managers performing identical functions exhibited similar activity profiles. Again, Stogdill and Shartle (1955) asked navy officers to keep a minute-by-minute log of their activities for a period of three days. After the logs were collected, the officers were asked to estimate the percent of time spent in different activities during the period. Correlations between logged time and estimated time were computed. The results indicated a fairly high correspondence between logged time and estimated time for objectively observable performances such as talking with other persons, reading and answering mail, reading and writing reports, and operating machines. Less objective, less readily observable forms of behavior such as planning and reflection failed to yield estimates that corresponded highly with logged time. Nor was there a high correlation between logged and estimated behavior for infrequent activities such as teaching and research.

*Effects of Rater*

Brooks (1955) asked ninety-six executives, their superiors, and their subordinates to rate the work performed by the executives on 150 functional items. Managers rated themselves higher than they were rated by subordinates in activities such as defining authority, delegating, planning, and showing how jobs related to the whole picture. Again, Sequeira (1964) reported that foremen and workers differed in perceptions of the foreman's role. Foremen perceived themselves as required to perform duties not legitimately belonging to their jobs. Among these duties were training new workers on the job, arranging wage agreements, and checking supplies. Workers expected foremen to do more in the way of settling personnel problems and grievances, clarifying work difficulties and improving work methods and conditions. In a study of eleven Indian plants in three industries (textiles, processing, and engineering) Yoga (1964) found such required supervisory functions in the three types of industries.

## TIME USE OF MANAGERS

Stogdill, Shartle, Wherry, and Jaynes (1955) hypothesized that executive performance would vary with respect to (1) type of position; (2) level of position within the organization structure; and (3) type of organization. In order to test this hypothesis, it was necessary to quantify various aspects of work performance. Shartle suggested that executive work could most meaningfully be quantified in terms of amount of time devoted to various performances.

### Navy and Business Executives

Stogdill and Shartle (1955) compared the time use profiles of 470 navy officers and sixty-six business executives. Both groups spent more time (about 34 percent) with subordinates than with superiors or peers. Both devoted about 15 to 20 percent of their time to inspections, examining reports, and writing reports. They spent somewhat more time in planning than in other major administrative functions. The profiles suggested a high degree of similarity in administrative work between military and business organizations. Similarly, Jaynes (1956) analyzed variations in performances between twenty-four officers in four submarines and twenty-four officers occupying identical positions in four landing ships. He reported that variance in performance was more closely related to the type of position than to the type of organization in which the position was located.

*Industrial Analyses.* In a study of executives in Sweden, S. Carlson (1951) found that they spent about 20 percent of their time in internal and external inspections and almost 40 percent of their time in acquiring information. The remainder of their time was divided about equally between advising and explaining, making decisions, and giving orders. Most of the executives felt overworked, complaining that they had little time for family or friends.

Fleishman (1956) used the same kinds of data to analyze the differences between military and industrial organizations. He found that differences between patterns of peformance in industrial and naval organizations were generally no greater than differences within the two types of organizations.

### Factor Analyses of Time Use Profiles

Stogdill, Shartle, Wherry, and Jaynes (1955) studied 470 navy officers in forty-five different positions or job categories. The officers were located in forty-seven different organizations. Data were obtained from all officers on the percent of their working time devoted to thirty-five performances; personal contacts (eleven items), individual effort (ten items), and major reponsibilities (fourteen items). Eleven additional items, including level in organization, military rank, scope of responsibility, scope of authority, and leader behavior variables were also given quantitative scores.

The scores for all officers occupying a given position in the same kind of organization were averaged to obtain a score for that particular position and type of organization. For example, the scores of nine commanding officers in submarines were averaged to obtain a profile of scores for the position commanding officer, submarines. The total sample of 470 officers was divided into 120 such groupings by position and type of organization. The scores for the 120 groups were then intercorrelated and factor-analyzed. Eight factors emerged. The results of the factor analysis brought together on the same factor those positions with the most similar performance profiles.

*Position Clusters.* Using the same data, Stogdill, Wherry, and Jaynes (1953) computed average scores on each variable for the specialties with high loadings on each factor to cluster positions according to time use. Eight factors emerged: (1) high-level policy making; (2) administrative coordination; (3) methods planning; (4) representation of member interests; (5) personnel services; (6) professional consultation; (7) maintenance services; and (8) inspection. The eight clusters of time use involved were (1) public relations officers (writing for publication, consulting outsiders, reflection and representation); (2) legal or accounting officers (consulting juniors, professional consultation, interpretation); (3) personnel administration officers (attending meetings, planning interviewing personnel); (4) technical supervisors (teaching, supervising, using machines, computing); (5) planners, such as operations officers (scheduling, preparing procedures, reading technical publications, interviewing personnel, consulting peers); (6) maintenance administrators (interpretation, consultation, attending meetings, technical performances); (7) commanders and directors (representation, inspection, preparing reports); (8) coordinators such as executive or staff officers (consulting juniors, supervising, scheduling, examining reports and personnel).

The factor analysis served to identify eight types of positions or functional specialties characterizing the 120 groups of officers. Some of the specialties were highly loaded on a single factor with only low or moderately high loadings on several factors. In certain cases, similar specialties in different organizations exhibited similar profiles of factor loadings.

### Time-By-Function

T. A. Mahoney (1955) plotted the profiles of fifty company presidents against those of sixty-six business executives reported by Stogdill, Shartle, Wherry, and Jaynes (1955). The two profiles were almost identical. T. A. Mahoney (1961) analyzed the performance of 348 business executives in terms of eight functions. The performances with the highest percent of time devoted to each were as follows: supervision (39 percent); planning (18 percent); generalist (14 percent); investigation (8 percent); coordination (6 percent); negotiation (5 percent); evaluation (4 percent); and miscellaneous (7 percent). In terms of amount of time devoted to a single function, the preceding results suggest that supervision, planning, and general functions tended to dominate the performance of business executives in the sample.

### ANALYSES OF WORK DONE

Wallace and Gallagher (1952) analyzed the job activities and behaviors of 171 production supervisors in five plants. They collected 3,765 behavioral incidents. These were analyzed in terms of topic involved, location of the incident, person contacted, and nature of the foreman's behavior during the incident. The incidents were classified under forty-one major topics. Similarly, Flanagan (1951) applied the critical incidents technique to a study of the jobs of air force officers and research executives. Incidents were classified under the following major headings: supervision, planning and direction, handling administrative details, exercise of responsibility, exercise of personal responsibility, and proficiency in a given specialty.

*Naval Officers*

Stogdill, Scott, and Jaynes (1956) asked navy officers to use Work Analysis Forms developed by Stogdill and Shartle (1958) to indicate "What I Do" and "What I Ought to Do." Junior officers also indicated their perception of what their senior officer does and ought to do. Seniors expected and were expected to spend more time than juniors on such activities as attending conferences, consulting superiors, examining reports, planning, and coordination. Seniors expected and were expected to spend less time than juniors in activities such as writing reports, reading technical publications, scheduling and routing, research, and technical and professional operations.

Comparisons of relations between self-descriptions and self-expectations indicated areas of agreement and disagreement. Both juniors and seniors tended to report that they should spend more time than they did in inspection, research, planning, public relations, reflection, reading technical periodicals, and writing for publication. Activities in which both seniors and juniors reported that they should do less than they did included consulting assistants and superiors, interviewing personnel, reading and answering mail, preparing charts, supervising, interpreting, and scheduling.

*Civilian Managers*

Sheriff (1969) used the Work Analysis Forms in a comparative study of three levels of management in six diverse organizations. As would be expected, top managers spent more time than middle managers in consultation with subordinates, while managers at the bottom spent more time with superiors and peers. Middle managers fell between the other two groups in contacts with superiors, peers, and subordinates. In regard to individual effort, time spent in examining reports and thinking increased with level of position, while time spent in writing reports, computation, and use of machines decreased with level. At the same time, with respect to major functions, preparing procedures, coordinations, and evaluation increased with level of position. Time spent in supervision and personnel activities progressively decreased with level of position. Haas, Porat, and Vaughan (1969) also used an adaptation of the Work Analysis Forms in a comparative study of three levels of organization. Time spent in planning and coordination was greatest in top-level positions; negotiating, in middle-level positions; and supervising, in lower level positions. All levels combined spent more time than they considered ideal in investigation, but less than they thought ideal in planning.

*Factor Analyses of Work Done*

Factorial studies of leader performance in groups and organizations have proved unusually productive in providing data on functions of leaders. Measurements are usually obtained on a large number of variables. The variable scores are intercorrelated and factor-analyzed. Each factor brings together the specific variables that measure a given aspect of general behavior. Concern with the general aspects of behavior rather than with its specific details facilitates the interpretation of performance in terms of functions. Thus, for example, Berkowitz (1953a) asked members of aircrews to describe the behavior of the aircraft commander in terms of thirteen items. These items were then intercorrelated and factor-analyzed. The factors were identified as maintaining standards of performance, behavior in a nurturant manner, acting upon an awareness of situational needs, and maintaining crew coordination and teamwork.

Hemphill (1960) studied ninety-three business executives located in five companies. The positions represented three levels of organization and five specialties (research and development, sales, manufacturing, general administration, and industrial relations). Data were obtained on 575 items classified as (1) position activities; (2) position responsibilities; (3) position demands and restrictions; and (4) position characteristics. Correlations were computed between positions (1) within each organization; (2) within each level of organization; and (3) within each specialty. The results indicate a greater degree of similarity between positions in the same specialty but in different organizations than between positions within the same level of organization. Hemphill also factor-analyzed the correlations between the 575 items. Ten factors emerged: (1) providing a staff service for a nonoperations area; (2) supervising work; (3) business control; (4) technical—markets and product; (5) human, community, and social affairs; (6) long-range planning; (7) exercise of broad power and authority; (8) business reputation; (9) personal demands; and (10) preservation of assets.

A factor analysis of time use by Stogdill, Shartle, Wherry, and Jaynes (1955) based on correlations between naval officers' profiles produced many factors exhibiting considerable apparent similarity: (1) professional consultants; (2) technical supervisors; (3) coordinators; (4) personnel administrators; (5) schedule, procedure markets; (6) directors; and (7) maintenance administrators. Even though business and military organizations are responsible for different types of operations and materials, the results suggested a basic core of performance clusters common to both types of organizations.

Wofford (1967, 1970, 1971) reached a somewhat simpler set of more psychologically defined factors to describe a manager's behavior: (1) order and group achievement—neatness and accuracy in planning, organizing, and controlling; (2) personal enhancement—use of power and pressure to achieve employee compliance; (3) maintenance of interpersonal relationships—personal interaction as a leader; (4) security and maintenance—reactions to, or the avoidance of, insecurity feelings; and (5) dynamic and achievement orientation—aggression and setting specific goals.

*First-Line Supervisors.* Following Hemphill's (1960) work on the dimensions of managerial jobs, Prien (1963) constructed the Supervisor Position Description Questionnaire with items written by job analysts guided by an outline of general supervisory functions. Thirty supervisors indicated the extent to which each of the items was descriptive of their work. Prien extracted seven factors: (1) employee supervision; (2) employee contact and communications; (3) union–management relations; (4) manpower coordination and administration; (5) work organization, planning, and preparation; (6) manufacturing process supervision; and (7) manufacturing process administration.

Using a similar methodology, Dowell and Wexley (1978) factor-analyzed the responses of 251 supervisors regarding the importance of eighty-nine work activities of first-line supervisors. The factor structure obtained from the intercorrelations among ratings of importance was highly congruent with the factor structure obtained from the intercorrelations among the ratings of amount of time spent in an activity. The seven dimensions along which first-line supervisors could be ordered were: (1) working with subordinates—direct contact with subordinates, informing employees of levels of performance expected, instructing workers in safe working habits, seeing that safety equipment is used, instructing workers in the proper use of materials and equipment, observing subordinates' work activities, listening to employees' ideas and problems, and settling disciplinary problems or potential grievances; (2) organizing work of subordinates—talking with supervisors in other departments regarding levels of production, scheduling overtime, shifting people to other jobs to maintain production levels, establishing priorities on "down" equipment and assigning employees to specific jobs; (3) work planning and scheduling—consulting with off-going supervisor about shift conditions, reading records of previous shifts' activities and planning production levels for shift, and completing reports on shift conditions at the end of the shift; (4) maintaining efficient/quality production—checking quality of production, finding causes of low production or poor quality, determining production levels, determining quality, kinds, and causes of waste, and soliciting suggestions from subordinates regarding improvements in work methods; (5) maintaining safe/clean work areas—communicating Occupational Safety and Health Act (OSHA) regulations to workers, checking to see that walkways and fire exits are clear, completing maintenance records, and inspecting work areas for cleanliness; (6) maintaining equipment and machinery—diagnosing problems with machines, adjusting machines, checking maintenance work when completed, inspecting machines for proper working order, and setting up machines; and (7) compiling records and reports—compiling miscellaneous reports, distributing tools or equipment, keeping personal record of job incidents, performing routine checks of safety devices, and notifying people of schedule changes.

There was little variation in judged importance among supervisors assigned to different production and housekeeping functions except in the obvious maintenance of efficient production, although they did vary systematically on the amount of time spent on different activities. For example, according to Dowell and Wesley (1978), shipping supervisors stood apart from production supervisors in the time spent in work planning and scheduling and in maintaining equipment and machinery.

*Higher-Level Managers.* With a heavier emphasis on functional responsibilities of different managerial positions, Tornow and Pinto (1976) completed a similar analysis for higher-level managers emerging with thirteen dimensions on which executives could be differentiated and evaluated: (1) product, marketing, and financial strategy planning—long-range thinking and planning; (2) coordination of other organizational units and personnel—coordinating the efforts of others over whom one exercises no direct control; (3) internal business control—reviewing and controlling the allocation of manpower and other resources, cost reduction, performance goals, budgets, and employee relations practices; (4) products and services responsibility—planning, scheduling, and monitoring products and services delivery; (5) public and customer relations—promoting the company's products and services, the goodwill of the company, and general public relations; (6) advanced consulting—application of technical expertise to special problems, issues, questions, or policies; (7) autonomy of action—discretion in the handling of the job, making decisions that are most often not subject to review; (8) approval of financial commitments—authority to obligate the company; (9) staff service—fact gathering, data acquisition and compilation, and record keeping for higher authority; (10) supervision—getting work done efficiently through the effective use of people; (11) complexity and stress—handling information under time pressure to meet deadlines, frequently taking risks, interfering with personal or family life; (12) advanced financial responsibility—preservation of assets, making investment decisions and large-scale financial decisions that affect the company's performance; (13) broad personnel responsibility—management of human resources and the policies affecting it.

Both studies strongly support the complex rather than the simple nature of the formal leader's job.

## MANAGERIAL ROLE PROCESSES

Pursuing a radically different longitudinal study of managerial activities, Mintzberg (1973) obtained information about five chief executives and their organizations along with a calendar of their scheduled appointments for a month. Additional data were collected during a week of structured observations including anecdotal data about specific activities, chronological records of activity patterns, a record of incoming and outgoing mail, and a record of the executive's verbal contacts with others.

Executives were found to work at an unrelenting pace on a wide variety of tasks. They were subject to frequent interruptions. Specific, well-defined activities of current importance were preferred rather than work on general functions of less certainty and less immediate relevance. Verbal was preferred over written contact with others. (Many large-scale communication studies such as by Klauss and Bass (1981) corroborate this tendency for interpersonal interaction in large organizations by managers to be primarily verbal rather than written.)

### Role Differences

Based on these data, Mintzberg divided managerial activities into interpersonal, informational, and decisional roles. The interpersonal category contained three specific roles: (1) in the figurehead role, managers perform symbolic duties of a legal or social nature because of their obligations as head of the organization; (2) in the leader role, managers establish the work atmosphere within an organization and motivate subordinates to achieve organizational goals; (3) in the liaison role, managers develop and maintain webs of contacts outside the organization to obtain favors and information.

The informational category also included three roles: (1) in the monitor role, managers act as collectors of all information relevant to the organization; (2) in the disseminator role, managers transmit information from the outside to members in the organization; (3) in the spokesman role, managers transmit information from inside the organization to outsiders.

Lastly, there were four specific decisional roles: (1) managers adopt the entrepreneurial role when they initiate controlled change in their organization to adapt to the changing conditions in the environment; (2) managers are disturbance handlers when forced to deal with unexpected changes; (3) managers adopt the role of resource allocators when they make decisions concerning the use of organizational resources; (4) managers act in the role of negotiators when they are involved in major negotiations with other organizations or individuals.

The ten roles were an integrated set. Formal authority supports the three interpersonal roles, which in turn result in three informational roles. The authority and information roles enable the manager to play the four decisional roles.

### Controversial Implications

Possibly most controversial about Mintzberg's observations were his conclusions that managers don't behave according to textbook requirements for orderliness, planning, optimum decisions, and maximum efficiency. Rather, managerial processes, according to Mintzberg, are characterized by brevity, variety, and discontinuity. Managers rely on judgment and intuition rather than formal analysis, making it difficult to observe clearly their decision-making processes. Kurke and Aldrich (1979) supported Mintzberg's conclusions in a complete replication with four chief executive officers for one week. However, Snyder and Glueck (1977), who also replicated Mintzberg's study, found their managers to have been more planful than Mintzberg's.

Mintzberg claims that managers are oriented toward action, not reflection. There is a certain amount of ritual and regular duties. Since personal communication is favored over written documents, managers spend a good deal of time on the telephone or in meetings. Klauss and Bass (1981) found that this tendency is increased when dealing with peers. Contact is by telephone if peers are at a distance and face-to-face if close. But if the communication is with persons higher or lower in the organizational hierarchy, the tendency is greater to write a memo.

### Simulation Analysis of Managerial Process

Guided by Mintzberg's (1973) conclusions, Shapira and Dunbar (1978) simulated the chief executive's job as head of a firm of 6,000 employees with an inbasket test completed by fifty-four MBA students at Hebrew University. The "chief executive" could exercise each of the roles in dealing with the sixteen memos of the inbasket and with the agenda he/she had prepared. A small space analysis indicated that the ten managerial roles could be described meaningfully with two clusters. The first cluster was made up of the liaison, disseminator, spokesman, and figurehead roles. These were concerned primarily with information generation and transmission. The cluster corresponded with Mintzberg's (1975) notion of the executive as the general nerve center of the organization unit.

The second cluster of roles, entrepreneur, negotiator, leader, disturbance handler, monitor and resource allocator, was concerned primarily with the active formulation and execution of decisions.

## ANTECEDENT CONDITIONS AFFECTING TIME USE AND WORK DONE BY MANAGERS

### Organizational Effects

Changes in the manager's organization will result in considerable changes in his or her activities. Thus, in a study of production foremen in four plants, Wikstrom (1967) found that, whereas in the past supervisors tended to make decisions like workers, the introduction into the organization of numerous specialists who influenced production in various ways now required supervisors to coordinate and sequence manufacturing processes. Since the supervisors must coordinate the impact of various specialists, they had to assume managerial functions and decision responsibilities. Similarly, K. W. Harris

(1968), who studied twenty-three school superintendents, each with more than twenty-five years of tenure in the same position, found that they spent less time than common a quarter-century earlier on curriculum and pupil personnel problems and more time on problems involving buildings, finance, and school–community relations.

Organizational demand characteristics make an obvious difference in manager's activities. Katzell, Barrett, Vann, and Hogan (1968) studied the relationship between nine executive role patterns and various dimensions of organization. The data were provided by 194 middle management personnel in the U.S. army. The role performances most highly associated with variations in the organization were controlling, staffing, and time spent with other persons. Organizational dimensions most highly related to variation in role performance were level and mission of the organization and executive's span of control and job classification.

Alexander (1979) studied 225 managers in production, marketing, and accounting, noting that marketing and accounting managers reported themselves higher in requiring Mintzberg's informational roles of monitor, disseminator, and spokesperson than did the production managers. Fewer differences were seen in requirements in other roles.

### Effects of Hierarchical Level

In the preceding discussions about analyses of time spent and work done, organizational level has already been seen to be a major determinant. Further evidence and observations are available. Thus, Barnard (1938) noted that top management is concerned with broad policies, objectives, and plans. These purposes and objectives become more specific as they filter down to lower levels where the work is actually done (Barnard, 1938). In addition, according to W. A. Scott (1967), unlike middle and lower management, top managers are both the ultimate teacher and the judge of subordinates. They must be sensitive to the interactions among people below and to their material resources. But at lower levels in the organizational hierarchy, Whyte (1956) observed that the primary function is to perceive one's task accurately and conform to it. Technology and controls are most important. Nevertheless, if the broad objectives and policies set at the top are to be operationalized and successfully carried out, managers at lower levels must exhibit considerable initiative (Fiedler & Nealey, 1966).

Many other differences in activity and function were seen between managers at different levels in the organization by Pfiffner and Sherwood (1960). First-line supervisors more often are in direct personal contact with subordinates, whereas middle managers see their subordinates less often. Middle managers spend more time with their own superiors than do supervisors. Middle managers use formal communications in their work to a greater extent than do first-line supervisors.

At each level, the manager's constituents and interests are different. At the top, the manager is concerned with sponsors, clients, and the community as well as with his or her own subordinates. At the bottom, the first-level supervisors are concerned with the interests of their superiors, their peers, and their subordinates as well as others such as union stewards or outside inspectors. In all, managers spend relatively little of their time with their superiors according to Brewer and Tomlinson (1963–1964) and, as just noted above, much time may be spent with a wide variety of other parties, not just subordinates (M. W. McCall, 1974, 1977).

Argyris (1964a) observed that job objectives and interpersonal factors play more important roles in influencing the managers' effectiveness higher in the hierarchy. Nealy and Fiedler (1968) added more specifically that the typical functions of first-line supervisors are production, on-the-job training, control of materials and supplies, and maintenance. Second-level supervisors are concerned with cost control, setting standards, selection and placement, coordination of work units, and formal training.

*Supporting Evidence.*   In Alexander's (1979) previously cited study, hierarchical level made a considerable difference in seven of the Mintzberg role requirements. With increasing level, there were increasing requirements for the roles of figurehead, liaison, monitor, disseminator, spokesperson, and entrepreneur. The negotiation role was seen as required most by middle managers.

Dubin and Spray (1964) analyzed the logs kept by executives over a two-week period. Lower-level executives were more likely than those on higher levels to concentrate time on a single activity. Face-to-face communication was the most frequent form of interaction for all. High-level executives more often initiated than received contacts.

T. A. Mahoney (1961) concluded from several studies (for example, L. Strong, 1956; *Fortune,* 1946) that the higher the level of managers' positions, the more hours per week they devoted to their job and the more time they spent in planning and organizing rather in the technical work of the organization. This was confirmed in the previously cited survey of 452 managers in thirteen firms by Mahoney, Jerdee, and Carroll (1965). Whereas supervising was the main function of 51 percent of lower-level supervisors, it was the main function of only 36 percent of middle managers and 22 percent of top managers. On the other hand, top managers were more likely to be generalists and planners in comparison to lower-level managers. Figure 17.2 shows how managers could be typed according to their main function. It can be seen that the type of manager depends on organizational level.

*Time Lag between Decision and Consequences.*   Jaques (1956) advanced the hypothesis that high-level administrative work is characterized by long-time lags between the time a decision is made and the time that the effects of the decision have an impact on the organization. If so, high-level managers would personally exhibit comparatively high degrees of future orientation and tolerance for delayed outcomes in their time perspectives. But in a study of 141 managers at six levels of a plant, Goodman (1967) failed to find that future orientation and preference for delayed gratification were highly related to the level of an executive's position. However, Jaques's proposition was supported in an investigation of four levels of supervisors and managers in British industry. Martin (1959) observed that in a sample of British managers at four levels, from foreman at the bottom to works manager at the top of the same factory, almost all decisions of a shift foreman at the bottom of the hierarchy were about matters that occurred within a two-week period. On the other hand, only 3.3 percent of the decisions of the works manager involved questions of short duration. Fifty percent of the decisions of the works manager involved policies with time perspectives of one year or longer. No one at lower levels was involved in decisions involving such periods of time.

Despite Goodman's (1967) negative results, most other observers agreed with Martin that the time perspective of managers at higher levels requires them to live with more uncertainty and lack of feedback, to consider longer-range goals, and to be able to remain for long periods without evaluation of the effects of their decisions. Decisions at the highest levels involve especially high uncertainty and risk. Thus, W. A. Scott (1967)

**FIGURE 17.2.  Distribution of Assignments among Job Types at Each Organizational Level**

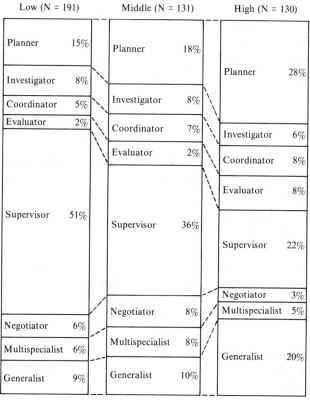

NOTE: *Totals do not add up to 100 percent because of rounding.*

SOURCE: *Mahoney, Jerdee, and Carroll (1965).*

observed that "top management must have the ability to detach itself from the internal imperatives of coordination and to reflect on the general purposes and objectives of the company in its industry and society." Top managers by the nature of their role, are often detached from outside judgment or objective criteria against which they can appraise their approach to problems, their decisions, and their philosophy. The production worker can be appraised against tangible output and the lower-level manager against departmental performance. The long time span of decision and the subjectivity of the job of the top manager make appraisals more difficult.

## CONSEQUENCES OF MANAGERIAL ACTIVITIES

*Work Overload*

The sense of being overworked is a common executive response. For instance, S. Carlson (1951) found that most Swedish executives queried reported being overloaded with little time for family or friends. Yet a *Business Management* (Anonymous,

1968) survey of 179 company presidents and board chairmen found that the average executive worked approximately sixty-three hours per week but did not feel overworked, although over 70 percent felt that they did not have enough time for thinking and planning. W. E. Moore (1960) found that detailed chores involving problems in communication and operations interfered with the effective use of managerial time. But Jaques (1966) reported that hard work and long hours were not sufficient conditions for producing stress symptoms in executives. Rather, stress conditions are generated from within the manager as responses to impossible achievement standards or overly difficult tasks.

### Effective Managerial Process

Functional differences can be observed in managers assigned to the same line and staff positions as a consequence of their differential effectiveness. Thus, Heizer (1969) asked 200 managers to write incidents of effective and ineffective managerial behavior. Effective managers differed significantly from ineffective managers in planning, coordination, delegation, and staffing. In the same way, Kavanagh, MacKinney, and Wolins (1970) reported that the extent to which the department head fulfills the functions of planning, investigating, coordinating, evaluating, supervising, and representing was related to the job satisfaction of the supervisors below the department head.

Effective managers differ from ineffective ones in how they define their own roles in the larger organizational context. Thus, Ghiselli and Barthol (1956) found that successful supervisors differ from unsuccessful ones in perceiving themselves as planful, loyal to the company and to subordinates, and feeling the responsibility of working with people to achieve organizational goals. Unsuccessful supervisors saw themselves as good fellows, well-liked, responsible for production, and able to rely upon ingenuity and resourcefulness rather than planning or loyalty to company or employees to get the job done. Successful supervisors identified with their work group and its members, whereas unsuccessful supervisors were interested in making a living.

Campbell, Dunnette, Lawler, and Weick (1970) proposed a person-process-product model of managerial effectiveness. The "person" in the model refers to the managers' competencies such as discussed in Chapter 6. The "product" is an organizational result such as productivity. The "process" is the manager's on-the-job activities. All three components, person-process-product, need to be understood in evaluating the manager's effectiveness, which depends on identifying and judging observable actions and behavior leading to the accomplishment of the organization's objectives (Porter, Lawler & Hackman, 1975).

Most studies of managerial effectiveness have centered on managerial competence and organizational results; relatively few studies have focused on the effectiveness of managerial process. One such study was by E. Williams (1968), who compared the activity patterns and preferences of thirty effective and thirty ineffective executives. The effective executives scored significantly higher in responsibility, human relations, decision making, and problem solving. Although the two samples differed in time devoted to organizing and controlling, the less effective executives spent less time in planning and also rated organizing and controlling significantly higher in importance than did the effective executives. Apparently, the comparative deficiency in planning in the ineffective executives was accompanied by a perceived need for higher degrees of control.

*An Application.* An examination of the effectiveness of managerial process was completed by Morse and Wagner (1978). They used a modified list of nine of Mintzberg's (1973) managerial roles to classify managerial activities: (1) strategic problem solving; (2) resource managing; (3) conflict handling; (4) organizing; (5) information handling; (6) motivating; (7) providing for growth and development; (8) coordinating; and (9) managing the organization's environment. After several refinements by means of factor analysis, they constructed a list of fifty-one activities which could be used by managers to evaluate another manager with whom they worked closely. By rating the extent of each activity, a colleague could evaluate a manager's behavior. Six extracted factors covered the original nine or activities as follows: *(1) managing the organization's environment and its resources*–managers are proactive and stay ahead of changes in their environment; they base plans and actions pertaining to the organization's resources on clear, up-to-date, accurate knowledge of the objectives of the company; *(2) organizing and coordinating*–managers suit the amount of formal rules and regulations in their organization to the tasks to be done and to the abilities and personalities of the people doing them; these managers are not difficult to get along with and not difficult to coordinate with; *(3) information handling*–managers make sure that information entering the organization is processed by formal reports, memos, and word of mouth on a timely basis so that it is usable, current, and provides rapid feedback; they make sure that the person who has to use the information clearly understands it; *(4) providing for growth and development*–managers insure, through career counseling and careful observation and recording, that their subordinates are growing and developing in their skill for performing their work; they guide subordinates by commendation of good performance; *(5) motivating and conflict handling*–managers transmit their own enthusiasm for attaining organizational goals to others; they are not plagued by recurring conflicts of a similar nature which get in the way of associates' efforts to perform their jobs; *(6) strategic problem solving*–managers periodically schedule strategy and review sessions involving the design of projects to improve organizational performance and to solve organizational problems; they spend considerable amounts of time looking at their organization for opportunities to improve performance or for problem situations.

Evaluations of 231 managers by colleagues were higher among better performing managers on all six dimensions in three of six offices according to objective end result criteria such as net profit, budgeting data, and customer billing volume. The evaluations were correlated between .41 and .65 with superiors' rankings of how well the managers were performing. Multiple regression analyses suggested that, overall, the managerial activities of most consequence to end results were managing the organization's environment and resources and motivation and conflict handling. But consequences depended on the organization's objectives. Thus, in one firm engaged in data processing, accounting and handling financial records for clients, information handling, and strategic problem solving had the highest beta weights in multiple regression analysis of the contribution of scores on the six dimensions of managers and their appraised performance by their superiors (Morse & Wagner, 1978).

Effective managerial process may be a matter of style, the issue to which we turn next.

# 18

## DEMOCRATIC VERSUS AUTOCRATIC LEADERSHIP

### INTRODUCTION

Leaders and managers vary in how they deal with their subordinates. A great many different concepts have been used to describe how they vary. They involve either work-related or person-related behavior. Many seem to have a notion of autocracy at one extreme and democracy and relations orientation at the other, first examined as such in the seminal investigation of Lewin and Lippitt (1938).

The listing of different, but correlated, ways of describing the extremes include the following:

| Source (by year) | Work Related and/or Authoritarian, Autocratic | Person-Related and/or Equalitarian, Democratic |
|---|---|---|
| (1938) Lewin and Lippitt | Authoritarian, autocratic | Democratic |
| (1950) Katz et al. | Production-oriented | Employee-oriented |
| (1951) Hemphill et al. | Initiating structure | Considerate |
| (1957a,b) Fleishman | Production emphasis | Employee emphasis |
| (1958) Kahn | Path-goal structuring, modifying goals, enabling achievement | Direct need satisfaction |
| (1960) Cartwright and Zander | Goal achievement-oriented | Group maintenance-oriented |
| (1960) MacGregor | Theory X | Theory Y |
| (1960) Bass | Coercive, persuasive | Permissive |
| (1964) Blake and Mouton | "9, 1" (production, not employee concerned) | "1, 9" (employee, not production concerned) |
| (1964) Day and Hamblin | Punitive | Non-punitive |
| (1961a) R. Likert | High performance, technical, close in supervision | Supportive, group methods, general in supervision |
| (1962) Blau and Scott | Distant, formal, aloof, cold | Close, informal, warm |
| (1965) F. C. Mann | Administrative, technical | Human relations-oriented |
| (1966) Bowers and Seashore | Work facilitative, goal emphasizing | Interaction facilitative, supportive |
| (1966a,b) P. J. Burke | Directive | Nondirective |
| (1967b) Bass | Task, self-oriented | Interaction-oriented |
| (1967a) Fiedler | Task-oriented | Relations-oriented |

| Source (by year) | Work Related and/or Authoritarian, Autocratic | Person-Related and/or Equalitarian, Democratic |
|---|---|---|
| (1967) R. Likert | System I, II | System III, IV |
| (1969a) Heller | Coercive, directive | Joint decision making |
| (1970) Wofford | Order, achievement, personal enhancement | Personal attraction, security and maintenance |
| (1971) Yukl | Decision centralization, initiation | Considerate |
| (1974) D. R. Anderson | Traditional, prescriptive | People-centered, supportive |
| (1974) Bass and Valenzi | Directive, negotiative (manipulative), persuasive | Consultative, participative, delegative |
| (1974) Vroom and Yetton | A (decisions) | C, G (decisions) |
| (1976) Flowers | Closed | Open |
| (1976) Keller and Szilagyi | Nonrewarding | Rewarding |

Sweney, Fiechtner, and Samores (1975) completed a factor analysis of the leadership focus of 103 male employed part-time college students which corroborated the high degree of complexity to be found in examining autocratic and democratic leadership. Factors included authoritarian role preference, authoritarian role pressure, equalitarian role preference, equalitarian role pressure, balanced manager, people-oriented manager, assumed similarity between opposites, contemptuous indulgence, supportive values, people tolerance, and organizational tolerance.

Nevertheless, the same persons who display one type of, say, initiation of structure, are likely to be seen as displaying authoritarian behavior, work facilitation, and persuasion as well. The same persons who display one type of democratic behavior are likely to be seen as supportive, considerate, and people-oriented as well, but the correlation is far from perfect.

### Conceptual versus Empirical Communality

Fiske (1979) suggested that the study of a particular act by different persons can reach different conclusions than the study of the same persons who continue to perform a particular act. Bass, Valenzi, Farrow, and Solomon (1975) found that according to subordinates describing their superiors, direction and negotiation were positively correlated. Even more highly intercorrelated were consultation, participation, and delegation. However, forty-six judges, using response allocation procedures, could readily and reliably discriminate between the specific behaviors involved in direction and negotiation as well as between the behaviors involved in consultation, participation, and delegation. Leaders who were consultative also tended to be participative and delegative. Nevertheless, the three kinds of styles are distinctive and may to some degree have different antecedents and consequences. Factorial independence of each of the styles would make research with them easier; however, maintaining conceptually distinct but correlated styles remains viable and useful in the same way that we continue to separate analyses of body height and body weight, although they also are empirically correlated.

*Caveat.* Leaders can also tend toward inactivity. Whereas any of the preceding styles require activity, laissez-faire leadership or abdication do not. They call for doing little or nothing with subordinates.

Furthermore, each leader tends to use a variety of different styles. W. A. Hill (1973) found that only 14 percent of 124 observed supervisors used only one style in four different situations. Similarly, McDonnell (1974) found that when 226 respondents were asked to choose whether they would be autocratic, consultative, participative, or laissez-faire, each respondent used a different style of reacting depending on which of twelve problem situations was presented for consideration. Yet, Hollander (1978) observed that political leaders often try to project a consistent image to a wide audience based on a particular style uniform across situations. Most, in fact, do change from before to after election, and from one constituency to another.

### Distinctions

In this and the next four chapters, we will look at the following dichotomies of leadership: democratic versus autocratic, participative versus directive, relations- versus task-oriented, showing consideration versus initiation, and laissez-faire leadership versus motivation to manage. What are the distinctions among these dichotomies?

Democratic versus autocratic leadership is the most multifaceted. It refers to the way power is distributed, whose needs are met, and which way decisions are made. Participative versus directive leadership refers primarily to how decisions are made. Relations- versus task-oriented leadership focuses on whose needs are met. Consideration versus initiation of structure is a behaviorally factor-derived dichotomy. Depending on how they are measured, consideration and initiation refer to how decisions are made and to the structuring of tasks and goals and role relationships. Laissez-faire leadership and motivation to manage refer to the extent to which leadership is avoided or attempted.

Karmel (1978) drew attention to the ubiquity of initiation and consideration in the study of leadership and efforts to theorize about it. What she primarily offered to add was the importance of the total amount of both kinds of leader activity in contrast to leader inactivity. Thus, she brought us back full-circle to Lewin and Lippitt (1938), who conceptualized leadership as authoritarian (initiating), democratic (considerate), or laissez-faire (inactive rather than active).

### Two Clusters of Leader Focus

Although investigations use many terms that are not fully overlapping in meaning, generally correlations will be high among those described in one or another of the "leader or task focused" ways involving initiating structure. That is, the same leaders who are described as autocratic or authoritarian (Lewin & Lippitt, 1938) will also be described as directive (Heller, 1969a; Bass & Barrett, 1981), "Theory X" (McGregor, 1960), coercive and persuasive (Bass, 1960), concerned with production (Blake & Mouton, 1964), lone decision makers (Vroom & Yetton, 1974), initiators of structure (Fleishman, 1953c), production-centered (R. Likert, 1961a), goal emphasizers and work facilitators (Bowers & Seashore, 1966), and task-oriented (Fiedler, 1967a).

Similarly, a second relatively independent "follower-focused" cluster will overlap consideration of followers in many different ways. This second cluster will emerge around leaders who are considerate (Fleishman, 1953c), democratic (Lewin & Lippitt, 1938), consultative and participative (Bass, 1976), employee-centered (R. Likert,

1961a), concerned with people (Blake & Mouton, 1964), supportive and facilitating interaction (Bowers & Seashore, 1966), relations-oriented (Fiedler, 1967a), joint decision makers (Heller, 1969a), "Theory Y" ideologists (McGregor, 1960), and group decision makers (Vroom & Yetton, 1974).

A task-focused leader initiates structure, provides the information, determines what is to be done, issues the rules, promises rewards for compliance, and threatens punishments for disobedience. The follower-focused leader solicits advice, opinions, and information from followers and checks decisions or shares decision making with followers. The leader-focused or task-focused leader uses his or her power to obtain compliance with what the leader has decided. The follower-focused leader uses his or her power to set the constraints within which followers are encouraged to join in deciding what is to be done.

*Three Types of Advocates.* Theorists fall into three groups. There are partisans for the leader- or task-focused approach such as Miner (1968) or the classical "scientific managers." There are theorists such as R. Likert (1967) and Seashore and Bowers (1963) who support a follower focus. A third group, which includes Fiedler (1967a), Heller (1969a), Vroom and Yetton (1974), and Bass (1976), are likely to argue that it all depends on the environment, the organization, the task, and the particular leader and particular followers involved.

## AUTOCRATIC AND DEMOCRATIC LEADERSHIP

Why do we emerge with just two clusters? Possibly because there are only two ways of changing subordinates' behavior (apart from using drugs or physical force). The leader must alter either the subordinate's information, understanding, and ability to cope with the task at hand or the subordinate's motivation to deal with the task. When the leader has more relevant knowledge than the followers, task-focused direction provides for the necessary transfer of information. Powerful leaders can arouse motivation. But in many situations where followers have as much or more information than the leader and/or where power is more widely shared, motivation of followers is more likely to depend on involving them in decisions about handling the task and their concerns about it and themselves.

### Fundamental Character

The duality has been seen down through history. How should humankind be led? How should humankind be governed? How should humankind be guided? Two views prevailed (based on opposing doctrines about human nature). Either human nature was cursed by original sin or human nature was blessed with the inherent ability to find salvation. If humankind was essentially bad, it had to be controlled, directed, and uplifted by authority. If humankind was essentially good, it must be given the freedom in which to learn, to grow, and to overcome.

### Contribution and Concern

In distinguishing between leader- or task-focused and follower-focused leadership, two differentiations have been emphasized: contribution to decision making and focus of concern. The primitive task-directed leader, say, the ''bull-of-the-woods,'' the early twentieth-century shop foreman, the exploitative authoritarian (Likert, 1961a), makes the decisions for his group and is concerned with what is needed to get the job done, not with the needs of his subordinates, except possibly for their economic needs. A more sophisticated task-focused leader reserves decisions for himself or herself and still is more concerned about getting the job done than the needs of his/or her subordinates for, say, autonomy and growth. A follower-focused leader encourages contributions of subordinates to the decision process and pays attention to their needs.

### The Differences in Processes and Expected Outcomes

The first experiments to deal with the subject contrasted the effects of the authoritarian leader with those of the democratic leader. The authoritarian or autocratic leader dictated what was to be done and was unconcerned about group member needs for autonomy and development. The democratic leader shared the decision making with subordinates and was concerned about their needs to contribute to deciding on what was to be done. The authoritarian leader was personal in praise or aloof of each member; the democratic leader was factual and rational. The authoritarian leader remained aloof; the democratic leader de-emphasized social distance from the members.

Following experiments with authoritarian and democratic leadership, subsequent studies tended to concentrate on one of four aspects of the discrimination between authoritarian and democratic leadership: (1) whether decision making was or was not shared by the leader; (2) whether or not the follower was of primary concern to the leader; (3) whether social distance was maintained; and (4) whether punishment and coercion were employed.

*Combinations.* Conceptually, each is different. Yet, as we have already suggested, the same persons who display one aspect of democratic behavior are also likely to display the others. That is, the participative leader is likely to be more concerned about the needs of his or her group than is the directive leader. But combinations are possible. The benevolent autocrat is dictatorial yet concerned about the needs of his or her subordinates. The participative manager may encourage group decision making but place more emphasis on getting the job done than on the needs of the group.

We will see that generally autocracy or democracy is preferable to neither and that objectives, task demands, interpersonal, and personal relations must be considered in determining which way is optimal. Increased follower understanding and motivation both call for leader action rather than inaction.

### Problems in Reviewing the Evidence

Some researchers have taken greater care than others in defining and ''purifying'' the patterns of leader behavior to be studied. It has been difficult to determine in a few studies whether a given pattern of behavior should be included as democratic, participative, considerate, or relations-oriented.

A further difficulty arises from the definition and measurement of follower satisfaction and group productivity. Some studies measure global satisfaction, whereas others measure satisfaction with leadership, the job, the group, or the organization. Some researchers count units of output as measures of productivity. Others use ratings of quantity or quality of output as productivity measures. Thus, there is little commonality from study to study in the definitions of satisfaction and productivity.

Several outstanding analyses have produced complex and curvilinear relationships, yielding real insight into a problem. Modifier variables have to be taken into account.

*Cause-Effect.* We face the "chicken-or-the-egg" issue. One-time concurrent studies of leadership and its consequences may in reality be a one-time study of leadership and its antecedent conditions. Leaders may be autocratic because their work groups are unproductive. Leaders can afford to be democratic because their groups are productive. The needed longitudinal studies are few; the one-time studies are many. R. Likert's (1967) research with moving organizations in a more democratic direction suggests that the results may not become immediately apparent. One or two years may elapse before a change exerts any measurable effects on organizational performance.

*Results Reflect Implicit Theories.* In Chapter 16, we observed that followers condition a leader's behavior, that is, the leader of a productive group can afford to be more considerate of his or her subordinates than the leader of a poorly performing group. In addition, Mitchell, Larson, and Green (1977) showed that subordinates' descriptions of a leader's initiation and consideration are erroneously confounded with the perceived quality of his or her group's success. What is cause and what is effect is complicated by the extent to which the correlations reflect the implicit leadership theories of the raters. That is, we may assume that subordinates will be more productive under a particular pattern of supervision. They may make their report about the supervisor as a consequence of how they see the group performing (Rush, Thomas, & Lord, 1977). Thus, in Mitchell, Larsen, and Green's study, knowledge that a group performed well caused increases in the rated consideration and initiating structure of that group's supervisor, whereas knowledge that a group performed poorly caused large decreases in rated consideration and initiating structure. These distortions in leadership ratings due to knowledge of performance also occurred when raters of high- or low-performing leaders were exposed to identical and highly salient leadership behaviors (Lord, Binning, et al., 1978).

## DEMOCRATIC VERSUS AUTOCRATIC LEADERSHIP

### Types of Autocratic Leadership

MacIver (1947) and Bass (1960) noted that autocratic leaders may depend upon their power to coerce and their ability to persuade. An able leader successfully persuades others to follow him or her because they expect that following the leader's suggestions will result in solving the problems the group faces. A powerful person successfully coerces others to follow him or her because the power of the leader's position or the power of the leader as a person makes others expect that the leader will reward them for compliance or punish them for rejection. An able leader can indirectly reinforce the behavior of others. Such a leader can provide the cues aiding in their goal attainment. A powerful leader can directly reinforce the behavior of others by granting or denying rewards or punishments for the others' behavior (Bass, 1960). These types of autocratic leadership were described by F. C. Bartlett (1926), who observed that leaders in any complex social group maintain their success, on the one hand, because of the social prestige (the status) of their position or because of their personal capacity to impress and dominate and, on the other, by virtue of personal capacity to persuade their followers. Parten (1932), observing the spontaneous play of nursery school children using one-minute sampling, found two types of leadership possible in the situation: persuasive leadership employing diplomatic, "artful" suggestion and leadership through personal power using brute force to dominate others. Similarly, Zillig (1933) observed the same two types of leader in the German classroom: leaders who dominate and leaders who direct and guide.

### Types of Democratic Leadership

Democratic leadership usually requires more maturity and some education in its processes. Some leaders may be identified as democratic based on their use of parliamentary procedures and majority decision making. Others may consult, strive for consensus, pursue an open, trusting, follower-oriented relationship.

### The Prototype Experiment

The first major research undertaken to study leadership as a two-way process of interaction between leader and followers was published by Lewin and Lippitt (1938). This experiment explored the "effects of democratic and authoritarian group atmospheres upon the behavior of the group members." Reporting on the same study, Lippitt (1940) defined what was meant by democratic and authoritarian leader behavior. By means of careful coaching and practice, the authoritarian leader was trained to determine all policy for group members, to dictate the methods and stages of goal attainment one step at a time, to direct the actions and interactions of group members, and to praise in a personal manner. The democratic leader was trained to encourage group members to determine their own policies, to give them perspective by explaining in advance the steps toward goal attainment, to award them freedom to initiate their own tasks and interactions, and to praise them in an objective manner. The leaders were adults. The group members were 10-year-old boys and girls, closely matched on several control variables. Two groups of five members each worked on hobby projects. The behavior of leaders and members was recorded by trained observers.

Both leaders and group members initiated more actions in the authoritarian groups. Members of authoritarian groups made more submissive reactions to the leader, however, and treated him less as an equal than was the case in the democratic group. In the authoritarian group, members became progressively more submissive to the leader, demanding attention and approval. Although members of the authoritarian group tended to respond to the leader rather than to initiate interaction with each other, they hesitated to approach him because to do so might further reduce their personal power and freedom of movement. The democratic form of leadership, on the other hand, tended to increase the freedom of action of group members. The members of democratic groups exhibited less tension and hostility, and their subgroups were more cohesive and enduring than was the case for authoritarian groups.

Laissez-faire leadership was also studied in this prototype experiment, but its effects will be discussed later.

## EFFECTS OF DEMOCRATIC VERSUS AUTHORITARIAN LEADERSHIP

### Effects on Performance

Results have been mixed in the short-term and concurrent studies of the effects of autocratic and democratic leadership on group performance when the performance objectives are immediate productivity and/or problem solution rather than developing team capabilities, and motivation.

*Autocratic Better.* Torrance (1953) reported that crews given feedback by highly authoritarian methods exhibited greater improvement in performance than those given feedback by less highly structured methods. Hise (1968), studying simulated business groups, found that productivity was positively related to close rather than general supervision. M. E. Shaw (1955) obtained results indicating that speed and accuracy of group performance in a highly structured communications network were significantly higher under autocratic than under democratic leadership. In a study of groups in a formal organization, Shepherd and Weschler (1955) found that psychosocial distance between leader and followers was associated with fewer communication difficulties. Working closely together was related to greater difficulty in communication. Bergum and Lehr (1963) studied monitoring (detection) performance under different conditions of supervision. They found that vigilance performance could be maintained at fairly high levels under authoritarian conditions.

Even in the short run, whether or not autocratic leadership pays off will depend on the extent to which the leader has more knowledge or control of resources. On the face of it, democratic approaches are indicated when subordinates are in possession of as much or more of what is needed to accomplish the collective task. This can be demonstrated by an exercise such as PAXIT (Shackleton, Bass & Allison, 1975). Autocratic leadership can be productive if the trainee assigned the autocratic leader role happens, by chance, to know more about the problem to be solved than the person playing the subordinate role. Cammalleri, Hendrick, Pittman, et al. (1973) clearly demonstrated this effect using the Lost on the Moon Exercise. When autocratic leaders had possession of the correct answer, they could better ensure highly accurate group outcomes than could democratic leaders. But autocratic leaders with misinformation could also lead their groups further astray than democratic leaders with the same degree of misinformation.

*Democratic Better.* Comrey, Pfiffner, and Beem (1952) studied employees at six levels of organization in the U.S. Forest Survey. Supervisors of more effective departments were described as sympathetic, democratic, interacting socially, and sharing information. Similarly, Comrey, High, and Wilson (1955a, 1955b) studied supervisors and workers in an aircraft factory. Supervisors of effective groups were characterized by adequate authority, communication downward, sympathy, lack of arbitrariness, and lack of hypercritical attitudes toward employees. Argyle, Gardner, and Ciofi (1958) also reported higher rates of productivity, reduced personnel turnover, and reduced absenteeism under democratic, nonpunitive supervision in work groups in seven British factories. Zweig (1966) found that democratic supervisors were rated by higher management as more effective than supervisors exhibiting less democratic styles of behavior. Similarly, Hall and Donnell (1979) reported that the fastest advancing managers were least likely to subscribe to Theory X beliefs; the slowest advancing were more likely to do so.

Results obtained by Day and Hamblin (1964) indicated that close supervision was associated with reduced productivity and a nonsignificant reduction in group harmony. They studied twenty-four groups of four members each who had to follow elaborate blueprints to assemble models of molecules of pegs, springs, and various colored balls. In this complex task, they were subjected to either punitive or nonpunitive supervision as well as to close or general supervision. Punitive and close supervision, in contrast to nonpunitive and general supervision, tended to increase subjects' feelings of aggression toward their coworkers as well as toward their supervisor, significantly lowering productivity.

In earlier chapters we have already observed that supervisors tend to avoid punitive action. They mainly tend to do so when confronted with poor subordinate performance. But Maier and Danielson (1956) reported that even when disciplinary rules call for punishment, foremen tend to avoid it. They perceive it will reduce rather than increase productivity even when it is used to control rule violations. In fact, Keller and Szilagyi (1976) found that punitive leadership primarily increased role ambiguity. Nevertheless, in a military setting involving a survey of 30,735 U.S. army superiors, peers and subordinates of officers, and noncom leaders, Penner, Malone, Coughlin, and Herz (1973) found that leaders who established a high level of discipline were likely to be rated much higher in their overall performance by their superiors.

More subtle effects were obtained by Schmitt (1969), who studied the effects of punitive supervision on worker productivity. Results indicated that magnitude of the penalty imposed on the better paid of two tasks affected the amount of time spent on the tasks when the penalties occurred at unequal intervals but not at equal ones. Under unequal intervals of punishment, the higher the penalties, the less time spent on the punished task and the greater the time spent on the unpunished but lower-paying task. Numerous other experiments point to the deleterious main and side effects of punitive supervision in contrast to absence from such conditions. French (1957) examined the effects of the supervisor who obtains compliance by using the power to punish. Paid participants worked at a simple task of sorting IBM cards according to the total number of holes they contained. The assignment was supposedly part of a research project. Participants were fined for failure to maintain speed and accuracy of performance up to standard. In comparison to participants rewarded extra when they reached and maintained the standard, participants punished by fines for failure were more likely to show signs of resistance to maintaining production. After four working periods had occurred, punishment for failure became detrimental to speed and accuracy. There was a greater desire of participants to leave the work. They also were more likely to want to do something else and to make suggestions for changing the work situation. They also showed greater feelings of aggression, liked their supervisor less, and were less likely to accept the supervisor as competent to evaluate their work. In a similar experiment, Raven and French (1958b), levied fines when participants failed to conform to demands of supervisors. This led the participants to resist by overconforming to the suggestions of their supervisors. That is, metaphorically, if participants were ordered against their will to "polish the silverware," they rubbed so hard that they rubbed off all the silver.

Other experiments by deCharms and Hamblin (1960) yielded similar results, finding that punitive supervision resulted in increased worker tension and lower productivity.

*Alternatives Better.* Ziller (1957) observed greater problems for members led democratically. Neither autocratic nor democratic leadership was as effective as a type of leadership that consistently reinforced correct member performance by approval and suggested improvements. Spector and Suttell (1956) demonstrated that this resulted in better group achievement than an authoritarian type that made decisions for the group or a democratic type that permitted maximum member participation.

Wehman, Goldstein, and Williams (1977) reported results from an experiment in which four leadership styles were varied to study effects on eighty undergraduates' individual risk-taking behavior in group settings. Democratic and authoritarian leadership styles significantly depressed a shift toward risk in groups when compared to laissez-faire-led groups and no-designated-leader groups. Georgopolos (1965) observed productivity to be associated with a pattern of supervisory behavior that employees regarded as "just right" and "not too strict."

D'Angelo (1973) reported that a "human resources" style which involves "striving to continually expand the areas over which the manager's subordinates have self-direction and self-control" was associated with more effective work groups before and after an organizational development program for 103 sales managers and their 360 salesmen subordinates. This was in contrast to less effective autocratic or human relations styles.

*No Differences.* Still other investigators obtained no significant differences in productivity between democratically and autocratically led groups. Thus, Spector and Suttell (1956) found no differences in group performance under democratic and autocratic leadership. Likewise, Lyle (1961) found no significant differences in performance of groups under democratic and autocratic leadership. There was a tendency for democratic groups to work faster under restricted communication, while authoritarian groups worked faster under open communication. Results obtained by S. Adams (1952) indicated that bomber crews performed more effectively under medium than under high or low degrees of democratic leadership. Sales (1964) obtained no significant difference in performance scores of groups with democratic and autocratic leaders.

Johnson and Smith (1953) studied classes taught traditionally and under democratic leadership. No significant differences were found in achievement gains or in student evaluations.

Mullen (1965, 1966b) failed to find group productivity related to supervisory style. Likewise, T. A. Mahoney (1967) found no relationship between democratic supervision and measures of organizational effectiveness in a study of industrial organizations. Similarly, Swartz (1973) found that whether or not football coaches were autocratic, democratic, or laissez-faire was unrelated to their success in winning games. G. H. Graham (1969) conducted one class democratically according to Theory Y and another autocratically according to Theory X. The two groups did not differ in examination scores. The top quartile of students did better under class freedom, however, whereas the remaining students made better grades under instructor control.

### Effects on Satisfaction

Ordinarily, satisfaction and morale are likely to be higher with democratic supervision.

*Democratic Better.* Beam (1975) showed that all navy enlisted personnel, regardless of the level of technology or physical activity in which they were involved, had a strong desire to be treated democratically. Mohr (1971) obtained similar results in 144 work groups from thirteen local health departments, as did Pennings (1975) in forty branch offices of a large U.S. brokerage firm. Satisfaction was strongly associated with democratic supervision in these as well as in most other large-scale, long-term studies.

Baumgartel (1957) studied attitudes and motivations of scientists in government R & D labs under three leadership conditions (democratic, authoritarian, and laissez-faire). He found that scientists working under the democratic leadership held the most favorable attitudes and greater job motivation, whereas least favorable attitudes were found with persons working under authoritarian leadership. In the same way, Harnquist (1956) observed that group members tended to feel more satisfied under democratic than under autocratic leadership. Ziller (1957) also found members least satisfied under autocratic leadership. Again, Mullen (1965, 1966b) reported that employee satisfaction was associated with democratic supervision. But no relation was obtained between supervisory style and employee requests for transfer. In another study of personnel turnover, Ley (1966) found that authoritarian behavior of the supervisor was the factor most frequently associated with subordinates' quitting the job.

Mandell and Duckworth (1955) reported that overall morale of sixty-four trade employees in civil service was high if they said that their "supervisor lets them know how they are doing." In a series of surveys to be discussed in more detail later, R. Likert (1961a) found that public utilities employees revealed higher job satisfaction when their supervisors were more "personal" than "institutional" in their dealings, when they were more "downward" or employee-oriented, and when they trained subordinates for better jobs. Supervisors of high-morale groups differed from supervisors of low-morale groups in that they reviewed their subordinates' work more frequently, welcomed discussion of mutual problems with subordinates, carried on group discussions, and kept subordinates posted on new information.

D'Angelo (1973), cited earlier, found that sales managers who believed themselves to be practicing a democratic, human relations style brought about more change in their subordinates in an organizational development program than those practicing autocratic or "human resources" leadership. Finally, H. H. Meyer (1968) studied two plants, one managed according to McGregor's Theory Y, the other according to Theory X. Workers under the more democratic (Theory Y) type of management reported higher responsibility, risk, reward, warmth, and identity—items suggestive of group cohesiveness and member satisfaction.

*No Differences.* Some studies have failed to find democratic or autocratic supervision having any significant effect on satisfaction. Thus, in a study of experimental groups of students, Hamblin, Miller, and Wiggins (1961) reported no relationship between authoritarian leadership and group morale. Again, J. D. White (1963) examined the relation of democratic or autocratic leadership to power and morale in boards of directors. The power of subordinates was found higher in boards under democratic than under autocratic leadership. But subordinates' morale was not related to leadership or power differences.

### ANTECEDENT CONDITIONS THAT MODERATE THE EFFECTS

We have already noted in Chapter 8 that autocratic leadership works better with authoritarian personalities and in authoritarian cultures. Other potential personal and interpersonal modifiers have been discussed in Chapters 9 through 13. In Chapters 23 through 28, we will look at how situational modifiers affect the results. Many studies demonstrate that the effects of authoritarian versus democratic leadership depend on these antecedent conditions. Illustrative are those by Day and Hamblin (1964), Patchen (1962), McCurdy and Eber (1953), Foa (1957), Vroom and Mann (1960), Calvin, Hoffman, and Harden (1957), R. C. Anderson (1959), and Snadowsky (1969).

### Follower Expectations and Orientation

McCurdy and Eber (1953) studied groups composed of democratic and authoritarian participants. Their leaders were coached in democratic and autocratic patterns of behavior. Democratically led groups were somewhat less effective than autocratically led groups in speed of problem solutions, but the differences were not statistically significant. However, authoritarian participants performed somewhat less effectively under democratic than autocratic leadership.

According to French, Morrison, and Levinger (1960), autocratic leadership is likely to generate dissatisfaction and hostility on the part of subordinates unless they see it as a legitimate part of the supervisor's role. Thus, Foa (1957) studied groups of workers under democratic and autocratic leadership. Groups with authoritarian and democratic expectations were about equally well satisfied with democratic leaders. But when leaders were autocratic, crews with authoritarian expectations were better satisfied than those with democratic expectations. Hemphill (1949) noted that arbitrary inconsistency and reversal of opinion on the part of the leader are easier tolerated in groups that lack well-established rules and regulations, well-defined goal direction, and strong inter-member cohesiveness.

### Immediate Work Group Characteristics

Vroom and Mann (1960) studied industrial work groups that varied in size and in style of supervision. They found that workers in small groups who preferred equalitarian leaders exhibited high rates of interaction between workers and supervisors. Workers exhibited more positive attitudes toward autocratic leaders in large groups where members interacted less frequently with each other and with their leaders. Calvin, Hoffman, and Harden (1957) constructed experimental groups that differed in member scores on tests of intelligence and leader authoritarianism–equalitarianism. Dull members in authoritarian groups were more effective than dull members in equalitarian groups. But the performance of groups composed of bright members did not differ under authoritarian and equalitarian conditions.

Kruglanski (1969) reported that managers tended to supervise less closely those subordinates whom they trusted. But circularity occurs. Strickland (1967) found that laboratory "supervisors" came to mistrust "subordinates" whom they had to monitor closely and increased their trust in "subordinates" whom they did not have to watch closely. In the same way, McFillen (1978) and McFillen and New (1978) failed to find any significant relationship between supervisory rewards or punishment and subordinate performance, but subordinate performance caused a difference in closeness of supervision. Low-performing subordinates were more closely supervised. Finally, McFillen and

New (1979) demonstrated experimentally that not only is mistrust increased under close supervision, but the supervisor attributes more success to the closely rather than the generally supervised subordinate who succeeds and more failure when the closely supervised subordinate fails.

### Immediate Task Demands

According to Rudin (1964), a punitive style of supervision leads to high performance on simple tasks and to poor performance on complex tasks. Schmitt (1969) observed that punishment administered at unequal time intervals tended to result in less work on punished tasks and in more work on unpunished tasks.

R. C. Anderson's (1959) survey of leadership in experimental groups disclosed that groups under autocratic leaders required less time in planning phases, but were less efficient in task solution phases. Consistent with what we said earlier, democratic leadership resulted in greater member satisfaction in both phases of problem solving. Subsequently, Doyle (1971) found that in group problem solving tasks, equalitarian leadership was most effective in the analysis phase of problem solving, while in the final, synthesizing phase, where coordination becomes more important, groups with powerful leaders were particularly effective. Becker and Baloff (1969) also suggested that the optimum form of power distribution in group activities and the style of leadership it produces may depend on whether the task involves information processing or the generation of ideas.

In a laboratory experiment involving complex mechanical tasks under close or general supervision and punitive or nonpunitive styles, Day and Hamblin (1964) found that close supervision produced a large increase in aggressive feelings toward the supervisor. Close supervision did not affect satisfaction with the task, but production was significantly lower. The punitive style also resulted in increased aggressive feelings toward the supervisor, again without any effect on satisfaction with task. As with the close supervision, punitive supervision led to a decrease in production. On the other hand, Patchen (1962) obtained a positive relationship between close supervision and higher performance in manual type work when there was strong group cohesiveness and where the supervisor was seen as rewarding rather than punitive. Thus, while close supervision is considered usually as part of a more autocratic style, its effects may depend more on whether it also includes a punitive rather than nonpunitive component. (A benevolent autocrat would be more rewarding and less punitive.)

### Falling Dominoes Again

As we have seen in Chapter 16, managers' behavior toward subordinates depends on how their superiors act toward them. Thus, D. Katz (1951) found that highly productive groups had less close supervision from their foremen who in turn were less closely supervised by their superiors. Hunt et al. (1975) observed that whether upper-level management is autocratic or not has an impact on what sort of leadership style at lower levels is most effective. In the same way, Morse (1953) studied employees and supervisors in an office situation and found that although general supervision and delegation of authority facilitated worker satisfaction with the work group, they did not foster job satisfaction or satisfaction with the company unless the supervisor's orientation toward employees was reinforced by higher management.

## COMPARISONS OF AUTOCRATIC AND DEMOCRATIC SYSTEMS OF MANAGEMENT WITH EMPHASIS ON LARGE-SCALE SURVEYS OF LONG-TERM CONSEQUENCES

### The Michigan Studies

The outstanding application of democratic as opposed to autocratic influence processes in organization has been the massive effort of Rensis Likert and his associates at the University of Michigan.

The first study was completed by Katz, Maccoby, and Morse (1950) in the home office of a large insurance company. Twenty-four work groups were studied, half high and half low in productivity. Each highly productive unit was matched with another low in productivity. Differences in supervisory behavior between the high and low productivity units were assessed by means of interviews with both supervisors and their subordinates. Highly productive supervisors more frequently were employee-centered rather than production-centered. They were more likely to exercise general rather than close supervision and they were more likely to differentiate their roles from those of their subordinates in terms of the duties they performed.

Next, Katz, Maccoby, Gurin, and Floor (1951) studied railroad maintenance-of-way workers. Again, the more productive supervisors were found to be more employee-centered and to exercise more general supervision than those who were less productive. However, no difference in role differentiation was found.

The line of investigation was continued by Morse and Reimer (1956), who showed that although autocratic methods contributed more to increased productivity in an insurance firm during the first year of an experimental effort to change, a sizable drop in performance followed in subsequent years due to the adverse impact of the autocratic approach on human factors. Examples are replete of the extent to which the harmful attitudinal and performance effects of an autocratic leader linger long after the leader has left the organization. These coercive effects often do not surface until the autocratic leader has departed since one of his or her techniques may include repressing dissent by means of threats to such dissidence (R. H. Solomon, 1976).

These studies led to the formulation of a rationale for organizational improvement. This rationale relied partly on democratizing the leadership patterns in the organization, predicated on the efficacy of democratic over autocratic processes, and it borrowed heavily from the original Lewin and Lippitt (1938) concepts and results.

### Rationale

Likert (1961a) conceived of four systems of interpersonal relationships in large organizations: (1) exploitative autocratic; (2) benevolent autocratic; (3) consultative; and (4) democratic.

These systems varied as System 1 to System 4 on a variety of criteria. Likert proposed and demonstrated that moving organizations away from System 1 and 2 and toward System 3 and 4 would result, given sufficient time for effects to take place, to increase both employee productivity and employee satisfaction.

The Profile of Organizational Characteristics (POC)—based on survey questionnaire results—generates a measure of the extent to which the organization is perceived as somewhere on the dimension from System 1 to System 4.

*Leadership in Democratic Systems 3 and 4.* With reference to leadership and influence processes in these systems, supervisors and subordinates trust each other a great deal, supervisors are very supportive, very easy to talk to, and virtually always get subordinates' ideas to try to make constructive use of them. There is emphasis on economic and task achievement motivation as well as personal worth.

Subordinate participation in goal setting is encouraged along with bottoms-up communication. Subordinates are influential in determining goals, tasks, and methods. Decisions and controls are decentralized.

*Leadership in Autocratic Systems 1 and 2.* The exploitative autocrat emphasizes threats, fear, and punishment with some promise of reward. The benevolent autocrat emphasizes more positive and less negative reinforcement.

Top-down communication is stressed. Subordinates have little influence on goals and methods. Decisions and controls are centralized and are made person-to-person.

Specifically, Likert applied Bowers and Seashore's (1966) four dimensions of leader behavior to distinguish among autocratic and democratic leaders. System 4 leaders were highest and system 1 leaders lowest on: (1) support—friendly, pays attention to what one is saying, listens to subordinates' problems; (2) team building—encourages subordinates to work as a team, encourages the exchange of opinions and ideas; (3) goal emphasis—encourages best efforts, maintains high standards; and (4) help with work—shows ways to do a better job, helps subordinates plan, organize, and schedule, offers new ideas and solutions to problems. Figure 18.1 shows the major elements differentiating the systems.

The correlations among the scales of leader, peer, subordinate, and organizational behaviors shown in Figure 18.1 range between .4 and .8. Correlations with performance range from .3 to .6 (R. Likert, 1977), that is, in the more than 500 studies completed, positive associations generally have been found between organizations moving toward or being at System 3 or 4 rather than System 1 or 2 and measures of the organizations' performance. Although it is impossible to attribute particular effects to changes in leadership style, given the pattern of large-scale, long-term changes reported by R. Likert (1977b) associated with changes in leadership and organizational development, it seems most plausible to attribute some of these effects, at least, to the changes in leadership.

### Industrial Studies

The more than 500 studies completed by 1977 were carried out in petroleum, automotive, pharmaceuticals, investment banking, insurance, delivery service, publishing, utilities, textiles, office equipment, heavy equipment, packaging, paper making, and railroad companies. Research also has been done in government, hospitals, schools, colleges, correctional institutions, military organizations, and voluntary organizations. Data have been obtained from more than 20,000 managers at all hierarchical levels and more than 200,000 nonsupervisory employees.

R. Likert (1975) reported that the shift away from System 4 and toward System 1 between 1969 and 1970 at a General Motors plant resulted in substantial increases in direct labor efficiency in 1971 and 1972 and although indirect labor efficiency declined between 1970 and 1971, it sharply increased between 1971 and 1972.

## FIGURE 18.1. Profile of Organizational Characteristics

| Organizational Variables | System 1 | System 2 | System 3 | System 4 | Item No. |
|---|---|---|---|---|---|
| How much confidence and trust is shown in subordinates? | Virtually none | Some | Substantial amount | A great deal | 1 |
| How free do they feel to talk to superiors about job? | Not very free | Somewhat free | Quite free | Very free | 2 |
| How often are subordinates' ideas sought and used constructively? | Seldom | Sometimes | Often | Very frequently | 3 |
| Is predominant use made of 1 fear, 2 threats, 3 punishment, 4 rewards, 5 involvement? | 1, 2, 3, occasionally 4 | 4, some 3 | 4, some 3 and 5 | 5, 4, based on group | 4 |
| Where is responsibility felt for achieving organization's goals? | Mostly at top | Top and middle | Fairly general | At all levels | 5 |
| How much cooperative teamwork exists? | Very little | Relatively little | Moderate amount | Great deal | 6 |
| What is the usual direction of information flow? | Downward | Mostly downward | Down and up | Down, up, and sideways | 7 |
| How is downward communication accepted? | With suspicion | Possibly with suspicion | With caution | With a receptive mind | 8 |
| How accurate is upward communication? | Usually inaccurate | Often inaccurate | Often accurate | Almost always accurate | 9 |
| How well do superiors know problems faced by subordinates? | Not very well | Rather well | Quite well | Very well | 10 |
| At what level are decisions made? | Mostly at top | Policy at top, some delegation | Broad policy at top, more delegation | Throughout but well integrated | 11 |
| Are subordinates involved in decisions related to their work? | Almost never | Occasionally consulted | Generally consulted | Fully involved | 12 |
| What does decision-making process contribute to motivation? | Not very much | Relatively little | Some contribution | Substantial contribution | 13 |
| How are organizational goals established? | Orders issued | Orders, some comments invited | After discussion, by orders | By group action (except in crisis) | 14 |
| How much covert resistance to goals is present? | Strong resistance | Moderate resistance | Some resistance at times | Little or none | 15 |
| How concentrated are review and control functions? | Very highly at top | Quite highly at top | Moderate delegation to lower levels | Widely shared | 16 |
| Is there an informal organization resisting the formal one? | Yes | Usually | Sometimes | No—same goals as formal | 17 |
| What are cost, productivity, and other control data used for? | Policing, punishment | Reward and punishment | Reward, some self-guidance | Self-guidance, problem-solving | 18 |

SOURCE: *Adapted from Appendix 11 in* The Human Organization: Its Management and Value *by Rensis Likert. Copyright © 1967 by McGraw-Hill, Inc. Used with the permission of McGraw-Hill Book Company.*

These results need to be understood in terms of the differential impact of autocratic and democratic systems on immediate as compared to long-term labor costs. In three continuous-processing plants, autocratically imposed belt tightening produced immediate reductions in costs in one organization of 600, but at the expense of deteriorating employee motivation, satisfaction with company policy, and leadership as reflected in increased grievances, turnover, work stoppages, failure to meet delivery dates, and decreased quality, which in one study took three to five years to show up clearly. The immediate savings of $250,000 actually produced losses of $450,000 due to less motivated, more hostile, and less individually productive employees as a result of the autocratic imposition (R. Likert, 1977b). Consistent with this, Dunnington, Sirota, and Klein (1963) found that when engineered work standards were imposed on an IBM manufacturing plant managers and supervisors, the employees in these plants resented the pressure, and the same kinds of adverse trends occurred in the measurements of the human consequences as reported for the continuous-processing plants. Yet, they did find that employees whose particular supervisors were more democratic, showed much less resentment of the work standards than did employees whose supervisors were more autocratic. The employees working for democratic supervisors felt less resentful because the democratic supervisors were more likely to try to do something if an employee complained that the work standard was unreasonable.

*Generality Effects.* Contingency research to be discussed in Chapter 23 supports the need for different organizational structures for different kinds of industry (for example, Woodward, 1965; Lawrence & Lorsch, 1967a,b). Assembly plants have organizational structures different from oil refineries. Nevertheless, R. Likert (1977) notes that "within each kind of plant or industry, the higher-performing plant or department is likely to be closer to System 4 in its structure and leadership-interaction processes, and the lower performing plant or department closer to System 1 in its management system." Similar results have been reported by Likert, 1967; Likert and Likert, 1976; Marrow, Bowers, and Seashore, 1968; McCullough, 1975; Mohr, 1971; Roberts et al., 1968; and Toronto, 1972.

### Effects on Business Organizations

Results from thirty studies in thirty-five companies involving some 260 sections, departments, or similar organizational units containing more than 50,000 employees were reported by R. Likert (1961a), Likert (1967), Likert and Likert (1976), and Likert and Fisher (1977), demonstrating the efficacy of democratic as opposed to autocratic systems of management.

Nineteen of the studies as summarized by Likert (1977b) were comparisons of democratic organizations closer to System 4 in their leadership and management with those closer to the autocratic System 1. The differences in productivity and earnings favoring System 4 over System 1 ranged from 14 to 75 percent. In eleven "before–after" studies in which management was helped to shift in the democratic direction toward System 3, productivity and earnings showed improvements from 15 to 40 percent emerging one or two years after the shift. In two comparisons where control groups were available, no such improvements were obtained for the control groups.

These improvements continued if the democratic shift was maintained. In departments of one or two hundred persons the improvement resulted usually in annual savings of $50,000 to $100,000. In a large plant of 6,000 employees the annual savings were more than $5,000,000.

Guest (1962a) observed similar results for productivity, quality, and safety when a new manager of the poorest performing of six plants shifted the organization toward a democratic, theory Y, leadership.

For fifteen business firms, Taylor and Bowers (1972) reported the relations between their measures of organizational climate derived from their survey of organizations and various organizational outcomes obtained from six months prior to the survey to eighteen months afterward. Relations with efficiency reached as high as .8 and were somewhat lower with reduced rates of absenteeism, minor injuries, ill health, and grievances.

Other studies have shown that democratic approaches in organizations have a favorable effect on the physical and mental health of the persons in those organizations (Caplan, Cobb, et al., 1975).

The effectiveness of supervisors and purchasing managers was seen by White (1971a, 1972b) to be associated with the extent to which they were more democratic and less autocratic. Hollman (1973) and Tanimoto (1977) found that the effectiveness of management-by-objectives as seen by subordinates was greater when practiced by a more democratic rather than a more autocratic manager.

### Effects on Governmental Agencies

In a federal agency, White (1972b) observed that effective county office managers and line and staff headquarters managers used a more democratic style. Heslin (1966) found that the high producing units in a federal government agency engaged in automatic data processing were closer to Likert's System 4 in their management as seen by the employees than were the low producing units. Operating bureaus of the Department of State were seen to provide better budgeting, space, travel, and personnel services if their managements (according to their own subordinates) were closer to System 4 than to System 1 (Warwick, 1975).

R. Likert (1977b) reported that city managers, when asked to compare the highest producing unit with a matched lowest producing unit they knew well, described the highest unit as between Systems 3 and 4 and the lowest unit as pursuing a benevolent autocratic (System 2) management.

### Effects on Military Organizations

In navy data from twenty ships and eighteen shore stations, Bowers (1975) found a strong relationship between an individual's intention to re-enlist (which is a good predictor of actual re-enlistment) and the extent to which the ship or station was closer to System 4 and further from System 1.

R. Likert (1977b) reported that among fourteen navy crews, absence of mishaps (accidents and disasters due to operational failure of aircraft serviced) was associated with the extent to which supervisors facilitated the work and team development.

D. E. Johnson (1969) found that those air force ROTC units judged to be operating closer to System 4 rather than System 1 among ninety-three units were also seen by higher authority as better performing units.

### Effects on Educational Institutions

Summarizing forty of these studies in school systems, R. Likert (1977b) concluded that school surveys for members of the Board of Education, superintendents, central staff, principals, department heads, teachers, students, and parents demonstrated that school systems closer to System 4, when compared to those closer to System 1, exhibited better communications (Lepkowsky, 1970), cooperation, and coordination. They were more flexible and innovative (Broman, 1974; Ladouceur, 1973; Naumann-Etienne, 1975; Gehrman, 1970) and overall more effective (Riedel, 1974; Ferris, 1965). Their personnel felt a greater sense of self-actualization and satisfaction from their work (Wagstaff, 1970; Smallridge, 1972; Chung, 1970; M. C. Smith, 1975; D. E. Thompson, 1971; Brindisi, 1976; Feitler & Blumberg, 1971; Morall, 1974; Byrnes, 1973; Carr, 1971; C. E. Shaw, 1976; Prieto, 1975). They were judged as achieving superior educational results. They had better board–employee relations (R. C. Key, 1974) and union–management relations (Haynes, 1972; Bernhardt, 1972). Their students were more highly motivated and attained higher educational achievement for given IQ and socioeconomic levels (A. K. Gibson, 1974; Belasco, 1973). Their students had more favorable attitudes, were less dissatisfied, and were much less likely to engage in disruptive behavior or acts of aggression against the schools (Morall, 1974; Cullers, Hughs, and McGreal, 1973).

Again, for twelve studies in institutions of higher education, Likert (1977b) concluded that institutions having administrations closer to System 4 than to System 1, experienced more favorable outcomes. Faculty were more satisfied with administrative decision making (A. B. Smith, 1971; Gardner, 1971; Lasher, 1975; Javier, 1972), lack of need for collective bargaining (Cline, 1974), commitment to college objectives (T. G. Fox, 1973; Laughlin, 1973), and innovativeness (Bowers, 1976; Hanna, 1973). More favorable student outcomes were also obtained with System 4 (Bowers, 1976; Gilbert, 1972).

### Effects on Other Not-for-Profit Organizations

Munson (reported by Likert, 1977b) studied in eight hospitals the relation of the management system used by head nurses, as seen by the nurses reporting to them, and the satisfactions that the nurses felt. Based on data from 351 nurses in fifty-five patient teams, Munson found that except for satisfaction with task variety, the closer the head nurse was to System 4 in management style as seen by the nurses, the greater was satisfaction of the nurses with their work. H. C. White (1971b, 1971c, 1971d) reported similar results for peers describing effective and ineffective supervisors they had known. Again, System 4 leadership was seen to be more effective in three outpatient clinics than System 1 management, according to an unpublished report by the National Tuberculosis and Respiratory Disease Association and by Ketchel (1972), who studied the effectiveness of volunteer health planning in seventeen Ohio counties.

Studying the management systems of three community-based reintegration centers in Ohio, McGruder (1976) concluded that the most democratic center was also most effective as measured by graduation along with low absconding and reincarceration rates in comparison to the most autocratic center as seen by residents and staff on Likert's Profile of Organizational Characteristics.

Marchant (1976) obtained data on Likert's Profile of Organizational Characteristics from staffs of twenty-two research-oriented university libraries. Staffs were more satisfied and faculty evaluations of service were higher, the closer the libraries were to System 4 and the further they were from System 1.

Haggard (as reported by Likert, 1977b) found a positive correlation for a YMCA in the extent to which its management shifted from System 2 in 1970 to System 3 in 1971–1973 and to System 4 in 1974, growth in number of persons served (increased from 11,064 to 23,794), and growth in budget (increased from $173,000 to $303,000).

What about democratic leadership accounts for the results? In the next chapter, we examine further the decision processes involved.

# 19

## PARTICIPATIVE VERSUS DIRECTIVE LEADERSHIP

### INTRODUCTION

To direct or to consult? This is probably the single most central question for managers in their role as supervisors. Should they give directions and tell subordinates how to do the work or should they share with subordinates the needs for solving problems or handling situations and involve them in working out what and how to do what needs to be done?

Research results indicate that most managers do both depending on circumstances but in differing amounts. Tannenbaum and Schmidt (1958) suggested that direction and participation are two halves of a continuum with many gradations possible in between. At one extreme of the continuum, the supervisor may give directions and orders without even explaining why to subordinates. The supervisor expects unquestioning compliance. Participation by subordinates is minimal. At the next gradation, the supervisor accompanies directions with detailed explanations. The supervisor expects to persuade and manipulate the subordinates or to bargain with them. At the third level (in between direction and participation) is the supervisor who consults with subordinates before deciding what is to be done. Full participation of both superior and subordinates occurs at the fourth gradation when both join in deciding what is to be done. At the fifth level, the superior delegates the task and how it is to be handled to the subordinates. The superior's own participation becomes minimal. Within the constraints set, whatever the subordinates decide is acceptable to the supervisor. Finally, supervisors may abdicate completely from their responsibilities. (We will discuss this laissez-faire leadership in Chapter 22.) Participative leadership implies that the leader permits or encourages group members to participate actively in discussion, problem solving, and decision making. Directive leadership implies that the leader plays the active role in problem solving and decision making and expects group members to be guided by his or her decisions.

Participation and direction were seen by Tannenbaum and Schmidt (1958) to be based on how much authority was used by the superior relative to how much freedom was permitted subordinates. Bass (1960) noted that participative leadership required a leader with power who was willing to share it. With his or her power, the leader sets the boundaries within with subordinate participation or consultation is welcomed. This contrasts with the powerless leader or the leaderless situation where a struggle for status among group members will ensue (Chapter 13).

This dimension has been the dependent measure (or close to it) in a number of efforts to determine empirically (Sadler & Hofstede, 1972; Heller and Yukl, 1969; and Bass & Valenzi, 1974) and rationally (Vroom & Yetton, 1974) the antecedent conditions that prompt the leader to be more or less participative and the antecedent conditions that make greater or lesser participative leadership more effective and satisfying. Table 19.1 shows the comparable conceptualizations of this same dimension, the degree of participative versus directive decision-making leadership.

## Meanings

Participation has two distinct meanings, one encompassing the other. First, it may refer to a simple distinct way of leader–subordinate decision making in which there is power-equalization by the leader and a sharing of final decision making of the leader with subordinates. Consensus is sought. In this instance we will always note the specific style in italics.

Participation is also commonly used as a general expression to refer to the half of the continuum of decision making in which subordinates are involved in some way in the decision process either because they are consulted individually or in a group by their leader (who makes the final decision) or they share with the leader in making the final decision, or they are delegated responsibility by the leader for making the decision. We will not italicize "participation" when we intend its general meaning.

In the same way, direction or directiveness has one meaning as a distinct style in which the leader decides and announces his decision without consulting subordinates beforehand. Such direction can be with or without explanation. We will italicize "direction" when used in this way. Directiveness can also refer generally to that portion of the decision-making continuum in which in lieu of giving orders the leader may manipulate, sell, persuade, negotiate, or bargain. When used in this sense, it will not be italicized. Sometimes, it is referred to as supervisory.

Holding frequent group meetings does not necessarily imply participation. Guetzkow and Kriesberg (1950) found that leaders may use meetings to "sell" their own solutions as well as to aid problem solving, assume acceptance of their solutions, and to explain their own preferences. These executives see meetings as a way to transmit information and to make announcements rather than as an opportunity for sharing information and opinions or for reaching decisions.

## Related Styles

We have already noted that participative decision making is a characteristic of democratic leadership. Direction is more often found in autocratic leaders. Clearly, participation is also likely to be seen with general rather than close supervision, power equalization, delegation, and nondirective leadership. Directive leadership is more likely to be exhibited by the same leaders who are also close supervisors, who do a lot of structuring and are manipulative and persuasive.

*Relations with Consideration and Initiation of Structure.* Many elements of consideration (Chapter 21) are part of participative decision-making leadership: asking subordinates for their suggestions before going ahead, getting the approval of subordinates

**TABLE 19.1**
**Conceptions of the Dimension of Participative versus Directive Leadership**

| Leader: | Tannenbaum and Schmidt (1958) | Sadler and Hofstede (1969) | Heller and Yukl (1969) | Bass and Valenzi (1975) | Vroom and Yetton (1974) |
|---|---|---|---|---|---|
| directive { | decides and announces decision | tells | own decision—no explanation | directive | AI |
| | "sells" decision | sells | own decision—with explanation | persuasive—manipulative | |
| | presents ideas and invites questions | consults | consultation | consultative | AII, CI |
| participative { | presents tentative decisions subject to modification | consults | consultation | consultative | AII, CI |
| | presents problems, gets suggestions, makes decisions | consults | consultation | consultative | AII, CI |
| | defines limits and asks group to make decision | joins | joint decision making | participative | GII |
| | permits followers to function within limits | | delegation | delegative | |

on important matters, treating one's subordinates as equals, making subordinates feel at ease when talking with the leader, putting subordinates' suggestions into operation, and remaining easily approachable. Similarly, many elements of direction are to be found on the scale of initiation of structure: making attitudes clear, assigning subordinates to particular tasks, and deciding in detail what shall be done and how it is to be done. Consideration also involves support and concern for employee welfare. Initiation also concerns production emphasis. These will be treated separately in Chapter 20 when we look at relations-oriented versus task-oriented leadership.

*Relations to Social versus Political Approaches to Leadership.* Bass (1968c) contrasted MBA students' and managers' beliefs in how to succeed in business. Two social factors emerged: share decision making and emphasize candor, openness, and trust. These factors coincide with ideal participative decision making as proposed by Argyris (1962), and Bennis (1964). The factors included making open and complete commitments, establishing mutual goals, and organizing group discussions.

The persuasive, manipulative emphasis was seen in political factors involving withholding information, bluffing, making alliances, publicly supporting but privately opposing particular views, compromising, and using delaying and diversionary tactics (Martin and Sims, 1956; Jameson, 1945).

### Frequency

On the one hand, the popular stereotype of the ideal leader is the decisive, directive, heroic order-giver. On the other hand, if one concentrates on the behavioral science literature, fully shared, participative decision making would seem most commonly advocated. Actually, both Heller and Yukl (1969) and Bass and Valenzi (1974) have shown that neither extreme is the one reported most frequently by subordinates. Rather, consultation is most frequently reported. Thus, on a scale of frequency ranging from zero (never) to five (a great deal), according to over 400 subordinates from a variety of organizations, the frequency with which superiors were observed exhibiting each of the styles of behavior was as follows: consultation, 3.10; *participation,* 2.65; delegation, 2.46; *direction* with reasons, 1.97; *direction* without reasons, 1.90; manipulation, 1.88 (Bass & Valenzi, 1974). The most powerful autocrats may also be strong advocates of consultation. Lenin (Bass & Farrow, 1977) was seen by his biographers as a frequent consultant of his immediate subordinates. Mao Zedung (quoted by J. M. Burns, 1978, p. 238) urged party leaders to be consultative and instructed carefully on how to carry out a doctrine stressing consultation: "We should never pretend to know what we don't know, we should not feel ashamed to ask and learn from people below, and we should listen carefully to the views of the cadres at the lower levels. Be a pupil before you become a teacher; learn from the cadres at the lower levels before you issue orders."

Naturally, there are exceptions. For instance, McKenna (n.d.) found that for 212 chief accountants *direction* was more popular than consultation. *Participation* and delegation were very low in occurrence. Manipulation and negotiation were reported least frequently. This may be due to the greater subtlety of manipulative behavior. It is more difficult to discern when it happens and, inherently as well as empirically, there is less reliability in judgments about it than other decision-making styles. Subordinates feel they are being manipulated when they think managers know in advance what they will decide and what they want the subordinates to do. The manager strikes bargains and plays favorites. Such manipulative behavior tends to be exhibited by directive managers but not by managers who generally tend to be participative (Bass, Valenzi, Farrow & Solomon, 1975).

### Multiplicity of Styles

Few managers are seen to use only one style; most are seen to use a variety of styles ranging from extreme direction to extreme participation. For 124 middle- and first-level supervisors, W. A. Hill (1973) found that only 14 percent of the supervisors were seen as likely to use the same one of four styles in four hypothetical situations. Bass and Valenzi (1974) obtained sharper results with 124 subordinates who described how frequently their superiors actually used six styles ranging from deciding without explanation to delegating decisions to subordinates. A manager was classified as exhibiting a *single* managerial style if the subordinate indicated that only one of these styles was displayed by the manager "very often" or "always" and the remaining styles "never" or "seldom." A manager was classified as exhibiting a *dual* approach if managers were described by subordinates as displaying two styles "very often" and/or "always" and the others, "never" or "seldom." A manager was classified as exhibiting a multi-managerial approach if displaying three or more of the six styles "sometimes," "fairly often," "very often," and/or "always." Of 124 subordinates, three or 2.4 percent indicated that their superior exhibited a single style, one or 0.8 percent indicated that the superior exhibited a dual approach, 117 or 94.4 percent indicated that their boss exhibited a multistyle approach, and 3 or 2.4 percent were unclassifiable.

Vroom and Yetton (1973), using a completely different method, emerged with similar results. Several thousand managers indicated the decision-making style they would employ if confronted with different kinds of cases requiring or not requiring quality solutions and subordinate acceptance. Only about 10 percent of the variance in response could be attributed to general tendencies of the managers to be more directive or more participative. Thirty percent depended on whether quality solutions and subordinate acceptance were required. Hill and Schmitt (1977) tested a shortened version of Vroom and Yetton's method and found that 37 percent of leader decision style variance was due to case requirement effects and 8 percent was due to the effects of individual differences. The results tend to be relatively insensitive to the hierarchical levels dealt with in the cases (Jago, 1978).

### Interrelations among Gradations

Another way of noting the fact that the same managers exhibit many of the same styles of decision making is to examine the intercorrelations among them. Consultation, *participation,* and delegation are highly intercorrelated. That is, consultative managers also tend to be highly *participative* and delegative. The intercorrelations were above .6 for a sample of 343 to 396 respondents. Even the extent to which managers are *directive* tends to correlate positively with the extent to which they are manipulative or negotiative, .25, consultative, .31, *participative, .28,* and delegative, .13. That is, empirically opposite to all of the styles is inactivity, laissez-faire leadership. Nevertheless, each style was conceptually independent of every other style according to a scale allocation analysis by forty-one manager and student judges. Although empirically correlated, the five style variables were generally conceptually independent. Consultation was clearly seen as a different pattern of behavior than, say, delegation; nevertheless, the same managers who were most likely to consult were also more likely to delegate (Bass, Valenzi, Farrow & Solomon, 1975).

## WHETHER LEADERS CAN AND WILL BE DIRECTIVE OR PARTICIPATIVE

We have already noted that a variety of samples and methods discloses that supervisors say they prefer and are seen by their subordinates to be consultative most often, involving their subordinates to some extent in the decision process but reserving the final decision for themselves. But the whole range from *direction* to delegation in varying amounts is seen to be used by a given manager.

What predisposes the supervisor to pursue one approach rather than another? Both deductive and inductive research points to a variety of factors of consequence including: attributes of the supervisor and of the subordinates, their policies, goals, tasks, and assignments, and the organizational and external environment in which the group of subordinates and the supervisor are embedded.

### Effects of the Leaders Themselves

Some argue that direction or participation will depend on the nature of the situation; others state that it depends on the leader's judgment of the situation (Vroom & Yetton, 1973). Still others argue that it is the leader's persistent personality that is most significant (Fiedler, 1967a). Yet, others find that personality has more effect on direction and situation has more effect on participation (Farrow & Bass, 1977). Both the contingency and the noncontingency theorists may be right. Frequency of direction may be mainly a matter of personality; frequency of participation may mainly hinge on contingent factors.

Although situational contingencies seem more important, supervisory decision-making style will depend to some extent on personality. Farrow and Bass (1977) found for seventy-seven managers described by their 407 subordinates that situational factors as seen by the managers or by the subordinates were irrelevant in determining whether or not a manager would be *directive*. According to path analysis, managers who were most frequently *directive* according to their subordinates were managers who were highly assertive and regarded people as fundamentally unfair. Furthermore, such managers were highly satisfied with their own jobs. These results transcended various organizational, intrapersonal, and personal attributes of the subordinates. On the other hand, the amount of participation seen by subordinates depended on the extent to which the manager perceived that the subordinates had discretionary opportunities and had highly interdependent tasks. Whether the managers had short- or long-term objectives was a key variable in determining whether they were seen by their subordinates to be manipulative and negotiative. (Manipulativeness coincided with short-term objectives.)

Vroom (1960a) found that managers with authoritarian personalities, as measured by the *F* scale of Adorno et al. (1950), were more directive. The lower their need for independence and the higher their degree of authoritarianism, the higher was their directiveness. Beliefs in the legitimacy of the manager's prerogatives to plan, direct, and control had similar effects. Managers who characterized themselves on personality inventories as unwilling to believe that people were fairminded were more likely to be *directive* according to their subordinates. Those who felt people were fairminded tended to be participative (Farrow & Bass, 1977). This is consistent with the expectation that McGregor's (1960) Theory X managers will be directive since they believe that employees cannot be trusted.

Heller and Yukl (1969) reported in a study of 203 British managers at all levels in sixteen organizations that senior managers, particularly those in their positions for a considerable amount of time, were more likely to share in decision making with their subordinates. Again, younger managers tended to be more directive while older managers tended to be more participative in a study of 200 managers by Pinder, Pinto, and England (1973).

Bass, Valenzi, and Farrow (1977) found among seventy-six managers a correlation of − .37 between their educational level and their tendency to be participative.

*Power and Direction.* Leaders who are esteemed and valued by subordinates, who are acknowledged as experts, and who are seen by subordinates to control rewards which they can allocate among them if desired can be directive (Raven, 1965b; Mulder, 1971). Their powers and influence tend to be highly intercorrelated (Dieterly & Schneider, 1974). If we experimentally suddenly increase the power of leaders in an experiment, we increase the amount they can be directive and, in fact, they do tend to increase their directiveness (Shiflett, 1973).

### Effects of the Subordinates, Followers, and the Immediate Group Led

Some level of agreement between the leader and the led about procedures, interests, and norms is necessary before effective participation can take place (Heller, 1969). Relevance is required.

*Relevance of Participation.* Subordinates or followers vary in how much they would like to participate in decisions. In a number of samples in several countries, Heller (1971, 1976) reported that participation is used by managers more frequently when decisions are more important to their subordinates than to the firm. Again, in a review of the literature overall, Hespe and Wall (1976) noted that workers wanted to participate more than they actually were given the opportunity to do. But, they expressed the greatest interest in participating in decisions directly relating to performance of their jobs, followed by matters concerning their immediate work units, with a very weak interest in participation in general policy decisions. This was corroborated by Long (1979) who found that workers in a Canadian trucking company that became wholly owned by its employees saw that their participation and interest in doing so had increased with the employee takeover. According to Maier (1965), if subordinates are seeking personal growth, if subordinates are seeking to be more creative, if subordinates are highly interested in the objectives of the task at hand, participative approaches will be preferred by subordinates. On the other hand, subordinates may prefer a great deal of guidance and attention from their supervisor until they have mastered the job, particularly if it does not involve much creativity from them but only attention to routine details which must be learned (Bennis, 1966c).

*Subordinate Personality.* Associated with lack of preference to participate is the authoritarian-submissive personality syndrome (Adorno et al., 1950). Followers with authoritarian rather than equalitarian attitudes are likely to reject participative leadership. A survey of Philadelphia residents by Sanford (1951) disclosed that highly authoritarian personalities wanted powerful, prestigious leaders who would strongly direct them.

*Subordinate Competence.* Managers apparently view participative approaches as too risky because of managerial reservations about the competence and commitment of lower-level employees (Rosen & Jerdee, 1977). Lowin (1968) showed that subordinates perceiving lack of competence for the tasks to be completed were more appreciative of directive supervision than when they considered themselves competent. Similarly, Heller (1969) found that whenever managers reported a big skill differential between themselves and their subordinates, they were more likely to use *direction*. Skill differentials of particular importance were technical ability, decisiveness, and intelligence. Managers were more likely to engage in participation when subordinates were esteemed by the managers for their expertise and personal qualities.

Based on a study of members of 144 work groups in thirteen local health agencies, Mohr (1977) concluded that supervisory participation probably depended on subordinate training and technical and professional level. But the results were masked when they depended on subordinates' perceptions of how much they participated.

*Subordinate Competence and Power Relative to the Leader's.* Bass and Valenzi (1974) proposed that the frequency of a particular leadership style can be accounted for by the power differences between manager and subordinates and by the differences in their competence or the information available to them.

Shapira (1976) confirmed through small-space analysis the validity of the deductions as a whole, namely, that given managers' power ($P_m$), subordinates' power ($P_s$), managers' information ($I_m$), and subordinates' information ($I_s$), then: *direction* is more likely if $P_m > P_s$ and $I_m > I_s$; *manipulation* or *negotiation* is more likely if $P_m < P_s$ and $I_m > I_s$; *consultation* is more likely if $P_m > P_s$ and $I_m < I_s$; and *delegation* is more likely if $P_m < P_s$ and $I_m < I_s$.

Heller (1976) also found that participative leadership was favored at senior organizational levels where subordinate competence was high.

### Effects of Constraints and Objectives

Policies, goals, task requirements, and functions furnish constraints on how directive or participative a leader can be. They will also furnish objectives which will be seen by the leader to be met more satisfactorily by either direction or participation. Both leader and subordinates may be bound by rules, constrained by regulations, by time demands, by schedules over which they have no control, or by fixed requirements for methods and solutions. Decision requirements may be highly programmed. More group acceptance and change may be desired or required. The manager may see as objectives long-range rather than quick payoffs, the development of subordinates, the creation of a capable and effective operation for the long run rather than short-run results. Or the emphasized objective may be maximum productivity at minimum costs now. According to Vroom (1976), it "seemed unlikely" that the same leadership style model would be appropriate where one's objective was the conservation of time rather than the long-term development of subordinates. If the cost of the time required of subordinates is more expensive than the value of the outcomes of their participation, directive approaches are more likely to be observed (Tannenbaum & Massarik, 1950).

*Function.* Marketing is usually under shorter time constraints than is research. Within working units in marketing, directive styles may more often than not be appropriate, whereas in research they are likely to be less appropriate (Lawrence & Lorsch, 1967a,b). Heller and Yukl (1969) found that production and finance managers tended to use directive decision making, whereas general and personnel managers were more participative. This was seen as probably due to the fact that managers in accounting, finance, and production had more standardized, programmed types of jobs, permitting less freedom and flexibility and allowing for less meaningful participation by subordinates. In fact, when accounting managers were faced with unprogrammed decisions they tended to be more participative. McKenna (n.d.) found that consultation and *participation* are more likely to be used instead of *direction* or delegation when chief accountants must make unprogrammed decisions rather than programmed decisions and decisions dealing with personnel rather than with tasks. Service managers see themselves facing more unprogrammed decisions. Child and Ellis (1973) found in a study of 787 managers that managers in service organizations saw their roles as less formal, less well-defined, and less routine compared to manufacturing managers.

*Hierarchical Level.* Blankenship and Miles (1968) reported that level of position is more important than span of control or organization size in managerial decision behavior. Upper-level managers not only report greater freedom from their superiors in decisions but tend to involve their subordinates more in decisions than managers at lower levels. At higher levels, managers are concerned with longer-range problems and policies, norms, and values. They are dealing with more creative, more educated, higher-status subordinates who expect more opportunity to participate. There is more interest in long-term commitments from subordinates as well as in the development of subordinates. At lower levels, managers are dealing with more routine types of work, more clearly defined objectives, and with subordinates of lower status and fewer expectations about participating in the decision process (Selznick, 1957).

This is consistent with the conclusions that leaders are more prone to engage in participation with more highly qualified subordinates (Mohr, 1977) and more skilled subordinates (Heller, 1969) if the leaders are more highly educated (Bass, Valenzi & Farrow, 1977) and older (Pinder, Pinto & England, 1973). Conversely, in their intensive study of the worker on the assembly line, Walker and Guest (1952) emphasized the extent to which supervision was likely to be more directive when tasks to be performed were extremely routine.

*Riskiness of Decisions.* The riskiness of a decision to a supervisor is decreased if it is to be implemented on a trial basis. In a simulation with 143 bank employees under such conditions, Rosen and Jerdee (1978) found greater willingness of leaders to engage in participation when decisions were to be implemented on a trial basis than when decisions were seen to imply permanent solutions.

The risk of decisions is increased for top managers facing intense competition from the outside marketplace. Here, the top manager tends to be more directive and highly controlling in some decisions, say about production, purchasing, and cost control, and more participative in others such as those dealing with raising capital, research and development, policy changes, and marketing strategies (Khandwalla, 1973).

*Task Manageability.* Mohr (1971) found that although the degree of "task manageability" did not increase participation in a manager's style, task interdependence of subordinates did.

*Technology.* Woodward (1965) studied the impact of technology on decision processes in 100 British firms. She concluded that in companies involved in mass or batch production, decision making was more likely to be directive but usually not precedent-setting. On the other hand, in continuous-processing industries, such as petroleum refining, decisions were more likely to be made by committees with considerable participation and with long-term implications.

### Effects of the Environment Outside Immediate Work Group

Managers differ in what aspects of the outside environment they regard as most important to their work, and as a consequence they behave differently inside the organization. Bass, Valenzi, and Farrow (1977) asked seventy-six managers to describe the importance of economic, political, social, and legal influences on the work of their 277 immediate subordinates. These subordinates, in turn, described the frequency with which their own manager displayed *direction,* negotiation, consultation, *participation,* and delegation. Managers who tended to see economic events such as inflation and taxes as having stronger effects on their work situation were more likely to be *directive* or negotiative. Managers who tended to see political, social, or legal issues as more important were more likely to be consultative or *participative.*

*Higher Authority.* If rules and regulations set by higher authority restrict subordinates' decisions, then supervisors dominate the group and make the decisions, according to a survey by Hemphill, Seigel, and Westie (1951). Higher authority indirectly can prevent participation in decisions by subordinates by demanding immediate answers from supervisors with no opportunity allowed for workers to be consulted. Thus, whether or not supervisors can be participative with their subordinates depends on the extent to which secrecy concerning products, techniques, and business strategies is required of its employees by higher authority. If people in the organization are supposed to know only "what they need to know," employees cannot be asked to participate in or be consulted about decisions where much of the information required to discuss and consider such decisions cannot be revealed to them (Tannenbaum & Massarik, 1950).

*Top Management.* The number of hierarchical levels at which participation is encouraged will increase the tendency of supervisors to be participative throughout the system. Particularly important is acceptance of the ideology by the sponsors of the organization and its top management (Marrow, Bowers & Seashore, 1968).

L. B. Ward's (1965) large-scale survey of top managements in the United States suggested strongly that the religious affiliation represented by top management in a firm affected the firm's personnel policies. Leadership at lower levels was more likely to be participative where top management was not restricted to members of one religious group. Where restricted to one religion, participation was most likely in all-Jewish-led firms and least likely in all-Catholic-led firms.

*Organizational Size.* Blankenship and Miles (1968), Wofford (1971), and McKenna (n.d.) reported systematic trends between size of organization and the leadership style observed in it. On the whole, larger firms' managers exhibited more participation and less directiveness. However, third variables may be responsible, such as more education among managers of larger firms, policy differences, and so forth.

## GENERAL EFFECTS OF DIRECTIVE AND PARTICIPATIVE LEADERS

We have seen that the leader, the led, and the constraints and objectives of the task along with surrounding conditions influence whether a leader will be directive or participative. We now examine what effects can be expected as a consequence. We will review the effects on: (1) decision acceptance, successful influence, and increased cohesiveness; (2) subordinate satisfaction; (3) subordinate involvement and commitment; and (4) decision quality and productivity.

### Effects on Acceptance

In general, available evidence supports the contention that participative leadership promotes acceptance of decisions and agreement to a greater extent than does directive leadership. When participative leadership is practiced in a group, R. Likert (1961a,b) finds that each member has the opportunity to gain in recognition and a sense of self-worth. This also creates conditions allowing each subordinate to observe how everyone else in the group feels about a matter under consideration. Such conditions reduce the individual's resistance to suggestions and change of opinion. Thus, Bennett (1955) found that students were much more likely to volunteer to serve as experimental subjects if they perceived that almost all other members of their class volunteered. Observing near-consensus and the opportunity to make public decisions increased volunteering more than did opportunity for discussion. In a more tightly controlled experiment, Pennington, Haravey, and Bass (1958) showed that follower acceptance and change was greatest when both discussion and group decision were permitted, less when only discussion or announcements of group opinion were allowed, and least when only secret balloting was used.

Participatory leaders, instructed primarily to inhibit hasty decisions and domination of the group by any one member, were contrasted by Preston and Heintz (1949) with "supervisory leaders" directed to keep the group on the task. With more shared participation under participatory leaders, members as a whole showed more agreement with each other than members without the opportunity to interact as much. The latter were more likely to be coerced, to show less acceptance of decisions privately than publicly. Again, Pennington, Haravey, and Bass (1958) found that groups under participative leadership achieved greater coalescence and opinion change than those denied discussion and decision. Bovard (1951a,b) observed that group-centered teams shifted their perceptions toward a common group norm more readily than leader-centered groups. Group-centered units also facilitated higher degrees of member interaction than leader-centered groups. Hare (1953) found that although both participative and supervisory styles of leadership produced significant changes in amount of agreement among group members, participative leaders found themselves more in agreement with group rankings than did directive leaders. Likewise, Levine and Butler (1952) found participative leadership and group decision more successful in producing behavior change than a lecture or control condition.

In application, T. P. Wilson (1968) reported that prisoners make better cooperative adaptation to prison life under participative rather than bureaucratic management. In the same way, French, Kay, and Meyer (1966) observed that management participation in an appraisal system facilitated goal acceptance, group cohesiveness, and favorable attitudes toward the appraisal system. Jacobson, Charters, and Lieberman (1951) showed that workers who are involved in decision making by their foremen but not by their shop stewards tend to share management values and goals; workers who are involved in decisions by their stewards but not by their foremen tend to share union goals and standards.

In a demonstration during World War II with housewives' meat-buying behavior, Lewin (1947) pointed the way toward the use of participative leadership to overcome resistance to change. Coch and French (1948) illustrated how a combination of participation in goal setting and job redesign resulted in increased productivity of three groups of garment workers, with no such change obtained for a control group.

On the other hand, P. J. Burke (1966a,b) as well as Katzell, Miller, Rotter, and Venet (1970) found that leadership direction could enhance group cohesiveness. Thiagarajan and Deep (1970) studied groups in which supervisors played three roles—involved, neutral, and uninvolved. The directive leader was more influential than the persuasive leader, and the persuasive leader more than the participative one.

In an experiment with forty-seven executives, Bass (1967a) reported that the simulated advisory staff of a head shifted and coalesced more if the head announced his opinion, particularly if he did so at the beginning of the problem-solving meeting. However, T. A. Hill (1973) found consensus in student groups more likely to be achieved when the leader was least opinionated. More will be said about the effects of directiveness on acceptance when we examine how contingencies modify the effects of participation and direction.

### Effects on Subordinate and Follower Satisfaction

Preston and Heinz's (1949) previously mentioned study revealed greater subordinate satisfaction under participatory than under supervisory leaders. Again, Bass, Burger, et al. (1979) found that for an international sample of 1,641 managers engaged as subordinates in a training simulation, 51.7 percent preferred working again with a participative rather than either of two kinds of directive supervisors (chance choice was 33.3 percent). Zimet and Fine (1955) contrasted content lectures given fifteen chief school administrators with group-centered participative discussion. Although initially more defensive behavior appeared with discussion, subsequent sessions reduced hostility, yielded increased warm, friendly behavior, and more favorable attitudes toward themselves and others outside the meeting. Likewise, Ziller (1954) found that aircrews were more satisfied with decisions to simulated problems if they discussed the problem and afterwards their participative leader stated an opinion. They were less satisfied when the decision was made authoritatively by a more directive leader. Again according to

Aspegren (1963), participatory leadership produced higher levels of member satisfaction and task motivation than either directive or laissez-faire leadership. Storey (1954) studied groups with participative leadership and groups with directive leadership. Members of participative groups were better satisfied with group procedures, decisions reached, and intermember acceptance, although no significant differences were found in satisfaction with leadership.

A. S. Tannenbaum (1963) reported increased satisfaction among 200 clerks as a consequence of their increased opportunity to participate. Morse, Reimer, and Tannenbaum (1951) noted increased satisfaction with a new organizational arrangement that promoted more self-determination and group decision making by lowering by one echelon the authority to make and execute various decisions. What the supervisor had decided previously was now delegated to subordinates. In the same way, Mann and Baumgartel (1952) found that employees who felt free to discuss job-related and personal problems with their supervisors were better satisfied with the company, exhibited less absenteeism, and enjoyed membership in more cohesive work groups. Baumgartel (1956, 1957) found that scientists in research laboratories exhibited higher degrees of task motivation and job satisfaction under participatory than under directive supervisors. Again, Mann, Indik, and Vroom (1963) reported that worker satisfaction was highly related to participation in decision making. Employee satisfaction and task motivation were especially low under directive supervision. In the same way, absences of white-collar workers related to how free they said they felt to discuss their job with their supervisor. Of men absent four or more times during a six-month period, only 29 percent said they felt very free to talk with their boss, while 57 to 69 percent of those absent less often said they felt very free to hold such discussions (Likert, 1961a).

Consistent with what has been presented above, Weschler, Kahane, and Tannenbaum (1952) found that a research group led by a directive leader was less satisfied with its job. Dissatisfaction and high levels of job tension were also reported by Alutto and Belasco (1972), to be associated with "decision making deprivation."

*Mixed Results.* Analyses by Farrow, Valenzi, and Bass (1980) for approximately 1,400 subordinates describing their 350 managers found that the manager's consultation correlated .34 with subordinates' satisfaction with their jobs and .53 with subordinates' satisfaction with their supervisors. Managerial *participation* as seen by the subordinates correlated .25 with their job satisfaction and .41 with their satisfaction with the leader. Comparable correlations for delegation were .32 and .46. However, *direction* also was positively correlated with satisfaction (.17 and .38). Only negotiation or manipulation was negatively related to job satisfaction ($-.16$) and satisfaction with the leader ($-.16$).

Pheysey and Payne (1970) found no relation between member satisfaction and amount of participation. Page and McGinnies (1959) showed a motion picture to groups of subjects who discussed the film under two styles of leadership. The directive leader was rated by the members as significantly more interesting, satisfying, purposeful, frank, industrious, and persuasive than the nondirective leader. Levy (1954a,b) also found member satisfaction higher under directive than under nondirective leadership. Berkowitz (1953b) observed decision-making groups in business and government organizations. He found that group cohesiveness and member satisfaction decreased with leadership hearing and increased with directive leadership.

### Effects on Subordinate and Follower
### Involvement, Commitment, and Loyalty

According to D. Katz (1951), workers tend to enter or withdraw psychologically from groups as a function of their ability to make decisions in the respective groups.

Kahn and Tannenbaum (1957) and Tannenbaum and Smith (1964) surveyed organized workers and members of women's clubs. Member participation was facilitated by leadership that encouraged consultation and participation in activities. Member loyalty to the organization was also strengthened by participation in activities. In the same way, in a study of Tennessee Valley Authority (TVA) technicians and laboratory testers, Patchen (1970) found that participative management led to increased individual integration into the organization. Individuals became more involved in the work project when they were engaged in participative decision making. Siegel and Ruh (1973) reported similar results in a study of manufacturing employees. Participative leadership was positively related to employee job involvement.

Opportunity to participate can be a mixed blessing. According to a nation-wide survey by Gurin, Veroff, and Feld (1960), participation in the decision-making process increases both one's involvement in one's job and frustration with it. A. S. Tannenbaum (1963) studied 200 clerks given greater responsibility to make decisions. Despite their general increase in satisfaction, the clerks felt less of a sense of accomplishment at the end of the work day. They were also less satisfied with their present level in the organization. In acquiring an increased feeling of responsibility for the work, the clerks developed standards of achievement which were harder to satisfy.

### Effects on Task Performance

Mixed results are the result when we look at the effects of participation and direction, generally, on subordinate task performance and on task outcome.

*Effects on Decision Quality.* Experiments generally show that group decisions are superior to decisions reached by the average member of that group, although it is also true that the group decision may not be as good as that of the best member in the group. But how often is the supervisor the best? If this could be guaranteed, then decision quality might be better when decisions were made by the supervisor alone (Bass, 1960).

When sixty-six air force officers wrote decisions prior to discussion and then met as an ad hoc staff to write the decisions, the decisions written by the staff were superior to the average quality of decisions written by individuals without discussion. At the same time, the quality was the same after discussion whether the decision was written by the staff or by the commander who had listened to the staff discussion. Group discussions contributed to better decision making, whether or not the final decision was written by the group or by the person leading the group (Lorge, Fox, Davitz & Brenner, 1958). Maier (1950), Maier and Solem (1952), Solem (1953), Hoffman, Harburg, and Maier (1962), Blake and Mouton (1962), Hoffman, Burke, and Maier (1965), and Hoffman and Maier (1967) also studied the quality of decisions made by discussion groups. Quality of decision was higher under participation than under a directive style of leadership that discouraged discussion. Lanzetta and Roby (1960) found that both time and error scores were better under participative than under directive leadership.

*Effects on Productivity.* If one searches for universal answers about the immediate effects of participation and direction on productivity, about every possible alternative emerges. Katzell, Miller, Rotter, and Venet (1970) studied small problem-solving groups. Higher leader directiveness was positively associated with greater group effectiveness. Kidd and Christy (1961) found that error avoidance was greatest under directive leadership. Schumer (1962) obtained results which indicated that both the quality and quantity of productivity were enhanced by a directive form of leadership. Similarly, Torrance (1952) contrasted five types of critiques following sixteen minutes of problem-solving activity by aircrews in survival school in order to see which resulted in greatest improvement in ability to solve subsequent problems. The largest gains were made when an expert directed the critique; next best was guided discussion (participative leadership); least gain was found with free discussion (laissez-faire leadership) where no control was exerted.

Schlesinger, Jackson, and Butman (1960) found that committees are more effective in problem solution under directive than under nondirective leadership. Again, Stagner (1969) studied a large sample of corporation executives by questionnaire. Corporate profit was associated with more formality, more centralization of decision making, and less personalized management.

Likert (1977b), aiming toward long-range effects, involved various business and industrial groups in "Management by Group Objectives." MBGO generates participative sharing of data and group goal setting. A 27 percent increase over the previous year in profits from a retail sales division was reported. Such participation by teams of foremen resulted in a rise in productivity of 15 percent and a decrease in scrap of 7 to 14 percent in an auto assembly plant.

In an early study reported by the Survey Research Center (1948), work groups were more productive among those first-line supervisors in an insurance company who encouraged their workers to participate in decisions. Indik, Georgopoulos, and Seashore (1961) showed that among 975 delivery men at twenty-seven parcel delivery stations, the ease and freedom they felt in communicating with their superiors at a station correlated between .39 and .48 with the average deliveries the men completed daily relative to the standard time allotted for completion.

Participative leadership needs to have a focus to affect productivity. Lawrence and Smith (1955) studied checkers and mail openers over a five-week period. Groups of each held participative discussions about their work or set group goals. Only the goal-setting groups showed increased productivity, although both types of meetings were equally satisfying to the participants.

The amount of participation by subordinates seems to reach an optimum. If actual participation is greater than expected, R. Likert (1959) noted that dissatisfaction would result. Ivancevich (1979) found that performance suffered when participation was above or below optimum.

A number of studies reported no differences. McCurdy and Eber (1953) observed that groups in which free communication and decision making were practiced did not perform more effectively than those in which the leader made all the decisions. Tomekovic (1962) obtained no differences in productivity between participative and nonparticipative groups. Spector and Suttell (1956) reported that groups under participative and those under directive leadership did not differ in productivity.

In a study of twenty small shoe manufacturing firms, Willits (1967) found that neither the degree of delegation by the president nor the extent of executive participation in decision making was related to measures of company success. Heyns (1948) and W. M. Fox (1957) also found no differences of consequence.

Finally, both participation and direction were seen to benefit task performance. According to Weschler, Kahane, and Tannenbaum (1952), a research group perceived itself to be less productive than one led by a participative leader. However, the leader's boss thought the group led by the directive leader was more productive. Lange and Jacobs (1960) and Lange, Campbell, Katter, and Shanley (1958) found that both directive patterns of leader behavior and encouraging participation were positively and significantly related to group performance ratings. Similar, Farrow, Valenzi, and Bass (1980) found effectiveness according to approximately 250 managers and 1,400 subordinates correlated positively with amount of *direction* (.23) of the managers as seen by the subordinates. Effectiveness also correlated positively with various participatory approaches: consultation (.33), *participation* (.23), and delegation (.22). Only negotiation or manipulation by managers was negatively related to effectiveness (− .25).

### Effects on the Manager's Rate of Advancement

Hall and Donnell (1979) calculated the rate at which managers had been promoted by comparing their organizational level to their age. Over 2,000 subordinates indicated the extent to which the 731 managers allowed and encouraged their subordinates to participate in making and influencing work-related decisions. While slowly and moderately advancing managers were seen to permit or encourage very little participation, faster advancing managers did a lot of this.

## EFFECTS OF DIRECTIVE AND PARTICIPATIVE LEADERSHIP AS A FUNCTION OF CONTINGENCIES

What we have seen is that generally participative leadership enhances decision quality and is more satisfying, but in the short run, at least, it may be less conducive to productivity than directive leadership. Various contingencies must be taken into account to more fully predict and understand the impact of direction and participation. These contingencies include the differences between the leaders themselves and their followers, the task objectives, and the environmental constraints under which they must operate.

Three bases for understanding exist here. First, we can draw empirical inferences from surveys in which correlations have been run between leader style and productivity or satisfaction under different contingencies. Second, we can draw further inferences from experiments in which each leader style has been introduced under each contingency. Third, beginning with several acceptable assumptions consistent with what we have said earlier about the impact of participation on follower acceptance and about decision quality, we can present a deductive model (Vroom & Yetton, 1974) prescribing which leader style is likely to be more effective as well as empirical data supporting the propositions derived from the model.

### Leader–Follower Relations

*Power.* Kipnis (1958) studied groups of children under different conditions of leadership, reward, and threat. Both reward and threat produced more public compliance than the control condition. Participative leadership induced more children to change their beliefs when leadership was associated with power to reward. Under threat of punishment for noncompliance, significantly fewer children changed their beliefs under participative leadership than under lecture conditions. The participative leader was better liked than the lecturer if he did not threaten. Similarly, Patchen (1962) found that directive supervision resulted in high group output only if the group was also cohesive as well as directed by a supervisor who was seen to be a rewarding figure.

*Information.* Bass (Bass & Ryterband, 1979) asked eighteen wives of managers to meet with one of the managers (not their own spouse) to reach decisions about either company affairs or household affairs. Managers were either directive or participative in a counterbalanced design. The housewives felt responsibility for the household discussion regardless of the leader's style; they felt responsibility for the discussion about the company with the participative leader but not with the directive leader. Considerable hostility was reported by the wives for the directive leader dealing with household affairs. This also was the least satisfying experience for them. The wives did not react negatively when leaders directed the decision-making process if the problem concerned company issues. However, they were quite put out when the male leaders attempted to direct the discussion about household operating efficiency.

Communication network experiments to be reported in Chapter 28 demonstrated that if leaders are in the center of a network, so that they are in two-way contact with all the people at the periphery, their network will be more effective if they are directive. On the other hand, if the leaders occupy peripheral positions their network will be most effective if they are more participative (Shaw, 1954a).

*Personality.* In Vroom's (1959) study of 108 supervisors in a retail parcel delivery service, productivity was found correlated with felt influence on decisions among equalitarians much more than among authoritarians. Satisfaction on the job was increased by participation, but only for subordinates with equalitarian rather than authoritarian attitudes. A. S. Tannenbaum (1958) noted that followers predisposed toward participation tended to be satisfied under conditions of increased involvement. Those who were predisposed toward dependency, however, reacted adversely to increased participation.

Passive followers favored a more directive leader in Page and McGinnies's (1959) comparison of discussion groups led by directive and participative leaders. Likewise, in simulations (Bass, Burger, et al., 1979) apathetic subordinates are relatively more comfortable with directive supervisors.

Bass, Valenzi, and Farrow (1977) developed discriminant functions for 244 managers and the 992 subordinates of work groups above and below the median in effectiveness who had responded to a questionnaire about the system of inputs, relations, and outputs under which they perceived themselves to operate. Effectiveness (as seen by managers and subordinates) was more likely with delegative supervision (as seen by subordinates) if the managers tended to regard the world as fairminded and if the subordinates were introspective but not assertive. The same was true for the effectiveness of *participative* leadership except that in addition, assertive manager personality contributed to it. Consultation was more effective with introspective, unassertive subordinates and assertive managers. Manipulation and negotiation were noneffective with introspective managers and subordinates. Personality was of no consequence to the effectiveness of *direction*. Different configurations of other contingencies contributed to more group effectiveness and subordinate satisfaction. Some variables such as trust, harmony, and commitment contributed to effectiveness regardless of leadership, but harmony was more important for consultation than *participation*. Trust was more important for *participation* than for consultation.

### Constraints and Goals

Hemphill (1949) found that directive behavior on the part of a leader is most readily accepted in groups with closely restricted membership, stratified status structure, and lack of dependence of members on the group. On the other hand, Murnigham and Leung (1976) found that leader participation helped performance only when the task was seen as important by the subordinates.

*Task Requirements.*   Shaw and Blum (1966) manipulated task requirements by using three problems which were rated high, medium, or low on a solution multiplicity dimension using scale values determined by M. E. Shaw (1963b). The results showed that directive leadership was more effective in structured task situations while nondirective leadership was more effective in less structured conditions. Roby, Nicol, and Farrell (1963) obtained results which indicated that problems requiring reaction to environmental changes are more quickly solved under participative conditions. Problems requiring coordinated action are solved more efficiently under directive leadership.

Decision-making style within an organization is influenced by whether the organization must deal with a stable or turbulent market. Firms operating in turbulent markets are more effective if they encourage participation and decision making at the lowest possible levels (Emery & Trist, 1965). Burns and Stalker (1961) contrasted the relatively stable environment of a rayon mill with the more unstable conditions faced by firms in the electronics industry. For the mill in its stable environment, a "mechanistic" system with directive supervision was most effective. In the electronics field with its rapidly changing environment, a more participative, "organic" system seemed most effective. Similar conclusions were reached by Lawrence and Lorsch (1967a,b). For a container firm in the stable environment, effective decision-making processes within the firm were likely to be directive; in the more turbulent environment of a plastics firm, effective decision processes were more likely to be participative.

*Falling Dominoes Effects.*   Effectiveness of participatory leadership at lower levels in an organization will depend on its being practiced also at higher levels as well as in adjacent departments. Otherwise, conflict emerges (Lowin, 1968). Likert's (1967a) organization of overlapping groups in which every manager is a linchpin linking the participatory group of the manager and his or her subordinates with the participatory group of the manager's boss, the manager's peers, and the manager facilitates avoidance of such conflict.

*Objectives.*   When leaders overstep their authority by forcing an arbitrary decision on the group, the expected resistance and hostility may fail to materialize if the leaders' behavior actually facilitates achievement of the group's goals. Whether leaders reach their objectives depends on whether the style of leadership they choose meets the needs of their subordinates to attain their goals and whether it clarifies for them the paths to their goals (House & Mitchell, 1974). Participation may meet subordinate needs but may fail to achieve clarification of goals without some direction. If the task has a practical rather than a theoretical outcome, directive supervision may be more effective. Korten (1968) observed that if the final product of a task was practical, more directive supervision was in order. On the other hand, if the outcome was theoretical, participation was of more utility.

If the supervisors' time perspective is short, if they have some immediate objectives to be obtained, they are likely to find it most effective to be directive. Alternatively, if an important objective is the long-term efficiency of their groups, participation is more likely to pay off (Hahn & Trittipoe, 1961).

## A DEDUCED MODEL FOR IDENTIFYING APPROPRIATE LEADERSHIP STYLE CONTINGENT ON WHETHER DECISION QUALITY OR SUBORDINATE ACCEPTANCE IS REQUIRED

Which style is appropriate and most conducive to success (achieving subordinate compliance) and effectiveness (achieving mutual objectives and group goals)? R. Likert (1977a) argues that if long-term measures of effectiveness are the criteria of consequence, then a democratic approach, including shared participative decision making, is universally more effective as long as the leader is task-oriented. There are no contingencies for Likert. On the other hand, summarizing the previous literature, based mainly on short-term laboratory studies and surveys, Bass and Barrett (1981) noted that participative leadership is contraindicated when interaction is restricted by the task, when higher authority disapproves, when maximum output is demanded, when subordinates do not expect to participate, when leaders are unready for participation, and in emergencies. Similarly, for situations with short-term perspectives, when effectiveness means quality and/or subordinate acceptance, Vroom and Yetton (1973) have deduced what style is most conducive to effectiveness given known demand characteristics of the situation. They have buttressed their arguments with efforts to show adequate correspondence between their deductions and what can be induced empirically from managers' preferred and actual styles in dealing with problems containing various combinations of the demand characteristics.

Vroom and Yetton laid out the direction-to-participation continuum as follows:

AI: You solve problem or make decision yourself using information available to you.

AII: You obtain necessary information from subordinates, then decide on solution to problem yourself. Subordinates are not asked to generate or evaluate alternative solutions.

CI: You share the problem with relevant subordinates *individually,* getting their ideas and suggestions. Then you make the decision, which may or may not reflect your subordinates' influence.

CII: You share the problem with your subordinates *as a group,* collectively obtaining their ideas and suggestions. Then you make the decision, which may or may not reflect your subordinates' influence.

GII: You share the problem with your subordinates as a group. Together you generate and evaluate alternatives and attempt to reach a solution. You do not try to influence the group to adopt ''your'' solution and you are willing to accept and implement any solution which has the support of the entire group.

The responses can be judgementally scaled according to the greater opportunities for subordinates to influence outcomes as follows: AI = 0; AII = .625; CI = 5.0; CII = 8.125, and GII = 10.0.

The situational demand characteristics and the requirements of the problem the leader faces can be described by affirmative or negative answers to the following seven questions:

1. Is there a quality requirement such that one solution is better than another?
2. Does the leader have sufficient information to make a high quality decision?
3. Is the problem structured?
4. Is acceptance of decision by subordinates critical to effective implementation?
5. If the leader were to make the decision by himself or herself, is it reasonably certain that it would be accepted by the subordinates?
6. Do subordinates share the organizational goals to be obtained in solving this problem?
7. Is conflict among subordinates likely in preferred solutions?

Seven rules are imposed to limit various leader styles to those feasible sets which can be deduced in order to protect the quality of the solution and acceptance of the decision: (1) AI is eliminated as a possible choice for the leader when solution quality is important and the leader lacks information; (2) GII is eliminated from the feasible set of leader styles if quality is important and subordinates do not share organizational goals; (3) AI, AII, and CI are eliminated when quality is important, the leader lacks information, and the problem is unstructured; (4) if subordinate acceptance of the solution is critical, AI and AII are eliminated from the feasible set; (5) if subordinate acceptance is critical and subordinates are likely to conflict about the solution, AI, AII, and CI are eliminated (a group approach is necessary to resolve conflicts); (6) if acceptance but not quality is critical, then AI, AII, CI, and CII are eliminated; (7) if acceptance is critical and subordinates share organizational goals, AI, AII, CI, and CII are eliminated (shared participation will emerge as the only suitable leadership style).

Figure 19.1 shows the decision-tree which must be followed given the situational characteristics and the rules for eliminating choices of leadership styles. For example, in Figure 19.1, if the leader's answer to question 1 is that the problem does not require a quality solution, the leader's next decision is about whether subordinate acceptance is important (question 4). If a directive decision (5) is seen to be unacceptable, the appropriate style for the leader to choose is GII, group participation.

*Empirical Verifications*

Leaders were asked to describe, in written form, a recent problem which they had had to solve in carrying out their leadership role. They then specified the method (AI, AII, CI, CII, or GII) which came closest to the one which they had actually used in

**FIGURE 19.1. Decision Process Flowchart (Feasible Set)**

A. Does the problem possess a quality requirement?
B. Do I have sufficient information to make a high-quality decision?
C. Is the problem structured?
D. Is acceptance of the decision by subordinates important for effective implementation?
E. If I were to make the decision by myself, am I reasonably certain that it would be accepted by my subordinates?
F. Do subordinates share the organizational goals to be attained in solving this problem?
G. Is conflict among subordinates likely in preferred solutions?

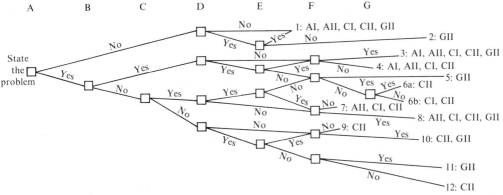

dealing with that problem. They described the problem in terms of its quality and situational demand characteristics. Diagnosed situation, not respondent personality, determined what methods had been used, with some degree of correspondence to what would have been prescribed by the Vroom and Yetton decision-tree.

These problems were used to prepare thirty to fifty-four standardized cases which were then given to several thousand managers to diagnose in terms of the seven questions and decide which style they would use. As noted earlier, most of the differences in style used depended on case differences rather than individual differences among the managers. Vroom and Yetton concluded that on the average managers said they would (or did) use exactly the same decision process as their decision-tree model in about 40 percent of the situations. In the two-thirds of the situations, their behavior was consistent with the feasible set of methods proposed in the model. In other words, in only about one-third of the situations did their behavior violate at least one of the seven rules underlying the model.

Nevertheless, Vroom and Yetton also noted that the model called for more variance in style than recalled or proposed by the average manager. Thus, if managers used the model as the basis for choosing their leadership styles, all would become both more directive and more participative. They would employ direction more frequently in situations in which their subordinates were unaffected by the decision and would use participative approaches more frequently when their subordinates' cooperation and support were critical and/or their information and expertise were required. All of this is predicted on the short-term objective of minimizing the time of leader and subordinates. As we will note later, another model is required if long-term objectives to develop subordinates are involved.

Vroom and Jago (1978) followed up with a study of ninety-six managers who were unaware of the decision-tree model. Managers from a variety of organizations described 181 situations and their leader behavior in these situations. The model was then employed to predict ratings of the technical quality, subordinate acceptance, and the overall effectiveness of the final leadership styles chosen by the managers. The managers noted the extent to which their chosen leadership styles in the situation they described had been effective in terms of resulting in a quality solution and subordinate acceptance. The logical Vroom-Yetton decision-tree came up with prescribed leader styles that matched what the managers reported they actually did in 117 (65 percent) of the 181 situations. Among the 117, eighty (68 percent) were judged as effective in the situation and thirty-seven (32 percent) were judged as ineffective leadership performances.

In sixty-four cases the chosen leadership style was outside Vroom and Yetton's feasible sets for the situation described. Here, only fourteen (22 percent) were seen by the managers to be effective leadership behavior and fifty (78 percent) were seen as ineffective. Effectiveness was less, the more often Vroom and Yetton's seven rules were violated, particularly when subordinate acceptance was involved.

*Caveat.* Field (1979) suggested that these results should be accepted with caution. They are too dependent on self-reports. Weissenberg and Kavanagh (1972) found little relation between what leaders said they should do and what subordinates say they actually do. Field suggested returning to an earlier, simpler, fourfold model developed by Maier (1970b) based on earlier creativity and problem-solving experiments (Maier, 1960; Maier, 1963; Maier & Danielson, 1956; Maier & Hoffman, 1960, 1964; Maier & Maier, 1957; Maier & Solem, 1962): Type I problem has a quality requirement, acceptance is likely to be obtained easily, and the decision should be made by the leader; Type II problems do not have a quality requirement but acceptance is critical; therefore, these problems should be resolved by group decision; Type III problems do not have quality or acceptance requirements and should be decided by tossing a coin; participative approaches with this type of problem generate unnecessary conflicts; Type IV problems require both quality and acceptance and are solved by using persuasion but better yet group discussion. Field also noted that in Figure 19.1 the decision process CII is in the feasible set for nineteen of the twenty-three situations included in the four types of problems. But in the four situations where CII is not in the feasible set, GII is in the feasible set. A more parsimonious rule proposed by Field to protect decision quality and acceptance is: "If acceptance of the decision by subordinates is critical to effective implementation and it is not reasonably certain that subordinates would accept an autocratic decision, but they share organizational goals (or decision quality is not important), use GII; otherwise, use CII." This simple model uses only four situation demand characteristics instead of seven, and uses only two leadership styles, CII or GII, rather than the five of the Vroom-Yetton model. Also, this simple model offers a balance between the short-term time efficient model and the long-term group development model.

Field thus concludes that what needs to be prescribed is either consultation with the group of subordinates or shared participatory leadership with the group unless there is certainty that a directive decision would be acceptable to subordinates. This, in turn, may depend on whether the leader is relations- or task-oriented, the subject of the next chapter.

# 20

## RELATIONS-ORIENTED AND TASK-ORIENTED LEADERSHIP

## INTRODUCTION

### Task Orientation

Leaders differ in their concern for the group's goals and the means to achieve them. Those with strong concern are seen as task-oriented (Bass, 1967b; Fiedler, 1967a) concerned with production (Blake & Mouton, 1964), in need of achievement (McClelland, 1961; Wofford, 1970), production-oriented, (Katz, et al., 1950), production-emphasizing (Fleishman, 1957), goal-achieving (Cartwright & Zander, 1960), and work-facilitative and goal emphasizing (Bowers & Seashore, 1966). Such leaders are likely to keep their distance psychologically from their followers and to be more cold and aloof (Blau & Scott, 1962). When coupled with an inability to trust subordinates, such concern for production is likely to manifest itself in close, controlling supervision (McGregor, 1960).

### Relations Orientation

Leaders also differ in their concern about the group members in the extent to which they pursue a human relations approach and try to maintain friendly, supportive relations with followers. Those with such strong concern are identified as relations-oriented (Katz et al., 1950), emphasizing employees (Fleishman, 1957), concerned for group maintenance (Cartwright & Zander, 1960; Wofford, 1970), concerned for people (Blake & Mouton, 1964), people-centered (D. R. Anderson, 1974), interaction-facilitative and supportive (Bowers & Seashore, 1966), interaction-oriented (Bass, 1967b), and in need of affiliation (McClelland, 1961). Usually associated with a relations orientation is a sense of trust in subordinates, less felt need to control them, and more general rather than close supervision (McGregor, 1960).

### Related Concepts

As noted in Chapter 18, relations and task orientation are components of democratic and autocratic leadership. Although the various conceptualizations of task orientation have similar-sounding labels, their intercorrelations are not necessarily high. In fact, they may point to different attributes of an individual. Thus, the direct assessment of eighty-one industrial personnel's task orientation—using the Orientation Inventory which asks examinees for their preferred activities—correlated only .32 with need for achievement as measured by the Thematic Apperception Test tapping the projected fantasies of the same examinees (Dobruszek, 1967). In the same way, Fiedler's (1967a) determination of task orientation based on leaders' rejection of the coworker with whom they have found it most difficult to work, does not correlate highly with other approaches to measuring task orientation. (In fact, the least preferred coworker, LPC, measure seems so unique, that we will treat research on it mostly separately in a section by itself in this chapter.) Thus, it is necessary to review results in the light of variations due to how orientations are measured. Furthermore, while measurements for research use, such as those of Fiedler (1967a) or Bass (1967b) often artificially force separation into task- or relations-oriented categories, conceptually leaders may have strong concerns for both task and relations, or for neither. At the same time, observers can accurately discriminate among the ratings for emerging task and socioemotional leadership earned by interacting members of experimental task groups (Stein, Geis & Damarin, 1973).

## ANTECEDENTS CONTRIBUTING TO TASK ORIENTATION AND RELATIONS ORIENTATION

As before, leadership style tends to depend on the leader's personal characteristics as well as situational contingencies such as characteristics of the followers and the organization and task goals and constraints within which the leadership occurs.

### Leader Personality

Klebanoff (1976) measured task orientation and relations orientation by within-group observer and peer rankings of the task- or relations-oriented behavior displayed by 160 participants in forty small groups working on tasks. Task-oriented leaders were more likely to have been first-born children, felt more personal autonomy, and tended to participate more. Helmich and Erzen (1975) surveyed 108 corporation presidents and found that task-oriented leaders lacked fulfillment as presidents. The needs of relations-oriented presidents were better met.

*Orientation Inventory Results.* Items clustering on the Orientation Inventory (Bass, 1962c) for the highly task-oriented examinee included: to be wise, to have the feeling of a job well done, to have bright, interesting friends, and to be a leader who gets things done. Interaction-oriented preferences included: to have fun with friends, to have helpful friends, to work cooperatively, to make more friends, and to be an easy-to-talk-to leader.

Personal factors significantly associated with task orientation included: self-sufficient, resourceful, controlled will-power, aloof, not sociable, sober-serious, tough-realistic, and aggressive-competitive (Bass & Dunteman, 1963) as well as restraint, ascendance, masculinity, objectivity, thoughtfulness, endurance, need for achievement, and heterosexuality (Bass, 1965b). Task orientation was higher among males than females, and among those with greater maturity, education, status, and technical training. Task-oriented students were more likely to volunteer and to persist at tasks voluntarily until completion (Frye & Spruill, 1965). They were self-reinforcers (Marston, 1964) and more likely to be seen as helpful to others in sensitivity training groups (Bass & Dunteman, 1963).

Personal factors significantly associated with relations orientation (interaction orientation) as measured by the Orientation Inventory included: socially group-dependent, warm, sociable, and need for affiliation (Bass & Dunteman, 1963). Interaction orientation correlated also with wanting to be controlled by others, to be close to others, to receive affection from others, to include others, and to be included with others (Bass, 1965b).

Task orientation has been found to correlate as high as .41 and interaction orientation as low as − .32 with intelligence as measured by the Army General Classification Test (Dobruszek, 1967).

### Followers and Their Performance

Cause and effect cannot be separated from a study of 112 engineering employees by Jones, James, and Bruni (1975). But their results are suggestive of follower influence on leader behavior, although the reverse is also tenable (as with the Katz, Maccoby, and Morse [1950] results mentioned below). Jones, James, and Bruni obtained correlations from .41 to .55 between employee confidence and trust in their supervisors and the extent to which their supervisors were seen to be high in support, goal emphasis, work facilitation, and interaction facilitation.

*Prior Follower Performance.* In earlier chapters we noted that poor subordinate performance appears to cause much of the observed leader punitiveness. In the same way, good subordinate performance appears to increase tendencies for their leaders to be relations-oriented. In a study of routine clerical workers and their supervisors in a life insurance company, Katz, Maccoby, and Morse (1950) found that supervisors of high producing sections were significantly more likely to be employee-oriented rather than production-oriented. Barrow (1975) showed that increasing subordinate performance in a laboratory setting resulted in the leader becoming significantly more supportive. Decreasing subordinate performance caused the leader to become more task-oriented. This is consistent with Bass, Binder, and Breed's (1967) findings for the performance of a simulated organization discussed below.

*Prior Organizational Effectiveness.* Commonly observed as well as deplored (for instance, Likert, 1977b) is the extent to which human relations concerns are abandoned when an enterprise's profits are seriously eroded. Akin to a stress response, task orientation is increased at the expense of relations orientation. Bass, Binder, and Breed (1967) demonstrated this phenomenon in a simulated budgeting exercise. Whether or not their company had just finished a profitable year strongly influenced the concern of decision makers for employee satisfaction and well-being and the willingness to accept more employee-centered solutions to problems in safety, labor relations, and management development. MBA students were shown a firm's year-end profit and loss statement, one showing that an $86,000 net loss had occurred and another that moderate or large profits had been earned. Three-quarters of the students in the profitable circumstances recommended buying safety equipment. Only half of the students in the unprofitable enterprise and only 25 percent of those in the firm losing money in the previous year were willing to spend the required funds to settle a strike quickly. Goals emphasized in the profitable situation were employee welfare, goodwill, and satisfactory operations. Goals stressed in the firm which had experienced a loss were meeting competition and raising profits.

*Follower Personality.* As noted in Chapter 8, Sanford (1951) found in a survey of Philadelphia residents that equalitarians wanted leaders who were warm and generally supportive. But authoritarians preferred leaders who would serve their special interests. Indirectly, we infer that more relations-oriented leadership would be demanded by highly self-oriented followers, by followers with personal problems, by followers in need of nurturance, and by followers seeking affection.

## GENERAL CONSEQUENCES OF RELATIONS-ORIENTED AND TASK-ORIENTED LEADERSHIP

Three kinds of evidence are available. First, we can examine the extent to which relations- and task-oriented leaders are seen to be more or less meritorious by others. Second, we can review their differential impact on subordinate satisfaction. Third, we can detail their differential effects on group performance.

### Evaluations as a Leader

Reports published on correlations of evaluations as leader and relations or task orientation generally found both orientations of positive importance.

*Relations Orientation.* Shartle (1934) used interviews and questionnaires in a comparative study of supervisors rated as either effective or ineffective. Effective supervisors did not differ from their ineffective peers in technical skills, but they were found to excel in ability to interact effectively and in interest in people. Similarly, Katzell, Barrett, Vann, and Hogan (1968) found that executives whose roles emphasized administrative rather than technical performances received higher performance ratings from their superiors.

Mann and Dent (1954b) studied supervisors rated according to promotability by higher levels of management. Highly promotable supervisors were described by their employees as being good at handling people, approachable, willing to go to bat for employees, letting them know where they stand, pulling for both company and workers rather than either alone, and using general rather than close supervision. The supervisors saw their superiors as good at handling people, letting them know where they stand, and permitting freedom in making decisions.

H. H. Meyer (1951) observed that effective supervisors regarded others as individuals with motives, feelings, and goals of their own. They did not avoid interactional stress. Similarly, Kay and Meyer (1962), using both questionnaire and observational methods, found that higher rated foremen were less production-oriented and gave general rather than close supervision. Again, Walker, Guest, and Turner (1956) observed that effective supervisors established personal relationships with employees, stuck up for them, and absorbed the pressures from higher levels of authority. In the same way, A. N. Turner (1954) reported that workers regarded as good supervisors those who did not pressure their subordinates unnecessarily, were fair, friendly, and understanding, and did not tell them to quit if they didn't like conditions.

Among the seventeen Americans on the 1963 Mount Everest expedition, all of whom were highly task-oriented, those most interaction-oriented and highest on FIRO-B Expressed Inclusion were rated highest in leadership. "The qualities of being emotionally responsive, affectionate, warm, inviting in manner, of placing primary value on the emotional give-and-take in face-to-face relations were important. The men reacted negatively to emotional constriction, to too much emphasis on method, efficiency, productivity, and the imposition of high impersonal standards'' (Lester, 1965). However, when interaction orientation scores are high at the expense of task orientation scores such as when ipsative scoring is used, task rather than interaction or relations orientation is likely to correlate with merit as a leader.

*Task Orientation.* Rubenowitz (1962) reported that job-oriented supervisors were regarded by higher management as more effective than person-oriented supervisors. Shortly after, Kelly (1964) found that the technical features of executive behavior outweighed the effects of personal style.

According to Dunteman (1966), task orientation as measured by the Orientation Inventory correlated with promotability ratings based on three days of assessment of ninety-six supervisors (but correlations were negative among younger, temporary supervisors and journeymen so assessed). For both sixty-six first-line and twenty-seven second-line supervisors, task orientation significantly contributed to their high on-the-job performance ratings by their own supervisors (Dunteman & Bass, 1963).

Many other studies will be enumerated in Chapter 25 showing that leaders who are concerned about the task in those situations where such concern is relevant are likely to be evaluated highly by others.

### Impact on Subordinate Satisfaction

The majority of reports indicates that subordinate satisfaction with their leaders is linked to their leaders' relations-oriented attitudes and behavior.

*Organizational Surveys.* Hoppock (1935) analyzed the early literature on job satisfaction. Results indicated that workers tended to feel more satisfied when supervisors understood their problems and helped when needed. Ronan (1970), in a survey of more than 10,000 managerial, supervisory, and hourly personnel, obtained similar findings as did Roberts, Miles, and Blankenship (1968) and Hain and Widgery (1973).

Stagner, Flebbe, and Wood (1952) found that railroad workers were better satisfied when their supervisors were good at handling grievances and communicating with employees. Likewise, Bose (1955) observed that workers under employee-centered supervisors had more group pride than those under work-centered supervisors. Mann and Hoffman (1960) found that in two plants, one automated, the other not, employees were more satisfied with supervisors who were considerate of their feelings, recognized good work, were reasonable in their expectations, and stood up for their subordinates.

Stampolis (1958) showed that the higher employees rated their supervisor in fairness, authority, ability to handle people, giving credit, readiness to discuss problems, and keeping employees informed, the less the employees expressed a desire for unionization of their company. Bass and Mitchell (1976) reported similar results for professional and scientific workers.

Wager (1965) found that a supportive style of leadership assisted the supervisor in fulfilling and satisfying employees' role expectations. In an aircraft factory, where team leaders devoted much of their time to facilitating the work of their team members and attending to their personal problems, indicators of dissatisfaction such as absenteeism and turnover were lower (Mayo & Lombard, 1944).

*Experiments.* Most experimental studies likewise concluded that member satisfaction was positively associated with leader relations-oriented behavior. Wischmeier (1955) found that group-centered rather than task-centered discussions resulted in a warm, friendly group atmosphere. T. Gordon (1955) also found that group-centered discussion was associated with member sense of belonging, respect for others, ability to listen to and understand others, and loss of self-defensiveness. Similarly, Thelen and Whitehall (1949) and Schwartz and Gekoski (1960) reported that follower-oriented leadership enhanced satisfaction. Again, Maier and Danielson (1956) reported that an employee-oriented solution for a disciplinary problem produced greater satisfaction in groups of problem solvers than one bound by legalistic restrictions.

Heyns (1948) coached one set of leaders in playing a positive, supportive role which emphasized agreement, mutual liking, and cooperation. Another set was coached in a negative role to display overt misunderstanding of members with no effort to develop group cohesiveness. The two styles produced no significant difference in quality of group decision or member satisfaction; however, the groups with positive leaders exhibited evidences of greater cohesiveness. W. M. Fox (1954) repeated Heyn's research, using scenarios to coach the leaders in their roles. Groups with positive leaders exhibited higher degrees of cohesiveness and member satisfaction, but were slower in problem solution. With a different group of participants, W. M. Fox (1957) also found that positive leadership was associated with member satisfaction and group cohesiveness.

*Social Distance.* Several investigations focused on the impact of psychological closeness or distance on satisfaction which we noted may be a component of relations orientation. As expected, Julian (1964) found job satisfaction high with psychological proximity between the leader and the led. However, Blau and Scott (1962) and E. P. Shaw (1965) reported that group cohesiveness was strengthened by distance between leader and followers, whereas Sample and Wilson (1965) found cohesiveness unrelated to social distance. Likewise, Sorcher (1966) found no relationship between psychological distance and group productivity.

*Both Orientations.* Both socioemotional and task-oriented leadership of residence hall leaders each measured separately were linked by MacDonald (1969) to student satisfaction. Litwin and Stringer (1968) also noted in an experiment that member satisfaction was higher under leaders with a strong need for affiliation and achievement but not power. However, under leaders with a high need for affiliation, the groups exhibited warmth and regard. Under leaders with a high need for achievement, groups exhibited much conflict. Consistent with this, in a survey of several thousand employees, R. Likert (1955) found their job satisfaction to decrease as supervisory pressure for production increased.

### Leader Orientation and Impact on Follower Performance

Again, generally both relations orientation and task orientation are found to be positively associated with group productivity, goal attainment, and follower performance but there are many exceptions, as will be noted below, pointing to the need for a contingent approach. Some situations call for more relations-oriented leadership, others for more task-oriented leadership, although it may be that in a majority of circumstances both types of leadership are optimal.

*Relations-Orientation Effects.* Pandey (1976) reported that relations-oriented leaders fostered the generation of more ideas in the groups they led than did task-oriented leaders (measured by LPC). Katz, Maccoby, and Morse (1950) and Roberts, Miles, and Blankenship (1968) found that group performance was higher under an employee-oriented style than under a more disinterested style of supervision. Philipsen (1965a,b) also found that human relations leadership correlated positively with group effectiveness. But, in a study of skilled tradesmen, Wilson, Beem, and Comrey (1953) established that supervisors of both high and low performing shops were described as more helpful, sympathetic, consistent, and self-reliant than those in medium performing shops.

Indik, Georgopoulos, and Seashore (1961) studied the employees of a transportation company. Results indicated that high levels of group performance were associated with satisfaction with supervisors' supportiveness, open communication, mutual understanding, and worker autonomy on the job. As observed in Chapter 18, R. Likert (1961a, 1967, 1977b) concluded from many survey studies that supportive attitudes toward employees, combined with group loyalty toward management, was associated with increased employee productivity and desire for responsibility. With the introduction of a human relations approach to management, along with high performance goals, long-term gains in productivity were achieved.

Nevertheless, numerous exceptions have been reported, particularly in short-range analyses, and qualification of Likert's conclusions is needed. Thus, Lundquist (1957) obtained results indicating that whether or not supervisors were worker-oriented, frequency of their interaction with workers increased their effectiveness. Weitz and Nuckols (1953) found that supervisors' scores on a test measuring human relations orientation were not related to group productivity or turnover. MacKinney, Kavanagh, Wolins, and Rapparlie (1970) found that both production-oriented and employee-oriented management were unrelated to employee satisfaction. Carp, Vitola, and McLanathan (1963) obtained results showing that supervisors of effective postal teams maintained their social distance from subordinates which reduced the surfacing of emotional problems.

In a study of simulated management groups, Kaczka and Kirk (1967) established that team profitability was associated with relations-oriented leadership. It also resulted in less pressure toward task accomplishment and lower group cohesiveness. Andrews and Farris (1967) found that innovation among scientific personnel was highest when their supervisors were moderate rather than low or high in their human relations leadership tendencies. Finally, C. A. Dawson (1969), studying the achievement of school children observed that the children performed equally well under "cold" or "warm" leadership.

*Task-Orientation Effects.* R. Likert (1955) reported that a survey of several thousand workers indicated a tendency for productivity to be higher in the presence of higher supervisory pressure for production. Similarly, Litwin (1968) noted that experimental groups with leaders high in need for achievement were much more productive than those with leaders high in need for affiliation or power. Again, Dunteman and Bass (1963) studied foremen who differed in interaction orientation and task orientation. Groups working under task-oriented leaders were more productive than those under interaction-oriented leaders. Likewise, Mann, Indik, and Vroom (1963) showed that worker productivity was associated with the supervisor's task orientation. R. Cooper (1966) also demonstrated that first-line supervisors judged by their own bosses to be higher in "task relevance" tended to have more productive and more task-motivated subordinates.

For fourteen navy airplane maintenance groups, R. Likert (1977a) reported strong associations with the extent to which supervisors facilitated the work by helping with advanced scheduling and offering new ideas to solve job problems and the extent to which airplanes serviced by the groups avoided accidents and disasters due to operational failures.

*Effectiveness of Both Orientations Combined.* Blake and Mouton (1964) argued that maximum leadership effectiveness occurs only when the leader, both highly concerned for production and highly concerned for people, integrates the human and task requirements of the job. The exclusively task-oriented manager is seen to treat employees as machines to the detriment of employee commitment, growth, and morale. The exclusively people-oriented manager is seen to run a country club to the detriment of productivity. Kahn and Katz (1953), Oaklander and Fleishman (1964), and Likert (1977a), among many others, came to similar conclusions. Thus, for example, Medalia and Miller (1955) observed that human relations leadership and employee satisfaction interact to influence group effectiveness. Again, Patchen (1962) reported that the leader who maintained high performance norms and encouraged efficiency along with attempts to obtain rewards for followers was likely to have a high-performing group. However, sustaining high performance standards alone and attempts to obtain rewards for followers alone each had a negative effect on productivity. Both patterns of behavior must be combined in order to affect productivity in a positive direction. In contrast, Andrews and Farris (1967) found no evidence that innovation was higher when supervisors were high in both task and human relations functions. Human relations skills had little moderating effect on the generally positive relationships between the leader's carrying out of task functions and innovation. The most innovation occurred under supervisors neither high nor low in their attention to human relations regardless of task functions completed.

## SITUATIONAL CONTINGENCIES AFFECTING CONSEQUENCES OF RELATIONS AND TASK ORIENTATION

Situational contingencies need to be examined for their moderating effects on the impact of relations- and task-oriented leadership on follower satisfaction and productivity.

### Follower Effects

In a study of community hospitals, F. C. Mann (1965) observed that the satisfaction of the nurses was related to the human relations skills of their supervisors, while that of the nursing supervisors was related to the administrative skills of their superiors. But the satisfaction of the technicians was related to their supervisors' technical and human relations skills.

Tannenbaum and Allport (1956) studied two departments of women workers. One was given more responsibility and authority for their work and decisions about it. In the second department, line authority was emphasized. A personality test was administered initially and scored as to the suitability of the workers' personality to the situation in which they worked. One year later an attitude test was administered. Significantly more suited than unsuited workers in the situation with more authority and responsibility wanted it to continue. But suited and unsuited workers did not differ in attitude toward the program if they had not been given authority and responsibility.

Seashore (1954) found that supportive leadership with cohesive followers paid off in higher productivity. However, follower cohesiveness also resulted in lower productivity where supervisors were unsupportive.

*Need for Achievement.* The followers' need for achievement was found by a number of investigators to make a difference in the way the followers reacted to particular styles of leadership. W. W. Burke (1965) discovered that followers high in need for achievement with socially close leaders rated their situation as more tense regardless of the nature of the task than did high need achievement followers under socially distant leaders. Followers without need for achievement with socially distant leaders reported more tension than low need achievement followers with socially close leaders. High need achievement followers rated socially close leaders high in authoritarianism, while low need achievement followers did the same for socially distant leaders. Misumi and Seki (1971) also studied leadership style effects on performance of students high or low in need for achievement. Achievement-oriented students performed best under a leader high in both task orientation and maintenance orientation. In groups lacking in need for achievement, performance was best under a task-oriented leader.

*Dogmatism.* Weed, Mitchell, and Moffitt (1976) studied the effects of task versus relations orientation as a function of subordinate personality and task type on group performance and satisfaction with supervision. Compared were leaders who scored high in human relations and high in task orientation, low in human relations and high in task orientation, and high in human relations and low in task orientation. Each leader worked with subordinates high or low in dogmatism. Subordinates varied in task and relations orientation, as well. Subordinates, regardless of their personality and regardless of the task, were significantly more satisfied with leadership behavior that was high in human relations orientation.

### Constraints and Goals

Several studies obtained results suggesting that style of supervision interacted with situational variables to influence productivity and job satisfaction. For example, Lundquist (1957) reported that foremen who are worker-oriented produce better results in smaller rather than larger groups.

*Task Effects.* W. W. Burke (1965) found that group performance in a coding task was more effective under a production-oriented leader, but in a decision task was more effective under a relations-oriented leader. In the just cited experiment by Weed, Mitchell, and Moffitt (1976), the task was varied in ambiguity and difficulty. The interacting effects of leader style—relations- or task-oriented—and subordinate relations or task orientation were strongest on difficult and ambiguous rather than clear and easy tasks. That is, the compatibility of leader and follower personality made a difference only if the task was difficult and ambiguous.

Wofford (1971) obtained results indicating that a relations-oriented manager is likely to be more effective in terms of productivity and morale of the group led in simple, centralized, structured operations. Schacter, Festinger, Willerman, and Hyman (1961) generated contrary evidence in an experiment with work groups matched in age, productivity, seniority, and disciplinary records. For three weeks, managers were friendly, helpful, and praising for the favored group and were threatening, reproving, and deliberately annoying in their demands to the unfavored group. The favorable and unfavorable relations ceased at the end of three weeks, when minor changes in work were instituted.

Table 20.1 shows the percentage of assembled units requiring repair during each phase of the experiment. When employees continued to work on old and familiar tasks, the unfavorable supervision had only slight effects on performance. But when a changeover occurred, requiring work on new, unfamiliar tasks, repair rates of the unfavored group jumped much higher than did those of the favored group. Equally important, while the favored group rapidly returned to its normal repair record by the end of the third week after the changeover, the unfavored group continued to exhibit a repair rate three times worse than what had been their normal record before the onset of the unfavorable supervisory relations. Unlike survey results, this experiment demonstrated that unfavorable supervisory human relations cause decrements primarily when new learning is required, not when accustomed tasks are performed.

*Functions.* Woodward (1958) reported that friendly supervisors were rated as more effective in service departments. They were rated as less effective in production departments. Consistent with this, B. Schneider (1973) noted that in social service agencies, in the relations with their subordinates, supervisors set examples for how they expect their subordinates to relate to clients of the agencies. Satisfied clients mirrored friendly, concerned, supervisory relations with subordinates. Schneider found that good customer relations with a bank reflected good relations of bank tellers with their superiors. Relations-oriented supervision would seem particularly indicated in service operations.

The manager and the coach of English football teams differ greatly in their function. The manager has little continuous contact with the players; the coach maintains a high degree of contact. Cooper and Payne (1967) found a correlation of .72 between the task orientation of the team coach and the success of the teams in winning games. But the same correlation was close to zero for managers.

**TABLE 20.1**
**Quality of Work before and after Changeover of Work Groups**
**Subjected to Favored and Unfavored Supervisory Treatment**

| | Percentage of Assembled Units Requiring Repair | |
|---|---|---|
| Phase of Experiment | *Favored Group* | *Unfavored Group* |
| During first week of contrived disturbance | 10.6 | 11.8 |
| During second two weeks of contrived disturbance | 11.7 | 14.7 |
| First week after changeover | 21.1 | 31.4 |
| Second week after changeover | 13.8 | 28.0 |
| Third and fourth weeks after | 11.6 | 29.0 |

Source: Schacter, Willerman, Festinger and Hyman, 1961, p. 206.

*Community.*   Blood and Hulin (1967) reported that workers in communities where one would expect adherence to middle-class norms (for example, small communities) tended to accept a human relations style of leadership. Workers in large, industrialized communities where one would expect alienation from middle-class norms did not respond as positively to a human relations style of supervision.

### Interactions with Other Leader Behaviors

The effects of what else the leader does moderates the impact of task or relations orientation.

Thus, working with elementary school teachers, Larkin (1975) showed that teachers who were task-oriented in their behavior created high morale among pupils regardless of how much they also resorted to power. But teachers low in task-oriented behavior who used power did generate rebellious climates. Among supervisors of technical personnel, participative approaches (provision of freedom) resulted in the most innovation if the supervisors were low in task or human relations orientation (Andrews & Farris, 1967). In an experiment with small groups of ROTC students, Anderson and Fiedler (1964) found that those under task-oriented leaders were most productive and satisfied when the leaders were participative but satisfaction was greater when relations-oriented leaders were directive. Similarly, Pandey (1976) showed that the behavior and effectiveness of relations- and task-oriented leadership of discussion groups depended on whether the leaders were appointed, elected, or rotated since elected and rotational leaders tended to be more participative in comparison to appointed leaders.

## FIEDLER'S CONTINGENCY MODEL OF LEADERSHIP

Fiedler's (1967a) contingency model of leadership is the most widely researched on leadership. At the same time, it is the most widely criticized. It is presented here as part of our discussion of relations- and task-oriented leadership. Nevertheless, at the time of this writing, controversy continues about what is being measured by LPC—Fiedler's Least Preferred Coworker questionnaire. This, in turn, affects the ability to understand its varying relation to effectiveness in different situations. On the surface, LPC measures what respondents report characterizes their feelings about a person with whom they can work least effectively.

### Development of the LPC Measurement

Starting in the early 1950s, Fiedler (1953a,b,c) began studying the success of therapists as a function of their accuracy and assumed similarity to their patients. This research was then extended to leaders and the effectiveness of the groups they led (Fiedler, 1954a, 1954b, 1955, 1956). A measure of Assumed Similarity between Opposites (ASo) was developed. ASo scores were obtained by computing the difference between two sets of semantic differential ratings. One set was the leader's description of his or her Least Preferred Coworker (LPC). The other set were ratings of the leader's Most Preferred Coworker. ASo scores were viewed as indicators of "leadership style" and were correlated with group performance. Predictions of outcomes from scores were mixed in success.

Eventually, the Most Preferred Coworker was abandoned as an assessment and attention focused on LPC. In its most recent version, the examinee is asked to think of everyone with whom he or she has ever worked and then to describe the one person with whom he or she could work least well. This description of one's least-preferred coworker is made by marking eighteen items such as:

friendly :___:___:___:___:___:___:___:___: unfriendly

cooperative :___:___:___:___:___:___:___:___: uncooperative

The other item pairs are rejecting–accepting, tense–relaxed, distant–close, cold–warm, supportive–hostile, boring–interesting, quarrelsome–harmonious, gloomy–cheerful, open–guarded, backbiting–loyal, untrustworthy–trustworthy, considerate–inconsiderate, nasty–nice, agreeable–disagreeable, insincere–sincere, and kind–unkind. The favorable pole of each scale is scored as 8 and the unfavorable pole is scored as 1 (Fiedler, Chemers & Mahar, 1976). The sum of the item scales constitutes the individual's LPC score. A relatively high LPC score (favoring the least preferred coworker) has most generally been conceived by Fiedler (1967a, 1970b) to be indicative of a relationship-motivated person, whereas a low LPC score (rejecting the least preferred coworker) has been conceived to be indicative of a task-motivated person.

### Measurement Properties of LPC

A good deal of evidence is available concerning the internal consistency and stability of LPC. Validity remains a complex question.

*Internal Consistency.* For earlier versions of LPC, Rice (1978a) obtained a mean split-half reliability of .88 for a variety of investigations. Fox, Hill, and Guertin (1973), Shiflett (1974), and Yukl (1970) discovered separate interpersonal and task factors in these earlier LPC scales, but the secondarily scored task factor was seen to be relatively unimportant. Therefore, a newer eighteen-item scale was designed to minimize task factor items and as a consequence was somewhat higher in internal consistency (Fiedler, 1978). In five studies with the newest eighteen-item version, Rice (1979) reported coefficient alpha's of .90, .91, .79, .84, and .89.

*Stability.* Rice (1978a) found twenty-three reports of test–retest reliability ranging from .01 to .91 with a median of .67. Stability indexed by high test–retest correlations were obtained by Chemers and Skrzypek (1972), Fiedler, O'Brien, and Ilgen (1969), Hardy, Sack, and Harpine (1973), Hardy (1971), Hardy (1975), and Hardy and Bohren (1975), where test and retest were separated by several weeks, at least. However, intervening time itself was not strongly associated with stability (as might have been expected) in an analysis of test–retest reliability of studies ranging in intervening times from several days to over two years (Rice, 1978a). Stability can be maintained over extended intervals of time. Bons (1974) obtained a retest reliability for forty-five higher-level army leaders over a five-month period of .72, and Prothero and Fiedler (1974) obtained a retest correlation of .67 for eighteen faculty members of a school of nursing over a sixteen- to twenty-four-month period. But LPC is not necessarily invariant as an attribute of an individual. Fishbein, Landy, and Hatch (1969), E. J. Frank (1973), and Stinson and Tracy (1974) obtained results suggesting that it was a transitory attitude. It appears sensitive to major life changes such as being subjected to stressful contact assignments (Bons, Bass & Komorita, 1970). Temporary shifting can be induced by unsatisfactory work experiences in laboratory experiments. Where instability has been found, it has been attributed to "implicit instructions" of training interventions as to how one should adapt toward poor coworkers (Rice, 1978a). Nevertheless, Schriesheim and Kerr (1977a) pointed out that a significant proportion of persons also changed category from high or low LPC or vice versa. Also, in spite of the satisfactory median test–retest results, Schriesheim, Bannister, and Money (1979) remained unconvinced of LPC stability because of the wide variation in test-retest results.

*Parallel Form Reliability.* Rice (1978a) reported one study in which scales of different item content and different format were fairly well correlated with each other. Different versions of LPC employed have contained differing amounts of task-oriented items (eliminated in the most recent version), and are likely to lack parallel form reliability. This may account for some of the variations in correlations of the LPC version used with other tests and measures of group effectiveness in attempts to determine the meaning of LPC (Schriesheim, Bannister & Money, 1979). But Rice (1979) argued that earlier evidence in which items and formats had been changed yielded correlations of .79, .78, and .66, suggesting that highly correlated parallel forms could be constructed.

*Factor Validity.* As noted earlier, Shiflett (1974) and Yukl (1970) among others demonstrated that the earlier versions of LPC contained two factors, one associated with interpersonal relations; the other, with task-oriented items.

*Content Validity.* If LPC is a measure of the degree to which an individual rejects completely those with whom he or she cannot work, an attitude reflected by describing the least preferred coworker on attributes not directly related to their work, then task-oriented items such as bright–dull, reduce content validity (Schriesheim, Bannister & Money, 1979). The latest eighteen-item version omits such items.

Studies by Fiedler (1967a) and Schriesheim (1979b) have found LPC scores relatively free of social desirability, unlike so many other personality measures.

### Construct Validity

Fiedler and Chemers (1974) observed that "for nearly 20 years, we have been attempting to correlate [LPC] with every conceivable personality trait and every conceivable behavior observation score. By and large these analyses have been uniformly fruitless." But Rice (1978b), who sampled sixty-six out of 114 studies involving over 2,000 empirical relationships between LPC and other variables, felt he succeeded in laying out the nomological network of empirical relationships and concluded more optimistically that although it remains unclear as to whether LPC is a measure of social distance, personal need, cognitive complexity, or motivational hierarchy (as will be discussed later), not in doubt is the interpersonal relations versus task orientation of LPC scores.

The inconsistent results can be seen if one examines LPC's correlations with biographical data and then compares what Bass (1967b) reported about the correlations of direct measures of relations orientation and task orientation. In agreement with Bass's review, low LPC (task orientation) was higher with increasing age (Fiedler & Hoffman, 1962) and with experience (Bons, Bass & Komorita, 1970). But opposite to Bass's conclusions, high LPC (relations orientation) was positively correlated with managerial level (Alpander, 1974) and Protestant rather than Catholic affiliation (Fiedler & Hoffman, 1962). Above and beyond these results, no significant relations of biodata and LPC were found by Eagly (1970), Lawrence and Lorsch (1967a), Nealey and Blood (1968), Shiflett (1974), Posthuma (1970), and A. R. Bass, Fiedler, and Krueger (1964).

Schriesheim and Kerr (1974) have critically noted, as new evidence has emerged, that LPC has been redefined as an orientation toward work, an attitude, a cognitive complexity measure (E. J. Frank, 1973), the ability to conceptually differentiate (Foa, Mitchell & Fiedler, 1971), or an index of a goal hierarchy (Fiedler, 1972a). However, this could be a virtue rather than a fault. (Theoretical constructs like ether should wither away leaving behind empirical facts like the electrical discharge in lightning.) But critics fail to see that the new data justify the new interpretations (Hosking, 1978). For example, Evans and Dermer (1974) correlated LPC scores for 112 business students, managers, and systems analysts with two measures of differentiation and cognitive complexity and found that low LPC scores were associated with cognitive simplicity. Nevertheless, high LPC scores were not unequivocally related to cognitively complexity.

*Interpretive Meaning.* Fiedler (1978) inferred that for the individual who describes his or her least preferred coworker in negative, rejecting terms, the completion of the task is of such overriding importance that it completely colors the perception of all other personality traits attributed to the LPC:

> If I cannot work with you, if you frustrate my need to get the job done, then you can't be any good in other respects. You are unfriendly, unpleasant, tense, distant, etc.
>
> The relationship-motivated individual who sees his or her LPC in relatively more positive terms says, "Getting a job done is not everything. Therefore, even though I can't work with you, you may still be friendly, relaxed, interesting, etc.; in other words, someone with whom I could get along quite well on a personal basis. Thus, the high LPC person looks at the LPC in a more differentiated manner—more interested in the personality of the individual than merely in whether this is or is not someone with whom one can get a job done. (p. 61)

But a high LPC score, Fiedler (1978) notes, does not always predict that a leader will behave with concern for relations orientation nor will low LPC scores of a leader always predict that the leader will push for production, for task completion, or for more structuring. Low LPC scores do not relate much to decision style either.

*LPC, Leader Attitudes, and Decision Making.* McKenna (n.d.) obtained correlations between LPC and style of decision making of 212 chief accountants, as follows: directive—without explanation, $-.12$; directive with explanation, $-.01$; consultative, .06; participative, .03; and delegative, .13. However, Vroom and Yetton (1973) and Sashkin, Taylor, and Tripathi (1974) reported high LPC to relate to preference for participation in resolving conflict. Nebeker and Hansson (1972) found high LPC scores to correlate with judgments about the amount of freedom children should be given in using facilities. Also, as expected, Alpander (1974) obtained positive relations between LPC and judged importance of people-oriented management functions. But in reverse of expectations, Steiner and McDiarmid (1957) found high LPC coinciding with authoritarian beliefs, while LPC was found unrelated significantly to authoritarianism or dogmatism by Evans and Dermer (1974), Fishbein (1969b), Sashkin et al. (1974), and A. R. Bass, Fiedler, and Krueger (1964).

*LPC and Observed Leader Behavior.* Observers and other group members found low LPC to coincide, as expected, with initiating structure and task-oriented leader behavior and high LPC to coincide with relations-oriented behavior in a number of studies (Green, Nebeker & Boni, 1974; Gruenfeld, Rance & Weissenberg, 1969; W. M. Fox, 1974; Yukl, 1970; Meuwese & Fiedler, 1965; Chemers & Skrzypek, 1972; Blades & Fiedler, 1973; Sample & Wilson, 1965; and Sashkin, 1972). Complete reversals (Nealy & Blood, 1968) and negative results were also reported (Evans, 1973; Fiedler, 1967a; Fiedler, O'Brien & Ilgen, 1969; Graen, Orris & Alvarez, 1971; Stinson, 1972; L. R. Anderson, 1964). Interactions with situations had to be considered (W. W. Burke, 1965; Chemers, 1969; Fiedler, 1967a, 1972a; W. K. Graham, 1973; Nealy & Blood, 1968; Rice & Chemers, 1975; Shiflett & Nealy, 1972; Shima, 1968; Green & Nebeker, 1974; Fiedler, 1971b,c,d). LPC scores did not relate much either to initiation or to consultation (Yukl, 1970).

Mitchell (1970a) found that, as expected, high LPC leaders gave more weight to interpersonal relations. Gottheil and Lauterbach (1969) studied military cadets and squads competing in field exercises and found that low LPC (ASo) in the leader was associated with group performance, while high LPC was associated with morale. But contrary to what one might have expected, LPC scores were higher (were relations-oriented) for leaders working under short-term rather than long-term spans (Muller, 1970). Such complete reversals of results and the weakness of LPC scores as indicators of leader behavior led Vroom (1976) to suggest caution in characterizing leadership style on the basis of LPC score alone. But for Fiedler (1967a) it all depends on combining LPC scores with measures of the situation in which the high or low LPC persons find themselves. At any rate, while LPC may prove to discriminate among leaders in ways of consequence to their effectiveness in different contingencies, LPC is not directly symptomatic of the other styles of leadership behavior discussed earlier or yet to be discussed. Hence, the results with LPC must stand alone.

### Support for Alternative Meanings of LPC

As already noted, LPC has gone through a series of interpretations based on empirical studies of its characteristics.

*Social Distance.* At first, Fiedler (1957, 1958) interpreted LPC—then called Assumed Similarity between Opposites (ASo), an index almost perfectly correlated with LPC—as a generalized index of psychological closeness. Low LPC persons were conceived to be more socially or psychologically distant from other group members than were high LPC persons. The assumed similarity data were drawn from person perception research conducted in therapeutic settings. Fiedler (1953a, 1953b) suggested that respondents showed greater assumed similarity between themselves and group members they liked than between themselves and disliked members. Analyses suggested that LPC was a measure of emotional and psychological distance since high LPC persons conformed more in the face of social pressure and were more closely involved with other group members. But following a review of studies of reactions of others to high and low LPC persons, Rice (1978b) concluded that the data were contradictory.

*Relations and Task Orientation.* Fiedler (1964, 1967a) proposed that high LPC persons have strong needs to attain and maintain successful interpersonal relationships. Low LPC persons have strong needs for successful task performance. Four sets of data generally gave some support for this interpretation (although we have noted the many reversals). Behavior of low LPC leaders tended to be task-oriented; behavior of high LPC leaders was generally relations-oriented. Members of groups with high and low LPC leaders tended to exhibit task-oriented and relations-oriented leadership. Higher levels of satisfaction and lower levels of anxiety were among followers in groups with high LPC leaders. Finally, data suggested that low LPC persons gain self-esteem and satisfaction from successful task performance and high LPC persons gain self-esteem and satisfaction from successful interpersonal relations.

*Cognitive Complexity.* Foa, Mitchell, and Fiedler (1971) and Hill (1969a) argued that high LPC persons are more cognitively complex than low LPC persons. They based their proposal on finding positive correlations between LPC and several measures of cognitive complexity. Also, there was greater differentiation (that is, lower correlations) among the factor scores of the LPC scale for high LPC persons. In addition, greater responsiveness to interpersonal factors in the judgments and behavior of high LPC persons had been observed.

Although LPC was found correlated significantly with intelligence in only one of fourteen analyses, in seven of eleven other analyses, LPC was related to specific cognitive tendencies. Thus, Mitchell (1970a,b) found that high LPC leaders gave more weight to power and structure in making discriminations, whereas low LPC leaders gave more weight to interpersonal relations. Foa, Mitchell, and Fiedler (1970) observed that the high LPC leader performed better in situations presenting difficulties in either interpersonal or task relations, thus requiring a high degree of cognitive differentiation between them. Jacoby (1968) found positive correlations between LPC and scores on the Remote Associates Test, a test of creativity. Similarly, Triandis, Mikesell, and Ewen (1962) reported a possibly positive correlation between LPC and judged creativity of two written passages. The findings concerning field independence–dependence as measured by the Embedded Figures Test are less consistent (Weissenberg & Gruenfeld, 1966; Gruenfeld and Arbuthnot, 1968). Furthermore, the following studies failed to support LPC as a measure of cognitive complexity: Fiedler (1954a,b), Fishbein, Landy, and Hatch (1969b), Nealy and Blood (1968), Shiflett (1974), Shima (1968), and Larson and Rowland (1974).

*Motivational Hierarchy.* To account for its variabilities, Fiedler (1972a) saw the need for a "hierarchical" measure of relations or task orientation. Since the high LPC person needs to be related and socially connected to others, he or she will show concern for good interpersonal relations when the situation is tense and anxiety-arousing and when his or her relations with coworkers seem tenuous. But when goals of being related are secure, the relationship-motivated, high LPC person will then seek self-oriented admiration of others and the attainment of prominence. In leader work groups such goals can be attained by showing concern for the task-relevant aspects of the group interaction. In the same way, the major objective of the low LPC person is to accomplish a task and earn self-esteem by doing a good job (D. W. Bishop, 1964). But when task accomplishment presents no problem, friendly, good interpersonal relations with coworkers will be sought in part because the low LPC person believes that good interpersonal relations are conducive to task accomplishment (Fiedler, 1971b).

Nevertheless, this, like previous interpretations, remains controversial. Green and Nebeker (1977) presented data to support it. But evidence by Rice and Chemers (1975) failed to support predictions based on a motivational hierarchy. LPC as a measure of cognitive complexity better fit their results. Similarly, Kunczik (1976a,b) found no support for the motivational hierarchy in studies of the relation of ASo with various personality measures among 1,590 German army recruits and 148 group leaders. Schriesheim and Kerr (1977b) concluded that neither sufficient theoretical nor empirical support has emerged for this interpretation of LPC.

*Value-Attitude.* Based on a review of available evidence, Rice (1978b) agreed that the data did not support the shifting in orientation required by the motivational hierarchy concept of LPC. Rather, the data better fit a simpler conceptualization of LPC as a value and an attitude. For LPC was more consistently and strongly related to attitudes and judgments than to behavioral manifestations. Therefore, LPC is seen as an attitude that reflects differences toward interpersonal relations and task accomplishment. One can make some general statements about the behavior of high and low LPC leaders, but situational variables have a strong influence.

How can Fiedler and Chemers's own beliefs in the uniqueness of LPC be reconciled with Rice's conclusion that LPC is a value-attitude assessment? One problem was Rice's strategy of building his summary around published relationships statistically significant at the 5 percent level. As David Bakin has quipped, significant relationships are more likely to be published than nonsignificant ones. The total universe of studies is probably far greater than what Rice compiled. And with so many in the significant pool at the margin of significance, without attention to the strength of relationships found, it is difficult to accept Rice's evidence as compelling. However, Rice concluded as a consequence of his analysis that LPC was most strongly linked (that is, significant results at the 5 percent level were obtained) with values and attitudes. But even here, only 27 percent of the 313 relationships were significant. Yet even among these, some expected and reasonable inferences could be made with some conviction. Thus, as would be expected from relations-oriented individuals, high LPC persons were found to make more favorable judgments of other group members than did low LPC persons in eighteen of twenty analyses. These include more favorable judgments about the leader, coworkers, and followers in general (Wearing & Bishop, 1967; Hunt, 1971; Wood & Sobel, 1970; Alpander, 1974; Godfrey, Fiedler & Hall, 1959; and Cronbach, Hartmann & Ehart, 1953). Low LPC persons tended to be more favorable than high LPC persons in judgments of their best friends, more preferred coworkers, and loyal subordinates (Godfrey et al., 1959; Jones & Johnson, 1972; A. R. Bass, Fiedler & Krueger, 1964; Bons, Bass & Komorita, 1970; Fiedler, 1958, 1962, 1964, 1967a; Gottheil & Vielhaber, 1966; Shiflett, 1974). Negative results were reported by Chemers (1969), Gottheil and Lauterbach (1969), Hutchins and Fiedler (1960), Steiner and Peters (1958), and Bishop (1967).

Rice (1978b) concluded from this that low LPC persons discriminated more sharply among other group members on task competence than did high LPC persons. LPC was related to judgments about oneself. Low LPC persons judged themselves significantly more favorably than did high LPC persons in thirty-four of 102 analyses, particularly for direct evaluations (88 percent of the relationships were statistically significant) (Bons, Bass & Komorita, 1970; W. M. Fox, 1974; A. R. Bass, Fiedler & Krueger, 1964; D. R. Anderson, 1964; Shiflett, 1974; Fiedler, 1972a; W. W. Burke, 1965; Ayer, 1968).

A complete reversal (not necessarily unexpected) occurred in a Japanese study (Shima, 1968) and negative results were reported by Fiedler (1967a), Gottheil and

Lauterbach (1969), Gottheil and Vielhaber (1966), Gruenfeld and Arbuthnot (1968), Sashkin, Taylor, and Tripathi (1974), Steiner and McDiarmid (1957), Bishop (1967), Strickland (1967), and Golb and Fiedler (1955).

Evidence for the valuing of task success by low LPC persons was seen in the defensiveness shown in their attributions about the cause of task failure and evaluation of the group in terms of the task-relevant ability of the group. In addition, low LPC persons are more optimistic about achieving task success and about earning important rewards as a consequence. At the same time, high LPC persons are more optimistic about interpersonal success and the expectation that interpersonal success will lead to important outcomes (Fiedler, 1967a, 1972a).

Taking everything into account, based on these mixed results, Rice (1978b) agreed with Fiedler that low LPC persons value task success and high LPC persons value interpersonal success. But Fiedler, with his motivational hierarchy, puts the premium on situational considerations determining how such orientations will manifest itself. That is, the main effects of LPC on leader behavior are seen by Fiedler to be weak in comparison to the effects of the interaction of LPC with the favorableness of the situation to the leader.

### Situational Control

In Fiedler's (1967a, 1978) exposition, low (task-oriented) LPC leaders performed better and ran more effective groups when the quality of leader–member relationships, the degree of task structure, and the position power of the leader were either altogether highly favorable or altogether highly unfavorable to the leader. High LPC (relations-oriented) leaders are most effective when one departs from either of these extremes in favorability and control. Eight situations (octants I through VIII) were envisaged by Fiedler, one for each combination of poor or good member relations, low or high structure, and weak or strong leader power. The extremes of octants I and VIII are clearly determined, but octants II and III, for instance, would change place if one gave more weight to task structure than to leader position power, which was subsequently done. The eight octants of the situational control dimension are shown along the horizontal axis of Figure 20.1.

*Weighting.* The relative importance of the three situational factors to a leader's situational control is reflected in a continuous scale constructed by Nebeker (1975) which weights standardized scores for each of the three situational variables as follows: leader situational control = 4(leader–member relations) + 2(task structure) + (positive power).

Theoretical combinations by Fiedler required for octant analysis, that is, octant II is more favorable to the leader than octant III, etcetera, fit empirical multiple regression analyses by Nebeker (1975). Beach and Beach (1978) also reported findings supporting an independent, additive view of the three variables. Beach and Beach (1978) asked students to estimate the probability of success and the situational favorability of a series of hypothetical leadership situations. Situations were presented as having either good or poor leader-member relations, high or low task structure, and high or low position power. A correlation of .89 was obtained between the estimated probability of the leader's success and the degree of situational favorability. A multiple correlation was then

**FIGURE 20.1.** **The Contingency Model of Leadership Effectiveness Based on Original Studies**

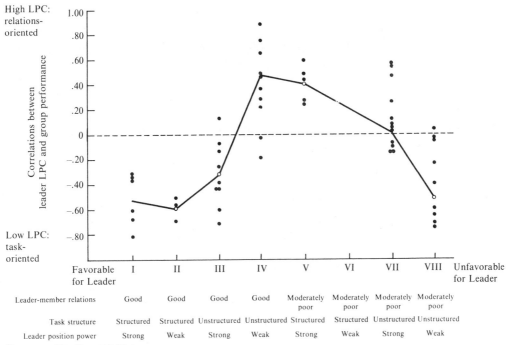

compared with situational favorableness or control as the criterion and the three situational control subscales as predictors. Beta weights obtained were .45 for leader–member relations, .33 for task structure, and .11 for position power, roughly 11:4:1, comparable to the Nebeker formula of 4:2:1.

Further support for the linkage of situational favorability and situational certainty and control come from a study by Mai-Dalton (1975). Participants were asked to complete a leader's In-Basket Test. In moderate-control situations in which high LPC leaders tend to be most effective, these individuals were also most likely to ask for additional information, while low LPC persons manifested most information-searching behavior in high-control situations.

*Measurement.* In Fiedler's original studies, the quality of interpersonal relations were measured by sociometric choices and related measures of liking. Open-hearth steel crews were judged as highly structured and boards of directors or transient student groups as unstructured. The leader's power was judged as high for managers of gasoline stations and as low for the informal leaders of basketball teams. Subsequently, Fiedler developed specific scales to provide measurements of the three variables for any leader–group situation. Other situational variables which have been assumed to determine the leader's situational control include stress, cultural and linguistic heterogeneity, and the leader's amount of experience (Ayer, 1968; Meuwese & Fiedler, 1965; Fiedler, 1966; Fiedler, Meuwese & Oonk, 1961; and Fiedler, O'Brien & Ilgen, 1969).

A group atmosphere scale was developed which correlated .88 with earlier methods of estimating leader–member relations. A recent task structure scale obtained judgments about whether the goal was clearly stated, whether there was only one way to accomplish the task, whether there was one correct answer, and whether results are easy to check for correctness. A leader's position power scale asks such questions as: can the leader evaluate subordinates and recommend rewards, punishments, promotions, and demotions (Fiedler, Chemers & Mahar, 1976). Schriesheim (1979) found the group atmosphere scale free of social desirability, but the position power scale correlated .42 with social desirability.

*Meaning.* Situational favorability with its high degree of control and influence implies that the leader is certain that his or her decisions and actions will have predictable results, will achieve the desired goals, and will satisfy the leader (Fiedler, 1978). At the favorable high control extreme and the unfavorable low extreme, the leader knows where he or she stands in relation to the group. In-between relations are more cloudy for the leader.

*Critique.* Schriesheim and Hosking (1978) found a number of problems with the measurement of situational favorability or situational control. The three variables are assumed to interact in a relatively simple way to determine the amount of influence the leader has over the group, an assumption supported by Beach and Beach's (1978) results. McMahon (1972) questioned the way in which these variables have been measured. Without Beach and Beach's (1978) data, Schriesheim and Kerr (1977a, 1977b) noted that no sufficient justification has been presented for the manner in which the variables were weighted or combined to form a single metric. Although Fiedler (1978) acknowledged the importance of other variables to situational control, he relied on just these three among the many moderator variables of consequence (Filley, House & Kerr, 1976).

### Interaction of Situational Favorability and LPC

Between 1953 and 1964, Fiedler and his associates studied leadership effectiveness in a variety of groups. A "contingency hypothesis" was tested from the results of those studies. Fiedler (1964) plotted the correlations and their medians between LPC scores (actually ASo) and group performance for the different octants—the different levels of situational favorability. Positive median correlations between LPC of the leader and effectiveness of the group showed that the high LPC leaders performed better than did low LPC leaders. Negative median correlations indicated that the low LPC leaders were superior. Fiedler theorized that the curvilinear relation (as seen in Figure 20.1) was an indication that low LPC leaders were more effective than high LPC leaders in very favorable and very unfavorable situations, whereas in situations of intermediate favorability, high LPC leaders were most effective. Such interacting effects of the LPC scores of leaders of U.S. army combat engineer training squads and squad performance were reported by Wearing and Bishop (1974), for example.

### Validity of the Model

Fiedler (1971b), Fiedler and Chemers (1974), Mitchell, Biglan, Oncken, and Fiedler (1970), and Fiedler (1978) have reviewed efforts to validate the contingency model.

*Field Studies.* Typical field validation tests of the model were completed with basketball teams, student surveying teams, bomber crews, tank crews, open-hearth shops, farm supply cooperatives, training groups, departments of a large physical science research laboratory, a chain of supermarkets, and a heavy machinery manufacturing plant. W. Hill (1969) reported analyses in a large electronics firm with assembly line instructors. Fiedler, O'Brien, and Ilgen (1969) worked with public health volunteer groups in Honduras. Shima (1968) studied Japanese student groups; Mitchell (1970b), participants in a church leadership workshop; and Fiedler (1971c), trainees of an executive development program.

*Field Experiments.* A number of experiments and controlled field studies also tested the model. Fiedler (1966) studied ninety-six experimentally assembled groups of Belgian sailors. Half the groups in this study were led by petty officers and half by recruits; half the groups began with structured tasks (routing a ship convoy through ten and then twelve ports), while the other half began with unstructured tasks (writing a recruiting letter).

A controlled experiment was completed by Skrzypek (1969) at West Point. Here, leaders were chosen on the basis of sociometric choices by the members to determine in advance whom the members would choose as a leader. Then half the groups were assembled with preferred leaders and half with nonpreferred leaders. This West Point study, with carefully preselected leaders, replicated the predicted median correlations. The generally supportive results are displayed in Figure 20.2. Similarly, Gruenfeld,

**FIGURE 20.2. Median Correlations Between Leader Performance and Group Performance for the Original Studies, Validation Studies, and the Chemers and Skrzypek (1972) Study**

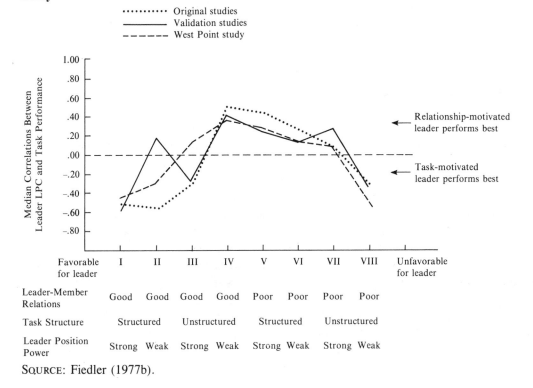

SOURCE: Fiedler (1977b).

Rance, and Weissenberg (1969) studied leaders under high, medium, or low support in experimental groups. Low LPC leaders behaved in a more dominant manner than high LPC leaders regardless of group support, but especially under medium support.

*Laboratory Experiments.* Exceptions to the predicted relations were found in octant II (good member relations–structured–weak power), where the correlations between LPC and group effectiveness in the laboratory studies were positive rather than negative as predicted. The same occurred in laboratory experiments by Hardy (1971, 1975) and Hardy, Sack, and Harpine (1973), who obtained LPC scores one or two weeks prior to their experiment. In two of these studies, leader–member relations were experimentally manipulated by assigning subjects to groups on the basis of preassessed sociometric scores (Hardy, 1975; Hardy et al., 1973).

*Octant Studies.* As shown in Table 20.2, a large number of studies have assessed the hypothesized relationships for various octants. Generally supportive have been: D. R. Anderson (1964), W. W. Burke (1965), Chemers and Skrzypek (1972), Cleven and Fiedler (1956), Csoka (1974, 1975), Cummins (1970), Eagly (1970), Fiedler (1954, 1955, 1966, 1967, 1972), Fiedler and Meuwese (1963), Fiedler, Meuwese, and Oonk (1961), Fiedler, O'Brien, and Ilgen (1969), Green and Nebeker (1977), Hardy (1971), Hawkins (1962), W. Hill (1969), Hovey (1974), Hunt (1967, 1971), Hutchins and Fiedler (1960), Ilgen and O'Brien (1974), Julian (1964), Kunczik (1976a,b), L. K. Michaelson (1973), Muller (1970), Nealy and Blood (1968), Reavis and Derlega (1976), Rice and Chemers (1973, 1975), Sashkin (1972), Sample and Wilson (1965), Schneier (1978), and Ziller (1963).

Illustrative of additional supportive selected octant analyses are dissertation studies of 122 child study teams and their chairpersons in public schools by Jacobs (1976), sixty-four groups of secondary school juniors by Smith (1974), and forty task-oriented three-person experimental groups by Maher (1976). Beebe (1975) manipulated leader position power by instruction, structure, and task assignments. Only good leader–member relations were involved in order to determine the effectiveness of thirty-seven three-person groups for octants II and IV. The correlation of LPC and group productivity was .01 in octant II and .40 in octant IV, both nonsignificant. Nevertheless, the octant IV result was near the usual obtained in many other studies.

*Negative Results.* Generally unsupportive of the contingency model have been studies by Shiflett and Nealy (1972), Lanaghan (1972), Graen, Orris, and Alvares (1971), Vecchio (1977), and Utecht and Heier (1976), among others.

In fifty-nine Illinois elementary schools, analyses of school effectiveness, principal effectiveness, and teacher satisfaction as a function of the behavior of the principals by Lanaghan (1972) provided support for Fiedler's contingency model predictions in only six of eighty situations analyzed (at the 5 percent level of confidence). In seven other situations, results for relations and task orientation were opposite to what would have been predicted by the model. Shiflett and Nealy (1972) compared three-man college groups with very high intellectual ability and with moderate ability on performance in creative tasks in octants III and IV (weak and strong position power). The results of the moderate ability groups supported the prediction of the model, but those of very high ability gave contradictory and nonsignificant findings.

Two laboratory experiments by Graen, Orris, and Alvares (1971) also failed to find the expected outcomes. But Fiedler (1971a) and Chemers and Skrzypek (1972)

**TABLE 20.2**
**Summary of Field and Laboratory Studies Testing the Contingency Model**

| | Octant I | Octant II | Octant III | Octant IV | Octant V | Octant VI | Octant VII | Octant VIII |
|---|---|---|---|---|---|---|---|---|
| **Field Studies** | | | | | | | | |
| Hunt (1967) | −.64* | | | | .21 | | .30 | |
| | −.51 | | | | | | −.30 | |
| Hill (1969) | | .60 | −.80 | | | | | |
| Fiedler, O'Brien, and Ilgen (1969) | | −.10 | −.29 | .00 | | −.24 | .62 | −.51 |
| O'Brien and Fiedler (unpublished) | | −.21 | | .47 | | .67[b] | | −.14 |
| Tumes (1972) | −.47 | −.46 | | .62 | | −.45 | | |
| **Laboratory experiments[a]** | | | | | | | | |
| Belgian Navy (Fiedler, 1966) | −.72 | .37 | −.16 | .08 | .03 | .07 | .26 | −.37 |
| | −.77 | .50 | −.54 | .13 | | .14 | −.27 | .60 |
| Shima (1968) | | .26 | | .71 | | | | |
| Mitchell (1970) | | .24 | | .43 | | | | |
| | | .17 | | .38 | | | | |
| Fiedler Executives | | .34 | | .51 | | | | |
| Chemers and Skrzypek (1972) | −.43 | −.32 | .10 | .35 | .28 | .13 | .08 | −.33 |
| Rice and Chemers (1973) | | | | | | .30 | | −.40 |
| Sashkin (1972) | | | −.29 | | | | | |
| Schneier (1978) | | −.55[e] | | | | | | |
| Median, all studies | −.59 | −.10 | −.29 | .40 | .19 | .13 | .17 | −.35 |
| Median, field studies | −.51 | −.21 | −.29 | .47 | .21 | −.24 | .30 | −.33 |
| Median, laboratory experiments | −.72 | .21 | −.23 | .38 | .16 | .14 | .08 | −.35 |
| Medians in original studies | −.52 | −.58 | −.33 | .47 | .42 | | .05 | −.43 |

Number of correlations in the expected direction: 38
Number of correlations opposite to expected direction: 9
p by binomial test: .01

SOURCE: Fiedler (1971a). Copyright 1971 by the American Psychological Association. Reprinted with permission. Revised by Fiedler (1978), p. 68.
*The correlation between leader's LPC and group effectiveness.

attributed these failures to methodological manipulations inadequate to test the model. Utecht and Heier's (1976) and Vecchio's (1977) results also failed to support the model, but Fiedler (1978) found that the assignment by Vecchio of leaders to mixes of class-mates whom they ranked favorably and unfavorably was an invalid manipulation of good and poor relations. Fiedler (1977) also pointed out that much research designed to test the model has failed to use favorable and unfavorable situations different enough from each other to provide a valid test. Fiedler (1978) concluded that results from field research on work groups uniformly supported the model, but that experimental group research was less supportive.

### Criticisms and Rejoinders

In studies where only an approximate classification of situations—favorable, intermediate, or unfavorable to the leader—was employed, twenty-six of thirty-five correlations of LPC and group effectiveness were as predicted by the model (Fiedler, 1971b). But critics fault these conclusions. Some correlation coefficients were based on subsamples in the same study where one subsample might have had good and the other poor leader–member relations (Ashour, 1973; Graen, Alvares, Orris & Martella, 1970). More general criticisms are that most of the validations are based on concurrent measurement of LPC, leader–member relations, and group performance scores. Leader–member relations measures and even LPC scores may be affected by the group's performance (Vroom, 1976). This cause–effect criticism can be leveled at a good percentage of leadership research, not just results with Fiedler's model (Kerr & Schriesheim, 1974), but Katz and Farris (1976) actually found specific evidence that group performance can cause variations in leader's LPC scores.

Rice (1976) could find only one clear significant pattern relating LPC to group performance among 140 significant relations reported in the literature. When the leader described leader–member relations favorably, low LPC leaders were clearly more effective; twenty-three of twenty-six significant effects (88 percent) under such conditions showed low LPC leaders to be more effective than high LPC leaders. When leaders described leader–member relations as poor, there was no clear pattern. This could be seen as evidence that group performance affected the leader's judgment of the quality of relations with members. But a longitudinal study of eighty intramural basketball teams over a nine-week season by Konar-Goldband, Rice, and Monkarsh (1979) concluded that earlier LPC scores and initial group atmosphere did predict subsequent group performance according to the contingency model. Increments in performance beyond initial levels were most likely for groups with low LPC leaders and good group atmosphere. An additional 7 percent of the variance in performance was accounted for by the interaction of prior group atmosphere and leader LPC. At the same time, they also found that 10 percent of the increments in group atmosphere beyond initial levels was accounted for by LPC interacting with initial group performance. They concluded that a systems approach allowing for cause and effects to flow in both directions was required.

*When Effectiveness Criterion is Restricted.* Particularly supportive conclusions can be reached if the criterion measure of effectiveness is limited to superior's evaluations of the performance of high and low LPC persons in carrying out their tasks as leaders. Rice (1978b) reviewed relevant findings by octants. Almost all predictions are correct. Table 20.3 displays Rice's results.

**TABLE 20.3**
**Extent to Which Contingency Model Fits**
**Obtained Correlations of LPC and Superior Appraisals**
**as a Function of Situational Favorability**

| Octant: | I | II | III | IV | V | VI | VII | VIII |
|---|---|---|---|---|---|---|---|---|
| Predicted direction: | Neg | Neg | Neg | Pos | Pos | Pos | Pos | Neg |
| Correlation of superior's appraisal and LPC in direction predicted by model | 14 | 1 | 18 | — | 12 | 0 | 2 | 16 |
| Total number of analyses | 17 | 1 | 18 | — | 12 | 1 | 2 | 16 |

SOURCE: Rice (1978b).

*Octant Differences.* As noted earlier, octant II, in toto, gave mixed and widely diverging results. However, Fiedler (1978) argued that octant II, requiring a structured task with a powerless leader, may be created experimentally but is unlikely to exist in the field. Fiedler (1978) suggested that leaders placed under such circumstances will find the situation unmanageable. This, of course, fails to explain what is causing the varying results of octant II. A more important question is why octant II, for example, is less favorable to a leader than octant III. In both, two of three variables favor the leader. What is required is differential weighting of the variables. The difference in task structure between octant II and octant III must be given more weight toward favorability than the leader's position power as weak or strong. This weighting was provided by Nebeker (1975) and Beach and Beach (1978). However, except for permitting the graphics to remain the same, a rationale and evidence is needed to support the logic that task structure is twice as important to a leader's control than is the leader's power of position. The same problem exists between octants IV and V where leader–member relations must be given more weight than task structure (as has been done).

*Variance.* Empirically troublesome to some critics is the wide divergence of individual correlation coefficients in each octant as can be seen in Figure 20.1 and Table 20.2. The median for octant IV, for instance, may be .40 in Table 20.2, but the range of results varies from .00 to .71. And interpreting some of the sudden shifts, say, from octant III to octant IV of the median of − .29 to the median of .40 is another problem for which explanations are offered, but not necessarily accepted. Hosking (1978) believes that the most supportable inference about all octants except octant I is that the medians are random departures from zero. Schriesheim and Kerr (1977b) review additional studies which agree with Hosking. Schriesheim and Hosking (1978) conclude that

> when the relevant studies are critically examined, and a distinction drawn between those that constitute adequate tests of the model and those that do not, the results are far from encouraging. Examining both the size and direction of the correlations in each of the eight octants of the situational favorableness dimension, reveals that Fiedler's model really has little empirical support [p. 500].

However, Strube and Garcia (n.d.), using R. Rosenthal's (1978, 1979) meta-analyses of the contingency model felt that all but octants III and VII in Fiedler's original validation were supportable. Octant VI was ignored.

Fiedler (1971a, 1971b, 1973, 1978) has systematically dealt with criticisms of his methodology, of the statistical strength of evidence, of the conceptual meaning of the three variables defining situational favorability, and of the construct assessed by the LPC scales. He even anticipated many of the criticisms (Mitchell, Biglan, Oncken & Fiedler, 1970). As T. R. Mitchell (1972) noted, if the validity of the hypothesized curvilinear relationship is to be tested, all eight octants must be assessed in a given study. Despite the difficulty of obtaining sufficient participants when the group rather than the individual is the unit of analysis, research designs must have adequate sample sizes and resulting statistical power (T. R. Mitchell, 1972).

### Other Situational Variables of Consequence

In a cross-cultural situation, Chemers (1969) trained leaders in the culture of their followers or in the geography of the country. Low LPC leaders were more supportive and developed a more enjoyable group atmosphere in the culture-trained situation than the high LPC leaders in the geography-trained situation. These findings agreed with Fiedler's model in that in favorable situations, high LPC leaders should tend to be concerned with the task, while low LPC leaders should tend to behave in a relationship-oriented manner. In unfavorable situations, the high LPC leaders should be concerned with relations; the low LPC leaders, with task (Cummins, 1970).

*Task.* Whether members of groups were co-acting (side-by-side performance) or interacting did not seem to influence Hunt's (1967) or W. Hill's (1969) supportive but nonsignificant findings.

*Verbal Behavior.* Follower behavior, as well as effectiveness, depends on the favorability of the situation and the leader's LPC. Fiedler (1967a) found that group members made more task-related comments in favorable situations and fewer in unfavorable situations under a high LPC leader. The reverse was true for the low LPC leader. The group made more person-related comments in the unfavorable situation and fewer in the favorable situation under the high LPC leader.

*Follower's LPC.* Follower's LPC also may make a difference. Schuster and Clark (1970) studied first- and second-level supervisors in post offices. Under high LPC second-level supervision, high LPC first-level supervisors were better satisfied than their low LPC peers. With low LPC second-level supervisors, high and low LPC first-level supervisors did not differ in satisfaction.

Hunt (1971) assembled groups with a manager and two supervisors each with two workers to play a business game. Manager–supervisor interaction effects did not account for variance in team performance. However, manager and supervisor effects alone were each significantly related to performance. Low LPC managers and high LPC supervisors had the best performing groups, while the poorest performing groups were those with high LPC managers and low LPC supervisors. The two-level interaction effect also predicted worker satisfaction better than either LPC effect alone.

*Leadership Experience.* The leader's experience changes the situational favorability to the leader (Bons & Fiedler, 1976). Tasks become more routine, leaders get to know their subordinates, and usually leaders can work better with them with continued experience. In addition, the leader learns the expectations of higher authority.

Although the effectiveness of leaders, as a whole, does not necessarily improve with experience (Fiedler, 1970; Fiedler, 1972a), the contingency model predicts that leadership experience will have different effects on the performance of high and low LPC leaders. In a study of infantry squads by Fiedler, Bons, and Hastings (1975a), twenty-eight sergeants who served as squad leaders were evaluated at the time the units were formed and after they had had five months of experience. The sergeants' judgments about their situational control increased over the five months, as expected. The high LPC leaders performed better at first when they had little experience and situational control than five months later. As predicted by the model, the low LPC leaders performed relatively better after they had five months experience and gained in situational control. Similar results were found by Godfrey, Fiedler, and Hall (1959) for the general managers of thirty-two consumer cooperatives, by McNamara (1968) for Canadian elementary and secondary school principals, and by Hardy and Bohren (1975) for college teachers.

Training of leaders generates similar dynamics and results (Chemers, Rice, Sundstrom, and Butler, 1975; Fiedler, 1972a) which will be discussed in Chapter 33.

*Organizational Shifting.* Changes in organization can have similar effects on situational favorability and control as increase in experience. Bons and Fiedler (1976) tested the contingency model using experienced army squad leaders who were given new subordinates, new bosses, or new jobs.

In the stable condition of continuing with the same bosses, subordinates, and jobs, the experienced leaders who were low in LPC were unaffected, but continued stability evidenced a decline in the performance of high LPC leaders as situational control became extreme. The converse occurred for high LPC leaders. But when change in boss, subordinates, or job moved leaders from moderate to low situational control, again the low LPC leader did better.

### Implications

The Contingency Model offers a remedial plan for increasing leader effectiveness different from all other leadership theories. Blake and Mouton (1964), Vroom and Yetton (1974), or R. Likert (1977a) would see the need to educate leaders to improve their styles. In the case of Blake and Mouton, it would be toward "9–9," the one best way. For Likert, it would be toward a democratic style. For Vroom and Yetton, it would depend on the problem situation. But Fiedler (1978) sees an entirely different course of action. Because a leader's LPC is what matters, and LPC is relatively unchanging, then either one must identify and select leaders of high or low LPC to fit given situations or leaders need to know their LPC scores and in what situations they are most effective in order to change the situation rather than themselves. Fiedler argues that changing leader–member relations or task structure or a leader's position power is easier than changing a leader's personality. Leader Match (Fiedler, Chemers & Mahar, 1976), a training program that tries to do this will be discussed in Chapter 33. There are also implications of the Contingency Model for leadership under stressful conditions, which will be examined in Chapter 26.

# 21

## CONSIDERATION AND INITIATING STRUCTURE

### INTRODUCTION

In 1945, Shartle (1950b) organized the Ohio State Leadership Studies. Shartle's background had been the study of job requirements and job performance. At that time nothing existed in the way of satisfactory leadership theory. Research before World War II had sought to identify the different traits of leadership. However, analysis of this research by Bird (1940), W. O. Jenkins (1947), and Stogdill (1948; Chapter 4 of this Handbook) concluded that (1) little success had been attained in attempts to select leaders in terms of traits; (2) numerous traits differentiated leaders from followers; (3) traits demanded in a leader varied from one situation to another; and (4) the trait approach ignored the interaction between the leader and his or her group.

Since the personality trait approach was deemed to have proved fruitless, an attempt was made to study the behaviors rather than the traits of leaders—in other words, to describe individuals' behavior while they acted as leader of a group or organization. Hemphill (1949a) had already initiated such work at the University of Maryland. After joining the Ohio State Leadership Studies, Hemphill and his associates developed a list of approximately 1,800 items describing different aspects of leader behavior. The items were sorted by staff members into nine different categories or hypothetical subscales, with most items assigned to several subscales. However, staff members agreed that 150 items could be assigned to one subscale only. These items were used to develop the first form of the Leader Behavior Description Questionnaire—the LBDQ (Hemphill, 1950a; Hemphill & Coons, 1957).

Several factor-analytic studies by Halpin and Winer (1957) of item intercorrelations produced two factors identified by Hemphill as Consideration and Initiation of Structure in Interaction. Factor analysis of intercorrelations between the subscale scores also tended to yield two factors, and occasionally a third weak factor. The items and the subscales composed of the items measured two different patterns of behavior, rather than nine, as originally hypothesized.

### Two Factors of Leader Behavior Description

*Consideration.* This factor comprised the extent to which a leader exhibited concern for the welfare of the other members of the group. Considerate supervisors expressed appreciation for good work, stressed the importance of job satisfaction, main-

**358**

tained and strengthened self-esteem of subordinates by treating them as equals, made special efforts for subordinates to feel at ease, were easy to approach, put subordinates' suggestions into operation, and obtained approval of subordinates on important matters before going ahead.

The inconsiderate superior criticized subordinates in public, treated them without considering their feelings, threatened their security and refused to accept suggestions or to explain actions.

*Initiation of Structure.* This second factor referred to the extent to which a leader initiated activity in the group, organized it, and defined the way work was to be done. The initiation of structure included·such behavior as insisting on maintaining standards and meeting deadlines, deciding in detail what will be done, and how it should be done. Particularly relevant were defining and structuring the leader's own role and those of the subordinates toward goal attainment.

## PSYCHOMETRIC PROPERTIES

### Three Questionnaires

A form consisting of forty items was developed to measure the two factors of consideration and initiation: the Leader Behavior Description Questionnaire or LBDQ. An industrial version, the Supervisory Behavior Description Questionnaire (SBDQ) by Fleishman (1953c) followed along with a revised Form XII-LBDQ (Stogdill, 1963a).

Intentions, particularly about initiation of structure, differed somewhat in the development of each version. The LBDQ contained fifteen items which asked subordinates to describe the actual structuring behavior of their leader—the leader's behavior in delineating relationships with subordinates, in trying to establish well-defined patterns of communications, and in ways to get the job done (Halpin, 1957b). The SBDQ consisted of twenty items also asking subordinates about their leader's actual structuring behavior. Initiation of structure as measured by the SBDQ was intended to reflect the extent to which the leader organizes and defines interactions among group members, establishes ways to get the job done, schedules, criticizes, and so on (Fleishman, 1972). SBDQ items for initiation of structure were mainly drawn from traits originally conceptualized as domination and production emphasis, while LBDQ items came mostly from original conceptualizations about communication and organization (Schriesheim, House & Kerr, 1976).

The revised LBDQ-XII has ten items measuring initiation of structure—the actions of the leaders that clearly define their own role and let followers know what is expected of them (Stogdill, 1963a).

### Reliability and Validity

As noted by Taylor, Crook, and Dropkin (1961) and Philipsen (1965a), descriptions of the consideration and initiation of structure by leaders are highly stable and consistent from one situation to another. According to Schriesheim and Kerr's (1974) review of the psychometric properties of the LBDQ and SBDQ, they do maintain the high internal consistency that was the basis for their construction. Results range from about .7 to more than .8. That is, items on the consideration behavior scale of each instrument correlate highly with all the other consideration items and do not correlate with items on the initiation scale. Conversely, items on the initiation of structure scale, independent of the consideration items, are highly intercorrelated with all the other structuring items. Schriesheim (1979a) found for 308 public utilities employees that the consideration and initiation scales were significantly robust so that it did not make much difference in a supervisor's scores if one asked a subordinate to describe how the supervisor behaved toward him or her personally (the dyadic approach) or how the supervisor behaved toward the whole work group—the standard approach. Yet the scales leave a lot to be desired. The scales suffer from halo effects and may be plagued by a variety of other response errors, such as leniency and social desirability, as well as a response set to agree rather than disagree (Schriesheim, Kinicki & Schriesheim, 1979). Unknown is whether they are valid measures of true consideration and initiation of structure. Most importantly, as research with these instruments continued, it became apparent that much of what leaders do had been missed. A great deal of leader behavior was being lost in the emphasis on just two factors to account for all the common variance among items describing a leader's behavior. For LBDQ-XII, a variety of additional factored scales were constructed, possibly lacking complete independence from structuring and consideration, yet likely to include much of the missing information of consequence about a leader's behavior.

*Comparison of the Three Forms.* Although all three versions have been used extensively and each has been subjected to further factor analyses (Bish & Schriesheim, 1974; Szilagyi & Sims, 1974; Tscheulin, 1973), a direct comparison of all three became possible after a survey and factor-analytic study of 242 hourly employees by Schriesheim and Stogdill (1975). This comparison study was necessary since, as Korman (1966) and others had noted, the content of the scales varied causing differences in outcomes. The original LBDQ and particularly the SBDQ contained extraneous items such as "needling subordinates for greater effort" measuring punitive, arbitrary, coercive, and dominating behaviors which affected scores on initiation of structure. The LBDQ-XII was considered most free of such autocratic items (Schriesheim & Kerr, 1974). As has usually been found, internal consistency reliabilities were high for scores on both factors derived from the items drawn according to their use in the LBDQ, SBDQ, or LBDQ-XII. For consideration and initiation, reliabilities were .93 and .81 for the LBDQ, .81 and .68 for the SBDQ, and .90 and .78 for the LBDQ-XII. (The reliability of .68 for initiation of structure on the SBDQ was raised to .78 by removing three SBDQ punitive items from the scoring of the scale.) Primary factors extracted indicated that all three versions of leader behavior descriptions contained some degree of arbitrary punitive performance ("the leader demands more than we can do"). But as expected, the pattern was most marked in the SBDQ. A hierarchical factor analysis disclosed the existence of a higher-order factor of rater bias, which appeared in all three questionnaires.

*Other Psychometric Problems*

The items ask about how the leader acts toward the work group rather than toward specific individuals. Critics such as Graen and Schiemann (1978) assume the existence of large variations in the leader's behavior toward different individual members of the work group. But the previously cited findings of Schriesheim (1979a) suggest that the matter has been overblown. Nevertheless, D. M. Lee (1976) asked eighty students to judge the initiation and consideration of their English professors over an eight-week period. Results indicated that individuals differed widely in the cues they used as the basis of their ratings of the same professors.

Other criticisms are that the questionnaires fail to weight the timing, appropriateness, importance, and specificity or generality of responses. They may assess job circumstantial requirements rather than the leader as a person with discretionary opportunities to behave in the manner indicated.

*Leniency Effects.* Seeman (1957) has reported that the LBDQ scales suffered from halo effects. Even making items more detailed was of no help in reducing such halo. Schriesheim, Kinicki, and Schriesheim (1979) completed five studies of the extent to which consideration and initiation of structure were biased by leniency effects. They inferred from the results that leniency response bias, the tendency to describe others in favorable but probably untrue terms, did not particularly affect descriptions of initiation of structure. But even though consideration and leniency are conceptually distinct, they concluded that: (1) consideration items were not socially neutral and were susceptible to leniency; (2) consideration reflected an underlying leniency factor when applied in a field setting; (3) leniency explained much or most of the variance in consideration.

Leniency may explain why consideration tends to correlate higher with other evaluative variables than does initiation of structure (Fleishman, 1973).

*Implicit Theories.* It has been suggested by D. J. Schneider (1973), among others, that respondents report their implicit theories and stereotypes about leaders and leaders' behavior rather than the behavior of the specific leader they are supposed to be describing with the LBDQ. Thus, Eden and Leviathan (1975) noted that leader behavior descriptions using the Survey of Organizations (Chapter 18) of a fictitious manager resulted in a factor structure highly similar to that obtained from descriptions of real managers reported by Taylor and Bowers (1972). In the same way, Rush, Thomas, and Lord (1977) found a high degree of congruence between factor structures obtained from descriptions of a fictitious supervisor using LBDQ-XII and descriptions of real leaders from a field study by Schriesheim and Stogdill (1975). In both studies, the authors concluded that since practically identical factor structures emerged for fictitious and real, specific leaders, the actual behavior of a leader is relatively unimportant for behavior descriptions since descriptions are based mainly on implicit theories or stereotypes. In turn, we might suggest that the tendency to project such results tells us more about the subordinate than about the leader being rated. But this tendency to project or to use stereotypes occurs as a consequence of ambiguity and absence of specific information about the leader to be rated. Schriesheim and DeNisi (1978) studied 110 bank employees and 205 manufacturing plant workers, who used LBDQ-XII to describe supervisors in general after first describing their own supervisor. The investigators found the expected identity of the factors structures emerging from the general and specific descriptions when each was analyzed separately. However, separate real and imaginary factors emerged when an analysis was made of the combined data which gave the opportunity for statistical differentiation. As before, in both real and imaginary descriptions, initiation of structure and consideration were correlated above .50 with reliabilities ranging from .84 to .87.

Particularly important, Schriesheim and DeNisi found that while satisfaction with one's real supervisor correlated between .51 and .75 with descriptions of the actual consideration and initiation of the real supervisors, such satisfaction with one's real supervisor correlated only .23 and − .03 with scores for initiating structure and consideration for the stereotypes of the supervisor described by the banking employees, and .29 and .19 with the manufacturing workers' stereotypes of supervisory behavior. Leniency scores were expected to, and did, correlate more highly with the LBDQ-XII descriptions of real rather than stereotypes of supervisors.

Subsequent experimentation by Schriesheim and DeNisi with 360 undergraduates strongly supported the contention that as more specific information became available to respondents, their LBDQ responses became more accurate and were less likely to depend on implicit theories and stereotypes. These results are consistent with Bass, Valenzi, et al. (1975), who showed that subordinates describing the same real leader were in much more significant agreement with each other than with subordinates describing other leaders.

*Lack of Relation to Self-Rated Leader Behavior and Opinions.* As reported by Solomon (1976a) for self-rated directive versus participative leadership, D. T. Campbell (1956), Bass (1957a), Besco and Lawshe (1959), Graham and Gleno (1970), and T. R. Mitchell (1970) reported little relation between leaders' self-descriptions of their initiation and consideration and their subordinates' LBDQ descriptions of the leaders. There is a similarly low relation between what leaders say they should do using the Leadership Opinion Questionnaire (LOQ) and what they do do according to LBDQs by their subordinates (Schriesheim & Kerr, 1974).

### Relation between Consideration and Initiation Structure

Theoretically, given the original orthogonal factor structure, initiation and consideration should be independent, but such is not the case. Schriesheim, House, and Kerr (1976) re-examined Weissenberg and Kavanagh's (1972) review data along with work published subsequently. In eleven of thirteen studies using the LBDQ, a positive correlation was reported. The median correlation for the thirteen analyses was .45. Likewise for the LBDQ-XII for ten studies, the median correlation was .52 between initiation of structure and consideration. But eleven of the sixteen studies that used the SBDQ, with its autocratic, arbitrary items dealing with initiation of structure, yielded negative correlations as low as − .57 between consideration and initiation. The median correlation was − .05.

## ALTERNATIVE AND ADDITIONAL SCALES

### Industrial Example

Oldham (1976), among others, developed alternative and additional scales of leader behavior. These included: personally rewarding, personally punishing, setting goals, designing feedback systems, placing personnel, and designing job systems. These scales were higher in relation to effectiveness than were measures of consideration and initiation of structure.

*Educational Example*

Halpin and Croft (1962) also were not satisfied that leader behavior could be adequately described with just two factors. Using items containing additional content about school principals, as well as LBDQ items, they extracted four factors to account for the common variance in the obtained descriptions of school principals' behavior: aloofness-formality and social distance; production emphasis—pushing for results; thrust—personal hard work and task structure; and consideration—concern for comfort and welfare of followers. These scales for describing the leader behavior of school principals were supplemented by four scales used to describe the behavior of teachers as follows: disengagement—clique formation, withdrawal; hindrance—frustration from routine and overwork; esprit—high morale, enthusiasm; and intimacy—mutual liking and teamwork.

When 71 schools were classified into six categories according to school climate, an open school climate was found associated with teacher esprit under a principal high in thrust. An autonomous climate produced teacher intimacy under an aloof leader. A controlled climate resulted in teacher hindrance under a principal who pushed for production. A familiar climate was associated with teacher disengagement under a considerate principal. A climate with potential resulted in teacher disengagement under a principal attempting to solve the problem by exhibiting consideration along with an emphasis on production. A closed climate also resulted in teacher disengagement under an aloof principal. The above results yielded considerably more insight into the dynamic interplay between school climate, leader behavior, and teacher response than could be produced by the use of just two factors to describe leader behavior.

## PSYCHOMETRIC PROPERTIES OF ADDITIONAL SCALES OF LEADERSHIP BEHAVIOR DESCRIPTION QUESTIONNAIRE—FORM XII

*Description*

Based on a theoretical analysis of the differentiation of roles in groups, Stogdill (1959) proposed ten additional patterns of behavior involved in leadership, conceptually independent of consideration and initiation of structure, which should be included in LBDQ-XII along with consideration and initiation of structure: (1) representation—speaks and acts as representative of the group; (2) reconciliation—reconciles conflicting organizational demands and reduces disorder to system; (3) tolerance of uncertainty—is able to tolerate uncertainty and postponement without anxiety or upset; (4) persuasiveness—uses persuasion and argument effectively, exhibits strong convictions; (5) tolerance of freedom—allows followers scope for initiative, decision and action; (6) role retention—actively exercises leadership role rather than surrendering leadership to others; (7) production emphasis—applies pressure for productive output; (8) predictive accuracy—exhibits foresight and ability to predict outcomes accurately; (9) integration—maintains a closely knit organization, resolves intermember conflicts; (10) influence with supervisors—maintains cordial relations with superiors, has influence with them, is striving for higher status.

Saris (1969) developed items for a subscale which he identified as responsibility reference. Yukl (1971) also produced an additional subscale designed to measure decision centralization.

### Interdescriber Agreement

In the study of a governmental organization (Day, 1968), high-ranking administrators were described by two male and two female subordinates. Correlations were computed to determine the extent to which pairs of subordinates agreed in descriptions of their immediate superiors. The greatest agreement was shown by pairs of female subordinates describing their female superiors. Their agreement was represented by correlations ranging from .39 (integration) to .73 (retention of the leadership role). The least agreement was shown by pairs of male subordinates describing their female superiors. Their correlations ranged from − .02 (tolerance of freedom) to .53 (retention of the leadership role). Pairs of female subordinates exhibited higher degrees of agreement than did male subordinates in descriptions of male superiors. The only exceptions were for representation, production emphasis, integration, and influence with superiors.

In general, the scales with the highest degrees of interdescriber agreement across groups of describers were demand reconciliation, tolerance of uncertainty, persuasiveness, role retention, predictive accuracy, and influence with superiors. The scales with the lowest degrees of agreement across samples were representation, tolerance of freedom, and integration.

### Differential Validities

To test the differential validity of several subscales of LBDQ-XII, Stogdill (1969), with the assistance of a playwright, wrote a scenario for each of six subscales (consideration, structure, representation, tolerance of freedom, production emphasis, and superior orientation). The items in a subscale were used as a basis for writing the scenario for that pattern of behavior. Experienced actors played the roles of supervisor and workers. Each role was played by two different actors, and each actor played two different roles. Motion pictures were made of the role performances. Observers used LBDQ-XII to describe the supervisor's behavior. No significant differences were found between two different actors playing the same role. Still, the actors playing a given role were described as behaving significantly more like that role than the other roles.

Since each role was designed to portray the behaviors represented by the items on a respective subscale and since the same items were used by observers to describe enactment of the role, Stogdill concluded that the scales measured what they purported to measure.

### Factor Validation

Data collected by Stogdill, Goode, and Day (1963a,b, 1964, 1965) used several subscales to obtain descriptions of the leader behavior of United States senators, corporation presidents, presidents of international labor unions, and presidents of colleges and universities. For leaders in each type of locale, the scores for the subscales were intercorrelated and factor-analyzed. In general, the results suggested that each factor was strongly dominated by a single subscale. However, two factors, production emphasis and tolerance for uncertainty, contained substantial loadings from more than one subscale in some locales, as shown in Table 21.1.

For example, senators and corporation presidents who push for production also emphasize structuring. More tolerant senators appear to work more to reduce conflicting demands than those senators lacking in tolerance. All the other factors emerged only with one scale loaded highly in all locales, as shown in Table 21.2. For example, the representation factor emerged in each of the four factor analyses for each of the four locales with only the representation subscale correlated highly with it in all four analyses. The representation subscale correlated with the representation factor, .80, .94, .92, and .92, in the four locales. Similarly, as seen in Table 21.2, the role retention subscale correlated only with its own retention factor, .89, .93, .81, and .92.

Surprisingly, reconciliation of conflicting demands failed to emerge as a factor differentiating college presidents since this seems to be one of their main functions. Orientation to superiors, of course, did not fit with a senator's role, nor did union presidents differ in orientation to higher authority. Finally, the leader behavior of senators and college presidents did not differ enough in description by their followers to generate the factor of predictive accuracy in their respective analyses.

**TABLE 21.1**
**Correlations of Subscales with Factors A and B in LBDQ-XII**

| | Factor A. Production Emphasis | | | |
|---|---|---|---|---|
| Subscale | *Senate* | *Corporation* | *Union* | *College* |
| Production emphasis | .97 | .95 | .94 | .91 |
| Structuring | .58 | .48 | — | — |
| | Factor B. Tolerance of Uncertainty | | | |
| Subscale | *Senate* | *Corporation* | *Union* | *College* |
| Tolerance of uncertainty | .93 | .95 | .94 | .94 |
| Demand reconciliation | .47 | — | — | — |

*Further Factor Studies of LBDQ-XII*

Slightly different results emerged when all the items of LBDQ-XII were intercorrelated and factor-analyzed for three additional locales. Ten factors emerged as follows: (1) general persuasive leadership; (2) tolerance of uncertainty; (3) tolerance of follower freedom of action; (4) representation of the group; (5) influence with superiors; (6) production emphasis; (7) structuring expectations; (8) consideration (I); (9) consideration (II); and (10) retention of the leadership role.

The most numerous and most highly loaded items on the first, a general factor, were measures of persuasiveness. Other subscales with items on the factor were about reconciliation of conflicting demands, structuring expectations, retention of the leadership role, influence with superiors, consideration, and production emphasis. These items represented the followers' general impression of the leaders. (This probably comes close to what we will say in Chapter 22 about laissez-faire leadership versus the motivation to

**TABLE 21.2**

**Correlations of the Subscale with the Factor with the Same Name**

| | Factor | Senate | Corporation | Union | College |
|---|---|---|---|---|---|
| C | Representation | .80 | .94 | .92 | .92 |
| D | Role retention | .89 | .93 | .81 | .95 |
| E | Tolerance of freedom | .97 | .89 | .97 | .89 |
| F | Persuasiveness | .95 | .90 | .74 | .77 |
| G | Consideration | .69 | .94 | .90 | .86 |
| H | Structuring | .67 | .71 | .71 | .82 |
| I | Demand reconciliation | .63 | .83 | .76 | a |
| J | Superior orientation | a | .96 | a | .94 |
| K | Predictive accuracy | a | .77 | .80 | a |

[a] Scale loaded below .40.

manage actively.) The items dealt with being persuasive, as well as being able to reconcile conflicting demands, structure expectations regarding the task to be performed, hold the leadership role, and influence the superiors. In fulfilling these functions, leaders were seen as considerate of followers' welfare.

Each of the remaining factors tended to be composed of items from a single subscale. Some contained stray items from other subscales. Consideration broke down into two separate factors, to be discussed later in connection with J. A. Miller's (1973b) hierarchical analysis.

The first nine factors showed similar loadings across the three organizations. Retention of the leadership role appeared as a separate factor only in the state government organization. All subscales except those dealing in the tolerance of uncertainty, tolerance of freedom, and representation contributed some items to the general factor. However, all subscales except persuasiveness and demand reconciliation emerged as separate factors differentiated one from the other. These findings indicate that leader behavior is indeed complex in structure and that followers are able to differentiate between different aspects of behavior. Although persuasiveness and demand reconciliation did not emerge as separate factors, their high loadings on the general factor provided valuable additional insight into the nature of leadership, strongly suggesting that this general factor may be particularly useful given what will be said in the next chapter about laissez-faire leadership, its opposite.

*Two Higher-Order Dimensions.* A. F. Brown (1967) used the LBDQ-XII to obtain descriptions of 170 principals by 1,551 teachers in Canadian schools. He found that two factors accounted for 76 percent of the total factor variance. The loadings for the two factors, when plotted against each other, assumed a circumflex form. Production emphasis, structure, and representation clustered about one axis; tolerance of uncertainty, tolerance of freedom, and consideration clustered about the other. The loadings for the remaining factors fell between the clusters at the extremes of the orthogonal axes.

A plot of factor loadings obtained for university presidents (Stogdill, Goode & Day, 1965) produced similar results. Representation, structure, production emphasis, and persuasiveness clustered around one axis; freedom, uncertainty, and consideration clustered around a second axis.

Marder (1960) obtained a somewhat different pattern of loadings when military rather than educational leaders were studied. The data consisted of 235 descriptions of army officers by enlisted men. Productivity and initiation of structure centered around one axis; freedom and uncertainty, around the other. Consideration was displaced toward the central cluster of items.

*Alternative Analyses and Outcomes.* There are different schools of thought regarding the use of factor analysis. One school maintains that as much of the total factor variance as possible should be explained in terms of a general factor. Another school holds that rotational procedures, such as the varimax which reduces the magnitude of the general factor, are legitimate. The former school, while admitting that systems of events in the real world may involve more than two factors, maintains that human perception contains a large element of bias and halo which should be removed in the general factor before attempting to determine the structure of measurements representing the real world. The second school argues that the apparent halo in the general factor has its equivalent in the opacity of the real world and that the purpose of research is to reduce this opacity by making full use of all the structure differentiated by human perception. Such structure as perceived should not be permitted to remain hidden in the general factor.

If one prefers a two-factor theory of leader behavior, initiation of structure and production emphasis appear to define one of the factors. Tolerance of freedom and tolerance of uncertainty tend to define the other. Consideration makes some contribution to the second factor, while representation and persuasiveness contribute to the first.

A two-factor solution, which leaves a considerable amount of the total variance unexplained, can always be obtained in the analyses of leader behavior descriptions. Nevertheless, a multifactor solution should not be rejected until its consequences have been thoroughly explored and it has been proved untenable. Furthermore, we can reconcile the dilemma, as J. A. Miller (1973b) and Schriesheim and Stogdill (1975) did, by recourse to hierarchical factor analysis. The former exploited rotation and differentiation; the latter, the general evaluative bias factor. Finally, the high positive association of consideration and initiation of structure as measured by LBDQ-XII suggests that a single, general factor, solution may be warranted. Nevertheless, with reference to the contents of the LBDQs, the two-factor framework for describing leader behavior, consideration and initiation of structure, emerge consistently from factor analyses when no additional constraints are placed on the analyses.

### Refining Initiation and Consideration

But consideration and initiation of structure can be finely factored in a number of ways by adding more detailed behaviors and pursuing reconceptualizations about initiation and consideration. Stogdill (1963a) added a variety of new content dealing with different domains of leader behavior to obtain the nine additional LBDQ scales for LBDQ-XII. More detail about initiation and consideration can also result in more intensification of analysis. Yukl (1971) demonstrated the feasibility of a three-factor approach (consideration, initiation of structure, and decision centralization). Another three-factor approach—initiating structure, participation, and decision making—was pursued by R. H. Johnson (1973). Wofford (1971) expanded the framework of leader behavior to five factor-analytically derived behavior dimensions (group achievement and order, personal enhancement, personal interaction, dynamic achievement, security, and mainte-nance). Using several thousand members of a nation-wide business fraternity describing their leaders on both a new instrument, the FFTQ, and the comparable scales of the LBDQ-XII, Yukl and Hunt (1976) demonstrated some degree of communalities between scales purporting to deal with similar dimensions; yet overall they revealed an unfortu-nate lack of equivalence.

*Hierarchical Factor Analysis.* Because of earlier reported findings of such lack of equivalence (Korman, 1966; Lowin, 1968; Yukl, 1971; House, 1972), to better un-derstand the similarities and differences in the measures of consideration and initiation of structure, R. A. Miller (1973b) assembled 160 items from nine frequently referenced standard instruments used in published research concerning leadership behavior. Particu-lar attention was given to the Ohio State LBDQ, LOQ, and SBDQ items and to the leadership items in the Michigan Institute for Social Research Survey of Organizations (Taylor & Bowers, 1972), both because of the extensive previous work devoted to the development of these items and because of the widespread prominence of the classifica-tion systems deriving from their use (Bowers & Seashore, 1966), as already noted in Chapters 18 and 20. The original item pool included items from the following: the LBDQ (Halpin & Winer, 1957); Survey of Organizations (Taylor & Bowers, 1972); interaction process analysis (Bales, 1950); the Job Descriptive Index (Smith, Kendall & Hulin, 1969); the Orientation Inventory (Bass, 1963); scale anchors used to describe a ''continuum of leadership behavior'' (Tannenbaum & Schmidt, 1958); six categorical statements describing a continuum of decision-making styles (Vroom & Yetton, 1974); the five bases of social power (French & Raven, 1959); and adjectives used by Fiedler (1967a) for measuring LPC. Miller drew seventy-three nonduplicative items from the pool of 160 that were most specific and that were descriptive rather than evaluative, and then collected data from 300 respondents from ten organizations including social agen-cies, industrial firms, and military organization.

The hierarchical solution was achieved by first completing a factor analysis stipu-lating a two-factor solution. Then, the process was repeated stipulating a three-factor solution, then a four-factor solution, and so on (Zavala, 1971). Miller then successively rotated all twelve principal components, using the varimax (orthogonal) rotation algo-rithm. At each level, interpretable solutions reflecting familiar leader behavior factors emerged. The two-factor solution clearly paralleled consideration and initiation of struc-ture.

Other clearly identifiable factors discovered in previous research emerged in suc-cessive levels of analysis, each calling for an additional factor. Production and goal emphasis and close supervision split apart as subfactors of initiating structure in the four-factor solution. Participation emerged at level six, information-sharing at seven, and supporting (the narrowly interpersonal interpretation of consideration) at level eight. Enforcing rules and procedures emerged as a subfactor of close supervision at level nine, and so forth. The emergence of the factors and their hierarchical linkages are shown in Figure 21.1.

A subsequent higher-order factor analysis based on an oblique solution obtained a higher-order factor of consideration and another of initiation of structure. Miller con-cluded from his hierarchical and higher-order analyses that consideration was not a behavior description but rather a motivational inference.

It can be seen from Figure 21.1 that consideration includes what ordinarily is regarded as concern for the welfare of subordinates such as supportive behavior and sharing of information, but it also appears to link to participative group decision making, to abdication, and to delegation.

## IDEAL LEADER BEHAVIOR DESCRIPTIONS

### Ideal Form—What a Leader Should Do

Hemphill, Seigel, and Westie (1951) developed an ideal form of the LBDQ asking respondents to describe how their leader *should* behave, not, as on the LBDQ, how their

**FIGURE 21.1.  The Hierarchical Structure of Leadership Behaviors**

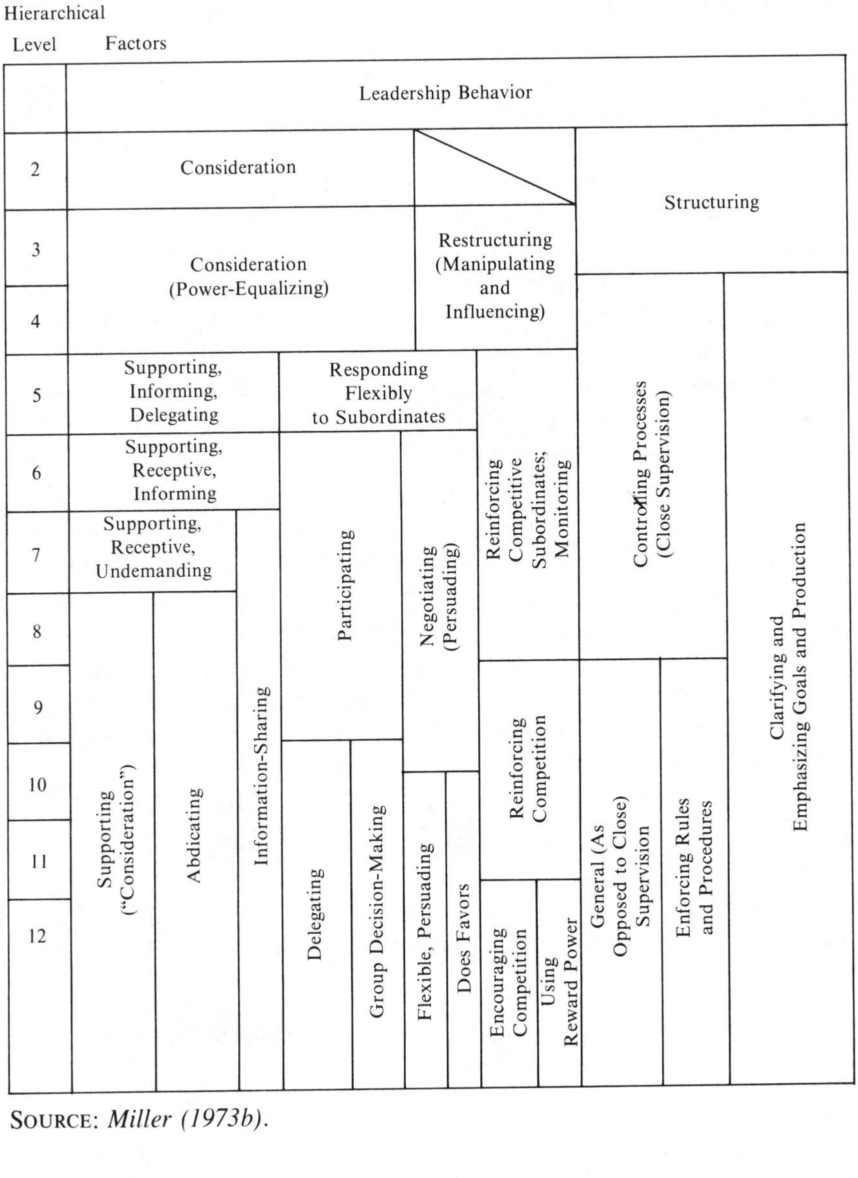

SOURCE: *Miller (1973b).*

leader was actually seen to behave. Thus, for example, in a study of fifty principals, J. E. Hunt (1968) found that teachers described principals as lower in actual consideration and structure than they believed ideal. Such discrepancies between subordinates' descriptions of what their leaders should do and what they actually did were more highly related to various measures of group performance than were desired or observed behavior alone. Such discrepancies were a measure of dissatisfaction with the leader's performance and as a consequence were more strongly related to various group outcomes.

Stogdill, Scott, and Jaynes (1956) studied a large military research organization in which executives and their subordinates each described themselves on the real and ideal forms of the LBDQ. In addition, subordinates described their superiors on the real and ideal forms. When superiors were really high in structuring according to their subordinates, the subordinates described them as having less responsibility than they should, as delegating more than they should, and as devoting more time than they should to teaching. When superiors were really high in consideration according to their subordinates, the subordinates expected them to assume more responsibility than they were perceived to assume, to devote more time than necessary to scheduling, and to devote less time to teaching and mathematical computation. When superiors were really high in initiating structure as seen by their subordinates, they perceived themselves devoting more time than they should to evaluation, consultating peers, and teaching, and not enough time to professional consultation. When superiors were described as actually high in consideration, subordinates perceived themselves as having more responsibility than they should. They also reported that they ought to devote more time than they do to coordination, professional consultation, and writing reports, but less time in preparing charts. Leader initiation of structure was more highly related to subordinates' actual work performance. Leader consideration, on the other hand, was more highly related to subordinates' expectations about their work performance. These results suggest that leader initiation is related to subordinates' objective behavior, while leader consideration exerts its impact on followers' expectations and values. Furthermore, the results suggest that consideration and structure are differentially related to leaders' work performance and produce an impact upon the performance of subordinates. When superiors are described as really high in initiation of structure, their subordinates feel that superiors ought to have more responsibility and to delegate less. However, when superiors are high in actual consideration, subordinates feel that they themselves are overburdened with responsibilities.

*Leadership Opinion Questionnaire.* Fleishman's (1957b) Leadership Opinion Questionnaire (LOQ) differed from the "ideal" form developed by Hemphill and revised by Halpin (1957c) in that Fleishman's LOQ scale for initiation of structure contained several items that were found afterward (Stogdill, Goode & Day, 1962) to measure production emphasis. Production emphasis correlates with initiating structure but is not identical with it.

Following a review, Schriesheim and Kerr (1974) felt that the test-retest reliability of the LOQ had been adequately demonstrated over a one- to three-month period.

## ANTECEDENTS AND CORRELATES OF CONSIDERATION AND INITIATION OF STRUCTURE

The internal consistency and test–retest reliability of the various scales of leader behavior description may be satisfactory but content differences make it mandatory in order to understand their effects, to distinguish whether the measures were based on the LBDQ, SBDQ, LOQ, or LBDQ-XII. We now turn to an examination of antecedent conditions that influence the extent to which a particular leader behavior is exhibited and the concurrent conditions that are associated with such behavior. A clear-cut example of the impact of organizational context on the behavior of the individual leaders within it was provided by Stanton (1960) with the case of two medium-sized firms. Authoritarian policies were dominant in one company. It was interested only in profits. Subordinates had to understand what was expected of them. Personal qualities of leadership were emphasized. All company information was restricted to management except where it clearly applied to an employee's job. The second firm had democratic policies. It was concerned about employee well-being as well as profits. Participation was stressed as a matter of policy. There was a maximum effort to inform employees about company matters. Supervisors under democratic policies favored more consideration; supervisors under authoritarian policies favored more initiation.

### Interpreting Concurrent Analyses

Most of the research available consists of surveys in which leader behavior and other variables about the leader or the situation were measured concurrently. We infer that a relatively invariant attribute such as the intelligence of the leader is an antecedent to the leader's display of consideration or initiation as seen by colleagues. The leader's educational level is likewise obviously antecedent to the leader's behavior. The leader behavior cannot cause a change in his or her intelligence or educational level. With less confidence, we will make similar inferences about situational influences on leader behavior, because the leader can influence the situation just as the situation is influencing the leader. If we find a concurrent association between company policy and the leader behavior of the first-line supervisor, it seems more reasonable to infer that the policy influenced the supervisors, although it is also possible that the policy reflects the continuing behavior of the supervisors. If we find an association between leader behavior and conflict in the work group, it is more likely that the leader is a source of the conflict. Nevertheless, the continuing conflict is likely to be influencing the leader's behavior.

The national origin of the leader's organization can be antecedent to the leader's behavior, but it is impossible to conceive that the average leader's behavior in the organization would affect the origin of the organization. But suppose we obtain a positive association between a leader's consideration and an absence of conflict within a group. The most plausible hypothesis is likely to be that the leader's behavior contributes to an absence of conflict, but the harmony within the group makes it possible for the leader to be more considerate. Therefore, in examining these concurrent results, we will leave to the reader the need to try to appreciate the most appropriate meaning to draw from the reported associations. We will reserve for a later section the findings on leader behavior and such criteria of leader effectiveness as subordinate productivity, satisfaction, cohesion, and role clarity. Again, it can be seen that although such criteria can be a consequence of leader behavior, they may influence the leader's as well.

*Motivation and Ability.* In a study of ROTC cadets, Fleishman (1957a) found that candidates' attitudes toward consideration and initiation were not related to their intelligence or level of aspiration. But in a study of eighty-seven school principals described by 726 teachers, Rooker (1968) found that principals with strong need for achievement were described as high in tolerance of freedom and reconciliation of conflicting demands. However, Tronc and Enns (1969) found that promotion-oriented executives tended to emphasize structure over consideration to a greater degree than executives less highly oriented toward promotion. And in a study of college deans, Lindemuth (1969) reported that their consideration was related to their scholarship, propriety, and practicality.

*Values and Attitudes.* Fleishman (1957a) did find that the leader's endorsement of authoritarian attitudes was negatively related to initiation of structure ($r = -.29$), but it was not related to consideration ($r = -.03$). Similarly, Stanton (1960) found no relation between consideration and authoritarianism. In the same way, Flocco (1969), who studied 1,200 school administrators, showed that consideration and initiating structure were unrelated to personality test scores on dogmatism.

Fleishman (1957b) also found that supervisors favoring consideration tend to make high scores on a personality scale of benevolence, whereas those favoring initiation are more meticulous and sociable. Also, Fleishman and Peters (1962) found that for supervisors independence was correlated negatively with both initiation of structure ($r = -.27$) and consideration ($r = -.27$); benevolence was positively but not significantly correlated with initiation of structure ($r = .19$) and consideration ($r = .35$). Consideration was more highly related than structure to ratings of social adjustment and charm, according to Marks and Jenkins (1965). Again, Litzinger (1965) reported that those managers favoring initiation of structure tended to value support (being treated with understanding and encouragement), whereas those favoring consideration tended to place low value on independence.

Newport (1962) studied forty-eight cadet flight leaders, each described on the LBDQ by seven flight members. Those leaders described as equally high in showing consideration and structuring differed from those described as equally low on the two scales as follows: (1) strong desire for individual freedom of expression; (2) little resistance to social pressure; (3) strong desire for power; (4) strong in cooperativeness; and (5) strong in aggressive attitudes.

In line with expectations, in a study of nursing supervisors, R. M. Anderson (1964) found that those who preferred nursing care activities were described as high in consideration. Those supervisors who preferred coordinating activities were not described high in structuring. According to analyses by Stromberg (1967), school principals with emergent value systems were perceived by teachers as high in initiating structure, whereas those with traditional value orientations were perceived as high in consideration. Durand and Nord (1976) noted that forty-five managers in a midwestern textile and plastics firm were seen by their subordinates as higher on both initiation of structure and consideration if the managers were externally rather than internally controlled, that is, if the managers believed that personal outcomes were due to forces outside their own control rather than to their own actions.

*Cognitive Complexity.* A number of studies of the influence of cognitive complexity and leader behavior have been completed with positive findings, particularly when using the additional LBDQ-XII scales. W. R. Kelley (1968) reported that school superintendents high in cognitive complexity were also described as high in predictive accuracy and reconciliation of conflicting demands. Again, Streufert, Streufert, and Castore (1968) obtained significant differences between emergent leaders who varied in perceptual complexity scores in a negotiations game. Leaders lower in cognitive complexity scored higher on initiating structure, production emphasis, and reconciliation. Leaders higher in cognitive complexity scored higher on tolerance of uncertainty, retaining the leadership role, consideration, and predictive accuracy. Results obtained by Weissenberg and Gruenfeld (1966) indicated that supervisors scoring high in field independence endorsed less consideration than did those who were field-dependent. However, Erez (1979) found for forty-five Israeli managers with engineering backgrounds that self-described consideration was positively related to field independence and to social intelligence, whereas initiating structure was negatively related to these two factors. However, Rowland and Scott (1968) failed to find any relation between LOQ consideration and social sensitivity of supervisors.

*Personality.* Fleishman and Salter (1963) measured empathy in terms of supervisors' ability to guess how their subordinates would fill out a self-description questionnaire. Empathy was significantly related to employee descriptions of the supervisors' consideration but not to their structuring. L. V. Gordon (1963a) showed that personal ascendancy was positively and significantly related to initiating structure ($r = .38$) but negatively related to consideration ($r = -.21$). Neither leader behavior score was related to responsibility, emotional stability, or sociability. Sociability, however, was correlated .21 with initiating structure, while the correlation with consideration was $-.06$. But many investigators found LBDQ and LOQ scores unrelated to personality measures. For example, Greenwood and McNamara (1969), who studied 593 managerial and premanagerial personnel in an assessment program involving manufacturing exercises, reported that managerial attitudes toward consideration and structure were not related to personality test scores or attitudes. Likewise, T. O. Bell (1969) found consideration and structure unrelated to the personality test scores of school superintendents, to superintendent attitude toward change, and to innovativeness in the school district. J. P. Siegel (1969), too, reported that neither consideration nor initiation of structure was significantly related to personality measures.

### Other Personal Attributes

Initiation and consideration are greater among more satisfied leaders. Their decision tendencies and attempts to lead are also related.

*Leader Satisfaction.* Managers who are more satisfied with their circumstances tend to earn higher scores in their leader behavior, according to Siegel (1969). Again, A. F. Brown (1966) reported that highly satisfied school principals were described higher than dissatisfied principals on all subscales except tolerance of uncertainty.

*Decision Making.* Risky decision making by supervisors was studied by Rim (1965) who reported that male supervisors scoring high on both consideration and initiating structure and head nurses scoring high in structure tended to make riskier decisions. Men and women scoring high in both attitudes tended to be influencers in the group and to lead toward riskier decisions. However, Trimble (1968) found that for a sample of teachers who described their principals as higher in consideration than in initiating structure, neither of the principals' scores was related to the principals' perceptions of their own decision-making behavior.

*Emergence as a Leader.* Attempts to lead as manifest in one's emergence as a leader in a leaderless group discussion was negatively related to consideration ($r = -.25$) and positively related to initiation of structure ($r = .32$), according to Fleishman (1957a). Seeman (1957) noted that a school principal's leadership was seen to be a matter of how much consideration, initiation of structure, communication, and willingness to change was exhibited and to what degree domination and social distance was avoided.

Foote (1970) studied managerial staff members in television stations. Those managers who tended to describe themselves on LBDQ-XII scales as high in responsibility and authority tended to be described high in tolerance of freedom. Those delegating most freely were described high in production emphasis and low in representation orientation toward superiors.

Finally, when Capelle (1967) asked fifty student leaders and fifty nonleaders to fill out the Leadership Opinion Questionnaire, he found that leaders scored significantly higher than nonleaders on both consideration and structure. But G. W. Bryant (1968) observed that appointed and sociometrically chosen leaders (college students in ROTC) did not differ significantly in their conceptions of the ideal leader.

### Relations to Other Leader Styles

Chapters 18, 19, and 20 have been devoted to democratic versus autocratic, participative versus directive, and relations-oriented versus task-oriented leader styles. It should come as no surprise that consideration and initiation are related to other leader styles as well.

*Democratic and Autocratic Styles.* Although factorially independent, the various consideration and initiation scales contain the conceptually mixed bag of authoritarian and democratic leadership behaviors (Chapter 18). Each scale contains a variety of authoritarian or democratic elements. Although they empirically cluster on one side or the other, they are conceptually distinct elements. The industrial version, SBDQ, particularly, added strongly directive behaviors ("he rules with an iron hand") to its initiating structure scale (House & Filley, 1971).

Yunker and Hunt (1976) correlated the four Bowers-Seashore factors of support, interaction facilitation, goal emphasis, and work facilitation with the LBDQ for seventy-four business fraternity presidents. Support correlated .74 with consideration and .41 with initiation. Interaction facilitation correlated .66 with consideration and .61 with initiation of structure. On the other hand, goal emphasis correlated .64 with consideration and .76 with initiation, while work facilitation correlated .56 with consideration and .64 with initiation of structure. Clearly present is a large general factor of leadership permeating all of these scales, which adds credence to what we will present in the next chapter, namely, that the most important dimension empirically may be whether or not leadership per se is displayed. This becomes most apparent when the LBDQ rather than the LOQ is employed. Weissenberg and Kavanagh (1972) concluded from a review that although managers think they should behave as if consideration and initiating structure are independent, in thirteen of twenty-two industrial studies and in eight of nine military studies, a significant positive correlation was found between these two independent factors of leader behavior on the LBDQ as completed by subordinates, particularly if LBDQ-XII was the version employed in the survey (Schriesheim & Kerr, 1974). This fits with our general contention that conceptually, initiation of structure is readily distinguishable from consideration, just as autocratic and democratic or relations-oriented and task-oriented leadership can be conceptually discriminated. But empirically, the same leaders who are high on one factor are likely to be high on the other.

*Task and Relations Orientation.* The initiating structure scale emphasized task concern (insists on maintaining standards, sees that subordinates work to full capacity, emphasizes the meeting of deadlines) as well directiveness (makes attitudes clear, decides in detail what should be done and how it should be done). The consideration scale emphasized follower orientation (stresses the importance of people and their satisfaction at work, sees that subordinates are rewarded for a job well done, makes subordinates feel at ease when talking with them) as well as participative decision making (puts subordinates' suggestions into operation, gets approval of subordinates on important matters before going ahead). Social distance was also minimized for considerate leaders (treats subordinates as equals, easy to approach).

Conceptually in opposition to structuring would be destructuring behavior (J. A. Miller, 1973a), that is, reducing the request for consistent patterns of relations within the group. Lack of initiation of structure would imply allowing conditions to continue without structure and avoiding giving directions or being task-oriented. Conceptually opposite to consideration would be exploitative, unsupportive, unconcerned leader behavior (Bernardin, 1976). Among fifty-five corporation presidents, a correlation of .55 was found between their task-oriented production emphasis and their tendency to initiate structure according to a member of their staffs. Similarly, the presidents' consideration correlated .49 with the relations-oriented representation of their subordinates' interests and .41 with toleration of freedom of action among their subordinates (Stogdill, Goode & Day, 1963a).

Meuwese and Fiedler (1965) reported that leaders who are high and low on Fiedler's LPC measure tend to differ significantly on specific items of the LBDQ, but not in the total scores for consideration and initiating structure. W. K. Graham (1968) found that high (relations-oriented) LPC leaders were described higher in consideration and structure than low (task-oriented) LPC leaders. Moreover, Yukl (1968) noted that low LPC leaders tended to be described as high in structure and low in consideration. Yukl (1971) and Kavanagh (1975) concluded that task-oriented behavior is implicit in initiating structure, but subordinates can still influence the superior's decisions.

## GENERAL EFFECTS ON PRODUCTIVITY, SATISFACTION, AND OTHER CRITERIA OF EFFECTIVE LEADERSHIP

As noted earlier, except for a few recent cross-lagged analyses and experiments, most of the results to be reported here comes from concurrent surveys of leader behavior and criteria such as subordinate productivity and satisfaction. Although we tend to infer that productivity and satisfaction are a consequence of leader behavior, the effective outcomes modify the leader's behavior to some extent as well. Thus, Greene and Schriesheim (1977) completed a rare longitudinal study suggesting that more initiating structure by a leader can contribute to good group relations which, in turn, possibly may result in higher productivity by the group.

*First Evidence*

Using an early version of the scales, Hemphill, Siegel, and Westie (1951) found that organizing behavior (structure) and membership behavior (consideration) were both significantly related to group cohesiveness. Likewise, Christner and Hemphill (1955) noted that both consideration and structure were positively related to measures of group cohesiveness. In addition, Hemphill and Coons (1957) found that descriptions of both consideration and structure, when made by subordinates, were positively related to ratings of unit effectiveness, but leaders' self-descriptions of consideration and structure were not related significantly to effectiveness.

In an extensive analysis of twenty-seven organizations of seven types involving more than 1,300 supervisors and 3,700 employees, Stogdill (1965a) found that supervisory consideration was related to employee satisfaction with the company and to measures of group and organization cohesiveness. But, as with authoritarian and democratic leadership, neither supervisory consideration nor initiation of structure was consistently related to group productivity. Organizational differences had to be considered.

*Industrial Studies: Leader Behavior*

Generally, the reworded version of the LBDQ, the Supervisory Behavior Description Questionnaire (SBDQ), was used in the industrial studies that contained the autocratic elements mentioned earlier.

*General Results.* Fleishman (1957a) studied foremen in a production plant. Effective foremen were described as high in initiation and low in consideration. But absenteeism was greater with initiation and lower with consideration, suggesting that job satisfaction was higher under considerate foremen. Fleishman, Harris, and Burtt (1955) found that absenteeism, grievances, and personnel turnover (dissatisfaction) were higher under structuring than under consideration among lower-skilled blue collar workers. Gekoski (1952) found that initiating structure, but not consideration of superiors, was related positively to group productivity measures in a clerical situation.

Lawshe and Nagle (1953) obtained a high positive correlation for a small sample of work groups between group productivity and employees' perceptions of how considerate their supervisor was. In a study of foreman leadership, Besco and Lawshe (1959) found that superiors' descriptions of foreman consideration and initiating structure were both related positively to unit effectiveness ratings. Subordinates' descriptions of foreman consideration, but not initiation, were positively related to effectiveness.

Trieb and Marion (1969) studied two chains of retail grocery stores. Supervisory consideration, as described by workers, was positively related to productivity, cohesiveness, and satisfaction in both chains. Supervisory initiation of structure was related positively to productivity of their subordinates and cohesiveness in one chain, but not in the other.

In a study of two companies, House and Filley (1971) found supervisory consideration in both companies related significantly to satisfaction with company, job, and freedom of action. In both companies, initiating structure was also related significantly to satisfaction with company, job, and family attitudes toward company and job. Again, Fleishman and Simmons (1970) showed that the effectiveness of Israeli supervisors was positively related to their initiation of structure and consideration.

M. G. Evans (1968) reported that both supervisory consideration and structure were positively related to worker goal importance and job satisfaction. Under high supervisory consideration, a strong positive relationship existed between supervisory initiation of structure and group performance. In a later study, M. G. Evans (1970a) found that supervisory consideration and structure were related to worker perceptions of opportunity for satisfaction of security needs, but not to actual satisfaction with job security. Supervisory initiation of structure and consideration were unrelated to satisfaction of social, esteem, autonomy, and self-actualization needs. But using an early version of the LBDQ (Fleishman, Harris & Burtt, 1955), Hammer and Dachler (1973) showed that the leader's consideration was positively related to subordinates' perceptions that their job performance was instrumental in their obtaining desired outcomes. At the same time, the leader's initiation of structure was negatively related to such perceptions.

In a study of insurance sales supervisors, W. K. Graham (1970) found that supervisory consideration was positively associated with group performance. In a similar setting—seven retail discount department stores—Hodge (1976) studied the behavior of twenty-one second-level managers as reported on the LBDQ by 188 first-line managers. The subordinates' need satisfactions were positively associated with the higher-level managers' initiation of structure. Surprisingly, the relation was negative with consideration. These results were similar to what Patchen (1962) found for supervision of manual workers but contrary to that reported by Fleishman and Harris for similar types of workers.

*Interaction and Curvilinearity of Results.* Fleishman and Harris (1962) found that foremen consideration and initiating structure interacted to affect employee grievances and turnover. Medium and high degrees of consideration, along with low degrees of structure by foreman, were associated with the lowest rates of employee turnover and grievances. At the same time, Skinner (1969) obtained results indicating that industrial foremen scoring high in consideration experienced lower than average grievance and turnover rates among their subordinates. As did Fleishman and Harris, Skinner concluded that supervisory consideration bears a curvilinear relationship to employee turnover and grievances. As consideration increases, grievances decrease to a point, then level off. But supervisory structure was also curvilinearly related to grievances.

*Superior, Peer, and Subordinate Evaluations.* Brooks (1955) found that all the items measuring consideration and structure differentiated excellently rated managers from those rated average or below average in effectiveness. At the same time, Marks and Jenkins (1965) reported that descriptions of initiating structure were more highly related than consideration to global ratings of effectiveness (efficiency, leadership, motivation, and resourcefulness).

Korman (1966) reviewed the research in which consideration and structure scores of industrial supervisors were related to various criteria of supervisory effectiveness and work group performance. Generally, peer ratings of group performance were found to be unrelated to the peer ratings of supervisors' consideration and initiation of structure. However, evaluations of the supervisor by superiors and subordinates, as well as various objective criteria, tended to be related significantly to the supervisor's leader behavior as described by subordinates. These findings appear reasonable in that a supervisor's peers in an organization are not as well placed to evaluate the supervisor's performance accurately as are his or her superiors.

*Industrial Studies with the Additional LBDQ-XII Scales.* D. R. Day (1961) obtained 165 descriptions of executives in an aircraft manufacturing firm. Leader effectiveness correlated with a general factor as well as LBDQ-XII predictive accuracy, persuasiveness, role enactment, and demand reconciliation. According to R. E. Hastings (1964), leaders high in initiating structure and production emphasis supervised research teams rated high in volume of work. If the leaders were high in orientation to superiors, their groups were low in harmony. Leaders high in representation and role retention tended to supervise teams high in enthusiastic effort, while leaders high in persuasiveness supervised teams that were high in quality of work.

M. Beer (1964) used LBDQ-XII to test McGregor's (1960) hypothesis that employees become motivated and are enabled to satisfy their higher-order needs (for autonomy, esteem, and self-actualization) only when supervisors allow them freedom from organizational structure and pressure. He found that employees' satisfaction of need for autonomy, esteem, and self-actualization was positively related to supervisory consideration and tolerance of freedom. However, contrary to hypothesis, the leader behaviors resulting in higher-order need satisfaction were not the ones that led to strong motivation. Initiating structure was the leader behavior associated with strong employee motivation.

### Industrial Studies: Leader Attitudes

Findings were mixed here. Bass (1956) found that the effectiveness ratings by superiors of fifty-three supervisors were significantly related to their attitudes toward consideration ($r = .29$) expressed two years previously. However, attitudes toward initiation of structure were unrelated ($r = -.09$) to later effectiveness. In a replication (Bass, 1958), a significant correlation of .32 was found between attitude toward consideration and effectiveness ratings by superiors three years later. But Bass (1957a) also reported that neither attitudes toward consideration nor initiation of structure were related to peer ratings of sales supervisors on criteria such as popularity, problem-solving ability, and value to the company. At the same time, Fleishman and Peters (1962) found no relation between LOQ measures of supervisors' attitudes toward leadership and their rated effectiveness as supervisors. Rowland and Scott (1968) also noted that LOQ measures of supervisory consideration were unrelated to employee satisfaction.

According to T. C. Parker (1963), 1,760 employees of a wholesale pharmaceutical company in eighty decentralized warehouses were more satisfied with their supervision, their recognition, and their job security when their supervisors felt that consideration and initiation were important, as measured by the LOQ. The correlations of subordinates' satisfaction and supervisors' attitudes were .51 with supervisory consideration and .22 with supervisory initiation. But there was no relation to such objective measures of group performance as productivity and order-filling errors. Favoring initiation of structure was correlated .23 with pricing errors. Spitzer and McNamara (1964) also reported that attitudes toward consideration and structure were not related to an objective criterion (salary) of managerial success, nor were such attitudes related to superiors' ratings of executive success. Findings by Gruenfeld and Weissenberg (1966) indicated that supervisors scoring high in attitude toward consideration and structure were more favorably inclined toward personal development of their subordinates than those with low scores.

*Military Studies*

The first extensive use of the LBDQ was with air force personnel. Christner and Hemphill (1955) found that changes in the attitudes of crew members toward each other over a period of time were related to the leader behavior of the crew commander. When crew members described their commander as high in consideration, they increased their ratings of each other in friendliness, mutual confidence, conversation on duty, and willingness for combat. Crews describing their commander as high in initiating structure increased their ratings of each other in friendship and confidence. Halpin (1954) also found that superiors tended to evaluate positively those air crew commanders described high in initiating structure and to evaluate negatively those described high in consideration. In training, crew member satisfaction was positively related to consideration ($r = .48$) and negatively related to initiating structure ($r = -.17$). For the same crews in combat, however, both consideration ($r = .64$) and initiating structure ($r = .35$) were positively related to crew member satisfaction. In a later study, Halpin (1957a) found that superiors' ratings of commanders' combat effectiveness were not related to crew members' descriptions of the commanders' consideration. Superiors' ratings, however, were positively and significantly related to commanders' initiation of structure. Significantly, crew members' ratings of their commander on confidence and proficiency, friendship and cooperation, morale and satisfaction were positively related to both consideration and initiation of structure by their commander.

At the same time, Hooper (1968, 1969) obtained results indicating that the attitudes of air force cadets toward consideration and structure were not significantly related to their effectiveness ratings; the two scales, however, differentiated significantly between those scoring high and those scoring low on a composite leadership criterion. Again, Fleishman (1957a) found that both consideration and structure scores of ROTC leaders were positively and significantly related to peer ratings of value to the group, but superiors' ratings were not related to either pattern of behavior. Finally, in a study of trainee leaders, Hood (1963) found that they reported more affiliation and less communication when their own leaders were higher in initiating structure and consideration. Enlisted personnel attained higher scores on a pencil-paper test of military leadership when their leaders structured the situation and pushed for production. However, such higher attainment was not related to their leaders' consideration.

*Group Effects.*  C. H. Rush (1957) reported the effects of leader behavior on other dimensions of the performance of 212 aircrews. Crew members described the leader behavior of the crew leader and also described the crews on Hemphill and Westie's (1950) Group Dimension Descriptions. Leader consideration was associated with more crew intimacy and harmony, and less crew control and stratification. High leader initiation of structure was related to more crew harmony and procedural clarity, and to less crew stratification.

*Educational Studies*

A variety of investigations have been completed for the leader behavior of college administrators, school administrators, and school principals.

*High Education Administrators.*  Hemphill (1955) used the LBDQ to study the leadership of academic department heads in a university. The department head's reputation for administrative competence correlated .36 with consideration and .48 with initiation of structure. But Lindemuth (1969) failed to establish any relations between a college dean's initiation of structure and various measures of organizational climate.

*School Administrators.* Superintendents who were rated as effective leaders by both staff and school board members were described high in both consideration and initiation of structure (Halpin, 1956).

H. J. Bowman (1964) asked school principals to describe the leader behavior of higher-level school executives and themselves. Principals perceived themselves as exercising high degrees of responsibility and authority and as delegating extensively when they described their own superiors as high in consideration but not in initiation of structure. Again, for 1,200 school administrators studied by Flocco (1969), those described higher in consideration and initiating structure by staff subordinates were rated more effective. Rated ineffective were those administrators who described themselves as higher in consideration and initiating structure relative to descriptions obtained from their staff subordinates.

*School Principals.* Results obtained by Fast (1964) indicated that teachers' expectations regarding consideration and structure by their principal were unrelated to satisfaction. However, teachers' satisfaction was associated positively with their descriptions of principals' actual consideration and initiation of structure.

A. F. Brown (1967) and Greenfield (1968) concluded from a review of Canadian studies that pupil performance was associated with principals' LBDQ scores. Keeler and Andrews (1963) studied the relation of principals' leadership to pupil performance and staff cohesiveness in Canadian public schools. Both consideration and initiation of structure by the principals, as described by teachers, were significantly and positively related to pupils' examination scores on a province-wide examination. Initiation of structure by the principal was positively related to staff cohesiveness, but consideration was not. Nevertheless, A. F. Brown (1966) reported that effective principals were higher in scores on all LBDQ-XII scales. In the same way, Seeman (1957) found performance evaluations of the school principal's leadership positively related to consideration, structure, communication, and willingness to change and negatively related to domination and social distance. Again, Stromberg (1967) obtained a significant relation between teacher morale and the attitudes of their principals toward consideration and initiation of structure.

C. C. Wall (1970) studied four principals who scored high and four who scored low in dialog, decision making, and action on the LBDQ-XII. Effective principals were described higher than ineffective principals in consideration and tolerance of freedom. Ineffective principals were described as high in production emphasis. Teachers in seven of the eight schools believed that the principals ought to initiate more structure than they were perceived to do. Teachers in the ineffective schools studied by Wall believed that the principals should exhibit more persuasion and demand more reconciliation and more integration of the group than they were perceived to do. Mansour (1969) found that these discrepancies between the expected and actual behavior of principals were negatively related to teachers' job satisfaction and participation. According to Fast (1964), the consideration and initiation of structure behavior of principals, as described by teachers, were positively related to teacher satisfaction, although expected behavior was not.

However, the greater the discrepancy between expected and observed principal behavior, the lower was teacher satisfaction.

Among different schools, Punch (1967) found that the principal's initiation of structure was positively related and the principal's consideration was negatively related to a measure of school bureaucracy. At the same time, Mathews (1963) reported that the initiation of structure and consideration of principals was significantly related to Hemphill and Westie's (1950) measures of their staffs' stratification, control, homogeneity, viscidity, hedonic tone, and participation.

Hills (1963) obtained 872 teacher descriptions of fifty-three principals. Both consideration and initiating structure were highly correlated with two representative functions: (1) representing interests of the teachers to higher levels of organization; and (2) representing teachers' interests to the schools' clientele. Hills concluded that consideration and initiation of structure were not solely concerned with internal leadership, but were reflected in the manner with which the leader dealt with outsiders and higher levels of authority.

On the other hand, Rasmussen (1976) failed to establish any significant relations between twenty-five successful and unsuccessful elementary schools, teacher satisfaction, and the principal's behavior on the LBDQ. Again, Bailey (1966) studied four principals described by their superintendents and four teachers as higher in consideration than in initiating structure. Four other principals were described as higher in initiating structure than in consideration. Each principal and four teachers played a decision-making game. Although leader consideration was significantly related to teachers' satisfaction with the decision and support of it, neither the leader's consideration nor initiating structure scores were significantly related to the ability of a group to arrive at a decision or to perceptions that teachers had helped in making the decision.

*School Teachers.* In a large-scale Canadian study, Greenfield and Andrews (1961) obtained results indicating that the consideration and initiation of structure by teachers were positively and significantly related to the scores of their pupils on tests of school achievement.

### Hospital Studies

In a study of nurses and their supervisors, Nealy and Blood (1968) found that subordinate satisfaction was related to the consideration scores of both first- and second-level supervisors. Supervisory initiation of structure contributed to subordinate job satisfaction at the first, but not at the second level of supervision. Oaklander and Fleishman (1964) observed that both high consideration and initiation of structure endorsed by hospital administrators were related to low stress in the units they supervised.

A path analysis by Sheridan and Vredenburgh (1979) for 372 nurses, practical nurses, and nursing aides describing the behavior of their head nurses, disclosed a positive effect of the head nurses' initiation of structure on subordinates' group relations consistent with results by Greene and Schriesheim (1977). But these group relations, in turn, did not affect subordinate performance or turnover rates. Yet, the head nurses' consideration had a direct positive effect on subordinate performance as well as an indirect effect in that leader consideration reduced felt job tension. However, such job tension was slightly positively associated with job performance. (This fits with Weed,

Mitchell, and Moffitt's (1976) laboratory results that leader consideration makes for a pleasant working situation although it may not contribute to group productivity.)

### Other Studies in Not-for-Profit Organizations

Cunningham (1964) observed that the most effective agricultural agents and 4-H club agents were above the median in both LBDQ consideration and initiation of structure.

For 501 police officers in a major city department, consideration by their supervisors was found by Bernardin (1976) to be positively and linearly related to the police officers' satisfaction but not to their performance or absenteeism. Additional descriptive data about the supervisors were required, which were not provided by the LBDQ, such as the supervisors' specific reward orientation and punitiveness in order to account for the results more adequately. But for eighty professional mental health workers and their directors, Denton (1976) found significant and direct relations between both supervisory consideration and initiation, on the one hand, and their subordinates' job satisfaction and satisfactory client relations.

Stogdill (1965a) studied ten regional organizations in a department of state government. He noted that throughout the ten organizations, when executives described their superiors, those described high in representation on LBDQ-XII tended to manage groups rated high in support of the organization, and their subordinates tended to be satisfied with their pay. Tolerance of uncertainty in superiors was related to group harmony. Superiors high in initiating structure supervised subordinates satisfied with the organization. When employees described first-line supervisors, Stogdill found that those supervisors described as high in initiation of structure, consideration, and "influence upstairs" tended to supervise employees who were satisfied with the organization. Those supervisors described as high in initiating structure supervised groups rated strong in drive. Employees who described their supervisors as tolerant of freedom expressed satisfaction with their own freedom on the job.

In a study of trainees, Hood (1963) found that they reported more affiliation and less communication when their leaders were high both in initiating structure and in consideration. Furthermore, the trainees attained higher scores on a pencil-paper test when their leaders structured the situation and pushed for production. But such increased attainment was not related to the leader's consideration.

Osborn and Hunt (1975a,b) obtained data indicating that most aspects of member satisfaction in sixty business fraternity chapters were positively associated with their president's initiation and consideration. But at the same time, Yunker and Hunt (1976) reported results from seventy-four business fraternities finding correlations of only .12 and .10 between LBDQ assessments of the chapter presidents' initiation and consideration and chapter efficiency in fulfillment of specified requirements.

## CONTINGENCIES IN THE EFFECTS OF CONSIDERATION AND INITIATION OF STRUCTURE

We have seen that, generally, supervisory consideration seems to be associated with subordinate satisfaction with their supervisors. Subordinates are also likely to have fewer absences and are less likely to quit. But the correlations between a leader's initiation of structure and subordinate satisfaction and productivity vary in outcome depending on the instruments used, and the constraints and goals in the situation. The personnel involved may be particularly important. Followers in a wide variety of groups consider it legitimate for the leader to exercise influence on matters related to task performance and work environment (Fleishman & Peters, 1962). At higher executive levels, initiation of structure is seen in planning, innovation, and coordination. At lower levels, it is seen in the push for production (Brooks, 1955).

While too much such initiation often increases the likelihood of grievances, absenteeism, and turnover (Fleishman & Harris, 1962), a certain amount of pointing out the "paths to successful effort" (Bass, 1965c) is characteristic of the effective supervisor. It yields the greatest effectiveness and satisfaction in his or her work group. This optimum is likely to be greatest when workers are untrained and/or unmotivated—for example, lacking in cohesiveness. Untrained personnel need more help; trained ones prefer less.

The variety of mixed results noted in reviews by Vroom (1976), L. R. Anderson (1966a), Campbell Dunnette, Lawler, and Weick (1970), and Korman (1966) suggests the need to specify conditions in order to better understand the effects of initiation and consideration (House, 1971; Kerr, Schriesheim, Murphy & Stogdill, 1974). For example, although initiation of structure usually has been found associated with subordinate role clarity, it is less frequently correlated with performance, and it varies greatly from study to study in its correlation with satisfaction (Fleishman, 1973). While we have already seen differences between studies in different organizational settings, we now need to attend to the less common investigations systematically conducted under two or more conditions or where the consideration-to-effects linkage or the initiation-to-effects linkage is examined as modified by contingent variables.

### Instrumentation

As we have noted earlier, the differences in results obtained can be accounted for to a considerable degree by whether the investigator used the LBDQ, the SBDQ, the LBDQ-XII, or the LOQ.

Schriesheim, House, and Kerr (1976) did a masterful detective job in reconciling the mixed results obtained with the various versions of the LBDQ and SBDQ in measuring initiation of structure. First, they pointed out that the LBDQ of Halpin (1957b) contained fifteen items which asked subordinates to describe the actual initiating of structure behavior of their leader to establish well-defined patterns of communications and to set up ways to get the job done. But the revised LBDQ-XII (Stogdill, 1963a) contained ten items measuring initiation of structure which dealt with the actions of the leaders in clearly defining their own roles and informing followers about what was expected of them. Even more substantial differences were found in the leader behavior tapped by the SBDQ and the LBDQ in comprehensive item-by-item analyses for 242 employees describing their supervisors. In addition to role clarification by the leader, as we noted earlier, the SBDQ included a cluster of items measuring punitive, autocratic, and production-oriented behaviors such as "he rules with an iron hand" or "he needles foremen under him for greater effort." Thus, the three scales—SBDQ and the earlier and later versions of the LBDQ—differed markedly in content. The LBDQ forms largely reflected communication and organization elements; the SBDQ, on the other hand, consisted mainly of domination and production content.

Initiation of structure in all instruments involved role clarification behaviors as an essential component. A specific aspect of role clarification—established methods to get the work done—is mentioned in the LBDQs, but other aspects such as scheduling and criticizing are found only in the SBDQ. Schriesheim, House, and Kerr concluded that:

> When measured by the SBDQ, leader Initiation of Structure is generally positively related to performance ratings by superiors of manufacturing first-level supervisors and to ratings of their work group's performance. However, it is negatively related to satisfaction of the first-level supervisors' subordinates (Fleishman, Harris & Burtt, 1955; Fleishman & Harris, 1962; Harris & Fleishman, 1955; Skinner, 1969). This generalization also holds with regard to noncommissioned . . . infantry officers and air force officers (Stouffer, 1949, Moore, 1953; Moore & Smith, 1956), with Initiating Structure being measured in these studies by a form containing items similar to the autocratic behavior of the SBDQ. A similar although much weaker pattern of relationships has been found concerning non-manufacturing supervisors of clerical workers doing routine tasks by Fleishman *et al.* (1955), and by Lowin, Hrapchak and Kavanagh (1969) using selected items from the SBDQ in a laboratory experiment.
>
> When the revised LBDQ Initiating Structure scale is used to measure leader behavior of first-line supervisors of non-manufacturing employees performing routine tasks, correlations with subordinate satisfaction are positive, although generally so low as to be, at best, only marginally significant (Beer, 1966; Hunt & Hill, 1971; Hunt, Hill & Reaser, 1971; Hunt & Liebscher, 1973; Dessler, 1973) using a very modified version of the revised LBDQ [Schriesheim, House & Kerr, 1976, p. 301].

Demonstration of the differences were obtained when Meheut and Siegel (1973) divided the initiation of structure items of the SBDQ into those concerned with role clarification and those concerned with autocratic leader behavior. They obtained a correlation of .26 between leader role clarification and subordinate satisfaction, but $-.21$ between leader autocratic behavior and subordinate satisfaction.

*Other Difficulties.* Other sources of error accounting for variations in results with the SBDQ, according to Schriesheim, House, and Kerr, are the failure to provide opportunity to describe the timing or appropriateness of structuring to the particular task or to the context in which respondents work, even though empirical evidence indicates that this may be more important than the frequency of specific leader behaviors (for example, W. K. Graham, 1968; Sample & Wilson, 1965). In addition, leaders who have adequate knowledge of their subordinates' task demands may vary the amount of initiation of structure and also the kind and timing of structure provided. Some tasks require more structure during the goal-setting (goal clarification) stage, whereas others require more path clarification and performance feedback. Furthermore, some subordinates need more administrative structure to relate their work to other employees, whereas others could benefit more from technical guidance. The leader may have no control over standards. His or her initiation of structure may depend on circumstances outside the leader's purview. "He decides what shall be done and how it shall be done" may reflect physical impossibilities for leaders in some situations. Other initiation of structure items, such as "he tries out his ideas in the group" are less likely to be affected by circumstances.

Some items deal with specific behavior, others with general tendencies. Such initiation of structure items as "he schedules the work to be done" refer to specific actions; items such as "he encourages overtime work" relate to general practices. Even further removed from specific behaviors, and more concerned with skills, traits, and personality attributed of the leader are such items as "he makes accurate decisions" or "he is a very persuasive talker."

### Organizational Contingencies

The impact of a leader's initiation and consideration will depend on the organization in which it occurs. House, Filley, and Gujarati (1971) found that both leader consideration and initiating structure acted to moderate employee satisfaction with freedom on the job, job security, and family attitudes in one firm, but not in another. Similarly, Larson, Hunt, and Osborn (1974) found that leader consideration was related in one mental health state institution to performance of groups, but structure was more highly related in another.

The importance of the higher authority represented by the organization can be inferred indirectly from results obtained in a progressive petrochemical refinery and in a national food-processing firm where the extent to which supervisors felt they should be considerate was positively correlated with how highly they were rated by their superiors (Bass, 1956, 1958). Yet, in other companies no such correlation was found (Rambo, 1958). Obviously, in some firms or agencies considerate supervisors would be rated poorly by their superiors, while in other firms or agencies the reverse would be true.

*Military-Civilian Differences.*   Holloman (1967) studied military and civilian personnel in a large air force organization and found that superiors did not perceive military and civilian supervisors to be different in observed consideration and initiation of structure although they expected military supervisors to rank higher in initiation of structure and lower in showing consideration than civilian supervisors. Unexpectedly, Holloman found that subordinates perceived the military supervisor to be higher in consideration, as well as in initiating structure, than the civilian supervisor. This was true for both military and civilian subordinates. Thus, in comparison to civilian supervisors, military supervisors were seen to display more leadership by both their civilian and military subordinates.

Halpin (1955b) administered the ideal LBDQ to educational administrators and aircraft commanders. Subordinates described their leaders on the real form of the LBDQ. The educators exhibited more consideration and less initiation of structure than commanders both in observed behavior and ideal behavior. But, in both samples, the leaders' ideals of how they should behave was not highly related to their actual behavior as described by subordinates.

*Differences in Function.*   Fleishman, Harris, and Burtt (1955) noted that the leader's greater initiation of structure contributed to absences and grievances in manufacturing departments and to heightened turnover rates in nonmanufacturing departments. At the same time, Fleishman, Harris, and Burtt found that supervisors in manufacturing departments or in other departments working under time constraints were likely to receive higher merit ratings from their own supervisors if they tended to exhibit more initiation of structure, whereas the reverse was true for supervisors in service departments. In addition, in the nonmanufacturing service departments, the more considerate supervisors were seen as more proficient. Rambo (1958) also observed that executives in different functional departments of an organization differed in consideration and initiation of structure.

Cunningham (1964) studied county agricultural agents and 4-H club agents. Agent consideration was significantly related to effectiveness for agricultural agents, but initiation of structure was not. Initiating structure was significantly related to effectiveness for 4-H club agents, but consideration was not. However, as noted earlier, the most effective agents were those described above the median in both consideration and structure. Mannheim, Rim, and Grinberg (1967) reported that manual workers tolerated more initiation of structure by their supervisors than did clerical workers. Only clerical workers tended to reject the high-structuring supervisor when they expected low structure. When high consideration was expected, both groups chose the leader conforming to their expectations.

Hunt and Liebscher (1973) showed that leader consideration was more strongly associated with subordinate satisfaction in a construction bureau than in a bureau of design of a state highway department. Leader initiation of structure did not vary as much in its effects on satisfaction. D. R. Day (1961) found that upper-level marketing executives were described high in tolerance of freedom and low in structuring; upper-level engineering executives were described as low in tolerance of freedom and high in initiation; manufacturing executives were rated as high and personnel executives as low in tolerance of uncertainty.

*Leader in the Middle.* Relations between rated leadership, subordinate satisfaction, and group performance depend strongly on who does the rating. Although Rambo (1958) failed to find any significant differences in leader initiation and consideration between executives in different echelons of the hierarchical structure, hierarchical differences were seen by Halpin (1956a) when examining attitudes of individuals at different levels about the leader in between. He studied the leadership of school superintendents described by staff members, school board members, and self on both real and ideal forms of the LBDQ. Halpin found that board members agreed among themselves and staff members agreed among themselves in descriptions of the superintendents' behavior, but the two groups differed significantly in perceptions. Staff members saw the superintendent as less considerate than he or board members saw him. He was described higher in initiating structure by board members than by staff or self. Staff and board members differed significantly relative to how considerate the superintendent should be, but they did not differ significantly regarding the extent to which he should initiate structure. Boards expected the superintendent to act in a more considerate manner than the staff considered ideal. There was a nonsignificant tendency for board members to expect more initiation of structure than either staff members or the superintendents considered ideal.

Other studies in educational institutions by raters of a leader in the middle were completed by Sharpe (1956), Carson and Schultz (1964), and Luckie (1963). Sharpe studied the leadership of principals described by teachers, staff members, and self. The three groups held similar ideals of leader behavior. But teachers and staff members perceived the principals as deviating less from the ideal norms than did the principals themselves. Occupants of high-status positions perceived the principals as deviating more from the ideal norms than did those in lower-status positions. Carson and Schultz

(1964) obtained descriptions of junior college deans by college presidents, department heads, student leaders, and the deans themselves. The greatest discrepancies were found between presidents and student leaders in regard to both their perceptions and expectations of the dean's behavior. The evidence suggested that the greatest source of role conflict for the dean was based on discrepant expectations of the dean's behavior. Luckie (1963) obtained 434 descriptions of fifty-three directors of instruction by superintendents, staff members, and self. Results indicated that directors behave at a lower level of consideration than superintendents, self, and staff members rate ideal. Superintendents and staff members expected the director to exhibit higher degrees of structure than superintendents considered ideal.

The conflict of the leader in the middle seems to reside in the question of how considerate to be, not how much structure to provide. Graen, Dansereau, and Minami (1972b) obtained data indicating that at lower organizational levels, both superiors and subordinates evaluated the leader in between them more highly if the leader initiated more structure. But leader consideration had more of an impact on subordinates than on superiors.

Lawrie (1966) used the real and ideal consideration and structure scales in a study of superiors' and subordinates' expectations of supervisors in two departments. Convergence between real and expected behavior as described by subordinates was not related to ratings of foreman effectiveness. However, in one of the two departments, the ability of foremen to predict superiors' expectations and discrepancy between foremen and superiors' expectations were related to effectiveness ratings.

*Other Conflicts for the Leader.* Various kinds of conflict between the group and external agents as well as within the group moderate the extent to which consideration and initiation will be effective. R. Katz (1977) found that considerate leadership was most effective when the group faced external conflict; initiation of structure by the leader was most effective in dealing with internal interpersonal conflict.

Stumpf (n.d.) completed a path analysis for the questionnaire data from 144 professionals in a government R & D organization. Leader behavior was not directly related to subordinate job satisfaction or performance but only through two moderating or intervening variables which linked leader consideration and initiation to job satisfaction and performance. Leader initiation of structure correlated with skill-role compatibility, which in turn correlated with subordinate job satisfaction. Thus, the R & D professionals' satisfaction with their jobs depended on the extent to which their skills were not in conflict with the demands of their roles, which in turn depended on the structuring of the situation by their supervisors.

*Influence "Upstairs."* Leaders' influence among higher authorities has been found to affect the impact of their initiation of structure and consideration on their subordinates' satisfaction and performance. Consideration involves promises of rewards. Influence "upstairs" may be needed to "deliver on promises." Initiation of structure involves setting forth goals and plans. Influence "upstairs" adds to the leader's ability to do so with authority and credibility. In one of two companies studied, House, Filley, and Gujarati (1971) found the expected strong positive relation between a supervisor's influence with higher authority and increase in the correlation of the supervisor's consideration with subordinate satisfaction. (As had been found by Wager, 1965, earlier, the greater a supervisor's influence with higher authority, the greater the supervisor's tendency to be considerate in both companies studied.) Presumably, the influential leader can offer support and rewards with more certainty of providing them. Again, the more influential supervisor exhibited more initiation of structure in only one of the firms studied, but generally employees were more satisfied with most aspects of their jobs if their supervisors were more influential with higher authority.

*Falling Dominoes Again.* The falling dominoes effect we discussed at length in Chapter 16 has been observed by, Hunt, Hill, and Reaser (1973) for results with LBDQ-XII. In a school for the mentally retarded, an increase was found in the association of considerate supervision and the performance of their aides when the LBDQ scores of the second-level and first-level supervisors were combined. In the same vein, Hunt, Osborn, and Larson (1975), with data from three mental institutions, showed that leaders' consideration had more of a positive impact on group performance if the leaders' superiors were high in authoritarianism. Contrary to the possible compensatory effects, however, group performance here was higher if leader structuring was low. This same lack of initiation of structure by the leaders yielded the highest group performance when the leaders' superiors were equalitarian.

In his first study with the LOQ, Fleishman (1953a) found that the higher the supervisors' position in the plant hierarchy, the less considerate they felt they should be and the more structure they felt should be initiated. These attitudes had impact below them. Foremen whose superiors expected them to lead with less consideration and with more structuring had high grievance rates.

*Existing Structure.* J. A. Miller (1973a) pointed out that more initiation of structure by a leader should be productive in situations in which more structure of relations is needed for subordinates to accomplish their tasks. Such increased initiation of structure would be contraindicated in a highly structured setting. Thus, for a supervisor to tell skilled crafts personnel how to do their job is expected to be detrimental to performance. As J. A. Miller (1973a) deduced, Badin (1974) found that when first-line supervisors did initiate structure a great deal in forty-two work groups in a manufacturing firm, effectiveness was reduced in the already highly structured one of the forty-two groups. The correlation of group effectiveness and initiating structure by the leader was − .56. But in the less structured of the forty-two work groups, effectiveness of the groups was correlated .20 with the extent to which their first-line supervisors initiated structure. Consistent with these results, Hsu and Newton (1974) showed that supervisors of unskilled employees (less structured in their approach to tasks?) were able to initiate more structure than supervisors of skilled employees in the same manufacturing plant. In the same way, subordinates in a textile and plastics firm who felt that their success was outside their own control, tended to see their supervisors as initiating more structure, but they also felt that their supervisors were less considerate (Durand & Nord, 1976).

### Group and Member Contingencies

The size and cohesiveness of the group led and subordinate attitudes and leader's tenure also moderate the effects of the leader's initiation and consideration.

*Size of Unit Led.* Ordinarily we would expect that as the size of the unit led is enlarged, to be effective as before, a leader would have to display more initiation of structure (Bass, 1960). Consideration of the concerns for all subordinates by the leader would be expected to become increasingly difficult to maintain as the unit enlarged. Corollary results consistent with this expectation were found by Badin (1974), who showed that in the smaller of forty-two work groups, initiation of structure by the leader correlated negatively with the productivity of 489 manufacturing employees. However, the amount of a supervisor's initiation of structure was unrelated to productivity in larger groups.

Osborn and Hunt (1975c), in the previously cited study of presidents of business fraternity chapters, found that size of chapter moderated the positive effects of initiation and consideration on member satisfaction. However, Sheridan and Vredenburgh (1979) failed to find any relation between unit size and head nurses' leader behavior, although size correlated with perceived job tension which in turn related to subordinate performance.

*Dyadic versus All-Group Relationships.*  By the late 1970s, considerable research had concentrated on the dyadic leader–subordinate relationship (Graen & Schiemann, 1978), instead of on the leader and the primary work group (Hunt, Osborn & Schriesheim, 1978). Nevertheless, as we noted in Chapter 16, there was a failure to reveal substantive differences in results from standard leader–group investigations. In the case of the LBDQ, for 308 managerial and clerical employees, Schriesheim (1979) found correlations of .77 and .89 between dyadic and group LBDQ descriptions of supervisors for initiation and consideration, respectively.

*Cohesion.*  Among 308 low- and middle-level managerial and clerical employees in forty-three work groups in a public utility, J. F. Schriesheim (1980), using a modification of the LBDQ-XII, asked subordinates to indicate how their superior acted toward them as individuals rather than toward the group as a whole. She showed that, in line with expectations, when work group cohesion was low, leader initiation of structure was positively related to satisfaction with supervision, role clarity, and subordinates' self-rated performance. But when cohesiveness was high in the work group, leader consideration was related to the measures of satisfaction, clarity, and performance.

*Interaction of Effects.*  The interacting effects of consideration and initiation of structure were observed to vary depending on the situation and how the factors combined (for instance, Cummins, 1971). Graen, Dansereau, and Minami (1972a) found among 660 members of management of a large corporation that for those members who saw their leader as either high or low in structuring, the relationship between their leader's consideration behavior and their performance evaluation was positive. But for those who saw their leader as intermediate in structuring, the relationship between their leader's consideration and their performance was near zero.

Filley, House, and Kerr (1976) studied three companies to test the Fleishman and Harris (1962) hypothesis that leader initiation of structure acts as a mediator of the relationship between consideration and job satisfaction. Initiating structure was positively and significantly related to satisfaction with the company in all three organizations. Consideration was significantly related to satisfaction with company and freedom of action in all organizations. The data failed to support the mediating hypothesis. Leader initiation of structure was positively rather than negatively related to employee satisfaction. Similarly, as will be examined more fully in Chapter 25, M. G. Evans (1970a) tested the path-goal hypothesis in two organizations. He found that consideration and initiation of structure did not interact in path-goal facilitation but, rather, that consideration and initiation of structure each acted separately to enhance path-goal in-strumentality.

*Attitudes of Subordinates.* As might have been expected from what we have seen in the effects of autocratic leader behavior compounded with authoritarian subordinates, Weed, Mitchell, and Moffitt (1976) found that leaders who initiated more structure with dogmatic subordinates were likely to achieve higher levels of performance, while more consideration by the leader yielded greater performance among subordinates low in dogmatism. In the previously mentioned path analysis by Sheridan and Vredenburgh (1979), the greater job experience of the nursing personnel was found related to less considerate leadership from the head nurses, which in turn increased tension and had mixed effects on performance.

M. Beer's (1964) industrial study of the effects of leader behavior on subordinate need fulfillment disclosed that subordinates high in need for self-actualization, esteem, autonomy, production emphasis, and consideration were positively motivated by leader initiation of structure, contrary to the hypothesis that leader consideration would be more effective in motivating subordinates.

*Other Leader Attributes.* Assuming that one of the primary functions of a lower-level leader is to maintain subordinate job performance at a level acceptable to the leader's superior, Mayes (1979) studied how leader need for achievement and need for affiliation moderated the relations between subordinate job performance and the leader's consideration and initiating of structure. For 180 leader–subordinate dyads, the leader's need for achievement significantly moderated the relationship between subordinate job performance and leader initiating structure.

Another illustration of a contingent effect due to the leader was provided by Miklos (1963), who observed that the longer the tenure of principals high in initiation of structure, the greater the consensus among teachers in their role expectations for teach-ers, and the greater the agreement between teachers and principals. Agreement between teachers and principals was highest when principals were described high in both consid-eration and initiating structure.

## CAUSAL EFFECTS

### Cross-Lagged Analyses

Path analyses can help to suggest whether considerate and structuring leaders promote satisfaction and productivity or whether leaders of satisfied and productive subordinates can afford to be considerate and tend to initiate more structure (Bass, 1965c; Lowin & Craig, 1968). However, only the few longitudinal studies with cross-lagged analyses provide us with some confidence that the leader behavior as gauged from survey data results in subsequent improved subordinate satisfaction and productiv-ity. Reciprocal causality seems to be present in the few causal studies completed to date (Greene, 1973, 1974, 1975, 1979a).

Greene (1975) asked first-line managers in insurance, marketing, finance, and research and engineering to describe their own consideration and initiation of structure on the LBDQ. Two subordinates of each of the managers rated their own work satisfac-tion. Peers of these subordinates rated the subordinates' productivity. The measures were picked up on successive occasions one month apart. Cross-lagged comparisons were made of leader behavior at time 1 correlated with subordinate satisfaction or productivity at time 2, contrasted with subordinate satisfaction or performance at time 1 correlated with leader behavior at time 2. The results strongly suggested that considerate leadership resulted subsequently in increased subordinate satisfaction. At the same time, subordinates' productivity resulted subsequently in their managers' increased consideration for them. Finally, subordinates' productivity resulted subsequently in a reduction in the managers' initiation of structure as well.

### Experimental Effects

Even greater confidence about the cause and effects of initiation and consideration comes from the rare experiment when the leader's initiation and/or consideration is arbitrarily manipulated experimentally and measurements are taken of the subsequent effects on subordinates. (Of course, the short-term experiment itself is fraught with threats to its validity.) Thus, Dawson, Messé, and Phillips (1972) arranged for teachers to deliberately increase their initiation of structure. Student work productivity improved as a consequence. When the teachers subsequently increased their consideration deliberately, student work group productivity again was increased as a consequence.

In a laboratory experiment by Gilmore, Beehr, and Richter (1979), forty-eight participants were subjected to either low or high consideration and low or high structure by specially coached student supervisors working in groups of four members each. The LBDQ was completed by participants but failed to discriminate the behavior of the four types of supervisors, even though the leader behavior itself had differential effects on the quality of performance of the subordinates. Such performance quality was highest with leaders who were high in initiation of structure but were low in consideration. On the other hand, neither amount of initiation nor consideration was related to various measures of participant satisfaction.

### Conclusions

We conclude by observing that the several components variously involved in different versions of scales to measure leader consideration and initiation must be taken into account to fully appreciate their antecedents, and effects on subordinate performance. Role and task clarification have positive effects; the autocratic elements in the earlier LBDQs do not. Consideration, likewise, may contribute differentially in different situations to satisfaction and effectiveness as a consequence of its several components, including participatory and consultative decision making as well as concern for the welfare of subordinates.

The discrepancy between empirical correlations and conceptual discriminations—the mixture of conceptually distinct items of behavior that the same leaders tend to exhibit—requires looking at more of the LBDQ scales than just initiation and consideration in any single study to understand what is happening. In different settings one could guess that different elements such as influence higher up, production emphasis, and so on would have the greatest effects or interaction with initiation and consideration in their impact on productivity and satisfaction. Since the subscales of LBDQ-XII are differentially related to different dimensions of member satisfaction and group performance in the interest of uncovering some heretofore hidden complexities of leader behavior and leader influence, it would seem desirable to explore the possibilities of a multifactor approach rather than rest content with a two-factor solution. At the same time, as we shall see in the next chapter, such a multifactor approach must have room for a general leadership activity factor.

# 22

## LAISSEZ-FAIRE LEADERSHIP VERSUS MOTIVATION TO MANAGE

## INTRODUCTION

What we have seen in the immediately preceding chapters is that despite the conceptual distinctions between participative and directive leadership, task and relations orientation, and consideration and initiating structure, empirically, if we base our assessments on subordinates' descriptions and do not force the emergence of differences, the same leaders who are seen high on direction, task orientation, and initiating structure are also seen to exhibit a good deal of participation, relations orientation, and consideration. Thus, Jones, James, and Bruni (1975) for 112 managers found that leader supportiveness correlated .64 with goal emphasis and .74 with work facilitation. Likewise, interaction facilitation correlated .58 with goal emphasis and .70 with work facilitation. Schriesheim, House, and Kerr (1976) found a median correlation for ten studies of .52 between LBDQ-XII initiation and consideration. Directive and participative decision styles seem less highly interrelated. Farrow, Valenzi, and Bass (1980) reported that frequency of leader *direction* as seen by their over 1,200 subordinates correlated .13 with negotiation, .26 with consultation, .13 with *participation,* and .11 with delegation. However, consultation, *participation,* and delegation ranged from .55 to .71 in intercorrelation. Errors of leniency and halo may be involved. Even so, what we have is a strong tendency to describe leaders as more or less active in several dimensions. This may be due to real behavioral tendencies of leaders as well as to subordinates' perceptual biases. Nevertheless, subordinate perceptions of their leaders may be just as influential as the actual behavior of the leaders.

### Relation to Satisfaction and Effectiveness

More leader activity, regardless of style, is usually associated with more satisfaction and effectiveness. Thus, Bass, Valenzi, Farrow, and Solomon (1975) found overall correlations ranging from .3 to .6 between leader behavior as seen by subordinates and judged effectiveness of the leader's work unit regardless of whether the leader was directive or participative. When *direction,* consultation, *participation,* and delegation were added simply, their composite correlated .36 and .61 with effectiveness and satisfaction respectively. Similarly, Likert's System 4 combined participative management with "high performance, no-nonsense goals, orderly systematic goal setting processes

**393**

and rigorous assessment of progress in achieving those goals'' (Likert & Likert, 1976). Path analyses reported by R. Likert (1973) demonstrated that managerial leadership, whether task- or relations-oriented, contributed both directly and indirectly to subordinate satisfaction and productive efficiency. For large samples, the direct correlations between total leadership, subordinate satisfaction, and total productive efficiency were .49 and .42 respectively. In addition, total managerial leadership correlated .42 with a good organizational climate, .23 with peer leadership, and .27 with good group process. The latter, in turn, correlated between .25 and .67 with subordinate satisfaction and total productive efficiency.

In similar fashion, Blake and Mouton (1964) argued for the optimality of ''9–9'' leadership concerned both with production and with people. Hall and Donnell (1979) confirmed this by showing that the 190 out of 1,878 managers who were the fastest in their career advancement were likely to be high in both relations orientation and task orientation according to their subordinates. And the slowest 445 managers were clearly laissez-faire in style, low in both relationship and task orientation. However, the 1,243 moderately advancing managers were high in task orientation, but low in relationship orientation.

Fleishman and Simmons (1970) concluded that leadership combining higher consideration and initiation of structure was most likely to optimize a number of effectiveness criteria for a variety of supervisory jobs. In agreement, Karmel (1978) has concluded that combined initiation and consideration—the total activity of leaders in contrast to their inactivity—may be the most important of dimensions to investigate. A powerful general factor can be produced if one so decides by selection of appropriate factor-analytical routines. However, Larson, Hunt, and Osborn (1976) found (probably because of the high correlation between consideration and initiation) that for fourteen sample predictions of overall satisfaction and four predictions of overall performance, generally, consideration or initiation alone yielded higher correlations than consideration added or multiplied by initiation. It may be that because of the metrics involved pooling of different decision styles or new measures of generalized leadership activity will be more predictive. Nystrom (1978) also failed to obtain positive results with ''hi–hi'' leadership but here the failure could have been due to the use of the SBDQ to measure initiation of structure.

### Laissez-Faire and Motivation to Manage

In all, little evidence has appeared on such generalized leadership activity. Rather, studies have focused either on its opposite, laissez-faire leadership, or on what motivates someone to manage.

Laissez-faire leadership was seen by Bradford and Lippitt (1945) as descriptive of leaders who avoid attempting to influence their subordinates and shirk their supervisor duties. They have no confidence in their ability to supervise. They bury themselves in paper work and stay away from subordinates. They may condone ''license.'' They leave too much responsibility with subordinates, set no clear goals toward which they may work, and do not make decisions to help their group to make decisions. They tend to let things drift.

Laissez-faire leadership should not be confused with democratic, relations-oriented, participative, or considerate leader behavior. The second and opposite approach, which has been studied extensively by Miner (1978) deals with the active end of the spectrum by positing that managers are likely to be more successful to the degree that they are motivated to engage in six prescribed managerial roles: (1) maintain good relations with superiors; (2) compete for advancement and recognition; (3) be an active and assertive father figure (even if they are women managers); (4) exercise power over subordinates with appropriate use of positive and negative sanctions; (5) be a visible "standout" from his or her subordinates; and (6) accept responsibility for administrative details.

## LAISSEZ-FAIRE LEADERSHIP

### Research Beginnings

As already noted in Chapter 18, Lewin, Lippitt, and White (1939), Lippitt and White (1943), and White and Lippitt (1960) compared democratic, authoritarian, and laissez-faire leadership by adults instructed by the investigators on how to lead boys' clubs. Laissez-faire leaders gave group members complete freedom of action, provided them with materials, refrained from participating except to answer questions when asked, and did not make evaluative remarks. This was in contrast to autocratic leaders, who displayed a much greater frequency of order giving, disrupting commands, praise and approval, and nonconstructive criticism. It also contrasted with democratic leaders who gave suggestions and stimulated self-guidance. Laissez-faire leaders exceeded the other two patterns only in giving information. Under laissez-faire conditions the groups were less well-organized, less efficient, and less satisfying to members than under democratic conditions. Work was of poorer quality and less work was done. There was more play and more frustration, disorganization, discouragement, and aggression than under democratic leadership. When groups of boys were required to carry out various projects under a high degree of laissez-faire leadership, they exhibited a strong tendency to want to get things organized and to want to know where they stood. When an autocratic leader was followed by a laissez-faire leader, the group exhibited an initial outburst of aggressive, uncontrolled behavior. This form of behavior subsided during the second and third meetings. Similar outbursts were not observed after the transition from laissez-faire to other forms of leadership. Although not stimulating as much aggression as the autocratic condition, laissez-faire leadership was disliked because it was accompanied by less sense of accomplishment, less clearness of cognitive structure, and less sense of group unity.

### Follow-Up Studies

These original observations have been supported in a variety of survey and experimental studies. In a study of railroad section groups, Katz, Maccoby, Gurin, and Floor (1951) found that the supervisors of unproductive groups avoided exercising the leadership role and relinquished it to members of the work group. These supervisors also did not differentiate their role from the worker role. Like their subordinates, they engaged in production work rather than spend their time in supervisory functions. Again, Berrien (1961) studied groups that differed in adaptation to work change. Poorly adapted groups felt little pressure from their superiors and appeared to attribute their poor performance to lax discipline. In the same way, Muringhan and Leung (1976) found that undergraduate participants in an experiment led by uninvolved leaders were less productive in quality and quantity of problems solved and lower in satisfaction in comparison to participants led by an involved leader.

Pelz (1956) reported that the laissez-faire pattern of leadership was negatively related to productivity in a research organization. Similarly, Farris (1972) demonstrated that the less innovative of twenty-one NASA scientific groups had less peer and managerial leadership. Leadership was less task- or relations-oriented and less consultative or participative.

Baumgartel (1957) studied directive, laissez-faire, and participative patterns of leader behavior. Group members under the laissez-faire leadership reported more isolation from the leader and less participation in decision making than those under directive leadership. The results suggested that laissez-faire leadership contributed to low group cohesiveness. Kidd and Christy (1961) studied three patterns of behavior: laissez-faire, active monitoring, and participative leadership. Although processing speed was found to be greatest under laissez-faire leadership, error avoidance was greatest under active monitoring. Aspegren (1963) compared laissez-faire leadership, directive, and participative patterns and showed that laissez-faire leadership was associated with lower task motivation and lower satisfaction with superiors. Similarly, W. S. MacDonald (1967) studied three styles of leadership (laissez-faire, dominant, and democratic) in the Job Corps. Laissez-faire leadership was associated with the highest rates of truancy and delinquency and with slowest modifications in performance.

*Direction and Consultation Rather Than Laissez-Faire.* Managers take the major responsibility for decision making when they are directive and consultative. This is opposite to what they do as laissez-faire leaders. When data collected by Farrow, Valenzi, and Bass (1980) from 1,300 subordinates and their 340 managers describing the pooled direction and consultation of the managers was correlated with group effectiveness as seen by both managers and subordinates, the correlation with effectiveness (.41) was higher than that obtained for direction (.28) or consultation (.37) alone. Even more extreme, the combined direction-consultation index correlated .61 with satisfaction, and consultation alone correlated .52. But nothing was added to the relationship of leader behavior to subordinate job satisfaction by combining direction and consultation.

*Laissez-Faire and Dissatisfaction.* Arensberg and McGregor (1942) completed a case study of an engineering department without supervisors. A management committee approved plans and checked progress. Management considered this arrangement to offer ideal conditions for creative work. Employees, however, felt insecure and constrained in this overly permissive environment. Argyris (1954) conducted a case study in a bank in which management recruited the ''right kind'' of supervisor who was interested in security and predictability, disliked hostility and aggression, and wanted to be left alone. The bank's recruitment policy fostered in employees a norm of low work standards and unexpressed dissatisfaction.

*Problem Solving.* Maier and Maier (1957) experimented with discussion under free and more systematic styles of leadership. Free discussion produced decisions of lower quality than systematic, controlled, step-by-step discussion. Freer approaches to problem solving were found less effective and less satisfying, and also yielded less participant commitment than systematic problem solving. Thus, when Maier and Solem (1962) compared fifty free-discussion groups with ninety-six groups of four participants each who used problem solving in systematic steps, the free problem solvers were less likely to generate quality solutions than the systematic groups. Only 12 percent of the free problem-solving groups created integrated solutions that met the criteria of success, whereas almost half of the systematic groups did so. Maier and Thurber (1969) reported similar results.

### Subordinate Autonomy, Satisfaction, and Productivity

Evidence can also be mustered to support the contention that employees who feel a great deal of freedom to do their work as they like tend to be more satisfied and productive. Thus, March (1955) analyzed patterns of interpersonal control in fifteen primitive communities. Productivity was found related to degree of group autonomy. A. K. Rice (1953) studied a weaving shed in India. A type of reorganization providing greater worker autonomy resulted in increased efficiency and decreased damage.

Morse and Reimer (1956) arranged for the authority of operative employees to be increased in two departments to strengthen autonomy. Satisfaction was increased as a consequence. Productivity increased as well. O'Connell (1968) changed the responsibilities and behavior patterns of first-line supervisors in an insurance company. Despite the fact that the supervisors became bogged down in paperwork to a greater degree than expected, sales improved and lapse rates declined to some degree.

Meltzer (1956) reported that scientists are most productive when they have freedom to control their own research activities. Pelz and Andrews (1966a,b) studied scientists and engineers in several laboratories. They found that the most effective scientists were self-directed and valued freedom, but at the same time they welcomed coordination as well as guidance from other members of the organization. Similar results were reported for two divisions of a research laboratory by Weschler, Kahane, and Tannenbaum (1952) and by Tannenbaum, Weschler, and Massarik (1961).

Indik (1965b) studied ninety-six organizations of three types. Workers' freedom to set their own work pace was associated with productivity and job satisfaction. Trow (1957) reported that experimental groups with high degrees of autonomy provided greater member satisfaction than those in which members were dependent upon a centralized group structure.

*There Is No Contradiction: Laissez-Faire Leadership Does Not Necessarily Imply Effective Autonomy for Subordinates.*   How do we reconcile the two sets of findings that (1) laissez-faire leadership is detrimental to subordinate performance and (2) subordinate autonomy enhances performance? The answer lies in what is needed by the subordinates to do their job well. If they are skilled, professional, or self-starting sales people, what may be needed is participative leadership. The boundary conditions need to be specified either by the leader, the organization, or even the task itself. Within these boundaries, the already competent and motivated subordinates should be permitted by their leader to complete their work in the manner they think best. This kind of leadership, as Bass (1960) noted, paradoxically requires that the leader exercise authority to permit or deny freedom of action. This is not laissez-faire leadership where the leader does nothing unless asked by colleagues and even then may procrastinate or fail to respond. The laissez-faire leader will be nonactive or reactive rather than proactive. The extreme laissez-faire leader will not provide those clear boundaries. Rather than feeling free to carry on their jobs as they see fit, subordinates will feel uncertain about their own authority, responsibilities, and duties. The laissez-faire leader may work alongside subordinates or withdraw into paperwork. Decisions will be avoided rather than shared.

Supporting this distinction between working under laissez-faire leadership and being provided with freedom are results reported by Farris (1972), who in a study of twenty-one research teams found that providing freedom for subordinates was positively related to innovation when the superior preceded his own decision making with consultation with his subordinates (the correlation was .7). Among supervisors making little use of consultation, however, such provision of freedom was uncorrelated with innovation.

Further indirect support comes from a review of leaderless groups by Desmond and Seligman (1977). In twenty-eight studies reviewed, those groups obtaining positive results were with more intelligent participants and were likely to be more highly structured by audiotapes, directed instruction, and instrumented feedback. That is, the freedom of the leaderless group could result in productivity if participants had more competence to deal with the situation and obtained the necessary instructions to clarify the boundary conditions within which they could carry on.

### Is Any Style of Active Leadership Better Than Laissez-Faire Nonactivity?

Sharp, operationally defined distinctions between the various leader styles are seldom available. But we have seen in one example (Chapter 21) how greatly the relation between initiation of structure and satisfaction changes as a consequence of removing the autocratic punitive elements from the scale of initiation. Laissez-faire inactivity—unwillingness to accept responsibility, give directions, provide support, and so on—consistently is negatively related to productivity, satisfaction, and cohesiveness. Sheer activity is likely to be correlated with successful leadership and influence (Chapter 6). The question is if such successful influence necessarily results in increased group performance, satisfaction, and cohesiveness. This appears to vary depending on whether the work-related leadership behavior is autocratic, directive, task-oriented, or structuring and whether the person-related leadership behavior is democratic, participative, relations-oriented, or considerate. This is aside from the many contingencies described in Chapters 18 through 21 which also may have to be taken into account.

Stogdill (1974) reviewed a mix of surveys and experiments, mostly containing concurrent analyses of leader behavior and outcomes, more often than not in temporary, short-term, groups and without reference to possible contingent conditions. Stogdill (1974) concluded that both the democratic leadership cluster (participation, relations-orientation, consideration) and the work-related cluster (direction, task-orientation, structuring but not autocratic) were more likely to be positively than negatively related to group productivity, satisfaction, and cohesiveness. Follower satisfaction was particularly likely to be found related to active person-oriented leader behavior that was democratic, participative, and relations-oriented or considerate. It was also seen in ten of fourteen studies as positively related to structuring.

Participative and considerate patterns of leader behavior tended to be related positively to group cohesiveness. In all available studies, leader behavior that structured follower expectations was consistently related to group cohesiveness. Other work-oriented styles—autocratic, restrictive, socially distant, and directive—were less so. Again, only the considerate and participative behaviors in the person-oriented cluster were found to be consistently related to group cohesiveness. Thus, leadership activity as such does not always guarantee group performance, satisfaction, and cohesion. In fact, highly active but coercive, autocratic leadership was found to contribute more to group dissatisfaction and lack of cohesiveness than to group productivity. The qualities of the leadership activity must be taken into account. For the leader, doing something is usually but not always better than doing nothing.

A further examination of the qualities of importance to active leadership in contrast to laissez-faire leadership is seen in a role theory—Miner's motivation to manage.

## THE MOTIVATION TO MANAGE

Building on role theory and psychoanalytic theory and the empirical results of Kahn (1956) and Fleishman, Harris, and Burtt (1955), Miner (1965) originated a theory of managerial role motivation. This theory was directed specifically toward role-taking propensities within the ideal large organization formalized and rationalized to function bureaucratically. Miner argued that people who "repeatedly associate positive rather than negative emotion" with various managerial role prescriptions are more likely to meet existing organizational effectiveness.

### Roles and Requisite Motivation

The six managerial role prescriptions presented by Miner along with the required motivation for success as a manager were as follows:

1. Managers must behave in ways that do not provoke negative reactions from their superiors. In order to represent their group upward in the organization and to obtain support for their actions, managers should maintain good relationships with those above them. A generally positive attitude toward those holding positions of authority is required.

2. Since a strong competitive element is built into managerial work, managers must compete for the available rewards, both for themselves and for their groups. If they do not, they may lose ground as functions are relegated to lower their status. Without willingness to compete, promotion is improbable. To meet this role requirement, managers should be favorably disposed toward engaging in competition.

3. There is a parallel between managerial role requirements and the assertiveness traditionally demanded of the masculine role. Both a manager and a father are supposed to take charge, to make decisions, to take such disciplinary action as may be necessary, and to protect others. Even women managers will be expected to follow an essentially masculine behavior pattern as traditionally defined (more about this in Chapter 30). A desire to meet the requirements of assertive masculinity will generally lead to success in meeting certain role prescriptions of the managerial job.

4. Managers must exercise power over subordinates and direct their behavior in a manner consistent with organizational and personal objectives. Managers must tell oth-

ers what to do when necessary, and enforce their words through appropriate use of positive and negative sanctions. The person who finds such directive behavior difficult and emotionally disturbing will have difficulty meeting this managerial role prescription.

5. Managers must stand out from their groups and assume positions of high visibility. They cannot use the actions of their subordinates as a guide for their own behavior as managers. Rather, they must deviate from their immediate groups and do things that will inevitably invite attention, discussion, and perhaps criticism from those reporting to them. When the idea of standing out from the group, of behaving in a different manner, and of being highly visible elicits feelings of unpleasantness, then behavior appropriate to the role will occur less often than needed.

6. Managers must "get the work out" and keep on top of routine demands. Administrative requirements of this kind are found in all managerial work, although the specific activities will vary somewhat from one situation to another. To meet these prescriptions a manager must at least be willing to deal with routines and ideally gain some satisfaction from it.

*Contradictions.* As can be seen, Miner did not mince words. He argued that in a typical bureaucratic hierarchy what is needed for leadership is an authority-accepting, upward-oriented, competitive, assertive, masculine, power-wielding, tough-minded person who will attend to detail. In preparing his role prescriptions, he was selective about which facts about leadership he incorporated and which facts he ignored. A positive attitude toward authority may characterize the authoritarian–submissive behavior (Chapter 8). An organization of submissive managers would not seem one of promise for innovation and effectiveness.

Competitive behavior presents many costs to the organization. Managers in competition with their peers hide necessary information from each other and fail to see the subordinate goals whose attainment is important to all concerned. Competition means that managers negotiate with their peers instead of solving problems with them. Decisions are based on power rather than merit—again, a consequence not calculated to add to organizational effectiveness.

It is true that visibility may help one's own advancement, but concern for such visibility may conflict with good team support from subordinates who might feel exploited.

The stern father image and the willingness and need to use sanctions seem to contradict most of the evidence about the costs of coercion and autocratic leader behavior. If attention to detail means inclusion of sanctions, this prescription can easily be overdone if the manager fails to have a sense of priorities.

Despite these contradictions, considerable support for Miner's theory has been amassed.

### Measuring Motivation to Manage

The Miner Sentence Completion Scale (MSCS) was used to measure managerial role motivation (Miner, 1965). The MSCS contains forty items; thirty-five are scored. The scale is a projective measure. A majority of the items refer to situations that are either outside the work environment entirely or not specifically related to the managerial job. Examinees are unaware of what is being measured so that distortion of responses to present themselves in a good light as managers is unlikely. A multiple choice version is available (Miner, 1977b).

Subscales for motivation to take each of the prescribed managerial roles can be obtained.

*Psychometric Criticisms of MSCS.* Brief, Aldag, and Chacko (1976, 1977) have been critical of the scoring reliability of the sentence completion in the original MSCS. But Miner (1978) has shown that when more experienced raters are used, agreement as measured by correlations among scorers runs from .83 to .98. Experienced scorers also are more in agreement in the mean score assigned.

The multiple choice version of MSCS eliminates this issue. Correlations between item scores on the original and multiple choice versions were .68, .71, and .38 for three samples of production and office managers, although subscales tend to be less consistent from one version to the other.

Brief, Aldag, and Chacko also criticized the lack of correlation of the MSCS with the Personal Values Questionnaire (England, 1976) and the Self-Description Inventory (Ghiselli, 1971) which also have been found to correlate with managerial success. But Miner (1978) finds more problems with the PVQ and SDI as standards than with the MSCS.

*Concurrent Validity.* Miner (1965) found that the higher their total MSCS scores, the higher were the grade level performance ratings and the rated potentials of eighty-one to 100 R & D managers in a petrochemical firm. For seventy department store managers, total MSCS scores related significantly to their grade level and potential but not to their rated performance. Again, Gantz, Erickson, and Stevenson (1977a) reported that total MSCS scores related significantly to peer ratings of the supervisory potential of 117 scientists and engineers in a government R & D laboratory. For 101 personnel and industrial managers, Miner and Miner (1977) reported a significant relation between total MSCS scores and a composite measure of their success, compensation, and position level. Similar relations with position levels were found by Miner (1977a) for 142 personnel and industrial relation managers and for 395 managers from a variety of firms.

With eighty-two school administrators in a large city, Miner (1967) found total MSCS to relate significantly with their compensation, rated performance, and potential, but not with their grade level. However, grade level was significantly related to total MSCS scores of forty-four women department store managers (Miner, 1977a), and fifty and thirty-seven textile managers respectively (Southern, 1976).

With student samples, Miner and Crane (1977) obtained positive findings relating MSCS scores to promotion into management of forty-seven MBA students, to selection among forty fraternity presidents (Steger, Kelley, Chouiniere, and Goldenbaum, 1977), and to selection among 190 for student offices. Miner, Rizzo, Harlow, and Hill (1977) also reported positive findings for undergraduate students in a simulated bureaucratic organization.

Less consistently significant results were obtained for subscale scores. Motivation for the role most often associated with criteria of managerial success was the desire to enter into competitive situations. Least often associated were assertive motivation, the desire to stand out and to perform routine administrative functions.

*Predictive Validity.* Total MSCS scores forecast changes in grade level and performance ratings of forty-nine to eighty-one petrochemical R & D and marketing managers (Miner, 1965). Lacey (1977) found that total MSCS scores were significantly able to predict promotion into management of ninety-five scientists and engineers. Lardent (1977) likewise showed that total MSCS scores for 251 cadets forecast graduation from officer candidate school.

### Validity Contingent on Bureaucratic Hierarchy

Since the role prescriptions were applicable only to traditional bureaucratic hierarchies, Miner (1965) proposed and found that total MSCS scores should be unrelated to success of professionals outside such highly structured organizations. Although it is impossible to prove the hypothesis, his argument was supported by his failure (Miner, 1977a) to find significant relations between MSCS scores and various criteria of success of twenty-four to fifty-one managerial consultants, forty-nine business school faculty members, thirty-six to fifty-seven school administrators in small and medium-size cities and consolidated districts, and sixty-five oil dealer salesmen (Miner, 1962).

More convincing support for this argument was obtained by Miner, Rizzo, Harlow, and Hill (1977), who showed that in simulated low-structure situations, in which eighty-nine students worked on various case projects in small teams of four to seven, MSCS scores were unrelated to emergence as leader. On the other hand, in line with Miner's theory, in a high-structure situation where students chose to work on current problems in assigned positions in a simulated six-level divisionalized organization, total MSCS scores of higher-level leaders were highest; nonleaders and those who opted to work outside the organization were lowest.

*Caveat.* Even restricting Miner's motivation to manage to traditional hierarchies fails to account for the contrast between his prescriptions for the managerial role and those, say, of Likert (Chapter 18). Conspicuously absent from Miner's results are criteria of subordinate satisfaction, production, cohesiveness, and growth. As we have noted in Chapter 21, subordinate satisfaction may be strongly associated with considerate leader behavior, but the leaders' superiors may evaluate the leaders more favorably for their production emphasis. Again, in Chapter 19, we saw that one leader style, negotiation or manipulation, was related to salary attained (usually superior-determined) adjusted for age, seniority, education, function, and so on. Yet, negotiative behavior was the one leader style likely to be negatively related to subordinate satisfaction and the effectiveness of work groups.

Thus, individual managers may be most successful pursuing the role prescriptions set forth by Miner, but in the absence of evidence, we can only guess, given Likert's long-range studies, that organizations are likely to suffer from the consequences in subordinate grievances, absences, turnover, and dissatisfaction as well as vertical and lateral communication blockages and filtering. Nevertheless, Miner may be performing an extremely important service in helping us to see a fundamental conflict: the integration of the long-term objectives of the individual manager and those of the organization, as called for by Argyris (1964).

part

# SITUATIONAL ASPECTS OF LEADERSHIP

# 23

## LEADERSHIP, ORGANIZATION, AND ENVIRONMENT

## INTRODUCTION

We have just seen how Miner's motivation to manage appears relevant only in highly bureaucratic or authoritarian settings. Similarly, there is some optimum rather than absolutely high level of activity of quality leadership which will depend on the constraints and challenges faced by the group led. If the performance of American presidents were rated on Osgood's semantic differential scales—active–inactive, strong–weak, and good–bad—no doubt generally activity, strength, and goodness would go together. However, the 1950s may have been best served by a less active President Eisenhower, whereas a more active T. R. Roosevelt might have created more problems than he would have solved.

Both situational demands and personal attributes of the leader must be considered in trying to understand the likely effectiveness of the leader.

### Trait versus Situation

As we have already noted in our earlier historical review of leadership theory, the trait approach was not enough for understanding leadership. Above and beyond personal attributes of consequence, the situation could make a difference. Whereas some types of leadership are reported and/or expected of leaders in all situations, other leader behaviors are more specific to particular types of situations (Hemphill, 1950a). For instance, according to a survey by Hemphill, Siegel, and Westie (unpublished), when the group has a high degree of control over its members, the leader is expected to dominate and actually does so. Contrarily, in groups where members participate to a high degree, these expectations and reports of domination do not occur.

Some leader behavior is a function of individual differences; other leader behavior appears to depend mainly on the situation. Thus, Stogdill's (1951b) study of transferred naval officers suggested that some behavior of the transferee in the new situations was characteristic of himself rather than of the position. This included his tendency to delegate authority; to spend time in public relations; to evaluate, read, and answer mail; to read technical publications; and to spend time with outsiders. Other behavior, characteristic of the situation, included the amount of personal contact time; time spent with superiors; and time spent in supervision, coordination, and writing reports.

*Interaction of Traits and Situation.* In Chapter 4, we saw that Stogdill had located 124 studies indicating that patterns of leadership traits differ with the situation. For example, Sward (1933) characterized subgroups of 125 campus leaders as follows: (1) bright, relatively unmotivated, unsocial, self-confident campus editors; (2) rather insecure, intellectualistic, very intelligent debaters; (3) strongly socialized, intellectually mediocre campus politicians; and (4) extroverted women leaders. Results of the 124 studies suggested that "if there are general traits which characterize leaders, the patterns of such traits are likely to vary with the leadership requirements of different situations." W. O. Jenkins (1947) also reviewed a large number of studies indicating that the traits required in a leader are related to demands of the situation. Subsequently, DuBrin (1963) found that a leadership inventory consisting of both trait and situational items correlated significantly with a leadership criterion, whereas neither set of items alone was significantly related to the criterion. Again, O. L. Campbell (1961) reported significant differences between leaders in eight different situations when described on the consideration and initiating structure scales of the Leader Behavior Description Questionnaire (LBDQ).

*Situational Factors.* Subsequently, much has been learned about how task demands and the immediate group members modify what type of leadership will occur. Less well studied has been the impact of the external environment and the organization. Yet, it is clear that they exert important effects on leader behavior. Increasing attention has been devoted in recent years to these effects for two reasons. Katz and Kahn's (1966) introduction of systems theory to the study of leadership and social interaction was one reason. The second reason was the sharp increase in government legislative intervention into the world of work and the relations among employers and employees.

As noted in Chapter 21, Kerr, Schriesheim, Murphy, and Stogdill (1974) reviewed how situational elements determined whether consideration or initiation of structure was more effective. Among the situational variables found to modify significantly whether initiation of structure and/or consideration yielded satisfaction and productivity were subordinates' need for information, their job level, their expectations of leader behavior, and their perceived organizational independence. Also important were how similar the leaders' attitudes and behavior were to the managerial style of higher management and the leaders' upward influence. In addition, task effects, including whether there were pressures to produce and provisions for intrinsic satisfaction, were significant.

In this chapter we will focus on organizational and outside environmental factors that influence leader–subordinate relations inside the organization. Subsequent chapters will examine group, task, and other factors.

## THE ENVIRONMENT OUTSIDE THE ORGANIZATION

### Stable versus Turbulent Environment

Systems theory suggests that what takes place outside a system is likely to affect what takes place inside it. This emphasis on organizations as open systems contrasts with the earlier approaches of economists, engineers, or behaviorists. We now pay more attention to the environmental forces that interact with the organization and modify in a continuing way what is going on inside it. Thus, if a business operates in a stable environment, all its departments can look very similar in structure. If the environment is unstable, much greater differences emerge among the various divisions of the firm (Lawrence & Lorsch, 1967b).

Failure of organizational structures to change in response to changing environmental processing requirements led J. A. Miller (1974), who studied leader behavior in ten organizations, to propose and find support for the argument that the optimum degree of initiation of structure by the leader depends on how much the processes demand such structure when the organization has not already provided it.

Osborn, Hunt, and Bussom (1977), like Miller, proposed to extend Ashby's (1957, 1960) Law of Requisite Variety to understand the relation between environmental demands on the organization and the organization's structure. The organization must possess as much regulatory variety as can be expected from the environment. Internal variety of structure should vary directly with environmental variety of demand. Organizations in environments with numerous disturbances should, therefore, contain an equally sophisticated capability to vary important internal characteristics. Osborn, Hunt, and Bussom tested whether the consistency of leader behavior matching environmental conditions was more valid than an alternative model suggesting that the leader's behavior offsets and compensates (as Miller argued). In sixty business fraternity chapters, within-chapter variation across selected environmental dimensions gave a measure of environmental variety. Five leadership dimensions from LBDQ-XII for each chapter leader yielded a measure of leadership variety. Overall chapter performance was best when environmental variety was low and was matched by low leadership variety. Performance was worst when environmental variety was low and was mismatched with high leadership variety. Again, leadership variety that matched high environmental variety was associated with better chapter performance but the effects were much smaller.

*Market Stability.* An attribute of the outside environment likely to influence a leader behavior inside an organization is the stability of the market in which a firm or agency operates. Other attributes are the current economic situation and outsiders' expectations (Bass & Barrett, 1981). Thus, with reference to the organization's market, if the firm operates in a stable market place, less total leadership is needed. Matters can be programmed and policies can be set, and leadership will be required only if programs and policies are not properly pursued. Leadership, when needed, can be directive. In a turbulent market, more leadership will be needed, particularly consultation on a continuing basis.

Burns and Stalker (1961) interviewed key people in twenty organizations in a variety of industries. They classified the management methods as either "mechanistic" or "organic." The mechanistic style was found more appropriate for dealing with stable environments and the organic style was more suited to changing environments. The mechanistic organization was characterized by vertical communication patterns with decision and influence centered at the top levels, while organic forms featured lateral communication and less rigidly defined jobs.

Effective firms in a rapidly changing, complex environment involved lower-level managers in joint departmental decisions. Managers who possessed the competence and knowledge to deal with the environment had more decision-making influence than those who did not. Effective firms in relatively stable environments concentrated decision making and influence at the top level of management. Managers in such stable environments found satisfaction from being able to get a quick decision from higher levels.

The executives in one company (sales engineering) were required to deal with a heterogeneous, changing environment, while in the other company (clothing) the environment was constant and executives were required to deal with the same customers, suppliers, and regulatory bodies repeatedly. The demand for direct interaction with the environment was greater for the sales engineering company, whereas in the clothing company interaction was accomplished indirectly, mainly in written form.

The autonomy of executives was lower in the environment where differentiation of customers was less, feedback was greater, and communication with the environment was indirect. All these characteristics were associated with the clothing company. Executives were less involved in decision making and more concerned with routine tasks. Their autonomy was more restricted both horizontally and vertically as compared to the sales engineering executives whose environmental surroundings were the opposite of those of the clothing firm (Burns & Stalker, 1961).

Firms which must operate in turbulent fields are more likely to share power of decision making inside their organization, according to a study by Emery and Trist (1965). In agreement, Lawrence and Lorsch (1967a) compared decision making observed in the stable container industry with decision making in the more turbulent plastics industry. Again, in the stable environment the decision-making processes within the container firm were likely to be directive; in the more turbulent environment of the plastics firm, decision processes were more likely to be consultative.

### Economic, Political, Social, and Legal Influences

Using factored questionnaires, Bass, Valenzi, and Farrow (1977) asked seventy-six managers to rate the extent to which economic, political, social, and legal forces outside their organization influenced themselves and their immediate subordinates. Each of their 277 subordinates, in turn, described the leadership behavior of their managers. Production, accounting, and finance managers saw economic forces as most important; service, sales, and marketing managers saw economic forces as less important than political, social, or legal forces. But even after partialing out the effects of managers' personality, background characteristics, and managerial function, managers who perceived external economic forces as important to their supervisor–subordinate relations tended to be more *directive* and manipulative according to their subordinates. On the other hand, managers who themselves felt that external political, social, and legal forces were more important tended to be more consultative according to their subordinates.

In a follow-up analysis, Farrow, Valenzi, and Bass (1980) examined 250 managers in profit organizations and ninety-five in nonprofit organizations. In the nonprofit firms, leadership style as seen by subordinates was affected more by the managers' perceptions of outside environmental influences. For example, perceptions of strong economic influences were correlated $-.30$, $-.25$, and $-.21$ with consultation, *participation,* and delegation in the nonprofit organizations. The same correlations in the profit-making organizations were $-.05$, $-.11$, and $-.02$.

Studies of legislative leadership by Peabody (1976) and Rosenthal (1974) suggested that a variety of environmental forces strongly affect the stability of political leadership. The same variables can be seen operating even more intensively in the private sector, where market forces and technological changes often dramatically affect leadership stability and succession (Bryson & Kelley, 1978). Performance reviews in the form of annual elections for the Board of Directors, periodic audits, and stockholders' meetings by outsiders can influence the actions of organizational leadership (M. P. Allen, 1974). These reviews can affect the stability of the dominant coalition inside the organization. A change in law, in resources, or in competing organizations also may force changes in leadership (Pfeffer, 1972b). Client groups, unions, professional associations, and regulatory agencies affect how and what will be discussed and decided, both in legislatures and in private organizations, especially on visible and emotional questions. Features, publicity, and exposés can be used to support or destroy the leadership in both locations (Ilchman & Uphoff, 1969).

### Socioeconomic Status of Community

Osborn and Hunt (1979) created an index based on community median family income, mean educational level, tendency to vote, and socioeconomic conditions. For sixty chapters of a national business fraternity, they obtained a correlation of .40 between community status and chapter leaders' initiation of structure and .68 between socioeconomic status and the leaders' consideration as measured by the LBDQ.

### Treatment by Outsiders

Pettigrew (1973) observed that developing and maintaining a network of contacts inside and outside the organization forms the basis by which many leaders help their subordinates reach desired objectives. Furthermore, Koulack (1977) involved forty-four undergraduates in simulated bargaining situations. Leaders who did all the bargaining were treated by outgroup members either with friendliness or with hostility. The leaders treated in a friendly manner by outgroup members were rated as more effective by ingroup members.

### Reference Groups

Another influence on leaders and members of any group is exerted by those with whom they compare themselves—their outside reference groups.

Hyman's (1942) conception of the reference group has contributed much to group theory and research. Hyman asked subjects to estimate their status along several dimensions—social, economic, intellectual, physical, and the like. He found that individuals estimated some aspects of status in relation to family members, others in relation to friends or work peers, and still others in relation to people in general. Small reference groups were usually more important than people in general in estimating and determining satisfaction with status. Satisfaction with income was highly dependent upon the reference group with which the individuals compared themselves.

*Relations to Leadership.* Merton (1949) showed that different reference group identifications were associated with variations in patterns of leader behavior. In a community study, eighty-six informants identified 379 individuals as persons of some influence. The thirty most influential members of the community were interviewed. Of these, sixteen were classified as "locals" and fourteen as "cosmopolitans" in their reference group identifications. The two groups differed as follows:

| *Locals* | *Cosmopolitans* |
|---|---|
| Local patriots | Interested in world at large |
| Reluctant to leave community | Willing to leave community |
| Reared locally | Mostly newcomers |
| Desire to know many people | Selective in choice of organizations |
| Members of local fraternal and business groups | Members of national professional societies |
| Influence rests on complex network of personal relationships | Influence derived from prestige and professional position |
| Understand the community | Know their job |

*Culture.* Particularly important is the national culture from which the leaders and the followers are drawn. We will devote Chapter 32 to examine such cultural effects.

*Multiple Reference Groups.* People usually see themselves as members of several reference groups if asked ''What are you?'' In Texas, a Texas resident might say American first. Outside Texas, the Texas resident might first say Texan, then American, businessman, father, Episcopalian. Each is a reference group. The effects are complex. Thus, when Catholic and Jewish girls were brought together by Festinger (1949) in a small club and asked to elect officers before religion was identified, both groups voted as much for nonmembers as members of their own religion. In a control situation in which religious identities were disclosed, 64 percent of Catholic votes were for Catholic girls, but the Jewish girls continued to vote equally as often for members of either religion. However, in a large group where the voters could not be identified, when the nominees' religions were known, Jewish girls showed the same tendency to vote for members of their own religion as did Catholic girls. The same effects were observed when confederates were alternately identified as Catholics and Jews for the benefit of different groups of voters in order to rule out any influences of the individual nominee on the outcomes.

To understand and predict a person's interpersonal behavior in a designated social situation, one has to determine his or her various reference groups. For example, two people collide in a crowded street. They each may ignore the collision, they may beg each other's pardon, or one may shove the other. What each person does to some extent will depend upon whether the interacting persons are male or female, white or black, upper, middle, or lower class, and whether the situation is in North America or Zambia.

*Religious Affiliations.* L. B. Ward (1965) completed a large-scale survey of top managements in the United States that suggested that the religious affiliation represented by top management in a firm affected the personnel policies promoted within the firm. Personnel practices were more likely to be liberal where top management was not restricted to members of one religious group. Policies were more likely to be liberal if top management was exclusively Jewish than if it was exclusively Protestant. Most conservative were exclusively Catholic managements.

### Real Outside Relationships

Leaders usually belong to more groups than do followers. Leaders integrate the various subgroups of a larger group and mediate between membership groups and the wider community. Thus J. B. Marks (1959) found that leaders maintained significantly more extra-clique friendship links than did followers. Leaders tended to mediate between their own groups and the surrounding social environment. Again, Schiffman and Gaccione (1974) found that the opinion leaders in the nursing home industry were administrators who interacted more often with administrators from other nursing homes. However, the leaders who identified with group norms were more strongly supported by members than the leader who identified with external groups.

Effects of leaders' outside connections are well-known. Interlocking company directorates take considerable advantage of such linkages. In the same way, social service organizations were found to be more effective and better financed and to provide higher quality of service when their boards were composed of high-status (business leaders) rather than middle-status (middle management and professional) members (Zald, 1967).

*Organizational Affiliations.* Emergent leadership within an initially leaderless group tends to be related to the leader's status in society and in various formal organizations. Bass and Wurster (1963b) reported that in discussion groups involving industrial supervisors emergent leadership was highly related to the leaders' rank in the hierarchy of their company. Results obtained by Chapple and Donald (1946) also supported this point of view. In the same way, Crockett (1955), studying decision-making conferences in business and government, observed that emergent leaders tended to hold comparatively high rank in their own organizations.

## THE SURROUNDING ORGANIZATION

It is obvious that the relations between a supervisor and a subordinate are strongly influenced by the policies and climate of the larger organization in which their small group forms a part. Examples are replete of such studies in education, health organizations, industry, and elsewhere. For instance, Halpin and Croft (1962) developed scales for the measurement of different aspects of a school's organizational climate, leadership, and teacher response. Sheridan and Vredenburgh (1978) showed that the head nurses' consideration and initiation of structure in a hospital setting could be explained partly by turnover among staff members and administrative climate as measured by an instrument developed by Pritchard and Karasick (1973). J. L. Franklin (1975) examined similar relations in a broader organizational context.

To examine the linkage of leadership to organization, it will be convenient to consider organizations in terms of the Aston model which focused on two major characteristics of the organization: structuring of activities (prescribed work roles) and centralization of decision making (limits on discretion). These represent the two major strategies of administrative control (Pugh, Hickson, Hinings & Turner, 1968).

### Structuring of Activities

Using data from 215 governmental departments, M. W. Meyer (1975) found that the stability of organizational structure was lower when leadership had changed a great deal in the past, when leaders were dependent on higher authority, and when close contact was maintained with superiors.

*Functional Requirements.* Further evidence along these lines by O'Connor and

Farrow (1979) demonstrated the importance for satisfaction of matching the amount of structure required by the research and production managers and the preferences of managers in these respective functions.

Heller (1969a), in a survey of British managers, found that those in personnel and general management functions typically used less directive procedures than colleagues in finance and production. Managers who led groups in purchasing, stores, and sales tended to be in between. This is consistent with earlier work by Fleishman, Harris, and Burtt (1955), who noted that foremen in manufacturing departments of other departments working under time constraints were likely to receive higher merit ratings if they tended to initiate structure more often, while the reverse was true for foremen in service departments. In addition, in the nonmanufacturing service departments, considerate supervisors were seen as more proficient. More initiation contributed to greater absenteeism and grievances mainly in manufacturing departments and to turnover in service departments.

Manufacturing usually demands more routinization and coordination than do service functions. In a study of 787 managers, Child and Ellis (1973) found that managers in service organizations compared to manufacturing organizations saw their roles as less formal, less well-defined, and less routine.

*More on the Effects of Organizational Differences in Structure.* Leadership and interpersonal behavior were seen to depend on how much constraint was imposed by the situation and by the organizational structure. For example, Hare (1957) observed that self-oriented and group-oriented leaders among groups of boys did not differ in aggression on the supervised playground at school, but self-oriented leaders were significantly more aggressive in the unsupervised neighborhood. There were more differences between situations than between leadership styles. Disagreement was higher in both styles on the playground, while tension and antagonism were higher in the neighborhood.

Elsewhere, more delegation by the superior was seen if work roles were clearly prescribed and much discretion was permitted. Pellegrin (1953), Philipsen and Cassee (1965), and Weinberg (1965) observed that institutional requirements determined the characteristics of members who were accepted as leaders. Based on questionnaire responses from 395 white-collar employees and managers from the engineering division of a public utility, Hunt, Osborn, and Schuler (1978) concluded that the amount of approval of subordinates by a manager was predicted by the organization's general communication and planning adequacy and by the extent to which the manager received orders out of the chain of command. The manager's disapproval of subordinates was also affected by these out-of-the-chain-of-command orders over which the manager had no control. Altogether, five organizational practices concerned with enhancing communications, promoting job clarity, and providing clear standards affected the leaders' supportive behavior toward their subordinates.

E. L. Miller (1966b) reported that craft union officials expressed a greater need for other-directed behavior than did officials of industrial unions. However, in both types of unions, the relative emphasis on other-directed behavior was less in the higher positions. This behavior tended to vary not only with type of organization but with level of position in the structure.

For seventy-eight executives described by 407 subordinates, with stepwise regression, Bass, Farrow, Valenzi, and Solomon (1975) found that in organizations described as more trusting, more *participative* leadership behavior was observed. Organizations described as more orderly tended to yield more delegation, whereas in organizations seen by subordinates as having clear goals, the managers were described as more *directive,* more likely to consult with their subordinates, and to share decision making with them. In a followup with over 1,200 subordinates describing their superior's leader behavior and aspects of the organization, Farrow, Valenzi, and Bass (1980) found that *direction* was most frequent when organizational constraints were high and consultation was most frequent when organizational goals were clear and trust levels were high. *Direction* and consultation were greater when more organization order was present. Under these same organizational conditions of more clarity, trust, and order, less leader manipulation was observed. Blain (1964) surveyed twenty-four companies in England. The tightness of organizational structure was found highly related to the organizational functions to be performed.

*Structural Complexity.* As the complexity of the organization increases, the dynamics within it must change. For example, the number of possible coalitions increases. Further, as Bryson and Kelley (1978) have noted, the greater the complexity, the more leadership positions there will be. The positions will be arranged hierarchically, with additional carefully delineated roles and responsibilities, and additional power attached to each position as one moves higher in the hierarchy.

Complexity is likely to have an indirect effect on the pattern of succession. The greater the complexity, the more levels any candidate needs to climb to reach the top of the hierarchy. Complexity probably also has an effect on the nature of accession to office. As complexity increases, so does factionalism (Tichy, 1973; Tushman, 1977).

Hunt, Osborn, and Martin (1979) completed a line of investigation of that part of a leader's behavior that is nondiscretionary, that is determined by the structured relationships and requirements imposed by the organization, and that part that is discretionary. Studying sixty-eight army telecommunication units, they found that greater complexity in the structure of the unit was associated with more discretionary leadership. In addition, discretionary leadership was related to both performance and satisfaction.

Appelbaum (1977) showed that those leaders involved in the structural complexity represented by government bureaucracy tended to be oriented more toward Theory X in their outlook and to be more concerned than normal about their safety needs and less concerned about ego and self-actualizing needs. However, Farrow, Valenzi, and Bass (1980) reported that leaders in private, profit-making firms exhibited significantly more *direction,* manipulation, consultation, and delegation than counterparts in mainly governmental not-for-profit agencies.

*Secrecy.* An obvious condition that limits whether managers can be participative with their subordinates is the extent to which secrecy concerning products, techniques, and business strategies are required by the organization. Employees cannot be asked to participate in decisions if much of the information required to discuss such decisions cannot be revealed to them (Tannenbaum & Massarik, 1950).

*Tall versus Flat Structures.* Worthy (1950) maintained that flat, decentralized organizations resulted in greater employee satisfaction than tall, centralized structures. Richardson and Walker (1948) studied a company (IBM) in which the number of vertical levels of organization was reduced and concluded that reduction of social distance between management and workers resulted in improved satisfaction and teamwork. Again,

Porter and Lawler (1964) studied managers in tall or flat organizations. Managers in small companies were better satisfied with a flat structure, while those in large companies were better satisfied with a tall structure. Porter and Lawler (1965) surveyed the published literature on the relationship between job satisfaction and organizational structure. Neither centralization–decentralization, tall–flat structure, nor total organizational size was found consistently related to job satisfaction. Carzo and Yanouzas (1969) studied experimental organizations with tall and flat structures. Tall structures required more time to process decisions; flat structures required more time to coordinate efforts and resolve conflicts. But tall organizations were superior in profits and rate of return.

### Centralization and Decentralization

Some case studies have suggested that increases in worker authority and autonomy come about as a result of managerial policy and action. Such policy is not dependent upon decentralization, but it is perhaps more easily enforced by higher management when working through few rather than many levels of authority (Cordiner, 1952; Newman & Logan, 1965; Zald, 1964). Decentralization was advocated as a method for reducing the concentration of authority in high-level positions and for filtering it down to employees (Kruisinga, 1954; Kline & Martin, 1958). But the reasons that motivate managerial decisions to decentralize are usually concerned with problems of coordination. As organizations become larger, with many geographically dispersed subunits involving numerous products, the problem of coordination and responding to local change induces a tendency toward decentralization (Chandler, 1956, 1962; National Industrial Conference Board, 1948).

Centralization of legislative leadership was seen by Bryson and Kelley (1978) as likely to give greater enforcement power to the leadership and more stability. But more conflicts are also likely due to the lack of sharing of information (A. Rosenthal, 1974). Consensual decision making becomes less frequent (Pettigrew, 1972; Mechanic, 1962). Adversary relationships will be greater (R. A. Gordon, 1961) unless statesmen appear at the top of the centralized leadership (Selznick, 1951). However, centralization promotes coups (S. Kahn, 1970).

*Interview and Survey Evidence.* In a survey of 217 executives in 109 firms, Stagner (1969) found that decentralization was not related to profitability from sales. However, profitability from capital was significantly higher in centralized than in decentralized firms.

Baum (1961) studied a government agency and found that decentralization, was accompanied by an increase of decision-making authority in the higher levels of administration. Baker and France (1954) studied the personnel and industrial relations departments of a sample of firms. Top managers tended to prefer the decentralization of industrial relations functions so that local problems arising in a specific plant could be solved as they arose. Union officials, on the other hand, preferred centralization of industrial relations functions as an aid in industry-wide bargaining. Similarly, M. Whitehill (1968) surveyed companies in the meat-packing industry and found that union negotiations with centralized structures (main office contacts) resulted in more benefits for employees than negotiations with decentralized structures (local plant contacts). Blau (1968) studied 250 government agencies and found that decentralization was most prevalent in those agencies employing large numbers of highly qualified personnel. The presence of automation and poorly qualified personnel in large agencies was accompanied by more vertical levels of organization and by tighter management control.

Dale (1955) concluded that little in the way of reliable data has accumulated on the actual effects of decentralization. T. A. Mahoney (1967) surveyed 283 organizations, obtaining managers' perceptions on 114 variables. Decentralization was found correlated negatively with most criteria of organizational effectiveness. Nevertheless, Newman and Summer (1961) outlined a set of guides for determining the degree of decentralization to be considered by an organization. Finally, W. T. Morris (1967) formulated forty propositions and a set of mathematical models for evaluating the factors involved in and the consequences of decentralization.

## SUPERIORS AND SUBORDINATES AS REFERENCE GROUPS FOR LEADERS

In Chapter 13, we discussed how supervisors in the middle of the hierarchy handle the potential conflicts inherent in having both their supervisors and their subordinates as reference groups.

### Measurement of Orientation toward Superiors

D. T. Campbell and associates (1955, 1957, 1958, 1961) developed various methods for measuring orientation toward, or identification with superiors and subordinates. Campbell, Burwen, and Chapman (1955) analyzed items assigned to seventeen subscales. The subscales were not highly correlated, nor were they highly related to measures of authoritarianism or aptitude for service. The most promising subscales were identification with discipline, superior–subordinate orientation, and eagerness for responsibility and advancement. Burwen and Campbell (1957a) found that attitude test scores did not predict differences in superior–subordinate orientation in a role-playing situation. Scores on an information test based on leadership research were not highly related to authoritarianism or other measures of superior–subordinate orientation (Campbell & Damarin, 1961).

Campbell and McCormack (1957) compared attitudes of air force and civilian personnel. Colonels were found significantly less oriented toward superiors than were majors or college men, and majors were less so than air force cadets or their instructors. Air force majors and lieutenant-colonels were significantly more subordinate-oriented than the other groups tested.

Chapman and Campbell (1957a) studied small groups performing verbal and manual tasks. Scales for measuring superior–subordinate attitudes, identification with discipline, alienation, authoritarianism, and cooperation were administered. Superior rather than subordinate orientation correlated .21 with authoritarianism, .08 with alienation, .25 with identification with discipline, and − .20 with cooperation. Teams led by superior-oriented leaders were somewhat more productive than those led by subordinate-oriented leaders on the motor task, but not on the verbal task. Group members with high superior-oriented scores were rated high in popularity and those with high scores on authoritarianism were rated low in popularity.

*Identification with Superiors or Subordinates and Performance
and Satisfaction of Leaders and Followers*

Lawler, Porter and Tannenbaum (1968) found that interactions with superiors were more favorably valued than those with subordinates. In addition, the managers reacted more favorably to interactions that they initiated than to those initiated by others. Results obtained by Pelz (1952) in his study of industrial work groups indicated that first-line supervisors who are subordinate-oriented tended to be evaluated positively by workers, but only if they were perceived to have sufficient influence with superiors so that they could satisfy workers' expectations. Balma, Maloney, and Lawshe (1958a, b) studied more than 1,000 foremen in nineteen plants. They found that foremen who identified themselves with management were rated as having significantly more productive groups than those who were lacking in identification with superiors. But employee satisfaction with a foreman was not related to the foreman's orientation. Again, R. S. Barrett (1963) discovered that foremen who perceived themselves as similar to immediate superiors in approach to problems tended to feel free to do things in their own way. Henry (1949) and others found that rapidly promoted executives tended to identify themselves with their superiors as a primary organization reference group. Finally, Fleishman and Peters (1962) observed that top-level managers tended to identify the effectiveness of lower-level managers with that of their immediate middle-level superiors.

*Perceived Similarity Effects*

Porter and Kaufman (1959) devised a scale for determining the extent to which supervisors describe themselves as similar to top management. Self-perceptions similar to top management were associated with interaction patterns perceived by peers as similar to the interaction patterns of managers in high-level positions.

Subordinates whose attitudes and role perceptions were similar to those of superiors were preferred by their superiors (Miles, 1964a) and rated by them as more effective (V. F. Mitchell, 1968). In turn, subordinates resembling their superiors in the personality traits ''sociable'' and ''stable'' were better satisfied than those resembling their superiors less closely.

We now move from examining influences on the leader from outside the immediate group led to those from the inside.

# 24

## INTRODUCTION

In Chapter 16 we explored the interacting nature of leader–follower relations. Here, we concentrate further on effects of the group qua group on its leadership. Group activities transcend those of its individual members. For example, group norms can survive even if all the members are changed. Members isolated from each other behave very differently than when all are gathered together.

### Mutuality Involved

What a leader may do will depend on the group (Carter, Haythorn, Shriver & Lanzetta, 1951; Barnlund, 1962). At the same time, what the group will do will depend on the leader. The leader can influence the group's drive, its cohesion, its goal selection, and its goal attainment. In turn, the impact of leader–group interactions on the individual members is substantial. Individual subordinates may react differently to a leader when alone with the leader than when in a group with the leader. The group narrows the range of possible leader–individual subordinate interactions in the interests of equity and time, and because of group expectations about the leader. Leader reactions to the group may have a stronger impact on its members than reactions to them as individuals. Supervisors are evaluated based on the performance of their group rather than of individual members (Schriesheim, Mowday & Stogdill, 1979).

Group properties—the means and variances in individual member attributes—make a difference in the type of leadership and its effects. Thus, Dyson, Godwin, and Hazelwood (1976) were able to link member consensus about decisions in homogeneous but not heterogeneous groups. D. G. Bowers (1969) found that the leader's importance will be greater for work groups composed of some persons rather than others. Among 1,700 work groups from twenty-two organizations, groups made up of longer-service, older, and less educated members attached greater importance to the supervisor and his or her direct influence on their behavior. The effects were particularly relevant in administrative, staff, production, and marketing groups. In better educated, shorter-service, younger groups, especially those largely female such as clerical and service groups, less importance was given to the role of the supervisor and greater importance to the behavior of peer members in the group. Variations in groups likely to affect what the leader can and will do include group motivation, cohesiveness, size, and status. Chapters 10, 13, and 16 have looked at some of these effects from different perspectives.

The leadership contribution to group productivity is likely to be reduced by faulty group interaction processes (Steiner, 1972) or enhanced by "assembly bonus effects" (Collins & Guetzkow, 1964) that occur mainly with difficult tasks (Shaw & Ashton, 1976). That is, above and beyond individual members' capabilities to deal with the task they face, faulty leader–group interactions may result in a performance worse than if the members had been free to work alone and uninfluenced; when members form a well-led group, their performance may be greater than what might have been expected from a simple pooling of their individual capabilities (Bass, 1980).

Based upon a review of the literature, Stogdill (1959, 1972) identified three possible main effects of the leader on organized groups: productivity, drive, and cohesiveness. A rational model (Figure 24.1) presented by Schriesheim, Mowday, and Stogdill (1979) suggests that group drive and group cohesiveness interact with each other to generate group productivity. Supportive or relations-oriented leadership behavior interacts with instrumental or task-oriented leadership behavior (see Chapter 20) to promote group drive and cohesiveness. All this occurs in the context of the group's development.

## THE GROUP'S DEVELOPMENT

As shown in Figure 24.1, the stage at which the group is in its development as a group is important to the leadership effects. For example, different leaders emerged in

**FIGURE 24.1.  Model Linking Leadership to Group Outcomes**

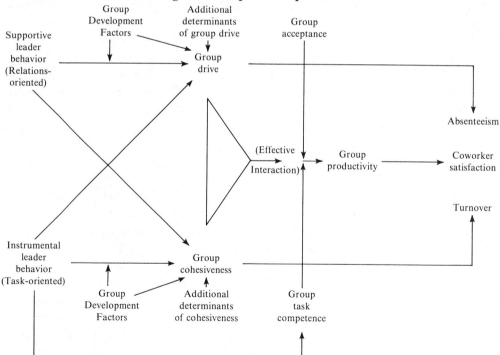

SOURCE: *Adapted from Schriesheim, Mowday, and Stogdill (1979). Modifications are shown in parentheses. Feedback effects of group outcomes on leadership not shown.*

successive stages of therapy in a psychiatric ward (S. Parker, 1958). Again, Sterling and Rosenthal (1950) reported that leaders and followers change with different phases of the group process. The same leaders reoccur when the same phases return. Kinder and Kolmann (1976) found that in 23-hour marathon groups, gains in self-actualization were greatest when initially highly structured leader roles were maintained early in the group's development and then switched to low-structured leadership roles later in the group's development. Similarly, Okanes and Stinson (1974) concluded that more Machiavellian persons were chosen as informal leaders early in the development when groups could still improvise. Later, when the groups had become more highly structured, Machiavellians were less likely to be chosen as leaders.

### Phases in Group Development

In one of the early studies of group development, Bales (1950) observed that groups exhibit phases of problem-solving behavior. Bales and Strodtbeck (1951), Heinicke and Bales (1953), Borgatta and Bales (1953b), and Philip and Dunphy (1959) demonstrated that, after an initial introductory polite stage, the second phase in group development tends to involve a great deal of tension growing out of member competition for leadership and stabilization of status structure. Tuckman (1965) reviewed some sixty studies involving experimental, training, and therapeutic groups. An analysis of these studies suggested the following stages of development: (1) forming, characterized by testing and orientation task; (2) storming, characterized by intragroup conflict, status differentiation, and emotional response; (3) norming, characterized by the development of group cohesion, norms, and intermember exchange; and (4) performing, marked by functional role interrelations and effective task performance. These stages overlap in some groups and alternate in others (Heinen & Jacobsen, 1976). Geier (1967) completed a study detailing the first two stages. In a study of unstructured experimental groups, Geier (1967) instructed some participants on a group task. Members entered their groups without an assigned role. The leader was that member perceived by a consensus of members as having made the most successful attempt to influence the group. Stage 1 involved a rapid and painless elimination of contenders with negative characteristics. The second stage involved an intense struggle for leadership and further elimination. Only two of eighty members made no effort to gain leadership. Those who were uninformed, unparticipative, rigid, and hindered goal attainment were eliminated first. Attempts to recruit lieutenants and member support were most obvious in stage 2. Lieutenant roles developed in eleven of sixteen groups. Of the eleven lieutenants, seven had been contenders for leadership in stage 1.

Groups are unable to engage in effective task performance when they are prevented from developing a differentiated role structure (Borgatta & Bales, 1953b). Groups with high degrees of consensus about their leadership are more effective and better satisfied than those lacking in consensus.

Stogdill (1972) suggested that group cohesiveness, drive, and productivity are closely related with the developmental stages of groups. In the third stage, when roles have been accepted and communication has improved, group cohesiveness emerges. In the fourth and final stages of effective task performance, group productivity is seen. The arousal and tensions of the second stage most closely reflects group drive, but group drive appears in every stage. The specific tasks which the group is motivated to perform, however, may differ across the stages. Thus, for instance, in the second stage, group drive is directed toward evolving a structure for the group; in the third stage group drive operates to develop greater cohesiveness; in the last stage, group drive is directed toward the successful completion of the group task. Leadership functions would depend on the stage of a group's development. Relations-oriented leader behavior would most closely correspond to the group's need to develop cohesiveness in the third stage; task-oriented leader behavior would facilitate group task accomplishment in the fourth stage of development.

### Effects of Changes and Instability

Hall and Williams (1966) found that established groups were more effective than ad hoc groups in the solution of problems, the use of member resources, and the handling of intermember conflict. Trow (1960) systematically varied the rate of member turnover in problem-solving groups. Performance effectiveness of groups decreased with the increase in rate of turnover. Rogers, Ford, and Tassone (1961) also reported a decrement in experimental group performance with increase in member turnover. Various training methods employed to counteract the effects of turnover were unsuccessful. B. D. Fine (1970) studied 151 members of an unstable manpower pool and 582 workers assigned to stable groups in a refinery. The groups did not differ significantly in coordination, communication, participation, decision making, satisfaction, or mental health. Unstable groups were higher than stable groups in motivation and conflict resolution. Leaders of stable groups were significantly higher in interaction facilitation, but not in support, goal emphasis, or work facilitation. Leaders of unstable groups exercised less control and the workers expressed less need for freedom.

H. Feldman (1937) and J. M. Jackson (1953b) studied the effects of switching the supervisors of highly effective and highly ineffective work groups. Previously ineffective groups improved their performance under effective supervisors. The performance of previously effective groups declined under supervisors of previously ineffective groups.

Flament (1956) and Pryer, Flint, and Bass (1962) reported that groups tended to remain effective as long as they did not change leaders. Early agreement about who should lead tended to increase group effectiveness in highly motivated groups. E. R. Carlson (1960) found that a group is better satisfied with its leaders and with the group as a whole when it does not contain cliques. If the discussion leader of a therapy group failed to provide task structure, members striving to arrive at structure sought a leader among themselves (Bion, 1961).

### The Group's History

According to J. R. Gibb (1961) the developmental history of the group must be taken into account. The role boundary set for an individual—his or her limits—encompasses the acts that group members will accept from him or her. Boundary is established by fairly stable role expectations. In group experiments by Gibb, one leader with a permissive leadership style was followed by another with a restrictive style and vice versa. In other groups, one leader was followed by another with the same style.

Group members accepted and responded more readily to leaders who followed other leaders with the same prescribed range of behaviors. They were also less defensive and more productive in problem solving. Expectations were built quickly, with minimum cues, and survived over long periods.

*Conformity to Boundary Expectations.* Members frequently chosen in sociometric tests tended to stay within the realistic boundaries prescribed by the group. Individuals less frequently chosen were more likely to violate boundary specifications. Perhaps those who were chosen more often had wider behaviors and more role space in which to move. Role actions outside the role boundary were responded to by pretending not to see or hear the behavior, ignoring it, subtle fighting, open rebellion, isolating the member, or forcing his or her withdrawal.

*Role Repertoire.* The adequacy of role repertoire was found a function of (1) adequate diagnosis of the situation; (2) adequate hypothesis about the requisite role for high influence entry into the group; and (3) adequate role-taking skill once an appropriate hypothesis has been formulated about entry. Given powerful norms, groups tend to select goals and perform activities commensurate with the norms. In order to exert influence, the behavior and goals of the leader must be consonant with group goals. A high group defense level prevents effective exercise of influence.

*Reduced Defensiveness.* Groups undergo four levels of increasing maturity and reduced defensiveness, according to J. R. Gibb (1964). First, they learn to trust each other; second, with increasing trust they learn how to make effective decisions; third, better decisions make possible better control over choice of goals; and fourth, these better goals make for better use of the group's resources.

*Changes in Performance.* Heinicke and Bales (1953) observed that emergent leaders tended to rate high in initiating suggestions and opinions in the first and second sessions, while in the second session they engaged in an active status struggle. After consolidating their position in the second session, they became less active in the third and fourth sessions, permitting other members to play more active roles. But the leader's opinions and suggestions remained accepted and they did not have to make as much effort to win their points.

*Leadership and Stable Structure.* A stable structure of relations must be developed for a group to become cohesive (Sherwood & Walker, 1960; Tuckman, 1965; Heinen & Jacobsen, 1976). Leaders have important effects on a group's development of a stable structure (Heslin & Dunphy, 1964). As Schriesheim, Mowday, and Stogdill (1979) noted and we have detailed in earlier chapters, during the early stages of a group's development members may want and accept more direction. At this time, leaders may exert greater impact on stabilizing group role structures and thus have a greater impact on group cohesiveness.

## EFFECTS OF GROUP DRIVE AND GROUP COHESIVENESS ON LEADERSHIP

### Group Drive

Group drive was conceived by Stogdill (1972) as group arousal, motivation, freedom, enthusiasm or esprit, and the intensity with which members invest expectation and energy on behalf of the group. Similarly, Steiner (1972) defined group motivation as the willingness of members to contribute their resources to the collective effort. Zander (1971) found such motivation to depend on members' desires to achieve success and avoid failure, the value to them of successful outcomes as well as previous history of success (Zander, 1968), and pressures for high performance (Zander, Medow & Dustin, 1964).

Group drive can be relatively negative. Thus, Ingham, Levinger, Graves, and Peckham (1974) observed that individuals did not work quite as hard when paired with one or two others than when they worked individually (Zander, 1971).

### Group Cohesiveness

C. E. Shaw (1976) noted three ways to define group cohesiveness: member attraction to the group, the level of group morale, and the coordination attitudes among the members of a group. Festinger (1950) viewed group cohesiveness broadly as a group property resulting from all the forces acting on members to remain in the group. Bass (1960) equated group cohesiveness with the attraction of the members to the group and how much they esteemed each other. Cartwright (1965) added individual needs, expectancies from group membership, and alternatives offered elsewhere. But Stogdill (1972) limited the concept of group cohesiveness to the extent to which members reinforce each others' expectations about the value of maintaining the identity of the group.

### Impact of Group Drive and Group Cohesiveness and Other Group Variables on Leadership Behavior

Except for the impact of stress on leader behavior which we shall detail in Chapter 26, there have been relatively few studies dealing with how leaders are affected by their group's motivation and cohesiveness. Farrow, Valenzi, and Bass (1980), in the previously quoted analysis of 1,200 to 1,400 subordinates' descriptions of their groups and leaders, found that directive and delegative leadership was seen more frequently when subordinate commitment to the group was high. Also, consultation by the group leader was more frequent in work groups described by their members as harmonious and free of conflict (Bass, Farrow, Valenzi & Solomon, 1975).

*Group Drive.* The willingness to expend effort for the group affected the leadership process. Thus, Gustafson (1968) manipulated commitment for members of discussion groups by varying the extent to which course grades depended on group performance. Less role differentiation (leaders, task specialists, and social-emotional specialists) was perceived by members with both strong or weak commitment: that is, the three functions were not differentiated, but the group showed less social-emotional behavior in groups with strong commitment. Similarly, Borgatta, Cottrell, and Wilker (1959) studied groups that differed in member expectations about the value of group activities. The higher the initial expectation, the higher the final level of satisfaction for groups as a whole. Leaders of low-expectation groups changed their assessments more than leaders of high-expectation groups.

The motivation of members affected the success of their leaders. Bass, Flint, and Pryer (1957b) demonstrated that when all members are equal in status an individual is more likely to attain success as a group leader if he or she attempts more leadership than others. However, among highly motivated members, attempted leadership was found to exert little effect on success in influencing the group decision. In the same way, Hemphill and associates (1957) showed that group members attempt to lead more frequently when the rewards for problem solution are relatively high and there is a reasonable expectation that efforts to lead will contribute to task accomplishment. Durand and Nord (1976) observed that those subordinates in a textile and plastics firm who felt that their success or failure was in the hands of forces outside their own control and therefore were presumably lower in group motivation tended to see their supervisors as initiating more structure and less consideration.

*Cohesiveness.* The ease of the flow of influence between leader and follower was expected to be associated with cohesive social relations (Turk, Hartley & Shaw, 1962). Theodorson (1957) found that the roles of task leader and social leader were combined in cohesive groups but were separated in poorly integrated groups. Weak group cohesiveness provided a condition under which a leader who scored high in sociability attempted to develop cooperation through increased interaction, while an individual who was low in sociability tended to remain passive (Armilla, 1967).

Gergen and Taylor (1969) demonstrated that high-status participants, when presented to a group in a "solidarity setting," tended to meet group expectations. However, they failed to meet expectations when they were presented in a "productivity setting." When no expectations were present, low-status participants in the productivity context presented themselves more positively. In the solidarity condition they became more self-demeaning. In the absence of expectations, the high-status participants did not behave differently under the two settings.

Acceptance of the group leadership is linked to identification with the in-group. Thus, Bulgarians or Yemenites identified themselves first as Jewish so therefore they could more easily accept Israeli leadership. On the other hand, Israeli immigrants who identified first as German, American, or Moroccan were more likely to accept Israeli leadership only if their self-evaluation was not rooted in the old country (Eisenstadt, 1952).

*Agreement on Who Shall Lead.* Whether or not the immediate group is in agreement on who shall lead it affects the leadership process. Agreement among the members about who should lead, associated with greater group cohesiveness (Shelley, 1960a), and increased the frequency of leadership attempts (Banta & Nelson, 1964). Bales and Slater (1955) found that three different member roles tended to emerge in groups without consensus on who shall lead: an active role, a task specialist, and a best-liked person. In groups with high consensus about who should be the leader, the active and task specialist roles were performed by the same member. Harrell and Gustafson (1966) reported that groups without consensus tended to exhibit an active task specialist along with a best-liked member. Role differentiation occurred less in both their high- and low-consensus groups than in the Bales and Slater study. In addition, attractive groups and those with the most interesting tasks tended to exhibit the least role differentiation.

*Cooperativeness.* Groups with cooperative members, as compared with groups with competitive members, were more likely to develop leaders, evaluate fellow members more favorably, show less hostility, and solve their problems as a group more rapidly (Raven & Eachus, 1963). This is consistent with conventional wisdom suggesting that competition should be encouraged between groups but not within groups.

*Compatible Members.* Groups composed of compatible rather than incompatible members were better able to elect a competent leader or to use the resources and abilities of members by electing a leader who allowed enough freedom to high-ability members for expression and influence on group performance (W. C. Schutz, 1955). Lester (1963) found that the emergent leader among the highly task-oriented members of the American Mount Everest expedition was more relations-oriented.

Thelen and associates (1954) factor-analyzed the self- and group descriptions made by members of a discussion group. Five clusters of members were identified. Cluster A, composed of members who rejected fighting and pairing, made significantly more leadership attempts than any other group. It preferred structure and cohesiveness which prevents undue domination and intimacy. Cluster B, with ego needs for intimate relationships, showed little interest in status differences. Cluster C, which preferred to avoid power struggles or responsibility, rejected competition for leadership. Cluster AC, which rejected fighting, supported the leader and looked to him to support their status needs. Cluster BC, which accepted fighting, supported the leader and attempted to mediate conflicts in order to maintain group cohesion.

Other group variables affecting group leadership include its size, status, norms, and goals.

## EFFECTS OF SIZE OF THE GROUP ON LEADERSHIP

### Opportunities to Lead

The size of the group affects emergence as a leader. Bass and Norton (1951) reported that the opportunity to adopt leadership functions in a group decreases as the number of members increases. In groups ranging in size from two to twelve, relative stratification increased directly with increases in size, with a maximum in groups of six members. In agreement, Hare (1962) reviewed several studies which suggest that as size of the group increases, individual members have less opportunity to talk and to attempt to lead and fewer members initiate leadership acts. In parallel, Warner and Hilander (1964) studied 191 voluntary organizations in a community. Member involvement and participation decreased as the size of the organization increased. Evidence that the opportunity for leadership tends to decrease as the size of the group increases was also provided by Dawe (1934), Bales, Strodtbeck, Mills and Roseborough (1951), and Stephan (1952).

As group size increases, more differences appear among members in their tendencies to be talkative and in their attempts to influence (Bales & Slater, 1955). But Kidd (1958), contrary to most researchers, found no relation between group size and increase of influence in groups of two, four, or six members. Also, Blankenship and Miles (1968) noted that the size of unit led was less important to the decision behavior of executives than their organizational level.

### Changing Leadership Style

*Requirements.* Hemphill (1950b) studied groups with leaders considered superior by the group members. He found that as the size of the group increased, the members made greater demands on the leader. Larger groups made significantly stronger demands for leader strength, reliability, predictability, job competence, coordination, impartial enforcement of rules, and structure along with less consideration of the individual.

Chapin and Tsouderos (1955) studied 91 organizations by the case history method. They concluded that as organizations increase in size and differentiation there is a tendency for rank-and-file members to become more passive and further removed from the policy-making centers and for the executives to become further removed from the activities which they plan and initiate. The long lines of command impose problems in communication. Goodstadt and Kipnis (1970) found that as group size increased, supervisors tended to spend less time with poor workers and to give fewer pay raises to good workers.

Pelz (1951) observed that small groups were better satisfied with the leader who took their part, while large groups (ten or more members) were better satisfied with the leader who supported the organization. Medalia's (1954) results indicated that, as the size of the work unit increased, the workers' perception of their leader as "human relations minded" decreased. Similarly, in 100 randomly selected chapters of the League of Women Voters, J. Likert (1958) found that officers engaged in more activities as the chapters increased in size, but presidents exhibited less interest in members' ideas. Consistent with all of the above findings, Schriesheim and Murphy (1976) found through a subgroup moderator analysis that leader initiation of structure was related to satisfaction of members in larger work groups and consideration was related to satisfaction in smaller groups.

### Changing Personal Requirements

Hare (1952) studied boys in groups ranging from five to twelve members. Leaders were found to yield more influence on decisions in the smaller groups, but the leader's skill level was not related to influence. The larger groups demanded more skill from the leader, and in large groups leader skill was positively correlated with amount of change toward group consensus.

Thomas and Fink (1963) reviewed several studies which suggested that as groups enlarged, the leader had to deal with more other leaders, more role differentiation, more role specialization, and more cliques. Slater (1958) noted that stabilization of a group's role structure became increasingly difficult with increased group size. In a comprehensive summary of personal factors found associated with leadership in natural and experimental groups, R. D. Mann (1959) noted that in groups of seven or under in size, intelligence seemed a little more important to leadership than adjustment, but in larger groups adjustment increased slightly and intelligence decreased slightly in correlation with leadership.

### Span of Control

As the size of the group increases, the number of interactional relationships between members increases at an extremely rapid rate. Graicunas (1937) demonstrated that a leader with two subordinates, when interacting with them singly and in combination and considering contacts initiated by the leader and the subordinates, can be involved in six possible relationships. With four subordinates, the number of relationships is 44; with six subordinates, the number of relationships is 222. Graicunas concluded that executives should not have more than four or five assistants reporting to them directly due to the time required by personal contacts. Surveys of industrial executives by Dale (1952), F. W. Mahler (1961), J. H. Healy (1956), and Entwisle and Walton (1961) indicated that corporation presidents may have from one to twenty-five assistants reporting to them. The average in the several surveys ranged from five to nine immediate assistants. A review of the literature on the relation of span of control to group size was completed by House and Miner (1969).

Guion (1953) and G. D. Bell (1967) found that first-line supervisors tended to supervise fewer subordinates as the complexity of the job increased. Contrary to hypothesis, span of control was not related to closeness of supervision (G. D. Bell, 1967; Udell, 1967). J. H. Healy (1956) found, however, that for chief executives of corporations there was greater involvement of subordinates in policy making as number of subordinates increased. The number of assistants tended to increase with growth in size of the firm. His results suggested that individuals differ in interaction capacity and that many who become leaders of very large organizations are able to interact with twelve to fifteen or more assistants without feeling overburdened or pressured for time. Indik (1964) surveyed 116 organizations ranging in size from fifteen to 3,000 members, finding that as organizations increase in size they take on more and more operative members before adding new supervisors. Thus, the number of individuals supervised by the chief executive tends to increase as the organization grows.

### Confounding with Other Factors

Indik (1963, 1965a) cautioned that most generalizations about the effects of size are confounded by other factors, such as the nature of the task, communications, co-ordinations, and the degree to which members are attracted to the organization. For instance, Seashore (1954), in a survey of 5,871 workers from 228 factory groups ranging in size from five to fifty found that the smaller groups were also more cohesive. The same was true for conference groups studied by N. E. Miller (1950). Satisfaction is also likely to be higher among employees in smaller groups (Worthy, 1950; D. Katz, 1949). Further complicating the matter, Porter and Lawler (1964) indicated that the effect of group size on satisfaction depends on the organization's structure.

Worthy (1950) suggested that employee morale is higher in "flat" organizations with few status levels than in "tall" organizations with several status levels. Porter and Lawler (1964) found, however, that employee morale was not clearly related to tall or flat structure. Size and structure interacted to affect satisfaction. Job satisfaction was high in small, flat structures and in large, tall structures. The satisfaction of self-actualization needs was higher in the former; satisfaction of social and security needs was high in the latter type of structure.

## GROUP STATUS

Stogdill (1962) advanced the hypothesis that negotiations between groups will be carried on most effectively when representatives are equal in status. Manheim (1960) studied experimental groups that varied in status and had either appointed or emergent leaders. Two groups sent notes to each other to reach agreement on solution of a problem. The lowest degree of conflict occurred when both groups had high status and appointed leaders. Conflict increased in rank order under the following conditions: (1) both groups with low status and emergent leaders; (2) both with low status and appointed leaders; (3) and both with high status and emergent leaders. Even greater conflict occurred when a high-status group negotiated with low-status group, both with emergent leaders. Most conflict occurred when a high-status group with an appointed leader negotiated with a low-status group with an emergent leader. These results suggest that not only the status of the leader but also the relative status levels of the groups are important in intergroup negotiations.

## GROUP NORMS AND LEADERSHIP

### Relevance to Leadership

The group's definition of its task, goals, and paths to its goals strongly affects what a leader can accomplish in the group as well as who will emerge as leader. In turn, the leader often has an impact on group outcomes by influencing the group's norms and goals. Sherif's conception of the social norm exerted a marked influence on leadership research. In an autokinetic experience, Sherif (1936) seated a participant in a darkened room and asked the person to observe a spot of light projected on a screen. The participant reported the distance that the light appeared to move. The average distance for several trials was recorded as the participant's individual norm. When the participant was later placed with other individuals who uniformly reported a distance varying markedly from that reported by the participant, the latter tended to change estimates to conform with the group norm. Asch (1952) obtained similar results when participants were asked to judge the length of lines after numerous confederates of the experimenter had rendered judgments that defied the senses. It was the norm and not any single emergent leader that influenced the participant.

### Conformity and Deviation

Festinger (1950) suggested that the pressure on a member to communicate with others in the group increased with increased discrepancy in opinion between members regarding an item and with increased cohesiveness of the group. In addition, Festinger (1954) suggested that group members tended to compare themselves with others closest to themselves in opinion or ability. When a discrepancy existed, the individual tended to move closer to the group norm. When there was a range of opinion, the extreme deviate tended to be rejected if he or she refused to yield.

Schachter (1951) found that the extreme deviate tended to be rejected by other members of the group. Gerard (1953) and Berkowitz and Howard (1959) obtained results indicating that leaders directed most of their communications to the deviates. If the deviate was unreceptive to accepting the majority point of view, there was a tendency psychologically to expel the deviate from the group. Raven (1959a) reported that experimental group deviates would change more toward the norm than nondeviates when their opinions were expressed both privately and in public.

*The Leader and Norm Conformity*

Thibaut and Strickland (1956) obtained results indicating that as the group pressure to conform increases (often pushed by the leader), the percent of members whose judgments change to conformity increase under group set and decrease under task set. At the same time, McKeachie (1954) reported that member conformity to group norms and liking for the group were greater in leader-oriented than in group-oriented student classes.

Newcomb (1943) conducted a study of social values on a college campus. He found that the most influential members most nearly represented the dominant values of the campus. Those who conformed in conduct but not in attitude possessed social skills but maintained close home and family ties. Those who conformed in attitude but not in conduct tended to lack social skills but regarded attitude conformity as a mark of community acceptance and superior intelligence. In the same way, Sharma (1974) found that Indian student activists prominent as leaders of demonstrations were concerned primarily with student issues, not social change. They tended rather to reflect in attitude the values toward religion, caste, marriage and family of their communities. Subsequently, Scioli, Dyson, and Fleitas (1974) found that when conformity was demanded by college groups, the most dominant members became its instrumental leaders. Similarly, Merei (1949) formed groups composed of very submissive nursery school children. When placed in separate rooms, each group developed its own role structure, rules for play, and routine of activities. After these had become stabilized, a strong leader in play activities was introduced to each group. Although rather widely successful in gaining leadership positions, the new members were not able to change the norms and procedural rules of the group.

Consistent with the above findings, Bates (1952) indicated that the closer individuals come to realizing in their behavior the norms of the group, the higher is their likely position as leaders in the group. However, Borgatta (1955b), Jones, Gergen, and Jones (1963), Kates and Mahone (1958), E. M. Mumford (1959), Katz, Libby, and Strodtbeck (1964), Tannenbaum and Bachman (1966), and Turk (1961) found that group leaders ranked higher in assimilation of group norms because they were highly influential in the formation of the norms. Hare (1962) reviewed several studies which suggested that although leaders may be influential in establishing group norms, once the norms are adopted they are expected to observe the norms.

*Modifiers*

In a study of modernization in India which sampled 606 heads of households engaged in agriculture, Trivedi (1974) found that although opinion leaders may accept innovations in agriculture, they adhere to traditional religious beliefs and convictions. They differentiate agricultural from religious activities more fully in the process.

O. J. Harvey (1960) found that formal leaders conformed more to group norms than informal (sociometric) leaders or other group members, especially under conditions of uncertainty. Mulder (1960) also found that the judgment of leaders was most influenced by other members when they, the leaders, were appointed in an ambiguous situation; least influenced were the informal leaders in the same situation. When the discrepancy between leader judgment and group judgment was gradual, the formal leaders relied more on the situation and less on other members in making their estimations. In the ambiguous situation, the leaders relied more on judgments of other members as a standard for their own evaluation.

### When the Leader Can Deviate

The fact that leaders tend to be prime exemplars of the group value system is not to suggest that they are slaves to the group norm (Rittenhouse, 1966). In fact, they may deviate considerably from the norm in various aspects of their conduct. Rasmussen and Zander (1954), in a study of sociometric cliques among teachers, found that leaders were less threatened than followers by deviation from subgroup norms. Leaders appeared secure enough that they feel they could depart from the norms without jeopardizing their status. Again, Harvey and Consalvi (1960) found that the second-status member in a group was significantly more conforming than the top or bottom member. The leader conformed the least, but not significantly less than the lowest status member. Again, Hughes (1946) observed that members of industrial work groups let "rate busters" know in forceful terms that their violation of group norms would not be tolerated. However, the group leader was allowed more freedom to deviate from certain group norms than other members whose positions were less secure.

### The Leader's Need for Early Conformity

As we have detailed in Chapter 16, Hollander (1958, 1960, 1964) suggested that the early conformity of leaders to the norms of their group gains for them "idiosyncracy credits" enabling them to deviate from the norms at later dates without group disapproval. A large body of research (Hollander, 1964) supported this hypothesis. The lesson here for would-be leaders who wish to bring about changes in a group is that first they usually must accept the group's current norms to be accepted by the group. Practical politicians often can bring about more change by first identifying with a country's current norms, then moving the country ahead with statesmanship that takes the country to where it would not have gone without the politician's direction. F. D. Roosevelt leading the isolationist United States into World War II is illustrative.

*Importance of Acceptance.* Biddle, French, and Moore (1953), in a study of air force personnel, found that the closer the attitude of crew chiefs were to the air force attitude, the stronger were their attempts to lead. Chiefs who accepted their role as supervisor used their influence to further institutional goals and purposes. However, the amount of leadership attempted was not related to the extent to which the chiefs were accepted by crew members. Crew chiefs accepted by their groups, however, deviated further from the air force norm than those who were not accepted, suggesting that greater acceptance enables such crew chiefs to deviate from the official air force attitude. Raven, Kelley, and Shapiro (1954, 1959) obtained results which indicated that highly accepted members of a group were better able to deviate from group norms than those who were not accepted. Also, Dittes and Kelley (1956) studied groups in which members were led to believe that they rated either high, average, or low in acceptance by other members. Those who believed they were average in acceptability conformed to the group norm, while those rated high tended not to conform. Those rated low in acceptability were intermediate in conformity.

*Leadership and Group Goals*

The group purpose or goal is without doubt the predominant norm of a group. Studies of experimental groups indicate that members readily accept, or commit themselves, to the defined task. They appear to develop other norms in support of the task norm. Once the members understand and agree upon the group goal, it operates as a norm in terms of which they evaluate each other for leadership potential.

Goode and Fowler (1949) observed in a small industrial plant that the informal groups supported the company's production goals despite low job satisfaction among workers. The authors attributed this outcome to clear statements of group goals, clear definition of member roles, and strong, congruent pressures toward conformity from within and outside the group.

*Leaders Are More Concerned.* Medow and Zander (1965) found that group members in positions of centrality—and therefore more likely to exert leadership— exhibit more concern for group goals than members in peripheral positions. They select goals in terms of the group's probability for success, are more insistent that the group be correct, exhibit a stronger desire for group success, and perceive themselves to have more influence than other members.

A leader can help maintain interest in a task goal. Zander and Curtis (1965) reported that group members whose task performance was poorer than they expected tend to lower their aspirations. But they did not downgrade or reject the task as much when a leader was present rather than absent.

Those exerting leadership tend to feel more responsible for group outcomes. E. Pepitone (1952) also found that the more responsible a member's role, the greater his or her concern for success of the group. D. M. Shaw (1960) also observed that the member with the larger share in the group task exhibited more concern than other members for success of the group. E. J. Thomas (1957) reported that when members were highly interdependent for task performance, those able to facilitate the performance of other members worked harder for the group.

*Parochialism of Leaders.* Vroom (1960b) studied the attitudes and goal perceptions of executives in a large firm. Actual goals consisted of the average of the statements made by twenty-three top-ranking executives about the organization's goals. Vroom found that the more positive the executives' attitudes toward the organization, the greater the correspondence between the organization's goals and their perception of these goals. But, Browne (1950c) and Dearborn and Simon (1958) found that top-ranking executives of a business firm tended to perceive organizational goals in terms of the functions of their own departments. This is consistent with Bass, Valenzi, and Farrow's (1977) finding that managers' departmental functions determined whether or not they saw economic or noneconomic goals as more important.

*Leaders Assist Goal Clarification.* Absence of a leader to clarify task requirements and group goals result in much time being spent by groups in concern for such clarity and orderliness. Members of unorganized groups (J. R. P. French, 1941) and members of groups under a laissez-faire type of leadership (Lippitt, 1940) frequently expressed a desire to get things organized, to buckle down to work, and to stick to the job that was supposed to be done.

In sum, members readily commit themselves to the goals of a group. The greater a member's responsibility for goal attainment, the stronger his or her commitment to the goals. Leaders exhibit more concern than followers about group success. Goals are used by members as criteria for evaluation of group performances. Once members agree upon their expectations for a group, these expectations operate as a norm that induces a strong pressure for compliance, making routine leadership easier. It also makes leadership that attempts to move the group away from its chosen paths more difficult.

The group variables discussed so far should be considered suggestive rather than exhaustive. Many other group variables affecting leadership transcending individual member attributes can be readily proposed: the age of the group, its charter or sponsors, its temporary versus permanent character, its ease of entry, and so on. Each of these is likely to affect who emerges as leader and what leadership style is most likely to succeed.

## IMPACT OF THE LEADER ON GROUP DRIVE AND COHESIVENESS

### Impact on Group Drive

The evidence that leadership affects group drive is sparse, according to a review by Schriesheim, Mowday, and Stogdill (1979). Nevertheless, Greene and Schriesheim (1977) examined leader behavior, group drive, and cohesiveness, using a longitudinal design with 123 work groups. With cross-lagged correlational, cross-lagged path, and corrected dynamic correlational analyses, instrumental (task-oriented) and supportive (relations-oriented) leader behavior were both found causally antecedent to group drive.

Indirect evidence of the importance of instrumental leader behaviors for group drive stems from Zander's (1971) work on group level of aspiration. The group leader's feedback on performance, centrality of member work role, and reward practices have a positive impact on the group's desire to achieve success.

### Impact on Group Cohesiveness

The review by Schriesheim, Mowday, and Stogdill (1979) noted that democratic, participative, and relations-oriented leader behavior was found to contribute to group cohesiveness in studies by Lewin (1939), Lippitt (1940), R. Likert (1961, 1967), Mann and Baumgartel (1952), among others. Again, task-oriented, directive leader behavior was seen to increase cohesiveness according to Berkowitz (1953a), P. J. Burke (1966a,b), Katzell, Miller, Rotter, and Venet (1970), Keeler and Andrews (1963), and Stogdill (1965a). Both types of leader behavior were important to group cohesiveness in still other investigations (Christner & Hemphill, 1955; Greene & Schriesheim, 1977; Hemphill, Siegel & Westie, 1951; Trieb & Marion, 1969).

### Group Moderators of Leader Impact on Subordinates

How leadership behavior affects the group depends to some extent on characteristics of the group. The same leadership that might contribute to satisfied and productive subordinates in one kind of group may fail to do so in another.

Job involvement and commitment to the Protestant work ethic did not, as expected, reduce the impact of perceived leader behavior on job satisfaction. But for a total of 131 hourly employees in a manufacturing firm in the midwest who completed anonymous mailed questionnaires, significant differences appeared in the impact of job satisfaction and adherence to the Protestant ethic on the relation of leader behavior to job satisfaction (Brief & Aldag, 1977). O'Reilly and Roberts (1978) showed that low supervisor influence and low subordinate mobility aspirations reduced the impact of leader behavior on satisfaction and performance.

According to Farrow, Valenzi, and Bass (1980), consultative leadership would yield more subordinate satisfaction if the leader felt that members were highly committed to the group and its goals. House and Dessler (1974) suggested that the leader might need to structure such groups less tightly.

J. Likert's (1958) study showing how the size of League of Women Voters chapters influenced the chapter presidents, found that in turn, members were more active when the president was interested in their ideas (as in smaller chapters) and when the officers of the chapter felt that members should have relatively high degrees of influence in policies and activities. Members participated less actively in chapter activities when they felt pressure from the president, but participated more actively under pressure from peers and project discussion leaders.

We now turn from variables about the group and its members to the tasks faced by the group, the constraints on the group, the barriers in the paths to its goals, and how these interact with the leader's behavior.

# 25

## TASK DETERMINANTS OF LEADERSHIP

### LEADER COMPETENCE AND TASK REQUIREMENTS

Task requirements affect who emerges as leader, how the leader behaves, and what kinds of leader behavior result in greater productivity and follower satisfaction. Some of the earliest research on leadership in small groups was carried out in the Soviet Union by Chevaleva-Ianovskaia and Sylla (1929) who observed in 888 spontaneous preschool groups that no leadership arose unless special problems occurred. This was a precursor by forty years of path-goal theory which we will examine here. After reviewing the problem dimensions of consequence, we will see how well path-goal theory accounts for available research evidence.

#### Differential Selection

Caldwell and Wellman (1926) showed that the basis of choice varied for the activities for which leaders were chosen by their junior high school classmates. For example, physical abilities determined selection of athletic leaders. Nevertheless, scholarship was high among chosen leaders in all situations examined (one wonders what results for scholarship would be obtained in typical American high schools in the 1980s). Dunkerley (1940) found that college women chosen as intellectual leaders were superior in judgment, initiative, and intellectual ability; women chosen as social leaders were superior in dress and appearance. Those chosen as religious leaders were least neurotic, while those chosen as social leaders were most neurotic.

#### Transfer Effects

Although there is some consistency in a leader's performance in different situations, there is also systematic change in what happens when a leader is transferred. For instance, Stogdill, Shartle, Scott, Coons, and Jaynes (1956) studied twenty navy officers who were to be transferred to new positions and the twenty officers whom they were to replace. After several months in their new positions, transferred officers were found to resemble officers whom they replaced in patterns of work performance, but not in patterns of interpersonal behavior. In other words, there was a tendency for patterns of interpersonal behavior to be transferred from one situation to another, but patterns of work performance were changed in response to the task requirements of the new situations. In a similar way, in small-group experimental study, Carter, Haythorn, Shriver, and Lanzetta (1951) found that the behavior of leaders differed from one situation to another depending upon requirements of the group task.

The individual who emerges as leader in one group tends to acquire leadership status when placed in other groups, particularly if the different groups are performing similar tasks. A change in task may permit new leaders to emerge. Barnlund (1962) rotated group members through six tasks and through groups with changing membership. The highest degree of leadership transferability occurred between literary and construction tasks; the lowest degree between coordination and mathematical tasks. Changes in both task and group membership were found to condition emergence of leadership by specific individuals.

Contrary to the several studies described above, Borg and Tupes (1958) and Blake, Mouton, and Fruchter (1954) reported consistency of behavior in the same leader performing in different groups with varying tasks. Nevertheless, the general trend of the research reviewed supports the hypothesis that groups tend to accept as leaders those members who exhibit characteristics and abilities that will facilitate the accomplishment of the group's specific task. Results from a smaller number of studies support the view that leaders tend to change certain aspects of their behavior in response to changes in group task demands. But the concern of recent leadership theorists and researchers interested in the moderating effects of task requirements on the leader's performance as motivator of subordinates has tended to ignore the leader's task capabilities.

### Leader Ability and Task Requirements

Carter and Nixon (1949a) performed a complicated experiment in which the leader performance of 100 high school boys was measured by teacher ratings, student nominations, school activity records, and observer ratings in three group tasks. A seven-hour battery of tests was also administered. Mechanical ability test scores were related to leadership in mechanical tasks on all criteria. Numerical test scores and persuasiveness were related to leadership in intellectual tasks, while work fluency and clerical test scores were related to leadership in clerical tasks on all criteria. Reasoning test scores were positively related and musical interest scores were negatively related to leadership in all tasks on all criteria.

Clifford and Cohn (1964) correlated described attributes of group members with number of sociometric nominations for nine different leadership positions. Nominations for the role of planner were significantly related to ideas, orders, smart, friendly, liked, empathy, and good influence. Nominations for swimming captain were significantly correlated with being good at swimming and being a good influence. A different pattern of characteristics was associated with each role. None of the characteristics was significantly related to the roles of banquet chairman or wish to be a leader.

Experimenters observed the effects of task ability on leadership processes by varying the information they provided and by varying the difficulty of the problems they posed to members. Thus, Hemphill, Pepinsky, Shevitz, Jaynes, and Christner (1956) reported that individuals given task-relevant information before the experiment scored higher in attempted leadership in assembly and construction tasks but not in strategy and discussion tasks.

*Competence Relative to Subordinates' Abilities.* The competence of the leader for the task and how the leader behaves as a consequence is moderated by the subordinates' ability to handle the task with the leader's intervention. If supervisors believe that their subordinates have the requisite skill, the supervisors are more likely to be participative or delegative (Heller, 1969a). It seems equally true that if in fact the subordinates do have the skills, productivity and subordinate satisfaction will be greater if supervisors permit full or partial subordinate participation in the decision process.

### Leader Personality and Task Requirements

Wardlow and Greene (1952) reported that adolescent girls making high scores on tests measuring adjustment to school, home, and health were preferred by peers in an intellectual task. Girls recording high scores on social adjustment and preference for social activities were rejected as participants in a social situation. Megargee, Bogart, and Anderson (1966) asked pairs of participants, one high and one low in dominance test scores, to perform two different tasks. When instructions emphasized the task, the dominant participants did not emerge as leaders significantly more often than did their partners. When leadership was emphasized in the instructions, however, the dominant member emerged as leader in 90 percent of the pairs.

B. B. Roberts (1969) administered a battery of personality tests to leaders and followers studied under different conditions. Concrete and practical-thinking persons were chosen as leaders in structured tasks by all group members, but for unstructured tasks they were chosen only by the practical and concrete chooser. The theoretically oriented member was chosen as leader in unstructured tasks by abstract, theoretical followers. W. W. Burke (1965) found that followers working under a socially distant leader rated their groups as more satisfying and productive in a decision task than on a code-solving task. Dubno (1963) obtained results which indicated that group effectiveness was higher when quality rather than speed of task performance was emphasized and when the group leaders reached decisions more quickly than other members. However, Hoyt and Stoner (1968) failed to confirm that the risky decisions made by groups are due to the leadership of risk-prone members. With leadership effects held constant, group discussion still produced group decisions riskier than the mean of the individual decisions of members.

## TASK DIMENSIONS OF CONSEQUENCE
## TO LEADERSHIP PERFORMANCE

Valenzi, Miller, et al. (1972) reviewed previous research on the impact of leader behavior on task requirements and concluded that degree of task structure, routineness, complexity, interdependency, and intellectual rather than manipulative requirements systematically alter the amount and kind of leadership that will be most effective. Based on this review, a survey followed. Using stepwise regression analyses, Bass, Farrow, Valenzi, and Solomon (1975) found for seventy-eight managers described by their 407 subordinates that tasks with clear objectives promoted more *direction* and consultation. Routine tasks were associated with less participative leadership; more complex tasks, with negotiative leadership and more frequent delegation. Other dimensions isolated were autonomy or discretionary opportunities. If subordinates engaged in planning, co-ordination, and other managerial activities, again delegation was reported more frequently among their leaders. The correlation of superior–subordinate relations to structure was particularly strong. With much structure, more *direction* was seen. This was confirmed in an unpublished followup by the author with 340 managers and over 1,300 subordinates.

### Structure

Leadership of groups with structured versus unstructured tasks have been considered in a great many studies (for example, Fiedler, 1964; Hunt, 1967; Shaw & Blum, 1966; Wofford, 1971).

Structure may refer to the extent to which role relations are loosely or tightly arranged. Task structure refers to the extent to which what needs to be done is specified. For example, Lawrence and Lorsch (1967) assumed task structure went from lowest to highest as one moved from fundamental research to applied research, to sales, and finally to production. In six organizations, they found that production personnel (whose work was most certain) and fundamental research personnel (whose tasks were least certain) both preferred task-oriented leaders, whereas members in the sales subsystem (which had moderately certain work) preferred more interpersonal socially oriented leaders.

*Fiedler's Contingency Model.*   A tenet of Fiedler's (1967a) contingency model detailed in Chapter 20 was based on the effect of task structure. Task structure creates a more favorable situation for the leader. A task-oriented leader will be more effective when there is either a great deal of task structure or very little task structure. A relations-oriented leader will be more effective if task structure is moderate. Although the conclusions remain controversial (for instance, Graen, Alvares, Orris & Martella, 1970; Graen, Orris & Alvares, 1971), an impressive body of empirical support was presented in Chapter 20. However, the effects of task structure may be much less than other sources of situational elements favoring the leader (W. Hill, 1969a).

*Some Effects on Leader Behavior.*   Wofford (1971) observed that unstructured as compared to structured tasks elicited more achievement-oriented and organizing managerial behavior. But Lord (1975) found that the degree of task structure was negatively related to the occurrence of facilitative leader behavior. An unexpected curvilinear effect emerged. Instrumental leadership was most effective with tasks moderate in structure.

Structured problems were seen by Shaw and Blum (1966) to be better served by directive supervision. They found that when the problem on which five-person groups were working was highly structured so that clear procedures could be followed, directive supervision led to quick results. Yet when leaders did initiate structure a great deal, as seen in a study by Badin (1974) of forty-two work groups in a manufacturing firm, effectiveness was reduced if the groups were already highly structured. The correlation of effectiveness and initiating structure was −.56. But in the less structured of the forty-two work groups, effectiveness of the groups was greater if the first-line supervisors initiated structure. The correlation was .20.

*Role Clarity.*   The degree of members' role clarity and lack of role ambiguity are a way to discern how much structure exists in a group. Kinicki and Schriesheim (1978) studied 173 freshmen's role clarity in sixteen classes as measured by Rizzo, House, and Lirtzman's (1970) scale: clear, planned objectives, clear responsibilities, clear expectations, and clear explanations of what has to be done. Students were more satisfied with relations-oriented teachers, particularly when role clarity was low. But, likewise, students were more productive with directive teachers only when role clarity was low, not when it was high. Valenzi and Dessler (1978) showed that among 284 employees in two electronics firms the impact of leader initiation of structure was unrelated to role ambiguity of subordinates. Again, satisfaction was uniformly high when role ambiguity was low; the leadership did not matter. But leader consideration promoted significantly more employee satisfaction when employee role ambiguity was high. However, in a previously cited study in nineteen black social service agencies, Schriesheim and Murphy (1976) failed to find that role clarity moderated the relationship between any kind of leader behavior and subordinate satisfaction and performance.

To try to make sense out of this mix of evidence, more will be said about the extent to which structure affects the impact of leadership on performance and satisfaction when we review path-goal theory later in this chapter.

### Clarity of Objectives

To some extent, clear objectives may be able to substitute for structured relationships or clear role relationships in getting the job done, particularly if little coordination is required. Assuming that members are competent and motivated to attain the objectives, if they can operate independently, little else is needed for their effective performance other than clear objectives. A negative correlation of $-.15$ between the amount of structure observed and clarity of objectives was found for 1,350 subordinates and their 340 managers by Farrow, Valenzi, and Bass (1980).

Nagata (1965) observed that groups with goal-relevant tasks enabled leaders to exercise more influence on other members than groups with low goal orientation. Regression analyses by Bass, Farrow, and Valenzi (1977) for 250 managers and their 924 subordinates suggested that work group effectiveness was significantly greater if the managers themselves had clear objectives, if they felt that the groups were free of conflict, and if they exhibited more leadership regardless of style, according to their subordinates.

### Autonomy and Discretionary Opportunities

Unpublished data of Bass for over 1,300 subordinates describing 340 managers indicated that delegation and negotiation were highest when subordinates had more discretionary opportunities. Leaders were also less likely to be *directive* under such conditions, according to a study by Bass, Valenzi, et al. (1975). Johns (1978) found a correlation of .29 between leader initiation of structure and job satisfaction when 232 union employees reported that autonomy was high and a correlation of .01 when they indicated that autonomy was low. In somewhat the reverse, leader consideration and job satisfaction was only .20 when autonomy was high, but it was .52 when autonomy was low.

*Routineness versus Task Variety*

The degree of routineness has been viewed as an important task variable affecting optimum leader performance: uniform, recurring, repetitive tasks are distinguished from those involving considerable variability in requirements (Valenzi, Miller, et al., 1972).

In their classic study of the worker on the assembly line, Walker and Guest (1952) emphasized the extent to which supervision was likely to be more directive when tasks to be performed were extremely routine. Likewise, Bass, Valenzi, Farrow, and Solomon (1975) reported more directive leadership as well as less supervisory delegation in work groups carrying on routine tasks.

In a study involving sixteen departments in ten organizations, R. H. Hall (1962) distinguished between uniform, easily routinized, standardized, traditional skills and activities in contrast to nonuniform, difficult to routinize, and creative activities. He found that departments and hierarchical levels which were more nonroutine in nature were less bureaucratic than those departments and levels which were oriented toward routine activities. In nonroutine situations, the atmosphere was more personal, had less hierarchical emphasis and fewer procedures and regulations. Finally, consistent with all of the above, Heller and Yukl (1969) found that production and finance managers (supervising more routinized work) tended to use centralized decision making while general and personnel managers (with less routinized work) were more participative.

*Variety as a Moderator.* Hackman and Oldham's (1975) Job Diagnostic Survey included job variety as an important variable likely to relate to work motivation. Using ratings based on it, Johns (1978) showed that with variety, leader initiation of structure generated job satisfaction and lowered turnover intentions. Without variety, leader structuring was unrelated to satisfaction and increased intentions to quit. Consideration was strongly associated with satisfaction regardless of whether the job was varied or routine. Yet, only when variety was absent did lack of consideration associate with intentions to quit.

In a study which distinguished uniform from nonuniform tasks, Pelz (cited in Litwak, 1961), found a higher correlation between motivation to work and productivity when those engaged in nonuniform tasks were permitted by their supervisor to make their own job decisions. But for those involved with uniform tasks, there was a higher correlation between motivation and productivity when freedom to make decisions was restricted. Katz, Maccoby, and Morse (1950) found that supervisors of high-producing sections were significantly more likely to give general rather than close supervision despite the fact that they were supervising routine clerical work in a life insurance company. In a subsequent study of less routine railroad work (Katz, Maccoby, Gurin & Floor, 1951), degree of closeness of supervision showed little difference between foremen of high and low producing sections. In these and the many other related studies that followed (see Chapter 18), Likert could find no diminution in the utility of participative (System 4) leadership in routine jobs as compared to those with more variety.

*Task Complexity*

G. D. Bell (1967) saw task complexity in terms of degree of predictability of work demands, amount of discretion exercised, extent of responsibility, and number of different tasks performed. Among supervisors in a hospital, he found that the more complex the subordinates' task, the narrower was the supervisor's span of control, the more complex was the supervisor's job, and the lower was the supervisor's span of control. Hence both the supervisor's and the subordinate's task complexity tended to decrease span of control. But Bell also found closeness of supervision to be unrelated to span of control.

Alderfer (1969) found that when job enlargement was introduced, subordinates' satisfaction decreased with the amount of respect shown them by their superiors. Barrow (1976) observed in a simulation using 120 male college students as leaders that more initiating structure was caused by increasing complexity of the task, but autocratic behavior (as we have noted several times before) was generated by poor worker performance rather than by increasing task complexity, while considerate leadership was evoked by rising worker performance levels. Relevant to these results, Wofford (1971) found that a personal-interaction (relations-oriented) manager was more effective for complex operations, whereas the self-oriented, autocratic manager was more suited to situations with simple work schedules.

In examining by factor analysis 104 different experimental tasks, M. E. Shaw (1963b) disclosed three factors of consequence each of which conceptually but not empirically may be seen as contributing to the effects of task complexity. The three factors were: (1) task difficulty—the number of operations, skills, and knowledge required to complete the task; (2) solution multiplicity—more than one solution is correct; and (3) cooperation requirements—integrated efforts are required.

*Task Difficulty.* C. G. Morris (1966a,b) found that as task difficulty increased for groups, the interaction process (both leaders and followers) increased in trying to structure answers, propose solutions, and seek evaluations, but tasks of intermediate difficulty generated the highest frequency of attempts to structure the problem. Easy tasks produced more irrelevant interactions. At the same time, Nagata (1966) found that groups with easy tasks exhibited more role differentiation and permitted leaders to exercise more influence than groups with difficult tasks. However, Bass, Pryer, Gaier, and Flint (1958) found that attempts to lead were observed less frequently on easy problems.

*Solution Multiplicity.* Shaw and Blum (1966) noted that directive supervision was more effective if the problem called for convergence on a single solution, whereas participation paid off when multiple divergent solutions were required.

*Complexity, Group Drive, and Productivity.* Just as there are optimum levels of motivation for given levels of task complexity for individuals, so group drive can be too high or too low for a group task of intermediate complexity. High group drive produced high productivity on simple but not on complex group tasks, according to Zander (1971).

*Cooperation Requirements.* For M. E. Shaw's (1963b) third factor, O'Brien (1969b) theorized that cooperation requirements should be matched with the amount of difference in power between superior and subordinates. Thus, power equalization and participative leadership would be appropriate for tasks requiring a great deal of cooperation, whereas a power differential between superior and subordinates would be more effective in situations where subordinates carry out tasks independently of each other.

Vroom and Mann's (1960) results were illustrative. They studied drivers and positioners in a delivery company. The positioner's job required a high degree of interdependence and considerable interaction with coworkers as well as with the supervisor.

The driver's job involved little interpersonal interaction and considerable independene in work activity. In line with expectations, the positioners favored democratic leaders and the drivers preferred authoritarian leaders. But Bass, Valenzi, Farrow, and Solomon (1975) failed to find any significant correlations between leader styles and task interdependence of work group members. Unpublished larger-scale followup data indicated that more *directive* and consultative leadership were asssociated with task interdependence. Negotiative leadership was greater when members worked more independently of each other.

Kabanoff and O'Brien (1979) studied leadership when members either had to collaborate (work simultaneously with each other on every subtask) or coordinate their efforts (work on subtasks arranged in an order of precedence). Groups which had to coordinate were more productive. They were even more so when leaders were more task competent. But leader task competence was irrelevant to productivity in the collaborative task situation. According to Hill and Hughes (1974), there is a greater emphasis on the leaders' socioemotional function than their task function in the collaborative situation. As a consequence, their task competence is less important.

### Socioemotional versus Task Requirements

As just observed, a distinction of importance to understanding what competence will be demanded of a leader, particularly in nonproductive groups such as therapeutic groups, sensitivity training groups, social clubs, and gangs, is whether socioemotional or task requirements are emphasized. In productive groups usually both need to be. Fiedler (1967a) built his theory of contingent leadership on this (see Chapter 20).

Slater (1955) found that the most frequent type of role differentiation in discussion groups consisted of divorcing task functions from socioemotional functions. In groups achieving a high degree of consensus on problem solutions, the highest participator usually received the highest rating on task ability. In low-consensus groups, the highest participator was not rated high in ability. When task demands were high, being liked was not highly related to leadership. Here, socioemotional skills were not highly valued. But Gustafson and Thomas (1970) found relatively little such role differentiation in experimental groups. However, they did note that task-oriented followers preferred leaders who contributed to group task accomplishment. In the same way, V. Williams (1965) observed that some types of group structures were able to operate effectively without differentiation of task specialists from socioemotional specialists.

A. S. Miles (1970) reported that student leaders who rated high on both task ability and socioemotional ability were considered most influential on the campus. To sort out the effects, Olmsted (1954) gave one set of groups instructions designed to induce socioemotional concerns for group processes and member satisfaction. The directions for a second set of groups emphasized task accomplishment and impersonal relations between members. The most talkative members in the task-directed groups talked longer than their counterparts in the socioemotional groups, perhaps as the result of a group norm relative to intensity of participation. Task-directed groups tended to develop stable leadership status structures, while socioemotional groups continued longer to jockey for position.

*Phases in Group Problem-Solving*

Task requirements change as a group solves problems. For the divergent generation of alternatives, broad participation is needed. As a consequence, democratic leaders were seen by Doyle (1971) to be most effective in this phase of problem solving. But in the convergent, final synthesizing phase, where coordination becomes more important, groups with leaders of high status were particularly effective. Becker and Baloff (1969) also suggested that the optimum leader–subordinate relations may depend on whether the immediate group task involves information processing, generation of alternatives, or decision making. Likewise, given these changing requirements during the course of group problem solving, Valenzi, Miller, et al. (1972) concluded that effective leadership for one phase of problem solving may be different for another phase.

Ghiselli (1966a) observed experimental groups at various stages of task performance. Poor initial performance was associated with a heavy concentration in the group of confident decision makers, the presence of an outstandingly capable decision maker, and strong group cohesiveness. The presence of a strongly self-confident decision maker, however, along with highly intelligent followers, was associated with better group performance in later stages of group development.

Sample and Wilson (1965) also studied groups in different phases of problem solving. Task-oriented leaders quickly structured the group procedures during the planning phase and were then able to play a more relaxed role in the operational phase. Relations-oriented leaders, on the other hand, tended to hold group discussion sessions during the planning stage and the work did not get organized. As a result, they attempted to organize procedures during the operational stage, with only partial success. Thus, groups under task-oriented leaders tended to perform more effectively.

*Type of Task*

Carter and Nixon (1949b) found that different participants emerged as leaders depending on which of these tasks were involved: intellectual, clerical, or mechanical assembly. Carter, Haythorn, and Howell (1950) studied the effects of six types of tasks (reasoning, intellectual construction, clerical, discussion, motor cooperation, mechanical assembly) on leadership in initially leaderless groups. There was some generality of leadership performance across all tasks. However, two clusters of tasks emerged that made a difference in who emerged as leader: intellectual tasks and tasks involving doing things with one's hands.

C. G. Morris (1966a,b) varied task activity along with task difficulty, as mentioned earlier, for 108 groups. Variance in leader behavior was related more to type of task than to task difficulty. Discussion tasks elicited significantly more leader structuring of problems and explanatory and defensive comments. Production tasks resulted in more answer structuring, solution proposals, disagreement, and procedural comments. Problem-solving tasks were similar to discussion tasks but led to more irrelevant activity and less problem structuring.

Not unexpectedly, Bass, Valenzi, Farrow, and Solomon (1975) found that the more subordinates' work involved planning, coordination, evaluation, and other managerial activities, the more frequently was their superior likely to delegate decision making to them. Unpublished followup analyses on a larger scale added that they were also given more direction.

Korten (1968) suggested that if the final product of a task was practical, more directive supervision was in order. On the other hand, if the outcome was theoretical, then participation was likely to be more useful.

Consistent with what we have said about task complexity and cooperation requirements, Shaw and Blum (1966) required groups of five members each to perform three tasks seeking different types of solutions. Directive supervision was more effective when the problem called for a single final decision or involved the convergence of judgments into some final product. On the other hand, when the problem was divergent in solution and required multiple alternatives for a final answer, participative approaches were more effective.

*Decision Quality Emphasized.* There is voluminous evidence that groups achieve better solutions to problems than their average member working alone—although the group solution may not be as good as the best single solution achieved by the members working alone. This assembly bonus effect occurs unless individual members already alone have the requisite information to solve the problem and/or unless adding members adds interference rather than nonredundant information. Thus, according to Heller (1969), the primary reason that managers in fifteen firms reported using participative leadership was to improve the technical quality of the decisions. In fact, some form of consultation is mandatory in highly technically oriented organizations, for the technical expertise available does not fully reside with the supervisors but is distributed among their subordinates.

## PATH-GOAL THEORY

Beginning with Georgopoulos, Mahoney, and Jones (1957) and popularized by M. G. Evans (1970a) and House (1971), path-goal theory stimulated the search to explain how the nature of the group's task systematically affects whether consideration, initiation of structure, or their interplay makes more of a contribution to the group's satisfaction and effectiveness. Bass (1965c) argued for initiation, suggesting that effective leaders ''point out the paths to successful effort,'' but results have been mixed. Rightfully, the theory has been modified on a continuing basis by experimental failures. According to T. R. Mitchell (1979), a current version calls for the leader to provide subordinates with coaching, guidance, and the rewards necessary for satisfaction and effective performance. Valued rewards should be contingent on effective performance— this was called reinforcement leadership by Spector and Suttell (1956). (Such reinforcement leadership has already been discussed at length in Chapter 15.) Focus is on ways for the leader to influence subordinates' perceptions of the clarity of the paths to goals and the desirability of the goals themselves. Leadership behavior that is best suited for increasing motivation depends on subordinate personal characteristics and task demands, as we have seen in this and many preceding chapters.

Translated into experiments, considerate leader behavior (or supportive, relations-oriented leadership) is expected to correlate more highly with satisfaction and productivity in structured rather than unstructured situations. Initiation of structure is expected to correlate more highly with satisfaction and productivity in unstructured rather than structured situations. This is a restatement of the conventional wisdom that "chaos is the midwife of dictatorship" (Durant, 1957). Unfortunately, we are more likely to see more initiation of structure when it is less needed, when the group task is already structured.

### Source of Measurements

Most often, the measures of leader behavior are obtained from the LBDQ-XII, less so from the SBDQ. The various studies relate consideration and initiation of structure to job satisfaction and performance with various personal and task factors serving as moderators.

Many studies have used House and Dessler's (1974) measure of task structure. This ten-item questionnaire, completed by subordinates, examines the extent to which task characteristics are simple, repetitive, and unambiguous. Johns (1978) argued for a much broader measurement to include Hackman and Oldham's (1975) index based on variety, identity, job significance, autonomy, and feedback from the job.

### Supportive Results

Reviews of the empirical literature are available in House and Mitchell (1974) and Schriesheim and Kerr (1974). Both reviews tend to support the theory. Earlier, House (1971) found support aposteriori in several studies cited in earlier chapters (Fleischman, Harris & Burtt, 1955; Halpin, 1954; Rush, 1957; Mulder & Stemerding, 1963; Mulder, Ritsema & de Jong, 1970; and Sales, 1972). In specific apriori tests of the theory, House found that the more autonomous the subordinates, the more leader initiation correlated with subordinate satisfaction and the less it correlated with their performance. Leader consideration correlated more with subordinate satisfaction and performance as task scope decreased. Subordinate satisfaction was associated with the extent leader initiation reduced role ambiguity. Also supportive were direct tests of the theory by Dessler (1973) who found that with consideration held constant, as task ambiguity decreased, initiation correlated less with subordinate satisfaction and role clarity. Meheut and Siegel (1973) found that leader initiation that was role clarifying was positively related to subordinate satisfaction with MBO. Finally, House and Dessler (1974) demonstrated that task structure generally determined whether leader initiation and consideration would contribute to subordinate satisfaction, positive expectations, and role clarity.

Schriesheim and DeNisi (1979) studied how task variety, feedback, and dealing with others moderated the impact of initiating structure on satisfaction with supervision among two samples. The first consisted of 110 employees working in a medium-size bank located in the midwest. The second sample consisted of 205 employees of a medium-size manufacturer located in the midwest. Task variety was expected to require more initiation of structure for satisfaction and supervision. Such initiation would be redundant with routine jobs (House & Dessler, 1974) and when feedback was already structured and subordinates dealt a lot with others. The results confirmed the moderating effect of all three task variables, mainly at satisfactory levels of statistical significance.

Schriesheim and Murphy (1976) found that job stress, like lack of structure, acted to moderate the initiating structure/job satisfaction relationship, as expected. Again, Johns (1978) found that job scope moderated the leader behavior/satisfaction relationships, as expected.

*Mixed Results*

Szilagyi and Sims (1974) studied relationships between leader behavior and subordinate satisfaction and performance, unmoderated by the subordinates' role ambiguity. Data were obtained from fifty-three administrative, 240 professional, 117 technical, and 231 service personnel at multiple occupational skill levels in a hospital. Although the results supported path-goal propositions concerning the relationship between leader initiating structure and subordinate satisfaction, they failed to do so for the relationship between leader initiating structure and subordinate performance. Similarly, Stinson and Johnson (1975) tested hypotheses derived from the path-goal theory of leadership that the relationships between leader initiating structure and satisfaction variables and role clarity variables are more positive under conditions of low task structure, low task repetitiveness, and high task autonomy than under high task structure, high task repetitiveness, and low task autonomy. Leader consideration, subordinate satisfaction and role clarity were expected to be more positively related under structured, repetitive, dependent conditions than under unstructured, unrepetitive, autonomous conditions. Subjects were military officers, civil service personnel, and project engineers. The results were consistent with path-goal theory in respect to consideration but tended to counter the theory regarding initiating structure.

Consistent with the myriad findings reported in Chapter 21, consideration still is generally found to result in higher subordinate satisfaction (Johns, 1978; Miles & Petty, 1977). Also, generally, initiation of structure still frequently increases tensions, especially when consideration is low, (Miles & Petty, 1977; Schriesheim & Murphy, 1976) and when the initiation of structure measure continues to contain coercive, threatening items along with direction and order-giving. In turn, this linkage of direction and coercion is a consequence of dependence on empirical rather than conceptual analyses for developing measurements. There is a common tendency for autocrats to want to structure situations, but conceptually one can direct without being a threatening autocrat. Pure direction without coercion correlates positively with subordinate satisfaction. For over 1,300 subordinates of their 340 managers, the correlation is .38 according to Farrow, Valenzi, and Bass (1980).

Using three levels of task structure, Greene (1979a) showed in a first study that, as expected, instrumental (structuring) leader behavior was correlated positively with satisfaction and performance if low and medium task structure existed for 119 engineers, scientists, or technicians. (Dyadic analysis was employed. Subordinate performance was evaluated by two peers). But such leader structuring was negatively correlated with satisfaction and minimally with performance when medium and high task structure were present in the situation. Considerate or supportive leadership, as expected from the theory, increased in relation to intrinsic satisfaction with increasing task structure. But the relationship with extrinsic satisfaction with task structure was medium and broke down when subordinate performance was examined.

The second, a longitudinal study (Greene, 1979b), tested several assumptions about causation underlying both versions of the theory. The findings supported the theory, except, again, for the hypotheses concerning subordinate performance. Downey, Sheridan, and Slocum (1975) found only partial support for the path-goal predictions and J. P. Siegel (1973) and Szilagyi and Sims (1974) found none. Dessler and Valenzi (1977) failed to find moderator effects across supervisory levels. T. R. Mitchell (1979) concluded that the findings were stronger for the consideration hypothesis than for the structuring hypothesis and stronger for satisfaction as a criterion than for performance.

*Efforts to Reconcile the Theory with the Mixed Results*

Schriesheim and VonGlinow (1977) first noted that path-goal predictions of job satisfaction were less likely to be supported when a more coercive measure such as the SBDQ scale of initiation of structure had been used (for example, Downey, Sheridan & Slocum, 1975, 1976, and J. P. Siegel, 1973). Schriesheim and VonGlinow then demonstrated with 230 maintenance workers that if a coercion-loaded scale was used, reverse results were obtained for the path-goal predictions for job satisfaction. But when coercion-free scales (LBDQ and LBDQ-XII) or items from them were used, path-goal predictions were confirmed if task structure and role clarity were used to moderate relations between leader consideration, initiation of structure, and job satisfaction.

A second source of contradictory findings results from the fact that leaders tend to be more directive when it is easier for them to do, so such as when roles are clear, conditions are structured, and jobs are routine (Bass, Valenzi, Farrow & Solomon, 1975). But such direction is unnecessary for productivity when conditions are already structured. Rather, such direction is needed more by the group when conditions are unstructured. In such unstructured situations, the group wants some direction from the leader, not just the leader's sympathy.

Personality factors need to be taken into account also in the structured situation, given Farrow and Bass' (1977) finding that directive leaders tend primarily to be satisfied authoritarians.

Subordinate personality also needs to be considered. Griffin (1979) proposed a set of prescriptions combining path-goal theory and subordinate need for achievement and self-actualization. Griffin called for achievement-oriented, consultative leadership for self-actualizing subordinates with "big" jobs. But for self-actualizers on routine jobs of little scope, supportive leadership (consideration without consultation) was required. For "big" jobs performed by occupants uninterested in self-actualization, directive leadership (structuring without threat) was seen as most needed. For routine jobs, with job occupants lacking in need for self-actualization, delegation by the leader (a fifth style introduced by Griffin as "maintenance leader behavior") was suggested.

As we shall see in what follows next, task demands figure strongly in the occurrence of stress.

# 26

## THE PHENOMENON OF STRESS

In terms of what has been presented in Chapters 24 and 25, stress occurs in a group when the situation is overly complex (unclear, ambiguous) or demanding relative to the group's competence or structural adequacy. In addition, the group's drive may be too high. Emotional arousal, frustration, anxiety, defensiveness, and other forms of inadequate emotional reactions result. The condition is likely to generate directive leader behavior. Group performance and satisfaction are likely to be greater if the leader can provide the missing structure, define common objectives, and suggest solutions or help to reduce the group's drive level.

### Stress and Ordinary Coping Behavior

Ordinary adjustment of an individual, group, or organization to dissatisfaction with the current state of affairs is to examine fully what prevents reaching the more desired state, consider various alternative courses of action, and take appropriate steps to do so. But if motivation is high, if obstacles are severe, or if remaining in the current state is threatening to welfare or survival, malfunctionings occur in the coping process. There may be no time to deliberate about choices among actions. There may be communication outages, information overloads, and autonomic energy mobilization. There is emotional arousal. As observed by Lazarus (1966), anxiety and stress narrow the individual's focus and limit his or her ability to think creatively. In addition, many studies indicate that anxiety and stress impair memory as well as cognitive functions (Weschler, 1955). For example, when Sorokin (1943) examined reports of the reactions of groups and communities to calamity such as famine, war, and revolution, he found that calamity tended to intensify emotional arousal, distort cognitive processes, focus attention upon the calamity and away from other features of the environment, hasten disintegration of the self, and decrease rationality of behavior. Leadership requirements under such conditions of stress take on a character different from when stress is absent. The questions for us here are:

What do leaders do differently as a consequence of stress?
What can they do differently?

What should they do differently if they want to successfully influence other members?

What should they do differently to promote group goal attainment, member satisfaction and group survival?

### Multifaceted Stress

A variety of quite different antecedent conditions may give rise to stress in groups. To some degree, the observed and appropriate leadership behavior will depend on what particular antecedents were involved. Bass, Hurder, and Ellis (1954) identified four emotionally arousing stress experiences differing from each other in antecedents: (1) frustration is likely to be felt where highly prized positive goals are unattainable due to inability or difficulties on the path to the goals; (2) fear is the experience when escape from noxious conditions is threatened by obstacles in the path; (3) anxiety is aroused when these paths, obstacles, and goals become unclear—fear and frustration turn to anxiety with increasing uncertainty; (4) conflicts occur when one faces incompatible goal choices. Potentially high risks and costs compete with anticipated benefits of a course of action.

After examining the physiological reactions and the cognitive and psychomotor performance of 200 college men under experimentally induced frustration, fear, anxiety, and conflict, Bass, Hurder, and Ellis concluded that performance under these various stress conditions would decrease or increase in contrast to no stress depending on which tasks and skills were involved, which type of stress was imposed, and the initial level of arousal of the participants. Individual differences were also large. Yet, the study of leadership under stressful conditions has often treated stress as a homogeneous situation.

In the same way, Kahn, Wolfe, Quinn, Snoek, and Rosenthal (1964) showed that two distinct sources of stress could be identified in organizations: role conflict and role ambiguity, each with different antecedents and consequences. House and Rizzo (1972a, b) and Rizzo, House, and Lirtzman (1970) also conceived role conflict and role ambiguity as critically distinct phenomena. When the Job-Related Tension Index of Kahn, Wolfe, et al. (1964) was completed by 113 Canadian managers for R. E. Rogers (1977), four factors were extracted from the results: (1) sense of insufficient authority and influence upstairs; (2) self-doubts; (3) too heavy work load; and (4) having to make unpopular decisions against their own better judgment.

### Stress and Motivation

As already noted, stress occurs when group drive is too high for the task demands. When blocked from obtaining a goal or from escaping from a noxious condition, stress increases with increasing motivation to obtain the goal or escape the situation. Since cohesiveness and commitment imply heightened motivation to attain goals, more stress should be seen in cohesive as compared to noncohesive groups. This was found by French (1951) who frustrated groups of cohesive teammates and groups of strangers, lower in cohesiveness. The more cohesive teams showed more fear and frustration. Similarly, Festinger (1949) reported more complaints suggestive of stress appearing among more cohesive groups. Also, M. E. Wright (1943) found that more cohesive pairs of friends exhibited more aggression when frustrated than pairs lower in cohesiveness.

Given high motivation, perceived inability to obtain goals or escape danger increases the likelihood of stress. Groups unable to interact easily or lacking the formal or informal structure to react quickly are likely to experience stress (Bass, 1960). Panic ensues when members of a group lack superordinate goals—goals that transcend the self-interests of each individual participant. Mintz (1951) found that when members of an experimental group sought uncoordinated individual reward (or avoiding individual punishment), panic was likely to ensue in a crisis. If the group was organized and perceived a single goal for all, such panic did not materialize. Similarly, in an analysis of anxiety in aerial combat, D. G. Wright (1946) concluded that an aircrew could cope with stress when a common threat was perceived and when a common goal and action toward it were maintained with an apparent plan of action.

### Stress and Structure

The inability to respond adequately, underreadiness to react, lack of training, and inexperience characterize the stressed individual when highly motivated to ecape threat or to obtain highly valued goals. Increased preparedness and overlearning are ways of helping the individual to cope with anticipated stessful situations. At the group or organizational level, reliability and predictability of group response becomes necessary. Everyone needs to know what everyone else is likely to do. Roles must be clear and free of conflict and ambiguity. Structure, through informal or formal organization, becomes important. When a group does not have the necessary structure to meet emergencies and likely stressful conditions, initiation of such a structure by a strong leader is seen as needed and useful to the group.

Path-goal formulations (Chapter 25) examine such requisite leader behavior when worker roles are unclear. When subordinates have clear perceptions of their work roles, leader initiation of structure is redundant. For subordinates with less clear role perceptions, leader initiation of structure should help subordinates to perform their jobs and thus increase their satisfaction and performance.

The need for structure at the macro-level as well as the individual level was seen by Sorokin (1943). In times of disaster, ideal human conduct is associated with a well-integrated system of values, in conformity with the ethical values of the larger society and with little discrepancy between value and conduct. Individuals who exhibit social and delinquent behavior (murder, assault, robbery, looting, and the like) tend to be guided by self-centered, materialistic, disillusioned ideologies. But their lack of integration into a larger organized effort is also involved. The wanton massacre of penitentiary inmates in New Mexico in early 1980 by berserk fellow prisoners was partly attributable to the lack of organization of the prisoner rebellion as well as sudden complete availability of drugs.

In J. R. P. French's (1941) previously cited investigation, he studied eight organized groups (with elected leaders) and eight unorganized groups. Frustration was produced by requiring the groups to work on unsolvable problems. Unorganized groups showed a greater tendency to split into opposing factions. Previous organization of the group was associated with greater social freedom, cohesiveness, motivation, and equality of participation. The greater the differentiation of function, the greater was the interdependence and unity of the group as a whole.

*A Response-to-Conflict Model*

Janis and Mann (1977) looked at responses under stress induced by conflict in the face of an impending threat and the risks and costs of taking action to avoid it. They argued that the completely rational approach to an authentic warning of impending danger would be a thorough examination of objectives, of values, and of alternative courses of action. Costs and risks would be weighed. A final choice would be based on a cost-benefit analysis. Included would be development, careful implementation, and contingency planning. But such vigilance, thorough search, appraisal, and contingency planning are likely to be short-circuited as a consequence of emotional arousal and socioemotional phenomena generated by the impending threat. Various defective reactions to the danger warnings are likely to happen.

*Unconflicted Adherence to the Steady State.* This is one inadequate reaction based on the hasty decision that the threat involves fewer serious costs and risks than taking action. People remain in their homes despite slowly rising flood waters and warnings to evacuate. An inadequate analysis ignoring appropriate information sees the costs of evacuation as greater than the risks of remaining. This is less likely from sudden threats such as tornado warnings. Analogously, the energy crisis built for twenty years in the face of much inertia of response to cope with it adequately. But in 1941, full national commitment and mobilization to the Japanese threat signaled by Pearl Harbor was instantaneous.

*Hasty Change.* If the costs and risks for taking action are perceived to be low, a new course of action is adopted, often too hastily, again without adequate examination of the potential threat, risks, and long-term implications. Rapid decisive leadership is valued highly under conditions of threat to the group. Executives and politicians incrementally "put out one fire after another" drifting into a new policy to cope with a threat rather than formulating a new policy based on a thorough search, appraisal, and plan (Lindbloom, 1959).

*Defensive Avoidance.* Where risks of change are seen to be high and the current course of action is maintained because of pessimistic fatalism and a sense that no better course can be found, the various Freudian mechanisms such as rationalization, displacement, fantasy, and denial provide psychological defenses to avoid the threat in the absence of coping with the danger rationally. Particularly common to managers in large organizations, according to Janis (1972), are procrastination, shifting responsibility (buck-passing) and bolstering—social support for quickly seizing on the least objectionable choice. These are defective ways of dealing with a threat.

*Hypervigilance (Panic).* If the threat contains time pressures and deadlines, if individual motivation to escape the threat is high, hypervigilance (panic) may set in. Defective search is illustrated by the failure to take the time to choose a satisfactory escape route from a fire. Instead, a person in panic, in a highly suggestible state, simply starts imitating what everybody else is doing, failing to anticipate the consequences of blocking the common exit choice. A. L. Strauss (1944) analyzed the literature on panic. He found that the major factors in panic are (1) conditions weakening individuals physically; (2) reduced mental ability and lessened capacity to act rationally; (3) heightened emotionality, tension, and imagination which facilitate impulsive action; (4) heightened suggestibility and contagion which may precipitate flight; and (5) loss of contact with leaders and predisposition to follow those at hand.

## STRESS AND EMERGENCE AS A LEADER

Stress differences make a difference in who emerges as leader. Initiating structure, clarifying goals, exhibiting task orientation, and direction are leader behaviors that tend to increase in importance when groups and organizations are under stress.

Lanzetta (1953) found a lower than usual correlation (.51) between the tendency to emerge as a leader at each of three different levels of group stress. Different leaders emerged to some extent in the same groups as more stressful conditions were imposed. In the same way, results obtained by Hamblin (1958b) indicated that members of experimenal groups, when facing genuine crisis situations, tended to replace their old leaders with new ones if the old leaders were unable to cope with the crisis.

### Rapid Decisions Sought from Leaders

In emergencies, subordinates want to be told what to do, and in a hurry, when danger threatens. They perceive no time to consider alternatives. Rapid, decisive leadership is demanded (Hemphill, 1950b). Five hundred groups were described on questionnaires by members on a variety of dimensions formulated by Hemphill. The adequacy of various leadership behaviors was correlated with group characteristics. Hemphill concluded that if leaders fail to make decisions quickly, their adequacy will tend to be judged low in frequently changing and emergency groups.

Considerable evidence is available to support the contention that leaders speed up their decision making as a consequence of stress. Failure to do so leads to their rejection as leaders (Sherif & Sherif, 1953; Korten, 1962). Acceptance of their rapid, arbitrary decisions without consultation, negotiation, or participation is also increased. A leader who can react quickly in emergencies will be judged as better by followers than one who cannot.

A field investigation by Torrance and staff (1955) reported that aircrews who were "forced down" and faced simulated survival difficulties in "enemy" territory tended to turn to immediate but ineffective solutions to their problems and to concede more to comfort, as stress increased. For example, as hardship increased, they began electing to travel on roads in "enemy" territory instead of traveling over routes where they were less likely to be seen.

Flanagan, Levy, et al. (1952) found that, according to respondents, "taking prompt action in emergency situations" was a critical behavior differentiating those judged to be better officers from those judged as worse in performance. Large-scale surveys of the American soldier during World War II by Stouffer, Suchman, Devinney, Starr, and Williams (1949) confirmed that particularly at lower levels in the organization, the military stressed rapidity of response to orders from higher authority despite the fact that the unit actually operated a relatively small amount of the time under battlefield conditions.

### Groups under Stress Favor Directive Leadership

Hertzler (1940) examined thirty-five historical dictatorships and concluded that they arose during crises and when sudden change was required.

Similarly, where rapid decisions are called for, executives are likely to become more directive than participative (Lowin, 1968). Consistent with this, the more organizations wish to be prepared for emergency action, the more they are likely to stress a high degree of structure, attention to orders, and authoritarian direction. Fodor (1976, 1978) demonstrated that industrial supervisors exposed to the stress of simulated, disturbing subordinates became more autocratic in dealing with the situation. College students did likewise (Fodor, 1973). From half to two-thirds of 181 airmen, asked for their opinions about missile teams, rescue teams, scientific teams, or other small crews facing emergencies, strongly agreed that they should respond to the orders of the commander with less question than usual. In an emergency, the commander was expected to "check more closely to see that everyone is carrying out his responsibility." A majority felt that "the commander should not be 'just one of the boys' " (Torrance, 1956/1957).

During the unstable period of a union's organization as it goes from one emergency to the next, militant, decisive aggressive leadership is demanded. In terms of Osgood's semantic differential factors, under stress, strength and activity take on more importance for leadership. After the struggle for survival is over and the union is recognized, the leadership required changes in the direction of greater willingness to compromise and to cooperate (Selekman, 1947).

*Effects of External Threat.* For centuries, political leaders have used real or imagined external threat as the way to increase the cohesiveness among their followers and gain unquestioning support for their own dictates.

The common scenario begins with economic weakness and dislocation, followed by international complications, revolution and/or civil war, and finally a breakdown of political institutions. The dictator organizes ready-made immediate solutions that soothe, flatter, and exalt the public. Defensive avoidance is promoted. Blame is directed elsewhere.

Thus, as Janis and Mann (1977) have noted, threat generates the desire for prompt decisive action. Leadership becomes centered in one or a few who gain increased power to decide for the group. The price for the rapid, arbitrary dictation is the cost in lost freedoms and abuses and corruption by placing power in the hands of the dictator.

### Intergroup Conflict Effects

A reversal of effects seems to occur when conflict due to intergroup competition arises. Here, in-group cohesiveness increases and in-group–out-group differences are magnified, but rather than more initiation of structure, according to Oaklander and Fleishmen (1964), endorsement of consideration becomes greater. Since in most staged intergroup competitions, in-group cohesiveness increases greatly, deviants are not tolerated for long, and the strongest members are sent forth to do battle with the "enemy" (Blake & Mouton, 1962b), it is difficult to account for Oaklander and Fleishman's findings that leaders favor more consideration under such conditions. Thus, Mulder and Stemerding (1963) found, as expected, that when individuals feel threatened from outside, they will exhibit a tendency to lean on strong leadership.

The in-group and out-group relations of leaders in organizations under the stress of the prospect of their own demise was studied by Hayashida (1976). The leaders of 146 students in an evangelical Christian organization with stated beliefs diverging from the cosmopolitan campus culture were found to be the ones most likely to isolate themselves formally and informally from the rest of the campus. Evidently, they coped with intergroup conflict by avoiding it. In 1979-1980 we saw two classical examples of how external threats (the holding of the American diplomatic staff in Tehran and the Soviet invasion of Afghanistan) dramatically increased follower support for the leader, President Carter, and his attempts to deal with the threats. Ranks were closed, dissension was muted, and rapid leader decision making was sought and accepted by followers with little examination of the causes, intensity, and risks of the threats as well as the costs of taking actions to deal with them. If anything, Carter failed to come on as strongly and decisively as demanded. In the face of crises, nations condemn the vacillating, indecisive leader and applaud the would-be hero-savior (Hook, 1943). When calamity threatens, followers want immediate action to escape. Leader influence attempts will be accepted and complied with more readily than in the absence of such stress. Thus, Berkowitz (1953b) found that both government and industrial groups were more likely to accept leadership when the problem was urgent. Holding a participative discussion to generate a high-quality decision with group commitment may be both impossible and unacceptable. The commitment will come from the followers' restriction of the options they think they have. The leader who shows initiative, inventiveness, and decisiveness is valued most (Barnard, 1948). Although business and government leaders may be seen to consult and share decisions with subordinates in times of crises (Berkowitz, 1953b), it is likely that to some degree they seek bolstering from their subordinates and try to spread the responsibility for the decision from themselves to their group.

*Short-Term Effects.* Helmreich and Collins (1967) observed that participants facing a fearful experimental situation exhibited a decrease in preference for the company of peers and favored being in a leader-dominated group. Polis (1964) also found that under stress, individuals tended to manifest a need for strong leadership and to continue their association with the group. In the same way, A. L. Klein (1976) observed in an experimental study of panic conditions of too many people trying to escape through the same door, that the stressed group preferred a strong leader rather than the one who under low stress was the more highly acceptable elected leader. Acceptance and election, which under conditions of low stress gave the accepted legitimate leader control of the group's fate was replaced under high stress by the group turning to a less legitimate but stronger leader, seen to be endowed with more competence.

*Long-Term Effects.* Hall and Mansfield (1971) studied the longer-term effects of stress and the response to it in three research and development organizations. The stress was caused by a sudden drop in available research funds resulting in strong internal pressures for reduced spending and increased search for new funds. Response to the stress was increased top management control with reduced consultation with researchers. The effect over two years on the researchers was decreased identification with the organization, decreased need satisfaction and perceptions of less favorable job opportunities, although research performance was unaffected.

### Increased Susceptibility to Influence

Response to leader initiation of structure, leader direction, and autocratic behavior is facilitated by the increased susceptibility to influence of followers made anxious or fearful or suffering severe deprivations. Thus, Hamblin (1958b) found followers more willing to accept leader influence during crises than during noncrisis periods. They gave leaders more responsibility and were seen as more competent when panic was induced experimentally. Wispé and Lloyd (1955) concluded that the less secure, more anxious of forty-three sales agents were more in favor of having decisions made for them by their superiors.

Japanese internees were subjected to isolation, loss of subsistence, threat to loved ones, enforced idleness, and physiological stress due to internment during World War II in California. As a consequence, the internees were apathetic and blindly obedient to influence (Leighton, 1945). Similarly, Fisher and Rubinstein (1956) reported that experimental participants deprived of sleep for forty-eight to fifty-four hours were more susceptible than normal to social influence and showed significantly greater shifts in autokinetic judgments.

### Authoritarians under Stress

Individuals more predisposed toward direction, initiation of structure, and autocratic behavior are more likely to try to take charge when their groups are stressed. They will preempt the leadership role from members more likely to want to consult with others before taking action. Given the authoritarian–submissive syndrome, the same authoritarians who make hasty decisions for the group in stressful situations presumably, if assigned subordinate roles, will be more ready to submit unquestioningly to the dictates of whoever has been assigned the leader role. Since, under stress, the success and acceptance of leaders depends on their decisiveness, boldness, and willingness to initiate actions rapidly, socially bold and authoritarian members less concerned with consultation and the seeking of group opinion are more likely to emerge as leaders during stress. Thus, Lanzetta (1953) found that aggressive members were more likely to emerge as successful leaders when laboratory groups were stressed by harassment and space and time restrictions in comparison to the situation when no stress was induced. Along similar lines, Ziller (1954) concluded that leaders who accepted responsibility for group action under conditions of uncertainty and risk were also relatively unconcerned about what the group thought about the issues and were higher in authoritarian attitudes.

## STRESS AND EFFECTIVENESS AS A LEADER

### Transformational Leadership Needed

A transactional leader (Chapter 2) can be influential in groups under stress. Such a leader can supply solutions for immediate member needs as perceived by them. There will be immediate satisfaction with such leadership but not long-term positive effectiveness. What is required is a transformational leader who can evoke higher-level needs, such as for the common good, who can move the group into a fully vigilant search for long-term solutions.

Rather than autocratic, rapid decision making demanded of the leader by the ready-to-be-influenced group, effective leadership in stressful situations depends on whether the group is failing to fully consider a potential threat either by inertia, by reacting too hastily, by acting defensively, or by overreacting in panic (Janis & Mann, 1977). Considering also the distinctions of Bass, Hurder, and Ellis (1954) between frustration, fear, anxiety, and conflict, to be effective under stress the leader must be able to rise above what the group sees as its immediate needs and appropriate reactions. The leader must arouse an inert group about the significance of threats and the group's lack of preparedness. The leader must alter the inert group's willingness to live with frustration rather than make efforts to deal more adequately with obstacles in its path to positive goals. Again, to be effective, a leader may need to calm the demands for hasty change. An effective leader may need to identify and publicize the inadequacy of pseudo-solutions. The effective leader may need to provide adequate structure, direction, and superordinate goals for the hypervigilant group in a state of panic. Clearly, effective leadership for a group under stress is transformational leadership. Thus, Strauss (1944) found that factors that reduce panic are (1) calm, intelligent leadership; (2) group discipline and morale; (3) rational action according to a plan; (4) prior training; (5) sound physical health; and (6) attention directed toward a realistic appraisal of conditions and alternatives. For the anxious, directing attention to the specifics of their problems may be indicated just as providing a full analysis of costs and benefits of competing goals may be needed by groups facing such conflicts among goals. Each is so different a type of leader response that the lack of uniformity and the results of research on stress and effective leadership cannot be summed up in one simple proposition, although it would seem that the leader needs to some degree to be transformational, active, directive, and structuring. However, the nature of conflict—socioemotional, interpersonal, or task-related—may make some difference in the extent to which initiation of structure by the leader will contribute to effectiveness (Guetzkow & Gyr, 1954; Likert & Likert, 1976). Thus, if the leader has the ability and authority and if the situation generates stress, pressure, and tension to achieve success, directive leadership is still the most likely to be effective, according to Rosenbaum and Rosenbaum (1971).

In dealing particularly with inertia or defensive avoidance among followers, the leader's role will involve challenging outworn decisions and stimulating the followers to rise up beyond their own self-serving rationalizations. Followers need to be made aware of their rationalizations and defense mechanisms that conflict with their true values and interests (Rokeach, 1971; Reed & Janis, 1974). Radical speakers attempt this by confronting audiences with the contradictions and inconsistencies in popular, accepted points of view.

Leaders can organize group efforts of followers in ways which will help to promote vigilance, thorough search, thorough appraisal, and contingency planning to avoid defective coping with threat. Bolstering can be minimized by encouraging "devil's advocates." As noted in Chapter 24, heterogenity rather than homogeneity can be pursued in selecting members for the group so as to promote creativity. Reassessment meetings can be held (Janis & Mann, 1977).

*Survival Studies*

The detrimental effect of inadequate leadership performance to groups under stress was observed by Torrance (1961) who conducted an extensive, outstanding program of research on military groups undergoing training for survival. The following leadership behaviors and group conditions were found to produce an adverse effect on group survival: (1) conflict between various echelons of leadership; (2) failure of the formal leader to accept the informal leadership structure; (3) formation of cliques, some with resources and others without; (4) isolation of the leader from the remainder of the group; (5) reduction of the power of the group with resulting hostility toward the leader; (6) abdication of leadership roles or functions customarily performed; (7) unwillingness of the designated leader to act outside of authority; (8) attempt to function without a designated leader; (9) failure of the leader to fulfill group expectations; and (10) failure of the leader to resolve feelings of isolation and loneliness. Stress resulting from differences in values between members or between leader and members, failure of members to inform others realistically about what they were doing, and failure to give mutual support and to sacrifice personal goals for group goals also tended to jeopardize survival. These findings indicate that group survival under extreme hardship is dependent on competent exercise of the leadership role, maintenance of group unity and goal direction, and maintenance of communication. Under conditions of extreme hardship and stress, a group's chances of survival are enhanced when it has a leader who maintains its integrity, keeps it realistically informed of the situation confronting it, fulfills the expectations of members, is willing to act outside the bounds of stated authority, maintains its commitment and goal direction, and is able to transform members' personal concerns into concerns for achieving group goals.

### Conflict, Initiation of Structure, and Effectiveness

Among eighty-four randomly selected faculty members from twenty departments of two universities, R. Katz (1977) found that both affective and substantive conflict contributed to felt tension (.49 and .47) and perceived lack of departmental effectiveness ($-.28$ and $-.29$) as measured by rated academic quality and quantity of education provided students. The correlation between initiation of structure in a department and its effectiveness was .63 when affective conflict was high and only .29 when affective conflict was low. The correlation between initiation and effectiveness was .51 when substantive conflict was high and .38 when substantive conflict was low.

R. Katz (1977) partially confirmed these findings with an experiment in which participants were hired to perform routine tasks under low and high affective conflict. For a routine coding task, initiating structure correlated $-.62$ with productivity when stress was absent and .46 under high affective conflict. But such clear results failed to materialize with a cross-checking task. Again, initiating structure was negatively related to effectiveness ($-.36$) when stress was low. But it was also negative when stress was high ($-.12$). Consistent with this, Katz, Phillips, and Cheston (1976) demonstrated that "forcing" may be more effective in resolving interpersonal conflicts than "problem solving." Additional support comes from French, Kay, and Meyer (1966), who found that management participation in appraisal systems improved performance under conditions of low threat but affected performance adversely under conditions of high threat.

LaRocco and Jones (1978) concluded that although leadership support and interaction facilitation contributed to such desired outcomes for 3,725 U. S. Navy enlisted personnel as job satisfaction and satisfaction with the Navy, direct attention was needed to alleviate the effects of stress, presumably by the structuring of work and goal emphasis, increasing role clarity, and reducing role ambiguity.

Consistent with these results, fifty-four subordinates of nineteen unit heads in a national black social services organization who perceived little on-the-job anxiety generated a correlation of − .45 between their unit head's observed initiation of structure (LBDQ-XII) and a seventeen-item measure of unit performance (Schriesheim and Murphy, 1976). But the correspondence correlation was .15 for subordinates perceiving strong job anxiety. For leader consideration, the figures were reversed, .41 between consideration and peformance when anxiety was low and − .24 when anxiety was high. The state of anxiety was seen as the perceptual manifestation of objective stress conditions (Spielberger, 1972). A twenty-item State Anxiety subscale of the State-Trait Anxiety Inventory (Spielberger, Gorsuch & Lushene, 1970) was employed by Schriesheim and Murphy to measure on-the-job anxiety.

### Stress, Intelligence and Experience

Fiedler, Potter, Zais, and Knowlton (1979) reviewed the results of four studies in military organizations examining the significance of subordinate leaders' intelligence and experience in coping with conflict with their own superior officer. Among those 158 infantry squad leaders who perceived a very high degree of stress in their relations with their immediate superiors, their experience, but not their tested intelligence, correlated with their rated performance as a squad leader (Fiedler & Leister, 1977b). When perceived stress was low, experience correlated between − .20 and .00 with rated performance; when perceived stress was high, experience correlated between .39 and .66 with rated performance. For forty-five army first sergeants studied by Knowlton (1979), correlations between their rated performance and their intelligence correlated between .51 and .78 when little conflict was perceived between themselves and their superiors. The correlations ranged from − .04 to .24 when such perceived conflict was high. Similar findings were obtained by Potter (1978) for 130 Coast Guard officers and by Zais (1979) among the battalion line and staff officers in nine army battalions.

The positive impact of experience on coping with stress is not unexpected, but the reverse effects for intelligence are yet to be explained. In a bureaucracy, it may be that the highly intelligent subordinate leader is a threat to superiors who in turn downgrade such subordinates' performance. Stress may be more disturbing to the potentially more creative, intelligent, subordinate leader. A leader in conflict with higher authority is likely to have less "influence upstairs," reducing the leader's likely effectiveness and ability to use his or her intelligence.

### Task, Stress, and Effective Leadership

The task makes a difference in the effects of leadership in groups under stress. Dubno (1968) assembled experimental groups, some with fast decision time leaders and others with slow decision time leaders. Congruent groups were those with fast decision leaders and tasks demanding pressure for speed and fast decision making. Incongruent groups were those with slow decision leaders, but with tasks demanding speed of performance and quick decisions. With appointed leaders, the most effective groups were those with slow decision leaders urging them to arrive at high-quality solutions under pressure for speed. For groups with emergent leaders, the most effective were those with fast decision leaders urging high quality of performance.

The task was also seen to make a difference by Butler and Jones (1979). For 776 U. S. Navy ship personnel, when risks of accident were high and hazards due to equipment were evident (as among engineering personnel), leadership was unrelated to accident performance (presumably, structure was already very high). But, in the work settings of deck personnel, where environmental hazards were less evident and personnel were less experienced and hence less clear and competent about tasks, hazards, and goals, the occurrence of accidents was lower where leaders were seen to emphasize goals and facilitate interaction. More of any kind of leadership (support, goal emphasis, and work and interaction facilitation) seemed to reduce multiple accidents of deck personnel.

Further illustrating the importance of task in the analysis of stress, Sample and Wilson (1965) found that groups with task-oriented leaders performed better than those with person-oriented leaders under conditions of stress, but not under routine conditions. However, reversed results were obtained by Fiedler, O'Brien, and Ilgen (1969) in a study of American volunteers in Honduras, who found that task-oriented leaders were more effective in relatively stress-free villages, whereas relations-oriented leaders exerted a more therapeutic effect in more stressful villages. The reversal may be a function of how task orientation was measured.

### Long-Range Planning

Immediately increasing role clarity, reducing ambiguities, and initiating needed structure are not the only effective leader responses to stress. By planning ahead, by anticipating potential crises and preparing the group in advance for them, leaders will be more effective than if they engage in short-range efforts. Studies of leader behavior in a public utility company, an insurance office, an automobile plant, and in heavy industry found that supervisors of groups with better production records more often exhibited long-range planning and anticipated future problems rather than limited themselves to day-to-day operations (D. Katz, 1951).

### SURVIVAL OF SOCIAL SYSTEMS

Prolonged stress from internal or external challenges too great for the group to deal with will result in the demise of the group. What leads to some groups dying and others surviving over long periods of time? Research on both animal and human social systems indicates that the survival capacity of a group under stress is closely dependent upon a type of leadership that is able to maintain its integrity, drive, and goal direction. Lanzetta (1955), Lanzetta, Haefner, Langham, and Axelrod (1954), and Torrance (1961) reported that groups under threat tended to strengthen their cohesiveness and at the same time became less forceful and active in task performance. Thus, increased cohesiveness and decreased task activity appear to operate as defensive survival measures.

Southwick and Siddiqi (1967) observed a colony of fifteen rhesus monkeys over a period of several months. Following the injury and disability of the dominant male, the group's home range was reduced from forty to less than ten acres. The injured leader retained his position until his death, suggesting the operation of social tradition in the group. With emergence of a new leader the group increased its range of activities.

F. E. Parker (1923, 1927) sent questionnaires to some 3,000 consumer cooperative societies. Among those that had failed, the most frequent reasons were: (1) inefficient leadership and management; (2) declining interest and cooperative spirit among the members; (3) factional disputes among the members; and (4) member interference with management. Blumenthal (1932) attributed the decline of social and fraternal groups in small towns to the departure of young people (and consequently best leadership potential) to the cities.

Munro (1930) studied community service organizations. He found that ineffective organizations less likely to survive were characterized by overorganization and duplication of services, ineffective leadership and lack of political sagacity, unwise policies and tactics, and spasmodic work. On the other hand, among rural communities observed over a period of ten years, consistent with what we have said earlier about the utility of shared goals and cohesiveness for survival, Kolb (1933) found that groups held together by a religious purpose tended to survive longest. Likewise, Sorokin (1943) concluded that communities surviving calamity tend to be strongly committed to an integrative ideology of religion.

Kolb and Wileden (1927) reported that special interest groups in rural communities exhibited the following stages: (1) statement or purpose; (2) promotion and recruitment; (3) frequent and enthusiastic meetings; (4) acceptance of organizational form; (5) adoption of a program; (6) use of factions with competition for leadership; (7) conflict with other groups in the community; (8) decline in member interest; (9) differentiation of function; (10) irreconcilable differences between leaders and followers; and (11) decline and demise.

A historical account of Paris, Illinois, in the first half of the nineteenth century by Alcorn (1974) from an analysis of 1,850 census data suggested that both demographic change and stability of leadership and values existed side by side during the turbulent period of the town's rapid growth. Political, economic, and reform leaders all were present and overlapping. They were wealthier, older, and more likely to be professional or commercial in occupation.

### Utopian Communities

During the nineteenth century, the eastern United States witnessed the rise and decline of numerous utopian communities founded upon ideals of brotherhood and communal life. For example, Ballou (1897) documented the history of the Hopedale Community, founded in 1839 with thirty-two members. It reached its peak in 1854 with 229 residents and declined rapidly thereafter. There were only 110 residents (members and nonmembers) in 1856. The members, until 1842, had no individual property rights and were required to work solely for the community. Ballou attributed the decline of the community to reliance on a few heavy investors who withdrew their funds, lack of skilled and experienced leaders, and a continual influx of undisciplined recruits.

In a study of the origin and development of various communal colonies, Gide (1930) concluded that the only ones able to survive for any considerable period of time were those in which a strong leader was able to maintain discipline and control founded upon religious principles as the primary motivating factors in the group objective. May and Doob (1937) arrived at similar conclusions.

To conclude, strong commitment to a common religious or ideological purpose tends to facilitate group survival. Utopian and cooperative societies tend to survive so long as they are held together by a leader able to reconcile differences between contending factions and keep the group integrated around a common purpose. Of course, a whole community can commit suicide when led to it by a highly charismatic, paranoid leader, as was the case in Jonestown, Guyana, in 1978. And Hitler pleaded for a Götterdämmerung in 1945 for all Germany, turning in frustration from his fantasy of Odin as Savior to Odin as Destroyer.

# 27

## LEADERSHIP AND INTERPERSONAL SPACE

### LEADERSHIP AND PHYSICAL SPACE

It is not surprising that the traditional Eskimo culture was highly individualistic rather than cooperative or competitive (Mead et al., 1937). The low population density of the Arctic meant that opportunity for contact between people was low. And with contact opportunities absent, the amount of influence and leadership was severely limited. James Worthy believes that the rise of civilizations required the development of management which could occur only with more dense settlements. Stable agriculture, animal husbandry, and fishing were needed to support the requisite density of population in which such organizing leadership was possible as well as necessary for civilizations to emerge.

### Interaction Potential

Bass (1960) proposed the concept of interaction potential as the likelihood that particular individuals would interact with each other. The more they could interact, the greater was the likelihood that one could influence or lead the other. Such potential to interact was greater if, among other things, the individuals were geographically and socially close. Thus, Schrag (1954) noted that physical proximity is an important determinant of leadership among prison inmates.

### Physical Proximity

The respective physical locations of individuals make a difference. The group discussant who grabs the chalk and controls the blackboard at a meeting can influence what ideas are singled out for attention. Thus, before the advent of the telephone, rural leaders were likely to be those settled at the crossroads. As telecommunications developed, physical proximity became less important for leadership. Bass, Klauss, and DeMarco (1977) have shown that as physical distance increases, there is a direct increase in the use of the telephone instead of a face-to-face meeting to contact colleagues at one's own organizational level. But as hierarchical distance—levels between a manager and a colleague—increases, there is an increase in use of memos instead of face-to-face contact. Beyond this, neither hierarchical nor physical distance had much effect on perceived communication styles, credibility, or satisfaction with focal persons for 577 civilian colleagues in the Naval Materiel Command.

**462**

*Choice and Acceptance.* Willerman and Swanson (1952) found that sorority girls living in the same house chose each other as friends significantly more often than did girls who lived in town. Thus, propinquity was shown to be a factor in mutual choice. Maisonneuve (1952) and Priest and Sawyer (1967) also found propinquity a factor in interpersonal choice along with Gullahorn (1952) who studied the interactions of girls seated in rows separated by filing cabinets. Interaction within rows was greater than that across rows. Within rows, girls related more with those near them than with those seated at a distance. When distance did not operate as a factor, friendship was the next most important influence on choice for interaction.

Streufert (1965) indicated that attitudes toward a member who deviates from group norms becomes more unfavorable as interaction distance decreases, while attitude toward a conforming member becomes more favorable as interaction distance decreases.

Propinquity between persons may also be a consequence rather than a cause of influence processes. Willis (1966) observed that individuals stand closer to one another when talking to friends and assume greater distance when talking to strangers or persons of high status. Mehrabian (1968) noted that female participants maintain significantly more eye contact in conversation with high-status than with low-status partners.

Little (1965) observed pairs of individuals in various situations. The distance between pairs of individuals in interaction was found to increase as their relationship changed from that of friend to acquaintance to stranger. Physical distance tended to increase as the impersonality of the situation increased from living room to office to street corner.

### Location

A. M. Rose (1968) identified job occupants who because of their physical locations take on "ecologically influential" roles of leadership. Their leadership is not based on personal, social, or psychological traits. They are influential because they occupy a position that permits them to mediate ideas among several societal groups. Beauticians, barbers, bartenders, and traveling salespeople are examples of such leaders.

*Seating Arrangement.* A considerable amount of research has been completed on the extent to which one's influence in a small discussion group is related to the location of one's seat in relation to the rest of the group. Traditionally, the appointed leader took his or her place at the head of the table with those near in status to the appointed leader grouped around the leader. Low-status people, as in feudal times, gather "below the salt." This pattern is maintained in informal groups according to a variety of studies. Leaders in small discussion groups tend to gravitate toward the head of the table (Sommer, 1959, 1961; Lott & Sommer, 1967; LeCuyer, 1976). In simulated juries, Strodtbeck and Hook (1961) found that those who sat at the end of the table were more likely to be elected jury foreman.

For V-shaped arrangements, those with external status gravitate toward the apex (Bass & Klubeck, 1952). When the leader does not occupy the head position, other members tend to sit opposite rather than alongside him or her. Leaders tend to seat themselves symmetrically around one end of the table (Sommer, 1961). Members as a whole tend to seat themselves closer to status peers than to members who are higher or lower than themselves in status (Lott & Sommer, 1967). Group members sitting at end positions of a rectangular arrangement participate more and are rated as wielding more influence than those at side positions (Strodtbeck & Hook, 1961). LeCuyer (1976) found with French undergraduates that the leader's position at the end of a rectangular table enhanced the leader's ability to direct the group.

Both centrality of seating position and distance affect interaction rate. The more dominant members of a group tend to choose central seats and to do most of the talking (Hare & Bales, 1963).

Although H. Harris (1949) suggested that a semicircular or V-arrangement, such as a panel discussion, isolates those at the ends and spotlights those at the center, Bass and Klubeck (1952) failed to find any such differences when the outside status of participants was taken into account. Howells and Becker (1962) seated two group members on one side of a table and three members on the opposite side. A greater number of leaders than would be expected by chance emerged on the two-seat side. C. D. Ward (1968) studied groups of strangers seated in a circle with several empty seats. Those individuals facing the largest number of other members were most likely to be judged as leaders by other group members.

Participation is affected by seating arrangements. Steinzor (1950) noted that when members of a discussion group were seated in a circle, an individual seated opposite rather than alongside tended to speak next when a group member stopped talking. Similarly, Festinger, Schachter, and Back (1950) showed that individuals positioned opposite each other interacted more than those standing side by side. But Hearn (1957) found that the leader's activity affected the interaction pattern of group members. In groups under active leadership, members tended to interact with individuals seated on either side. Under passive leadership, members tended to address more comments to those seated opposite than to those seated at either side.

Sommer (1959) found that persons in neighboring seats interacted more than persons in distant locations. Those in corner positions interacted more than those side by side or opposite one another. Felipe (1966) also found that spatial arrangements affected interaction rate.

Seating arrangements are also a consequence of the purposes of meetings. Sommer (1965) reported that casual groups prefer corner seating, cooperating groups sit side by side, co-acting groups sit at a distance, and competing groups opposite one another. For more on the effects of propinquity and location, the reader may refer to reviews by Mehrabian (1968), Sommer (1967, 1969), Barker (1968), Klopfer (1969), Dogan and Rokkan (1969), and M. Patterson (1968).


## LEADERSHIP AND PSYCHOSOCIAL DISTANCE

Status differences can be either accented or minimized in the search for organizational effectiveness. Status differences can give rise to psychological and social distances, although such distance is not necessary or even desirable for organizational effectiveness, according to behavioral theorists such as J. R. Gibb (1964) and Argyris (1962) who see more virtue in close, personal relations between those differing in status. However, Martin and Simms (1956), Jameson (1945), and Pfiffner (1951), argued strongly in favor of maintaining such psychosocial distance in organizations to promote organizational effectiveness.

In a questionnaire on "how to succeed in business" administered to 107 MBA students, Bass (1968c) found an orthogonal factor supporting the maintenance of social distance and prerogatives. The factor was correlated with the perceived importance of emphasis on personal gain, with less human or social concern in simulated budgeting decisions, and with strong economic values. Managers saw somewhat less utility in maintaining social distance than did MBA students. Night school students showed the largest decline in favoring maintenance of social distance as a consequence of human relations training programs (Bass, 1970).

### Advantages of Maintaining Distance

Proponents who argue in favor of maintaining psychosocial distance from followers, suggest that leaders thereby enhance their power and effectiveness. They do this by limiting access to themselves, accenting the difference between their own status, esteem, ability, and power and those of their followers and by various symbolic separations. (Emperors, sultans, and kings vied with each other as to the height of their thrones above their audience chambers, so they could literally talk down to their subjects from "on high.") Such social distance may either promote the legitimacy of leader and follower roles or be a consequence of it (see Chapter 13).

By maintaining psychosocial distance, a leader can remain impartial, task-directed, and free of emotional concern for individual followers. A general can order individual groups of soldiers to almost certain death for the sake of expected victory. A manager who would have difficulty discharging an incompetent personal secretary might find it easier to lay off a hundred employees several levels below in the hierarchy. Barnard (1946a) suggested that maintaining psychosocial distance in an organization serves several necessary functions in addition to that of coordination. It protects members from the need to compete for leadership. It acknowledges the importance of the individual's special contribution. It protects the integrity of the individual in that it acknowledges certain rights, privileges, and obligations that pertain to his or her position. It obviates the necessity of unfavorable comparisons between individuals who differ in training and ability.

### Costs of Maintaining Distance

But the costs of such psychosocial distancing are high: more defensive behavior by followers, loss of contact, poorer quality of communications, poorer goal selection, less commitment to group goals, incipient revolt, and organizational rigidity. Barnard (1946a) observed that psychosocial distance can limit the adaptability of the organization, distort the system of distributive justice, and exalt the symbolic function at the expense of efficient performance.

There seems to be some optimum in psychosocial distance between leader and subordinates. Carp, Vitola, and McLanathan (1963) found that effective leaders had a perceptual set enabling them to maintain optimal psychological distance from subordinates, neither so close that they were hampered by emotional ties nor so distant that they lost emotional contact. The optimum appears to vary from one situation to another, according to Fiedler as we have noted in Chapter 20.

### Distance from Least Preferred Coworker

When one describes a least preferred coworker as different from oneself, one is indicating one's psychosocial distance from that least preferred coworker. In Chapter 20, we discussed Fiedler's (1967a) model and measurements of LPC and the evidence that those who perceive such social distance from their least preferred coworkers are more effective leaders in situations which are either extremely favorable or extremely unfavorable to the leader.

### Discussion of Personal Affairs

It is often easier to discuss intimate problems with a total stranger whom one expects never to see again than with friends and relatives. Festinger, Pepitone, and Newcomb (1952) studied groups of students required to discuss personal family matters. They confirmed that members experienced less restraint under deindividuation—a kind of enforced psychosocial distance—minimizing the degree of attention they paid to one another. Deindividuation constituted a satisfying state of group affairs associated with increased group attractiveness when it was present. In the same way, Rosenbaum (1959) found that participants preferred to maintain a greater psychosocial distance between themselves and their partners when potentially unfavorable evaluations might be fed back to them than when no such information was anticipated. Desire for psychosocial distance, however, was not affected by group success or failure.

### Task, Achievement Motivation, and Social Distance of Leaders

W. W. Burke (1965) studied different combinations of leaders and followers, each differentiated as to scores on social distance and need for achievement. In a group situation varying in tenseness, followers with a strong need for achievement under a socially close leader rated the situation as more tense than followers with strong need for achievement under a socially distant leader. Weak need achievement followers rated the situation less tense under socially close than under socially distant leaders. Thus, strong need achievement followers were more comfortable under social distance, while weak need achievement followers were more comfortable with social closeness. Strong need achievement followers rated socially close leaders as more autocratic than high social distance leaders. Weak need achievement followers rated socially distant leaders as more autocratic. Socially distant leaders were rated more effective in a coding task and socially close leaders were rated more effective in a human relations task. In all, followers with a socially distant leader considered their groups less productive and less satisfying than those under socially close leaders.

### Friendship and Acceptance of Inequality

Morgan and Sawyer (1967) found that schoolboys prefer strict equality in distribution of rewards, both with friends and with others. (Repeatedly, one sees this when involved in experimental gaming with college students.) Nevertheless, although preferring equality, friends are willing to accept inequality if one thinks that the other might want it. Nonfriends are less willing to accept inequality. Knowing what the other expects facilitates one's ability to reach an agreement.

### Territoriality and Leadership

Territoriality is one of the major phenomena of interest to students of animal behavior. One of the primary functions of leadership in animal societies appears to involve location and protection of territory (Allee, 1945, 1951; Allee et al., 1949). It has its counterpart in the attitudes of delinquent gangs about their own "turf."

### The Differential Effects of Status and Social Difference

The existence of status differences does not necessitate maintaining social distance. General Joseph Stilwell, among others, was known for his tendency to wear an unmarked private's uniform, lead infantry marches on foot, and eat in the enlisted men's mess (Tuchman, 1971). Seeman (1960) studied status differences and status preferences in twenty-seven public school systems and found that teachers who perceived wide differences between their own status and that of the principal tended to describe the principal high in change behavior and leadership but low in domination. Principals who rated themselves high in status and saw sharp differences between their own status and that of teachers were described by teachers as high in communication and change behavior, low in separatism, and high in leader effectiveness. These results suggested that social status and psychosocial distance are differentially valued in the public school situation. In an earlier study, Seeman (1950) found that teachers who favored wide status differences in society and in organizations tended to prefer a directive rather than a group-oriented style of leadership. More teachers than anticipated favored wide status differences and directive leadership. Rettig, Despres, and Pasamanick (1960) obtained results which indicated that persons in professional positions perceiving wide status differences between occupations tended to attach greater importance to personal freedom and overestimated their own status less than did status equalizers.

Results of the research discussed above support at least three of Barnard's hypotheses. Status differences and psychosocial distance tend to be valued when the consequences of close personal interaction are likely to be unpleasant. Psychosocial distance is valued when participants in interaction are likely to be compared with each other on an evaluative basis. Maintenance of status differences is associated with effective leadership and group performance under specified circumstances, as already discussed in more detail in Chapter 10.

Social distance and status differences can be increased or decreased by the communication network available or imposed. This is the subject of the next chapter.

# 28

## OPEN VERSUS CLOSED CHANNELS

In Chapter 16, we dealt at length with the mutual influence of leaders and followers. Whether such can occur depends on how open or closed the channels of communication are between them. Thus, those who had access to the political leaders and decision makers in a community were themselves found more likely to be influential in the community (Bockman & Gayk, 1977). Again, according to J. R. P. French (1956), group members could influence each other more readily if they were in open communication with each other.

### Information Available

The transfer and processing of information from subordinates and elsewhere has become a dominant facet of management (Sayles, 1964). Whether a manager will act in a planned or involuntary way will depend on the manager's acquisition and use of information (Glube & Margerison, 1976). Bass, Valenzi, Farrow, and Solomon (1975) found the differential amount of information available to managers and their subordinates an important factor in the manager's style. If the boss possessed more information than the subordinates, significantly more frequent *direction* was seen by the subordinates. But where the subordinates possessed more information on what needed to be done, significantly more consultation, *participation,* and delegation was seen.

### Communications and Effectiveness

Open, easy, ready communications not only contribute to the extent the leader and the group can influence each other, but also to the extent they will be effective.

Based on research with B-29 aircrews, Roby and Forgays (1953) argued that crews who could direct information faster at "decision stations" could solve problems faster. In a report on maintenance in four medium bomber wings, Bates (1953) inferred that in the two better performing maintenance systems, there was more contact between subgroups. Philips (1954) observed that among twenty-four groups of five third-graders playing a modified version of "Twenty Questions," task efficiency correlated positively with the amount of task-oriented communication and interests in discussing the question. Torrance (1954) noted that plane crews were most likely to survive if communications

**468**

were resumed among the scattered crew members, leading to a clarification of the situation. A survey of 500 work groups suggested that communication ease resulted in increased efficiency (Bass, 1954b). Conversely, in interviews of Naval Research Laboratory teams engaged in a series of ordnance tests, Weschler and Shepard (1954) found that when the existence of difficulties of communication were expressed in interviews, a lack of understanding and satisfaction was also likely to be found.

*Effects of Regular Meetings.* Dyer and Lambert (1953) found that in two medium bomber wings, regular meetings of personnel were scheduled in the wing with a better record of performance and effectiveness but not in the less effective wing. In addition, the wing executive officer of the superior wing was a more active communicator of information to others in the wing. Habbe (1952) noted that in an individual plant with regularly scheduled meetings of work groups, workers felt freer to talk about their problems with the foreman and favored more such meetings than workers of a plant without such regular meetings.

## LEADERSHIP IN EXPERIMENTAL COMMUNICATION NETWORKS

### Origins

As we have noted in Chapter 27, physical arrangements give rise to who can communicate with whom, thereby affecting the potential leadership process. Bavelas (1950) originated a laboratory experiment to study the effects of systematic changes in who among five participants could communicate directly with each of the other participants. Bavelas dealt poker hands to the five members of a group. The members could communicate with each other only by written messages. The object was to select the one best poker hand from the combined cards of all members. The groups differed in communication channels, as shown in Figure 28.1.

In the circle arrangement, the members had an equal opportunity to send messages to and receive messages from the member to their left and the member to their right. In the chain, members could, if they wished, send messages toward the person in the center. In the wheel, four of the members had equal opportunities to send messages toward the person in the center. In the Y, three members could send messages to a fourth person in a central position, but the fifth member was required to communicate with the center position through another member.

### The Standard Design

Subsequently, a standardized task was developed by Leavitt (1951) that was free of potential biases due to differences among members with poker playing knowledge. At the beginning of each trial, each of five participants was given a card on which were printed five of six symbols. One symbol was missing from each card. Each member lacked a different symbol. The problem each time was to have the group discover and record the one symbol that everyone had in common. The participants were seated around a circular table and were separated from each other by five vertical partitions. They passed messages to each other through open interconnecting slots. These were the only ways of communicating among participants. What was analyzed was the pattern of messages that developed and the speed with which the problem was solved when a

**FIGURE 28.1.  Communications Networks**

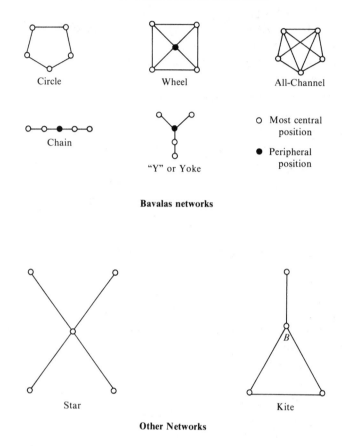

Circle

Wheel

All-Channel

Chain

"Y" or Yoke

O  Most central
position

●  Peripheral
position

**Bavalas networks**

Star

Kite

**Other Networks**

particular network of channels was open for use. Many other common problems came to be used with constraints on communications as described (Leavitt, 1951). Reviews of the method and research outcomes can be found in Cartwright and Zander (1960), Glanzer and Glaser (1961), and Mulder (1963).

*Centrality*

In Chapter 27, we noted the importance of a central location for rural leadership (in the absence of telephones) or the extent to which a bartender at a neighborhood bar occupies a kind of leadership due to the centrality of his location. Bavelas experimented with several arrangements for which he developed an index of network centrality for the different communication nets shown in Figure 28.1. Centrality was seen to be greatest in the wheel, and decreased in the following order: Y, chain, and circle.

Individual centrality can exist in three ways. A person in a network can be more or less geographically central (his or her position in space), more or less central in terms of the interaction of the network (his or her information centrality), or more or less central in terms of the decisions of the network (his or her centrality in the decisions to be made). The greater the inequalities in the communication opportunities of group members, the more the members will differ in centrality (Bass & Ryterband, 1979).

*Network Development*

Leavitt (1951) found that speed in solving problems, agreement on who is the leader, satisfaction with the group, and development of an organization were highly correlated with the centrality index of the communication network. That is, it took the least time to solve problems, agree on leadership, and so on in the Y, more so in the chain, and the most time in the circle. The circle experienced difficulty in developing a stable structure for problem solving.

*Role Differentiation.* Consistent informal roles emerged within the restrictions of the formal networks, more so in some networks, less so in others. Little informality was possible in the wheel network. The highly restricted wheel network rapidly developed a stable hierarchy conforming to the formal demands of the system. Here, the central person sent out information to all participants once he or she had received information from all. On the other hand, all-channel groups could display much more variety in the informal organizations they built, particularly in distributing answers. Some evolved a system in which each person sent answers to every other member, while others developed patterns identical to the wheel or to the chain. Those groups that were formally restricted to circle communication networks had the greatest difficulty in developing and maintaining a single formal pattern of communications. Over many trials, they tended to fluctuate in the particular patterns of communications they used, especially in exchanging answers (Guetzkow & Simon, 1955). Usually, a network that began with a central position or informally developed a centralizing procedure was able to complete the task faster with fewer errors (Mulder, 1960). However, as we said above, such centralization was likely to give rise to less satisfying peripheral jobs as well as less opportunity for members as a whole to modify their own organization, to learn about how the organization operated, to be flexible, and to be creative when new challenges were imposed upon the group (Bass & Ryterband, 1979).

*Central Functions.* Persons occupying central positions carry out tasks different from the tasks of those occupying peripheral positions. For example, only the person in the central position spends a great deal of time compiling data, forming solutions, and transmitting answers. Those in peripheral positions spend more of their time receiving information (Guetzkow & Simon, 1955).

Using seventy-six groups of five participants with Leavitt designs, Guetzkow (1960, 1961) found that three types of roles tended to emerge. The central person tended to receive information, formulate answers, and send answers. The peripheral person sent his or her own missing information and received answers. The relayer passed on own and other information and relayed answers. The wheel and all-channel nets tended to develop two-level structures consisting of one central person and four peripheral persons. One third of the circle groups developed three-level structures consisting of a central person, two relayers, and two peripheral persons. Two-thirds of the circle groups did not develop organized structures of mutually supporting roles. Groups with differentiated role structures solved the problem faster than those that remained undifferentiated. Central persons and relayers perceived structure more accurately than peripherals in all except the all-channel groups. They also sent more messages proposing organization and nominated themselves more often as a leader.

Cohen, Robinson, and Edwards (1969) studied groups required to solve experimental problems of organization. Centralized problem-solving systems were developed by all subgroups in both wheel and all-channel networks.

*Stability of Leadership.* A. M. Cohen (1962) observed greater continuity of leadership in communication networks when members could elect their leaders. Cohen and Bennis (1961) studied groups with changing structures. Groups that had changed from a wheel to a circle network tended to organize themselves into a more efficient chain system, but with different leaders than were present in the wheel. Groups with elected leaders retained them longer than those not permitted to elect leaders.

### Emergence of Leadership

Bales (1953) observed that the one group member able to control the communication network was most likely to emerge as leader. Emergence of leadership was more frequent in the star with its one central position than in other networks (Shaw & Rothschild, 1956). M. L. Goldberg (1955), Shaw, Rothschild, and Strickland (1957) and Cohen, Bennis, and Wolkon (1961) confirmed that the group member occupying a position of centrality was most likely to emerge as leader. Abrahamson (1969), however, removed the partitions that prevented group members from seeing each other. In the face-to-face situation, central members emerged as leaders only when no personality liability was present. Abrahamson concluded that centrality is a dominant factor in emergence only when physical isolation prevents personality factors from having an impact.

### Involvement

Zander and Forward (1968) found that participants in positions of centrality developed a stronger desire for group success than when in a peripheral position. But individual differences in motivation affected the results. Occupying a central position, a participant whose need to avoid personal failure exceeded the need for personal success tended to become more concerned about group performance than when the needs were reversed in strength.

### Satisfaction

Centralized groups typically have one member at their hub. In routine tasks, the more centralized the structure, the more efficiently members solve problems, but the less they are satisfied (Cohen, 1964).

Shaw and Rothschild (1956) found that member satisfaction differed with group structure only to the extent that the occupant of the central position in a star design showed greater satisfaction. Using the same designs, Shaw, Rothschild, and Strickland (1957) determined that member satisfaction was a joint function of centrality and amount of member support. Central members, more than peripheral members, tried to change the opinion of those who disagreed. But if the central members failed, they changed more than peripheral members. Member satisfaction was found to differ with position in the system (Cohen, Robinson & Edwards, 1969). It was somewhat higher in decentralized organizations. More specifically, Vannoy and Morrissette (1969) obtained results which suggested that satisfaction with a role in the network is related to its centrality, whereas satisfaction with the group is related to group effectiveness.

In an experimental effort to detect what underlying elements were of consequence, Trow (1957) studied groups of participants matched on scores of need for autonomy. Some members were led to believe that they occupied positions of centrality, others that they occupied positions of dependency. The autonomous situation provided greater satisfaction than the dependent situation. The effect of centrality on satisfaction was positive, but not significant.

### Effects of Group Task

Communications networks in an organization can result from the demands of authority, the demands for information, the demands of particular tasks, the bonds of friendship, or the more formal status characteristics of organizations. The purpose served by a network will affect how information is transmitted within it. For example, communication in an authority network will typically be more formalized than those in a friendship network (Bass & Ryterband, 1979). Heise and Miller (1951) concluded that the task faced by the network is a determinant of the leadership and the group behavior likely to occur. The uniqueness of the solution, the number of decisions to be made, and the amount of previous structure all are involved. For example, G. B. Cohen (1969) studied groups performing an information processing task. Centrality was found to facilitate performance most in highly interdependent tasks.

The centralized networks produce the fastest solutions with the fewest errors in the simplest kind of problem-solving situation, such as finding the common symbol. But the superiority of the centralized star, wheel, or yoke disappears when the problem is made more complex by adding ''noise'' to the communications. For instance, when participants have to solve anagram problems where they may or may not need information from each other, noise—complicated and possibly irrelevant information in the communication system—causes the disappearance of differences in the efficiency of the various nets. Thus, the effectiveness of a communication network depends on the characteristics of the task. No one network is always best (Glanzer & Glaser, 1961).

### Information Distribution

Trow (1957) analyzed the interacting effects of providing the occupant of a position in a communications network with access to communication channels to others and with access to information. Perceived status was more a matter of access to communication channels than to knowledge. On the other hand, Guetzkow (1954) found that persons in central positions showed better knowledge and understanding of the network than persons in peripheral positions. Changing the information available to members had an effect similar to that of changing the centrality of their position or the channels available to the position (M. E. Shaw, 1954a). In a followup of this earlier finding, M. E. Shaw (1963a) studied the influence of the availability of information in various networks. Group members with an informational advantage were found to enter the discussion earlier, to initiate more task-oriented communications, to find their suggestions accepted more frequently, and to be rated by others as contributing more to the group task than members with no prior information relative to the problem. Likewise, Gilchrist, Shaw, and Walker (1954) varied the information available to the four members of a wheel network. Centrality of position was directly related to emergence of leadership and member satisfaction. But variations in availability of information were not related to centrality.

### Contingent Factors

Planning opportunities make a difference. Thus, members are more likely to learn how to use their own position to the best advantage of the group when the groups are given the opportunity for planning between trials, particularly if they are connected with each other by open channels (Guetzkow & Dill, 1957). They are also likely to develop different communication patterns, depending on the amount and type of prior experience they have had with alternative networks (A. R. Cohen, 1964).

The placement of persons of lower or higher status or esteem in key positions can alter the outcomes of communication networks. For G. B. Cohen (1969), the presence of high-status members in positions of centrality facilitated performance. Nevertheless, low-status members became more effective in positions of centrality. Cohen concluded that in a pluricentral social system the various centers of influence should have an easy communicative access to all parts of the organization. Consistent with this, Mohanna and Argyle (1960) assigned sociometrically popular and unpopular participants to wheel and circle networks. Wheel groups with esteemed central members learned faster than other groups and required less time and fewer messages to solve the problem. (As we noted in Chapter 13, efficiency is increased and conflict is reduced in organizations when one's esteem is congruent with the importance of the position to which one is assigned.)

### Network and Effective Leadership Style

The type of communication network imposed upon the group determines which kind of leadership will be most effective. When the central member of the wheel or yoke network and a designated member in the all-channel network are instructed to be coercive, to use the power of their position to require compliance rather than to be persuasive, and to use logic and information to convince, all three types of networks make fewer information errors. However, the relative superiority of coercion over persuasion is particularly greatest in the wheel network, to a lesser extent in the yoke network, and least apparent in the all-channel network. But, under all three conditions, as might be expected, members are less satisfied with coercion than with persuasion. In the all-channel and yoke networks, the same or similar amounts of decision errors occur with persuasive and coercive leadership. Only in the wheel are there fewer errors of decision under coercive rather than persuasive leadership (Shaw & Blum, 1966; Shepard, 1956).

M. E. Shaw (1955) compared democratic and authoritarian (order-giving) leaders of the different communication networks. Networks made less of a difference than leadership style. Speed and accuracy of performance were greater under authoritarian than under democratic leadership. Member satisfactions and nominations for leadership, however, were greater under a democratic style of leadership.

## Personal Factors

The placement of individuals with particular personal attributes in central positions or the use of participants who have some strong personal characteristics may systematically affect communication network outcomes. However, M. E. Shaw (1960) failed to find that the homogeneity of members of a network in such attributes as intelligence, acceptance of authority, and individual prominence changed depending on whether centralized or decentralized structures resulted in more satisfaction and efficiency.

*Need for Autonomy.* Trow (1957) observed that the stronger the desire of participants for autonomy, the higher was the correlation between satisfaction of the participants with the extent to which believed they occupied positions of centrality.

*Ascendance.* Berkowitz (1956) selected participants scoring very high and others scoring very low on a personality test of ascendance. The participants were assigned to different positions in a star network. Socially bold participants in central positions tended to complete their work before other group members on the first trial, while those lacking such boldness in central positions completed their work after other members had finished. However, these differences disappeared by the end of the third trial. All participants in central positions, regardless of the extent of their ascendancy, were better satisfied than those in peripheral positions. Low ascendants in central positions were more passive than high ascendants in peripheral positions during the first trial, but not during the third trial.

*Repressors and Worriers.* Cohen and Foerst (1968) studied groups composed of repressors (members who repress or deny anxiety) and sensitizers (members who react to anxiety and worry). Leadership was found significantly more continuous in the repressor than in the sensitizer groups. Repressor groups developed centralized systems earlier than sensitizer groups. Nevertheless, both types, when given the opportunity, rejected the all-channel network in favor of the centralized structure.

## Implications for Organizational Leadership

Results of the above research indicate that groups with a position of centrality are more efficient than those without differentiated role structures. Members who occupy a position of centrality enabling them to exercise control over the flow of information are most likely to emerge as a leader. They are also better satisfied with the group than are more peripheral members. Several studies suggest that personality factors may mitigate the relation between centrality and leadership. But a highly submissive member may become a more active participant in the group activities when placed for a time in a position of centrality.

Organizations are composed of networks and contain one or more of the types described earlier. Moreover, the networks in a particular organization will be interrelated and may vary from well-structured networks carrying regular task-related messages to loose informal nets (Guetzkow, 1965).

In real-world organizations, communications are involved in the exercise of authority, information exchange, specific task completion, friendship, or status. Communications networks based on authority and those based on information typically may have opposite directions of information flow. That is, those nets based on authority have information flowing from those persons in a position of authority downward to subordinates. In contrast, many networks based on information have their primary flow upward from those providing information to those collecting that information for use in decision making. The potential for conflict (Chapter 13) is great as a consequence.

Network experiments can be used to simulate some particular organizational problem. In one such simulation, five participants represented each of five separate departments of a manufacturing company: sales, research and development, planning and production, organization methods, and purchasing and subcontracting. All participants received complete information about the procedures of the company and a functional description of their respective departments. They were also given information necessary to contribute to the decision-making process in their respective departmental roles. The purpose of the simulation was to discover, within a time limit of five fifteen-minute periods, the best working combination of product design, delivery time, and price so as to be able to accept or reject a customer's order. The participants were given sufficient time to discuss as a team how to organize the different department roles. Only written communication could be passed among the five department heads. The participants were left to form their own network (Hesseling & Konnen, 1969). Analysis focused on what kinds of networks emerged in such circumstances.

It may be impossible to translate these laboratory and simulation findings directly to large organizations. Yet these laboratory networks are analogous to real organizational ones. The chain is seen in the vertical and horizontal serial communication linkages in an organization shown in Figure 28.2. The meeting of the board of directors is an all-channel network. The typical line organization is a yoke. For many specific operations in an organization, persons will find themselves at the hub of the wheel (Dubin, 1958).

**FIGURE 28.2.  Examples of Operational Networks**

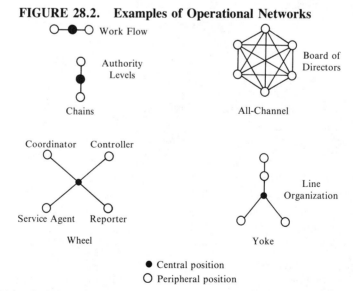

SOURCE: R. Dubin, Stability of human organizations. In M. Haire (Ed.), *Modern Organizational Theory*. New York: Wiley, 1959, 1962.

# 29

## THE PERSISTENCE AND TRANSFER OF LEADERSHIP

### PERSISTENCE AND CHANGES IN LEADERSHIP

In Chapters 4 through 10, we analyzed the extent to which leadership could be seen as an attribute of the individual. In Chapters 23 through 28, we examined various situational elements that needed to be considered. Now, we look at the extent to which individual consistency is observed in leadership over time and from one situation to another. We shall also consider antecedents and consequences of the leadership succession process.

Although tasks and goals can be extremely different from situation to situation, some amount of interpersonal competence is required from any leader. So there is likely to be some amount of generalizability in who emerges as leader in different situations. Cowley (1928, 1931) and Bogardus (1928, 1931) observed that great leaders obtained their leadership first in one situation and then transferred that leadership to other similar situations and finally, some gained sufficient esteem and experience in these earlier efforts to succeed as leaders in almost any situation they entered. For J. M. Burns (1978), political offices serve as steppingstones to other offices. They may also immobilize or destroy political careers.

### Evidence of Persistence Due to Trait Persistence

Some generality across situations is commonly found for the consistency from childhood to adulthood of intelligence and various personality traits. This suggests that consistency will be found as well in trait-associated early leadership tendencies and adult leadership potential. For example, C. M. Cox's (1926) analyses of the biographies of 300 outstanding military, religious, and political leaders frequently found traits of behavior above normal in the childhood of these men, such as desire to excel, intelligence, insight, self-esteem and forcefulness—traits usually related to leadership.

### Childhood and Adolescent Influences

Bass (1960) examined how certain childhood and adolescent relationships at home, in school, and elsewhere result in tendencies during the formative years to emerge as a leader. Of possible significance are parental relations, birth order, family size, and experiences with peers. Mother as a source of interaction experience plays a dominant role. Thus, B. M. Bishop (1951) noted that when interacting with a neutral adult, children tend to transfer to the new situation the pattern of interaction they have developed with their mothers. If their mothers were directive, interfering, and critical, the children tended to be inhibited, reluctant, or noncooperative in their interactions with others. Negativism and rebellion against authority if fostered in interaction with parents turn into aggressive behavior expressed in fighting, threatening, and boasting against other or in withdrawal into fantasy. The normal, maturing child can accept parental and school authority and is cooperative with family and teacher (L. B. Murphy, 1947).

*Birth Order.* As compared with their siblings, the oldest child in the family has been reported as being less dominant, less aggressive, less self-confident, and less inclined toward leadership due to the inexperience and insecurity of the parents with their first-born child and the need for the oldest child to adjust from an only-child family to a family where attention toward children must be divided (Goodenough & Leahy, 1927). In comparison with their siblings, youngest children have been reported as being more disobedient, more persistent, and more likely to be pampered and helped when help is no longer necessary as well as disregarded when family or personal decisions are to be made (Hurlock, (1950). As a consequence, younger siblings are expected to attempt more leadership as an adult than the older siblings (Bass, 1960).

Maller (1931) found that the tendency of a child to work in a group for a group goal rather than alone for an individual prize is greatest among children with three or four siblings and is less among children of smaller or larger families. Cooperativeness was rated highest among these children at the optimum family size, but persistence was greatest among children from the largest families.

*Home Life.* Children from homes where the children participate in decisions were found by A. L. Baldwin (1949) to be more active, socially outgoing, intelligent, curious, original, constructive, and domineering. C. T. Meyer (1947) conluded that sociability and cooperativeness were greater when parents were clear and consistent, explained decisions to their children, offered opportunities for decision making, had rapport with their children, and better understood their children's problems.

Conflicting demands by the mother and father promoted behavior in the children detrimental to the children's effective and successful interaction with others, according to Meyers (1944), who also found that the most nervous behavior in children occurred when parents issue conflicting negative demands. Disobedience was greatest when parents conflicted in positive demands.

*Parents as Models.* W. A. Anderson (1943) provided data suggesting the significance of parents' leadership behavior as a model for their children. In a rural New York area, Anderson found that the social participation of an individual is a "family trait." If father participated, so did mother. If both participated, children usually did so also.

Lack of parental models also made a difference. Comparison of children reared in orphanages with children raised by parents was suggestive of the importance of parental interaction or lack of it. Public nursery school children were found by H. H. Anderson (1937) to interact more with others and to initiate and attempt more leadership than children from a nursery in an orphanage. But Bass (1954a) reported failure of an experimental confirmation effort. College students rated the extent to which each of their parents had been considerate of them when they were children and the extent to which the parents initiated interactions with them. Then, the students' success as a leader in an initially leaderless discussion was correlated with their ratings of their parents' behavior. No significant correlations emerged.

For more on the experiential opportunities during adolescence that are likely to affect leadership behavior as an adult, see Bass (1960, pp. 199–205).

### Effects of Changes in Age of Leaders and Followers

Although there is persistence in leadership, systematic changes take place also as a function of age. The emerging leader can be observed in primary school at an early age (Mey, 1936). Leadership is attempted to satisfy the desire to influence others. Such emergent leaders tend to be tyrants or stimulators. But later, attempts to organize become more common. With maturation, consistency in attempts and successful leadership increase, while rivalry among would-be leaders decreases (Toki, 1935). Increasing age brings changes in the behavior making for success as a leader. During the 1930s at least, among 12-year-old girls, leaders were daring and humorous, but among 15-year-old girls, the friendly, enthusiastic, and happy ones were more successful leaders (Tryon, 1939).

Observations of the spontaneous play of nursery school children by a one-minute sampling procedure indicated the existence of two approaches to leading others: persuasion and coercion. The emphasis on coercion was observed to change to a persuasive appeal to ideals among European adolescents (Winkler-Hermaden, 1927).

Horrocks and Thompson (1946) studied the friendship choices of boys and girls from age 10 to 17. The sociometric tests were repeated two weeks later. Boys and girls of the same age did not differ in choice fluctuations. However, older boys and girls tended to name the same individual both times as friends, while younger children showed less overlap on the two lists. These results suggested that sociometric choices tended to stabilize in later adolescence.

### Persistence in School and Onward

I. J. Levi (1930) obtained a correlation of .19 in leadership activity of students in elementary school and these same students in high school. But the correlation was .52 when their leadership performance in junior high school was compared with performance in high school. D. P. Page (1935) found that first-year leadership rank at West Point correlated .67 with fourth-year leadership rank.

Several early studies also determined that leadership in elementary school, high school, and college was predictive of later leadership in adult business and social activities. J. R. Shannon (1929), I. J. Levi (1930), Clem and Dodge (1933), D. P. Page (1935), and Courtenay (1938) found that leadership in extracurricular activities was more highly related to various criteria of adult success than were scholarship or academic achievement. In other words, leadership rather than scholarship was best predictive of later leadership. Williams and Harrell (1964) reported a significant correlation (.24) between leadership in undergraduate activities and later business success as measured by salary level. Roskens (1958) found significant correlations, ranging from .37 to .63, between college leadership and postcollege leadership. Postcollege leadership was not highly related to grades in college or to parents' occupational status.

*Persistence of Successful Leadership in Experimental Groups*

As early as 1904, Terman (1904) reported an experimental verification of the consistency of leadership behavior in school children from one problem to the next. Borgatta, Couch, and Bales (1954) observed that new groups were more effective if they contained "great men" identified in old groups for their ability, assertiveness, and social success. The "great men" continued to be influential in the new groups. Highly esteemed, active, able persons continue to succeed as leaders in groups of different membership faced with similar tasks. Blake, Mouton, and Fruchter (1954) reported that leadership contribution to group decisions and dominance as rated by different observers in different situations yield consistent individual differences among raters despite the variation in situation and group composition. They also noted that, as task and group were altered, self-ratings and ratings of others were most consistent when concerned with leadership and interest. They were less consistent when concerned with the effectiveness and satisfaction of others.

In the same way, in small experimental group settings, Borgatta, Couch, and Bales (1954) found that initially effective leaders tended to emerge as leaders in group after group to which they were assigned. Bass and Norton (1951) analyzed test–retest performance in initially leaderless discussions held a week apart. The test–retest measures of successful leadership was .90. Carter, Haythorn, and Howell (1950) studied the emergence of leadership in groups of college students performing the same task again after about four months. The test–retest correlations ranged from .39 (discussion) to .88 (motor coordination) depending on the nature of the task.

Rosenberg, Erlick, and Berkowitz (1955) studied small groups required to cooperate in tilting an apparatus in such a manner as to move a small bar up a ramp. The persistence of leadership was highly significant from one reassembly of members to another. Gordon and Medland (1965a) obtained peer nominations and ratings in small military units before and eight weeks after the reconstitution of the units. Peer nominations for leadership were highly correlated (.80 to .90) for the two situations.

Attempted leadership also shows consistencies across situations. Hemphill, Pepinsky, et al. (1954) found an average correlation of .45 between assessments of attempted leadership in four different tasks: reasoning, instruction, assembly, and strategy.

*Changing Functions.* As groups develop, leaders serve different functions. So the same successful leaders will emerge again as the same functions are needed. Sterling and Rosenthal (1950) reported that leaders and followers change roles in different phases of group development, with the same leaders tending to emerge as similar phases of group process recur.

*Persistence of Leadership Effectiveness in Industry*

Considerable evidence is available concerning the tendency of the same leaders to be effective given the same task requirements with new groups. An impressive set of field studies of first-line supervisors is illustrative.

H. Feldman (1937) studied twenty-two work groups that shared in savings on operating costs. One year after the project began, supervisors of groups with high savings were assigned to groups with low savings, and vice versa. The order of merit of the supervisors remained practically the same. Many of the differences among groups were associated with the leader—not the group led. Supervisors were then shifted by chance. Again, the relative order of performance of the groups depended on who led the groups. Those with previously low savings records later made high savings, while those with high previous savings later made low savings. J. M. Jackson (1953b) had the supervisors of high-morale telephone line crews change places with the supervisors of low-morale crews. A retest of the crews four months later showed a significant shift in morale scores, with the previously low groups scoring high and the previously high groups scoring low. Each foreman tended in his second group to receive a score similar to that obtained in his first group. No significant changes occurred in a set of control groups. Wyndham and Cooke (1964) also studied work groups in which the supervisors exchanged places. Previously ineffective groups improved in performance under previously effective supervisors. Previously effective groups declined in performance under supervisors of previously ineffective groups. Likewise, F. L. W. Richardson (1961) studied work groups in which the only way found to improve productivity and morale was by transferring troublesome leaders out of their groups.

*Associated Effects.* N. A. Rosen (1969) obtained ratings of worker preference for eight foremen in an upholstering shop. Foremen high and low in preference then changed places. The greater the worker consensus in weeks 1 to 10 that the new foreman "is our leader," the greater was the increase in productivity and cohesiveness in weeks 11 to 16. The findings suggested that the new foremen were evaluated in terms of their ability to help the group. In a second experiment, N. A. Rosen (1970a) found that cohesiveness dropped in the most cohesive groups and increased in the least cohesive groups. Groups that liked their previous foremen tended to like the new ones. In a third experiment (N. A. Rosen, 1970b), large changes in foreman preference were associated with large gains in productivity following reassignment, while small changes in preference were associated with small gains or losses in productivity. More will be said later about the associated effects of the leadership of successors and their predecessors.

## TASK EFFECTS ON SUCCESS AND EFFECTIVENESS OF PERSISTENCE

### A Transfer Model

Borrowing from the general psychology of transfer, Bass (1960) developed a model to account for conditions for positive and negative transfer of leadership behavior. Among the major propositions were that:

- Positive transfer (transfer facilitating performance) from an old to a new situation will be greater, the more the new situation is similar to the old one and the more the new situation calls for the same leader behavior as the old one to attain goals.
- Negative transfer (transfer detrimental to performance) will be greater, the more the new situation, different from the old one and requiring new modes of leadership, is responded to with the old ways of behaving to achieve goals. The new

situation is responded to as if it were similar to the old when it actually is not. It is perceived as requiring the old ways of leader behavior when actually new ways are necessary.

There is considerable experimental evidence to confirm the positive transfer of leadership, some of which has already been cited, but although negative transfer is often seen, it has seldom been easy to demonstrate experimentally.

### Effects of Similar Tasks

Katz, Blau, Brown, and Strodtbeck (1957) reported that groups exhibited a tendency to return to the same leader when the task performed in time 2 is similar to that performed in time 1. Again, as noted earlier, Bass and Norton (1951) reported a correlation of .90 between successful leadership displayed by members of leaderless group discussions held a week apart. The composition of the groups and the problems discussed were the same. When one discussion was an examination and the other not, the correlation remained as high as .86 (Bass, 1954), but the correlation dropped to .75 when two members of each group of seven were coached on how to emerge as leaders between test and retest situations.

### Effects of Changes in Membership

As long as the task stays the same in a new situation, recomposing the group membership does not seem to reduce the positive transfer effects greatly. Various experimental attempts have been made to determine whether the same individuals will emerge as leaders when members are reassigned to new groups with varying combinations of leaders and followers. Bass (1949) found a correlation of .72 between initial leadership status attained by group members in leaderless discussion groups and leadership status attained in reassembled discussion groups. Bass and Wurster (1953a) obtained correlations ranging from .51 to .66 between measures of leadership status in groups that differed in member composition and problem to be discussed. Even when in addition to changing group composition, a year instead of a week intervened between test and retest of the tendency to emerge as a discussion leader, the correlation still was .53 (Bass & Coates, 1952). Arbous and Maree (1951) obtained a median correlation of .67 between the extent to which administrative candidates displayed successful leadership when they were appointed discussion leaders and the extent to which they displayed successful leadership in initially leaderless discussions. Similar research by Carter, Haythorn, Meirowitz, and Lanzetta (1951) yielded a correlation of .55. When, in addition to changing the composition of the membership, the type of discussion problem was varied systematically, the correlation in consistency of success was still .58 (Bass & Coates, 1953).

Bass (1960) analyzed the results of eight studies that reported eighteen correlations between successful performance in initially leaderless group discussions and successful performance as a leader in ''real life.'' The correlations ranged from − .25 to .68, with a median of .38.

Subtle effects can be seen in changes that occur. Cloyd (1964) found that the same group members tended to perform the same function in successive groups. At the same time, different functions, if needed, were not performed by the same member. Analysis of leaders' comments in discussions with differing purposes indicated to J. T. Wood (1977) that the same leaders can be successful in a variety of discussion situations with divergent goals, members, and constraints if they adapt their oral behaviors to meet varying goals and compensate for failures at previous meetings. Other members also readjust.

*Compensatory Performance.* Haythorn (1952) combined and recombined the members of experimental groups. Members were rated on aggressiveness, initiative, confidence, submissiveness, sociability, leadership, and the like. Haythorn found that when one member in a group was rated high on one of these variables, other members were all rated low. It appeared that when one member exhibited a high degree of a given behavior the other members attempted to adapt to the situation by reducing their behaviors in the same area of role performance. Again, I. S. Bernstein (1964) removed the dominant male from a group of rhesus monkeys. During the month of his removal the remaining males increased their dominance and social activities. Upon his return, the dominant male assumed his former position and the other males exhibited a reduction in social activities.

*Opinion Leadership.* Positive transfer of successful opinion leadership has also been measured, using the multitrait, multimethod approach of Campbell and Fiske (1959). Jacoby (1974) found that opinion leaders' influence overlapped in different areas, and the degree of overlap of influence increased with the increase in the similarity of opinion issues.

### Effects of Different Tasks

As posited by the transfer model, transfer of leadership behavior decreases when tasks differ from an old to a new situation, especially when a change from a purely intellectual performance to purely manual-mechanical activities is involved. An examination of situational data collected in the screening of OSS candidates (OSS, 1948) supports the proposition. Positive transfer as evidenced by the correlation of leadership ratings of other situational test performances with rated performance in leaderless discussions dropped as the other tests became more dissimilar from free discussions. The correlation was .56 with leadership displayed in a debate, .48 with leadership in a personal interview, .47 with leadership in solving a problem of crossing a brook, and .30 with leadership in cooperatively constructing a giant toy.

Carter, Haythorn, and Howell (1950) found that although leaders in reasoning tasks also tended to emerge as leaders in intellectual and clerical tasks, they did not do so in mechanical tasks. Leaders in mechanical tasks tended to emerge as leaders in motor coordination and discussion tasks, but not in intellectual tasks. In an earlier study, Carter and Nixon (1949a) found a tendency for the same person to emerge as leader in clerical and intellectual tasks, but not in mechanical tasks. Thus, no transfer or even a negative transfer seems most likely when the transfer of leadership to be effected is from tasks of the ''head'' to tasks of the ''hand.''

*Negative Transfer*

Although negative transfer is a theoretical possibility as well as observable in real life, it is difficult to create experimentally. The manual-mechanical tasks, indeed, have to be completely free of any discussion, any verbal or intellectual components, or any interaction requirements. All individual traits likely to promote positive transfer need to be controlled such as general ability, interpersonnel competency, and external status and external esteem of the participants in the groups shifted from "head" to "hand" tasks.

Nevertheless, many observers have described how earlier success in an old situation fixes the behavior of the leader, making him or her less effective in a new, different situation requiring a new approach to problems. The technical supervisor who has been a successful leader in a situation demanding precision exactness, when promoted to general management, fails to deal with the challenge of decision making in the absence of complete information (Pearse, Worthington & Flaherty, 1954). The business executive fails in efforts to transfer profit-making practices to running a government agency (Fishman, 1952). Merton (1940) singles out the stereotyped bureaucrat who adopts measures as a leader in keeping with past training. Under new conditions, not recognized as significantly different, the very soundness of the training leads to the adoption of wrong procedures. Furthermore, continued success in day-to-day routines makes the bureaucrat unable to change or see the need to change when the conditions under which the bureaucracy was organized are changed.

The garrison commander may not do as well when in a front-line command. Conversely, an effective general like Ulysses S. Grant is a disaster as president. The effective leader in emergencies (Chapter 26) may be unsuccessful and ineffective elsewhere. Thus, Elkin, Halpern, and Cooper (1962) observed that the same individuals tended to emerge as leaders in experimentally created mobs. But such mob leaders were not popular under other circumstances.

What is likely to make a leader effective in the early development of a T-group seems to reverse in later stages of development. Data from 158 members and leaders of twenty T-groups showed that trainers who were considered low in control and affection needs tended to elicit the most favorable reactions during an early period in group life and the most negative reactions at a later time.

Shifting leaders from situations favorable to themselves in which they have experienced effectiveness to situations unfavorable to themselves should foster negative transfer. Their earlier success should result in their continuing to attempt leadership in the new situation with consequential decrement in effective outcomes. Such has been demonstrated by Fiedler and associates (see Chapter 20).

## LEADERSHIP SUCCESSION

The process of succession is an examination of the transfer process from another vantage point. Antecedents that promote more effective replacement of one leader by another and the consequences of replacing one leader with another provide a further opportunity to see how positive and negative transfer of leadership may occur (Gordon & Rosen, n.d.).

*Antecedents*

The rate of change in leaders is affected by the personality of the group, size of the organization, and its effectiveness. Groups composed of individuals with complex personalities changed their leaders more often than groups of personally simple individuals (Schroder, Streufert & Weeden, 1964).

Grusky (1961) found that the rate of succession of chief executive officers was directly related to the firm's size. However, Gordon and Becker (1964) found the relationship less clear. Kriesberg (1964) suggested that differences among industry and differences in technology had to be taken into account.

Well-known is the extent to which managers of baseball teams with the poorest season's records are most likely to be changed (Grusky, 1963). Path analyses by Allen, Panian and Lotz (1979) confirmed that poor records rather than other related elements resulted in replacing managers of baseball teams. Hamblin (1958b) demonstrated that groups change leaders informally if the leaders do not have a way of helping the groups out of crises. Goldman and Fraas (1965) found subordinates more likely to choose leaders who earlier had been more successful with the group's task. But Daum (1975) failed to find such results.

*Choice of Insiders or Outsiders.* Conflict is avoided inside the organization by choosing outsiders. The Balkan countries upon winning their independence from Turkey often chose petty German princes for their new kings to avoid conflict among the leading noble families as well as to obtain Great Power support. Similarly, Birnbaum (1971) showed that state universities tend to recruit their presidents from the lower administration levels of other state universities rather than from community colleges nearby, thus promoting both transfer from elsewhere and restricting conflict inside their own universities. The tendency to go outside for a new manager was greater where the previous year's performance of baseball teams had been bad (Allen, Panian & Lotz, 1979).

*Consequences*

Changes in the leadership have a variety of effects depending on the rate of succession, whether insiders or outsiders.

*Group Effectiveness.* Changing leaders, all other things being equal, seems to yield decreased group performance (Pryer, Flint & Bass, 1962), but some of this may be due to the costs to performance of personnel turnover in general (Trow, 1960; Rogers, Ford & Tassone, 1961). In seventeen groups studied by Pryer, Flint, and Bass, those groups gaining in effectiveness exhibited correlations of .70 and .33 in consistency of leadership status. Among failing groups, the same correlations were $-.08$ and .01.

Gamson and Scotch (1964) felt that the impact of a change in manager of baseball teams was minimal. The firing of a baseball manager was only a ritual. Nevertheless, Allen, Panian and Lotz's (1979) previously cited path-analytic examination of managerial succession over a fifty-four-year period showed that baseball teams that replaced a manager during the season performed worse subsequently.

As cited before, Grusky (1963) had found that baseball teams with the poorest records had the highest rates of changing managers. Allen, Panian, and Lotz (1979) then showed that such higher rates subsequently resulted in poorer team performance. But contrary to expectations, inside succession was less disruptive to performance than bringing in a new manager from the outside. And Eitzen and Yetman (1972) found no relation between the turnover of coaches of basketball teams and team performance records over forty years. Lieberson and O'Connor (1972) failed to establish any simple relationship between turnover of CEOs over twenty years with sales and profits. Different industries and organizations yielded different results.

*Leader Style.* Helmich (1974) established that the origin and style of a successor to 140 presidents of manufacturing firms influenced the changes that occurred in the organization. More specifically, he showed that rapid change resulted in more task-oriented leadership behavior, particularly during the early tenure of successors. It follows that with more such continuing changes in CEOs, task orientation would dominate over time in such organizations.

*Abruptness of Change.* Gordon and Rosen (n.d.) noted that particularly detrimental to group effectiveness are leadership changes that come with little advance notice.

### A Succession Model

Gordon and Rosen (n.d.) have proposed a model for the dynamics of succession involving a set of variables antedating the arrival and entry of the new leader into the organization, postarrival variables of consequence, and the interaction between the two sets of variables. Included in the prearrival variables are the successor's background, competence, motivation, and orientation, whether the successor came from inside or outside, how well the successor was known in advance by the organization, the organization's previous general experience with the succession process, as well as specific involvement in selecting the new leader. The new leader's mandate is also important. Postarrival variables include much of what we have identified in preceding chapters about what factors influence leader–follower relationships and how they, in turn, affect productivity and satisfaction.

We now move on to take into account the effects of sex, race, and culture on leaders and followers.

part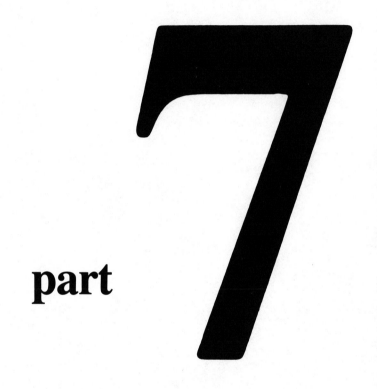

# SPECIAL
# CONDITIONS

# 30

## WOMEN AND LEADERSHIP

## SOCIETAL CONSIDERATIONS

### Changing Situation

Sex as a difference of consequence in the study of leadership was almost completely absent in Stogdill's (1974) review (Chapter 4) and followup (Chapter 5), although it was seen as a useful subject for future research. Early research by Hall and Locke (1938) and E. Livingstone (1953) found that women, particularly in industry, were often reluctant to assume supervisory responsibilities. The times, indeed, are "a-changing." After two decades of social turbulence, the women's liberation movement, and cultural changes along with federal legislation prohibiting sex discrimination in employment practices (specifically, Title VII of the Civil Rights Act, 1964, and the Affirmative Action program of the Equal Opportunity Commission) as well as the large increase of women into the world of work, the issue of women as leaders now looms large in research and policy consideration. Indicative was the steadily increasing percentage of nationally representative samples surveyed between 1937 and 1978 in Gallop polls of people willing to vote for a woman for president: 1937—31 percent, 1949—48 percent, 1958—52 percent, 1967—57 percent, and 1978—76 percent (New York Times, 1980). In 1974, Michigan State University reported twice the proportion of women students in business as it had in 1969. Stanford University noted a similar doubling in a three-year period from 1971 to 1974 (Chambers, 1974). In the period of 1971 to 1976, the number of women enrolled in MBA programs in American universities tripled (L. Werner, 1979).

By the end of 1979, nearly 51 percent of all females 16 years and over in this country were working, an almost 10 percent increase since 1967. Six percent were managers or administrators, compared to 15 percent of male workers (U.S. Department of Labor, 1979). But women mainly occupied first-level managerial positions (Baron, 1977; R. A. Patterson, 1975). As of 1975, they made up less than 5 percent of middle management and less than 2 percent of executives in business (M. W. Meyer, 1975).

By 1980, 8 percent of the U.S. armed forces were women, a greater percentage than in any other country. The figure is expected to climb to 12 percent in five years. There is now a female commanding general of a large army post (Newsweek, 1980).

*Society in Transition*

It may be that the period between 1960–2000 is one of transition for women in leadership, at the end of which the issue will disappear for different reasons. The cultural factors supporting differences in leader behavior associated with sex differences in leaders and/or followers may have disappeared by then. We are already seeing some shifting away from sex-role stereotypes for both women (Kravetz, 1976) and men (Tavris, 1977). This chapter and the next should be read as possibly of only transitory consequence.

It goes without saying that the role of women in society is primarily culturally determined. Child-bearing has its obvious universal effects, but most of what women can and do do is culture-based. Thus, in a survey of 224 mainly subsistence-level societies, Murdock (1937) showed that although generally men hunt and trap and women gather and prepare food, few occupations were entirely relegated anywhere to only one sex. (An exception was hunting sea-mammals which would be hard on pregnant women.)

In the United States by 1977, over 75 percent of women disagreed that some work is meant for men and other work is meant for women. This was an increase of 21 percentage points from 1962. Younger women in 1977 were even more likely to disagree, suggesting that even more extreme rejection of the duality of work roles is likely in the future (Thornton & Freedman, 1979).

*Disadvantaged Opportunities for Leadership*

Leadership opportunities for women in the past tended to be limited to women's institutions: sororities, nunneries, and all-girl schools (but even presidents of colleges for women often were men). In mixed organizations, women were generally expected to take subordinate roles (O'Leary, 1974; Schein, 1973, 1975), except where their position was legitimized by inheritance, the lack of male heirs, or marriage. According to Eskilson and Wiley (1976), the same occurs when in an experiment women are legitimized in a leadership position by a bogus test rather than placed there by chance. Those seen as legitimate engage in more task-oriented behavior and initiate more leadership than those seen as assigned to the role by chance. Although women form the vast majority of public school teachers, they are a small minority of higher-level school administrators (Estler, 1975).

*Handicaps.* Even when women are promoted into management, they continue to face a variety of handicaps limiting their upward mobility. For example, homemaking requirements when married may call for husbands willing to share homemaking duties. Job rotation for management development requiring relocation of one's husband is more difficult. Lack of as much experience in team sports as men have had limits the ability of women to participate effectively in management teams, according to Hennig and Jardim (1977). They do not know the rules (Harragan, 1977). "Old boy" networks make it more difficult for women executives to obtain necessary information to fulfill the monitoring role of the manager effectively.

Women do not frequent men's athletic clubs. They may be excluded from some social clubs. They may be unable to entertain visitors at which time important information may be gathered and sometimes important decisions are made. In Finland, male executives may gather in a sauna to negotiate with male union leaders. Bayes and Newton (1978) observed that ordinarily a woman leader and her subordinates have little social experience perceiving a woman with legitimate power to control and protect the boundaries of an adult group, to stand alone as a figure of authority, and to evaluate output of other adults. Success for a woman as a manager is seen by Hennig and Jardim (1977) and by Trahey (1977) to require competing with men in a system that the men understand better and with which they are more familiar and comfortable. Carpeno (1976) found that for 100 professional staff members of a regional high school system, statements about female leaders indicated doubt and uneasiness about their future. Frank and Katcher (1977) concluded from a survey of 104 male and forty-four female medical students that the men tended to stereotype the women's behavior and to exclude them from positions of leadership in anatomy dissection groups.

Illustrative of how differential opportunities make for the difference observed in women's emergence as leaders, Mottl (1977) studied through interviews the different career paths of white and black women reform leaders. The school bureaucracy was immediately accessible to white women who became involved as teachers and middle class mothers. Black women leaders began and ended up in community organizations. Easy entry from home into school politics was related to the closeness of school, particularly elementary school, to family life.

*Women as Assistants.* What we are accustomed to is women in auxiliary and service roles. Numerous surveys and observers' analyses substantiate that being a woman legitimizes the performance of a service role as a nurse, secretary, or administrative assistant (O'Leary, 1974; Schein, 1973, 1975; Kanter, 1977). R. S. Weiss (1956) noted this in a study of the allocation and acceptance of responsibility in a government agency.

Women are counseled accordingly. Weisman, Morlock, Sack, and Levine (1976) observed that counseling of women who were denied entry into medical school was different from counseling of men denied entry. Men were encouraged to reapply to other medical schools or to try to obtain a Ph.D. in a related field. Women were reminded of the obstacles they would continue to face if they tried to continue in medicine. They were encouraged to change to more sex-role-accepted professions such as nursing. Such inadequate career counseling as well as a lack of successful female role models were seen as key factors in reducing women's choice of higher-status careers by Heinen, McGlauchin, Legeros, and Freeman (1975) and Lannon (1977).

*Disadvantageous Stereotypes.* Women are seen as poor prospects for managerial positions for a number of reasons. A factor analysis of 176 male managers' responses to a survey of their attitudes toward women in the world of work was completed by Bass, Krusell, and Alexander (1971). The factors included: (1) women lack career orientation; (2) women lack leadership potential; (3) women are undependable and; (4) women are emotionally less stable. The perceived lack of career orientation links with the stereotype that women are less concerned about their jobs. The other stereotypes are built around a mixture of fact and fancy which we will address later in the chapter.

*Discrimination and Obstacles.* Women's entry into management is also handicapped by male administrators' tendencies to discriminate against female employees in personnel decisions involving selection, promotion, and supervision (Rosen & Jerdee, 1973, 1974). Such discriminatory practices have been justified on the basis of higher female absenteeism, higher female turnover, and their lack of geographical mobility, particularly if married or with children (Robie, 1973). Absenteeism and turnover rates among females are higher than those for males at all age levels (U.S. Department of Labor, 1977), often as a consequence of child care problems and problems because of husband's relocating. In the movement to upgrade women at work, adequate day care for children, more challenging jobs for women, and the opportunity for the individual woman to decide about relocation instead of being treated as a class are prerequisites.

*Status, Sex, and Leadership.* Women in our society remain handicapped in their efforts to obtain leadership by their lower status as compared to men. The lower status of women in American society is seen by the effect of the entrance of large numbers of women into an occupation. The occupation's prestige and desirability is lowered (Touhey, 1974). Prestige of occupants is linked with having large majorities of men (Bartol & Bartol, 1975). Lockheed (1976) has noted that the lack of influence of women found in small group research has been attributed to sex-role socialization. Yet, much of it really is a consequence of the lower status of women.

In Chapter 10, we noted the extent to which one's success as a leader is associated with the status one is accorded. Illustrative of the impact of sex was Megargee's (1969) finding that when participants were paired with their own sex, those scoring high in dominance tended to assume leadership but when paired with the opposite sex, males assumed leadership even when the males were very submissive. In most cultures, the male position has higher status than the females. But considerable variation exists, ranging from those societies where men and women are almost equal in status, as is the case among the Arapesh, to those where the women are higher in status as, for example, among the Tchambuli. Where women are higher in status than men, they are more likely to lead. The higher-status woman is dominant; the man less responsible and more dependent. The woman makes the choice; the man is chosen (Mead, 1935). Strodtbeck (1951) contrasted three cultural groups within the United States—Navaho, Mormon, and "American"—by arranging discussions between husband and wives drawn from the three groups. Husbands were most likely to lead in discussions in the patriarchal Mormon culture where their status over women is higher. Husbands were least likely to lead in the discussions between the Navahos, where women traditionally have more status and are more active and demanding.

Even among two different geographical regions presumably with the same general culture, differences in status and leadership appeared. New York college girls reported "playing dumb" much more frequently when on a date than did West Coast college girls (Wallin, 1950).

### Socialization, Sex, and Leadership

In our society, we are socialized primarily within the nuclear family in a culture that defines sex roles as total roles that define our sense of self and our behavior. The sex role pertains to all aspects of life and takes precedence over situation-specific work roles if they are incompatible. Dominance and independence are associated with the masculine roles; submissiveness, passivity, and nurturance, with the feminine. Desirable femininity, culturally defined, emphasizes giving and the avoidance of aggressiveness and domination. (Broverman, Broverman, Clarkson, Rosenkrantz & Vogel, 1970). Even the exceptions seem to be a consequence of the differences in the nuclear family in which the woman was raised. Vogel, Broverman, Broverman, Clarkson, and Rosenkrantz (1970) and Almquist (1974) found that women who chose nontraditional careers historically occupied by men were raised in families in which the mother worked full time. Generally, the nuclear family is likely to discourage women from choosing nontraditional careers. Goodale & Hall (1976) found that high school students of both sexes had similar aspirations for college and career choice, yet male students indicated significantly more parental interest and pressure to pursue their aspiration.

Broverman, Vogel, Broverman, Clarkson, and Rosenkrantz (1972) asked 100 college students to indicate on which characteristics, attitudes and behaviors men and women differed. A second group then rated the extent to which the items mentioned most frequently by the first group were typical of adult men or women. The female role stereotype that emerged found the woman to be less aggressive, dependent, and emotional. She did not hide her emotions, was subjective, easily influenced, submissive, and enjoyed art and literature but not math and science. She was excitable in minor crises, passive, not competitive, illogical, home-oriented, unskilled in business, sneaky, unfamiliar with the ways of the world. Her feelings were easily hurt. She was unadventurous, indecisive, cried easily, almost never acted as a leader, and lacked self-confidence. She was uncomfortable about being aggressive, unambitious, unable to separate feelings from ideas, conceited about appearance, talkative, tactful, gentle, aware of other's feelings, religious, interested in her own appearance, neat, quiet, strong in need for security, and easily expressed tender feelings.

### Management and Sex-Role Stereotypes

The female sex role stereotype labels women as less competent and warmer emotionally than men. The stereotype of the effective manager matches the masculine stereotype of competence and toughness—lacking in warmth. As we have documented in Chapter 22, Miner (1965) reflected the accepted stereotype that there are parallel role requirements for being a manager and being a man. Both need to be able to take charge, to make decisions, to be assertive and to take disciplinary action. Women managers must follow masculine behavior patterns, according to Miner. The stereotyped concepts of women and leaders are viewed as incompatible (Schein, 1973, 1975). Surveys report large differences in the attributes of women and those of successful middle managers. Survey data also indicate popular beliefs that women make inferior leaders (Bowman, Worthy & Greyser, 1965). Women themselves tend to subscribe to the difference in stereotypes for managers and for women. O'Leary (1974) and McClelland (1965b) both found that women as a group described themselves as different from or even opposite to men as a group on traits supposedly required for management. In confirmation, Frantzve (1979) found a positive relation between masculinity scores on the Bem Sex-Role Inventory and the tendency to emerge as a leader in forty-nine initially leaderless discussions mixed in sex.

*Subordinate Reactions.* According to Bayes and Newton (1978), subordinates respond to a woman leader partly as an individual and partly according to the cultural stereotype of woman. The responses of subordinates to women leaders may be due to the socialized expectations about women, in general, resulting in likely conflict with the more appropriate response to the woman as manager, involved in a role which is seen as primarily masculine. But Kanter (1977) and Alban and Seashore (1978) argued that the stereotyped female role requirement to deal effectively with people offsets the disadvantages to a woman of the submissive, nurturing role requirements. Similarly, Larwood and Wood (1977) pointed out, in agreement with what we have detailed in preceding chapters, that the effective manager can make use of both supposedly masculine competence, task orientation, and initiative and the supposedly more feminine concern for people, feelings, and relationships. But the strength of popular beliefs cannot be ignored. Thus, Powell and Butterfield (1979) found that among 694 business students, the good manager was still described in masculine terms.

Stereotypes have their effects on behavior. We expect women to be more submissive, so we have trouble taking orders from women, no matter what they are like individually. Women leaders themselves are in conflict when facing divergence in what is expected from them in their role as managers and in their role as females. But do the stereotypes reflect reality? Do women actually differ from men in traits of consequence to leadership as they differ in stereotype? A variety of answers emerges. For example, women are supposed to be less task-oriented than men. Such was actually found true when the Orientation Inventory (Bass, 1967b), a direct measure, was used for male and female counterparts from adolescence to middle age, and for many student and occupational groups, except for one group of Berkeley senior women. But the opposite was found when LPC (Chapter 20), a more disguised method, was used by J. M. Ward (1977) to determine the task and relations orientation of thirty-six male and thirty-six female students.

All this may work to a woman manager's advantage. If women managers are not expected to perform well and are seen to operate under handicaps (Terborg & Ilgen, 1975), then if they do perform well, their performance may be attributed to extra effort and competence and as more worthy of reward than comparable male managers.

## MALE–FEMALE DIFFERENCES IN LEADERSHIP POTENTIAL

### Motivation to Lead

Status and sex-role stereotyping handicap the elevation of women to leadership positions. However, socialization as a female itself contributes to reduced motivation to attain higher-level posts (Estler, 1975). On the average, women's self-confidence is lower than that of male counterparts. According to Maccoby and Jacklin (1974), females have less confidence in their abilities across a wide variety of activities such as achieving good grades in tasks requiring manual dexterity, in solving puzzles, and in the ability to deal with emergencies. In fact, women's self-confidence is increased with the incorporation of more of the stereotyped masculine traits into their own self-concept (Spence, Helmreich & Stapp, 1975). In the desire to project stereotyped femininity (Ireson, 1976), females, more so than males, will predict lower performance for themselves than warranted by their intelligence (Crandall, Katkovsky & Preston, 1962) and will present themselves as dependent and incompetent (Vaught, 1965). Lack of self-esteem is strongly associated with avoiding attempts to lead (Chapter 10). But whether or not women avoid attempting to climb the executive ladder because they fear failure remains controversial (Tresemer, 1976; Wood & Greenfeld, 1976; Horner, 1970; O'Leary, 1974; Zuckerman & Wheeler, 1975).

*Intelligence.* Shields (1975) and Wittig (1976) reviewed the many studies of male–female differences on the subject and could find no support for any differences in intellectual characteristics except possibly in spatial visualization (important in math and science), which difference Block and Kolakowski (1973) attributed possibly to a sex-linked chromosome.

### Other Trait Differences of Consequence to Leadership

Caution is required about accepting reports of male–female trait differences without considering society at the time they appeared. However, the available data do suggest that females actually differ from their male counterparts in the same situation on many traits of consequence to leadership. Lockheed and Hall (1976) concluded that men and women actually differ in activity, influence, and task orientation in small group experiments. Purcell (1960) found that women exhibit stronger loyalty to company than do men. According to Kehoe (1976), the need for dominance in women appears unrelated to their verbal output (attempts to lead) as it does in men in initially leaderless groups.

A. R. Marks (1954) compared the interests of male and female high school leaders. Girl leaders showed more social, heterosexual, and adult-disapproved interests than did their nonleader control group. Boy leaders exhibited more nonconforming interests than nonleaders by scoring lower in mechanical interests. According to Sandler and Scalia (1975), first-born females were more likely to serve as leaders in a church congregation, but this was not true for males.

*Change Structure and Authority.* Trumbo (1961) found that women express significantly less favorable attitudes toward change than men. According to a study by Kuenzli (1959), low-income female adults from rural areas preferred little structure, but high-income urban women preferred high structure. However, when Denmark and Diggory (1966) tested the hypothesis that women would endorse higher degrees of authoritarian leader behavior than men, the opposite was found, but the differences were not statistically significant.

*Self-Disclosure.* Aries (1976) noted that women revealed more information about themselves and their feelings than did men in mixed groups. Men were more open only in all-male groups. But Eisman (1975) failed to find that self-disclosure among members was related to the participants' sex. Regardless of whether they were in same-sex or mixed groups, women were observed by Wheelan (1975) to make more maintenance than substantive statements in contrast to men.

*Trait Differences between Male and Female Managers.* Miner (1974) found no differences between sexes on motivation to manage (see Chapter 22) within a sample of store managers and school administrators. Further illustrating the impermanence of sex differences in leader behavior, Miner (1965) found that the motivation of women changed with training and experience in a similar way to that seen for men. Similar results were reported by Morrison and Sebald (1974). Female executives were similar to male executives on self-esteem, motivation, and mental ability. Female executives differed from women employees in general in the same way that male executives differed from men employees in general. Bartol (1976a), Brief and Aldag (1975), Brief and Oliver (1976), and Matteson, McMahon, and McMahon (1974) reported similar results. But contrary evidence was obtained by R. S. Schuler (1975). Schwartz and Waetjen (1976) reported that women managers were observed by their own supervisors to be less confident, more conservative, and less risk-taking than their male counterparts. An interview study by Hennig and Jardim (1977) agreed with these findings and also observed that female managers were more passive, inflexible, noncompetitive and less career-oriented than men.

Greater lack of self-confidence among women managers was seen by N. M. Wood (1975) in their tendency to attribute personal failure to their lack of ability. Nevertheless, after reviewing the evidence, Terborg (1977) concluded that on the whole, women who become managers have motives similar to those of male managers. In this same vein, Pfeffer and Shapiro's (1978) findings suggested that managerial women are different from women in general. They are less likely to have traditional female characteristics and more likely, either by temperament or by accommodation to the stereotyped male role, to be analytical, rationally oriented, and personally competitive (Lannon, 1977). Bartol (1978) has likewise distinguished between women managers and women in general, finding that career-oriented women see themselves as more broadminded, dominating, efficient, and independent than noncareer women.

Consistent with these results, in developing a leadership orientation scale for the Women's Strong Vocational Interest Blank, Casey (1975) found that women leaders varied significantly from women nonleaders in interests. The leaders responded positively to items suggesting positions of eminence, freedom of thought, challenge, and interpersonal contact; the nonleaders responded more positively to items suggesting artistic preferences.

*Implications.* Larwood and Wood (1977) agree that women have been found to differ from men in traits of consequence to leadership such as need for achievement, fear of success, assertiveness, self-esteem, need for power, need for dominance, self-reliance, dependence, risk preferences, and competitiveness which may result in women, when placed in leadership roles, failing to seek their maximum advantage and reaching compromises too quickly when cooperation is required. But they interpret the results of experimental findings of such sex differences as transitory evidence of the relative lack of familiarity of the women with the tasks involved.

They see women more likely to withdraw psychologically from organizations when facing obstacles to promotion to higher management levels. Role conflict with homemaking may be a second source of psychological withdrawal from the organization. In comparison to men who will initiate competition for the whole reward, women are seen to be more likely to engage in retaliatory competition entering competition only when others reject initial efforts to cooperate (Terhune, 1970; J. A. Wall, 1976).

DeSanctis, White, and Crino (1981) note that in the late 1960s, the implication was drawn that women had to adapt to a managerial model that conformed to the male stereotype of our culture. Women's traits had to be altered so that they could become more consistent with those of male managers. But more recently, it is seen that with the personality differences between men and women, the two sexes can complement each other in management. Mixed sex teams should be more creative. The leader behavior of women in contrast to male counterparts in the same situation may be positively enhanced by their greater recognition and response to the needs of others and greater sensitivity to interpersonal cues. To the degree that women are less assertive, they may make better leaders in situations where such assertiveness would be threatening, arousing competitiveness and defensiveness in followers (Larwood & Wood, 1977).

## MALE–FEMALE DIFFERENCES IN LEADERSHIP STYLE

Contrary to what might be expected from what we have said so far about male–female socialization and trait differences, the preponderance of available evidence is that no consistently clear pattern of differences can be discerned in the supervisory style of female as compared to male leaders, although individual studies have been able on occasion to find some positive indications, but not necessarily in the same directions.

### When Sex Has Made a Difference in Style

Although earlier we noted that women, in general, are more relations- than task-oriented than men and that there is some evidence in leaderless studies that females tend toward person-oriented rather than task-oriented leadership styles, studies by Bond and Vinacke (1961), Uesgi and Vinacke (1963), Gamson (1965), and Lirtzman and Wahba (1972) reported contrary results for coalition formation among females in a competitive high-risk game.

Heinmen, McGlauchin, Legeros, and Freeman (1975) suggested that women managers have particular difficulty in dealing with interpersonal conflict among subordinates due to their socialization which encourages them to avoid confrontation. In a study by Rosenfeld and Fowler (1976), some differences emerged for self-described ideal leader scores of eighty-nine men and eighty-nine women in the behaviors of democratic men and women, although the results for the autocratic styles were the same for both groups. Democratic women emphasized being helpful, affectionate, nurturing, open-minded, and accepting blame; democratic men emphasized being mature, forceful, competent, moral, utilitarian, analytical, and valuing people. Morsink (1966) found that female principals when they were described by both male and female staff members scored significantly higher on LBDQ-XII (Chapter 21) than male principals on representation, persuasiveness, production emphasis, predictive accuracy, integration of the group, and influence with superiors.

In an unpublished study in the 1970s, Sleeth and Humphreys found slight differences between 122 men and 122 women students at a large urban university in self-descriptions of their leader behavior as scored on the LBDQ and Hersey and Blanchard's (1977) Leader Effectiveness and Adaptability Description, as well as assertiveness and endorsement of the work ethic. The women reported themselves to be slightly higher in consideration and the men reported themselves higher in task rather than relations orientation. Similarly, among fifty-one first- and second-level women supervisors, more consideration than initiating of structure was seen in self-descriptions (DiMarco & Whitsitt, 1975). In reverse, Eskilson (1975) reported that women who emerged as leaders of three-person laboratory groups showed more intensive involvement with the task than men who emerged as leaders.

*Lack of Difference*

We have seen that women do differ from men on a wide variety of attributes associated with emergence as a leader, but the differences tend to blur if we contrast women and men who already have achieved status as leaders. Once legitimized as a leader, women actually do not behave differently from men. Most often, only modest, if any, effects of sex on leader style have been reported (Bartol, 1973; 1974; Bartol & Butterfield, 1976; Bartol & Wortman, 1975, 1976; Chapman, 1975; Day & Stogdill, 1972; Osborn & Vicars, 1976; Petty & Lee, 1975; Roussel, 1974; Wexley & Hunt, 1974). This is true whether the leaders are describing themselves or are being described by their subordinates and whether the setting is a field or laboratory study. Thus, Osborn and Vicars (1976) found no sex differences in the initiation of structure or the amount of consideration of supervisors according to their subordinates in residences for the mentally retarded. Again, among 100 male and 100 female executives at the same middle-management level in federal agencies, Muldrow and Bayton (1979) found no differences in handling six personnel decision tasks, although the women described themselves as less likely to take risks. And, Carpeno (1976) found no differences due to sex on the LOQ (Chapter 21) among 100 high school professionals. Sex is still an important consideration, but it may be confounded with other variables in superior–subordinate relationships. Thus, Hansen (1974) could find no significant differences in support or goal facilitation of supervisors associated with their sex; nevertheless, subordinates of both sexes were more dissatisfied if their supervisor was a woman. This might have been due to women supervisors themselves reporting they had less autonomy or, as found in other studies, women supervisors having less influence with higher authority.

As a consequence, as we shall detail more fully later, the same style displayed by a female as a male supervisor may have different effects on subordinates' satisfaction with their supervision (Rosen & Jerdee, 1973; Petty & Lee, 1975).

## SEX EFFECTS CONTINGENT ON GROUP AND SITUATION

After a review of available evidence, Chapman and Luthans (1975) concluded that in general, leadership style was not a function of sex differences. Instead, the question of whether men and women differ in leadership style needs to be considered in the context of the group and situation involved. Thus, female leaders were least likely to perform as leaders when leading two males in three-person groups and were most likely to exhibit leadership in all-female groups (Eskilson, 1974). Consistent with these results in mixed groups of males and females, Aries (1976) observed that males displayed more leadership than females in contrast to same-sex situations. Likewise, Megargee (1966) found in a study of various combinations of dominant and submissive men and women in two experimental tasks that dominant men paired with submissive men and women and dominant women paired with submissive women tended to appoint themselves as leaders. Dominant women paired with submissive men tended to appoint the men as leaders. These results were interpreted as indicating the unwillingness of dominant women to assume overt leadership over male partners. Wheelan (1975) reported that for seventy-two female and seventy-two male undergraduates, women were ranked lower than men in leadership in mixed-sex six-person groups despite the fact that women participated more. Haccoun, Haccoun, and Sallay (1978) found nondirective styles favored for women. The sex of both supervisor and subordinate involved determined group performance.

Among 144 undergraduates in forty-eight three-person groups, Eskilson and Wiley (1976) observed that although typical sex role expectations resulted in male leaders receiving more requests for leadership, both sexes addressed more directive behavior toward their own sex groups.

Petty and Lee (1975) found that male subordinates of female supervisors rated their supervisors as lower in consideration and higher in initiating structure than did female subordinates of female supervisors or subordinates of either sex of male supervisors. Unknown is whether the ratings reflected actual differences in female supervisory behavior toward female and male subordinates or differences in the way subordinates perceived the same supervisory behavior by female and male supervisors.

### Subordinates' Attitudes toward Women as Leaders

If the subordinates' sex is not considered, generally little difference has been found in actual subordinate satisfaction with female as compared to male supervisors (Bartol, 1974, 1975; Bartol & Wortman, 1976; Maier, 1970a; Osborn & Vicars, 1976; Petty & Miles, 1976; Reif, Newstrom & St. Louis, 1976). However, Yerby (1975) reported that subordinate attitudes were a complex interaction of the sex composition of the subordinate groups and the leader's sex. In a laboratory study of seventy-two teams of male cadets led by males or females, Rice, Bender, and Vitters (1980) found that male subordinates with traditional attitudes toward women were lower in overall team morale when led by women. Traditionalists attributed group success more to luck and less to the leader's hard work when led by a woman. For those subordinates with liberal attitudes, the leader's sex did not matter as much. At the same time, male subordinates, as a whole, felt that women leaders contributed more to the group's performance, while the expert ability of male leaders was more important to their own individual performance. This was consistent with Garland and Price's (1977) results. They found that men with favorable views toward women managers attributed success to factors such as ability and effort and avoided attributions of success to luck and task difficulty.

Bowman, Worthy, and Greyser (1965) found that among 2,000 active executives, 86 percent of men and 77 percent of women reported that men were uncomfortable working for women executives. Consistent with what we have reported earlier about stereotypes of women's lack of leadership potential (Bass, Krusell & Alexander, 1971), 41 percent of the men were unfavorable toward women as managers. Women also generally preferred working for a man (Robie, 1973), but this was not so for women at higher education levels, who were more favorable to women managers, and younger college women who indicated they were looking forward to working for a woman (Koff, 1973; Terborg, Peters, Ilgen & Smith, 1977).

Petty and Lee (1975) reported a tendency for male subordinates to be more dissatisfied with female supervisors who were high in initiating structure and more satisfied when both male and particularly female supervisors were more considerate. Petty and Miles (1976) noted among social service agency personnel that considerate leader behavior by female supervisors (as well as initiating structure by male supervisors) was most conducive to subordinate satisfaction with supervision. But when much larger samples were employed by Petty, Odewahn, Bruning, and Thomason (1976), satisfaction with supervision was positively correlated with all leader behavior except production emphasis. No differences were found between correlations due to supervisor sex or subordinate sex. In the same way, Bartol (1974) failed to find that dominant (counterstereotype) women had a detrimental effect on subordinate satisfaction in a study of 100 undergraduates in twenty-four same-sex and mixed-sex teams of four members playing a business game.

*Subordinates' Perceptual Distortions.* Subordinates tend to be more lenient in judging women leaders. According to results obtained by Jacobson and Effertz (1974), women leaders in experimental small groups with seventy-two undergraduates were judged less harshly than male leaders when performance levels did not meet expectations. Another distortion was observed by Elrick (1977) in a case study of a "self-analytic" learning group of six women and nine men. A tendency was found to deny that early in the group's development a woman was leading the group.

## WOMEN'S SUCCESS AS LEADERS

When women emerge or are assigned to positions of leadership, to what extent can they succeed as leaders, supervisors, and managers, that is, achieve and maintain influence over followers and subordinates?

### Antecedent Conditions

Lonetto and Williams (1974) found that the personal factors involved in working for success as a leader were the same for women as for men. For thirty-one male and thirty-one females in three-person undergraduate groups, Lonetto and Williams found that regardless of the sex of the group, the same factors, such as a member's intelligence and self-orientation, were related to their emergence as leaders. In the same way, Kanter (1977) noted that when all-male and all-female groups were given a specific assignment, the interaction patterns and leadership styles within each group were similar. Among a group of experienced managers, Gaudreau (1975) could find no differences in leadership competencies associated with their sex.

*Subordinate and Peer Acceptance.* We have already noted the industrial surveys suggesting that even women workers generally prefer male superiors. But studies in the late 1970s of college women suggested that they preferred women as bosses. As for opinion leadership, much change has occurred between 1935 and 1975 consistent with the change in willingness to vote for a woman as president, which we mentioned earlier. On most topics, men by 1975 exhibited no preferences in selecting opinion leaders based on sex, but women showed a distinct preference for women leaders except on political issues (Richmond & McCroskey, 1975).

As with more educated subordinates, peer managers also are more favorably inclined toward women as managers than subordinates in general. A survey by M. M. Wood (1976) of approximately 100 male and female managers found that most managers felt that women are winning increased acceptance in the business environment.

### Attributes of the Successful Woman Manager

What characterizes the woman who succeeds in obtaining and holding a position as a manager? Many, particularly early in their experience, identify with the masculine stereotype of the successful manager (Hennig, 1971). In a study of twenty-seven women in middle management in a variety of organizations, Banfield (1976) found that all but two incorporated masculine characteristics. Seventeen were identified as masculine in self-concept and role behavior and only one as feminine. The other nine were androgynous. In the same way, 684 business students (both male and female) described the good manager in masculine rather than androgynous terms on the Bem Sex-Role Inventory (Powell & Butterfield, 1979). In agreement, Schein (1975) found that women saw a good manager more unlike themselves than did men.

Larwood and Kaplan (1979) surveyed eighty women bank officers concerning strategies for success. Ability to make decisions and demonstration of competence were thought most important. Successful officers were distinguished from unsuccessful ones by their greater interest in learning from male models and in their decision-making ability. They reported themselves successful despite a lower evaluation of their own self-confidence. At the same time, the women middle managers studied by Banfield (1976) emphasized their human relations skills, participative decision making, sacrifice of femininity, and reluctance to assert themselves. As a group, they revealed well-integrated personalities with high levels of self-esteem.

According to Litterer (1976), the successful woman executive is characterized by the ability to move socially between informal male and female groups. She can be part of the important informal communication networks of both groups.

*Career Paths.* Sex is a determinant of the differential road to success in organizations. Although larger firms have the best developed affirmative action programs and more standardized promotion programs where sex bias can be avoided (Donnelly, 1976), historically, according to Bowman, Worthy, and Greyser (1965), women have been more successful as managers in smaller firms. In larger firms, most women enter managerial ranks in staff rather than line positions. Here they can become specialists and earn credit and acceptance from male colleagues for their skills, expertise, and task competence (Hennig & Jardim, 1977; Jacobson & Kock, 1977).

*Sources of Failure.* Failure to perform well results in reduced self-confidence and motivation and serves to reinforce the negative stereotypes about women's potential for management (Schwartz & Waetjen, 1976). The two main reasons for women failing as managers, according to a survey of 100 male managers, were their unwillingness to help other women and their tendency to be overdemanding at times, particularly of other women (M. M. Wood, 1976). They are at first expected to behave in a feminine manner by showing their subordinates more consideration and less direction than expected from male leaders (Bartol & Butterfield, 1976). But, Staines, Tavris, and Jayaratne (1973) noted that women who have achieved high status tend to reveal the "queen bee syndrome." They regard lower-status women negatively.

*Special Tactics for Women*

Special tactics are suggested by Larwood and Wood (1977) for the woman manger for promoting her success in an organization. Even more than male managers, she needs to ensure her superiors of her competence by earning the right credentials and receiving competitive job offers and outside acclaim (M. M. Wood, 1975). Learning how to befriend, give, and receive help from men without letting it become a sexual encounter is important. There is need to act and dress more like a manager and less like a secretary (Donnelly, 1976). She can take a visible seating position at meetings (Donnelly, 1976—see Chapter 27). She can make sure to inform superiors about her activities. Depending on the situation, women need to be able to play the female role or the managerial role whichever is appropriate (Harragan, 1977; Trahey, 1977; M. M. Wood, 1975). (Analogously, a management professor talks to graduate students and colleagues in different language than to business groups.) Like male managers, women managers can profit from an apprentice role with several superiors. Women may exploit their stereotypic differences by requesting assignments to ensure that "the woman's point of view is represented." (To the extent that heterogeneity in groups promotes creativity, adding women to an all-male management committee has its advantages.)

*Necessary Adjustments.* Women managers have a higher degree of job satisfaction than nonsupervisory women (Keaveny, Jackson & Fossum, 1976). They appear to enjoy their positions and to hold the same expectations of them as do male supervisors (Brief & Oliver, 1976). Many other studies have found little or no difference in the job satisfaction of female as compared to male leaders (Bartol, 1974, 1975; Bartol & Wortman, 1976; Herrick, 1973; and Jacobson & Effertz, 1974). This is despite Litterer's (1976) finding that almost all in one sample of women executives reported they had been discriminated against.

Kavanagh and Halpern (1977) found that life and job satisfaction were correlated for university men in general and for women at lower job levels, but it was uncorrelated for women at higher levels of university leadership. This may be partly due to the fact that women executives are likely to lack a spouse, like most male managers have, to assist with the social and home-care demands on the female executive's time (Harlan, 1976). Women executives are only one-third as likely to be married as male counterparts and are less likely to have children (Jusenius, 1976). But those that are married and are mothers face role conflicts which are best handled by what Hall (1972) described as structural role redefinition, changing the demands of the conflicting role of homemaker and manager. This is in contrast to trying to meet the conflicting demands of both.

*The "Casting Couch."* Almost all women executives surveyed by Litterer (1976) had experienced sexual advances from male executives, but practically none reported having an affair with someone in their own organization. The traditional casting couch demand on an entertainer for career success evidently is present but not required for success as a woman in management.

## EFFECTIVENESS OF WOMEN LEADERS

Does sex of the leader make a difference in whether the group attains its objectives and satisfies its needs? Is group productivity and satisfaction affected by the sex of its leader? As Rice, Bender, and Vitters (1980) commented, answering these questions is complicated by the extent to which most available studies depend on subjective ratings which tend to contain sex bias rather than objective performance effects.

### Group Performance and Sex of the Leader

Results, mainly from laboratory studies, suggest that sex of the leader generally is not a consistent factor in determining group productivity (Bartol, 1978). Nor does individual effectiveness of performance of managers appear to be associated consistently with their sex (Larwood, Wood & Inderlied, 1978). For example, Bullard and Cook (1975) found no difference in team productivity as a consequence of the sex of 168 female and 168 male undergraduate groups or whether the leaders were relations- or task-oriented on the LPC (Chapter 20). Nor was the pleasantness of the group's atmosphere affected. B. A. Hall (1975) reported no difference in women undergoing assertiveness training as a function of the sex of the group leader.

Taylor and Ilgen (1979) completed a survey of employees with female and male supervisors and could find no difference in the employees' satisfaction with their supervision associated with the sex of their supervisors. But in comparison to employees working under male supervisors, the employees working for female managers did feel their supervisors had less reward power.

Contrary to what they had hypothesized, Eskilson and Wiley (1976) found in a study with 144 undergraduates that female-led groups were more productive than those led by males. Several studies, however, point to negative effects of women in leadership posts. In an employee attitude survey, Hansen (1974) found that women supervisors had less impact than men supervisors on departmental climate as evidenced by the correlations between attitudes of the supervisor and ratings of group climate. Roussel (1974) examined the effects of the sex of forty department heads on teacher ratings of departmental climate in ten high schools. Departments headed by men were rated higher in esprit and intimacy and departments headed by women were rated higher in hindrance.

Yerby (1975) assigned 192 male and female undergraduates to small-problem solving groups according to their positive or negative attitudes toward female leadership. All groups were led by women. Group performance was associated with the attitudes of its members toward females as leaders. Such attitudes also resulted in lower group morale of male subordinates under female leaders. Rice, Bender, and Vitters (1980) completed a laboratory study of 288 West Point cadets assigned to seventy-two four-person groups led by females and males with all roles as subordinates taken by males. Groups with male leaders did better on two assigned tasks than did groups led by females.

*Status Reversal Conflict.* By placing women in leadership positions over men, we generate status reversal conflict, particularly for men with traditional attitudes toward the role of women, with the consequential negative impact on the men's performance (as with Yerby's results above). Whyte (1949) described such a status reversal in restaurants where waitresses give orders to countermen. Although the countermen accept such orders, they do so with resentment and hostility.

*Subordinate Coping with Conflict.* Zammuto, London, and Rowland (1979) studied how dormitory resident advisers dealt with their supervisors as a consequence of whether either or both were men or women. The results suggest that sex may affect their working relationships. When in conflict with their supervisors, both female and male subordinates were less likely to withdraw when in conflict with female rather than male supervisors. Also, highly committed male subordinates were more likely to try to smooth over differences, to compromise, and to confront if the supervisor was female.

*Same-Sex Supervision.*  Eisman (1975) found that in marathon encounter groups, where one goal is to promote disclosure for therapeutic value, more such disclosure occurred when groups were led by the opposite instead of the same sex. But most studies, dealing with short-term, less emotionally involved performances found the contrary to be true. Same-sex supervision was better. When supervised by a woman rather than a man, females performed better on mechanical tasks (Larwood, O'Carroll & Logan, 1977), standard math tests (Pedersen, Shinedling & Johnson, 1968), and math work problems (Hoffman & Maier, 1967). However, contrary to expectations, Frantzve (1979) failed to find much effect on whether male or female emerged as leader in initially leaderless groups as she systematically varied the number of females from 0 to 6 in six-person groups.

### Subordinate Satisfaction and Sex of the Leader

We have noted earlier the expected conflict between fulfilling the stereotyped role of a woman and the role of a manager. Yet, subordinate satisfaction was unrelated to whether or not their supervisors fulfilled appropriate sex-role stereotypes (Bartol & Wortman, 1975; Osborn & Vicars, 1976). It is difficult to divorce subordinate attitudes and expectations about women leaders from subordinate job satisfaction under female as opposed to male leaders. Nevertheless, a majority of studies have reported little difference in job satisfaction of subordinates as a function of the sex of the supervisor (Bartol, 1974, 1975; Bartol & Wortman, 1975; N. R. F. Maier, 1970a; Osborn & Vicars, 1976). Petty and Lee (1975) reported that male subordinates with female supervisors were lower in satisfaction with their work and with their supervisors. Since women are expected to exhibit more consideration and generally do, Petty and Lee suggested that when female supervisors display lack of consideration, it has more of an effect on subordinate dissatisfaction than similar inconsiderate behavior by male supervisors. However, Bartol and Wortman (1975) and Osborn and Vicars (1976) reported that subordinate job satisfaction was unrelated to perceptions of leaders fulfilling appropriate sex role stereotypes. Even when, as in a study by Goetz and Herman (1976) of subordinates of department managers in a large retail store chain, it was found that employees working for women managers were more satisfied with supervision than employees working for men, the sex effects could be accounted for mainly by other differences such as commission versus noncommission payment plans, and composition of the work unit. In the same way, Osborn and Vicars (1976) reported that the effects of the sex of the supervisor could be explained by other factors.

*Rated Performance as Managers.*  Deaux (1976) found no difference in the rated performance of men and women retail store managers. M. M. Wood (1975, 1976) and Wood and Greenfeld (1976) also found little difference in rated performance of men and women managers in several field analyses. Schwartz and Waetjen (1976) reported that 95 percent of employers of female managers rated their job performance as excellent, very good, or good (probably no different than their leniency-prone ratings of male managers). A survey by M. M. Wood (1976) suggested that male managers tended to rate their female peers highly in decision making, competence, and ability to handle emotions. Women were seen to bring fresh outlooks to business problems and to offer useful insights into marketing problems dealing with female customers. They were regarded as tending to reduce intense feelings of competition between male managers. However, R. A. Patterson (1975) in an analysis using 192 male middle managers, found females to receive lower ratings than males on evaluations of performance and promotability.

Rosen and Jerdee (1973) completed three experiments with in-baskets to examine cross-sex role behavior by women supervisors. Although friendly, helpful leadership was rated as more effective whether the supervisor was male or female, a reward style was evaluated as more effective for male than for female supervisors. At the same time, Petty and Lee (1975) obtained results suggesting that consideration by female supervisors is more highly related to subordinate satisfaction than is consideration by male supervisors. Petty and Lee inferred that more such consideration is expected from women, and when it fails to materialize, it is more likely to affect subordinate satisfaction. But an unpublished survey of the 276 subordinates of eighteen chain store managers by Adams failed to find differential subordinate satisfaction with supervision due to the sex of the manager or to an interaction of sex with initiation and consideration.

### Caveat

Along with the rise of feminism and affirmative action, opportunity seems an important element in the sudden flood of sex–leadership experiments. Students are a readily available supply of subjects. Women have reached parity with men in college attendance. In a culture rapidly changing from a time when smart women played dumb to a time when assertiveness training is now commonplace for women, it would seem important that before another hundred male–female experiments are completed, careful consideration about the dynamics and dimensions of importance are required.

We guess that the confusion of masculinity with aggressiveness needs to be sorted out along with female overreaction and we need to question if the college student in transitory experimental male–female interaction is at all representative of male–female interactions of adults in more permanent organizational relationships. Similar arguments apply to the study of black leaders, the subject that follows.

# 31

## BLACKS AND LEADERSHIP

INTRODUCTION

In the next chapter, we will look at leadership in other cultures. But blacks in the United States are not members of another culture. Rather, blacks form an American subculture, tied to the majority's institutions without clear boundaries marking it off from the larger white society and sensitive to the norms and values of the majority culture (Liebow, 1967). Blacks have adopted the cultural patterns of the dominant white society (Baldwin, Glazer, et al., 1966). Pinkney (1969) finds black overconformity to white middle class standards of behavior. But the status ascribed by whites to blacks remains low. As Bass, Cascio, McPherson, and Tragash (1976) noted in a factor-analytic study of 315 managers' responses to a racial awareness questionnaire, people vary in their perception that the "system" is biased against blacks and that blacks are excluded from the mainstream. Even potential black leaders may restrict themselves. Thus, Gump (1975) found among black and white female college students that the black women were more likely to see their future role as wife and mother, whereas the white women were oriented more toward their own career development than toward fulfilling a traditional woman's role.

Among 359 black executives surveyed by E. E. Jennings (1980), 45 percent still believed that racial prejudice was the most important reason impeding their further career progress.

A 300-year legacy of master–slave relationship is giving way by fits and jumps prompted by war, civil strife, legislation, and education to the rise of blacks into positions of leadership in sizable numbers. The 359 black executives in Jennings's survey are located primarily in large organizations, mainly in manufacturing, real estate, insurance, or finance in the same functions that provide faster career success for whites—marketing, manufacturing, and finance. Higher education and personal contact were important to their being recruited.

Experimental research lags behind. Moreover, the little of it available prior to the mid-1960s has little relevance to understanding black and white attitudes and behavior in the 1980s. For example, consider Goode and Fowler's (1949) finding that the tough, autocratic, primitive foreman was most effective for maximizing productivity among marginal, predominantly black workers in a Detroit bumper grinding and polishing shop.

We will first examine the situational constraints and personal factors associated with the emergence of blacks as leaders. Then, we will consider their performance and

**508**

satisfaction and the extent to which such performance is contingent on the racial composition of their subordinates. We will also look at white supervision of black subordinates.

## EMERGENCE OF BLACKS AS LEADERS

There is a rich store of biographical literature on black political, community, educational, and religious leaders ranging from the leaders of slave insurrections like Nat Turner to the reform leaders Frederick Douglass and Martin Luther King, Jr. To work within the "system" (Booker T. Washington), to modify it (W. E. B. du Bois), or to destroy it (Malcolm X) have been the different goals of the emergent, charismatic, political leaders. But entry into leadership positions in business and industry, except for a few black service-oriented industries such as insurance and undertaking, is mainly a consequence of the equal opportunities legislation of the 1960s. Entry into military leadership was stimulated by President Truman's orders to integrate the armed forces in the late 1940s. There followed continuing increases in the proportion of blacks, particularly in the all-volunteer army, of which blacks are projected to make up 42 percent in the early 1980s. Nevertheless, despite their high proportions in some types of organizations such as labor unions, they continue to be underrepresented in positions of leadership. For example, Lamm (1975) found that among thirty union locals with black members in the San Francisco Bay Area only ten had blacks in leadership positions in proportion to their numbers among the membership; in ten, blacks were proportionally underrepresented among the leadership, and in ten, there were no black leaders.

When community leaders were named by 1,507 black residents interviewed by Larson (1975), the need was demonstrated to look for such leaders in individual black groups and neighborhoods and not for the city as a whole.

### Constraints on the Rise of Black Leaders in American Society in General

*Educational Gap.*  Although the gap in black and white educational level has been reduced, it still remains substantial. In 1970, one of ten whites had completed at least four years of college, but less than one in twenty blacks had done so. Only 15 percent of blacks aged 55–64 had completed high school compared to 45 percent of whites. Among those 20 and 21 years old, 82 percent of the whites and 50 percent of the blacks had completed high school. (Manpower Report, 1970). Lack of educational attainment, coupled with inferior quality of education available, continues to keep the proportions of blacks at less than those of whites in comparable positions of political, educational, military, and industrial leadership.

*Socioeconomic Status.*  Socioeconomic status, one key to leadership, remains much lower for blacks compared to whites in almost every respect. Incomes are lower and unemployment rates are higher. Nevertheless, it is a mistake to equate impoverishment with race. Half of blacks do *not* live in slums. There is a small black upper class and a larger middle class, although the preponderance falls into a large lower class. This is unlike the white class structure. Whites mainly see themselves as middle class with small proportions in the upper and lower classes (St. C. Drake & Cayton, 1966). Frazier (1966) described black "high society" of black professionals and businessmen as characterized by conspicuous consumption and excessive club formations based on their exclusion from their counterpart white society.

*Family Life.* Contrary to white stereotypes about blacks, Farley and Hermalin (1971) found that the majority of both black and white families are in stable families with sound husband–wife relationships and with the children residing with both parents. Nevertheless, for the population as a whole, black family life is less stable than white. Black children living with both parents declined from 75 to 67 percent during the 1960s. The white rate remained at 91 or 92 percent (U.S. Department of Commerce, 1971). Black women were more likely to encounter marital discord than white women. In 1970, 19 percent of all black women who were at one time married were either divorced or separated as compared with 6 percent of white women (U.S. Department of Commerce, 1971). Moynihan's (1965) well-publicized analysis concluded from these types of differences that black fathers, often transients, failed to provide their children with support, discipline, or direction. The National Urban League (1971) countered with pointing with pride to five strengths of black families: their adaptability of family roles, strong kinship bonds, strong work orientation, strong religious orientation, and strong achievement orientation.

An interesting question is whether absence of father as a role model for children raised only by their mother reduces their leadership potential in either childhood or later life. Actually, strong, dominant mothers have been most significant for many world leaders. Fatherless children may have to take on initiatives and responsibilities earlier, although evidence suggests that fatherless boys lacking a masculine role model with which to identify develop personalities marked by impulsivity, academic failure and indifference, immature dependency and effeminacy (I. Katz, 1974). This ignores the potential role models provided by older street gang leaders, older brothers, and so on.

The educational impact of fatherlessness seems minimal. Whiteman and Deutsch (1968) found no relationship between black children's reading skills and family intactness. Again, in the national survey by Coleman et al. (1966) the presence or absence of a father was not a factor in the scholastic attitudes or achievement of lower-class black or white students. Also, Feld and Lewis (1967) found practically no relationship between family intactness and school anxiety.

*The Slum Subculture.* But any study of blacks as leaders would be incomplete if it ignored that large subset of blacks who are in the disadvantaged poor. The slum subculture contains its own ethos which is a more important determinent of behavior than being black. Characteristics of this subculture include the absence of a sheltered childhood, early initiation into sex, female-centered families, authoritarianism, marginality, helplessness, resignation, fatalism, dependence, inferiority, lack of impulse control, inability to defer gratification, a belief in male superiority, and tolerance for psychological pathology (H. Lewis, 1965). There are strategies for survival in the slums, according to Rainwater (1966), and presumably black leaders in the ghetto become masters of such strategies. First, to obtain immediate gratification, one needs to make oneself interesting and attractive to others in order to manipulate and to seduce others, even though one really has little to exchange. The second strategy is to resort to force and violence. Concerns center on trouble with the law, toughness and masculinity, cleverness in manipulating others, excitement and thrills, and luck and autonomy (W. B. Miller, 1965). At the same time, lower class black youth miss the socialization experiences to prepare them for the world of work as are obtained by white working class youth (Himes, 1965).

### Conditions Promoting the Rise of Black Leadership

King and Bass (1974) listed several factors affecting the movement of blacks into management and leadership positions. First, when opportunities are made available in temporary, undervalued group settings, blacks may actually be overselected for leadership positions. Thus, Fenelon (1966) found that in laboratory experiments in psychology, using pairs of high- and low-dominant white and black coeds performing a clerical task in which one participant had to assume the role of leader, the other of follower, contrary to expectations, black women assumed the leader role twice as often as white women no matter what their relative dominance scores.

Second, when higher authority or political climate demanded it, such as occurred earlier in the military and more recently in industrial and educational organizations, blacks have been advanced into higher-level positions. Black generals, company presidents, and university chancellors are now appearing. Affirmative action has opened opportunities for black advancement and made visible black movement into higher-status positions. The legal impediments to political leadership have changed drastically since the restrictions on black voting rights were lifted in 1964. Particularly where blacks form majority or large minority voting blocs such as in the Deep South or inner cities, blacks have succeeded in being elected to office. Some black politicians have gained large white constituencies.

### Personal Attributes Associated with Black Leadership

*Black Values and Black Leadership.* As indicated in Chapter 10, individuals who "typify the group norm" will be more esteemed than those rejecting or departing from it. Grossack (1954) found that blacks attracted to black activities and valuing the Negro race as such, were more esteemed by fellow blacks than those indifferent to black activities, rejecting blacks, or disliking black heroes. And so it follows, as Kirkhart (1963) showed, that black college students accept for group leadership and external leadership positions those who identify themselves with their own ethnic group. Dellums (1977) felt that black political leaders must fully identify with "black politics," a commitment to the eradication of the oppression of minorities. Lamm (1975) noted that black union leaders, despite their own high incomes, identified themselves with the black working class and had more favorable attitudes toward blacks. They were also more antiwhite and antisemitic in attitude. Fifty percent were identified as "Race Men." Compared with 27 percent of the black middle class who were identified as "Uncle Toms" (subscribing to white value structure), only 6 percent of these black union leaders could be so identified.

*Personal Motivation and Black Leadership.* Indirectly, one sees likely differences in black and white leadership potential in the differences in the personal values declared by black and white college students. According to Fichter (1966) and Bayer and Boruch (1969), in comparison to white college students, black students placed more emphasis on being helpful to others and to society. They were less concerned than whites about experiencing leadership, making money, and autonomy. Traditionally, high-status, open occupations with little interaction and competition with whites were sought, such as roles as black educators (Porat & Ryterband, 1974). But this broadened by the late 1960s (Bayer & Boruch, 1969) as affirmative action opened new opportunities in the professions and industry. Some of this shift may be due to the decline of teaching opportunities in the 1970s, a profession to which black college students in the 1960s aspired in far greater proportions than white students.

But among those blacks who attain leadership and management positions, little difference has been found in their values in contrast to their white counterparts. Watson and Barone (1976) failed to detect such differences in self-concept on England's (1967a) Personal Values Questionnaire or in need for achievement and need for affiliation.

Again, Dexter and Stein (1955) found little difference among campus women leaders as a function of race in masculinity, personality, and speed of association. Similarly, W. R. Allen (1975) could find no significant differences between black and white naval squad leaders in level of aspiration and expectancy of success, although black leaders chose themselves as best squad leader in their company more often than did white leaders. Black leaders scored lower than white leaders on Rotter's Internal–External Control Scale.

Watson and Barone (1976) noted that black managers were lower in power motivation. Yet, in a study of twenty-three black and seventy-five white supervisors, Miner (1977c) found the black supervisors to be higher in motivation to manage (namely, good relations with superiors, competitive, masculine, assertive, visible, and willing to deal with routines, as detailed in Chapter 22).

Lack of black self-esteem and its implication for black leadership (Proshansky & Newton, 1968) has to be discounted as a factor in the 1980s considering the rapid increase in the 1970s of successful black models in sports, TV, and politics and the sudden demand for qualified black professionals and managers in the white world of work stimulated by affirmative action programs.

Some differences have been found in the few available studies in what about their jobs is important to black managers and professionals compared to white managers and professionals. Thus, Alper (1975) observed that both black and white newly hired college graduates rated growth orientation more favorably than the contextual conditions surrounding the job. However, the black graduates gave the contextual elements significantly higher ratings than did the white graduates. Similarly, Vinson and Mitchell (1975) showed that black managers assigned higher ratings than white managers to the importance of obtaining autonomy, self-fulfillment, friendship, and promotion.

*Job Satisfaction of Black Leaders.* Overall, satisfaction that their needs were being met was lower among black leaders and professionals than among their white counterparts. Slocum and Strawser (1972) found that black CPAs reported higher need deficiencies than other CPAs. Black CPAs felt significantly more deprived in compensation, opportunity to help people, opportunity for friendship, feeling of self-esteem, opportunity for independent thought and action, and feeling of self-fulfilment. E. E. Jennings (1980) reported that black executives felt their progress as a group had been slower than that of women and was likely to be slower over the next fifteen years. Finally, O'Reilly and Roberts (1973) reported that overall job satisfaction was significantly higher for white than for nonwhite female registered nurse supervisors.

*Individual Competence and Black Leadership.* In a typical study of black–white intelligence, the mean for blacks is substantially lower than the mean for whites. Nevertheless, 25 percent of the blacks obtain higher scores than 50 percent of the whites. There are always some blacks available for positions of leadership regardless of the validity or sources of the mean black–white differences (Elliot & Penner, 1974). And such leadership, for instance in the black community, is related to ability as reflected in educational level attained. Thus, J. J. Cobb (1974) showed that those blacks nominated as the most influential members in their black community were well-educated in diverse fields. Black executives surveyed by E. E. Jennings (1980) were similar to their white counterparts in educational level.

## PERFORMANCE OF BLACKS VERSUS WHITES AS LEADERS

### Importance of Subordinate's Race

Examination of black as compared to white supervisors requires specifying whether the subordinates are black or white. Thus, a study by Rosen and Jerdee (1977) illustrated the expectation that effective supervisory style depends on the ethnic composition of the group supervised. Rosen and Jerdee administered a decision exercise to 148 business students. The students evaluated the extent to which participative decision-making styles were appropriate when supervising work groups of varying organizational status and minority composition. Significantly less participation was seen likely to be efficacious with minority subordinates and subordinates of lower organizational status. Such subordinates were judged to be less competent and less concerned with the organization's goals. In a similar type of opinion gathering, Shull and Anthony (1978) found that among twenty-one black and fifty-six white participants in a supervisory training program, the blacks were less willing to accept harsh punishment for violation of organizational rules than were whites, especially when there was a history of good performance. Otherwise, there was little difference in the way blacks and whites thought they would respond in handling disciplinary problems and resolve role conflict situations.

Somewhat different findings emerged when Stogdill and Coady (1970) used the Ideal Form of the LBDQ in a study of two vocational high schools. Consideration was the most highly regarded pattern by white students, while initiating structure was most preferred by the black students.

Another line of evidence that indirectly indicates that race will affect interactions between leaders and subordinates comes from studies reviewed by Sattler (1970) on the influence of race on behavior in interviews. Respondents tended to give socially desirable responses to interviewers of races other than their own, responses which were socially "correct" or acceptable, whether or not they reflected their true feelings. Lower class respondents were even more likely to be sensitive to the interviewer's race than were middle and upper class respondents.

*Hard-Core Unemployed as Subordinates.* Although many whites are numbered among the hard-core unemployed, blacks are heavily overrepresented. Therefore, the literature about their supervision has relevance, particularly the possibly extra need for supervisors to be both generally supportive as well as controlling. This was demonstrated by Friedlander and Greenberg (1971) and by the National Industrial Conference

Board (1970). Both studies found that the hard-core unemployed wanted supervisory support in terms of friendliness, courtesy, and encouragement. The need for supervisors to intervene with the interpersonal difficulties of the hard-core unemployed (Goodman, 1969; Hodgson & Brenner, 1968; Morgan, Blonsky & Rosen, 1970) and possibly to provide close supervision (Triandis & Malpass, 1971) was suggested even though such close supervision might prove dissatisfying (Goodale, 1973). Beatty (1974) found generally positive correlations between the extent to which twenty-one hard-core unemployed black women described their supervisor's consideration on the SBDQ and their earnings and performance over a two-year period. Supervisory initiation on the SBDQ (which includes autocratic items, as noted in Chapter 21) was negatively associated with the black women's work peformance. Consistent with this were W. S. MacDonald's (1967) results in Job Corps Centers (with large percentages of black trainees). Verbal reproof and positive incentives had little value in shaping behavior in contrast to setting and policing goals and applying sanctions for infractions by the group. Such infractions dropped 60 percent in two weeks.

### Black Supervisor with Black Subordinates

Traditionally, blacks were limited to leading other blacks. Black supervisors with mainly black subordinates were expected by King and Bass (1974) to be highly concerned about how their subordinates felt about them. Therefore, they were expected to be less directive than white supervisors of blacks. However, as we noted in Chapter 26, for nineteen black social service agency heads supervising fifty-four counselors of black inner city clients, Schriesheim and Murphy (1976) found that more such consideration was helpful, but mainly in low-stress job settings, whereas more initiation of structure was helpful when stress was high in this situation of blacks supervising blacks.

Black leaders often face the problem of having to earn the trust of their black subordinates as the latter see them as having been coopted into the white power structure (M. L. King, 1968). Delbecq and Kaplan (1968) studied the managerial effectiveness of local leaders in neighborhood opportunity centers in an urban ghetto. Clients served by the centers felt the directors were conservative, unwilling to permit community involvement in decision making, and ineffective in negotiations with leaders in the larger community. Subordinates in the centers sought immediate change and action through social protest, marches, and rallies. The directors tended to see such subordinate activism as a threat to their own self-esteem and to their leadership position. They knew that higher authority was opposed to demonstrations and they were therefore "men in the middle" between conflicting demands from subordinates and higher authority. At the same time, King and Bass (1974) suggested that in comparison to white supervisors, black supervisors of black subordinates may have more difficulty in identifying with white higher authority than with their black work group. Yet, the black supervisor may need additional symbols of authority as well as higher-level support to make his or her position credible.

Black supervisors of black subordinates in particular may have to be able to converse fluently in the "street language" of their subordinates and the general American English of their superiors and to be flexible about both (Kochman, 1969).

*Black Supervisor with White Subordinates*

King and Bass (1974) suggested that in comparison to whites supervising whites, black supervisors with mainly white subordinates were expected to engage more often in general rather than close supervision and to allow or encourage subordinates to initiate boss–subordinate interactions. This would serve to reduce possible feelings of status incongruity (see Chapter 13) among the white subordinates. The job of black supervisors of white subordinates may be made more difficult, according to Richards and Jaffee (1972), by white subordinates of black leaders who may go out of their way to hinder the effectiveness of black supervisors. For this and other reasons, King and Bass (1974) suggest it is particularly important for black supervisors of whites to have the full support of higher authority.

*Subordinate Defensiveness.* The minority–majority status inversion when blacks supervise whites may generate, for status-conscious whites, a conflict between wanting to avoid the black supervisor and the need to interact with him or her (Blalock, 1959). Such whites may also suffer from a sense of status loss themselves as a consequence of the required interaction with a black superior (Blalock, 1967). Even if the black leader has status as an expert, hostility and status loss may be experienced, particularly by lower-status white subordinates (Winder, 1952).

*Leader Visibility.* King and Bass (1974) also noted that the small number of black leaders in organizations, particularly blacks who supervise whites, makes them more visible than white counterparts. This, King and Bass suggested, should cause them greater anxiety about succeeding, greater sensitivity to negative data regarding activities supervised and possible overreaction to such data, and greater need for external confirmation of the value of the group's and the leader's performance.

*Style.* Richards and Jaffee (1972) described a laboratory study in which groups consisting of two white undergraduate males and a supervisor played a business game. Trained observers rated white supervisors significantly higher than black supervisors on human relations skills and administrative-technical skills. Ratings were based on check lists of effective and ineffective behaviors, as well as overall graphic ratings. Observers also used Bales's Interaction Process Analysis to assess leader and subordinate behavior. The white supervisors of the all-white subordinate groups engaged in significantly more showing of solidarity, giving suggestions, and giving orientation, lending support to the King and Bass (1974) hypothesis that white supervisors will be more directive and less passive about relationships than black supervisors when dealing with predominantly white subordinates. However, Bartol, Evans, and Stith (1978) suggest that the data are possibly biased since all the observers were white.

*White Supervisor with Black Subordinates*

In their speculations about the leadership styles of black and white supervisors as a function of the racial composition of the groups they supervised, King and Bass (1974) expected white supervisors to be more directive and less consultative when supervising groups with predominantly black subordinates than when supervising groups with white subordinates. They would be more likely to undervalue the capabilities of black subordinates. Such rejection of black workers, in turn, would produce poor performance (I. Katz, 1968, 1970). White supervisors would want black subordinates to respect them rather than to like them and to be concerned primarily with pleasing (probably white) higher authority. Furthermore, King and Bass suggested that

> Whites supervising blacks often reflect . . . in private conversations, a feeling of walking on eggshells. This feeling may well be reflected in (a) greater censoring of responses and reactions by white supervisors when most of their subordinates are black, (b) less spontaneity in supervisory–subordinate relations, and (c) less certainty on the part of white supervisors as to how rigidly to enforce company rules on procedures.
>
> Reciprocally, black subordinates may be less willing to discuss personal problems with a white as opposed to a black supervisor. This statement is consistent with Sattler's (1970) research review, which indicates that black clients prefer black counselors [King & Bass, 1974, p. 256].

Kraut (1975) also noted that white managers often are apprehensive about supervising new black subordinates, but they frequently react by giving special help to the new black employees. White supervisors' concerns about black subordinates range from fear of customer reactions to how to handle mixed race social events.

*Black Subordinates' Concerns.* But the shoe is also on the other foot. Surveys and commentary suggest that new black professional employees experience many stresses above and beyond what would be expected for white employees and their new, usually white superiors (E. W. Jones, 1973; T. R. Mitchell, 1969; Nason, 1972; C. H. Williams, 1975). Moreover, when blacks are involved in intellectual-type task assignments, their performance tends to be affected adversely if they are led to believe that it is being compared with that of equivalent white groups (Katz & Greenbaum, 1963; Katz, Epps & Axelson, 1964), especially if anxiety levels are high.

### Black or White Leaders with Mixed Groups of Black and White Subordinates

When subordinates comprise a mixed group of black and white employees, King and Bass (1974) suggest that the group will lack cohesion, and this, as noted in Chapter 19, should result in more directive behavior by supervisors, black or white. Conversely, where subordinates are racially homogeneous, cohesion probably will be higher and will result in more participative supervisory styles by both black and white supervisors.

One might also apply Fiedler's (Chapter 20) contingency theory with somewhat different expectations, assuming that a situation is most favorable to the supervisor when subordinates are of the same race and most unfavorable when all subordinates are of a different race. Task-oriented supervision would, therefore, be expected to be most effective when either condition prevailed, whereas relations orientation would be most effective with a racially mixed group of subordinates.

*Differences between Black and White Leaders.* Experiments prior to the early 1960s of biracial teams working on intellectual-type problem-solving tasks showed that blacks spoke less than whites and blacks spoke more to whites than to other blacks (Katz, Goldston & Benjamin, 1958; Katz & Benjamin, 1960). But, probably reflecting the societal shifts in the 1960s, Fenelon and Megargee (1971) obtained contrary results.

They studied sixty female college students who scored either high or low in dominance. Both black and white women assumed the leadership role. When interacting with the other race, white women yielded to the black, apparently to avoid the implication of prejudice.

Hill and Hughes (1974) and Hill and Ruhe (1974) used a laboratory experiment in which undergraduate student participants had to compare black and white leaders under conditions where the subordinate dyads were black, white, or both. Bales Interaction Process Analyses observations generally failed to differ significantly except in one instance. Results of observations by trained black and white observers showed no significant differences in supervisory behavior between black and white leaders. But black and white leaders of black dyads were significantly less directive than leaders of white or mixed dyads on a fairly structured knot-tying task. (Of the three tasks, the knot-tying task was expected to require the most directive behavior from the leaders who possessed the knot-tying knowledge.) Hill and Ruhe (1974) reported no difference in the total time talked by each supervisor during the three tasks regardless of the racial composition of the subordinate pairs. Similar results were obtained by Allen and Ruhe (1976) for supervision of mixed dyads involved in ship-routing and knot-tying tasks.

Consistent with King and Bass's (1974) suggestion that white supervisors would be more directive with their black subordinates, Kipnis, Silverman, and Copeland (1973) found that although they mentioned similar kinds of problems with their black and white subordinates, white supervisors in mixed situations reported using more coercion, such as suspensions, more frequently when dealing with black than with white subordinates.

Somewhat different findings were reported by Hill and Fox (1973) based on a study of seventeen racially mixed Marine rifle squads in a training battalion. White squad leaders reported giving proportionately more reprimands, but also more praise, to white subordinates than to black subordinates. In addition, white leaders reported giving more praise to white subordinates than did black leaders.

Using 288 male naval recruits, W. R. Allen (1975) formed sixty-four experimental tetrads, 25 percent black, 50 percent black, and 75 percent black. Supervisors were black or white. The leaders, regardless of whether they were black or white, experienced increasing supervisory difficulties as the relative proportion of blacks increased in the groups supervised. But subordinates' SBDQ descriptions of the consideration or initiation of their leaders failed to account for any of the results. Furthermore, black leaders were less expressive in their behavior and were generally more inhibited. White supervised groups performed tasks faster than black supervised groups. These results were explained by Allen as due to status incongruence and social stress.

W. S. Parker (1976) administered the Survey of Organizations (see Chapter 18) to a sample of seventeen white supervisors and all the sixteen black supervisors in three plants with a total of 427 supervisors and 7,286 hourly employees. There were a total of seventy-two black and thirty-six white subordinates for the thirty-three supervisors. Smaller percentages of Chicano supervisors and subordinates were also involved in the racially mixed work groups. When the four leadership effectiveness measures derived from the Survey of Organizations were examined, significant differences were found between black and white supervisors. Compared to white supervisors, black supervisors were rated significantly more favorably by their subordinates for managerial support, goal emphasis, and work facilitation. The difference for interaction facilitation was in the same direction, but was not statistically significant. Furthermore, according to Parker, blacks achieved higher ratings from their black and white subordinates because black supervisors were seen as giving more support, as stimulating a contagious enthusiasm for doing a good job, emphasizing the task to be completed, and removing roadblocks to doing a good job. But when white subordinates were the minority in their work group, they tended to rate their white supervisor more favorably on managerial support than in the situation in which white subordinates were in a majority in their own work group. This was the only exception to the general finding that subordinates did not give more favorable ratings to supervisors of their own race. We will shortly look further at this issue.

*Subordinate Reactions to Black Leaders.*  Some evidence exists indicating that when black supervisors adopt a close and punitive style of leadership with mixed black and white subordinates, in comparison to the white subordinates, the black subordinates are likely to be more vocal in opposing the leaders. But the white subordinates may show their dissatisfaction by reducing output (Mayhand & Grusky, 1972). Thus, whites in this situation might be more accommodating in attitude but not in behavior to coercive black supervisors.

Contrary to King and Bass's expectations, Schott (1970) found that among non-white principals with integrated staffs, faculty job satisfaction was highly related to reconciliation of demands, tolerance of uncertainty, persuasiveness, tolerance of freedom, role assumption, consideration, predictive accuracy, and integration of the group by the principals.

## ARE PERFORMANCE EVALUATIONS OF BLACK LEADERS BIASED?

A world-wide leadership survey was completed by the U. S. Army in each of its major commands. Data were obtained by asking about one-third of the 30,735 respondents to complete a written questionnaire describing the leadership of their immediate superior; another third to complete the questionnaire describing the leadership of one of their immediate subordinates; and the final third to complete the questionnaire, describing their own leadership. In addition to various demographic items and a single measure of satisfaction with the overall performance of the individual described, the questionnaire used in the study included a list of forty-three specific items of behavior commonly observed in army leaders. About half of these forty-three behaviors were derived fairly directly from the SBDQ and LBDQ (see Chapter 21). For each behavior, three questions were asked: "How often does he?," "How often should he?," and "How important was this to you?" The first question is a measure of perceived actual performance, the second a statement of expectations, and the third an indicator of the criticality of the behavior as perceived by the respondent.

Table 31.1 shows a summary analysis of data reported by Penner, Malone, Coughlin, and Herz (1973) on differences of supervisors, self, and subordinates in their overall satisfaction with white and nonwhite officers and noncoms. It can be seen that at the three higher officer levels, superiors gave higher evaluations to white than to non-white leaders. Subordinates did the reverse, favoring nonwhites. Self-ratings of satisfac-

**Table 31.1**
**Mean Satisfaction with Overall Performance of U.S. Army Leaders**

| | Raters | | |
|---|---|---|---|
| Rank of Ratee | *Superiors* | *Self* | *Subordinates* |
| *Field Grade Officers* | | | |
| White | 5.65 (715)* | 5.58 (1,867) | 5.45 (3,843) |
| Nonwhite | 5.24 (63) | 5.61 (122) | 5.66 (375) |
| *Company Grade Officers* | | | |
| White | 5.36 (1,227) | 5.16 (2,240) | 5.07 (2,129) |
| Nonwhite | 5.26 (155) | 5.13 (128) | 5.24 (441) |
| *Senior NCOs* | | | |
| White | 5.32 (2,116) | 5.45 (1,988) | 5.00 (1.943) |
| Nonwhite | 5.22 (314) | 5.45 (505) | 5.22 (548) |
| *Junior NCOs* | | | |
| White | 5.02 (3,265) | 4.95 (2,385) | 4.78 (1,117) |
| Nonwhite | 5.08 (697) | 5.05 (695) | 4.81 (251) |

*Numbers in parentheses refer to the number of leaders rated.
Adapted from Penner, Malone, Coughlin, and Herz (1973).

tion generally were the same for whites and nonwhites. Since the percentage of non-whites decreased with increasing level of raters so that in each instance more subordinates than superiors were nonwhite, the results could be a consequence of over-valuing leaders of one's own race.

*Differential Reactions.* Among the lists of ten behaviors correlated most highly with self-satisfaction with overall performance, white and nonwhite field grade officers differed in that the list for nonwhite field grade officers contained seven negative correlations and that of white field grade officers contained only one. In evaluating themselves, the nonwhite field grade officer was satisfied with his own overall performance if he avoided doing negative things such as "hesitating to take action," "failing to show appreciation for priorities of work," or "making it difficult for subordinates to use initiative." On the other hand, the white field grade officer was satisfied with his own overall performance if he did positive things such as "being technically competent to perform his duties," "seeking additional and more important responsibilities," "being aware of the state of his unit's morale and doing all he can to make it high." Penner, Malone, et al. attributed this difference to the discrimination experienced by the non-white officer in the 1950s and early 1960s when he first entered service, when it was more important for the nonwhite officer to avoid making mistakes than it was for him to stand out in a positive manner.

### Further Evidence of Bias

A variety of different kinds of bias have been demonstrated, but the effects have been decidedly mixed. Hamner, Kim, et al. (1974) asked participants to rate workers shown performing on video tape according to an objective criterion of effectiveness. Raters and workers included whites and blacks of both sexes. Although generally high performers were rated as more effective than low performers, they also found that blacks rated blacks higher than whites, whites rated whites higher than blacks, and greater differences were seen between high and low performing whites than between high and low performing blacks.

Bigoness (1976) found that raters tended to give higher ratings to blacks than whites when performance was poor, yet rated high-performing whites and blacks similarly. Bartol, Evans, and Stith (1978) concluded after reviewing studies by Huck and Bray (1976), Drucker and Schwartz (1973), Richards and Jaffee (1972), and Beatty (1973) that there was a tendency to evaluate black leaders more heavily on relations-oriented rather than task-oriented factors. Thus, for example, Beatty (1973) found that sponsoring employers' perceptions of social behaviors, such as friendliness and acceptance by others, had a greater influence on the employers' performance ratings of new black supervisors than did perceptions of the new blacks' task-related behaviors. At the same time, Richards and Jaffee (1972) obtained results suggesting that subordinates with more liberal attitudes were more likely to give their black supervisors higher ratings, especially on human relations skills, than were subordinates with less liberal attitudes.

Burroughs (1970) studied black and white girls in discussion groups. White followers rated black leaders higher when they exhibited a high quality of performance. But Hall and Hall (1976) found no differences due to race or sex of undergraduates' ratings of a case of an effective personnel administrator. Although Richards and Jaffee (1972) found that as a whole white trained observers judged black leaders more harshly than white leaders, Vinson and Mitchell (1975) reported the opposite. They noted that black managers received higher performance ratings from mostly white superiors than did white managers. Schmidt and Johnson (1973) found no differences in peer evaluations among supervisory trainees, whereas among naval squad leaders W. R. Allen (1975) found that white leaders received significantly higher ratings from white subordinates than from black subordinates. But the reverse was not true for black leaders. Black subordinates chose their black leader as best squad leader in the company more often than black subordinates chose their white leader. Finally, Cox and Krumboltz (1958) and Dejung and Kaplan (1962) found in early nonsupervisory situations that ratees received significantly higher evaluations from persons of their own race. In the same way, Flaugher, Campbell, and Pike (1969) found that black medical technicians were rated significantly higher by black than by white supervisors.

*Some Implications*

No simple answers emerge to the question about whether racial considerations bias performance evaluations. As long as we must depend on subjective evaluations of black and white leaders, it will be necessary to be sensitive to the potential for bias in their evaluations, although often such bias may fail to show up in particular instances. One can imagine some circumstances where superiors will "lean over backward" to give unearned higher evaluations to black supervisors. In other situations, prejudice may cause lower-than-deserved ratings. Black subordinates and superiors may feel the need to overvalue members of their own race or may set extra high standards for them. When student participants make such ratings in transitory experimental settings, are they biased more by generalized feelings about race than when a long-time colleague rates a familiar associate's performance? Finally, individual differences may override any possible generalizations. Thus, Bass, Cascio, McPherson, and Tragash (1976) collected the responses of 315 managers and professional employees in a large light manufacturing establishment on 109 racial awareness items. Factor analysis revealed that respondents differed among themselves in the extent to which they agreed that the effectiveness of blacks in leadership and management is generally affected because (1) the system is biased; (2) implementation of affirmative action policies is limited; (3) black employees are incompetent in general; (4) black employees lack real inclusion; and (5) black employees need to build self-esteem.

# 32

# LEADERSHIP IN DIFFERENT CULTURES

## INTRODUCTION

Can we generalize the results of leadership research from one culture to another? How transferable are managers with experience and education from one country to another? Do managerial decision-making practices and leadership styles vary in different cultures? These are the kinds of questions we will attempt to answer in this chapter. (For additional coverage, particularly on leadership in children, in education, and in small groups, the reader should consult Triandis's (1980) Handbook of Cross-Cultural Psychology, volumes IV, V.) We will also consider unique or unusual leadership practices that appear to be associated with a particular cultural background. Leadership under such circumstances requires examining the unusual institutions of that culture. But this does not preclude the discovery of universal tendencies, that is, tendencies common to a wide variety of cultures and countries. For example, using standard survey procedures in twelve countries and country clusters ranging from the United States and Britain to India and Japan, Bass, Burger, et al. (1979) found that managers everywhere wanted to be more proactive and to get work done by using less authority. In the same way, managers with higher rates of career advancement everywhere saw themselves as higher in effective intelligence. Nevertheless, more often than not, it was concluded that national boundaries did make a difference in the speed of promotion of managers as well as in their goals, risk preferences, pragmatism, interpersonal competence, effective intelligence, emotional stability, and leadership style and in the degree to which these attributes were associated with speed of promotion.

### Early Research and Reviews

Harbison and Myers (1959) published a collection of field studies in various countries dealing with comparative management and leadership. This was followed by Haire, Ghiselli, and Porter's (1966) survey comparison of managers in fourteen countries. Available two- or more-country comparisons made possible reviews by Nath (1969), Boddewyn and Nath (1970), K. H. Roberts (1970), and Barrett and Bass (1976). Other works of consequence included those by Fayerweather (1959), McClelland (1961), and Farmer and Richman (1964).

Studies generally tended to be based on interviews, but Nath (1969) uncovered twenty survey reports, mostly of students compared across two countries.

*The Unit of Study*

The cultural units we tend to compare are somewhat arbitrary. National boundaries make a convenient difference which may or may not be coterminous with cultural boundaries. The Dutch-speaking Flemings are culturally closer in many respects to their Dutch neighbors in the Netherlands than to their Wallonian French-speaking Belgian countrymen. Nevertheless, it is the national boundaries, not the cultural boundaries that determine educational institutions, legal forces, political effects, and economic considerations of consequence to understanding leadership and management. On the other hand, cultural boundaries are likely to have the greater impact on values, sentiments, ideals, language, and role models. Not surprisingly, Weissenberg (1979) was able to show that German-speaking managers varied significantly in judging the importance of six of eleven of their life goals depending on whether they came from Austria, West Germany, or German Switzerland. Thus, among the nationals from the three countries, the Austrians put relatively more emphasis on service; the West Germans on leadership, independence, and prestige, and the Swiss on wealth and duty.

At the same time, countries tend to cluster by culture. Thus, North American managers (excluding French Canada) tend to cluster with their British cousins on numerous dimensions of leader behavior and attitudes. Ronen and Kraut (1977) demonstrated meaningful clusters in a smallest-space analysis of Haire, Ghiselli, and Porter's (1966) fourteen-country leadership data, as shown in Figure 32.1.

As can be seen, the United States and Britain form a cluster joined by Canada, Australia, New Zealand, and South Africa in other studies, as do Latin Europe and Northern Europe. The less developed countries of India, Chile, and Argentina group together also. Japan lies between the Northern European and the Anglo-American clusters.

*Within-Culture Differences.* Despite these cultural clusters, we should recognize considerable differences possible between these countries of similar culture on designated dimensions. For example, Hines and Wellington (1974) found with both entrepreneurs and middle managers that those native to Britain were much higher in need for achievement than those native to Australia and New Zealand. Countries may be clustered by geography, similar languages, and the like, yet be quite different from each other in many ways of consequence to leadership. Although seemingly connected geographically, actually Latin America reflects wide variations in culture and linkages to the Old World. Mexico is characterized by its mestizo majority; Argentina, by its diverse European ethnic groups. Venezuela is thoroughly Latin; Chile more North European. Portuguese, Indian, and African influences have the strongest impact on Brazil. Nevertheless, certain Latin American patterns cross national boundaries. Communalities are found. For instance, standards of Anglo-American efficiency appeared lacking to Heller (1969b) in South American Boards of Directors. He saw common values and habits in Argentina and Chile, each with their own different subculture, deleterious to organizational effectiveness. In fifty-nine out of sixty-eight business organizations he observed, board meetings were held without precirculated minutes and agendas. Consequently, the boards spent some 38 percent of their time reexamining the same subject matter which they had previously discussed. There was a noticeable failure to carry out decisions which had been reached by the boards. Heller also noted that the managers in these

**FIGURE 32.1. Smallest-space Analysis Map of Fourteen Countries**

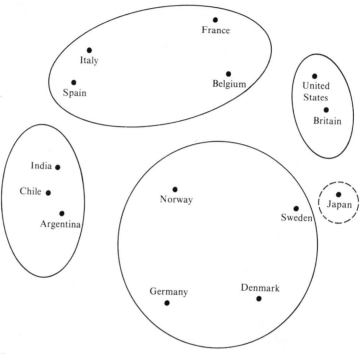

SOURCE: *Ronen and Kraut (1977).*

countries as compared to North American and British managers tended to equate authority with rapid decision making and to stress its importance. Whereas the Anglo-American commonly will try to gather more information before making a decision, Heller sensed that senior management was expected to make quick decisions in Argentina, Chile, and Uruguay. Adding to the inefficiency of decision making are a Latin American propensity to rely on intuition, emotional arguments, and justifications, according to McCann (1964). Thought proceeds in a series of direct perceptions of truths. The truths concern the object being contemplated independent of any demonstrated reasoning process. They are neither verifiable nor repeatable. The tendency is toward action which is improvised. Actions are taken without conscious planning. When planning is done, projects may be considered completed after they have been planned (projectismo).

But the overly rapid decision making observed by Heller in Argentina, Chile, and Uruguay is not universal. In fact, in Brazil, the opposite tendency was noted by Harbron (1965). Traditional Brazilian managers running inherited family factories practice *jeitinhos,* finding little solutions and avoiding dealing with big problems for which they have had no experience. They are characterized by languid, compromising "wait and see" attitudes (Harbron, 1965).

*Other Factors.* At the same time, within the same culture, it should be obvious that wide differences in leader behavior are likely to emerge. Chowdhry and Pal (1960) warned against focusing on an overall pattern or values among people within one country which could obscure the differences between subgroups within that country. Further, focusing on overall value patterns between countries could miss the communalities among similar subgroups within these countries. Thus, Singh, Arya, and Reddy (1965) reported that patterns of leader behavior in Indian villages differ with socioeconomic status, caste, and occupation. Again, cultural effects may be washed out by more powerful transcending organizational effects of the multinational corporation. For example, to see if the original Early Identification of Management Potential (EIMP) assessment program in the United States could be validated cross-nationally, the analyses were replicated with 800 Exxon managers from Norway, Denmark, and the Netherlands (Laurent, 1970). Success as a manager was measured by salary adjusted for age and organization salary structure. Table 32.1 shows the extent to which results generalized across four countries.

The same traits and measurements of ability were predictive of success of a United States manager and were also predictive of success of managers in other countries working in the same multinational corporation. Similar results were obtained in Venezuela and elsewhere by Cassens (1966a, b) using the same biographical information blank for selecting Exxon executives with samples of nearly 400 Latin-Americans working in their native country and 200 North American managers. Several reasons may be involved. First, universal traits could be involved for relatively uniform tasks. Second, Exxon may tend to recruit ''Americanized'' Europeans and Latins. Third, socialization processes which occur after one enters an organization may result in uniformalities in requirements that transcend cultures.

### Origins of Leaders

In nonindustrial societies, whether or not the village head was elected, inherited, or was appointed to the post was found by Greenbaum (1977) to be unrelated to family, economic, or other societal factors in an analysis of 616 societies described in Murdock's Ethnographic Atlas (1967). But differences between countries are the rule rather than the exception when we seek the origins of their leaders in the public and private sectors. Thus, countries may vary in the extent to which their managements are drawn from all social classes or from the upper or lower portions of society. At the one extreme, McClelland (1961) noted that 54 percent of Turkey's business leaders came from its upper middle and upper classes. At the other extreme, in a socialist country such as Poland, 96 percent of managers reported that they came from the working or lower middle classes. In between was a country like the United States where managers were drawn from uniformly all classes. As Table 32.2 shows, neither the working classes nor

**TABLE 32.1**
**Forecasting Accuracy of a Battery of Tests and Measurements for the Early Identification of Exxon Managers in Four Different Countries**

| Test | United States | Norway | Denmark | Netherlands |
|------|---------------|--------|---------|-------------|
| Part A | .44 | .59 | .61 | .55 |
| Part B | .64 | .65 | .57 | .62 |
| Part C | .33 | .29 | .34 | .27 |
| Part D | .52 | .43 | .34 | .45 |

Adapted from Laurent (1970).

**TABLE 32.2**
**Social Class Background of Managers in Turkey, Mexico, Italy, United States, and Poland (Percent)**

| | Turkey Private | Turkey Public | Mexico Private | Italy Public | Italy Private | United States Private | Poland |
|---|---|---|---|---|---|---|---|
| | N = 39 | N = 24 | N = 69 | N = 49 | N = 61 | N = 158 | N = 25 |
| 1–3. Working class | 0 | 4 | 12 | 2 | 8 | 22 | 40 |
| 4. Lower middle class | 18 | 54 | 30 | 53 | 49 | 26 | 56 |
| 5. Middle class | 28 | 25 | 39 | 22 | 26 | 32 | 4 |
| 6. Upper middle and upper class | 54 | 17 | 19 | 22 | 16 | 20 | 0 |

Unclassifiable cases not included (for example, military or government service backgrounds) or inadequate information.
(1) Unskilled, (2) semiskilled, and (3) skilled laborers, foremen, public service workers, and tenant farmers.
(4) Clerical or sales occupations, small farm owners, small business.
(5) Minor professional (high-school teachers, medical technicians), medium business, and large farms with paid help.
(6) major professionals, executives, and owners.

SOURCE: McClelland (1961).

the aristocracy and upper classes are the prime sources of private sector management in Mexico or Italy. Public sector managers in Turkey have much more different class backgrounds than private sector managers but they are much more similar in background in Italy.

*Differences in History and Institutions.* Cross-country comparisons of the differences in the origins of leaders need to consider what are often almost unique circumstances within a given country. For instance, religion and history (Roman Catholic ethos and a return of the French entrepreneur to France after 1763) have been seen to retard the emergence of French Canadians as leaders in industry and business (Pelletier, 1966).

This book is essentially a review of what we know about the antecedents and effects of leadership in the United States, supported a bit by relevant work elsewhere, particularly in Britain. In many ways, studies of leadership in the United States, with its cultural emphasis on individualism, action rather than contemplation, pragmatism, and equalitarianism, cannot capture the diversity of relationships found in other countries, influenced by their own histories and institutional peculiarities.

In many ways, the U. S. experience has been a unique one for leadership development. The military historian S. L. A. Marshall (1964) noted the surprise in 1917 to the trainers of the American Expeditionary Force to be sent to France that the U. S. draftees responded naturally to discipline and that a high percentage of them were potential leaders. Getting this army ready was not the formidable task originally envisaged based on European experience. In decided contrast to the United States, in Britain, managing in business or industry (other than finance) was not the occupation of a gentleman. The eldest son inherited the estate; the younger sons went into the armed services or the church. Middle class sons went into the professions, the civil service, or the family business. Until recently, a businessman who wanted a title had to work hard for public causes, devoting less time to business and more to public service. But business is now finally becoming respectable; finance always was (R. Stewart, 1966).

In Britain, public school education (actually private, elitist boarding schools) has been important for industrial leadership, particularly in finance (Copeman, 1955) as well as for leadership in the civil service, foreign service, the military, and the Church of England. Little change occurred in the importance of the public schools and Oxford and Cambridge between 1939 and 1971, according to an analysis of the educational backgrounds of 3,682 of the British elite by D. P. Boyd (1974). Social class traditions and entrance into management as a consequence of social class and academic (nonmanagement) education remain strong. This is coupled with a lack of mobility. Each department in an organization is a self-contained unit in which members frequently spend much of their whole career. In consequence they are exposed to a limited range of management attitudes and ideas. They become so immersed in the way of thinking of their department that they are unlikely to be able to think outside this pattern of beliefs (R. Stewart, 1966).

*Communalities.* Some common patterns have been observed across what at first would appear to be extremely different cultural settings. Wilkinson (1964) noted that Confucian China and Victorian England emphasized the same developmental requirements for leaders in the public sector. Good manners, good form, and classical cultural training better fitted amateurs for governmental service in comparison to an expert, technical, or professional education. Civil servants were drawn from the landed gentry and those of middle class origin who went to the same schools and adopted upper class accent, dress, and mannerisms. Of course, particularly in the People's Republic of China, public sector leadership now originates quite differently. A detailed study by M. Sheridan (1976) of five prominent women Party leaders in the PRC indicated that they came from manual and service worker backgrounds. They earned merit in their political, familial, and work roles and became models for others.

*Dissenting Minorities.* Curiously, despite their public service leadership, it was not the established landed gentry in Britain that sparked industrialization and the moves toward modernity. Generally, the leaders of industry came from dissenting minorities. In England, leaders of the industrial revolution were drawn out of proportion from the Methodist and other dissenting religious groups. In Roman Catholic France, until the Revocation of the Edict of Nantes in 1685, the source was the Protestant Huguenots. In Colombia, it was the Antioquian miners rather than the landowning latifundists. In India, it was the Parsees. In Southeast Asia, it was the Chinese, and in the western world, the Jews have played a major role (Hagen, 1962).

*Meritocracies.* In France and Belgium, education, a source of income from property, and bourgeois origins underlie leadership of industry and government. Elite cadres dominate the management of business and government based on educational achievement not ordinarily attained by children from the working classes. Particularly important is an engineering degree from the highly selective *grandes écoles.* Leadership in nonremunerative high prestige fields is pursued by those with property income. In Japan also, graduation from a highly selective and prestigious university is a key to success in business or government.

Strong class divisions characterize the Soviet union. Party officials, the military, and industrial and scientific technocrats are the upper classes. The workers and peasants are the lower classes. In a production-oriented economy, engineering or technical training is almost mandatory for career advancement in industry. Still a different and changing pattern is seen in Germany. Since World War II, there have been increasing opportunities to advance from working class origins into positions of top leadership in business and government service. Before 1945, leadership was dominated by the landed aristocracy and the military (Granick, 1962).

*Latifundismo,* the leadership of a country by the few large landowning families is still strong in many Latin American countries and a prime cause of revolutionary action. In some countries, leading the social change are the middle class technocrats of public and private enterprise. Thus, Mexico is a "guided democracy" run by self-made millionaires, an industrial elite, top government bureaucrats, and political figures with middle class origins. On the other hand, business and government leadership in Chile springs from a landed aristocracy. In countries such as Argentina and Peru, the rise of the middle class industrial manager occurred with the post-1945 industrial expansion (Harbron, 1965). Lauterbach (1963) observed in interviews in thirteen Latin American countries that family relationships are important to emergence as a leader, particularly outside the major industrial centers. Second, there is lack of specialization. The same person, family, or executive office can administer a wide variety of enterprises. Immediate objectives predominate. Competition is accepted in the abstract but is a bothersome condition to be restrained by public or private action.

*Family.* In India, the managing agency system was the basis for the development of large-scale indigenous private and public enterprise as well as foreign subsidiaries. The agency promoted, financed, and managed the organization for London capital. The agency was rigidly structured, highly characterized, personal, and likely to be a family unit or dominated by one. The karta or head of the extended Indian family is responsible for and has authority over its other members. Children are taught obedience to their elders. A high degree of authority is exercised and obedience demanded in the Indian family system. There is a lack of delegation in management. Yet there are subtle constraints preventing the head from giving directions without consultation with senior members of the family (Chowdhry & Tarneja, 1961). At the same time, it is difficult for nonfamily members to advance into upper management positions. There is a sharp gap between middle and upper management, unlike, say, the situation in firms in the United States.

## ATTITUDES AND TRAITS OF CONSEQUENCE TO LEADERSHIP ASSOCIATED WITH CULTURE AND COUNTRY

Managerial values embedded in a culture affect organizational leadership goals and strategies (Dill, 1958; Haire, Ghiselli & Porter, 1966; Negandhi & Reimann, 1972). In the search for generalizations about how leadership is affected by cultural differences, a variety of culture-based values, beliefs, norms, and ideals are salient.

### Cultural Dimensions

Three dimensions of particular consequence that have been studied are: traditionalism versus modernity, particularism versus universalism, and pragmatism versus idealism. Also likely to differ across cultures and countries are competitiveness, risk preferences, sense of duty, interpersonal competencies, communication skills, effective intelligence, and needs such as for achievement, affiliation, and power. Interests, goals, and objectives also differ, likewise contributing to differences in leadership style (Dawson, Haw, Leung & Whitney, 1971; Negandhi & Estafen, 1967).

*Traditionalism versus Modernity.* Inkeles (1966) focused attention on this dimension. Traditionalism places emphasis on family, class, revealed truths, reverence for the past, and ascribed status. Modernism places emphasis on merit, rationality, and progress. Traditionalism remains strong in India or Afghanistan; modernism is dominant in the United States or Sweden. The traditional leader is more likely to be the oldest, usually male, head of the family. As a culture group receives more education, it shifts toward modern attitudes, but at a certain point there is a reversion by the most educated to a semitraditional point of view. There is an elite-led revival of traditionalism, such as has been seen in Iran and elsewhere in the Islamic world.

A traditionalistic leader in a traditional society meets with less opposition than one who is pushing modernity. A modernist leader like Kemal Atatürk in a traditional society like Osmanli Turkey often must resort to autocratic and coercive methods to promote change.

Valuing modernity rather than tradition is likely to be accompanied by a reduction in the sense of obligations to family and friends. The more traditional French Canadian manager is more likely to choose family over business obligations when they are in conflict. The less traditional English Canadian will do the reverse (Auclair, 1968). Differential effects on successful leadership are likely to follow. The strong traditionalist is unlikely to be willing or able to lead his or her followers toward modernity but rather will be more influential when attempting to turn the clock back.

Along with traditionalism in 138 Botswana students, Ulin (1976) also measured their elitism, prejudice, anomie, and authoritarianism. The students were ambivalent about traditionalism and authoritarianism, but showed strong anomic and elitist convictions. They held strong anti-Asiatic prejudices and weaker antiwhite attitudes, but they were not biased against other tribes of Africans.

*Particularism versus Universalism.* A particularistic value orientation implies institutionalized obligations of friendship, whereas the universalistic value orientation stresses institutionalized obligations to society and puts less stress upon interpersonal considerations (Parsons & Shils, 1959). Particularism with reference to work is likely to be more common in a Latin developing country; universalism, in the Anglo-American world. Zurcher (1968) contrasted Mexican, Mexican-American, and American bank officers and employees. As expected, Mexicans were more particularistic than Mexican-Americans; and Mexican-Americans were more particularistic than the Anglo-Americans. Beyond this, the officers as a whole were more universalistic than the line employees. Such universalism correlated with job satisfaction and plans to continue working in the bank (Zurcher, Meadow & Zurcher, 1965).

*Pragmatism versus Idealism.* Pragmatists look for what will work; idealists search for the truth. Pragmatists are opportunistic. Curiously, Webster's Third International Dictionary includes in the definition of pragmatic ''active and skilled in business.'' England and associates (England, 1967a, 1972; England, Agarwal & Dhingra, 1973; England & Koike, 1970; England & Weber, 1972; England & Lee, 1974) found pragmatism, as measured by their Personal Values Questionnaire, related to success as managers in the United States, Australia, India, and Japan. The career success of these approximately 2,000 managers was indexed by their income adjusted for their age. In all four countries, successful managers were more likely to hold pragmatic values emphasizing productivity, profitability, and achievement. Similarly, among 5,122 managers who were administered Exercise Objectives (Bass, 1975a) by Bass, Burger, et al. (1979) on all five budgeting decisions, a somewhat greater percentage favored the pragmatic solutions not to spend money for safety, to settle a strike, to improve management morale, to improve the quality of a product, or to clean up a stream the company was polluting. Palmer, Veiga, and Vora (n.d.) showed that the decision to reject expenditures in Exercise Objectives by U. S. and Indian managers was higher among those higher in pragmatic values (economic, political, theoretical) and lower in those with altruistic or idealistic values (social, aesthetic, religious). But wide cross-cultural variations occurred. Whereas 71 percent of Latin Americans, 65 percent of U. S., and 65 percent of Indian managers chose to clean up the stream, less than 50 percent of European or Japanese managers did the same. In a replication by Palmer, Veiga, and Vora (n.d.), 61 percent of U. S. and 82 percent of Indian managers chose to clean up the stream.

Among the nationals of twelve countries studied by Bass, Burger, et al. (1979), significant interactions were found between nationality and managerial rate of advancement and the tendency to be pragmatic about two of the budgeting decisions. Sixty-four percent of all slower-climbing managers favored accepting a costly wage agreement to settle a strike immediately, as compared with only 60 percent of all faster-climbing managers, but the tendency was reversed in Belgium, Germany-Austria, Italy, and particularly India, where 63 percent of the faster-climbing managers opted to settle the strike and only 32 percent of the slower-rising managers did so. The political implications and potentials for violence may have rendered the decision to settle quickly more pragmatic rather than idealistic there. In fact, 100 percent of Indian managers in Palmer, Veiga, and Vora's study elected to settle the strike, but only 63 percent of United States managers did the same.

Again, in eight of twelve nationalities, those managers higher in rate of advancement gave the more pragmatic response to delay spending money to control the stream pollution, but the tendency was reversed in Belgium, Scandinavia, Iberia, and Latin America where more of the faster-climbing managers reacted idealistically. However, with the U. S., British, Dutch, French, and Japanese managers, on both issues of strike settlement and controlling stream pollution, the faster-climbing managers uniformly were more reluctant to spend money to handle the problems immediately.

Personal acquisitiveness rather than social concerns also vary across countries. Wide variations among the same twelve national groupings studied by Bass, Burger, et al. were found in a multinational survey of IBM personnel completed by Hofstede (1978). Factor scores for the same national groupings varied greatly in how they responded to quesions dealing with national norms for personal acquisitiveness in contrast to social concerns. Japanese personnel were most acquisitive and Scandinavians were most socially concerned. Factor scores were as follows: Japan, 95; Germany, 73; Italy, 70; Britain, 66; United States, 62; Latin America, 61; Belgium, 54; India, 50; France, 43; Iberia, 37; Netherlands, 14; Scandinavia, 10.

In a study of student leaders and nonleaders in India, Kumar (1965) found that unlike American or European results usually found, Indian student leaders scored high on theoretical and religious interests, while nonleaders scored high on economic and social values. But Govindarajan (1964) observed that high school leaders were more interested than nonleaders in professional and technical jobs. They mentioned salary, prestige, and status as reasons for job choice more frequently.

Compensation decisions vary across countries. Evidence of cross-cultural differences in pragmatism among managers comes from Bass, Burger, et al. (1979) and their analysis of the responses to Exercise Compensation of 4,255 managers from twelve national groups. Respondents had to decide the percent salary increase to recommend for each of ten engineers differing in merit, job context, personal problems, and so on. Although the 4,255 managers as a whole recommended only 82 percent as much of an increase for the engineer in the 10th percentile in merit as for the engineer at the 50th percentile in meritorious performance, the Indian managers gave him 103 percent of the average performing engineer's increase. Only in India was the poor performer given more of an increase than the average performer. Thiagarajan suggested that whereas in the developed countries, salary increases are rewards for meritorious performance, in India, a salary increase is seen as a stimulator. Ryterband and Thiagarajan (1968) reported a similar tendency for Colombian in contrast to U. S. and Scandinavian managers. According to Bass, Burger, et al. (1979), Japanese managers stood out at the other end of the scale in deciding what to award the engineer in the 90th percentile in merit. They suggested 138 percent of the average award in contrast to the 162 percent favored by the 4,255 managers as a whole. For each individual manager of the 4,255 in the sample, the standard deviation in his recommendations for eight engineers in the 50th percentile in merit were calculated. The results confirmed (except for Japan) earlier findings by Ryterband and Thiagarajan (1968), that managers from more developed countries tend to find salary differentials for people doing the same job justified only by merit differences among the job occupants. In the less developed countries, family, job insecurity, alternative offers, lack of job prestige, and so on justify differentials.

Attitudes toward merit and competence were reflected also in the differential decisions of Greek and U. S. personnel directors and students rating hypothesized applicants for positions in accounting and finance. Triandis (1963) asked 100 Illinois students, 100 Greek students, thirty-two Illinois personnel directors, and twenty Greek personnel directors to rate thirty-two candidates, systematically differing in competence, age, sex, race, religion, sociability, and wealth in different combinations. For the Illinois personnel directors, 54 percent of the variance in the ratings of the candidates was accounted for by whether candidates were described as highly competent or barely competent. But such competence accounted for only 24.8 percent of the ratings of the Greek personnel directors. Competence was even more important to the American students; sociability was particularly important to the Greek students.

*Pervasiveness of Pragmatism.* Despite the national variations, the relatively high level of pragmatism everywhere among managers needs to be kept in mind. This pervasiveness of the pragmatic orientation among managers was found in an analysis of American and Indian managers' responses to the same Personal Values Questionnaire (Thiagarajan, 1968). The studies of England and associates also showed that the managers from different countries were more like each other than like compatriots who were not managers. Thus, the pragmatic orientation is almost totally absent among theology students regardless of cultural background (England, 1970). The managers in all the countries surveyed were only secondarily moralistic.

### In-Group and Out-Group Relations

Bass (1977) demonstrated by using Exercise Organization (Bass, 1975d) that in general productivity and satisfaction are greater when we complete plans developed in our own group than when we carry out plans assigned by another group. But there were considerable national variations. Overall, objective efficiency differences favored self-planning compared with carrying out others' plans: U. S., 13.7; Irish, 12.8; French, 11.8; Colombians, 8.8; British, 8.5; Italians, 8.0; Japanese, 7.9; Belgians, 6.1; Dutch, 5.5; Swiss, 5.2; Danes, 1.1; and Germans, −2.0. U. S. managers profited the most from working on their own plan rather than a plan assigned to them by another group but it did not matter whose plan Danes and Germans used. Yet, most managers saw their own plans as better still than those assigned by another group to their own group (Bass, Burger, et al., 1979). Most exaggerated in this competitive effect were the French as well as managers who were slower in rate of advancement.

*Loyalty to In-Group.* The Japanese operate their large organizations with lack of clarity about the nature of one's job and area of authority. One-quarter of the larger firms had no organization chart. According to a 1960 survey, only one-third had rules delineating the authority for the chief of the general affairs division or for the chief of the accounting division (Keizai Doyukai, 1960). When Japanese are asked what their job is, they are likely to reply that they are members of a particular company instead of saying what they do (Tsutomu, 1964). Associated with this is a lack of career specialization (Mannari & Abbeglen, 1963). The ambiguous organization works effectively because of the group orientation of its members, the willingness to work organically with each other, taking into account not only a particular role requirement but also who happens to be filling it. The group orientation is accompanied by strong peer pressure (Abbeglen, 1958). Hesseling and Konnen (1969) reported that during a decision-making simulation, Japanese managers were extremely critical of their peers as compared to Dutch managers. The Japanese managers appeared to combine behaviors in this situation which to Westerners may seem incompatible.

Well-known are the life-time employment assignments in Japan. However, Abegglen (1958) noted that generally the employer is more obligated than the employee. According to Marsh and Mannari (1971), quit rates and piracy of managers indicated that there actually is considerably movement from one firm to another among Japanese employees. For example, during one decade, one-fourth of the Japanese manufacturing employees left their place of employment annually; two-thirds of these, voluntarily. But, despite these facts, both Japanese managers and workers tend to believe that they have permanent employment, and organizational loyalty is high. Promotions take place at regular intervals but an ''up-or-out'' policy actually results in either continued promotion upward or early retirement (Kezai Doyukai, 1960). In comparison to responses of successful U. S., Australian, and Indian managers, England and Lee (1974) found that successful Japanese managers were most likely to emphasize loyalty. Among the twelve nationalities studied by Bass, Burger, et al., the life goal of duty—dedication to ultimate values, ideals, and principles—was among the top three in importance for 46 percent of Japanese and 34 percent of Indian managers, at one extreme, and 7 to 9 percent of German, Austrian, Scandinavian, and British managers, at the other. Japanese workers tend to merge their company and family life. Thus, whereas 56 percent of the Japanese workers in the early 1960s perceived the company to be at least equal in importance to their personal life, only 24 percent of the Americans felt the same way (Whitehill, 1964). Later, according to a questionnaire administered by Whitehill and Takezawa (1968) to approximately 2,000 Japanese workers, 57 percent thought of their company as ''a part of my life at least equal in importance to my personal life,'' whereas only 22 percent of the United States workers responded similarly.

In the same way, the values of a culture affect individual expectations of organizational rewards (England & Koike, 1970). In the United States, workers see themselves receiving wages in exchange for services, but in the Orient, compensation is an obligation of the employer, who is responsible for employee welfare. Compensation is less likely to be related to the services performed than to the individual's needs. Performance appraisal becomes difficult to introduce under such circumstances (Gellerman, 1967).

Loyalty to close friends takes on special relationships in a number of countries and can markedly affect influence patterns. Particularism flourishes. For example, in the Philippines, *pakikisama* expresses all-encompassing friendship. It results in intense loyalty to one boss and the formation of cliques. In Greece, one speaks of *philotimo*— the strong bond of affection and loyalty between friends, again with its effects on clique formation. In Nigeria, loyalty to other members of one's tribe transcends objective considerations with strong loyalty patterns. Objective merit ratings, promotions, and salary recommendations based on performance become impossible. Ratings will reflect tribal relationships rather than performance.

*Labor and Management.*  In a study of attitudes in Israel and Australia, Rim and Mannheim (1964) found considerable homogeneity of attitude within management groups and within union leader groups regarding specific issues in labor–management relations. The older the enterprise, the greater the mutuality of attitudes between management and labor leaders.

### Personal Motives, Values, Goals and Orientation

Nowotny (1964) focused attention on the differences between European and U. S. management philosophies. Nowotny attributed emphasis on stability, convention, quality, and diversity to the European respect for the past. The U. S. management's differential focus on the future results in emphasis on vitality, mobility, informality, abundance, quantity, and organization. In the same way, Barrett and Ryterband (1968) found that managers from developing countries such as Colombia and India assigned less importance to meeting competition than did managers from the United States, Britain, and the Netherlands. Managers from developed countries put greater stress on the objectives of growth and competition. Conversely, maintaining satisfactory organizational operations appeared to be more important to those from the developing countries (Barrett & Ryterband, 1968).

*Needs for Achievement, Affiliation, and Power.*  Illustrative of the many available studies, McClelland (1961) reported systematic differences among approximately 200 managers from the United States, Italy, Turkey, and Poland in their *n* achievement, *n* affiliation, and *n* power scores. In *n* achievement, countries ranked: United States (highest), Poland, Italy, and Turkey; in *n* affiliation: Italy, Turkey, United States, and Poland; and in *n* power: United States, North Italy, Turkey, South Italy, and Poland. As we noted in Chapter 9, McClelland showed with U. S. executives that *n* achievement correlated significantly with entrepreneural drive. Further support for this result was obtained in a variety of studies in other countries, including Turkey (Bradburn, 1963), Nigeria (LeVine, 1966), Brazil (Angelini, 1966), Iran (Tedeschi & Kian, 1962), South Africa (Morsbach, 1969), India (Singh, 1969, 1970), and Trinidad (Mischel, 1961). McClelland and Winter (1971) were also able to demonstrate among Indian and Mexican businessmen that a program which increased *n* achievement also resulted in increasing their entrepreneural activities (see Chapter 33).

*Relations and Task Orientation.*  The self-, interaction and task orientation (Bass, 1967b) of leaders and nonleaders have been studied in many different countries such as Poland (Dobruszek, 1967), Britain (Cooper, 1966; R. Cooper & Payne, 1967), and India (Muttayya, 1977) with results generally similar to what was found in U. S. samples (Chapter 9). For example, Muttayya found that among 275 diverse formal and informal Indian leaders and nonleaders, leaders were more task-oriented, as expected. But self-orientation among leaders was associated with less commitment to principled public conduct and more concern for economic equality.

Within-country differences in orientation of leaders were seen as more significant in Italy by Gallino (1975). Three types of Italian managers were conceived: the liberal, the lay humanist, and the Christian Socialist. These types will vary in how they conceive the manager's role and functions, how subordinates should be trained, the use of formal organization techniques, their models of economic development, their investment preferences, and their attitude toward the work force and worker representation.

The "liberal" is more often found in the older, established private companies operating in relatively traditional productive and technological sectors; the lay humanist, in the newer, recently established private companies operating in advanced productive and technological sectors; and the Christian Socialist, in companies run fully or partly by the state. The liberal is task-oriented and profit-maximizing; the lay humanist is more concerned about relations and people; and the Christian Socialist is oriented toward the public good and the collectivity.

*Life Goals.* In Exercise Life Goals (Bass, 1975e), 3,082 managers from the twelve nationalities surveyed by Bass, Burger, et al. rated the importance of eleven life goals to themselves. Although high percentages of managers everywhere ranked self-realization as first, second, or third, the Japanese were highest (74 percent) and the Indians were lowest (42 percent) in this tendency. Leadership was most important to Germans and Austrians (51 percent) and least so for the Dutch (20 percent) for whom expertness (50 percent) was most important. Expertness was lowest for the Italians (22 percent) relative to the other eleven groups. Stereotypes to the contrary, the British managers were highest in emphasizing pleasure (29 percent), while the Spaniards (9 percent) and Latin Americans (10 percent) were relatively low in stressing pleasure.

When nationalities were compared, wealth was most important to the Indian and American managers and least important to the Japanese. Independence was most important to the Germans and Austrians and least important to the Indians. Prestige was most important to the Latin Americans and least so to the Japanese for whom duty (already mentioned) was most important. Service was most important to the Italians and French and security to the Scandinavians and British.

*Risk Tendencies and Preferences.* Bass, Burger, et al. (1979) noted which of twelve nationalities were above or below the median on eighteen indicators of risk tendencies or risk preferences. U. S. managers were above the median on 89 percent of the eighteen indicators. Results for the remaining eleven nationalities were as follows: Japanese, 67 percent; Dutch, French, and Scandinavians, 61 percent; Latin Americans, 60 percent; British and Indians, 50 percent; Italians, Spanish, and Portuguese, 44 percent; Belgians, Germans, and Austrians, 39 percent.

### Need Satisfaction

Haire, Ghiselli, and Porter (1966) surveyed approximately 3,600 managers from fourteen countries. Mozina (1969) used the same questionnaire to survey 500 managers from Yugoslavia, as did Clark and McCabe (1970) for over 1,300 Australian managers and Badawy (n.d.) for middle managers in Saudi Arabia.

In agreement with the Bass, Burger, et al. findings (1979), Maslow's (1954) higher-level needs such as for self-actualization and esteem were judged important by managers everywhere. But the satisfaction of these higher-level needs was deemed inadequate, although the lowest-level physiological needs, of relatively little importance, were seen to be fairly well satisfied. The need for security, considered to be important, was relatively highly fulfilled in line with expectations.

But again, broad national variations emerged. Managers from the developing countries perceived all the needs to be more important to them than did managers from developed countries and reported a greater sense of unfulfillment. At the other extreme, the North European countries tended to place the least importance upon all the needs.

Consistent with what was concluded in Chapter 9, the perception of one's degree of need fulfillment depends everywhere on one's level of satisfaction and hierarchial rank in the organization. Especially in Japan, lower management consistently indicated greater dissatisfaction in all areas surveyed than did upper management.

*Perceived Stress and Conflict.* Rogers (1977) found that whereas for U. S. managers, decision making was the more important source of stress, for Canadian managers both work load and decision making were equally frequent sources of stress. But even sharper differences appeared when English and French Canadian managers were analyzed by Auclair (1968). Male French Canadian managers placed a higher value on their role as the head of the family than did English Canadian managers. Consequently, the French Canadian manager perceived a great deal of stress placed upon him due to the conflicting role demands of family and business. In comparison, the English Canadian manager placed less value upon his role in the family and experienced less conflict with role demands from his business organization.

Various kinds of role conflict faced by supervisors (Chapter 13) may by exacerbated in India where, on the one hand, Bhatt and Pathak (1962) found industrial supervisors more production-oriented than human-relations oriented, and on the other, Sequeira (1964) reported that Indian workers expected foremen to do more in the way of settling personnel problems and grievances, clarifying work difficulties, and improving work methods and conditions. In other respects, as well, foremen perceived themselves as required to perform duties not legitimately belonging to their jobs, such as training new men on the job, arranging wage agreements, and checking supplies. Yoga (1964) found similar results in eleven Indian plants in three types of industries (textiles, processing, and engineering).

An in-depth interview survey of thirty managers in the Paris area was conducted by COFREMCA (1978). What seemed particularly salient in their attitudes and values was a conflict between the valuing of their own work and their self-actualization as professionals, the lack of warmth and understanding in work relations, insecurity among the older managers, and competitiveness—particularly in large firms.

The Soviet manager faces fundamental conflicts in contradictory demands from an inflexible system of production quotas determining rewards and punishments for performance. These demands are intertwined with conflicts and defenses rooted in Russia's Mongol and Byzantine-influenced past—entrenched bureaucracy and emphasis on secrecy, characteristic of the pre-Soviet regime (Pipes, 1974). These are reflected in Lenin's own model of close-knit mutually supportive working relationships with immediate subordinates whose advice may be sought but who are expected to conform to their superiors' dictates (Bass & Farrow, 1977). Loyalty and support for one's superiors is exchanged for their protection from the larger outside system (Ryapolov, 1966). Leaders and their immediate subordinates become excessively dependent on each other to buffer the demands of the larger system (Granick, 1960).

Central planning pits the small group of leaders and immediate subordinates against the arbitrary, distant, demanding central authority. To survive within the system, the small groups must back each other up as unauthorized activities such as plan falsification are carried out in order to meet quotas. For example, central planning overestimates of available supplies resulting in shortages of vital parts may require hiring *tolkhachi* who live permanently near bases of supply to obtain necessary materials, even shipping it by briefcase, if necessary (Ryapolov, 1966). Assembled items may be declared ready for shipment and distribution even though they are lacking in quality because of missing parts. If a higher-up in the larger system wants to ''get'' the plant director, the success of the director's coverup will depend on the loyalty to him of his immediate subordinates.

Unlike his Soviet counterpart who must conceal productive capacity, hoard resources, sacrifice product quality, or even falsify reports to meet inflexible production quotas from central planning, the Chinese plant director does not face the same demands from central authority in the People's Republic of China. Rather, more such pressure is likely to arise from the plant work force coupled with much greater flexibility to adjust plans, even weekly, based on experience. Democratic centralism in China involves mass worker participation in the management of enterprises and receives strong support from factory party cadres, according to Richman (1967).

### Variations in Competences in Different Countries

Various abilities associated with leadership have been found to vary across countries. These include social perceptual skills, interpersonal competence, effective intelligence, and efficient work habits. These are only illustrative. Space prohibits any examination of the wide variety of industrial aptitude tests used in many countries to forecast successful leader behavior.

*Social Perceptual Skills.* Bass, Alexander, et al. (1971) and Bass, Burger, et al. (1979) calculated empathy and projection scores for managers from twelve national groupings based on the managers' rankings of their own life goals as well as those of the other members of their training group. The similarity of their self-rankings was also obtained. The British (.35) and Japanese (.30) were highest in empathy and the Latin Americans (.03) lowest in such accuracy. The British (.62) and Dutch (.62) were highest in projection; the Indians (.31) and Iberians (.34) were lowest. To a considerable degree, the results were attributable to the actual similarity of self-rankings.

The average similarity of self-rankings among participants was only .15 in India with its sixteen major language groups and many religions and castes. It was even lower for the United States (.11) with its multiplicity of ethnic, racial, and religious groups and lowest for Latin America (.05) where data included managers drawn from recent European immigrant groups from many countries, old Spanish or Portuguese stock, as well as mestizos and other multiethnics. In general, in Europe, with greater uniformity of religion, language, and centralized education, the average similarities ranged from .23 for France to .39 for Britain. Japan (.27) was also more homogeneous.

Managers everywhere assumed themselves to be more similar to their colleagues than they actually were. The distortion was greatest for U. S. managers and Latin Americans. At the other extreme, Iberian managers' projections were close to actual similarity.

*Interpersonal Competence.* A factor analysis of sixty self-ratings on Exercise Self-Appraisal (Bass, 1975f) of actual and preferred behavior by Bass, Burger, et al. (1979) revealed for over 1,000 managers seven factors involved with interpersonal competence: (1) preferred awareness; (2) actual awareness; (3) submissiveness; (4) reliance on others; (5) favoring group decision making; (6) concern for good human relations; and (7) cooperative peer relations. With reference to the first factor dealing with preferences for awareness of the feelings of others, self-understanding, accepting feedback from others, listening to others, and concern for the welfare of subordinates, Spanish and Portuguese managers stood out as highest and Germans and Austrians as lowest among the twelve national groupings on the preferences correlated with the factor. Germans and Austrians were also lowest on the second factor of actual awareness.

Indian managers were most concerned about rules; Japanese, the least so. They felt the least conflict about the more ambiguous (in western eyes) organizational arrangements to which they are accustomed. Indian managers saw themselves as most dependent on higher authority and German/Austrian managers as least dependent. Italian managers saw themselves lowest in depending on others in problem solving; and as expected. Japanese were highest in this regard as well as in actual, and preference to initiate others when problem solving. U. S. managers stood out in the preference for group decision making. Spain, Portugal, and Italy were lowest in this regard. In keeping with stereotypes, French managers were lowest in reported actual cooperative peer relations; the Dutch were highest. On other specific ratings such as willingness to discuss feelings with others, again the French managers were lowest among the twelve national groupings; the Italian and Japanese, highest in this self-rating.

Self-ratings which discriminated faster- from slower-climbing managers varied from one country to another. In France, Spain, and Portugal, the faster-climbing managers were more concerned than the slower climbers about their dependence on higher authority. The more rapidly promoted French managers also showed greater preference for imitation than average for French managers. Faster-climbing managers were less favorable to imitation in the Netherlands, Scandinavia, Spain, and Portugal.

*Effective Intelligence.* In Bass, Burger, et al.'s (1979) analysis of the results from twelve national groupings for Exercise Self-Appraisal, the Japanese were highest in the desire to be objective rather than intuitive. The Japanese preference for persistence was even more extreme relative to other nationalities. Again, to be proactive rather than reactive was most strongly favored by the Japanese. The same was true for preferring long-term rather than short-term views. Moreover, the Japanese managers also saw themselves as actually very high (in comparison to the results for other countries) in actual objectivity, persistence, proactivity, and long-term thinking. The French tended to be most critical of themselves in their self-appraisals of actual objectivity, persistence, proactivity and long-term thinking.

In Exercise Communications (Bass, 1975g), Leavitt's one-way/two-way problem is completed. Senders transmit verbally a pattern of six dominoes when two-way communications are permitted. If communications are one way only, receivers must reconstruct the pattern without seeing the original and cannot ask questions. Consistent with their actual and preferred self-appraisals, the objective results of Exercise Communication showed the Japanese managers to be highest in number of correct placements, both in one-way and two-way communications. Their faster-climbing managers, in particular, were able to achieve this degree of accuracy in the fastest time for one-way communications. Close behind them in accuracy with one-way communications were the Germans and Austrians.

Indian managers did poorest. They were relatively slow and inaccurate. These results can be accounted for possibly by the Japanese familiarity with ideographic communication (in which case Chinese and Koreans should also do well) and the fact that for Indian managers, English, the language of business, is their second or third language.

## DIFFERENCES IN LEADERSHIP ACROSS CULTURES

### Leadership Requisites Vary across Cultures

Mead's (1930, 1935, 1939) anthropological studies clearly showed that what it takes to be a leader varies across cultures. The aggressive, efficient, ambitious Manus leader in Oceania would have been rejected by the Dakota Indians who valued mutual welfare, conforming to the group, generosity, and hospitality. Individualism, lack of political integration, and lack of need to comply with leadership characterized the Bachiga of Central Africa, while obedience, respect for the chief, and cooperative effort with little room for rivalry was the norm among the Bathonga. With their consciousness of position and conformity to rank in a clear hierarchy, the Samoans followed a completely different style of leadership than pursued by the individualistic Eskimos. For the traditional Eskimo, no person's importance was considered relative to another. Leadership among the Iroquois was achieved through behavior socially rewarding to others, such as generosity, cooperation, and hospitality. But among the Kwakiutl, the ideal chieftain was one who could successfully compete financially against other chiefs. What appeared to be demanded of the leader was quite different among the Arapesh of New Guinea, who have no strict ownership of land or scale of success, and the Ifugao of the Philippines, where land ownership has been concentrated and where the landowner is the ideal of success. Thus, it is not surprising that the patterns of leader–subordinate behavior in industrialized society show considerable variation as we move across countries and across cultures. Although such extreme effects of cultural differences may not be seen in the modern industrialized world, nevertheless considerable differences emerge in what is seen by managers as required for success in top, middle, and lower management.

*Traits Judged Important for Top, Middle, and Lower Management.* Bass, Burger, et al. (1979) analyzed the choices of managers from twelve country groups in their selection, from a list of twenty-five, of the five most important traits and the five least important traits required for top, middle, and lower management using Exercise Supervise (Bass, 1975c), developed from original lists by L. W. Porter (1959). Indexes reflecting the choices of 3,401 managers yielded significant variations across countries in many of the attributes for the three management levels. For example, managers everywhere else called for more imagination for successively higher management levels, but the Dutch saw no difference in this requirement for lower and middle managers. Being systematic was judged most important for lower-level managers in Italy, Spain, Portugal, and Latin America, but more necessary for middle managers everywhere else. Managers everywhere were expected to be more careful, the lower their organizational level. But the Dutch felt it was most important for middle management. The French judged it most important for lower and middle management to be sharpwitted. The U. S. and British managers put a premium on being resourceful; the Japanese saw intuition as far more important than logic. Sociability was seen as important for top managers by faster accelerating managers more than by slower ones in Holland, Belgium, Italy, Spain, Portugal, Latin America, and India. Slower-rising managers saw such sociability as more important for top management in Britain, Scandinavia, and France.

*Required Superior–Subordinate Relations.* Luther's concept of the "calling," serving God by doing one's best in one's occupation, continues to influence strongly the extent to which the German subordinate expects to carry out decisions once they have been indicated. We have already mentioned the required informal mutual defense pacts that provide for the survival of both superiors and subordinates in the Soviet system. We have also noted the extent to which in some cultures, such as the Japanese, the organization takes on particular importance in life. This in turn affects what is required of Japanese superior–subordinate relations.

The supervisor has different relevance to the worker in Japan. Not only is the supervisor likely to be more involved in the subordinate's off-the-job life, but the supervisor will be accorded more status off the job. Whereas 44 percent of Japanese workers would offer their supervisor their seat on a crowded bus, only two percent of Americans said they would do so (Whitehill & Takezawa, 1968).

In the Soviet Union, the need to "beat the system" may produce mutual suspicion between superior and subordinate. Both may face cuts in pay of 25 percent below base salary if performance is not up to expectations (Anonymous, 1970).

*Required Masculinity.* In Chapter 30, we noted that U. S. data strongly indicated that masculinity was seen to be required for success in management by both male and female respondents. No doubt, similar results can be obtained in many other countries. But among 1,600 Australian high school students, Bottomley and Sampson (1977) reported comparable results only for male respondents. Unlike the boys, a majority of Australian girls believed that men and women could be equally competent on four leadership tasks.

### Styles of Leadership

In parallel with Chapters 18 through 22, we can consider national and cultural similarities and differences in required, preferred, and observed leadership that is autocratic or democratic, participative or directive, relations-oriented or task-oriented, considerate or structuring, and active or laissez-faire.

*Autocratic versus Democratic Leadership.* Subscription to democratic leadership was found surprisingly high by Haire, Ghiselli, and Porter (1966) across the fourteen countries they studied. But, compared to U. S. managers, there was little acceptance elsewhere of what would be required for such democratic leadership such as agreement that employees as well as supervisors have the potential to exhibit initiative, share leadership, and contribute to the problem-solving process in organizations. They concluded, based on data from the early 1960s, that in most other countries, introducing democratic leadership outside the United States would be "a little like building the techniques and practices of a Jeffersonian democracy on a basic belief in the divine right of kings."

Kenis (1977) compared the attitudes toward leadership of 150 Turkish and 147 American first-line supervisors in branch banks in Ankara and Istanbul. The Turks favored more authoritarian and directive leadership in contrast to the Americans who favored more participative leadership and consideration. Kenis attributed his results to the authoritarianism inherent in the Turkish culture.

As we noted in Chapter 8, authoritarianism as measured by the $F$ scale influences the acceptance of autocratic rather than democratic behavior. The $F$ scale has been administered to student groups in many different countries. Thus, as just noted, Turkish students are likely to score higher and American students are likely to score lower on the scale. Indian students usually score high also (Meade & Whittaker, 1967). Therefore, as suggested by Sinha (1976), authoritative leadership is optimum in India. It features task orientation and strong personal involvement and effort by the leader. More democratic processes are possibly only after the structure has become firm for the employees and moderate productivity has been achieved.

Singh and Arya (1965) studied forty sociometrically identified leaders in a village in India. Given the strong authoritarian norm, it was not surprising that leaders were found significantly more authoritarian than nonleaders. Leaders preferred task-oriented leaders to other types. But both leaders and nonleaders rejected the self-interested leader.

Paternalism, featuring the autocratic patron and compliant followers, takes a variety of forms in Latin America. Paternalism dominates indigenous Brazilian industry. The traditional worker identifies with the *patrão,* the patriarchial owner to whom he is a ward, not a member of an organization. M. Nash (1958) described first-line supervision within the large padrone system in a rural Guatemalan factory as one in which the immediate supervisor, of local origin, has limited authority, suggests rather than orders, and is identified as a member of the work force. On the other hand, before unionization, the foreign engineer and the owner or their white-collar surrogates treated workers like children, physically abusing them, as well as dealing directly with their complaints.

Nationalities vary in their willingness to trust others and how they deal with a lack of trust. In Italy, trust may be publicly expressed but privately denied, for Italy's history has been characterized by oppressive surface regimentation first by foreign occupiers, then by domestic autocratic governments. But strong defenses of liberty of the individual and his or her family have been maintained. Outer and inner acceptance have been separated by making the world truly a stage in which the relations between the leader and the led play a dramatic part. Trust levels influence willingness to work with democratic leaders, according to a Peruvian study by Williams, Whyte, and Green (1966), who found the trust level generally low among Peruvians.

Within countries, organization and status affect willingness to trust others. Senner (1971) found Brazilian bankers similar to American college students in that both groups were more trusting than Peruvian white-collar workers. The bankers' trust levels reflected their above average socioeconomic status in Brazil. Again, Negandhi and Prasad (1971) found that managers in U. S. subsidiaries in India showed more trust in their subordinates than managers in indigenous Indian firms.

Hofstede (1978) factored results with survey questionnaires of IBM personnel in forty countries, clearly showing wide variations in national norms about autocratic supervisory–subordinate relations. Contrary to stereotypes, Germany was relatively low, with a factor score of 77. At the other extreme was India, with a factor score of 15. Examples of other results were Britain, 35; the Netherlands, 38; the United States, 40; Italy, 50; Japan, 54; Belgium, 65; and France, 68. Nevertheless, all managers who role-played subordinates in Exercise Supervise preferred to return to a democratic rather than to an autocratic supervisor in Bass, Burger, et al.'s twelve-nation groupings. However, there was considerable variation in the choice across nationalities. Surprisingly, highest in preference were the French; lowest, the Japanese. But preference by those who played supervisory roles to work again with passive, nonparticipating subordinates was highest among Indian managers and lowest among the Japanese.

R. Likert (1963) as well as Blake and Mouton (1970) argued that a democratic, actively task- and relations-oriented leadership is most likely to be effective in any productive organization regardless of culture or country. We have seen wide variations in leader preferences and behavior, but the argument is that, regardless of culture, there is one best way to lead. Nevertheless, autocratic rather than democratic leadership was seen as more effective in some locations. An experimental replication of the classic Lewin, Lippitt, and White (1939) study of leadership in India by Meade (1967) found that both productivity and satisfaction in boys' groups were higher under autocratic than under nonautocratic leadership in India. Again, in a study of Israeli naval officers and crews, Foa (1957) concluded that authoritarian commanders should be in charge of subordinates with authoritarian expectations.

The complexities and ambiguities of the Japanese organizational and social setting suggest that the leadership results of investigators such as Misumi and Seki (1971), demonstrating that supervisory style differentially affected groups either high or low in $n$ achievement may not be generalizable to non-Japanese managers. Yet Misumi (1974), following Likert's (Chapter 18) System 4 strategy, successfully completed a project that started in 1970 in a large shipyard in Japan using group meetings for group problem solving, goal setting, and decision making in an effort to reduce accidents among 4,000 workers. An index of accidents per man hours worked ($\times$ $10^5$) declined from thirty in 1969 to twelve in 1973.

*Participative and Directive Leadership.* A survey by Sirota (1968) of IBM employees about their supervision in forty-six countries indicated preference for consultation and joint decision making, although directive leadership was seen as more common. As we would expect from the reviews in Chapter 19 and 22, the managers who consulted were viewed most favorably by subordinates and the managers who persuaded and especially the ones with "no style" were seen least favorably, particularly in Britain. Interestingly, participative managers in Britain were not seen as good counselors. Many subordinates objected to the number of meetings they called (Sadler, 1970). Consistent with these results, Chaney (1966) found that whereas more productive U. S. scientists had more frequent communications with their superiors and their colleagues, the reverse was true for British scientists—the more productive ones had less frequent communications with their superiors.

As seen in an analysis by Sadler and Hofstede (1972) of IBM employees from Australia, Britain, Brazil, and Japan (shown in Table 32.3), the preferred management style for the majority of IBM employees was consultative, but there were distinct differences among countries. For example, in Brazil, an additional 29 percent of the employees preferred participative leadership. At the same time, consultation was considerably higher in preference in Australia and Britain than in Brazil or Japan. Little participative leadership was perceived anywhere. These results were consistent with data gathered through the Management Styles Survey in the United States, Spain, Sweden, Finland, and India (Bass, Valenzi, et al., 1975). Consultation is preferred over participation everywhere and is more frequently seen everywhere. In all the countries in the IBM survey and in those just mentioned, directive supervision was favored less by the vast majority of subordinates. Participative leadership was self-appraised (in Exercise Self-

**TABLE 32.3**
**Preferred and Perceived Leadership Styles of IBM Employees (Percent)**

| Manager | Australia | Britain | Brazil | Japan |
|---|---|---|---|---|
| Preferred | | | | |
| Directive | 1 | 5 | 8 | 1 |
| Persuasive | 25 | 25 | 21 | 42 |
| Consultative | 65 | 61 | 42 | 44 |
| Participative | 9 | 9 | 29 | 13 |
| Perceived | | | | |
| Directive | 22 | 14 | 23 | 19 |
| Persuasive | 32 | 30 | 24 | 26 |
| Consultative | 30 | 34 | 17 | 26 |
| Participative | 5 | 8 | 12 | 10 |
| None of these | 11 | 14 | 24 | 19 |

SOURCE: Adapted from Sadler and Hofstede (1972).

Appraisal) as highest among Italian managers and lowest among the Dutch and Japanese. Preference for participation was highest among Italians and Japanese (Bass, Burger, et al., 1979). But these figures need to be discounted.

Compared with their subordinates, IBM managers themselves thought they did more consulting. Among a multinational sample of 178 managers, 71 percent saw themselves as using a "consulting" leadership style, but only 29 percent of their employees agreed with them (Sadler & Hofstede, 1972). A contradiction probably contributed to the discrepancy. Noted earlier was Haire, Ghiselli, and Porter's (1966) finding in their fourteen-country study that whereas 3,600 managers professed favorable beliefs toward participative leadership and sharing information, they also believed that the average individual preferred to be directed and wanted to avoid responsibility. Similar results were reported by Clark and McCabe (1970) for an additional 1,300 managers in Australia and by Cummings and Schmidt (1972) for a small sample of Greek managers. These national differences in such preferences were seen with considerable consistency across studies. Preference as a receiver in Exercise Communication of one-way communication correlated across nationalities .82 with the Haire, Ghiselli, and Porter (1966) survey measure of propensity to share information and objectives (Barrett & Franke, 1969).

According to analyses by Bass, Burger, et al. (1979) of Exercise Communications data from twelve national groupings, the U. S. and Japanese managers were highest in seeing two-way communications as less frustrating than one-way communications. On the other hand, relatively least frustrated by one-way communications were the Belgians, German/Austrians, and French. All Japanese managers sampled preferred two-way communications both as senders and receivers. Almost identical results occurred for U. S. managers. The Dutch, Belgians, German, Austrians, French, and Indians seemed somewhat more tolerant of one-way communications as senders, but not as receivers. The Japanese were most satisfied with two-way communications, and the relative differential preference for two-way over one-way was lowest for the French.

A. S. Tannenbaum (1974) contrasted the extent to which subordinate plant employees participated both informally and formally in decision making in Italy, Austria, the United States, Yugoslavia, and the Israeli kibbutz. As expected, satisfaction with job as well as mental adjustment was closest in match between subordinates and superiors in Yugoslavia and Israel, where workers formally participate in organizational decision processes, and most distant in Italy, where employees participate neither formally nor informally, as in the United States.

Participation may take on different character in a country like Japan from what is ordinarily practiced elsewhere. To a western observer, leader–subordinate relations may seem authoritarian–submissive in which complete subordinate obedience is given to decisions announced by the leader. Actually, leadership in Japan as seen in the *Ringi* method is a blend of full consultation all around and seeming intolerance for deviation when consensus has been reached.

In traditional Japan, negative votes in a group were rare. Members faced loss of esteem, ridicule, and offense to others if they deviated from the "will of the group" as announced by the group leader. The leader in turn had to divine intellectually and emotionally, "with his belly," what the group needed and wanted as a group (Kerlinger, 1951). The description is still valid for modern Japan.

Coch and French (1948) had found a marked increase in productivity on the part of American work groups who were permitted to participate in goal-setting decisions affecting them. This was in contrast to findings with control groups not permitted to participate. But the same experiment failed with Norwegian factory workers because Norwegian workers, lower in autonomy needs, did not see participation as legitimate to the extent that American workers did (French, Israel & Ås, 1960). Again, in Puerto Rico, when the manager of a new Harwood Manufacturing plant began to encourage employee participation in problem-solving meetings, turnover increased sharply. It was found that the workers had decided that if management was so ignorant of the answers to its problems that it had to consult employees, the company was poorly managed and was unlikely to survive (Marrow, 1964). In the same way, Israeli sailors were more satisfied with expected legitimate directive leadership than with participative leadership (Foa, 1953).

Bass and Franke (1972) administered the Organizational Success Questionnaire to 1,064 university students from six countries in their native languages. The students were applying for summer jobs in other countries. Student nationality strongly influenced how the students from the six countries varied in their endorsement of participative and political, manipulative approaches to success in getting ahead in management.

The participative responses as a whole correlated .89 for the six countries with Haire, Ghiselli, and Porter's (1966) manager's preferences for sharing information and objectives. Endorsement of participative approaches for the six countries correlated .77 with the countries' national wealth as measured by GNP per capita.

But nationalities varied in specific endorsements. As seen in Table 32.4, for example, the Germans were highest in endorsing openly committing themselves, but they were lowest in finding it important to share in decision making.

*Relations-Oriented and Task-Oriented Leadership.* Considerable agreement across countries was reported by Blake and Mouton (1970) in what managers regard as ideal. Among almost 2,500 managers during GRID seminars from the United States, South Africa, Canada, Australia, the Middle East, and South America, most agreed that the "9–9" management style (maximal concern with both production and people) was the ideal for their company. But much of the uniformity across countries could be

**TABLE 32.4**
**Responses of 1,009 Students to the Organizational Success Questionnaire**

Leadership Style

*Participative*

| Foster mutual trust (grand M = 4.68) | | Arrange group discussion (grand M = 3.71) | | Establish mutual objectives (grand M = 4.31) | |
|---|---|---|---|---|---|
| Sweden | 4.84 | France | 3.95 | United States | 4.58 |
| Netherlands | 4.81 | Britain | 3.74 | France | 4.31 |
| United States | 4.78 | United States | 3.67 | Sweden | 4.29 |
| West Germany | 4.69 | Sweden | 3.62 | Britain | 4.26 |
| France | 4.66 | West Germany | 3.43 | West Germany | 4.20 |
| Britain | 4.54 | Netherlands | 3.27 | Netherlands | 4.13 |

| Share in decision making (grand M = 3.60) | | Level with others (grand M = 4.14) | | Openly commit oneself (grand M = 3.28) | |
|---|---|---|---|---|---|
| France | 3.88 | Sweden | 4.42 | West Germany | 3.93 |
| Sweden | 3.88 | France | 4.36 | Sweden | 3.63 |
| Britain | 3.46 | West Germany | 4.25 | France | 3.55 |
| United States | 3.44 | United States | 4.13 | United States | 3.16 |
| Netherlands | 3.33 | Britain | 3.86 | Netherlands | 3.00 |
| West Germany | 3.30 | Netherlands | 3.50 | Britain | 2.56 |

*Manipulative*

| Maintain social distance (grand M = 1.48) | | Withhold information (grand M = 2.83) | | Compromise but delay (grand M = 0.91) | |
|---|---|---|---|---|---|
| Netherlands | 2.47 | Britain | 3.42 | West Germany | 1.11 |
| Britain | 1.56 | United States | 3.17 | France | 0.99 |
| France | 1.50 | Netherlands | 2.80 | Britain | 0.98 |
| United States | 1.40 | West Germany | 2.74 | Netherlands | 0.81 |
| West Germany | 1.21 | France | 2.41 | United States | 0.69 |
| Sweden` | 1.09 | Sweden | 2.34 | Sweden | 0.62 |

| Make political alliances (grand M = 2.61) | | Initiate but retard actions (grand M = 0.56) | | Bluff (grand M = 2.50) | |
|---|---|---|---|---|---|
| France | 3.81 | Netherlands | 0.77 | Netherlands | 3.48 |
| Sweden | 2.92 | France | 0.69 | Sweden | 3.02 |
| West Germany | 2.55 | Britain | 0.57 | Britain | 2.63 |
| Netherlands | 1.97 | West Germany | 0.50 | France | 2.33 |
| Britain | 1.70 | United States | 0.43 | West Germany | 2.25 |
| United States | 1.67 | Sweden | 0.18 | United States | 2.19 |

NOTE: Items are listed in order of general endorsement.
SOURCE: Adapted from Bass & Franke, 1972, p. 315. Copyright © 1972 by the American Psychological Association. Reprinted by permission.

attributed to course indoctrination. When they described their own actual behavior, managers from Japan and South America reported more concern for production than for people.

In Bass, Burger, et al.'s (1979) twelve-nation data for Exercise Self-Appraisal, Italian managers saw themselves as most concerned about their subordinates and the Spanish and Portuguese actually were highest in such preference to be so concerned. Lowest in felt need to be concerned for subordinates were the Japanese. Lowest in preference to be concerned were the Germans and Austrians. Actual task orientation (rather than human relations concerns) was self-appraised as highest among the Germans and Austrians. The Dutch managers tended toward the human relations approach. Preference for a human relations orientation was highest as well for Dutch managers, while preference for task orientation was highest among the Japanese.

Gopala and Hafeez (1964) reported for an Indian sample of superiors that high educational attainment was associated with favorable attitudes toward employees, while lack of education was associated with a production orientation.

*Initiation versus Consideration.* In the Bass, Burger, et al. (1979) twelve-nation data for Exercise Supervise, there was an overall trend to see the need for more consideration, the lower the manager's organizational level. But the French regarded being considerate as relatively unimportant at all levels of management as did Latin Americans; the Germans and Austrians thought it highly important for lower, middle, and top management. Consideration was emphasized by fast-rising managers as compared to slow-climbing managers in Italy, Spain, Portugal, and the United States; it was deemphasized in Belgium, Scandinavia, France, Latin America, and India.

Matsui, Ohtsuka, and Kikuchi (1978) were able to replicate and extend Fleishman and Peters (1962) U. S. results with seventy-nine Japanese supervisors, finding that considerate supervisors (as seen by their subordinates on the SBDQ) were higher in benevolence on L. V. Gordon's Survey of Interpersonal Values. Initiation of structure was lower if supervisors were higher in valuing independence.

L. R. Anderson (1966) studied discussion groups composed of American and Indian graduate students. The leader's effectiveness as rated by American students was positively correlated to both consideration and structure. But ratings of the leader's effectiveness by Indian students were correlated to the leader's consideration scores only.

Culture may affect the psychometric properties involved in measuring attitudes toward initiation and consideration. K. F. Mauer (1974) administered the leadership opinion questionnaire to a sample of 190 mine overseers and shift bosses in the South African gold mining industry. Neither a varimax rotation nor an orthogonal target rotation of the two extracted factors approximated the findings of U. S. and Canadian researchers. An oblique target rotation produced the closest, although relatively unsatisfactory, solution. The correlation between the factors was much higher than that found in other studies.

*Active versus Laissez-Faire Leadership.* Despite the existence of workers' councils and institutionalized industrial democracy in Yugoslavia, Rus (1970) confirmed the findings of A. S. Tannenbaum (1968) in the United States that both managers and workers have similar perceptions of the distribution of influence in an organization.

In the Exercise Self-Appraisal data of Bass, Burger, et al. (1979), self-appraised actual ability to influence was highest among the Dutch and lowest among the French.

Preference for such ability to influence was highest among the Japanese, U. S., German, and Indian managers. Lowest in such preferences were the Dutch and French.

Endorsement of active intervention in contrast to laissez-faire behavior was seen by Bass and Franke (1972) to relate to a country's economic growth rate. They obtained a correlation of .93 in the ranking of six industralized countries between the rate of economic growth of the country for nine preceding years and the extent to which students from those countries endorsed both participative and political approaches to career success in management.

In Spain, Filella (1971) factor-analyzed 77 managers' self-descriptions and their subordinates' descriptions of the managers' directive, negotiative, consultative, participative, and delegative behavior as measured by the Bass and Valenzi Management Styles Questionnaire (Chapter 19) along with Reddin's managers' self-descriptions on eight types such as missionary, deserter, and so on (Chapter 3). Consistent with earlier findings about the relative lack of validity of managers' self-described leader behavior, a strong first factor of subordinates' descriptions of Bass-Valenzi styles emerged, but none of the Reddin self-descriptions were loaded on it. Consistent with what was concluded in Chapter 22, all five subordinate-rated styles loaded .80 to .93 on this first general leadership activity factor. The remaining factors dealt exclusively with the managers' self-perceptions (which were totally unrelated to the subordinates' descriptions of the manager). Whereas managers saw themselves as high or low on a variety of Reddin's types, subordinates only saw managers who were more or less generally active as leaders.

## LEADERSHIP IN THE MULTINATIONAL FIRM

Little has been reported about the specific leader–subordinate relations among supervisors and subordinates who differ in nationality. They may be operating together at parent country headquarters, in a host country, or a third country. Either leader or subordinate may be a parent country national (PCN), host country national (HCN) or third country national (TCN).

Of considerable importance to the leader–subordinate relationships is the firm's organization and methods of decision making. Perlmutter (1969) saw three possibilities that were likely to have an impact on PCN, HCN and TCN leadership relations.

- Ethnocentric: The home country is superior to the foreign organization in all respects and all decisions and methods will be controlled by the home country. PCNs monopolize the power and status.
- Polycentric: The organization is host country-oriented since foreign cultures are different and local people are able to make the best decisions about the firm's progress. HCNs are more equal in power to PCNs.
- Geocentric: The organization is world-oriented and a balanced view is taken of the local national interests and the objectives of the multinational firm. Managerial positions are filled by people having the most talent regardless of national background. TCNs have as much status and power as PCNs or HCNs.

According to Perlmutter, as a multinational organization matures, it moves from ethnocentric to geocentric organizational patterns. Presumably, cultural origins become less significant in the decision-making process with increasing maturity.

### Differences in Satisfaction

Illustrative of the significance of identity as an PCN, HCN, or TCN was a job satisfaction survey completed by Peter (1969) for Shell, a British-Dutch multinational. Non-Europeans were much more dissatisfied with the company's image than were Europeans. Moreover, among all nationals, the British and Dutch were relatively most satisfied with the company as a place to work and with opportunities to obtain responsibility and authority.

### PCN Emphasis on Uniformity

According to Zeira (1975) who interviewed 248 HCNs and parent country headquarters personnel management, PCNs and TCNs tended to impose parent country headquarters' managerial patterns on their host country peers and subordinates. According to the headquarters' personnel directors, multinational uniformity facilitated comparisons of managers in subsidiaries in different countries and their career advancement. Uniformity was also thought to keep up the firm's reputation in different countries and make it easier to introduce policy changes. HCNs disagreed. A majority felt that PCNs maintained uniformity of policies and practices for their own self-interests. HCNs believed that PCNs (and TCNs) at higher management levels in the local subsidiaries were unmotivated to make local improvements and to meet local needs. PCNs were seen to be insensitive to expectations of local HCNs resulting in many conflicts. HCNs were particularly critical of the tendency of multinational firms to centralize decisions, making it impossible to adapt to the needs of the local marketplace. HCNs mistrusted their PCN superiors and felt that promotion to higher level was prevented by their not being nationals of the parent country.

Because the PCNs were representatives of their multinational corporations, they could achieve entry into the upper class social life of the local communities beyond what they could reach in their previous positions at international headquarters at home. PCNs obtained special benefits as part of their compensation abroad, which made it possible for them to enjoy a standard of living considerably higher than that of their local peers and higher than what they could expect upon their return home to headquarters.

### Reasons for PCN Failure

A survey of 105 U. S. multinational firms by Tung (n.d.) suggested that the most important reasons for a PCN's failure to function effectively in a foreign environment were: (1) the inability of the manager's spouse to adjust to a different physical or cultural environment and other family-related problems; (2) the manager's inability to adapt to a different physical or cultural environment; (3) lack of emotional maturity; (4) inability to cope with the larger responsibilities posed by the overseas work; (5) lack of technical competence for the job assignment; and (6) lack of motivation to work overseas. Lack of company attention to proper selection and training were particularly important sources of failure. Ratings of the reported rigor of selection, training, and preparation of personnel for overseas assignments correlated $-.63$ with failure rates reported by the 105 firms.

*Staffing with HCNs*

More HCNs are used in developed countries than in developing countries where qualified HCNs are less readily available. Nevertheless, when efforts are made to locate, select, and train HCNs, dramatic increases can be achieved in the percent of HCN managers in a developing country as was illustrated by Nestlé, the Swiss multinational firm, in its Ivory Coast subsidiary (Salmons, 1977).

Multinational firms can attract potentially more productive and accommodating types of HCNs into their ranks than comparable domestic firms. For example, Vansina and Taillieu (1970) showed that highly task-oriented Flemish business school graduates preferred to work for American or German companies rather than for their own Belgian organizations.

Other reasons for staffing with HCNs include: familiarity with culture, knowledge of language, reduced costs, and good public relations. TCNs are most likely to be used as a consequence of their competence and technical expertise. PCNs, likewise, are selected for technical competence and are more likely to be used when starting up a foreign enterprise. Whether PCNs, TCNs, or HCNs are successful is likely to depend on their training and development, the subject of the next chapter.

part

# APPLICATIONS AND IMPLICATIONS

# 33

## LEADERSHIP TRAINING AND MANAGEMENT DEVELOPMENT

### INTRODUCTION

The leaders and administrative officials of the British Empire at its zenith received from their public schools a general education in self-discipline, team work, and group loyalty, which created an aura of command and habits of superiority with "a façade of crisp decisiveness." Their classical education included nothing about modern science, technology, modern languages, or the social sciences. Little attention was paid to innovation and creativity, but a skill and capacity for social role-taking coupled with a sense of self-esteem and a need for achievement were sufficient to make for reasonably effective leaders and officials for the world arena (J. M. Burns, 1978). As has been mentioned in the preceding chapter, D. P. Boyd (1974) indicated that most British leaders still originate from the public schools. The question remains, have we developed better specific methods for leadership training? This chapter is a review of leadership training and management development procedures and their research evaluation.

### Training in the Context of Development

Training for leadership occurs in the context of the current stage of development in which the leader is found. Based on analogies from developmental learning over the adult life cycle, Bryson and Kelley (1978) suggested that leaders go through stages. A developmental learning process occurs in which capacities and skills gained in one stage prepare the leader for new and bigger tasks and responsibilities in later stages. One learns to be a leader by serving as a leader, and one is promoted to higher levels of leadership responsibilities based on past performance and promise of future performance.

*A Life-Long Process.* As J. M. Burns (1978) has noted, to understand the leadership performance of great persons such as Woodrow Wilson, one needs not only to examine their early childhood development but also to analyze the social and political challenges encountered in middle and later life and to see how such experiences provided opportunities for further increases in political maturity.

*Locales.* Learning and opportunities to serve at higher levels of responsibility are facilitated by training. Training for leadership has been widely used in industry, the armed services, and public and private service agencies. The earliest reports of leadership training in industry and the armed services were concerned primarily with state-

553

ments regarding the need for and value of training, descriptions of programs, and discussions of problems (W. T. Foster, 1929; Greenly & Mapel, 1943; R. S. Miller, 1943; Dietz, 1943; MacKechnie, 1944; and McFeely & Mussmann, 1945). The outpouring of such statements continues unabated in the *Training and Development Journal,* the *European Journal of Training Personnel,* and so on. But it was among the educators that actual research on training for leadership was first reported.

### Early Research on Training for Leadership

The earliest research on training for leadership appeared in primary and secondary school settings (E. L. Thorndike, 1916; G. C. Meyers, 1923; E. W. Hastings, 1926; Crouch, 1926; A. M. Nash, 1927; Lavoy, 1928). For example, Fretwell (1919) gave elected leaders in junior high school responsibility for managing athletic and playground activities. A leadership club was formed to plan and discuss activities. Fretwell concluded that the experience provided opportunity for leadership and initiative. In the same way, Mayberry (1925) concluded that participation in student government provided training in social purpose, initiative, and cooperation.

*Controlled Experiments.* Eichler and Merrill (1933) asked each member of high school classes to rate each other on leadership. Experimental and control groups were paired on the basis of the ratings. Experimental groups were given lectures on leadership methods or participated in discussions about leadership. New ratings were collected. The experimental groups gained more than the control groups in such ratings of leadership, but not to a significant degree. G. G. Thompson (1944) studied nursery school children under two programs. In one, the teacher acted in an impersonal manner and gave help only when needed. In the second, the teacher took an active part in play and helped children in their adjustment to each other. Children in the second group showed significant gains in ascendance, social participation, and leadership.

McCandless (1942) studied two cottages of boys in a training school. Both began with adult supervisors, but the experimental cottage became self-governing. Sociometric ratings of intermember popularity were highly correlated with dominance at the beginning. Four months later, the most dominant boys lost in popularity in the experimental cottage, but not in the control cottage.

Zeleny (1940b) compared recitation and group discussion as methods of teaching sociology. Students in the discussion classes gained more in dominance and sociability than those in the recitation classes and also recorded slightly higher gains in knowledge of the subject. Again, Zeleny (1941, 1950) gave student leaders instruction in techniques of leadership and guided practice in the use of these techniques. Students found the training interesting and felt that it helped them adapt better to the social demands made upon them. This early research thus focused on the leadership training process.

### PROCESSES EMPLOYED

For convenience, we will first concentrate on the processes and techniques applied to training for leadership; then we will consider the contents and purposes of such training.

Training for leadership in any organizational context can be provided in many different ways. Individuals may receive training on or near their job. They may be coached by their immediate superior. They may be given guided job experience on a planned basis. They may train as an understudy, "assistant to" a higher position. They may serve a formal management apprenticeship or leadership internship. They may rotate through a variety of jobs by planned transfers. They may be placed in a special trainee position or be given special project assignments.

Off-the-job leadership training can be obtained by participation in trade and professional associations and civic projects and from formal classrooms or workshops. Within these, didactic and experiential training may be given by lecture, case or problem discussion groups, and role playing. Simulation using "in baskets" and games are also popular. Computer-assisted instruction and programmed instruction are also being employed along with less structured sensitivity training. Stimulated by social learning theory, behavior role modeling which integrates didactic with experiential techniques has become increasingly popular.

On the job, coaching, job rotation, apprenticeships, process consultation, and survey feedback are employed.

### Lectures and Discussion

Among available methods to be examined here, lectures are the least popular with training directors (Carroll, Paine & Ivancevich, 1972). Discussion groups are relied on heavily in most leadership training programs even when many lecture, film and other didactic presentations are used. Lectures (or their surrogates—films, videotapes, and TV) can arouse audiences, provide information, and stimulate thinking. But most comparisons of lecture versus discussion approaches to instructing leaders to change their ways of behaving (for example, Levine & Butler, 1952) suggest that discussion of issues in small groups is likely to be more effective, particularly if attitudes must be changed before the new ways will be accepted and adopted by the trainees.

According to L. A. Allen (1957), discussion provides experience in working with others to reach decisions. The experience can promote the potential leadership of the members by preparing them to use the group discussion as a means for reaching effective decisions. Again, Riegel (1952) suggested that case discussions, in particular, can provide experience in objective ways of thinking about common leadership problems. The need to study issues in terms of possible causes and effects is emphasized. Trainees exchange and evaluate each other's solutions to such problems. They develop an awareness of the need for more than single, simple answers to complex problems.

*Some Positive Findings.* Maier (1953), among others, demonstrated the effectiveness of training using problem-solving discussions. He compared the performance of 176 trained supervisors with 144 untrained ones. The supervisors with eight hours of training in group decision making were found more likely to bring about acceptance of change in their groups. Argyris (1965) used lectures and case discussions in the laboratory training of senior executives. No significant change followed the lectures but some measures of skill in interpersonal relations improved after the case discussions.

Discussions may be ineffective poolings of ignorance or they can be adequately stimulated, directed, and provided with resources to promote learning. Mann and Mann (1959c) compared the effects of free discussion groups and task-directed groups on behavior as described by members. Task-directed discussion groups changed significantly more than free discussion groups in friendliness, desirability as a friend, leadership, avoiding goal attainment, cooperativeness, and general adjustment.

*No Differences Found.* Despite expectations favoring discussion over lecture, numerous reports of failure to confirm expectations have been reported. For instance, DiVesta (1954) compared lectures and group discussions as vehicles for training in human relations. They were found equally effective. However, the discussion groups did show slight gains in favorable attitudes toward initiating structure. Again, Mahoney, Jerdee, and Korman (1960) compared case analysis, group discussion, and lectures as methods for training in management development. No significant difference between methods was found. All groups gained in a test of knowledge, probably as a result of practice.

*Both Discussion and Lecture Can Be Useful.* Experiments have focused on the wrong issue. Discussion and lecture are suitable for different objectives, different situations, and different personnel. As a result of a research survey on leader training, Filley and Jessee (1965) developed a set of hypotheses suggesting conditions under which more didactic, trainer-oriented training and more discussionlike, trainee-oriented training will be effective. This will be seen later in this chapter.

House (1965) studied attitudes of forty-three managers toward trainee-oriented and trainer-oriented training. More than half (twenty-four) preferred a combination of the two methods, while twelve preferred trainee-oriented and seven preferred trainer-oriented training. Thus discussion can reinforce lectures. Discussion is useful when a lecture needs clarification and amplification. Learning from a lecture or film is facilitated if they are followed by small ''buzz groups'' to share opinions, raise questions, and consider alternatives. Buzz group conclusions can be shared with other groups and the trainer. This promotion of two-way communication increases motivation of trainees and enables them to test their understandings.

### Role Playing

Various behavior adjustment methods developed by psychiatrists and social and clinical psychologists were adapted to the training of leaders. Psychodrama and sociodrama (Lippitt, 1943a; Moreno, 1955; Lippitt, Bradford & Benne, 1947) require participants (alone or with other actors) to act out various leadership problems under different conditions of audience participation in discussion. Role playing requires one member to play the role of leader and other members to play follower roles (J. R. P. French, 1944b; Symonds, 1947; Zander, 1947; Wolozin, 1948; Speroff, 1957; A. F. Klein, 1956; Corsini, Shaw & Blake, 1961). ''Acting out'' solutions to problems without a script was thought to promote transference from learning situations to leadership performance on the job. Bradford and Lippitt (1952) suggested that interpersonal skills may be hard to teach by only providing verbal or intellectual reasons for behaving in a certain way without actually helping to produce the ability to behave in the desired way. Didactic approaches by themselves may reduce rather than increase successful leadership by resulting in frustration and anxiety.

Many uses were seen possible from role playing. Trainees might practice what they eventually had to do. Role playing might serve as a diagnostic technique. Group discussion following the role playing might focus on examining specific interchanges experienced in the role plays. Different ways of solving problems could be tested by role players. Other trainees could gain vicariously from observing the success or failure of various attempts during role plays. Role players could learn from feedback about their leadership effectiveness during the role plays. Standards could be set for handling specific situations (J. R. P. French, 1944b; Stahl, 1953, 1954). Having to verbalize a position would promote shifting toward that new point. Hence, role reversal might be useful.

*Role Reversal.* When supervisors appear unable to appreciate the views of subordinates, they may be asked to play the role of a subordinate while someone else plays supervisor. Supervisors in such role reversals may gain insight into what is affecting their subordinates (Bradford & Lippitt, 1952; Speroff, 1954).

*Multiple Role Playing.* An audience is divided into small teams, each member of which receives instructions to play a particular role. Following the role plays within each team, the audience reassembles and shares experiences (Maier & Zerfoss, 1952). The different teams can be given different instructions, so the effects of these differences on what occurs during the interactions among the players is revealed during the critique by the audience reassembled as a whole.

*Availability.* Role plays can be packaged for self-administration. For example, PAXIT (Shackleton, Bass & Allison, 1975) provides participants with experience and results comparing the five leadership styles: directive, negotiative, consultative, participative, and delegative presented in Chapter 19. Corsini, Shaw, and Blake (1961) have surveyed the various role-playing methods including an annotated bibliography of 102 references.

*Positive Findings.* As was expected, Lonergan (1958) and Lawshe, Brune, and Bolda (1958) observed that participants in role playing tended to regard it as beneficial in increasing their understanding of human relations problems. Furthermore, the latter found that about twice as many participants preferred the leader role to the follower role. Similarly, Mann and Mann (1959a,b) demonstrated that experience in role playing improved role-playing ability as judged by self, other role players, and observers. They compared ratings of participant behavior under role playing and group discussion. Students improved more in interpersonal adjustment after role playing than after group discussion.

Role playing appears to add to leadership skills in dealing with human relations problems. For example, Solem (1960) arranged for small teams drawn from 440 supervisors to meet either in twenty-two case discussion groups or in 23 multiple role-playing exercises. They discussed or role-played one of two problems, one concerning the assignment of a new truck to a crew of utility repairmen and the other about how to change a work procedure. When role playing, one participant took the part of the crew foreman and one of the repairmen. In the case discussion, they just talked about solutions to the problem. A change-of-work-procedure problem was handled similarly. Among the role-playing teams, 46 percent developed integrated, new solutions to the problems. That is, instead of assigning a new truck to the man with the oldest truck, they replaced the oldest truck but enabled each crewman to switch to a newer truck. But only 15 percent of the case discussants did likewise.

*Contingencies.* The positive effects of role playing tend to depend on a variety of circumstances. Thus, for instance, Lawshe, Bolda, and Brune (1959) studied five groups under different conditions of feedback. They found that role playing and subsequent discussion increased sensitivity and employee orientation when participants were required to criticize their own performance and when the human relations point of view was presented to them in a strong, emotional manner. Again, Harvey and Beverly (1961) found that role playing had a significant positive effect on opinion change, but authoritarian participants gained more from role playing than did those low in such authoritarianism. However, Elms and Janis (1965) found a high degree of counternorm attitude acceptance occurring only under conditions of overt role playing (as opposed to nonovert role playing) and large monetary reward (as opposed to little reward). Trittipoe and Hahn (1961) studied participants in role-playing groups and problem-solving groups. Both observers and followers rated participants higher in role playing *if* they were also rated higher in problem solving. In turn, those rated higher in both were rated higher in leadership and class standing.

*Negative Results.*    Some experiments less favorable to role playing also were completed. Mann and Mann (1960) compared role playing and task-oriented group experience. Contrary to hypothesis, participants in the task-oriented problem-solving groups changed more in leadership and general adjustment than those in the role-playing groups. In addition, Hanson, Morton, and Rothaus (1963) found that role-playing situations involving evaluation of followers' personality traits induced a critical posture in the leader and a submissive role for followers, whereas working on a problem in goal setting and planning permitted followers to play a more active role. In a study of 200 officer trainees, Tupes, Carp, and Borg (1958) found that role-playing scores were not related to ratings of leadership effectiveness but to personality scores.

*Role Playing Combined with Videotaping.*    Videotape feedback of role plays has become commonplace in leadership training. Illustrative of the use of videotape replay was a training program of American overseas advisers. They viewed a videotape of their interactions with an actor trained to play the role of a foreigner. The trainees' performance was critiqued as they watched the tape. Learning was more effective and was retained longer in comparison to a control group which only read the training manual about the same issues (P. H. King, 1966).

### Simulation

Other facsimiles of the real leadership situation are created by means of the inbasket technique and by games.

*In-Baskets.*    Participants are given a booklet that essentially reproduces the contents of a manager's in-basket along with some general information about the organization in which they are located. They must decide what actions to take to dispose of the items before leaving on a trip (Frederiksen, 1962). Good performance is associated with a good sense of priorities, planning ahead, and appropriate use of available information (Zoll, 1969). Butler and Keys (1973) reported comparisons between thirty-three first-line supervisors taking a course on the traditional fundamentals of supervision and thirty supervisors who carried out a series of group discussions based on responses to the in-basket items. The "fundamentals" groups showed no significant improvement in tested knowledge on "How Supervise" (File & Remmers, 1971) or the Supervisory

Inventory on Human Relations (Kirkpatrick, 1954). But the in-basket discussion group improved significantly on both instruments. Commensurate with the significant knowledge gains registered by the "in-basket" participants, the responses from their subordinates back on the job over a two-month period indicated significant changes in their perceptions of their supervisor's behavior, particularly on "people orientation" and innovation on Marvin's (1968) Management Matrix. Little or no such change was found for those given the traditional course on principles of leadership.

*Games.* Organizational, institutional, and business games are living cases. Trainees must make sequential decisions and then live with them (Leavitt & Bass, 1964). Outcomes from leadership performance have fairly rapid consequences. Success and failure are more fully objective and observable than is true for role playing in general. Over 30,000 executives had participated in one or more of the hundred-or-so business games that appeared in the first five years following the introduction in 1956 by the American Management Association of its Top Management Decision Simulation (L. Stewart, 1962). This prototype business game and most of its successors confront teams of players with sets of decisions requiring them to decide at each successive play how much to budget for raw materials, plant, equipment, advertising, research, and labor. Players usually need to make decisions on what prices to set for their products, whether to borrow money, to build plants, and negotiate with suppliers and union officials. When the game is used for leader training, teams may compete against each other or against a computer model.

Organizational games such as UPPOE, described by Bass (1964), create leadership problems. Player-managers must literally obtain the cooperation of player-workers to produce for a "market" paper products made by cutting, assembling, and stapling. Players can be hired and fired; they can speed up, slow down, or strike. Tangible products and raw materials are processed, bought, and sold.

Despite their widespread use, evaluations are hard to come by, although Raia (1966) has shown that a business game, simple or complex, can add more to performance on a final exam about case problems than discussions and readings about the cases.

### Computer-Assisted and Programmed Instruction

Hausser, Blaiwes, Weller, and Spencer (1976) described computer-assisted instruction (CAI) in teaching interpersonal skills to U.S. Navy commanders. With the PLATO system and an instructional programming language, TUTOR, Hausser and Spencer (1975) applied CAI to interpersonal skill training in feedback, communication, goal setting, problem solving, decision making, effective rewards and punishments, and the use of power and authority. Compared to controls who received the same pre- and posttest assessments and were involved in the same duties as recruiting officers, considerably greater skill learning was obtained with CAI. Costs of CAI remain high so that despite its potential, applications to leadership training may continue to be limited.

Videotapes and films can be included as part of computer-regulated programs and their advantages can be incorporated in training.

*Programmed Instruction.* Some effort has been made to use Programmed Instruction (PI) to teach effective human relations. For example, the American Management Association has sponsored PRIME, a programmed textbook for training supervisors. "Cultural assimilators," programmed texts, have been developed and evaluated for their effectiveness in teaching for leadership training and good human relations across cultures (Fiedler, 1968). However, it is quite difficult to write an effective program if what is to be taught involves shadings of opinion, sensitivity to fuzzy socioemotional issues, and unclear ideas as to the order of steps in which learning can take place (Bass & Barrett, 1981).

Nevertheless, Hynes, Feldhusen, and Richardson (1978) found in a controlled experimental study of a three-stage program to train high school students to be better leaders that PI coupled with lectures in the first stage yielded improvements in understanding and attitudes whereas experiential approaches in the second and third stages failed to do so.

### Sensitivity Training

It was at a social workers' conference on leadership in 1946 that Kurt Lewin and his M.I.T. graduate students stumbled into sensitivity training serendipitously. Conferees found the students' observations about the interpersonal processes they saw occurring more valuable than the formal leadership subjects they had been discussing. The idea took root that all participants in discussion groups could become observers and that the sharing of their observations would provide insight into leadership processes in general as well as into specific individual learning about one's adequacy in interaction with others. The learning process was facilitated by eliminating the formal agenda prior to the beginning of a group's convening (Bradford, Gibb & Benne, 1964). The social vacuum that was created as a consequence increased the individual members' differential abilities and willingness to attempt to initiate structure, which was not provided by the group trainer who on the surface at least abdicated from the leadership role. The situation gave participants the opportunity to try out new ways of carrying out various leadership functions and task and maintenance activities of use to the group. The feedback from the other participant-observers reinforced those new attempts that worked well and indicated the inadequacy of other less successful attempts to lead. For this reason, the situation was seen as a "laboratory," a place for experimenting. Trainers establish themselves as ambiguous authority figures, provide group members with information needed for analysis of group processes, and encourage participation and openness. Trainers do not structure group discussion but instead throw the entire burden of initiative upon group members. Feedback sessions are used to suggest that the demand for trainer direction and structure acts to inhibit the examination of group process and the development of insight into role relationships.

*Theory.* Theoretical supports are diverse. They include analytic theory, Bion's (1948, 1961) fight or flight analyses, Lewin's (1939) topological existentialism, Moreno's (1955) sociopsychological focus, Berne's (1964) transactional analysis, Perls's (1969) Gestalt therapy, and Maslow's (1965) humanistic psychology.

*Variants.* Numerous variants have been developed. Sensitivity training, using T (for training) groups itself during the 1950s and onward, focused on interpersonal learning. The encounter group which arose in the 1960s was designed to provide a more intensive experience in openness, self-examination of hostilities, defenses, and feelings, self-awareness, and personal growth.

Training may begin with a task and structure, then gradually become less structured. A marathon nonstop training weekend may be used. Two or more trainers meeting with a much larger-than-ordinary cluster group may be employed. Many organizations have developed their own unique programs, incorporating some aspects of the sensitivity training laboratory (Morton & Bass, 1964).

*Objectives.* The numerous variants of the sensitivity training program all attempt to accomplish one or more of the following changes in attitude or behavior on the part of the trainee leaders: (1) greater sensitivity to follower needs and desires; (2) greater openness and sharing of information; (3) greater sharing of decision-making responsibilities with followers; (4) more intimate, friendly, and equalitarian interaction with followers; and (5) less structuring, personal dominance, and pushing for productive output. Most of the research concerned with the effects of sensitivity training has attempted to determine whether such change has occurred.

*Changes in Trainee's Attitudes.* A majority of studies completed indicate that sensitivity training results in significant change in interpersonal attitudes. Change is in the direction of a more favorable attitude toward subordinates, a stronger human relations orientation, and greater awareness of interpersonal dynamics. For example, Bunker and Knowles (1967) and P. B. Smith (1964, 1975) reported significant attitude changes in participants as a consequence of laboratory training. Schutz and Allen (1966) found that compared to controls the effects of laboratory training resulted in more change in attitudes and personality. Tests administered before and six months after training indicated change in response to other people, feelings about others, behavior and feeling toward self, and perceptions of others' behavior and feelings toward self. The participants indicated greater friendliness, sensitivity, and tolerance toward others after training.

Golembiewski and Carrigan (1970) conducted a mild reinforcement session one year after the initial sensitivity training of managers. Attitude change persisted over a period of eighteen months for the group with reinforcement. But Belasco and Trice (1969b) reported that such changes associated with training were small. Training combined with testing was more effective than training alone in producing change. The most significant changes were in morale, self-concept, and role expectations.

Asquith and Hedlund (1967) administered a before and after questionnaire to twenty management trainees in a chemical firm. Improvement in attitudes was obtained in the scale for human relations practices, but the participants exhibited no significant change in attitude toward consideration, initiating structure, supervision, or management. Blake and Mouton (1966) studied managers and union officers from the same plant. Training in the Managerial Grid resulted in significant attitude improvement for both groups. But H. B. Stephenson (1966), Biggs, Huneryager, and Delaney (1966) and Asquith and Hedlund (1967) all obtained results indicating that laboratory training produced no significant changes in attitude toward leader behaviors as measured by such instruments as the LOQ (Chapter 21). Similarly, Kernan (1963) obtained before and after responses to attitude and personality items from two experimental groups and a control group. No significant changes in attitude or personality were found for the T-groups or the control group.

*Changes in Trainee Perceptions.* In line with the primary objectives calling for training to increase perceptual sensitivity, a content analysis by R. H. Solomon (1976a) found leaders' statements of the effects of undergraduate laboratory training to include increased personal awareness, along with improved interpersonal relations, and improvements as well as frustrations in their leadership skills. Bass (1962b) asked training group members to record their self-perceived moods at five different intervals during sensitivity training. Skepticism decreased. Concentration and depression increased for awhile, then leveled off. But anxiety did not increase as expected.

Several studies have been concerned with changes in self-concept and in perception of others. T. Gordon (1955) found that leader trainees tended to describe their behavior in terms very similar to their conception of an ideal leader. Laboratory training produced change toward greater conformity with ideal behavior. Burke and Bennis (1961) reported that perceptions of actual self and ideal self were closer at the end than at the beginning of training. Perceptions of self and others tended to converge. According to French, Sherwood, and Bradford (1966), the individual's perception of his or her self-identity is changed by sensitivity training. Bass (1962a) found significant increases in perceptual sensitivity to interpersonal relations after training. Sensitivity was positively related to peer ratings of influence in the group. But Greiner, Leitch, and Barnes (1968) were unable to demonstrate that training in the Managerial Grid (instrumented sensitivity training to be described later) produced significant change in trainee perceptions of behavior. Likewise, Kassarjian (1965) reported no significant change in orientation toward self or others as a result of sensitivity training.

*Changes in Trainee Behavior.* Typical of improvements reported were those found when each participant's supervisor, two of his peers, and two of his subordinates were interviewed in the sixth week and again in the sixth month following training by Boyd and Ellis (1962) at the Hydroelectric Power Commission of Ontario. Controls were also interviewed in the same manner. Improvements were noted in 64 percent of the sensitivity trainees and only 23 percent of the controls. The trainees changed more than the controls in increased listening, better interpersonal understanding, better contributions at meetings, increased tolerance and flexibility, and, to a lesser extent, in self-confidence and effective expression. Similarly, Bunker (1965) questioned trainees and their coworkers one year after participation in a laboratory training program. Participants were reported by coworkers to have gained significantly more than a control group in interpersonal skills, openness, and understanding of social relationships. Again, Morton and Bass (1964) studied ninety-seven managers who listed more than 350 incidents of behavior change during the six months following a laboratory in management development. The most frequently mentioned changes dealt with improved working relationships and self-understanding. M. B. Miles (1965) reported data indicating that training resulted in unfreezing of participation and greater receptivity to feedback, but earlier M. B. Miles (1960) had been unable to establish any associated change in consideration and structure. Bechanan and Brunstetter (1958) used T-group methods to train sixty engineers in supervisory positions. Questionnaires were then administered to subordinates of the trained group and a control group. Two-thirds of the trained group were described by subordinates as being more desirable supervisors.

R. Harrison (1962) asked participants in laboratory training to describe themselves and ten associates before and after training. The trained group increased the number of interpersonal and emotional words used to describe themselves but not to describe others. Three months after training, R. Harrison (1966) found that 115 laboratory trainees used more terms describing awareness of interpersonal relations and fewer terms expressing manipulation of behavior. In similar fashion, Oshry and Harrison (1966) administered before and after tests to middle managers. The items in which changes occurred suggested that after training the managers saw themselves as more human and less impersonal, saw a closer connection between meeting personal needs and getting work done, saw themselves as a significant part of the problem, yet saw no connection between their new perceptions and how to translate them into action. These effects were strongest for those participating most intensely in the laboratory training. Harrison and Lubin (1965a) studied person-oriented and work-oriented subjects in homogeneous and heterogeneous training groups. Person-oriented members were rated as behaving more expressively and warmly and as forming stronger ties to their homogeneous group. Contrary to hypothesis, work-oriented members were perceived as learning more than person-oriented members. Members perferring low structure exceeded those preferring high structure in "understanding self" and "understanding others." The high-structure group members felt themselves capable and active in discussion but avoided examination of interpersonal relations.

*Effects on Group and Organizational Performance.* The preceding studies were designed to determine whether sensitivity training results in change in leader attitude or behavior. The most pragmatic criterion of the effect of training, however, is whether or not it results in change in the performance or response of the group supervised by the leaders. Unfortunately, outcomes are multivariate. Thus, Blake, Mouton, and Fruchter (1962) factor-analyzed various measures of quasi T-group outcomes. Group cohesion and group accomplishment were found to load on separate factors. T-groups may increase cohesion at the expense of, say, productivity.

Blake, Mouton, Barnes, and Greiner (1964) studied the management of a large petroleum company engaged in Grid (quasi T-group) training. They concluded that employee productivity increased as a result of management change toward a 9–9 leadership style (Chapter 20). Miles, Milavsky, Lake, and Beckhard (1965) found that sensitivity training resulted in both managerial attitude change and improved departmental productivity. Beckhard (1966) and Kuriloff and Atkins (1966) also attributed improved operating efficiency to the effects of T-group programs. Unfortunately, the controls in these studies were inadequate. The research was conducted during a long economic upswing when, in general, businesses were increasing their profits.

Friedlander (1967) compared four work groups that participated in team training with eight similar groups that did not. The trained groups improved in problem solving, mutual influence, and personal involvement. But there were no significant changes in interpersonal trust, leader approachability, or evaluation of training sessions.

Weschler and Reisel (1959) studied a sensitivity training group over a period of one year. An emotionality index increased steadily through thirty sessions, but group productivity varied from week to week.

*Contraindications.* There is evidence that sensitivity, training groups' subsequent task performance is impaired. Deep, Bass, and Vaughn (1967) studied ninety-three business students assigned to simulated companies to play a business game. Some had undergone sensitivity training as intact groups fifteen weeks earlier. Others came from diverse sensitivity training groups. Intact groups performed significantly more poorly than those composed of separately trained members, but they described themselves as higher in cooperation and openness. Going further, Hellebrandt and Stinson (1971) found that T-group trainees did worse than controls. Stinson (1970) studied five control groups, five groups trained as intact teams, and five composed of members assigned to different training groups. They were equated on the basis of gross profits earned in a prior business game. The fragmented and control groups outperformed the intact groups in gross profit but declined in cohesiveness. The intact groups were high in cohesiveness but low in productivity. Underwood (1965), in a study of fifteen training and fifteen control groups, found that the T-groups changed more than the controls, but training had an adverse effect on productivity.

Mosvick (1971) analyzed ten studies of scientists and engineers, eight using control groups. In four of the latter (Moon & Hariton, 1958; Miner, 1960; Carron, 1964; and Mosvick, 1966), the subjects were trained by lectures and discussion. The other four groups (Buchanan & Brunstetter, 1958; Kernan, 1963; Underwood, 1965; and Asquith & Hedlund, 1967) were given T-group training. Standard methods of training in human relations were found more effective than T-group methods with technically oriented supervisors.

*Transfer of Sensitivity Training.* Pugh (1965), among others, called attention to the problem of transferring what is learned in the artificially contrived T-group setting to the real world. As just noted, intact T-groups who subsequently served as teams in a business game did worse than controls or T-groups which were split up before being reassembled as teams for the game (Hellebrandt & Stinson, 1971; Deep, Bass & Vaughan, 1967). Similarly, in a massive analysis of field data, D. G. Bowers (1973) found strong indications in twenty-three organizations of negative effects of the T-group on the subsequent improvement of the organization's performance in contrast to survey feedback without the T-group experience. Oshry and Harrison (1966) found that new diagnostic orientations learned by middle managers as a result of sensitivity training could not be converted into action back on the job because they saw no clear connection between the new perceptions and the job. Bass (1967c) and Bass and Barrett (1981) enumerated what may be needed for transfer of sensitivity training. Increased use, in parallel with sensitivity training groups, of simulations of the back-home organization involving supervisory, managerial, and organizational problems as the subject of inter-action and discussion are suggested. Real organizational issues can be brought into the laboratory. After the program is completed, the T-groups can continue back home. Another approach used by Bamforth (1965) as a consequence of the failure of the within-plant T-group members with whom he worked to transfer their learning to on-the-job problems was to change the role of a T-group trainer to that of a consultant to functioning, formal work-group meetings, where he helped the groups to recognize their boss-subordinate difficulties, anxieties about using or not using authority, colleague relations, role classifications, communications difficulties, resistance to the disclosure of initially unrecognized dynamics, and other sociopsychological problems.

*Cohesion versus Productivity.* To a considerable degree, the belief that organizational productivity increases as a result of sensitivity training tends to rely on inadequately controlled studies. Where controls are more adequate, sensitivity-trained groups and their leaders may prove less productive or the same in performance as control groups (Weschler & Reisel, 1959). Group learning and problem solving have been found higher under some sensitivity-trained leaders but not among others (Maloney, 1956).

Generalizations about the effects of sensitivity training are made difficult because of the many variations, referred to earlier, which are now employed. Although testimonials do not provide evidence of consequence, Wedel (1957) surveyed 333 former participants in laboratory training and found that they tended to regard the instruction as valuable in improving their human relations skills.

Buchanan (1969) found that only two of sixty-six studies analyzed made adequate use of control groups. However, from a review of the literature, Campbell and Dunnette (1968) concluded that laboratory training did change behavior in the laboratory, but as we have just noted there was less conclusive evidence for transfer of such training to the job situation. More recently, P. B. Smith (1975) was able to collect a sufficient number of studies that had satisfactory controls, repeated measure designs, and minimal time duration of twenty hours of training. Unfortunately, pretest sensitization of participants and rater awareness of who participated in training still could not be controlled in most of these studies. He found seventy-eight reports of significant effects of training on one or more scores after training. But only thirty-one studies employed designs which assessed the persistence of the effects. However, twenty-one did report long-term effects supporting the conclusions that a high degree of cohesiveness usually appears at the conclusion of sensitivity training groups (Stinson, 1970). Yet the impact on productivity depends on individual differences (Cooper & Levine, 1978), and the "back home" circumstances to which the training is to be transferred (Bass, 1967c; Argyris, 1969). (More will be said about this later.)

Reviews by House (1967, 1968) and findings presented by Goodall (1971) agreed that sensitivity training does induce change, particularly in attitude. It also induces anxiety, confusion, and uncertainty.

*Ethical Concerns.* K. F. Taylor (1967) charged that sensitivity training was based on questionable objectives—development of group cohesiveness, confidence in compliance with the norms of the training culture, and disruption of the trainee's personal integrity. Similarly, Lakin (1969) questioned the ethical basis of laboratory training on the grounds that untrained and improperly trained leaders are often employed, and that the method takes advantage of group pressure to impose trainers' values upon the trainee, uses scapegoating and demands for consensus and conformity to accomplish its objectives, and invades the individual's privacy. Goldstein (1980) complained about the absence of adequate theory to account for the varying results such as reported by P. B. Smith (1975, 1976). P. B. Smith concluded that we do not know if the effects occur in all types of groups, why effects are detected with some measures and not others, and why certain effects occur at all. Fortunately, the potential casualties likely are sufficiently small and controllable to be at acceptance limits, assuming the potential gains from sensitivity training are as large as expected (Cooper, 1975). For further critiques, the reader may wish to consult Odiorne (1963), Stock (1964), Marrow (1964), Coghill (1967), Golembiewski and Blumberg (1970), and Back (1972).

### Instrumented and "Packaged" Sensitivity Training

Bass (1977) saw the standardization of technique as the way to increase the reliability and reduce the variability of results with sensitivity training. Standardized processes can be provided using instrumented, self-administered, repeated questionnaires for data gathering, analysis, discussion, role plays, in-baskets, cases, audiotaped or video-taped instructions, and other types of experiential exercises for sensitivity training. They either match the general T-group or focus on more specific socioemotional learning experiences. Seven standards are proposed for developing such "ready-to-use" learning programs: (1) predevelopment scientific review of what is known about the processes; (2) identification of the behavioral dimensions of consequence that are the subjects of learning; (3) effective reinforcement; (4) reliable and valid measures of change; (5) adequate followup; (6) control of necessary antecedent conditions and associated consequences; and (7) adequate norms.

Blake and Mouton (1962) pioneered "the most radical innovation in T-group training" (Weschler & Schein, 1962): they removed the trainer. The Managerial Grid (Blake & Mouton, 1964) which emerged was widely adopted as a substitute for sensitivity training with trainers. Self-administered, "instrumental" training was seen as giving trainees greater responsibility for learning, as having more transfer potential, as giving participants more respect for systematic data analysis and as cheaper to conduct (Shepard, 1964).

Berzon, Reisel, and Davis (1969) evaluated a ten-session audiotape program for self-directed personal growth groups entitled PEER (Planned Experiences for Effective Relating). They reported a positive change in self-concept. Worden (1976) found that although no immediate personality differences could be detected between experimentals and controls, twenty-five of sixty-seven youths subjected to PEER reported in a six-month followup that they had made use of leadership skills learned in PEER. Similarly, Vicino, Krusell, et al. (1973) evaluated the effects of PROCESS (Krusell, Vicino, et al., 1971), a program of eight exercises (twelve in a 1980 revision) self-administered by booklet for personal and interpersonal development. A field experiment using a holdout control procedure yielded results indicating that the undergraduate participants improved their concept of themselves, were more able to see themselves as their peers did, and reacted favorably to the total experience. Similar results were obtained with 219 members of a women's religious order.

*Behavior Modeling*

This is a composite method based on social learning theory. In contrast to the more "mindless" Skinnerian operant learning, Bandura (1977) argued with experimental support that learning is facilitated if models are provided in advance of the consequences of engaging in a specific behavior. Action is foresightful. People are more attentive and active in organizing what is to be learned if they are provided models in advance. In observational learning, anticipation of a reinforcer also influences not only what is observed but also what goes unnoticed. Learning from the model is increased when the consequence of a model's behavior is highly valued. Goldstein and Sorcher (1974) showed how this theoretical approach could be applied to training first-line supervisors. Pilot experiments followed; they were generally supportive (Kraut, 1976; Moses & Ritchie, 1976; King & Arlinghaus, 1976). More convincing evidence was provided by Latham and Saari (1979). For two hours each week for nine weeks, for twenty supervisors, training dealt with: (1) orienting a new employee; (2) giving recognition; (3) motivating a poor performer; (4) correcting poor work habits; (5) discussing potential disciplinary action; (6) reducing absenteeism; (7) handling a complaining employee; (8) reducing turnover; and (9) overcoming resistance to change.

Each session followed the same plan after an introduction: (1) a film showing a model supervisor effectively handling a situation followed by a set of three to six learning points that were shown in the film immediately before and after the model was presented; (2) group discussion of the effectiveness of the model in exhibiting the desired behaviors (to promote retention); (3) practice in role-playing the desired behaviors in front of the entire class; and (4) feedback from the class on the effectiveness of each trainee in demonstrating the desired behaviors.

The learning points shown in the film were posted in front of the trainee playing the role of supervisor. The learning points to handle a complaint included avoiding responding with hostility or defensiveness; asking for and listening openly to the employee's complaint; restating the complaint for thorough understanding; recognizing and acknowledging the employee's viewpoint; when necessary, stating one's position nondefensively; and setting a specific date for a followup meeting.

Positive reactions to the program were sustained over an eight-month period. In contrast to twenty supervisors in a holdout control group, experimental trainees scored significantly higher on a test of the knowledge necessary to transfer the principles learned in class to different types of job-related problems. The trainees were also more effective in role plays resolving supervisor–employee problems and in earning higher superior job performance evaluations one year after training compared to the control group although they had been equivalent in rated performance with the control group one month before training.

Despite the sound theoretical underpinnings and seeming effectiveness of behavior role modeling, caution in its uncritical adoption was urged by Hakel (1976), McGehee and Tullar (1978), and Locke (1977).

*Specific Leader Skill Training.* In addition to behavior role modeling to cope with specific leader problems, one also sees much training on skills necessary to fulfill a leader's responsibilities adequately. Goldstein (1980) noted the continuing work on rater training and improving of performance evaluation by supervisors. He also found that much of what is available evaluating leader skill training, such as how to handle disciplinary problems, is anecdotal. But illustrative of controlled experimental evaluations of leadership skill training was a small sample investigation by Douglas (1977), who examined the efficacy of systematically training group leaders using operationally defined leadership skills in a group interaction. Compared to an alternate placebo group, results indicated that leaders trained to use both the Reflective-Supportive and the Command-Response styles employed these styles consistently and appropriately. The trained leaders also used the associated verbal responses more consistently and appropriately than the leaders in the placebo condition. Another finding was that leaders' behaviors overlap regardless of the theoretical orientation, suggesting that leadership skills can be taught systematically across theoretical orientations. Training leaders to use one verbal response style does not interfere with the leader's ability to use another leadership style. Leaders can improve their skills in both supportive and confrontive behaviors to help group members explore their intrapersonal and interpersonal feelings and attitudes.

*On-the-Job Leadership Training*

Formal training efforts can center on the leaders in their assignments and can be as effective as other kinds of training. Thus, Baxter (1953) found no significant differences between on-the-job training and the conference method for training supervisors.

*Coaching.* This is probably the most common of management training procedures. Superiors use consultation to solicit subordinate reactions, then offer advice on how the subordinates should deal with the question. The subordinate may represent the superior at a meeting and receive coaching afterwards. Coaching may occur in the context of management by objectives.

Any senior person may serve as coach or mentor as the role is being increasingly called (M. C. Johnson, 1980). If the trainee's problems are emotional or personal, coaching is not as likely to be effective as less directive approaches such as sensitivity training. Coaching is expected to be ineffective if relations between coached subordinate and superior are ambiguous because the subordinate does not trust the coach. Coaching is expected to be less effective if the superior sees the subordinate as a rival, if the dependent needs of the subordinate are ignored, if the superior is intolerant or does not allow sufficient time for coaching. Coaches need to avoid withholding information to maintain their power out of hostility toward their subordinates or to feel more secure (Tannenbaum, Kallejian & Weschler, 1954). Coaching is expected to work well if the subordinate can identify with the coach and if the coach provides a good model, if coach and sobordinate can be open and trusting with each other, if both accept responsibilities fully, and if the subordinate is provided with suitable rewards and recognition for improvement (H. Levinson, 1962). Coaches will be more effective also if they set clear standards, if they appreciate their subordinates' interests and abilities, if they practice delegation coupled with appropriate followup, and if they encourage completion of assignments (Goodacre, 1963). Coaching thrives in a "climate of confidence," a climate in which subordinates respect the integrity and capability of their superiors. Coaching is expected to take greatest advantage of the possibilities of individualized instruction. It can concentrate on those specific stimulus situations subordinates find hardest to deal with. It can attend to those specific performances subordinates find hardest to improve. It may provide the kind and quality of feedback which can have great impact on subordinates (Mace, 1950).

Coaching has been successfully applied to leadership and human relations training. Wexley and Jaffee (1969) compared ten control groups, ten groups with approval of leader after first session, and ten groups with coaching of the leader during the training session. Both observers and followers reported significant change in the leader in the direction of greater human relations orientation for those who were coached. Similarly, Maloney (1956) reported that group cohesiveness and participation but not group learning were improved when a leader followed a precisely coached method for implementing discussion.

*Job Rotation.* Management development may be built around job rotation—transferring trainees from one job to another to provide a succession of educational experiences. Lawler (1964) reported in a survey of 1,958 lower and middle managers that they tended to be more satisfied with their jobs if they remained in the same position for relatively shorter periods of time. They were more satisfied, in particular, with their opportunities for self-actualization if they were moved more frequently. Increased family and housing difficulties in the 1970s, caused by frequent relocation, may have changed this attitude. Firms may have need to develop substitute training approaches to meet the objectives of job rotation. Rotation is expected to increase identification with the whole organization rather than with a single area. Comparison of the British tendency to maintain narrow specialization in a single department with the Japanese tendency to be ready to work anywhere in the firm might shed further light on this and its effects. But little experimental evidence is available about any of the expected effects of rotation. Maier, Hoffman, and Read (1963) studied superior–subordinate communications in situations where the supervisor had formerly occupied the job of his subordinate. In comparison with a control group in which the superior had not occupied the job of his subordinate, it was found that previous occupancy of the job did not facilitate superior–subordinate communication.

*Survey Feedback.* Feedback about performance on the job is critical if learning is to occur from work experiences. This is why survey feedback from peers, subordinates, and clients as well as superiors based on standardized questionnaires (see Chapter 18) can play an important part in leadership training. R. D. Mann (1961) found more change in supervisors of experimental than control departments as a consequence of survey feedback. D. G. Bowers (1973) reported that survey feedback promoted more improvement than other developmental interventions such as sensitivity training or individual consultation (R. H. Solomon, 1976).

## PURPOSES AND CONTENT OF TRAINING OF LEADERS

Training programs have been developed and evaluated to train individuals to be more successful leaders and how to use each of the major styles of leadership enumerated in Chapters 18 through 22. Thus, the University of Michigan's pioneering survey research feedback programs served to reduce autocratic and increase democratic leader behavior (Chapter 18). Vroom and Yetton (1973) centered their attention on a program that teaches when various forms of participation or direction are rationally more appropriate (Chapter 19). Fiedler and Mahar (1979b) summarized twelve validity studies of the efficacy of a program to train managers to deal with the situations they face as a function of their own LPC scores (Chapter 20). Numerous programs beginning with Fleishman (1953b) focused on increasing the consideration behavior of supervisors (Chapters 21). And Miner (1965) trained managers in how to increase motivation to manage (Chapter 22).

### Training in Succeeding as a Leader

In research reports, training procedures are seldom described in detail. For this reason it is difficult to determine the extent to which participants are given direct training in methods that may be used to gain and hold a position of leadership. However, several studies have shown that direct training in the techniques of leadership tends to improve trainees' leadership and effectiveness in groups.

*Opportunity to Emerge as Leader.* Jennings (1952b) studied two groups of twenty production supervisors over sixteen training sessions. The experimental group was subdivided into discussion groups to solve case problems. At the end of the first session the emergent leaders were removed and placed in a separate group. Thus, new leaders were forced to emerge in the second session. These were also removed and placed in the leadership pool. Successive sessions permitted the rise of new leaders. In the control group the discussion leader presented a problem and helped the group arrive at a solution. Six months later, more members of the experimental group than of the control group were rated above average in effectiveness.

*Discussion Leadership Training.* Training can also improve the likelihood that discussions will be effective. Thus, Maier (1953) demonstrated that discussion groups with skilled leaders produced better decisions than those with unskilled leaders. Maier (1950) studied groups of foremen with a leader and three followers with and without training. Leaders of experimental groups (N = 44) were given eight hours of lectures, discussions, and role playing. The control groups (N = 36) were untrained. Maier found that the trained leaders had more success in inducing their groups to accept change and compromise than the untrained leaders. Subsequently, Maier and Hoffman (1960) demonstrated that groups with trained leaders produced discussions of higher quality than those with untrained leaders. Again, Maier and Hoffman (1964) and Maier and Solem (1962) found that leaders using a problem-solving approach helped their groups to achieve solutions of higher quality than did leaders who applied financial incentives or concentrated on a solution. Barnlund (1955) also demonstrated that trainees, given discussion leadership training, in comparison with controls, improved in leadership quality in group discussion, regulated participation more, and exhibited greater ability to resolve conflict in group discussion.

*Individual Differences.* Some individuals profit more from leadership training than others. Klubeck and Bass (1954) studied 140 girls from seven sororities. They were divided into twenty groups composed of one member from each of the seven sororities. The groups engaged in leaderless discussion problems. Observers rated each girl on leadership, influence on discussion, and other behaviors. Average scores were used to rank the girls from 1 to 7 in each group. Between the first and second leaderless group discussion sessions, some of the girls were given private instruction on how leaders behave. Trained girls who initially ranked 3 in their groups gained significantly more than those who received no training. Trained girls who initially ranked 6 in their groups did not gain significantly more than those without training. Girls initially ranking higher in leadership profited more from training than those ranking low.

### Training Emphasizing Democratic Leadership and Human Relations

Eichler and Merrill (1933) and Zeleny (1941) found that students gain from direct training in such leadership. Similarly, Spector (1958) found significant improvement in human relations attitudes among air force cadets as a result of training. Bavelas (1942) trained three adult leaders in community center activities in democratic leadership. Three controls received no training. The trained leaders greatly reduced the number of leader-initiated activities and the giving of orders and increased the number of activities in which children exercised responsibility. The control group made no such changes. Under trained leaders, the children showed more interest, enthusiasm, and initiative in planning projects. Lippitt (1949) gave community leaders in intergroup relations a two-week workshop in group discussion, role playing, and sociodrama. Both participants and observers reported that the trainees became more proficient in handling problems of intergroup relations as a result of the workshop. Again, Maier and Hoffman (1961) demonstrated that supervisors trained in human relations compared with those without such training led groups to a more effective and creative solution of a problem in changing work methods. Similarly, Baum, Sorensen, and Place (1970) found that workers' answers to a questionnaire indicated an increase in actual and desired organizational control after their supervisors had completed a course. The change was in the direction of more democratic control.

*Improved Leader Skills and Knowledge.* Early on, leadership training programs (for example, Canter, 1949; Katzel, 1948; Maier, 1948; Mold, 1947; and Vonachen et al., 1946) stressed increasing the supervisor's human relations knowledge, skills, and ability, especially with reference to problems of interaction among his or her subordinates, as one of the basic goals of training.

Katzell (1948) found that seventy-three superiors scored significantly higher on a test of human relations attitudes (How Supervise) after a training course of eight weeks. Canter (1951), using the same test, studied supervisors in insurance companies. Significant gains were found in scores on how to supervise, general facts and principles, and estimates of group opinion. He also found that large gains in understanding psychological principles in supervising others and better insight into subordinates' attitudes were obtained through supervisory training. Again, Goodacre (1955) and Neel and Dunn (1960) administered tests of knowledge of human relations practices to members of training groups. Significant gains in knowledge were obtained in both studies. But Hand and Slocum (1970) reported no change either in knowledge of human relations, self-actualization, motivation, interpersonal relations, or participation as a consequence of a training program for middle managers.

*Associated Changes.* Results by R. D. Miller (1969) indicated that leadership training also resulted in improved attitude toward the importance of the leadership role. Papaloizos (1962) reported that about one-third of the participants in a human relations training program exhibited favorable change in attitude toward subordinates. Following similar training, Mayo and DuBois (1963) found that the gain in leadership ratings was correlated positively with final course grades but not with other criteria. In the same way, A. K. Healy (1962) found that training in democratic leadership enabled school children to gain in exercise of the leadership role and in sociometric score. The status of sociometric isolates was improved in the democratic setting. Academic achievement also improved. Likewise, Cassel and Shafer (1961) gave students direct training in human relations and leadership. Test scores revealed significant gains in leadership and social insight but not in sociometric preference or personality tensions and needs. But House and Tosi (1963) found that a training course of forty weeks produced no important advantage for management trainees over a control group in job satisfaction and other measures of performance.

To improve self-perception was the objective of several democratic leadership training studies. Although Gassner, Gold, and Snadowsky (1964) found no significant increase between actual and ideal self for either experimental or control groups, the experimental group increased significantly in knowledge of democratic leadership, but the control group did not. Trice (1959) reported significant changes in self-perception in a trained group but not in a control group. Members of the experimental group who changed the most described themselves as more flexible after training. In a study of middle management human relations training, Hand and Slocum (1970) found that only acceptance of self and others was significantly improved in an immediate posttest. But there were no significant changes ninety days later.

Improved decision making was also often targeted for improvement. Employing eighty-three undergraduates trained in human relations techniques and seventy-five who were not, Madden (1977) reported that leaders who received human relations training made significantly more accurate postdiscussion decisions than untrained leaders, but they were no different in their satisfaction with the decision-making process.

*Leader Match.* In Fiedler's Contingency Model (Chapter 20), leaders' effectiveness depends on the leaders' LPC scores and on whether the situation is favorable. Since LPC is seen as a kind of invariant personality attribute, it follows that leadership effectiveness can best be increased by teaching leaders how to make situations more favorable to themselves. Fiedler, Chemers, and Mahar (1976) developed a four–six hour self-paced programmed instruction workbook, *Leader Match.* It teaches leaders how to (1) assess their own leadership style based on their LPC scores; (2) assess the amount of situational favorability; and (3) change the situation so that it matches their style. Fiedler and Mahar (1979b) reviewed twelve studies demonstrating the validity of the training effort. Five studies were conducted in civilian organizations and seven were conducted in military settings. The performance evaluations were collected from two to six months after training. Some included measures before and after training. The performance evaluations of 423 trained leaders were compared with those of 484 leaders without Leader Match training who were randomly assigned to control groups. Generally, although not uniformly, supportive results were obtained. For example, Fiedler and Mahar (1979b) completed a field experiment with 190 ROTC cadets. Leader Match training was administered to cadets before they attended four weeks of advanced summer camp where they were selected at random to serve in several different leadership positions for twenty-four hour periods. Analysis of commissioned and noncommissioned officer evaluations of performance as well as peer ratings showed that the 155 male and thirty-five female cadets with training tended to perform better than the 176 male and thirty-nine female cadets in the control group. Similar findings were obtained by Csoka and Bons (1978), Leister, Borden, and Fiedler (1977), Fiedler, Mahar, and Schmidt (1976), and Chemers and Mahar (1978). Nevertheless, Schriesheim and Hosking (1978) remain troubled with Leader Match since they find too many problems remaining with the Contingency Model itself to warrant using it for remedial actions by specific individuals in specific situations.

### Training Emphasizing Participative and/or Directive Leadership

Sensitivity training has been seen by Argyris (1969) as central to the development in leaders of receptivity to participative management. Sensitivity training, according to Argyris, moves people to become trusting, open, and experimenting with their own ideas and feelings and to own up to them. Moreover, such people can help others to become more so. Without sensitivity training, supervisors will be more inclined to remain directive in their leadership. Those who have been through sensitivity training will be more comfortable with participative approaches with their subordinates.

*Rational Training.* Vroom and Yetton (1973) saw what was needed quite differently. In Chapter 19, we described their rational model for choosing which leadership style to use. The Vroom and Yetton training program encourages trainees to see the discrepancies between their own way of dealing with a set of standardized cases and the rational model's solution. Detailed analyses are also provided trainees in answer to such questions as:

- What circumstances cause the trainee to behave in directive fashion; what circumstances cause the trainee to behave participatively?
- What rules of the model did the trainee violate most frequently and least frequently?
- Does the leadership style displayed by the trainee reflect more concern with getting decisions that are high in quality or with getting decisions that are accepted?
- Does the leadership style reflect more concern about time pressure or about development of subordinates?

Jago and Vroom (1975) have also pursued survey feedback for training by asking subordinates of the trainees to indicate how they think their superior would respond to each case problem.

*Empirical Approach.* Survey feedback has also been used by Bass (1976) to teach about direction and participation and when each is appropriate based on empirical findings about the individual trainees themselves and the system in which they are embedded. Bass-Valenzi survey feedback (Chapter 19) of a trainee's management styles (direction, participation, and so on, along with other variables) as seen by one's subordinates provide trainees with the basis of examining the discrepancies between normative results and the trainee's own behavior as described by his or her subordinates. R. H. Solomon (1976) reported positive effects on library directors and their work groups as a consequence of the Bass-Valenzi data feedback.

*Other Studies.* Training efforts to promote participative or directive leadership were described by A. J. Franklin (1969), Herod (1969), and House (1962). Franklin administered a test of knowledge of group theory to groups of disadvantaged youth. Test scores after training were related to group cohesiveness, but not to a significant degree. Herod (1969) demonstrated that a group-centered training program for college women resulted in enhancement of participative leadership practices after training. At the end of four months, however, the leaders had regressed to their original positions. House (1962) trained one group in a participative style of leadership and another in a directive style. The more directive method along with elevated course requirements was associated with a significant decrease in absences and a significant increase in the number of trainees completing the course.

### Training Emphasizing Consideration and/or Initiating Structure

Fleishman (1953b) examined the initiation and consideration scores of International Harvester supervisors following a training program. Consideration scores increased in means and variances. Heightened consideration scores subsequently maintained themselves only if supervisors returned to superiors who were similarly higher in consideration. Harris and Fleishman (1955) administered the LBDQ to thirty-nine foremen before and after a course in human relations. At the same time, the questionnaire was administered to a control group of foremen who had not taken the course. The control group exhibited greater stability of behavior over time than the experimental group, suggesting that training was effective in changing behavior as perceived by subordinates. However, the trainee group exhibited greater change in initiating structure than in consideration. Similarly, Biggs, Huneryager, and Delaney (1966) found that a two-week training course resulted in more favorable attitudes toward consideration and less favorable attitudes toward initiating structure. Before training, those high in structure were also in greater need for affection and expression of control than those low in favoring structure. After training, they differed in need to express control, but not in need for affection. Again, Carron (1964) found that supervisors became less strongly oriented toward structuring and authoritarianism as a result of a training effort. Herod (1969) and M. B. Miles (1965) obtained results from a training program that produced a more considerate attitude toward group processes but no significant change in attitude toward consideration and structure.

Hand and Slocum (1972) also conducted a training program to raise supervisors' consideration scores. Eighteen months later, they found supervisors' job performance more highly rated as a consequence. Stroud (1959) reported that supervisors after training were described by their superiors as more considerate. Again, Schwartz, Stillwell, and Scanlon (1968) studied two groups of insurance supervisors. One group moved toward more consideration and less production emphasis after training. The second group moved toward more initiation of structure. Finally, Deitzer (1967) studied two groups of district sales managers in an insurance company before, four weeks after, and twelve weeks after a training program to increase consideration and initiation of structure. The control group outperformed the experimental group after training on all criterion variables—number of new agents recruited, volume of new policies sold by the agent working under the manager, and the like. Manager consideration was positively related to volume of sales both four and twelve weeks after training. Initiation of structure was related to sales twelve weeks later.

Several researchers used the LOQ to measure change in leader attitude as a result of training. Carron (1964) found that attitudes toward initiating structure and authoritarianism decreased immediately after training, but that there were no significant changes seventeen months later. Ayers (1964) found that feedback did little to enhance the effects of training as measured by attitudes toward consideration and initiation of structure. Similarly, H. B. Stephenson (1966) administered the LOQ to 449 management trainees and observed that training in management development produced no significant change in attitude.

*Multidimensional Training for Leaders and Followers.* Stogdill (1970) developed a set of films, each depicting a different pattern of LBDQ-XII leader behavior: consideration, initiation of structure, tolerance of freedom, and production emphasis. The films were shown to thirty-five sorority presidents. Each film was followed by a discussion period designed to induce insight into the whys and wherefores of the patterns of behavior. Leaders were described by five sorority members before training and three months after on the LBDQ-XII. The results suggested that leader behavior was more logically related to group performance after training than before. Stogdill and Bailey (1969) showed the four films to small groups of boys in three vocational high schools along with a fifth film on representation. After seeing each movie, groups discussed the supervisor's behavior. The investigators found that discussion of the movies exerted a favorable effect on response to supervision. In another experiment, Stogdill, Coady, and Zimmer (1970) attempted to influence student attitudes toward the different supervisory roles by use of the films. Results suggested that discussion of the films affected student adjustment to supervision. Insight and understanding facilitated favorable response to supervision.

### Motivation to Manage

By means of lecture, Miner (1961) successfully increased the favorableness of attitudes of seventy-two R & D supervisors toward accepting responsibility for their leadership role above and beyond their professional roles. He further reported that training resulted in more favorable attitudes toward supervisory work and obtained a small positive correlation between favorable attitude change and change toward more effective supervisory performance (Miner, 1960, 1965). Finally, both college students and business managers taking a course with Miner (1965) improved in attitude toward acceptance of responsibility, authority, and willingness to initiate remedial action. Managers had significantly better promotion records than a control group five years later.

## PROGRAMMATIC APPLICATIONS

### Management Development

Management development usually refers to the total, long-term off-the-job and on-the-job educational process; supervisory training refers to shorter courses. A full-blown program may accomplish much more than what might be possible with shorter, independent training courses. Thus, Guetzkow, Forehand, and James (1962) reported that a one-year management development course changed behavior significantly more than training courses of short duration.

Management development programs serve other organizational functions. Recruiting is facilitated if prospective applicants know that such a program is available. An organizational growth strategy can be maintained efficiently when candidates for newly opening positions are already in training. In turn, the growth strategy makes for more promotion possibilities as a source of reward for managers at lower levels and may reduce defensive competition for promotion (Luttwak, 1976).

*Evaluative Impressions.* The National Industrial Conference Board (NICB, 1964) surveyed 167 firms' experience with management development. In evaluating the effectiveness of such programs, 57 percent expressed the belief that they were valuable, but only 14 percent reported evidence in support of this belief. Other evaluative studies were reported by Jerkedal (1967), K. R. Andrews (1966), Merrell (1965), Oberg (1966), Roethlisberger (1954), Basil (1964), Habbe (1950), and Wikstrom (1961). A handbook (Taylor & Lippitt, 1975) and a text (Herbert & Yost, 1978) on management education and development are also available.

The National Industrial Conference Board (1963) surveyed 1,074 recently recruited college graduates who had attended management development programs sponsored by their employers. About 40 percent of those who had hoped that the training would prepare them for promotion felt disappointed and regarded the training as of little value to themselves or to the company. They preferred instruction preparing them for specific jobs over that in human relations and general management. But executives with experience have a different point of view. K. R. Andrews (1966) received 6,000 replies from executives who had attended thirty-nine different university programs in management development. Although about 85 percent saw no relationship between attending the courses and subsequent advances in salary, the benefits they most frequently mentioned were increased understanding of self and others, greater tolerance for differences in opinion, and heightened awareness of alternative solutions to problems. Structured lectures and didactic teacher-led classwork were regarded as more valuable than unstructured group discussions and informal contacts with faculty and students.

*Attitude and Self-Reported Change.* Leadership training of some sort figures strongly in most management development programs, although consideration may be given to training in many other nonsupervisory management functions (see Chapter 17). In fact, M. W. McCall (1976) sees that too much emphasis has been placed on leadership training and not enough on the many other varied aspects of managerial work.

Numerous examples of successful attitude change as a consequence of training and development programs have appeared. For instance, C. W. Nelson (1967) conducted a training course for top-level managers in a plant. They, in turn, conducted a similar course for their lower-level managers. Significant change in attitude occurred. A retest one year later showed that effects persisted. Similarly, E. H. Schein (1967) demonstrated that a two-year course in management education produced a significant change in human relations attitudes. Again, Valiquet (1968) reported a significant change in attitude and behavior among managers participating in a one-year training program. R. S. Barrett (1965) found significant change in attitudes, but not in performance, following training of executives.

Bakke (1959) studied sixty-seven manager trainees in Norway. The trainees reported expanded understanding of other people, self, and social trends. They also reported greater self-confidence in dealing with superiors, peers, and subordinates. Similarly, Waaler (1962) studied another 194 executives in a management development program in Norway. Trainees from the "best" firms, when compared with those from the "poorest" firms, reported greater nearness, warmth, and understanding of their employees, more informality with employees, greater predictability of behavior, letting employees know what to expect, and reduced pressure on subordinates.

### Specialized Leadership Training

Training programs to lead scientists, engineers, and technicians or to lead military personnel are programs to which much specialized effort has been devoted. The MBA is another specialized program aimed at preparing students for general business leadership. Other specialized programs prepare leaders to work with minorities and in other cultures.

*Technical Supervisors.* Moon and Hariton (1958) gave fifty engineering supervisors thirty hours of instruction on methods of self-impovement and greater job efficiency. Lectures were followed by role-playing sessions in which each participant acted out problems in human relations. A questionnaire administered to sixty-seven subordinates of the trained group and to sixty-seven subordinates of untrained supervisors indicated greater improvement for the trained group in understanding the subordinate as an individual, expressing recognition for good work, giving subordinates an opportunity to express their side of a story, and showing more interest in the employees' progress. Carron (1964) administered training over a period of six months to twenty-three scientists in supervisory positions, using lectures, discussions, and role playing. A battery of tests was administered immediately before and after training to the experimental and a control group, and again seventeen months later. The experimental group decreased significantly in authoritarianism and initiating structure, whereas the control group did not. Mosvick (1966) examined four different training methods in a study of fifty-five engineers in supervisory positions. Three attitude scales and two behavioral measures were administered before and after training to experimental and control groups. The trained group showed significant change in behavior, but not in attitudes, and improved in ability to analyze a simulated communication conflict situation.

*Military Leaders.* The heaviest continuing investment in leadership training occurs at all levels for military leaders. Space prohibits any detailed examination of the special classroom and field exercises that are featured in such training. A typical evaluative study was reported by Hood, Showel, and Stewart (1967). They compared squad leaders who received leader preparation training with a control group of leaders. The trained leaders received higher effectiveness ratings, their squads showed higher esprit, and their followers scored higher on proficiency tests. Descriptions by followers indicated that trained leaders initiated more structure, exercised better control of field exercises, and demonstrated more adequacy in briefing and giving information. Their followers were less willing to re-enlist, however, and showed less favorable attitudes toward the army. Again, in a study of infantry leaders, Rittenhouse (1968) found that graduates of NCO Infantry Leaders Schools exceeded a control group in rate of promotion and number of awards, but not in leadership evaluations. Another typical analysis was by Lange, Rittenhouse, and Atkinson (1968) who presented films of leadership situations followed by group discussion as a method of training military leaders. Groups discussing the films were more effective than control groups in solving leadership problems.

Showel, Taylor, and Hood (1966) found that automated instruction was as effective as conventional methods in training noncommissioned officers in the army. Hood et al. (1967) evaluated three methods for training noncommissioned officers. Recycling consisted of lectures and discussions of leadership principles, followed by a repetition of the course. The integrated system involved lectures, group discussions, films, and role playing of human relations problems. The short course presented formal training in a four-week leader preparation course. Written and performance tests of proficiency at the end of recycling were significantly higher than for the control group. The integrated system and the short course also produced higher scores on written tests, but the differences were not statistically significant.

*MBA Education.* Training of one and usually two years leading to the Master's Degree in Business Administration is broadly based in those institutions following guidelines of the American Assembly of Collegiate Schools of Business. Students receive instruction in applied behavioral science, applied mathematics and applied economics as well as in the functional areas of production, marketing, finance, and accounting. A major problem for graduates appears to be the lack of opportunity to ply their trade. For example, Hilgert (1965) surveyed MBA graduates out of school an average of eight years. Sixty-one percent were in middle or top management. Seventy-three percent felt their MBA skills were used only marginally or not at all. Gutteridge (1973) reported that employers regarded the MBA's advantage over the non-MBA as only temporary. Herbert (1972) found no clear effect of MBA learnings on job performance. But according to Herbert (1977), eighty-two supervisors of MBAs and non-MBAs gave MBAs better reputational ratings on technical skills, initiative, responsibility, motivation, judgment, and problem solving, but not on better human relations or supervisory skills. No significant staff–line interactions were found.

*Leadership Training for and about Minorities.* "Awareness" training mainly for white, male managers about special issues of working with women, blacks, and the disadvantaged has become commonplace (Awareness, 1968). In some instances, heightened awareness has produced overreactions and backlash (L. A. Johnson, 1969). One of the few such programs that has received extensive evaluation was reported by Bass, Cascio, McPherson, and Tragash (1976). Following identification of five factors differentiating issues of awareness of managers about affirmative action for black employees (Chapter 31), PROSPER (Bass, Cascio & McPherson, 1972) was developed. It begins with a pretraining assessment on the five factors. Next, a case of an insubordinate black engineer and in-basket decisions follow. Each player then is assigned a role as one of five different managers in a firm gathered to discuss the case. Each of the roles is built around one of the five factors. Participants verbalize favorable positions on one of the factors while they hear favorable information about the other four. Significant score increases were achieved by 2,293 managers. After three to five months, 298 managers still showed some of the increase on all five factors. Cascio and Bass (1976) further analyzed the specific role-playing effects of PROSPER, which were in the direction of expectations. PROFAIR, a comparable attitude change program for working with women (Bass, 1971) was developed out of a survey of attitudes toward working with women.

Special programs to train black leaders are illustrated by Katz and Cohen's (1962) "assertion" training to increase self-confidence among blacks. Beatty (1973) completed a study about the training of blacks as supervisors and the importance of their superiors' expectations.

Assertiveness training for women has become a fad and fashion (Fensterheim, 1972). Heinen et al. (1975) increased self-awareness and self-confidence in nineteen of twenty women managers. Numerous programs to train women as leaders have been conducted. As DeSanctis et al. (1981) observe, these programs are predicated on the supposition that women leaders have unique problems (Chapter 30). These issues cannot be effectively resolved through changing the organization. The woman leader needs to adjust to the organization. Nevertheless, a survey of 101 women and 121 male managers by Alpander and Gutmann (1976) indicated that both sexes perceived similar training needs. Be that as it may, Brenner (1972) developed recommendations for designing special enrichment programs for women by using male role training for women so that they learn to adopt more acceptable managerial characteristics.

Hart (1975) designed and evaluated a training program in leadership for adult women based on the Hersey-Blanchard life cycle theory (1972). Training that focused on interpersonal skills, leadership theory, life style, and importance of motivation to be a leader resulted in increasing the self-esteem and self-confidence of trainees in contrast to controls. Compared to controls, trainees also perceived themselves as better able to make decisions, more active, more in control of their lives, and having a greater knowledge of listening skills.

*Training Leaders for Foreign Assignments.* Space prohibits much discussion here about preparing managers for overseas assignments. Lack of such preparation is extremely costly (Tung, n.d.). Based on surveys and interviews, Zeira (1975) suggested that multinational firms need to equip parent-country nationals and third-country nationals who are expected to serve as managers abroad with adequate knowledge of the complex human problems of international enterprises and with self-confidence to adapt their leader behavior to the needs of the subsidiary. Tung (n.d.) found that twenty-six of 105 U.S. multinationals ran training programs to prepare personnel for overseas assignments. About half of these mentioned environmental briefings, cultural orientations, and language training. A few used culture assimilators, sensitivity training, and field experience.

Mitchell and Foa (1969) studied American leaders with non-American followers. They found that leaders were rated as more effective when they were trained in the norms of the follower group. Again, Chemers, Fiedler, Lekhyananda, and Stolurow (1966) demonstrated that training leaders in the culture of a foreign nation, as opposed to information on the geography of the nation, resulted in higher levels of group performance and rapport in tasks involving subjects from two different cultures. L. R. Anderson (1965) trained leaders in their own culture's style of leadership or in the style characteristic of another culture, then assigned them to intercultural task groups. Those trained in other cultural styles led groups that were more effective in creativity tasks but not in negotiation tasks.

In line with Fiedler's Contingency Model, Chemers (1969) found that intercultural training tended to modify the situation in the direction of making it more favorable for the task-oriented leader, who then showed more consideration than the relations-oriented leader.

*Transformational Leadership.* We are dealing with both method and content of leadership training, and the method often provides a leadership model which may be central to what is learned. J. M. Burns (1978) holds that transformational leadership (Chapter 2) requires a broad educational process. It cannot be manipulative, but rather should be a joint search for truth by teacher and students.

> [Teachers] help students define moral values not by imposing their own moralities on them but by positing situations that pose hard moral choices and then encouraging conflict and debate. They seek to help students rise to higher stages of moral reasoning and hence to higher levels of principled judgment . . . students are helped to respect the fairness, equity, honesty, responsibility, and justice for which they speak [Burns, 1978, p. 449].

## FACTORS AFFECTING TRAINING OUTCOMES

Several researchers have investigated factors that influence the outcome of leadership training, for all individuals do not react alike to the process. Personal attributes of trainee, composition of the training group, followup strategies, behavior of the trainer, and congeniality of the environment to which the person returns have been found to influence behavior after instruction. The effects of sensitivity training seem particularly likely to depend on these kinds of contingent variables to result in changes in behavior, attitudes, and organizational performance, but not necessarily in the same direction for each trainee. Thus, Lennung and Ahlberg (1975) compared seventeen managers receiving sensitivity training with an untrained control sample in the gains five to seven months after training. Most striking were the greater variances in attitudes, awareness, and observed and objectively measured behaviors, suggesting that training effects depended on individual differences in situations to which trainees returned.

### Attributes of the Trainees

Zenger (1974) made a strong case for integrating the assessment of managers with their training. Trainee differences in motivation figured in Gruenfeld's (1966) report that participants who paid part of their tuition devoted themselves more intensely to the program, found it more difficult, and benefited more as measured by a rating scale and test of values.

Schein and Bennis (1965) studied a complex of organizational and personal variables related to perceived and observed change following laboratory training. Verified change was defined as change reported by trainee and two associates in the organization. Security and power of position in the organization and unfreezing during training were significantly related to verified behavior change. Prior anticipation of change was negatively related to verified change.

### Composition of Training Group

Composition of sensitivity training groups has figured strongly in evaluative studies. Illustrating this type of experiment, Harrison and Lubin (1965b) studied participants in homogeneous and heterogeneous groups. The finding that most learning occurred in heterogeneous groups was interpreted as suggesting that member feelings of cohesiveness and emotional satisfaction may not be appropriate criteria for evaluating the effects of training groups, since ordinarily much more conflict tends to be experienced in heterogeneous groups once the polite façades have been removed.

### Followup Reinforcing Practice and Feedback

To transfer to the job what has been learned during training, trainees need to receive continuing opportunities to practice what has been learned. This in turn needs to be coupled with feedback or self-reinforcement about the trainees' practice efforts. Wexley and Nemeroff (1975) described a self-feedback mechanism for promoting transfer of leadership training to the job. For six weeks following training, trainees completed a daily behavioral checklist to record their own supervisory behaviors. On each day, they noted whether they had done such things as: praised subordinates; thanked subordinates for suggestions and told them how they would be followed up; called subordinates together to discuss mutual assistance; gave help, as requested; assigned jobs and did not interfere until completion. Further transfer was promoted by the trainer who met twice for individual consultation with trainees on the job to review progress and to arrange for trying out and evaluating the effects of newly learned behaviors.

### Behavior of the Trainer

The trainer is likely to be important to the outcomes of most training programs, but particularly to sensitivity training outcomes. Casualties in training have been linked to hostile trainers, for instance. Amount of learning has been affected as well. Lieberman, Yalom, and Miles (1973) studied 206 trainees led by different types of encounter group trainers. Casualties were greatest (12 percent) when the trainers were autocratic, aggressive, charismatic, and convinced of their own beliefs. Other types of trainers with high casualty rates were impersonal, uncaring trainers (11 percent), highly controlling trainers (10 percent), and laissez-faire types (8 percent). On the other hand, there were few or no casualties when the laboratory was trainerless and conducted by instrumented audiotape or when trainers were benevolent, caring, group-oriented or participative. Learning was also likely to be greater with such trainers. Learning correlated $-.33$ with casualty rates, contrary to expectations.

According to C. L. Cooper (1969), participants in sensitivity training tended to identify with the trainers when the latter were seen as attractive. As a result, they became more like the trainers in attitude and behavior as training progressed. Psathas and Hardert (1966) obtained results indicating that the trainer in sensitivity training groups sends implicit norms which indicate to members what the norms of the group should be. Thus, the trainer plays a significant role in determining the group's values and norms. Zigon and Cannon (1974) found similarly that students in group discussions whose appointed leaders were seen as genuine and respected were more likely to transfer what was learned in the groups.

Much of the rationale for instrumented self-guided training is based on the known variance in outcomes that are due to differences among trainers in motivation and skill.

### Congruence of Training and Organizational Environment

Organizational factors affecting the effectiveness of supervisory training include the organizational climate, the trainer's immediate superior, upper management, and various other components.

*Organizational Climate.* Zaleznik (1951) explained the failure of a human relations training program to help trainees solve their work problems on the basis of inadequate initial diagnosis of supervisory difficulties and on the irrelevance of training to the problems. Sykes (1962) conducted a case study of a firm in which participants in a management development program regarded the training as unsuccessful because top management was unwilling to correct grievances and unsatisfactory conditions toward which they had become sensitized during the discussion sessions. Again, a deterioration in human relations resulted from an attempt at supervisory training when a program conflicted with unionism, when recruitment for a program was inadequate, and when a program itself was seen as an effort to indoctrinate a captive audience (Form & Form, 1953).

Both House (1968) and Glube and Margerison (1976) concluded that the organizational climate is extremely important in the development of managers. Baumgartel and Jeanpierre (1972) studied 240 managers who had participated in a management development program. The respondents came from 200 different industrial and commercial firms. Whether managers could apply what they had learned in training was seen to depend on freedom to set personal goals, consideration of higher management of the feelings of lower management, the organization's stimulation and approval of innovation and experimentation, the organization's desire for executives to make use of knowledge given in management courses, and free and open communication among management groups.

*Immediate Superior.*   Most important to whether training will modify behavior back on the job is the trainee's immediate superior. F. C. Mann (1951) found that foremen who changed more as a consequence of training in leadership received more encouragement from their superiors, expected greater personal benefit from training, felt more secure in their relations with their superiors, and perceived greater opportunity to try out new ideas on the job. Consistent with this, Hariton (1951) observed that supervisory training increased employee satisfaction when the supervisors were encouraged by their superiors to use the principles they had learned in training. Similarly, Fleishman (1953b) found that foremen trained in a human relations orientation appeared to experience role conflict when they returned to their jobs under superiors exhibiting a markedly different pattern of behavior. They were most likely to maintain their consideration scores if they returned to superiors who favored such behavior. Supervisors given training in the value of exhibiting consideration as supervisors were, after returning to their jobs, more likely to continue exhibiting considerate behavior, according to their associates, if the supervisors indicated that their superior expected such behavior from them. When supervisors with the training returned to jobs with perceptions of a superior who did not expect such behavior, the supervisors experienced conflict revealed in greater discrepancies between what they said they should do and what they actually did do. In the long run, as Harris and Fleishman (1955) observed, supervisory training to increase consideration behavior resulted in shifting some trainees' behavior in one direction and some in another when training and subsequent environmental conditions were taken into account. Fleishman, Harris, and Burtt (1955) reported that the impact of human relations training upon supervisors after returning to their work depended on the attitudes and behavior of their superiors. Foremen tended to endorse a considerate attitude toward employees and to be described high in consideration if their superiors endorsed considerate attitudes and behaved in a considerate manner. There was a nonsignificant tendency for foremen to be described high in initiating structure when their superiors exhibited a similar pattern of behavior. Those foremen who returned from training to work under a superior low in consideration and high in initiating structure experienced the greatest role conflict, as measured by the discrepancy between their actual behavior and their ideas about how they ought to behave. No such relationship was found for control foremen who had not taken the training course in human relations. Thus, the foremen's leader behavior tended to be more highly conditioned by the behavior of their superiors than by the type of training they received.

Haire (1948), Fleishman (1953b), W. Mahler (1952), and many others have suggested that for training to be effective the entire management of the organization should be subjected to the same or similar program. It is self-defeating to train lower-level managers in a style of supervision incompatible with that of their superiors.

*Other Factors.* Other organizational and interpersonal elements also are important. Steele, Zane, and Zalkind (1970) reported that perceived pressures from associates, particularly peers, were negatively correlated with consultants' ratings of trainee involvement in changed activities twenty months after instruction. In the same way, Carroll and Nash (1970) reported that forty-five foremen in a management development program felt the training was more applicable to the job when they were more highly motivated toward promotion, satisfied with the organization, and had sufficient freedom to perform their functions.

Training often must be supported by other specific organizational actions to result in the desired training effects. For instance, a supervisory training program to reduce employee absenteeism actually lowered absenteeism only when quantitative data about the absences of their own subordinate personnel were fed back to supervisors following training (Mann & Sparling, 1956). Similarly, training programs for women managers were seen to require buttressing by encouraging upper-level management to be supportive of female middle managers along with providing husbands with an understanding of the importance of their support in assuring the success of their wives on the job (Brenner, 1972).

# 34

## LOOKING BACK

This chapter will highlight what has been presented in the earlier chapters. A prospectus of what lies ahead will then follow.

### LEADERSHIP THEORY AND RESEARCH

#### Concepts of Leadership

Leadership, a universal phenomenon, has been a subject of research from a theoretical and from a problem point of view. A host of definitions have been developed depending on the interests and needs of the developer. Leadership has been seen as the focus of group processes, as a personality attribute, as the art of inducing compliance, as an exercise of influence, as a particular kind of act, as a form of persuasion, as a power relation, as an instrument in goal attainment, as an effect of interaction, as a differentiated role, and as initiation of structure. Definitions can broadly include many of these aspects or they can be narrow. A distinction may be made between headship and leadership. One complex definition that has evolved, particularly to help understand a wide variety of research findings, delineates effective leadership as interaction between members of a group that initiates and maintains improved expectations and competence of the group to solve problems or attain goals.

#### Theories and Models

The long history of reliance on Great Man theories naturally led to the search for traits of leadership and trait theories. In reaction there arose an equally strong emphasis on environmental theories. Finally, syntheses were achieved in theories of interacting persons and situations built around psychoanalysis, role attainment, reinforced change, paths to goals, or contingencies of leader and situation.

Theories have been built on the assumption that humankind is inherently good or inherently evil, on exchange relationships, on behavioral, perceptual, or cognitive bases. Empirical and rational problem solving and systems analysis have also been used.

#### Types and Functions of Leadership

Early in the scientific process, efforts are made to classify phenomena. Investigators have focused attention on classifications of crowds, institutions, industries, and

**584**

community leaders. They have also attempted educational, political, and legislative classifications. An important distinction is the difference between transactional and transformational leaders. The former concentrate on an exchange relation of what the leader and follower each want. The latter strive to arouse and satisfy higher-level needs of the followers. Various sociopsychological classifications of small-group leaders are also available; many of these can be seen in terms of either task or relations orientation.

Many functional typologies are also available. Those for organizational leaders appear quite distinct from those for experimental small groups.

## THE LEADER AS A PERSON

### Traits of Leadership

Research on the characteristics of leaders indicates that personality is an important factor in emergence as a leader and in maintaining the role. Early theoretical attempts to define leadership in terms of personality produced a reaction by some writers who denied the importance of this quality and who said that leadership is determined by the demands of the situation. Most recent theorists maintain that leader characteristics and situational demands interact to determine the extent to which a given leader will prove successful in a group.

Stimulated by the personnel testing and selection programs begun in World War I, researchers sought to identify the distinguishing traits of leaders. Leaders were found to score higher than followers in a wide variety of characteristics, including intelligence and ability, personality, task motivation and performance, and social competence.

Research results suggest that the traits and abilities required of a leader tend to vary from one situation to another. The best predictor of leadership is prior success in this role. But previously successful leaders may fail when placed in a situation that imposes demands incompatible with their personality or that has a stabilized pattern of interaction and performance.

### Activity, Competence, and Emergence as a Leader

The member who talks and participates most actively in the group's activities is the one most likely to emerge as a leader. Leaders differ from followers in this ability to initiate and sustain interaction. Yet the members of a group are more discriminating in choice of leaders than in choice of friends. Fewer members are chosen for leader than for friend. Ratings of leader effectiveness are highly related to nominations for leadership, but not to nominations for friendship.

Group members tend to make more attempts to influence the group when their prestige is high, their control is high, they are highly motivated, they are highly esteemed, they are promised rewards, they have a reasonable expectation of task success, their influence attempts are accepted by members, and they are perceived by members as competent in the group task.

Group members who possess information enabling them to contribute more than other members to the solution of the group task tend to emerge as leaders. However, a would-be leader with excess of information or too proficient, may be handicapped. Leaders can be too able.

Observational studies have identified several patterns of leader behavior not anticipated by the trait theorists. Emergent leaders in experimental and in natural groups tend to be valued because their spontaneity is contagious and they stimulate spontaneity in others. They widen the field of participation for others and expand the area of group freedom for decision and action. They protect the weak and underchosen, encourage participation of less capable members, are tolerant of the deviate, and accept rather than reject a wide range of member personalities.

### Insight and Empathy

In comparison to others, leaders do not appear to exhibit a higher degree of *generalized* insight into the feelings of motivation of followers. But considerable positive evidence has been amassed about insight of leaders into the feelings and understandings of the *localized* situation and their own immediate followers. Often, many contingencies force qualification of the results. A variety of measurement problems further complicate outcomes.

### Authoritarianism

Measuring the authoritarianism of both leaders and followers has been most helpful in understanding their leadership preferences, performance, and satisfaction, particularly as a function of the structure and size of the groups involved. There is a tendency for authoritarian personalities to be rejected in sociometric choice. But this tendency does not necessarily prevent authoritarians from performing as leaders in task-oriented, emergent groups as well as in formal organizations. The personalities of leaders and followers interact. Authoritarian followers tend to evaluate leaders in terms of status, power, and position, whereas equalitarians evaluate their leaders as persons in terms of behavioral and personality cues. Authoritarian followers tend to feel more comfortable in large, structured groups with directive leaders. Equalitarians tend to react more favorably in small, less highly structured groups with equalitarian leaders. Equalitarian followers are somewhat more hostile toward leaders in high-status positions. Thus, the degree to which a leader is accepted and the degree of member satisfaction under authoritarian and equalitarian leaders generally is dependent upon a matching of leader personality and follower personality along with a congruent group structure.

### Values, Needs, and Satisfactions

Leaders differ in their values for many reasons. They may be selected into organizations because of their values. They may assimilate the organization's values after joining. Their profession and locale will also make for obvious differences.

However, the most important values to be found among leaders generally are task orientation and the need for self-actualization and autonomy. Their performance is associated with their pragmatism, risk preferences, and valuing of short-term maximization or long-term gain.

Pay is a strong motivator, but its effects are relative. Identification with the organization is also a strong motivator along with commitment to one's organization's goals.

But dual loyalty is commonplace. Satisfaction with the role of leader is associated with earnings and status with its accompanying power and control. Particularly important is role clarity. Although exceptions can be found, the higher one's status in an organization, the greater one's job satisfaction.

### Status, Esteem, and Charisma

More esteemed members can be more persuasive if their esteem depends on their being perceived as able to solve the group's problems. They can be more coercive if their accorded status depends on their personal control of what is desired by others in the group. Such members will attempt more leadership. However, continued direction, particularly if it is coercive, may lead to resentment and a loss of esteem.

Individuals tend to choose friends similar to themselves in social status. The group member, however, tends to prefer the high-status persons for positions of leadership. Members interact with them more frequently than with the low-status members, accept them more readily as authority figures, more readily justify their actions on behalf of the group, and exhibit more tolerance of their deviant behavior. The high-status members are permitted to suggest innovative changes in the group, but they are not expected to interrupt or otherwise to behave inconsiderately toward low-status members.

Members of a group quickly size up the leadership potential of a new member. Status evaluations made upon first acquaintance are rather highly correlated with evaluations made several weeks later. Groups tend to choose not only leaders but also other members whose values, interests, and personalities are similar to their own. Leaders tend to be regarded as more attractive than members of lower status. Both the positive and negative actions of high-status members tend to be regarded as legitimate.

Group members tend to evaluate themselves in terms of the reactions of their fellow members. The more attractive the group, the greater its impact upon the members' evaluations of themselves. For this reason, a loss of status is damaging to the members' self-respect, particularly if the downward mobility is interpreted as evidence of decreased liking by other group members. A loss of status may be accompanied by a decline in performance, reduced liking for task and group, and feelings of hostility. On the other hand, an opportunity for rise in status may be rejected by ordinary members if it involves radical changes in responsibility and style of living that are in conflict with their self-concept and system of values. Leaders appear willing to accept the responsibilities as well as the rewards of high status.

## POWER AND LEGITIMACY

### Power

Social power has been defined as an influence relation. Studies of power are concerned with the means whereby and the extent to which one individual has the potential to influence others. The most thoroughly researched sources of power are personal—expert and reference (liking and respect)—and positional—reward, coercive, and legitimate. Power represents but one aspect of role differentiation. It is not synonymous with leadership. The concept leaves unexplained much variance associated with the leadership role.

The more powerful members of a group tend to be better liked than less powerful members. They attempt more influence and exercise more of it, and their influence is more accepted. Groups tend to be better satisfied when more powerful members occupy the leadership positions.

Followers react differently to different sources of power, tending to be influenced by the expert's opinion. Followers seek to be liked by those with power. The threat of punishment tends to induce compliance, but leaders using coercive power are less attractive than those using other forms of power. Reward power tends to be responded to either by development or contractual agreements or by formation of coalitions that tend to equalize the bargaining positions of participants in the power structure. Appointment or election to a position tends to legitimize it to a greater degree than acquisition of a position by force or by emergence in interaction.

All sources of power yield influence. In real life situations the leader probably draws consciously or unconsciously upon multiple sources of power. Reward and coercive power are probably the sources most easily manipulated by leaders. They have less control over referent power—the extent to which group members like them and are attracted to them (H. H. Jennings, 1950; Borgatta & Bales, 1953b). Degree of expertness can usually be improved by study or training. By their conduct, leaders can increase or decrease the perceived legitimacy of their position.

Self-confidence, self-esteem, and knowledge of task enable subordinates to resist influence attempts. Ingratiation may to some extent mitigate exercise of power over followers. Interacting with peers and support provided by reference groups tend to strengthen follower resistance to power. The influence of a leader can be weakened by formation of coalitions and cliques with bargaining power. Followers can reduce the extent to which they are subject to influence by asking and receiving a clear definition of the situation. The power of a leader is weakened by the presence of members whose values and goals are in opposition to those of the leader and the organization, and thus challenge the legitimacy of the leadership role.

The advantage in a power situation, however, appears to reside with the holder of power. For every source of power, countermeasures can be utilized by followers to reduce the extent to which they are subject to influence. Thus, social power implies a relationship in which participants are bound together by interdependency, influence, and exchange. In the absence of mutual obligation that participants will honor, there is no stable basis for exercise of power.

*Power Distribution*

The overall power available to the group rather than to its individual members strongly affects member conformity to persistence and change in attitudes and behavior. How power is distributed in the group is associated with its structure of role relations.

Group members exhibit a desire for structure, especially under conditions of stress, threat, and task pressure. But power sharing is also desired. The extent to which structure is desired tends to vary with the personality of the individual and the demands of the situation. Group members tend to feel better satisfied under moderate degrees of structure than under overly structured or totally unstructured conditions. But they prefer too much structure over none at all. Groups tend to be more productive and more cohesive in structured rather than unstructured situations. Formal structure does not necessarily block satisfaction of needs for autonomy and self-actualization. Some degree of structure is necessary for the satisfaction of follower needs.

An opportunity to discuss a proposed change facilitates its acceptance by members who will be affected by it. Participation in planning and decision making regarding the change induces a still higher degree of acceptance. As a consequence, power sharing programs and restructuring, both voluntary and mandated, have become common.

### Conflict and Legitimacy

Role ambiguity and lack of a clear task definition are associated with lowered job satisfaction and reluctance to initiate action. Middle managers and first-line supervisors experience more role ambiguity than top managers.

The necessity of playing contradictory roles may be stressful, but individuals seem able to play a variety of roles without apparent stress. Greater pressure ensues when contradictory demands are made upon the same role. Disagreement between leaders and their superiors on the definition of the leader's role is a potent source of role conflict as are contradictory demands.

Workers are better satisfied and more productive when their supervisors are able to predict the reactions of their superiors. The failure of a superior to support supervisors results in lowered self-esteem on the part of the supervisors and in reduced esteem for them by their subordinates. Disagreement between supervisors and their superiors as to the supervisors' role results in greater anxiety and disagreement between the supervisors and their subordinates.

The supervisors' influence is increased when their subordinates acknowledge the legitimacy of their role. How legitimate the subordinates see the severity with which their supervisors apply sanctions for subordinate noncompliance tends to influence subordinate compliance. Compliance will also depend upon the leader's personality. Such legitimation of the leader role appears to depend upon the degree of consensus with which the members perceive the role. One function of high status may be the maintenance of stability in definition of roles.

The leadership role is subject to a variety of conflicting expectations. The extent to which the leader is able to fulfill these expectations tends to determine the degree to which the groups concerned will legitimize the leadership role.

### Responsibility, Authority, and Delegation

Members of organizations tend to accept rather than reject authority. Furthermore, they tend to resist a reduction in their own authority. Scope of responsibility and authority tends to increase as level in organizational hierarchy increases. Responsibility tends to be more highly related to amount of education than to age or time in position. Leaders with more authority tend to describe their own superiors as more considerate leaders. Delegation is not highly related to leader behavior, but in some organizations leaders who delegate freely are described as inconsiderate. Follower satisfaction is not highly related to leader responsibility, authority, or delegation. When superiors are high in responsibility and authority, their subordinates tend to delegate less freely, perhaps due to the greater demands for coordination and control made upon the subordinates by superiors with much responsibility and authority.

In large organizations, free delegation by superiors results in free delegation by subordinates down to the lowest levels of supervision. In small organizations, however, free delegation by superiors is accompanied by restricted delegation among first-line supervisors. The responsibility of superiors tends to influence the performance of subordinates, but their authority produces its strongest impact on subordinate expectations. Large amounts of both responsibility and authority on the part of superiors are perceived by subordinates to increase demands made upon them for coordination. When superiors delegate freely, subordinates report that they are overburdened with responsibilities and need more authority than they possess. Delegation is not viewed as an unmixed blessing by subordinates when they have critical or burdensome duties to perform. The responsibility, more than the authority, of superiors appears associated with lowered follower satisfaction and performance. But it should be clear that the responsibility, authority, and delegative tendencies of any one leader must be understood within the context of the larger organizational setting in which the leader must operate.

## LEADER–FOLLOWER INTERACTION

### Reinforcement and the Propensity to Interact

Mutual esteem, familiarity, intimacy, homogeneity and other situational and status variables increase the propensity to interact.

Leadership attempts are made more frequently under high than under low probabilities of reinforcement. Positive reinforcement is more effective than negative reinforcement. Success in attempting to lead appears to reinforce the expectation of further success in leading. Nonleaders, when their attempts at leadership are reinforced, tend to exhibit a higher rate of leadership acts and their leadership improves in the eyes of fellow group members.

Possessing the ability to offer rewards or to reinforce the expectations of other group members constitutes an advantage toward emerging as a leader. An individual is better liked when he or she is able to fulfill, rather than disappoint, the expectations of other group members.

### Interdependence of Leaders and Followers

Leadership and followership are reciprocal. Different patterns of interaction among superiors vary in their effects upon the performance and expectations of subordinates. When superiors interact with subordinates and with members within their own subgroup, their subordinates report a loss of responsibility but feel overburdened with planning. When superiors interact with members other than their own subordinates and subgroup members, however, their subordinates feel under pressure to increase efforts in planning, coordination, inspection, and preparing procedures. These counterbalancing reactions appear logically consistent.

The relationships between interactions, performance, and expectations change to some extent as the group undergoes change. For this reason, these findings do not apply to all groups in general or to the same group under all circumstances.

Impersonal, as opposed to more highly personalized, performance tends to have an integrative effect upon interactions among subordinates. The tendency of superiors to interact with their subordinates also tends to produce an integrative effect among them. But the great variety of counteracting effects suggests that leaders may be required to thread their way with considerable discrimination in order to keep their subordinates working with them as a cohesive group. The interaction patterns of superiors influence not only the interaction patterns of subordinates but also their work and the kinds of problems they have to solve.

Leaders play a mediating and connecting role between their followers and their own superiors. Their attempts to ally themselves with their subordinates and to work in behalf of their subordinates tend to result in follower dissatisfaction unless the leaders have enough influence with superiors to obtain the benefits sought for subordinates. Leaders must have influence "upstairs" in order to be successful. Under conditions of stress and rapid change, however, good relations between the leaders and their superiors may widen the gap between the leaders and their followers.

Groups operate more successfully and experience less stress when task structure, leader personality, and follower personality are compatible. For example, groups with task-oriented leaders perform better than those with person-oriented leaders under conditions of stress and high task structure, expecially when followers are also task-oriented. Followers low in task orientation experience less tension under person-oriented leaders and with tasks of low or medium structure.

Leaders act as models, cues, and molders of expectations and satisfaction. Leaders' behavior often is a reaction to the followers' competence, maturity, interpersonal behavior, and objectives.

## MANAGEMENT AND STYLES OF LEADERSHIP

### Management in the Working Situation

The manager or administrator does much more than just supervise subordinates. However, the manager's effectiveness to a considerable degree depends on getting work done through others. Interpersonal skills are needed at all levels according to various time uses and position analyses of the work done.

A manager's hierarchical level affects the time for which decisions are to be made and the lag in feedback about the effects. Work overload is a common experience at all levels as are systematic differences in effective and ineffective performance as a manager.

### Democratic versus Autocratic Leadership

A large cluster of styles can be included in democratic leadership and/or person-related behaviors: employee-oriented, considerate, concerned with need satisfaction, maintenance oriented, "1–9," rewarding and nonpunitive, supportive, relations-oriented, open, close, informal, warm, System 4, and people-centered. Included in autocratic leadership and/or work-related behaviors are opposites to the above: job-centered, structuring, task-oriented, "9–1," punitive, closed, distant, formal, cold, System 1, and work-centered.

All other things being equal, generally the patterns of leader behavior included in democratic leadership are more satisfying and more effective than those associated with autocratic leadership. This is particularly so if the democratic leadership can also include the task orientation and concern for goals and production without loss of employee orientation. The positive effects of democratic leadership are also more likely to be seen if long-term employee development and commitment are important to productivity. But numerous conditions, such as the authoritarianism of subordinates or the culture, increase the utility of autocratic methods.

The positive effects of democratic approaches are most apparent if we depend on the results of large-scale field surveys and lagged productivity measurements rather than small-group laboratory experiments with immediate, concurrent effects.

A sharper picture of leadership effects can be seen as we look at more distinctive components of democratic leadership such as participation, relations orientation, and consideration for subordinates.

### Participative versus Directive Leadership

This focuses on the extent to which decisions are made by the superior, the subordinate, or both. Although conceptual distinctions are clearly maintained between direction, negotiation, and participation, most leaders exhibit all these modes with different frequency. Many antecedent conditions add to the variance found in these patterns. Participation is indicated when subordinate acceptance, satisfaction, and commitment are important and where subordinates have the required information. But direction can also be effective when structure is needed, when the leader has the necessary information, when decision quality is more important than subordinate commitment, and so on. Both empirical and rational models are available for specifying the conditions under which either more direction or more participation is appropriate.

### Relations-Oriented and Task-Oriented Leadership

Particularly important are the leaders' personality and the subordinates' attitudes to the task and relations orientation of leaders. In general, the leader who is more highly rated by superiors and peers, who is most satisfying to subordinates, and whose approach results in good group performance is likely to be both relations-oriented and task-oriented. But many situational contingencies moderate the effects. Best known is Fiedler's contingency model stating that task orientation (as measured by LPC) works best in situations either extremely favorable or extremely unfavorable to the leader; relations orientation works best in situations in between such favorableness (or control of the leader). Despite a vast array of publications on the reliability, validity, and meaning of LPC and situational favorableness or control and despite many supportive tests of the model, the validity of the model is still contested.

### Consideration and Initiating Structure

Again, personal and situational variables of considerable variety relate to the appearance of leader consideration and initiation of structure. The latter becomes more important when less structure is available to the group. Psychometric reviews of results using the original and revised LBDQ and the SBDQ indicate that the generally negative association between task-oriented initiation of structure as measured by the SBDQ and satisfaction and morale become positive when the coercive elements are removed. But leniency is likely to continue to bias results. Self-ratings seem unlikely to indicate what leaders do or will do according to their subordinates. Many contingencies can be cited as moderators of the relationships. A variety of expanded and alternative factor structures are available for a more detailed study of leader behavior with LBDQ XII.

Causal analyses by cross-lagged surveys and experimentation suggest that consideration both increases subordinate satisfaction and is increased by it. Initiation of structure by the leader (if structure is low) improves subordinate performance, which in turn increases the leader's subsequent consideration and reduces the leader's initiation of structure.

### Laissez-Faire Leadership versus Motivation to Manage

Uniformly, laissez-faire leaders are downgraded by their subordinates. Productivity, cohesiveness, and satisfaction suffer under such leadership. But this should not be confused with the positive effects of legitimate autonomy for subordinates. In contrast to laissez-faire, active, responsible, masculine assertiveness and related behaviors are required for success as a manager in the typical hierarchy, although possibly not to the extremes proposed in Miner's model. An integration of findings about various types of leaders' active intervention suggests that all such activity is not necessarily more efficacious to the group than nonactive laissez-faire leadership. Rather, person-oriented behaviors tend to promote follower satisfaction; they may or may not contribute to group productivity. Work-oriented behaviors restricting member participation and applying pressure for production may or may not further group productivity. Those maintaining role differentiation and clarifying expectations tend to further productivity; however, only the work-oriented pattern that structures and clarifies expectations promotes follower satisfaction and group cohesiveness. The person-oriented behaviors that contribute to group cohesiveness are those facilitating member freedom for participation and ensuring the welfare and comfort of followers.

The stucturing of expectations is the only pattern that contributes positively to group productivity, cohesiveness, and satisfaction. This pattern of behavior is the central factor in leadership where leadership is defined as the initiation and maintenance of structure in expectation and interaction. It is doubtful that leaders in most situations can be of positive value to the group's performance, satisfaction, and cohesiveness without this kind of active leader structuring unless all such structure has already been provided by other means.

## SITUATIONAL ASPECTS

### Organizational and Environmental Determinants

How the leader and subordinates relate to each other within the group depends upon societal influences, real outside relationships, and reference groups in the minds of both. For example, leaders who see economic externalities as most important tend to be more directive; leaders who see social or political influences from the outside as more important tend to be more participative. The surrounding organization and its policies, size, and structure are of particular consequence to leader–subordinate interaction. The leader's discretionary and nondiscretionary behavior also depends on organizational and environmental considerations.

### The Immediate Group

Leader-subordinate relations depend on the phase of the group's development in which the leadership is occurring as well as the group's history.

As newly formed groups progress, they find it necessary to resolve contests for influence and to develop role structure and cohesiveness before they can engage in effective task performance. Leaders are expected to provide role structure, maintain goal direction, and resolve interpersonal problems. If leaders fail to fulfill their expected roles, new leaders tend to emerge.

Group drive and cohesiveness contribute to the success or failure of goal attainment. Cohesive groups can either effectively further the leader's and the organization's aims or sabotage them.

The larger the group, the more difficult it becomes for a randomly selected member to acquire leadership. Large groups make greater demands on the leader than small ones. Particularly important to this are the group's norms. Groups develop norms that define appropriate conduct for members. Once a norm has become stabilized in the mutual expectations of members, members bring strong pressures to bear on the individual who deviates from the norm. Deviates who persist in their nonconformity tend to be rejected. The more cohesive the group, the greater the pressure it exerts in an effort to induce conformity to its norms.

The greater the extent to which group members absorb the norms and values of a group, the greater the probability of their emergence as leaders. As leaders, they tend to act as a strong exponent of group norms and tend to conform to them. However, leaders who have consolidated their position may be granted considerable latitude in departing from group norms. The goals of a group operate as group norms in terms of which members evaluate group performance. Leaders exhibit stronger concern and commitment to the group goal and work harder for group success than do followers. Goals are used by members as criteria for evaluation of group performances. Expectations operate as a norm that induces a strong pressure for compliance.

Leaders usually belong to more groups than other members and tend to facilitate integration of the group into the larger community. Their acceptance by a group is increased if they identify themselves with the membership group rather than with external reference groups. In a structured hierarchy, those leaders identifying with superiors and with the organization tend to be rated as more effective and are better satisfied with their jobs than those identifying with subordinates or with external reference groups.

### Task Determinants

Task requirements systematically affect what happens in the group. Task requirements of consequence are structure, clarity, provisions for discretion, routineness, variety, complexity, difficulty, and socioemotional elements.

Path-goal theory has been widely tested and modified to account for the impact of the task on optimum leader–subordinate relations. Currently, it suggests that in order to obtain effective subordinate performance and satisfaction the leader must provide structure if it is missing and must supply rewards contingent on adequate subordinate performance. To do this, leaders must clarify the paths to the goals and the desirability of the goals for the subordinates.

### Stress

Stress situations can be categorized in a variety of ways, and emergent and effective leadership will vary accordingly. Groups may be frustrated by unattainable goals. They may be in fear of impending dangers. They may be anxious because of unclear and ambiguous demands. They may be in conflict over competing demands or with other groups. Groups may be in a state of inertia perceived as less risky and costly than actively responding to warnings of danger. They may be aroused to respond impulsively, defensively, or in panic. Threats to survival may be internal or external, substantive or interpersonal.

The emergent leader will do what is immediately required to provide the group with ways of coping with the stress. Rapid direction, initiation of structure, and task-oriented leadership will make the leader more likely to succeed. Groups will be more susceptible to such influence.

Both demagogues and statesmen and -women can exhibit such success as leaders in times of crisis. Transactional and transformational leadership both can be successful. The transactional demagogue can assure inert followers that the warnings are unimportant and persuade impulsive followers that simple solutions are acceptable. He can convince defensive followers by bolstering and shifting responsibility and he can sway panicking followers with other-worldly solutions. The demogogue can successfully lead the popular, easier search for internal subversives when complex external problems are paramount. The effective leader (who, of course, must also successfully influence followers) is a transforming statesman who addresses the inert followers by shaking them out of their torpor in the face of impending dangers or by rousing them to work toward seemingly unobtainable goals. The transforming statesman shows followers the inadequacies of simple solutions and defensive avoidance. Superordinate goals are provided for the hypervigilant, and motivation and initiation of structure are provided for adequate search, appraisal of alternatives, and contingency plans.

The survival of a group is dependent upon a type of leadership able to keep members and subgroups working together toward a common purpose, maintain productivity at a level sufficient to sustain the group or to justify its existence, and satisfy member expectations regarding leader and group. Competent leadership is especially needed in times of crisis to unite the efforts of members and strengthen group cohesiveness around a common purpose. A group that desires to survive will prevent leaders of contending factions from destroying the legitimacy of the group.

### Interpersonal Space

Studies of interpersonal space indicate that individuals interact more frequently with those located close to them than with those farther away. The member who occupies the head position at the table tends to assume leadership. Leaders tend to gravitate toward head positions and are expected to do so. Members occupying head positions tend to be more influential than those occupying side or peripheral positions. Members tend to maintain greater physical distance between themselves and members of high or low status than between themselves and status peers. Status differences and social distance tend to be valued when consequences of social interaction may be unpleasant, when participants in interaction are likely to be compared on an evaluative basis, and when effective group performance is desired by group members.

Individuals who live or work in close proximity to each other also exhibit a higher rate of mutual sociometric choice than those situated at a greater distance from each other.

Personal interaction and group achievement tend to be facilitated by some degree of psychosocial distance between leader and followers. Individuals prefer greater social distance between themselves and their competitors than between themselves and those with whom they cooperate.

### Communication Networks

Research on experimental communication nets indicates that the member who occupies a position of centrality tends to emerge as leader. He or she has greater access to communication than other members and is thus better able to coordinate and direct group activities. Groups with positions of centrality are more efficient than those with undifferentiated role structures. The member who occupies a position of centrality is better satisfied with the group than are members in peripheral positions. Personal factors such as the need for autonomy and ascendancy moderate effects. The results have implications for parallel real-world organizational networks.

The openness of channels is directly related to the information available to a leader and therefore to the leader's ability to exert influence. Regular meetings usually (but not always) provide more continuing communications, promoting group performance.

### Persistence and Transfer of Leadership

Strong evidence has been found supporting the view that leadership is transferable from one situation to another. Although the nature of task demands may limit transferability, there is a tendency for the leader in one group to emerge in this capacity when placed in other groups.

Leadership in high school and college tends to be predictive of leadership in adult life. When members of experimental groups are successively reassigned to new groups, the same individuals tend to emerge as leaders. This effect is enhanced when the task is similar from group to group.

When successful and unsuccessful leaders change places, formerly ineffective groups tend to gain in performance and morale under successful leaders, while formerly effective groups tend to decline in performance and morale under unsuccessful leaders.

Groups that change leaders frequently or experience high rates of personnel turnover tend to suffer a reduction in productivity. But such reductions may be the cause of rapid turnover of leaders. Moderators of the effect may include whether successors are insiders or outsiders and how abruptly changes are made.

## SPECIAL SITUATIONS

### Women

Situational changes are occurring rapidly. Earlier research may need to be discounted. Despite the many continuing handicaps to movement into positions of leadership due to socialization and stereotyping, progress is being made. Characteristics usually linked to masculinity are still demanded for effective management. Many of the differences in male and female leadership tend to be accounted for by other controllable or modifiable factors, although women will continue to face conflicts in their decisions to play roles as wives and mothers as well as managers and leaders.

### Blacks

Again, much change has occurred in recent years suggesting the need to discount earlier studies. Constraints still ride heavily on black leaders as compared to whites. Leadership styles are affected by whether leaders and subordinates are black or white. Relatively little is known as yet about black leaders supervising whites or mixed groups although some evidence is beginning to appear.

### Leadership in Different Cultures

Cultural dimensions of consequence to leadership include traditionalism, particularism, and idealism in a given society compared to valuing modernity, universalism, and pragmatism. In-group, out-group feelings also are important. In the same way, needs for achievement, affiliation, and power of subordinates and supervisors have different effects on their relations in difficult cultures.

Although some argue that there is one best way to manage, considerable evidence points to autocratic leader behavior being more effective in authoritarian cultures, and democratic styles, in democratic cultures. The same is seen for direction versus participation, task versus relations orientation, and initiation versus consideration.

Within the multinational firm, leader–subordinate relations will be affected by whether the firm is ethnocentric, polycentric, or geocentric and whether the individuals involved are from the parent country of the organization, the host country, or a third country.

## APPLICATIONS AND IMPLICATIONS

### Leadership Training and Management Development

Looser, experiential approaches have been favored over highly structured didactic lectures but new kinds of highly structured experiences such as provided by behavior modeling have demonstrated desired training effects. Nevertheless, sensitivity training continues to be widely practiced. Considerable research is available about its effects. Positive results depend to some extent on opportunities for the transfer of learning into appropriate organizational settings.

On-the-job leadership training such as coaching seems to be widely practiced but is underresearched. Studies are available about some of the training effects of most of the leadership styles advocated in Chapters 18 through 22. Special attention is now being given to examining ways to train leaders to work effectively with minorities and the disadvantaged. Specific programs to prepare people for foreign assignments have also been evaluated.

Research indicates, not unexpectedly, that the effectiveness of training depends on the trainee, the trainer, the composition of the training group, followup reinforcement and feedback, and particularly on whether there is congruence between the training and the organizational environment for which the trainee is being prepared.

## A SUMMING UP

The real test of leadership lies not in the personality or behavior of the leaders, but in the performance of the groups they lead. Groups, when free to do so, appear to select as leaders members who create the expectation that they will be able to maintain goal direction, facilitate task achievement, and ensure group cohesiveness. Whether objectives are long-term to develop the group or short-term to maximize current performance will make a decided difference. The behaviors furthering task accomplishment are not necessarily the same as those fostering cohesiveness. Some leaders are extremely effective in furthering task achievement. Others are exceptionally skilled in the art of building member satisfaction and intermember loyalty, which strengthen group cohesiveness. The most valued leaders are able to do both.

# 35

## ISSUES FOR THE EIGHTIES AND BEYOND

### CONSIDERATIONS IN LOOKING AHEAD

First, we can look ahead by extrapolation. What can be seen is more longitudinal research and fewer one-time, cross-sectional studies. We should also be seeing more field studies and laboratory studies that are integrated with them. At the same time, there should appear more sophisticated evaluations of the leader's interaction processes, not only with subordinates but also with superiors, peers, and clients.

Second, leadership research is influenced considerably by what is happening in society as a whole. The majority of the American work force has shifted from manufacturing to service. Opportunities to increase productivity increasingly depend on effective human relationships and the development of personnel. In the same way, even when at lower levels humans are replaced with robots and computers, more higher level personnel specialists, supervisors, and team development are likely to be required. Industrial democracy is likely to become a fact of life in the United States as it is now in Western Europe. The percentage of relations-oriented personnel in the U.S. labor force has dramatically increased with the sharp increase in the employment of women. A plural society of varied ethnicity and race is replacing the ideal of an amalgamated society. The multinational firm with its world-wide outlook continues to expand. Foreign investment in the United States has risen sharply as well. We are likely to see leadership research continuing to reflect these societal developments. Thus, Pascarella and Cook (1978) see that a premium will be placed on the middle managers' abilities to deal with the human factor. More statesmanship will be required of top managers.

The turnover and low quality of the all-volunteer armed services may focus attention on new approaches to promoting stability and cohesiveness through better leadership. Educational leadership in the 1980s is also likely to take a sharp turn in the face of declining enrollments. A more energy-conserving world generates both a requirement for better relations and a mounting concern for productivity. More research will be needed on how these are best merged. Increasingly, there will be less toleration of laissez-faire leadership. But care will have to be exerted to avoid a drift back to promoting autocratic behavior in the guise of active leadership, particularly if unemployment and job insecurity remain high. The world of computerized management information systems—the organization predicted over twenty years ago by Leavitt and Whistler (1958) for the 1980s—has arrived. Yet, there is little research on how managers' interactions with each other, with superiors, peers, subordinates, and clients have been altered.

**599**

To date, behavioral research on management information systems has been unimpressive, but a breakthrough in empirical research spearheaded by new models may be in the offing.

The third consideration is the possibility of revolutionary paradigms. We have already seen the rapid impact of social learning theory (Chapter 33). Uses for catastrophe theory from mathematics may be found that have a larger appreciation of natural discontinuities in leader–follower relationships. The social science of leadership may be influenced by new ways of looking at phenomena developed in twentieth-century physics. For example, a willingness to accept two distinct ways of dealing with the same phenomenon may lead leadership theorists to treat simultaneously the leader's and subordinates' rationales for what is happening. Cause-and-effect analyses may be seen as the exception to mutual interactions between leader and group outcomes.

Given the issues that have dominated leadership research in the past decade, the expected continuing societal change, and possibly revolutionary shifts in thinking, what shall we expect to see dominating in the near future?

## METHODOLOGICAL ISSUES

### Causal Relations

It is becoming increasingly clear that it may be as plausible to accept the hypothesis that the considerate, supportive supervisor is so because the subordinates' performance is good as to argue that consideration results in improved subordinate performance (Bass, 1965c).

Of eighty-nine leadership studies between 1970 and 1975 reviewed by Hunt, Osborn, and Schriesheim (1977), 24 percent of the field studies and almost all the laboratory studies concentrated on causal relations. Despite the shortcomings of laboratory studies, they still make causal data collection convenient; something much more difficult to accomplish in the field. However, it is edifying to see the increasing effort to search in field studies for causal relationships by cross-lag analyses. But care needs to be exerted particularly about the need for highly reliable measures. Regression strategies such as path analysis require strong enough relationships to permit the testing of alternative models.

### Laboratory versus Field Studies

Substantively, the bulk of studies have been about supervisory behavior and reactions to it. In the field, actual managers and their associates in a wide variety of organizations have served as the focus. In the laboratory, superior–subordinate relations have been simulated. A fundamental question has been posed about whether the temporariness of laboratory relations is so different from the ongoing, real-life leader–subordinate relationship that such laboratory situations cannot faithfully represent the real-world relationship. Osborn and Vicars (1976) noted a particular source of error in trying to generalize the function of sex roles from laboratory studies of leader–follower relations. Short-term laboratory situations tend to evoke participant behavior based on available stereotypes. Extensive interpersonal contact in real life provides a more realistic basis for behavior. Laboratory studies are likely to yield deceptive results overstating the total influence of sex-role stereotyping.

Hunt, Osborn, and Schriesheim (1977), reviewing six major journals for leadership articles between 1970 through 1975 found that seventy-two of the eighty-nine were field studies; only seventeen were laboratory investigations. Clearly, exclusive reliance on laboratory studies should be avoided. Another reason for such avoidance was noted by Bass (1974) as Meehl's paradox: the more aseptic and controlled the laboratory study, the greater its precision in outcome. For physics, such greater precision increases confidence in the generality of the finding; in social science, it does just the opposite. Ideally, laboratory studies should be planned in conjunction with field work before and after.

### The Erroneous Law of Small Numbers

The law of large numbers states that large random samples will be highly representative of the population from which they are drawn. The law of small numbers assumes erroneously that small samples will be similarly representative. Tversky and Kahneman (1971) demonstrated that such belief in the law of small numbers leads to highly inflated estimates of the amount of information contained in small-sample studies. Schmidt and Hunter (1980) see that much of the variation from situation to situation in observed relationships in small samples can be accounted for as random departures from a relatively simple overall generalization. This is in contrast to inducing from the variations a generalization needing qualification and explanation as a consequence of the observed situational variations in outcomes. For example, in examining the relationship between individual competence and job performance, Schmidt, Hunter, and Urry (1976) showed that sample sizes were almost always too small to produce acceptable levels of statistical power. Thus, if the true relation between, say, intelligence test scores and success as a leader is really .30 or .40, any sample of 30 to 50 would yield a result statistically significant from zero only 25 to 50 percent of the time. For statistical power of .90, to statistically reject 90 percent of the time the zero relationship when the true one is .30 or .40, sample sizes of 200 or 300 are needed. Thus, we may look at ten small-sample studies of intelligence test scores as they relate to leadership performance and find half statistically significant and half lacking in such significance. Then, we try to develop a generalization to account for the different findings, when in fact the differences can be accounted for by the law of large numbers. The obvious implication is our need to be cautious in interpreting the meaning of situational variance when the data from the different situations are based on small samples. With contingent analyses using small samples, we will err considerably in rejecting the null hypothesis at the 5 percent level of confidence that no differences exist between different contingencies. Thus, Hunter and Schmidt (1978) noted that 28 percent of the time (at the 5 percent level of confidence) we could find ourselves erroneously inferring differential relationships between, say, intelligence and performance for black leaders as compared to white leaders when no true difference exists if we depend upon sample sizes of thirty each. The problem is far from academic. In the study of leadership of eighty-nine reports between 1970 and 1975 reviewed by Hunt, Osborn, and Schriesheim (1977), 20 percent used samples as small as thirty or even less in analyses of data. The problem is compounded in dealing with leadership because ordinarily only small samples of leaders are available unless the organization is very large. We may need to reexamine carefully how much contingent results occur because of the low power of the sampling upon which many are based.

Some of the remaining controversy about Fiedler's contingency model might be settled if we had access to all the available LPC scores of leaders along with standardized data about the favorability of the situation to the leader and the effectiveness of the group. Two large samples could be drawn for cross-validations for each octant. Two large sample correlations would substitute for the median of the smaller sample correlations usually reported. We would, of course, be required to ignore other contaminating differences between the samples.

### Measurement Problems

*Limitations.*   As we have already ventured in Chapter 3, we need to be conscious about the serious limitations in our measurements. Elaborate theories may spin out tales of curvilinear complexity and multiplicative effects implying that $y = ax + by + cxy$. Yet, fifty years of such analyses including $cxy$ have generally proved to add little beyond error to the equation. Theory building should not go too far beyond what is empirically possible. As Korman (1973) noted, contingency hypotheses should be entertained in a theory only if they are empirically supported and necessary. Although contingency models intuitively are more appealing than main-effect models, the robustness of simple linear models (Yntema & Torgerson, 1961) suggest caution in moving to contingency models.

*Simple versus Complex Hypothesis Testing.*   As noted in Chapter 3, we face a dilemma. On the one hand, Lieberman (1976a) noted that "the chain of relationships between leader behavior and outcome is long and complex." We miss much of what needs to be understood if we simply try to relate leader behavior, particularly generalized leader behavior, to final group outcomes. The relation must be considered in terms of the group's norms, cohesiveness, and so on, as well as the leader's characteristics. Member expectation may be more important in determining group outcomes than anything the leader can do. Multivariate analyses, complex models, and contingent and moderator analyses need to be used. On the other hand, L. G. Cronbach (1975) saw the likelihood that second- or higher-order interactions are likely to render inconsistent any simple moderator effects from sample to sample. Like Bass (1974), he argued for more openness to experience and greater clinical understanding of data, using less complex models that demand less mathematical rigor. Similarly, Korman and Tanofsky (1975) added that a priori models are difficult to use because of the difficulties of accurately estimating necessary parameters. Yet, empirical models may be fraught with psychometric errors. But they conclude that both kinds of models can be helpful in identifying the important elements for study rather than the final true relationships.

*Theoretical Biases.*   Theoretical preferences and preconceptions already mentioned have limited the range of research. Reviews of leadership research and opinion, of which hundreds are available, tend to consider the same small collection of studies over and over again. Thus, the same misconceptions have been perpetuated year after year during the past three decades. Additional research has not alleviated the problem because much of it is formulated in terms of a few widely publicized hypotheses. When research fails to support popular hypotheses, it tends to be ignored on the grounds that the research instruments were inadequate or the sample was poorly selected. These questions are not raised, of course, when positive results are obtained. As we have noted earlier, negative research results are much less likely to be published. Thus, it appears that the accretion of new publications has done little to change opinion regarding the nature of the relationship between leader behavior and group performance.

*Leniency Effects.* The quality of leadership measures is likely to see improvement as a consequence of Schriesheim, Kinicki, and Schriesheim's (1979) demonstration of the strong leniency effect in the LBDQ-XII consideration scale. Similar leniency is likely to be found in related measures of leaders' relations orientation, participation, and support. Such leniency may account for much of the association between subordinates' descriptions of their leaders' consideration and the subordinates' satisfaction. Measures of initiating structure free of coercion and measures of consideration free of leniency (if such is possible) will provide more precise measurements against which to pit situational and personal variables for study.

*Errors in Leaders' Self-Ratings.* Repeatedly in earlier chapters, we have seen little or no relation between leaders' self-descriptions compared to those of their subordinates. Leaders' self-ratings are suspect. They have consistently been found to relate poorly or not at all with various dependent variables (Schriesheim & Kerr, 1977b). Most are probably contaminated by social desirability (Schriesheim & Kerr, 1974). They contain self-serving, self-vindicating biases and are likely to generate descriptions of what leaders think is expected of them in their organization and society rather than an accurate portrayal of their behavior relative to other leaders. Not uncommon is the manager who assures everyone that there is always full consultation on subordinates' problems since the manager's door is always open. Then there is the democratic manager who announces that the organization is going to be democratic or else sanctions will be imposed.

Training and research efforts will over time make greater use of superiors', peers', and subordinates' ratings and less of leaders' self-ratings of their purported behavior. But, as will be discussed later, leaders' perceptions, attributions, cognitions, and opinions will continue to be of considerable research importance as a link to what the leader actually does.

### Dyadic versus Group Relations

Some suggestions have appeared that the felt need to describe leaders' performance in terms of their one-on-one relationships with each of their subordinates is more conceptually pleasing than empirically fruitful. However, the dyadic approach can be applied with considerable utility to a variety of research questions. For example, sanctioning and punitive leader behavior seems to be the result rather than the cause of inadequate subordinate performance. It follows that dyadic analysis should reveal strong differential dealings of supervisors with their subordinates based on the leaders' differential judgments about each of their subordinates. Indeed, we are likely to find experimental support for Hollander's (1978) important observation that leaders have ''A'' lists and ''B'' lists of subordinates. The As are closer; Bs are more distant. Work-oriented leaders are likely to relegate the more incompetent of their subordinates to the B list and to treat them more punitively. But the As will be expected to be more loyal and obedient and will be required to maintain higher standards of performance. Person-oriented leaders may exert extra effort with their black sheep, seeing their most competent subordinates as sources of conflict by their deviation in performance in excess of group norms. The linkages to LPC are apparent.

No doubt we shall see an increasing use of dyadic analyses of a leader's relations with individual peers, individual superiors, and relevant others.

### Focus on Perception or Behavior

Considerable exploitation about attribution phenomena can be applied with profit to the leader–follower relationship. The leader's behavior toward subordinates appears to be strongly determined by the reasons (ability or motivation) the leader gives for the subordinate's performance—how much it is a matter of luck, situation, or the subordinate's control. In the same way, subordinates' attributions of the reasons for the leader's behavior will strongly relate to the subordinates' satisfaction. The leader judged by subordinates as willing but incompetent seems to be more forgivable than the leader judged competent but unwilling.

As we have already noted, conscious perceptions can determine the leader's subsequent efforts. Thus, Nebeker and Mitchell (1974) found that differences in leadership behavior could be explained by the leader's expectations that a certain style of leadership would be effective in a given situation. At the same time, subordinates' descriptions of their leader's behavior may be distorted by their implicit theories about leadership, particularly when they lack real information about the situation and are inclined therefore to fall back on stereotypes (Schriesheim & deNisi, 1978).

*Behavioral Accounts Are Still Needed.* Purely behavioral explanations cannot be dismissed. One can look at leadership as a perceptual phenomenon under certain conditions or a behavioral phenomenon under others and accurately explain what is happening in both instances. Leadership research has been heavily dependent on subordinates' reported perceptions of their leader's behavior. Yet, Gilmore, Beehr, and Richter (1979) demonstrated in a laboratory setting that although participants failed to perceive that their leaders (instructed to be high or low in initiation and consideration) actually differed in their behavior, actual (but not perceived) high initiation coupled with high consideration by the leaders resulted in higher work quality, as expected. Least quality occurred when actual leader initiation of structure was high but leader consideration was low. It is clear that we need more studies that do not depend solely on subordinate observations and descriptions.

### SUBSTANTIVE ISSUES

### Personality

Research designed solely to isolate the characteristics of leaders has reached the point of diminishing returns. Perhaps there are dimensions of leader personality and behavior yet to be discovered. However, factor-analytic studies do not offer a great deal of encouragement to the researcher who hopes to invent a uniquely new trait. Newly defined traits are likely to load rather heavily on factors already identified.

Nevertheless, personality is now to be seen as interacting with situational variables to account for leadership and group performance. It may have more importance in some situations than others and more with some people than with others. It may be dominant in cultural settings where, to be a leader, one must epitomize the authoritarianism rooted in the culture. As we noted earlier, autocrats may behave that way because of their personalities; democrats may behave the way they do as a consequence of other immediate situational and personal considerations.

Research designed to test the effect on the group of leader characteristics interacting with follower characteristics generally has been effective for producing valuable insights into leader–follower relations. The research on different combinations of authoritarian leaders and followers by Haythorn, Couch, Haefner, Langham, and Carter (1956b), Calvin, Hoffmann, and Harden (1957), and Frey (1963) suggests designs that could be used to test the effects of other leader–follower characteristics. The study of self-interaction- and task-oriented leaders and followers by Bass, Dunteman, et al. (1963) suggests another useful approach.

There is a scarcity of research that tests the interaction of leader personality, values, and behaviors with follower personality, values, and behaviors and the effect of such interaction upon the group. Results of several studies suggest that extreme homogeneity in leader–follower characteristics may be dysfunctional to exercise of leadership and group performance. This hypothesis needs to be tested for each of a number of personality, value, and behavior variables.

### Emergence of the Leadership Role

Research on emergence of the leadership role includes some of the most sophisticated experiments on the subject. It exhibits a high degree of originality in its theoretical basis and in conceptualization of experimental strategies. At the same time, research on interpersonal perception presents uniform evidence that individuals quickly perceive status differences and evaluate others for leadership potential. A problem in need of investigation might be phrased as follows: "What range of leader personality traits will be acceptable to a group that is highly homogeneous with respect to a given personality trait?"

Experiments on interpersonal reinforcement indicate that reinforcement of leadership tends to strengthen the status of the reinforced individual. We are just beginning to see research to determine the effects of reinforcing given patterns of behavior, such as directive or participative, in behavior modeling.

Various personal characteristics (rate of talking and interaction, interaction capacity, task ability, dominance, exclusive possession of information, initiation of spontaneity, provision of group freedom, and acceptance of group members) have been found associated with emergence as a leader. It has not been demonstrated, however, that these are the same variables that enable the leader to retain his or her role. There is a need for research isolating the factors that facilitate retention of a position of leadership once it has been attained.

Various group factors, such as size, structure, and task, tend to influence the emergence of leadership. One important question yet to be resolved concerns the effect of member homogeneity versus heterogeneity on acceptance of a leader with a given pattern of behavior, personality, or values. Research on interpersonal space and communication nets also provides an opportunity to study the interaction of status (or centrality) with other variables such as personality, behavior, and values.

Research on social norms and reference groups leaves important questions unanswered. For example, are there behaviors that can be exhibited by a leader whose values differ from those of the group that will enable him or her to act as an effective leader of the group? Conversely, to what extent will value similarity between leader and followers act to stabilize the position of a leader whose personality or behavior is inimical to the group?

In all, it appears that there is an abundance of evidence on factors contributing toward emergence as a leader. There is a dearth of research on factors that enable a leader to consolidate his or her position once it has been obtained.

### Leadership and Social Power

The assertion by several authors that leadership is nothing but a form of social power has tended to obscure important relationships between leadership and power and has no doubt restricted the range of research on the problem.

Little research has been done so far on the interaction of leader behavior and personality with power. Questions such as the following remain to be answered. Will a group respond positively to a leader with high (or low) power who exhibits one of the task-oriented patterns of behavior as opposed to a leader who exhibits one of the person-oriented styles of behavior? If so, how will the personality structure of the group members and the urgency of the group task affect the response? Are there patterns of leader personality that may mitigate in some degree the adverse effects of coercive and reward power? Will coercive power and strong control be more readily accepted under high than under low degrees of leader–follower value similarity? What factors tend to legitimize different forms of power among group members? What factors tend to legitimize different forms of power in the eyes of observers who are not members of the group?

Research on power equalization has been attended by serious difficulties. Appropriate control organizations are seldom available for comparative purposes when some form of power equalization is introduced into a firm. External forces are almost impossible to control. The effects of social, political, and economic factors may be stronger than any variations that the experimenter may introduce into a firm. Use of the experimental group would provide greater control in research on power equalization.

Research on role conflict, conducted almost entirely in formal organizations, is also deficient with respect to experimental controls. Here again, it would be advantageous to study role conflict in experimental groups where conflict-inducing demands could be varied and controlled. Research is needed to determine the extent to which various styles of leader personality and behavior are subject to role conflict.

A small number of competently executed studies is available on legitimization of the leadership role. The importance of the subject merits a much higher rate of activity in this area. In future research, it would be desirable to determine the effect of variations in follower characteristics as well as variations in leader characteristics. One would like to know, as an example, for what types of follower a given characteristic or pattern of behavior tends to legitimize the leadership role. In addition, it would be useful to know under what conditions a given pattern of leadership behavior would be regarded as legitimate or illegitimate and by what type of follower. From a practical point of view, the problem of leader legitimation is one that should be given high priority in future research.

### Leader–Follower Interactions

The research on leader–follower interactions ranks very high in interest value as well as in originality and sophistication of research design. The complex designs developed for investigation of conditional relationships are of particular value. They should be more widely used to permit a study of relationships between variables that have not been previously combined.

But given the erroneousness of the law of small numbers, much care needs to be taken in selecting interactive variables for consideration because we need a large bank of data to validate the particular differential outcome. At the same time, a small number of variables (authoritarianism, democratic leadership, consideration, initiating structure, and LPC, for example) has been overworked at the expense of other variables that are equally important and about which little is known.

Originality and research competence should not be judged on the basis of inventing idiosyncratic new concepts likely to be insignificant variants of concepts already identified. It should be evaluated rather on the rigor and execution of research exploring relationships between known variables that have not been previously combined.

In view of the emphasis upon the interaction concept in theoretical discussions, it is surprising that only a few studies have been made of the effects of interaction. The "Work With" sociometry (Stogdill & Haase, 1957) provides a measure of interaction structures that could be applied to a variety of research designs. Research on responsibility and authority indicates that it is erroneous to equate these concepts with power and authoritarianism. Much existing confusion should be clarified by further research. The available findings suggest, for example, that responsibility is a more likely source of organizational pathology than authority. These results contradict popular hypotheses. Could it be possible that the hypothesis is unfounded?

### The Overlapping Dimensions of Leader Style

In Chapter 18, we listed the many dimensions that have been proposed for describing how leaders differ in their style. Relations between some of them have been clarified and altered. Borrowing from work motivation theory, researchers have purged scales of initiating structure of their coercive components and have relabeled them as instrumental (to task success). Consideration, similarly, particularly when limited to dyadic analysis, concentrates on the subordinate's needs rather than the automatic use of group methods. As such, it takes on the label of supportive leadership.

Chapters 18 through 21 have noted the similarity and the differences in leaders' behaviors and their effects. To some degree, all research on leadership styles can be conceived as about democratic, autocratic, or laissez-faire leadership, taking us back to where it all began in 1938 with Lewin and Lippitt's seminal experiment. Each of these styles is described by either the amount of activity of the leaders or the extent the leaders are oriented toward being completely work-oriented or completely person-oriented. The leaders' performance will be better if they are more active than inactive. But activity does not guarantee effective satisfied and cohesive groups. Thus, leaders tend to be more autocratic and directive when it is easier and more comfortable for them to do so because of their own personalities and because goals are clear and structure is given. But they really need to be directive and structuring when the opposite pertains about goal clarity and structure. Leaders tend to be more democratic, participative, relations-oriented and considerate when concerned about the need for subordinate input and reaction. Again, personality plays a part but their activity as leaders is likely to be seen by them as needed.

It should be clear that factor analyses can establish only how leaders distribute themselves empirically in a given cluster in the eyes of observers of their performance. However, leaders in real-life positions tend to display all three clusters of styles, but in differing amounts. The clusters are conceptually distinct as well.

One can stress the utility of consultation (the manager's most frequent style anyway) as a useful style in general. But as Vroom (1976b) notes, concrete situations may demand otherwise. And leaders do change their styles in response to situational conditions (Hill & Hughes, 1974).

The differential effects of work-related and person-related clusters of leadership styles suggest that a central need is a response allocation analysis to sort out conceptually the different styles from each other as well as more factoral analyses to see the empirical communalities among the styles. Somehow, we need to take into account the generally negative impact on the group of the inactivity of the laissez-faire leader with the possibly but not necessarily positive impact of various types of active intervention by the leader.

### Concentration of Effort with Standardized Measures

Despite the many different but closely parallel conceptualizations of leader style, Fiedler's LPC scale and the LBDQ in some form have dominated leadership research in the past twenty years. This use of common instruments has made possible opportunity for a great deal of comparison across studies. We have already noted how even small changes in the study of instruments may lead to large differences in outcomes. Yet, this concentration has kept the research establishment from looking at many other, possibly more important aspects of leader behavior.

A much wider diversity of environmental, task, group, interpersonal, and personal variables have been employed, usually in multivariate fashion, as antecedent conditions, correlates, or moderators. A balance is needed. Minimally, researchers need to avoid inventing new measures of the same attribute when old ones with satisfactory reliability and validity are available.

*Other Concentrations.* Research on the relation of leader behavior to group productivity has included person-oriented and work-oriented behaviors about equally. However, in studies of follower satisfaction, person-oriented behaviors have been included twice as often as task-oriented behaviors. The effects of work-oriented behaviors require a more extensive investigation. Person-oriented behaviors have been related more often to group cohesiveness than task-oriented behaviors. Here again, there is a deficiency of research on the effects of work-oriented behaviors. In regard to both follower satisfaction and group cohesiveness, it should be noted that structuring expectations does not have the same effect as other forms of work-oriented behavior.

Research on group survival has been concerned mostly with observed groups in the open society. An excellent opportunity provided by the military situation has not been sufficiently exploited. Despite the difficulty of studying experimental groups over long periods of time, there is a need for experimental studies of factors related to group survival.

### A Less Ordered Role

Suggestions continue to appear that leadership research—in addition to its narrowness—has been concentrating on the wrong thing.

The aim of science is to understand. Understanding is checked by prediction. Adequate prediction can produce control. Practitioners are anxious to provide such control when understanding is far from perfect. Leadership research is faulted because it fails to provide immediately such improvements in control. Basic research should be judged on whether it contributes to understanding. The failure of adequate understanding to provide suitable control of behavior may also be partly a consequence of the unpredictable and uncontrollable elements in the real-world performance of leaders. As Mintzberg (1973) observed, instead of a systematic, steady, orderly attack on one problem at a time, the practicing manager is more likely to be observed devoting short bursts of time unsystematically responding despite frequent interruptions to a diversity of demands from superiors, peers, clients, and subordinates as well as dealing with the tasks at hand (hence, the popularity of training in time management.) Given the large array of diverse situations which are the daily regimen of the general manager, M. W. McCall (1977) suggests that much of leadership style research to determine which type is most effective in particular conditions may remain an impractical academic exercise because the demand characteristics of the manager's role result in optimizing his or her performance by "proficient superficiality" (Mintzberg, 1973).

### Transformational versus Transactional Leadership

M. W. McCall (1977) has suggested that we have concentrated research on the nitty-gritty, readily observable, usually short-time, leader–subordinate relations because it is easier to do so and have ignored the much more important aspects of leadership to be seen in the charismatic movers and shakers of our time. Mueller (1980) sees the need for "more leaders and fewer executives." Persons are needed who can "initiate structure in group expectation and show us how to master and motivate institutions and individuals within a complex environment experiencing excessive internal and external stresses and changes."

Given what has been said about transformational leadership by J. M. Burns (1978) (see Chapter 2), we think the time is ripe to pursue the examination of such questions as: In what ways can a leader move subordinates toward the acceptance of superordinate goals? How can followers be aroused into self-transcendence? How does a leader move a group from complacency, hasty responses, inertia, or defensiveness in the face of threat to complete and adequate vigilance? If a group is focused primarily on its lower-level safety and security needs, how does a leader move it toward concern for recognition and achievement? If a group is under stress too high for coping with the complexity of the situation, how does the leader steady and calm the group?

We have been unwilling or unable to put the quantitative research spotlight on famous charismatics such as Churchill, Ghandi, de Gaulle, the Roosevelts, Mao Zedung or Ho Chi Min perhaps because such performance is seen as exceptional and therefore not of much relevance to understanding or improving the performance of the everyday leader or perhaps it is because of the seeming inability to reproduce the effects in the laboratory or in simulation. But surely we should be able to abstract some of the elements in the dynamic interplay of such leaders with their followers. Bass and Farrow (1977) showed the feasibility of using standardized survey questionnaires to study indirectly the interaction of such leaders and their immediate subordinates. Judges read the biographies of famous historical personages, then completed the Bass-Valenzi Management Styles Questionnaire as if they were the subordinates. With the increasing interest in political psychology, efforts of this kind can be expected to increase.

It would be instructive to gather behavioral data on an identified current group of charismatic business, military, church, and government leaders nominated by their subordinates because of the strong emotional bonding that has been established between the leaders and their subordinates and because the subordinates credit the leader for their transformed need structure and goal attainments. No doubt, we would see that the subordinates' own personalities played a part as well as other contingent factors.

We may be avoiding a study of transformational leadership because when seen in the everyday manager, it is often merely autocratic, coercive behavior dressed in charismatic clothes (Culbert & McDonough, 1980). Publicly, subordinates fully comply; privately, they reject the leader and display all the side effects of the use of coercive power (Chapter 11).

One interested in researching the transformational leader will probably have to be prepared to make use of psychodynamic variables associated with charisma mentioned in Chapters 10 and 11. Managers, ministers, battalion commanders, teachers, coaches, and directors can be found who fit the description of persons to whom followers form deep emotional attachments and who in turn inspire their followers to transcend their own interests for superordinate goals, for goals higher in level than previously recognized by the followers. Even in hardened bureaucracies, there are leaders with knowledge of the system, good connections and the ability to mobilize and husband resources, who keep their eyes on the bigger issues and take the risks required for "creative administration," which gives them the idiosyncracy credit necessary to arouse in subordinates complete faith and trust in the leader and willingness to strive for the higher goals set forth as challenges for the group by the leader.

The question is: Can we take what J. M. Burns (1978) saw primarily as transforming leadership at the mass level and apply the concept to the small-group situation? Are there analogues in the small group for the intellectual, reform, revolutionary, and heroic leaders who transform societies? How can we obtain the benefits without the associated costs of heroic leadership characterized by followers' strong belief in the leader as a person, apart from his/her competence, followers' faith that the leader will make it possible for the group to succeed, and their willingness to give the leader power to act in crises? Such a leader inspires, legitimizes, guides, enlarges the arena of action, and manages conflict successfully. The result is a followership transformed into something greater than before.

R. K. Mueller (1980), chairman of the board of Arthur D. Little, describes "leading-edge" leadership. Such leadership deals with "fuzzy futures." It is able to simplify problems and to jump to the (correct) crux of complex matters while the rest of the crowd is still trying to identify the problem. He sees the need for research on this "rapid reification." He also sees the need for leadership research on how "to integrate and relate a charismatic component with the logical and intuitive attributes which are vital to leading-edge leadership."

In terms of directing attention to a big chunk of the more important aspects of leadership, it is perhaps time to agree with K. Lewin (1951) that behavior is a function of both person and environment and to move on to search for what it means to group drive, subordinate motivation, and performance to initiate structure effectively or to consult or delegate.

We need to examine the conditions that promote the emergence of the transformational leader and how to facilitate this emergence. We need to determine the consequences of moving from emphasis on social change, which characterizes the transactional leader, to leadership that mobilizes and directs members toward higher objectives. We need to study the costs and clear and obvious dangers as well as the benefits of transformational leadership.

We need to learn how to train the average supervisor in the sensitivities and interpersonal competencies required of a transformational leader. We need to determine how to select potential transformational leaders who may not show up as well on many currently available predictors of transactional leaders. We need to overcome the parochialism that has characterized empirical leadership research, which has been focused on the easier-to-study transactional leadership.

### Leaders as Organizational Politicians

Although the evidence (possibly as a consequence of social desirability) points to a general rejection of Machiavellian approaches (withholding information, bluffing, agreeing but delaying, and maintaining social distance (Bass, 1968c), organizational decisions often can be understood as a consequence of coalition formation and negotiations and other political processes (March & Simon, 1958; Culbert & McDonough, 1980). Decisions are based on the relative power of those involved rather than on the merits of the issue. But Culbert and McDonough (1980) see effective brokering inside and outside their own group as a challenge for leaders. Inside, such brokering should try to negotiate arrangements within their subordinate group that makes for the best possible mix of subordinates serving their own self-interests as well as meeting the needs of the group. Externally, the leader as representative can often do much to increase the group's resources and opportunities through effective negotiations with outsiders. Whereas such negotiating behavior with individual subordinates seems to be counterproductive as a leadership style (Chapter 19), playing the role of broker successfully still seems worthy of further exploration. The effective political use of authority and power is still a highly underresearched area.

*Horizontal versus Vertical Relations.* By now, the need to focus more attention on the manager's horizontal interactions with peers in other units and with clients has become a platitude (Dubin, 1962b). Much of leaders' success with their subordinates may depend on how well they negotiate arrangements with other units. Conceptualizing organizations as a collection of constituencies (March & Simon, 1958) remains a powerful source for understanding the individual leader's performance.

### Criteria of Leader Effectiveness

Hunt, Osborn, and Schriesheim (1977) noted in a review of eighty-nine studies published between 1970 and 1975 that 61 percent used only a single criterion, with some emphasis on performance (43 percent). However, a greater use of multiple criteria was noted in field studies. Most (81 percent) used criteria obtained from a different informational source than the predictors.

Studies have been conducted on the response of follower beliefs, satisfaction, and behavior, as well as group productivity, drive, and cohesiveness to leader behavior. However, certain variables such as group productivity and follower satisfaction have been overemphasized at the expense of other variables. For instance, group drive, which presumably should be affected by transformational leadership, in particular, has been widely neglected as a variable in group performance.

*Misdirection in Evaluation.* Well-known are the stories about executives who introduce belt-tightening measures into a department, ride roughshod over subordinates to reduce costs and maximize immediate productivity, and are promoted to repeat the process higher up, leaving behind a shambles of dissatisfaction and conflict to be blamed on their successor. Conversely, Shartle (1956) observed that ten years too late a firm might discover it had fired its most effective manager. As M. W. McCall (1977) has suggested, we need to broaden the criteria of consequence and to attach appropriate longer-term value of leadership to organizational and subordinate development. Human resources accounting is an effort in this direction. As managerial accountants increasingly become interested in the behavioral side of a firm's assets and liabilities, we should see increasing opportunities to measure such effects (Caplan & Landekich, 1974). But considerable care will be required to weed out the cause–effect relationships.

*More Attention Needed to Linkages.* Why does leader behavior affect group outcomes? Why do group outcomes affect a leader's behavior? There is a functional dependency between leadership and group performance. Leadership serves the functions of maintaining role structure, role freedom, goal direction, and cohesive group action in task performance. In the emergent situation, leadership is created by the group in response to its own necessities even though an impatient member may impose himself or herself upon the group before the group expresses a demand for such services. In formal organizations, the necessity is acknowledged by the appointment or election of leaders. Effective task peformance is dependent upon the presence of one or more leadership roles in the group. In the group situation, leadership is without meaning except as it serves the function of facilitating group performance or survival.

The dependence of group performance upon a leadership role does not specify the patterns of behavior that should be exhibited in the role. However, the role has three functions to perform for the group to be effective. The leader is required to (1) maintain role structure and goal direction; (2) provide role freedom and group drive; and (3) maintain group cohesiveness and norm conformity. The behaviors that produce these outcomes differ from group to group depending upon variations in member characteristics, task characteristics, and group characteristics.

Research on the relation of leadership to group performance has investigated several patterns of leader behavior in relation to group productivity and cohesiveness. Comparatively few studies are available on the relationship of these patterns of behavior to group drive or arousal. Future research on leadership should incorporate measures of group performance. Measures of group drive, productivity, and cohesiveness should be included. Stogdill (1972) reviewed sixty studies that indicated that the level of group drive conditions the relationship between productivity and cohesiveness. Under routine operating conditions and low drive, productivity and cohesiveness tend to be negatively related, while they tend to be positively related under high drive. Seemingly paradoxical findings are readily explained when group drive is studied along with productivity and cohesiveness.

### Leadership as Determined by Contingent Factors

We have seen a few efforts to identify the nondiscretionary forces that shape the leader's behavior. Much more is needed for knowing what is and is not under a leader's control. Such knowledge should serve to reduce subordinates' unrealistic expectations about the leader as well as the leader's own experiences of violated expectations. In selection and placement testing, we should be able to generate higher validity coefficients between personality attributes and that portion of leader behavior that is discretionary.

*Systems Approach.* Katz and Kahn (1966) pointed the way. Bass (1976), among others, described a systems approach that looks at the leader as someone embedded in a system with multiple inputs from the environment, the organization, the immediate work group supervised, the task, the leader's behavior, and relationships with subordinates and outputs in terms of effective performance and satisfactions. Hunt, Osborn, and Schriesheim (1977) see this kind of systems view of contingent variables as particularly important for future research.

But the vast array of variables must continually face pruning. For experimentation to be manageable, different aspects of the total process of leader–follower interactions are singled out for study. Models are built focusing on one aspect or another that are not necessarily inconsistent with each other. In fact, the potential exists for considerable integration among models. In the broadest sense, behavioral theorists focus on stimulating conditions, behavioral repertoires, and reinforcements contingent on subordinate performance. At the other extreme are those who focus on perceptions, causal attributions, and expectations. For design purposes, both overstate their case.

## APPLICATIONS RESEARCH

### Contingency Applications

Despite continuing criticisms, applications of Fiedler's model (Chapter 20) are becoming prolific sources of further examinations and validation with considerable success. Causal, longer-term, larger-scale studies are likely to appear during the coming decade.

Vroom and Yetton's rational model (Chapter 19) should be the source of considerable research interest in the 1980s. Less well-known but with considerable potential is the empirical approach using regression analyses by Bass, Valenzi, and Farrow (1977) to determine prescriptions for a leader increasing or decreasing the frequency of a particular style as a function of differing contingencies in the situation.

### Leadership Development, Training, and Persistence

On the one hand, we can point with pride to the large array of positive evidence about the efforts to train leaders and the success experienced (Chapter 33). On the other hand, it is still possible to decry all its continuing inadequacies. M. W. McCall (1977) sees that training efforts have concentrated too much on the leader's relation to subordinates (although sensitivity training and intergroup exercises would seem to have much relevance to peer relationships). More experiential exercises, tested for their transfer value to the job, are needed.

Leader development is a continuing process. We need to learn a lot more about how experience with subordinates, peers, and superiors shape one's subsequent leadership performance. Research on the persistence and transfer of leadership has produced a convincing body of evidence which indicates that past success as a leader yields an advantage in gaining future leadership. Unless some powerful new research design is forthcoming, repetitions of this line of inquiry are not likely to yield much in the way of new insights. However, increasing empirical attention to the replacement and succession problem would seem to have great utility. There are many differences here to be explored. Does the successor ignore the former occupant's performance, see it competitively or attempt to build on it? Is the former occupant involved in the choice of the successor? Does the former occupant help or hinder the succession process? When occupants are "lame ducks" and must give up office in a designated amount of time, how does this shape their objectives, planning, power?

On the one hand, Stogdill (1974) faulted training research as focused too much on the extent to which training produces attitude and behavioral change in the trainees. More evidence was demanded on its impacts on the follower group. Yet, we still need to link particular training efforts with particular behavioral changes. The training may understandably increase a trainee's sensitivities; nevertheless, such increased sensitivities may be counterproductive on the job. Sensitivity training may incapacitate the leader for coping with strong opposition, threat, and challenge to the legitimacy of his or her status. What is at fault here is not the training as such, but an inadequate analysis of the situational demands on the leader. We are beginning to see much greater precision in such analyses. Over time, we expect to see much more intensive application of sophisticated analyses of the manager's, administrator's, and leader's roles.

Evidence of the utility of focus on specific behavioral training and its specific effects is to be found in the attention now being paid to behavioral objectives, behavioral modeling, and applications of social learning theory.

More attention needs to be paid to the various threats to the validity of training designs (Bass & Barrett, 1981). For example, if possible, superiors should be blind to who has received training and who has not. Trainees should be blind to their serving as controls (as in holdout designs).

A most important problem that has been ignored entirely concerns the effects of training on retention of the leadership role. What kind of training strengthens or weakens an individual's chances of retaining the leadership position?

In many studies of leadership training, it is impossible to determine the method or combination of methods employed. Both the method of training and the content taught should be outlined in detail.

What experiences are necessary to make an effective leader? Does one need to be trained in theology to make an effective pope? Does one need to be a lawyer to be an effective legislative leader? Does one need legislative experience to be an effective president?

### Special Interests

Studies of black and women leaders will continue to increase reflecting their movement into management. Extensive commentaries should be replaced by more empirical studies, particularly if we consider how quickly outdated such findings can become. Because of the emotional content involved, care needs to be taken not to accept at face value leaders' and subordinates' cross-race and cross-sex opinions and descriptions. At the same time, more attention has to be paid to the underlying feelings of rejection, contempt, guilt, threat, and so on, which do not surface because of superficial socialization, social desirability responses, or mistrust of the investigators. This is another reason why empirical monitoring of such dimensions as self-confidence of blacks, women, and Spanish-speaking people is essential. It should be recognized that an effective, polite, mutual acceptance can be maintained at one level while underneath a wall of misunderstanding is maintained.

Little is known about Anglo-Spanish leader–subordinate relations. Yet the Spanish-surnamed group is fast becoming the largest U.S. minority. Research here will be made particularly difficult by the wide differences among the Chicanos, the Puerto Ricans, the Cuban-Americans and the large immigrant groups from elsewhere in Latin America.

So far the preponderance of evidence endorses the need by minority members serving as leaders in majority environments to emulate the original white, male manager. However, more and timely research will be needed on the accommodations made by minority members to the duality of their roles as both manager and minority member. It is also a completely different matter for community leaders who ordinarily need to identify more strongly with their own subculture than do their followers.

A SUMMING UP

A review of the preceding chapters suggests that some topics and research designs have been overworked while other important questions remain relatively unexplored. The period 1950 to 1965 was marked by an enormous amount of original, creative research. The same period witnessed a wasteful repetition of testing shopworn hypotheses accompanied by a general disregard for negative results. Naïve, uncritical theorizing is likely to retard the process of discovery. Fortunately, much research published since 1965 exhibits a just regard for scientific objectivity.

*Accomplishments*

New, complex, and effective research designs are now available. These designs would be equally useful for testing other relationships that have not been explored. The production of critically needed information could be greatly accelerated by feeding new combinations of variables into research designs demonstrated to be effective.

The preceding suggestions for future research indicate that the possibilities are far from exhausted. In fact, only a beginning has been made. Leadership presents a lively, challenging field for research.

A prime necessity is to break loose from the existing trend toward repeating what has been done over and again in the past. A second necessity is use of the complex, more inclusive research designs. To these necessities should be added the desirability of combining variables that have not been studied in relation to each other. It is especially desirable that one or more measures of follower or group reaction be included.

The complex designs are comparatively costly in terms of time and number of participants required. However, they optimize the probabilities of productive, meaningful research. When one considers the magnitude of the unknown in comparison with what is known about leadership, it is apparent that relatively powerful designs are needed to speed the process of discovery.

In suggesting needs for future research, an attempt has been made to strike a middle ground between restrictive specificity and unstructured generality. Each scientist desires freedom to conceptualize his or her own research but creative pooled effort is become increasingly necessary as the difficulty in keeping up with research developments in more than one field become increasingly difficult. It has been the aim in this chapter to identify areas where productive research is still to be done. Within these areas, there remains scope for unbounded degrees of originality and creative effort.

*Optimism or Pessimism?*

The optimist sees the wine bottle as half full; the pessimist sees it as half-empty (and sour to boot). It is easier to be destructive than constructive, particularly when one lacks information. In every research field there are always ''know-nothings'' who argue that the past years have essentially been a waste and it is now necessary to start afresh. Miner (1975) proposed to abandon the concept of leadership altogether. M. W. McCall (1977) saw leadership remaining enigmatic as a subject because of its many definitions, but in Chapter 1 we noted that the differences were evolving in a systematic fashion and, at any rate, they do not seem to detract from model and theory building. The many models and theories which sprang forth in the 1960s and 1970s are not as divergent and conflicting as one might expect. In fact, what we really need are ways of juxtaposing one with another to test which one yields more plausible explanations. Fiedler and associates test Fiedler's contingency theory; Vroom and associates test their deductive model; Likert produces massive amounts of support for System 4. It should not be too hard to locate points of theoretical disagreement and to develop critical experiments. To some extent, the problem may be that each theoretical point of view is supported by a different array of measurements and situational circumstances. Part of the problem may also be that situational factors determine some kinds of leadership behavior but not others. Autocratic leaders, rigid, inflexible and self-assured, may try to lead in any situation in which they are placed. Democratic leaders may attempt leadership only if they feel competent and supported in the particular situation.

Different styles may work equally well in different situations. These styles in fact, may consist of nondiscretionary behavior determined by organizational and environmental matters not within the leader's control.

It is one thing to say we know nothing because we do not obtain consistent results. The lack of consistency may be attributable to lack of knowledge. Yet, it may be that to achieve consistency of results requires accounting for a complexity of variables and as we do so we increase our understanding of what is happening. What are needed are better measurement, a broader appreciation of which situational variables are more important and which are less so (Korman, 1974), and, as we noted earlier, larger samples.

Some disparage the thousands of research studies of leadership completed with the supposed lack of progress. Yet, when we compare our understanding of leadership in 1980 with what it was thirty years earlier, we can agree with T. R. Mitchell (1979) that "there seems to be progress in our field. Theory and research are developing and much of what is being done is being used in practice. There is reason for controlled optimism. Yet the challenges are still there for the years ahead."

# REFERENCES

The following is a list of the most widely quoted journals in this reference list:

| *Abbreviations* | *Journals* |
|---|---|
| *Acad. Mgmt. J.* | *Academy of Management Journal* |
| *Acad. Mgmt. J.* | *Academy of Management Journal* |
| *Acta Psychol.* | *Acta Psychologica* |
| *Admin. sci. Quar.* | *Administrative Science Quarterly* |
| *Adv. Mgmt.* | *Advanced Management* |
| *Alberta J. educ. Res.* | *Alberta Journal of Educational Research* |
| *Amer. J. Psychol.* | *American Journal of Psychology* |
| *Amer. J. Sociol.* | *American Journal of Sociology* |
| *Amer. Psychologist* | *American Psychologist* |
| *Amer. sociol. Rev.* | *American Sociological Review* |
| *Année Psychol.* | *Année Psychologique* |
| *Behav. Sci.* | *Behavioral Science* |
| *Child Develop.* | *Child Development* |
| *Dissertation Abstr.* | *Dissertation Abstracts* |
| *Dissertation Abstr. Internat.* | *Dissertation Abstracts International* |
| *Educ. psychol. Measmt.* | *Educational and Psychological Measurement* |
| *Educ. Res.* | *Educational Research* |
| *Educ. res. Bull.* | *Educational Research Bulletin* |
| *Genet. psychol. Monogr.* | *Genetic Psychology Monographs* |
| *Harvard bus. Rev.* | *Harvard Business Review* |
| *Harvard educ. Rev.* | *Harvard Educational Review* |
| *Hum. Relat.* | *Human Relations* |
| *Infantry J.* | *Infantry Journal* |
| *Internat. J. Psychol.* | *International Journal of Psychology* |
| *J. abnorm. soc. Psychol.* | *Journal of Abnormal and Social Psychology* |
| *J. appl. behav. Sci.* | *Journal Applied Behavior Science* |
| *J. appl. Psychol.* | *Journal of Applied Psychology* |
| *J. clin. Psychol.* | *Journal of Clinical Psychology* |
| *J. comp. physiol. Psychol.* | *Journal of Comparative and Physiological Psychology* |
| *J. consult. Psychol.* | *Journal of Consulting Psychology* |
| *J. educ. Psychol.* | *Journal of Educational Psychology* |
| *J. educ. Res.* | *Journal of Educational Research* |
| *J. exp. Psychol.* | *Journal of Experimental Psychology* |

| *Abbreviations* | *Journals* |
|---|---|
| J. exp. soc. Psychol. | Journal of Experimental Social Psychology |
| J. gen. Psychol. | Journal of General Psychology |
| J. genet. Psychol. | Journal of Genetic Psychology |
| J. indus. Psychol. | Journal of Industrial Psychology |
| J. math. Psychol. | Journal of Mathematical Psychology |
| J. Pers. | Journal of Personality |
| J. pers. soc. Psychol. | Journal of Personality and Social Psychology |
| J. Psychol. | Journal of Psychology |
| Mgmt. Sci. | Management Science |
| Org. behav. hum. Perform. | Organizational Behavior and Human Performance |
| Percept. mot. Skills | Perceptional and Motor Skills |
| Personnel guid. J. | Personnel and Guidance Journal |
| Personnel Mgmt. | Personnel Management |
| Personnel pract. Bull. | Personnel Practice Bulletin |
| Personnel Psychol. | Personnel Psychology |
| Psychonomic Sci. | Psychonomic Science |
| Psychol. Bull. | Psychological Bulletin |
| Psychol. Issues | Psychological Issues |
| Psychol. Monogr. | Psychological Monographs |
| Psychol. Rec. | Psychological Record |
| Psychol. Rep. | Psychological Reports |
| Psychol. Rev. | Psychological Review |
| Rev. educ. Res. | Review of Educational Research |
| Sm. grp. Beh. | Small Group Behavior |
| Soc. Forces | Social Forces |
| Sociol. soc. Res. | Sociology and Social Research |
| Sociometry | Sociometry |
| Speech Monogr. | Speech Monographs |
| Teach. Coll. Rec. | Teachers College Record |
| Train. Directors J. | Training Directors Journal |
| Train. develop. J. | Training and Development Journal |

**Aaronovich, G. D., & Khotin, B. I.** The problem of imitation in monkeys. *Novoye v Refleksologii i Fiziologii Nervnoy Systemi*, 1929, *3*, 378–390.

**Abegglen, J. C.** *The Japanese factory: aspects of its social organization.* New York: Free Press, 1958.

**Aboud, J.** The interactive effect of group cohesion and supervisory style on the productivity of college students on a motor skill test. *Dissertation Abstr.*, 1968, *29*, 1853.

**Abrahamson, M.** *Interpersonal accommodation.* Princeton, N.J.: Van Nostrand, 1966.

**Abrahamson, M.** *The professional in the organization.* Chicago: Rand McNally, 1967.

**Abrahamson, M.** Position, personality, and leadership. *Psychol. Rec.*, 1969, *19*, 113–122.

*ABS* [**American Behavioral Scientist**] *Guide to recent publications in the social and behavioral sciences, The.* New York: American Behavioral Scientist, 1965.

**Ackerson, L.** *Children's behavior problems: relative importance and intercorrelations among traits.* Chicago: University of Chicago Press, 1942.

**Ackoff, R. L., & Emery, F. E.** *On purposeful systems.* Chicago: Aldine-Atherton, 1972.

**Adair, J.** *Action centered leadership.* New York: McGraw-Hill, 1973.

**Adams, E. F.** Influences of minority supervisors on subordinate attitudes. Unpublished ms., 1976.

**Adams, J. S.** Wage inequities, productivity and work quality. *Indus. Relat.*, 1963, *3*, 9–16.

**Adams, J. S., & Romney, A. K.** A functional analysis of authority. *Psychol. Rev.*, 1959, *66*, 234–251.

**Adams, S.** Effect of equalitarian atmospheres upon the performance of bomber crews. *Amer. Psychologist*, 1952, *7*, 398.

**Adams, S.** Status congruency as a variable in small group performance. *Soc. Forces*, 1953, *32*, 16–22.

**Adams, S., & Fyffe, D.** *The corporate promotables.* Houston: Gulf, 1969.

**Adjutant General's Department.** *The personnel system of the United States Army.* Washington, D.C.: U.S. Army, 1919.

**Adorno, T. W., Frenkel-Brunswik, E., Levinson, D. J., & Sanford, R. N.** *The authoritarian personality.* New York: Harper, 1950.

**Aiken, E. G.** Changes in interpersonal descriptions accompanying the operant conditioning of verbal frequency in groups. *J. verbal Learn. verbal Behav.*, 1965a, *4*, 243–247.

**Aiken, E. G.** Interaction process analysis changes accompanying operant conditioning of verbal frequency in small groups. *Percept. mot. Skills.* 1965b, *21*, 52–54.

**Aiken, W. J., Smits, S. J., & Lollar, D. J.** Leadership behavior and job satisfaction in state rehabilitation agencies. *Personnel Psychol.*, 1972, *25*, 65–73.

**AIR (American Institute for Research).** Situational problems for leadership training. Part IV—categorized bibliography of leadership research literature. Washington, D.C.: American Institute for Research, 1961 (mimeo).

**Akin, G.** Grounded theory doesn't come easily: a response to Dunn and Swierczek. *J. appl. behav. Sci.*, 1978, *15*, 557–559.

**Alban, B. T., & Seashore, E. W.** Women in authority: an experienced view. *J. appl. behav. Sci.*, 1978, *14*, 21.

**Albrecht, P. A., Glaser, E. M., & Marks, J.** Validation of a multiple-assessment procedure for managerial personnel. *J. appl. Psychol.*, 1964, *48*, 351–360.

**Albrook, R. C.** Participative management: time for a second look. *Fortune*, May 1967, 166–170; 197–200.

**Alcorn, R. S.** Leadership and stability in mid-nineteenth century America: a case study of an Illinois town. *J. Amer. His.*, 1974, *61*, 685–702.

**Alderfer, C. P.** An organizational syndrome. *Admin. sci. Quar.*, 1967, *12*, 440–460.

**Alderfer, C. P.** Job enlargement and the organizational context. *Personnel Psychol.*, 1969, *22*, 418–426.

**Alderfer, C. P.** Management development and intergroup relations. *Exp. publ. System, Amer. psychol. Assn.*, 1970, No. 206A.

**Alderfer, C. P.** *Existence, relatedness, and growth: human needs in organizational settings.* New York: Free Press, 1972.

**Alexander, L. D.** The effect of level in the hierarchy and functional area on the extent to which Mintzberg's managerial roles are required by managerial jobs. *Dissertation Abstr.*, 1979, *40*, 2156A.

**Alford, R. R., & Scoble, H. M.** Community leadership, education, and political behavior. *Amer. sociol. Rev.*, 1968, *33*, 259–272.

**Alkire, A. A., Collum, M. E., Kaswan, J., & Love, L. R.** Information exchange and accuracy of verbal communication under social power conditions. *J. pers. soc. Psychol.*, 1968, *9*, 301–308.

**Allee, W. C.** Social biology of subhuman groups. *Sociometry*, 1945, *8*, 21–29.

Allee, W. C. *Cooperation among animals, with human implications*. New York: Schuman, 1951.

Allee, W. C., et al. *Principles of animal ecology*. Philadelphia: Saunders, 1949.

Allegro, J. T., Bagchus, P. M., & Hofstee, W. K. Konstruktie van een gedwongen keuze-leiderschapsschaal (LOS). *Nederlands Tijdschrift Psychol. Grensgebieden*, 1970, *25*, 451–463.

Allen, L. A. Does managerial development develop managers? *Personnel*, 1957, *34*, 18–25.

Allen, L. A. *Management and organization*. New York: McGraw-Hill, 1958.

Allen, M., Panian, S., & Lotz, R. Managerial succession and organizational performance: a recalcitrant problem revisited. *Admin. sci. Quar.*, 1979, *24*, 167–180.

Allen, L., & Sutherland, R. *Role conflict and congruences*. Austin, Texas: Hogg Foundation, 1963.

Allen, M. P. The structure of interorganizational elite cooptation. *Amer. sociol. Rev.*, 1974, *39*, 393–406.

Allen, W. R. A comparative analysis of black and white leadership in a naturalistic setting. *Dissertation Abstr. Internat.*, 1975, *36*, 2516.

Allen, W. R. Black and white leaders and subordinates: leader choice and ratings, aspirations and expectancy of success. In D. Frederick & J. Guiltinan (Eds.), *New challenges for the decision sciences*. Amherst, Mass.: Northeast Region of the American Institute for Decision Sciences, 1975.

Allen, W. R., & Ruhe, J. A. Verbal behavior by black and white leaders of biracial groups in two different environments. *J. appl. Psychol.*, 1976, *61*, 441–445.

Allport, F. H. *Social psychology*. Boston: Houghton Mifflin, 1924.

Allport, F. H. A structuronomic conception of behavior: individual and collective. *J. abnorm. soc. Psych.*, 1962, *64*, 3–30.

Allport, G. W., Vernon, P. E., & Lindzey, G. *A study of values*. Boston: Houghton Mifflin, 1960.

Allswang, J. M., & Bova, P. NORC Social Research 1941–64: an inventory of studies and publications in social research. Chicago: University of Chicago, National Opinion Research Center, 1964.

Almquist, E. M. Sex stereotypes in occupational choice: the case for college women. *J. vocat. Behav.*, 1974, *5*, 13–21.

Alpander, G. G. Planning management training programs for organizational development. *Personnel J.*, 1974, *53*, 15–21.

Alpander, G. G., & Guttman, J. E. Contents and techniques of management development programs for women. *Personnel J.*, 1976, *55*, 76–79.

Alper, S. W. Racial differences in job and work environment priorities among newly hired college graduates. *J. appl. Psychol.*, 1975, *60*, 132–134.

Alsikafi, M., Jokinen, W. J., Spray, S. L., & Tracy, G. S. Managerial attitudes toward labor unions in a southern city. *J. appl. Psychol.*, 1968, *52*, 447–453.

Altman, I. Aspects of the criterion problem in small group research, II. Analysis of group tasks. *Acta Psychol.*, 1966, *25*, 199–221.

Altman, I., Pendleton, C., & Terauds, A. *Annotations of small group research studies*. Arlington, Va.: Human Sciences Research, 1960 (mimeo).

Alutto, J. A., & Belasco, J. A. A typology for participation in organizational decision making. *Admin. sci. Quar.*, 1972, *17*, 117–125.

Alvarez, R. Informal reactions to deviance in simulated work organizations. *Amer. sociol. Rev.*, 1968, *33*, 895–912.

Anderhalter, O. F., Wilkins, W., & Rigby, M. K. Peer rating relationships between officer and peer-candidate predictions of effectiveness as a company grade officer in the U.S. Marine Corps and the ability to predict estimated officer effectiveness of peers. St. Louis: Washington University, Department of Psychology, Technical Report No. 2, 1952.

**Anderson, B., & Nilsson, S.** Studies in the reliability and validity of the critical incident technique. *J. appl. Psychol.*, 1964, *48*, 398–413.

**Anderson, C. L.** *Community health.* St. Louis, Mo.: C. V. Mosby Co., 1969.

**Anderson, C. R., Hellriegel, D., & Slocum, J. W., Jr.** Managerial response to environmentally induced stress. *Acad. Mgmt. J.*, 1977, *20*, 260–272.

**Anderson, C. R., & Schneier, C. E.** Locus of control, leader behavior and leader performance among management students. *Acad. Mgmt. J.*, 1978, *21*, 690–698.

**Anderson, D. R.** Leadership effectiveness in education as related to congruence between human behavior types and leadership styles. *Dissertation Abstr. Internat.*, 1974, *34*, 6887.

**Anderson, H. H.** An experimental study of dominative and integrative behavior in children of pre-school age. *J. soc. Psychol.*, 1937, *8*, 335–345.

**Anderson, H. H.** Domination and integration in the social behavior of young children in an experimental play situation. *Genet. psychol. Monogr.*, 1937, *19*, 341–408.

**Anderson, H. H.** Domination and social integration in the behavior of kindergarten children and teachers. *Genet. psychol. Monogr.*, 1939, *21*, 287–385.

**Anderson, H. H.** An examination of the concepts of domination and integration in relation to dominance and ascendance. *Psychol. Rev.*, 1940, *47*, 21–37.

**Anderson, H. H., & Brewer, J. E.** Studies of teachers' classroom personalities, II: effects of teachers' dominative and integrative contacts on children's classroom behavior. *Appl. psychol. Monogr.*, 1946, No. 8.

**Anderson, L. R.** *Some effects of leadership training on intercultural discussion groups.* Urbana: University of Illinois, Group Effectiveness Research Laboratory, Technical Report, 1964.

**Anderson, L. R.** Some effects of leadership training on intercultural discussion groups. *Dissertation Abstr.*, 1965, *25*, 6796.

**Anderson, L. R.** Initiation of structure, consideration, and task performance in intercultural discussion groups. Urbana: University of Illinois, Group Effectiveness Research Laboratory, unpublished report, 1966a.

**Anderson, L. R.** Leader behavior, member attitudes, and task performance of intercultural discussion groups. *J. soc. Psychol.*, 1966b, *69*, 305–319.

**Anderson, L. R., & Fiedler, F. E.** The effect of participatory and supervisory leadership on group creativity. *J. appl. Psychol.*, 1964, *48*, 227–236.

**Anderson, L. R., Karuza, J., & Blanchard, P. N.** Enhancement of leader power after election or appointment to undesirable leader roles. *J. Psychol.*, 1977, *97*, 59–70.

**Anderson, N.** *The hobo: the sociology of the homeless man.* Chicago: University of Chicago Press, 1923.

**Anderson, R. C.** Learning in discussions—a resume of the authoritarian—democratic studies. *Harvard educ. Rev.*, 1959, *29*, 201–215.

**Anderson, R. M.** Activity preferences and leadership behavior of head nurses. *Nursing Res.*, 1964, *13*, 239–242, 333–337.

**Anderson, W. A.** The family and individual social participation. *Amer. sociol. Rev.*, 1943, *8*, 420–424.

**Andreoli, V. A.** Effect of a leader's threat to behavioral freedom. Unpublished doctoral dissertation, University of North Carolina, Chapel Hill, 1975.

**Andrews, F. M., & Farris, G. F.** Supervisory practices and innovations in scientific teams. *Personnel Psychol.*, 1967, *20*, 497–515.

**Andrews, F. M., & Farris, G. F.** Time pressure and performance of scientists and engineers: a five-year panel study. *Org. behav. hum. Perform.*, 1972, *8*, 185–200.

**Andrews, I. R., & Henry, M. M.** Management attitudes toward pay. *Indus. Relat.,* 1963, *3*, 29–40.

**Andrews, J. D. W.** The achievement motive and advancement in two types of organizations. *J. pers. soc. Psychol.,* 1967, *6*, 163–168.

**Andrews, K. R.** *The effectiveness of university management development programs.* Boston: Harvard University, Graduate School of Business Administration, 1966.

**Andrews, L. C.** *Leadership and military training.* Philadelphia: Lippincott, 1918.

**Andrews, R. E.** *Leadership and supervision, a survey of research findings: a management report.* Washington, D.C.: U.S. Civil Service Commission, 1955.

**Angelini, A. L.** Measuring the achievement motive in Brazil. *J. soc. Psychol.,* 1966, *68*, 35–44.

**Anikeeff, A. M.** The effect of job satisfaction upon attitudes of business administrators and employees. *J. soc. Psychol.,* 1957, *45*, 277–281.

**Anonymous.** Informal social organizations in the Army. *Amer. J. Sociol.,* 1945/1946, *51*, 365–370.

**Anonymous.** How to succeed. *Bus. Week,* April 9, 1955, p. 128.

**Anonymous.** How 179 chief executives waste their time. *Bus. Mgmt.,* March 1968, *33*, 12–14.

**Anonymous.** Russia sets program of wage incentives in scientific work. *Wall Street Journal,* June 1, 1970, p. 12.

**Anonymous.** Women and business: agenda for the seventies. *Business environment studies.* New York: General Electric Co., 1972.

**Anonymous.** Would you vote for a woman for president? *New York Times,* April 21, 1980, p. B1.

**Ansbacher, H. L.** German military psychology. *Psychol. Bull.,* 1942, *39*, 370–392.

**Ansbacher, H. L.** Attitudes of German prisoners of war: a study of the dynamics of national-socialistic followership. *Psychol. Monogr.,* 1948, *62*, 1–42.

**Antia, K.** Job satisfaction: facts versus fiction. *Exp. publ. System, Amer. psychol. Assn.,* 1969a, No. 113A.

**Antia, K.** Cognitive factors in an organization—a new era in emergence. *Exp. publ. System, Amer. psychol. Assn.,* 1969b, No. 096A.

**Appelbaum, S. H.** The motivation of government administrators within a closed climate. *Akron bus. eco. Rev.,* 1977, *8*, 26–32.

**Aral, S. O., & Whelan, R. K.** *Leadership styles in urban societies.* Tucson: University of Arizona, Institute of Government Research, 1974.

**Arbous, A. G., & Maree, J.** Contributions of two group discussion techniques to a validated test battery. *Occup. Psychol.,* 1951, *25*, 73–89.

**Arensberg, C. M., & McGregor, D.** Determination of morale in an industrial company. *Appl. Anthrop.,* 1942, *1*, 12–34.

**Arensberg, C. M., & Tootell, G.** Plant sociology: real discoveries and new problems. In M. Komarovsky. *Common frontiers of the social sciences.* New York: Free Press, 1957.

**Argyle, M., & Dean, J.** Eye-contact, distance, and affiliation. *Sociometry,* 1965, *28*, 289–304.

**Argyle, M., Gardner, G., & Ciofi, F.** Supervisory methods related to productivity, absenteeism, and labour turnover. *Hum. Relat.,* 1958, *11*, 23–40.

**Argyris, C.** Some characteristics of successful executives. *Personnel J.,* 1953, *32*, 50–63.

**Argyris, C.** Human relations in a bank. *Harvard bus. Rev.,* 1954, *32*, 63–72.

**Argyris, C.** *Personality and organization.* New York: Harper, 1957.

**Argyris, C.** *Understanding organizational behavior.* Homewood, Ill.: Dorsey, 1960.

**Argyris, C.** Organizational leadership. In L. Petrullo & B. M. Bass (Eds.), *Leadership and interpersonal behavior.* New York: Holt, Rinehart & Winston, 1961.

**Argyris, C.** *Interpersonal competence and organizational effectiveness.* Homewood, Ill.: Irwin-Dorsey, 1962.

**Argyris, C.** In defense of laboratory education. *Train. Directors J.,* 1963, *17,* 21–30.

**Argyris, C.** *Integrating the individual and the organization.* New York: Wiley, 1964a.

**Argyris, C.** T-groups for organizational effectiveness. *Harvard bus. Rev.,* 1964b, *42,* 60–74.

**Argyris, C.** Explorations in interpersonal competence—II. *J. appl. behav. Sci.,* 1965, *1,* 255–269.

**Argyris, C.** The incompleteness of social-psychological theory: examples from small group, cognitive consistency, and attribution research. *Amer. Psychologist,* 1969, *24,* 893–908.

**Argyris, C.** *Intervention theory and method.* Reading, Mass.: Addison-Wesley, 1970.

**Argyris, C.** Personality and organization theory revisited. *Admin. sci. Quar.,* 1973, *18,* 141–167.

**Argyris, C.** *Increasing leadership effectiveness.* New York: Wiley, 1976.

**Aries, C.** Interaction patterns and themes of male, female, and mixed groups. *Sm. grp. Behav.,* 1976, *7,* 7–18.

**Arlen, E.** *Leadership and human relations: a bibliographic review.* Chicago: University of Chicago, Industrial Relations Center, 1957.

**Armilla, J.** Predicting self-assessed social leadership in a new culture with the MMPI. *J. soc. Psychol.,* 1967, *73,* 219–225.

**Aronoff, J., & Messé, L. A.** Motivational determinants of small-group structure. *J. per. soc. Psychol.,* 1971, *3,* 319–324.

**Aronson, E., & Cope, V.** My enemy's enemy is my friend. *J. pers. soc. Psych.,* 1968, *8,* 8–12.

**Aronson, E., & Worchel, P.** Similarity versus liking as determinants of interpersonal attractiveness. *Psychonomic Sci.,* 1966, *5,* 157–158.

**Arrington, R. E.** Time sampling in studies of social behavior: a critical review of techniques and results with research suggestions. *Psychol. Bull.,* 1943, *40,* 81–124.

**Arvey, R. D., & Ivancevich, J. M.** Punishment in organizations: a review, propositions, and research suggestions. *Acad. Mgmt. Rev.,* 1980, *5,* 123–132.

**Arvey, R. D., & Neel, C. W.** Moderating effects of employee expectancies on the relationship between leadership consideration and job performance of engineers. *J. vocat. Behav.,* 1974, *4,* 213–222.

**Asch, S. E.** Forming impressions of personalities. *J. abnorm. soc. Psychol.,* 1946, *41,* 258–290.

**Asch, S. E.** *Social psychology.* New York: Prentice-Hall, 1952.

**Ashbrook, J. B.** Ministerial leadership in church organization. *Ministry Studies,* 1967, *1,* 3–32.

**Ashby, W. R.** Variety, constraint, and the law of requisite variety (1956). In W. Buckley (Ed.), *Modern systems research for the behavioral scientist.* Chicago: Aldine, 1968.

**Ashby, W. R.** *An introduction to cybernetics.* New York: Wiley, 1957.

**Ashby, W. R.** *Design for a brain.* New York: Wiley, 1960.

**Ashour, A. S.** Further discussion of Fiedler's contingency model of leadership effectiveness. *Org. behav. hum. Perform.,* 1973, *9,* 369–376.

**Ashour, A. S.** The contingency model of leadership effectiveness: an evaluation. *Org. behav. hum. Perform.,* 1973, *9,* 339–355.

**Ashour, A. S., & England, G.** Subordinate's assigned level of discretion as a function of leader's personality and situational variables. *Exp. publ. System, Amer. psychol. Assn.,* 1971, *12,* No. 466–1.

**ASME (American Society of Mechanical Engineers).** *50 years progress in management, 1910–1960.* New York: American Society of Mechanical Engineers, 1960.

**Aspegren, R. E.** A study of leadership behavior and its effects on morale and attitudes in selected elementary schools. *Dissertation Abstr.,* 1963, *23,* 3708.

**Asquith, R. H., & Hedlund, D. E.** Laboratory training and supervisory attitudes. *Psychol. Rep.,* 1967, *20,* 618.

**Assael, H.** Constructive role of interorganizational conflict. *Admin. sci. Quar.,* 1969, *14*, 573–582.

**Atkinson, J. W. (Ed.).** *Motives in fantasy, action and society.* Princeton, N.J.: Van Nostrand, 1958.

**Atkinson, J. W., & Walker, E. L.** The affiliation motive and perceptual sensitivity to faces. *J. abnorm. soc. Psychol.,* 1956, *53*, 38–41.

**Auclair, G.** Managerial role conflict: a cross-cultural comparison. *Proceedings of the 76th Annual Convention of the American Psychological Association,* 1968.

**Ausubel, D. P.** Socioempathy as a function of sociometric status in an adolescent group. *Hum. Relat.,* 1955, *8*, 75–84.

**Ausubel, D. P., & Schiff, H. M.** Some intrapersonal and interpersonal determinants of individual differences in socioemphatic ability among adolescents. *J. soc. Psychol.,* 1955, *41*, 39–56.

Awareness training. *Indust. relat. News,* New York: Industrial Relations Counselors, 1968.

**Ayer, J. G.** Effects of success and failure of interpersonal and task performance upon leader perception and behavior. Urbana: University of Illinois, Group Effectiveness Research Laboratory, Technical Report No. 26, 1968.

**Ayers, A. W.** Effect of knowledge of results on supervisor's post-training test scores. *Personnel Psychol.,* 1964, *17*, 189–192.

**Bachman, J. G.** Faculty satisfaction and the dean's influence: an organizational study of twelve liberal arts colleges. *J. appl. Psychol.,* 1968, *52*, 55–61.

**Bachman, J. G., Smith, C. G., & Slesinger, J. A.** Control, performance, and satisfaction: an analysis of structural and individual effects. *J. pers. soc. Psychol.,* 1966, *4*, 127–136.

**Bachrach, A. J., Candland, D. K., & Gibson, J. T.** Group reinforcement of individual response experiments in verbal behavior. In I. A. Berg & B. M. Bass (Eds.), *Conformity and deviation.* New York: Harper, 1961.

**Back, K. W.** Interpersonal relations in a discussion group. *J. soc. Issues,* 1948, *4*, 61–65.

**Back, K. W.** Influence through social communication. *J. abnorm. soc. Psychol.,* 1951, *46*, 9–23.

**Back, K. W.** *Beyond words: the story of sensitivity training and the encounter movement.* New York: Basic Books, 1972.

**Backman, C. W., & Secord, P. F.** The effect of perceived liking on interpersonal attraction. *Hum. Relat.,* 1959, *12*, 379–384.

**Backner, B. L.** "Attraction-to-group," as a function of style of leadership, follower personality, and group composition. *Dissertation Abstr.,* 1961, *22*, 628.

**Badawy, M. K.** Managerial attitudes and need orientations of mideastern executives: an empirical cross-cultural analysis. Cleveland, Ohio: Cleveland State University, unpublished ms, undated.

**Badin, I. J.** Some moderator influences on relationships between consideration, initiating structure, and organizational criteria. *J. appl. Psychol.,* 1974, *59*, 380–382.

**Bailey, H. D.** An exploratory study of selected components and processes in educational organizations. Doctoral dissertation, University of California, Berkeley, 1966.

**Baker, B. O., & Block, J.** Accuracy of interpersonal prediction as a function of judge and object characteristics. *J. abnorm. soc. Psychol.,* 1957, *54*, 37–43.

**Baker, H., & France, R. R.** *Centralization and decentralization in industrial relations.* Princeton, N.J.: Princeton University, Industrial Relations Section, 1954.

**Baker, R. A., Ware, J. R., Spires, G. H., & Osborn, W. C.** The effects of supervisory threat on decision making and risk taking in a simulated combat game. *Behav. Sci.,* 1966, *11*, 167–176.

**Bakke, E. W.** *A Norwegian contribution to management development.* Bergen: Norwegian School of Economics & Business Administration, 1959.

**Baldwin, A. L.** The effects of home environment on nursery school behavior. *Child Develop.,* 1949, *20*, 49–62.

**Baldwin, J., Glazer, N., Hook, S., Myrdal, G., & Podhoretz, N.** Liberalism and the Negro: a round-table discussion. In B. E. Segal (Ed.), *Racial and ethnic relations.* New York: Thomas Y. Crowell, 1966.

**Baldwin, L. E.** A study of factors usually associated with high school male leadership. Columbus: Ohio State University, Master's thesis, 1932.

**Bales, R. F.** *Interaction process analysis.* Reading, Mass.: Addison-Wesley, 1950.

**Bales, R. F.** The equilibrium problem in small groups. In T. Parsons, R. F. Bales, & E. A. Shils (Eds.), *Working papers in the theory of action.* New York: Free Press, 1953.

**Bales, R. F.** Task roles and social roles in problem-solving groups. In E. E. Maccoby, T. M. Newcomb, & E. L. Hartley (Eds.), *Readings in social psychology.* New York: Holt, Rinehart & Winston, 1958a.

**Bales, R. F.** Role and role conflict. In E. E. Maccoby, T. M. Newcomb, & E. L. Hartley (Eds.), *Readings in social psychology.* New York: Holt & Co., 1958b.

**Bales, R. F., & Cohen, S. P.** *SYMLOG.* New York: Free Press, 1980.

**Bales, R. F., & Slater, P. E.** Role differentiation in small decision-making groups. In T. Parsons et al. (Eds.), *Family, socialization, and interaction processes.* New York: Free Press, 1955.

**Bales, R. F., & Strodtbeck, F. L.** Phases in group problem-solving. *J. abnorm. soc. Psychol.,* 1951, *46*, 485–495.

**Bales, R. F., Strodtbeck, F., Mills, T., & Roseborough, M. E.** Channels of communication in small groups. *Amer. social Rev.,* 1951, *16*, 461–468.

**Balk, W. L.** Status perceptions of management "peers." *Acad. Mgmt. J.,* 1969, *4*, 431–437.

**Ballou, A.** *The Hopedale community.* Lowell, Mass.: Thompson & Hill, 1897.

**Balma, M. J., Maloney, J. C., & Lawshe, C. H.** The role of the foreman in modern industry. II. Foreman identification with management, work group productivity, and employee attitude toward the foreman. *Personnel Psychol.,* 1958a, *11*, 367–378.

**Balma, M. J., Maloney, J. C., & Lawshe, C. H.** The role of the foreman in modern industry. III. Some correlates of foreman identification with management. *Personnel Psychol.,* 1958b, *11*, 535–544.

**Baltzell, E. D.** *Philadelphia gentlemen: the making of a national upper class.* New York: Free Press, 1958.

**Baltzell, E. D.** *Puritan Boston and Quaker Philadelphia.* New York: Free Press, 1980.

**Balyeat, R. R.** Leader and administrative behavior exhibited by participants of the Administrator Change Agent Program, the University of Tennessee, 1968–1970. *Dissertation Abstr. Internat.,* 1972, *32*, 6024.

**Bamforth, K.** T-group methods within a company. In G. Whitaker (Ed.), *ATM occasional papers 2.* Oxford: Basil E. Blackwell, 1965.

**Bandura, A.** *Social learning theory.* Englewood Cliffs, N.J.: Prentice-Hall, 1977.

**Bandura, A., & Huston, A. C.** Identification as a process of incidental learning. *J. abnorm. soc. Psychol.,* 1961, *63*, 311–318.

**Bandura, A., Ross, D., & Ross, S. A.** "Vicarious" reinforcement and imitation. Stanford, Calif.: Stanford University, unpublished ms., 1962a.

**Bandura, A., Ross, D. & Ross, S. A.** An experimental test of the status envy, social power, and the secondary reinforcement theories of identificatory learning. Stanford, Calif.: Stanford University, unpublished ms., 1962b.

**Bandura, A., Ross, D., & Ross, S. A.** A comparative test of the status envy, social power, and secondary reinforcement theories of identificatory learning. *J. abnorm. soc. Psychol.,* 1963, *67*, 527–534.

**Banfield, E. E.** Women in middle management positions: characteristics, training, leadership style, limitations, rewards, and problems. *Dissertation Abstr. Internat.,* 1976, *37*, 1952–1953.

**Banfield, E., & Wilson, J. Q.** *City politics.* Cambridge, Mass.: Harvard University Press, 1963.

**Bankart, C. P., & Lanzetta, J. T.** Performance and motivation as variables affecting the administration of rewards and punishments. *Rep. res. soc. Psychol.,* 1970, *1*, 1–10.

**Banks, O.** *The attitudes of steelworkers to technical change.* Liverpool: Liverpool University Press, 1960.

**Banta, T. J., & Nelson, C.** Experimental analysis of resource location in problem-solving groups. *Sociometry,* 1964, *27*, 488–501.

**Barber, J. D.** *The law makers.* New Haven: Yale University Press, 1965.

**Barber, J. D.** *Power in committees: an experiment in the government process.* Chicago: Rand McNally, 1966.

**Bare, R.** A factor analytic description of the performance of enlisted personnel. *USN Bur. Naval pers. tech. Bull.,* 1956, No. 56–1, 1–37.

**Barker, R. G.** The social interrelations of strangers and acquaintances. *Sociometry,* 1942, *5*, 169–179.

**Barker, R. G.** *Ecological psychology.* Stanford, Calif.: Stanford University Press, 1968.

**Barnard, C. I.** *The functions of the executive.* Cambridge, Mass.: Harvard University Press, 1938.

**Barnard, C. I.** *Dilemmas of leadership in the democratic process.* Princeton, N.J.: Princeton University Press, 1939.

**Barnard, C. I.** Functions and pathology of status systems in formal organizations. In W. F. White (Ed.), *Industry and society.* New York: McGraw-Hill, 1946a.

**Barnard, C. I.** The nature of leadership. In S. D. Hoslett (Ed.), *Human factors in management.* New York: McGraw-Hill, 1946b.

**Barnard, C. I.** *Organization and management.* Cambridge, Mass.: Harvard University Press, 1948.

**Barnard, C. I.** Functions of status systems in formal organizations. In R. Dubin (Ed.), *Human relations in administration.* Englewood Cliffs, N.J.: Prentice-Hall, 1951.

**Barnard, C. I.** A definition of authority. In R. K. Merton, A. P. Gray, B. Hockey, & H. C. Selvin (Eds.), *Reader in bureaucracy.* New York: Free Press, 1952.

**Barnes, L. B.** *Organizational systems and engineering groups: a comparative study of two technical groups in industry.* Boston: Division of Research, Harvard Business School, 1960.

**Barnes, R. M., & Englert, N. A.** *Bibliography of industrial engineering and management literature to January 1, 1946* (5th ed.). Dubuque, Iowa: W. C. Brown, 1946.

**Barnlund, D. C.** Experiments in leadership training for decision-making groups. *Speech Monogr.,* 1955, *22*, 1–14.

**Barnlund, D. C.** Consistency of emergent leadership in groups with changing tasks and members. *Speech Monogr.,* 1962, *29*, 45–52.

**Baron, A. S.** Selection, development and socialization of women. *Business Quar.,* 1977, *42*, 61.

**Barrett, G. V., & Bass, B. M.** Cross-cultural issues in industrial and organizational psychology. In M. D. Dunnette (Ed.), *Handbook of industrial and organizational psychology.* Chicago: Rand McNally, 1976.

**Barrett, G. V., & Franke, R. H.** Communication preference and performance: a cross-cultural comparison. *Proceedings of the 77th Annual Convention of the American Psychological Association,* 1969.

**Barrett, G. V., & Ryterband, E. C.** Cross-cultural comparisons of corporate objectives on *Exercise Objectives. Proceedings of the 76th Annual Convention of the American Psychological Association,* 1968.

**Barrett, R. S.** Performance suitability and role agreement: two factors related to attitudes. *Personnel Psychol.,* 1963, *16*, 345–357.

**Barrett, R. S.** Impact of the executive program on the participants. *J. indus. Psychol.,* 1965, *3*, 1–13.

**Barrett, R. S.** The influence of the supervisor's requirements on ratings. *Personnel Psychol.,* 1966, *19*, 375–388.

**Barrow, J. C.** An empirical framework of leadership effectiveness and investigation of leader–subordinate–task causality relationships. *Dissertation Abstr. Internat.,* 1975, *35*, 3631.

**Barrow, J. C.** Worker performance and task complexity as causal determinants of leader behavior, style, and flexibility. *J. appl. Psychol.,* 1976, *61*, 433–440.

**Barrow, J. C.** The variables of leadership: a review and conceptual framework. *Acad. Mgmt. Rev.,* 1977, *2*, 231–251.

**Barsini, L.** *The Italians.* London: Atheneum, 1964.

**Bartlett, C. J.** Dimensions of leadership behavior in classroom discussion groups. *J. educ. Psychol.,* 1959, *50*, 280–284.

**Bartlett, F. C.** The social psychology of leadership. *J. Natl. Inst. indus. Psychol.,* 1926, *3*, 188–193.

**Bartol, K. M.** *Male and female leaders in small work groups.* East Lansing: Michigan State University Press, 1973.

**Bartol, K. M.** Male vs. female leaders: the effect of leader need for dominance on follow satisfaction. *Acad. Mgmt. J.,* 1974, *17*, 225–233.

**Bartol, K. M.** The effect of male versus female leaders on follower satisfaction and performance. *J. bus. Research,* 1975, *3*, 33–42.

**Bartol, K. M.** Relationship of sex and professional training area to job orientation. *J. appl. Psychol.,* 1976a, *61*, 368–370.

**Bartol, K. M.** Expectancy theory as a predictor of female occupational choice and attitude toward business. *Acad. mgmt. J.,* 1976b, *19*, 669–675.

**Bartol, K. M.** The sex structuring of organizations: a search for possible causes. *Acad. Mgmt. Rev.,* 1978, *3*, 805–815.

**Bartol, K. M., & Bartol, R. A.** Women in managerial and technical positions: the United States and the Soviet Union. *Indus. lab. relat. Rev.,* 1975, *28*, 524–534.

**Bartol, K. M., & Butterfield, D. A.** Sex effects in evaluating leaders. *J. appl. Psychol.,* 1976, *61*, 446–454.

**Bartol, K. M., Evans, C. L., & Stith, M. T.** Black vs. white leaders: a comparative review of the literature. *Acad. Mgmt. Rev.,* 1978, *3*, 293–304.

**Bartol, K. M., & Wortman, M. S.** Male versus female leaders: effects on perceived leader behavior and satisfaction in a hospital. *Personnel Psychol.,* 1975, *28*, 533–547.

**Bartol, K. M., & Wortman, M. S.** Sex effects in leader behavior self-descriptions and job satisfaction. *J. Psychol.,* 1976, *94*, 177–183.

**Bartol, K. M., & Wortman, M. S., Jr.** Sex of leader and subordinate role stress: a field study. *Sex Roles,* 1979, *5*, 513–518.

**Bar-Yosef, R., & Schild, E. O.** Pressures and defenses in bureaucratic roles. *Amer. J. Sociol.,* 1966, *71*, 665–673.

**Basil, D. C.** *Executive development: a comparison of small and large enterprise.* Minneapolis: University of Minnesota Press, 1964.

**Bass, A. R.** Some determinants of supervisory and peer ratings. *Dissertation Abstr.,* 1964, *24*, 5526.

**Bass, A. R., Fiedler, F. E., & Krueger, S.** *Personality correlates of assumed similarity (ASo) and related scores.* Urbana: University of Illinois, Group Effectiveness Research Laboratory, Technical Report 19, 1964.

**Bass, B. M.** An analysis of the leaderless group discussion. *J. appl. Psychol.,* 1949, *33*, 527–533.

**Bass, B. M.** Effects of the nature of the problem on LGD performance. *J. appl. Psychol.,* 1953, *37*, 96–99.

**Bass, B. M.** The leaderless group discussion. *Psychol., Bull.,* 1954a, *51*, 465–492.

**Bass, B. M.** Feelings of pleasantness and work group efficiency. *Personnel Psychol.,* 1954b, *7*, 81–91.

**Bass, B. M.** Authoritarianism or acquiescence? *J. abnorm. soc. Psychol.,* 1955a, *51*, 616–623.

**Bass, B. M.** Interrelations among measurements of leadership and associated behavior. Baton Rouge: Louisiana State University, unpublished report, 1955b.

**Bass, B. M.** Behavior in groups. III. Consistent differences in the objectivity measured performance of members and groups. Baton Rouge: Louisiana State University, unpublished report, 1955c.

**Bass, B. M.** Leadership opinions as forecasts of supervisory success. *J. appl. Psychol.,* 1956, *40*, 345–346.

**Bass, B. M.** Leadership opinions and related characteristics of salesmen and sales managers. In R. M. Stogdill & A. E. Coons (Eds.), *Leader behavior: its description and measurement.* Columbus: Ohio State University, Bureau of Business Research, 1957a.

**Bass, B. M.** Behavior in groups. Baton Rouge: Louisiana State University, *Third Annual Report,* 1957b.

**Bass, B. M.** Leadership opinions as forecasts of supervisory success: a replication. *Personnel Psychol.,* 1958, *11*, 515–518.

**Bass, B. M.** *Leadership, psychology, and organizational behavior.* New York: Harper, 1960.

**Bass, B. M.** Some observations about a general theory of leadership and interpersonal behavior. In L. Petrullo & B. M. Bass (Eds.), *Leadership and interpersonal behavior.* New York: Holt, Rinehart & Winston, 1961a.

**Bass, B. M.** Conformity, deviation, and a general theory of interpersonal behavior. In I. A. Berg & B. M. Bass (Eds.), *Conformity and deviation.* New York: Harper, 1961b.

**Bass, B. M.** Some aspects of attempted, successful, and effective leadership. *J. appl. Psychol.,* 1961c, *45*, 120–122.

**Bass, B. M.** Reactions to *Twelve Angry Men* as a measure of sensitivity training. *J. appl. Psychol.,* 1962a, *46*, 120–124.

**Bass, B. M.** Mood changes during training laboratory. *J. appl. Psychol.,* 1962b, *46*, 361–364.

**Bass, B. M.** *Orientation Inventory.* Palo Alto: Consulting Psychologists Press, 1962c.

**Bass, B. M.** Amount of participation, coalescence, and probability of decision making discussions. *J. abnorm. soc. Psychol.,* 1963, *67*, 92–94.

**Bass, B. M.** Business gaming for organizational research. *Mgmt. Sci.,* 1964, *10*, 545–556.

**Bass, B. M.** Orientation and reactions to coercive, persuasive, and permissive leadership. Pittsburgh: University of Pittsburgh, Office of Naval Research, Technical Report No. 4, 1965a.

**Bass, B. M.** Social behavior and the orientation inventory. Pittsburgh: University of Pittsburgh, Office of Naval Research, Technical Report No. 9, 1965b.

**Bass, B. M.** *Organizational Psychology.* Boston: Allyn & Bacon, 1965c.

**Bass, B. M.** A plan to use programmed group exercises to study cross-cultural differences in management behavior. *Internat. J. Psychol.,* 1966a, *1*, 315–322.

**Bass, B. M.** Effects on the subsequent performance of negotiators of studying issues or planning strategies alone or in groups. *Psychol. Monogr.,* 1966b, *80*, No. 6.

**Bass, B. M.** Some effects on a group of whether and when the head reveals his opinion. *Org.*

*behav. hum. Perform.,* 1967a, *2*, 375–382.

**Bass, B. M.** Social behavior and the orientation inventory: a review. *Psychol. Bull.,* 1967b, *68*, 260–292.

**Bass, B. M.** The anarchist movement and the T group: some possible lessons for organizational development. *J. appl. behav. Sci.,* 1967c, *3*, 211–227.

**Bass, B. M.** Ability, values, and concepts of equitable salary increases in exercise compensation. *J. appl. Psychol.,* 1968a, *52*, 299–303.

**Bass, B. M.** A preliminary report on manifest preferences in six cultures for participative management. Rochester: University of Rochester, Management Research Center, Technical Report No. 21, 1968b.

**Bass, B. M.** How to succeed in business according to business students and managers. *J. appl. Psychol.,* 1968c, *52*, 254–262.

**Bass, B. M.** When planning for others. *J. appl. behav. Sci.,* 1970, *6*, 151–171.

**Bass, B. M.** *PROFAIR—an affirmative action program for women employees.* Scottsville, N.Y.: Transnational Programs Corporation, 1971.

**Bass, B. M.** The substance and the shadow. *Amer. Psychologist,* 1974, *29*, 870–886.

**Bass, B. M.** *Exercise objectives.* Scottsville, N.Y.: Transnational Programs, 1975a.

**Bass, B. M.** *Exercise compensation.* Scottsville, N.Y.: Transnational Programs, 1975b.

**Bass, B. M.** *Exercise supervise.* Scottsville, N.Y.: Transnational Programs, 1975c.

**Bass, B. M.** *Exercise organization.* Scottsville, N.Y.: Transnational Programs, 1975d.

**Bass, B. M.** *Exercise life goals.* Scottsville, N.Y.: Transnational Programs, 1975e.

**Bass, B. M.** *Exercise self appraisal.* Scottsville, N.Y.: Transnational Programs, 1975f.

**Bass, B. M.** *Exercise communication.* Scottsville, N.Y.: Transnational Programs, 1975g.

**Bass, B. M.** *Exercise organization.* Scottsville, N.Y.: Transnational Programs, 1975h.

**Bass, B. M.** *PEX—a program of exercises in management and organizational development.* Scottsville, N.Y.: Transnational Programs Corporation, 1975i.

**Bass, B. M.** *Program of exercises for management and organizational psychology.* Scottsville, N.Y.: Transnational Programs, 1975j.

**Bass, B. M.** A systems survey research feedback for management and organizational development. *J. appl. behav. Sci.,* 1976, *12*, 215–229.

**Bass, B. M.** Utility of managerial self-planning on a simulated production task with replications in twelve countries. *J. appl. Psychol.,* 1977, *62*, 506–509.

**Bass, B. M.** Team productivity and individual member competence. *Sm. grp. Behav.,* 1980, *11*, 431–504.

**Bass, B. M.** Individual capability, team response, and productivity. In E. A. Fleischman & M. D. Dunnette (Eds.), *Human performance and productivity.* New York: Erlbaum, 1981.

**Bass, B. M., Alexander, R. A., Barrett, G. V., & Ryterband, E. C.** Empathy, projection, and negation in seven countries. In L. E. Abt. & B. F. Reiss (Eds.), *Progress in clinical psychology: industrial applications.* New York: Grune & Stratton, 1971.

**Bass, B. M., & Barrett, G. V.** *Man, work and organizations: an introduction to industrial and organizational psychology.* Boston: Allyn & Bacon, 1972.

**Bass, B. M., & Barrett, G. V.** *People, work and organizations: an introduction to industrial and organizational psychology.* Boston: Allyn & Bacon, 1981.

**Bass, B. M., Binder, M. J., & Breed, W.** Profitability and good relations: which is cause and which is effect? Pittsburgh: University of Pittsburgh, Management Research Center, Brief No. 4, 1967.

**Bass, B. M., Burger, P. C., Doktor, R., & Barrett, G. V.** *Assessment of managers: an international comparison.* New York: Free Press, 1979.

**Bass, B. M., Cascio, W. F., & McPherson, J. W.** *PROSPER—an affirmative action for black employees.* Scottsville, N.Y.: Transnational Programs Corporation, 1972.

Bass, B. M., Cascio, W. F., McPherson, J. W., & Tragash, H. J. PROSPER—training and research for increasing management awareness about affirmative action in race relations. *Acad. Mgmt. J.*, 1976, *19*, 353–369.

Bass, B. M., & Coates, C. H. Forecasting officer potential using the leaderless group discussion. *J. abnorm. soc. Psychol.*, 1952, *47*, 321–325.

Bass, B. M., & Coates, C. H. Situational and personality factors in leadership in ROTC. Baton Rouge: Louisiana State University, 1953 (mimeo).

Bass, B. M., & Dunteman, G. Behavior in groups as a function of self, interaction, and task orientation. *J. abnorm. soc. Psychol.*, 1963, *66*, 419–428.

Bass, B. M., Dunteman, G., Frye, F., Vidulich, R., & Wambach, H. Self, interaction, and task-orientation inventory scores associated with overt behavior and personal factors. *Educ. psychol. Measmt.*, 1963, *23*, 101–116.

Bass, B. M., & Farrow, D. L. Quantitative analyses of biographies of political figures. *J. Psychol.*, 1977a, *97*, 281–296.

Bass, B. M., & Farrow, D. L. The importance of manager and subordinate personality in contingency leadership analysis. *Proceedings of the Western Academy of Management*, 1977b.

Bass, B. M., Farrow, D. L., & Valenzi, E. R. A regression approach to identifying ways to increase leadership effectiveness, Rochester: University of Rochester, U.S. Army Research Institute for the Behavioral and Social Sciences, Technical Report No. 77–3, 1977.

Bass, B. M., & Flint, A. W. Some effects of power, practice and problem difficulty on success as a leader. Baton Rouge: Louisiana State University, Technical Report No. 18, 1958a.

Bass B. M., & Flint, A. Comparison of the construct validation of three objective measures of successful leadership. Baton Rouge: Louisiana State University, 1958b (mimeo).

Bass, B. M., Flint, A. W., & Pryer, M. W. Group effectiveness as a function of attempted and successful leadership. Baton Rouge: Louisiana State University, 1957a (mimeo).

Bass, B. M., Flint, A. W., & Pryer, M. W. Effects of status-esteem conflict on subsequent behavior in groups. Baton Rouge: Louisiana State University, 1957b (mimeo).

Bass, B. M., & Franke, R. H. Societal influences on student perceptions of how to succeed in organizations: a cross-national analysis. *J. appl. Psychol.*, 1972, *56*, 312–318.

Bass, B. M., Gaier, E. L., & Flint, A. W. Attempted leadership as a function of motivation interacting with amount of control. Baton Rouge: Louisiana State University, unpublished report, 1956.

Bass, B. M., Hurder, W. P., & Ellis, N. Human stress tolerance. Baton Rouge: Louisiana State University, USAF Aero-Medical Lab, Final Technical Report, 1954.

Bass, B. M., Klauss, R., & DeMarco, J. J. Factors influencing communication style. Syracuse: Syracuse University, Technical Report No. 4, 1977.

Bass, B. M., & Klubeck, S. Effects of seating arrangement of leaderless group discussions. *J. abnorm. soc. Psychol.*, 1952, *47*, 724–727.

Bass, B. M., Krusell, J., & Alexander, R. A. Male managers' attitudes toward working women. *Amer. behav. Scientist*, 1971, *15*, 221–236.

Bass, B. M., & Leavitt, H. J. Some experiments in planning and operating. *Mgmt. Sci.*, 1963, *9*, 574–585.

Bass, B. M., McGehee, C. R., Hawkins, W. C., Young, P. C., & Gebel, A. S. Personality variables related to leaderless group discussion behavior *J. abnorm. soc. Psychol.*, 1953, *48*, 120–128.

Bass, B. M., & Mitchell, C. W. Influences on the felt need for collective bargaining by business and science professionals. *J. appl. Psychol.*, 1976, *61*, 770–773.

Bass, B. M., & Norton, Fay-Tyler, M. Group size and leaderless discussions. *J. appl. Psychol.*, 1951, *35*, 397–400.

**Bass, B. M., Pryer, M. W., Gaier, E. L., & Flint, A. W.** Interacting effects of control, motivation, group practice, and problem difficulty on attempted leadership. *J. abnorm. soc. Psychol.*, 1958, *56*, 352–358.

**Bass, B. M., & Rosenstein, E.** Integration of industrial democracy and participative management: U.S. and European perspectives. In B. T. King, S. S. Streufert, & F. E. Fiedler (Eds.), *Managerial control and organizational democracy*. Washington, D.C.: Victor Winston & Sons, 1977.

**Bass, B. M., & Ryterband, E. C.** Organizational psychology (2d ed.). Boston: Allyn & Bacon, 1979.

**Bass, B. M., & Shackleton, V. J.** Industrial democracy and participative management: a case for synthesis. *Acad. Mgmt. Rev.*, 1979, *4*, 393–404.

**Bass, B. M., & Thiagarajan, K. M.** Differential preferences for long-vs. short-term payoffs in India and the United States. *Proceedings of the XVIth International Congress of Applied Psychology*. Amsterdam: Swets & Zeitlinger, 1969.

**Bass, B. M., & Valenzi, E. R.** *PROFILE*. Scottsville, N. Y.: Transnational Programs Corporation, 1973.

**Bass, B. M., & Valenzi, E. R.** Contingent aspects of effective management styles. In J. G. Hunt & L. L. Larson (Eds.), *Contingency approaches to leadership*. Carbondale: Southern Illinois University Press, 1974.

**Bass, B. M., Valenzi, E. R., & Farrow, D. L.** External environment related to managerial style. Rochester: University of Rochester, U.S. Army Research Institute for the Behavioral and Social Sciences, Technical Report No. 77–2, 1977. (Also in The *Proceedings of International Conference on Social Change and Organizational Development*, Dubrovnik, Yugoslavia, March 1–3, 1977).

**Bass, B. M., Valenzi, E. R., & Farrow, D. L.** Discriminant functions to identify ways to increase leadership effectiveness. *Proceedings of the 15th Annual Eastern Academy of Management*, 1978.

**Bass, B. M., Valenzi, E. R., Farrow, D. L., & Solomon, R. J.** Management styles associated with organizational, task, personal, and interpersonal contingencies. *J. appl. Psychol*, 1975, *60*, 720–729.

**Bass, B. M., & Vaughan, J. A.** *The psychology of learning for managers*. New York: American Foundation for Management Research, 1965.

**Bass, B. M., & White, O. L.** Situation tests. III. Observers' ratings of leaderless group discussion participants as indicators of external leadership status. *Educ. psychol. Measmt.*, 1951, *11*, 355–361.

**Bass, B. M., & Wurster, C. R.** Effects of the nature of the problem on LGD performance. *J. appl. Psychol.*, 1953a, *37*, 96–99.

**Bass, B. M., & Wurster, C. R.** Effects of company rank on LGD of oil refinery supervisors' performance. *J. appl. Psychol.*, 1953b, *37*, 100–104.

**Bass, B. M., Wurster, C. R., & Alcock, W.** A test of the proposition: we want to be esteemed most by those we esteem most highly. *J. abnorm. soc. Psychol.* 1961, *63*, 650–653.

**Bass, B. M., Wurster, C. R., Doll, P. A., & Clair, D. J.** Situational and personality factors in leadership among sorority women. *Psychol. Monogr.*, 1953, *67*, 1–23.

**Batchelder, R. L., & Hardy, J. M.** *Using sensitivity training and laboratory method: an organizational case study in the development of human resources*. New York: Association Press, 1968.

**Bates, A. P.** Some sociometric aspects of social ranking in a small, face-to-face group. *Sociometry*, 1952, *15*, 330–342.

**Bates, F. L.** The coordination of maintenance activities in bomb wings: synchronization and performance. *Inst. res. soc. Sci.*, University of North Carolina, 1953.

**Baum, B. H.** *Decentralization of authority in a bureaucracy.* Englewood Cliffs, N.J.: Prentice-Hall, 1961.

**Baum, B. H., Sorenson, P. F., & Place, W. S.** The effect of managerial training on organizational control: an experimental study. *Org. behav. hum. Perform.,* 1970, *5,* 170–182.

**Baumgartel, H.** Leadership, motivations, and attitudes in research laboratories. *J. soc. Issues,* 1956, *12,* 24–31.

**Baumgartel, H.** Leadership style as a variable in research administration. *Admin. sci. Quar.,* 1957, *2,* 344–360.

**Baumgartel, H., Bennis, W. G., & De Nitish, R.** *Readings in group development for managers and trainers.* New York: Asia Publishing House, 1967.

**Baumgartel, H., & Goldstein, J. W.** Need and value shifts in college training groups. *J. appl. behav. Sci.,* 1967, *3,* 87–101.

**Baumgartel, H., & Jeanpierre, F.** Applying knowledge in the back home setting. *J. appl. behav. Sci.,* 1972, *8,* 674–694.

**Bavelas, A.** Morale and the training of leaders. In G. Watson (Ed.), *Civilian morale.* Boston: Houghton Mifflin, 1942.

**Bavelas, A.** Some problems of organizational change. *J. soc. Issues,* 1948, *4,* 48–52.

**Bavelas, A.** Communication patterns in task-oriented groups. *J. Acoust. Soc. Amer.,* 1950, *22,* 725–730.

**Bavelas, A.** Leadership: man and function. *Admin, sci. Quar.,* 1960, *4,* 491–498.

**Bavelas, A., Hastorf, A. H., Gross, A. E., & Kite, W. R.** Experiments on the alteration of group structure. *J. exp. soc. Psychol.,* 1965, *1,* 55–70.

**Baxter, B.** A training evaluation study. *Personnel Psychol.,* 1953, *6,* 403–417.

**Baxter, B., & Cassidy, R.** *Group experience, the democratic way.* New York: Harper, 1943.

**Bayer, A. E., & Boruch, R. F.** The black student in American colleges. Washington, D.C.: American Council on Education, research report No. 4(2), 1969.

**Bayes, M., & Newton, P. M.** Women in authority: a sociopsychological analysis. *J. appl. behav. Sci.,* 1978, *14,* 7–20.

**Beach, B. H., & Beach, L. R.** A note on judgments of situational favorableness and probability of success. *Org. behav. hum. Perform.,* 1978, *22,* 69–74.

**Beam, H. H.** Effectiveness and satisfaction as a function of managerial style and technological complexity in a Navy work environment. Doctoral dissertation, University of Michigan, Ann Arbor, 1975.

**Beatty, R. W.** Blacks as supervisors: a study of training job performance and employer expectations. *Acad. Mgmt. J.,* 1973, *10,* 191–206.

**Beatty, R. W.** Supervisory behavior related to job success of hard-core unemployed over a two-year period. *J. appl. Psychol.,* 1974, *59,* 38–42.

**Beatty, R. W., & Schneier, C. E.** Training the hard-core unemployed through positive reinforcement. *Hum. resource Mgmt.,* 1972, *11,* 11–17.

**Bechard, J. E.** The college of education at Michigan State University as an organization: a survey of the perceptions of its students, faculty and administrators. Doctoral dissertation, Michigan State University, East Lansing, 1971.

**Bechtel, R. B., & Rosenfeld, H. M.** Expectations of social acceptance and compatibility as related to status discrepancy and social motives. *J. pers. soc. Psychol.,* 1966, *3,* 300–349.

**Bechterew, W., & Lange, A.** Die Ergebnisse des Experiments auf dem Gebiete der kollektiven Reflexologie. *Zsch. f. angew. Psychol.,* 1924, *24,* 224–254. (Reported in G. Murphy and L. Murphy, *Experimental social psychology.* New York: Harper, 1931.)

**Becker, S. W., & Baloff, N.** Organization structure and complex problem solving. *Admin. sci. Quar.,* 1969, *14,* 260–271.

**Beckhard, R.** An organization improvement program in a decentralized organization. *J. appl.*

*behav. Sci.*, 1966, *2*, 3–25.

**Beckhard, R.** *Organizational development: strategies and models.* Reading, Mass.: Addison-Wesley Co., 1969.

**Bedrosian, H.** An analysis of vocational interests at two levels of management. *J. appl. Psychol.*, 1964, *48*, 325–328.

**Beebe, R. J.** The least preferred co-worker score of the leader and the productivity of small interacting task groups in octants II and IV of the Fiedler contingency model. *Dissertation Abstr. Internat.*, 1975, *35*, 3642.

**Beer, M.** Leadership, employee needs, and motivation. Doctoral dissertation, Ohio State University, Columbus, 1964.

**Beer, M.** Needs and need satisfaction among clerical workers in complex and routine jobs. *Personnel Psychol.*, 1968, *21*, 209–222.

**Beer, M., Buckhout, R., Horowitz, M. W., & Levy, S.** Some perceived properties of the differences between leaders and nonleaders. *J. Psychol.*, 1959, *47*, 49–56.

**Beer, S.** *Decision and control.* New York: Wiley, 1966.

**Belasco, J. A.** Educational innovation: the impact of organizational and community variables on performance contract. *Mgmt. Sci.*, 1973, *20*, 498–506.

**Belasco, J. A., & Trice, H. M.** *The assessment of change in training and therapy.* New York: McGraw-Hill, 1969a.

**Belasco, J. A., & Trice, H. M.** Unanticipated returns of training. *Train. develop. J.*, 1969b, *23*, 12–17.

**Bell, D.** *Work and its discontents.* Boston: Beacon Press, 1956.

**Bell, G. B.** The relationship between leadership and empathy. Doctoral dissertation, Northwestern University, Evanston, Ill., 1951.

**Bell, G. B., & French, R. L.** Consistency of individual leadership position in small groups of varying membership. *J. abnorm. soc. Psychol.*, 1950, *45*, 764–767.

**Bell, G. B., & Hall, H. E.** The relationship between leadership and empathy. *J. abnorm. soc. Psychol.*, 1954, *49*, 156–157.

**Bell, G. B.** Determinants of span of control. *Amer. J. Sociol.*, 1967, *73*, 100–109.

**Bell, T. O.** A study of personality characteristics of school superintendents in relation to administrative behavior. *Dissertation Abstr.*, 1969, *29A*, 2049–2050.

**Bell, W., Hill, R. J., & Wright, C. R.** *Public leadership: a critical review with special reference to adult education.* San Francisco: Chandler, 1961.

**Bellingrath, G. C.** *Qualities associated with leadership in extracurricular activities of the high school.* New York: Teachers College Contributions to Education, 1930.

**Bellows, R. M.** *Creative leadership.* Englewood Cliffs, N.J.: Prentice-Hall, 1959.

**Bellows, R. M., Gilson, T. Q., & Odiorne, G. S.** *Executive skills: their dynamics and development.* Englewood Cliffs, N.J.: Prentice-Hall, 1962.

**Bender, I. E., & Hastorf, A. H.** The perception of persons: forecasting another person's responses on three personality scales. *J. abnorm. soc. Psychol.*, 1950, *45*, 556–561.

**Benne, K. D.** *A conception of authority.* New York: Teachers College, Columbia University, 1943.

**Benne, K. D., Bradford, L. P., & Lippitt, R.** The laboratory method. In L. P. Bradford, J. R. Gibb, & K. D. Benne (Eds.), *T-group theory and laboratory method.* New York: Wiley, 1964.

**Benne, K. D., & Sheats, P.** Functional roles of group members. *J. soc. Issues*, 1948, *4*, 41–49.

**Bennett, E.** *Human factors in technology.* New York: McGraw-Hill, 1963.

**Bennett, E. B.** Discussion, decisions, commitment, and consensus in "group decision." *Hum. Relat.*, 1955, *8*, 251–273.

**Bennis, W. G.** Leadership theory and administrative behavior: the problems of authority. *Admin. sci. Quar.*, 1959, *4*, 259–301.

**Bennis, W. G.** Revisionist theory of leadership. *Harvard bus. Rev.*, 1961, *39*, 26–36, 146–150.

**Bennis, W. G.** Effecting organizational change: a new role for the behavioral scientist. *Admin. sci. Quar.*, 1963, *8*, 125–165.

**Bennis, W. G.** Goals and meta-goals of laboratory training. In W. G. Bennis *et al.* (Eds.), *Interpersonal dynamics, essays and readings on human interaction.* Homewood, Ill.: Dorsey Press, 1964.

**Bennis, W. G.** Theory and method in applying behavioral science to planned organizational change. *J. appl. behav. Sci.*, 1965, *1*, 337–360.

**Bennis, W. G.** *Changing organizations.* New York: McGraw-Hill, 1966a.

**Bennis, W. G.** Changing organizations. *J. appl. behav. Sci.*, 1966b, *2*, 247–263.

**Bennis, W. G.** Organizational developments and the fate of bureaucracy. *Indus. relat. Rev.*, 1966c, *7*, 41–55.

**Bennis, W. G.** *Organizational development: its nature, origins, and prospects.* Reading, Mass.: Addison-Wesley, 1969.

**Bennis, W. G.** *American bureaucracy.* Chicago: Aldine, 1970.

**Bennis, W. G.** *The unconscious conspiracy: why leaders can't lead.* New York: Amacom, 1976.

**Bennis, W. G., Benne, K. D., & Chin, R.** *The planning of change: readings in the applied behavioral sciences.* New York: Holt, Rinehart & Winston, 1962.

**Bennis, W. G., Berkowitz, N., Affinito, M., & Malone, M.** Authority, power, and the ability to influence. *Hum. Relat.*, 1958, *11*, 143–155.

**Benoit-Smullyan, E.** Status, status types, and status interrelations. *Amer. sociol. Rev.*, 1944, *9*, 151–161.

**Bentz, V. J.** The Sears experience in the investigation, description, and prediction of executive behavior. Chicago: Sears, Roebuck, unpublished report, 1964.

**Bentz, V. J.** Leadership, a study of social interaction. Unpublished ms., undated.

**Berelson, B., & Steiner, G. A.** *Human behavior: an inventory of scientific findings.* New York: Harcourt, Brace & World, 1964.

**Berg, I. A., & Bass, B. M.** *Conformity and deviation.* New York: Harper, 1961.

**Bergen, H. B.** Finding out what employees are thinking. *Conference Board Mgmt. Rec.*, April 1939, 53–58.

**Berger, C. R.** The effects of influence feedback and need influence on the relationship between incentive magnitude and attitude change. *Dissertation Abstr. Internat.*, 1969, *30*, 385–386.

**Bergum, B. O., & Lehr, D. J.** Effects of authoritarianism on vigilance performance. *J. appl. Psychol.*, 1963, *47*, 75–77.

**Berkowitz, L.** An exploratory study of the roles of aircraft commanders. *USAF Hum. Resour. Res. Cent. res. Bull.*, 1953a, No. 53–65, 1–27.

**Berkowitz, L.** Sharing leadership in small, decision-making groups. *J. abnorm. soc. Psychol.*, 1953b, *48*, 231–238.

**Berkowitz, L.** Group standards, cohesiveness, and productivity. *Hum. Relat.*, 1954, *7*, 509–519.

**Berkowitz, L.** Personality and group position. *Sociometry*, 1956a, *19*, 210–222.

**Berkowitz, L.** Social desirability and frequency of influence attempts as factors in leadership choice. *J. Pers.*, 1956b, *24*, 424–435.

**Berkowitz, L.** Group norms among bomber crews: patterns of perceived crew attitudes, "actual" crew attitudes, and crew liking related to aircrew effectiveness in Far Eastern combat. *Sociometry*, 1956c, *19*, 141–153.

**Berkowitz, L.** Liking for the group and the perceived merit of the group's behavior. *J. abnorm. soc. Psychol.*, 1957a, *54*, 353–357.

**Berkowitz, L.** Effects of perceived dependency relationships upon conformity to group expectations. *J. abnorm. soc. Psychol.*, 1957b, *55*, 350–354.

**Berkowitz, L.** Some factors affecting the reduction of overt hostility. *J. abnorm. soc. Psychol.*, 1960, *60*, 14–21.

**Berkowitz, L.** *Advances in experimental social psychology*, vol. 4. New York: Academic Press, 1969.

**Berkowitz, L.** *Advances in experimental social psychology*, vol. 5. New York: Academic Press, 1970.

**Berkowitz, L., & Connor, W. H.** Success, failure, and social responsibility. *J. pers. soc. Psychol.*, 1966, *4*, 664–669.

**Berkowitz, L. & Daniels, L. R.** Responsibility and dependency. *J. abnorm. soc. Psychol.*, 1963, *66*, 429–436.

**Berkowitz, L., & Daniels, L. R.** Affecting the salience of the social responsibility norm; effects of past help on the response to dependency relationships. *J. abnorm. soc. Psychol.*, 1964, *68*, 275–281.

**Berkowitz, L., & Haythorn, W.** The relationship of dominance to leadership choice. Crew Research Laboratory, AF Personnel & Training Reserve Center, Randolph AF Base, LN-55-8, 1955.

**Berkowitz, L., & Howard, R. C.** Reactions to opinion deviates as affected by affiliation need (n) and group member interdependence. *Sociometry*, 1959, *22*, 81–91.

**Berkowitz, L., & Levy, B. I.** Pride in group performance and group-task motivation. *J. abnorm. soc. Psychol.*, 1956, *53*, 300–306.

**Berkowitz, L., & Lundy, R. M.** Personality characteristics related to susceptibility to influence by peers or authority figures. *J. Pers.*, 1957, *25*, 306–316.

**Berkowitz, L., & Macaulay, J. R.** Some effects of differences in status level and status stability. *Hum. Relat.*, 1961, *14*, 135–148.

**Berlew, D. E., & Hall, D. T.** The socialization of managers: effects of expectations on performance. *Admin. sci. Quar.*, 1966, *11*, 207–223.

**Berlyne, D. E.** Novelty and curiosity as determinants of exploratory behavior. *Brit. J. Psychol.*, 1950, *41*, 68–80.

**Berlyne, D. E.** The arousal and satiation of perceptual curiosity in the rat. *J. compar. physiol. Psychol.*, 1955, *48*, 238–246.

**Bernard, J.** Political leadership among North American Indians. *Amer. J. Sociol.*, 1928, *34*, 296–315.

**Bernard, L. L.** *An introduction to social psychology*. New York: Holt, 1926.

**Bernard, L. L.** Leadership and propaganda. In J. Davis & H. E. Barnes. *An introduction to sociology*. New York: Heath, 1927.

**Bernardin, H. J.** The influence of reinforcement orientation on the relationship between supervisory style and effectiveness criteria. *Dissertation Abstr. Internat.*, 1976, *37*, 1018.

**Bernardin, H. J., & Alvares, K. M.** The effects of organizational level on perceptions of role conflict resolution strategies. *Org. behav. hum. Perform.*, 1975, *14*, 1–9.

**Berne, E.** *Games people play*. New York: Grove Press, 1964.

**Bernhardt, R. G.** A study of the relationships between teachers' attitudes toward militancy and their perceptions of selected organizational characteristics of their schools. Doctoral dissertation, Syracuse University, Syracuse, N.Y., 1972.

**Bernstein, I. S.** Group social patterns as influenced by removal and later reintroduction of the dominant male Rhesus. *Psychol. Rep.*, 1964, *14*, 3–10.

**Bernstein, M. D.** Autocratic and democratic leadership in an experimental group setting: a modified replication of the experiments of Lewin, Lippitt, and White, with systematic observer variation. *Dissertation Abstr. Internat.*, 1971, *31*, 6712.

**Bernstein, M. H.** *The job of the federal executive.* Washington, D.C.: Brookings Institution, 1958.

**Berrien, F. K.** Homeostasis theory of groups—implications for leadership. In L. Petrullo & B. Bass (Eds.), *Leadership and interpersonal behavior.* New York: Holt, Rinehart & Winston, 1961.

**Berscheid, E., & Walster, E.** *Interpersonal attraction.* Reading, Mass.: Addison-Wesley, 1969.

**Berzon, B., Reisel, J., & Davis, D.** PEER: an audio-tape program for self-directed small groups. *J. hum. Psychol.*, 1969, *9*, 71–87.

**Besco, R. O., & Lawshe, C. H.** Foreman leadership as perceived by superiors and subordinates. *Personnel Psychol.*, 1959, *12*, 573–582.

**Besco, R. O. Tiffin, J., & King, D. C.** Evaluation techniques for management programs. *J. Amer. soc. train. Directors*, 1959, *13*, 13–27.

**Beutler, L. E., Jobe, A. M., & Elkins, D.** Outcomes in group psychotherapy: using persuasion theory to increase treatment efficiency. *J. consult. clin. Psychol.*, 1974, *42*, 547–553.

**Bhanos, A. P.** The entroper: an information theory analysis of democratic leadership and group behavior. INSEAD Monograph, 1973 (unpublished).

**Bhatt, L. J., & Pathak, N. S.** A study of functions of supervisory staff and the characteristics essential for success as viewed by a group of supervisors. *Manas*, 1962, *9*, 25–31.

**Bhushan, L. I.** A scale of leadership preference. *Psychol. Studies*, 1969, *14*, 28–34.

**Bibby, D. L.** An enlargement of the job for the worker. In *Proceedings of the 17th Conference, Texas Personnel and Management Associations.* Austin: University of Texas, 1955.

**Biddle, B. J., French, J. R. P., & Moore, J. V.** Some aspects of leadership in the small work group. Ann Arbor: University of Michigan, Institute for Social Research, 1953 (mimeo).

**Biddle, B. J., & Thomas, E. J.** *Role theory: concepts and research.* New York: Wiley, 1966.

**Bierstedt, R.** An analysis of social power. *Amer. sociol. Rev.*, 1950, *15*, 730–736.

**Biggane, J. F., & Stewart, P. A.** Job enlargement: a case study. *Personnel Admin.*, 1965, *10*, 22–32, 39–40.

**Biggs, D. A., Huneryager, S. G., & Delaney, J. J.** Leadership behavior: interpersonal needs and effective supervisory training. *Personnel Psychol.*, 1966, *19*, 311–320.

**Bigoness, W. J.** Effect of applicant's sex, race, and performance on employer's performance ratings: some additional findings. *J. appl. Psychol.*, 1976, *61*, 80–84.

**Binder, A., Wolin, B. R., & Terebinski, S. J.** Leadership selection when uncertainty is minimal. *Psychonomic Sci.*, 1965, *3*, 367–368.

**Binder, A., Wolin, B. R., & Terebinski, S. J.** Learning and extinction of leadership preferences in small groups. *J. math Psychol.* 1966, *3*, 129–139.

**Binet, A.** *La suggestibilité.* Paris: Schleicher, 1900.

**Bingham, W. V.** Leadership. In H. C. Metcalf, *The psychological foundations of management.* New York: Shaw, 1927.

**Bingham, W. V., & Davis, W. T.** Intelligence test score and business success. *J. appl. Psychol.*, 1924, *8*, 1–22.

**Bion, W. R.** Experiences in groups. *Hum. Relat.*, 1948, *1*, 314–320, 487–496.

**Bion, W. R.** *Experiences in groups.* New York: Basic Books, 1961.

**Bird, C.** *Social psychology.* New York: Appleton-Century, 1940.

**Birnbaum, R.** Presidential succession: an inter-institutional analysis. *Educ. Record*, 1971, Spring, 133–145.

**Bish, J., & Schriesheim, C.** An exploratory dimensional analysis of form XII of the Ohio State leadership scales. *Proceedings of the Academy of Management*, 1974.

**Bishop, B. M.** Mother–child interaction and the social behavior of children. *Psychol. Monogr.,* 1951, *65,* No. 328.

**Bishop, D. W.** Relations between tasks and interpersonal success and group member adjustment. Urbana: University of Illinois, Master's thesis, 1964.

**Bishop, D. W.** Group member adjustment as related to interpersonal and task success and affiliation and achievement motives. Urbana: University of Illinois, Group Effectiveness Research Laboratory, Technical Report No. 23, 1967.

**Bishop, R. C., & Hill, J. W.** Job enlargement vs. job change and their effects on contiguous but non-manipulated work groups. *Exp. publ. System, Amer. Psychol. Assn.,* 1969, No. 107A.

**Bishop, R. C., & Hill, J. W.** Effects of job enlargement and job change on contiguous but nonmanipulated jobs as a function of workers' status. *J. appl. Psychol.,* 1971, *55,* 175–181.

**Bither, S. W.** *Personality as a factor in management team decision making.* University Park, Pa.: College of Business Administration, Pennsylvania State University, 1971.

**Bjerstedt, A.** The interpretation of sociometric status scores in the classroom. *Nordisk Psykologi,* 1956, *1–2,* 8–14.

**Blackmar, F. W.** Leadership in reform. *Amer. J. Sociol.,* 1911, *16,* 626–644.

**Blades, J. W.** The influence of intelligence, task ability and motivation on group performance. *Dissertation Abstr. Internat.,* 1976, *37,* 1463.

**Blades, J. W., & Fiedler, F. E.** Participative management, member intelligence, and group performance. Seattle: University of Washington, Organizational Research, Technical Report No. 73–40, 1973.

**Blain, I.** *Structure in management.* London: National Institute of Industrial Psychology, 1964.

**Blake, R. R., & Mouton, J. S.** *Group dynamics–key to decision making.* Houston: Gulf, 1961a.

**Blake, R. R., & Mouton, J. S.** Perceived characteristics of elected representatives. *J. abnorm. soc. Psychol.,* 1961b, *62,* 693–695.

**Blake, R. R., & Mouton, J. S.** Power, people and performance reviews. *Advan. Mgmt.,* 1961c, *26,* 13–17.

**Blake, R. R., & Mouton, J. S.** Union–management relations: from conflict to collaboration. *Personnel,* 1961d, *38,* 38–51.

**Blake, R. R., & Mouton, J. S.** The instrumented training laboratory. In I. R. Weschler & E. H. Schein (Eds.), *Issues in training.* Washington, D.C.: NTL-NEA, 1962a.

**Blake, R. R., & Mouton, J. S.** The intergroup dynamics of win-lose conflict and problem-solving collaboration in union–management relations. In M. Sherif (Ed.), *Intergroup relations and leadership.* New York: Wiley, 1962b.

**Blake, R. R., & Mouton, J. S.** *The managerial grid.* Houston: Gulf, 1964.

**Blake, R. R., & Mouton, J. S.** A 9.9 approach for increasing organizational productivity. In E. H. Schein & W. G. Bennis (Eds.), *Personal and organizational change through group methods.* New York: Wiley, 1965.

**Blake, R. R., & Mouton, J. S.** Some effects of managerial grid seminar training on union and management attitudes toward supervision. *J. appl. behav. Sci.,* 1966, *2,* 387–400.

**Blake, R. R., Mouton, J. S., Barnes, J. S., & Greiner, L. E.** Breakthrough in organizational development. *Harvard bus. Rev.,* 1964, *42,* 133–155.

**Blake, R. R., Mouton, J. S., & Bidwell, A. C.** Managerial grid. *Advanc. Mgmt.,* 1962, *1,* 12–15.

**Blake, R. R., Mouton, J. S., & Fruchter, B.** The consistency of interpersonal behavior judgments made on the basis of short-term interactions in three-man groups. *J. abnorm. soc. Psychol.,* 1954, *49,* 573–578.

**Blake, R. R., Mouton, J. S., & Fruchter, B.** A factor analysis of training group behavior. *J. soc. Psychol.,* 1962, *58,* 121–130.

**Blalock, H. M.** Status consciousness: a dimensional analysis. *Soc. Forces,* 1959, *37,* 243–248.

**Blalock, H. M., Jr.** *Toward a theory of minority-group relations.* New York: Wiley, 1967.

**Blankenship, L. V., & Miles, R. E.** Organizational structure and managerial decision behavior. *Admin. sci. Quar.,* 1968, *13,* 106–120.

**Blau, P. M.** Patterns of interaction among a group of officials in a government agency. *Hum. Relat.,* 1954a, *7,* 337–348.

**Blau, P. M.** Cooperation and competition in a bureucracy. *Amer. J. Sociol.,* 1954b, *59,* 530–535.

**Blau, P. M.** *The dynamics of bureaucracy.* Chicago: University of Chicago Press, 1955.

**Blau, P. M.** Patterns of deviation in work groups. *Sociometry,* 1960, *23,* 245–261.

**Blau, P. M.** *Exchange and power in social life.* New York: Wiley, 1964.

**Blau, P. M.** The hierarchy of authority in organizations. *Amer. J. Sociol.,* 1968, *73,* 453–467.

**Blau, P. M., & Scott, W. R.** *Formal organizations.* San Francisco: Chandler, 1962.

**Blauner, R.** *Alienation and freedom: the factory worker and his industry.* Chicago: University of Chicago Press, 1964.

**Bleda, P. R., Gitter, G. A., & D'Agostino, R. B.** Enlisted men's perceptions of leader attributes and satisfaction with military life. *J. appl. Psychol.,* 1977, *62,* 43–49.

**Block, D. R., & Kolakowski, D.** Further evidence of sex-linked major-gene influence on human spatial visualizing ability. *Amer. J. hum. Genet.,* 1973, *25,* 1–14.

**Blood, M. R., & Hulin, C. L.** Alienation, environmental characteristics, and worker responses. *J. appl. Psychol.,* 1967, *51,* 284–290.

**Blum, R.** The study of groups. Washington, D.C.: George Washington University, Human Resources Research Office, 1953 (mimeo).

**Blumberg, L. U.** Community leaders: the social bases and social-psychological concomitants of community power. *Dissertation Abstr.,* 1955, *15,* 638.

**Blumenthal, A.** *Small town stuff.* Chicago: University of Chicago Press, 1932.

**Blumenthal, W. M.** *Codetermination in the German steel industry.* Princeton, N.J.: Princeton University, Industrial Relations Section, 1956.

**Bockman, S., & Gayk, W. F.** Political orientations and political ideologies. *Pacific sociol. Rev.,* 1977, *20,* 536–552.

**Boddewyn, J., & Nath, R.** Comparative management studies: an assessment. *Mgmt. internat. Rev.,* 1970, *10,* 3–11.

**Bogard, H. M.** Union and management trainees: a comparative study of personality and occupational choice. *J. appl. Psychol.,* 1960, *44,* 56–63.

**Bogardus, E. S.** *Essentials of social psychology.* Los Angeles: University of Southern California Press, 1918.

**Bogardus, E. S.** World leadership types. *Sociol. soc. Res.,* 1928, *12,* 573–599.

**Bogardus, E. S.** Leadership and attitudes. *Sociol. soc. Res.,* 1929, *13,* 377–387.

**Bogardus, E. S.** Leadership and social situations. *Sociol. soc. Res.,* 1931, *16,* 164–170.

**Bogardus, E. S.** *Leaders and leadership.* New York: Appleton-Century, 1934.

**Bohleber, M. E.** Conditions influencing the relationships between leadership style and group structural and population characteristics. *Dissertation Abstr.,* 1967, *28,* 776–777.

**Boise, W. B.** Supervisors' attitudes toward disciplinary actions. *Personnel Admin.,* 1965, *28,* 24–27.

**Bolda, R. A.** Employee attitudes related to supervisory and departmental effectiveness. *Engng. indus. Psychol.,* 1959, *1,* 31–39.

**Bollett, R. M.** The effect of leader presence on change in a personal growth group. *Dissertation Abstr. Internat.,* 1972, *32,* 4340.

**Bolman, L.** Some effects of trainers on their groups: a partial replication. *J. appl. behav. Sci.,* 1973, *9,* 534–539.

**Bond, J. R., & Vinacke, W. E.** Coalitions in mixed-sex triads. *Sociometry,* 1961, *24,* 61–75.

**Bonjean, C. M.** Community leadership: a case study and conceptual refinement. *Amer. J. Sociol.,* 1963, *67,* 672–681.

**Bonjean, C. M.** Class, status, and power reputation. *Sociol. soc. Res.,* 1964, *49,* 69–75.

**Bonjean, C. M.** Mass, class, and the industrial community: a comparative analysis of managers, businessmen, and workers. *Amer. J. Sociol.,* 1966, *72,* 149–162.

**Bonner, H.** *Group dynamics.* New York: Ronald Press, 1959.

**Bonney, M. E.** The consistency of sociometric scores and their relationship to teacher judgments of social success and to personality self-ratings. *Sociometry,* 1943, *6,* 409–424.

**Bonney, M. E.** A study of mutual friendships on the elementary, high school and college levels. *Sociometry,* 1946a, *9,* 21–47.

**Bonney, M. E.** A study of the sociometric process among sixth-grade children. *J. educ. Psychol.,* 1946b, *37,* 359–372.

**Bonney, M. E.** Popular and unpopular children: a sociometric study. *Sociometry Monogr.,* 1947a, No. 9.

**Bonney, M. E.** Sociometric study of agreement between teacher judgments and student choices. *Sociometry,* 1947b, *10,* 133–146.

**Bonney, M. E.** A study of friendship choices in college in relation to church affiliation, in-church preferences, family size, and length of enrollment in college. *J. soc. Psychol.,* 1949, *29,* 153–166.

**Bonney, M. E., & Powell, J.** Differences in social behavior between sociometrically high and sociometrically low children. *J. educ. Res.,* 1953, *46,* 481–495.

**Bons, P. M.** The effect of changes in leadership environment on the behavior of relationship and task-motivated leaders. Doctoral dissertation, University of Washington, Seattle, 1974.

**Bons, P. M., Bass, A. R., & Komorita, S. S.** Changes in leadership style as a function of military experience and type of command. *Personnel Psychol.,* 1970, *23,* 551–568.

**Bons, P. M., & Fiedler, F. E.** Changes in organizational leadership and the behavior of relationship- and task-motivated leaders. *Admin. sci. Quar.,* 1976, *21,* 433–472.

**Borg, W. R.** Leadership reactions in situational tests. *Amer. Psychologist,* 1956, *11,* 379.

**Borg, W. R.** The behavior of emergent and designated leaders in situational tests. *Sociometry,* 1957, *20,* 95–104.

**Borg, W. R.** Prediction of small group role behavior from personality variables. *J. abnorm. soc. Psychol.,* 1960, *60,* 112–116.

**Borg, W. R., & Tupes, E. C.** Personality characteristics related to leadership behavior in two types of small group situational problems. *J. appl. Psychol.,* 1958, *42,* 252–256.

**Borg, W. R., Tupes, E. C., & Carp, A.** Relationships between physical proficiency and measures of leadership and personality. *Personnel Psychol.,* 1959, *12,* 113–126.

**Borgatta, E. F.** Analysis of social interaction and sociometric perception. *Sociometry,* 1954, *17,* 7–32.

**Borgatta, E. F.** Analysis of social interaction: actual, role playing, and projective. *J. abnorm. soc. Psychol.,* 1955a, *51,* 394–405.

**Borgatta, E. F.** Attitudinal concomitants to military statuses. *Soc. Forces,* 1955b, *33,* 342–347.

**Borgatta, E. F.** Small group research—a trend report and bibliography. *Current Sociol.,* 1960, *9,* 173–272.

**Borgatta, E. F.** Role-playing specifications, personality, and performance. *Sociometry,* 1961, *24,* 218–233.

**Borgatta, E. F.** A systematic study of interaction process scores, peer and self-assessments, personality and other variables. *Genet. psychol. Monogr.,* 1962, *65,* 219–291.

**Borgatta, E. F., & Bales, R. F.** Interaction of individuals in reconstituted groups. *Sociometry,* 1953a, *16,* 302–320.

**Borgatta, E. F., & Bales, R. F.** Task and accumulation of experience as factors in the interaction of small groups. *Sociometry*, 1953b, *16*, 239–252.

**Borgatta, E. F., & Bales, R. F.** The consistency of subject behavior and the reliability of scoring in interaction process analysis. *Amer. sociol. Rev.*, 1953c, *18*, 566–569.

**Borgatta, E. F., & Cottrell, L. S.** On the classification of groups. In J. L. Moreno (Ed.), *Sociometry and the science of man*. New York: Beacon House, 1956.

**Borgatta, E. F., Cottrell, L. S., & Mann, J. H.** The spectrum of individual interaction characteristics: an interdimensional analysis. *Psychol. Rep.*, 1958, *4*, 279–319.

**Borgatta, E. F., Cottrell, L. S., & Wilker, L.** Initial expectation, group climate, and the assessments of leaders and members. *J. soc. Psychol.*, 1959, *49*, 285–296.

**Borgatta, E. F., Couch, A. S., & Bales, R. F.** Some findings relevant to the great man theory of leadership. *Amer. sociol. Rev.*, 1954, *19*, 755–759.

**Borgatta, E. F., & Eschenbach, A. E.** Factor analysis of Rorschach variables and behavior observations. *Psychol. Rep.*, 1955, *1*, 129–136.

**Borgatta, E. F., & Evans, R. R.** Behavioral and personality expectations associated with status positions. *Multivariate beh. Res.*, 1967, *2*, 153–173.

**Borgatta, E. F., Ford, R. N., & Bohrnstedt, G. W.** The Work Components Study (WCS): a revised set of measures for work motivation. *Multivariate beh. Res.*, 1968, *3*, 403–413.

**Borgatta, M. L.** Power structure and coalitions in three person groups. *J. soc. Psychol.*, 1961, *55*, 287–300.

**Borowiec, W. A.** Persistence and change in the gatekeeper role of ethnic leaders: the case of the Polish-American. *Pol. Anthrop.*, 1975, *1*, 21–40.

**Bose, S. K.** Employee morale and supervision. *Indian J. Psychol.*, 1955, *30*, 117–125.

**Bottomley, M., & Sampson, S.** The case of the female principal: sex role attitudes and perceptions of sex differences in ability. *Austr. New Zea. J. Sociol.*, 1977, *13*, 137–140.

**Boulanger, F., & Fischer, D. G.** Leadership and the group-shift phenomenon. *Percep. mot. Skills*, 1971, *33*, 1251–1258.

**Bovard, E. W., Jr.** Social norms and the individual. *J. abnorm. soc. Psychol.*, 1948, *43*, 62–69.

**Bovard, E. W.** Group structure and perception. *J. abnorm. soc. Psychol.*, 1951a, *46*, 398–405.

**Bovard, E. W.** The experimental production of interpersonal affect. *J. abnorm. soc. Psychol.*, 1951b, *46*, 521–528.

**Bovard, E. W.** Clinical insight as a function of group process. *J. abnorm. soc. Psych.*, 1952, *47*, 534–539.

**Bowden, A. O.** A study of the personality of student leaders in the United States. *J. abnorm. soc. Psychol.*, 1926, *21*, 149–160.

**Bowden, G. T.** The adaptive capacity of workers. *Harvard bus. Rev.*, 1947, *25*, 527–542.

**Bowers, D. G.** Self-esteem and the diffusion of leadership style. *J. appl. Psychol.*, 1963, *47*, 135–140.

**Bowers, D. G.** Self-esteem and supervision. *Personnel Admin.*, 1964a, *27*, 23–26.

**Bowers, D. G.** Organizational control in an insurance company. *Sociometry*, 1964b, *27*, 230–244.

**Bowers, D. G.** Development techniques and organizational climate: an evaluation of the comparative importance of two potential forces for organizational change. Technical Report. Office of Naval Research, 1971.

**Bowers, D. G.** OD techniques and their results in 23 organizations: the Michigan ICL study. *J. appl. behav. Sci.*, 1973, *9*, 21–43.

**Bowers, D. G.** *Navy manpower: values, practices, and human resources requirements*. Ann Arbor: Institute for Social Research, 1975.

**Bowers, D. G.** *Systems of organization*. Ann Arbor: University of Michigan Press, 1976.

**Bowers, D. G., & Franklin, J.** *Survey guided development: data based organizational change.* Ann Arbor: University of Michigan, Institute for Social Research, 1975.

**Bowers, D. G., & Seashore, S. E.** Predicting organizational effectiveness with a four-factor theory of leadership. *Admin. sci. Quar.,* 1966, *11,* 238–263.

**Bowers, D. G., & Seashore, S. E.** Peer leadership within work groups. *Personnel Admin.,* 1967, *30,* 45–50.

**Bowers, J. J.** Relationship between organizational variables and contemporary practices in small private liberal arts colleges in the State of Ohio. Doctoral dissertation, Ohio State University, Columbus, 1976.

**Bowers, R. V.** *Studies on behavior·in organizations: a research symposium.* Athens: University of Georgia Press, 1966.

**Bowin, R. B.** Attitude change toward a theory of managerial motivation. In J. B. Miner (Ed.), *Motivation to manage.* Atlanta: Organizational Measurement Systems Press, 1977.

**Bowman, G. W., Worthy, N. B., & Greyser, S. A.** Are women executives people? *Harvard bus. Rev.,* 1965, *43,* 14–28; 164–178.

**Bowman, H. J.** Perceived leader behavior patterns and their relationships to self-perceived variables—responsibility, authority, and delegation. *Dissertation Abstr.,* 1964, *25,* 3340.

**Bowman, L. E.** An approach to the study of leadership. *J. appl. Sociol.,* 1927, *11,* 315–321.

**Boyce, M. W.** Management by committee. *Personnel pract. Bull.,* 1964, *20,* 47–51.

**Boyd, B. B., & Jensen, J. M.** Perceptions of the first-line supervisor's authority: a study in superior–subordinate communication. *Acad. Mgmt. J.,* 1972, *15,* 331–342.

**Boyd, D. P.** Research note: the educational background of a selected group of England's leaders. *Sociology,* 1974, *8,* 305–312.

**Boyd, J. B., & Ellis, J.** *Findings of research into senior management seminars.* Toronto: Personnel Research Department, The Hydro-Electric Power Commission of Ontario, 1962.

**Boyd, N. K.** Negotiation behavior by elected and appointed representatives serving as group leaders or as spokesmen under different cooperative group expectations. Doctoral dissertation, University of Maryland, 1972.

**Boyles, B. R.** The interaction between certain personality variables and perceived supervisory styles and their relation to performance and satisfaction. *Dissertation Abstr.,* 1968, *28* (11-B), 4788–4789.

**Bradburn, N. M.** N achievement and father dominance in Turkey. *J. abnorm. soc. Psychol.,* 1963, *67,* 464–468.

**Bradford, L. P., & French, J. R. P.** Introduction: the dynamics of the discussion group. *J. soc. Issues,* 1948, *4,* 2–8.

**Bradford, L. P., Gibb, J. R., & Benne, K. D.** *T-group theory and laboratory method.* New York: Wiley, 1964.

**Bradford, L. P., & Lippitt, R.** Building a democratic work group. *Personnel,* 1945, *22,* 142–148.

**Bradford, L. P., & Lippitt, R.** Role-playing in management training. In M. J. Dooher & V. Marquis (Eds.), *The development of executive talent.* New York: American Management Association, 1952.

**Bradshaw, H. H.** Need satisfaction, management style, and job level in a professional hierarchy. *Exp. publ. System, Amer. Psychol.. Assn.,* 1970, *8,* No. 289–1.

**Brainard, S. R., & Dollar, R. J.** Personality characteristics of leaders identifying with different student subcultures. *Coll. Student Personnel,* 1971, *12,* 200–203.

**Bramwell, B. S.** The order of merit: the holders and their kindred. *Eugenics Rev.,* 1944, *36,* 84–91.

**Brandon, A. C.** Status congruence and expectations. *Sociometry,* 1965, *28,* 272–288.

**Brass, D. J., & Oldham, G. R.** Validating an in-basket test using an alternative set of leadership scoring dimensions. *J. appl. Psychol.*, 1976, *61*, 652–657.

**Braun, D. D.** Alienation and participation: a replication comparing leaders and the "mass." *J. pol. mil. Sociol.*, 1976, *4*, 245–259.

**Bray, D. W., Campbell, R. J., & Grant, D. L.** *Formative years in business: a long-term AT&T study of managerial lives.* New York: Wiley-Interscience, 1974.

**Bray, D. W., & Grant, D. L.** The assessment center in the measurement of potential for business management. *Psychol. Monogr.*, 1966, *80*, No. 625.

**Brayfield, A. H., & Crockett, W. H.** Employee attitudes and employee performance. *Psychol. Bull.*, 1955, *52*, 396–424.

**Brenner, M. H.** Management development for women. *Personnel J.*, 1972, *51*, 165–169.

**Brewer, E., & Tomlinson, J. W. C.** The manager's working day. *J. indus. Eco.*, 1963/1964, *12*, 191–197.

**Bridges, E. M., Doyle, W. F., & Mahan, D. F.** Effects of hierarchical differentiation on group productivity, efficiency, and risk taking. *Admin. sci. Quar.*, 1968, *13*, 305–319.

**Brief, A. P., & Aldag, R. J.** Male–female differences in occupational values within majority groups. *J. vocat. Behav.*, 1975, *6*, 305–314.

**Brief, A. P., & Aldag, R. J.** Work values as moderators of perceived leader behavior-satisfaction relationships. *Sociol. work. Occup.*, 1977, *4*, 99–112.

**Brief, A. P., Aldag, R. J., & Chacko, T. I.** The Miner sentence completion scale: a psychometric appraisal. *Proceedings of the Institute of Decision Sciences*, 1976, 171–172.

**Brief, A. P., Aldag, R. J., & Chacko, T. I.** The Miner sentence completion scale: an appraisal. *Acad. Mgmt. J.*, 1977, *20*, 635–643.

**Brief, A. P., & Oliver, R. L.** Male–female differences in work attitudes among retail sales managers. *J. appl. Psychol.*, 1976, *61*, 526–528.

**Brim, O. G.** The acceptance of the new behavior in child-rearing. *Hum. Relat.*, 1954, *7*, 473–491.

**Brindisi, J. G.** Role satisfaction of community school council members. Doctoral dissertation, Florida Atlantic University, Boca Raton, 1976.

**Brinker, P. A.** Supervisor's and foremen's reasons for frustration. *Personnel J.*, 1955, *34*, 101–103.

**Brinton, C.** Clubs. In *Encyclopaedia of the social sciences*. New York: Macmillan, 1930.

**Brogden, H. E., & Thomas, W. F.** The primary traits in personality items purporting to measure sociability. *J. Psychol.*, 1943, *16*, 85–97.

**Broich, K.** Führeranforderungen in der Kindergruppe. *Z. angew. Psychol.*, 1929, *32*, 164–212.

**Broman, W. K.** The relationship of administrative processes to the innovativeness of public secondary schools. Doctoral dissertation, State University of New York at Buffalo, Buffalo, 1974.

**Bronfenbrenner, U.** Some familial antecedents of responsibility and leadership in adolescents. In L. Petrullo & B. M. Bass (Eds.), *Leadership and interpersonal behavior*. New York: Holt, Rinehart & Winston, 1961.

**Bronfenbrenner, U., Harding, J., & Gallwey, M.** A review and theoretical framework for the study of interpersonal perception. In D. C. McClelland (Ed.), *Talent and society*. Princeton, N.J.: Van Nostrand, 1958.

**Brooks, E.** What successful executives do. *Personnel*, 1955, *32*, 210–225.

**Broverman, I. K., Broverman, D. M., Clarkson, F. E., Rosenkrantz, P. S., & Vogel, S. R.** Sex-role stereotypes and clinical judgments of mental health. *J. consult. clin. Psychol.*, 1970, *34*, 1–7.

**Broverman, I. K., Vogel, S. R., Broverman, D. M., Clarkson, F. E., & Rosenkrantz, P. S.** Sex-role stereotypes: a current appraisal. *J. soc. Issues*, 1972, *28*, 59–78.

**Brown, A. F.** Reactions to leadership. Mimeo report, 1966.

**Brown, A. F.** Reactions to leadership. *Educ. Admin. Quar.*, 1967, *3*, 62–73.

**Brown, D. S.** Subordinates' views of ineffective executive behavior. *Acad. Mgmt. J.*, 1964, *7*, 288–299.

**Brown, J. F.** *Psychology and the social order*. New York: McGraw-Hill, 1936.

**Brown, J. S.** Risk propensity in decision making: a comparison of business and public school administrators. *Admin. sci. Quar.*, 1970, *15*, 473–481.

**Brown, M.** *Leadership among high school pupils*. New York: Teachers College Contribution Education, 1933.

**Brown, M.** Leadership among high school pupils. *Teach. Coll. Rec.*, 1934, *35*, 324–326.

**Brown, S. C.** Some case studies of delinquent girls described as leaders. *Brit. J. educ. Psychol.*, 1931, *1*, 162–179.

**Browne, C. G.** A study of executive leadership in business. I. The R, A, and D scales. *J. appl. Psychol.*, 1949, *33*, 520–526.

**Browne, C. G.** An exploration into the use of certain methods for the study of executive function in business. *Dissertation Abstr.*, 1950a, *58*, 51–57.

**Browne, C. G.** Study of executive leadership in business. II. Social group patterns. *J. appl. Psychol.*, 1950b, *34*, 12–15.

**Browne, C. G.** Study of executive leadership in business. III. Goal and achievement index. *J. appl. Psychol.*, 1950c, *34*, 82–87.

**Browne, C. G.** Study of executive leadership in business. IV. Sociometric pattern. *J. appl. Psychol.*, 1951, *35*, 34–37.

**Browne, C. G., & Cohn, T. S.** *The study of leadership*. Danville, Ill.: Interstate, 1958.

**Browne, C. G., & Neitzel, B. J.** Communication, supervision, and morale. *J. appl. Psychol.*, 1952, *36*, 86–91.

**Browne, C. G. & Shore, R. P.** Leadership and predictive abstracting. *J. appl. Psychol.*, 1956, *40*, 112–116.

**Browning, R. P., & Jacob, H.** Power motivation and political personality. *Pub. opin. Quar.*, 1964, *28*, 75–90.

**Bruce, M. M.** The prediction of effectiveness as a factory foreman. *Psychol. Monogr.*, 1953, *67*, 1–17.

**Brumback, G. B., & Vincent, J. W.** Factor analysis of work performed data for a sample of administrative, professional, and scientific positions. *Personnel Psychol.*, 1970, *23*, 101–107.

**Brumbach, R. B.** Authenticity and theories of administrative behavior. *Admin. sci. Quar.*, 1971, *16*, 108–112.

**Brunner, E. DeS.** *Village communities*. New York: Doubleday Doran, 1928.

**Bryant, D. W.** A simulation depicting concepts of leadership. *Dissertation Abstr. Internat.*, 1972, *32*, 6548.

**Bryant, G. W.** Ideal leader behavior descriptions of appointed and sociometrically chosen student leaders. *Dissertation Abstr.*, 1968, *28*, 3497.

**Bryson, J., & Kelley, G.** A political perspective on leadership emergence, stability, and change in organizational networks. *Acad. Mgmt. Rev.*, 1978, *3*, 712–723.

**Buchanan, P. C.** Evaluating the effectiveness of laboratory training in industry. In *Explorations in human relations training and research*. Washington, D.C.: National Training Laboratories, 1965.

**Buchanan, P. C.** Laboratory training and organization development. *Admin. sci. Quar.*, 1969, *14*, 466–480.

**Buchanan, P. C., & Brunstetter, P. H.** A research approach to management improvement. *J. Amer. Soc. Train. Directors*, 1959, *13*, 18–27.

**Buck, V. E.** Job pressures on managers: sources, subjects, and correlates. *Dissertation Abstr.*, 1963, *24*, 2164–2165.

**Buckley, H. A.** Organizational congruence in perceptions of leader effectiveness. *Dissertation Abstr. Internat.*, 1970, *31*, 2337.

**Buckley, W. (Ed.),** *Modern systems research for the behavioral scientist.* Chicago: Aldine Pub. Co., 1968a.

**Buckley, W.** Society as a complex adaptive system. In W. Buckley (Ed.), *Modern systems research for the behavioral scientist.* Chicago: Aldine Pub. Co., 1968b.

**Buckley, W. F.** Lets define that "leadership" that Kennedy says we need. *Press-Bulletin*, Binghamton, N.Y., September 22, 1979.

**Bucklow, M.** A new role for the work group. *Admin. sci. Quar.*, 1966, *11*, 59–78.

**Bugental, D. E.** A study of attempted and successful social influence in small groups as a function of goal-relevant skills. *Dissertation Abstr.*, 1964, *25*, 660.

**Bugental, J. F., & Lehner, G. F. J.** Accuracy of self-perception and group-perception as related to two leadership roles. *J. abnorm. soc. Psychol.*, 1958, *56*, 396–398.

**Bullard, P. D., & Cook, P. E.** Sex and workstyle of leaders and followers: determinants of productivity. *Psychol. Rep.*, 1975, *36*, 545–546.

**Bundel, C. M.** Is leadership losing its importance? *Infantry J.*, 1930, *36*, 339–349.

**Bunker, D. R.** Individual applications of laboratory training. *J. appl. behav. Sci.*, 1965, *1*, 131–148.

**Bunker, D. R.** The effect of laboratory education upon individual behavior. In E. H. Schein & W. G. Bennis (Eds.), *Personal and organizational change through group methods.* New York: Wiley, 1965.

**Bunker, D. R., & Knowles, E. S.** Comparison of behavioral changes resulting from human relations laboratories of different lengths. *J. appl. behav. Sci.*, 1967, *3*, 505–523.

**Bureau of Business Research.** *Leader behavior description questionnaire*–form XII. Columbus: Ohio State University, College of Commerce and Administration, 1962.

**Burgess, R. L.** Communication networks: an experimental reevaluation. *J. exp. soc. Psychol.*, 1968, *4*, 324–337.

**Burke, P. J.** Authority relations and disruptive behavior in the small group. *Dissertation Abstr.*, 1966a, *26*, 4850.

**Burke, P. J.** Authority relations and disruptive behavior in small discussion groups. *Sociometry*, 1966b, *29*, 237–250.

**Burke, P. J.** The development of task and social-emotional role differentiation. *Sociometry*, 1967, *30*, 379–392.

**Burke, P. J.** Participation and leadership in small groups. *Amer. sociol. Rev.*, 1974, *39*, 832–843.

**Burke, R. J.** A plea for systematic evaluation of training. *Train. develop. J.*, 1969, *23*, 24–29.

**Burke, R. L., & Bennis, W. G.** Changes in perception of self and others during human relations training. *Hum. Relat.*, 1961, *14*, 165–182.

**Burke, R. L., & Wilcox, D. S.** Effects of different patterns and degrees of openness in superior–subordinate communication on subordinate job satisfaction. *Acad. Mgmt. J.*, 1969, *3*, 319–326.

**Burke, W. W.** Leadership behavior as a function of the leader, the follower, and the situation. *Dissertation Abstr.*, 1964, *24*, 2992.

**Burke, W. W.** Leadership behavior as a function of the leader, the follower, and the situation. *J. Pers.*, 1965, *33*, 60–81.

**Burks, F. W.** Some factors related to social success in college. *J. soc. Psychol.*, 1938, *9*, 125–140.

**Burnett, C. W.** Leadership on the college campus. *Educ. res. Bull.*, 1951a, *30*, 34–41.

**Burnett, C. W.** Validating campus leadership. *Educ. res. Bull.*, 1951b, *30*, 67–73.

**Burnham, L. E., & Lee, H. E.** *Correlations between seven leadership criteria and selected variables.* Stanford, Calif.: Stanford University, 1963.

**Burns, J. H.** *Psychology and leadership.* Fort Leavenworth, Kansas: Command and General Staff School Press, 1934.

**Burns, J. M.** *Leadership.* New York: Harper & Row, 1978.

**Burns, T.** The direction of activity and communication in a departmental executive group. *Hum. Relat.*, 1954, *7*, 73–97.

**Burns, T., & Stalker, G. M.** *The management of innovation.* Chicago: Quadrangle Books, 1961.

**Burnstein, E.** An analysis of group decision involving risk (''the risky shift''). *Hum. Relat.*, 1969, *22*, 381–395.

**Burnstein, E., & Zajonc, R. B.** Individual task performance in a changing social structure. *Sociometry*, 1965a, *28*, 16–29.

**Burnstein, E., & Zajonc, R. B.** The effect of group success on the reduction of status incongruence in task-oriented groups. *Sociometry*, 1965b, *28*, 349–362.

**Burroughs, W. A.** A study of white females' voting behavior toward two black female collaborators in a modified leaderless group discussion. *Dissertation Abstr. Internat.*, 1970, *30*, 5063.

**Burroughs, W. A., & Jaffee, C. L.** Verbal participation and leadership voting behavior in a leaderless group discussion. *Psychol. Rec.*, 1969, *19*, 605–610.

**Bursk, E. C.** *Human relations for management: the newer perspective.* New York: Harper, 1956.

**Burwen, L. S., & Campbell, D. T.** A comparison of test scores and role-playing behavior in assessing superior vs. subordinate orientation. *J. soc. Psychol.*, 1957a, *46*, 49–56.

**Burwen, L. S., & Campbell, D. T.** The generality of attitudes toward authority and nonauthority figures. *J. abnorm. soc. Psychol.*, 1957b, *54*, 24–31.

**Butler, D. C., & Miller, N.** Power to reward and punish in social interaction. *J. exp. soc. Psychol.*, 1965, *1*, 311–322.

**Butler, J. L., & Keys, J. B.** A comparative study of simulation and traditional methods of supervisory training in human resource development. *Proceedings of the Academy of Management*, 1973.

**Butler, M. C., & Jones, A. P.** Perceived leader behavior, individual characteristics, and injury occurrence in hazardous work environments. *J. appl. Psychol.*, 1979, *64*, 299–304.

**Butler, R. P.** A study of the effects of incentive feedback and manner of presenting the feedback on leader behavior. *Dissertation Abstr. Internat.*, 1971, *31*, 4377–4378.

**Butler, W. P.** Job satisfaction among foremen—case study no. 2. *Personnel prac. Bull.*, 1961, *17*, 5–14.

**Butterfield, D. A.** An integrative approach to the study of leadership effectiveness in organizations. *Dissertation Abstr.*, 1969, *29*, 3122.

**Butterfield, D. A., & Bartol, K. M.** Evaluators of leader behavior: a missing element in leadership theory. In J. G. Hunt & L. L. Larson (Eds.), *Leadership: the cutting edge.* Carbondale: Southern Illinois University Press, 1977.

**Buttgereit, H.** Führergestalten in der Schulklass. *Z. f. angew. Psychol.*, 1932, *43*, 369–413.

**Byars, L. L., & Crane, D. P.** Training by objectives. *Train. develop. J.*, 1969, *23*, 38–48.

**Byham, W. C., Adams, D., & Kiggins, A.** Transfer of modeling training to the job. *Personnel Psychol.*, 1976, *29*, 345–349.

**Byrne, D.** Interpersonal attraction and attitude similarity. *J. abnorm. soc. Psychol.*, 1961, *62*, 713–715.

**Byrne, D.** Authoritarianism and response to attitude similarity-dissimilarity. *J. soc. Psychol.*, 1965, *66*, 251–256.

**Byrne, D.** *The attraction paradigm*. New York: Academic Press, 1971.

**Byrne, D., & Clore, G. L.** Predicting interpersonal attraction toward strangers presented in three different stimulus modes. *Psychonomic Sci.*, 1966, *4*, 239–240.

**Byrne, D., Clore, G. L., & Worchel, P.** Effect of economic similarity-dissimilarity on interpersonal attraction. *J. pers. soc. Psychol.*, 1966, *4*, 220–224.

**Byrne, D., & Griffitt, W.** A developmental investigation of the law of attraction. *J. pers. soc. Psychol.*, 1966a, *4*, 699–703.

**Byrne, D., & Griffitt, W.** Similarity versus liking: a clarification. *Psychonomic Sci.*, 1966b, *6*, 295–296.

**Byrne, D., Griffitt, W., & Golightly, C.** Prestige as a factor in determining the effect of attitude similarity-dissimiliarity on attraction. *J. Pers.*, 1966, *34*, 434–444.

**Byrne, D., & Nelson, D.** The effect of topic importance and attitude similarity-dissimilarity on attraction in a multistranger design. *Psychonomic Sci.*, 1965a, *3*, 449–450.

**Byrne, D., & Nelson, D.** Attraction as a linear function of proportion of positive reinforcements. *J. pers. soc. Psychol.*, 1965b, *1*, 659–663.

**Byrnes, J. L.** A study of certain relationships among perceived supervisory style, participativeness, and teacher job satisfaction. Doctoral dissertation, Syracuse University, Syracuse, N.Y., 1973.

**Calder, B. J.** An attribution theory of leadership. In B. M. Staw & G. R. Salancik (Eds.), *New directions in organizational behavior*. Chicago: St. Clair, 1977.

**Caldwell, O. W.** Some factors in training for leadership. In *Natl. Assn. Secondary School Principals, Fourth Yearbook*, 1920.

**Caldwell, O. W., & Wellman, B.** Characteristics of school leaders. *J. educ. Res.*, 1926, *14*, 1–15.

**Calvin, A. D., Hoffmann, F. K., & Harden, E. D.** The effect of intelligence and social atmosphere on group problem-solving behavior. *J. soc. Psychol.*, 1957, *45*, 61–74.

**Camealy, J. B.** Management development training: multiple measurement of its effect when used to increase the impact of a long term motivational program. *Dissertation Abstr.*, 1969, *29*, 4136–4137(A).

**Cammalleri, J. A., Hendrick, H. W., Pittman, W. C., Jr., Blout, H. D., & Prather, D. C.** Effects of different leadership styles on group accuracy. *J. appl. Psychol.*, 1973, *57*, 32–37.

**Cammann, C., & Nadler, D. A.** Fit control systems to your managerial style. *Harvard bus. Rev.*, 1976, *54*, 65–72.

**Campbell, D. P.** SVIB managerial orientation scores of outstanding men. *Personnel Psychol.*, 1969, *22*, 41–44.

**Campbell, D. T.** *A study of leadership among submarine officers*. Columbus: Ohio State University, Personnel Research Board, 1953.

**Campbell, D. T.** An error in some demonstrations of the superior social perceptiveness of leaders. *J. abnorm. soc. Psychol.*, 1955, *51*, 694–695.

**Campbell, D. T.** *Leadership and its effect upon the group*. Columbus: Ohio State University, Bureau of Business Research, 1956.

**Campbell, D. T.** Reforms as experiments. *Amer. Psychologist*, 1969, *24*, 409–429.

**Campbell, D. T., Burwen, L. S., & Chapman, J. P.** Assessing attitudes toward superiors and subordinates through direct attitude statements. Evanston, Ill.: Northwestern University Department of Psychology, 1955 (mimeo).

**Campbell, D. T., & Damarin, F. L.** Measuring leadership attitudes through an information test. *J. soc. Psychol.*, 1961, *55*, 159–176.

**Campbell, D. T., & Fiske, D. W.** Convergent and discriminant validation by the multi-trait multi-method matrix. *Psychol. Bull.*, 1959, *56*, 81–105.

**Campbell, D. T., & McCormack, T. H.** Military experience and attitudes toward authority. *Amer. J. Sociol.*, 1957, *62*, 482–490.

**Campbell, D. T., & Mehra, K.** Individual differences in evaluations of group discussions as a projective measure of attitudes toward leadership. *J. soc. Psychol.*, 1958, *47*, 101–106.

**Campbell, D. T., & Stanley, J. C.** *Experimental and quasi-experimental designs for research.* Chicago: Rand McNally, 1963.

**Campbell, E.** A sociometric study of day care children. Unpublished ms., undated.

**Campbell, H.** Some effects of joint consultation on the status and role of the supervisor. *Occup. Psychol.*, 1953, *27*, 200–206.

**Campbell, J. D.** Subjective aspects of occupational status. *Amer. Psychologist*, 1952, *7*, 308.

**Campbell, J. D., & Radke-Yarrow, M.** Interpersonal perception and behavior in children's groups. *Amer. Psychologist*, 1956, *11*, 416.

**Campbell, J. P.** Identification and enhancement of managerial effectiveness. IV. Management training. Greensboro, N.C.: Richardson Foundation, 1966 (mimeo).

**Campbell, J. P., & Dunnette, M. D.** Effectiveness of T-Group experiences in managerial training and development. *Psychol. Bull.*, 1968, *70*, 73–104.

**Campbell, J. P., Dunnette, M. D., Lawler, E. E., & Weick, K. E.** *Managerial behavior, performance, and effectiveness.* New York: McGraw-Hill, 1970.

**Campbell, J. W.** An attitude survey in a typical manufacturing firm. *Personnel Psychol.*, 1948, *1*, 31–39.

**Campbell, M. V.** Self-role conflict among teachers and its relationship to satisfaction, effectiveness, and confidence in leadership. Doctoral dissertation, University of Chicago, Chicago, 1958.

**Campbell, O. L.** The relationships between eight situational factors and high and low scores on the leadership behavior dimensions of instructional supervisors. *Dissertation Abstr.*, 1961, *22*, 786.

**Campbell, V., Lange, C. J., & Shanley, F. J.** Relationships among leader effectiveness ratings, intelligence and job knowledge. Washington, D.C.: Human Resources Research Office, *Bibliography of Publications,* June 1968.

**Campion, J. E.** Effects of managerial style on subordinates' attitudes and performance in a simulated organization setting. *Dissertation Abstr. Internat.*, 1969, *30*, 881.

**Canter, R. R., Jr.** An experimental study of a human relations training program. Doctoral dissertation, Ohio State University, Columbus, 1949.

**Canter, R. R.** A human relations training program. *J. appl. Psychol.*, 1951, *35*, 38–45.

**Capelle, M. H.** Concurrent validation of the Leadership Opinion Questionnaire for college student leadership. *Dissertation Abstr.*, 1967, *27*, 3607.

**Caplan, E. H., & Landekich, S.** *Human resource accounting: past, present and future.* New York: National Association for Accountants, 1974.

**Caplan, R. D., Cobb, S., French, J. R. P., Jr., Harrison, V., & Pinneau, S. R., Jr.** *Job demands and workers' health.* Washington, D.C.: U.S. Printing Office, 1975.

**Caplow, T.** A theory of coalitions in the triad. *Amer. sociol. Rev.*, 1956, *21*, 489–493.

**Caplow, T.** *Two against one: coalitions in triads.* Englewood Cliffs, N.J.: Prentice-Hall, 1968.

**Caplow, T., & Forman, R.** Neighborhood interaction in a homogeneous community. *Amer. sociol. Rev.*, 1950, *15*, 357–366.

**Carey, H. H.** Consultative supervision and management. *Personnel*, 1942, *18*, 286, 295.

**Carlson, E. R.** Clique structure and member satisfaction in groups. *Sociometry*, 1960, *23*, 327–337.

Carlson, H. B., & Harrell, W. An analysis of *Life's* "ablest congressman" poll. *J. soc. Psychol.*, 1942, *15*, 153–158.

Carlson, R. E., & James, L. R. Sampling managerial behavior: a functional time analysis. Life Insurance Agency Management Association, unpublished report, 1971.

Carlson, S. *Executive behavior.* Stockholm: Strombergs, 1951.

Carlyle, T. *Heroes and hero worship.* Boston: Adams, 1907 (original 1841).

Caro, R. *The power broker: Robert Moses and the fall of New York.* New York: Knopf, 1974.

Carp, F. M., Vitola, B. M., & McLanathan, F. L. Human relations knowledge and social distance set in supervisors. *J. appl. Psychol.*, 1963, *47*, 78–80.

Carpeno, L. Expectations of male/female leadership styles in an educational setting. *Dissertation Abstr. Internat.*, 1976, *37*, 1482.

Carpenter, C. R. Societies of monkeys and apes. In C. H. Southwick (Ed.), *Primate social behavior.* Princeton, N.J.: Van Nostrand, 1963.

Carpenter, H. H. The relationship between certain organizational structure factors and perceived needs satisfaction of classroom teachers. Doctoral dissertation, University of Houston, Houston, Texas, 1970.

Carpenter, H. H. Formal organizational structural factors and perceived job satisfaction of classroom teachers. *Admin. sci. Quar.*, 1971, *16*, 460–465.

Carr, R. W. A study of the job satisfaction of high school principals. Doctoral dissertation, University of Michigan, Ann Arbor, 1971.

Carrell, J. B. Sensitivity training: effects on perceived self-ideal of self congruence. *Dissertation Abstr. Internat.*, 1974, *34*, 3863–3864.

Carroll, S. J., & Nash, A. N. Some personal and situational correlates of reactions to management development training. *Acad. Mgmt. J.*, 1970, *13*, 187–196.

Carroll, S. J., Paine, F. T., & Ivancevich, J. J. The relative effectiveness of training methods— expert opinion and research. *Personnel Psychol.*, 1972, *3*, 495–509.

Carroll, S. J., & Taylor, W. H. The study of the validity of a self-observational central-signaling method of work sampling. *Personnel Psychol.*, 1968, *21*, 359–364.

Carroll, S. J., & Taylor, W. H. Validity of estimates by clerical personnel of job time estimates. *J. appl. Psychol.*, 1969, *53*, 164–166.

Carroll, S. J., & Tosi, H. L. Goal characteristics and personality factors in a management-by-objectives program. *Admin. sci. Quar.*, 1970, *15*, 295–305.

Carron, T. J., Human relations training and attitude change: a vector analysis. *Personnel Psychol.*, 1964, *17*, 403–422.

Carson, J. O., & Schultz, R. E. A comparative analysis of the junior college dean's leadership behavior. *J. exp. Educ.*, 1964, *32*, 355–362.

Carter, G. C. Student traits and progression through college. *J. educ. Psychol.*, 1949, *40*, 306–308.

Carter, L. F. Leadership and small group behavior. In M. Sherif & M. O. Wilson (Eds.), *Group relations at the crossroads.* New York: Harper, 1953.

Carter, L. F. Evaluating the performance of individuals as members of small groups. *Personnel Psychol.*, 1954, *7*, 477–484.

Carter, L. F., Haythorn, W., & Howell, M. A further investigation of the criteria of leadership. *J. abnorm. soc. Psychol.*, 1950, *45*, 350–358.

Carter, L. F., Haythorn, W., Meirowitz, B., & Lanzetta, J. T. The relation of categorizations and ratings in the observation of group behavior. *Hum. Relat.*, 1951, *4*, 239–254.

Carter, L. F., Haythorn, W., Shriver, B., & Lanzetta, J. T. The behavior of leaders and other group members. *J. abnorm. soc. Psychol.*, 1951, *46*, 589–595.

Carter, L. F., & Nixon, M. An investigation of the relationship between four criteria of leadership ability for three different tasks. *J. Psychol.*, 1949a, *27*, 245–261.

**Carter, L., & Nixon, M.** Ability, perceptual, personality, and interest factors associated with different criteria of leadership. *J. Psychol.*, 1949b, *27*, 377–388.

**Cartwright, D.** A field theoretical conception of power. In D. Cartwright (Ed.), *Studies in social power*. Ann Arbor: University of Michigan, Institute for Social Research, 1959a.

**Cartwright D.** *Studies in social power*. Ann Arbor: University of Michigan, Institute for Social Research, 1959b.

**Cartwright, D.** Influence, leadership, control. In J. G. March (Ed.), *Handbook of organizations*. Chicago: Rand McNally, 1965.

**Cartwright, D., & Zander, A.** *Group dynamics—research and theory*. Evanston, Ill.: Row, Peterson, 1960.

**Cartwright, D. C.** Achieving change in people: some applications of group dynamics theory. *Hum. Relat.*, 1951, *4*, 381–393.

**Cartwright, D. S., & Robertson, R. J.** Membership in cliques and achievement. *Amer. J. Sociol.*, 1961, *66*, 441–445.

**Carzo, R., & Yanouzas, J. N.** Effects of flat and tall organization structure. *Admin. sci. Quar.*, 1969, *14*, 178–191.

**Cascio, W. F.** Functional specialization, culture, and preference for participative management. *Personnel Psychol.*, 1974, *27*, 593–603.

**Cascio, W. F., & Bass, B. M.** The effects of role play in a program to modify attitudes toward black employees. *J. soc. Psychol.*, 1976, *92*, 261–266.

**Case, C. M.** Leadership and conjuncture. *Sociol. soc. Res.*, 1933, *17*, 510–513.

**Casey, T. J.** The development of a leadership orientation scale on the SVIB for women. *Meas. eval. Guid.*, 1975, *8*, 96–100.

**Cashman, J., & Graen, G.** The nature of leadership in the vertical dyad: the team building process. *Org. behav. hum. Perform.*, in press.

**Cassel, R. N.** A construct validity study of leadership and social insight tests for 200 college freshmen students. *J. genet. Psychol.*, 1961, *99*, 165–170.

**Cassel, R. N., & Haddox, G.** Comparative study of leadership test scores for gifted and typical high school students. *Psychol. Rep.*, 1959, *5*, 713–717.

**Cassel, R. N., & Sanders, R. A.** A comparative analysis of scores from two leadership tests for Apache Indian and Anglo–American youth. *J. educ. Res.*, 1961, *55*, 19–23.

**Cassel, R. N., & Shafer, A. E.** An experiment in leadership training. *J. Psychol.*, 1961, *51*, 299–305.

**Cassens, F. P.** Cross cultural dimensions of executive life history antecedents (biographical information). *Dissertation Abstr.*, 1966a, *27*, 291.

**Cassens, F. P.** Cross cultural dimensions of executive life history antecedents (biographical information). Greensboro, N.C.: Creativity Research Institute, Richardson Foundation, 1966b.

**Cates, J. N.** Disclosure of role conflict through critical incidents. *Sociol. soc. Res.*, 1965, *49*, 319–329.

**Cattell, J. McK.** *American men of science*. New York: Science Press, 1906.

**Cattell, R. B.** The concept of social status. *J. soc. Psychol.*, 1942, *15*, 293–308.

**Cattell, R. B.** New concepts for measuring leadership in terms of group syntality. *Hum. Relat.*, 1951, *4*, 161–184.

**Cattell, R. B.** *Factor analysis*. New York: Harper, 1952.

**Cattell, R. B.** On the theory of group learning. *J. soc. Psych.*, 1953, *37*, 27–52.

**Cattell, R. B.** A mathematical model for the leadership role and other personality-role relations. In M. Sherif & M. O. Wilson (Eds.), *Emerging problems in social psychology*. Norman: University of Oklahoma, 1957.

**Cattell, R. B.** Psychological theory and scientific method. In R. B. Cattell (Ed.), *Handbook of multivariate experimental psychology*. Chicago: Rand McNally, 1966.

**Cattell, R. B., Saunders, D. R., & Stice, G. F.** The dimensions of syntality in small groups. *Hum. Relat.*, 1953, *6*, 331–356.

**Cattell, R. B., & Stice, G. F.** The psychodynamics of small groups. Urbana: University of Illinois, Laboratory Personality Assessment & Group Behavior, 1953 (mimeo).

**Cattell, R. B., & Stice, G. F.** Four formulae for selecting leaders on the basis of personality. *Hum. Relat.*, 1954, *7*, 493–507.

**Caul, J. L.** A comparative study of student, teacher, and principal perceptions of organizational structure between middle schools with high levels and those with low levels of middle school concept implementation. Doctoral dissertation, Michigan State University, East Lansing, 1976.

**Centers, R.** Motivational aspects of occupational stratification. *J. soc. Psychol.*, 1948, *28*, 187–217.

**Centers, R., & Bugental, D. E.** Intrinsic and extrinsic job motivations among different segments of the working population. *J. appl. Psychol.*, 1966, *50*, 193–197.

**Chambers, P.** No easy path for women managers. *International Management*, 1974, *2*, 46–48.

**Chandler, A. D.** Management decentralization: a historical analysis. *Bus. hist. Rev.*, 1956, *30*, 111–174.

**Chandler, A. D.** *Strategy and structure.* Cambridge, Mass.: M.I.T. Press, 1962.

**Chaney, F. B.** A cross-cultural study of industrial research performance. *J. appl. Psychol.*, 1966, *50*, 206–210.

**Chaney, M. V., & Vinacke, W. E.** Achievement and nurturance in triads varying in power distribution. *J. abnorm. soc. Psychol.*, 1960, *60*, 175–181.

**Chapin, F. S.** Socialized leadership. *Soc. Forces*, 1924a, *3*, 57–60.

**Chapin, F. S.** Leadership and group activity. *J. appl. Sociol.*, 1924b, *8*, 141–145.

**Chapin, F. S.** Activities of college students: a study in college leadership. *School & Society*, 1926, *23*, 212–216.

**Chapin, F. S.** Research studies of extra-curricular activities and their significance in reflecting social changes. *J. educ. Sociol.*, 1931, *11*, 491–498.

**Chapin, F. S.** Sociometric stars as isolates. *Amer. J. Sociol.*, 1950, *56*, 263–267.

**Chapin, F. S., & Tsouderos, J. E.** Formalization observed in ten voluntary associations: concepts, morphology, process. *Soc. Forces*, 1955, *33*, 306–309.

**Chapman, J. B.** Comparisons of male and female leadership style. *Acad. Mgmt. J.*, 1975, *18*, 645–650.

**Chapman, J. B., & Luthans, F.** The female leadership dilemma. *Pub. personnel Mgmt.*, 1975, *4*, 173–179.

**Chapman, L. J., & Campbell, D. T.** An attempt to predict the performance of three-man teams from attitude measures. *J. soc. Psychol.*, 1957a, *46*, 277–286.

**Chapman, L. J., & Campbell, D. T.** Response set in the F scale. *J. abnorm. soc. Psychol.*, 1957b, *54*, 129–132.

**Chapple, E. D., & Donald, G., Jr.** A method of evaluating supervisory personnel. *Harvard bus. Rev.*, 1946, *24*, 197–214.

**Charters, W. W.** Teacher perceptions of administrator behavior. St. Louis: Washington University, 1964 (mimeo).

**Charters, W. W., & Gage, N. L.** *Readings in the social psychology of education.* Boston: Allyn & Bacon, 1963.

**Chemers, M. M.** Cross-cultural training as a means for improving situational favorableness. *Hum. Relat.*, 1969, *22*, 531–546.

**Chemers, M. M., Fiedler, F. E., Lekhyananda, D., & Stolurow, L. M.** Some effects of cultural training on leadership in heterocultural task groups. *Internat. J. Psychol.*, 1966, *1*, 301–314.

**Chemers, M. M., & Mahar, L.** Amigos two: a comparison of LEADER MATCH with alternative managerial training. Seattle: University of Washington, unpublished ms., 1978.

**Chemers, M. M., Rice, R. W., Sundstrom, E., & Butler, W.** Leader esteem for the least preferred co-worker score, training, and effectiveness: an experimental examination. *J. pers. soc. Psychol.*, 1975, *31*, 401–409.

**Chemers, M. M., & Skrzypek, G. J.** Experimental test of the contingency model of leadership effectiveness. *J. pers. soc. Psychol.*, 1972, *24*, 172–177.

**Cherry, C.** *On human communication.* Cambridge, Mass.: M.I.T. Press, 1957.

**Chesterfield, R., & Ruddle, K.** A case of mistaken identity: ill-chosen intermediaries in a Venezuelan agricultural extension programme. *Comm. develop. J.*, 1976, *11*, 53–59.

**Chevaleva-Ianovskaia, E., & Sylla, D.** Essai d'une etude sur les enfants meneurs. *J. Psychol.*, 1929, *26*, 604–612.

**Child, J.** Strategies of control and organizational behavior. *Admin. sci. Quar.*, 1973, *18*, 1–17.

**Child, J., & Ellis, T.** Predictors of variation in managerial roles. *Hum. Relat.*, 1973, *26*, 227–250.

**Chowdhry, K., & Newcomb, T. W.** The relative abilities of leaders and nonleaders to estimate opinions of their own groups. *J. abnorm. soc. Psychol.*, 1952, *47*, 51–57.

**Chowdhry, K., & Pal, A. D.** Production planning and organizational morale. In J. A. Rubenstein & C. J. Haberstroh (Eds.), *Some theories of organization.* Homewood, Ill.: Dorsey, 1960.

**Chowdhry, K., & Tarneja, R.** India. In *Developing better managers: an eight-nation study.* New York: National Industrial Conference Board, 1961.

**Christensen, L.** Validity of person-perception accuracy scores. *Percept. mot. Skills,* 1970, *30*, 871–877

**Christie, L., Luce, D., & Macy, J.** Communication and learning in task oriented groups. Cambridge, Mass.: M.I.T., Research Lab of Electronic, Technical Report No. 231, 1952.

**Christie, R.** Changes in authoritarianism as related to situational factors. *Amer. Psychologist,* 1952, *7*, 307–308.

**Christie, R.** Authoritarianism re-examined. In R. Christie & M. Jahoda (Eds.), *Studies in the scope and method of "The Authoritarian Personality."* New York: Free Press, 1954.

**Christie, R., & Cook, P.** A guide to published literature relating to the authoritarian personality through 1956. *J. Psychol.*, 1958, *45*, 171–179.

**Christie, R., & Geis, F. L. (Eds.).** Studies in Machiavellianism. New York: Academic Press, 1970.

**Christner, C. A., & Hemphill, J. K.** Leader behavior of B-29 commanders and changes in crew members' attitudes toward the crew. *Sociometry,* 1955, *18*, 82–87.

**Chung, K. S.** Teacher-centered management style of public school principals and job satisfaction of teachers. ERIC *Document Reproduction Service,* 1970 (Ms. No. ED042-259).

**Chyatte, C.** Personality traits of professional actors. *Occupations,* 1949, *27*, 245–250.

**Clark, A. W., & McCabe, S.** Leadership beliefs of Australian managers. *J. appl. Psychol.*, 1970, *54*, 1–6.

**Clark, A. W., & McCabe, S.** The motivation and satisfaction of Australian managers. *Personnel Psychol.*, 1972, *25*, 625–638.

**Clark, B. R.** Organizational adaptation and precarious values: a case study. *Amer. sociol. Rev.*, 1956, *21*, 327–336.

**Clark, R. A.** Analyzing the group structure of combat rifle squads. *Amer. Psychologist,* 1953, *8*, 333.

**Clarke, H. I.** Definition of a leader: Roosevelt? Toscanini? Hitler? Adams? Dillinger? *Group,* 1951, *13,* 7–11.

**Clausen, G.** Risk taking in small groups. Doctoral dissertation, University of Michigan, Ann Arbor, 1965.

**Cleeton, G. U., & Mason, C. W.** *Executive ability—its discovery and development.* Yellow Springs, Ohio: Antioch Press, 1934.

**Clelland, D. A., & Form, W. H.** Economic dominants and community power: a comparative analysis. *Amer. J. Sociol.,* 1964, *69,* 511–521.

**Clem, O. M., & Dodge, S. B.** The relation of high school leadership and scholarship to post-school success. *Peabody J. Educ.,* 1933, *10,* 321–329.

**Clements, R. V.** *Managers: a study of their careers in industry.* London: Allen & Unwin, 1958.

**Cleven, W. A., & Fiedler, F. E.** Interpersonal perceptions of open-hearth foremen and steel production. *J. appl. Psychol.,* 1956, *40,* 312–314.

**Clifford, C., & Cohn, T. S.** The relationship between leadership and personality attributes perceived by followers. *J. soc. Psychol.,* 1964, *64,* 57–64.

**Cline, T. A.** A study of the relationships between Colorado Community College faculty members' attitudes toward collective negotiations and their perceptions of the management styles used in their colleges. Doctoral dissertation, University of Colorado, Boulder, 1974.

**Cline, V. B., & Richards, J. M.** Accuracy of interpersonal perception—a general trait? *J. abnorm. soc. Psychol.,* 1960, *60,* 1–7.

**Cline, V. B., & Richards, J. M.** The generality and accuracy of interpersonal perception. *J. abnorm. soc. Psychol.,* 1961, *62,* 446–449.

**Cline, V. B., & Richards, J. M.** Cline & Richards' reply to O'Connor's methodological note. *J. abnorm. soc. Psychol.,* 1963, *66,* 195–196.

**Clingenpeel, R. E.** Leadership in a technical organization. *Dissertation Abstr. Internat.,* 1971, *32,* 3680–3681.

**Cloyd, J. S.** Functional differentiation and structure of informal groups, *Sociol. Quar.,* 1964, *5,* 243–250.

**Coates, C. H., & Pellegrin, R. J.** Executives and supervisors: contrasting self-perceptions and conceptions of each other. *Amer. sociol. Rev.,* 1957, *22,* 217–220.

**Cobb, J. J.** Leadership and decision-making in a black community: an inter-disciplinary analysis and study. *Dissertation Abstr. Internat.,* 1974, *34,* 4451.

**Cobb, K.** Measuring leadership in college women by free association. *J. abnorm. soc. Psychol.,* 1952, *47,* 126–128.

**Coch, L., & French, J. R. P.** Overcoming resistance to change. *Hum. Relat.,* 1948, *1,* 512–532.

**Cochran, W. G.** *Sampling techniques,* 2nd ed. New York: Wiley, 1963.

**Coffin, T. E.** A three-component theory of leadership. *J. abnorm. soc. Psychol.,* 1944, *39,* 63–83.

**COFREMCA.** A psychological study of the attitudes of French managers. *Internat. stud. mgmt. Org.,* 1978, *8,* 22–38.

**Coghill, M. A.** *Sensitivity training.* Ithaca, N.Y.: Cornell University, Industrial & Labor Relations Library, 1967.

**Cohen, A. M.** Changing small group communication networks. *Admin. sci. Quar.,* 1962, *6,* 443–462.

**Cohen, A. M., & Bennis, W. G.** Continuity of leadership in communication networks. *Hum. Relat.,* 1961, *14,* 351–367.

**Cohen, A. M., Bennis, W. G., & Wolkon, G. H.** The effects of continued practice on the behaviors of problem-solving groups. *Sociometry,* 1961, *24,* 416–431.

**Cohen, A. M., & Foerst, J. R.** Organizational behaviors and adaptations to organizational change of sensitizer and represser problem-solving groups. *J. pers. soc. Psychol.*, 1968, *8*, 209–216.

**Cohen, A. M., Robinson, E. L., & Edwards, J. L.** Experiments in organization embeddedness. *Admin. sci. Quar.*, 1969, *4*, 208–221.

**Cohen, A. R.** The effects of situational structure and individual self-esteem on threat-oriented reactions to power. Doctoral dissertation, University of Michigan, Ann Arbor, 1953.

**Cohen, A. R.** The effects of individual self-esteem and situational structure on threat-oriented reactions to power. *Dissertation Abstr.*, 1954, *14*, 727–728.

**Cohen, A. R.** Social norms, arbitrariness of frustration, and status of the agent of frustration in the Frustration-Aggression Hypothesis. *J. abnorm. soc. Psychol.*, 1955, *51*, 222–226.

**Cohen, A. R.** Upward communication in experimentally created hierarchies. *Hum. Relat.*, 1958, *11*, 41–53.

**Cohen, A. R.** Situational structure, self-esteem, and threat-oriented reactions to power. In D. Cartwright (Ed.), *Studies in social power*. Ann Arbor: University of Michigan, Institute for Social Research, 1959.

**Cohen, A. R.** Communication networks. *Personnel Admin.*, 1964, *27*, 18–24.

**Cohen, D., Whitmyre, J. W., & Funk, W. H.** Effect of group cohesiveness and training upon creative thinking. *J. appl. Psychol.*, 1960, *44*, 319–322.

**Cohen, D. J., & Lindsley, O. R.** Catalysis of controlled leadership in cooperation by human stimulation. *J. child Psychol.*, 1964, *5*, 119–137.

**Cohen, E.** Stimulus conditions as factors in social change. *Amer. Psychologist*, 1956, *11*, 407.

**Cohen, E.** The effect of members' use of a formal group as a reference group upon group effectiveness. *J. soc. Psychol.*, 1957, *46*, 307–310.

**Cohen, G. B.** *The task-tuned organization of groups*. Amsterdam: Swetz & Zeitlinger, 1969.

**Cohen, J.** *Secondary motivation*. Chicago: Rand McNally, 1970.

**Cohen, J.** Job satisfaction as a function of philosophy of work style among professionals and executives. *Dissertation Abstr.*, 1968, *29*, 1196.

**Cohn, T. S., Fisher, A., & Brown, V.** Leadership and predicting attitudes of others. *J. soc. Psychol.*, 1961, *55*, 199–206.

**Cole, C. T.** Rural leadership—its origin and development. *J. educ. Sociol.*, 1947, *21*, 184–188.

**Coleman, J. S. *et al.*** *Equality of educational opportunity*. U.S. Department of Health, Education, and Welfare, Washington, D.C.: U.S. Government Printing Office, 1966.

**Coles, L. W.** A study of the differential effects of two leadership training styles on United Methodist adult groups. *Dissertation Abstr. Internat.*, 1972, *32*, 4913.

**Collaros, P. A., & Anderson, L. R.** Effect of perceived expertness upon creativity of members of brainstorming groups. *J. appl. Psychol.*, 1969, *2*, 159–163.

**Collins, A. K.** Developing leadership in a small plant: a critical account of an experimental training program. Doctoral dissertation, Cornell University, Ithaca, N.Y., 1957.

**Collins, B. E., & Guetzkow, H.** *A social psychology of group processes for decision-making*. New York: Wiley, 1964.

**Collins, O., Dalton, M., & Roy, D.** Restriction of output and social cleavage in industry. *Appl. Anthropol.*, 1946, *5*, 1–14.

**Colmen, J. G., Fiedler, G. O., & Boulger, J. R.** Methodological considerations in determining supervisory training needs. *Amer. Psychologist*, 1954, *9*, 350.

**Colyer, D. M.** The good foreman—as his men see him. *Personnel*, 1951, *28*, 140—147.

**Comrey, A. L., High, W. S., & Wilson, R. C.** Factors influencing organizational effectiveness. VI. A survey of aircraft workers. *Personnel Psychol.*, 1955a, *8*, 79–99.

**Comrey, A. L., High, W. S., & Wilson, R. C.** Factors influencing organizational effectiveness. VII. A survey of aircraft supervisors. *Personnel Psychol.*, 1955b, *8*, 245–257.

**Comrey, A. L., Pfiffner, J. M., & Beem, H. P.** Factors influencing organizational effectiveness. I. The U.S. Forest Survey. *Personnel Psychol.*, 1952, *5*, 307–328.

**Conant, E. H., & Kilbridge, M. D.** An interdisciplinary analysis of job enlargement: technology, costs, and behavioral implications. *Indus. lab. relat. Rev.*, 1965, *18*, 377–395.

**Conant, R. C., & Ashby, R. W.** Every good regulator of a system must be a model of the system. *Internat. J. systems Sci.*, 1970, *1*, 89–97.

**Conference Research.** *Process of administrative conference.* University of Michigan, Ann Arbor, 1950.

**Conradi, E.** Song and call-notes of English sparrows when reared by canaries. *Amer. J. Psychol.*, 1905, *16*, 190–198.

**Conway, M.** *The crowd in peace and war.* New York: Longmans, Green, 1915.

**Cook, D. M.** The impact on managers of frequency feedback. *Acad. Mgmt. J.*, 1968, *11*, 263–277.

**Cooley, C. H.** *Human nature and the social order.* New York: Scribners, 1902.

**Cooley, W. W., & Lohnes, P. R.** *Multivariate data analysis.* New York: Wiley, 1971.

**Cooper, C. L.** The influence of the trainer on participant change in T-Group. *Hum. Relat.*, 1969, *22*, 515–530.

**Cooper, C. L.** How psychologically dangerous are T-groups and encounter groups? *Hum. Relat.*, 1975, *28*, 249–260.

**Cooper, C. L., & Levine, N.** Implicit values in experimental learning groups: their functional and dysfunctional consequences. In C. L. Cooper & C. Alderfer (Eds.), *Advances in experimental social processes.* New York: Wiley, 1978.

**Cooper, C. L., & Mangham, I. L. (Eds.).** *T-groups: a survey of research.* New York: Wiley, 1971.

**Cooper, R.** Leader's task relevance and subordinate behavior in industrial work groups. *Hum. Relat.*, 1966, *19*, 57–84.

**Cooper, R., & Payne, R.** Personality orientations and performance in football teams: leader's and subordinates' orientations related to team success. Birmingham, Eng.: University of Aston, Organizational Group Psychology, Report No. 1, 1967.

**Copeland, N.** *Psychology and the soldier.* Harrisburg, Pa.: Military Service Publ. Co., 1942.

**Copeland, N.** *The art of leadership.* London: Allen, 1944.

**Copeman, G. H.** *Leaders of British industry: a study of the careers of more than a thousand public company directors.* London: Gee, 1955.

**Cordiner, R. J.** *Problems of management in a large decentralized organization.* American Management Association, 1952.

**Corey, L. G.** People who claim to be opinion leaders: identifying their characteristics by self-report. *J. Marketing*, 1971, *34*, 48–53.

**Corsini, R. J., Shaw, M. E., & Blake, R. R.** *Roleplaying in business and industry.* New York: Free Press, 1961.

**Coste, M. M.** Caracterisation de la perception empathique du choix sociometrique. *R. Franc. Sociol.*, 1962, *3, 4*, 407–414.

**Couch, A., & Carter, L. F.** A factorial study of the related behavior of group members. *Amer. Psychologist*, 1953, *8*, 333.

**Courtenay, M. E.** Persistence of leadership. *School Rev.*, 1938, *46*, 97–107.

**Courtney, D., Greer, F. L., & Masling, J. M.** Leadership identification and acceptance. Philadelphia: Institute for Research in Human Relations, 1952 (mimeo).

**Courtney, D., Greer, F. L., Masling, J. M., & Orlans, H.** *Naval, neighborhood, and national leadership.* Philadelphia: Institute for Research in Human Relations, 1953.

**Cowley, W. H.** Three distinctions in the study of leaders. *J. abnorm. soc. Psychol.*, 1928, *23*, 144–157.

**Cowley, W. H.** Traits of face-to-face leaders. *J. abnorm. soc. Psychol.*, 1931, *26*, 304–313.

**Cox, C. M.** *The early mental traits of three hundred geniuses.* Standard: Stanford University Press, 1926.

**Cox, D.** *Women's attitudes to repetitive work.* London: National Institute of Industrial Psychology, 1953.

**Cox, J. A., & Krumboltz, J. D.** Racial bias in peer ratings of basic airmen. *Sociometry*, 1958, *21*, 292–299.

**Coyle, G. L.** *Group work with American youth.* New York: Harper, 1948.

**Cozan, L. W.** Job enlargement and employee satisfaction. *Personnel J.*, 1959, *38*, 95–96.

**Craf, J. R.** Measure of a man: officer candidate rating scale. *Occupations*, 1943, *22*, 214.

**Crandall, V. C.** Sex differences in expectancy of intellectual and academic reinforcement. In C. P. Smith. (Ed.), *Achievement-related motives in children.* New York: Russell Sage Foundation, 1969.

**Crandall, V. J., Katkovsky, W., & Preston, A.** Motivational and ability determinants of young children's intellectual achievement behaviors. *Child. Develop.*, 1962, *33*, 643–661.

**Crannell, C. W., & Mollenkopf, W. G.** Combat leadership. In F. Wickert (Ed.), *Psychological research on problems of redistribution.* Army Air Forces Aviation Psychology Program Research Reports No. 14, 1946.

**Crawford, A. B.** Extra-curriculum activities and academic work. *Personnel J.*, 1928, *7*, 121–129.

**Creager, J. A., & Harding, F. D.** A hierarchical factor analysis of foreman behavior. *J. appl. Psychol.*, 1958, *42*, 197–203.

**Criswell, J. H.** The sociometric study of leadership. In L. Petrullo & B. Bass (Eds.), *Leadership and interpersonal behavior.* New York: Holt, Rinehart & Winston, 1961.

**Crockett, W. H.** Emergent leadership in small, decision-making groups. *J. abnorm. soc. Psychol.*, 1955, *51*, 378–383.

**Crockett, W. H., & Meidinger, T.** Authoritarianism and interpersonal perception. *J. abnorm. soc. Psychol.*, 1956, *53*, 378–382.

**Cronbach, L. G.** Beyond the two disciplines of scientific psychology. *Amer. Psychologist*, 1975, *30*, 116–127.

**Cronbach, L. J.** Processes affecting scores on "understanding of others" and assumed "similarity." *Psychol. Bull.*, 1955, *52*, 117–193.

**Cronbach, L. J., & Glaser, G. C.** *Psychological tests and personnel decisions.* Urbana: University of Illinois Press, 1953.

**Cronbach, L. J., Hartmann, W., & Ehart, M. E.** Investigation of the character and properties of assumed similarity measures. Urbana: University of Illinois, Group Effectiveness Research Laboratory, Technical Report 7, 1953.

**Crouch, E. H.** Public school training for leadership. *Peabody J. Educ.*, 1926, *3*, 230–231.

**Crow, W. J.** The need for representative design in studies of interpersonal perception. *J. consult. Psychol.*, 1957a, *21*, 323–325.

**Crow, W. J.** The effect of training upon accuracy and variability of interpersonal perception. *J. abnorm. soc. Psychol.*, 1957b, *55*, 355–359.

**Crow, W. J., & Hammond, K. R.** The generality of accuracy and response sets in interpersonal perception. *J. abnorm. soc. Psychol.*, 1957, *54*, 384–390.

**Crowe, B. J., Bochner, S., & Clark, A. W.** The effects of subordinates' behavior on managerial style. *Hum. Relat.*, 1972, *25*, 215–237.

**Csoka, L. S.** A relationship between leader intelligence and leader rated effectiveness. *J. appl. Psychol.*, 1974, *59*, 43–47.

**Csoka, L. S.** Relationship between organizational climate and the situational favorableness dimension of Fiedler's contingency model. *J. appl. Psychol.*, 1975, *60*, 273–277.

Csoka, L. S., & Bons, P. M. Manipulating the situation to fit the leader's style—two validation studies of LEADER MATCH. *J. appl. Psychol.*, 1978, *63*, 295–300.

Csoka, L. S., & Fiedler, F. E. Leadership and intelligence: a contingency model analysis. *Proceedings of the 80th Annual Convention of the American Psychological Association,* 1972a, *7*, 439–440.

Csoka, L. S., & Fiedler, F. E. The effect of military leadership training: a test of the contingency model. *Org. behav. hum. Perform.*, 1972b, *8*, 395–407.

Culbert, S. A., & McDonough, J. J. *The invisible war.* New York: Wiley, 1980.

Cullers, B., Hughes, C., & McGreal, T. Administrative behavior and student dissatisfaction: a possible relationship. *Peabody J. Educ.*, 1973, *50*, 155–163.

Cummin, P. C. TAT correlates of executive performance. *J. appl. Psychol.*, 1967, *51*, 78–81.

Cummings, L. L., & ElSalmi, A. M. Empirical research on the bases and correlates of managerial motivation: a review of the literature. *Psychol. Bull.*, 1968, *70*, 127–144.

Cummings, L. L., & ElSalmi, A. M. The impact of role diversity, job level, and organizational size on managerial satisfaction. *Admin. sci. Quar.*, 1970, *15*, 1–10.

Cummings, L. L., & Schmidt, S. M. Managerial attitudes of Greeks: the roles of culture and industrialization. *Admin. sci. Quar.*, 1972, *17*, 265–272.

Cummings, L. L., & Scott, W. E. Academic and leadership performance of graduate business students. *Bus. Perspectives*, 1965, *1*, 11–20.

Cummins, R. C. An investigation of a model of leadership effectiveness. *Proceedings of the 78th Annual Convention of the American Psychological Association,* 1970, *5* (pt. 2), 599–600.

Cummins, R. C. Relationship of initiating structure and job performance as moderated by consideration. *J. appl. Psychol.*, 1971, *55*, 489–490.

Cummins, R. C. Leader-member relations as a moderator of the effects of leader behavior and attitude. *Personnel Psychol.*, 1972, *25*, 655–660.

Cunningham, C. J. Measures of leader behavior and their relation to performance levels of county extension agents. Doctoral dissertation, Ohio State University, Columbus, 1964.

Curtis, B., Smith, R. E. & Smoll, F. L. Scrutinizing the skipper: a study of behaviors in the dugout. *J. appl. Psychol.*, 1979, *64*, 391–400.

Curtis, Q. F., & Gibbard, H. A. The acquiring of membership in established groups. Morgantown: West Virginia University, Final Technical Report, 1955.

Cussler, M. *The woman executive.* New York: Harcourt, Brace & World, 1958.

Cyert, R. M., & March, J. G. *A behavioral theory of the firm.* Englewood Cliffs, N.J.: Prentice-Hall, 1963.

Dahl, R. A. The concept of power. *Behav. Sci.*, 1957, *2*, 201–215.

Dahl, R. A. *Who governs?* New Haven: Yale University Press, 1961.

Dahl, R. A. Power. In *International Encyclopedia of the Social Sciences,* vol. 12. New York: Macmillan and Free Press, 1968.

Dale, E. *Planning and developing the company organization structure.* New York: American Management Association, 1952.

Dale E. Centralization versus decentralization. *Advanced Mgmt.*, 1955, *20*, 11–16.

Dalton, G. W., Barnes, L. B., & Zaleznik, A. *The distribution of authority in formal organizations.* Boston: Harvard University, Graduate School of Business Administration, 1968.

Dalton, G. W., Lawrence, P. R., & Greiner, L. E. (Eds.). *Organizational change and development.* Homewood, Ill.: Irwin-Dorsey, 1970.

Dalton, M. Conflicts between staff and line managerial officers. *Amer. sociol. Rev.*, 1950, *15*, 342–351.

**D'Angelo, R. V.** The influence of three styles of leadership on the process and outcome of an organization development effort. Doctoral dissertation, University of California, Berkeley, 1973.

**Daniels, L. R., & Berkowitz, L.** Liking and response to dependency relationships. *Hum. Relat.*, 1963, *16*, 141–148.

**Dansereau, F., Cashman, J., & Graen, G.** Instrumentality theory and equity theory as complementary approaches in predicting the relationship of leadership and turnover among managers. *Org. behav. hum. Perform.*, 1973, *10*, 840.

**Dansereau, F., & Dumas, M.** Pratfalls and pitfalls in drawing inferences about leader behavior in organizations. In J. G. Hunt & L. L. Larson (Eds.), *Leadership: the cutting edge.* Carbondale, Ill.: Southern Illinois University Press.

**Dansereau, F., Graen, G., & Haga, W. J.** A vertical dyad linkage approach to leadership in formal organizations. *Org. behav. hum. Perform.*, 1975, *13*, 46–78.

**Danzig, E. R., & Galanter, E. H.** *The dynamics and structure of small industrial work groups.* Philadelphia: Institute for Research in Human Relations, 1955.

**Danzig, E. R., & Siegel, A. I.** *Emergent leadership in a civil defense evacuation exercise.* Philadelphia: Institute for Research in Human Relations, 1955.

**Darley, J. G., Gross, N., & Martin, W. E.** Studies of group behavior factors associated with the productivity of groups. *J. appl. Psychol.*, 1952, *36*, 396–403.

**Darley, J. M., & Berscheid, R.** Increased liking as a result of the anticipation of personal contact. *Hum. Relat.*, 1967, *20*, 29–40.

**Dashiell, J. F.** Personality traits and the different professions. *J. appl. Psychol.*, 1930, *14*, 197–201.

**Daugherty, R. A., & Walters, T. J.** Closure flexibility, field dependence, and student leadership. *Percept. mot. Skills*, 1969, *29*, 256–258.

**Daum, J. W.** Internal promotion: a psychological asset or debit? a study of the effects of leader origin. *Org. behav. hum. Perform.*, 1975, *13*, 404–413.

**Davenport, W. G., Brooker, G., & Munro, N.** Factors in social perception: seating position. *Percept. mot. Skills*, 1971, *33*, 747–752.

**Davies, D. R., & Tune, G. S.** *Human vigilance performance.* New York: American Elsevier, 1970.

**Davis, F. J.** Conceptions of official leader roles in the air force. *Soc. Forces*, 1954, *32*, 253–258.

**Davis, G.** The maturation of Theodore Roosevelt: the rise of an "affective leader." *His. child. Quar.*, 1975, *3*, 43–74.

**Davis, J. A.** A study of 163 communist leaders. *Amer. sociol. Soc.*, 1929, *24*, 42–45.

**Davis, J. A., & Warnath, C. F.** Reliability, validity, and stability of a sociometric rating scale. *J. soc. Psychol.*, 1957, *45*, 111–122.

**Davis, K.** Learning to live with informal groups. *Adv. Mgmt.*, 1951, *16*, 17–19.

**Davis, K.** Management by participation. *Mgmt. Rev.*, 1957, *46*, 69–79.

**Davis, K.** *Human relations at work.* New York: McGraw-Hill (1962), 1967.

**Davis, K.** The case for participative management. *Bus. Horizons*, 1963, *6*, 55–60.

**Davis, K.** Attitudes toward the legitimacy of management efforts to influence employees. *Acad. Mgmt. J.*, 1968, *11*, 153–161.

**Davis, L. E., & Valfer, E. S.** Studies in supervisory job design. *Hum. Relat.*, 1966, *19*, 339–352.

**Davis, L. E., & Werling, R.** Job design factors. *Occup. Psychol.*, 1960, *34*, 109–132.

**Davis, R. C.** *The fundamentals of top management.* New York: Harper, 1942.

**Davis, T. R. V., & Luthans, F.** Leadership reexamined: a behavioral approach. *Acad. Mgmt. Rev.*, 1979, *4*, 237–248.

**Davitz, J. R.** Social perception and sociometric choice of children. *J. abnorm. soc. Psychol.*, 1955, *50*, 173–176.

**Dawe, H. C.** The influence of size of kindergarten group upon performance. *Child Develop.*, 1934, *5*, 295–303.

**Dawson, C. A.** Leadership and achievement: the effects of teaching styles on first-grade children. *Dissertation Abstr.*, 1969, *29*, 2648–2649.

**Dawson, J. E.** Consideration and ICS: instructor leadership influencing student performance. East Lansing: Michigan State University, Human Learning Research Institute, 1970 (mimeo).

**Dawson, J. E., Messé, L. A., & Phillips, J. L.** Effect of instructor-leader behavior on student performance. *J. appl. Psychol.*, 1972, *56*, 369–376.

**Dawson, J. L. M., Haw, H., Leung, A., & Whitney, R. E.** Scaling Chinese traditional-modern attitudes and the GSR measurement of "important" versus "unimportant" Chinese concepts. *J. cross-cult. Psychol.*, 1971, *2*, 1–27.

**Day, C.** Industrial leadership. *Yale Rev.*, 1909, *18*, 21–33.

**Day, D. R.** Basic dimensions of leadership in a selected industrial organization. *Dissertation Abstr.*, 1961, *22*, 3760.

**Day, D. R.** *Descriptions of male and female leader behavior by male and female subordinates.* Urbana: University of Illinois, Department of Industrial Administration, 1968.

**Day, D. R., & Stogdill, R. M.** Leader behavior of male and female supervisors: a comparative study. *Personnel Psychol.*, 1972, *25*, 353–360.

**Day, R. C., & Hamblin, R. L.** Some effects of close and punitive styles of supervision. *Amer. J. Sociol.*, 1964, *69*, 499–510.

**Dean, L. R.** Union activity and dual loyalty. *Indus. labor relat. Rev.*, 1954, *7*, 449–460.

**Dearborn, DeW. C., & Simon, H. A.** Selective perception: a note on the departmental identifications of executives. *Sociometry*, 1958, *21*, 140–144.

**Deaux, K.** Self-evaluations of male and female managers. Unpublished ms., 1976.

**DeBolt, J. W., Liska, A. E., & Weng, B. R.** Replications of associations between internal locus of control and leadership in small groups. *Psychol Rep.*, 1976, *38*, 470.

**DeCarlo, C. R., & Robinson, O. W.** *Education in business and industry.* New York: Center for Applied Research in Education, 1966.

**DeCharms, R.** Affiliation motivation and productivity in small groups. *J. abnorm. soc. Psychol.*, 1957, *55*, 222–226.

**DeCharms, R., & Hamblin, R. I.** *Structural factors and individual needs in group behavior.* St. Louis, Mo.: Washington University, 1960.

**DeCharms, R., & Rosenbaum, M. E.** Status variables and matching behavior. *J. Pers.*, 1960, *29*, 492–502.

**Deep, S. D., Bass, B. M., & Vaughn, J. A.** Some effects on business gaming of previous quasi-T-group affiliations. *J. appl. Psychol.*, 1967, *51*, 426–431.

**Deets, L. E.** The origins of conflict in the Huttererische communities. *Publ. Amer. Social Soc.*, 1931, *25*, 125–135.

**DeGrazia, A.** *Human relations in public administration: an annotated bibliography from the fields of anthropology, industrial management, political science, psychology, public administration, and sociology.* Chicago: Public Administration Clearing House, 1949.

**DeGrove, J. M., & Kammerer, G. M.** Urban leadership during change. *Amer. Acad. Polit. Soc. Sci.*, 1964, *353*, 95–106.

**Deitzer, B. A.** Measuring the effectiveness of a selected management development program. Doctoral dissertation, Ohio State University, Columbus, 1967.

**Dejung, J. W., & Kaplan, H.** Some differential effects of race of rater and ratee on early peer ratings of combat attitude *J. appl. Psychol.*, 1962, *26*, 370–374.

**Delbecq, A. L., & Kaplan, S. J.** The myth of the indigenous community leader: a case study of managerial effectiveness within the "War on Poverty." *Acad. Mgmt. J.*, 1968, *11*, 11–25.

**Dellums, R. V.** Black leadership: for change or for status quo? *Black Scholar*, 1977, *8*, 2–5.

**DeLong, A.** Dominance-territorial criteria and small group structure. *Comparative group Studies*, 1971, *2*, 235–266.

**DeLong, A. J.** Seating position and perceived characteristics of members of a small group. *Cornell J. soc. Relat.*, 1970, *5*, 135–151.

**DeLora, J. R., & Barber, W. F.** Dimensions of occupational status-images as they relate to recruitment and retention of personnel. San Diego, Calif.: Bureau of Business Research, San Diego State College, 1963 (mimeo).

**Dember, W. N., & Earl, R. W.** Analysis of exploratory, manipulatory, and curiosity behaviors. *Psych. Rev.*, 1957, *64*, 91–96.

**Dennardt, R. B.** Leadership style, worker involvement, and deference to authority. *Sociol. soc. Res.*, 1970, *54*, 172–180.

**Denmark, F. L., & Diggory, J. C.** Sex differences in attitudes toward leaders' display of authoritarian behavior. *Psychol. Rep.*, 1966, *18*, 863–872.

**Dent, J. K.** Organizational correlates of the goals of business managements. *Personnel Psychol.*, 1959, *12*, 365–396.

**Dent, J. K., & Paz, R. de la.** Union security and management attitudes. *Personnel Psychol.*, 1961, *14*, 167–182.

**Denton, R. T.** The effects of differing leadership behaviors on the job satisfaction and job performance of professional mental health workers. *Dissertation Abstr. Internat.*, 1976, *37*, 3183.

**Department of Labor (U.S.).** *The Negroes in the United States: their economic and social situation.* Bulletin No. 1511, June, 1966.

**Department of Commerce (U.S.)** *The social and economic status of Negroes in the United States,* 1970. BLS Report No. 394, July, 1971.

**Derber, M.** Crosscurrents in workers' participation. *Indus. Relat.*, 1970, *9*, 123–136.

**Derber, M., Chalmers, W. E., Edelman, M. T., & Triandis, H. C.** *Plant union–management relations.* Urbana: University of Illinois Press, 1965.

**Desmond, R. E., & Seligman, M.** A review of research on leaderless groups. *Sm. grp. Behav.*, 1977, *8*, 3–24.

**Dessler, G.** A test of the path-goal theory of leadership. *Proceedings of the Academy of Management*, 1972.

**Dessler, G.** An investigation of the path-goal theory of leadership. Doctoral dissertation, Baruch College, City University of New York, New York, 1973.

**Dessler, G., & Valenzi, E. R.** Initiation of structure and subordinate satisfaction: a path analysis test of path-goal theory. *Acad. Mgmt. J.* 1977, *20*, 251–259.

**Deutsch, M.** An experimental study of the effects of cooperation and competition upon group process. *Hum. Relat.*, 1949, *2*, 199–232.

**Deutsch, M.** *The resolution of conflict: constructive and destructive processes.* New Haven: Yale University Press, 1973.

**Deutsch, M., & Gerard, H. B.** A study of normative and informational social influences upon individual judgment. New York: New York University, Technical Report, 1954.

**Deutschberger, P.** The structure of dominance. *Amer. J. Orthopsychiatr.*, 1947, *17*, 343–351.

**Devereux, E. C.** Community participation and leadership. *J. soc. Issues*, 1960, *16*, 29–45.

**Devine, R. P.** Opinion influence roles: opinion leaders, opinion followers, and isolates. *Dissertation Abstr. Internat.*, 1977, *37*(12A), 79770.

**DeVries, D. L.** Teams-games-tournament. n *Simulation and games,* in press.

**DeVries, M. F.** Crisis leadership and the paranoid potential: an organizational perspective. *Bull. Menninger Clinic*, 1977, *41*, 349–365.

**Dewhirst, H. D.** Impact of organizational climate on the desire to manage among engineers and scientists. *Personnel J.*, 1971, *50*, 196–203.

**Dexter, Emily S., & Stein, B.** The measurement of leadership in white and negro women students. *J. abnorm. soc. Psychol.*, 1955, *51*, 219–221.

**Dhanagare, D. N.** Perception of leader's competence and the rates of positive-negative reactions in work-groups. *Indian psychol. Rev.*, 1968, *4*, 126–133.

**Dickinson, Z. C.** *Compensatory industrial effort.* New York: Ronald, 1937.

**Diesing, P.** *Patterns of discovery in the social sciences.* Chicago: Aldine-Atherton, 1971.

**Dieterly, D. L., & Schneider, B.** The effect of organizational environment on perceived power and climate: a laboratory study. *Org. behav. hum. Perform.*, 1974, *11*, 316–337.

**Dietz, W.** Training new supervisors in the skill of leadership. *Personnel*, 1943, *19*, 604–608.

**Dill, W. R.** Environment as an influence on managerial autonomy. *Admin. sci. Quar.*, 1958, *2*, 409–443.

**DiMarco, N., & Whitsitt, S. E.** A comparison of female supervisors in business and government organizations. *J. vocat. Behav.*, 1975, *6*, 185–196.

**Dittes, F. E., & Kelley, H. H.** Effects of different conditions of acceptance upon conformity to group norms. *J. abnorm. soc. Psychol.*, 1956, *53*, 100–107.

**Dittes, J. E.** Attractiveness of group as function of self-esteem and acceptance by group. *J. abnorm. soc. Psychol.*, 1959, *59*, 77–82.

**DiVesta, F. J.** Instructor-centered and student-centered approaches in teaching a human relations course. *J. appl. Psychol.*, 1954, *38*, 329–335.

**DiVesta, F. J., Meyer, D. L., & Mills, J.** Confidence in an expert as a function of his judgments. *Hum. Relat.*, 1964, *17*, 235–242.

**Dobruszek, Z.** Badanie postaw kierowniczych za pomoca "Inwentarza postaw i pogladow" B. M. Bassa. (A study on the leadership attitudes with "Orientation inventory" of B. M. Bass.) *Przeglad psychologiczny*, 1967, *15*.

**Dobruszek, Z.** Leadership attitudes measured by the Bass Orientation Inventory. *Polish psychol. Bull.*, 1971, *2*, 31–35.

**Dodd, S. C.** Diffusion is predictable: testing probability models for laws of interaction. *Amer. sociol. Rev.*, 1955, *20*, 392–401.

**Dogan, M., & Rokkan, S.** *Quantitative ecological analysis in the social sciences.* Cambridge, Mass.: M.I.T. Press, 1969.

**Doll, R. E., & Gunderson, E. K.** The relative importance of selected behavioral characteristics of group members in an extreme environment. *Exper. publ. System. Amer. Psychol. Assn.*, 1969, No. 097A.

**Doll, R. E., & Longo, A. A.** Improving the predictive effectiveness of peer ratings. *Personnel Psychol.*, 1962, *15*, 215–220.

**Dommermuth, W. P.** *The road to the top: a study of the careers of corporation presidents.* Austin: University of Texas, Bureau of Business Research, 1965.

**Donnelly, C.** Keys to the executive powder room. *Money*, 1976, *5*, 28–32.

**Doroschenko, O.** Der Einfluss des Milieus auf den Inhalt und den Aufbau frei entstehender Kollektive in vorschulpflichtigen Alter. *Z. angew. Psychol.*, 1928, *30*, 150–167.

**Douglas, W. S.** An evaluation of experimental procedures for the systematic training of group leaders. *Dissertation Abstr. Internat.*, 1977, *36*, 4255.

**Douglis, M. B.** Social factors influencing the hierarchies of small flocks of the domestic hen; interactions between resident and part-time members of organized flocks. *Physiol. Zool.*, 1948, *21*, 147–182.

**Douvan, E.** Social status and success strivings. *J. abnorm. soc. Psychol.*, 1956, *52*, 219–223.

**Dowd, J.** *Control in human societies.* New York: Appleton-Century, 1936.

**Dowell, B. E., & Wexley, K. N.** Development of a work behavior taxonomy for first-line supervisors. *J. appl. Psychol.*, 1978, *63*, 563–572.

**Dowling, W. F.** At General Motors: systems 4 builds performance and profits. *Org. Dynam.*, 1975, *3*, 23–38.

**Downey, H. K., Sheridan, J. E., & Slocum, J. W., Jr.** Analysis of relationships among leader behavior, subordinate job performance and satisfaction: a path goal approach. *Acad. Mgmt. J.*, 1975, *18*, 253–262.

**Downey, H. K., Sheridan, J. E., & Slocum, J. W., Jr.** The path-goal theory of leadership: a longitudinal analysis. *Org. behav. hum. Perform.*, 1976, *16*, 156–176.

**Downing, J.** Cohesiveness, perception, and values. *Hum. Relat.*, 1958, *11*, 157–166.

**Downton, J. V.** *Rebel leadership: commitment and charisma in the revolutionary process.* New York: Free Press, 1973.

**Doyle, W. J.** The effects of leader achieved status on hierarchically differentiated group performance. *Dissertation Abstr. Internat.*, 1970, *30*, 2747.

**Doyle, W. J.** Effects of achieved status of leader on productivity of groups. *Admin. sci. Quar.*, 1971, *16*, 40–50.

**Drake, R. M.** A study of leadership. *Character & Pers.*, 1944, *12*, 285–289.

**Drake, St. C., & Cayton, H.** The world of the urban lower-class Negro. In R. J. Murphy & H. Elinson (Eds.), *Problems and prospects of the Negro movement.* Belmont, Calif.: Wadsworth, 1966.

**Draper, N. R., & Smith, H.** *Applied regression analysis.* New York: Wiley, 1966.

**Drought, N. E.** The operations committee: an experience in group dynamics. *Personnel Psychol.*, 1967, *20*, 153–163.

**Drucker, E. H., & Schwartz, S.** *The prediction of AWOL, military skills, and leadership potential.* Alexandria, Va.: Human Resources Research Organization, 1973.

**Drucker, P. F.** *Concept of the corporation.* New York: John Day, 1946.

**Drucker, P. F.** *The practice of management.* New York: Harper, 1954.

**Dubin, R.** *The world of work.* Englewood Cliffs, N.J.: Prentice-Hall, 1958.

**Dubin, R.** Business behavior behaviorally viewed. In G. B. Strother (Ed.), *Social science approaches to business behavior.* Homewood, Ill.: Dorsey Press, 1962a.

**Dubin, R.** Stability of human organizations. In M. Haire (Ed.), *Modern organizational theory.* New York: Wiley, 1962b.

**Dubin, R.** Supervision and productivity: empirical findings and theoretical considerations. In R. Dubin, G. C. Homans, F. C. Mann, & D. C. Miller (Eds.), *Leadership and productivity.* San Francisco: Chandler, 1965.

**Dubin, R., & Spray, S. L.** Executive behavior and interaction. *Indus. Relat.*, 1964, *3*, 99–108.

**Dubno, P.** Decision time characteristics of leaders and group problem solving behavior. *J. soc. Psychol.*, 1963, *59*, 259–282.

**Dubno, P.** Leadership, group effectiveness, and speed of decision. *J. soc. Psychol.*, 1965, *65*, 351–360.

**Dubno, P.** Group congruency patterns and leadership characteristics. *Personnel Psychol.*, 1968, *21*, 335–344.

**DuBrin, A. J.** Trait and situational approaches in the development of a leadership inventory. *J. indus. Psychol.*, 1963, *1*, 28–37.

**DuBrin, A. J.** Trait and interpersonal self descriptions of leaders and nonleaders in an industrial setting. *J. indus. Psychol.*, 1964, *2*, 51–55.

**Duffy, P. J.** Lateral interaction orientation: an expanded view of leadership. Doctoral dissertation, Southern Illinois University, Carbondale, 1973.

**Dulany, D.** Converging operations. Unpublished note, 1975.

**Dunkerley, M. D.** A statistical study of leadership among college women. *Stud. psychol. Psychiat.*, 1940, *4*, 1–64.

**Dunn, W. N., & Swierczek, F. W.** Planned organizational change: toward grounded theory. *J. appl. behav. Sci.*, 1976, *13*, 135–157.

**Dunnington, R. A., Sirota, D., & Kelin, S. M.** Research for organization theory and management action. *Proceedings of the Industrial Relations Research Association*, 1963.

**Dunnette, M. D.** Identification and enhancement of managerial effectiveness. II. Research problems and research results in the identification of managerial effectiveness. Greensboro, N.C.: Richardson Foundation, 1966 (mimeo).

**Dunnette, M. D.** The motives of industrial managers. *Org. behav. hum. Perform.*, 1967, *2*, 176–182.

**Dunnette, M. D., & Campbell, J. P.** Laboratory education: impact on people and organizations. *Indus. Relat.*, 1968, *8*, 1–27.

**Dunnette, M. D., Campbell, J. P., & Argyris, C.** *A symposium: laboratory training.* Minneapolis: University of Minnesota, Industrial Relations Center, 1968.

**Dunnette, M. D., Lawler, E. E., Weick, K. E., & Opsahl, R. L.** The role of financial compensation in managerial motivation. *Org. behav. hum. Perform.*, 1967, *2*, 175–216.

**Dunphy, D. C.** The social structure of urban adolescent peer groups. *Sociometry*, 1963, *26*, 230–246.

**Dunteman, G. H.** Self, interaction, and task-orientation scores and their relationship to promotability ratings. *J. indus. Psychol.*, 1966, *4*, 20–26.

**Dunteman, G., & Bass, B. M.** Supervisory and engineering success associated with self, interaction, and task orientation scores. *Personnel Psychol.*, 1963, *16*, 13–22.

**Durand, D. E., & Nord, W. R.** Perceived leader behavior as a function of personality characteristics of supervisors and subordinates. *Acad. Mgmt. J.*, 1976, *19*, 427–438.

**Durant, W.** *The reformation.* New York: Simon & Schuster, 1957.

**Durbrow, B. R.** Inter-firm executive mobility. Doctoral dissertation, Ohio State University, Columbus, 1971.

**Durham, L. E., & Gibb, J. R.** *An annotated bibliography of research, 1947–1960.* Washington, D.C.: National Training Laboratories, 1960.

**Durkheim, E.** *The division of labor in society.* New York: Free Press, 1947.

**Durojaiye, M. O.** Patterns of friendship and leadership choices in a mixed ethnic junior school: a sociometric analysis. *British J. educ. Psychol.*, 1969, *39*, 88–89.

**Dustin, D. S., & Davis, H. P.** Authoritarianism and sanctioning behavior. *J. pers. soc. Psychol.*, 1967, *6*, 222–224.

**Du Vall, E. W.** *Personality and social group work.* New York: Association Press, 1943.

**Dyer, J. L., & Lambert, W. E.** Coordination of flying activities in bomb wings: integration and performance. Chapel Hill: University of North Carolina, Institute for Research Social Science, 1953.

**Dyer, J. L., Lambert, W. E., & Tracy, G.** Attitudes toward selected elements of organization and the performance of bomb squadrons. Chapel Hill: University of North Carolina, Institute for the Research of the Social Sciences, 1953.

**Dyer, W. G.** *Modern theory and method in group training.* New York: Van Nostrand Reinhold, 1972.

**Dynes, R. R.** *Organized behavior in disaster.* Columbus: Ohio State University, Disaster Research Center, 1969.

**Dyson, J. W., Fleitas, D. W., & Scioli, F. P.** The interaction of leadership personality, and decisional environments. *J. soc. Psychol.*, 1972, *86*, 29–33.

**Dyson, J. W., Godwin, P. H., & Hazelwood, L. A.** Group composition, leadership orientation, and decisional outcomes. *Sm. grp. Behav.*, 1976, *7*, 114–128.

**Eaglin, R. G.** An experimental study of the effect of positive, negative, and no verbal reinforcers on assigned leaders in eight-member decision making groups. *Dissertation Abstr. Internat.*, 1970, *31*, 3688–3689.

**Eaglin, R. G.** The effect of verbal reinforcement on leader behavior. *J. coll. student Personnel*, 1973, *14*, 71–76.

**Eagly, A. H.** Leadership style and role differentiation as determinants of group effectiveness. *J. pers.*, 1970, *38*, 509–524.

**Eaton, J. W.** Controlled acculturation: a survival technique of the Hutterites. *Amer. sociol. Rev.*, 1952, *17*, 331–340.

**Eckerman, W. C.** The relationship of need achievement to production, job satisfaction, and psychological stress. *Dissertation Abstr.*, 1964, *24*, 3446.

**Edel, E. C.** A study in managerial motivation. *Personnel Admin.*, 1966, *29*, 31–38.

**Edel, E. C.** "Need for success" as a predictor of managerial performance. *Personnel Psychol.*, 1968, *21*, 231–240.

**Eden, D., & Leviathan, U.** Implicit leadership theory as a determinant of the factor structure underlying supervisory behavior scales. *J. appl. Psychol.*, 1975, *60*, 736–741.

**Edinger, L. J.** Political science and political biography (II): reflections in the study of leadership. *J. Politics*, 1964, *26*, 648–676.

**Edinger, L. J.** *Political leadership in industrialized societies.* New York: Wiley, 1967.

**Edwards, M. T.** Leader influence and task set. Buffalo: State University of New York, Master's thesis, 1973.

**Edwards, W.** The theory of decision making. *Psych. Bull.*, 1955, *51*, 380–417.

**Eichler, G. A.** Studies in student leadership. Doctoral dissertation, Pennsylvania State College, State College, 1934.

**Eichler, G. A., & Merrill, R. R.** Can social leadership be improved by instruction in its technique? *J. educ. Sociol.*, 1933, *7*, 233–236.

**Eisenberger, R.** Explanation of rewards that do not reduce tissue needs. *Psych. Bull.*, 1972, *77*, 319–339.

**Eisenstadt, S. N.** The process of absorption of new immigrants in Israel. *Hum. Relat.*, 1952, *5*, 223–246.

**Eisenstadt, S. N.** Studies in reference group behavior. 1. Reference norms and the social structure. *Hum. Relat.*, 1954, *7*, 191–216.

**Eisman, E. J.** The effects of leader sex and self-disclosure on member self-disclosure in marathon encounter groups. *Dissertation Abstr. Internat.*, 1975, *36*, 1429.

**Eitzen, R., & Yetman, N.** Managerial change, longevity, and organizational effectiveness. *Admin. sci. Quar.*, 1972, *17*, 110–116.

**Elkin, F., Halpern, G., & Cooper, A.** Leadership in a student mob. *Canad. J. Psychol.*, 1962, *16*, 199–201.

**Elkins, D.** Some factors related to the choice-status of ninety eighth-grade children in a school society. *Genet. psychol. Monogr.*, 1958, *58*, 207–272.

**Elliot, O., & Penner, D. D.** The impact of social structure and organizational change. In H. L. Fromkin & J. J. Sherwood (Eds.), *Integrating the organization.* New York: Free Press, 1974.

**Elliot, J. D.** Increasing office productivity through job enlargement. In *The human side of the office manager's job.* New York: American Management Association, 1953.

**Ellis, H.** *A study of British genius.* London: Hurst & Blackett, 1904.

**Ellis, R. A.** Social status and social distance. *Sociol. soc. Res.*, 1956, *40*, 240–246.

**Elms, A. C., & Janis, I. L.** Counter-norm attitudes induced by consonant vs. dissonant conditions of role-playing. *J. exp. res. Pers.*, 1965, *1*, 50–60.

**Elrick, M.** The leader, she: dynamics of a female-led self-analytic group. *Hum. Relat.*, 1977, *30*, 869–878.

**ElSalmi, A. M., & Cummings, L. L.** Managers' perceptions of needs and need satisfactions as a function of interactions among organizational variables. *Personnel Psychol.*, 1968, *21*, 465–477.

**Elson, J. A.** Abstracts of personnel research reports: *USAF PRL Tech. Rep.*, 1965, No. 65–23.

**Emerson, R. M.** Power-dependence relations: two experiments. *Sociometry,* 1964, *27*, 282–298.

**Emery, D. A.** Managerial leadership through motivation by objectives. *Personnel Psychol.*, 1959, *12*, 65–79.

**Emery, F. E., & Thorsrud, E.** *The form and content in industrial democracy.* London: Tavistock, 1969.

**Emery, F. E., & Trist, E. L.** The causal texture of organizational environments. *Hum. Relat.*, 1965, *18*, 21–32.

**Emmet, D.** *Rules, roles, and relations.* New York: St. Martin's Press, 1966.

**Engel, G. V.** Professional autonomy and bureaucratic organization. *Admin. sci. Quart.*, 1970, *15*, 12–21.

**England, G. W.** Personal value systems of American managers. *Acad. Mgmt. J.,* 1967a, *10*, 53–68.

**England, G. W.** Organizational goals and expected behavior of American managers. *Acad. Mgmt. J.,* 1967b, *10*, 107–117.

**England, G. W.** Personal value systems analysis as an aid to understanding organizational behavior: a comparative study in Japan, Korea, and the United States. Presented at the Exchange Seminar on Comparative Organizations, Amsterdam, 1970.

**England, G. W.** *Personal values systems of Australian managers.* Minneapolis: University of Minnesota, Industrial Relations Center, 1972.

**England, G. W.** *The manager and his values: an international perspective.* Cambridge, Mass.: Ballinger, 1976.

**England, G. W., Agarwal, N. C., & Dhingra, O. P.** *Personal value systems of Indian managers.* Minneapolis: University of Minnesota Press, 1973.

**England, G. W., & Koike, R.** Personal value systems of Japanese managers. *J. cross-cult. Psychol.*, 1970, *1*, 21–40.

**England, G. W., & Lee, R.** Organizational goals and expected behavior among American, Japanese, and Korean managers—a comparative study. *Acad. Mgmt. J.,* 1971, *14*, 425–438.

**England, G. W., & Lee, R.** The relationship between managerial values and managerial success in the United States, Japan, India, and Australia. *J. appl. Psychol.*, 1974, *59*, 411–419.

**England, G. W., & Weber, M. L.** Managerial success: a study of value and demographic correlates. Minneapolis: University of Minnesota, Center for the Study of Organizational Performance and Human Effectiveness, ONR Technical Report, 1972.

**Entwisle, D. R., & Walton, J.** Observations on the span of control. *Admin. sci. Quar.*, 1961, *5*, 522–533.

**Epstein, C. F.** Encountering the male establishment: sex status limits on women's careers in the professions. *Amer. J. Sociol.*, 1970, *75*, 965–982.

**Epstein, S.** An experimental study of some of the effects of variations in the clarity and extent of a supervisor's area of freedom upon his supervisory behavior. *Dissertation Abstr.*, 1956, *16*, 2513.

**Eran, M.** Relationship between self-perceived personality traits and job attitudes in middle management. *J. appl. Psychol.*, 1966, *50*, 424–430.

**Erez, M.** Correlates of leadership style: field-dependence, and social intelligence versus social orientation. Unpublished ms., 1979.

**Erikson, E.** *Insight and responsibility.* New York: Norton, 1964.

**Eskilson, A.** Sex composition and leadership in small groups. *Dissertation Abstr. Internat.*, 1975, *35*, 5694.

**Eskilson, A., & Wiley, M. G.** Sex composition and leadership in small groups. *Sociometry*, 1976, *39*, 183–194.

**Esser, N. J., & Strother, G. B.** Rule interpretation as an indicator of style of management. *Personnel Psychol.*, 1962, *15*, 375–386.

**Estler, S. E.** Women as leaders in public education. *Signs*, 1975, *1*, 363–386.

**Etkin, W. (Ed.)** *Social behavior and organization among vertebrates.* Chicago: University of Chicago Press, 1964.

**Etzioni, A.** Lower levels of leadership in industry. *Sociol. soc. Res.*, 1959, *43*, 209–212.

**Etzioni, A.** *A comparative analysis of complex organizations.* New York: Free Press, 1961.

**Etzioni, A.** Dual leadership in complex organizations. *Amer. sociol. Rev.*, 1965, *30*, 688–698.

**Evan, W. M., & Simmons, R. G.** Organizational effects of inequitable rewards: two experiments in status inconsistency. *Admin. sci. Quar.*, 1969, *4*, 224–237.

**Evan, W. M., & Zelditch, M.** A laboratory experiment on bureaucratic authority. *Amer. sociol. Rev.*, 1961, *26*, 883–893.

**Evans, G. C.** Validity of ascendance measurements in group interaction. *Psychol. Rep.*, 1960, *7*, 114.

**Evans, M. G.** The effects of supervisory behavior upon worker perception of their path-goal relationships. Doctoral dissertation, Yale University, New Haven, Conn., 1968.

**Evans, M. G.** Conceptual and operational problems in the measurement of various aspects of job satisfaction. *J. appl. Psychol.*, 1969, *53*, 93–101.

**Evans, M. G.** The effects of supervisory behavior on the path-goal relationship. *Org. behav. hum. Perform.*, 1970a, *5*, 277–298.

**Evans, M. G.** Leadership and motivation: a case concept. *Acad. Mgmt. J.*, 1970b, *13*, 91–102.

**Evans, M. G.** Leadership behavior: demographic factors and agreement between subordinate and self-descriptions. *Personnel Psychol.*, 1972, *25*, 649–653.

**Evans, M. G.** A leader's ability to differentiate: the subordinate's perception of the leader and subordinate's performance. *Personnel Psychol.*, 1973, *26*, 385–395.

**Evans, M. G.** Extensions of a path-goal theory of motivation, *Journal of Applied Psychology*, 1974, *59*, 172–178.

**Evans, M. G., & Dermer, J.** What does the least preferred co-worker scale really measure? A cognitive interpretation. *J. appl. Psychol.*, 1974, *59*, 202–206.

**Evenson, W. L.** Leadership behavior of high school principals. *Nat'l. Assn. Secondary School Principals Bull.*, 1959, *43*, 96–101.

**Exline, R. V.** Interrelations among two dimensions of sociometric status, group congeniality and accuracy of social perception. *Sociometry*, 1960, *23*, 85–101.

**Exline, R. V., & Ziller, R. C.** Status congruency and interpersonal conflict in decision-making groups. *Hum. Relat.*, 1959, *12*, 147–162.

**Falbo, T.** Multidimensional scaling of power strategies. *J. pers. soc. Psychol.*, 1977, *35*, 537–547.

**Fanelli, A. A.** A typology of community leadership based on influence and interaction within the leader subsystem. *Soc. Forces.*, 1956, *34*, 332–338.

**Farley, R., & Hermalin, A.** Family stability: a comparison of trends between blacks and whites. *Amer. Sociol. Rev.*, 1971, *36*, 1–17.

**Farmer, R. N., & Richman, B. M.** A model for research in comparative management. *Calif. mgmt. Rev.*, 1964, *1*, 55–68.

**Farris, G. F.** Colleagues roles and innovation in scientific teams. Cambridge, Mass.: Alfred P. Sloan School of Management, M.I.T. Working Paper No. 552–71, 1971a.

**Farris, G. F.** Executive decision making in organizations: identifying the key men and managing the process. Cambridge, Mass.: Alfred P. Sloan School of Management, M.I.T. Working Paper No. 551–71, 1971b.

**Farris, G. F.** Organizing your informal organization. *Innovation,* 1971c, No. 25, 2–11.

**Farris, G. F.** The effect of individual roles on performance in innovative groups. *R&D Mgmt.,* 1972, No. 3.

**Farris, G. F., & Lim, F. G.** Effects of performance on leadership, cohesiveness, influence, satisfaction, and subsequent perfofmance. *J. appl. Psychol.,* 1969, *53*, 490–497.

**Farrow, D. L.** A path-analytic approach to the study of contingent leader behavior. Doctoral dissertation, University of Rochester, Rochester, N.Y., 1976.

**Farrow, D. L., & Bass, B. M.** A phoenix emerges: the importance of manager and subordinate personality in contingency leadership analyses. Rochester: University of Rochester, Army Research Institute, Technical Report 77–1, 1977.

**Farrow, D. L., Bass, B. M., & Valenzi, E. R.** A manager's tendencies to be participative associated with his perceptions of the environment outside his organization. *Proceedings of the 37th Annual Meeting of the Academy of Management,* 1977.

**Farrow, D. L., & O'Connor E.** Environmental constraints, organizational structures and preferred patterns of managerial behavior. *Proceedings of the Southeastern Psychological Association,* 1977.

**Farrow, D. L., Valenzi, E. R., & Bass, B. M.** A regression approach to identifying ways to increase leadership effectiveness. *Proceedings of the 87th Annual Convention of the American Psychological Association,* 1979.

**Farrow, D. L., Valenzi, E. R., & Bass, B. M.** A comparison of leadership and situational characteristics within profit and non-profit organizations. *Proceedings of the Academy of Management,* 1980.

**Farrow, D. L., Valenzi, E. R., & Bass, B. M.** Managerial political behavior, executive success and effectiveness. *Proceedings of the Academy of Management,* 1981.

**Fast, R. G.** Leader behavior of principals as it relates to teacher satisfaction. University of Alberta, Master's thesis, 1964.

**Fathi, A.** Leadership and resistance to change: a case from an underdeveloped area. *Rural Sociol.,* 1965, *30*, 204–212.

**Faunce, D., & Beegle, J. A.** Cleavages in a relatively homogeneous group of rural youth: an experiment in the use of sociometry in attaining and measuring integration. *Sociometry,* 1948, *11*, 207–216.

**Fauquier, W., & Gilchrist, J.** Some aspects of leadership in an institution. *Child Develop.,* 1942, *13*, 55–64.

**Fay, P. J., & Middleton, W. C.** Judgment of leadership from the transmitted voice. *J. soc. Psychol.,* 1943, *17*, 99–102.

**Fayerweather, J.** *The executive overseas.* Syracuse, N.Y.: Syracuse University Press, 1959.

**Fearing, F.** Psychological studies of historical personalities. *Psychol. Bull.,* 1927, *24*, 521–539.

**Feffer, M., & Phillips, L.** Social attainment and performance under stress. *J. Pers.,* 1953, *22*, 284–297.

**Feil, M. H.** A study of leadership and scholastic achievement in their relation to prediction factors. Doctoral dissertation, Ohio State University, Columbus, 1950.

**Feierabend, R. L., & Janis, I. L.** An experimental comparison of two ways of organizing positive and negative arguments in persuasive communications. *Amer. Psychologist,* 1954, *9*, 362–363.

**Feinberg, M. R.** Relation of background experience to social acceptance. *J. abnorm. soc. Psychol.,* 1953, *48*, 206–214.

**Feitler, F. C.** A study of relationships between principal leadership styles and organizational characteristics of elementary schools. Doctoral dissertation, Syracuse University, Syracuse, N.Y., 1971.

**Feitler, F. C., & Blumberg, A.** Changing the organizational character of a school. *Elem. sch. J.,* 1971, *71*, 206–215.

**Feld, S., & Lewis, J.** The assessment of achievement anxieties in children. Mental Health Study Center, NIMH, manuscript, 1967.

**Feldman, H.** *Problems in labor relations.* New York: Macmillan, 1937.

**Feldman, R. A.** Three types of group integration: their relationship to power, leadership, and conformity behavior. *Dissertation Abstr.,* 1967, *27*, 2202–2203.

**Felipe, N.** Interpersonal distance and small group interaction. *Cornell J. soc. Relat.,* 1966, *1*, 59–64.

**Fenchel, G. H., Monderer, J. H., & Hartley, E. L.** Subjective status and the equilibration hypothesis. *J. abnorm. soc. Psychol.,* 1951, *46*, 476–479.

**Fenelon, J. R.** The influence of race on leadership prediction. Austin: University of Texas, Master's thesis, 1966.

**Fenelon, J. R., & Megargee, E. I.** The influence of race on the manifestation of leadership. *Exp. publ. system, Amer. Psychol. Assn.,* 1971, *10*, No. 380–12.

**Fensterheim, H., & Tresselt, M. E.** The influence of value systems on the perception of people. *J. abnorm. soc. Psychol.,* 1953, *48*, 93–98.

**Ferguson, L. W.** The L.O.M.A. merit rating scales. *Personnel Psychol.,* 1950, *3*, 193–216.

**Ferris, A. E.** Organizational relationships in two selected secondary schools: a comparative study. Doctoral dissertation, Columbia University, New York, 1965.

**Festinger, L.** The analysis of sociograms using matrix algebra. *Hum. Relat.,* 1949, *2*, 153–158.

**Festinger, L.** Informal social communication. *Psychol. Rev.,* 1950, *57*, 271–282.

**Festinger, L.** A theory of social comparison processes. *Hum. Relat.,* 1954, *7*, 117–140.

**Festinger, L., Cartwright, D., et al.** A study of a rumor: its origin and spread. *Hum. Relat.,* 1947, *1*, 464–486.

**Festinger, L., Gerard, H. B., Hymovitch, B., Kelley, H. H., & Raven, B.** The influence process in the presence of extreme deviates. *Hum. Relat.,* 1952, *5*, 327–346.

**Festinger, L., & Hutte, H. A.** An experimental investigation of the effect of unstable interpersonal relations in a group. *J. abnorm. soc. Psychol.,* 1954, *49*, 513–522.

**Festinger, L., & Kelley, H. H.** *Changing attitudes through social contact.* Ann Arbor: Research Center for Group Dynamics, 1951.

**Festinger, L., Pepitone, A., & Newcomb, T.** Some consequences of de-individuation in a group. *J. abnorm. soc. Psychol.,* 1952, *47*, 382–389.

**Festinger, L., Schachter, S., & Back, K.** *Social processes in informal groups: a study of a housing project.* New York: Harper, 1950.

**Festinger, L., & Thibaut, J.** Interpersonal communication in small groups. *J. abnorm. soc. Psychol.,* 1951, *46*, 92–99.

**Festinger, L., Torrey, J., & Willerman, B.** Self-evaluation as a function of attraction to the group. *Hum. Relat.,* 1954, *7*, 161–174.

**Fichter, J. H.** Career preparation and expectations of Negro college seniors. *J. Negro Educ.,* 1966, *35*, 322–335.

**Fiedler, F. E.** Quantitative studies in the role of therapists' feelings toward their patients. In O. H. Mowrer (Ed.), *Psychotherapy: theory and research.* New York: Ronald Press, 1953a.

**Fiedler, F. E.** The psychological distance dimension in interpersonal relations. *J. Pers.,* 1953b, *22*, 142–150.

**Fiedler, F. E.** Assumed similarity measures as predictors of team effectiveness in surveying. Urbana: University of Illinois, Bur. Res. Serv., Technical Report No. 6, 1953c.

**Fiedler, F. E.** Interpersonal perception and sociometric structure in prediction of small team effectiveness. *Amer. Psychologist,* 1954a, *8,* 365.

**Fiedler, F. E.** Assumed similarity measures and predictors of team effectiveness. *J. abnorm. soc. Psychol.,* 1954b, *49,* 381–388.

**Fiedler, F. E.** The influence of leader-keyman relations on combat crew effectiveness. *J. abnorm. soc. Psychol.,* 1955, *51,* 227–235.

**Fiedler, F. E.** Social perception and group effectiveness. Urbana: University of Illinois, Annual Technical Report, 1956.

**Fiedler, F. E.** A note on leadership theory: the effect of social barriers between leaders and followers. *Sociometry,* 1957, *20,* 87–94.

**Fiedler, F. E.** *Leader attitudes and group effectiveness.* Urbana: University of Illinois Press, 1958.

**Fiedler, F. E.** Leadership and leadership effectiveness traits: a reconceptualization of the leadership trait problem. In L. Petrullo & B. M. Bass (Eds.), *Leadership and interpersonal behavior.* New York: Holt, Rinehart & Winston, 1961.

**Fiedler, F. E.** Leader attitudes, group climate, and group creativity. *J. abnorm. soc. Psychol.,* 1962, *65,* 308–318.

**Fiedler, F. E.** A contingency model for the prediction of leadership effectiveness. Urbana: University of Illinois, Group Effectiveness Research Lab, Technical Report No. 10, 1963.

**Fiedler, F. E.** A contingency model of leadership effectiveness. In L. Berkowitz (Ed.), *Advances in experimental social psychology.* New York: Academic Press, 1964.

**Fiedler, F. E.** Engineering the job to fit the manager. *Harvard bus. Rev.,* 1965, *43,* 115–122.

**Fiedler, F. E.** The effect of leadership and cultural heterogeneity on group performance: a test of the contingency model. *J. exp. soc. Psychol.,* 1966, *2,* 237–264.

**Fiedler, F. E.** *A theory of leadership effectiveness.* New York: McGraw-Hill, 1967a.

**Fiedler, F. E.** The effect of inter-group competition on group member adjustment. *Personnel Psychol.,* 1967b, *20,* 33–44.

**Fiedler, F. E.** The effect of culture training on leadership, organizational performance, and adjustment. *Naval res. Rev.,* 1968, 7–13.

**Fiedler, F. E.** Leadership experience and leader performance: another hypothesis shot to hell. *Org. behav. hum. Perform.,* 1970a, *5,* 1–14.

**Fiedler, F. E.** Personality, motivational systems, and behavior of high and low LPC persons. Seattle: University of Washington, Technical Report No. 70–12, 1970b.

**Fiedler, F. E.** *Leadership.* New York: General Learning Press, 1971a.

**Fiedler, F. E.** Note on the methodology of the Graen, Orris, and Alveres studies testing the contingency model. *J. appl. Psychol.,* 1971b, *55,* 202–204.

**Fiedler, F. E.** Validation and extension of the contingency model of leadership effectiveness: a review of empirical findings. *Psychol. Bull., 1971c, 76,* 128–148.

**Fiedler, F. E.** Personality and situational determinants of leader behavior. Seattle: University of Washington, Department of Psychology, Technical Report, 1971d.

**Fiedler, F.** Personality, motivational systems and the behavior of high and low LPC persons. *Hum. Relat.,* 1972, *25,* 391–412.

**Fiedler, F. E.** Predicting the effects of leadership training and experience from the contingency model. *J. appl. Psychol.,* 1972a, *56,* 114–119.

**Fiedler, F. E.** The effects of leadership training and experience: a contingency model interpretation. *Admin. sci. Quar.,* 1972b, *17,* 453–470.

**Fiedler, F. E.** The contingency model—a reply to Ashour. *Org. behav. hum. Perform.,* 1973, *9,* 356–368.

**Fiedler, F. E.** The contingency model—new directions for leadership utilization. *J. contemp. Bus.,* 1974, *3,* 65–79.

**Fiedler, F. E.** What triggers the person-situation interaction in leadership. In D. Magnusson &

N. S. Endler (Eds.), *Personality at the crossroads: current issues in interactional psychology*. Hillsdale, N.J.: Erlbaum, 1977a.

**Fiedler, F. E.** A rejoinder to Schriesheim and Kerr's premature obituary of the contingency model. In J. G. Hunt & L. L. Larson (Eds.), *Leadership: the cutting edge*. Carbondale: Southern Illinois University Press, 1977b.

**Fiedler, F. E.** Situational control and dynamic theory of leadership. In B. King, F. E. Fiedler, and S. Streufert (Eds.), *Managerial control and organizational democracy*. Washington, D.C.: W. H. Winston & Sons, 1977c.

**Fiedler, F. E.** The contingency model and the dynamics of the leadership process. In L. Berkowitz (Ed.), *Advances in experimental social psychology*, vol. 11. New York: Academic Press, 1978.

**Fiedler, F. E., Bons, P. M., & Hastings, L.** The utilization of leadership resources. In W. T. Singleton & P. Spurgeon (Eds.), *Measurement of human resources*. London: Taylor & Francis, 1975.

**Fiedler, F. E., & Chemers, M. M.** *Leadership and effective management*. Glenview, Ill.: Scott, Foresman, 1974.

**Fiedler, F. E., Chemers, M. M., & Mahar, L.** *Improving leadership effectiveness: the LEADER MATCH concept*. New York: Wiley, 1976.

**Fiedler, F. E., Fiedler, J., & Camp, S.** Who speaks for the community? *J. appl. soc. Psychol.*, 1971, *1*, 324–333.

**Fiedler, F. E., Hartmann, W., & Rudin, S. A.** The relationship of interpersonal perception to effectiveness in basketball teams. Urbana: University of Illinois, Bur. Res. Serv., Technical Report No. 3, 1953.

**Fiedler, F. E., & Hoffman, E. L.** Age, sex, and religious background as determinants of interpersonal perception among Dutch children: a cross-cultural validation. *Acta Psychol.*, 1962, *20*, 185–195.

**Fiedler, F. E., & Leister, A. F.** Intelligence and group performance: a multiple screen model. *Org. behav. hum. Perform.*, 1977a, *20*, 1–14.

**Fiedler, F. E., & Leister, A. F.** Leader intelligence and task performance: a test of a multiple screen model. *Org. behav. hum. Perform.*, 1977b, *20*, 11–14.

**Fiedler, F. E., & Mahar, L.** A field experiment validating contingency model leadership training. *J. appl. Psychol.*, 1979a, *64*, 247–254.

**Fiedler, F. E., & Mahar, L.** The effectiveness of contingency model training: validation of LEADER MATCH. *Personnel Psychol.*, 1979b, *32*, 45–62.

**Fiedler, F. E., Mahar, L., & Schmidt, D.** *Four validation studies of contingency model training*. Seattle: University of Washington, Organizational Research, Technical Report 75-70, 1976.

**Fiedler, F. E., & Meuwese, W. A. T.** Leaders' contribution to task performance in cohesive and uncohesive groups. *J. abnorm. soc. Psychol.*, 1963, *67*, 83–87.

**Fiedler, F. E., Meuwese, W. A. T., & Oonk, S.** An exploratory study of group creativity in laboratory tasks. *Acta Psychol.*, 1961, *18*, 100–119.

**Fiedler, F. E., & Nealey, S. M.** *Second-level management*. Washington, D.C.: U.S. Civil Service Commission, 1966.

**Fiedler, F. E., O'Brien, G. E., & Ilgen, D. R.** The effect of leadership style upon the performance and adjustment of volunteer teams operating in successful foreign environment. *Hum. Relat.*, 1969, *22*, 503–514.

**Fiedler, F. E., Potter, E. H., III, Zais, M. M., & Knowlton, W. A., Jr.** Organizational stress and the use and misuse of managerial intelligence and experience. *J. appl. Psychol.*, 1979, *64*, 635–647.

**Fiedler, F. E., Warrington, W. G., & Blaisdell, F. J.** Unconscious attitudes as correlates of sociometric choice in social groups. *J. abnorm. soc. Psychol.*, 1952, *47*, 790–796.

**Field, R. H. G.** A critique of the Vroom-Yetton contingency model of leadership behavior. *Acad. Mgmt. Rev.*, 1979, *4*, 249–257.

**File, Q. W.** The measurement of supervisory quality in industry. *J. appl. Psychol.*, 1945, *29*, 323–337.

**File, Q. W., & Remmers, H. H.** How supervise? *The psychological corporation test catalog.* New York: Psychological Corporation, 1971.

**Filella, J. F.** Exercise life goals: guess work or interpersonal perception? Rochester: University of Rochester, Management Research Center, Technical Report No. 40, 1971.

**Filley, A. C.** *Interpersonal conflict resolution.* Glenview, Ill.: Scott, Foresman, 1975.

**Filley, A. C., & Grimes, A. J.** The bases of power in decision processes. *Proc. Acad. Mgmt.*, 1967.

**Filley, A. C., House, R. J., & Kerr, S.** *Managerial process and organizational behavior.* Glenview, Ill.: Scott, Foresman, 1976.

**Filley, A. C., & Jesse, F. C.** Training leadership style: a survey of research. *Personnel Admin.*, 1965, *28*, 14–21.

**Finch, F. H., & Carroll, H. A.** Gifted children as high school leaders. *Ped. Sem.*, 1932, *41*, 476–481.

**Fine, B. D.** Comparison of work groups with stable and unstable membership. *Exp. publ. System, Amer. Psychol. Assn.*, 1970, *9*, No. 333–1.

**Fine, S. A.** A functional approach to a broad scale map of work behavior. *Proceedings of the 71st Annual Convention of the American Psychological Association*, 1963.

**Finn, D.** *The corporate oligarch.* New York: Simon & Schuster, 1969.

**Firestone, I. J., Lichtman, C. M., & Colamosca, J. V.** Leader effectiveness and leadership conferral as determinants of helping in a medical emergency. *J. pers. soc. Psychol.*, 1975, *31*, 243–248.

**Fischer, P. H.** An analysis of the primary group. *Sociometry*, 1953, *16*, 272–276.

**Fishbein, M., Landy, E., & Hatch, G.** Some determinants of an individual's esteem for the least preferred co-worker: an attitudinal analysis. *Hum. Relat.*, 1969, *22*, 173–188.

**Fishbein, M., Landy, E., & Hatch, G.** A consideration of two assumptions underlying Fiedler's contingency model for prediction of leadership effectiveness. *Amer. J. Psychol.*, 1969, *82*, 457–473.

**Fisher, C. D.** Transmission of positive and negative feedback to subordinates: a laboratory investigation. *J. appl. Psychol.*, 1979, *64*, 533–540.

**Fisher, S., & Rubinstein, I.** The effects of moderate sleep deprivation on social influence in the autocratic situation. *Amer. Psychologist*, 1956, *11*, 411.

**Fishman, L.** Limitations of the business executive as government administrators. *J. Bus.*, 1952, *25*, 89–94.

**Fisk, G.** *The frontiers of management psychology.* New York: Harper, 1964.

**Fiske, D. W.** Two worlds of psychological phenomena. *Amer. Psychol.*, 1979, *34*, 733–739.

**Fiske, D. W., & Cox, J. A., Jr.** The consistency of ratings by peers. *J. appl. Psychol.*, 1960, *44*, 11–17.

**Fiske, D. W., & Maddi, S. R.** *Functions of varied experience.* Homewood, Ill.: Dorsey, 1961.

**Fitzsimmons, S. J., & Marcuse, F. L.** Adjustment in leaders and non-leaders as measured by the sentence completion projective technique. *J. clin. Psychol.*, 1961, *17*, 380–381.

**Flament, C.** Changements de roles et adaptation à la tache dans des groupes de travail utilisant divers réseaux de communications. *Année Psychol.*, 1956, *56*, 411–431.

**Flanagan, J. C.** Critical requirements: a new approach to employee evaluation. *Personnel Psychol.*, 1949, *2*, 419–425.

**Flanagan, J. C.** Defining the requirements of the executive's job. *Personnel*, 1951, *28*, 28–35.

**Flanagan, J. C.** The critical incident technique. *Psychol. Bull.,* 1954, 51, 327–358.

**Flanagan, J. C.** Leadership skills: their identification, development, and evaluation. In L. Petrullo & B. M. Bass (Eds.), *Leadership and interpersonal behavior.* New York: Holt, Rinehart & Winston, 1961.

**Flanagan, J. C.** *et al. Development of an objective form of the leaders reaction test.* Pittsburgh: American Institute for Research, 1952.

**Flaugher, R. L., Campbell, J. T., & Pike, L. W.** Ethnic group membership as a moderator of supervisor's ratings. *ETS Bulletin PR–69–5.* Princeton, N.J.: Educational Testing Service, 1969.

**Fleishman, E. A.** Leadership climate and supervisory behavior. Doctoral dissertation, Ohio State University, Columbus, 1951.

**Fleishman, E. A.** The measurement of leadership attitudes in industry. *J. appl. Psychol.,* 1953a, 37, 153–158.

**Fleishman, E. A.** Leadership climate, human relations training, and supervisory behavior. *Personnel Psychol.,* 1953b, 6, 205–222.

**Fleishman, E. A.** The description of supervisory behavior. *J. appl. Psychol.,* 1953c, 37, 1–6.

**Fleishman, E. A.** Differences between military and industrial organizations. In R. M. Stogdill & C. L. Shartle (Eds.), *Patterns of administrative performance.* Columbus: Ohio State University, Bureau of Business Research, 1956.

**Fleishman, E. A.** A leader behavior description for industry. In R. M. Stogdill & A. E. Coons (Eds.), *Leader behavior: its description and measurement.* Columbus: Ohio State University, Bureau of Business Research, 1957a.

**Fleishman, E. A.** The leadership opinion questionnaire. In R. M. Stogdill & A. E. Coons (Eds.), *Leader behavior: its description and measurement.* Columbus: Ohio State University, Bureau of Business Research, 1957b.

**Fleishman, E. A.** *Manual for the supervisory behavior description questionnaire.* Washington, D.C.: American Institutes for Research, 1972.

**Fleishman, E. A.** Twenty years of consideration and structure. In E. A. Fleishman & J. G. Hunt (Eds.), *Current developments in the study of leadership.* Carbondale: Southern Illinois University Press, 1973.

**Fleishman, E. A., & Harris, E. F.** Patterns of leadership behavior related to employee grievances and turnover. *Personnel Psychol.,* 1962, 15, 43–56.

**Fleishman, E. A., Harris, E. F., & Burtt, H. E.** *Leadership and supervision in industry.* Columbus: Ohio State University, Bureau of Educational Research, 1955.

**Fleishman, E. A., & Peters, D. R.** Interpersonal values, leadership attitudes, and managerial "success." *Personnel Psychol.,* 1962, 15, 127–143.

**Fleishman, E. A., & Salter, J. A.** Humanizing relationships in a small business. *Advan. Mgmt.,* 1961, 26, 18–20.

**Fleishman, E. A., & Salter, J. A.** Relation between the leader's behavior and his empathy toward subordinates. *J. indus. Psychol.,* 1963, 1, 79–84.

**Fleishman, E. A., & Simmons, J.** Relationship between leadership patterns and effectiveness ratings among Israeli foremen. *Personnel Psychol.,* 1970, 23, 169–172.

**Flint, A. W., Bass, B. M., & Pryer, M. W.** Esteem and successful leadership. Baton Rouge: Louisiana State University, Technical Report No. 11, 1957a.

**Flint, A. W., Bass, B. M., & Pryer, M. W.** *Esteem, status, motivation, and attraction to the group.* Technical Report No. 9. Baton Rouge: Louisiana State University, 1957b.

**Flocco, E. C.** An examination of the leader behavior of school business administrators. *Dissertation Abstr. Internat.,* 1969, 30, 84–85.

**Flowers, M. L.** Laboratory study of some implications of Janis' groupthink hypothesis. *Dissertation Abstr. Internat.,* 1976, 36, 4197.

**Flyer, E. S., Barron, E., & Bigbee, L.** Discrepancies between self-descriptions and group ratings as measures of lack of insight. *USAF Hum. Resour. Res. Cent. res. Bull.,* 1953, No. 53–55.

**Foa, U. G.** A test of the foreman-worker relationship. *Personnel Psychol.,* 1956, *9,* 469–486.

**Foa, U. G.** Relation of worker's expectation to satisfaction with supervisor. *Personnel Psychol.,* 1957, *10,* 161–168.

**Foa, U. G.** Some correlates of the empathy of the workers with the foreman. *J. appl. Psychol.,* 1960, *44,* 6–10.

**Foa, U. G., Mitchell, T. R., & Fiedler, F. E.** Differential matching. Seattle: University of Washington, Department of Psychology, 1970. Also: *Behav. Sci.,* 1971, *16,* 130–142.

**Fodor, E. M.** Group stress, ingratiation, and the use of power. *J. soc. Psychol.,* 1973, *91,* 345–346.

**Fodor, E. M.** Disparagement by a subordinate as an influence on the use of power. *J. appl. Psychol.,* 1974, *59,* 652–655.

**Fodor, E. M.** Group stress, authoritarian style of control, and use of power. *J. appl. Psychol.,* 1976, *61,* 313–318.

**Fodor, E. M.** Simulated work climate as an influence on choice of leadership style. *Pers. soc. psychol. Bull.,* 1978, *4,* 111–114.

**Fogarty, M. P.** *Personality and group relations in industry.* New York: Longmans Green, 1956.

**Foote, A. E.** Managerial style, hierarchical control, and decision making in public television stations. Doctoral dissertation, Ohio State University, Columbus, 1970.

**Ford, B. L., & McCaffrey, A.** An exploratory investigation of "power" among nursery-school children by the method of resource process analysis. *Cornell J. soc. Relat.,* 1966, *1,* 33–43.

**Forehand, G. A., & Guetzkow, H.** The administrative judgment test as related to descriptions of executive judgment behaviors. *J. appl. Psychol.,* 1961, *45,* 257–261.

**Forehand, G. A., & Gilmer, B. vH.** Environmental variation in studies of organizational behavior. *Psych. Bull.,* 1964, *62,* 361–382.

**Forlano, G., & Watson, G.** Relation between success in military training and intelligence, extroversion, and adequacy. *J. soc. Psychol.,* 1937, *8,* 243–249.

**Form, W. H.** Status stratification in a planned community. *Amer. sociol. Rev.,* 1945, *10,* 605–613.

**Form, W. H., & Form, A. L.** Unanticipated results of a foreman training program. *Personnel J.,* 1953, *32,* 207–212.

**Form, W. H., & Sauer, W. L.** Labor and community influentials: a comparative study of participation and imagery. *Indus. labor relat. Rev.,* 1963, *17,* 3–19.

*Fortune.* The management poll. *Fortune,* 1946, *34*(4), 5–6.

*Fortune.* A special issue on American youth. January 1969, 66–148.

**Foster, J. P.** Perceptions of principals' behavior as rated by teachers, students, and principals in junior high schools in Chattanooga, Tennessee. Doctoral dissertation, Virginia Polytechnic Institute and State University, Blacksburg, 1976.

**Foster, W. T.** Education for leadership in business. *School Soc.,* 1929, *29,* 734–736.

**Foundation for Research on Human Behavior.** Leadership patterns and organizational effectiveness. Ann Arbor, Mich.: Foundation for Research on Human Behavior, 1954.

**Fouriezos, N., Hutt, M., & Guetzkow, H.** Measurement of self oriented needs in discussion groups. *J. abnorm. soc. Psychol.,* 1950, *45,* 682–690.

**Fox, A. M.** Temperament and attitude correlates of leadership behavior. *Educ. psychol. Measmt.,* 1967, *27,* 1167–1168.

**Fox, D., Lorge, I.,** *et al.* Comparison of decisions written by large and small groups. *Amer. Psychologist,* 1953, *8,* 351.

**Fox, H., Walton, S. D., Kirchner, W. K., & Mahoney, T. A.** *Leadership and executive development: a bibliography.* Minneapolis: University of Minnesota Press, 1954.

**Fox, T. G.** The influence of manifest and latent social identities on medical school faculty attitudes. Doctoral dissertation, University of Michigan, Ann Arbor, 1973.

**Fox, V.** A study of the promotion of enlisted men in the army. *J. appl. Psychol.,* 1947, *31,* 298–305.

**Fox, W. M.** An experimental study of group reaction to two types of conference leadership. Doctoral dissertation, Ohio State University, Columbus, 1954.

**Fox, W. M.** Group reaction to two types of conference leadership. *Hum. Relat.,* 1957, *10,* 279–289.

**Fox, W. M.** Least preferred coworker scales: research and development. Gainesville: University of Florida, Technical Report No. 70–5, 1974.

**Fox, W. M., Hill, W. A., & Guertin, W. N.** Dimensional analyses of least preferred co-worker scales. *J. appl. Psychol.,* 1973, *57,* 192–194.

**Frank, E. J.** Cognitive complexity and leadership: the effect of perceptual sensitivity on leadership success. Doctoral dissertation, Purdue University, Lafayette, Ind., 1973.

**Frank, H. H., & Katcher, A. H.** The qualities of leadership: how male medical students evaluate their female peers. *Hum. Relat.,* 1977, *30,* 403–416.

**Frank, L. K.** Dilemma of leadership. *Psychiatry,* 1939, *2,* 343–361.

**Frank, R. S.** The relationship between dogmatism, preference for self-actualizing values, and indirect discussion leadership styles—as influenced by two group procedures. *Dissertation Abstr. Internat.,* 1971, *32,* 3025.

**Frankfort, H., Frankfort, H. A., Wilson, J. A., & Jacobsen, T.** *Before philosophy.* Baltimore: Penguin Books, 1949.

**Franklin, A. J.** The relationship between leadership training in group dynamics and the development of groups among disadvantaged youth. *Dissertation Abstr.,* 1969, *29,* 2090–2091.

**Franklin, J. L.** Relations among four social-psychological aspects of organizations. *Admin. sci. Quar.,* 1975, *20,* 422–433.

**Frantzve, J.** The influence of gender composition of leaderless group discussions on ratings of effectiveness. Doctoral dissertation, University of Georgia, Athens, 1979.

**Frazier, E. F.** "Society": status without substance. In R. J. Murphy & H. Elinson (Eds.), *Problems and prospects of the Negro movement.* Belmont, Calif.: Wadsworth, 1966.

**Frederiksen, N.** In-basket tests and factors in administrative performance. In H. Guetzkow (Ed.), *Simulation in social science: readings.* Englewood Cliffs, N.J.: Prentice-Hall, 1962.

**Frederiksen, N.** Factors in in-basket performance. *Psychol. Monogr.,* 1962, *76,* No. 541.

**Freeman, G. L., & Taylor, E. K.** *How to pick leaders.* New York: Funk & Wagnalls, 1950.

**Freeman, L. C., Fararo, T. J., Bloomberg, W., & Sunshine, M. H.** Locating leaders in local communities: a comparison of some alternative approaches. *Amer. sociol. Rev.,* 1963, *28,* 791–798.

**French, E. B., & Magee, J. J.** The incidence of the emotionally disturbed within the administrative units of a large organization. *Personnel Psychol.,* 1972, *3,* 535–543.

**French, E. G.** Motivation as a variable in work-partner selection. *J. abnorm. soc. Psychol.,* 1956, *53,* 96–99.

**French, J. R. P.** The disruption and cohesion of groups. *J. abnorm. soc. Psychol.,* 1941, *36,* 361–377.

**French, J. R. P.** Organized and unorganized groups under fear and frustration. *University Iowa, Stud. Child Welf.,* 1944a, *20,* 231–308.

**French, J. R. P.** Retraining an autocratic leader. *J. abnorm. soc. Psychol.,* 1944b, *39,* 224–237.

**French, J. R. P.** Field experiments: changing group productivity. In J. G. Miller. *Experiments in social process.* New York: McGraw-Hill, 1950.

**French, J. R. P.** A formal theory of social power. *Psychol. Rev.*, 1956, *63*, 181–194.

**French, J. R. P., Jr.** An experimental study of resistance to influence. In *Annual Report*. Ann Arbor: University of Michigan, Research Center Group, 1957.

**French, J. R. P., Israel, J., & Ås, D.** An experiment on participation in a Norwegian factory. *Hum. Relat.*, 1960, *13*, 3–19.

**French, J. R. P., Kay, E., & Meyer, H. H.** Participation and the appraisal system. *Hum. Relat.*, 1966, *19*, 3–20.

**French, J. R. P., Morrison, W., & Levinger, G.** Coercive power and forces affecting conformity. *J. abnorm. soc. Psychol.*, 1960, *61*, 93–101.

**French, J. R. P., & Raven, B.** The bases of social power. In D. Cartwright (Ed.), *Studies in social power*. Ann Arbor: University of Michigan, Institute for Social Research, 1959.

**French, J. R. P., Sherwood, J. J., & Bradford, D. L.** Change in self-identity in a management training conference. *J. appl. behav. Sci.*, 1966, *2*, 210–218.

**French, J. R. P., & Snyder, R.** Leadership and interpersonal power. In D. Cartwright (Ed.), *Studies in social power*. Ann Arbor: University of Michigan, Institute for Social Research, 1959.

**French, J. R. P., & Zander, A.** The group dynamics approach. In A. Kornhauser (Ed.), *Psychology of labor-management relations*. Champaign, Ill.: Industrial Relations Research Association, 1949.

**French, R. L.** Morale and leadership. In *Human factors in undersea warfare*. Washington, D.C.: National Research Council, 1949.

**French, R. L.** Verbal output and leadership status in initially leaderless discussion groups. *Amer. Psychologist*, 1950, *5*, 310–311.

**French, R. L.** Sociometric status and individual adjustment among naval recruits. *J. abnorm. soc. Psychol.*, 1951, *46*, 64–72.

**French, W. L., Bell, C. H., & Zawacki, R. A. (Eds.),** *Organizational development: theory, practice and research*. Dallas: Business Publications, 1978.

**Frenkel, E.** Studies in biographical psychology. *Char. Pers.*, 1936, *5*, 1–34.

**Fretwell, E. K.** Education for leadership. *Teach. Coll. Rec.*, 1919, *20*, 324–352.

**Freud, S.** *Group psychology and the analysis of ego*. London: International Psychoanalytical Press, 1922.

**Frey, M. W.** An experimental study of the influence of disruptive interaction induced by authoritarian-equalitarian, leader-follower combinations upon the decision-making effectiveness of small groups. *Dissertation Abstr.*, 1963, *25*, 897.

**Freyer, F. W.** *An evaluation of level of aspiration as a training procedure*. Englewood Cliffs, N.J.: Prentice-Hall, 1964.

**Friedlander, F.** Underlying sources of job satisfaction. *J. appl. Psychol.*, 1963, *47*, 246–250.

**Friedlander, F.** Importance of work versus nonwork among socially and occupationally stratified groups. *J. appl. Psychol.*, 1966a, *50*, 437–441.

**Friedlander, F.** Performance and interactional dimensions of organizational work groups. *J. appl. Psychol.*, 1966b, *50*, 257–265.

**Friedlander, F.** The impact of organizational training laboratories upon the effectiveness and interaction of ongoing work groups. *Personnel Psychol.*, 1967, *20*, 289–307.

**Friedlander, F., & Greenberg, S.** Effect of job attitudes, training, and organizational climate on performance of the hard-core unemployed. *J. appl. Psychol.*, 1971, *55*, 287–295.

**Friedlander, F., & Margulies, N.** Multiple impacts of organizational climate and individual value systems upon job satisfaction. *Personnel Psychol.*, 1969, *22*, 171–183.

**Friedlander, F., & Pickle, H.** Components of effectiveness in small organizations. *Admin. sci. Quar.*, 1968, *13*, 289–304.

**Friedman, G.** *The anatomy of work*. New York: Free Press, 1961.

**Friedman, S. T.** Relation of parental attitudes toward child rearing and patterns of social behavior in middle childhood. *Psychol. Rep.*, 1969, *24*, 575–579.

**Fromm, E.** *Escape from freedom.* New York: Farrar & Rinehart, 1941.

**Fruchter, B., & Skinner, J. A.** Dimensions of leadership in a student cooperative. *Multivariate beh. Res.*, 1966, *1*, 437–445.

**Frye, R. L., & Spruill, J.** Type of orientation and task completion of elementary-grade students. *J. genet. Psychol.*, 1965, *106*, 45–49.

**Fujii, D. S.** A dyadic, interactive approach to the study of leader behaviors. *Dissertation Abstr. Internat.*, 1977, *37*, 5415–5416.

**Fultiner, J. D.** School principals look at leader behavior: the problem of interpersonal needs. *Dissertation Abstr. Internat.*, 1972, *32*, 6036.

**Gage, N. L., & Exline, R. V.** Social perception and effectiveness in discussion groups. *Hum. Relat.*, 1953, *6*, 381–396.

**Gallino, L.** Three types of Italian top managers. *Internat. stud. mgmt. Org.*, 1975, *5*, 43–70.

**Gallo, P. S., & McClintock, C. G.** Behavioral, attitudinal, and perceptual differences between leaders and non-leaders in situations of group support and non-support. *J. soc. Psychol.*, 1962, *56*, 121–133.

**Galton, F.** *Hereditary genius.* New York: Appleton, 1869.

**Galton, F.** *English men of science: their nature and nurture.* New York: Appleton, Century, 1890.

**Gamson, W. A.** Experimental studies of coalition formation. In L. Berkowitz (Ed.), *Advances in experimental social psychology.* New York: Academic Press, 1965.

**Gamson, W. A.** *Power and discontent.* Homewood, Ill.: Dorsey, 1968.

**Gamson, W. A., & Scotch, N.** Scapegoating in baseball. *Amer. J. Sociol.*, 1964, *70*, 69–70.

**Gantt, H. L.** *Industrial leadership.* New Haven, Conn.: Yale University Press, 1916.

**Gantz, B. S., Erickson, C. O., & Stephenson, R. W.** Measuring the motivation to manage in a research and development population. In J. B. Miner (Ed.), *Motivation to manage.* Atlanta: Organizational Measurement Systems Press, 1977a.

**Gantz, B. S., Erickson, C. O., & Stephenson, R. W.** Some determinants of promotion in a research and development population. In J. B. Miner (Ed.), *Motivation to manage.* Atlanta: Organizational Measurement Systems Press, 1977b.

**GAP (Group for the Advancement of Psychiatry).** Problems of psychiatric leadership. *GAP Report,* 1974, *8*, 925–946.

**Garbin, A. P., & Bates, F. L.** Occupational prestige and its correlates: a re-examination. *Soc. Forces,* 1966, *44*, 295–302.

**Gardner, B. B., & Whyte, W. F.** The man in the middle. *Appl. Anthropol.*, 1945, *4*, 1–28.

**Gardner, C. A., Jr.** Faculty participation in departmental administrative activities. Doctoral dissertation, University of Michigan, Ann Arbor, 1971.

**Gardner, E. F., & Thompson, G. G.** *Social relations and morale in small groups.* New York: Appleton-Century-Crofts, 1956.

**Gardner, G.** Functional leadership and popularity in small groups. *Hum. Relat.*, 1956, *9*, 491–509.

**Gardner, J. W.** *Self-renewal,* New York: Harper & Row, 1965.

**Gardner, N. D.** *Group leadership.* Washington, D.C.: National Training and Development Service Press, 1974.

**Garland, H., & Price, K. H.** Attitudes toward women in management and attributions for their success and failure in managerial position. *J. appl. Psychol.*, 1977, *62*, 29–33.

**Garrison, K. C.** A study of some factors related to leadership in high school. *Peabody J. Educ.*, 1933, *11*, 11–17.

**Gartner, D., & Iverson, M. A.** Some effects of upward mobile status in established and ad hoc

**Gassner, S. M., Gold, J., & Snadowsky, A. M.** Changes in the phenomenal field as a result of human relations training. *J. Psychol.*, 1964, *58*, 33–41.

**Gates, T. J.** Change in selected personality variables of high ranking federal executives during a residential executive training program. *Dissertation Abstr. Internat.*, 1972, *32*, 6196.

**Gatzke, H. W.** Hitler and psychohistory. *Amer. his. Rev.*, 1973, *78*, 394–401.

**Gaudreau, P. A.** Investigation of sex differences across job levels. *Dissertation Abstr. Internat.*, 1975, *36*, 1957B.

**Gauthier, W. J., Jr.** The relationship of organizational structure, leader behavior of the principal and personality orientation of the principal to school management climate. Doctoral dissertation, University of Connecticut, Storrs, 1975.

**Gebel, A. S.** Self-perception and leaderless group discussion status. *J. soc. Psychol.*, 1954, *40*, 309–318.

**Gehrman, G. H.** An investigation of the relationship between participation and organizational climate: an empirical study of the perceptions of high school senior students, teachers, principals and district superintendents in innovative vs. noninnovative schools. Doctoral dissertation, University of Massachusetts, Amherst, 1970.

**Geier, J. G.** A descriptive analysis of an interaction pattern resulting in leadership emergence in leaderless group discussion. *Dissertation Abstr.*, 1963, *26*, 2919–2920.

**Geier, J. G.** A trait approach to the study of leadership in small groups. *J. Communicat.*, 1967, *17*, 316–323.

**Gekoski, N.** Predicting group productivity. *Personnel Psychol.*, 1952, *5*, 281–291.

**Gellerman, S. W.** Passivity, paranoia, and "pakikisama." *Columbia J. world Bus.*, 1967, *2*, 59–66.

**Gellert, E.** Stability and fluctuation in the power relationships of young children. *J. abnorm. soc. Psychol.*, 1961, *62*, 8–15.

**Gemmill, G. R., & Heisler, W. J.** Fatalism as a factor in managerial job satisfaction, job strain, and mobility. *Personnel Psychol.*, 1972, *25*, 241–250.

**George, E. I., & Abraham, P. A.** A comparative study of leaders and non-leaders among pupils in secondary schools. *J. psychol. Researches*, 1966, *10*, 116–120.

**George, J. R., & Bishop, L. K.** Relationship of organizational structure and teacher personality characteristics to organizational climate. *Admin. sci. Quar.*, 1971, *16*, 467–475.

**George, N.** *Supervisor's thinking on current issues.* Dayton, Ohio: National Management Association, 1958.

**George, W. L.** Mastery of men. *Harpers*, 1922, *144*, 657–665.

**Georgi, C.** *The literature of executive management.* New York: Special Libraries Association, 1963.

**Georgopoulos, B. S.** Normative structure variables and organizational behavior. *Hum. Relat.*, 1965, *18*, 155–169.

**Georgopoulos, B. S., Mahoney, G. M., & Jones, N. W.** A path-goal approach to productivity. *J. appl. Psychol.*, 1957, *41*, 345–353.

**Georgopoulos, B. S., & Tannenbaum, A. S.** A study of organization effectiveness. *Amer. sociol. Rev.*, 1957, *22*, 534–540.

**Gerard, H. B.** The effect of different dimensions of disagreement on the communication process in small groups. *Hum. Relat.*, 1953, *6*, 249–271.

**Gerard, H. B.** The anchorage of opinions in face-to-face groups. *Hum. Relat.*, 1954, *7*, 313–325.

**Gerard, H. B.** Some effects of status, role clarity, and group goal clarity upon the individual's relations to group progress. *J. Pers.*, 1957, *25*, 475–488.

**Gergen, K. J.** *The psychology of behavior exchange.* Reading, Mass.: Addison-Wesley, 1969.

**Gergen, K. J., & Taylor, M. G.** Social expectancy and self-presentation in a status hierarchy. *J. exp. soc. Psychol.*, 1969, *5*, 79–92.

**Gerth, H., & Mills, C. W.** A sociological note on leadership. In J. E. Hulett & R. Stagner (Eds.), *Problems in social psychology*. Urbana: University of Illinois Press, 1952.

**Gerth, H., & Mills, C. W.** *Character and social structure*. New York: Harcourt, Brace, 1953.

**Gesell, A. L., & Thompson, H.** *Infant behavior: its genesis and growth*. New York: McGraw-Hill, 1934.

**Getzels, J. W.** Conflict and role behavior in an educational setting. In W. W. Charters & N. L. Gage (Eds.), *Readings in the social psychology of education*. Boston: Allyn & Bacon, 1963.

**Getzels, J. W., & Guba, E. G.** Role, role conflict, and effectiveness: an empirical study. *Amer. sociol. Rev.*, 1954, *19*, 164–175.

**Getzels, J. W., & Guba, E. G.** Social behavior and the administrative process. *School Rev.*, 1957, *55*, 423–441.

**Ghiselli, E. E.** Traits differentiating management personnel. *Personnel Psychol.*, 1959, *12*, 535–544.

**Ghiselli, E. E.** Individuality as a factor in the success of management personnel. *Personnel Psychol.*, 1960, *13*, 1–10.

**Ghiselli, E. E.** The validity of management traits in relation to occupational level. *Personnel Psychol.*, 1963a, *16*, 109–113.

**Ghiselli, E. E.** Intelligence and managerial success. *Psychol. Rep.*, 1963b, *12*, 898.

**Ghiselli, E. E.** Maturity of self-perception in relation to managerial success. *Personnel Psychol.*, 1964, *17*, 41–48.

**Ghiselli, E. E.** Psychological properties of groups and group learning. *Psychol. Rep.*, 1966a, *19*, 17–18.

**Ghiselli, E. E.** *The validity of occupational aptitude tests*. New York: Wiley, 1966b.

**Ghiselli, E. E.** Interaction of traits and motivational factors in the determination of the success of managers. *J. appl. Psychol.*, 1968a, *52*, 480–483.

**Ghiselli, E. E.** Some motivational factors in the success of managers. *Personnel Psychol.*, 1968b, *21*, 431–440.

**Ghiselli, E. E.** *Explorations in managerial talent*. Pacific Palisades, Calif.: Goodyear, 1971.

**Ghiselli, E. E., & Barthol, R. P.** The validity of personality inventories in the selection of employees. *J. appl. Psychol.*, 1953, *37*, 18–20.

**Ghiselli, E. E., & Barthol, R. P.** Role perceptions of successful and unsuccessful superiors. *J. appl. Psychol.*, 1956, *40*, 241–244.

**Ghiselli, E. E., & Johnson, D. A.** Need satisfaction, managerial success, and organizational structure. *Personnel Psychol.*, 1970, *23*, 569–576.

**Ghiselli, E. E., & Lodahl, T. M.** The evaluation of foremen's performance in relation to the internal characteristics of their groups. *Personnel Psychol.*, 1958a, *11*, 179–187.

**Ghiselli, E. E., & Lodahl, T. M.** Patterns of managerial traits and group effectiveness. *J. abnorm. soc. Psychol.*, 1958b, *57*, 61–66.

**Ghiselli, E. E., & Siegel, J. P.** Leadership and managerial success in tall and flat organization structures. *Personnel Psychol.*, 1972, *25*, 617–624.

**Ghiselli, E. E., & Wyatt, T. A.** Need satisfaction, managerial success, and attitudes toward leadership. *Personnel Psychol.*, 1972, *3*, 413–420.

**Gibb, C. A.** The principles and traits of leadership. *J. abnorm. soc. Psychol.*, 1947, *42*, 267–284.

**Gibb, C. A.** Some tentative comments concerning group Rorschach pointers to the personality traits of leaders. *J. soc. Psychol.*, 1949, *30*, 251–263.

**Gibb, C. A.** The sociometry of leadership in temporary groups. *Sociometry*, 1950, *13*, 226–243.

**Gibb, C. A.** An experimental approach to the study of leadership. *Occup. Psychol.*, 1951, *25*, 233–248.

**Gibb, C. A.** Leadership. In G. Lindzey (Ed.), *Handbook of social psychology.* Cambridge, Mass.: Addison-Wesley, 1954.

**Gibb, C. A.** Leadership. In G. Lindzey & E. Aronson (Eds.), *The handbook of social psychology,* 2nd ed., vol. 4. Reading, Mass.: Addison-Wesley, 1969a.

**Gibb, C. A.** *Leadership: selected readings.* Baltimore: Penguin Books, 1969b.

**Gibb, C. A.** Leadership. Unpublished ms., undated.

**Gibb, J. R.** Factors producing defensive behavior within groups. Boulder: University of Colorado, Human Relations Lab, Annual Technical Report, 1954.

**Gibb, J. R.** Defense level and influence potential in small groups. In L. Petrullo & B. M. Bass (Eds.), *Leadership and interpersonal behavior.* New York: Holt, Rinehart & Winston, 1961.

**Gibb, J. R.** The T-group as a climate for trust formation. In L. P. Bradford, J. R. Gibb, & K. D. Benne (Eds.), *T-group theory and laboratory methods: innovation in re-education.* New York: Wiley, 1964.

**Gibb, J. R., Platts, G. N., & Miller, L. F.** *Dynamics of participative groups.* St. Louis: John S. Swift, 1951.

**Gibbard, G. S., Hartman, J. J., & Mann, R. D.** *Analysis of groups: contribution to the theory, research, and practice.* San Francisco: Jossey-Bass, 1974.

**Gibson, A. K.** The achievement of sixth grade students in a mid-western city. Doctoral dissertation, University of Michigan, Ann Arbor, 1974.

**Gibson, J. L., Ivancevich, J. M., & Donnelly, J. H., Jr.** *Organizations: structure, processes, behavior.* Dallas, Tex.: Business Publications, Inc., 1973.

**Gide, C.** *Communist and cooperative colonies.* New York: Crowell, 1930.

**Giffin, K., & Ehrlich, L.** The attitudinal effects of a group discussion on a proposed change in company policy. *Speech Monogr.,* 1963, *30,* 377–379.

**Gilbert, E. M.** Teaching styles prevalent in satisfying and dissatisfying college credit courses as perceived by adult students. Doctoral dissertation, Ohio State University, Columbus, 1972.

**Gilchrist, J. C.** The formation of social groups under conditions of success and failure. *J. abnorm. soc. Psychol.,* 1952, *47,* 174–187.

**Gilchrist, J. C., Shaw, M. E., & Walker, L. C.** Some effects of unequal distribution of information in a wheel group structure. *J. abnorm. soc. Psychol.,* 1954, *49,* 554–556.

**Gilman, G.** An inquiry into the nature and use of authority. In M. Haire (Ed.), *Organization theory in industrial practice.* New York: Wiley, 1962.

**Gilmore, D. C., Beehr, T. A., & Richter, D. J.** Effects of leader behaviors on subordinate performance and satisfaction: a laboratory experiment with student employees. *J. appl. Psychol.,* 1979, *64,* 166–172.

**Ginsburg, L. R.** Small group performance: the effects of the interaction of leader and member orientation on the effectiveness and attractiveness of small groups. *Dissertation Abstr. Internat.,* 1971, *32,* 3682.

**Gintner, G., & Lindskold, S.** Rate of participation and expertise as factors influencing leader choice. *J. pers. soc. Psychol.* 1975, *32,* 1085–1089.

**Ginzberg, E., & Reilley, E. W.** *Effecting change in large organizations.* New York: Columbia University Press, 1957.

**Gitter, A. G., Black, H., & Fishman, J. E.** Effect of race, sex, nonverbal communication and verbal communication on perception of leadership. *Sociol. soc. Res.,* 1975, *60,* 46–57.

**Gitter, A. G., Black, H., & Goldman, A.** Role of nonverbal communication in the perception of leadership. *Percept. mot. Skills,* 1975, *40,* 463–466.

**Gitter, A. G., Satow, Y., & Goldman, A.** Leadership: non-verbal communication and mode of presentation of stimuli. *CRC Report,* No. 25, Boston University, 1968.

**Gitter, A. G., & Walkley, J.** Nonverbal communication: leader–follower perception and mode of presentation. *CRC Report,* No. 21, Boston University, 1968.

**Given, W. B.** *Bottom-up management: people working together.* New York: Harper, 1949.

**Glanzer, M.** Curiosity, exploratory drive, and stimulus satiation. *Psych. Bull.,* 1958, *55,* 302–315.

**Glanzer, M., & Glaser, R.** Techniques for the study of group structure. II. Empirical studies of the effects of structure in small groups. *Psychol. Bull.,* 1961, *58,* 1–27.

**Glaser, B. G., & Strauss, A. L.** *The discovery of grounded theory.* Chicago: Aldine, 1967.

**Glaser, R., Schwartz, P. A., & Flanagan, J. C.** The contribution of interview and situational performance procedures to the selection of supervisory personnel. *J. appl. Psychol.,* 1958, *42,* 69–73.

**Gleason, W. J.** Predicting army leadership ability by modified leaderless group discussion. *J. appl. Psychol.,* 1957, *41,* 231–235.

**Glickman, A. S., Hahn, C. P., Fleishman, E. A., & Baxter, B.** *Top management development and succession: an exploratory study.* New York: Macmillan, 1969.

**Glube, R. H., & Margerison, C. J.** Managerial leadership. *J. europ. Training,* 1976, *5,* 76–101.

**Gluskinos, U. M., & Kestleman, B.** Management and union leaders' perception of work needs as compared with self-reported needs. Proceedings of the 78th Annual Convention of the American Psychological Association, 1970, *5,* 603–604.

**Goble, F.** *Excellence in leadership.* New York: American Management Association, 1972.

**Godfrey, E. P., Fiedler, F. E., & Hall, D. M.** *Boards, management, and company success.* Danville, Ill.: Interstate, 1959.

**Goetz, T. E., & Herman, J. B.** Effects of supervisor's sex and subordinate sex on job satisfaction and productivity. Washington, D.C.: American Psychological Assn., 1976.

**Goffman, I. W.** Status consistency and preference for change in power-distribution. *Amer. sociol. Rev.,* 1957, *22,* 275–281.

**Golb, E. F., & Fiedler, F. E.** A note on psychological attributes related to the score assumed similarity between opposites (ASo). Urbana: University of Illinois, Group Effectiveness Research Laboratory, Technical Report No. 12, 1955.

**Gold, H. A.** The importance of ideology in sociometric evaluation of leadership. *Group Psychother.,* 1962, *15,* 224–230.

**Gold, R.** Janitors versus tenants: a status-income dilemma. *Amer. J. Sociol.,* 1951/52, *57,* 486–493.

**Goldberg, H., & Iverson, M. A.** Inconsistency in attitude of high status persons and loss of influence: an experimental study. *Psychol. Rep.,* 1965, *16,* 673–683.

**Goldberg, M. L.** Leadership and self-attitudes. *Dissertation Abstr.,* 1955, *15,* 1457–1458.

**Goldberg, S. C.** Three situational determinants of conformity to social norms. *J. abnorm. soc. Psychol.,* 1954, *49,* 325–329.

**Goldberg, S. C.** Influence and leadership as a function of group structure. *J. abnorm. soc. Psychol.,* 1955, *51,* 119–122.

**Golden, O.** *Executive development: a bibliographic review.* Chicago: University of Chicago, Industrial Relations Center, 1955.

**Goldfarb, W.** Characteristics of 200 active merchant marine officers. In G. G. Killinger. Psychobiological program of WSA, 1949.

**Goldman, M., & Fraas, L. A.** The effects of leader selection on group performance. *Sociometry,* 1965, *28,* 82–88.

**Goldring, P.** Role of distance and posture in the evaluation of interactions. Proceedings of the 75th Annual Convention of the American Psychological Association, 1967, *2,* 243–244.

**Goldstein, A. P., & Sorcher, M.** *Changing supervisory behavior.* New York: Pergamon Press, 1974.

**Goldstein, I. L.** Training in work organizations. *Ann. Rev. Psychol.*, 1980, *31*, 229–272.

**Golembiewski, R. T.** Three styles of leadership and their uses. *Personnel*, 1961, *38*, 34–45.

**Golembiewski, R. T.** *Organizing men and power*. Chicago: Rand McNally, 1967.

**Golembiewski, R. T., & Blumberg, A.** *Sensitivity training and the laboratory approach: reading about concepts and applications*. Itasca, Ill.: Peacock, 1970.

**Golembiewski, R. T., & Carrigan, S. B.** The persistence of laboratory-induced changes in organization styles. *Admin. sci. Quar.*, 1970, *15*, 330–340.

**Gomberg, W.** The trouble with democratic management. *Transaction*, 1966, *3*, 30–35.

**Good, L. R., & Good, K. C.** Similarity to a group and desire for leadership status. *Psychol. Rep.*, 1974, *34*, 759–762.

**Goodacre, D. M.** The use of a sociometric test as a predictor of combat unit effectiveness. *Sociometry*, 1951, *14*, 148–152.

**Goodacre, D. M.** Group characteristics of good and poor performing combat units. *Sociometry*, 1953, *16*, 168–179.

**Goodacre, D. M.** Experimental evaluation of training. *J. personnel admin. indus. Relat.*, 1955, *2*, 143–149.

**Goodacre, D. M.** Stimulating improved management. *Personnel Psychol.*, 1963, *16*, 133–143.

**Goodale, J. G.** Effects of personal background and training on work values of the hard-core unemployed. *J. appl. Psychol.*, 1973, *57*, 1–9.

**Goodale, J. G., & Hall, D. T.** Inheriting a career: the influence of sex, values, and parents. *J. vocat. Behav.*, 1976, *8*, 19–30.

**Goodall, K.** Casualty lists from group encounters. *Psychol. Today*, 1971, *5*, 28.

**Goodchilds, J. D., & Smith, E. D.** The wit and his group. *Hum. Relat.*, 1964, *17*, 23–31.

**Goode, C. E.** Significant research on leadership. *Personnel*, 1951, *27*, 342–350.

**Goode, W. J.** Norm commitment and conformity to role-status obligations. *Amer. J. Sociol.*, 1960, *66*, 246–258.

**Goode, W. J., & Fowler, I.** Incentive factors in a low morale plant. *Amer. sociol. Rev.*, 1949, *14*, 618–624.

**Goodenough, F. L.** Inter-relationships in the behavior of young children. *Child Develop.*, 1930, *1*, 29–48.

**Goodenough, F. L., & Leahy, A. M.** The effect of certain family relationships upon the development of personality. *Ped. Sem.*, 1927, *34*, 45–71.

**Goodman, P. S.** An empirical examination of Elliott Jaques' concept of time span. *Hum. Relat.*, 1967, *20*, 155–170.

**Goodman, P. S.** Hiring, training, and retaining the hard-core. *Indus. Relat.*, 1969, *9*, 54–66.

**Goodstadt, B. E., & Hjelle, L. A.** Power to the powerless: locus of control and the use of power. *J. pers. soc. Psychol.*, 1973, *27*, 190–196.

**Goodstadt, B., & Kipnis, D.** Situational influences on the use of power. *J. appl. Psychol.*, 1970, *54*, 201–207.

**Gopala, K. K. M., & Hafeez, A.** A study of supervisors' attitude towards employees and production in relation to some personal factors. *Indian J. appl. Psychol.*, 1964, *1*, 78–83.

**Gorden, R. L.** Interaction between attitude and the definitions of the situation in the expression of opinion. *Amer. sociol. Rev.*, 1952, *17*, 50–58.

**Gordner, N. D.** *Group leadership*. Washington: National Training and Development Service Press, 1974.

**Gordon, C. W., & Adler, L. McK.** *Dimensions of teacher leadership in classroom social systems: pupil effects on productivity, morale, and compliance*. Los Angeles: University of California, Department of Education, 1963.

**Gordon, F. E., & Strober, M. H.** *Bringing women into management*. New York: McGraw-Hill, 1975.

**Gordon, G., & Becker, B.** Organization size and managerial succession: a re-examination. *Amer. J. Sociol.*, 1964, *70*, 215–222.

**Gordon, G. E., & Rosen, N.** Critical factors in leadership succession. Unpublished ms., undated.

**Gordon, L. V.** Personal factors in leadership. *J. soc. Psychol.*, 1952, *36*, 245–248.

**Gordon, L. V.** *Gordon Personal Inventory: Manual.* New York: Harcourt, Brace & World, 1963a.

**Gordon, L. V.** *Gordon Personal Profile: Manual.* New York: Harcourt, Brace & World, 1963b.

**Gordon, L. V.** Work Environment Preference Schedule—WEPS. Preliminary manual, 1966 (mimeo).

**Gordon, L. V.** Measurement of bureaucratic orientation. *Personnel Psychol.*, 1970, *23*, 1–11.

**Gordon, L. V.** *Measurement of interpersonal values.* Chicago: Science Research Associates, 1975.

**Gordon, L. V., & Medland, F. F.** The cross-group stability of peer ratings of leadership potential. *Personnel Psychol.*, 1965a, *18*, 173–177.

**Gordon, L. V., & Medland, F. F.** Leadership aspiration and leadership ability. *Psychol. Rep.*, 1965b, *17*, 388–390.

**Gordon, R. A.** *Business leadership in the large corporation.* Berkeley: University of California Press, 1961.

**Gordon, T.** Leadership: shall it reside in the leader or in the group? *Amer. J. Nurs.*, 1954, *54*, 1087–1088.

**Gordon, T.** *Group-centered leadership—a way of releasing the creative power of groups.* Boston: Houghton Mifflin, 1955.

**Gordon, T.** *Leadership effectiveness training, L.E.T.: the no-lose way to release the productive potential of people.* New York: Wyden Books, 1977.

**Gorman, A. H.** *The leader in the group: a conceptual framework.* New York: Teachers College, Columbia University, Bureau of Publications, 1963.

**Gorton, R. A.** *School administration: challenge and opportunity for leadership.* Dubuque, Ia.: W. C. Brown Co., 1976.

**Gottheil, E., & Lauterbach, C. G.** Leader and squad attributes contributing to mutual esteem among squad members. *J. soc. Psychol.*, 1969, *77*, 69–78.

**Gottheil, E., & Vielhaber, D. P.** Interaction of leader and squad attributes related to performance of military squads. *J. soc. Psychol.*, 1966, *68*, 113–127.

**Gough, H. G., McClosky, H., & Meehl, P.** A personality scale for social responsibility. *J. abnorm. soc. Psychol.*, 1952, *47*, 73–80.

**Gouldner, A. W.** Attitudes of "progressive" trade-union leaders. *Amer. J. Sociol.*, 1947, *52*, 389–392.

**Gouldner, A. W.** *Studies in leadership.* New York: Harper, 1950.

**Gouldner, A. W.** *Patterns of industrial bureaucracy.* Yellow Springs, Oh.: Antioch Press, 1954.

**Gouldner, A. W.** Cosmopolitans and locals: toward an analysis of latent social roles. *Admin. sci. Quar.*, 1957, *2*, 281–306.

**Gouldner, A. W.** The norm of reciprocity: a preliminary statement. *Amer. sociol. Rev.*, 1960, *25*, 161–178.

**Gourley, H. V.** Patterns of leadership in decision-making in a selected county. *Dissertation Abstr.*, 1963, *23*, 3717.

**Govindarajan, T. N.** Vocational interests of leaders and nonleaders among adolescent school boys. *J. psychol. Res.*, 1964, *8*(3), 124–130.

**Gowin, E. B.** *The executive and his control.* New York: Macmillan, 1915.

**Gowin, E. B.** *The selection and training of the business executive.* New York: Macmillan, 1918.

**Gowin, E. B.** *Developing executive ability.* New York: Ronald Press, 1919.

**Grace, H. A.** Conformance and performance. *J. soc. Psychol.*, 1954, *40*, 333–335.

**Graen, G.** Role making processes within complex organizations. In M. D. Dunnette (Ed.), *Handbook of industrial and organizational psychology*. Chicago: Rand McNally, 1976.

**Graen, G., Alvares, K., Orris, J. B., & Martella, J. A.** Contingency model of leadership effectiveness: antecedent and evidential results. *Psychol. Bull.*, 1970, *74*, 285–296.

**Graen, G., & Cashman, J. F.** A role making model of leadership in formal organizations: a developmental approach. In J. G. Hunt & L. L. Larson (Eds.), *Leadership frontiers.* Carbondale: Southern Illinois University Press, 1975.

**Graen, G., Cashman, J. F., Ginsburgh, S., & Schiemann, W.** Effects of linking-pin quality on the quality of working life of lower participants. *Admin. sci. Quar.*, 1977, *22*, 491–504.

**Graen, G., Dansereau, F., & Minami, T.** Dysfunctional leadership styles. *Org. behav. hum. Perform.*, 1972a, *7*, 216–236.

**Graen, G., Dansereau, F., & Minami, T.** An empirical test of the man-in-the-middle hypothesis among executives in a hierarchical organization employing a unit-set analysis. *Org. behav. hum. Perform.*, 1972b, *8*, 262–285.

**Graen, G., & Ginsburgh, S.** Job resignation as a function of role orientation and leader acceptance: a longitudinal investigation of organizational assimilation. *Org. behav. hum. Perform.*, 1977, *19*, 1–17.

**Graen, G., Orris, J. B., & Alvares, K. M.** Contingency model of leadership effectiveness: some experimental results. *J. appl. Psychol.*, 1971, *55*, 196–201.

**Graen, G., & Schiemann, W.** Leader-member agreement: a vertical dyad linkage approach. *J. appl. Psychol.*, 1978, *63*, 206–212.

**Graham, G. H.** Theories X and Y in the teaching of management. *Collegiate News Views*, 1969, *22*, 15–18.

**Graham, K. R., & Richards, M. D.** Relative performance deterioration, management and strategic change in rail-based holding companies. *Proceedings of the Academy of Management*, 1979.

**Graham, W. K.** Description of leader behavior and evaluation of leaders as a function of LPC. *Personnel Psychol.*, 1968, *21*, 457–464.

**Graham, W. K.** Comparison of job attitude components across three organizational levels. *Personnel Psychol.*, 1969, *22*, 33–40.

**Graham, W. K.** Leader behavior, esteem for least preferred co-worker, and group performance. *Exp. publ. System. Amer. Psychol. Assn.*, 1970, No. 192A. Also: *J. soc. Psych.*, 1973, *90*, 59–66.

**Graham, W. K., & Calendo, J. R.** Personality correlates of supervisory ratings. *Personnel Psychol.*, 1969, *22*, 483–487.

**Graham, W. K., & Gleno, T.** Perception of leader behavior and evaluation of leaders across organizational levels. *Exp. publ. system. Amer. Psychol. Assn.*, 1970, No. 144A.

**Graicunas, V. A.** Relationship in organization. In L. Gulick and L. Urwick (Eds.), *Papers on the science of administration*. New York: Institute of Public Administration, 1937.

**Granick, D.** *The Red executive*. Garden City, N.Y.: Doubleday & Co., 1960.

**Granick, D.** *The European executive*. New York: Doubleday, 1962.

**Granick, D.** Business and class in Europe. In D. Granick (Ed.), *The European executive*. New York: Doubleday & Co., 1962.

**Grant, D. L.** Leadership in the fraternity. *J. Higher Educ.*, 1932, *3*, 257–261.

**Grant, D. L.** A factor analysis of managers' ratings. *J. appl. Psychol.*, 1955, *39*, 283–286.

**Grant, D. L., & Bray, D. W.** Contributions of the interview to assessment of management potential. *J. appl. Psychol.*, 1969, *53*, 24–34.

**Grant, D. L., Katkovsky, W., & Bray, D. M.** Contributions of projective techniques to assessment of management potential. *J. appl. Psychol.*, 1967, *51*, 226–232.

**Graves, D.** Reported communication ratios and informal status in managerial work groups. *Hum.*

*Relat.*, 1972, *25*, 159–170.

**Gray, L. N., Richardson, J. T., & Mayhew, B. H.** Influence attempts and effective power: a re-examination of the unsubstantiated hypothesis. *Sociometry*, 1968, *31*, 245–258.

**Green, G. H.** Insight and group adjustment. *J. abnorm. soc. Psychol.*, 1948, *43*, 49–61.

**Green, N. E.** Verbal intelligence and effectiveness of participation in group discussion. *J. educ. Psych.*, 1950, *41*, 440–445.

**Green, S. G., & Mitchell, T. R.** Attributional processes of leaders in leader-member interactions. *Org. behav. hum. Perform.*, 1979, *23*, 429–458.

**Green, S. G., & Nebeker, D. M.** Leader behavior: autonomous or interactive? Seattle: University of Washington, Organizational Research, Technical Report No. 74–62, 1974.

**Green, S. G., & Nebeker, D. M.** The effects of situational factors and leadership style on leader behavior. *Org. behav. hum. Perform.*, 1977, *19*, 368–377.

**Green, S. G., Nebeker, D. M., & Boni, M. A.** Personality and situational effects in leader behavior. Seattle: University of Washington, Organizational Research, Technical Report No. 74–55, 1974.

**Greenbaum, L.** Cross-cultural study of the use of elections for selection of the village headman. *Behav. sci. Res.*, 1977, *12*, 45–59.

**Greenberg, J., & Leventhal, G. S.** Equity and the use of over-reward to motivate performance. *J. pers. soc. Psychol.*, 1976, *34*, 179–190.

**Greene, C. N.** Relationships among role accuracy, compliance, performance, evaluation, and satisfaction within managerial dyads. *Acad. Mgmt. J.*, 1972, *15*, 205–215.

**Greene, C. N.** A longitudinal analysis of relationships among leader behavior and subordinate performance and satisfaction. *Proceedings of the Academy of Management*, 1973.

**Greene, C. N.** The path-goal theory of leadership: a replication and an analysis of causality. *Proceedings of the Academy of Management*, 1974.

**Greene, C. N.** The reciprocal nature of influence between leader and subordinate. *J. appl. Psychol.*, 1975, *60*, 187–193.

**Greene, C. N.** A longitudinal investigation of performance-reinforcing leader behavior and subordinate satisfaction and performance. *Midwest Academy of Management Proceedings*, 1976a, 157–185.

**Greene, C. N.** Causal connections among cohesion, drive, goal acceptance, and productivity in work groups. *Proceedings of the Academy of Management*, 1976b.

**Greene, C. N.** Questions of causation in the path-goal theory of leadership. *Acad. Mgmt. J.*, 1979a, *22*, 22–41.

**Greene, C. N.** A longitudinal investigation of modifications to a situational model of leadership effectiveness. *Proceedings of the Academy of Management*, 1979b.

**Greene, C. N., & Organ, D. W.** An evaluation of casual models linking the received role with job satisfaction. *Admin. sci. Quar.*, 1973, *18*, 95–103.

**Greene, C. N., & Podsakoff, P. M.** Effects of withdrawal of a performance-contingent reward on supervisory influence and power. Bloomington: Indiana University, working paper, 1979.

**Greene, C. N., & Schriesheim, C.** Causal paths among dimensions of leadership, group drive, and cohesiveness: a longitudinal field investigation. *Proceedings of the Academy of Management*, 1977.

**Greenfield, T. B.** Research on the behavior of educational leaders: critique of a tradition. *Alberta J. educ. Res.*, 1968, *14*, 55–76.

**Greenfield, T. B., & Andrews, J. H. M.** Teacher leader behavior. *Alberta J. educ. Res.*, 1961, *7*, 92–102.

**Greenly, R. S., & Mapel, E. B.** The development of executive talent. *Personnel*, 1943, *19*, 628–634.

**Greenwood, J. M., & McNamara, W. J.** Leadership styles of structure and consideration and managerial effectiveness. *Personnel Psychol.*, 1969, *22*, 141–152.

**Greer, F. L.** Neighborhood leaders. In D. Courtney et al (Eds.), *Naval, neighborhood, and national leadership*. Philadelphia: Institute for Research in Human Relations, 1953.

**Greer, F. L.** Leadership identification and acceptance. *Inst. res. hum. relat. status Rep.*, May 1954.

**Greer, F. L.** *Leader indulgence and group performance*. Washington, D.C.: G. E. Co., 1960.

**Greer, F. L.** Leader indulgence and group performance. *Psychol. Monogr.*, 1961, *75*, No. 516.

**Greer, F. L., Galanter, E. H., & Nordlie, P. G.** Interpersonal knowledge and individual and group effectiveness. *J. abnorm. soc. Psychol.*, 1954, *49*, 411–414.

**Greiner, L. E., Leitch, D. F., & Barnes, L. B.** The simple complexity of organizational climate in a government agency. In R. Tagiuri & G. H. Litwin (Eds.), *Organizational climate*. Boston: Harvard University, Graduate School of Business Administration, 1968.

**Griffin, R. W.** Task design determinants of effective leader behavior. *Acad. Mgmt. Rev.*, 1979, *4*, 215–224.

**Griffitt, W. B.** Anticipated reinforcement and attraction. *Psychonomic Sci.*, 1968, *11*, 355.

**Griffitt, W. B.** Attitude evoked anticipatory responses and attraction. *Psychonomic Sci.*, 1969, *14*, 153–155.

**Gronlund, N. E.** Acquaintance span and sociometric status. *Sociometry*, 1955a, *18*, 62–68.

**Gronlund, N. E.** Sociometric status and sociometric perception. *Sociometry*, 1955b, *18*, 122–128.

**Gross, B. M.** What are your organization's objectives? A general systems approach to planning. *Hum. Relat.*, 1965, *18*, 195–215.

**Gross, E.** Dimensions of leadership. *Personnel J.*, 1961, *40*, 213–218.

**Gross, N., & Harrott, R. E.** *Staff leadership in public schools*. New York: Wiley, 1965.

**Gross, N., Martin, W. E., & Darley, J. G.** Studies of group behavior: leadership structures in small organized groups. *J. abnorm. soc. Psychol.*, 1953, *48*, 429–432.

**Gross, N., McEachern, A. W., & Mason, W. S.** Role conflict and its resolution. In B. J. Biddle & E. J. Thomas (Eds.), *Role theory: concepts and research*. New York: Wiley, 1966.

**Gross, N., Mason, W. S., & McEachern, A. W.** *Explorations in role analysis*. New York: Wiley, 1958.

**Grossack, M. M.** Cues, expectations, and first impressions. *J. Psychol.*, 1953, *35*, 245–252.

**Grossack, M. M.** Perceived Negro group belongings and social rejection. *J. Psychol.*, 1954, *38*, 127–130.

**Grossack, M. M.** Some effects of cooperation and competition upon small group behavior. *J. abnorm. soc. Psychol.*, 1954, *49*, 341–348.

**Grosser, D., Polansky, N., & Lippitt, R.** A laboratory study of behavioral contagion. *Hum. Relat.*, 1951, *4*, 115–142.

**Gruenfeld, L. W.** A study of the motivation of industrial supervisors. *Personnel Psychol.*, 1962, *15*, 303–314.

**Gruenfeld, L. W.** Effects of tuition payment and involvement on benefit from a management development program. *J. appl. Psychol.*, 1966, *50*, 396–399.

**Gruenfeld, L. W., & Arbuthnot, J.** Field independence, achievement values and the evaluation of a competency related dimension on the least preferred coworker (LPC) measure. *Percept. mot. Skills.* 1968, *27*, 991–1002.

**Gruenfeld, L. W., & Foltman, F. F.** Relationship among supervisors' integration, satisfaction, and acceptance of a technological change. *J. appl. Psychol.*, 1967, *51*, 74–77.

**Gruenfeld, L. W., Rance, D. E., & Weissenberg, P.** The behavior of task oriented (low LPC) and socially oriented (high LPC) leaders under several conditions of social support. *J. soc. Psychol.*, 1969, *79*, 99–107.

**Gruenfeld, L. W., & Weissenberg, P.** Supervisory characteristics and attitudes toward performance appraisals. *Personnel Psychol.*, 1966, *19*, 143–151.

**Grunstad, N. L.** The determination of leader behavior from the interaction of Fiedler's LPC and situation favorableness. Doctoral dissertation, Ohio State University, Columbus, 1972.

**Grusky, O.** Organizational goals and the behavior of informal leaders. *Amer. J. Sociol.*, 1959, *65*, 59–67.

**Grusky, O.** Corporate size, bureaucratization, and managerial succession. *Amer. J. Sociol.*, 1961, *67*, 261–269.

**Grusky, O.** Managerial succession and organizational effectiveness. *Amer. J. Sociol.*, 1963, *69*, 21–31.

**Grusky, O.** Managerial succession. *Amer. J. Sociol.*, 1963, *69*, 72–76.

**Guest, R. H.** Of time and the foreman. *Personnel*, 1956, *32*, 478–486.

**Guest, R. H.** Job enlargement, a revolution in job design. *Personnel Admin.*, 1957, *20*, 9–16.

**Guest, R. H.** *Organizational change: the effect of successful leadership.* Homewood, Ill.: Irwin-Dorsey, 1962a.

**Guest, R. H.** Managerial succession in complex organizations. *Amer. J. Sociol.*, 1962b, *68*, 47–56.

**Guest, R. H., Hersey, P., & Blanchard, K. H.** *Organizational change through effective leadership.* Englewood Cliffs, N.J.: Prentice-Hall, 1977.

**Guetzkow, H.** *Groups, leadership, and men; research in human relations.* Pittsburgh: Carnegie Press, 1951.

**Guetzkow, H.** *Organizational development and restrictions in communication.* Pittsburgh: Carnegie Institute of Technology, 1954.

**Guetzkow, H.** Differentiation of roles in task-oriented groups. In D. Cartwright & A. Zander (Eds.), *Group Dynamics.* Evanston, Ill.: Row, Peterson, 1960.

**Guetzkow, H.** Organizational leadership in task-oriented groups. In L. Petrullo & B. M. Bass (Eds.), *Leadership and interpersonal behavior.* New York: Holt, Rinehart & Winston, 1961.

**Guetzkow, H., & Dill, W. R.** Factors in the organizational development of task-oriented groups. *Sociometry*, 1957, *20*, 175–204.

**Guetzkow, H., Forehand, G. A., & James, B. J.** An evaluation of educational influence on administrative judgment. *Admin. sci. Quar.*, 1962, *6*, 483–500.

**Guetzkow, H., & Gyr, J.** An analysis of conflict in decision-making groups. *Hum. Relat.*, 1954, *7*, 367–382.

**Guetzkow, H., & Kriesberg, M.** *Executive use of the administrative conference.* New York: American Management Association, 1950.

**Guetzkow, H., & Simon, H. A.** The impact of certain communication nets upon organization and performance in task oriented groups. *Mgmt. Sci.*, 1955, *31*, 43–49.

**Guilford, J. P.** *Psychometric methods.* New York: McGraw-Hill, 1954.

**Guilford, J. P., & Guilford, R. B.** Personality factors D, R, T, and A. *J. abnorm. soc. Psychol.*, 1938, *34*, 21–36.

**Guilford, J. S.** Temperament traits of executives and supervisors measured by the Guilford Personality Inventories. *J. appl. Psychol.*, 1952, *36*, 228–233.

**Guion, R. M.** The employee load of first line supervisors. *Personnel Psychol.*, 1953, *6*, 223–244.

**Guion, R. M., & Gottier, R. F.** Validity of personality measures in personnel selection. *Personnel Psychol.*, 1965, *18*, 135–164.

**Gullahorn, J. T.** Distance and friendship as factors in the gross interaction matrix. *Sociometry*, 1952, *15*, 123–134.

**Gump, J. P.** Comparative analysis of black women's and white women's sex-role attitudes. *J. consult. clin. Psychol.*, 1975, *43*, 858–863.

**Gurin, G., Veroff, J., & Feld, S.** *Americans view their mental health: a nationwide interview study.* New York: Basic Books, 1960.

**Gurnee, H.** *Elements of social psychology.* New York: Farrar & Rinehart, 1936.

**Gusfield, J. R.** Functional areas of leadership in social movements. *Sociol. Quar.*, 1966, 7, 137–156.

**Gustafson, D. P.** The effect of commitment to the task on role differentiation in small unstructured groups. *Acad. Mgmt. J.*, 1968, 11, 457–458.

**Gustafson, D. P.** The effect of commitment to the task on role differentiation in small unstructured groups. *Dissertation Abstr.*, 1969, 29, 2357.

**Gustafson, D. P., & Harrell, T. W.** A comparison of role differentiation in several situations. *Org. behav. hum. Perform.*, 1970, 5, 299–312.

**Gutteridge, T. G.** MBA recruitment and utilization: a comparison of two perspectives. *Personnel J.*, 1973, 293–303.

**Guzzardi, W.** *The young executives.* New York: New American Library, 1965.

**Gyr, J. W.** Is a theory of direct visual perception adequate? *Psych. Bull.*, 1972, 77, 246–261.

**Haas, J. A., Porat, A. M., & Vaughan, J. A.** Actual versus ideal time allocations reported by managers: a study of managerial behavior. *Personnel Psychol.*, 1969, 22, 61–75.

**Habbe, S.** Job attitudes of life insurance agents. *J. appl. Psychol.*, 1947, 31, 111–128.

**Habbe, S.** *Company programs of executive development.* New York: National Industrial Conference Board, 1950.

**Habbe, S.** Does communication make a difference? *Mgmt. Rec.*, 1952, 14, 414–416, 442–444.

**Haccoun, D. M., Haccoun, R. R., & Sallay, G.** Sex differences in the appropriateness of supervisory styles: a nonmanagement view. *J. appl. Psychol.*, 1978, 63, 124–127.

**Hackman, J. R.** Toward understanding the role of tasks in behavioral research. *Acta Psych.*, 1969, 31, 97–128.

**Hackman, J. R., & Lawler, E. E.** Employee reactions to job characteristics. *J. appl. Psych. Monogr.*, 1971, 55, 259–286.

**Hackman, R. C., & Moon, R. G.** Are leaders and followers identified by similar criteria? *Amer. Psychologist*, 1950, 5, 312.

**Hackman, J. R., & Oldham, G. R.** Development of the job diagnostic survey. *J. appl. Psychol.*, 1975, 60, 159–170.

**Hafeez, A.** A study of ascendance-submission among engineering, humanities, and science students, employed engineers and supervisors. *Indian J. soc. Work*, 1971, 32, 95–98.

**Hage, J., & Aiken, M.** Relationship of centralization to other structural properties. *Admin. sci. Quar.*, 1967, 12, 72–92.

**Hage, J., & Aiken, M.** Routine technology, social structure, and organization goals. *Admin. sci. Quar.*, 1969, 14, 366–376.

**Hagen, E. E.** *On theory of social change.* Homewood, Ill.: Dorsey, 1962.

**Hahn, C. P.** *Collection of data for utilization of situational problems for training in those leadership behaviors essential for effective performance as a junior officer.* Washington, D.C.: American Institute for Research, 1959.

**Hahn, C. P., & Trittipoe, T. G.** Situational problems for leadership training: III. Review for petty officers of leadership research. Washington, D.C.: Naval Contract Report, Institute for Research, 1961.

**Haiman, F. S.** *Group leadership and democratic action.* Boston: Houghton Mifflin, 1951.

**Hain, T.** Determinants of changes in supervisory styles: an empirical test. *Proceedings of the Midwest Academy of Management*, 1972.

**Hain, T.** The development of a behavioral forecasting index. Detroit: General Motors Corporation, Unpublished technical report, 1974.

**Hain, T., & Tubbs, S.** Organizational development: the role of communication in diagnosis, change and evaluation. *Proceedings of the International Communication Association,* 1974.

**Hain, T., & Widgery, R.** Organizational diagnosis: the significant role of communication. *Proceedings of the International Communication Association,* 1973.

**Haire, M.** Some problems of industrial training. *J. soc. Issues,* 1948, *4,* 41–47.

**Haire, M., Ghiselli, E. E., & Porter, L. W.** Cultural patterns in the role of the manager. *Indus. Relat.,* 1963, *2,* 95–117.

**Haire, M., Ghiselli, E. E., & Porter, L. W.** *Managerial thinking.* New York: Wiley, 1966.

**Hakel, M. D.** Some questions and comments about applied learning. *Personnel Psychol.,* 1976, *29,* 361–369.

**Hakel, M. D., Hollman, D., & Dunnette, M. D.** Stability and change in the social status of occupations over 21 and 42 year periods. *Personnel Guid. J.,* 1968, *46,* 762–764.

**Halal, W. E.** Toward a general theory of leadership. *Hum. Relat.,* 1974, *27,* 401–416.

**Hall, B. A.** The effect of sex of the leader on the development of assertiveness in women undergoing group assertive training. Doctoral dissertation, University of Missouri, Kansas City, 1975.

**Hall, D. T.** A model of coping with role conflict: the role behavior of college educated women. *Admin. sci. Quar.,* 1972, *17,* 471–486.

**Hall, D. T., & Lawler, E. E.** Job characteristics and pressures and the organizational integration of professionals. *Admin. sci. Quar.,* 1970, *15,* 271–281.

**Hall, D. T., & Mansfield, R.** Organizational and individual response to external stress. *Admin. sci. Quar.,* 1971, *16,* 533–547.

**Hall, D. T., & Schneider, B.** Correlates of organizational identification as a function of career pattern and organizational type. *Admin. sci. Quar.,* 1972, *17,* 340–350.

**Hall, D. T., Schneider, B., & Nygren, H. T.** Personal factors in organizational identification. *Admin. sci. Quar.,* 1970, *15,* 176–190.

**Hall, F. S., & Hall, D. T.** Effects of job incumbents' race and sex on evaluations of managerial performance. *Acad. Mgmt. J.,* 1976, *19,* 476–481.

**Hall, H. E.** Empathy, leadership and art. Baton Rouge: Louisiana State University, Master's thesis, 1953.

**Hall, J., & Donnell, S. M.** Managerial achievement: the personal side of behavioral theory. *Hum. Relat.,* 1979, *32,* 77–101.

**Hall, J., & Williams, M. S.** A comparison of decision-making performances in established and ad hoc groups. *J. pers. soc. Psychol.,* 1966, *3,* 214–222.

**Hall, P., & Locke, H. W.** *Incentives and contentment: a study made in a British factory.* London: Pitman, 1938.

**Hall, R. H.** Intraorganizational structural variation: application of bureaucratic model. *Admin. sci. Quar.,* 1962, *7,* 295–308.

**Hall, R. L.** Social influence on the aircraft commander's role. *Amer. sociol. Rev.,* 1955, *20,* 292–299.

**Hall, R. L.** Predicting bomber crew performance from the aircraft commander's role. San Antonio, Tex.: Lackland Air Force Base, Crew Research Laboratory, 1956.

**Hall, R. L.** Group performance under feedback that confounds responses of group members. *Sociometry,* 1957, *20,* 297–305.

**Halpin, A. W.** *Studies in air crew composition. X. The combat leader behavior of B-29 aircraft commanders.* Columbus: Ohio State University, Personnel Research Board, 1953.

**Halpin, A. W.** The leadership behavior and combat performance of airplane commanders. *J. abnorm. soc. Psychol.,* 1954, *49,* 19–22.

**Halpin, A. W.** The leadership ideology of aircraft commanders. *J. appl. Psychol.,* 1955a, *39,* 82–84.

**Halpin, A. W.** The leader behavior and leadership ideology of educational administrators and aircraft commanders. *Harvard educ. Rev.,* 1955b, *25,* 18–32.

**Halpin, A. W.** *The leader behavior of school superintendents.* Columbus: Ohio State University, College of Education, 1956a.

**Halpin, A. W.** The behavior of leaders. *Educ. Leadership,* 1956b, *14,* 172–176.

**Halpin, A. W.** The leader behavior and effectiveness of aircraft commanders. In R. M. Stogdill & A. E. Coons (Eds.), *Leader behavior: its description and measurement.* Columbus: Ohio State University, Bureau of Business Research, 1957a.

**Halpin, A. W.** *Manual for the leader behavior description questionnaire.* Columbus: Ohio State University, Bureau of Business Research, 1957b.

**Halpin, A. W.** The observed leader behavior and ideal leader behavior of aircraft commanders and school superintendents. In R. M. Stogdill and A. E. Coons (Eds.), *Leader behavior: its description and measurement.* Columbus: Ohio State University, Bureau of Business Research, 1957c.

**Halpin, A. W.** *Theory and research in administration.* New York: Macmillan, 1966.

**Halpin, A. W., & Croft, D. B.** The organizational climate of schools. St. Louis: Washington University, 1962 (mimeo).

**Halpin, A. W., & Winer, B. J.** A factorial study of the leader behavior descriptions. In R. M. Stogdill & A. E. Coons (Eds.), *Leader behavior: its description and measurement.* Columbus: Ohio State University, Bureau of Business Research, 1957.

**Halsey, G. D.** How to be a leader. New York: Harper, 1938.

**Hamblin, R. L.** Group integration during a crisis. *Hum. Relat.,* 1958a, *11,* 67–76.

**Hamblin, R. L.** Leadership and crises. *Sociometry,* 1958b, *21,* 322–335.

**Hamblin, R. L., Miller, K., & Wiggins, J. A.** Group morale and competence of the leader. *Sociometry,* 1961, *24,* 295–311.

**Hammer, T. H., & Dachler, P.** The process of supervision in the context of motivation theory. College Park: University of Maryland, Department of Psychology, Technical Report No. 3, 1973.

**Hamner, W. C., Kim, J. S., Baird, L., & Bigoness, W. J.** Race and sex as determinants of ratings by potential employers in a simulated work-sampling task. *J. appl. Psychol.,* 1974, *59,* 705–711.

**Hanawalt, N. G., Hamilton, C. E., & Morris, M. L.** Level of aspiration in college leaders and nonleaders. *J. abnorm. soc. Psychol.,* 1943, *38,* 545–548.

**Hanawalt, N. G., Richardson, H. M., & Hamilton, R. J.** Leadership as related to Bernreuter personality measures: II. An item analysis of responses of college leaders and non-leaders. *J. soc. Psychol.,* 1943, *17,* 251–267.

**Hanawalt, N. G., & Richardson, H. M.** Leadership as related to the Bernreuter personality measures: IV. An item analysis of responses of adult leaders and non-leaders. *J. appl. Psychol.,* 1944, *28,* 397–411.

**Hand, H. H., & Slocum, J. W.** Human relations training for middle management: a field experiment. *Acad. Mgmt. J.,* 1970, *13,* 403–410.

**Hand, H. H., & Slocum, J. W.** A longitudinal study of the effects of a human relations training program on managerial effectiveness. *J. appl. Psychol.,* 1972, *56,* 412–417.

**Handy, C. B.** *Understanding organizations.* Baltimore: Penquin Books, 1976.

**Hanfmann, E.** Social structure of a group of kindergarten children. *Amer. J. Orthopsychiat.,* 1935, *5,* 407–410.

**Hankins, F. H.** Fraternal orders. In *Encyclopaedia of the social sciences.* New York: Macmillan, 1931.

**Hanna, N. E.** Organizational variables and innovativeness in collegiate nursing institutions: a comparative study. Doctoral dissertation, University of Michigan, Ann Arbor, 1973.

**Hannah, M. E.** Situational aspects of leadership in a high school. *Dissertation Abstr. Internat.*, 1974, *35*, 2990.

**Hansen, P.** Sex differences in supervision. Proceedings of the 82nd Annual Convention of the American Psychological Association, 1974.

**Hanson, P. G., Morton, R. B., & Rothaus, P.** The fate of role stereotypes in two performance appraisal situations. *Personnel Psychol.*, 1963, *16*, 269–280.

**Hansson, R. O., & Fiedler, F. E.** Perceived similarity, personality, and attraction to large organizations. *J. appl. soc. Psychol.*, 1973, *3*, 258–266.

**Harbison, F., & Myers, C.** *Management in the industrial world.* New York: McGraw-Hill, 1959.

**Harbron, J. D.** The dilemma of an elite group: the industrialist in Latin America. *Inter-Amer. eco. Affairs*, 1965, *19*, 43–62.

**Hardesty, D. L., & Jones, W. S.** Characteristics of judged high potential management personnel—the operations of an industrial assessment center. *Personnel Psychol.*, 1968, *21*, 85–98.

**Harding, L. W.** Twenty-one varieties of educational leadership. *Educ. Leadership*, 1949, *6*, 299–302.

**Hardy, R. C.** Effect of leadership style on the performance of small classroom groups: a test of the contingency model. *J. pers. soc. Psychol.*, 1971, *19*, 367–374.

**Hardy, R. C.** A developmental study of relationships between birth order and leadership style for two distinctly different American groups. *J. soc. Psychol.*, 1972, *87*, 147–148.

**Hardy, R. C.** A test of poor leader–member relations cells of the contingency model on elementary school children. *Child. Develop.*, 1975, *45*, 958–964.

**Hardy, R. C., & Bohren, J. F.** The effect of experience on teacher effectiveness: a test of the contingency model. *J. Psychol.*, 1975, *89*, 159–163.

**Hardy, R. C., Sack, S., & Harpine, F.** An experimental test of the contingency model on small classroom groups. *J. Psychol.*, 1973, *85*, 3–16.

**Hare, A. P.** A study of interaction and consensus in different sized groups. *Amer. sociol. Rev.*, 1952, *17*, 261–267.

**Hare, A. P.** Small group discussions with participatory and supervisory leadership. *J. abnorm. soc. Psychol.*, 1953, *48*, 273–275.

**Hare, A. P.** Situational differences in leader behavior. *J. abnorm. soc. Psychol.*, 1957, *55*, 132–135.

**Hare, A. P.** *Handbook of small group research.* New York: Free Press, 1962.

**Hare, A. P.** Bibliography of small group research 1959–1969. *Sociometry*, 1972, *35*, 1–150.

**Hare, A. P., & Bales, R. F.** Seating position and small group interaction. *Sociometry*, 1963, *26*, 480–486.

**Hare, A. P., Borgatta, E. F., & Bales, R. F.** *Small groups: studies in social interaction.* New York: Knopf, 1955.

**Hare, A. P., & Hare, R. T.** Family friendship within the community. *Sociometry*, 1948, *11*, 329–334.

**Hariton, T.** Conditions influencing the effects of training foremen in human relations principles. Doctoral dissertation, University of Michigan, Ann Arbor, 1951.

**Harlan, A.** Psychological coping patterns of male and female managers. *Proceedings of the Academy of Management*, 1976.

**Harlow, R. F.** *Social science in public relations: a survey and analysis of social science literature bearing upon the practice of public relations.* New York: Harper, 1957.

**Harmon, H. H.** *Modern factor analysis.* Chicago: University of Chicago Press, 1967.

**Harmon, H. H., & Jones, W. H.** Factor analysis by minimizing residuals (Minres). *Psycho-*

*metrika,* 1966, *31,* 351–368.

**Harnquist, K.** *Adjustment: leadership and group relations in a military training situation.* Stockholm: Almquist & Wiksell, 1956.

**Harper, S. F., & Golden, O. H.** *Executive development: a bibliographic review.* Chicago: University of Chicago, Industrial Relations Center, 1958.

**Harragan, M. L.** *Games mother never taught you.* New York: Rawson Associates Publishers, Inc., 1977.

**Harrell, T. W.** *Managers' performance and personality.* Cincinatti: South-Western, 1961.

**Harrell, T. W.** Personality differences between extreme performers during a fourth discussion session. Stanford, Calif.: Stanford University, Graduate School of Business, Technical Report No. 12, 1966.

**Harrell, T. W.** The personality of high earning MBA's in big business. *Personnel Psychol.,* 1969, *22,* 457–463.

**Harrell, T. W., & Alpert, B.** The need for autonomy among managers. *Acad. Mgmt. Rev.,* 1979, *4,* 259–267.

**Harrell, T. W., Burnham, L. E., & Lee, H. E.** Correlations between seven leadership criteria. Stanford, Calif.: Stanford University, Graduate School of Business, Technical Report No. 4, 1963.

**Harrell, T. W., Burnham, L. E., Hunt, R. S., & Lee, H. E.** Reliability and intercorrelations for thirteen leadership criteria. Stanford, Calif.: Stanford University, Graduate School of Business, Technical Report No. 8, 1964.

**Harrell, T. W., & Gustafson, D. P.** Discussion groups with a trend away from role differentiation. Stanford, Calif.: Stanford University, Graduate School of Business, Technical Report No. 13, 1966.

**Harrell, T. W., & Lee, H. E.** An investigation of the product moment intercorrelations among small group leadership criteria. Stanford, Calif.: Stanford University, Graduate School of Business, Technical Report No. 6, 1964.

**Harris, B. M.** Leadership prediction as related to measures of personal characteristics. *Personnel Admin.,* 1964, *27,* 31–34.

**Harris, C. R., & Heise, R. C.** Tasks, not traits—the key to better performance review. *Personnel,* 1964, *41,* 60–64.

**Harris, E. F., & Fleishman, E. A.** Human relations training and the stability of leadership patterns. *J. appl. Psychol.,* 1955, *39,* 20–25.

**Harris, H.** *The group approach to leadership testing.* London: Routledge & Kegan Paul, 1949.

**Harris, K. W.** Change in role requirements of superintendents over the last quarter-century. Doctoral dissertation, Ohio State University, Columbus, 1968.

**Harrison, C. W., Rawls, J. R., & Rawls, D. J.** Differences between leaders and nonleaders in six-to-eleven-year-old children. *J. soc. Psychol.,* 1971, *84,* 269–272.

**Harrison, R.** The impact of the laboratory on perceptions of others by the experimental group. In C. Argyris (Ed.), *Interpersonal competence and organizational effectiveness.* Homewood, Ill.: Dorsey, 1962.

**Harrison, R.** Cognitive change and participation in a sensitivity-training laboratory. *J. consult. Psychol.,* 1966, *30,* 517–520.

**Harrison, R.** Choosing the depth of organizational intervention. *J. appl. behav. Sci.,* 1970, *6,* 181–202.

**Harrison, R., & Lubin, B.** Personal style, group composition, and learning. Part I. *J. apply. behav. Sci.,* 1965a, *1,* 286–294.

**Harrison, R., & Lubin, B.** Personal style, group composition, and learning. Part II. *J. appl. behav. Sci.,* 1965b, *1,* 294–301.

**Harrow, M., Astrachan, B. M., Tucker, G. J., Klein, E. B., & Miller, J. C.** The T-group and study group laboratory experience. *J. soc. Psychol.*, 1971, *85*, 225–237.

**Harsanyi, J. C.** Measurement of social power, opportunity costs, and the theory of two-person bargaining games. *Behav. Sci.*, 1962a, *7*, 67–80.

**Harsanyi, J. C.** Measurement of social power in *n*-person reciprocal power situations. *Behav. Sci.*, 1962b, *7*, 81–91.

**Hart, L. B.** Training women to become effective leaders: a case study. *Dissertation Abstr. Internat.*, 1975, *35*, 6977.

**Hartley, R. E.** Relationships between perceived values and acceptance of a new reference group. *J. soc. Psychol.*, 1960a, *51*, 181–190.

**Hartley, R. E.** Norm compatibility, norm preference, and the acceptance of new reference groups. *J. soc. Psychol.*, 1960b, *52*, 87–95.

**Hartmann, H.** Codetermination in West Germany. *Indus. Relat.*, 1970, *9*, 137–147.

**Hartson, L. D.** The psychology of the club: a study in social psychology. *Pedagog. Sem.*, 1911, *18*, 353–414.

**Harvey, E.** Technology and the structure of organizations. *Amer. sociol. Rev.*, 1968, *33*, 247–259.

**Harvey, O. J.** An experimental approach to the study of status relations in informal groups. *Amer. sociol. Rev.*, 1953, *18*, 357–367.

**Harvey, O. J.** Reciprocal influence of the group and three types of leaders in an unstructured situation. *Sociometry*, 1960, *23*, 57–68.

**Harvey, O. J.** *Motivation and social interaction.* New York: Ronald Press, 1963.

**Harvey, O. J., & Beverly, G. D.** Some personality correlates of concept change through role playing. *J. abnorm. soc. Psychol.*, 1961, *63*, 125–130.

**Harvey, O. J., & Consalvi, C.** Status and conformity to pressure in informal groups. *J. abnorm. soc. Psychol.*, 1960, *60*, 182–187.

**Harville, D. L.** Early identification of potential leaders. *J. coll. student Personnel*, 1969, *10*, 333–335.

**Hastings, E. W.** Is pupil training for leadership a worth-while feature? *Amer. phys. educ. Rev.*, 1926, *31*, 1080–1085.

**Hastings, R. E.** Leadership in university research teams. *Dissertation Abstr.*, 1964, *24*, 2723.

**Hastorf, A. H.** The reinforcement of individual actions in a group situation. In L. Krasner & L. P. Ullmann (Eds.), *Research in behavior modification.* New York: Holt, Rinehart & Winston, 1965.

**Hastorf, A. H., Schneider, D., & Polefka, J.** *Person perception.* Reading, Mass.: Addison-Wesley, 1969.

**Hatch, R. S.** *An evaluation of a forced-choice differential accuracy approach to the measurement of supervisory empathy.* Englewood Cliffs, N.J.: Prentice-Hall, 1962.

**Hausman, H. J., & Strupp, H. H.** Non-technical factors in supervisors' ratings of job performance. *Personnel Psychol.*, 1955, *8*, 201–217.

**Hausser, D., Blaiwes, A. S., Weller, D., & Spencer, G.** Applications of computer-assisted instruction to interpersonal skill training. Orlando: NAVTRAEQUIPCEN Technical Report 74-C- 0100-1.

**Hausser, D., & Spencer, G.** *Application of computer-assisted instruction to interpersonal skill training.* Ann Arbor, Mich.: Institute for Social Research, 1975.

**Havighurst, R. J., & Russell, M.** Promotion in the armed services in relation to school attainment and social status. *School Rev.*, 1945, *53*, 202–211.

**Havighurst, R. J., & Taba, H.** *Adolescent character and personality.* New York: Wiley, 1949.

**Havron, M. D., & McGrath, J. E.** The contribution of the leader to the effectiveness of small military groups. In L. Petrullo & B. M. Bass (Eds.), *Leadership and interpersonal behavior.* New York: Holt, Rinehart & Winston, 1961.

**Hawkins, C. H.** A study of factors mediating a relationship between leader rating behavior and group productivity. *Dissertation Abstr.*, 1962, *23*, 733.

**Hayashida, C. T.** The isolation of leadership: a case study of precarious religious organization. *Rev. relig. Res.*, 1976, *17*, 141–152.

**Hayden, S. J.** Getting better results from post-appraisal interviews. *Personnel*, 1955, *31*, 541–550.

**Haynes, P. D.** A comparison of perceived organizational characteristics between selected work stoppage and non-work stoppage school districts in the state of Michigan. Doctoral dissertation, Western Michigan University, Kalamazoo, 1972.

**Haythorn, W. W.** The influence of individual group members on the behavior of coworkers and on the characteristics of groups. Doctoral dissertation, University of Rochester, Rochester, N.Y., 1952.

**Haythorn, W. W.** The influence of individual members on the characteristics of small groups. *J. abnorm. soc. Psychol.*, 1953, *48*, 276–284.

**Haythorn, W. W.** Relationships between sociometric measures and performance in medium bomber crews in combat. Crew Research Laboratory, AF Personnel & Training Reserve Center, Lackland AF Base, AFPTRC-TR-54-101, 1954a.

**Haythorn, W. W.** An analysis of role distribution in B-29 crews. *USAF Personnel Train. Res. Cent. res. Bull.*, No. AFPTRC-TR-54-104, 1954b.

**Haythorn, W. W.** The effects of varying combinations of authoritarian and equalitarian leaders and followers. *J. abnorm. soc. Psychol.*, 1956, *53*, 210–219.

**Haythorn, W. W., Couch, A., Haefner, D., Langham, P., & Carter, L. F.** The behavior of authoritarian and equalitarian personalities in groups. *Hum. Relat.*, 1956a, *9*, 57–74.

**Haythorn, W. W., Couch, A., Haefner, D., Langham, P., & Carter, L. F.** The effects of varying combinations of authoritarian and equalitarian leaders and followers. *J. abnorm. soc. Psychol.*, 1956b, *53*, 210–219.

**Hazel, J. T., Madden, J. M., & Christal, R. E.** Agreement between worker–supervisor descriptions of the worker's job. *J. indus. Psychol.*, 1964, *2*, 71–79.

**Healy, A. K.** Effects of changing social structure through child leaders. *Dissertation Abstr.*, 1962, *23*, 2233.

**Healy, J. H.** *Executive coordination and control.* Columbus: Ohio State University, Bureau of Business Research Monograph, 1956.

**Hearn, G.** Leadership and the spatial factor in small groups. *J. abnorm. soc. Psychol.*, 1957, *54*, 269–273.

**Heath, C. W.** *What people are: a study of normal young men.* Cambridge, Mass.: Harvard University Press, 1945.

**Heath, C. W., & Gregory, L. W.** What it takes to make an officer. *Infantry J.*, 1946, *58*, 44–45.

**Hefty, J. C.** The relationships between the value orientations, leader behavior, and effectiveness of secondary school principals in selected middle sized school systems. *Dissertation Abstr. Internat.*, 1972, *32*, 4286–4287.

**Hegarty, W. H.** Using subordinate ratings to elicit behavioral changes in supervisors. West Virginia University, undated.

**Heider, F.** *The psychology of interpersonal relations.* New York: Wiley, 1958.

**Heinen, J. S., & Jacobsen, E.** A model of task group development in complex organizations and a strategy of implementation. *Acad. Mgmt. Rev.*, 1976, *1*, 98–111.

**Heinen, J. S., McGlauchin, D., Legeros, C., & Freeman, J.** Developing the woman manager. *Personnel J.*, 1975, *54*, 282–286.

**Heinicke, C., & Bales, R. F.** Developmental trends in the structure of small groups. *Sociometry*, 1953, *16*, 7–38.

**Heintz, R. K., & Preston, M. G.** The dependence of the effect of the group on the individual upon the character of the leadership. *Amer. Psychologist*, 1948, *3*, 269–270.

**Heise, G. A., & Miller, G. A.** Problem-solving by small groups using various communication nets. *J. abnorm. soc. Psychol.*, 1951, *46*, 327–335.

**Heiss, J. S.** The dyad views the newcomer: a study of perception. *Hum. Relat.*, 1963, *16*, 241–248.

**Heizer, J. H.** A study of significant aspects of manager behavior. *Acad. Mgmt. J.*, 1969, *3*, 386–387.

**Heizer, J. H.** Manager action. *Personnel Psychol.*, 1972, *3*, 511–521.

**Helfrich, M. L., & Schwirian, K. P.** The American businessman—entrepreneur or bureaucrat? *Bull. bus. Res.*, 1968, *43*, 1, 6–9.

**Hellebrandt, E. T., & Stinson, J. E.** The effects of T-group training on business game results. *J. appl. Psychol.*, 1971, *77*, 271–272.

**Heller, F. A.** *Managerial decision making.* London: Human Resources Center, Tavistock Institute of Human Relations, 1969a.

**Heller, F. A.** The role of business management in relation to economic development. *Internat. J. compara. Sociol.*, 1969b, *10*, 292–298.

**Heller, F. A.** *Managerial decision making: a study of leadership styles and power sharing among senior managers.* New York: Harper & Row, 1972.

**Heller, F. A.** Research on five styles of managerial decision making. *Internat. stud. mgmt. Org.*, 1972, *11*, 85–104.

**Heller, F. A.** The decision process: an analysis of power-sharing at senior organizational levels. In R. Dubin (Ed.), *Handbook of work, organization and society.* Chicago: Rand McNally, 1976.

**Heller, F. A., & Clark, A. W.** Personnel and human resources development. *Ann. Rev. Psychol.*, 1976, *27*, 405–435.

**Heller, F. A., & Yukl, G.** Participation, managerial decision-making, and situational variables. *Org. behav. hum. Perform.*, 1969, *4*, 227–241.

**Helmich, D. L.** Predecessor turnover and successor characteristics. *Cornell J. soc. Relat.*, 1974, *9*, 249–260.

**Helmich, D. L.** Leader flows and organizational process. *Acad. Mgmt. J.*, 1978, *21*, 463–478.

**Helmich, D. L., & Erzen, P. E.** Leadership style and leader needs. *Acad. Mgmt. J.*, 1975, *18*, 397–402.

**Helmreich, R. L., & Collins, B. E.** Situational determinants of affiliative preference under stress. *J. pers. soc. Psychol.*, 1967, *6*, 79–85.

**Helson, H.** *Adaptation-level theory.* New York: Harper & Row, 1964.

**Hemphill, J. K.** The leader and his group. *J. educ. Res.*, 1949a, *28*, 225–229, 245–246.

**Hemphill, J. K.** *Situational factors in leadership.* Columbus: Ohio State University, Bureau of Educational Research, 1949b.

**Hemphill, J. K.** Leader behavior description. Columbus: Ohio State University, Personnel Research Board, 1950a (mimeo).

**Hemphill, J. K.** Relations between the size of the group and the behavior of "superior" leaders. *J. soc. Psychol.*, 1950b, *32*, 11–22.

**Hemphill, J. K.** Leadership in small groups. Columbus: Ohio State Leadership Studies, unpublished staff report, 1952 (out of print).

**Hemphill, J. K.** A proposed theory of leadership in small groups. Columbus: Ohio State University, Personnel Research Board, Technical Report, 1954 (unpublished).

**Hemphill, J. K.** Leadership behavior associated with the administrative reputations of college departments. *J. educ. Psychol.*, 1955, *46*, 385–401.

**Hemphill, J. K.** Job descriptions for executives. *Harvard bus. Rev.*, 1959, *37*, 55–67.

**Hemphill, J. K.** *Dimensions of executive positions.* Columbus: Ohio State University, Bureau of Business Research, 1960.

**Hemphill, J. K.** Why people attempt to lead. In L. Petrullo & B. M. Bass (Eds.), *Leadership and interpersonal behavior.* New York: Holt, Rinehart & Winston, 1961.

**Hemphill, J. K., & Coons, A. E.** Development of the Leader Behavior Description Questionnaire. In R. M. Stogdill & A. E. Coons (Eds.), *Leader Behavior: its description and measurement.* Columbus: Ohio State University, Bureau of Business Research, 1957.

**Hemphill, J. K., Griffiths, D. E., & Frederiksen, N.** *Administrative performance and personality: a study of the principal 'in a simulated elementary school.* New York: Teachers College, Columbia University, 1962.

**Hemphill, J. K., & McConville, C. B.** *The effect of ''human'' vs. ''machine'' set on group problem solving procedures.* Princeton, N.J.: Educational Testing Service, 1962.

**Hemphill, J. K., & Pepinsky, P. N.** *Leadership acts.* Columbus: Ohio State University, Personnel Research Board, 1955.

**Hemphill, J. K., Pepinsky, P. N., Kaufman, A. E., & Lipetz, M. E.** The effects of reward and expectancy on motivation to lead. *Amer. Psychologist,* 1956, *11,* 379.

**Hemphill, J. K., Pepinsky, P. N., Kaufman, A. E., & Lipetz, M. E.** Effects of task motivation and expectancy of accomplishment upon attempts to lead. *Psychol. Monogr.,* 1957, No. 451.

**Hemphill, J. K., Pepinsky, P. N., Shevitz, R. N., Jaynes, W. E., & Christner, C. A.** *Leadership acts. I. An investigation of the relation between possession of task relevant information and attempts to lead.* Columbus: Ohio State University, Personnel Research Board, 1954.

**Hemphill, J. K., Pepinsky, P. N., Shevitz, R. N., Jaynes, W. E., & Christner, C. A.** The relation between possession of task-relevant information and attempts to lead. *Psychol. Monogr.,* 1956, No. 414.

**Hemphill, J. K., & Sechrest, L. B.** A comparison of three criteria of aircrew effectiveness in combat over Korea. *J. appl. Psychol.,* 1952, *36,* 323–327.

**Hemphill, J. K., Seigel, A., & Westie, C. W.** An exploratory study of relations between perceptions of leader behavior, group characteristics, and expectations concerning the behavior of ideal leaders. Columbus: Ohio State University, Personnel Research Board, unpublished report, 1951.

**Hemphill, J. K., & Westie, C. M.** The measurement of group dimensions. *J. Psychol.,* 1950, *29,* 325–342.

**Hencley, S. P.** A typology of conflict between school superintendents and their reference groups. Chicago: University of Chicago, Doctoral Dissertation, 1960.

**Hencley, S. P.** The school superintendent and his role: a conflict typology. *Educ. res. Bull.,* 1961, *40,* 57–67.

**Henderson, D. B.** Identification and analysis of the relationship between self-actualization and leadership style in selected graduate students in educational administration. *Dissertation Abstr. Internat.,* 1977, *37,* 4894.

**Heneman, H. G.** An empirical investigation of expectancy theory predictions of job performance. *Proceedings of the Academy of Management,* 1971.

**Hennig, M.** What happens on the way up. *MBA,* 1971 (March), 8–10.

**Hennig, M., & Jardim, A.** *The managerial woman.* Garden City, N.Y.: Doubleday, 1977.

**Henning, D. A., & Moseley, R. L.** Authority role of a functional manager: the controller, *Admin. sci. Quar.,* 1970, *15,* 482–489.

**Henning, H.** Ziele und Möglichkeiten der experimentellen Charakterprüfung. *Jahrbuch d.*

*Charakterol.*, 1929, *6*, 213–273.

**Henry, W. E.** The business executive: the psycho-dynamics of a social role. *Amer. J. Sociol.*, 1949, *54*, 286–291.

**Henson, H. H.** *Analysis of leadership.* New York: Oxford University Press, 1934.

**Herbert, T. T.** Philosophy and design of graduate business programs: evaluative feedback and implications. *Proceedings of the Midwest Management Conference*, 1972.

**Herbert, T. T.** The MBA and job performance: evidence from appraisals. *Akron bus. eco. Rev.*, 1977, *8*, 35–40.

**Herbert, T. T., & Yost, E. B.** *Management education and development.* Westport, Conn.: Greenwood, 1978.

**Herman, J. E.** The objective environment and organizational attitudes. *Proceedings of the Midwest Academy of Management*, 1973.

**Herman, M. G., & Kogan, N.** Negotiation in leader and delegate groups. *J. Conflict Resolution*, 1968, *12*, 332–344.

**Herman, M. G., & Milburn, T. W. (Eds.).** *A psychological examination of political leaders.* New York: Free Press, 1977.

**Herod, J.** Characteristics of leadership in an international fraternity for women and influence on the leaders' attitudes of a group centered leader training experience. *Dissertation Abstr.*, 1969, *29*, 3461–3462.

**Herold, D. M.** Mutual influence processes in leader–follower relationships. Doctoral dissertation, Yale University, New Haven, Conn., 1974.

**Herold, D. M.** Two-way influence processes in leader–follower dyads. *Acad. Mgmt. J.*, 1977, *20*, 224–237.

**Heron, A. R.** *Sharing information with employees.* Stanford, Calif.: Stanford University Press, 1942.

**Herrick, J. S.** Work motives of female executives. *Pub. personnel Mgmt.*, 1973, *2*, 380–388.

**Herring, W. H.** A study of the effect of high and low congruence of role expectations by superiors, managers, and subordinates upon the performance of managers. *Dissertation Abstr. Internat.*, 1972, *37*, 3493.

**Hersey, P., & Blanchard, K. H.** Life cycle theory of leadership. *Train. develop. J.*, 1969a, *23*, 26–34.

**Hersey, P., & Blanchard, K. H.** *Management of organizational behavior.* Englewood Cliffs, N.J.: Prentice-Hall, 1969b.

**Hersey, P., & Blanchard, K. H.** The management of change. Change and the use of power. *Train. develop. J.*, 1972, *26*, 6–10.

**Hersey, P., & Blanchard, K. H.** *Management of organizational behavior: utilizing human resources.* Englewood-Cliffs, N.J.: Prentice-Hall, 1977.

**Hertzler, J. O.** Crises and dictatorships. *Amer. sociol. Rev.*, 1940, *5*, 157–169.

**Herzberg, F., Mausner, B., Peterson, R. O., & Capwell, D. F.** *Job attitudes: review of research and opinion.* Pittsburgh: Psychological Service of Pittsburgh, 1957.

**Herzberg, F., Mausner, B., & Snyderman, B. B.** *The motivation to work.* New York: Wiley, 1959.

**Heslin, J. A., Jr.** A field test of the Likert theory of management in an ADP environment. Washington, D.C.: American University, Master's thesis, 1966.

**Heslin, R., & Dunphy, D.** Three dimensions of member satisfaction in small groups. *Hum. Relat.*, 1964, *17*, 99–112.

**Hespe, G., & Wall, T.** The demand for participation among employees. *Hum. Relat.*, 1976, *29*, 411–428.

**Hesseling, P., & Konnen, E. E.** Culture and subculture in a decision-making exercise. *Hum. Relat.*, 1969, *22*, 31–51.

**Hetzler, S. A.** Variation in role-playing patterns among different echelons of bureaucratic leaders. *Amer. sociol. Rev.*, 1955, *20*, 700–706.

**Heyns, R. W.** Effects of variation in leadership on participant behavior in discussion groups. Doctoral dissertation, University of Michigan, Ann Arbor, 1948.

**Heyns, R. W.** Factors determining influence and decision satisfaction in conferences requiring pooled judgments. *Proceedings of the Administrative Conference,* Ann Arbor: University of Michigan, 1950.

**Hicks, C. F.** An experimental approach to determine the effect of a group leader's programmed nonverbal facial behavior upon group member's perception of the leader. *Dissertation Abstr. Internat.,* 1972, *32*, 4778–4779.

**Hicks, J. A., & Stone, J. B.** The identification of traits related to managerial success. *J. appl. Psychol.,* 1962, *46*, 428–432.

**Hickson, D. J., Pugh, D. S., & Pheysey, D. C.** Operations technology and organization structure: an empirical reappraisal. *Admin. sci. Quar.,* 1969, *14*, 378–397.

**High, W. S., Goldberg, L. L., & Comrey, A. L.** Factored dimensions of organizational behavior. II. Aircraft workers. *Educ. psychol. Measmt.,* 1955, *15*, 371–382.

**High, W. S., Goldberg, L. L., & Comrey, A. L.** Factored dimensions of organizational behavior. III. Aircraft supervisors. *Educ. psychol. Measmt.,* 1956, *16*, 38–53.

**High, W. S., Wilson, R. C., & Comrey, A. L.** Factors influencing organizational effectiveness. VIII. A survey of aircraft foremen. *Personnel Psychol.,* 1955, *8*, 355–368.

**Higham, J.** *Ethnic leadership in America.* Baltimore: Johns Hopkins Press, 1978.

**Hilgard, E. R., Sait, E. M., & Magaret, G. A.** Level of aspiration as affected by relative standing in an experimental social group. *J. exp. Psychol.,* 1940, *27*, 411–421.

**Hilgert, R. L.** The expectations of part-time MBA students. In *Proceedings: image and impact of education for business.* St. Louis: American Association of Collegiate Schools of Business, 1965.

**Hill, J. W., & Hunt, J. G.** An investigation of the relationship between employee need satisfaction and perceived leadership of two levels of management. Carbondale: Southern Illinois University, Department of Management, 1970 (mimeo).

**Hill, R. E.** The leadership role as a factor in commitment and satisfaction among registered nurses. *Dissertation Abstr. Internat.,* April 1971, *31*, 6314.

**Hill, T. A.** An experimental study of the relationship between the opinionatedness of a leader and consensus in group discussions of policy. Doctoral dissertation, Indiana University, Bloomington, 1973.

**Hill, T. E., & Schmitt, N.** Individual differences in leadership decision making. *Org. behav. hum. Perform.,* 1977, *19*, 353–367.

**Hill, W.** The validation and extension of Fiedler's theory of leadership effectiveness. *Acad. Mgmt. J.,* 1969a, *12*, 33–47.

**Hill, W.** A situational approach to leadership effectiveness. *J. appl. Psychol.,* 1969b, *53*, 513–517.

**Hill, W. A.** The LPC leader: a cognitive twist. *Proceedings of the Academy of Management,* 1969.

**Hill, W. A.** Leadership style: rigid or flexible? *Org. behav. hum. Perform.,* 1973, *9*, 35–47.

**Hill, W. H., & Fox, W. M.** Black and white marine squad leaders' perceptions of racially mixed squads. *Acad. Mgmt. J.,* 1973, *16*, 680–686.

**Hill, W. H., & Hughes, D.** Variations in leader behavior as a function of task type. *Org. behav. hum. Perform.,* 1974, *11*, 83–96.

**Hill, W. H., & Ruhe, J. A.** Attitudes and behaviors of black and white supervisors in problem solving groups. *Acad. Mgmt. J.,* 1974, *17*, 563–569.

**Hills, R. J.** The representative function: neglected dimension of leadership behavior. *Admin. sci.*

*Quar.*, 1963, *8*, 83–101.

**Himes, J. S.** Some work-related deprivations of lower-class Negro youths. In L. A. Ferman, J. A. Kornbluh, & A. Haber (Eds.), *Poverty in America*. Ann Arbor: University of Michigan Press, 1965.

**Hines, G. H., & Wellington, V. U.** Achievement motivation levels of immigrants in New Zealand. *J. cross-cult. Psychol.*, 1974, *5*, 37–47.

**Hinrichs, J. R.** Comparison of "real life" assessments of management potential with situational exercises, paper-and-pencil tests, and personality inventories. *J. appl. Psychol.*, 1969, *5*, 425–432.

**Hinton, B. L., & Barrow, J. C.** The superior's reinforcing behavior as a function of reinforcements received. *Org. behav. hum. Perform.*, 1975, *14*, 123–149.

**Hinton, B. L., & Barrow, J. C.** Personality correlates of the reinforcement propensities of leaders. *Personnel Psychol.*, 1976, *29*, 61–66.

**Hise, R. T.** The effect of close supervision on productivity of simulated managerial decision-making groups. *Bus. Studies*, North Texas State University, Fall 1968, pp. 96–104.

**Hites, R. W.** A questionnaire for measuring leader-identification. *Amer. Psychologist*, 1953, *8*, 368.

**Hites, R. W., & Campbell, D. T.** A test of the ability of fraternity leaders to estimate group opinion *J. soc. Psychol.*, 1950, *32*, 95–100.

**Hobert, R., & Dunnette, M. D.** Development of moderator variables to enhance the prediction of managerial effectiveness. *J. appl. Psychol.*, 1967, *51*, 50–64.

**Hobhouse, L. T., Wheeler, G. C., & Ginsberg, M.** *The material culture and social institutions of the simpler peoples*. London: Chapman & Hall, 1930.

**Hocking, W. E.** Leaders and led. *Yale Rev.*, 1924, *13*, 625–641.

**Hodge, J. W.** The relationship between styles of supervision and need satisfaction of two levels of management employees. *Dissertation Abstr. Internat.*, 1976, *37*, 1987.

**Hodgetts, R. M.** Leadership techniques in the project organization. *Acad. Mgmt.* 1968, *11*, 211–219.

**Hodgson, J. D., & Brenner, M. H.** Successful experience: training hard-core unemployed. *Harvard bus. Rev.*, 1968, *46*, 148–156.

**Hodgson, R. C., Levinson, D. J., & Zaleznik, A.** *The executive role constellation*. Boston: Harvard University, 1965.

**Hoffman, E. L., & Rohrer, J. H.** An objective peer evaluation scale: construction and validity. *Educ. psychol. Measmt.*, 1954, *14*, 332–341.

**Hoffman, L. R.** Similarity of personality: a basis for interpersonal attraction? *Sociometry*, 1958, *21*, 300–308.

**Hoffman, L. R.** Review of leadership and decision-making. *J. Bus.*, 1974, *47*, 593–598.

**Hoffman, L. R., Burke, R. J., & Maier, N. R. F.** Participation, influence, and satisfaction among members of problem-solving groups. *Psychol. Rep.*, 1965, *16*, 661–667.

**Hoffman, L. R., Harburg, E., & Maier, N. R. F.** Differences and disagreement as factors in creative group problem solving. *J. abnorm. soc. Psychol.*, 1962, *64*, 206–214.

**Hoffman, L. R., & Maier, N. R. F.** Valence in the adoption of solutions by problem-solving groups: II. Quality and acceptance as goals of leaders and members. *J. pers. soc. Psychol.*, 1967, *6*, 175–182.

**Hoffman, L. R., & Smith, C. G.** Some factors affecting the behaviors of members of problem-solving groups. *Sociometry*, 1960, *23*, 273–291.

**Hoffman, M. L.** Conformity to the group as a defense mechanism. *Amer. Psychologist*, 1956, *11*, 375.

**Hoffman, P. J., Festinger, L., & Lawrence, D. H.** Tendencies toward group comparability in competitive bargaining. *Hum. Relat.*, 1954, *7*, 141–159.

**Hoffman, R. H.** An analysis of factors affecting leadership in an industrial firm. Columbus: Ohio State University, MBA thesis, 1968.

**Hofstede, G.** Value systems in forty countries. *Proceedings of the 4th International Congress of the International Association for Cross-Cultural Psychology,* 1978.

**Hofstede, G.** Private correspondence, January 20, 1978.

**Hogue, J. P., Otis, J. L., & Prien, E. P.** Assessments of higher-level personnel: VI. Validity of predictions based on projective techniques. *Personnel Psychol.,* 1962, *15,* 335–344.

**Holden, R.** Relationships between perceived leadership perceptions of the ideal, and group productivity in small classroom groups. *Dissertation Abstr.,* 1954, *14,* 1994.

**Holding, D. H.** *Experimental psychology in industry.* Baltimore: Penguin, 1969.

**Hollander, E. P.** Authoritarianism and leadership choice in a military setting. *J. abnorm. soc. Psychol.,* 1954, *49,* 365–370.

**Hollander, E. P.** The friendship factor in peer nominations. *Personnel Psychol.,* 1956, *9,* 435–448.

**Hollander, E. P.** The reliability of peer nominations under various conditions of administration. *J. appl. Psychol.,* 1957, *41,* 85–90.

**Hollander, E. P.** Conformity, status, and idiosyncrasy credit. *Psychol. Rev.,* 1958, *65,* 117–127.

**Hollander, E. P.** Competence and conformity in the acceptance of influence. *J. abnorm. soc. Psychol.,* 1960, *61,* 365–369.

**Hollander, E. P.** Some effects of perceived status on responses to innovative behavior. *J. abnorm. soc. Psychol.,* 1961a, *63,* 247–250.

**Hollander, E. P.** Emergent leadership and social influence. In L. Petrullo & B. M. Bass (Eds.), *Leadership and interpersonal behavior.* New York: Holt, Rinehart & Winston, 1961b.

**Hollander, E. P.** *Leaders, groups, and influence.* New York: Oxford University Press, 1964.

**Hollander, E. P.** Validity of peer nominations in predicting a distant performance criterion. *J. appl. Psychol.,* 1965, *49,* 434–438.

**Hollander, E. P.** Leader style, competence, and source of authority as determinants of active and perceived influence. Buffalo: State University of New York, Technical Report, 1966.

**Hollander, E. P.** Style, structure, and setting in organizational leadership. *Admin. sci. Quar.,* 1971, *16,* 1–10.

**Hollander, E. P.** *Leadership dynamics: a practical guide to effective relationships.* New York: Free Press, 1978.

**Hollander, E. P., & Bair, J. T.** Attitudes toward authority-figures as correlates of motivation among aviation cadets, *J. appl. Psychol.,* 1954, *38,* 21–25.

**Hollander, E. P., Fallon, B. J., & Edwards, M. T.** Some aspects of influence and acceptability for appointed and elected leaders. *J. Psychol.,* 1977, *95,* 289–296.

**Hollander, E. P., & Julian J. W.** Leadership. In E. F. Borgatta and W. W. Lumbert. *Handbook of personality theory and research.* Chicago: Rand McNally, 1968.

**Hollander, E. P., & Julian, J. W.** Contemporary trends in the analysis of leadership processes. *Psychol. Bull.,* 1969, *71,* 387–397.

**Hollander, E. P., & Julian, J. W.** Studies in leader legitimacy, influence, and innovation. In L. Berkowitz (Ed.), *Advances in experimental social psychology,* vol. 5. New York: Academic Press, 1970.

**Hollander, E. P., Julian, J. W., & Perry, F. A.** Leader style, competence, and source of authority as determinants of actual and perceived influence. Buffalo: State University of New York, Technical Report No. 5, 1966.

**Hollander, E. P., & Sauaser, E. R.** A further consideration of peer nominations on leadership in the Naval Air Training Program. U.S. Naval Sch. Aviat. Med. Res. Rep., 1953.

**Hollander, E. P., & Webb, W. B.** Leadership, followership, and friendship: an analysis of peer nominations. *J. abnorm. soc. Psychol.,* 1955, *50,* 163–167.

**Hollingshead, A. B.** *Elmtown's youth; the impact of social classes on adolescents.* New York: Wiley, 1949.

**Hollingworth, L. S.** *Gifted children.* New York: Macmillan, 1926.

**Hollingworth, L. S.** What we know about the early selection and training of leaders. *Teach. Coll. Rec.,* 1939, *40,* 575–592.

**Hollman, R. W.** A study of the relationships between organizational climate and managerial assessment of management by objectives. Doctoral dissertation, University of Washington, Seattle, 1973.

**Holloman, C. R.** The leadership role of military and civilian supervisors in a military setting as perceived by supervisors and subordinates. *Dissertation Abstr.,* 1965, *26,* 2903–2904.

**Holloman, C. R.** The perceived leadership role of military and civilian supervisors in a military setting. *Personnel Psychol.,* 1967, *20,* 199–210.

**Holloman, C. R., & Hendrick, H. W.** Adequacy of group decisions as a function of decision-making process. *Acad. Mgmt. J.,* 1972, *15,* 175–184.

**Holmes, J. S.** Comparison of group leader and non-participant observer judgments of certain objective interaction variables. *Psychol. Rep.,* 1969, *24,* 655–659.

**Holt, R. T.** An exploratory study of the French cabinets of the first legislature of the Fourth Republic. Minneapolis: University of Minnesota, Technical Report 2, 1952a.

**Holt, R. T.** *An analysis of the problem of stability and cohesive membership in coalitions.* Minneapolis: University of Minnesota, Technical Report 3, 1952b.

**Holtzman, W. H.** Adjustment and leadership: a study of the Rorschach test. *J. soc. Psychol.,* 1952, *36,* 179–189.

**Homans, G. C.** *The human group.* New York: Harcourt, Brace, 1950.

**Homans, G. C.** Social behavior as exchange. *Amer. J. Sociol.,* 1958, *63,* 597–606.

**Homans, G. C.** *Social behavior: its elementary forms.* New York: Harcourt, Brace, 1961.

**Hood, P. D.** *Leadership climate for trainee leaders: the army AIT platoon.* Washington, D.C.: George Washington University, Human Resources Research Office, 1963.

**Hood, P. D., Showel, M., & Stewart, E. C.** *Evaluation of three experimental systems for noncommissioned officer training.* Washington, D.C.: George Washington University, Human Resources Research Office, 1967. Also: Preliminary assessment of three NCO leadership preparation training systems. *HumRRO Tech. Rep.,* 1967, No. 67–8.

**Hook, S.** *The hero in history.* New York: John Day, 1943.

**Hooker, E. R.** Leaders in village communities. *Soc. Forces,* 1928, *6,* 605–614.

**Hooper, D. B.** Differential utility of leadership opinions in classical and moderator models for the prediction of leadership effectiveness. Doctoral dissertation, Ohio State University, Columbus, 1968. Also: *Dissertation Abstr. Internat.,* 1969, *30,* 13.

**Hopfe, M. W.** Leadership style and effectiveness of department chairmen in business administration. *Acad. Mgmt. J.,* 1970, *13,* 301–310.

**Hopkins, T. K.** *The exercise of influence in small groups.* Totowa, N.J.: Bedminster Press, 1964.

**Hoppock, R.** *Job satisfaction.* New York: Harper, 1935.

**Hoppock, R., Robinson, H. A., & Zlatchin, P. J.** Job satisfaction researches of 1946–1947. *Occupations,* 1948, *27,* 167–175.

**Hornaday, J. A., & Bunker, C. S.** The nature of the entrepreneur. *Personnel Psychol.,* 1970, *23,* 47–54.

**Horne, H. H.** *The essentials of leadership.* Nashville, Tenn.: Cokesbury Press, 1931.

**Horner, M. S.** Femininity and successful achievement: a basic inconsistency. In J. M. Bardwick, E. Douvan, M. S. Horner, & D. Gutmann (Eds.), *Feminine personality and conflict.* Belmont, Calif.: Brooks/Cole, 1970.

**Horrocks, J. E., & Thompson, G. G.** A study of the friendship fluctuations of rural boys and girls. *J. genet. Psychol.*, 1946, *69*, 189–198.

**Horrocks, J. E., & Wear, B. A.** An analysis of interpersonal choice relationships of college students. *J. soc. Psychol.*, 1953, *38*, 87–98.

**Horsfall, A. B., & Arensberg, C. M.** Teamwork and productivity in a shoe factory. *Hum. Org.*, 1949, *8*, 13–26.

**Horwitz, M.** The recall of interrupted group tasks: an experimental study of individual motivation in relation to group goals. *Hum. Relat.*, 1954, *7*, 3–38.

**Horwitz, M., Goldman, M., & Lee, F. J.** Effects of two methods of changing a frustrating agent on reduction of hostility. Urbana: University of Illinois, Bureau of Educational Research, Preliminary Report, 1955.

**Hosking, D. M.** A critical evaluation of Fiedler's predictor measures of leadership effectiveness. Doctoral dissertation, University of Warwick, Warwick, England, 1978.

**Hostiuck, K. T.** The perceived pressure and perceived norm compatibility of reference groups as influences on executives' political behavior. Doctoral dissertation, Ohio State University, Columbus, 1970.

**House, R. J.** An experiment in the use of management training standards. *Acad. Mgmt. J.*, 1962, *5*, 76–81.

**House, R. J.** Managerial reactions to two methods of management training. *Personnel Psychol.*, 1965, *18*, 311–320.

**House, R. J.** T-group education and leadership effectiveness: a review of the empiric literature and a critical evaluation. *Personnel Psychol.*, 1967, *20*, 1–32.

**House, R. J.** Leadership training: some dysfunctional consequences. *Admin. sci. Quar.*, 1968, *12*, 556–571.

**House, R. J.** A path goal theory of leader effectiveness. *Admin. sci. Quar.*, 1971, *16*, 321–338.

**House, R. J.** Some new applications and tests of the path-goal theory of leadership. *Proceedings of the National Behavioral Organizational Conference*, 1972.

**House, R. J.** A 1976 theory of charismatic leadership. In J. G. Hunt & L. L. Larson (Eds.), *Leadership: the cutting edge*. Carbondale: Southern Illinois University Press, 1977.

**House, R. J., & Dessler, G.** The path goal theory of leadership: some post hoc and a priori tests. In J. G. Hunt and L. L. Larson (Eds.), *Contingency approaches to leadership*. Carbondale: Southern Illinois University Press, 1974.

**House, R. J., & Filley, A. C.** Leadership style, hierarchical influence, and the satisfaction of subordinate role expectations: a test of Likert's influence proposition. *J. appl. Psychol.*, 1971, *55*, 422–432.

**House, R. J., Filley, A. C., & Gujarati, D. N.** Leadership style, hierarchical influence, and the satisfaction of subordinate role expectations: a test of Likert's influence proposition. *J. appl. Psychol.*, 1971, *55*, 422–432.

**House, R. J., Filley, A. C., & Kerr, S.** Relation of leader consideration and initiating structure to R and D subordinates' satisfaction. *Admin. sci. Quar.*, 1971, *16*, 19–30.

**House, R. J., & Kerr, S.** Organizational independence, leader behavior, and managerial practices: a replicated study. *J. appl. Psychol.*, 1973, *58*, 173–180.

**House, R. J., & Miner, J. B.** Merging management and behavioral theory: the interaction between span of control and group size. *Admin. sci. Quar.*, 1969, *14*, 451–464.

**House, R. J., & Mitchell, T. R.** Path-goal theory of leadership. *J. contemp. Bus.*, 1974, *3*, 81–97.

**House, R. J., & Rizzo, J. R.** Toward the measurement of organizational practices: scale development and validation. *J. appl. Psych.*, 1972a, *56*, 388–396.

**House, R. J., & Rizzo, J. R.** Role conflict and ambiguity as critical variables in a model of organizational behavior. *Org. behav. hum. Perform.*, 1972b, *7*, 467–505.

**House, R. J., & Tosi, H. L.** An experimental evaluation of a management training program. *Acad. Mgmt. J.*, 1963, *6*, 303–315.

**House, R. J., Tosi, H. L., Rizzo, J. R., & Dunnock, R. C.** *Management development: design, evaluation, and implementation.* Ann Arbor: University of Michigan, Bureau of Industrial Relations, 1967.

**House, R. J., Wigor, L. A., & Schulz, K.** Psychological participation, leader behavior, performance and satisfaction: an extension of prior research and a motivation theory interpretation. *Proceedings of the Eastern Academy of Management,* 1970.

**Houser, J. D.** *What the employer thinks.* Cambridge, Mass.: Harvard University Press, 1927.

**Houston, G. C.** *Manager development: principles and perspectives.* Homewood, Ill.: Irwin, 1961.

**Hovey, D. E.** The low-powered leader confronts a messy problem: a test of Fiedler's theory. *Acad. Mgmt. J.,* 1974, *17,* 358–362.

**House, R. J.** Some new applications and tests of the path-goal theory of leadership. *Proceedings of the First National Behavioral Organizational Conference,* 1972.

**Howard, D. S.** Personality similarity and complementarity and perceptual accuracy in supervisor-subordinate relationships. *Dissertation Abstr.,* 1968, *28,* 4789–4790.

**Howell, C. E.** Measurement of leadership. *Sociometry,* 1942, *5,* 163–168.

**Howells, L. T., & Becker, S. W.** Seating arrangement and leadership emergence. *J. abnorm. soc. Psychol.,* 1962, *64,* 148–150.

**Howton, F. W.** *Functionaries.* Chicago: Quadrangle Books, 1969.

**Hoyt, G. C., & Stoner, J. A.** Leadership and group decisions involving risk. *J. exp. soc. Psychol.,* 1968, *4,* 275–284.

**Hsu, C. C., & Newton, R. R.** Relation between foremen's leadership attitudes and the skill level of their work groups. *J. appl. Psychol.,* 1974, *59,* 771–772.

**Huck, J. R., & Bray, D. W.** Management assessment center evaluations and subsequent job performance of white and black females. *Personnel Psychol.,* 1976, *29,* 13–30.

**Hughes, E. C.** Dilemmas and contradictions of status. *Amer. J. Sociol.,* 1945, *50,* 353–359.

**Hughes, E. C.** The knitting of racial groups in industry. *Amer. sociol. Rev.,* 1946, *11,* 512–519.

**Hulet, R. E.** Leadership behavior in independent and fraternity houses. *Dissertation Abstr.,* 1958, *19,* 1015.

**Hulin, C. L.** The measurement of executive success. *J. appl. Psychol.,* 1962, *46,* 303–306.

**Hulin, C. L.** Job satisfaction and turnover in a female clerical population. *J. appl. Psychol.,* 1966, *50,* 280–285.

**Hulin, C. L., & Blood, M. R.** Job enlargement, individual differences, and worker responses. *Psychol. Bull.,* 1968, *69,* 41–55.

**Humes, J. F.** The use and results of instructional demonstrations for supervisory training groups. *Amer. Psychol.,* 1947, *2,* 338–339.

**Hummel, R. P.** Psychology of charismatic followers. *Psychol. Rep.,* 1975, *37,* 759–770.

**Hunt, J. E.** Expectations and perceptions of the leadership behavior of elementary school principals. *Dissertation Abstr.,* 1968, *28,* 4852–4853.

**Hunt, J. G.** Fiedler's leadership contingency model: an empirical test in three organizations. *Org. behav. hum. Perform.,* 1967, *2,* 290–308.

**Hunt, J. G.** Leadership-style effects at two managerial levels in a simulated organization. *Admin. sci. Quar.,* 1971, *16,* 476–485.

**Hunt, J. G., & Hill, J. W.** *Improving mental hospital effectiveness: a look at managerial leadership.* Carbondale: Southern Illinois University, Technical Report No. 71–4, 1971.

**Hunt, J. G., & Hill, J. W.** Correlates of leadership behavior at two managerial levels in a mental institution. *J. appl. soc. Psychol.,* 1973, *3,* 174–185.

**Hunt, J. G., Hill, J. W., & Reaser, J. M.** *Consideration and structure effects in mental hospitals: an examination of two managerial levels.* Carbondale: Southern Illinois University, Technical Report No. 71–1, 1971.

**Hunt, J. G., Hill, J. W., & Reaser, J. M.** Correlates of leadership behavior at two managerial levels in a mental institution. *J. appl. Psychol.*, 1973, *3*, 174–185.

**Hunt, J. G., & Larson, L. L. (Eds.)** *Contingency approaches to leadership.* Carbondale: Southern Illinois University Press, 1974.

**Hunt, J. G., & Larson, L. L.** *Leadership frontiers.* Kent, Oh.: Kent State University Press, 1975.

**Hunt, J. G., & Larson, L. L.** *Leadership: the cutting edge.* Carbondale: Southern Illinois University Press, 1977.

**Hunt, J. G., & Liebscher, V. K. C.** Leadership preference, leadership behavior, and employee satisfaction. *Org. behav. hum. Perform.*, 1973, *9*, 59–77.

**Hunt, J. G., & Osborn, R. N.** A multiple approach to leadership for managers. In J. Stinson & P. Hersey (Eds.), *Leadership for practitioners.* Athens, Ohio: Ohio University, Center for Leadership Studies, 1978.

**Hunt, J. G., Osborn, R. N., & Larson, L. L.** Leadership effectiveness in mental institutions. Carbondale: Southern Illinois University, Department of Administrative Sciences, NIMH Final Technical Report, 1973.

**Hunt, J. G., Osborn, R. N., & Larson, L. L.** Upper level technical orientation and first level leadership within a noncontingency and contingency framework. *Acad. Mgmt. J.*, 1975, *18*, 476–488.

**Hunt, J. G., Osborn, R. N., & Martin, H. J.** A multiple influence model of leadership. Carbondale: University of Southern Illinois, Final Technical Report, 1979.

**Hunt, J. G., Osborn, R. N., & Schriesheim, C. A.** Omissions and commissions in leadership research. Unpublished ms., 1977.

**Hunt, J. G., Osborn, R. N., & Schriesheim, C. A.** Some neglected areas of leadership research. *Proceedings of the Midwest Academy of Management,* 1978.

**Hunt, J. G., Osborn, R. N., & Schuler, R. S.** Relations of discretionary and nondiscretionary leadership to performance and satisfaction in a complex organization. *Hum. Relat.*, 1978, *31*, 507–523.

**Hunt, J. G., & Schuler, R. S.** Leader reward and sanctions behavior relations with criteria in a large public utility. Carbondale: Southern Illinois University, working paper, 1976.

**Hunt, J. G., Sekaran, U., & Schriesheim, C. A. (Eds.),** *Leadership: Beyond establishment views.* Carbondale: Southern Illinois University Press, 1981.

**Hunter, E. C., & Jordan, A. M.** An analysis of qualities associated with leadership among college students. *J. educ. Psychol.*, 1939, *30*, 497–509.

**Hunter, F.** *Community power structure.* Chapel Hill: University of North Carolina Press, 1953.

**Hunter, F.** *Top leadership, U.S.A.* Chapel Hill: University of North Carolina Press, 1959.

**Hunter, J. E., & Schmidt, F. L.** Differential and single group validity of employment tests by race: a critical analysis of three recent studies. *J. appl. Psych.*, 1978, *63*, 1–11.

**Hunter, O. N.** Relationship between school size and discrepancy in perceptions of ten superintendents' behavior. Doctoral dissertation, Washington University, St. Louis, Mo., 1959.

**Hurlock, E. B.** *Child development.* New York: McGraw-Hill, 1950.

**Hurwitz, J. I., Zander, A. F., & Hymovitch, B.** Some effects of power on the relations among group members. In D. Cartwright & A. Zander (Eds.), *Group dynamics.* Evanston, Ill.: Row, Peterson, 1953.

**Husband, R. W.** Cooperative versus solitary problem solution. *J. soc. Psychol.*, 1940, *11*, 405–409.

**Huss, C.** *A study of planned organizational change in the structure and functioning of Indian hospitals.* Doctoral dissertation, School of Economics, Delhi University, Delhi, India, 1973.

**Hussein, A. L.** Factors emerging from favorableness judgments of basic interview data in six occupational fields. Doctoral dissertation, Ohio State University, Columbus, 1969.

**Hutchins, E. B., & Fiedler, F. E.** Task-oriented and quasi-therapeutic role functions of the leader in a small military group. *Sociometry*, 1960, *23*, 393–406.

**Hutchins, G. B.** Leadership, an opportunity and a challenge to industrial employees. *Ind. Mgmt.*, 1923, *66*, 76–77.

**Hyman, H. H.** The psychology of status. *Archives Psychol.*, 1942, No. 269.

**Hyman, H. H., & Singer, E.** *Readings in reference group theory and research*. New York: Free Press, 1968.

**Hynes, K., Feldhusen, J. F., & Richardson, W. B.** Application of a three-stage model of instruction to youth leadership training. *J. appl. Psychol.*, 1978, *63*, 623–628.

**IDE International Research Group.** Participation: formal rules, influence, and involvement. *Industrial Relat.*, 1979, *18*, 273–294.

**Ilchman, W. F., & Uphoff, N. T.** *The political economy of change*. Berkeley: University of California Press, 1969.

**Ilgen, D. R., & Fujii, D. S.** An investigation of the validity of leader behavior descriptions obtained from subordinates. *J. appl. Psychol.*, 1976, *61*, 642–651.

**Ilgen, D. R., & O'Brien, G.** Leader–member relations in small groups. *Org. behav. hum. Perform.*, 1974, *12*, 335–350.

**Ilgen, D. R., & Terborg, J. R.** Sex discrimination and sex-role stereotypes: are they synonymous? No! *Org. behav. hum. Perform.*, 1975, *14*, 154–157.

**Indik, B. P.** Some effects of organization size of member attitudes and behavior. *Hum. Relat.*, 1963, *16*, 369–384.

**Indik, B. P.** The relationship between organization size and supervisory ratio. *Admin. sci. Quar.*, 1964, *9*, 301–312.

**Indik, B. P.** Organization size and member participation: some empirical tests of alternative explanations. *Hum. Relat.*, 1965a, *18*, 339–350.

**Indik, B. P.** Three studies of organizational and individual dimensions of organizations. New Brunswick, N.J.: Rutgers, The State University, Technical Report No. 15, 1965b.

**Indik, B. P., & Berrian, F. K.** *People, groups, and organizations*. New York: Teachers College Press, 1968.

**Indik, B. P., Georgopoulos, B. S., & Seashore, S. E.** Superior-subordinate relationships and performance. *Personnel Psychol.*, 1961, *14*, 357–374.

**Ingham, A. G., Levinger, G., Graves, J., & Peckham, V.** The Ringlemann effect: studies of group size and group performance. *J. exp. soc. Psychol.*, 1974, *10*, 371–384.

**Ingmire, B. D.** Relationships between creativity scores and leadership behavior in a group of high school seniors. *Dissertation Abstr.*, 1968, *29*, 1365.

**Inkeles, A.** The modernization of man. In M. Weiner (Ed.), *Modernization*. New York: Basic Books, 1966.

**Inkson, J. H. K., Hickson, D. J., & Pugh, D. S.** Administrative reduction of variance in organizations and behavior. *Proceedings of the British Psychological Society*, 1968.

**Inkson, J. H. K., Payne, R. L., & Pugh, D. S.** Extending the occupational environment. *Occup. Psych.*, 1967, *41*, 33–49.

**Institute for Social Research.** *Task order 2*. Ann Arbor: University of Michigan, Annual Report, 1954.

**Ireson, C. J.** Effects of sex role socialization on adolescent female achievement. *Proceedings of the Pacific Sociological Association*, 1976.

**Irwin, F. A., & Poole, G. E.** Student leadership in community clubs. New Jersey S. T. C. Stud. Educ., 1940.

**Ivancevich, J. M.** An analysis of control, bases of control, and satisfaction in an organizational setting. *Acad. Mgmt. J.*, 1970, *13*, 427–436.

**Ivancevich, J. M.** An analysis of participation in decision making among project engineers. *Acad. Mgmt. J.*, 1979, *22*, 253–269.

**Ivancevich, J. M., & Baker, J. C.** A comparative study of the satisfaction of domestic U.S. managers and overseas U.S. managers. *Acad. Mgmt. J.*, 1970, *13*, 69–77.

**Ivancevich, J. M., & Donnelly, J. H.** Leader influence and performance. *Personnel Psychol.*, 1970, *23*, 539–549.

**Iverson, M. A.** Personality impression of punitive stimulus persons of differential status. *J. abnorm. soc. Psychol.*, 1964, *68*, 617–626.

**Izard, C. E.** Personality correlates of sociometric status. *J. appl. Psychol.*, 1959, *43*, 89–93.

**Izard, C. E.** Personality similarity and friendship. *J. abnorm. soc. Psychol.*, 1960, *61*, 47–51.

**Jack, L. M.** An experimental study of ascendant behavior in preschool children. *Univ. Iowa Stud. Child Welfare*, 1934, *9*, 5–65.

**Jackson, J. M.** The relation between attraction, being valued, and communication in a formal organization. Ann Arbor: University of Michigan, Institute for Social Research, 1953a (mimeo).

**Jackson, J. M.** The effect of changing the leadership of small work groups. *Hum. Relat.*, 1953b, *6*, 25–44.

**Jackson, M. L., & Fuller, F. F.** Influence of social class on students' evaluations of their teachers. *Proceed. 74th Annual Conv. Amer. psychol. Assn.*, 1966, 269–270.

**Jacobs, H. L.** A critical evaluation of Fiedler's contingency model of leadership effectiveness in its application to interdisciplinary task-groups in public school settings. *Dissertation Abstr. Internat.*, 1976, *36*, 4912.

**Jacobs, T. O.** *Leadership and exchange in formal organizations.* Alexandria, Va.: Human Resources Research Organization, 1970.

**Jacobson, E.** Foremen and stewards, representatives of management and the union. In H. Guetzkow (Ed.), *Groups, leadership, and men.* Pittsburgh: Carnegie Press, 1951.

**Jacobson, E., Charters, W. W., & Lieberman, S.** The use of role concept in the study of complex organizations. *J. soc. Issues*, 1951, *7*, 18–27.

**Jacobson, E., & Seashore, S. E.** Communication practices in complex organizations. *J. soc. Issues*, 1951, *7*, 28–29.

**Jacobson, M. B., & Effertz, I.** Sex roles and leadership, perceptions of the leaders and the led. *Org. behav. hum. Perform.*, 1974, *12*, 383–396.

**Jacobson, M. B., & Kock, W.** Women as leaders: performance evaluation as a function of method of leader selection. *Org. behav. hum. Perform.*, 1977, *20*, 149–157.

**Jacoby, J.** Creative ability of task-oriented versus person-oriented leaders. *J. Creative Behav.*, 1968, *2*, 249–253.

**Jacoby, J.** The construct validity of opinion leadership. *Pub. opin. Quar.*, 1974, *38*, 81–89.

**Jaffee, C. L.** Leadership attempting: why and when? *Psychol. Rep.*, 1968, *23*, 939–946.

**Jaffee, C. L., Cohen, S. L., & Cherry, R.** Supervisory selection program for disadvantaged or minority employees. *Train. develop. J.*, 1972, *26*, 22–27.

**Jaffee, C. L., & Lucas, R. L.** Effects of rates of talking and correctness of decision on leader choice in small groups. *J. soc. Psychol.*, 1969, *79*, 247–254.

**Jaffee, C. L., Richards, S. A., & McLaughlin, G. W.** Leadership selection under differing feedback conditions. *Psychonomic Sci.*, 1970, *20*, 349–350.

**Jaffee, C. L., & Skaja, N. W.** Conditional leadership in a two-person interaction. *Psychol. Rep.*, 1968, *23*, 135–140.

**Jago, A. G.** A test of spuriousness in descriptive models of participative leader behavior. *J. appl. Psychol.*, 1978, *63*, 383–387.

**Jago, A. G., & Vroom, V. H.** Perceptions of leadership style: superior and subordinate descriptions of decision-making behavior. In J. G. Hunt & L. L. Larson (Eds.), *Leadership frontiers.* Carbondale: Southern Illinois University Press, 1975.

**Jago, A. G., & Vroom, V. H.** Predicting leader behavior from a measure of behavioral intent.

*Proceedings of the American Institute for Decision Sciences,* 1974.

**Jain, S. C.** *Indian manager: his social origin and career.* Bombay: Somaiya Publications, 1971.

**Jambor, H.** *Discrepancies in role expectations for the supervisory position.* Doctoral dissertation, University of Minnesota, Minneapolis, 1954.

**James, G., & Lott, A. J.** Reward frequency and the formation of positive attitudes toward group members. *J. soc. Psychol.,* 1964, *62,* 111–115.

**James, J.** A preliminary study of the size determinant in small group interaction. *Amer. sociol. Rev.,* 1951, *16,* 474–477.

**James, W.** Great men, great thoughts and their environment. *Atlan. Mnthly,* 1880, *46,* 441–459.

**Jameson, S. H.** Principles of social interaction. *Amer. sociol. Rev.* 1945, *10,* 6–12.

**Janda, K. F.** Towards the explication of the concept of leadership in terms of the concept of power. *Hum. Relat.,* 1960, *13,* 345–363.

**Janis, I. L.** Psychological effects of warnings. In G. W. Baker & D. W. Chapman. (Eds.), *Man and society in disaster.* New York: Basic Books, 1962.

**Janis, I. L.** *Victims of groupthink.* Boston: Houghton Mifflin, 1972.

**Janis, I. L., & Feshbach, S.** Effects of fear-arousing communications. *J. abnorm. soc. Psychol.,* 1953, *48,* 78–92.

**Janis, I. L., & Mann, L.** *Decision making: a psychological analysis of conflict, choice, and commitment.* New York: Free Press, 1977.

**Jansen, D. G., Winborn, B. B., & Martinson, W. D.** Characteristics associated with campus social-political action leadership. *J. Counseling Psychol.,* 1968, *15,* 552–562.

**Jacques, E.** *The changing culture of a factory.* New York: Dryden Press, 1952.

**Jacques, E.** *Measurement of responsibility.* Cambridge, Mass.: Harvard University Press, 1956.

**Jaques, E.** Executive organization and individual adjustment. *J. Psychosomatic Res.,* 1966, *10,* 77–82.

**Jarrard, L. E.** Empathy: the concept and industrial applications. *Personnel Psychol.,* 1956, *9,* 157–167.

**Javier, E. O.** Academic organizational structure and faculty/administrator satisfaction. Doctoral dissertation, University of Michigan, Ann Arbor, 1972.

**Jaynes, W. E.** Differences between jobs and between organizations. In R. M. Stogdill & C. L. Shartle (Eds.), *Patterns of administrative performance.* Columbus: Ohio State University, Bureau of Business Research, 1956.

**Jencks, C.** *et al. Who gets ahead?* New York: Basic Books, 1979.

**Jenkins, D. H., & Blackman, C. A.** *Antecedents and effects of administration behavior.* Columbus: Ohio State University, College of Education, 1956.

**Jenkins, J. G.** The nominating technique, its uses and limitations. Unpublished ms. reported in D. Krech & R. S. Crutchfield (Eds.), *Theory and problems of social psychology.* New York: McGraw-Hill, 1948.

**Jenkins, J. G.** *et al. The combat criteria in naval aviation.* Washington, D.C.: United States Navy, Division of Aviation Medicine, Bureau of Medicine & Surgery, 1950.

**Jenkins, W. O.** A review of leadership studies with particular reference to military problems. *Psychol. Bull.,* 1947, *44,* 54–79.

**Jennings, E. E.** The frustrated foreman. *Personnel J.,* 1952a, *31,* 86–88.

**Jennings, E. E.** Forced leadership training. *Personnel J.,* 1952b, *31,* 176–179.

**Jennings, E. E.** The dynamics of forced leadership training. *J. personnel admin. indus. Relat.,* 1954, *I,* 110–118.

**Jennings, E. E.** Democratic supervision works only in the right climate. *Personnel J.,* 1955, *33,* 296–299.

**Jennings, E. E.** *An anatomy of leadership: princes, heroes, and supermen.* New York: Harper, 1960.

**Jennings, E. E.** *The executive: aristocrat, bureaucrat, democrat.* New York: Harper & Row, 1962.

**Jennings, E. E.** *The executive in crisis.* East Lansing: Michigan State University, 1966.

**Jennings, E. E.** *Executive success: stresses, problems, and adjustments.* New York: Appleton-Century-Crofts, 1967a.

**Jennings, E. E.** *The mobile manager: a study of the new generation of top executives.* Ann Arbor: University of Michigan, Bureau of Industrial Relations, 1967b.

**Jennings, E. E.** Profile of a black executive. Cited in World of Work Report, April 1980, p. 28.

**Jennings, H. H.** *Leadership and isolation.* New York: Longmans, Green (1943), 1950.

**Jennings, H. H.** Leadership—a dynamic re-definition. *J. educ. Sociol.*, 1944, *17*, 431–433.

**Jennings, H. H.** Leadership and sociometric choice. *Sociometry*, 1947, *10*, 32–49.

**Jensen, M. B., & Morris, W. E.** Supervisory ratings and attitudes. *J. appl. Psychol.*, 1960, *44*, 339–340.

**Jerdee, T. H.** Supervisor perception of work group morale. *J. appl. Psychol.*, 1964, *48*, 259–262.

**Jerkedal, A.** *Top management education: an evaluation study.* Stockholm: Swedish Council for Personnel Administration, 1967.

**Johns, G.** Task moderators of the relationship between leadership style and subordinate responses. *Acad. Mgmt. J.*, 1978, *21*, 319–325.

**Johnson, A. C., Peterson, R. B., & Kahler, G. E.** Historical changes in characteristics of foremen. *Personnel J.*, 1968, *47*, 475–481, 499.

**Johnson, D. E.** A comparison between the Likert management systems and performance in Air Force ROTC detachments. Doctoral dissertation, University of Minnesota, Minneapolis, 1969.

**Johnson, D. E.** *Concepts of air force leadership.* Maxwell AF Base, Alabama: Air University, 1970.

**Johnson, D. M., & Smith, H. C.** Democratic leadership in the college classroom. *Psychol. Monogr.*, 1953, *67*, No. 11.

**Johnson, D. W., & Johnson, F. P.** *Joining together: group theory and group skills.* Englewood Cliffs, N.J.: Prentice-Hall, 1975.

**Johnson, L. A.** *Employing the hard-core unemployed.* New York: American Management Association, 1969.

**Johnson, M. C.** Mentors—the key to development and growth. *Training and Develop. J.*, 1980, *34*, 55, 57.

**Johnson, P. O., & Bledsoe, J. C.** Morale as related to perceptions of leader behavior. *Personnel Psych.*, 1973, *26*, 581–592.

**Johnson, P. V., & Marcrum, R. H.** Perceived deficiencies in individual need fulfillment of career army officers. *J. appl. Psychol.*, 1968, *52*, 457–461.

**Johnson, R. H.** Initiating structure, consideration, and participative decision making: dimensions of leader behavior. Doctoral dissertation, Michigan State University, East Lansing, 1973.

**Johnson, R. J.** Relationship of employee morale to ability to predict responses. *J. appl. Psychol.*, 1954, *38*, 320–323.

**Johnson, R. J.** Two approaches to the prediction of group responses. *J. appl. Psychol*, 1963, *47*, 158–160.

**Johnson, R. W., & Ryan, B. J.** A test of the contingency model of leadership effectiveness. *J. appl. soc. Psychol.*, 1976, *6*, 177–185.

**Johnson, W. G.** On-the-job affirmation of self and stated level of job satisfaction and their relation to perceived supervisory climate. *Dissertation Abstr. Internat.*, 1969, *30*, 424.

**Jones, A. J.** *The education of youth for leadership.* New York: McGraw-Hill, 1938.

**Jones, A. P., James, L. R., & Bruni, J. R.** Perceived leadership behavior and employee confidence in the leader as moderated by job involvement. *J. appl. Psychol.*, 1975, *60*, 146–149.

**Jones, E. E.** Authoritarianism as a determinant of first-impression formation. *J. Pers.*, 1954, *23*, 107–127.

**Jones, E. E.** *Ingratiation.* New York: Appleton-Century-Crofts, 1964.

**Jones, E. E., & deCharms, R.** Changes in social perception as a function of the personal relevance of behavior. *Sociometry*, 1957, *20*, 75–85.

**Jones, E. E., Gergen, K. J., Gumpert, P., & Thibaut, J. W.** Some conditions affecting the use of ingratiation to influence performance evaluation. *J. pers. soc. Psychol.*, 1965, *1*, 613–625.

**Jones, E. E., Gergen, K. J., & Jones, R. E.** Tactics of ingratiation among leaders and subordinates in a status hierarchy. *Psychol. Monogr.* 1963, *77*, No. 566.

**Jones, E. W.** What it's like to be a black manager. *Harvard bus. Rev.*, 1973, *51*, 108–116.

**Jones, H. R., & Johnson, M.** LPC as a modifier of leader–follower relationships. *Acad. Mgmt. J.*, 1972, *15*, 185–196.

**Jones, R. E., & Jones, E. E.** Optimum conformity as an ingratiation tactic. *J. pers.*, 1964, *32*, 436–458.

**Jordan, A. M., & Hunter, E. C.** An analysis of quality associated with leadership among college students. *J. educ. Psychol.*, 1939, *30*, 497–509.

**Julian J. W.** Leader and group behavior as correlates of adjustment and performance in negotiation groups. *Dissertation Abstr.*, 1964, *24*, 646.

**Julian, J. W., & Hollander, E. P.** A study of some role dimensions of leader–follower relations. Buffalo: State University of New York, Technical report, No. 1, 1966.

**Julian, J. W., Hollander, E. P., & Regula, C. R.** Endorsement of the group spokesman as a function of his source of authority, competence, and success. *J. pers. soc. Psychol.*, 1969, *11*, 42–49.

**Jusenius, C. L.** Economics. *Signs*, 1976, *2*, 177–189.

**Justis, R. T.** Leadership effectiveness: a contingency approach. *Acad. Mgmt. J.*, 1975, *18*, 160–167.

**Kabanoff, B., & O'Brien, G. E.** Cooperation structure and the relationship of leader and member ability to group performance. *J. appl. Psych.*, 1979, *64*, 526–532.

**Kaczka, E. E., & Kirk, R. V.** Managerial climate, work groups, and organizational performance. *Admin. sci. Quar.*, 1967, *12*, 253–272.

**Kadushin, A.** Games people play in supervision. *Soc. Work*, 1968, *13*, 23–32.

**Kadushin, C.** Power, influence, and social circles: a new methodology for studying opinion makers. *Amer. sociol. Rev.*, 1968, *33*, 685–699.

**Kaess, W. A., Witryol, S. L., & Nolan, R. E.** Reliability, sex differences, and validity in the leadership discussion group. *J. appl. Psychol.*, 1961, *45*, 345–350.

**Kahn, R. L.** An analysis of supervisory practices and components of morale. In H. Guetzkow. *Groups, leadership, and men.* Pittsburgh: Carnegie Press, 1951.

**Kahn, R. L.** *Employee motivation.* Ann Arbor: University of Michigan, Bureau of Industrial Relations, 1956.

**Kahn, R. L.** The prediction of productivity. *J. soc. Issues.*, 1956, *12*, 41–49.

**Kahn, R. L.** Human relations on the shop floor. In E. M. Hugh-Jones (Ed.), *Human relations and modern management.* Amsterdam: North-Holland Publishing Co., 1958.

**Kahn, R. L.** Productivity and job satisfaction. *Personnel Psychol.*, 1960, *13*, 275–287.

**Kahn, R. L., & Boulding, E.** *Power and conflict in organizations.* New York: Basic Books, 1964.

**Kahn, R. L., & Katz, D.** Leadership practices in relation to productivity and morale. In D. Cartwright & A. Zander (Eds.), *Group dynamics*. New York: Harper & Row, 1953, 1960.

**Kahn, R. L., & Morse, Nancy C.** The relationship of productivity to morale. *J. soc. Issues.*, 1951, *7*, 8–17.

**Kahn, R. L., & Tannenbaum, A. S.** Leadership practices and member participation in local unions. *Personnel Psychol.*, 1957, *10*, 277–292.

**Kahn, R. L., Wolfe, D. M., Quinn, R. P., Snoek, J. D., & Rosenthal, R. A.** *Organizational stress: studies in role conflict and ambiguity*. New York: Wiley, 1964.

**Kahn, S.** *How people get power*. New York: McGraw-Hill, 1970.

**Kaiser, H. F.** The varimax criterion for analytic rotation in a factor analysis. *Psychometrika*, 1958, *23*, 187–200.

**Kamano, D. K., Powell, B. J., & Martin, L. K.** Relationship between ratings assigned to supervisors and their ratings of subordinates. *Psychol. Rep.*, 1966, *18*, 158.

**Kanareff, V. T., & Lanzetta, J. T.** Effects of task definition and probability or reenforcement upon the acquisition and extinction of imitative responses. *J. exp. Psychol.*, 1960, *60*, 340–348.

**Kanter, R. M.** Some effects of proportions on group life: skewed sex ratios and responses to token women. *Amer. J. Sociol.*, 1977, *82*, 965–990.

**Kanter, R. M.** *Men and women of the corporation*. New York: Basic Books, 1977.

**Kanungo, R.** Sociometric rating and perceived interpersonal behavior. *J. soc. Psychol.*, 1966, *68*, 253–268.

**Kanungo, S. C., Mathur, J. S., & Chatterjee, B. B.** Perceptions of leadership roles in rural settings. *Manas*, 1965, *12*, 127–143.

**Kaplan, A.** *The conduct of inquiry: methodology for behavioral science*. San Francisco: Chandler, 1964.

**Kaplan, H. R., Tausky, C., & Bolaria, B. S.** Job enrichment. *Personnel J.*, 1969, *48*, 791–798.

**Karasick, B., Leidy, T. R., & Smart, B.** Characteristics differentiating high school leaders from nonleaders. *Purdue Opinion Panel Poll Report*, 1968, *27*, 18.

**Karmel, B.** Leadership: a challenge to traditional research methods and assumptions. *Acad. Mgmt. Rev.*, 1978, *3*, 475–482.

**Kassarjian, H. H.** Social character and sensitivity training. *J. appl. behav. Sci.*, 1965, *1*, 433–440.

**Kates, S. L., & Mahone, C. H.** Effective group participation and group norms. *J. soc. Psychol.*, 1958, *48*, 211–216.

**Kast, F. E., & Rosenzweig, J. E.** General systems theory: applications for organization and management. *Acad. Mgmt. J.*, 1972, *15*, 447–465.

**Katz, D.** Employee groups: what motivates them and how they perform. *Advanced Mgmt.*, 1949, *14*, 119–124.

**Katz, D.** Survey research center: an overview of the human relations program. In H. Guetzkow, (Ed.), *Groups, leadership and men*. Pittsburgh: Carnegie Press, 1951.

**Katz, D., & Kahn, R. L.** Human organization and worker motivation. In L. R. Tripp (Ed.), *Industrial productivity*. Madison, Wis.: Industrial Relations Research Association, 1951.

**Katz, D., & Kahn, R. L.** *The social psychology of organizations*. New York: Wiley, 1966.

**Katz, D., Maccoby, N., Gurin, G., & Floor, L.** *Productivity, supervision, and morale among railroad workers*. Ann Arbor: University of Michigan, Institute for Social Research, 1951.

**Katz, D., Maccoby, N., & Morse, N. C.** *Productivity, supervision, and morale in an office situation*. Ann Arbor: University of Michigan, Institute for Social Research, 1950.

**Katz, E., Blau, P. M., Brown, M. L., & Strodtbeck, F. L.** Leadership stability and social change: an experiment with small groups. *Sociometry,* 1957, *20,* 36–50.

**Katz, E., & Lazarsfeld, P. F.** *Personal influence: the part played by people in the flow of mass communications.* New York: Free Press, 1955.

**Katz, E., Libby, W. L., & Strodtbeck, F. L.** Status mobility and reactions to deviance and subsequent conformity. *Sociometry,* 1964, *27,* 245–260.

**Katz, F. E.** Explaining informal groups in complex organizations: the case for autonomy in structure. *Admin. sci. Quar.,* 1965, *10,* 204–221.

**Katz, I.** Some motivational determinants of racial differences in intellectual achievement. *Internat. J. Psychol.,* 1967, *2,* 1–12.

**Katz, I.** Factors influencing Negro performance in the desegregated school. In M. Deutsch, I. Katz, & A. R. Jensen (Eds.), *Social class, race, and psychological development.* New York: Holt, Rinehart & Winston, 1968.

**Katz, I.** Experimental studies of Negro-white relationships. In L. Berkowitz (Ed.), *Advances in experimental social psychology,* vol. 5. New York: Academic Press, 1970.

**Katz, I.** Cultural and personality factors in minority group behavior: a critical review. In M. L. Fromkin & J. J. Sherwood (Eds.), *Integrating the organization.* New York: Free Press, 1974.

**Katz, I., & Benjamin, L.** Effects of white authoritarianism in biracial work groups. *J. abnorm. soc. Psychol.,* 1960, *61,* 448–456.

**Katz, I., & Cohen, M.** The effects of training Negroes upon cooperative problem solving in biracial teams. *J. abnorm. soc. Psychol.,* 1962, *64,* 319–325.

**Katz, I., Epps, E. G., & Axelson, L. J.** Effect upon Negro digit-symbol performance of anticipated comparison with whites and with other Negroes. *J. abnorm. soc. Psychol.,* 1964, *69,* 77–83.

**Katz, I., Goldston, J., & Benjamin, L.** Behavior and productivity in biracial work groups. *Hum. Relat.,* 1958, *11,* 123–141.

**Katz, I., & Greenbaum, G.** Effects of anxiety, threat, and racial environment on task performance of Negro college students. *J. abnorm. soc. Psychol.,* 1963, *66,* 562–567.

**Katz, R.** The influence of group conflict on leadership effectiveness. *Org. behav. hum. Perform.,* 1977, *20,* 265–286.

**Katz, R., & Farris, G.** Does performance affect LPC? Boston: Massachusetts Institute of Technology, unpublished paper, 1976.

**Katz, R., Phillips, E., & Cheston, R.** Methods of conflict resolution—a re-examination. Boston: Massachusetts Institute of Technology, unpublished ms., 1976.

**Katzell, R. A.** Testing a training program in human relations. *Personnel Psychol.,* 1948, *1,* 319–329.

**Katzell, R. A.** Contrasting systems of work organization. *Amer. Psychologist,* 1962, *17,* 102–111.

**Katzell, R. A., Barrett, R. S., Vann, D. H., & Hogan, J. M.** Organizational correlates of executive roles. *J. appl. Psychol.,* 1968, *52,* 22–28.

**Katzell, R. A., Miller, C. E., Rotter, N. G., & Venet, T. G.** Effects of leadership and other inputs on group processes and outputs. *J. soc. Psychol.,* 1970, *80,* 157–169.

**Kaufman, R. A., Hakmiller, K. L., & Porter, L. W.** The effects of top and middle management sets on the Ghiselli Self-Description Inventory. *J. appl. Psychol.,* 1959, *43,* 149–153.

**Kavanagh, M. J.** Subordinates' satisfaction as a function of their supervisor's behavior. *Dissertation Abstr. Internat.,* 1969, *30,* 1391–1392.

**Kavanagh, M. J.** Leadership behavior as a function of subordinate competence and task complexity. *Admin. sci. Quar.,* 1972, *17,* 591–600.

**Kavanagh, M. J.** Expected supervisory behavior, interpersonal trust and environmental preferences. Some relationships based on a dyadic model of leadership. *Org. behav. hum. Perform.*, 1975, *13*, 17–30.

Kavanagh, M. J., & Halpern, M. The impact of job level and sex differences on the relationship between life and job satisfaction. *Acad. Mgmt. J.*, 1977, *20*, 66–73.

Kavanagh, M. J., MacKinney, A. C., & Wolins, L. Satisfaction and morale of foremen as a function of middle manager's performance. *J. appl. Psychol.*, 1970, *54*, 145–156.

Kavanagh, M. J., & York, D. R. Biographical correlates of middle managers' performance. *Personnel Psychol.*, 1972, *25*, 319–332.

Kavcic, B., Rus, V., & Tannenbaum, A. S. Control, participation, and effectiveness in four Yugoslav industrial organizations. *Admin. sci. Quar.*, 1971, *16*, 74–86.

Kay, B. R. Key factors in effective foreman behavior. *Personnel*, 1959, *36*, 25–31.

Kay, B. R. Prescription and perception of the supervisory role: a rolecentric interpretation. *Occup. Psychol.*, 1963, *37*, 219–227.

Kay, E., French, J. R. P., & Meyer, H. H. A study of the performance appraisal interview. *Behavioral Research Science*. New York: General Electric, 1962.

Kay, E., & Meyer, H. H. The development of a job activity questionnaire for production foremen. *Personnel Psychol.*, 1962, *15*, 411–418.

Keaveny, T. J. The impact of managerial values on managerial behavior. *Dissertation Abstr. Internat.*, 1972, *32*, 6708.

Keaveny, T. J., Jackson, J. H., & Fossum, J. A. Sex differences in job satisfaction. *Proceedings of the Academy of Management*, 1976.

Keeler, B. T., & Andrews, J. H. M. Leader behavior of principals, staff morale, and productivity. *Alberta J. educ. Res.*, 1963, *9*, 179–191.

Kehoe, D. A. The interpersonal basis of consensus on emergent leadership in small discussion groups. *Dissertation Abstr. Internat.*, 1976, *36*, 5231–5232.

Keizai Doyukai 1958 Survey Report. The structure and function of top management of large enterprises in Japan. In N. Kazuo (Ed.), *Big business executives in Japan*. Tokyo: Diamond Press, 1960.

Keller, R. T., & Szilagyi, A. D. Employee reactions to leader reward behavior. *Acad. Mgmt. J.*, 1976, *19*, 619–626.

Kelley, H. H. The warm-cold variable in first impressions of personality. *J. Pers.*, 1950, *18*, 431–439.

Kelley, H. H. Communication in experimentally created hierarchies. *Hum. Relat.*, 1951, *4*, 39–56.

Kelley, H. H., & Arrowood, A. J. Coalitions in the triad: critique and experiment. *Sociometry*, 1960, *23*, 231–244.

Kelley, H. H., & Shapiro, M. M. An experiment on conformity to group norms where conformity is detrimental to group achievement. *Amer. sociol. Rev.*, 1954, *19*, 667–677.

Kelley, H. H., & Thibaut, J. W. Experimental studies of group problem solving and process. In G. Lindzey (Ed.), *Handbook of social psychology*. Cambridge, Mass.: Addison-Wesley, 1954.

Kelley, W.R. The relationship between cognitive complexity and leadership style in school superintendents. *Dissertation Abstr.*, 1968, *28*, 4910–4911.

Kelly, J. A study of leadership in two contrasting groups. *Sociol. Rev.*, 1963, *11*, 323–336.

Kelly, J. The study of executive behavior by activity sampling. *Hum. Relat.*, 1964, *17*, 277–287.

Kelman, H. C. Attitude change as a function of response restriction. *Hum. Relat.*, 1953, *6*, 185–214.

Kelman, H. C. Compliance, identification, and internalization: three processes of attitude change. *J. conflict Resol.*, 1958, *2*, 51–60.

**Kelman, H. C.** A social-psychological model of political legitimacy and its relevance to black and white student protest movements. *Psychiatry,* 1970, *33,* 224–246.

**Kenan, T. A.** A method of investigating executive leadership. Doctoral dissertation, Ohio State University, Columbus, 1948.

**Kenis, I.** A cross-cultural study of personality and leadership. *Grp. org. Studies,* 1977, *2,* 49–60.

**Kennedy, J. E., & O'Neill, H. E.** Job content and workers' opinions. *J. appl. Psychol.,* 1958, *42,* 372–375.

**Kerlinger, F. N.** Decision-making in Japan. *Social Forces,* 1951, *30,* 36–41.

**Kern, A. G., & Bahr, H. M.** Some factors affecting leadership climate in a state parole agency. *Pac. sociol. Rev.,* 1974, *17,* 108–118.

**Kernan, J. P.** Laboratory human relations training—its effect on the personality of supervisory engineers. Doctoral dissertation, New York University, New York, 1963.

**Kerr, C., Dunlop, J. T., Harbison, F., & Myers, C. A.** Industrialism and world society. *Harvard bus. Rev.,* 1961, *39,* 114–122.

**Kerr, S.** Ability- and willingness-to-leave as moderators of relationships between task and leader variables and satisfaction. *J. bus. Res.,* 1973, *1,* 115–128.

**Kerr, S.** On the folly of rewarding A, while hoping for B. *Acad. Mgmt. J.,* 1975, *18,* 769–783.

**Kerr, S., & Schriesheim, C.** Consideration, initiating structure, and organizational criteria—an update of Korman's 1966 review. *Personnel Psychol.,* 1974, *27,* 555–568.

**Kerr, S., Schriesheim, C. A., Murphy, C. J., & Stogdill, R. M.** Toward a contingency theory of leadership based upon the consideration and initiating structure literature. *Org. behav. hum. Perform.* 1974, *12,* 62–82.

**Kerr, W. A.** Labor turnover and its correlates. *J. appl. Psychol.,* 1947, *31,* 366–371.

**Kerr, W. A., & Speroff, B. J.** *Measurement of empathy.* Chicago: Psychometric Affiliates, 1951.

**Kessing, F. M., & Kessing, Marie M.** *Elite communication in Samoa: a study of leadership.* Stanford, Calif.: Stanford University Press, 1956.

**Kessler, C. C.** Differences between subordinates who are successful and less successful in meeting superiors' demands. *Dissertation Abstr.,* 1968, *28,* 3866–3867.

**Ketchel, J. M.** The development of methodology for evaluating the effectiveness of a volunteer health planning organization. Doctoral dissertation, Ohio State University, Columbus, 1972.

**Key, R. C.** A study of perceived organizational characteristics in persistent disagreement school districts and nonpersistent disagreement districts in the San Francisco Bay area. Doctoral dissertation, University of Southern California, Los Angeles, 1974.

**Key, V. O., Jr.** *Public opinion and American democracy.* New York: Knopf, 1961.

**Khandwalla, P.** Effect of competition on the structure of top management control. *Acad. Mgmt. J.,* 1973, *16,* 285–295.

**Khemka, K. C.** Perception of leadership status in a free operant group discussion situation as a function of the knowledge of reinforcement contingency. *Dissertation Abstr.,* 1968, *29,* 1189.

**Kidd, J. A., & Christy, R. T.** Supervisory procedures and work-team productivity. *J. appl. Psychol.,* 1961, *45,* 388–392.

**Kidd, J. S.** Social influence phenomena in a task-oriented group. *J. abnorm. soc. Psychol.,* 1958, *56,* 13–17.

**Kiernan, J. P.** A critical appreciation of Sundkler's leadership types in the light of further research. *Afr. Stud.,* 1975, *34,* 193–201.

**Kiesler, C. A., & Corbin, L. H.** Commitment, attraction, and conformity. *J. pers. soc. Psychol.,* 1965, *2,* 890–895.

**Kiesler, C. A., & Kiesler, S. B.** *Conformity.* Reading, Mass.: Addison-Wesley, 1969.

**Kiesler, C. A., Kiesler, S. B., & Pallak, M.** The reactions to norm violations. *J. Pers.,* 1967, *35,* 585–599.

**Kiessling, R. J., & Kalish, R. A.** Correlates of success in leaderless group discussion. *J. soc. Psychol.,* 1961, *54,* 359–365.

**Kight, S. S., & Smith, E. E.** Effects of feedback on insight and problem-solving efficiency in training groups. *J. appl. Psychol.,* 1959, *43,* 209–211.

**Kilbourne, C. E.** The elements of leadership. *J. Coast Artillery,* 1935, *78,* 437–439.

**Kilbridge, M. D.** Do workers prefer larger jobs? *Personnel J.,* 1960, *37,* 45–48.

**Kilbridge, M. D.** Do they want larger jobs? *Supervisory Mgmt.,* 1961, *6,* 25–28.

**Kim, J. S., & Schuler, R. S.** Contingencies of the effectiveness of participation in decision making and goal setting. *Proceedings of the Eastern Academy of Management,* 1976.

**Kincheloe, S. C.** The prophet as a leader. *Sociol. soc. Res.,* 1928, *12,* 461–468.

**Kinder, B. N., & Kolmann, P. R.** The impact of differential shifts in leader structure on the outcome of internal and external group participants. *J. clin. Psychol.,* 1976, *32,* 857–863.

**King, B., Streufert, S., & Fiedler, F. E. (Eds.).** *Managerial control and organizational democracy.* New York: Halsted Press, 1978.

**King, C. D., & van de Vall, M.** Dimensions of workers' participation in managerial decision-making. *Proceedings of the Industrial Relations Research Association,* 1969.

**King, C. E.** *Sociology of small groups.* New York: Pageant Press, 1962.

**King, D. C., & Bass, B. M.** Leadership, power, and influence. In H. L. Fromkin & J. J. Sherwood (Eds.), *Integrating the organization.* New York: Free Press, 1974.

**King, H. D., & Arlinghaus, C. G.** Interaction management validated in the steel industry. *Assess. Develop.,* 1976, III.

**King, M. L., Jr.** The role of the behavioral scientist in the civil rights movement. *J. soc. Issues,* 1968, *24,* 1–12.

**King, P. H.** *A summary of research in training for advisory roles in other cultures by the behavioral sciences laboratory.* Wright Patterson Air Force Base, Oh.: Aerospace Medical Research Laboratories, 1966.

**Kingsley, L.** Process analysis of a leaderless counter-transference group. *Psychol. Rep.,* 1967, *20,* 555–562.

**Kinicki, A. J., & Schriesheim, C. A.** Teachers as leaders: a moderator variable approach. *J. educ. Res.,* 1978, *70,* 928–935.

**Kipnis, D.** The effects of leadership style and leaderless power upon the inducement of an attitude change. *J. abnorm. soc. Psychol.,* 1958, *57,* 173–180.

**Kipnis, D.** Some determinants of supervisory esteem. *Personnel Psychol.,* 1960, *13,* 377–392.

**Kipnis, D.** Mobility expectations and attitudes toward industrial structure. *Hum. Relat.,* 1964, *17,* 57–72.

**Kipnis, D., & Cosentino, J.** Use of leadership powers in industry. *J. appl. Psychol.,* 1969, *53,* 460–466.

**Kipnis, D., & Lane, W. P.** Self-confidence and leadership. *J. appl. Psychol.,* 1962, *46,* 291–295.

**Kipnis, D., Silverman, A., & Copeland, C.** Effects of emotional arousal on the use of supervised coercion with black and union members. *J. appl. Psychol.,* 1973, *57,* 38–43.

**Kipnis, D., & Vanderveer, R.** Ingratiation and the use of power. *J. pers. soc. Psychol.,* 1971, *17,* 280–286.

**Kipnis, D., & Wagner, C.** Character structure and response to leadership. *J. exp. res. Pers.,* 1967, *1,* 16–24.

**Kirchner, W. K.** Differences between better and less effective supervisors in appraisal of their subordinates. *Amer. Psychologist,* 1961, *16,* 432–433.

**Kirchner, W. K., & Belenker, J.** What employees want to know. *Personnel J.*, 1955, *33*, 378–379.

**Kirchner, W. K., & Reisberg, D. J.** Differences between better and less effective supervisors in appraisal of subordinates. *Personnel Psychol.*, 1962, *15*, 295–302.

**Kirkhart, R. O.** Minority group identification and group leadership. *J. soc. Psychol.*, 1963, *59*, 111–117.

**Kirkpatrick, D. L.** Evaluating human relations programs for industrial foremen and supervisors. Doctoral dissertation, University of Wisconsin, Madison, 1954.

**Kirscht, J. P., & Dillehay, R. C.** *Dimensions of authoritarianism: a review of research and theory.* Lexington: University of Kentucky, 1967.

**Kirscht, J. P., Lodahl, T. M., & Haire, M.** Some factors in the selection of leaders by members of small groups. *J. abnorm. soc. Psychol.*, 1959, *58*, 406–408.

**Kiser, S. L.** *The American concept of leadership.* New York: Pageant Press, 1955.

**Klapp, O. E.** The creation of popular heroes. *Amer. J. Sociol.*, 1948, *54*, 135–141.

**Klaus, D. J., & Glasser, R.** Reinforcement determinants of team proficiency. *Org. behav. hum. Perform.*, 1970, *5*, 33–67.

**Klauss, R., & Bass, B. M.** *Impact of communication.* New York: Academic Press, 1981.

**Klebanoff, H. E.** Leadership: an investigation of its distribution in task-oriented small groups. *Dissertation Abstr. Internat.*, 1976, *36*, 3614.

**Klein, A. F.** *Role playing in leadership training and group problem solving.* New York: Association Press, 1956.

**Klein, A. L.** Changes in leadership appraisal as a function of the stress of a simulated panic situation. *J. pers. soc. Psychol.*, 1976, *34*, 1143–1154.

**Klein, A. L.** Changes in leadership appraisal as a function of the stress of a simulated panic situation and task outcome. *Dissertation Abstr. Internat.*, 1975, *36*, 1970.

**Klein, A. L.** Changes in leadership appraisal as a function of the stress of a simulated panic situation. *J. pers. soc. Psychol.*, 1976, *34*, 1143–1154.

**Klein, S. M.** Work pressure and group cohesion. *Dissertation Abstr.*, 1964, *24*, 3448.

**Klein, S. M., & Maher, J. R.** Education and satisfaction with pay. *Personnel Psychol.*, 1966, *18*, 195–208.

**Klein, S. M., & Maher, J. R.** Educational level, attitudes, and future expectations among first-level management. *Personnel Psychol.*, 1968, *21*, 43–53.

**Klein, S. M., & Maher, J. R.** Decision-making autonomy and perceived conflict among first-level management. *Personnel Psychol.*, 1970, *23*, 481–492.

**Klein, S. M., & Ritti, R. R.** Work pressure, supervisory behavior, and employee attitudes: a factor analysis. *Personnel Psychol.*, 1970, *23*, 153–167.

**Kline, B. E., & Martin, N. H.** Freedom, authority, and decentralization. *Harvard bus. Rev.*, 1958, *36*, 69–75.

**Klopfer, P. H.** *Behavioral aspects of ecology.* Englewood Cliffs, N.J.: Prentice-Hall, 1962.

**Klopfer, P. H.** *Habitats and territories: a study of the use of space by animals.* New York: Basic Books, 1969.

**Klubeck, S., & Bass, B. M.** Differential effects of training on persons of different leadership status. *Hum. Relat.*, 1954, *7*, 59–72.

**Knapp, D. E., & Knapp, D.** Effect of position on group verbal conditioning. *J. soc. Psychol.*, 1966, *69*, 95–99.

**Knickerbocker, I.** Leadership: a conception and some implications. *J. soc. Issues*, 1948, *4*, 23–40.

**Knight, M. E.** *The German executive: 1890–1933.* Stanford, Calif.: Stanford University Press, 1952.

**Knowles, E. S.** *A bibliography of research: 1960–1967.* Washington, D.C.: NTL Institute for Applied Behavioral Science, 1967.

**Knowles, H. P., & Saxberg, B. O.** *Personality and leadership.* Reading, Mass.: Addison-Wesley, 1971.

**Knowles, M. C.** Group assessment in staff selection. *Personnel pract. Bull.,* 1963, *19,* 6–16.

**Knowlton, W.** The effects of stress, experience, and intelligence on dyadic leadership performance. Doctoral dissertation, University of Washington, Seattle, 1979.

**Koch, H. L. et al.** Popularity in preschool children: some related factors and a technique for its measurement. *Child Develop.,* 1933, *4,* 164–175.

**Koch, S.** *Formulation of the person in the social context.* (Psychology: a study of a science, vol. 3.) New York: McGraw-Hill, 1959.

**Koch, S.** *Investigations of man as socius.* (Psychology: a study of a science, vol. 6.) New York: McGraw-Hill, 1963.

**Kochan, T. A., Schmidt, S. M., & de Cotiis, T. A.** Superior–subordinate relations: leadership and headship. *Hum. Relat.,* 1975, *28,* 279–294.

**Kochman, T.** "Rapping" in the black ghetto. *Trans-action,* 1969, *6,* 26–34.

**Koff, L. A.** Age, experience and success among women managers. *Mgmt. Rev.,* 1973, *62,* 65–66.

**Koford, C. B.** Group relations in an island colony of Rhesus monkeys. In C. H. Southwick. *Primate social behavior.* (Ed.), Princeton, N.J.: Van Nostrand, 1963.

**Kohs, S. C., & Irle, K. W.** Prophesying army promotion. *J. appl. Psychol.,* 1920, *4,* 73–87.

**Koile, E. A., & Draeger, C.** T-group member ratings of leader and self in human relations laboratory. *J. Psychol.,* 1969, *72,* 11–20.

**Kolaja, J., Able, R. L., Ferguson, J. P., Mathews, W. R., Jr., Porter, H. M., & Ramsey, L.** An organization seen as a structure of decision-making. *Hum. Relat.,* 1963, *16,* 351–357.

**Kolb, J. H.** Trends of country neighborhoods. *Agric. exp. Station, Univ. Wisc.,* 1933.

**Kolb, J. H., & Wileden, A. F.** Special interest groups in rural society. *Agric. exp. Station, Univ. Wisc.,* 1927.

**Kolstad, A.** Attitudes of employees and their supervisors. *Personnel J.,* 1944, *20,* 241–250.

**Konar-Goldband, E., Rice, R. W., & Monkarsh, W.** Time-phased interrelationships of group atmosphere, group performance, and leader style. *J. appl. Psychol.,* 1979, *64,* 401–409.

**Koontz, H., & O'Donnell, C.** *Principles of management.* New York: McGraw-Hill, 1955.

**Korman, A. K.** Job satisfactions of the first-line supervisors. *Personnel Admin.,* 1964, *27,* 35–37.

**Korman, A. K.** "Consideration," "Initiating Structure," and organizational criteria. *Personnel Psychol.,* 1966, *18,* 349–360.

**Korman, A. K.** The prediction of managerial performance: a review. *Personnel Psychol.,* 1968, *21,* 295–322.

**Korman, A. K.** Expectancies as determinants of performance. *J. appl. Psychol.,* 1971, *55,* 218–222.

**Korman, A. K.** On the development of contingency theories of leadership: some methodological considerations and a possible alternative. *J. appl. Psychol.,* 1973, *58,* 384–387.

**Korman, A. K.** Contingency approaches to leadership: an overview. In J. G. Hunt & L. L. Larson (Eds.), *Contingency approaches to leadership.* Carbondale: Southern Illinois University Press, 1974.

**Korman, A. K., & Tanofsky, R.** Statistical problems of contingency models in organizational behavior. *Acad. Mgmt. J.,* 1975, *18,* 393–397.

**Kornhauser, A. W., & Sharp, A. A.** Employee attitudes. *Personnel J.,* 1932, *10,* 393–404.

**Korten, D. C.** Situational determinants of leadership structure. *J. confl. Resol.*, 1962, *6*, 222–235.

**Korten, D. C.** Situational determinants of leadership structure. In D. Cartwright & A. Zander (Eds.), *Group dynamics: research and theory*. New York: Harper & Row, 1968.

**Kotter, J. P.** Power, success and organizational effectiveness. *Org. Dynam.*, 1978, *6*, 26–40.

**Koulack, D.** Effect of outgroup responses on perceptions of leader effectiveness. *Soc. Forces*, 1977, *55*, 959–965.

**Krauft, C., & Bozarth, J.** Democratic, authoritarian, and laissez-faire leadership with institutionalized mentally retarded boys. *Mental Retard.*, 1971, *9*, 7–10.

**Kraut, A. I.** Intellectual ability and promotional success among high level managers. *Personnel Psychol.*, 1969, *22*, 281–290.

**Kraut, A. I.** The entrance of black employees into traditionally white jobs. *Acad. Mgmt. J.*, 1975, *18*, 610–615.

**Kraut, A. I.** Developing managerial skills via modeling techniques: some positive research findings—a symposium. *Personnel Psychol.*, 1976, *29*, 325–369.

**Kravetz, D.** Sex role concepts of women. *J. consult clin. Psychol.*, 1976, *44*, 437–443.

**Krech, D., & Crutchfield, R. S.** *Theory and problems of social psychology*. New York: McGraw-Hill, 1948.

**Krejci, J.** Leadership and change in two Mexican villages. *Anthrop. Quart.*, 1976, *49*, 185–196.

**Kriesberg, L.** Careers, organization size, and succession. *Amer. J. Sociol.*, 1962, *68*, 355–359.

**Kriesberg, L.** Reply. *Amer. J. Sociol.*, 1964, *70*, 223.

**Krishnan, B.** The leadership qualities among the college students as assessed by the "L" scale of the Mysore Personality Inventory. *Psychol. Studies*, 1965, *10*, 23–36.

**Kroen, C. W.** Validation of Herzberg's theory of job motivation and its relationship to leadership style. *Dissertation Abstr.*, 1968, *28*, 5225–5226.

**Krout, M. H.** *Introduction to social psychology*. New York: Harper, 1942.

**Kruglanski, A. W.** Some variables affecting interpersonal trust in supervisor–worker relations. *Dissertation Abstr.*, 1969, *29*, 3219.

**Kruisinga, H. J.** *The balance between centralization and decentralization in managerial control*. Oxford: Blackwell, 1954.

**Krumboltz, J. D., Christal, R. E., & Ward, J. H.** Predicting leadership ratings from high school activities. *J. educ. Psychol.*, 1959, *50*, 105–110.

**Krusell, J., Vicino, F. L., Manning, M. R., Ryterband, E. C., Bass, B. M., & Landy, D. A.** *PROCESS—a program of self-administered exercises for personal and interpersonal development*. Scottsville, N.Y.: Transnational Programs Corporation, 1971, 1972, 1980.

**Kuenzli, A. E.** Preferences for high and low structure among prospective teachers. *J. soc. Psychol.*, 1959, *49*, 243–248.

**Kumar, P.** A study of value-dimensions in student leadership. *Psychol. Studies*, 1965, *10*, 73–79.

**Kumar, P.** Certain personal factors in student leadership. *J. Psychol. Researches*, 1966, *10*, 37–42.

**Kunczik, M.** The ASo-(LPC-)value in the contingency model of effective leadership: critical overview and suggestion of an alternative interpretation. *Kölner Zeitschrift für Soziologie und Sozialpsychologie*, 1974, *26*, 115–137.

**Kunczik, M.** Empirische Überprüfung des Kontingenzmodells effektiver Führung 1 (Empirical test of the contingency model of leadership effectiveness). *Kölner Zeitschrift für Soziologie und Sozialpsychologie*, 1976a, *28*, 517–536.

**Kunczik, M.** Empirische Überprüfung des Kontingenzmodells effektiver Führung. Teil 2; Überprufung anhand von Ausbildungsgruppen der Bundeswehr (Empirical test of the contingency model of leadership effectiveness. Part 2; Examination with the aid of the training groups of the federal armed services). *Kölner Zeitschrift für Soziologie und Sozialpsychologie*, 1976b, *28*, 738–754.

**Kuriloff, A. H.** An experiment in management—putting theory Y to the test. *Personnel J.*, 1963, *40*, 8–17.

**Kuriloff, A. H.** *Reality in management.* New York: McGraw-Hill, 1966.

**Kuriloff, A. H., & Atkins, S.** T group for a work team. *J. appl. behav. Sci.*, 1966, *2*, 63–93.

**Kurke, L. B., & Aldrich, H. E.** Mintzberg was right!: a replication and extension of "the nature of managerial work." *Proceedings of the Academy of Management*, 1979.

**Lacey, L.** Discriminability of the Miner sentence completion scale among supervisory and non-supervisory scientists and engineers. In J. B. Miner (Ed.), *Motivation to manage.* Atlanta: Organizational Measurement Systems Press, 1977.

**Ladouceur, J.** School management profile and capacity for change. Doctoral dissertation, University of Toronto, Toronto, 1973.

**LaGaipa, J. J.** Biographical inventories and style of leadership. *J. Psychol.*, 1969, *72*, 109–114.

**Lahat-Mandelbaum, B. S., & Kipnis, D.** Leader behavior dimensions related to students' evaluation of teaching effectiveness. *J. appl. Psych.*, 1973, *58*, 250–253.

**Laing, R. D., Phillipson, H., & Lee, A. R.** *Interpersonal perception: a theory and a method of research.* New York: Springer, 1966.

**Laird, D. A., & Laird, E. C.** *The new psychology for leadership.* New York: McGraw-Hill, 1956.

**Lakin, M.** Some ethical issues in sensitivity training. *Amer. Psychologist*, 1969, *24*, 923–928.

**Lambert, R.** Classement de portraits selon la valeur présumée au commandement et attribution de traits de personnalité. *Bull. Centre d'Etudes. Rech. Psychotech.*, 1971, *20*, 41–51.

**Lamm, H.** Intragroup effects on intergroup negotiation. *Eur. J. soc. Psychol.*, 1973, *3*, 179–192.

**Lamm, R.** Black union leaders at the local level. *Indus. Relat.*, 1975, *14*, 220–232.

**Lammers, C. J.** Power and participation in decision-making in formal organizations. *Amer. J. Sociol.*, 1967, *73*, 201–216.

**Lana, R. E., Vaughan, W., & McGinnies, E.** Leadership and friendship status as factors in discussion group interaction. *J. soc. Psychol.*, 1960, *52*, 127–134.

**Lanaghan, R. C.** Leadership effectiveness in selected elementary schools. Doctoral dissertation, University of Illinois, Urbana-Champaign, 1972.

**Land, K. C.** Principles of path analysis. In E. F. Borgatta (Ed.), *Sociological methodology.* San Francisco: Jossey-Bass, 1969.

**Landy, D., McCue, K., & Aronson, E.** Beyond Parkinson's Law: III. The effect of protractive and contractive distractions on the wasting of time on subsequent tasks. *J. appl. Psychol.*, 1969, *3*, 236–239.

**Lange, C. J., Campbell, V., Katter, R. V., & Shanley, F. J.** *A study of leadership in army infantry platoons.* Washington, D. C.: Human Resources Research Office, 1958.

**Lange, C. J., & Jacobs, T. O.** *Leadership in army infantry platoons: Study II.* Washington, D.C.: Human Resources Research Office, 1960.

**Lange, C. J., Rittenhouse, C. H., & Atkinson, R. C.** *Films and group discussions as a means of training leaders.* Washington, D.C.: Human Resources Research Office, June 1968.

**Langer, W. C.** *The mind of Adolf Hitler.* New York: Basic Books, 1972.

**Lannon, J. M.** Male vs. female values in management. *Mgmt. internat. Rev.*, 1977, *17*, 9–12.

**Lansing, F. W.** Selected factors of group interaction and their relation with leadership performance. *Internat. J. Sociometry*, 1957, *1*, 170–174.

**Lanzetta, J. T.** An investigation of group behavior under stress. Rochester: University of Rochester, Task Order V., 1953.

**Lanzetta, J. T.** Group behavior under stress. *Hum. Relat.*, 1955, *8*, 29–52.

**Lanzetta, J. T., Haefner, D., Langham, P., & Axelrod, H.** Some effects of situational threat on group behavior. *J. abnorm. soc. Psychol.*, 1954, *49*, 445–453.

**Lanzetta, J. T., & Haythorn, W. W.** Instructor-crew influence on attitude formation in student crews. San Antonio, Tex: AFPTRC-TR-54-79, 1954.

**Lanzetta, J. T., & Roby, T. B.** Group performance as a function of work-distribution patterns and task load. Crew Research Laboratory, AF Personnel & Training Reserve Center, Randolf AF Base, CRL-LN-55-4, 1955.

**Lanzetta, J. T., & Roby, T. B.** Effects of work-group structure and certain task variables on group performance. *J. abnorm. soc. Psychol.*, 1956, *53*, 307–314.

**Lanzetta, J. T., & Roby, T. B.** Group learning and communication as a function of task and structure "demands." *J. abnorm. soc. Psychol.*, 1957, *55*, 121–131.

**Lanzetta, J. T., & Roby, T. B.** The relationship between certain group process variables and group problem-solving efficiency. *J. soc. Psychol.*, 1960, *52*, 135–148.

**Lanzetta, J. T., Wendt, G. R., Langham, P., & Haefner, D.** The effects of an "anxiety-reducing" medication on group behavior under threat. *J. abnorm. soc. Psychol,* 1956, *52*, 103–108.

**Lapiere, R. T.** *Collective behavior.* New York: McGraw-Hill, 1938.

**LaPiere, R. T. & Farnsworth, P. R.** *Social psychology.* New York: McGraw-Hill, 1936.

**Lardent, C. L.** *An assessment of the motivation to command among U. S. army officer candidates.* Technical report to the U.S. Army Research Institute for the Behavioral and Social Sciences, 1977.

**Larkin, R. W.** Social exchange in the elementary school classroom: the problem of teacher legitimation of the social power. *Sociol. Educ.*, 1975, *48*, 400–410.

**LaRocco, J. M., & Jones, A. P.** Co-worker and leader support as moderators of stress-strain relationships in work situations. *J. appl. Psychol.*, 1978, *63*, 629–634.

**Larsen, K. S., & Larsen, K. J.** Leadership, group activity and sociometric choice in service sororities and fraternities. *Percept. mot. Skills*, 1969, *28*, 539–542.

**Larson, C. J.** Leadership in three black neighborhoods. *Phylon*, 1975, *36*, 260–268.

**Larson, L. L., Hunt, J. G., & Osborn, R. N.** Correlates of leadership and demographic variables in three organizational settings. *J. bus. Res.*, 1974, *2*, 335–347.

**Larson, L. L., Hunt, J. G., & Osborn, R. N.** The great hi-hi leader behavior myth: a lesson from Occam's razor. *Acad. Mgmt. J.*, 1976, *19*, 628–641.

**Larson, L. L., & Rowland, K. M.** Leadership style and cognitive complexity. *Acad. Mgmt. J.*, 1974, *17*, 37–45.

**Larwood, L., & Kaplan, M.** Women's strategies for success in management. *Proceedings of the Academy of Management*, 1979.

**Larwood, L., O'Carroll, M., & Logan, J.** Sex role as a mediator of achievement in task performance. *Sex Roles*, 1977, *3*, 109–114.

**Larwood, L., & Wood, M. M.** *Women in management.* Lexington, Mass.: D. C. Heath, 1977.

**Larwood, L., Wood, M. M., & Inderlied, S. D.** Training women for management: new problems, new solutions. *Acad. Mgmt. Rev.*, 1978, *3*, 584–593.

**Lasher, W. F.** *Academic governance in university professional schools.* Doctoral dissertation, University of Michigan, Ann Arbor, 1975.

**Lassey, W. R., & Fernandez, R. R.** *Leadership and social change.* La Jolla, Calif.: University Associates, 1976.

**Lasswell, H. D., & Kaplan, A.** *Power and society.* New Haven: Yale University Press, 1950.

**Lasswell, H. D., Lerner, D., & Rothwell, C. E.** *The comparative study of elites.* Stanford, Calif.: Stanford University Press, 1952.

**Latham, G. P., & Saari, L. M.** Importance of supportive relationships in goal setting. *J. appl. Psychol.*, 1979, *64*, 151–156.

**Laughlin, R. A.** A study of organizational climate perceived by faculty in Colorado community junior colleges. Doctoral dissertation, University of Colorado, Boulder, 1973.

**Laurent, H.** Research on the identification of management potential. In J. A. Myers (Ed.), *Predicting managerial success*. Ann Arbor: Foundation for Research on Human Behavior, 1968.

**Laurent, H.** Cross-cultural cross-validation of empirically validated tests. *J. appl. Psychol.*, 1970, *54*, 417–423.

**Lauterbach, A.** Management aims and development needs in Latin America. *Bus. his. Rev.*, 1963, *39*, 557–572, 577–588.

**Lauterbach, A.** *Men, motives, and money: psychological frontiers of economics*. Ithaca, N.Y.: Cornell University Press, 1954.

**Lavoy, K. R.** Leaders, born or made. *School Soc.*, 1928, *28*, 683–684.

**Lawler, E. E.** How long should a manager stay in the same job? *Personnel Admin.*, 1964, *27*, 6–8; 27.

**Lawler, E. E.** Managers' perceptions of their subordinates' pay and of their superiors' pay. *Personnel Psychol.*, 1965, *18*, 413–422.

**Lawler, E. E.** Identification and enhancement of managerial effectiveness: I. Current practices in industry and government for identifying and developing managers. Greensboro, N.C.: Richardson Foundation, 1966a (mimeo).

**Lawler, E. E.** Identification and enhancement of managerial effectiveness: III. The role of motivation in managerial effectiveness. Greensboro, N. C.: Richardson Foundation, 1966b (mimeo).

**Lawler, E. E.** Managers' attitudes toward how their pay is and should be determined. *J. appl. Psychol.*, 1966c, *50*, 273–279.

**Lawler, E. E.** How much money do executives want? *Personnel Mgmt. Abstr.*, 1967, *12*, 1–8.

**Lawler, E. E.** Job design and employee motivation. *Personnel Psychol.*, 1969, *22*, 426–435.

**Lawler, E. E., & Hackman, J. R.** Impact of employee participation in the development of pay incentive plans: a field experiment. *J. appl. Psychol.*, 1969, *53*, 467–471.

**Lawler, E. E., & Hall, D. H.** Relationship of job characteristics to job involvement, satisfaction, and intrinsic motivation. *J. appl. Psychol.*, 1970, *54*, 305–312.

**Lawler, E. E., & Porter, L. W.** Perceptions regarding management compensation. *Indus. Relat.*, 1963, *3*, 41–49.

**Lawler, E. E., & Porter, L. W.** Predicting managers' pay and their satisfaction with their pay. *Personnel Psychol.*, 1966, *19*, 363–374.

**Lawler, E. E., & Porter, L. W.** The effect of performance on job satisfaction. *Indus. Relat.*, 1967a, *7*, 20–28.

**Lawler, E. E., & Porter, L. W.** Antecedent attitudes of effective managerial performance. *Org. behav. hum. Perform.*, 1967b, *2*, 122–142.

**Lawler, E. E., Porter, L. W., & Tannenbaum, A.** Managers' attitudes toward interaction episodes. *J. appl. Psychol.*, 1968, *52*, 432–439.

**Lawler, E. J.** An experimental study of factors affecting the mobilization of revolutionary coalitions. *Sociometry*, 1975, *38*, 163–179.

**Lawrence, H.** The effectiveness of a group-directed vs. a worker-directed style of leadership in social group work. *Dissertation Abstr.*, 1968, *28*, 4712.

**Lawrence, L. C., & Smith, P. C.** Group decision and employee participation. *J. appl. Psychol.*, 1955, *39*, 334–337.

**Lawrence, P. R.** *The changing of organizational behavior patterns: a case study of decentralization*. Boston: Harvard Business School, 1958.

**Lawrence, P. R., & Lorsch, J. W.** *Organization and environment.* Cambridge: Harvard University Press, 1967a.

**Lawrence, P. R., & Lorsch, J. W.** Differentiation and integration in complex organizations. *Admin. sci. Quar.,* 1967b, *12,* 1–47.

**Lawrie, J. W.** Convergent job expectations and ratings of industrial foremen. *J. appl. Psychol.,* 1966, *50,* 97–107.

**Lawshe, C. H., Bolda, R. A., & Brune, R. L.** Studies in management training evaluation: II. The effect of exposures to role playing. *J. appl. Psychol.,* 1959, *43,* 287–292.

**Lawshe, C. H., Brune, R. L., & Bolda, R. A.** What supervisors say about role playing. *J. Amer. Soc. Train. Directors,* 1958, *12,* 3–7.

**Lawshe, C. H., & Nagle, B. F.** Productivity and attitude toward supervisor. *J. appl. Psychol.,* 1953, *37,* 159–162.

**Lazar, I.** Interpersonal perception—a selected review of the literature. Urbana: University of Illinois, 1953 (mimeo).

**Lazarsfeld, P., Berelson, B. & Gaudet, H.** *The people's choice,* 2nd ed. New York: Columbia University Press, 1948.

**Lazarus, R. S.** Psychological stress and the coping process. New York: McGraw-Hill, 1966.

**Learned, E. P., Ulrich, D. N., & Booz, D. R.** *Executive action.* Boston: Harvard University Press, 1951.

**Leavitt, H. J.** Some effects of certain communication patterns on group performance. *J. abnorm. soc. Psychol.,* 1951, *46,* 38–50.

**Leavitt, H. J.** Unhuman organization. *Harvard bus. Rev.,* 1962, *40,* 90–98.

**Leavitt, H. J., & Bass, B. M.** Organizational psychology. *Ann. rev. Psychol.,* 1964, *15,* 371–398.

**Leavitt, H. J., & Mueller, R. A. H.** Some effects of feedback on communication. *Hum. Relat.,* 1951, *4,* 401–410.

**Leavitt, H. J., & Whistler, T. L.** Management in the 1980's. *Harvard bus. Rev.,* 1958, *36,* 41–48.

**LeBon, G.** *The crowd.* New York: Macmillan, 1897.

**Lecuyer, R.** Social organizations and spatial organization. *Hum. Relat.,* 1976, *19,* 1045–1060.

**Lee, D. M.** Subordinate perceptions of leadership behavior: a judgmental approach. *Dissertation Abstr. Internat.,* 1976, *37,* 2555–2556.

**Lee, F. J., Horwitz, M., & Goldman, M.** Power over decision making and the response to frustration in group members. *Amer. Psychologist,* 1954, *9,* 413–414.

**Lee, H. C.** Do workers really want flexibility on the job? *Personnel,* 1965, *42,* 74–77.

**Lee, H. E., & Harrell, T. W.** *Relation between talking and sociometric choices.* Stanford, Calif.: Stanford University, Graduate School of Business, Technical Report, 1965.

**Lee, S. M.** Organizational identification of scientists. *Acad. Mgmt. J.,* 1969, *3,* 327–337.

**Lefkowitz, M., Blake, R. R., & Mouton, J. S.** Status factors in pedestrian violation of traffic signals. *J. abnorm. soc. Psychol.,* 1955, *51,* 704–706.

**Lehman, H. C.** The creative years in science and literature. *Sci. Mon.,* 1937, *45,* 65–75.

**Lehman, H. C.** Optimum ages for eminent leadership. *Sci. Mon.,* 1942, *54,* 162–175.

**Lehman, H. C.** The age of eminent leaders, then and now. *Amer. J. Sociol.,* 1947, *52,* 342–356.

**Lehman, H. C.** *Age and achievement.* Princeton, N.J.: Princeton University Press, 1953.

**Lehman, H. C., & Witty, P. A.** Play activity and school progress. *J. educ. Psychol.,* 1927, *18,* 318–326.

**Leib, A.** Vorstellungen und Urteile von Schölern über Führer in der Schulklass. *Z. angew. Psychol.,* 1928, *30,* 241–346.

**Leighton, A. H.** *The governing of men: general principles and recommendations based on* *experiences at a Japanese relocation camp.* Princeton, N.J.: Princeton University Press, 1945.

**Leik, R. K.** "Irrelevant" aspects of stooge behavior: implications for leadership studies and experimental methodology. *Sociometry,* 1965, *28,* 259–271.

**Leister, A., Borden, D., & Fiedler, F. E.** Validation of contingency model leadership training: LEADER MATCH. *Acad. Mgmt. J.,* 1977, *20,* 464–470.

**Lemann, T. B., & Solomon, R. L.** Group characteristics as revealed in sociometric patterns and personality ratings. *Sociometry,* 1952, *15,* 7–90.

**Lennerlöf, L.** The formal authority of the supervisor. *Psychol. res. Bull.,* 1965a, *5,* 2–31.

**Lennerlöf, L.** Attitudes to supervisory motivation. *Psychol. res. Bull.,* 1965b, *5,* 1–22.

**Lennerlöf, L.** *Supervision: situation, individual, behavior effect.* Stockholm: Swedish Council for Personnel Administration, 1968.

**Lennung, S. A., & Ahlberg, A.** The effects of laboratory training: a field experiment. *J. appl. behav. Sci.,* 1975, *11,* 177–188.

**Lenski, G. E.** Social participation and status crystallization. *Amer. sociol. Rev.,* 1956, *21,* 458–464.

**Leopold, L.** *Prestige.* London: Fisher & Unwin, 1913.

**Lepkowski, M. L., Sr.** Cooperative decision making as related to supportive relations and communication in the senior high school. Doctoral dissertation, University of Buffalo, Buffalo, N.Y., 1970.

**Lerea, L., & Goldberg, A.** The effects of socialization upon group behavior. *Speech Monogr.,* 1961, *28,* 60–64.

**Lerner, H. H.** Bibliography on leadership and authority in local communities. *Bull. World Fed. Ment. Health,* 1952, *4,* Suppl.

**Lerner, H.** Early origins of envy and devaluation of women: implications for sex role stereotypes. *Bull. Menninger Clinic,* 1974, *38,* 538–553.

**Lerner, M. J., & Becker, S.** Interpersonal choice as a function of ascribed similarity and definition of the situation. *Hum. Relat.,* 1962, *15,* 27–34.

**Lerner, M. J., Dillehay, R. C., & Sherer, W. C.** Similarity and attraction in social contexts. *J. pers. soc. Psychol.,* 1967, *5,* 481–486.

**Lesieur, F. G.** *The Scanlon plan.* Cambridge, Mass.: M.I.T. Press, 1958.

**Lester, J. T.,** Correlates of field behavior. Behavioral research during the 1963 Mount Everest expedition. *Tech Rept.* 1, Berkeley Institute of Psychological Research, San Francisco, 1965.

**Levi, A. M., & Benjamin, A.** Focus and flexibility in a model of conflict resolution. *J. conflict Resolution,* 1977, *21,* 405–525.

**Levi, I. J.** Student leadership in elementary and junior high school and its transfer into senior high school. *J. educ. Res.,* 1930, *22,* 135–139.

**Levi, M. A.** A comparison of two methods of conducting critiques. San Antonio, TX: AFPTRC-TR-54-108, 1954.

**Levi, M. A., Torrance, E. P., & Pletts, G. O.** Sociometric studies of combat air crews in survival training. *Sociometry,* 1954, *17,* 304–328.

**Levine, J., & Butler, J.** Lecture vs. group discussion in changing behavior. *J. appl. Psychol.,* 1952, *36,* 29–33.

**Levine, J., Laffal, J., Berkowitz, M., Lindemann, J., & Drevdahl, J.** Conforming behavior of psychiatric and medical patients. *J. abnorm. soc. Psychol.,* 1954, *49,* 251–255.

**LeVine, R.** *Dreams and deeds: achievement motivation in Nigeria.* Chicago: University of Chicago Press, 1966.

**Levine, S.** An approach of constructive leadership. *J. soc. Issues,* 1949, *5,* 46–53.

**Levinger, G.** The development of perceptions and behavior in newly formed social power relationships. In D. Cartwright (Ed.), *Studies in social power*. Ann Arbor: University of Michigan, Institute for Social Research, 1959.

**Levinger, G., Morrison, H. W., & French, J. R. P.** Coercive power and forces affecting conformity. *Amer. Psychologist*, 1957, *12*, 393.

**Levinson, D. J.** Role, personality, and social structure in the organizational setting. *J. abnorm. soc. Psychol.*, 1959, *58*, 170–180.

**Levinson, H.** A psychologist looks at executive development. *Harvard. bus. Rev.*, 1962, *40*, 69–75.

**Levinson, H.** *The exceptional executive: a psychological conception*. Cambridge, Mass.: Harvard University Press, 1968.

**Levinson, H.** Executive stress. New York: Harper & Row, 1970.

**Levy, B. I.** A preliminary study of informal crew conferences as a crew training adjunct. Crew Research Laboratory, AF Personnel & Training Reserve Center, Lackland AF Base, AFPTRC-TR-54-87, 1954a.

**Levy, B. I.** Some effects of periodic discussions upon the social characteristics of non-laboratory groups. *Amer. Psychologist*, 1954b, *9*, 569.

**Lewin, A., & Craig, J. R.** The influences of level of performance on managerial style: an experimental object-lesson in the ambiguity of correlation data. *Org. behav. hum. Perform.*, 1968, *3*, 440–458.

**Lewin, K.** Field theory and experiment in social psychology: concepts and methods. *Amer. J. Sociol.*, 1939, *44*, 868–896.

**Lewin, K.** Forces behind food habits and methods of change. *Bull. nat. res. Council*, 1943, *108*, 35–65.

**Lewin, K.** Frontiers in group dynamics: concept, method and reality in social science, social equilibria and social change. *Hum. Relat.*, 1947, *1*, 5–41.

**Lewin, K.** Group decision and social change (1944). In T. Newcomb & E. Hartley (Eds.), *Readings in social psychology*. New York: Holt, 1947.

**Lewin, K.** *Field theory in social science*, D. Cartwright (Ed.). New York: Harper & Row, 1951.

**Lewin, K., & Lippitt, R.** An experimental approach to the study of autocracy and democracy: a preliminary note. *Sociometry*, 1938, *1*, 292–300.

**Lewin, K., Lippitt, R., & White, R. K.** Patterns of aggressive behavior in experimentally created social climates. *J. soc. Psychol.*, 1939, *10*, 271–301.

**Lewis, G. F.** A comparison of some aspects of the backgrounds and careers of small businessmen and American business leaders. *Amer. J. Sociol.*, 1960, *65*, 348–355.

**Lewis, H.** Child rearing among low-income families. In L.A. Ferman, J. L. Kornbluh, & A. Haber (Eds.), *Poverty in America*. Ann Arbor: University of Michigan Press, 1965.

**Lewis, R., & Stewart, R.** *The managers: a new examination of the English, German, and American executive*. New York: New American Library, 1961.

**Ley, R.** Labor turnover as a function of worker differences, work environment, and authoritarianism of foremen. *J. appl. Psychol.*, 1966, *50*, 497–500.

**LIAMA.** "Realistic" job expectations and survival. Life Insurance Agency Management Association, 1964a, *2*, File No. 432.

**LIAMA.** Agent attitude: a study of attitudes and performance among ordinary agents. Life Insurance Agency Management Association, 1964b, *11*, File No. 440.

**Lichtenberg, P., & Deutsch, M.** A descriptive review of research on the staff process of decision-making. San Antonio, Tex.: AFPTRC-TR-54-129, 1954.

**Lichtman, C. M.** An interactional analysis of structural and individual variables in a work organization. *Dissertation Abstr.*, 1968, *29*, 675–676.

**Lichtman, C. M.** Some intrapersonal response correlates of organizational rank. *J. appl.*

*Psychol.*, 1970, *54*, 77–80.

**Lieberman, A.** The effects of principal leadership on teacher morale, professionalism, and style in the classroom. Doctoral dissertation, University of California, Los Angeles, 1969.

**Lieberman, M. A.** Change induction in small groups. *Ann. Rev. Psychol.*, 1976a, *27*, 217–250.

**Lieberman, M. A.** People-changing groups: the new and not so new. In S. Areli (Ed.), *The American handbook of psychiatry.* New York: Basic Books, 1976b.

**Lieberman, M. A., Yalom, I. D., & Miles, M. B.** *Encounter groups: first facts.* New York: Basic Books, 1973.

**Lieberman, S.** The relationship between attitudes and roles: a natural field experiment. *Amer. Psychologist*, 1954, *9*, 418–419.

**Lieberman, S.** The effects of changes in roles on the attitudes of role occupants. *Hum. Relat.*, 1956, *9*, 385–402.

**Lieberson, S., & O'Connor, J.** Leadership and performance. *Amer. sociol. Rev.*, 1972, *37*, 117–130.

**Liebow, E.** *Tally's corner.* Boston: Little, Brown, 1967.

**Likert, J.** *Leadership for effective leagues.* Washington, D.C.: League of Women Voters, 1958.

**Likert, R.** A technique for the measurement of attitudes. *Archives Psych.*, 1932, 140.

**Likert, R.** *Morale and agency management.* Hartford, Conn.: Life Insurance Sales Research Bureau, 1940.

**Likert, R.** *A program of research on the fundamental problems of organizational human behavior.* Ann Arbor: Survey Research Center, Institute for Social Research, 1947.

**Likert, R.** Developing patterns of management. I. *Amer. Mgmt. Assn., Genl. Mgmt. Series,* 1955, No. 178.

**Likert, R.** Developing patterns of management. II. *Amer. Mgmt. Assn. Genl. Mgmt. Series,* 1956, No. 182.

**Likert, R.** Effective supervision: an adaptive and relative process. *Personnel Psychol.*, 1958, *11*, 317–332.

**Likert, R.** Motivational approach to management development. *Harvard bus. Rev.*, 1959, *37*, 75–82.

**Likert, R.** *New patterns of management.* New York: McGraw-Hill, 1961a.

**Likert, R.** An emerging theory of organizations, leadership, and management. In L. Petrullo & B. M. Bass (Eds.), *Leadership and interpersonal behavior.* New York: Holt, 1961b.

**Likert, R.** Trends toward a world-wide theory of management. *Proceedings, COIS XIII. International Management Congress,* 1963, *2*, 110–114.

**Likert, R.** *The human organization.* New York: McGraw-Hill, 1967.

**Likert, R.** Human resource accounting: building and assessing productive organizations. *Personnel*, 1973, *50*, 8–24.

**Likert, R.** Improving cost performance with cross-functional teams. *Confer. bd. Rec.*, 1975, *92*, 51–59.

**Likert, R.** Management styles and the human component. *Mgmt. Rev.*, 1977a, *66*, 23–28; 43–45.

**Likert, R.** Past and future perspectives on system 4. *Proceedings of the Academy of Management,* 1977b.

**Likert, R., & Bowers, D. G.** Improving the accuracy of P/L reports by estimating the change in dollar value of the human organization. *Mich. bus. Rev.*, 1973, (March), 15–24.

**Likert, R., & Fisher, S.** MBGO: putting some team spirit into MBO. *Personnel*, 1977, *54*, 41–47.

**Likert, R., & Katz, D.** Supervisory practices and organizational structures as they affect employee productivity and morale. *Amer. Mgmt. Assn., Personnel Series,* 1948, No. 120.

**Likert, R., & Likert, J. G.** *New ways of managing conflict.* New York: McGraw-Hill, 1976.

**Likert, R., & Likert, J. G.,** A method for coping with conflict in problem-solving groups. *Grp. org. Stud.,* 1978, *3,* 427–434.

**Limerick, D. C.** Authority: an axis of leadership role differentiation. *Psychol. Africana,* 1976, *16,* 153–172.

**Lindbloom, C.** The science of "muddling through." *Public Admin. Rev.,* 1959, *19,* 79–99.

**Lindeman, E. C.** *Social education.* New York: New Republic, 1933.

**Lindemuth, M. H.** An analysis of the leader behavior of academic deans as related to the campus climate in selected colleges. Doctoral dissertation, University of Michigan, Ann Arbor, 1969.

**Lindgren, H. C.** *Effective leadership in human relations.* New York: Hermitage House, 1954.

**Lindzey, G.** *Handbook of social psychology.* Reading, Mass.: Addison-Wesley, 1954.

**Lindzey, G., & Aronson, E.** *Handbook of social psychology.* Reading, Mass.: Addison-Wesley, 1969.

**Lindzey, G., & Kalnins, D.** Theoretic apperception test: some evidence bearing on the "hero assumption." *J. abnorm. soc. Psychol.,* 1958, *57,* 76–83.

**Lindzey, G., & Urdan, J. A.** Personality and social choice. *Sociometry,* 1954, *17,* 47–63.

**Link, H. C.** The definition of social effectiveness and leadership through measurement. *Educ. psychol. Measmt.,* 1944, *4,* 57–67.

**Link, R.** Alienation. *Sweden Now,* 1971, June, 36–40.

**Linton, R.** *The cultural background of personality.* New York: Appleton-Century-Crofts, 1945.

**Lipetz, M. E., & Ossorio, P. G.** Authoritarianism, aggression, and status. *J. pers. soc. Psychol.,* 1967, *5,* 468–472.

**Lipham, J. M.** Personal variables related to administrative effectiveness. Doctoral dissertation, University of Chicago, Chicago, 1960.

**Lippitt, R.** An experimental study of the effect of democratic and authoritarian group atmospheres. *University Iowa Stud. Child Welf.,* 1940, *16,* 43–95.

**Lippitt, R.** The morale of youth groups. In G. B. Watson (Ed.), *Civilian morale.* Boston: Houghton Mifflin, 1942.

**Lippitt, R.** The psychodrama in leadership training. *Sociometry,* 1943a, *6,* 286–292.

**Lippitt, R.** From domination to leadership. *J. Natl. Assn. Dean's Women,* 1943b, *6,* 147–152.

**Lippitt, R.** *Training in community relations.* New York: Harper, 1949.

**Lippitt, R., Bradford, L. P., & Benne, K. D.** Sociodramatic clarification of leader and group roles as a starting point for effective group functioning. *Sociatry,* 1947, *1,* 82–91.

**Lippitt, R., Polansky, N., Redl, F., & Rosen, S.** The dynamics of power. *Hum. Relat.,* 1952, *5,* 37–64.

**Lippitt, R., Thelen, H., & Leff, E.** Unpublished memorandum, undated.

**Lippitt, R., Watson, J., & Westley, B.** *The dynamics of planned change.* New York: Harcourt, Brace, 1958.

**Lippitt, R., & White, R. K.** The social climate of children's groups. In R. G. Baker, J. S. Kounin, & H. F. Wright. *Child behavior and development.* New York: McGraw-Hill, 1943.

**Lippitt, R., & White, R.** Leader behavior and member reactions in three social climates. In I. D. Cartwright & A. Zander (Eds.), *Group dyanmics.* New York: Harper & Row, 1960.

**Lippitt, R., & Zander, A.** A study of boys' attitudes toward participation in the war effort. *J. soc. Psychol.,* 1943, *17,* 309–325.

**Lirtzman, S., & Wahba, M.** Determinants of coalitional behavior of men and women: sex roles or situational requirement *J. appl. Psychol.,* 1972, *56,* 406–411.

**Litterer, J. A.** Life cycle changes of career women: assessment and adaptation. *Proceedings of the Academy of Management,* 1976.

**Little, K. B.** Personal space. *J. exp. soc. Psychol.*, 1965, *1*, 237–247.

**Litwak, E.** Models of organization which permit conflict. *Amer. J. Sociol.*, 1961, *67*, 177–184.

**Litwin, G. H.** Climate and motivation: an experimental study. In R. Tagiuri & G. H. Litwin (Eds.), *Organizational climate*. Boston: Harvard University, Graduate School of Business Administration, 1968.

**Litwin, G. H., & Stringer, R. A.** *Motivation and organizational climate.* Boston: Harvard University, Graduate School of Business Administration, 1968.

**Litzinger, W. D.** Interpersonal values and leadership attitudes of branch bank managers. *Personnel Psychol.*, 1965, *18*, 193–198.

**Livingstone, E.** Attitudes of women operatives to promotion. *Occup. Psychol*, 1953, *27*, 191–199.

**Livingstone, S.** Pygmalion in management. *Harvard bus. Rev.*, 1969, *47*, 81–89.

**Lloyd, H.** *Biography in management studies.* New York: Humanities Press, 1964.

**Locke, E. A.** The myths of behavior mod in organizations. *Acad. Mgmt. Rev.*, 1977, *4*, 131–136.

**Lockheed, M. E., & Hall, K. P.** Conceptualizing sex as a status characteristic: applications to leadership training strategies. *J. soc. Issues*, 1976, *32*, 111–124.

**Lohmann, M. R.** *Top management committees: their functions and authority.* New York: American Management Association, 1961.

**Loken, R. D.** *Why they quit, a survey of Illinois employees who quit their jobs in 1949; retail, clerical, manufacturing.* Urbana: University of Illinois Press, 1951.

**Lonergan, W. G.** Management trainees evaluate role playing. *J. Amer. Soc. Train. Directors*, 1958, *12*, 20–25.

**Lonetto, R., & Williams, D.** Personality, behavioral and output variables in a small group task situation: an examination of consensual leader and non-leader differences. *Can. J. behav. Sci.*, 1974, *6*, 59–74.

**Long, R. J.** Desires for and patterns of worker participation in decision making after conversion to employee ownership. *Acad. Mgmt. J.*, 1979, *22*, 611–617.

**Lord, R. G.** Group performance as a function of leadership behavior and task structure. *Dissertation Abstr. Internat.*, 1975, *35*, 6155.

**Lord, R. G.** Group performance as a function of leadership behavior and task structure: toward an explanatory theory. *Org. behav. hum. Perform.*, 1976, *17*, 76–96.

**Lord, R. G.** Functional leadership behavior: measurement and relation to social power and leadership perceptions. *Admin. sci. Quar.*, 1977, *22*, 114–133.

**Lord, R. G., Binning, J., Rush, M. C., & Thomas, J. C.** Effect of performance and leader behavior on questionnaire ratings of leader behavior. *Org. behav. hum. Perform.*, 1978, *21*, 27–39.

**Lorge, I., Fox, D., Davitz, J., & Brenner, M.** A survey of studies contrasting the quality of group performance and individual performance, 1920–1957. *Psychol. Bull.*, 1958, *55*, 337–370.

**Lorsch, J. W.** Introduction to the structural design of organizations. In G. W. Dalton, P. R. Lawrence, & J. W. Lorsch (Eds.), *Organizational structure and design*. Homewood, Ill.: Dorsey Press, 1970.

**Lott, B. E.** Group cohesiveness: a learning phenomenon. *J. soc. Psychol.*, 1961, *55*, 275–286.

**Lott, B. E., & Lott, A. J.** The formation of positive attitudes toward group members. *J. abnorm. soc. Psychol.*, 1960, *61*, 297–300.

**Lott, D. F., & Sommer, R.** Seating arrangements and status. *J. pers. soc. Psychol.*, 1967, *7*, 90–95.

**Low, L.** Resolving employee resistance to new personnel policies: a case study. *Personnel Psychol.*, 1948, *1*, 185–196.

**Lowin, A.** Participative decision making: a model, literature, critique, and prescription for research. *Org. behav. hum. Perform.*, 1968, *3*, 68–106.

**Lowin, A., & Craig, J. R.** The influence of level of performance on managerial style: an experimental object-lesson in the ambiguity of correlation data. *Org. behav. hum. Perform.*, 1968, *3*, 440–458.

**Lowin, A., Hrapchak, W. J., & Kavanagh, M. J.** Consideration and initiating structure: an experimental investigation of leadership traits. *Admin. sci. Quar.*, 1969, *14*, 238–253.

**Lowry, R. P.** *Who's running this town? Community leadership and social change.* New York: Harper & Row, 1968.

**Loye, D.** *The leadership passion.* San Francisco: Jossey-Bass, 1977.

**Lucas, C.** Task performance and group structure as a function of personality and feedback. *J. soc. Psychol.*, 1965, *66*, 257–270.

**Luchins, A. S., & Luchins, E. H.** On conformity with judgments of a majority or an authority. *J. soc. Psychol.*, 1961, *53*, 303–316.

**Luckie, W. R.** Leader behavior of director of instruction. *Dissertation Abstr.*, 1963, *25*, 1960.

**Luecke, D. S.** The professional as organizational leader. *Admin. sci. Quar.*, 1973, *18*, 86–94.

**Luft, J.** *Of human interaction.* Palo Alto, Calif.: National Press, 1969.

**Luithlen, W. F.** Zur Psychologie der Initiative und der Führereigenschaften. *Z. f. angew. Psychol.*, 1931, *39*, 56–122.

**Lull, P., Fund, F., & Piersol, D.** What communication means to the corporation president. *Advan. Mgmt.*, 1955, *20*, 17–20.

**Lundberg, G. A., & Beazley, V.** Consciousness of kind in a college population. *Sociometry*, 1948, *11*, 59–74.

**Lundgren, D. C., & Knight, D. J.** Leadership styles and member attitudes in T groups. *Pers. soc. psychol. Bull.*, 1974, *74*, 263–266.

**Lundquist, A.** *Arbetsledare och arbetsgrupp.* Stockholm: Personal Administrativa Rådet, 1957.

**Lundy, R. M.** Assimilative projection and accuracy of prediction in interpersonal perceptions. *J. abnorm. soc. Psychol.*, 1956, *52*, 33–38.

**Lundy, R. M., Katkovsky, W., Cromwell, R. L., & Shoemaker, D. J.** Self acceptability and descriptions of sociometric choices. *J. abnorm soc. Psychol.*, 1955, *51*, 260–262.

**Lupfer, M. B.** Role enactment as a function of orientation, expectations, and duration of interaction. *Dissertation Abstr.*, 1965, *25*, 5376–5377.

**Luthans, F.** *Organizational behavior*, 2nd ed. New York: McGraw-Hill, 1977.

**Luthans, F., Walker, J. W., & Hodgetts, R. M.** Evidence on the validity of management education. *Acad. Mgmt. J.*, 1969, *4*, 451–457.

**Luttbeg, N. R.** The structure of beliefs among leaders and the public. *Publ. opinion Quar.*, 1968, *32*, 398–409.

**Luttwak, E. N.** *The grand strategy of the Roman empire.* Baltimore: Johns Hopkins, 1976.

**Lyda, M. L.** *Research studies in education: 1953–1963.* Bloomington, Ind.: Phi Delta Kappa, 1964.

**Lyle, J.** Communication, group atmosphere, productivity, and morale in small task groups. *Hum. Relat.*, 1961, *14*, 369–379.

**Lynd, R. S., & Lynd, H. M.** *Middletown.* New York: Harcourt, Brace, 1929.

**Lynton, R. P., & Pareek, U.** *Training for development.* Homewood, Ill.: Dorsey-Irwin, 1967.

**Maas, H. S.** Personal and group factors in leaders' social perception. *J. abnorm. soc. Psychol.*, 1950, *45*, 54–63.

**Macaulay, S.** Noncontractual relations in business. *Amer. sociol. Rev.*, 1963, *28*, 55–67.

**McCaffree, K. M.** Union membership policies and labor productivity among asbestos workers. *Indus. lab. relat. Rev.*, 1961, *14*, 227–234.

McCall, G. J., & Simmons, J. L. *Identities and interactions*. New York: Free Press, 1966.

McCall, M. W., Jr. The perceived cognitive role requirements of formal leaders. *Proceedings of the American Psychological Assoc.*, 1974.

McCall, M. W., Jr. Leadership research: choosing gods and devils on the run. *J. occup. Psychol.*, 1976, *49*, 139–153.

McCall, M. W., Jr. *Leaders and leadership: of substance and shadow.* Greensboro, N.C.: Center for Creative Leadership, Technical Report No. 2, 1977.

McCall, M. W., Jr., & Lombardo, M. M. (Eds.), *Leadership: where else can we go?* Durham, N.C.: Duke University Press, 1978.

McCandless, B. R. Changing relationships between dominance and social acceptability during group democratization. *Amer. J. Orthopsychiat.*, 1942, *12*, 529–535.

McCann, E. C. An aspect of management philosophy in the United States and Latin America. *J. Acad. Mgmt.*, 1964, *7*, 149–152.

McCarrey, M. W., & Edwards, S. A. Hierarchies of scientist goal objects: individual characteristics and performance correlates. *J. appl. Psychol.*, 1972, *3*, 271–272.

McClelland, D. C. *The achieving society.* Princeton, N.J.: Van Nostrand, 1961.

McClelland, D. C. Toward a theory of motive acquisition. *Amer. Psychologist*, 1965a, *20*, 321–333.

McClelland, D. C. Achievement motivation can be developed. *Harvard bus. Rev.*, 1965b, *43*, 6–24; 178.

McClelland, D. C. N achievement and entrepreneurship: a longitudinal study. *J. per. soc. Psychol.*, 1965c, *1*, 389–392.

McClelland, D. C. Does education accelerate economic growth? *Eco. develop. cult. Chge.*, 1966a, *14*, 257–278.

McClelland, D. C. Longitudinal trends in the relation of thought to action. *J. consult. Psychol.*, 1966b, *30*, 479–483.

McClelland, D. C., & Burnham, D. H. Power is the great motivator. *Harvard bus. Rev.*, 1976, *54*, 100–110.

McClelland, D. C., & Clark, R. A. Antecedent conditions for affective arousal. In D. C. McClelland, J. W. Atkinson, R. A. Clark, & E. L. Lowell (Eds.), *The achievement motive.* New York: Appleton-Century-Crofts, 1953.

McClelland, D. C., & Winter, D. G. *Motivating economic achievement.* New York: Free Press, 1969.

McClintock, C. G. Group support and the behavior of leaders and nonleaders. *J. abnorm. soc. Psychol.*, 1963, *67*, 105–113.

McClintock, C. G. The behavior of leaders, non-leaders, non-joiners, and non-leader joiners under conditions of group support and non-support. In R. V. Bowers (Ed.), *Studies on behavior in organizations.* Athens, Ga: University of Georgia Press, 1966.

Maccoby, E. E., Newcomb, T. M., & Hartley, E. L. *Readings in social psychology.* New York: Holt, Rinehart & Winston, 1958.

Maccoby, E. E., & Jacklin, C. N. *The psychology of sex differences.* Stanford: Stanford University Press, 1974.

Maccoby, M. *The gamesman.* New York: Bantam Books, 1978.

Maccoby, N. The relationship of supervisory behavior and attitudes to group productivity in two widely different industrial settings. *Amer. Psychologist*, 1949, *4*, 283.

McCormick, C. P. *Multiple management.* New York: Harper, 1938.

McCormick, C. P. *The power of people: multiple management up to date.* New York: Harper, 1949.

McCuen, T. L. Leadership and intelligence. *Education*, 1929, *50*, 89–95.

**McCullough, G. E.** The effects of changes in organizational structure: demonstration projects in an oil refinery. In L. E. Davis & A. B. Cherns (Eds.), *The quality of working life. Volume two: cases and commentary.* New York: Free Press, 1975.

**McCurdy, H. G., & Eber, H. W.** Democratic versus authoritarian: a further investigation of group problem-solving. *J. Pers.,* 1953, *22,* 258–269.

**McCurdy, H. G., & Lambert, W. E.** The efficiency of small human groups in the solution of problems requiring genuine cooperation. *J. Pers.,* 1952, *20,* 478–494.

**Macdonald, D. A.** The relationship between leadership orientation and group productivity and satisfaction: the residence hall section adviser and his section. *Dissertation Abstr. Internat.,* 1969, *30,* 391.

**MacDonald, W. S.** Responsibility and goal establishment: critical elements in Job Corps programs. *Percept. mot. Skills,* 1967, *24,* 104.

**MacDonald, W. S.** Social structure and behavior modification in Job Corps training. *Percept. mot. Skills,* 1967, *24,* 142.

**McDonnell, J. F.** An analysis of participative management as a choice of leadership style. *Dissertation Abstr. Internat.,* 1974, *35,* 1339.

**Mace, M. L.** *The growth and development of executives.* Boston: Harvard Business School, Division of Research, 1950.

**McFeely, W. M., & Mussmann, W. W.** Training supervisors in leadership. *Personnel,* 1945, *21,* 217–223.

**McFillen, J. M.** The role of power, supervision, and performance in leadership productivity. Columbus: Ohio State University, College of Administrative Sciences, working paper, 1978.

**McFillen, J. M., & New, J. R.** Situational determinants of supervisor attributes and behavior. Columbus: Ohio State University, College of Administrative Sciences, working paper, 1978.

**McFillen, J. M., & New, J. R.** Situational determinants of supervisor attributions and behavior. *Acad. Mgmt. J.,* 1979, *22,* 793–809.

**McGahan, F. E.** Factors associated with leadership ability. *Texas Outlook,* 1941, *25,* 37–38.

**McGehee, W., & Thayer, P. W.** *Training in business and industry.* New York: Wiley, 1961.

**McGehee, W., & Tullar, W. L.** A note on evaluating behavior modification and behavior modeling as industrial training techniques. *Personnel Psychol.,* 1978, *31,* 477–484.

**McGinnies, E., & Ferster, C. B.** *The reinforcement of social behavior.* Boston: Houghton Mifflin, 1971.

**McGrath, J. E., & Altman, I.** *Small group research: a synthesis and critique.* New York: Holt, Rinehart & Winston, 1966.

**McGregor, D.** Conditions of effective leadership in the industrial organization. *J. consult. Psychol.,* 1944, *8,* 55–63.

**McGregor, D.** *The human side of enterprise.* New York: McGraw-Hill, 1960.

**McGregor, D.** *Leadership and motivation.* Cambridge, Mass.: M.I.T. Press, 1966.

**McGregor, D.** *The professional manager.* New York: McGraw-Hill, 1967.

**McGregor, D., & Arensberg, C.** The genesis of attitudes toward management. *Psychol. Bull.,* 1940, *37,* 433–434.

**McGruder, J.** The community reintegration centers of Ohio: a case analysis in community based corrections. Doctoral dissertation, Ohio State University, Columbus, 1976.

**McGuire, C. Lammon, M., & White, G. D.** Adolescent peer acceptance and valuations of role behaviors. *Amer. Psychologist,* 1953, *8,* 397.

**McGuire, J. W.** *Interdisciplinary studies in business behavior.* Cincinnati: South-Western, 1962.

**Machiavelli, N.** *The prince.* New York: Modern Library, 1940.

**MacIver, R. M.** *The web of government.* New York: Macmillan, 1947.

**McKeachie, W. J.** Individual conformity to attitudes of classroom groups. *J. abnorm. soc. Psychol.,* 1954, *49,* 282–289.

**MacKechnie, A. R.** Importance and development of leadership in our small unit commanders. *Military Rev.,* 1944, *24,* 9–12.

**McKelvey, W. W.** Exceptational noncomplementarity and style of interaction between professional and organization. *Admin. sci. Quar.,* 1969, *14,* 21–32.

**McKenna, E.** A situational perspective of the leadership role of the chief accountant in industry. Unpublished paper, undated.

**McKenna, E. F.** Leadership styles in industry. Lancaster, Eng.: University of Lancaster, Master's thesis, 1972.

**MacKenzie, R. A.** The management process in 3-D. *Harvard bus. Rev.,* 1969, *47,* 80–87.

**MacKinney, A. C.** Conceptualizations of a longitudinal study of manager performance. Ames: Iowa State University, Industrial Relations Center, 1967 (mimeo).

**MacKinney, A. C.** The longitudinal study of manager performance: Phase I variables. Ames: Iowa State University, unpublished report, 1968.

**MacKinney, A. C., Kavanagh, M. J., Wolins, L., & Rapparlie, J. H.** Manager development project: summary of progress through June 1969. Ames: Iowa State University, 1970 (mimeo).

**MacKinney, A. C., Wernimont, P. F., & Galitz, W. O.** Has specialization reduced job satisfaction? *Personnel,* 1962, *39,* 8–17.

**MacKinney, A. C., Wolins, L., Kavanagh, M. J., & Rapparlie, J. H.** Manager development project. Progress through June 1971—a summary report. Dayton, Ohio: Wright State University, 1971.

**McLachlan, J. F.** Therapy strategies, personality orientation and recovery from alcoholism. *Can. psychiat. assoc. J.,* 1974, *19,* 25–30.

**McLarney, W. J.** *Management training.* Homewood, Ill.: Irwin, 1962.

**McLaughlin, F. E.** Personality changes through alternate group leadership. *Nurs. Res.,* 1971, *20,* 123–130.

**MacLennan, B. W.** The personalities of group leaders: implications for selection and training. *Internat. J. grp. Psychotherapy,* 1975, *25,* 177–183.

**McMahon, J. T.** The contingency theory: logic and method revisited. *Personnel Psychol.,* 1972, *25,* 697–710.

**McMartin, J. A.** Two tests of an averaging model of social influence. *J. pers. soc. Psychol.,* 1970, *15,* 317–325.

**McMurray, R. N.** The problem of resistance to change in industry. *J. appl. Psychol.,* 1947, *31,* 580–593.

**McMurry, R. W.** *The maverick executive.* New York: Amacom, 1974.

**McNamara, V. D.** Leadership, staff, and school effectiveness. Doctoral dissertation, University of Alberta, Alberta, 1968.

**MacNaughton, J. D.** A study of foremen's communication. *Personnel pract. Bull.,* 1963, *19,* 10–19.

**McNaul, J. P.** Behavioral patterns among professionals in a research and development environment. Doctoral dissertation, Stanford University, Stanford, Calif., 1969.

**McNerney, W. J.** *Hospital and medical economics.* Chicago: Hospital Research and Educational Trust, 1962.

**Madden, F. M.** The effect of human relations training on group leaders' decisions and members' satisfaction. *Dissertation Abstr. Internat.,* 1977, *38,* 52.

**Maher, J. P.** Situational determinants of leadership behavior in task-oriented small groups. *Dissertation Abstr. Internat.,* 1976, *37,* 693–694.

**Mahler, F. W.** The span of control in sixty Australian undertakings. *Personnel pract. Bull.*, 1961, *17*, 35–40.

**Mahler, W.** Trends in management training: a composite training and development program. In M. J. Dooher & V. Marquis (Eds.), *The development of executive talent*. New York: American Management Association, 1952.

**Mahoney, G. M.** *Supervisory and administrative practices associated with worker attitudes toward an incentive system*. Ann Arbor: University of Michigan, Institute for Social Research, 1953.

**Mahoney, T. A.** *What do managers do?* Minneapolis: University of Minnesota, Industrial Relations Center, 1955.

**Mahoney, T. A.** *Building the executive team*. Englewood Cliffs, N.J.: Prentice-Hall, 1961.

**Mahoney, T. A.** Managerial perceptions of organizational effectiveness. *Mgmt. Sci.*, 1967, *14*, 76–91.

**Mahoney, T. A., Frost, P., Crandall, N. F., & Weitzel, W.** The conditioning influence of organization size upon managerial practice. *Org. behav. hum. Perform.*, 1972, *8*, 230–241.

**Mahoney, T. A., Jerdee, T. H., & Carroll, S. I.** The job(s) of management. *Indus. Relat.*, 1965, *4*, 97–110.

**Mahoney, T. A., Jerdee, T. H., & Korman, A.** An experimental evaluation of management development. *Personnel Psychol.*, 1960, *13*, 81–98.

**Mahoney, T. A., Jerdee, T. H., & Nash, A. N.** *The identification of management potential*. Dubuque, Iowa: Brown, 1961.

**Mahoney, T. A., Sorenson, W. W., Jerdee, T. H., & Nash, A. N.** Identification and prediction of managerial effectiveness. *Personnel Admin.*, 1963, *26*, 12–22.

**Mahoney, T. A., & Weitzel, W.** Managerial models of organizational effectiveness. *Admin. sci. Quar.*, 1969, *14*, 357–365.

**Mai-Dalton, R.** The influence of training and position power on leader behavior. Seattle: University of Washington, Organizational Research, Technical Report No. 75–72, 1975.

**Maier, N. R. F.** A human relations program for supervisors. *Indus. labor relat. Rev.*, 1948, *1*, 443–464.

**Maier, N. R. F.** The quality of group decisions as influenced by the discussion leader. *Hum. Relat.*, 1950, *3*, 155–174.

**Maier, N. R. F.** An experimental test of the effect of training on discussion leadership. *Hum. Relat.*, 1953, *6*, 161–173.

**Maier, N. R. F.** Screening solutions to upgrade quality: a new approach to problem-solving under conditions of uncertainty. *J. Psychol.*, 1960, *49*, 217–231.

**Maier, N. R. F.** *Problem-solving discussions and conferences: leadership methods and skills*. New York: McGraw-Hill, 1963.

**Maier, N. R. F.** *Psychology in industry*. Boston: Houghton Mifflin, 1965.

**Maier, N. R. F.** Assets and liabilities in group problem solving: the need for integrative function. *Psychol. Rev.*, 1967, *74*, 239–249.

**Maier, N. R. F.** The subordinate's role in the delegation process. *Personnel Psychol.*, 1968, *21*, 179–191.

**Maier, N. R. F.** Male versus female discussion leaders. *Personnel Psychol.*, 1970a, *23*, 455–461.

**Maier, N. R. F.** *Problem solving and creativity in individuals and groups*. Belmont, Calif.: Brooks/Cole, 1970b.

**Maier, N. R. F.** *Psychology in industrial organizations*. Boston: Houghton Mifflin, 1973.

**Maier, N. R. F., & Danielson, L. E.** An evaluation of two approaches to discipline in industry. *J. appl. Psychol.*, 1956, *40*, 319–323.

**Maier, N. R. F., & Hoffman, L. R.** Using trained "developmental" discussion leaders to improve further the quality of group decisions. *J. appl. Psychol.*, 1960, *44*, 247–251.

**Maier, N. R. F., & Hoffman, L. R.** Quality of first and second solutions to group problem-solving. *J. appl. Psychol.*, 1960, *44*, 278–283.

**Maier, N. R. F., & Hoffman, L. R.** Organization and creative problem solving. *J. appl. Psychol.*, 1961, *45*, 277–280.

**Maier, N. R. F., & Hoffman, L. R.** Seniority in work groups: a right or an honor? *J. appl. Psychol.*, 1963, *47*, 173–176.

**Maier, N. R. F., & Hoffman, L. R.** Financial incentives and group decision in motivating change. *J. soc. Psychol.*, 1964, *64*, 355–368.

**Maier, N. R. F., & Hoffman, L. R.** Acceptance and quality of solutions as related to leader's attitudes toward disagreement in group problem solving. *J. appl. behav. Sci.*, 1965, *1*, 373–386.

**Maier, N. R. F., Hoffman, L. R., & Read, W. H.** Superior-subordinate communication: the relative effectiveness of managers who held their subordinates' positions. *Personnel Psychol.*, 1963, *16*, 1–12.

**Maier, N. R. F., & Maier, R. A.** An experimental test of the effects of "developmental" vs. "free" discussions on the quality of group decisions. *J. appl. Psychol.*, 1957, *41*, 320–323.

**Maier, N. R. F., & Solem, A. R.** The contribution of a discussion leader to the quality of group thinking: the effective use of minority opinions. *Hum. Relat.*, 1952, *5*, 277–288.

**Maier, N. R. F., & Solem, A. R.** Improving solutions by turning choice situations into problems. *Personnel Psychol.*, 1962, *15*, 151–158.

**Maier, N. R. F., Solem, A. R., & Maier, A. A.** *Supervisory and executive development: a manual for role playing.* New York: Wiley, 1957.

**Maier, N. R. F., & Thurber, J. A.** Problems in delegation. *Personnel Psychol.*, 1969, *22*, 131–139.

**Maier, N. R. F., & Zerfoss, L. F.** MRP: a technique for training large groups of supervisors and its potential use in social research. *Hum. Relat.*, 1952, *5*, 177–186.

**Maisonneuve, J.** Selective choices and propinquity. *Sociometry*, 1952, *15*, 135–140.

**Maller, J. B.** Size of family and personality of offspring. *J. soc. Psychol.*, 1931, *2*, 3–25.

**Maloney, R. M.** Group learning through group discussion: a group discussion implementation analysis. *J. soc. Psychol.*, 1956, *43*, 3–9.

**Mandell, M. M.** Supervisors' attitudes and job performance. *Personnel*, 1949, *26*, 182–183.

**Mandell, M. M.** Supervisory characteristics and ratings: a summary of recent research. *Personnel*, 1956, *32*, 435–440.

**Mandell, M. M., & Duckworth, P.** The supervisor's job: a survey. *Personnel*, 1955, *31*, 456–462.

**Mangee, C.** A study of the perceived behaviors of elementary school principals and the organizational climate of elementary schools. Doctoral dissertation, University of Michigan, Ann Arbor, 1976.

**Manheim, H. L.** Intergroup interaction as related to status and leadership differences between groups. *Sociometry*, 1960, *23*, 415–427.

**Manis, J. G., & Meltzer, B. N.** *Symbolic interaction: a reader in social psychology.* Boston: Allyn & Bacon, 1967.

**Mann, F. C.** Changing superior-subordinate relationships. *J. soc. Issues*, 1951, *7/8*, 56–63.

**Mann, F. C.** Studying and creating change. In W. Bennis, K. Benne, & R. Chin (Eds.), *The planning of change.* New York: Holt, Rinehart & Winston, 1961.

**Mann, F. C.** Toward an understanding of the leadership role in formal organization. In R. Dubin (Ed.), *Leadership and productivity.* San Francisco: Chandler, 1965.

**Mann, F. C., & Baumgartel, H.** *Absences and employee attitudes in an electric power company*. Ann Arbor: University of Michigan, Survey Research Center, 1952.

**Mann, F. C., & Baumgartel, H.** *The supervisor's concern with cost in an electric power company*. Ann Arbor: University of Michigan, Survey Research Center, 1953.

**Mann, F. C., & Dent, J. K.** The supervisor—member of two organizational families. *Harvard bus. Rev.*, 1954a, *32*, 103–112.

**Mann, F. C., & Dent, J. K.** *Appraisals of supervisors and attitudes of their employees in an electric power company*. Ann Arbor: University of Michigan, Survey Research Center, 1954b.

**Mann, F. C., & Hoffman, L. R.** *Automation and the worker: a study of social change in power plants*. New York: Holt, 1960.

**Mann, F. C., Indik, B. P., & Vroom, V. H.** *The productivity of work groups*. Ann Arbor: University of Michigan, Survey Research Center, 1963.

**Mann, F. C., & Sparling, J. E.** Changing absence rates: an application of research findings. *Personnel*, 1956, *32*, 392–408.

**Mann, F. C., & Williams, L. K.** Some effects of the changing work environment in the office. *J. soc. Issues*, 1962, *18*, 90–101.

**Mann, J. H.** The relationship between role playing ability and interpersonal adjustment. *J. gen. Psychol.*, 1960, *62*, 177–183.

**Mann, J. H., & Mann, C. H.** The effect of role-playing experience on role-playing ability. *Sociometry*, 1959a, *22*, 64–74.

**Mann, J. H., & Mann, C. H.** Role playing and inter-personal adjustment. *J. counsel. Psychol.*, 1959b, *6*, 148–152.

**Mann, J. H., & Mann, C. H.** The importance of group task in producing group-member personality and behavior changes. *Hum. Relat.*, 1959c, *12*, 75–80.

**Mann, J. H., & Mann, C. H.** The relative effectiveness of role playing and task oriented group experience in producing personality and behavior change. *J. soc. Psychol.*, 1960, *51*, 313–317.

**Mann, J. W.** Group relations in hierarchies. *J. soc. Psychol.*, 1961, *54*, 283–314.

**Mann, R. D.** A review of the relationships between personality and performance in small groups. *Psychol. Bull.*, 1959, *56*, 241–270.

**Mann, R. D.** Dimensions of individual performance in small groups under task and social-emotional conditions. *J. abnorm. soc. Psychol.*, 1961, *62*, 674–682.

**Mann, R. D., Gibbard, G. S., & Hartman, J. J.** *Interpersonal styles and group development: an analysis of the member-leader relationship*. New York: Wiley, 1967.

**Mannari, H., & Abegglen, J.** The educational background of Japan's industrial leaders. *Bessatsu chuo koron: keiei mondai*, 1963, Winter, 190–197.

**Mannheim, B. F., Rim, Y., & Grinberg, B.** Instrumental status of supervisors as related to workers' perceptions and expectations. *Hum. Relat.*, 1967, *20*, 387–396.

**Mansour, J. M.** Leadership behavior and principal–teacher interpersonal relations. *Dissertation Abstr. Internat.*, 1969, *30*, 526.

**Manton, E. J.** An analysis of the psychological consequences of organizational boundary relevance. *Dissertation Abstr. Internat.*, 1972, *32*, 6708–6709.

**Marak, G. E.** The evolution of leadership structure. *Sociometry*, 1964, *27*, 174–182.

**March, J. G.** Group autonomy and internal group control. *Soc. Forces*, 1955, *33*, 322–326.

**March, J. G.** Influence measurement in experimental and semi-experimental groups. *Sociometry*, 1956, *19*, 260–271.

**March, J. G.** *Handbook of organizations*. Chicago: Rand McNally, 1965.

**March, J. G., & Simon, H. A.** *Organizations*. New York: Wiley, 1958.

**Marchant, M. P.** *Participative management in academic libraries.* Westport, Conn.: Greenwood Press, 1976.

**Marchetti, P. V.** Some aspects of the manager–employee relationship in the retail grocery. *Amer. Psychologist,* 1953, *8,* 402.

**Marcus, P. M.** Expressive and instrumental groups: toward a theory of group action. *Amer. J. Sociol.,* 1960, *66,* 54–59.

**Marcus, P. M.** Group cohesion and worker productivity: a dissenting view. *Personnel Admin.,* 1962, *25,* 44–48, 57.

**Marder, E.** Leader behavior as perceived by subordinates as a function of organizational level. Columbus: Ohio State University, Master's thesis, 1960.

**Margiotta, F. D.** A military elite in transition: Air Force leaders in the 1980's. *Armed. for. Society,* 1976, *2,* 155–184.

**Margolin, J. B.** The application of Heider's theory to the effect of perceived cooperation or competition on the transfer of hostility.

**Marks, A. R.** An investigation of modifications of job design in an industrial situation and their effects on some measures of economic productivity. Doctoral dissertation, University of California, Berkeley, 1954.

**Marks, J. B.** Interests, leadership, and sociometric status among adolescents. *Sociometry,* 1954, *17,* 340–349.

**Marks, J. B.** Interests and group formation. *Hum. Relat.,* 1959, *12,* 385–390.

**Marks, M. R., & Jenkins, L. W.** "Initiate structure" and "Consideration"—their surprising and general relation to global ratings or rankings. Rochester, N.Y.: University of Rochester, Technical report No., 1965.

**Marple, C. H.** The comparative susceptibility of three age levels to the suggestion of group versus expert opinion. *J. soc. Psychol.,* 1933, *4,* 176–186.

**Marquis, D. G.** Individual responsibility and group decisions involving risk. *Indus. Mgmt. Rev.,* 1962, *3,* 8–23.

**Marquis, D. G., Guetzkow, H., & Heyns, R. W.** A social psychological study of the decision-making conference. In H. Guetzkow (Ed.), *Groups, leadership, and men.* Pittsburgh: Carnegie Press, 1951.

**Marrow, A. J.** *Behind the executive mask.* New York: American Management Association, 1964.

**Marrow, A. J.** Risks and uncertainties in action research. *J. soc. Issues,* 1964, *20,* 5–20.

**Marrow, A. J., Bowers, D. G., & Seashore, S. E.** *Management by participation.* New York: Harper & Row, 1968.

**Marrow, A. J., & French, J. R. P.** Changing a stereotype in industry. *Personnel,* 1946a, *22,* 305–308.

**Marrow, A. J., & French, J. R. P.** A case of employee participation in a non-union shop. *J. soc. Issues,* 1946b, *2,* 29–34.

**Marsh, R. M., & Mannari, H.** Lifetime commitment in Japan: roles, norms, and values. *Amer. J. Sociol.,* 1971, *76,* 795–812.

**Marshall, S. L. A.** *World War I.* New York: American Heritage, 1964.

**Marshall, H. R.** Factors relating to the accuracy of adult leaders' judgments of social acceptance in community youth groups. *Child Develop.,* 1958, *29,* 417–424.

**Marston, A.** Personality variables related to self-reinforcement. *J. Psychol.,* 1964, *58,* 169–175.

**Martin, A. R.** Morale and productivity: a review of the literature. *Pub. person. Rev.,* 1969, *30,* 42–45.

**Martin, N. H.** The levels of management and their mental demands. In W. L. Warner & N. H. Martin (Eds.), *Industrial man.* New York: Harper & Row, 1959.

**Martin, N. H., & Sims, J. H.** Thinking ahead: power tactics. *Harvard bus. Rev.*, 1956, *34*, 25–36; 140.

**Martin, R.** Decentralized school management: professional staff and client perception. Doctoral dissertation, University of California, Los Angeles, 1972.

**Martin, W. E., Gross, N., & Darley, J. G.** Studies of group behavior: leaders, followers, and isolates in small organized groups. *J. abnorm. soc. Psychol.*, 1952, *47*, 838–842.

**Marvin, P.** *Management goals: guidelines and accountability.* Homewood, Ill.: Dow Jones-Irwin, Inc., 1968.

**Marwell, G.** Types of past experience with potential work partners: their effects on partner choice. *Hum. Relat.*, 1966, *19*, 437–447.

**Masling, J. M.** The Bainbridge study. In D. Courtney (Ed.), *Naval, neighborhood, and national leadership.* Philadelphia: Institute for Research in Human Relations, 1953.

**Masling, J. M., Greer, F. L., & Gilmore, R.** Status, authoritarianism, and sociometric choice. *J. soc. Psychol.*, 1955, *41*, 297–310.

**Maslow, A. H.** *Motivation and personality.* New York: Harper, 1954.

**Maslow, A. H.** *Eupsychian management: a journal.* Homewood, Ill.: Dorsey Press, 1965.

**Mason, D. J.** Judgments of leadership based upon physiognomic cues. *J. abnorm. soc. Psychol.*, 1957, *54*, 273–274.

**Mason, W. A.** Sociability and social organization in monkeys and apes. In L. Berkowitz (Ed.), *Advances in experimental social psychology.* New York: Academic Press, 1964.

**Massarik, F., Tannenbaum, R., Kahane, M., & Weschler, I. R.** Sociometric choice and organizational effectiveness: a multi-relational approach. *Sociometry*, 1953, *16*, 211–238.

**Mathews, J. E.** Leader behavior of elementary principals and the group dimensions of their staffs. *Dissertation Abstr.*, 1963, *25*, 2318.

**Matsui, T., Ohtsuka, Y., & Kikuchi, A.** Consideration and structure behavior as reflections of supervisory interpersonal values. *J. appl. Psychol.*, 1978, *63*, 259–262.

**Matteson, M. T.** Attitudes toward women as managers: sex or role differences? *Psychol. Rep.*, 1976, *39*, 166.

**Matteson, M. T., McMahon, J. F., & McMahon, M.** Sex differences and job attitudes: some unexpected findings. *Psychol. Rep.*, 1974, *35*, 1333–1334.

**Matthews, D. R.** *The social background of political decision-makers.* New York: Random House, 1954.

**Matthews, J.** Research on the development of valid situational tests of leadership. 1. Survey of the literature. Pittsburgh: American Institute for Research, 1951 (mimeo).

**Mauer, J. G.** *Work role involvement of industrial supervisors.* East Lansing: Michigan State University, Bureau of Business & Economic Research, 1969.

**Mauer, K. F.** The utility of the leadership opinion questionnaire in the South African mining industry. *J. behav. Sci.*, 1974, *74*, 67–72.

**Mausner, B.** Studies in social interaction. III. Effect of variation in one partner's prestige on the interaction of observer pairs. *J. appl. Psychol.*, 1953, *37*, 391–393.

**Mausner, B.** The effect of prior reinforcement on the interaction of observer pairs. *J. abnorm. soc. Psychol.*, 1954a, *49*, 65–68.

**Mausner, B.** The effects of one partner's success in a relevant task on the interaction of observer pairs. *J. abnorm. soc. Psychol.*, 1954b, *49*, 557–560.

**Mausner, B.** Situational and personal factors in social interaction. Glenside, Pa.: Beaver College, Technical Report, 1966.

**Mausner, B., & Bloch, B. L.** A study of the additivity of variables affecting social interaction. *J. abnorm. soc. Psychol.*, 1957, *54*, 250–256.

**Mawhinney, T. C., & Ford, J. D.** The path goal theory of leader effectiveness: an operant interpretation. *Acad. Mgmt. Rev.*, 1977, *2*, 398–411.

**May, M. A., & Doob, L. W.** *Competition and cooperation.* New York: Social Science Research Council, Bulletin No. 25, 1937.

**May, O. P., & Thompson, C. L.** Perceived levels of self-disclosure, mental health, and helpfulness of group leaders. *J. couns. Psychol.,* 1973, *20,* 349–352.

**Mayberry, B. A.** Training for leadership by means of student government. *J. natl. educ. Assn.,* 1925, *14,* 186.

**Mayberry, H. T.** Measuring leadership qualities of officer candidates. *Texas personnel Rev.,* 1943, *2,* 79–83.

**Mayes, B. T.** Leader needs as moderators of the subordinate job performance-leader behavior relationship. *Proceedings of the Academy of Management,* 1979.

**Mayfield, E. C.** Management selection: buddy nominations revisited. *Personnel Psychol.,* 1970, *23,* 377–389.

**Mayhand, E., & Grusky, O.** A preliminary experiment on the effects of black supervisors on white and black subordinates. *J. black Stud.,* 1972, *2,* 461–470.

**Mayo, E., & Lombard, G. F. F.** Teamwork and labor turnover in the aircraft industry of Southern California. Cambridge, Mass.: Harvard Business School, No. 32, 1944.

**Mayo, G. C., & DuBois, P. H.** Measurement of gain in leadership training. *Educ. psychol. Measmt.,* 1963, *23,* 23–31.

**Mead, M.** *Growing up in New Guinea—à comparative study of primitive education.* New York: Morrow, 1930.

**Mead, M.** *Sex and temperament in three primitive societies.* New York: Morrow, 1935.

**Mead, M.** *From the South Seas—coming of age in Samoa.* New York: Morrow, 1939.

**Mead, M., Mirsky, M., Landes, R., Edel, M. M., Goldman, I., Quain, B., Mishkin, B., & Zessner, W.** *Cooperation and competition among primitive peoples.* New York: McGraw-Hill, 1937.

**Meade, R. D.** An experimental study of leadership in India. *J. soc. Psychol.,* 1967, *72,* 35–43.

**Meade, R. D., & Whittaker, J. D.** A cross-cultural study of authoritarianism. *J. soc. Psychol.,* 1967, *72,* 3–7.

**Mechanic, D.** Sources of power of lower participants in complex organizations. *Admin. sci. Quar.,* 1962, *7,* 349–364.

**Medalia, N. Z.** Unit size and leadership perception. *Sociometry,* 1954, *17,* 64–67.

**Medalia, N. Z.** Authoritarianism, leader acceptance, and group cohesion. *J. abnorm. soc. Psychol.,* 1955, *51,* 207–213.

**Medalia, N. Z., & Miller, D. C.** Human relations leadership and the association of morale and efficiency in work groups: a controlled study with small military units. *Soc. Forces,* 1955, *33,* 348–352.

**Medland, F. F., & Olans, J. L.** Peer rating stability in changing groups. USAPRO Technical Research Note, No. 142, 1964.

**Medow, H., & Zander, A.** Aspirations for the group chosen by central and peripheral members. *J. pers. soc. Psychol.,* 1965, *1,* 224–228.

**Megargee, E. I.** Prediction of leadership in a simulated industrial task. *J. appl. Psychol.,* 1966, *50,* 292–294.

**Megargee, E. I.** Influence of sex roles on the manifestation of leadership. *J. appl. Psychol.,* 1969, *53,* 377–382.

**Megargee, E. I., Bogart, P., & Anderson, B. J.** Prediction of leadership in a simulated industrial task. *J. appl. Psychol.,* 1966, *50,* 292–295.

**Mehaffey, T. D.** The effects of a T-group experience on clients with measured high and low dependency needs. *Dissertation Abstr. Internat.,* 1973, *33,* 3299–3300.

**Meheut, Y., & Siegel, J. P.** A study of leader behavior and MBO success. Toronto: University of Toronto, Faculty of Management Studies, unpublished paper, 1973.

**Mehrabian, A.** Inference of attitude from the posture, orientation, and distance of a communicator. *J. consult. clin. Psychol.*, 1968, *32*, 296–308.

**Mehrabian, A.** Significance of posture and position in the communication of attitude and status relationships. *Psychol. Bull.*, 1969, *71*, 359–372.

**Mehrabian, A.** *Tactics of social influence.* Englewood Cliffs, N.J.: Prentice-Hall, 1970.

**Meltzer, L.** Scientific productivity in organizational settings. *J. soc. Issues*, 1956, *12*, 32–40.

**Meltzer, L., & Salter, J.** Organization structure and the performance and job satisfaction of physiologists. *Amer. sociol. Rev.*, 1962, *27*, 351–362.

**Merei, F.** Group leadership and institutionalization. *Hum. Relat.*, 1949, *2*, 23–39.

**Merrell, V. D.** *An analysis of university sponsored executive development programs.* Los Angeles: UCLA, School of Public Administration, 1965.

**Merriam, C. E.** *Four American party leaders.* New York: Macmillan, 1926.

**Merriam, C. E., & Gosnell, H. E.** *The American party system.* New York: Macmillan, 1929.

**Merton, R. K.** Bureaucratic structure and personality. *Soc. Forces*, 1940, *18*, 560–568.

**Merton, R. K.** *Social theory and social structure.* New York: Free Press, 1949, 1957.

**Merton, R. K.** The social nature of leadership. *Amer. J. Nurs.*, 1969, *69*, 2614–2618.

**Merton, R. K., Gray, A. P., Hockey, B., & Selvin, H. C.** *Reader in bureaucracy.* New York: Free Press, 1952.

**Merton, R. K., & Kitt, A. S.** Contributions to the theory of reference group behavior. In R. K. Merton & P. F. Lazarsfeld (Eds.), *Studies in the scope and method of "The American Soldier."* New York: Free Press, 1950.

**Mesics, E. A.** *Training in organizations: business, industrial, and government.* Bibliography Series No. 4. Ithaca, N.Y.: Cornell University, New York State School of Industrial & Labor Relations, 1960.

**Mesics, E. A.** *An annotated bibliography on education and training in organizations.* Ithaca, N.Y.: Cornell University, New York State School of Industrial & Labor Relations, 1964.

**Metcalf, H. C.** *Business leadership.* New York: Pitman, 1931.

**Mettal, W. G.** Human relations training and creative problem-solving competence in adolescents. *Dissertation Abstr. Internat.*, 1973, *33*, 3288.

**Meuwese, W. A. T., & Fiedler, F. E.** *Leadership and group creativity under varying conditions of stress.* Urbana: University of Illinois, Group Effectiveness Research Laboratory, Technical Report, 1965.

**Mey, W.** Spontaneous and elective leadership in school classes. *Badag. stud. Krit.*, 1936, *12*, 1–82.

**Meyer, C. T.** The assertive behavior of children as related to parent behavior. *J. Home Econ.*, 1947, *39*, 77–80.

**Meyer, H. H.** Factors related to success in human relations aspect of work-group leadership. *Psychol. Monogr.*, 1951, *65*, No. 320.

**Meyer, H. H.** A comparison of foreman and general foreman conceptions of the foreman's job responsibility. *Personnel Psychol.*, 1959, *12*, 445–452.

**Meyer, H. H.** Achievement motivation and industrial climates. In R. Tagiuri & G. H. Litwin (Eds.), *Organizational climate.* Boston: Harvard University, Graduate School of Business Administration, 1968.

**Meyer, H. H.** The validity of the in-basket test as a measure of managerial performance. *Personnel Psychol.*, 1970a, *23*, 297–307.

**Meyer, H. H.** Improving supervisor–employee relations in the shop. Unpublished manuscript, 1970b.

**Meyer, H. H., & Walker, W. B.** Need for achievement and risk preferences as they relate to attitudes toward reward systems and performance appraisal in an industrial setting. *J. appl. Psychol.*, 1961, *45*, 251–256.

**Meyer, M. W.** The two authority structures of bureaucratic organization. *Admin. sci. Quar.*, 1968, *13*, 211–228.

**Meyer, M. W.** Leadership and organizational structure. *Amer. J. Sociol.*, 1975, *81*, 514–542.

**Meyers, A. K., & Miller, N. E.** Failure to find a learned drive based on hunger: evidence for learning motivated by "exploration." *J. comp. Physiol. Psychol.*, 1954, *47*, 428–436.

**Meyers, C. E.** The effect of conflicting authority on the child. *Univer. Iowa stud. child Welf.*, 1944, *20*, 31–98.

**Meyers, G. C.** Training for leadership. *School Soc.*, 1923, *17*, 437–439.

**Meyers, L. C.** Some effects of facilitator training on the attitudes and performances of people in leadership positions. *Dissertation Abstr. Internat.*, 1970, *31*, 2962–2963.

**Michaelson, F. J.** Some motivational aspects of leadership. Doctoral dissertation, Ohio State University, Columbus, 1951.

**Michaelson, L. K.** Leader orientation, leader behavior, group effectiveness, and situational favorability: an empirical extension of the contingency model. *Org. behav. hum. Perform.*, 1973, *9*, 226–245.

**Michels, R.** *Political parties.* New York: Macmillan, 1915.

**Michener, H. A., & Burt, M. R.** Components of "authority" as determinants of compliance. *J. personnel Psychol.*, 1975a, *31*, 606–614.

**Michener, H. A., & Burt, M. R.** Use of social influence under varying conditions of legitimacy. *J. pers. soc. Psychol.*, 1975b, *32*, 398–407.

**Michener, H. A., & Lawler, E. J.** Endorsement of formal leaders: an integrative model. *J. pers. soc. Psychol.*, 1975, *31*, 216–223.

**Middleton, W. C.** Personality qualities predominant in campus leaders. *J. soc. Psychol.*, 1941, *13*, 199–201.

**Miklos, E.** Dimensions of conflicting expectations and the leader behavior of principals. Doctoral dissertation, University of Alberta, Edmonton, 1963.

**Miles, A. S.** Dimensions of student leadership at Cornell University. *Dissertation Abstr. Internat.*, 1970, *30*, 2856.

**Miles, M. B.** Human relations training: processes and outcomes. *J. counsel. Psychol.*, 1960, *7*, 301–306.

**Miles, M. B.** Changes during and following laboratory training: a clinical experimental study. *J. appl. behav. Sci.*, 1965, *1*, 215–242.

**Miles, M. B., Milavsky, J. R., Lake, D. G., & Beckhard, R.** Organizational improvement: effects of management team training in Bankers Trust. New York: Bankers Trust Company, Personnel Division, unpublished monograph, 1965.

**Miles, P. L.** Leadership. *Infantry J.*, 1934, *41*, 183–188, 276–283.

**Miles, R. E.** Attitudes toward management theory as a factor in managers' relationship with their superiors. *Acad. Mgmt. J.*, 1964a, *7*, 308–314.

**Miles, R. E.** Conflicting elements in managerial ideologies. *Indus. Relat.*, 1964b, *4*, 77–91.

**Miles, R. E., & Ritchie, J. B.** Leadership attitudes among union officials. *Indus. Relat.*, 1968, *8*, 108–117.

**Miles, R. H., & Petty, M. M.** Leader effectiveness in small bureaucracies. *Acad. Mgmt. J.*, 1977, *20*, 238–250.

**Milgram, S.** Liberating effects of group pressure. *J. pers. soc. Psychol.*, 1965a, *1*, 127–134.

**Milgram, S.** Some conditions of obedience and disobedience to authority. *Hum. Relat.*, 1965b, *18*, 57–76.

**Milkovich, G. T., & Anderson, P. H.** Management compensation and secrecy policies. *Personnel Psychol.*, 1972, *25*, 293–302.

**Mill, C. R.** Personality patterns of sociometrically selected and sociometrically rejected male college students. *Sociometry*, 1953, *16*, 151–167.

**Miller, A. H.** *Military leadership.* New York: Putnam, 1920.

**Miller, D. C.** Using behavioral science to solve organizational problems. *Personnel Admin.,* 1968, *31,* 21–29.

**Miller, D. C., & Dirksen, J. L.** The identification of visible, concealed, and symbolic leaders in a small Indiana city: a replication of the Bonjean-Noland study of Burlington, North Carolina. *Soc. Forces,* 1965, *43,* 548–555.

**Miller, D. C., & Schull, F. A.** The prediction of administrative role conflict resolutions. *Admin. sci. Quar.,* 1962, *7,* 143–160.

**Miller, E. L.** Job attitudes of national union officials: perceptions of the importance of certain personality traits as a function of job level and union organizational structure. *Personnel Psychol.,* 1966a, *19,* 395–410.

**Miller, E. L.** Job satisfaction of national union officials. *Personnel Psychol.,* 1966b, *19,* 261–274.

**Miller, F. B.** Personnel research contributions by U.S. universities. Ithaca, N.Y.: Cornell University, New York State School of Industrial & Labor Relations, Bulletin No. 42, 1960.

**Miller, F. B., & Coghill, M. A.** *The historical sources of personnel work.* Ithaca, N.Y.: Cornell University, New York State School of Industrial & Labor Relations, 1961.

**Miller, F. G., & Remmers, H. H.** Studies in industrial empathy. II. Management's attitudes toward industrial supervision and their estimates of labor attitudes. *Personnel Psychol.,* 1950, *3,* 33–40.

**Miller, G. A.** Professionals in a bureaucracy: alienation among individual scientists and engineers. *Amer. sociol. Rev.,* 1967, *32,* 755–768.

**Miller, J. A.** Structuring/destructuring: leadership in open systems. Rochester, N.Y.: University of Rochester, Technical Report No. 64, 1973a.

**Miller, J. A.** A hierarchical structure of leadership behaviors. Rochester, N.Y.: University of Rochester, Management Research Center, Technical Report No. 66, 1973b.

**Miller, J. A.** Leadership in open systems. Doctoral dissertation, University of Rochester, Rochester, N.Y., 1974.

**Miller, J. G.** Toward a general theory for the behavioral sciences. *Amer. Psychologist,* 1955, *10,* 513–531.

**Miller, J. G.** The nature of living systems. *Behav. Sci.,* 1971, *16,* 277–301.

**Miller, J. G.** Living systems: the group. *Behav. Sci.,* 1971, *16,* 302–398.

**Miller, L., & Hamblin, R. L.** Interdependence, differential rewarding, and productivity. *Amer. sociol. Rev.,* 1963, *28,* 768–778.

**Miller, N. E.** Effects of group size on group process and member satisfaction. Ann Arbor: University of Michigan, Proc. Adm. Conf., 1950.

**Miller, P.** Democratic leadership in secondary education. Doctoral dissertation, Ohio State University, Columbus, 1951.

**Miller, P.** Leadership in secondary education. Columbus: Ohio State University, Personnel Research Board, 1953.

**Miller, R. B.** Task description and analysis. In R. M. Gagne (Ed.), *Psychological principles in system development.* New York: Holt, Rinehart & Winston, 1962.

**Miller, R. D.** A systems concept of training. *Train. develop. J.,* 1969, *23,* 4–14.

**Miller, R. E., & Murphy, J. V.** Social interactions of Rhesus monkeys: I. Food-getting dominance as a dependent variable. *J. soc. Psychol.,* 1956, *44,* 249–255.

**Miller, R. S.** Developing leadership in young officers. *Military Rev.,* 1943, *23,* 11–12.

**Miller, S. J.** *Prescription for leadership: training for the medical elite.* Chicago: Aldine-Atherton, 1970.

**Miller, W. B.** Focal concerns of lower-class culture. In L. A. Ferman, J. L. Kornbluh, & A. Haber (Eds.), *Poverty in America.* Ann Arbor: University of Michigan Press, 1965.

**Mills, T. M.** Power relations in three-person groups. *Amer. sociol. Rev.*, 1953, *18*, 351–357.

**Mills, T. M.** The coalition pattern in three-person groups. *Amer. sociol. Rev.*, 1954, *19*, 657–667.

**Mills, T. M.** *Group structure and the newcomer: an experimental study of group expansion.* Oslo, Norway: Oslo University Press, 1957.

**Mills, T. M.** *Group transformation: an analysis of a learning group.* Englewood Cliffs, N.J.: Prentice-Hall, 1964.

**Mills, T. M., & Rosenberg, S.** *Readings in the sociology of small groups.* Englewood Cliffs, N.J.: Prentice-Hall, 1970.

**Milner, E.** Student preferences concerning teaching method and class structuring. *Amer. Psychologist*, 1948, *3*, 233–234.

**Milton, O.** Presidential choice and performance on a scale of authoritarianism. *Amer. Psychologist*, 1952, *7*, 597–598.

**Miner, J. B.** The effect of a course in psychology on the attitudes of research and development supervisors. *J. appl. Psychol.*, 1960, *44*, 224–231.

**Miner, J. B.** The validity of the PAT in the selection of tabulating machine operation: an analysis of productive power. *J. proj. Techniques*, 1961, *25*, 330–333.

**Miner, J. B.** Conformity among university professors and business executives. *Admin. sci. Quar.*, 1962, *7*, 96–109.

**Miner, J. B.** Personality and ability factors in sales performance. *J. appl. Psychol.*, 1962, *46*, 6–13.

**Miner, J. B.** Occupational differences in the desire to exercise power. *Psychol. Rep.*, 1963, *13*, 18.

**Miner, J. B.** *Studies in management education.* New York: Springer, 1965.

**Miner, J. B.** *The school administrator and organizational character.* Eugene, Ore.: University of Oregon, Center for the Advanced Study of Educational Administration, 1967.

**Miner, J. B.** The early identification of managerial talent. *Personnel guid. J.*, 1968, *46*, 586–591.

**Miner, J. B.** Motivation to manage among women: studies of business managers and educational administrators. *J. vocat. Behav.*, 1974, *5*, 197–208.

**Miner, J. B.** *The uncertain future of the leadership concept: an overview.* Paper presented at the Southern Illinois Leadership Conference, 1975.

**Miner, J. B. (Ed.).** *Motivation to manage: a ten year update on the "studies in management education" research.* Atlanta: Organizational Measurement Systems Press, 1977a.

**Miner, J. B.** Implications of managerial talent projections for management education. *Acad. Mgmt. Rev.*, 1977b, *2*, 412–420.

**Miner, J. B.** Motivational potential for upgrading among minority and female managers. *J. appl. Psychol.*, 1977c, *62*, 691–697.

**Miner, J. B.** The Miner sentence completion scale: a re-appraisal. *Acad. Mgmt. J.*, 1978, *21*, 283–294.

**Miner, J. B., & Crane, D. P.** The continuing effects of motivational shifts among college students. In J. B. Miner (Ed.), *Motivation to manage.* Atlanta: Organizational Measurement Systems Press, 1977.

**Miner, J. B., & Miner, M. G.** Managerial characteristics of personnel managers. In J. B. Miner (Ed.), *Motivation to manage.* Atlanta: Organizational Measurement Systems Press, 1977.

**Miner, J. B., Rizzo, J. R., Harlow, D. N., & Hill, J. W.** Role motivation theory of managerial effectiveness in simulated organizations of varying degrees of structure. *J. appl. Psychol.*, 1974, *59*, 31–37. Also: In J. B. Miner (Ed.), *Motivation to manage.* Atlanta: Organizational Measurement Systems Press, 1977.

**Mintz, A.** Non-adaptive behavior. *J. abnorm. soc. Psychol.*, 1951, *46*, 150–159.

**Mintzberg, H.** *The nature of managerial work.* New York: Harper & Row, 1973.

**Mintzberg, H.** The manager's job: folklore and fact. *Harvard bus. Rev.*, 1975, *53*, 49–61.

**Mischel, W.** Preference for delayed reinforcement and social responsibility. *J. abnorm. soc. Psychol.*, 1961, *62*, 1–7.

**Mischel, W.** Predicting the success of Peace Corps volunteers in Nigeria. *J. pers. soc. Psychol.*, 1965, *1*, 510–517.

**Misshauk, M. J.** The relation of supervisor skill mix to employee satisfaction and productivity. Doctoral dissertation, Ohio State University, Columbus, 1968.

**Misumi, J.** Action research on the development of leadership, decision-making processes and organizational performance in a Japanese shipyard. *Proceedings of the 18th International Congress of Applied Psychology,* 1974.

**Misumi, J., & Seki, F.** Effects of achievement motivation on the effectiveness of leadership patterns. *Admin. sci. Quar.*, 1971, *16*, 51–59.

**Misumi, J., & Shirakashi, S.** An experimental study of the effects of supervisory behavior on productivity and morale in a hierarchical organization. *Hum. Relat.*, 1966, *19*, 297–307.

**Misumi, J., Takeda, T., & Seki, F.** An empirical study of the effects of managerial and supervisory behavior of PM pattern on productivity and morale, particularly need for achievement, in a hierarchical organization. *Jap. J. educ. soc. Psychol.*, 1967, *7*, 27–42.

**Misumi, J., & Tasaki, T.** A study on the effectiveness of supervisory patterns in a Japanese hierarchical organization. *Japanese psychol. Res.*, 1965, *7*, 151–162.

**Mitchell, B. N.** The black minority in the CPA profession. *J. Account.*, 1969, *128*, 41–48.

**Mitchell, T. R.** *Leader complexity, leadership style, and group performance.* Doctoral dissertation, University of Illinois, Urbana, 1969.

**Mitchell, T. R.** The construct validity of three dimensions of leadership research. *J. soc. Psychol.*, 1970a, *80*, 89–94.

**Mitchell, T. R.** Leader complexity and leadership style. *J. pers. soc. Psychol.*, 1970b, *16*, 166–174.

**Mitchell, T. R.** Cognitive complexity and group performance. *J. soc. Psychol.*, 1972, *86*, 35–43.

**Mitchell, T. R.** Organizational behavior. *Ann. rev. Psychol.*, 1979, *30*, 243–281.

**Mitchell, T. R., & Albright, D. W.** Expectancy theory predictions of the satisfaction, effort, performance, and retention of naval aviation officers. *Org. behav. hum. Perform.*, 1972, *8*, 1–20.

**Mitchell, T. R., Biglan, A., Oncken, G. R., & Fiedler, F. E.** The Contingency Model: criticism and suggestions. *Acad. Mgmt. J.*, 1970, *13*, 253–267.

**Mitchell, T. R., & Foa, U. G.** Diffusion of the effect of cultural training of the leader in the structure of heterocultural task groups. *Australian J. Psychol.*, 1969, *21*, 31–43.

**Mitchell, T. R., Larson, J. R., & Green, S. G.** Leader behavior, situational moderators and group performance: an attributional analysis. *Org. behav. hum. Perform.*, 1977, *18*, 254–268.

**Mitchell, T. R., Smyser, C. M., & Weed, S. E.** Locus of control: supervision and work satisfaction. *Acad. Mgmt. J.*, 1975, *18*, 623–630.

**Mitchell, T. R., & Wood, R. E.** An empirical test of an attributional model of leaders' responses to poor performance. Symposium on Leadership, Duke University, April, 1979.

**Mitchell, V. F.** The relationship of effort, abilities, and role perceptions to managerial performance. *Dissertation Abstr.*, 1968, *29*, 360.

**Mitchell, V. F.** Need satisfactions of military commanders and staff. *J. appl. Psychol.*, 1970, *54*, 282–287.

**Mitchell, V. F., & Porter, L. W.** Comparative managerial role perceptions in military and business hierarchies. *J. appl. Psychol.*, 1967, *51*, 449–452.

**Moede, W.** *Experimentelle Massenpsychologie.* Leipzig: Hirzel, 1920.

**Moffie, D. J., Calhoon, R., & O'Brien, J. K.** Evaluation of a management development program. *Personnel Psychol.*, 1964, *17*, 431–440.

**Mohanna, A. I., & Argyle, M.** A cross-cultural study of structured groups with unpopular central members. *J. abnorm. soc. Psychol.*, 1960, *60*, 139–140.

**Mohr, L. B.** Organizational technology and organizational structure. *Admin. sci. Quar.*, 1971, *16*, 444–459.

**Mohr, L. B.** Authority and democracy in organizations. *Hum. Relat.*, 1977, *30*, 919–947.

**Mold, H. P.** Outline of a complete training program. *Personnel J.*, 1947, *26*, 75–79.

**Mold, H. P.** Management builds itself—a case study in conference training. In M. J. Dooher & V. Marquis (Eds.), *The development of executive talent.* New York: American Management Association, 1952.

**Moment, D., & Zaleznik, A.** *Role development and interpersonal competence.* Boston: Harvard University, Graduate School of Business Administration, 1963.

**Monge, P. R., & Kirste, K. K.** Proximity, location, time, and opportunity to communicate. California State University, San Jose, 1975 (mimeo).

**Moon, C. G., & Hariton, T.** Evaluating an appraisal and feedback training program. *Personnel*, 1958, *35*, 37–41.

**Mooney, J. D., & Reiley, A. C.** *Onward industry! The principles of organization and their significance to modern industry.* New York: Harper, 1931.

**Moore, B. V.** The May conference on leadership. *Personnel J.*, 1927, *6*, 124–128.

**Moore, B. V., Kennedy, J. E., & Castore, G. F.** *The work, training, and status of supervisors as reported by supervisors in industry.* State College, Pa.: Pennsylvania State College, 1946.

**Moore, H. T.** The comparative influence of majority and expert opinion. *Amer. J. Psychol.*, 1921, *32*, 16–20.

**Moore, H. T., & Gilliland, A. R.** The measurement of aggressiveness. *J. appl. Psychol.*, 1921, *5*, 97–118.

**Moore, J. C.** Status and influence in small group interactions. *Sociometry*, 1968, *31*, 47–63.

**Moore, J. C.** Social status and social influence: process considerations. *Sociometry*, 1969, *32*, 145–158.

**Moore, J. V.** A factor analysis of subordinate evaluations of noncommissioned officer supervisors. *USAF Hum. Resour. Res. Cent. res. Bull.*, 1953, No. 53–6.

**Moore, J. V.** Factor analytic comparisons of superior and subordinate ratings of the same NCO supervisors. San Antonio, Tex.: Human Resources Research Center, Technical Report No. 53–24, 1953.

**Moore, J. V., & Smith, R. G.** Some aspects of noncommissioned officer leadership. *Personnel Psychol.*, 1953, *6*, 427–443.

**Moore, L. B.** Managerial time. *Mgmt. Rev.*, 1968, *9*, 77–85.

**Moore, L. H.** Leadership traits of college women. *Sociol. soc. Res.*, 1932, *17*, 44–54.

**Moore, L. H.** Leadership traits of college women. *Sociol. soc. Res.*, 1935, *20*, 136–139.

**Moore, L. I.** The FMI: dimensions of follower maturity. *Grp. org. Studies.*, 1976, *1*, 203–222.

**Moore, W. E.** *The professions: roles and rules.* New York: Russell Sage Foundation, 1970.

**Moos, M., & Koslin, B.** Political leadership reexamined: an empirical approach. *Publ. opin. Quar.*, 1951, *15*, 563–574.

**Morall, H. H.** The relationship between perceived participation in school management and morale of selected black and nonblack teachers and students in Volusia County, Florida senior high schools. Doctoral dissertation, University of Miami, Miami, 1974.

**Moranian, T., Gruenwald, D., & Reidenbach, R. (Eds.),** *Business policy and its environment.* New York: Holt, Rinehart & Winston, 1965.

**Mordechai, E.** Relationships between self-perceived personality traits and job attitudes in middle management. *J. appl. Psychol.,* 1966, *50,* 428–430.

**Moreno, J. L.** *Who shall survive?* Beacon, N.Y.: Beacon House, 1934, 1953.

**Moreno, J. L.** *Sociodrama: a method for the analysis of social conflicts.* Beacon, N.Y.: Beacon House, 1955.

**Moreno, J. L.** *The sociometry reader.* New York: Free Press, 1960.

**Moreno, J. L., Jennings, H. H., & Sargent, J.** Time as a quantitative index of interpersonal relations. *Sociometry,* 1940, *3,* 62–80.

**Morgan, B. S., Blonsky, M. R., & Rosen, H.** Employee attitudes toward a hard-core hiring program. *J. appl. Psychol.,* 1970, *54,* 473–478.

**Morgan, W. R., & Sawyer, J.** Bargaining, expectations, and the preference for equality over equity. *J. pers. soc. Psychol.,* 1967, *6,* 139–149.

**Morris, C. G.** Task effects on group interaction. *J. pers. soc. Psychol.,* 1966a, *4,* 545–554.

**Morris, C. G.** Effects of task characteristics on group process. *Dissertation Abstr.,* 1966b, *26,* 7477.

**Morris, C. G., & Hackman, J. R.** Behavioral correlates of perceived leadership. *J. pers. soc. Psychol.,* 1969, *13,* 350–361.

**Morris, C. G., & Fiedler, F. E.** Application of a new system of interaction analysis to the relationship between leader attitudes and behavior in problem solving groups. Urbana: University of Illinois, Department of Psychology, 1964.

**Morris, R. T., & Seeman, M.** The problem of leadership: an interdisciplinary approach. *Amer. J. Sociol.,* 1950, *56,* 149–155.

**Morris, W. T.** *Decentralization in management systems: an introduction to design.* Columbus: Ohio State University Press, 1967.

**Morrison, R. F., & Sebald, M.** Personal characteristics differentiating female executives from female nonexecutive personnel. *J. appl. Psychol.,* 1974, *59,* 656–659.

**Morrow, H. G.** Consensus of observed leader behavior and role expectations of the elementary school principal. *Dissertation Abstr. Internat.,* 1971, *31,* 5856.

**Morsbach, H.** A cross-cultural study of achievement motivation and achievement values in two South African groups. *J. soc. Psychol.,* 1969, *79,* 267–268.

**Morse, J. J., & Wagner, F. R.** Measuring the process of managerial effectiveness. *Acad. Mgmt. J.,* 1978, *21,* 23–35.

**Morse, N. C.** *Satisfactions in the white collar job.* Ann Arbor: University of Michigan, Institute for Social Research, 1953.

**Morse, N. C., & Reimer, E.** The experimental change of a major organizational variable. *J. abnorm. soc. Psychol.,* 1956, *52,* 120–129.

**Morse, N. C., Reimer, E., & Tannenbaum, A. S.** Regulation and control in hierarchical organizations. *J. soc. Issues,* 1951, *7,* 41–48.

**Morsink, H. M.** A comparison of the leader behavior of fifteen men and fifteen women secondary school principals in Michigan. Unpublished ms., 1966.

**Morton, R. B., & Bass, B. M.** The organizational training laboratory. *Train. Directors. J.,* 1964, *18,* 2–18.

**Moser, R. P.** The leadership patterns of school superintendents and school principals. *Administrator's Notebook, 1957, 6,* 1–4.

**Moses, J. L., & Boehm, V. R.** Relationship of assessment-center performance to management progress of women. *J. appl. Psychol.,* 1975, *60,* 527–529.

**Moses, J. L., & Ritchie, R. J.** Supervisory relationships training: a behavioral evaluation of a behavioral modeling program. *Personnel Psychol.*, 1976, *29*, 337–343.

**Moss, G.** How community leaders view extension. *J. Extension*, 1974, *12*, 8–15.

**Mostofsky, D. I. (ed.).** *Attention: contemporary theory and analysis.* New York: Appleton-Century-Crofts, 1970.

**Mosvick, R. K.** *An experimental evaluation of two modes of motive analysis instruction in an industrial setting.* Doctoral dissertation, University of Minnesota, Minneapolis, 1966.

**Mosvick, R. K.** Twenty years of experimental evaluation of human relations training in the United States and Great Britain, 1949–1969. St. Paul, Minn., Macalester College, unpublished report, 1969.

**Mosvick, R. K.** Human relations training for scientists, technicians, and engineers: a review of the relevant experimental evaluations of human relations training. *Personnel Psychol.*, 1971, *24*, 275–292.

**Mott, P. E.** *The characteristics of effective organizations.* New York: Harper & Row, 1972.

**Mottl, T. L.** School movements as recruiters of women leaders: Boston's school movements of the 1960's and 1970's. *Urban Educ.*, 1977, *12*, 3–14.

**Mouton, J. S., & Blake, R. S.** Issues in transnational organization development. In B. M. Bass, R. Cooper, & J. A. Haas (Eds.), *Managing for accomplishment.* Lexington, Mass.: D. C. Heath, 1970.

**Mowday, R. T.** Leader characteristics, self-confidence, and methods of upward influence in organizational decision situations. *Acad. Mgmt. J.*, 1979, *22*, 709–725.

**Moyer, D. C.** Teachers' attitudes toward leadership as they relate to teacher satisfaction. Doctoral dissertation, University of Chicago, Chicago, 1954.

**Moynihan, D. P.** Employment, income, and the ordeal of the Negro family. In T. Parsons & K. B. Clark (Eds.), *The Negro American.* Boston: Houghton Mifflin, 1965.

**Mozina, S.** Management opinion on satisfaction and importance of psychosocial needs in their jobs. *Proceedings of the Sixteenth International Congress of Applied Psychology*, 1969.

**Mudd, S. A.** Group sanction severity as a function of degree of behavior deviation and relevance of norm. *J. pers. soc. Psychol.*, 1968, *8*, 258–260.

**Mueller, R. K.** Leader-edge leadership. In *Human systems management.* 1980, *1*, 17–27.

**Mulder, M.** Power and satisfaction in task oriented groups. *Acta Psychol.*, 1959, *16*, 178–225.

**Mulder, M.** Communication structure, decision structure, and group performance. *Sociometry*, 1960, *23*, 1–14.

**Mulder, M.** *Group structure, motivation and group performance.* The Hague, Paris: Mouton, 1963.

**Mulder, M.** Power equalization through participation? *Admin. sci. Quar.*, 1971, *16*, 31–38.

**Mulder, M., Ritsema, V. E., & de Jong, R. D.** An organization in crisis and non-crisis situations. *Hum. Relat.*, 1971, *24*, 19–41.

**Mulder, M., & Stemerding, A.** Threat, attraction to group, and need for strong leadership. *Hum. Relat.*, 1963, *16*, 317–334.

**Mulder, M., Van Dijk, R., Stirwagen, T., Verhagen, J., Soutendijk, S., & Zwezerijnen, J.** Illegitimacy of power and positiveness of attitude towards the power person. *Hum. Relat.*, 1966, *19*, 21–37.

**Mulder, M., & Wilke, H.** Participation and power equalization. *Org. behav. hum. Perform.*, 1970, *5*, 430–448.

**Muldrow, T. W., & Bayton, J. A.** Men and women executives and processes related to decision accuracy. *J. appl. Psychol.*, 1979, *64*, 99–106.

**Mullen, J. H.** The supervisor assesses his job in management. *Personnel*, 1954, *31*, 94–108.

**Mullen, J. H.** Differential leadership modes and productivity in a large organization. *Acad. Mgmt. J.*, 1965, *8*, 107–126.

**Mullen, J. H.** Personality polarization as an equilibrating force in a large organization. *Hum. Org.,* 1966a, *25,* 330–338.

**Mullen, J. H.** *Personality and productivity in management.* New York: Columbia University Press, 1966b.

**Muller, H. P.** Relationship between time-span of discretion, leadership behavior, and Fiedler's LPC scores. *J. appl. Psychol.,* 1970, *54,* 140–144.

**Mumford, E.** Origins of leadership. *Amer. J. Sociol.,* 1906–1907, *12,* 216–240, 367–397, 500–531.

**Mumford, E.** *The origins of leadership.* Chicago: University of Chicago Press, 1909.

**Mumford, E. M.** Social behavior in small work groups. *Sociol Rev.,* 1959, *7,* 137–157.

**Munch, P. A.** Sociology of Tristan da Cunha: results of the Norwegian scientific expedition to Tristan da Cunha, 1937–1938. Oslo: I Kommisjon Hos Jacob Dybwad, No. 13, 1945.

**Munro, W. B.** Civic organization. In *Encyclopaedia of the Social Sciences.* New York, Macmillan, 1930.

**Munson, E. L.** *The management of men.* New York: Holt, 1921.

**Murchison, C.** The experimental measurement of a social hierarchy in Gallus Domesticus. *J. gen. Psychol.,* 1935, *12,* 3–39.

**Murdoch, P.** Development of contractual norms in a dyad. *J. pers. soc. Psychol.,* 1967, *6,* 206–211.

**Murdock, G. P.** Comparative data on the decision of labor by sex. *Social Forces,* 1937, *15,* 551–553.

**Murdock, G. P.** *Ethnographic atlas.* Pittsburgh: University of Pittsburgh Press, 1967.

**Murnighan, J. K., & Leung, T. K.** The effects of leadership involvement and the importance of the task on subordinates' performance. *Org. behav. hum. Perform.,* 1976, *17,* 299–310.

**Murphy, A. J.** A study of the leadership process. *Amer. sociol. Rev.,* 1941, *6,* 674–687.

**Murphy, L. B.** Social factors in child development. In T. M. Newcomb & E. L. Hartley (Eds.), *Readings in social psychology.* New York: Holt, 1947.

**Murray, V. V., & Corenblum, A. F.** Loyalty to immediate superior at alternate hierarchical levels in a bureaucracy. *Amer. J. Sociol.,* 1966, *72,* 77–85.

**Mussen, P. H., & Porter, L. W.** Personal motivations and self-conceptions associated with effectiveness and ineffectiveness in emergent groups. *J. abnorm. soc. Psychol.,* 1959, *59,* 23–27.

**Muttayya, B. C.** Personality and value orientations of Panchayat leaders, informal leaders and non-leaders: a comparative study. *Behav. sci. community Develop.,* 1977, *11,* 1–11.

**Myer, H. E., & Fredian, A. J.** Personality test scores in the management hierarchy: revisited. *J. appl. Psychol.,* 1959, *43,* 212–220.

**Myers, H. H., & Walker, W. B.** Need for achievement and risk preferences as they relate to attitudes toward reward systems and performance appraisal in an industrial setting. *J. appl. Psychol.,* 1961, *45,* 251–256.

**Myers, H. H., Walker, N. B., & Litwin, G. H.** Motive patterns and risk preferences associated with entrepreneurship. *J. abnorm. soc. Psychol.,* 1961, *63,* 570–574.

**Myers, M. S.** Conditions for manager motivation. *Harvard bus. Rev.,* 1966, *44,* 58–71.

**Myers, M. S.** Every employee a manager. *Calif. mgmt. Rev.,* 1968, *10,* 9–20.

**Nafe, R. W.** A psychological description of leadership. *J. soc. Psychol.,* 1930, *1,* 248–266.

**Nagata, Y.** The effects of task structure upon group organization process in terms of the relevance of the individual's goal oriented activities. *Japanese J. Psychol.,* 1965, *36,* 56–66.

**Nagata, Y.** Effects of task structure on the process of group organization in terms of the difficulty of the task. I. *Psychol. Rep.,* 1966, *18,* 566.

**Nagel, J. N.** Some questions about the concept of power. *Behav. Sci.,* 1968, *13,* 129–137.

**Nagle, B. F.** Productivity, employee attitude, and supervisor sensitivity. *Personnel Psychol.,*

1954, *7*, 219–232.

**Nahabetian, H. J.** The effects of a leader's upward influence on group member satisfaction and task facilitation. Doctoral dissertation, University of Rochester, Rochester, N.Y., 1969.

**Narain, R.** Two decades of studies of leadership traits. *Shiksha*, 1955, *8*, 80–94.

**Nash, A. M.** Training for leadership here and now. *Train. School Bull.*, 1927, *24*, 10–14.

**Nash, A. N.** Vocational interests of effective managers: a review of the literature. *Personnel Psychol.*, 1965, *18*, 21–37.

**Nash, J. B.** Leadership. *Phi Delta Kappan*, 1929, *12*, 24–25.

**Nash, M.** *Machine age Maya: the industrialization of a Guatemalan community.* Menasha, Wis.: American Anthropological Association, Memoirs No. 87, 1958.

**Nason, R. W.** Dilemma of black mobility in management. *Bus. Horizons*, 1972, *15*, 57–68.

**Nath, R.** A methodological review of cross-cultural management research. In J. Boddewyn (Ed.), *Comparative management and marketing.* Glenview, Ill.: Scott, Foresman, 1969.

**National Institute of Industral Psychology.** *Joint consultation in British industry.* London: Staples Press, 1952.

**National Research Council.** *Psychology for the fighting man.* New York: Penguin Books, 1943.

**National Urban League.** *The strengths of black families.* July, 1971.

**Naumann-Etienne, M.** Bringing about open education: strategies for innovation and implementation. Doctoral dissertation, University of Michigan, Ann Arbor, 1975.

**Nayar, P. K. B.** *Leadership bureaucracy and planning in India.* New Delhi: Associated Publishing House, 1969.

**Naylor, J. C., & Dickinson, T. L.** Task structure, work structure, and team performance. *J. appl. Psychol.*, 1969, *3*, 167–177.

**Nealey, S. M., & Blood, M. R.** Leadership performance of nursing supervisors at two organizational levels. *J. appl. Psychol.*, 1968, *52*, 414–422.

**Nealey, S. M., & Fiedler, F. E.** Leadership functions of middle managers. *Psychol. Bull.*, 1968, *5*, 313–329.

**Nebeker, D. M.** Situational favorability and environmental uncertainty: an integrative study. *Admin. sci. Quar.*, 1975, *20*, 281–294.

**Nebeker, D. M., & Hansson, R. O.** Confidence in human nature and leader style. Seattle: University of Washington, Organizational Research, Technical Report No. 72–37, 1972.

**Nebeker, D. M., & Mitchell, T. R.** Leader behavior: an expectancy theory approach. *Org. behav. hum. Perform.*, 1974, *11*, 355–367.

**Neel, R. G., & Dunn, R. E.** Predicting success in supervisory training programs by the use of psychological tests. *J. appl. Psychol.*, 1960, *44*, 358–360.

**Negandhi, A. R., & Estafen, B. D.** A research model to determine the applicability of American management know-how in differing cultures and/or environments. In S. B. Prasad (Ed.), *Management in international perspective. New York: Appleton-Century-Crofts, 1967.*

**Negandhi, A. R., & Prasad, S. B.** *Comparative management.* New York: Appleton-Century-Croft, 1971.

**Negandhi, A. R., & Reiman, B. C.** A contingency theory of organization re-examined in the context of a developing country. *Acad. Mgmt. J.*, 1972, *15*, 137–146.

**Nelson, C. W.** A new approach to the development of institutional leadership and communication: a challenge to deans. *J. Natl. Assn. Deans' Counselors*, 1967, *30*, 132–137.

**Nelson, P. D.** An evaluation of a popular leader. *USN MNPRU Rep. No. 63-9*, 1963.

**Nelson, P. D.** Similarities and differences among leaders and followers. *J. soc. Psychol.*, 1964a, *63*, 161–167.

**Nelson, P. D.** Supervisor esteem and personnel evaluations. *J. appl. Psychol.*, 1964b, *48*, 106–109.

**Nelson, P. D., & Berry, N. H.** Dimensions of peer and supervisor ratings in a military setting.

*USN MNPRU Rep. No. 66-1,* 1966.

**Newcomb, T. M.** *Personality and social change.* New York: Holt, Rinehart & Winston, 1943, 1957.

**Newcomb, T. M.** The prediction of interpersonal attraction. *Amer. Psychologist,* 1956, *11,* 575–586.

**Newcomb, T. M.** *The acquaintance process.* New York: Holt, Rinehart & Winston, 1961.

**Newcomb, T. M., Turner, R. H., & Converse, P. E.** *Social psychology.* New York: Holt, Rinehart & Winston, 1965.

**Newcomer, M.** *The big business executive: the factors that made him, 1900–1950.* New York: Columbia University Press, 1955.

**Newell, A., & Simon, H. A.** *Human problem solving.* Englewood Cliffs, N.J.: Prentice-Hall, 1972.

**Newman, W. H., & Logan, J.** *Business policies and central management.* Cincinnati: Southwestern, 1965.

**Newman, W. H., & Summer, C. E.** *The process of management: concepts, behavior, practice.* Englewood Cliffs, N.J.: Prentice-Hall, 1961.

**Newport, G.** A study of attitudes and leadership behavior. *Personnel Admin.,* 1962, *25,* 42–46.

**Newsome, R. R.** Risky decisions of leaders and their groups. *Dissertation Abstr. Internat.,* 1972, *32,* 4849.

**Newstetter, W. I., Feldstein, M. J., & Newcomb, T. M.** *Group adjustment.* Cleveland: Western Reserve University Press, 1938.

*Newsweek.* Women in the armed forces. February 18, 1980, 34–36, 39–42.

**NICB (National Industrial Conference Board).** *Decentralization in industry.* New York: National Industrial Conference Board, 1948.

**NICB (National Industrial Conference Board).** *College graduates assess their company training.* New York: National Industrial Conference Board, 1963.

**NICB (National Industrial Conference Board).** *Developing managerial competence: changing concepts and emerging practices.* New York: National Industrial Conference Board, 1964.

**NICB (National Industrial Conference Board).** *Managing programs to employ the disadvantaged.* Studies in Personnel Policy No. 219. New York: National Industrial Conference Board, 1970.

**Nichol, E. A.** Management through consultative supervision. *Personnel J.,* 1948, *27,* 207–217.

**Nie, N. H., Bent, D. H., & Hull, C. H.** *SPSS: statistical package for the social sciences.* New York: McGraw-Hill, 1970.

**Nie, N. H., Powell, G. B., Jr., E. Prewitt, K.** Social structure and political participation: developmental relationships. *Amer. pol. sci. Rev.,* 1969, *63,* 361–378, 808–832.

**Nimmo, D.** *The political persuaders.* Englewood Cliffs, N.J.: Prentice-Hall, 1970.

**Ninane, P.** Réactions des leaders de groupe aux décisions de leur supérieur hiérarchique. *Bull. d'Etudes, Recher. Psychol.,* 1970, *19,* 113–130.

**Ninane, P., & Fiedler, F. E.** Member reactions to success and failure of task groups. *Hum. Relat.,* 1970, *23,* 3–13.

**Nix, H. L., Dressel, P. L., & Bates, F. L.** Changing leaders and leadership structure: a longitudinal study. *Rural Sociol.,* 1977, *42,* 22–41.

**Nix, H. L., Singh, R. N., & Cheatham, P. L.** Views of leader respondents compared with random respondents' views. *J. Commun. dev. Society.* 1974, *5,* 81–91.

**Nolting, O. F.** *Management methods in city government.* Chicago: International City Managers Association, 1941.

**Nord, W. R.** Social exchange theory: an integrative approach to social conformity. *Psychol. Bull.,* 1969, *71,* 174–208.

**Norfleet, B.** Interpersonal relations and group productivity. *J. soc. Issues,* 1948, *4,* 66–69.

**Norman, A. K.** "Consideration" and "initiating structure" and organizational criteria. *Personnel Admin.*, 1964, *27*, 35–37.

**Norman, R. D.** The interrelationships among acceptance-rejection, self-other identity, insight into self, and realistic perception of others. *J. soc. Psychol.*, 1953, *37*, 205–235.

**Norman, W. T.** Toward an adequate taxonomy of personality attributes: replicated factor structure in peer nomination personality ratings. *J. abnorm. soc. Psychol.*, 1963, *66*, 574–583.

**Northway, M. L.** Some challenging problems of social relationships. *Sociometry*, 1946, *9*, 187–198.

**Northway, M. L., Frankel, E. B., & Potashin, R.** Personality and sociometric status. *Sociometry Monogr.*, 1947, *11*.

**Northwood, L. K.** The relative ability of leaders and non-leaders as expert judges of facts and opinions held by members of the community of which they are a part. *Dissertation Abstr.*, 1953, *13*, 898.

**Notcutt, B., & Silva, A. L. M.** Knowledge of other people. *J. abnorm. soc. Psychol.*, 1951, *46*, 30–37.

**Nowotny, O. H.** American vs. European management philosophy. *Harvard bus. Rev.*, 1964, *42*, 101–108.

**Null, E. J., & Smead, W. H.** Relationships between the political orientation of superintendents and their leader behavior as perceived by subordinates. *J. educ. Res.*, 1971, *65*, 103–106.

**Nunnally, J. C.** *Psychometric theory.* New York: McGraw-Hill, 1967.

**Nutting, R. L.** Some characteristics of leadership. *School Soc.*, 1923, *18*, 387–390.

**Nydegger, R. V.** Leadership status and verbal behavior in small groups as a function of schedule of reinforcement and level of information processing complexity. *Proceedings of the American Psychological Association*, 1971.

**Nye, J. R.** Role performance in situations of conflicting role definitions. *Dissertation Abstr.*, 1968, *29*, 1301.

**Nystrom, P. C.** Managers and the hi-hi leader myth. *Acad. Mgmt. J.*, 1978, *21*, 325–331.

**Oaklander, H., & Fleishman, E. A.** Patterns of leadership related to organizational stress in hospital settings. *Admin. sci. Quar.*, 1964, *8*, 520–531.

**Oberg, W.** The university's role in executive education: a report to the participating companies. East Lansing: Michigan State University, Graduate School of Business Administration, 1962.

**Obradovic, J.** Participation and work attitudes in Yugoslavia. *Indus. Relat.*, 1970, *9*, 161–169.

**Obradovic, J.** Workers' participation: who participates? *Indus. Relat.*, 1975, *14*, 32–44.

**O'Brien, G. E.** Group structure and measurement of potential leader influence. *Australian J. Psychol.*, 1969a, *21*, 277–289.

**O'Brien, G. E.** Leadership in organizational settings. *J. appl. behav. Sci.*, 1969b, *5*, 45–63.

**O'Brien, G. E.** Group structure and productivity. *Australian Military Forces res. Rep.*, 1970, No. *7-70*.

**O'Brien, G. E., & Harary, F.** Measurement of the interactive effects of leadership style and group structure upon group performance. *Aust. J. Psychol.*, 1977, *29*, 59–71.

**Obrochta, R. J.** Foremen–worker attitude patterns. *J. appl. Psychol.*, 1960, *44*, 88–91.

**O'Connell, J. J.** *Managing organizational innovation.* Homewood, Ill.: Irwin, 1968.

**O'Connor, E. J., & Farrow, D. L.** A cross-functional comparison of prescribed versus preferred patterns of managerial structure. *J. mgmt. Stud.*, 1979, *16*, 222–234.

**O'Connor, J.** *Characteristics of successful executives.* Hoboken: Stevens Institute of Technology, 1932.

**O'Connor, J. R.** The relationship of kinesic and verbal communication to leadership perception in small group discussion. *Dissertation Abstr. Internat.*, 1972, *32*, 6589.

**O'Connor, W. F.** A note on the Cline and Richards' studies on accuracy of interpersonal perception. *J. abnorm. soc. Psychol.*, 1963, *66*, 194–195.

**Odier, C.** Valeur et valence du chef. *Schweiz. Arch. Neurol. Psychiat.*, 1948, *61*, 408–410.

**Odiorne, G. S.** The trouble with sensitivity training. *Train. Directors J.*, 1963, *17*, 9–20.

**O'Donovan, T. R.** Differential extent of opportunity among executives and lower managers. *Acad. Mgmt. J.*, 1962, *5*, 139–149.

**Office of Strategic Services.** *Assessment of men: selection of personnel for Office of Strategic Services.* New York: Rinehart, 1948.

**Okanes, M., & Stinson, J. E.** Machiavellianism and emergent leadership in a management simulation. *Psych. Rep.*, 1974, *35*, 255–259.

**Oldham, G. R.** The motivational strategies used by supervisors: relationships to effectiveness indicators. *Org. behav. hum. Perform.*, 1976, *15*, 66–86.

**O'Leary, V. E.** Some attitudinal barriers to occupational aspirations in women. *Psychol. Bull.*, 1974, *81*, 809–826.

**Olive, B. A.** *Management: a subject listing of recommended books, pamphlets, and journals.* Ithaca, N.Y.: Cornell University, Graduate School of Business and Public Administration, 1965.

**Oliverson, L. R.** Identification of dimensions of leadership and leader behavior and cohesion in encounter groups. *Dissertation Abstr. Internat.*, 1976, *37*, 136–137.

**Olmstead, J. A.** *Development of leadership assessment simulations.* Arlington, Va.: U.S. Army Research Institute for the Behavioral and Social Sciences, 1974.

**Olmsted, D. W.** Organizational leadership and social structure in a small city. *Amer. Sociol. Rev.*, 1954, *19*, 273–281.

**Olmstead, D. W.** Inter-group similarities of role correlates. *Sociometry*, 1957, *20*, 8–20.

**Olmsted, M. S.** Orientation and role in the small group. *Amer. sociol. Rev.*, 1954, *6*, 741–751.

**Olsen, M. E.** *The process of social organization.* New York: Holt, Rinehart & Winston, 1968.

**O'Neill, H. E., & Kubany, A. J.** Observation methodology and supervisory behavior. *Personnel Psychol.*, 1957, *12*, 85–96.

**Opsahl, R. L., & Dunnette, M. D.** Role of financial compensation in industrial motivation. *Psychol. Bull.*, 1966, *66*, 94–118.

**O'Reilly, C. A. III, & Roberts, K. H.** Job satisfaction among whites and nonwhites: a cross-cultural approach. *J. appl. Psychol.*, 1973, *57*, 295–299.

**O'Reilly, C. A. III, & Roberts, K. H.** Supervisor influence and subordinate mobility aspirations as moderators of consideration ratings and structure. *J. appl. Psychol.*, 1978, *63*, 96–102.

**Orlans, H.** *Opinion polls on national leaders.* Institute for Research in Human Relations, Report No. 6, 1953.

**Orr, D. B.** A new method for clustering jobs. *J. appl. Psych.*, 1960, *44*, 44–49.

**Osborn, R. N., & Hunt, J. G.** An empirical investigation of lateral and vertical leadership at two organizational levels. *J. bus. Res.*, 1974, *2*, 209–221.

**Osborn, R. N., & Hunt, J. G.** An adaptive-reactive theory of leadership: the role of macro variables in leadership research. In J. G. Hunt & L. L. Larson (Eds.), *Leadership frontiers.* Carbondale: Southern Illinois University Press, 1975a. Also: Kent, OH: Kent State University, Comparative Administration Research Institute, 1975b.

**Osborn, R. N., & Hunt, J. G.** Relations between leadership, size, and subordinate satisfaction in a voluntary organization. *J. appl. Psychol.*, 1975b, *60*, 730–735b.

**Osborn, R. N., & Hunt, J. G.** Environment and leadership: discretionary and nondiscretionary leader behavior and organizational outcomes. Unpublished paper, 1979.

**Osborn, R. N., Hunt, J. G., & Bussom, R. S.** On getting your own way in organizational design: an empirical illustration of requisite variety. *Org. admin. Sci.*, 1977, *8*, 295–310.

**Osborn, R. N., Hunt, J. G., & Pope, R.** Lateral leadership, satisfaction, and performance. *Proceedings of the Academy of Management,* 1973.

**Osborn, R. N., Hunt, J. G., & Skaret, D. J.** Managerial influence in a complex configuration with two unit heads. *Hum. Relat.,* 1977, *30,* 1025–1038.

**Osborn, R. N., & Vicars, W. M.** Sex stereotypes: an artifact in leader behavior and subordinate satisfaction analysis? *Acad. Mgmt. J.,* 1976, *19,* 439–449.

**Oshry, B. I., & Harrison, R.** Transfer from here-and-now to there-and-then: changes in organizational problem diagnosis stemming from T-group training. *J. appl. behav. Sci.,* 1966, *2,* 185–198.

**OSS (Office of Strategic Services) Assessment Staff.** *Assessment of men: selection of personnel for the Office of Strategic Services.* New York: Rinehart, 1948.

***Oxford English Dictionary, The.*** London: Oxford University Press, 1933.

**Pacinelli, R. N.** Rehabilitation counselor job satisfaction as it relates to perceived leadership behavior and selected background factors. *Dissertation Abstr.,* 1968, *29,* 1863.

**Page, D. P.** Measurement and prediction of leadership. *Amer. J. Sociol.,* 1935, *41,* 31–43.

**Page, M. L.** The modification of ascendant behavior in pre-school children. *Univ. Iowa Stud. Child Welfare,* 1936, *12,* 69 pp.

**Page, R. H., & McGinnies, E.** Comparison of two styles of leadership in small group discussion. *J. appl. Psychol.,* 1959, *43,* 240–245.

**Paige, G. D.** *Political leadership.* New York: Free Press, 1972.

**Paige, G. D.** *The scientific study of political leadership.* New York: Free Press, 1977.

**Paine, F. T., Carroll, S. J., & Leete, B. A.** Need satisfactions of managerial level personnel in a government agency. *J. appl. Psychol.,* 1966, *50,* 247–249.

**Palm, L. B.** A study of videotaped behavior and its relationship to perceived leadership behavior. *Dissertation Abstr. Internat.,* 1976, *36,* 4930–4931.

**Palmer, D. D., Veiga, J. F., & Vora, J. A.** Managerial value profiles as predictors of policy decisions in a cross-cultural setting. Unpublished ms., undated.

**Palmer, F. H., & Myers, T. I.** Sociometric choices and group productivity among radar crews. *Amer. Psychol.,* 1955, *10,* 441–442.

**Palmer, G. J.** Task ability and effective leadership. *Psychol. Rep.,* 1962a, *10,* 863–866.

**Palmer, G. J.** Task ability and successful and effective leadership. *Psychol. Rep.,* 1962b, *11,* 813–816.

**Palmer, G. J., & McCormick, E. J.** A factor analysis of job activities. *J. appl. Psychol.,* 1961, *45,* 289–294.

**Palmer, W. J.** Management effectiveness as a function of personality traits of the manager. *Personnel Psychol.,* 1974, *27,* 283–295.

**Pandey, J.** Effects of leadership style, personality characteristics and method of leader selection on members' and leaders' behavior. *Eur. J. soc. Psychol.,* 1976, *6,* 475–489.

**Papaloizos, A.** Personality and success of training in human relations. *Personnel Psychol.,* 1962, *15,* 423–428.

**Parker, F. E.** *Consumers' cooperative societies in the United States in 1920.* Washington, D.C.: U.S. Department of Labor Bulletin No. 313, 1923.

**Parker, F. E.** *Cooperative movement in the United States in 1925 (other than experimental).* Washington, D.C.: U.S. Department of Labor Bulletin No. 437, 1927.

**Parker, S.** Leadership patterns in a psychiatric ward. *Hum. Relat.,* 1958, *11,* 287–301.

**Parker, T. C.** Relationships among measures of supervisory behavior, group behavior, and situational characteristics. *Personnel Psychol.,* 1963, *16,* 319–334.

**Parker, T. C.** The psychological environment and work group behavior. *Personnel Admin.,* 1965, *28,* 26–31.

**Parker, W. S., Jr.** Black–white differences in leader behavior related to subordinates' reactions. *J. appl. Psychol.,* 1976, *61,* 140–147.

**Parsons, T.** *The social system.* New York: Free Press, 1951.

**Parsons, T., & Shils, E. A. (Eds.),** *Toward a general theory of action.* Cambridge, Mass.: Harvard University Press, 1959.

**Parten, M. B.** Social participation among preschool children. *J. abnorm. soc. Psychol.,* 1932, *27,* 243–269.

**Parten, M. B.** Leadership among preschool children. *J. abnorm. soc. Psychol.,* 1933, *27,* 430–440.

**Partridge, E. DeA.** Leadership among adolescent boys. *Teach. Coll. Contrib. Educ.,* 1934, No. 608.

**Pascarella, P., & Cook, D. D.** Can you win? *Indus. Week,* 1978, *196,* 75–84.

**Patch, A. M.** Some thoughts on leadership. *Military Rev., Ft. Leavenworth,* 1943, *23,* 5–7.

**Patchen, M.** Supervisory methods and group performance norms. *Admin. sci. Quar.,* 1962, *7,* 275–294.

**Patchen, M.** Participation in decision-making and motivation. What is the relation? *Personnel Admin.,* 1964, *27,* 24–31.

**Patchen, M.** *Participation, achievement, and involvement on the job.* Englewood Cliffs, N.J.: Prentice-Hall, 1970.

**Patchen, M.** The locus and basis of influence on organizational decisions. *Org. behav. hum. Perform.,* 1974, *11,* 195–221.

**Patterson, M.** Spatial factors in social interactions. *Hum. Relat.,* 1968, *21,* 351–361.

**Patterson, M. L., & Holmes, D. S.** Social interaction correlates of the MPI extroversion-introversion scale. *Amer. Psychologist,* 1966, *21,* 724–725.

**Patterson, M. L., & Sechrest, L. B.** Impression formation and interpersonal distance. Evanston, Ill.: Northwestern University, unpublished manuscript, 1967.

**Patterson, R. A.** Women in management: an experimental study of the effects of sex and marital status on job performance ratings, promotability ratings and promotion decisions. *Dissertation Abstr. Internat.,* 1975, *36,* 3108–3109B.

**Patton, W. M.** Studies in industrial empathy: III. A Study of supervisory empathy in the textile industry. *J. appl. Psychol.,* 1954, *38,* 285–288.

**Payne, R.** Leadership and perceptions of change in a village confronted with urbanism. *Soc. Forces,* 1963, *41,* 264–269.

**Payne, R. L., & Pheysey, D. C.** Organization structure and sociometric nominations amongst line managers in three contrasted organizations. *European J. soc. Psychol.,* 1971, *1,* 261–284.

**Peabody, R. L.** Perceptions of organizational authority: a comparative analysis. *Admin. sci. Quar.,* 1962, *6,* 463–482.

**Peabody, R. L.** *Organizational authority: superior–subordinate relationships in three public organizations.* New York: Atherton Press, 1964.

**Peabody, R. L.** *Leadership in Congress.* Boston: Little, Brown, 1976.

**Peabody, R. L., & Rourke, F. E.** Public bureaucracies. In J. G. March (Ed.), *Handbook of service organizations.* New York: Atherton Press, 1964.

**Pearse, R. F., Worthington, E. I., & Flaherty, J. J.** A program for developing tool engineers into manufacturing executives. *ASTE Tool Engineering Conference Papers,* 22T5, Detroit, 1954.

**Peck, E. M.** A study of the personalities of five eminent men. *J. abnorm. soc. Psychol.,* 1931, *26,* 37–57.

**Peck, S. M.** *The rank-and-file leader.* New Haven, Conn.: College & University Press, 1966.

**Pedersen, D. M., Shinedling, M. M., & Johnson, D. L.** Effects of sex examiner and subject on children's quantitative test performance. *J. personality. soc. Psychol.*, 1971, *19,* 114–118.

**Peirce, J. R.** Effects of selected organizational variables on the behavioral style of the industrial supervisor. *Dissertation Abstr. Internat.*, 1970, *31,* 3047–3048.

**Pellegrin, R. J.** Status achievement in youth groups; elements of group adjustment in relation to social mobility. Doctoral dissertation, University of North Carolina, Chapel Hill, 1952.

**Pellegrin, R. J.** The achievement of high status and leadership in the small group. *Soc. forces,* 1953, *32,* 10–16.

**Pellegrin, R. J.** The interaction of physical and psychological distance in dyadic transactions. *Dissertation Abstr. Internat.*, 1969, *30,* 373.

**Pellegrin, R. J., & Coates, C. H.** Executives and supervisors: contrasting definitions of career success. *Admin. sci. Quar.*, 1957, *2,* 506–517.

**Pelletier, G.** Business management in French Canada. *Bus. Quar.-Can. Mgmt. J.,* 1966, Fall, 56–62.

**Pelz, D. C.** The effect of supervisory attitudes and practices on employee satisfaction. *Amer. Psychologist,* 1949, *4,* 283–284.

**Pelz, D. C.** Leadership within a hierarchical organization. *J. soc. Issues,* 1951, *7,* 49–55.

**Pelz, D. C.** Influence: a key to effective leadership in the first-line supervisor. *Personnel,* 1952, *29,* 209–217.

**Pelz, D. C.** The influence of the supervisor within his department as a condition of the way supervisory practices affect employee attitudes. In *Annual Review of Psychology, vol. 4.* Stanford, Calif.: Stanford University Press, 1953.

**Pelz, D. C.** Some social factors related to performance in a research organization. *Admin. sci. Quar.*, 1956, *1,* 310–325.

**Pelz, D. C., & Andrews, F. M.** Detecting causal priorities in panel study data. *Amer. sociol. Rev.*, 1964, *29,* 836–848.

**Pelz, D. C., & Andrews, F. M.** *Scientists in organizations: productive climates for research and development.* New York: Wiley, 1966a.

**Pelz, D. C., & Andrews, F. M.** Autonomy, coordination, and stimulation in relation to scientific achievement. *Behav. Sci.*, 1966b, *11,* 89–97.

**Penfield, R. V.** Identifying effective supervisors. *Personnel J.*, 1971, *50,* 209–212.

**Penner, D. D., Malone, D. M., Coughlin, T. M., & Herz, J. A.** Satisfaction with U.S. Army leadership. *U.S. Army War College, Leadership Monograph Series,* No. 2, 1973.

**Pennings, J. M.** The relevance of the structured-contingency model for organizational effectiveness. *Admin. sci. Quar.*, 1975, *20,* 393–407.

**Pennington, D. F., Haravey, F., & Bass, B. M.** Some effects of decision and discussion on coalescence, change, and effectiveness. *J. appl. Psychol.*, 1958, *42,* 404–408.

**Penzer, W. N.** Educational level and satisfaction with pay: an attemped replication. *Personnel Psychol.*, 1969, *22,* 185–199.

**Pepinsky, H. B., & Pepinsky, P. N.** Organization, management strategy, and team productivity. In L. Petrullo & B. M. Bass (Eds.), *Leadership and interpersonal behavior.* New York: Holt, Rinehart & Winston, 1961.

**Pepinsky, H. B., Pepinsky, P. N., Minor, F. J., & Robin, S. S.** Team productivity as related to the confirmation or contradiction by management of its commitments to an appointed leader. Columbus: Ohio State University, Personnel Research Board, 1957 (mimeo).

**Pepinsky, H. B., Pepinsky, P. N., Minor, F. J., & Robin, S. S.** Team productivity and contradiction of management policy commitments. *J. appl. Psychol.*, 1959, *43,* 264–268.

**Pepinsky, H. B., Pepinsky, P. N., & Pavlik, W. B.** Motivational factors in individual and group productivity: I. Successful task accomplishment as related to task relevant personal beliefs. Columbus: Ohio State University, Personnel Research Board, 1956 (mimeo).

**Pepinsky, P. N., Hemphill, J. K., & Shevitz, R. N.** Leadership acts. II. The relation between needs for achievement and affiliation and attempts to lead under conditions of acceptance and rejection. Columbus: Ohio State University Research Foundation, 1955 (mimeo).

**Pepinsky, P. N., Hemphil, J. K., & Shevitz, R. N.** Attempts to lead, group productivity, and morale under conditions of acceptance and rejection. *J. abnorm. soc. Psychol.*, 1958, *57*, 47–54.

**Pepinsky, P. N., Pepinsky, H. B., & Pavlik, W. B.** Motivational factors in individual and group productivity. III. The effects of task complexity and time presure upon team productivity. Columbus: Ohio State University, Personnel Research Board, 1956 (mimeo).

**Pepinsky, P. N., Pepinsky, H. B., & Pavlik, W. B.** The effects of task complexity and time pressure upon team productivity. *J. appl. Psychol.*, 1960, *44*, 34–38.

**Pepinsky, P. N., Pepinsky, H. B., Robin, S. S., & Minor, F. J.** The effects of induced orientation and type of task upon group performance and group member morale. Columbus: Ohio State University, Personnel Research Board, 1957 (mimeo).

**Pepitone, A.** Attributions of causality, social attitudes, and cognitive matching processes. In R. Taigiuri and L. Petrullo (Eds.), *Person perception and interpersonal behavior.* Stanford, Calif.: Stanford University Press, 1958.

**Pepitone, A.** *Attraction and hostility.* New York: Atherton Press, 1964.

**Pepitone, A., & Kleiner, R.** The effects of threat and frustration on group cohesiveness. *J. abnorm. soc. Psychol.*, 1957, *54*, 192–199.

**Pepitone, A., & Reichling, G.** Group cohesiveness and the expression of hostility. *Hum. Relat.*, 1955, *8*, 327–337.

**Pepitone, E.** Responsibility to the group and its effect on the performance of the members. Doctoral dissertation, University of Michigan, Ann Arbor, 1952.

**Peres, S. H.** Performance dimensions of supervisory positions. *Personnel Psychol.*, 1962, *15*, 405–410.

**Perlmutter, H. V.** Impressions of influential members of discussion groups. *J. Psychol.*, 1954, *38*, 223–234.

**Perlmutter, H. V.** The tortuous evolution of the multinational corporation. *Columbia J. world Bus.*, 1969, *4*, 9–18.

**Perls, F.** Gestalt theory, John O. Stevens (Ed.). Lafayette, Calif.: Real People Press, 1969.

**Perrow, C.** A framework for the comparative analysis of organizations. *Amer. sociol. Rev.*, 1967, *32*, 194–208.

**Perrucci, R., & Pilisak, M.** Leaders and ruling elites: the interorganizational bases of community power. *Amer. sociol. Rev.*, 1970, *35*, 1040–1057.

**Perry, D., & Mahoney, T. A.** In-plant communications and employee morale. *Personnel Psychol.*, 1955, *8*, 339–353.

**Person, H. S.** Leadership as a response to environment. *Educ. Rec. Supplmt. No. 6*, 1928, *9*, 10–21.

**Peter, H.** Cross-cultural survey of managers in ten countries. *Proceed. Amer. Psychol. Assn.*, 1969.

**Petersen, E., Plowman, E. G., & Trickett, J. M.** *Business organization and management.* Homewood, Ill.: Irwin, 1962.

**Petersen, P. B., & Lippitt, G. L.** Comparison of behavioral styles between entering and graduating students in officer candidate school. *J. appl. Psychol.*, 1968, *52*, 66–70.

**Peterson, R. B.** Worker participation in the enterprise: the Swedish experience. *Proceed. Industrial Relations Research Association*, 1969.

**Petrullo, L., & Bass, B. M.** *Leadership and interpersonal behavior.* New York: Holt, Rinehart & Winston, 1961.

**Pettigrew, A.** Information control as a power resource. *Sociology*, 1972, *6*, 187–204.

**Pettigrew, A. M.** *The politics of organizational decisions-making.* London: Tavistock, 1973.

**Petty, M. M., & Lee, G. K.** Moderating effects of sex of supervisor and subordinate on relationships between supervisory behavior and subordinate satisfaction. *J. appl. Psychol.*, 1975, *60*, 624–628.

**Petty, M. M., & Miles, R. H.** Leader sex-role stereotyping in a female-dominated work culture. *Personnel Psychol.*, 1976, *29*, 393–404.

**Petty, M. M., Odewahn, C. A., Bruning, N. S., & Thomason, T. L.** An examination of the moderating effects of supervisor sex and subordinate sex upon the relationships between supervisory behavior and subordinate outcomes in mental health organizations. Unpublished ms., 1976.

**Pfeffer, J.** Merger as a response to organizational interdependence. *Admin. sci. Quar.*, 1972a, *17*, 383–395.

**Pfeffer, J.** Interorganizational influence and managerial attitudes. *Acad. Mgmt. J.*, 1972b, *15*, 317–330.

**Pfeffer, J.** The ambiguity of leadership. *Acad. Mgmt. Rev.*, 1977, *2*, 104–112.

**Pfeffer, P., & Shapiro, S. J.** Personnel differences in male and female MBA candidates. *Business Quar.*, 1978, *43*, 77–80.

**Pfiffner, J. M.** A pattern for improved supervisory leadership. *Personnel*, 1948, *24*, 271–280.

**Pfiffner, J. M.** *The supervision of personnel: human relations in the management of men.* Englewood Cliffs, N.J.: Prentice-Hall, 1951.

**Pfiffner, J. M., & Sherwood, F. P.** *Administrative organization.* Englewood Cliffs, N.J.: Prentice-Hall, 1960.

**Pfiffner, J. M., & Wilson, R. C.** "Management-mindedness" in the supervisory ranks: a study of attitudes in relation to status. *Personnel*, 1953, *30*, 122–125.

**Pheysey, D. C., & Payne, R. L.** The Hemphill group dimensions description questionnaire: a British industrial application. Industrial Administration Research Unit, Birmingham: University of Aston, 1970 (mimeo).

**Pheysey, D. C., Payne, R. L., & Pugh, D. S.** Influence of structure at organizational and group levels. *Admin. sci. Quar.*, 1971, *16*, 61–73.

**Philip, H., & Dunphy, D.** Developmental trends in small groups. *Sociometry*, 1959, *22*, 162–174.

**Philips, B. N.** Relationship of process behavior to the task efficiency of small face-to-face groups. *Amer. Psychologist*, 1954, *9*, 449.

**Philipsen, H.** Het meten van leiderschap. *Mens en Onderneming*, 1965a, *19*, 153–171.

**Philipsen, H.** Medezeggenschap in de vorm van werkoverleg. In C. J. Lammers (Ed.), *Medezeggenschap en overleg in het bedriif.* Utrecht: Het Spectrum, 1965b.

**Philipsen, H., & Cassee, E. T.** Verschillen in de wijze van leidinggeven tussen drie typen organisaties. *Mens en Onderneming*, 1965, *19*, 172–174.

**Phillips, R. L.** A study of twenty-one variables relating to leader legitimation. Doctoral dissertation, Ohio State University, Columbus, 1972.

**Phillips, T. R.** Leader and led. *J. Coast Artillery*, 1939, *82*, 45–58.

**Pickle, H., & Friedlander, F.** Seven societal criteria of organizational success. *Personnel Psychol.*, 1967, *20*, 165–178.

**Pieper, F.** *Modular management and human leadership.* Minneapolis: Methods Press, 1958.

**Piersol, D. T.** Communication practices of supervisors in a midwestern corporation. *Advanced Mgmt.*, 1958, *23*, 20–21.

**Pigors, P.** Leadership and domination among children. *Sociologus*, 1933, *9*, 140–157.

**Pigors, P.** *Leadership or domination.* Boston: Houghton Mifflin, 1935.

**Pigors, P.** Types of leaders in group work. *Sociol. soc. Res.*, 1936, *21*, 3–17.

**Pinard, J. W.** Tests of perseveration. *Brit. J. Psychol.*, 1932, *23*, 5–19.

**Pinder, C., Pinto, P. R., & England, G. W.** Behavioral style and personal characteristics of managers. Minneapolis: University of Minnesota, Center for the Study of Organizational Performance and Human Effectiveness, Technical Report, 1973.

**Pinkney, A. P.** *Black Americans.* Englewood Cliffs, N.J.: Prentice-Hall, 1969.

**Pipes, R.** *Russia under the old regime.* New York: Weidenfeld and Nicolson, 1974.

**Pitkin, W. B.** *The psychology of achievement.* New York: Simon & Schuster, 1931.

**Plato.** *The republic.* Trans. by F. M. Cornford. New York: Oxford University Press, 1945.

**Poitou, J. P.** Pouvoir coercitif et interdépendence. *Année Psychol.,* 1969, *69,* 435–453.

**Polansky, N., Lippitt, R., & Redl, F.** An investigation of behavioral contagion in groups. *Hum. Relat.,* 1950a, *3,* 319–348.

**Polansky, N., Lippitt, R., & Redl, F.** The use of near-sociometric data in research on group treatment process. *Sociometry,* 1950b, *13,* 39–62.

**Polis, T.** A note on crisis and leadership. *Australian J. Psychol.,* 1964, *16,* 57–61.

**Pondy, L. R.** Organizational conflict: concepts and models. *Admin. sci. Quar.,* 1967, *12,* 296–320.

**Pondy, L. R.** Leadership is a language game. In M. McCall & M. Lombardo (Eds.), *Leadership: where else can we go?* Durham, N.C.: Duke University Press, 1976.

**Porat, A. M., & Ryterband, E. C.** Career performance, choice and attainment for members of minority groups. In H. L. Fromkin & J. J. Sherwood (Eds.), *Integrating the organization.* New York: Free Press, 1974.

**Porter, A.** Validity of socioeconomic origin as a predictor of executive success. *J. appl. Psychol.,* 1965, *49,* 11–13.

**Porter, L. W.** Differential self-perceptions of management personnel and line workers. *J. appl. Psychol.,* 1958, *42,* 105–108.

**Porter, L. W.** Self-perceptions of first-level supervisors compared with upper-management personnel and operative line workers. *J. appl. Psychol.,* 1959, *43,* 183–186.

**Porter, L. W.** A study of perceived need satisfaction in bottom and middle management jobs. *J. appl. Psychol.,* 1961a, *45,* 1–10.

**Porter, L. W.** Perceived trait requirements in bottom and middle managemet jobs. *J. appl. Psychol.,* 1961b, *45,* 232–236.

**Porter, L. W.** Job attitudes in management. I. Perceived deficiencies in need fulfillment as a function of job level. *J. appl. Psychol.,* 1962, *46,* 375–384.

**Porter, L. W.** Job attitudes in management: II. Perceived importance of needs as a function of job level. *J. appl. Psychol.,* 1963a, *47,* 141–148.

**Porter, L. W.** Job attitudes in management: III. Perceived deficiencies in need fulfillment as a function of line versus staff type of job. *J. appl. Psychol.,* 1963b, *47,* 267–275.

**Porter, L. W.** Job attitudes in management: IV. Perceived deficiencies in need fulfillment as a function of size of company. *J. appl. Psychol.,* 1963c, *47,* 386–397.

**Porter, L. W.** *Organizational patterns of managerial job attitudes.* New York: American Foundation for Management Research, 1964.

**Porter, L. W., & Ghiselli, E. E.** The self perceptions of top and middle management personnel. *Personnel Psychol.,* 1957, *10,* 397–406.

**Porter, L. W., & Henry, M. M.** Job attitudes in management. V. Perceptions of the importance of certain personality traits as a function of job level. *J. appl. Psychol.,* 1964a, *48,* 31–36.

**Porter, L. W., & Henry, M. M.** Job attitudes in management: VI. Perceptions of the importance of certain personality traits as a function of line versus staff type of job. *J. appl. Psychol.,* 1964b, *48,* 305–309.

**Porter, L. W., & Kaufman, R. A.** Relationships between a top-middle management self-description scale and behavior in a group situation. *J. appl. Psychol.,* 1959, *43,* 345–348.

**Porter, L. W., & Lawler, E. E.** The effects of "tall" versus "flat" organizational structures on managerial job satisfaction. *Personnel Psychol.,* 1964, *17,* 135–148.

**Porter, L. W., & Lawler, E. E.** Properties of organization structure in relation to job attitudes and behavior. *Psychol. Bull.,* 1965, *64,* 23–51.

**Porter, L. W., & Lawler, E. E.** *Managerial attitudes and performance.* Homewood, Ill.: Irwin-Dorsey, 1968.

**Porter, L. W., Lawler, E. E., & Hackman, J. R.** *Behavior in organizations.* New York: McGraw-Hill, 1975.

**Porter, L. W., & Mitchell, V. F.** Comparative study of need satisfactions in military and business hierarchies. *J. appl. Psychol.,* 1967, *51,* 139–144.

**Porter, L. W., & Siegel, J.** Relationships of tall and flat organization structures to the satisfaction of foreign managers. *Personnel Psychol.,* 1965, *18,* 379–392.

**Posthuma, A. B.** Normative data on the least preferred coworkers scale (LPC) and the group atmosphere questionnaire (GA). Seattle: University of Washington, Organizational Research, Technical Report 70–8, 1970.

**Potter, E. H.** The contribution of intelligence and experience to the performance of staff personnel. Doctoral dissertation, University of Washington, Seattle, 1978.

**Powell, G. N., & Butterfield, D. A.** The "good manager": masculine or androgynous? *Acad. Mgmt. J.,* 1979, *22,* 395–403.

**Powell, R. M.** Sociometric analysis of informal groups—their structure and function in two contrasting communities. *Sociometry,* 1952, *15,* 367–399.

**Powell, R. M.** An experimental study of role taking, group status, and group formation. *Sociol. soc. Res.,* 1956, *40,* 159–165.

**Powell, R. M.** *Race, religion, and the promotion of the American executive.* Columbus: Ohio State University, College of Administrative Science, 1969.

**Powell, R. M., & Nelson, D. H.** The business executive's self-image versus his image of the politician. *Personnel J.,* 1969, *48,* 677–682.

**Powell, R. M., & Stinson, J. E.** Individual and organization impact of laboratory training. *Acad. Mgmt. Proceedings,* 31st Annual Meeting, August 15–18, 1971.

**Powell, R. M., Thrasher, J. D., Darrough, D., et al.** The nature and extent of group organization in a girls' dormitory: a sociometric investigation. *Sociometry,* 1951, *14,* 317–339.

**Precker, J. A.** Similarity of valuings as a factor in selection of peers and near-authority figures. *J. abnorm. soc. Psychol.,* 1952, *47,* 406–414.

**Prentice, D. B., & Kunkel, B. W.** College contributions to intellectual leadership. *School Soc.,* 1930, *32,* 594–600.

**Prentice, W. C. H.** Understanding leadership. *Harvard bus. Rev.,* 1961, *39,* 143–151.

**Presthus, R. V.** Authority in organizations. *Pub. admin. Rev.,* 1960, *20,* 86–91.

**Presthus, R.** *Men at the top: a study in community power.* New York: Oxford University Press, 1964.

**Presthus, R.** *Behavioral approaches to public administration.* University, Ala.: University of Alabama Press, 1965.

**Preston, M. G., & Heintz, R. K.** Effects of participatory vs. supervisory leadership on group judgment. *J. abnorm. soc. Psychol.,* 1949, *44,* 345–355.

**Prestridge, V., & Wray, D.** Industrial sociology: an annotated bibliography. Champaign: University of Illinois, Institute of Labor and Industrial Relations, 1953 (mimeo).

**Price, B.** A study of leadership strength of female police executives. *J. Police sci. Admin.,* 1974, *2,* 219–226.

**Price, J. L.** *Organizational effectiveness: an inventory of propositions.* Homewood, Ill.: Irwin, 1968.

**Price, J. L.** *Cadres, commanders and commissars: the training of the Chinese communist leadership.* Boulder, Co.: Westview Press, 1976.

**Price, M. A.** A study of motivational factors associated with leadership behavior of young women in a private school. Doctoral dissertation, Ohio State University, Columbus, 1948.

**Prien, E. P.** Development of a supervisor position description questionnaire. *J. appl. Psychol.*, 1963, *47*, 10–14.

**Prien, E. P., & Culler, A. R.** Leaderless group discussion participation and inter-observer agreements. *J. soc. Psychol.*, 1964, *62*, 321–328.

**Prien, E. P., & Lee, R. J.** Peer ratings and leaderless group discussions for evaluation of classroom performance. *Psychol. Rep.*, 1965, *16*, 59–64.

**Prien, E. P., & Liske, R. E.** Assessments of higher level personnel. III. Rating criteria: a comparative analysis of supervisor ratings and incumbent self rating of job performance. *Personnel Psychol.*, 1962, *15*, 187–194.

**Priest, R. F., & Sawyer, J.** Proximity and peership: bases of balance in interpersonal attraction. *Amer. J. Sociol.*, 1967, *72*, 633–649.

**Prieto, A. C.** An investigation of the relationship between participative group management in elementary schools and the needs satisfaction of elementary classroom teachers. Doctoral dissertation, University of New Orleans, New Orleans, 1975.

**Pritchard, R., & Karasick, B.** The effects of organizational climate on managerial job performance and job satisfaction. *Org. behav. hum. Perform.*, 1973, *9*, 110–119.

**Prosh, F.** The basis on which students choose their leaders. *Amer. phys. educ. Rev.*, 1928, *33*, 265–267.

**Proshansky, H., & Newton, P.** The nature and meaning of Negro self-identity. In M. Deutsch, I. Katz, & A. Jensen (Eds.), *Social class, race, and psychological development*. New York: Holt, Rinehart & Winston, 1968.

**Proshansky, H. M., & Seidenberg, B.** *Basic studies in social psychology*. New York: Holt, Rinehart & Winston, 1965.

**Prothero, J., & Fiedler, F. E.** The effect of situational change on individual behavior and performance: an extension of the contingency model. Seattle: University of Washington, Organizational Research, Technical Report 74–59, 1974.

**Pryer, M. W., & Distefano, M. K.** Perceptions of leadership behavior, job satisfaction, and internal-external control across three nursing levels. *Nurs. Res.*, 1971, *20*, 534–537.

**Pryer, M. W., Flint, A. W., & Bass, B. M.** Group effectiveness and consistency of leadership. *Sociometry*, 1962, *25*, 391–397.

**Psathas, G., & Hardert, R.** Transfer interventions and normative patterns in the T Group. *J. appl. behav. Sci.*, 1966, *2*, 149–169.

**Psychological Services.** *Bibliography on military leadership: annotations of selected studies from scientific, technical, and related publications.* Maxwell Air Force Base, Ala.: Air Research & Development Command, Human Resources Research Institute, 1953.

**Puckett, E. S.** Productivity achievements: a measure of success. In F. G. Lesieur (Ed.), *The Scanlon plan*. Cambridge, Mass.: M.I.T. Press, 1958.

**Puffer, J. A.** Boys' gangs. *Ped. Sem.*, 1905, *12*, 175–213.

**Pugh, D.** T-group training from the point of view of organizational theory. In G. Whitaker (Ed.), *ATM occasional papers 2*. Oxford: Basil E. Blackwell, 1965.

**Pugh, D. S., Hickson, D. J., Hinings, C. R., & Turner, C.** Dimensions of organization structure. *Admin. sci. Quart.*, 1968, *13*, 65–105.

**Pugh, D. S., Hickson, D. J., Hinings, C. R., & Turner, C.** The context of organizational structures. *Admin. sci. Quar.*, 1969, *14*, 91–112.

**Punch, K. F.** Bureaucratic structure of schools and its relationship to leader behavior. Toronto: Ontario Institute for Studies in Education, unpublished ms, 1967.

**Punch, K. F.** Bureaucratic structure in schools and its relationship to leader behavior: an empirical study. *Dissertation Abstr.*, 1968, *29*, 448–449.

**Purcell, K., Modrick, J. A., & Yamahiro, R.** Item vs. trait accuracy in interpersonal perception. *J. gen. Psychol.*, 1960, *62*, 285–292.

**Purcell, T. V.** *The worker speaks his mind on company and union.* Cambridge, Mass.: Harvard University Press, 1953.

**Purcell, T. V.** Dual allegiance to union and management (a symposium). 2. Dual allegiance to company and union—packinghouse workers. A Swift-UPWA study in a crisis situation, 1949–1952. *Personnel Psychol.*, 1954, *7*, 45–58.

**Purcell, T. V.** *Blue collar man: patterns of dual allegiance in industry.* Cambridge, Mass.: Harvard University Press, 1960.

**Queener, E. L.** *Introduction to social psychology.* New York: Sloan, 1951.

**Quinn, R. P., & Kent, J. T.** Big fish, little fish: a "competitive" approach to organizational primary groups. *Proceed. Amer. Psychol. Assn.*, 1967.

**Rabow, J., Fowler, F., Bradford, D., Hofeller, M., & Shibuya, Y.** The role of social norms and leadership in risk-taking. *Sociometry*, 1966, *29*, 16–27.

**Rackham, N.** *Developing interactive skills.* Northampton, Eng.: Wellens Publishing Co., 1971.

**Racz, L. L.** A study of teacher alienation and its relationship to individual needs and leadership behavior. *Dissertation Abstr. Internat.*, 1971, *31*, 6319.

**Radke, M., & Klisurich, D.** Experiments in changing food habits. *J. Amer. diet. Assoc.*, 1947, *23*, 403–409.

**Radloff, R., & Helmreich, R.** *Groups under stress.* New York: Appleton-Century-Crofts, 1968.

**Raia, A. P.** A study of the educational value of management games. *J. Bus.*, 1966, *39*, 339–352.

**Raiffa, H., & Schlaifer, R.** *Applied statistical decision theory.* Boston: Harvard University, Graduate School of Business Administration, 1961.

**Rainey, H. G.** Reward expectancies, role perceptions, and job satisfaction among government and business managers: indications of commonalities and differences. *Proceedings of the Academy of Management*, 1979.

**Rainio, K.** *Leadership qualities: a theoretical inquiry and an experimental study on foremen.* Helsinki: Academiae Scientiarum Fennicae, 1955.

**Rainwater, L.** Crucible of identity: The Negro lower-class family. *Daedalus*, 1966, *95*, 172–216.

**Rambo, W. W.** The construction and analysis of a leadership behavior rating form. *J. appl. Psychol.*, 1958, *42*, 409–415.

**Randle, C. W.** How to identify promotable executives. *Harvard bus. Rev.*, 1956, *34*, 122–134.

**Raskin, A. H.** The workers' voice in German companies. *New York Times*, June 11, 1976, D7.

**Rasmussen, G., & Zander, A.** Group membership and self-evaluation. *Hum. Relat.*, 1954, *7*, 239–251.

**Rasmussen, R. L.** The principal's leadership behavior in unusually successful and unsuccessful elementary schools. *Educ. res. Quar.*, 1976, *1*, 18–29.

**Rath, K. C., & Sahoo, M. S.** Socio-economic status of Panchayat leaders and their role in agricultural production. *Soc. Cult.*, 1974, *5*, 25–28.

**Raube, S. A.** *Factors affecting employee morale.* New York: National Industrial Conference Board, 1947.

**Raudsepp, E.** Career satisfactions: money means less than sense of accomplishment. *Machine Design*, 1962, *34*, 99–102.

**Raven, B. H.** The dynamics of groups. *Rev. educ. Res.*, 1959a, *29*, 332–343.

**Raven, B. H.** Social influence on opinion and the communication of related content. *J. abnorm. soc. Psychol.*, 1959b, *58*, 119–128.

**Raven, B. H.** A bibliography of publications relating to the small group. Los Angeles: University of California, Department of Psychology, 1965a (mimeo).

**Raven, B. H.** Social influence and power. In I. D. Steiner & M. Fishbein (Eds.), *Current studies in social psychology*. New York: Holt, Rinehart & Winston, 1965b.

**Raven, B. H., & Eachus, H. T.** Cooperation and competition in means-interdependent triads. *J. abnorm. soc. Psychol.*, 1963, *67*, 307–316.

**Raven, B. H., & French, J. R. P.** An experimental investigation of legitimate and coercive power. *Amer. Psychologist*, 1957, *12*, 393.

**Raven, B. H., & French, J. R. P.** Group support, legitimate power, and social influence. *J. Pers.*, 1958a, *26*, 400–409.

**Raven, B. H., & French, J. R. P.** Legitimate power, coercive power, and observability in social influence. *Sociometry*, 1958b, *21*, 83–97.

**Raven, B. H., Kelley, H. H., & Shapiro, M. M.** An experiment on conformity to group norms where conformity is detrimental to group achievement. *Amer. Sociol. Rev.*, 1954, *19*, 667–677.

**Raven, B. H., & Shaw, J. I.** Interdependence and group problem-solving in the triad. *J. pers. soc. Psychol.*, 1970, *14*, 157–165.

**Read, P. B.** Source of authority and the legitimation of leadership in small groups, *Sociometry*, 1974, *37*, 180–204.

**Read, W. H.** Upward communication in industrial hierarchies. *Hum. Relat.*, 1962, *15*, 3–15.

**Ready, R. K.** Leadership in the 1960's. *California mgmt. Rev.*, 1964, *6*, 37–46.

**Reals, W. H.** Leadership in the high school. *School Rev.*, 1938, *46*, 523–531.

**Reavis, C. A., & Derlega, V. J.** Test of a contingency model of teacher effectiveness. *J. educ. Res.*, 1976, *69*, 221–225.

**Reddin, W. J.** *Managerial effectiveness*. New York: McGraw-Hill, 1970.

**Reddin, W. J.** An integration of leader-behavior typologies. *Grp. org. Stud.*, 1977, *2*, 282–295.

**Reddin, W. J.** Management style diagnosis test. Fredericton, N. B.: Organizational Tests, undated.

**Redl, F.** Group emotion and leadership. *Psychiat.*, 1942, *5*, 573–596.

**Redl, F.** Resistance in therapy groups. *Hum. Relat.*, 1948, *1*, 307–313.

**Reed, H. D., & Janis, I. L.** Effects of a new type of psychological treatment on smokers' resistance to warnings about health hazards. *J. consult. clin. Psychol.*, 1974, *42*, 748.

**Regula, C. R.** Quality and quantity of contributions as determinants of perceived ability. Buffalo: State University of New York, Department of Psychology, Technical Report, 1967.

**Regula, R. C., & Julian, J. W.** The impact of quality and frequency of task contributions on perceived ability. *J. soc. Psychol.*, 1973, *89*, 115–122.

**Reid, F. T.** Impact of leader style on the functioning of a decision-making group. *Archives gen. Psychiat.*, 1970, *23*, 268–276.

**Reider, N.** Psychodynamics of authority with relation to some psychiatric problems in officers. *Bull. Menninger Clinic*, 1944, *8*, 55–58.

**Reidy, R. J., Jr.** A comparative analysis of selected public elementary community school administrative systems and public elementary non-community school administrative systems using the Likert administrative systems model. Doctoral dissertation, University of Connecticut, Storrs, 1976.

**Reif, W. E., Newstrom, J. W., & St. Louis, R. D.** Sex as a discriminatory variable in organizational reward decisions. *Acad. Mgmt. J.*, 1976, *19*, 469–476.

**Reif, W. E., & Schoderbek, P. P.** Job enlargement: antidote to apathy. *Mgmt. personnel Quar.*, 1966, *5*, 16–23.

**Reilly, J. W., & Robinson, F. P.** Studies of popularity in colleges: II. Do dormitory arrangements affect popularity? *Educ. psychol. Measmt.*, 1947, *7*, 327–330.

**Reilly, R. R.** A study of the effects of task-irrelevant factors on leader selection. *Dissertation Abstr. Internat.*, 1970, *30*, 3551.

**Reilly, R. R., & Jaffee, C. L.** Influences of some task-irrelevant factors on leader selection. *Psychol. Rec.*, 1970, *20*, 535–539.

**Reininger, K.** Das soziale Verhalten von Schulneulingen. *Wien Arb. päd. Psychol.*, 1929, *7*, 14.

**Reitz, H. J.** Managerial attitudes and perceived contingencies between performance and organizational response. *Proceedings of the Academy of Management*, 1971.

**Remmelin, M. K.** Analysis of leaders among high school seniors. *J. exp. Educ.*, 1938, *6*, 413–422.

**Remmers, L. J., & Remmers, H. H.** Studies in industrial empathy: I. Labor leaders' attitudes toward industrial supervision' and their estimate of managements' attitudes. *Personnel Psychol.*, 1949, *2*, 427–436.

**Renck, R.** Morale in four key groups in industry. In *Conference on employee attitude surveys.* Chicago: University of Chicago, Industrial Relations Center, 1955.

**Renck, R.** *Morale in industrial organizations.* Chicago: University of Chicago, Industrial Relations Center, 1957.

**Rettig, S., Despres, L., & Pasamanick, B.** Status stratification and status equalization. *J. soc. Psychol.*, 1960, *52*, 109–117.

**Reynolds, F. J.** Factors of leadership among seniors of Central High School, Tulsa, Oklahoma. *J. educ. Res.*, 1944, *37*, 356–361.

**Reynolds, H. H.** Efficacy of sociometric ratings in predicting leadership success. *Psychol. Rep.*, 1966, *19*, 35–40.

**Rice, A. K.** Productivity and social organization in an Indian weaving shed. *Hum. Relat.*, 1953, *6*, 297–329.

**Rice, A. K.** *Productivity and social organization: the Ahmedabad experiment.* London: Tavistock, 1958.

**Rice, A. K.** *The enterprise and its environment.* New York: Humanities Press, 1963.

**Rice, A. K.** *Learning for leadership—interpersonal and inter-group relations.* New York: Humanities Press, 1965.

**Rice, R. W.** The esteem for least preferred co-worker (LPC) score: what does it measure? *Dissertation Abstr. Internat.*, 1976, *36*, 5360B–5361B.

**Rice, R. W.** Psychometric properties of the esteem for least preferred co-worker (LPC scale). *Acad. Mgmt. Rev.*, 1978a, *3*, 106–118.

**Rice, R. W.** Construct validity of the least preferred co-worker score. *Psychol. Bull.*, 1978b, *85*, 1199–1237.

**Rice, R. W.** Reliability and validity of the LPC scale: a reply. *Acad. Mgmt. Rev.*, 1979, *4*, 291–294.

**Rice, R. W., Bender, L. R., & Vitters, A. G.** Leader sex, follower attitudes toward women, and leadership effectiveness: a laboratory experiment. *Org. behav. hum. Perform.*, 1980, *25*, 46–78.

**Rice, R. W., & Chemers, M. M.** Predicting the emergence of leaders using Fiedler's contingency model of leadership effectiveness. *J. appl. Psychol.*, 1973, *57*, 281–287.

**Rice, R. W., & Chemers, M. M.** Personality and situational determinants of leaders' behavior. *J. appl. Psychol.*, 1975, *60*, 20–27.

**Richard, J. E.** A president's experience with democratic management. Chicago: University of Chicago, Industrial Relations Center, Occasional Paper No. 18, 1959.

**Richards, G. L., & Inskeep, G. C.** The middle manager—his continuing education and the business school. *Collegiate News and Views*, 1974, Spring, 5–7.

**Richards, S. A., & Cuffee, J. U.** Behavioral correlates of leadership effectiveness in interacting and counteracting groups. *J. appl. Psychol.*, 1972, *56*, 377–381.

**Richards, S. A., & Jaffee, C. L.** Blacks supervising whites: a study of interracial difficulties in working together in a simulated organization. *J. appl. Psychol.*, 1972, *56*, 234–240.

**Richardson, F. L. W.** *Talk, work, and action.* Ithaca, N.Y.: Cornell University, New York State School of Industrial & Labor Relations, 1961.

**Richardson, F. L. W., & Walker, C. R.** *Human relations in an expanding company.* New Haven, Conn.: Yale University, Labor & Management Center, 1948.

**Richardson, H. M.** Communality of values as a factor in friendships of college and adult women. *J. soc. Psychol.,* 1940, *11,* 303–312.

**Richardson, H. M., & Hanawalt, N. G.** Leadership as related to Bernreuter personality measures: I. College leadership in extracurricular activities. *J. soc. Psychol.,* 1943, *17,* 237–249.

**Richardson, H. M., & Hanawalt, N. G.** Leadership as related to Bernreuter personality measures: III. Leadership among men in vocational and social activities. *J. appl. Psychol.,* 1944, *28,* 308–317.

**Richardson, H. M., & Hanawalt, N. G.** Leadership as related to the Berneuter personality measures: V. Leadership among adult females in social activities. *J. soc. Psych.,* 1952, *36,* 141–153.

**Richardson, J. T.** Expertise, power, leadership and personal influence. An integration of theory and experimental evidence. *Dissertation Abstr.,* 1969, *29A,* 3221.

**Richardson, J. T., Mayhew, B. H., & Gray, L. N.** Differentiation, restraint, and the asymmetry of power. *Hum. Relat.,* 1969, *22,* 263–274.

**Richman, B.** Capitalists and managers in Communist China. *Harvard bus. Rev.,* 1967, *45,* 57–71, 78.

**Richman, B. M., & Farmer, R. N.** *Leadership, goals, and power in higher education.* San Francisco: Jossey-Bass, 1974.

**Richmond, A. H.** Conflict and authority in industry. *Occup. Psychol.,* 1954, *28,* 24–33.

**Richmond, V. P., & McCroskey, J. C.** Whose opinion do you trust? *J. Communication,* 1975, *25,* 42–50.

**Riecken, H. W.** Some problems of consensus development. *Rural Sociol.,* 1952, *17,* 245–252.

**Riecken, H. W.** Popularity and conformity to group norms. *Amer. Psychologist,* 1953, *8,* 420–421.

**Riecken, H. W.** The effect of talkativeness on ability to influence group solutions of problems. *Sociometry,* 1958, *21,* 309–321.

**Riedel, J. E.** *A comparison of principal, teacher and student perceptions of selected elementary school principals' effectiveness.* Doctoral dissertation, University of Southern California, Los Angeles, 1974.

**Riedesel, P. L.** Bales reconsidered: a critical analysis of popularity and leadership differentiation. *Sociometry,* 1974, *37,* 557–564.

**Riegel, J. W.** *Executive development: a survey of experience in fifty American corporations.* Ann Arbor: University of Michigan Press, 1952.

**Riegel, J. W.** *Employee interest in company success—how can it be stimulated and maintained?* Ann Arbor: University of Michigan, Bureau of Industrial Relations, 1955.

**Riley, M. W., & Cohn, R.** Control networks in informal groups. *Sociometry,* 1958, *21,* 30–49.

**Riley, M. W., & Flowerman, S. H.** Group relations as a variable in communications research. *Amer. sociol. Rev.,* 1951, *16,* 174–176.

**Rim, Y.** Leadership attitudes and decisions involving risk. *Personnel Psychol.,* 1965, *18,* 423–430.

**Rim, Y., & Mannheim, B. F.** Factors related to attitudes of management and union representatives. *Personnel Psychol.,* 1964, *17,* 149–165.

**Rinehart, J. B., Barrell, R. P., DeWolfe, A. S., Griffin, J. E., & Spaner, F. E.** Comparative study of need satisfactions in governmental and business hierarchies. *J. appl. Psychol.,* 1969, *3,* 230–235.

**Ring, K.** Some determinants of interpersonal attraction in hierarchical relationships: a motivational analysis. *J. Pers.*, 1964, *32*, 651–665.

**Ring, K., & Kelley, H. H.** A comparison of augmentation and reduction as modes of influence. *J. abnorm. soc. Psychol.*, 1963, *66*, 95–102.

**Rios, R. M.** The comparative effects of tape-led and leaderless groups. *Dissertation Abstr. Internat.*, 1972, *32*, 6769.

**Ritchie, J. B., & Miles, R. E.** An analysis of quantity and quality of participation as mediating variables in the participative decision making process. *Personnel Psychol.*, 1970, *23*, 347–359.

**Rittenhouse, C. H.** *A follow-up study of NCO leaders school graduates.* Washington, D.C.: Human Resources Research Office, 1968.

**Rittenhouse, J. D.** Conformity behavior in sixth grade leaders. *Dissertation Abstr.*, 1966, *26*, 6212.

**Rizzo, J. R., House, R. J., & Lirtzman, S. I.** Role conflict and ambiguity in complex organizations. *Admin. sci. Quar.*, 1970, *15*, 150–163.

**Roach, D. E.** Factor analysis of rated supervisory behavior. *Personnel Psychol.*, 1956, *9*, 487–498.

**Roach, J. M.** *Recent initiatives in labor–management co-operation.* National Center for Productivity and Quality of Working Life, 1976.

**Roadman, H. E.** An industrial use of peer ratings. *J. appl. Psychol.*, 1964, *48*, 211–214.

**Roberts, A. H., & Jessor, R.** Authoritarianism, punitiveness, and perceived social status. *J. abnorm. soc. Psychol.*, 1958, *56*, 311–314.

**Roberts, B. B.** The leader, group, and task variables of leader selection in college. *Dissertation Abstr.*, 1969, *29*, 2360–2361.

**Roberts, D. M.** *Leadership in teen-age groups.* New York: Association Press, 1950.

**Roberts, K., Miles, R. E., & Blankenship, L. V.** Organizational leadership, satisfaction, and productivity: a comparative analysis. *Acad. Mgmt. J.*, 1968, *11*, 401–414.

**Roberts, K. H.** On looking at an elephant: an evaluation of cross-cultural research related to organizations. *Psychol. Bull.*, 1970, *74*, 327–350.

**Robie, E. A.** Challenge to management. In E. Ginzberg & A. M. Yohalem (Eds.), *Corporate lib: women's challenge to management.* Baltimore: Johns Hopkins University Press, 1973.

**Robins, A. R., Willemin, L. P., & Brueckel, J. E.** Exploratory study of echelon differences in efficiency ratings. *Amer. Psychol.*, 1954, *9*, 457.

**Robinson, D. D.** Predicting police effectiveness from self reports of relative time spent in task performance. *Personnel Psychol.*, 1970, *23*, 327–345.

**Robinson, H. A.** Job satisfaction researches of 1953. *Personnel guid. J.*, 1954, *33*, 26–29.

**Robinson, H. A., Conners, R. P., & Whitacre, G. H.** Job satisfaction researches of 1964–65. *Personnel guid. J.*, 1966, *45*, 371–379.

**Roby, T. B.** The influence of subgroup relationships on the performance of group and subgroup tasks. *Amer. Psychol.*, 1952, *7*, 313–314.

**Roby, T. B.** Relationships between sociometric measures and performance in medium-bomber crews. San Antonio, Tex.: Lackland Air Force Base, Human Resources Research Center, 1953 (Res. Bull. 53–18).

**Roby, T. B.** The executive function in small groups. In L. Petrullo & B. Bass (Eds.), *Leadership and interpersonal behavior.* New York: Holt, Rinehart & Winston, 1961.

**Roby, T. B.** *Small group performance.* Chicago: Rand McNally, 1968.

**Roby, T. B., & Forgays, D. G.** A problem solving model of communication in B-29 crews. *HRRC Technical Report 53–32.* San Antonio, Tex., 1953.

**Roby, T. B., & Lanzetta, J. T.** Considerations in the analysis of group tasks. *Psych. Bull.*, 1958, *55*, 88–101.

**Roby, T. B., Nicol, E. H., & Farrell, F. M.** Group problem solving under two types of executive structure. *J. abnorm. soc. Psychol.*, 1963, *67*, 550–556.

**Rock, M. L., & Hay, E. N.** Investigation of the use of tests as a predictor of leadership and group effectiveness in a job evaluation situation. *J. soc. Psychol.*, 1953, *38*, 109–119.

**Roe, A.** *The psychology of occupations.* New York: Wiley, 1956.

**Roethlisberger, F. J.** *Management and morale.* Cambridge, Mass.: Harvard University Press, 1941.

**Roethlisberger, F. J.** The foreman: master and victim of double talk. *Harvard bus. Rev.*, 1945, *23*, 283–298.

**Roethlisberger, F. J.** The territory and skill of the administrator. In L. Sayles (Ed.), *Addresses on industrial relations, 1954 series.* Ann Arbor: University of Michigan, Bureau of Industrial Relations Bulletin No. 22, 1954.

**Roethlisberger, F. J., Lombard, G. F. F., & Renken, H. O.** *Training for human relations: an interim report.* Boston: Harvard University, Graduate School of Business Administration, 1954.

**Roethlisberger, F. J., & Dickson, W. J.** *Management and the worker.* Cambridge, Mass.: Harvard University Press, 1947.

**Roff, M.** A study of combat leadership in the air force by means of a rating scale: group differences. *J. Psychol.*, 1950, *30*, 229–239.

**Rogers, M. S., Ford, J. D., & Tassone, J. A.** The effects of personnel replacement on an information-processing crew. *J. appl. Psychol.*, 1961, *45*, 91–96.

**Rogers, R. E.** Components of organizational stress among Canadian managers. *J. Psychol.*, 1977, *95*, 265–273.

**Rohde, K. J.** Dominance composition as a factor in the behavior of small leaderless groups. Doctoral dissertation, Northwestern University, Evanston, Ill., 1951.

**Rohde, K. J.** The relation of authoritarianism of the aircrew member to his acceptance by the airplane commander. *Amer. Psychologist*, 1952, *7*, 310–311.

**Rohde, K. J.** Individual executive ability as a factor in the performance of small groups. Columbus: Ohio State University, Personnel Research Board, Technical Report No. 17, 1954a.

**Rohde, K. J.** Variations in group composition with respect to individual task ability as a factor in group behavior. Columbus: Ohio State University, Personnel Research Board, Technical Report No. 18, 1954b.

**Rohde, K. J.** An evaluation of the extent to which task ability of the man in charge of a group is determinative of that group's success in performing the task. *Amer. Psychologist*, 1954c, *9*, 569.

**Rohde, K. J.** Theoretical and experimental analysis of leadership ability. *Psychol. Rep.*, 1958, *4*, 243–278.

**Rokeach, M.** Long-range experimental modification of values, attitudes and behavior. *Amer. Psychologist*, 1971, *26*, 453–459.

**Ronan, W. W.** Individual and situational variables relating to job satisfaction. *J. appl. Psychol.*, 1970, *54*, 1–31.

**Ronen, S., & Kraut, A. I.** Similarities among countries based on employee work values and attitudes. *Columbia J. world Bus.*, 1977, *12*, 89–96.

**Ronken, H. O., & Lawrence, P. R.** *Administering changes.* Boston: Harvard University, Graduate School of Business Administration, 1952.

**Rooker, J. L.** The relationship of need achievement and need affiliation to leader behavior. *Dissertation Abstr.*, 1968, *28*, 4426.

**Rose, A. M.** Alienation and participation: a comparison of group leaders and the "Mass." *Amer. sociol. Rev.*, 1962, *27*, 834–838.

**Rose, A. M.** The ecological influential: a leadership type. *Sociol. soc. Res.*, 1968, *52*, 185–192.

**Rose, R.** The emergence of leaders. *New Society*, 1963, *2, 55*, 12–13.

**Roseborough, M. E.** Experimental studies of small groups. *Psychol. Bull.*, 1953, *50*, 275–303.

**Rosen, B., & Jerdee, T. H.** The influence of sex-role stereotypes on evaluation of male and female supervisory behavior. *J. appl. Psychol.*, 1973, *57*, 44–48.

**Rosen, B., & Jerdee, T. H.** Influence of sex role stereotypes on personnel decisions. *J. appl. Psychol.*, 1974, *59*, 9–14.

**Rosen, B., & Jerdee, T. H.** Influence of subordinate characteristics on trust and use of participative decision strategies in a management simulation. *J. appl. Psychol.*, 1977, *62*, 628–631.

**Rosen, B., & Jerdee, T. H.** Effects of decision permanence on managerial willingness to use participation. *Acad. Mgmt. J.*, 1978, *21*, 722–725.

**Rosen, H.** Managerial role interaction: a study of three managerial levels. *J. appl. Psychol.*, 1961a, *45*, 30–34.

**Rosen, H.** Desirable attributes of work: four levels of management describe their job environments. *J. appl. Psychol.*, 1961b, *45*, 156–160.

**Rosen, H., & Rosen, R. A. H.** *The union member speaks.* New York: Prentice-Hall, 1955.

**Rosen, H., & Weaver, C. G.** Motivation in management: a study of four managerial levels. *J. appl. Psychol.*, 1960, *44*, 386–392.

**Rosen, N. A.** How supervise?—1943–1960. *Personnel Psychol.*, 1961, *14*, 87–100.

**Rosen, N. A.** *Leadership change and work-group dynamics.* Ithaca, N.Y.: Cornell University Press, 1969.

**Rosen, N. A.** Open systems theory in an organizational subsystem: a field experiment. *Org. behav. hum. Perform.*, 1970a, *5*, 245–265.

**Rosen, N. A.** Demand characteristics in a field experiment. *J. appl. Psychol.*, 1970b, *54*, 163–168.

**Rosen, S.** Some effects of previous patterns of aggression on interpersonal relations in new groups. *Amer. Psychologist*, 1954, *9*, 459.

**Rosen, S., Levinger, G., & Lippitt, R.** Perceived sources of social power. *J. abnorm. soc. Psychol.*, 1961, *62*, 439–441.

**Rosenbaum, L. L., & Rosenbaum, W. B.** Morale and productivity consequences of group leadership style, stress, and type of task. *J. appl. Psychol.*, 1971, *55*, 343–348.

**Rosenbaum, M. E.** Social perception and the motivational structure of interpersonal relations. *J. abnorm. soc. Psychol.*, 1959, *59*, 130–133.

**Rosenberg, M., & Pearlin, L. I.** Power-orientations in the mental hospital. *Hum. Relat.*, 1962, *15*, 335–350.

**Rosenberg, S., Erlick, D. E., & Berkowitz, L.** Some effects of varying combinations of group members on group peformance measures and leadership behaviors. *J. abnorm. soc. Psychol.*, 1955, *51*, 195–203.

**Rosenfeld, E.** Social stratification in a "classless" society. *Amer. sociol. Rev.*, 1951, *16*, 766–774.

**Rosenfeld, J. M., & Smith, M. J.** Participative management: an overview. *Personnel J.*, 1967, *46*, 101–104.

**Rosenfeld, L. B., & Fowler, G. D.** Personality, sex, and leadership style. *Commun. Monogr.*, 1976, *43*, 320–324.

**Rosenstein, E.** Histadrut's search for a participation program. *Indus. Relat.*, 1970, *9*, 170–186.

**Rosenstein, E.** Workers' participation in management: problematic issues in the Israeli system. Binghamton: State University of New York, Systems Research Working Paper, 1976.

**Rosenthal, A.** *Legislative performance in the States: explorations in committee behavior.* New York: Free Press, 1974.

**Rosenthal, R.** Combining results of independent studies. *Psychol. Bull.*, 1978, *85*, 185–193.

**Rosenthal, R.** The "file-drawer" problem and tolerance for null results. *Psychol. Bull.*, 1979, *86*, 638–641.

**Roskens, R. W.** The relationship between leadership participation in college and after college. *Dissertation Abstr.*, 1958, *19*, 473.

**Roslow, S.** Nation-wide and local validation of the P.Q. or Personality Quotient Test. *J. appl. Psychol.*, 1940, *24*, 529–539.

**Ross, I. C., & Zander, A.** Need satisfaction and employee turnover. *Personnel Psychol.*, 1957, *10*, 327–338.

**Ross, M. G., & Hendry, C. E.** *New understandings of leadership.* New York: Association Press, 1957.

**Rossel, R. D.** Instrumental and expressive leadership in complex organizations. *Admin. sci. Quar.*, 1970, *15*, 306–316.

**Rothe, H. F.** Output rates among butter wrappers: II. *J. appl. Psychol.*, 1946, *30*, 320–327.

**Rothe, H. F.** Output rates among machine operations: I. Distributions and their reliability. *J. appl. Psychol.*, 1947, *31*, 484–489.

**Rothe, H. F.** The relation of merit ratings to length of service. *Personnel Psychol.*, 1949, *2*, 237–242.

**Rothe, H. F.** Does higher pay bring higher productivity? *Personnel*, 1960, *37*, 20–38.

**Rothe, H. F.** Output rates among machine operators: III. A non-incentive situation in two levels of business activity. *J. appl. Psychol.*, 1961, *45*, 50–54.

**Rothe, H. F., & Nye, C. T.** Output rates among coil winders. *J. appl. Psychol.*, 1958, *42*, 182–186.

**Rothe, H. F., & Nye, C. T.** Output rates among machine operators: II. Consistency related to methods of pay. *J. appl. Psychol.*, 1959, *43*, 417–420.

**Rothman, R. A., & Perrucci, R.** Organizational careers and professional expertise. *Admin. sci. Quar.*, 1970, *15*, 282–293.

**Rotter, J. B.** Generalized expectancies for internal versus external control of reinforcement. *Psychol. Monogr.*, 1966, *80*, no. 609.

**Roucek, J. S.** The social value of women's club work. *Sociol. soc. Res.*, 1934, *18*, 453–461.

**Roussel, C.** Relationship of sex of department head to department climate. *Admin. sci. Quar.*, 1974, *19*, 211–220.

**Rowland, K. M., & Scott, W. E.** Psychological attributes of effective leadership in a formal organization. *Personnel Psychol.*, 1968, *21*, 365–377.

**Roy, N. K., Jaiswal, N. K., & Shankar, J.** Socio-economic characteristics of leaders and followers in a rural society. *Soc. Cult.*, 1974, *5*, 43–48.

**Rubenowitz, S.** Job-oriented and person-oriented leadership. *Personnel Psychol.*, 1962, *15*, 387–396.

**Rubin, G. J.** A modified contingency model for leadership effectiveness. *Dissertation Abstr. Internat.*, 1972, *32*, 6710–6711.

**Rubin, I. M., & Goldman, M.** An open system model of leadership performance. *Org. behav. hum. Perform.*, 1968, *3*, 143–156.

**Ruch, F. L.** *Bibliography on military leadership.* Los Angeles: Psychological Services, 1953.

**Rudin, S. A.** Leadership as psychophysiological activation of group members: a case experimental study. *Psychol. Rep.*, 1964, *15*, 577–578.

**Rudin, S. A. et al.** Some empirical studies of the reliability of social perception scores. Urbana: University of Illinois, 1952 (mimeo).

**Rudraswamy, V.** An investigation of the relationships between perceptions of status and leadership attempts. *J. Indian Acad. appl. Psychol.*, 1964, *1*, 12–19.

**Runyon, K. E.** Some interactions between personality variables and management styles. *J. appl. Psychol.*, 1973, *57*, 288–294.

**Rupe, J. C.** When workers rate the boss. *Personnel Psychol.*, 1951, *4*, 271–290.

**Rus, V.** Influence structure in Yugoslav enterprise. *Indus. Relat.*, 1970, *9*, 149–160.

**Rush, C. H.** Leader behavior and group characteristics. In R. M. Stogdill & A. E. Coons (Eds.), *Leader behavior: its description and measurement.* Columbus: Ohio State University, Bureau of Business Research, 1957.

**Rush, C. H., Jr.** Group dimensions of air crews. Columbus: Ohio State University, Personnel Research Board, undated.

**Rush, M. C., Thomas, J. C., & Lord, R. G.** Implicit leadership theory: a potential threat to the internal validity of leader behavior questionnaires. *Org. behav. hum. Perform.*, 1977, *20*, 93–110.

**Rushlau, P. J., & Jorgensen, G. Q.** *Interpersonal relationships: a review.* Salt Lake City: University of Utah, Regional Rehabilitation Research Institute, 1966.

**Russell, B.** *Power.* London: Allen & Unwin, 1938.

**Ryapolov, G.** I was a Soviet manager. *Harvard bus. Rev.*, 1966, *44*, 117–125.

**Rychlak, J. F.** Personality correlates of leadership among first level managers. *Psychol. Rep.*, 1963, *12*, 43–52.

**Ryterband, E. C., & Barrett, G. V.** Managers' values and their relationship to the management of tasks: a cross-cultural comparison. In B. M. Bass, R. C. Cooper, & J. A. Haas (Eds.), *Managing for accomplishment.* Lexington, Mass.: D. C. Heath, 1970.

**Ryterband, E. C., & Thiagarajan, K. M.** Managerial attitudes toward salaries as a function of social and economic development. Rochester, N.Y.: University of Rochester, Management Research Center, Technical Report No. 24, 1968.

**Sabath, G.** The effect of disruption and individual status on person perception and group attraction. *J. soc. Psychol.*, 1964, *64*, 119–130.

**Sadler, P. J.** Leadership style, confidence in management, and job satisfaction. *J. appl. behav. Sci.*, 1970, *6*, 3–19.

**Sadler, P. J., & Hofstede, G. H.** Leadership styles: preferences and perceptions of employees of an international company in different countries. *Mens en Onderneming*, 1972, *26*, 43–63.

**Sakoda, J. M.** Factor analysis of OSS situational tests. *J. abnorm. soc. Psychol.*, 1952, *47*, 843–852.

**Salaman, G.** A historical discontinuity: from charisma to routinization. *Hum. Relat.*, 1977, *30*, 373–388.

**Salancik, G. R., Calder, B. J., Rowland, K. M., Leblebici, H., & Conway, M.** Leadership as an outcome of social structure and process: a multidimensional analysis. In J. G. Hunt & L. L. Larson (Eds.), *Leadership frontiers.* Carbondale: Southern Illinois University Press, 1975.

**Saleh, S. D., & Otis, J. L.** Age level and job satisfaction. *Personnel Psychol.*, 1964, *17*, 425–430.

**Saleh, S. D., Prien, E. P., Otis, J. L., & Campbell, J. T.** The relation of job attitudes, organization performance, and job level. *J. indus. Psychol.*, 1964, *2*, 59–65.

**Sales, S. M.** A laboratory investigation of the effectiveness of two industrial supervisory dimensions. Ithaca, N.Y.: Cornell University, Master's thesis, 1964.

**Sales, S. M.** Supervisory style and productivity: review and theory. *Personnel Psychol.*, 1966, *19*, 275–286.

**Sales, S. M.** Authoritarianism: But as for me, give me liberty, or give me a big, strong leader I can honor, admire, respect and obey. *Psychology Today*, 1972, *8*, 94, 143.

**Salmons, S.** Africans get a taste for the top. *Internat. Mgmt.*, 1977, *32*, 39–41.

**Salter, J. T.** *Boss rule: portraits in city politics.* New York: McGraw-Hill, 1935.

**Sample, J. A., & Wilson, T. R.** Leader behavior, group productivity, and rating of least preferred co-worker. *J. pers. soc. Psychol.*, 1965, *1*, 266–270.

**Sampson, E. E.** *Approaches, contexts, and problems: a book of readings of social psychology.* Englewood Cliffs, N.J.: Prentice-Hall, 1964.

**Sampson, E. E., & Brandon, A. C.** The effects of role and opinion deviation on small group behavior. *Sociometry*, 1964, *27*, 261–281.

**Sampson, R. V.** *The psychology of power.* New York: Random House, 1968.

**Sanders, E. P.** Evolutionary performance, managerial abilities, and change: an explanatory investigation of organizations. *J. appl. Psychol.*, 1968, *52*, 362–365.

**Sanderson, D., & Nafe, R. W.** Studies in rural leadership. *Publ. Amer. sociol. Soc.*, 1929, *23*, 163–175.

**Sandler, B. E., & Scalia, F. A.** The relationship between birth order, sex, and leadership in a religious organization. *J. soc. Psychol.*, 1975, *95*, 279–280.

**Sanford, F. H.** *Authoritarianism and leadership: a study of the follower's orientation to authority.* Philadelphia: Institute for Research in Human Relations, 1950.

**Sanford, F. H.** Leadership identification and acceptance. In H. Guetzkow (Ed.), *Groups, leadership and men.* Pittsburgh: Carnegie Press, 1951.

**Sarachek, B.** Greek concepts of leadership. *Acad. Mgmt. J.*, 1968, *11*, 39–48.

**Sarbin, T. R., & Jones, D. S.** The assessment of role-expectations in the selection of supervisory personnel. *Educ. psychol. Measmt.*, 1955, *15*, 236–239.

**Sargent, J. F., & Miller, G. R.** Some differences in certain communication behaviors of autocratic and democratic leaders. *J. Communication*, 1971, *21*, 233–252.

**Saris, R. J.** The development of a 13th subscale to the Leader Behavior Description Questionnaire—Form XII entitled "Responsibility Deference." Doctoral dissertation, University of Idaho, 1969.

**Sashkin, M.** Leadership style and group decision effectiveness: correlational and behavioral tests of Fiedler's contingency model. *Org. behav. hum. Perform.*, 1972, *8*, 347–362.

**Sashkin, M., Taylor, F. C., & Tripathi, R. C.** An analysis of situational moderating effects on the relationships between least preferred co-worker and other psychological measures. *J. appl. Psychol.*, 1974, *59*, 731–740.

**Sattler, J. M.** Racial "experimenter effects" in experimentation, testing, interviewing, and psychotherapy. *Psychol. Bull.*, 1970, *73*, 137–160.

**Saunders, J., Davis, J., & Monsees, D. M.** Opinion leadership in family planning. *J. heal. soc. Behav.*, 1974, *15*, 217–227.

**Sayles, L. R.** *Behavior of industrial work groups.* New York: Wiley, 1958.

**Sayles, L. R.** *Individualism and big business.* New York: McGraw-Hill, 1963.

**Sayles, L. R.** *Managerial behavior.* New York: McGraw-Hill, 1964.

**Schachter, S.** Deviation, rejection, and communication. *J. abnorm. soc. Psychol.*, 1951, *46*, 190–207.

**Schachter, S., Ellertson, N., McBride, D., & Gregory, D.** An experimental study of cohesiveness and productivity. *Hum. Relat.*, 1951, *4*, 229–238.

**Schachter, S., Willerman, B., Festinger, L., & Hyman, R.** Emotional disruption and industrial productivity. *J. appl. Psychol.*, 1961, *45*, 201–213.

**Schanck, R. L.** A study of a community and its groups and institutions conceived of behavior of individuals. *Psychol. Monogr.*, 1932, *43*, No. 2.

**Scheffler, I., & Winslow, C. N.** Group position and attitude toward authority. *J. soc. Psychol.*, 1950, *32*, 177–190.

**Schein, E. H.** Attitude change during management education. *Admin. sci. Quar.*, 1967, *11*,

601–628.

**Schein, E. H., & Bennis, W. G.** *Personal and organizational change through group methods.* New York: Wiley, 1965.

**Schein, E. H., & Lippitt, G. L.** Supervisory attitudes toward the legitimacy of influencing subordinates. *J. appl. behav. Sci.,* 1966, *2,* 199–209.

**Schein, E. H., & Ott, J. S.** The legitimacy of organizational influence. *Amer. J. Sociol.,* 1962, *67,* 682–689.

**Schein, V. E.** The relationship between sex role stereotypes and requisite management characteristics. *J. appl. Psychol.,* 1973, *57,* 95–100.

**Schein, V. E.** Relationships between sex role stereotypes and requisite management characteristics among female managers. *J. appl. Psychol.,* 1975, *60,* 340–344.

**Schendel, D. G., Patton, G. R., & Riggs, J.** Corporate turnaround strategies: a study of profit decline and recovery. *J. gen. Mgmt.,* 1976, *3,* 3–11.

**Schenk, C.** Leadership. *Infantry J.,* 1928, *33,* 111–122.

**Schiff, H.** Judgmental response sets in the perception of sociometric status. *Sociometry,* 1954, *17,* 207–227.

**Schiffman, L. G., & Gaccione, V.** Opinion leaders in institutional markets. *J. Mkting,* 1974, *38,* 49–53.

**Schiller, M.** A new approach to leadership assessment. *Personnel Psychol.,* 1961, *14,* 75–86.

**Schlacter, J. L.** Increased participation in the decision-making process among field crews in the Ohio Department of Highways: a field study. Doctoral dissertation, Ohio State University, Columbus, 1969.

**Schlesinger, L., Jackson, J. M., & Butman, J.** Leader–member interaction in management committees. *J. abnorm. soc. Psychol.,* 1960, *61,* 360–364.

**Schmid, J., & Leiman, J. M.** The development of hierarchical factor solutions. *Psychometrika,* 1957, *22,* 53–61.

**Schmidt, F. L., & Hunter, J. E.** The future of criterion-related validity. *Personnel Psych.,* 1980, *33,* 41–58.

**Schmidt, F. L., Hunter, J. E., & Urry, V. W.** Statistical power in criterion-related validity studies. *J. appl. Psychol.,* 1976, *61,* 473–485.

**Schmidt, F. L., & Johnson, R. H.** Effect of race on peer ratings in an industrial setting. *J. appl. Psychol.,* 1973, *57,* 237–241.

**Schmitt, D. R.** Punitive supervision and productivity: an experimental analog. *J. appl. Psychol.,* 1969, *2,* 118–123.

**Schneider, A. L.** A study of characteristics of outstanding first line supervisors. Columbus: Ohio State University, Master's thesis, 1969.

**Schneider, B.** Relationships between various criteria of leadership in small groups. *J. soc. Psychol.,* 1970, *82,* 253–261.

**Schneider, B.** Organizational climate: individual preferences and organizational realities. *J. appl. Psychol.,* 1972, *56,* 211–217.

**Schneider, B.** The perception of organizational climate: the customer's view. *J. appl. Psychol.,* 1973, *57,* 248–256.

**Schneider, D. J.** Implicit personality theory: a review. *Psychol. Bull.,* 1973, *79,* 294–309.

**Schneider, J.** The cultural situation as a condition for the achievement of fame. *Amer. sociol. Rev.,* 1937, *2,* 480–491.

**Schneier, C. E.** The contingency model of leadership: an extension to emergent leadership and leader's sex. *Org. behav. hum. Perform.,* 1978, *21,* 220–239.

**Schock, B. F., & Matthews, L. B.** Identifying extension opinion leaders. *J. Extension,* 1974, *12,* 16–24.

**Schoderbek, P. P.** The use of job enlargement in industry. *Personnel J.,* 1968, *47,* 796–801.

**Schoderbek, P. P., & Reif, W. E.** *Job enlargement: key to improved performance.* Ann Arbor: University of Michigan, Bureau of Industrial Relations, 1969.

**Schoen, D. R.** Human relations: boon or bogle? *Harvard bus. Rev.*, 1957, *35*, 41–47.

**Schoennauer, A. W.** Behavior patterns of executives in business acquisitions. *Personnel Admin.*, 1967, *30*, 27–32.

**Schopler, J., & Matthews, M. W.** The influence of the perceived causal locus of partner's dependence on the use of the interpersonal power. *J. pers. soc. Psychol.*, 1965, *2*, 609–612.

**Schott, J. L.** The leader behavior of non-white principals in inner-city elementary schools with integrated teaching staffs under conditions of high and low morale. Doctoral dissertation, Purdue University, Lafayette, Ind., 1970.

**Schrag, C.** Leadership among prison inmates. *Amer. sociol. Rev.*, 1954, *19*, 37–42.

**Schrage, H.** The R & D entrepreneur: profile of success. *Harvard bus. Rev.*, 1965, *43*, 56–61.

**Schregle, J.** Forms of participation in management. *Indust. Relat.*, 1970, *9*, 117–122.

**Schriesheim, C. A.** The similarity of individual directed and group directed leader behavior descriptions. *Acad. Mgmt. J.*, 1979a, *22*, 345–355.

**Schriesheim, C. A.** Social desirability and leader effectiveness. *J. soc. Psychol.*, 1979b, *108*, 89–94.

**Schriesheim, C. A., Bannister, B. D., & Money, W. H.** Psychometric properties of the LPC scale: an extension of Rice's review. *Acad. Mgmt. Rev.*, 1979, *4*, 287–290.

**Schriesheim, C. A., & DeNisi, A. S.** The impact of implicit theories on the validity of questionnaires. Unpublished ms., 1978.

**Schriesheim, C., & DeNisi, A. S.** Task dimensions as moderators of the effects of instrumental leader behavior: a path-goal approach. *Proceedings of the Academy of Management*, 1979.

**Schriesheim, C. A., & Hosking, D.** Review essay of Fiedler, F. E., Chemers, M. M., & Mahar, L. Improving leadership effectiveness: the leader match concept. *Admin. sci. Quar.*, 1978, *23*, 496–505.

**Schriesheim, C. A., House, R. J., & Kerr, S.** Leader initiating structure: a reconciliation of discrepant research results and some empirical tests. *Org. behav. hum. Perform.*, 1976, *15*, 297–321.

**Schriesheim, C. A., & Kerr, S.** Psychometric properties of the Ohio State leadership scales. *Psychol. Bull.*, 1974, *81*, 756–765.

**Schriesheim, C. A., & Kerr, S.** R.I.P. LPC: a response to Fiedler. In J. G. Hunt & L. L. Larson (Eds.) *Leadership: the cutting edge.* Carbondale: Southern Illinois University Press, 1977a.

**Schriesheim, C. A., & Kerr, S.** Theories and measures of leadership: a critical appraisal of present and future directions. In J. G. Hunt & L. L. Larson (Eds.), *Leadership: the cutting edge.* Carbondale: Southern Illinois University Press, 1977b.

**Schriesheim, C. A., Kinicki, A. J., & Schriesheim, J. F.** The effect of leniency on leader behavior descriptions. *Org. behav. hum. Perform.*, 1979, *23*, 1–29.

**Schriesheim, C. A., Mowday, R. T., & Stogdill, R. M.** Crucial dimensions of leader–group interactions. In J. G. Hunt & L. L. Larson (Eds.), *Cross-currents in leadership.* Carbondale: Southern Illinois University Press, 1979.

**Schriesheim, C. A., & Murphy, C. J.** Relationships between leader behavior and subordinate satisfaction and performance: a test of some situational moderators. *J. appl. Psychol.*, 1976, *61*, 634–641.

**Schriesheim, C. A., & Stogdill, R. M.** Differences in factor structure across three versions of the Ohio State leadership scales. *Personnel Psychol.*, 1975, *28*, 189–206.

**Schriesheim, C., & Von Glinow, M. A.** The path-goal theory of leadership: a theoretical and empirical analysis. *Acad. Mgmt. J.*, 1977, *20*, 398–405.

**Schriesheim, J. F.** The social context of leader–subordinate relations: an investigation of the effects of group cohesiveness. *J. appl. Psychol.*, 1980, *65,* 183–193.

**Schriver, W. R.** The prediction of worker productivity. *Hum. Org.*, 1966, *25,* 339–343.

**Schroder, H. M., Streufert, S., & Weeden, D. C.** The effect of structural abstractness in interpersonal stimuli on the leadership role. Princeton, N.J.: Princeton University, Office of Naval Research Technical Report No. 3, 1964.

**Schubert, M. L.** A comparison of the effects of two models of sensitivity training on "level of experiencing." *Dissertation Abstr. Internat.*, 1973, *34,* 1264.

**Schul, B. D.** *How to be an effective group leader.* Chicago: Nelson-Hall, 1975.

**Schuler, E. A.** A study of the consistency of dominant and submissive behavior in adolescent boys. *J. genet. Psychol.*, 1935, *46,* 403–432.

**Schuler, R. S.** Sex, organizational level, and outcome importance: where the differences are. *Personnel Psychol.*, 1975, *28,* 365–376.

**Schuler, R. S.** Participation with supervisor and subordinate authoritarianism: a path goal reconciliation. *Admin. sci. Quar.*, 1976, *21,* 320–325.

**Schultz, B.** Characteristics of emergent leaders of continuing problem-solving groups. *J. Psychol.*, 1974, *88,* 167–173.

**Schultz, G. P.** Worker participation on production problems. *Personnel*, 1951, *28,* 201–210.

**Schulze, R. O.** The role of economic dominants in community power structure. *Amer. sociol. Rev.*, 1958, *23,* 3–9.

**Schumer, H.** Cohesion and leadership in small groups as related to group productivity. *Dissertation Abstr.*, 1962, *22,* 3735–3736.

**Schuster, J. R., & Clark, B.** Individual differences related to feelings toward pay. *Personnel Psychol.*, 1970, *23,* 591–604.

**Schutz, A.** *The phenomenology of the social world.* Evanston, Ill.: Northwestern University Press, 1967.

**Schutz, W. C.** What makes groups productive? *Hum. Relat.*, 1955, *8,* 499–465.

**Schutz, W. C.** On group composition. *J. abnorm. soc. Psychol.*, 1961a, *62,* 275–281.

**Schutz, W. C.** The ego, FIRO theory, and the leader as completer. In L. Petrullo & B. M. Bass (Eds.), *Leadership and interpersonal behavior.* New York: Holt, Rinehart & Winston, 1961b.

**Schutz, W. C.** *Leaders of schools: FIRO theory applied to administrators.* La Jolla, Calif.: University Associates, 1977.

**Schutz, W. C., & Allen, V. L.** The effects of a T-Group laboratory on interpersonal behavior. *J. appl. behav. Sci.*, 1966, *2,* 265–286.

**Schwartz, E. B., & Waetjen, W. B.** Improving the self-concepts of women managers. *Business Quar.*, 1976, *41,* 20–27.

**Schwartz, F. C., Stillwell, W. P., & Scanlon, B. K.** Effects of management development on manager behavior and subordinate perception. *Train. develop. J.*, 1968, *22*(4), 38–50; *22*(5), 24–30.

**Schwartz, M. M., Jenusaitis, E., & Stark, H. F.** A comparison of the perception of job-related needs in two industry groups. *Personnel Psychol.*, 1966, *19,* 185–194.

**Schwartz, M. M., & Levine, H.** Union and management leaders: a comparison. *Personnel Admin.*, 1965, *28,* 44–47.

**Schwartz, M. M., Stark, H. F., & Schiffman, H. R.** Responses of union and management leaders to emotionally toned industrial relations terms. *Personnel Psychol.*, 1970, *23,* 361–367.

**Schwartz, S.** *Tank crew effectiveness in relation to the supervisory behavior of the tank commander.* Washington, D.C.: George Washington University, Human Resources Research Office, 1968.

**Schwartz, S. L., & Gekoski, N.** The Supervisory Inventory: a forced-choice measure of human relations attitude and technique. *J. appl. Psychol.*, 1960, *44*, 233–236.

**Schwartzbaum, A., & Gruenfeld, L.** Factors influencing subject–observer interaction in an organizational study. *Admin. sci. Quar.*, 1969, *14*, 443–449.

**Schwirian, K. P., & Helfrich, M. L.** Economic role and community involvement of business executives. *Sociol. Quar.*, 1968, *9*, 64–72.

**Schwyhart, W. R., & Smith, P. C.** Factors in the job involvement of middle managers. *J. appl. Psychol.*, 1972, *56*, 227–233.

**Scientific American.** The big business executive: 1964. *Scientific American*, 1965.

**Scioli, F. P., Dyson, J. W., & Fleitas, D. W.** The relationship of personality and decisional structure to leadership. *Sm. grp. Behav.*, 1974, *5*, 3–22.

**Scontrino, M. P.** The effects of fulfilling and violating group members' expectations about leadership style. *Org. behav. hum. Perform.*, 1972, *8*, 118–138.

**Scott, E. L.** *Leadership and perceptions of organization.* Columbus: Ohio State University, Bureau of Business Research, 1956.

**Scott, W. A.** Attitude change through reward of verbal behavior. *J. abnorm. soc. Psychol.*, 1957, *55*, 72–75.

**Scott, W. A.** *Organization theory: a behavioral analysis for management.* Homewood, Ill.: Irwin, 1967.

**Scott, W. E.** Some motivational determinants of work behavior. *Indiana bus. info. Bull.*, 1965, *54*, 116–131.

**Scott, W. E.** Leadership: a functional analysis. In J. G. Hunt & L. L. Larson (Eds.), *Leadership: the cutting edge.* Carbondale: Southern Illinois University Press, 1977.

**Scott, W. H.** *Industrial leadership and joint consultation.* Liverpool: University Press of Liverpool, 1952.

**Scott, W. R.** Reactions to supervision in a heteronomous professional organization. *Admin. sci. Quar.*, 1965, *10*, 65–81.

**Seashore, S. E.** *Group cohesiveness in the industrial work group.* Ann Arbor: University of Michigan, Institute for Social Research, 1954.

**Seashore, S. E., & Bowers, D. G.** *Changing the structure and functioning of an organization.* Ann Arbor: University of Michigan, Institute for Social Research, 1963.

**Seashore, S. E., & Bowers, D. G.** Durability of organization change. *Amer. Psychologist*, 1970, *25*, 227–233.

**Sechrest, L. B., & Hemphill, J. K.** Motivational variables in the assuming of combat obligation. *J. consult. Psychol.*, 1954, *18*, 113–118.

**Secord, P. F., & Backman, C. W.** Interpersonal congruency, perceived similarity, and friendship. *Sociometry*, 1964, *27*, 115–127.

**Seeman, M.** Some status correlates of leadership. In A. G. Grace (Ed.), *Leadership in American education.* Chicago: University of Chicago Press, 1950.

**Seeman, M.** Role conflict and ambivalence in leadership. *Amer. sociol. Rev.*, 1953, *18*, 373–380.

**Seeman, M.** A comparison of general and specific leader behavior descriptions. In R. M. Stogdill & E. A. Coons (Eds.), *Leader behavior: its description and measurement.* Columbus: Ohio State University, Bureau of Business Research, 1957.

**Seeman, M.** Social mobility and administrative behavior. *Amer. sociol. Rev.*, 1958, *23*, 33–642.

**Seeman, M.** *Social status and leadership—the case of the school executive.* Columbus: Ohio State University, Educational Research Monograph No. 35, 1960.

**Segard, C. P.** Thirty-three essentials of leadership. *Indus. Psychol.*, 1927, *3*, 270.

**Seidman, J., London, J., & Karsh, B.** Why workers join unions. *Ann. Amer. acad. pol. soc. Sci.*, 1951, *274*, 75–84.

**Seiler, D. A., & Williams, W. E.** Assessing engineer's early job adjustment: a longitudinal approach. *Personnel Psychol.*, 1972, *25*, 687–896.

**Seiler, J. A.** *Systems analysis in organizational behavior.* Homewood, Ill.: Irwin-Dorsey Press, 1967.

**Seldman, M. L.** An investigation of aspects of marathon-encounter group phenomena: types of participants and differential perceptions of leaders. *Dissertation Abstr. Internat.*, 1971, *32*, 3652.

**Selekman, B. M.** *Sharing management with the workers.* New York: Russell Sage Foundation, 1924.

**Selekman, B. M.** *Labor relations and human relations.* New York: McGraw-Hill, 1947.

**Seligman, L. G.** *Leadership in a new nation.* New York: Atherton Press, 1964.

**Sells, S. B.** The nature of organizational climate. In R. Tagiuri & G. L. Litwin (Eds.), *Organizational climate: explorations of a concept.* Cambridge, Mass.: Harvard University Press, 1968.

**Selvin, H. C.** *The effects of leadership.* New York: Free Press, 1960.

**Selznick, P.** An approach to a theory of bureaucracy. *Amer. sociol. Rev.*, 1943, *8*, 47–54.

**Selznick, P.** Foundations of the theory of organization. *Amer. sociol. Rev.*, 1948, *13*, 25–35.

**Selznick, P.** *Leadership in administration: a sociological interpretation.* Evanston, Ill.: Row, Peterson, 1957.

**Senger, J.** Managers' perceptions of subordinates' competence as a function of personal value orientation. *Acad. Mgmt. J.*, 1971, *14*, 415–423.

**Senner, E. E.** Trust as a measure of the impact of cultural differences on individual behavior in organizations. *Proceed. Amer. Psychol. Assn.*, 1971.

**Sequeira, C. E.** Characteristics of effective supervisor. *Manas*, 1962, *9*, 1–12.

**Sequeira, C. E.** Functions of a supervisor. *Indian J. appl. Psychol.*, 1964, *1*, 46–54.

**Sergiovanni, T. J., Metzcus, R. H., & Burden, L.** Toward a particularistic approach to leadership style: some findings. *Amer. educ. res. J.*, 1969, *6*, 62–80.

**Sexton, W. P.** Organizational necessities and individual needs: an empirical study. Doctoral dissertation, Ohio State University, Columbus, 1966.

**Sexton, W. P.** Organizational and individual needs: a conflict? *Personnel J.*, 1967, *46*, 337–343.

**Sgro, J. A., Worchel, P., Pence, E. C., & Orban, J. A.** Perceived leader behavior as a function of the leader's interpersonal trust orientation. *Acad. Mgmt. J.*, 1980, *23*, 161–165.

**Shackleton, V. J., Bass, B. M., & Allison, S. N.** *PAXIT.* Scottsville, N.Y.: Transnational Programs, 1975.

**Shainwald, R. G.** The effect of self-esteem on opinion leadership. *Dissertation Abstr. Internat.*, 1974, *34*, 3635.

**Shannon, C. E., & Weaver, W.** *The mathematical theory of communication.* Urbana: University of Illinois Press, 1949.

**Shannon, J. R.** The post-school careers of high school leaders and high school scholars. *School Rev.*, 1929, *37*, 656–665.

**Shapira, Z.** A facet analysis of leadership styles. *J. appl. Psychol.*, 1976, *61*, 136–139.

**Shapira, Z., & Dunbar, R. L. M.** Testing Mintzberg's managerial roles classification using an in-basket simulation. 1978.

**Shapiro, M. I.** Initiating structure and consideration: a situationist's view of the efficacy of two styles of leadership. *Dissertation Abstr. Internat.*, 1971, *31*, 4382–4383.

**Shapiro, R. J., & Klein, R. H.** Perceptions of the leaders in an encounter group. *Sm. grp. Behav.*, 1975, *6*, 238–248.

**Sharma, C. L.** Practices in decision-making as related to satisfaction in teaching. Doctoral

Dissertation, University of Chicago, 1955.

**Sharma, S. L.** Social value orientations of activist student leaders: a comparative study. *Indian J. soc. Work*, 1974, *35*, 67–71.

**Sharpe, R. T.** Differences between perceived administrative behavior and role-norms as factors in leadership evaluation and group morale. *Dissertation Abstr.*, 1956, *16*, 57.

**Shartle, C. L.** Some psychological factors in foremanship. Doctoral Dissertation, Ohio State University, Columbus, 1933.

**Shartle, C. L.** A clinical approach to foremanship. *Personnel J.*, 1934, *13*, 135–139.

**Shartle, C. L.** Organization structure. In W. Dennis (Ed.), *Current trends in industrial psychology*. Pittsburgh: University of Pittsburgh Press, 1949a.

**Shartle, C. L.** Leadership and executive performance. *Personnel*, 1949b, *25*, 370–380.

**Shartle, C. L.** Leadership aspects of administrative behavior. *Advanced Mgmt.*, 1950a, *15*, 12–15.

**Shartle, C. L.** Studies of leadership by interdisciplinary methods. In A. G. Grace (Ed.), *Leadership in American education*. Chicago: University of Chicago Press, 1950b.

**Shartle, C. L.** Leader behavior in jobs. *Occupations*, 1951a, *30*, 164–166.

**Shartle, C. L.** Studies in naval leadership. In H. Guetzkow (Ed.), *Groups, leadership, and men*. Pittsburgh: Carnegie Press, 1951b.

**Shartle, C. L.** *Executive performance and leadership*. Englewood Cliffs, N.J.: Prentice-Hall, 1956.

**Shartle, C. L.** Work patterns and leadership style in administration. *Personnel Psychol.*, 1960, *13*, 295–300.

**Shartle, C. L.** Leadership and organizational behavior. In L. Petrullo & B. M. Bass (Eds.), *Leadership and interpersonal behavior*. New York: Holt, Rinehart & Winston, 1961.

**Shartle, C. L., Brumback, G. B., & Rizzo, J. R.** An approach to dimensions of value. *J. Psychol.*, 1964, *57*, 101–111.

**Shartle, C. L., & Stogdill, R. M.** *Studies in naval leadership: methods, results, and applications*. Columbus: Ohio State University, Personnel Research Board, Technical Report, 1953.

**Shartle, C. L., & Stogdill, R. M.** *Manual for value scale—business firm*. Columbus: Ohio State University, Bureau of Business Research, 1966.

**Shartle, C. L., Stogdill, R. M., & Campbell, D. T.** *Studies in naval leadership*. Columbus: Ohio State University Research Foundation, 1949 (out of print).

**Shaver, E. L.** *Science of leadership*. Boston: Pilgrim Press, 1931.

**Shaw, C. E.** A comparative study of organizational climate and job satisfaction at selected public and Catholic secondary schools in Connecticut. Doctoral dissertation, University of Connecticut, Storrs, 1976.

**Shaw, D. M.** Size of share in task and motivation in work groups. *Sociometry*, 1960, *23*, 203–208.

**Shaw, E. P.** The social distance factor and management. *Personnel Admin.*, 1965, *28*, 29–31.

**Shaw, M. E.** Some effects of unequal distribution of information upon group performance in various communication nets. *J. abnorm. soc. Psychol.*, 1954a, *49*, 547–553.

**Shaw, M. E.** Some effects of problem complexity upon problem solving efficiency in different communication nets. *J. exp. Psychol.*, 1954b, *48*, 211–217.

**Shaw, M. E.** A comparison of two types of leadership in various communication nets. *J. abnorm. soc. Psychol.*, 1955, *50*, 127–134.

**Shaw, M. E.** Some effects of individually prominent behavior upon group effectiveness and member satisfaction. *J. abnorm. soc. Psychol.*, 1959a, *59*, 382–386.

**Shaw, M. E.** Acceptance of authority, group structure, and the effectiveness of small groups. *J. Pers.*, 1959b, *27*, 196–210.

**Shaw, M. E.** A note concerning homogeneity of membership and group problem solving. *J. abnorm. soc. Psychol.*, 1960, *60*, 448–450.

**Shaw, M. E.** A serial position effect in social influence on group decisions. *J. soc. Psychol.*, 1961, *54*, 83–91.

**Shaw, M. E.** Some effects of varying amounts of information exclusively possessed by a group member upon his behavior in the group. *J. gen. Psychol.*, 1963a, *68*, 71–79.

**Shaw, M. E.** Scaling group tasks: a method for dimensional analysis. Gainesville: University of Florida, Technical report No. 1, 1963b.

**Shaw, M. E.** *Group dynamics.* New York: McGraw-Hill, 1971.

**Shaw, M. E., & Ashton, N.** Do assembly bonus effects occur on disjunctive tasks? A test of Steiner's theory. *Bull. Psychonomic Soc.*, 1976, *8*, 469–491.

**Shaw, M. E., & Blum, J. M.** Effects of leadership style upon group performance as a function of task structure. Gainesville: University of Florida, 1964 (mimeo).

**Shaw, M. E., & Blum, J. M.** Effects of leadership style upon group performance as a function of task structure. *J. pers. soc. Psychol.*, 1966, *3*, 238–242.

**Shaw, M. E., & Gilchrist, J. C.** Intra-group communication and leader choice. *J. soc. Psychol.*, 1956, *43*, 133–138.

**Shaw, M. E., & Harkey, B.** Some effects of congruency of member characteristics and group structure upon group behavior. *J. pers. soc. Psychol.*, 1976, *34*, 412–418.

**Shaw, M. E., & Penrod, W. T.** Does more information available to a group always improve group performance? *Sociometry*, 1962, *25*, 377–390.

**Shaw, M. E., & Rothschild, G. H.** Some effects of prolonged experience in communication nets. *J. appl. Psychol.*, 1956, *40*, 281–286.

**Shaw, M. E., Rothschild, G. H., & Strickland, J. F.** Decision processes in communication nets. *J. abnorm. soc. Psychol.*, 1957, *54*, 323–330.

**Shaw, M. E., & Shaw, L. M.** Some effects of sociometric grouping under learning in a second grade classroom. *J. soc. Psychol.*, 1962, *57*, 453–458.

**Sheldon, W. H.** Social traits and morphologic type. *Personnel J.*, 1927, *6*, 47–55.

**Shelley, H. P.** Focused leadership and cohesiveness in small groups. *Sociometry*, 1960a, *23*, 209–216.

**Shelley, H. P.** Status consensus, leadership, and satisfaction with the group. *J. soc. Psychol.*, 1960b, *51*, 157–164.

**Shepard, H. A.** Superiors and subordinates in research. *J. Bus.*, 1956, *29*, 261–267.

**Shepard, H. A.** Explorations in observant participation. In L. P. Bradford, J. R. Gibb, & K. D. Benne (Eds.), *T-group theory and laboratory method.* New York: Wiley, 1964.

**Shepherd, C., & Weschler, I. R.** The relation between three interpersonal variables and communication effectiveness: a pilot study. *Sociometry*, 1955, *18*, 103–110.

**Sheppard, D. I.** Relationship of job satisfaction to situational and personality characteristics of terminating employees. *Personnel J.*, 1967, *46*, 567–571.

**Sheridan, J. E., & Vredenburgh, D. J.** Predicting leadership behavior in a hospital organization. *Acad. Mgmt. J.*, 1978, *21*, 679–689.

**Sheridan, J. E., & Vrendenburgh, D. J.** Structural model of leadership influence in a hospital organization. *Acad. Mgmt. J.*, 1979, *22*, 6–21.

**Sheridan, M.** Young women leaders in China. *Signs*, 1976, *2*, 59–88.

**Sherif, M.** *The psychology of social norms.* New York: Harper, 1936.

**Sherif, M.** *Intergroup relations and leadership.* New York: Wiley, 1962.

**Sherif, M.** *Social interaction: process and products.* Chicago: Aldine, 1967.

**Sherif, M., & Sherif, C. W.** *Groups in harmony and tension.* New York: Harper, 1953.

**Sherif, M., & Sherif, C. W.** *An outline of social psychology.* New York: Harper, 1956.

**Sherif, M., & Sherif, C. W.** *Reference groups: explorations into conformity and deviations of* *adolescents.* New York: Harper & Row, 1964.

**Sherif, M., White, B. J., & Harvey, O. J.** Status in experimentally produced groups. *Amer. J. Sociol.,* 1955, *60,* 370–379.

**Sherif, M., & Wilson, M. O.** *Group relations at the crossroads.* New York: Harper, 1953.

**Sherif, D. R.** *Administrative behavior: a quantitative case study of six organizations.* Iowa City: University of Iowa, Center for Labor & Management, 1969.

**Sherwood, C. E., & Walker, W. S.** Role differentiation in real groups: an extrapolation of a laboratory small-group research finding. *Sociol. soc. Res.,* 1960, *45,* 14–17.

**Shevitz, R. N.** An investigation of the relation between exclusive possession of information and attempts to lead in small groups. Doctoral dissertation, Ohio State University, 1955.

**Shields, S. A.** Functionalism, Darwinism, and the psychology of women. *Amer. Psychologist,* 1975, *30,* 739–754.

**Shiflett, S. C.** The contingency model of leadership effectiveness: some implications of its statistical and methodological properties. *Behav. Sci.,* 1973, *18,* 429–440.

**Shiflett, S. C.** Stereotyping and esteem for one's best preferred co-worker. *J. soc. Psychol.,* 1974, *93,* 55–65.

**Shiflett, S. C., & Nealey, S. M.** The effects of changing leader power: a test of situational engineering.'' *Org. behav. hum. Perform.,* 1972, *7,* 371–382.

**Shils, E. A.** Primary groups in the American army. In R. A. Merton & P. F. Lazarsfeld. *Studies in the scope and method of ''The American Soldier.''* New York: Free Press, 1950.

**Shils, E. A.** Authoritarianism: ''Right'' and ''Left.'' In R. Christie and M. Jahoda (Eds.), *Studies in the scope and method of ''The Authoritarian Personality.''* New York: Free Press, 1954.

**Shils, E. A., & Janowitz, M.** Cohesion and disintegration in the Wehrmacht in World War II. *Pub. opin. Quar.,* 1948, *12,* 280–315.

**Shima, H.** The relationship between the leader's modes of interpersonal cognition and the performance of the group. *Japanese psychol. Res.,* 1968, *10,* 13–30.

**Showel, M.** Interpersonal knowledge and rated leader potential. *J. abnorm. soc. Psychol.,* 1960, *61,* 87–92.

**Showel, M., Taylor, E. & Hood, P. D.** *Automation of a portion of NCO leadership preparation training.* Washington, D.C.: Human Resources Research Organization, 1966.

**Shrauger, S., & Altrocchi, J.** The personality of the perceiver as a factor in person perception. *Psychol. Bull.,* 1964, *62,* 289–308.

**Shriver, B.** *The behavioral effects of changes in ascribed leadership status in small groups.* Doctoral dissertation, University of Rochester, Rochester, N.Y., 1952.

**Shull, F., & Anthony, W. P.** Do black and white supervisory problem solving styles differ? *Personnel Psychol.,* 1978, *31,* 761–782.

**Shultz, G. P.** *Leaders and followers in an age of ambiguity.* New York: New York University Press, 1975.

**Siegel, A. L., & Ruh, R. A.** Job involvement, participation in decision-making, personal background and job behavior. *Org. Behav. Hum. Perf.,* 1973, *9,* 318–327.

**Siegel J. P.** A study of the relationship among organizational factors, personality traits, job, and leadership attitudes. *Dissertation Abstr.,* 1969, *29,* 2662–2663.

**Siegel, J. P.** Reconsidering ''consideration'' in a leadership-path-goal interpretation of satisfaction and performance. Toronto: University of Toronto, unpublished ms., 1973.

**Siegel, S.** *Nonparametric statistics for the behavioral sciences.* New York: McGraw-Hill, 1956.

**Siegenthaler, J. K.** Decision-making in Swiss labor unions. *Proceedings of the Industrial Relations Research Association,* 1969.

**Sikula, A. F.** Values, value systems, and their relationships to organizational effectiveness. *Proceedings of the Academy of Management,* 1971.

**Simmons, R. G.** The role conflict of the first-line supervisor: an experimental study. *Amer. J. Sociol.*, 1968, *73*, 482–495.

**Simon, H. A.** *Administrative behavior: a study of decision-making process in administrative native organization.* New York: Macmillan, 1947.

**Simon, H. A.** *Models of man.* New York: Wiley, 1957.

**Simpson, D. B., & Peterson, R. B.** Leadership behavior, need satisfactions, and role perceptions of labor leaders: a behavioral analysis. *Personnel Psychol.*, 1972, *25*, 673–686.

**Simpson, R. H.** *A study of those who influence and of those who are influenced in discussion.* New York: Teachers College Contributions to Education, 1938.

**Simpson, R. L.** Vertical and horizontal communication in formal organizations. *Admin. sci. Quar.*, 1959, *4*, 188–196.

**Sims, H. P.** The leader as a manager of reinforcement contingencies: an empirical example and a model. In J. G. Hunt & L. L. Larson (Eds.), *Leadership: the cutting edge.* Carbondale: Southern Illinois University Press, 1977.

**Sims, H. P.** Further thoughts on punishment in organizations. *Acad. Mgmt. Rev.*, 1980, *5*, 133–138.

**Sims, H. P., & Szilagyi, A. D.** A causal analysis of leader behavior over three different time lags. *Eastern Academy of Management Proceedings, 1978.*

**Singer, J. E.** The effect of status congruence and incongruence on group functioning. *Dissertation Abstr.*, 1966, *27*, 1932.

**Singh, N. P.** n/Ach among successful-unsuccessful and traditional-progressive agricultural entrepreneurs of Delhi. *J. soc. Psychol.*, 1969, *79*, 271–272.

**Singh, N. P.** n/Ach among agricultural and business entrepreneurs of Delhi. *J. soc. Psychol.*, 1970, *81*, 145–149.

**Singh, S. N., & Arya, H. P.** Value-orientations of local village leaders. *Manas*, 1965, *12*, 145–156.

**Singh, S. N., Arya, H. P., & Reddy, S. K.** Different types of local leadership in two north Indian villages. *Manas*, 1965, *12*, 97–107.

**Singleton, T.** A study of managerial motivation development among college student leaders. Doctoral dissertation, Georgia State University, Atlanta, 1976.

**Singleton, T.** Managerial motivation development: college student leaders. In J. B. Miner (Ed.), *Motivation to manage.* Atlanta: Organizational Measurement Systems Press, 1977.

**Sinha, D., & Kumar, P.** A study of certain personality variables in student leadership. *Psychol. Studies, 1966, 11*, 1–8.

**Sinha, J. B.** The authoritarian leadership: a style of effective management. *Indian J. indus. Relat.*, 1976, *2*, 381–389.

**Sirota, D.** Some effects of promotional frustration on employees' understanding of, and attitudes toward, management. *Sociometry*, 1959, *22*, 273–278.

**Sirota, D.** International survey of job goals and beliefs. *Proceedings of the International Congress of Applied Psychology*, 1968.

**Sisson, E. D.** Forced choice—the new army rating. *Personnel Psychol.*, 1948, *1*, 365–381.

**Skinner, E. W.** Relationships between leadership behavior patterns and organizational-situational variables. *Personnel Psychol.*, 1969, *22*, 489–494.

**Skrzypek, G. J.** The relationship of leadership style to task structure, position power, and leader-member relations. West Point, N.Y.: U.S. Military Academy, U.S. Army Hospital, Technical Report No. 34, 1969.

**Slater, P. E.** Role differentiation in small groups. *Amer. sociol. Rev.*, 1955, *20*, 300–310.

**Slater, P. E.** Contrasting correlates of group size. *Sociometry*, 1958, *21*, 129–139.

**Sleeth, R. G., & Humphreys, L. W.** Differences in leadership styles among future managers: a comparison of male and females. Unpublished ms., undated.

**Slocum, J. W.** Organizational climate: fact or fiction. *Proceedings of the Midwest Academy of Management,* 1973.

**Slocum, J. W., Miller, J. D., & Misshauk, M. J.** Needs, environmental work satisfaction, and job performance. *Train. develop. J.,* 1970, *24,* 12–15.

**Slocum, J. W., & Strawser, R. H.** Racial differences in job attitudes. *J. appl. Psychol.,* 1972, *56,* 28–32.

**Slusher, A., Van Dyke, J., & Rose, G.** Technical competence of group leaders, managerial role, and productivity in engineering design groups. *Acad. Mgmt. J.,* 1972, *15,* 197–204.

**Smallridge, R. J.** A study of relationships between perceived management system of elementary schools and the personal needs satisfaction of teachers. Doctoral dissertation, George Peabody College for Teachers, Nashville, Tenn., 1972.

**Smelser, W. T.** Dominance as a factor in achievement and perception in cooperative problem solving interactions. *J. abnorm. soc. Psychol.,* 1961, *62,* 535–542.

**Smith, A. B.** Role expectations for and observations of community college department chairmen: an organizational study of consensus and conformity. Doctoral dissertation, University of Michigan, Ann Arbor, 1971.

**Smith, A. J.** Similarity of values and its relation to acceptance and the projection of similarity. *J. Psychol.,* 1957, *43,* 251–260.

**Smith, A. J.** Perceived similarity and the projection of similarity: the influence of valence. *J. abnorm. soc. Psychol.,* 1958, *57,* 376–378.

**Smith, B. L., & Smith, C. M.** *International communication and political opinion: a guide to the literature.* Princeton, N.J.: Princeton University Press, 1956.

**Smith, C. G., & Ari, O. N.** Organizational control structure and member consensus. *Amer. J. Sociol.,* 1964, *69,* 623–638.

**Smith, C. G., & Tannenbaum, A. S.** Organizational control structure: a comparative analysis. *Hum. Relat.,* 1963, *16,* 299–316.

**Smith, C. G., & Tannenbaum, A. S.** Some implications of leadership and control for effectiveness in a voluntary association. *Hum. Relat.,* 1965, *18,* 265–272.

**Smith, E. E.** The effects of clear and unclear role expectations on group productivity and defensiveness. *J. abnorm. soc. Psychol.,* 1957, *55,* 213–217.

**Smith, E. E.** Congruence of self-perception variables for emergent leaders and non-leaders of small task groups. *Dissertation Abstr. Internat.,* 1969, *30,* 2899.

**Smith, E. E., & Kight, S. S.** Effects of feedback on insight and problem solving efficiency in training groups. *J. appl. Psychol.,* 1959, *43,* 209–211.

**Smith, F. J., & Kerr, W. A.** Turnover factors as assessed by the exit interview. *J. appl. Psychol.,* 1953, *37,* 352–355.

**Smith, G. A.** *Managing geographically decentralized companies.* Boston: Harvard Business School, 1958.

**Smith, G. A., & Matthews, J. B.** *Business, society, and the individual: problems in responsible leadership of private enterprise organizations operating in a free society.* Homewood, Ill.: Irwin, 1967.

**Smith, H.** *The Russians.* New York: Ballantine, 1976.

**Smith, H. C.** Music in relation to employee attitudes, piece work production, and industrial accidents. *Appl. psychol. Monogr.,* 1947, No. 14.

**Smith, H. C.** *Psychology of industrial behavior.* New York: McGraw-Hill, 1964.

**Smith, H. C.** *Sensitivity to people.* New York: McGraw-Hill, 1966.

**Smith, H. L., & Krueger, L. M.** *A brief summary of literature on leadership.* Bloomington: Indiana University, School of Education Bulletin, 1933.

**Smith, L. M.** Social psychological aspects of school building design. St. Louis: Washington University, 1967 (mimeo).

**Smith, M.** Personality dominance and leadership. *Sociol. soc. Res.*, 1934, *19*, 18–25.

**Smith, M.** Leadership: the management of social differentials. *J. abnorm. soc. Psychol.*, 1935a, *30*, 348–358.

**Smith, M.** Comparative study of Indian student leaders and followers. *Soc. Forces*, 1935b, *13*, 418–426.

**Smith, M.** Classifications of eminent men. *Sociol. soc. Res.*, 1937, *21*, 203–212.

**Smith, M.** Control interaction. *J. soc. Psychol.*, 1948, *28*, 263–273.

**Smith, M., & Nystrom, W. C.** A study of social participation and of leisure time of leaders and non-leaders. *J. appl. Psychol.*, 1937, *21*, 251–259.

**Smith, M. B., Bruner, J. S., & White, R. W.** Opinions and personality. New York: Wiley, 1956.

**Smith, M. C.** The relationship between the participative management style of elementary school principals as perceived by their teacher and level of teacher morale. Doctoral dissertation, University of Southern California, Los Angeles, 1975.

**Smith, McG.** Mending our weakest links. *Adv. Mgmt.*, 1942, *7*, 77–83.

**Smith, N. R.** *The entrepreneur and his firm: the relationship between type of man and type of company.* East Lansing: Michigan State University, Graduate School of Business Administration, 1967.

**Smith, P. B.** Differentiation between sociometric rankings. *Hum. Relat.*, 1963, *16*, 335–350.

**Smith, P. B.** Attitude changes associated with training in human relations. *British J. soc. clin. Psychol.*, 1964, *3*, 104–112.

**Smith, P. B.** *Group processes: selected readings.* Middlesex, England: Penguin, 1970.

**Smith, P. B.** Controlled studies of the outcome of sensitivity training. *Psychol. Bull.*, 1975, *82*, 597–622.

**Smith, P. B.** Why successful groups succeed: the implications of T-group research. In C. L. Cooper (Ed.), *Developing social skills in managers.* New York: Wiley, 1976.

**Smith, P. C., Kendall, L. M., & Hulin, C. L.** *The measurement of satisfaction in work and retirement.* Chicago: Rand McNally, 1969.

**Smith, P. B., Moscow, D., Berger, M., & Cooper, C.** Relationships between managers and their work associates. *Admin. sci. Quar.*, 1969, *14*, 338–345.

**Smith, R. G.** The effects of leadership style, leader position power, and problem solving method on group performance. *Dissertation Abstr. Internat.*, 1974, *35*, 773–774.

**Smith, S., & Haythorn, W. W.** Effects of compatibility, crowding, group size, and leadership seniority on stress, anxiety, hostility, and annoyance in isolated groups. *J. pers. soc. Psychol.*, 1972, *22*, 67–79.

**Smith, W. P.** Power structure and authoritarianism in the use of power in the triad. *J. Pers.*, 1967a, *35*, 65–89.

**Smith, W. P.** Reactions to a dyadic power structure. *Psychonomic Sci.*, 1967b, *7*, 373–374.

**Smith, W. P.** Precision of control and the use of power in the triad. *Hum. Relat.*, 1968, *21*, 295–310.

**Smits, S. J., & Aiken, W. J.** *A descriptive study of supervisory practices as perceived by counselors in state vocational rehabilitation offices.* Bloomington: Indiana University, School of Education, 1969.

**Smuckler, R. H., & Belknap, G. M.** *Leadership and participation in urban political affairs.* East Lansing: Michigan State University, 1956.

**Smythe, H. H.** Changing patterns in Negro leadership. *Soc. Forces*, 1950, *29*, 191–197.

**Snadowsky, A. M.** Group effectiveness as a function of communication network, task complexity, and leadership type. *Dissertation Abstr. Internat.*, 1969, *30*, 2155.

**Snedden, D.** Aspirational notions of leadership. *School Society*, 1930, *31*, 661–664.

**Snoek, J. D.** Role strain in diversified role sets. *Amer. J. Sociol.*, 1966, *71*, 363–372.

**Snyder, N., & Glueck, W. F.** Mintzberg and the planning literature: an analysis and reconciliation. *Proceedings of the Academy of Management,* 1977.

**Snyder, R., French, J. R. P., & Hoehn, A. J.** Experiments on leadership in small groups. Chanute AF Base, Ill.: Pers. Train. Res. Cent. Res. Rep., 1955.

**Sofer, C.** Reaction to administrative change: a study of staff relations in three British hospitals. *Hum. Relat.,* 1955, *8,* 291–316.

**Sofer, C.** *Men in mid-career: a study of British managers and technical specialists.* New York: Cambridge University Press, 1970.

**Sofranko, A. J., & Bridgeland, W. M.** Agreement and disagreement on environmental issues among community leaders. *Cornell J. soc. Relat.,* 1975, *10,* 151–162.

**Sola Pool, de, I.** The head of the company: conceptions of role and identity. *Behav. Sci.,* 1964, *9,* 147–155.

**Solem, A. R.** The influence of the discussion leader's attitude on the outcome of group decision conferences. *Dissertation Abstr.,* 1953, *13,* 439.

**Solem, A. R.** An evaluation of two attitudinal approaches to delegation. *J. appl. Psychol.,* 1958, *42,* 36–39.

**Solem, A. R.** Human relations training: comparison of case study and role playing. *Personnel Admin.,* 1960, *23,* 29–37.

**Solem, A. R., Onachilla, V. J., & Heller, K. Z.** The posting problems technique as a basis for training. *Personnel Admin.,* 1961, *24,* 22–31.

**Solomon, L.** The influence of some types of power relationships and game strategies upon the development of interpersonal trust. *J. abnorm. soc. Psychol.,* 1960, *61,* 223–230.

**Solomon, L. N., Berzon, B., & Davis, D. P.** A personal growth program for self-directed groups. *J. appl. behav. Sci.,* 1970, *6,* 427–452.

**Solomon, L. N., Berzon, B., & Weedman, C. W.** The programmed group: a new rehabilitation resource. *Internat. J. grp. Psychotherapy,* 1968, *18,* 199–219.

**Solomon, R. H.** Personality changes in leaders and members of personality laboratories. *Dissertation Abstr. Internat.,* 1976, *36,* 5285–5286.

**Solomon, R. J.** An examination of the relationship between a survey feedback O.D. technique and the work environment. *Personnel Psychol.,* 1976, *29,* 583–594.

**Sommer, R.** Studies in personal space. *Sociometry,* 1959, *22,* 247–260.

**Sommer, R.** Leadership and group geography. *Sociometry,* 1961, *24,* 99–110.

**Sommer, R.** Further studies of small group ecology. *Sociometry,* 1965, *28,* 337–348.

**Sommer, R.** Small group ecology. *Psychol. Bull.,* 1967, *67,* 145–152.

**Sommer, R.** *Personal space: the behavioral basis of design.* Englewood Cliffs, N.J.: Prentice-Hall, 1969.

**Sorcher, M.** The interaction between participation, urgency and group leader status in small decision-making groups. *Dissertation Abstr.,* 1966, *26,* 6213.

**Sorcher, M., & Goldstein, A. P.** A behavior modeling approach in training. *Personnel Admin.,* 1972, *35,* 35–41.

**Sord, B. H., & Welsch, G. A.** *Managerial planning and control as viewed by lower levels of supervision.* Austin: University of Texas, Bureau of Business Research, 1964.

**Sorokin, P. A.** *Social mobility.* New York: Harper, 1927a.

**Sorokin, P. A.** Leaders of labor and radical social movements in the United States and foreign countries. *Amer. J. Sociol.,* 1927b, *33,* 382–411.

**Sorokin, P. A.** *Man and society in calamity.* New York: Dutton, 1943.

**Sorokin, P. A., & Berger, C. Q.** *Time budgets of human behavior.* Cambridge, Mass.: Harvard University Press, 1939.

**Sorokin, P. A., & Zimmerman, C. C.** Farmer leaders in the United States. *Soc. Forces,* 1928, *7,* 33–46.

**Sorrentino, R. M., & Boutillier, R. G.** The effect of quantity and quality of verbal interaction on ratings of leadership ability. *J. exp. soc. Psychol.*, 1975, *11*, 403–411.

**South, E. B.** Some psychological aspects of committee work. *J. appl. Psychol.*, 1927, *11*, 348–368.

**Southern, L. J. F.** An analysis of motivation to manage in the tufted carpet and textile industry of northwest Georgia. Doctoral dissertation, Georgia State University, Atlanta, 1976.

**Southwick, C. H.** *Primate social behavior.* Princeton, N.J.: Van Nostrand, 1963.

**Southwick, C. H., & Siddiqi, M. R.** The role of social tradition in the maintenance of dominance in a wild Rhesus group. *Primates*, 1967, *8*, 341–353.

**Spaulding, C. B.** Types of junior college leaders. *Sociol. soc. Res.*, 1934, *18*, 164–168.

**Spector, A. J.** Factors in morale. *Amer. Psychologist*, 1953, *8*, 439–440.

**Spector, A. J.** Expectations, fulfillment, and morale. *J. abnorm. soc. Psychol.*, 1956, *52*, 51–56.

**Spector, A. J.** Changes in human relations attitudes. *J. appl. Psychol.*, 1958, *42*, 154–157.

**Spector, A. J., Clark, R. A., & Glickman, A. S.** Supervisory characteristics and attitudes of subordinates. *Personnel Psychol.*, 1960, *13*, 301–316.

**Spector, P., & Suttell, B. J.** Research on the specific leader behavior patterns most effective in influencing group performance. Washington, D.C.: American Institute for Research, 1956.

**Spence, J. T., Helmrich, R., & Stapp, J.** Ratings of self and peers on the sex role attributes and their relation to self-esteem and conceptions of masculinity and femininity. *J. pers. soc. Psychol.*, 1975, *32*, 29–39.

**Spencer, L. M.** The Navy leadership and management education and training program, undated.

**Speroff, B. J.** The group's role in role playing. *J. indust. Train.*, 1953, *7*, 3–5.

**Speroff, B. J.** Rotational role playing used to develop executives. *Personnel J.*, 1954, *33*, 49–50.

**Speroff, B. J.** Job satisfaction and interpersonal desirability values. *Sociometry*, 1955, *18*, 69–72.

**Speroff, B. J.** The ''behind-the-back'' way in training leaders. *Personnel J.*, 1957, *35*, 411–412, 435.

**Spicer, E. H.** *Human problems in technological change.* New York: Russell Sage Foundation, 1952.

**Spielberger, C. D.** Anxiety as an emotional state. In C. D. Spielberger (Ed.), *Anxiety: current trends in theory and research,* vol. 1. New York: Academic Press, 1972.

**Spielberger, C. D., Gorsuch, R. L., & Lushene, R. E.** *Manual for the state-trait anxiety inventory.* Palo Alto, Calif.: Consulting Psychologist Press, 1970.

**Spiller, G.** The dynamics of greatness. *Sociol. Rev.*, 1929, *21*, 218–232.

**Spitzer, M. E., & McNamara, W. J.** A managerial selection study. *Personnel Psychol.*, 1964, *17*, 19–40.

**Spriegel, W. R., & Mumma, E. W.** *Training supervisors in human relations.* Austin: University of Texas, Bureau of Business Research, 1961.

**Springer, D.** Ratings of candidates for promotion by co-workers and supervisors. *J. appl. Psychol.*, 1953, *37*, 347–351.

**Springer, D.** Why employees refuse promotion: a case study. *Personnel*, 1956, *32*, 457–462.

**Spruill, V. J., Frye, R. L., & Butler, J. R.** Differences in leadership stereotypes between deviants and normals. *J. soc. Psychol.*, 1969, *79*, 255–256.

**Sprunger, J. A.** The relationship of group morale estimates to other measures of group and leader effectiveness. Columbus: Ohio State University, Master's thesis, 1949.

**Srinivasan, V., Shocker, A. D., & Weinstein, A. G.** Measurement of a composite criterion of managerial success. *Org. behav. hum. Perform.*, 1973, *9*, 147–167.

**Srole, L.** Social integration and certain corollaries: an exploratory study. *Amer. sociol. Rev.*, 1956, *21*, 709–716.

**Stagner, R.** Stereotypes of workers and executives among college men. *J. abnorm. soc.*

*Psychol.*, 1950, *45*, 743–748.

**Stagner, R.** Dual allegiance to union and management. 1. Dual allegiance as a problem in modern society. *Personnel Psychol.*, 1954, *7*, 41–46.

**Stagner, R.** Personality variables in union-management relations. *J. appl. Psychol.*, 1962, *46*, 350–357.

**Stagner, R.** Corporate decision making: an empirical study. *J. appl. Psychol.*, 1969, *53*, 1–13.

**Stagner, R., Chalmers, W. E., & Derber, M.** Guttman-type scales for union and management attitudes toward each other. *J. appl. Psychol.*, 1958, *42*, 293–300.

**Stagner, R., Derber, M., & Chalmers, W. E.** The dimensionality of union–management relations at the local level. *J. appl. Psychol.*, 1959, *43*, 1–7.

**Stagner, R., Flebbe, D. R., & Wood, E. V.** Working on the railroad: a study of job satisfaction. *Personnel Psychol.*, 1952, *5*, 293–306.

**Stahl, G. R.** Training directors evaluate role playing. *J. indus. Train.*, 1953, *7*, 21–29.

**Stahl, G. R.** A statistical report of industry's experience with role playing. *Group Psychotherapy*, 1954, *6*, 202–215.

**Staines, G., Tavris, C., & Jayaratne, T. E.** The Queen Bee Syndrome. In C. Tavris (Ed.), *The female experience*. Del Mar, Calif.: CRM, 1973.

**Stampolis, A.** Employees' attitudes toward unionization, management, and factory conditions. Atlanta: Georgia State College of Business Administration, 1958 (mimeo).

**Standard & Poors.** *Register of corporations, directors and executives.* New York: Standard & Poors, 1967.

**Stander, N. E.** A longitudinal study of some relationships among criteria of managerial performance as perceived by superiors and subordinates. *J. indust. Psychol.*, 1965, *3*, 43–51.

**Stanley, D. T., Mann, D. E., & Doig, J. W.** *Men who govern: a biographical profile of federal political executives.* Washington, D.C.: Brookings, 1967.

**Stanton, E. S.** Company policies and supervisors' attitudes toward supervision. *J. appl. Psychol.*, 1960, *44*, 22–26.

**Stark, H. F.** Trade union administration: theory and practice. Doctoral dissertation, Rutgers University, New Brunswick, N.J., 1958.

**Stark, S.** Toward a psychology of charisma: III. Intuitional empathy, Vorbilder, Fuehrers, transcendence-striving, and inner creation. *Psychol. Rep.*, 1977, *40*, 683–696.

**Starr, C. G.** Civilization and the Caesars Ithaca: Cornell Univ. Press, 1954.

**Steele, F. I., Zane, D. E., & Zalkind, S. S.** Managerial behavior and participation in a laboratory training process. *Personnel Psychol.*, 1970, *23*, 77–90.

**Steger, J. A., Kelley, W. B., Chouiniere, G., & Goldenbaum, A.** A forced choice version of the Miner sentence completion scale and how it discriminates campus leaders and nonleaders. In J. B. Miner (Ed.), *Motivation to manage*. Atlanta: Organizational Measurement Systems Press, 1977.

**Stein, R. T.** Accuracy in perceiving emergent leadership in small groups. *Proceedings of the Amer. Psychol. Assn.*, 1971.

**Stein, R. T.** Identifying emergent leaders from verbal and nonverbal communications. *J. pers. soc. Psychol.*, 1975, *32*, 125–135.

**Stein, R. T.** Accuracy of process consultants and untrained observers in perceiving emergent leadership. *J. appl. Psychol.*, 1977, *62*, 755–759.

**Stein, R. T., Geis, F. L., & Damarin, F.** Perception of emergent leadership hierarchies in task groups. *J. pers. soc. Psychol.*, 1973, *28*, 77–87.

**Steiner, I. D.** *Current studies in social psychology*. New York: Holt, Rinehart & Winston, 1965.

**Steiner, I. D.** Models for inferring relationships between group size and potential group productivity. *Behav. Sci.*, 1966, *11*, 273–283.

**Steiner, I. D.** *Group process and productivity*. New York: Academic Press, 1972.

**Steiner, I. D.** *Task-performing groups.* Morristown, N.J.: General Learning Press, 1974.

**Steiner, I. D., Dodge, J. S.** A comparison of two techniques employed in the study of interpersonal perception. *Sociometry,* 1957, *20,* 1–7.

**Steiner, I. D., & Field, W. L.** Role assignment and interpersonal influence. *J. abnorm. soc. Psychol.,* 1960, *61,* 239–245.

**Steiner, I. D., & McDiarmid, C. G.** Two kinds of assumed similarity between opposites. *J. abnorm. soc. Psychol.,* 1957, *55,* 140–142.

**Steiner, I. D., & Peters, S. C.** Conformity and the A-B-X model. *J. Pers.,* 1958, *26,* 229–242.

**Steinman, J. I.** Some antecedents of participative decision making. Doctoral dissertation, University of California, Berkeley, 1974.

**Steinmetz, L. L.** Leadership styles and systems management: more direction, less confusion. *Personnel J.,* 1968, *47,* 650–654.

**Steinzor, B.** The spatial factor in face to face discussion groups. *J. abnorm. soc. Psychol.,* 1950, *45,* 552–555.

**Stephan, F. E.** The relative rate of communication between members of small groups. *Amer. sociol. Rev.,* 1952, *17,* 482–486.

**Stephenson, H. B.** The effect of a management training program on leadership attitude and on-the-job behavior. *Dissertation Abstr.,* 1966, *27,* 1512.

**Stephenson, T. E.** The leader–follower relationship. *Sociol. Rev.,* 1959, *7,* 179–195.

**Sterling, T. D., & Rosenthal, B. G.** The relationship of changing leadership and followership in a group to the changing phases of group activity. *Amer. Psychologist,* 1950, *5,* 311.

**Stewart, A. J., & Rubin, Z.** The power motive in the dating couple. *J. pers. soc. Psychol.,* 1974, *34,* 305–309.

**Stewart, B. R.** *Leadership for agricultural industry.* New York: McGraw-Hill, 1978.

**Stewart, G. T.** Charisma and integration: an eighteenth century North American case. In *Comparative studies in society and history.* Cambridge: At the University Press, 1974.

**Stewart, L.** Management games today. In J. M. Kibbee, C. J. Craft, & B. Nanus (Eds.), *Management games.* New York: Rinehart, 1962.

**Stewart, P. A.** *Job enlargement.* Iowa City: University of Iowa, Center for Labor & Management, 1967.

**Stewart, R.** The socio-cultural setting of management in the United Kingdom. *Internat. labor Rev.,* 1966, *94,* 108–131.

**Stewart, R.** *Managers and their jobs.* London: Macmillan, 1967.

**Stimpson, D. V., & Bass, B. M.** Dyadic behavior of self-, interaction-, and task-oriented subjects in a test situation. *J. abnorm. soc. Psychol.,* 1964, *68,* 558–562.

**Stinson, J. E.** The differential impact of participation in laboratory training in collaborative task effort in intact and fragmented groups. Doctoral dissertation, Ohio State University, Columbus, 1970.

**Stinson, J. E.** "Least preferred coworker" as a measure of leadership style. *Psychol. Rep.,* 1972, *30,* 930.

**Stinson, J. E., & Hellebrandt, E. T.** Group cohesiveness, productivity, and strength of formal leadership. *J. soc. Psychol.,* 1972, *87,* 99–105.

**Stinson, J. E., & Johnson, T. W.** The path-goal theory of leadership: a partial test and suggested refinement. *Acad. Mgmt. J.,* 1975, *18,* 242–252.

**Stinson, J. E., & Tracy, L.** Some disturbing characteristics of the LPC score. *Personnel Psychol.,* 1974, *24,* 477–485.

**Stires, L. K.** Leadership designation and perceived ability as determinants of the tactical use of modesty and self-enhancement. *Dissertation Abstr. Internat.,* 1970, *30A,* 3551.

**Stock, D.** A survey of research on T groups. In L. P. Bradford, J. R. Gibb, & K. D. Benne. *T-group theory and laboratory method.* New York: Wiley, 1964.

**Stogdill, R. M.** Personal factors associated with leadership: a survey of the literature. *J. Psychol.*, 1948, *25*, 35–71.

**Stogdill, R. M.** The sociometry of working relations in formal organizations. *Sociometry*, 1949, *12*, 276–286.

**Stogdill, R. M.** Leadership, membership and organization. *Psychol. Bull.*, 1950, *47*, 1–14.

**Stogdill, R. M.** The organization of working relationships: twenty sociometric indices. *Sociometry*, 1951a, *14*, 366–374.

**Stogdill, R. M.** Studies in naval leadership, Part II. In H. Guetzkow. *Groups, leadership, and men*. Pittsburgh: Carnegie Press, 1951b.

**Stogdill, R. M.** Leadership and morale in organized groups. In J. E. Hulett & R. Stagner (Eds.), *Problems in social psychology*. Urbana: University of Illinois, 1952.

**Stogdill, R. M.** Interactions among superiors and subordinates. *Sociometry*, 1955, *18*, 552–557.

**Stogdill, R. M.** *Leadership and structures of personal interaction*. Columbus: Ohio State University, Bureau of Business Research, 1957a.

**Stogdill, R. M.** *The RAD Scales: manual*. Columbus: Ohio State University, Bureau of Business Research, 1957b.

**Stogdill, R. M.** *Individual behavior and group achievement*. New York: Oxford University Press, 1959.

**Stogdill, R. M.** Intragroup-intergroup theory and research. In M. Sherif (Ed.), *Intergroup relations and leadership*. New York: Wiley, 1962.

**Stogdill, R. M.** *Manual for the Leader Behavior Description Questionnaire—Form XII*. Columbus: Ohio State University, Bureau of Business Research, 1963a.

**Stogdill, R. M.** *Team achievement under high motivation*. Columbus: Ohio State University, Bureau of Business Research, 1963b.

**Stogdill, R. M.** *Managers, employees, organizations*. Columbus: Ohio State University, Bureau of Business Research, 1965a.

**Stogdill, R. M.** *Manual for job satisfaction and expectation scales*. Columbus: Ohio State University, Bureau of Business Research, 1965b.

**Stogdill, R. M.** The structure of organization behavior. *Multivariate behav. Res.*, 1967, *2*, 47–61.

**Stogdill, R. M.** *Leadership: a survey of the literature. I. Selected topics*. Greensboro, N.C.: Smith Richardson Foundation, 1968.

**Stogdill, R. M.** Validity of leader behavior descriptions. *Personnel Psychol.*, 1969, *22*, 153–158.

**Stogdill, R. M.** Effects of leadership training on the performance of sororities. Columbus: Ohio State University, unpublished report, 1970.

**Stogdill, R. M.** Group productivity, drive, and cohesiveness. *Org. behav. hum. Perform.*, 1972, *8*, 26–43.

**Stogdill, R. M., & Bailey, W. R.** *Changing the response of vocational students to supervision: the use of motion pictures and group discussion*. Columbus: Ohio State University, Center for Vocational & Technical Education, 1969.

**Stogdill, R. M., Bailey, W. R., Coady, N. P., & Zimmer, A.** Improving response to supervision. *Train. devel. J.*, 1971, *25*, 16–22.

**Stogdill, R. M., & Coady, N. P.** Preferences of vocational students for different styles of supervisory behavior. *Personnel Psychol.*, 1970, *23*, 309–312.

**Stogdill, R. M., Coady, N. P., & Zimmer, A.** *Response of vocational students to supervision: effects of reinforcing positive and negative attitudes toward different supervisory roles*. Columbus: Ohio State University, Center for Vocational & Technical Education, 1970.

**Stogdill, R. M., & Coons, A. E.** *Leader behavior: its description and measurement*. Columbus: Ohio State University, Bureau of Business Research, 1957.

**Stogdill, R. M., & Goode, O. S.** Effects of the interactions of superiors upon the performances and expectations of subordinates. *Internat. J. Sociometry,* 1957, *1,* 133–145.

**Stogdill, R. M., Goode, O. S., & Day, D. R.** New leader behavior description sub-scales. *J. Psychol.,* 1962, *54,* 259–269.

**Stogdill, R. M., Goode, O. S., & Day, D. R.** The leader behavior of corporation presidents. *Personnel Psychol.,* 1963a, *16,* 127–132.

**Stogdill, R. M., Goode, O. S., & Day, D. R.** The leader behavior of United States senators. *J. Psychol.,* 1963b, *56,* 3–8.

**Stogdill, R. M., Goode, O. S., & Day, D. R.** The leader behavior of presidents of labor unions. *Personnel Psychol.,* 1964, *17,* 49–57.

**Stogdill, R. M., Goode, O. S., & Day, D. R.** The leader behavior of university presidents. Columbus: Ohio State University, Bureau of Business Research, unpublished report, 1965.

**Stogdill, R. M., & Haase, K. K.** Structures of working relationships. In R. M. Stogdill (Ed.), *Leadership and structures of personal interaction.* Columbus: Ohio State University, Bureau of Business Research, 1957.

**Stogdill, R. M., & Koehler, K.** *Measures of leadership structure and organization change.* Columbus: Ohio State University, Personnel Research Board, 1952.

**Stogdill, R. M., & Scott, E. L.** Responsibility and authority relationships. In R. M. Stogdill (Ed.), *Leadership and structures of personal interaction.* Columbus: Ohio State University, Bureau of Business Research, 1957.

**Stogdill, R. M., Scott, E. L., & Jaynes, W. E.** *Leadership and role expectations.* Columbus: Ohio State University, Bureau of Business Research, 1956.

**Stogdill, R. M., & Shartle, C. L.** Methods for determining patterns of leadership behavior in relation to organization structure and objectives. *J. appl. Psychol.,* 1948, *32,* 286–291.

**Stogdill, R. M., & Shartle, C. L.** *Methods in the study of administrative leadership.* Columbus: Ohio State University, Bureau of Business Research, 1955.

**Stogdill, R. M., & Shartle, C. L.** *Patterns of administrative performance.* Columbus: Ohio State University, Bureau of Business Research, 1956.

**Stogdill, R. M., & Shartle, C. L.** *Manual for the Work Analysis Forms.* Columbus: Ohio State University, Bureau of Business Research, 1958.

**Stogdill, R. M., Shartle, C. L., Scott, E. L., Coons, A. E., & Jaynes, W. E.** *A predictive study of administrative work patterns.* Columbus: Ohio State University, Bureau of Business Research, 1956.

**Stogdill, R. M., Shartle, C. L., Wherry, R. J., & Jaynes, W. E.** A factorial study of administrative behavior. *Personnel Psychol.,* 1955, *8,* 165–180.

**Stogdill, R. M., Wherry, R. J., & Jaynes, W. E.** Patterns of leader behavior: a factorial study of navy officer performance. Columbus: Ohio State University, 1953.

**Stoland, E.** Peer groups and reactions to power figures. *Amer. Psychologist,* 1954, *9,* 478.

**Stoltz, R. E.** Factors in supervisors' perceptions of physical science research personnel. *J. appl. Psychol.,* 1959, *43,* 256–258.

**Stone, G. G., Gage, N. L., & Leavitt, G. S.** Two kinds of accuracy in predicting another's responses. *J. soc. Psychol.,* 1957, *45,* 245–254.

**Stone, P., & Kamiya, J.** Judgments of consensus during group discussion. *J. abnorm. soc. Psychol.,* 1957, *55,* 171–175.

**Stone, R. C.** Status and leadership in a combat fighter squadron. *Amer. J. Sociol.,* 1946, *51,* 388–394.

**Stone, S. (Ed.),** *Management for nurses.* St. Louis: C. V. Mosby, 1976.

**Stoodley, B. H.** *Society and self: a reader in social psychology.* New York: Free Press, 1962.

**Storey, A. W.** A study of member satisfaction and types of contributions in discussion groups with responsibility-sharing leadership. *Dissertation Abstr.,* 1954, *14,* 737.

**Stotland, E.** Peer groups and reactions to power figures. In D. Cartwright (Ed.), *Studies in social power*. Ann Arbor: University of Michigan, Institute for Social Research, 1959.

**Stotland, E.** *The psychology of hope*. San Francisco: Jossey-Bass, 1969.

**Stotland, E., Cottrell, N. B., & Laing, G.** Group interaction and perceived similarity of members. *J. abnorm. soc. Psychol.*, 1960, *61*, 335–340.

**Stotland, E., Thorley, S., Thomas, E., Cohen, A., & Zander, A.** The effects of group expectations and self-esteem upon self-evaluation. *J. abnorm. soc. Psychol.*, 1957, *54*, 55–63.

**Stotland, E., Zander, A., & Natsoulas, T.** Generalization of interpersonal similarity. *J. abnorm. soc. Psychol.*, 1961, *62*, 250–256.

**Stouffer, S. A.** An analysis of conflicting social norms. *Amer. sociol. Rev.*, 1949, *14*, 707–717.

**Stouffer, S. A., Suchman, E. A., DeVinney, L. C., Star, S. A., & Williams, R. M., Jr.** *The American soldier: adjustment during army life*. Princeton, N.J.: Princeton University Press, 1949.

**Stouffer, S. A., & Toby, J.** Role conflict and personality. *Amer. J. Sociol.*, 1951, *56*, 395–406.

**Strauss, A. L.** The literature on panic. *J. abnorm. soc. Psychol.*, 1944, *39*, 317–328.

**Strauss, G.** Some notes on power equalization. In H. J. Leavitt (Ed.), *The social science of organizations*. Englewood Cliffs, N.J.: Prentice-Hall, 1963.

**Strauss, G.** The personality vs. organization theory. In D. R. Hampton, C. E. Summer, & R. A. Webber (Eds.), *Organizational behavior and the practice of management*. Glenview, Ill.: Scott, Foresman, 1963.

**Strauss, G.** Participative management: a critique. *ILR Res., Cornell Univ.*, 1966, *12*, 3–6.

**Strauss, G., & Rosenstein, E.** Workers' participation: a critical view. *Indus. Relat.*, 1970, *9*, 197–214.

**Stray, H. F.** Leadership traits of girls in girls' camps. *Sociol. soc. Res.*, 1934, *18*, 241–250.

**Streufert, S.** Communicator importance and interpersonal attitudes toward conforming and deviant group members. *J. pers. soc. Psychol.*, 1965, *2*, 242–246.

**Streufert, S., Streufert, S. C., & Castore, C. H.** Leadership in negotiations and the complexity of conceptual structure. *J. appl. Psychol.*, 1968, *52*, 218–223.

**Strickland, L. H.** Need for approval and the components of the ASo score. *Percept. mot. Skills*, 1967, *24*, 875–878.

**Stringer, L. A.** Sensitivity training: an alternative to the T-group method. *Teachers College Record*, 1970, *71*, 633–640.

**Strodtbeck, F. L.** Husband–wife interaction over revealed differences. *Amer. J. Sociol.*, 1951, *16*, 468–473.

**Strodtbeck, F. L., & Hare, A. P.** Bibliography of small group research: from 1900 through 1953. *Sociometry*, 1954, *17*, 107–178.

**Strodtbeck, F. L., & Hook, L. H.** The social dimensions of a twelve man jury team. *Sociometry*, 1961, *24*, 397–415.

**Stromberg, R. P.** Value orientation and leadership behavior of school principals. *Dissertation Abstr.*, 1967, *27*, 2811.

**Strong, E. K.** *Vocational interests of men and women*. Stanford, Calif.: Stanford University Press, 1943.

**Strong, L.** Of time and top management. *Mgmt. Rev.*, 1956, *45*, 486–493.

**Stroud, P. V.** Evaluating a human relations training program. *Personnel*, 1959, *36*, 52–60.

**Strube, M. J., & Garcia, J. E.** A meta-analytic investigation of Fiedler's contingency model of leadership effectiveness. Salt Lake City, Utah: University of Utah, undated.

**Strunk, O.** Empathy: a review of theory and research. *Psychol. Newsltr., NYU*, 1957, *9*, 47–57.

**Strupp, H. H., & Hausman, H. J.** Some correlates of group productivity. *Amer. Psychologist*, 1953, *8*, 443–444.

**Stryker, P.** How participative can management get? *Fortune,* 1956, *54,* 134–136, 217–218, 220.

**Stryker, P.** *The character of the executive.* New York: Harper & Row, 1960.

**Student, K. R.** Supervisory influence and work-group performance. *J. appl. Psychol.,* 1968, *52,* 188–194.

**Stumpf, S.** Leadership behaviors in managing scientists and engineers: a path analytic approach. Unpublished ms., undated.

**Sturmthal, A.** The workers' councils in Poland. *Indus. lab. relat. Rev.,* 1961, *14,* 379–396.

**Sturmthal, A.** *Workers' councils: a study of workplace organization on both sides of the Iron Curtain.* Cambridge, Mass.: Harvard University Press, 1964.

**Suchman, J.** Social sensitivity in the small task-oriented group. *J. abnorm. soc. Psychol.,* 1956, *52,* 75–83.

**Survey Research Center.** Productivity, supervision, and employee morale. Ann Arbor: University of Michigan, 1948.

**Susman, G. I.** The concept of status congruence as a basis to predict task allocations in autonomous work groups. *Admin. sci. Quar.,* 1970, *15,* 164–175.

**Suttell, B. J., & Spector, P.** *Research on the specific leader behavior patterns most effective in influencing group performance.* Washington, D.C.: American Institute for Research, November 1955.

**Svalastoga, K.** Note on leaders' estimates of public opinion. *Publ. opin. Quar.,* 1950, *14,* 767–769.

**Swain, R. L.** Catalytic colleagues in a government R&D organization. Boston: M.I.T., Master's thesis, 1971.

**Sward, K.** Temperament and direction of achievement. *J. soc. Psychol.,* 1933, *4,* 406–429.

**Swartz, J. L.** Analysis of leadership styles of college level head football coaches from five midwestern states. Doctoral dissertation, University of Northern Colorado, Greeley, 1973.

**Sweitzer, R. E.** Role expectations and perceptions of school principals. Stillwater: Oklahoma State University, Technical Report, 1963.

**Sweney, A. B., Fiechtner, L. A., & Samores, R. J.** An integrative factor analysis of leadership measures and theories. *J. Psych.,* 1975, *90,* 75–85.

**Swigart, J. S.** A study of the qualities of leadership and administrative qualifications of thirty-eight women executives. Columbus: Ohio State University, Master's thesis, 1936.

**Swingle, P. G.** Exploitative behavior in non-zero-sum games. *J. pers. soc. Psychol.,* 1970a, *16,* 121–132.

**Swingle, P. G.** *The structure of conflict.* New York: Academic Press, 1970b.

**Switzer, K. A.** Peasant leadership: comparisons of peasant leaders in two Colombian states. *Internat. J. compar. Sociol.,* 1975, *16,* 291–300.

**Sykes, A. J. M.** The effect of a supervisory training course in changing supervisors' perceptions and expectations of the role of management. *Hum. Relat.,* 1962, *15,* 227–243.

**Sykes, A. J. M.** A study in changing the attitudes and stereotypes of industrial workers. *Hum. Relat.,* 1964, *17,* 143–154.

**Symonds, P. M.** Role playing as a diagnostic procedure in the selection of leaders. *Sociatry,* 1947, *1,* 43–50.

**Szilagyi, A. D.** Causal inference between leader reward behavior and subordinate goal attainment, absenteeism, and work satisfaction. Houston, Tex.: University of Houston, working paper, 1979a.

**Szilagyi, A. D.** Reward behavior of male and female leaders: a causal inference analysis. *J. vocat. Behav.,* 1979b.

**Szilagyi, A. D., & Sims, H. P.** The cross-sample stability of the supervisory behavior description questionnaire. *J. appl. Psychol.,* 1974a, *59,* 767–770.

**Szilagyi, A. D., & Sims, H. P.** An exploration of the path-goal theory of leadership in a health care environment. *Acad. Mgmt. J.*, 1974b, *17*, 622–634.

**Tabb, J. Y., & Goldfarb, A.** *Workers' participation in management expectations and experience.* Elmsford, N.Y.: Pergamon, 1970.

**Taft, R.** The ability to judge people. *Psychol. Bull.*, 1955, *52*, 1–23.

**Tagiuri, R.** Value orientations and the relationship of managers and scientists. *Admin. sci. Quar.*, 1965, *10*, 39–51.

**Tagiuri, R.** Person perception. In G. Lindzey & E. Aronson (Eds.), *The handbook of social psychology, vol. 3.* Reading, Mass.: Addison-Wesley, 1969.

**Tagiuri, R., & Kogan, N.** The visibility of interpersonal preferences. *Hum. Relat.*, 1957, *10*, 385–390.

**Tagiuri, R., Kogan, N., & Long, L. M. K.** Differentiation of sociometric choice and status relations in a group. *Psychol. Rep.*, 1958, *4*, 523–526.

**Tagiuri, R., & Petrullo, L.** *Person perception and interpersonal behavior.* Stanford, Calif.: Stanford University Press, 1958.

**Talland, G. A.** The assessment of group opinion by leaders and their influence on its formation. *J. abnorm. soc. Psychol.*, 1954, *49*, 431–434.

**Talland, G. A.** Rate of speaking as a group norm. *Hum. Org.*, 1957, *15*, 8–10.

**Tanimoto, R. H.** A field study of MBO in a utility company. Malibu, Calif.: Pepperdine University, School of Business and Management, MBA thesis, 1977.

**Tannenbaum, A. S.** The concept of organizational control. *J. soc. Issues*, 1956a, *12*, 50–60.

**Tannenbaum, A. S.** Control structure and union functions. *Amer. J. Sociol.*, 1956b, *61*, 536–545.

**Tannenbaum, A. S.** The relationship between personality and group structure. In R. Likert (Ed.), Effective supervision: an adaptive and relative process. *Personnel Psychol.*, 1958, *11*, 317–322.

**Tannenbaum, A. S.** An event-structure approach to social power and to the problem of power comparability. *Behav. Sci.*, 1962, *7*, 315–331.

**Tannenbaum, A. S.** Control in organizations: individual adjustment and organizational performance. Seminar on his research in management controls, Palo Alto, Calif.: Stanford University, 1963.

**Tannenbaum, A. S.** *Social psychology of the work organization.* San Francisco: Wadsworth, 1966.

**Tannenbaum, A. S.** *Control in organizations.* New York: McGraw-Hill, 1968.

**Tannenbaum, A. S.** *Hierarchy in organizations: an international comparison.* San Francisco: Jossey-Bass, 1974.

**Tannenbaum, A. S., & Allport, F. H.** Personality structure and group structure: an interpretative study of their relationships through event-structure analysis. *J. abnorm. soc. Psychol.*, 1956, *53*, 272–280.

**Tannenbaum, A. S., & Bachman, J. G.** Attitude uniformity and role in a voluntary organization. *Hum. Relat.*, 1966, *19*, 309–323.

**Tannenbaum, A. S., & Georgopoulos, B. S.** The distribution of control in formal organizations. *Soc. Forces*, 1957, *36*, 44–50.

**Tannenbaum, A. S., & Smith, C. G.** Effects of member influence in an organization: phenomenology versus organization structure. *J. abnorm. soc. Psychol.*, 1964, *69*, 401–410.

**Tannenbaum, D. E.** Relation of executive leadership to the factor of external authority: a study of board-executive relationships in five family agencies. *Dissertation Abstr.*, 1959, *22*, 1239.

**Tannenbaum, R., Kallejian, V., & Weschler, I. R.** Training managers for leadership. *Instructions on industrial relations*, UCLA, 1954, No. 35.

**Tannenbaum, R., & Massarik, F.** Participation by subordinates in the managerial decision-making process. *Canad. J. econ. pol. Sci.*, 1950, *16*, 408–418.

**Tannenbaum, R., & Schmidt, W. H.** How to choose a leadership pattern. *Harvard bus. Rev.*, 1958, *36*, 95–101.

**Tannenbaum, R., Weschler, I. R., & Massarik, F.** *Leadership and organization.* New York: McGraw-Hill, 1961.

**Tansik, D. A.** Influences of organizational goal structure upon participant evaluations. *Proceedings of the Academy of Management*, 1971.

**Tarnapol, L.** Personality differences between leaders and nonleaders. *Personnel J.*, 1958, *37*, 57–60.

**Tarnowieski, D.** *The changing success ethic.* New York: American Management Association, AMACOM survey report series, 1973.

**Taub, R. P.** *Bureaucrats under stress.* Berkeley: University of California Press, 1969.

**Taussig, F. W., & Barker, W. S.** American corporations and their executives: a statistical inquiry. *Quar. J. Econ.*, 1925, *40*, 1.

**Taussig, F. W., & Joslyn, C. S.** *American business leaders: a study in social origins and social stratification.* New York: Macmillan, 1932.

**Tavris, C.** Men and women report their views on masculinity. *Psychol. Today*, 1977, *10*, 34–42, 82.

**Taylor, B., & Lippitt, G. L. (Eds.).** *Management development and training handbook.* London: McGraw-Hill, 1975.

**Taylor, D. W., Berry, P. C., & Block, C. H.** Does group participation when using brainstorming facilitate or inhibit creative thinking? *Admin. sci. Quar.*, 1958, *3*, 23–47.

**Taylor, J. C.** *The conditioning effects of technology on organizational behavior in planned social change.* Ann Arbor: University of Michigan, Institute for Social Research, Technical Report, 1969.

**Taylor, J. C.** *Technology and planned organizational change.* Ann Arbor: University of Michigan, Institute for Social Research, 1971.

**Taylor, J. C., & Bowers, D. G.** *Survey of organizations: toward a machine-scored standardized questionnaire instrument.* Ann Arbor: Institute for Social Research, 1972.

**Taylor, K. F.** Some doubts about sensitivity training. *Australian Psychol.*, 1967, *1*, 171–179.

**Taylor, M., Crook, R., & Dropkin, S.** Assessing emerging leadership behavior in small discussion groups. *J. educ. Psychol.*, 1961, *52*, 12–18.

**Taylor, M. S., & Ilgen, D. R.** Employees' reactions to male and female managers: is there a difference? *Proceedings of the Academy of Management*, 1979.

**Tead, O.** The technique of creative leadership. *In Human nature and management.* New York: McGraw-Hill, 1929.

**Tead, O.** *The art of leadership.* New York: McGraw-Hill, 1935.

**Tedeschi, J. T., & Kian, M.** Cross-cultural study of the TAT assessment for achievement motivation: Americans and Persians. *J. soc. Psychol.*, 1962, *58*, 227–234.

**Tedeschi, J. T., Lindskold, S., Horai, J., & Gahagan, J. P.** Social power and the credibility of promises. *J. pers. soc. Psychol.*, 1969, *13*, 253–261.

**Teller, L.** *Worker participation in business management.* Washington, D.C.: Government Printing Office, 1961.

**Tenopyr, M. L.** The comparative validity of selected leadership scales relative to success in production management. *Personnel Psychol.*, 1969, *22*, 77–85.

**Terauds, A., Altman, I., & McGrath, J. E.** *A bibliography of small group research.* Arlington, Va.: Human Sciences Research, 1960.

**Terborg, J. R.** Women in management: a research review. *J. appl. Psychol.*, 1977, *62*, 647–664.

**Terborg, J. R., & Ilgen, D. R.** A theoretical approach to sex discrimination in traditionally masculine occupations. *Org. behav. hum. Perform.*, 1975, *13*, 352–376.

**Terborg, J. R., Peters, L. H., Ilgen, D. R., & Smith, F.** Organizational and personal correlates of attitudes toward women as managers. *Acad. Mgmt. J.*, 1977, *20*, 89–100.

**Terhune, K. W.** The effects of personality in cooperation and conflict. In P. Swingle (Ed.), *The structure of conflict*. New York: Academic Press, 1970.

**Terman, L. M.** A preliminary study of the psychology and pedagogy of leadership. *Ped. Sem.*, 1904, *11*, 413–451.

**Terman, L. M.** *Mental and physical traits of a thousand gifted children*. Stanford, Calif.: Stanford University Press, 1925.

**Terreberry, S.** The evolution of organizational environments. *Admin. sci. Quar.*, 1968, *12*, 590–613.

**Terrell, G., & Shreffler, J.** A developmental study of leadership. *J. educ. Res.*, 1958, *52*, 69–72.

**Thelen, H. A.** *Dynamics of groups at work*. Chicago: University of Chicago Press, 1954.

**Thelen, H. A. et al.** *Methods for studying work and emotionality in group operation*. Chicago: University of Chicago, Human Dynamics Laboratory, 1954.

**Thelen, H. A., Hawkes, T. H., & Strattner, N. S.** *Role perception and task performance of experimentally composed small groups*. Chicago: University of Chicago, Graduate School of Education, 1965.

**Thelen, H. A., & Whitehall, J.** Three frames of reference: the description of climate. *Hum. Relat.*, 1949, *2*, 159–176.

**Theodorson, G. A.** The relationship between leadership and popularity roles in small groups. *Amer. sociol. Rev.*, 1957, *22*, 58–67.

**Thiagarajan, K. M.** A cross-cultural study of the relationships between personal values and managerial behavior. Rochester: University of Rochester, Management Research Center, Technical Report No. 23, 1968.

**Thiagarajan, K. M., & Deep, S. D.** A study of supervisor–subordinate influence and satisfaction in four cultures. *J. soc. Psychol.*, 1970, *82*, 173–180.

**Thibaut, J. W.** An experimental study of the cohesiveness of underprivileged groups. *Hum. Relat.*, 1950, *3*, 251–278.

**Thibaut, J. W., & Coules, J.** The role of communication in the reduction of interpersonal hostility. *J. abnorm. soc. Psych.*, 1952, *47*, 770–777.

**Thibaut, J. W., & Faucheux, C.** The development of contractual norms in a beginning situation under two types of stress. *J. exp. soc. Psychol.*, 1965, *1*, 89–102.

**Thibaut, J. W., & Gruder, C. L.** Formation of contractual agreements between parties of unequal power. *J. pers. soc. Psychol.*, 1969, *11*, 59–65.

**Thibaut, J. W., & Kelley, H. H.** *The social psychology of groups*. New York: Wiley, 1959.

**Thibaut, J. W., & Riecken, H. W.** Some determinants and consequences of the perception of social causality. *J. Pers.*, 1955a, *24*, 113–133.

**Thibaut, J. W., & Riecken, H. W.** Authoritarianism, status, and the communication of aggression. *Hum. Relat.*, 1955b, *8*, 95–120.

**Thibaut, J. W., & Strickland, L. H.** Psychological set and social conformity. *J. Pers.*, 1956, *25*, 115–129.

**Thomas, E. J.** Effects of facilitative role interdependence on group functioning. *Hum. Relat.*, 1957, *10*, 347–366.

**Thomas, E. J., & Fink, C. F.** Effects of group size. *Psychol. Bull.*, 1963, *60*, 371–384.

**Thomas, J. M.** The sensitivity hypothesis in laboratory education: its effect on the organization. *Proceedings of the Industrial Relations Research Association*, 1969.

**Thompson, D. E.** Favorable self-perception, perceived supervisory style, and job satisfaction. *J. appl. Psychol.*, 1971, *55*, 349–352.

**Thompson, G. G.** The social and emotional development of pre-school children under two types of educational programs. *Psychol. Monogr.*, 1944, *56*, 1–29.

**Thompson, J.** *Organizations in action.* New York: McGraw-Hill, 1967.

**Thompson, J. D.** Authority and power in "identical" organizations. *Amer. J. Sociol.*, 1956, *62*, 290–301.

**Thompson, J. D.** Organizations in action: social science bases of administrative theory. *Proceedings of the Amer. Psychol. Assn.*, 1969.

**Thorndike, E. L.** Education for initiative and originality. *Teach. Coll. Rec.*, 1916, *17*, 405–416.

**Thorndike, E. L.** The relation between intellect and morality in rulers. *Amer. J. Sociol.*, 1936, *45*, 321–334.

**Thorndike, E. L.** How may we improve the selection, training and life-work of leaders? *Teach. Coll. Rec.*, 1939, *40*, 593–605.

**Thorndike, E. L.** Human nature and the social order. New York: Macmillan, 1940.

**Thorndike, R. L.** On what type of task will a group do well? *J. abnorm. soc. Psychol.*, 1938, *33*, 409–413.

**Thornton, A., & Freedman, D.** Consistency of sex role attitudes of women, 1962–1977: evidence from a panel study. *Amer. sociol. Rev.*, 1979, *44*, 831–842.

**Thornton, G. C.** The relationship between supervisory and self-appraisals of executive performance. *Personnel Psychol.*, 1968, *21*, 441–455.

**Thorsrud, E., & Emery, F. E.** Industrial democracy in Norway. *Indus. Relat*, 1970, *9*, 187–196.

**Thrasher, F.** *The gang.* Chicago: University of Chicago Press, 1927.

**Throop, R. K.** An explanatory survey of teacher job satisfaction: a path analysis. Doctoral dissertation, Syracuse University, Syracuse, N.Y., 1972.

**Thurstone, L. L.** *A factorial study of perception.* Chicago: University of Chicago Press, 1944.

**Thurstone, L. L., & Chave, E. J.** *The measurement of attitude.* Chicago: University of Chicago Press, 1929.

**Tichy, N.** An analysis of clique formation and structure in organizations. *Admin. sci. Quar.*, 1973, *8*, 194–208.

**Timaeus, E., & Lück, H. E.** Stereotype Erwartungen bei der Wahrnehmung von Führungskräften in der Wirtschaft. *Psychol. Rundschau*, 1970, *21*, 39–43.

**Timmons, W. M.** Some outcomes of participation in dramatics: II. Likeability and cooperativeness: relationships between outcomes. *J. soc. Psychol.*, 1944, *19–20*, 35–51.

**Tinbergen, N.** *Social behavior in animals.* London: Methuen Monograph, 1953.

**Titus, C. H.** *The process of leadership.* Dubuque, Iowa: Brown, 1950.

**Titus, H. E., & Goss, R. G.** Psychometric comparison of old and young supervisors. *Psychol. Rep.*, 1969, *24*, 727–733.

**Titus, H. E., & Hollander, E. P.** The California F-Scale in psychological research. *Psychol. Bull.*, 1957, *54*, 47–64.

**Toby, J.** Some variables in role conflict analysis. *Soc. Forces*, 1952, *30*, 323–327.

**Toch, H., & Smith, H. C.** *Social perception.* Princeton, N.J.: Van Nostrand, 1968.

**Toki, K.** Führer-Gefolgschaftsstruktur in der Schulklasse. (Leader-follower structure in school classes.) *Jap. J. Psychol.*, 1935, *10*, 27–56.

**Tomekovic, T.** Levels of knowledge of requirements as a motivation factor in the work situation. *Hum. Relat.*, 1962, *15*, 197–216.

**Tornow, W. W., & Pinto, P. R.** The development of a managerial job taxonomy: a system for describing, classifying, and evaluating executive positions. *J. appl. Psychol.*, 1976, *61*, 410–418.

**Toronto, R. S.** General systems theory applied to the study of organizational change. Doctoral dissertation, University of Michigan, Ann Arbor, 1972.

**Torrance, E. P.** Survival research. *HRRL Memo. Rep. No. 29*, 1952.

**Torrance, E. P.** Methods of conducting critiques of group problem-solving performance. *J. appl. Psychol.*, 1953, *37*, 394–398.

**Torrance, E. P.** Some consequences of power differences on decisions in B-26 crews (Res. Bull. 54–128). San Antonio, Tex.: USAF Personnel & Training Research Center, 1954.

**Torrance, E. P.** The behavior of small groups under the stress conditions of "survival." *Amer. sociol. Rev.*, 1954, *19*, 751–755.

**Torrance, E. P.** Some consequences of power differences in permanent and temporary three-man groups. In P. Hare, E. F. Borgatta, & R. F. Bales (Eds.), *Small groups*. New York: Knopf, 1955a.

**Torrance, E. P.** Perception of group functioning as a predictor of group performance. *J. soc. Psychol.*, 1955b, *42*, 271–281.

**Torrance, E. P.** Group decision-making and disagreement. *Soc. Forces*, 1956/57, *35*, 314–318.

**Torrance, E. P.** An experimental evaluation of "no-pressure" influence. *J. appl. Psychol.*, 1959a, *43*, 109–113.

**Torrance, E. P.** The influence of experienced members of small groups on the behavior of the inexperienced. *J. soc. Psychol.*, 1959b, *49*, 249–257.

**Torrance, E. P.** A theory of leadership and interpersonal behavior under stress. In L. Petrullo & B. Bass (Eds.), *Leadership and interpersonal behavior*. New York: Holt, Rinehart & Winston, 1961.

**Torrance, E. P., & Aliotti, N. C.** Accuracy, task effectiveness, and emergence of a social-emotional resolver as a function of one- and two-expert groups. *J. Psychol.*, 1965, *61*, 161–170.

**Torrance, E. P., & Mason, R.** The indigenous leader in changing attitudes and behavior. *Internat. J. Sociometry*, 1956, *1*, 23–28.

**Torrance, E. P., & Mason, R.** Instructor effort to influence: an experimental evaluation of six approaches. *J. educ. Psychol.*, 1958, *49*, 211–218.

**Torrance, E. P., & Staff.** Survival research. A report of the fourth year of development. Reno, Nev.: Stead AFB, CRL Field Unit No. 2, 1955.

**Tosi, H.** A reexamination of personality as a determinant of the effects of participation. *Personnel Psychol.*, 1970, *23*, 91–99.

**Tosi, H.** Organization stress as a moderator in the relationship between influence and role response. *Acad. Mgmt. J.*, 1971, *14*, 7–20.

**Tosi, H.** The effect of interaction of leader behavior and subordinate authoritarianism. *Personnel Psychol.*, 1973, *26*, 339–350.

**Tosi, H., Aldag, R., & Storey, R.** On the measurement of the environment: an assessment of the Lawrence and Lorsch environment uncertainty questionnaire. *Admin. sci. Quar.*, 1973, *18*, 27–36.

**Touchet, R. E.** Leadership action: the transmission of information exclusively possessed. Privately published, 1949.

**Touhey, J.** Effects of additional women professionals on ratings of occupational prestige and desirability. *J. pers. soc. Psychol.*, 1974, *29*, 86–89.

**Trahey, J.** *Women and power*. New York: Avon Books, 1977.

**Trapp, E. P.** Leadership and popularity as a function of behavioral predictions. *J. abnorm. soc. Psychol.*, 1955, *51*, 452–457.

**Trattnor, J.** Comparison of three methods for assembling aptitude test batteries. *Personnel Psychol.*, 1963, *16*, 230.

**Tresemer, D.** Do women fear success? *Signs*, 1976, *1*, 863–874.

**Triandis, H. C.** Differential perception of certain jobs and people by managers, clerks and workers in industry. *J. appl. Psychol.*, 1959a, *43*, 221–225.

**Triandis, H. C.** Categories of thought of managers, clerks, and workers in an industry. *J. appl. Psychol.*, 1959b, *43*, 338–344.

**Triandis, H. C.** A critique and experimental design for the study of the relationship between productivity and satisfaction. *Psychol. Bull.*, 1959c, *56*, 309–312.

**Triandis, H. C.** Comparative factorial analysis of job semantic structures of managers and workers. *J. appl. Psychol.*, 1960, *44*, 297–302.

**Triandis, H. C.** Factors affecting employee selection in two cultures. *J. appl. Psychol.*, 1963, *47*, 89–96.

**Triandis, H. C.** Interpersonal relations in international organizations. *Org. behav. hum. Perform.*, 1967, *2*, 26–55.

**Triandis, H.** (Ed.), *Handbook of cross-cultural psychology.* Boston: Allyn & Bacon, 1980.

**Triandis, H. C., & Malpass, R. S.** Studies of black and white interaction in job settings. *J. appl. soc. Psychol.*, 1971, *1*, 101–117.

**Triandis, H. C., Mikesell, E. H., & Ewen, R. B.** Some cognitive factors affecting group creativity. Urbana: University of Illinois, Group Effectiveness Research Laboratory, Technical Report 5, 1962.

**Triandis, H. C., Vassiliou, V., & Thomanek, E. K.** Social status as a determinant of respect and friendship acceptance. *Sociometry*, 1966, *29*, 396–405.

**Trice, H. M.** A methodology for evaluating conference leadership training. *ILR Res., Cornell Univ.*, 1959, *5*, 2–5.

**Trieb, S. E.** An analysis of supermarket managerial leadership and its relation to measures of organizational effectiveness. Doctoral dissertation, Ohio State University, Columbus, 1967.

**Trieb, S. E., & Marion, B. W.** *Managerial leadership and the human capital of the firm.* Columbus: Ohio State University, College of Agriculture, 1969.

**Trimble, C.** Teachers' conceptions of leadership behavior of principals as related to principal's perception of this involvement in the decision-making process. *Dissertation Abstr.*, 1968, *28*, 4432–4433.

**Triplett, N.** The dynamogenic factors in pacemaking and competition. *Amer. J. Psychol.*, 1898, *9*, 507–533.

**Triplett, N.** The psychology of conjuring perceptions. *Amer. J. Psychol.*, 1900, *11*, 439–510.

**Trist, E. L., & Bamforth, V.** Some social and psychological consequences of the longwall method of coal-getting. *Hum. Relat.*, 1951, *4*, 3–38.

**Trist, E. L., Higgin, G. W., Murray, H., & Pollock, A. B.** *Organizational choice.* London: Tavistock, 1963.

**Trittipoe, T., G., & Hahn, C. P.** Situational problems for leadership training. Part I—Development and evaluation of situational problems. Washington, D.C.: American Institute for Research, 1961 (mimeo).

**Trivedi, D. N.** Modernization, rationality, opinion leadership or compartmentalization of spheres of activity. *Man in India*, 1974, *54*, 271–280.

**Tronc, K., & Enns, F.** Promotional aspirations and differential role perceptions. *Alberta J. educ. Res.*, 1969, *15*, 169–183.

**Trow, D. B.** Autonomy and job satisfaction in task-oriented groups. *J. abnorm. soc. Psychol.*, 1957, *53*, 204–209.

**Trow, D. B.** Membership succession and team performance. *Hum. Relat.*, 1960, *13*, 259–269.

**Trow, D. B.** Executive succession in small companies. *Admin. sci. Quar.*, 1961, *6*, 228–239.

**Trow, D. B., & Herschdorfer, G.** An experiment on the status incongruence phenomenon. Binghamton: State University of New York, Technical Report, 1965.

**Troxell, J. P.** Elements in job satisfaction: a study of attitudes among different occupational and status groups. *Personnel*, 1954, *31*, 199–205.

**Trumbo, D. A.** Individual and group correlates of attitudes toward work related change. *J. appl. Psychol.*, 1961, *45*, 338–344.

**Tryon, C. M.** Evaluations of adolescent personality by adolescents. *Monogr. soc. res. child Develop.*, 1939, *4*, No. 4.

**Tscheulin, D.** Leader behavior measurement in German industry. *J. appl. Psychol.*, 1973, *57*, 28–31.

**Tsutomu, O.** *Bijinesu man (Business man)*. Tokyo: San'ichi shobō, 1964.

**Tubbs, S. L., & Baird, J. W.** *The open person.* Columbus, Ohio: Charles E. Merrill, 1976.

**Tubbs, S. L., & Hain, T.** Managerial communication and its relation to total organizational effectiveness. *Proceedings of the Academy of Management*, 1979.

**Tubbs, S. L., & Moss, S.** Organizational communication. In Tubbs, S. L., & Moss, S. (Eds.), *Human Communication.* New York: Random House, 1978.

**Tubbs, S. L., & Porter, R. G.** *Predictors of grievance activity.* Detroit: General Motors Corporation, Unpublished Technical Report, 1978.

**Tubbs, S. L., & Widgery, R. N.** When productivity lags, check at the top: are key managers really communicating? *Mgmt. Rev.*, 1978, *67*, 20–25.

**Tuchman, B. W.** *Stilwell and the American experience in China, 1911–45.* New York: Macmillan, 1971.

**Tuckman, B. W.** Developmental sequence in small groups. *Psychol. Bull*, 1965, *63*, 384–399.

**Tumes, J.** The contingency theory of leadership: a behavioral investigation. *Proceedings of the Eastern Academy of Management*, 1972.

**Tung, R. L.** U.S. multinationals: a study of their selection and training procedures for overseas assignments. Unpublished ms., undated.

**Tupes, E. C., Carp, A., & Borg, W. R.** Performance in role playing situations as related to leadership and personality measures. *Sociometry*, 1958, *21*, 165–179.

**Turk, H.** Instrumental values and the popularity of instrumental leaders. *Soc. Forces*, 1961, *39*, 252–260.

**Turk, H., Hartley, E. L., & Shaw, D. M.** The expectation of social influence. *J. soc. Psychol.*, 1962, *58*, 23–29.

**Turk, T., & Turk, H.** Group interaction in a formal setting: the case of the triad. *Sociometry*, 1962, *25*, 48–55.

**Turner, A. N.** Foreman—key to worker morale. *Harvard bus. Rev.*, 1954, *32*, 76–86.

**Turner, A. N.** Interaction and sentiment in the foreman–worker relationship. *Hum. Org.*, 1955, *14*, 10–16.

**Turner, A. N.** Foreman, job, and company. *Hum. Relat.*, 1957, *10*, 99–112.

**Turner, A. N., & Lawrence, P. R.** *Industrial jobs and the worker.* Boston: Harvard University, Graduate School of Business Administration, 1965.

**Turner, A. N., & Miclette, A. L.** Sources of satisfaction in repetitive work. *Occup. Psychol.*, 1962, *36*, 215–231.

**Turner, N. W.** *Effective leadership in small groups.* Valley Forge, Pa.: Judson Press, 1977.

**Turner, W. W.** Dimensions of foreman performance: a factor analysis of criterion measures. *J. appl. Psychol.*, 1960, *44*, 216–223.

**Tushman, M. L.** A political approach to organizations: a review and rationale. *Acad. Mgmt. Rev.*, 1977, *2*, 206–216.

**Tutoo, D. N.** The mask effect of some variables on leadership assessment. *Manas*, 1970, *17*, 77–83.

**Tversky, A., & Kahneman, D.** Belief in the law of small numbers. *Psychol. Bull.*, 1971, *76*, 105–110.

**Udell, J. G.** An empirical test of hypothesis relating to span of control. *Admin. sci. Quar.*, 1967, *12*, 420–439.

**Uesgi, T. T., & Vinacke, W. E.** Strategy in a feminine game. *Sociometry*, 1963, *26*, 75–88.

**Uhlman, F. W., & Fiedler, F. E.** Choices of fraternity presidents for leadership and maintenance roles. *Psychol. Rep.*, 1958, *4*, 498.

**Ulin, R. D.** African leadership: national goals and the values of Botswana University students. *Compara. Educ.*, 1976, *12*, 145–155.

**Ulrich, D. N., Booz, D. R., & Lawrence, P. R.** *Management behavior and foreman attitude.* Boston: Harvard University, Graduate School of Business Administration, 1950.

**Underwood, W. J.** Evaluation of laboratory training. *Train. Directors J.*, 1965, *19*, 34–40.

**Updegraff, H.** *Inventory of youth in Pennsylvania.* Washington, D.C.: American Youth Commission of the American Council on Education, 1936.

**Uris, A.** *Techniques of leadership.* New York: McGraw-Hill, 1953.

**Uris, A.** Job stress and the executive. *Mgmt. Rev.*, 1958, *47*, 4–12.

**Urry, V. W., & Nicewander, W. A.** Factor analysis of the commander's evaluation report. *U.S. Army Enlisted Evaluation Center tech. res. Study*, 1966.

**Urwick, L. F.** *Leadership and morale.* Columbus: Ohio State University, College of Commerce & Administration, 1953.

**Urwick, L. F.** *Leadership in the twentieth century.* New York: Pitman, 1957.

**U.S. Army.** *The personnel system of the United States Army*, vol. 2. Washington, D.C.: Adjutant General's Office, 1919.

**USA, AGO, PRB.** A trend study of officer efficiency ratings for the period 1922–1945. *PRS Rep. 896*, 1952.

**USAF, ATC, HRRC.** *Aspects of noncommissioned officer leadership.* Lackland AFB, Tex.: Technical Report No. 52–3, 1952.

**U.S. Department of the Army.** *The executive: philosophy, problems, practices. A bibliographic survey.* Washington, D.C.: Government Printing Office, 1966.

**U.S. Department of Defense.** *Project one hundred thousand: characteristics and performance of "new standards" men.* Washington, D.C.: Assistant Secretary of Defense, Manpower, and Reserve Affairs, 1969.

**U.S. Department of Commerce.** The social and economic status of Negroes in the United States, 1970. BLS Report No. 394, July 1971.

**U.S. Department of Labor.** The Negroes in the United States: their economic and social situation. Bulletin No. 1511, June 1966.

**U.S. Department of Labor.** *Manpower report of the President*, 1970.

**U.S. Department of Labor, Bureau of Labor Statistics.** *U.S. working women: a data book.* Washington, D.C.: U.S. Bureau of Statistics, 1977.

**U.S. Department of Labor.** *Women in the labor force: some new data series.* Washington, D.C.: U.S. Bureau of Statistics, 1979.

**U.S. Interagency Advisory Group.** *Annotated bibliography on conference leadership and participation.* Washington, D.C.: U.S. Civil Service Commission, 1958.

**Utecht, R. E., & Heier, W. D.** The contingency model and successful military leadership. *Acad. Mgmt. J.*, 1976, *19*, 606–618.

**Utterback, W. E.** The influence of style of moderation on the outcomes of discussion. *Quar. J. Speech*, 1958, *44*, 149–152.

**Vagts, A.** Age and field command. *Military Rev.*, Ft. Leavenworth, 1942, *22*, 36–38.

**Valenzi, E. R., & Bass, B. M.** The Bass-Valenzi Management Styles Profile: a computerized systems survey feedback procedure. *Proceedings of the Academy of Management,* 1975.

**Valenzi, E. R., & Dessler, G.** Relationships of leader behavior, subordinate role ambiguity and subordinate job satisfaction. *Acad. Mgmt. J.,* 1978, *21,* 671–678.

**Valenzi, E. R., Miller, J. A., Eldridge, L. D., Irons, P. W., Solomon, R. J., & Klauss, R. E.** Individual differences, structure, task, and external environment and leader behavior: a summary. Rochester, N.Y.: University of Rochester, Management Research Center, Technical Report No. 49, 1972.

**Valiquet, M. I.** Individual change in management development programs. *J. appl. behav. Sci.,* 1968, *4,* 313–325.

**Van de Vall, M., & Bolas, C.** Applied social discipline research or social policy research: the emergence of a professional paradigm in sociological research. *Amer. Sociol.,* 1980, *15,* 128–137.

**Van de Ven, A. H.** On the nature, formation, and maintenance of relations among organizations. *Acad. Mgmt. Rev.,* 1976, *2,* 34–53.

**Van Dusen, A. C.** Measuring leadership ability. *Personnel Psychol.,* 1948, *1,* 67–79.

**Van Laningham, G.** The study of college leaders. Terre Haute: Indiana State College, Master's thesis, 1939.

**Van Meir, E. J.** Leadership behavior of male and female elementary principals. *Dissertation Abstr. Internat.,* 1972, *32,* 3643.

**Vannoy, J., & Morrissette, J. O.** Group structure, effectiveness, and individual morale. *Org. behav. hum. Perform.,* 1969, *4,* 299–307.

**Vansina, L. S., & Taillieu, T. C.** Comparative study of the characteristics of Flemish graduates planning their careers in national or international organizations. In B. M. Bass, R. C. Cooper, & J. A. Haas (Eds.), *Managing for accomplishment.* Lexington, Mass.: D. C. Heath, 1970.

**Van Zelst, R. H.** Worker popularity and job satisfaction. *Personnel Psych.,* 1951, *4,* 405–412.

**Van Zelst, R. H.** Sociometrically selected work teams increase production. *Personnel Psychol.,* 1952, *5,* 175–185.

**Van Zelst, R. H.** Empathy test scores of union leaders. *J. appl. Psychol.,* 1952, *36,* 293–295.

**Vaughan, W., & McGinnies, E.** Some biographical determiners of participation in group discussion. *J. appl. Psychol.,* 1957, *41,* 179–185.

**Vaught, G. M.** The relationship of role identification and ego strength to sex differences in the rod-and-frame test. *J. Pers.,* 1965, *33,* 271–283.

**Vecchio, R. P.** LPC as a measure of socio-emotional and task orientation. Unpublished ms. 1974.

**Vecchio, R. P.** Effects of interpersonal attraction, leadership style, and authoritarianism on decision making. *Proceedings of the Midwest Psychological Association,* 1975.

**Vecchio, R. P.** An empirical examination of the validity of Fiedler's model of leadership effectiveness. *Org. behav. hum. Perform.,* 1977, *19,* 180–206.

**Vecchio, R. P.** A dyadic interpretation of the contingency model of leadership effectiveness. *Acad. Mgmt. J.,* 1979, *22,* 590–600.

**Vengroff, R.** Popular participation and the administration of rural development: the case of Botswana. *Hum. Organ.,* 1974, *33,* 303–309.

**Verba, S.** *Small groups and political behavior: a study of leadership.* Princeton, N.J.: Princeton University Press, 1961.

**Veroff, J.** Development and validation of a projective measure of power motivation. *J. abnorm. soc. Psychol.,* 1957, *54,* 1–8.

**Veroff, J., Atkinson, J. W., Feld, S. E., & Gurin, G.** The use of thematic apperception to assess motivation in a nationwide interview study. *Psychol. Monogr.,* 1960, No. 12.

**Vertreace, W. C., & Simmins, C. H.** Attempted leadership in the leaderless group discussion as a function of motivation and ego involvement. *J. per. soc. Psychol.*, 1971, *19*, 285–289.

**Vicino, F., & Bass, B. M.** Lifespace variables and managerial success. *J. appl. Psychol.*, 1978, *63*, 81–88.

**Vicino, F. L., Krusell, J., Bass, B. M., Deci, E. L., & Landy, D. A.** The impact of PROCESS: self-administered exercises for personal and interpersonal development. *J. appl. behav. Sci.*, 1973, *9*, 737–757.

**Vielhaber, D. P., & Gottheil, E.** First impressions and subsequent ratings of performance. *Psychol. Rep.*, 1965, *17*, 916.

**Vinacke, W. E., & Arkoff, A.** An experimental study of coalitions in the triad. *Amer. sociol. Rev.*, 1957, *22*, 406–414.

**Vinson, E., & Mitchell, T. R.** Differences in motivational predictors and criterion measures for black and white employees. *Proceedings of the Academy of Management*, 1975.

**Viteles, M. S.** *Motivation and morale in industry*. New York: Norton, 1953.

**Viteles, M. S.** The long-range impact of a programme of humanistic studies for business executives on managerial attitudes and behavior. *Internat. rev. appl. Psychol.*, 1971, *20*, 5–24.

**Vogel, S. R., Broverman, I. K., Broverman, D. M., Clarkson, F. E., & Rosenkrantz, P. S.** Maternal employment and perception of sex roles among college students. *Devel. Psychol.*, 1970, *3*, 381–384.

**Vonachen, H. A., et al.** A comprehensive mental hygiene program at Caterpillar Tractor Co. *Indust. Med.*, 1946, *15*, 179–184.

**Von Bertalanffy, L.** General systems theory. *General systems*. Yearbook of the Society for the Advancement of General System Theory, 1956, *1*, 1–10.

**Von Bertalanffy, L.** General system theory—a critical review. *General systems. Yearbook of the Society for the Advancement of for General Systems Research*, 1962, *7*, 1–20.

**Vough, C.** *Tapping the human potential: a strategy for productivity*. New York: AMACOM, American Management Association, 1975.

**Vroom, V. H.** Some personality determinants of the effects of participation. *J. abnorm. soc. Psychol.*, 1959, *59*, 322–327.

**Vroom, V. H.** *Some personality determinants of the effects of participation*. Englewood Cliffs, N.J.: Prentice-Hall, 1960a.

**Vroom, V. H.** The effects of attitudes on perception of organizational goals. *Hum. Relat.*, 1960b, *13*, 229–240.

**Vroom, V. H.** Ego-involvement, job satisfaction, and job performance. *Personnel Psychol.*, 1962, *15*, 159–178.

**Vroom, V. H.** *Work and motivation*. New York: McGraw-Hill, 1964.

**Vroom, V. H.** *Motivation in management*. New York: American Foundation for Management Research, 1965.

**Vroom, V. H.** Organizational choice: a study of pre- and post-decision processes. *Org. behav. hum. Perform.*, 1966, *1*, 212–225.

**Vroom, V. H.** Decision making and the leadership process. *J. contem. Bus.*, 1974, *3*, 47–64.

**Vroom, V. H.** A new look at managerial decision making. *Org. Dynamics*, 1974, *5*, 66–80.

**Vroom, V. H.** Can leaders learn to lead? *Org. Dynam.*, 1976a, *4*, 17–28.

**Vroom, V. H.** Leadership. In M. D. Dunnette (Ed.), *Handbook of industrial and organizational psychology*. Chicago: Rand McNally, 1976b.

**Vroom, V. H., & Jago, A. G.** Decision making as a social process: normative and descriptive models of leader behavior. *Decision Sci.*, 1974, *5*, 743–769.

**Vroom, V. H., & Jago, A. G.** On the validity of the Vroom-Yetton model. *J. appl. Psychol.*, 1978, *63*, 151–162.

**Vroom, V. H., & Mann, F. C.** Leader authoritarianism and employee attitudes. *Personnel*

*Psychol.*, 1960, *13*, 125–140.

**Vroom, V. H., & Pahl, B.** Relationship between age and risk taking among managers. *J. appl. Psychol.*, 1971, *55*, 399–405.

**Vroom, V. H., & Yetton, P. W.** *Leadership and decision-making.* Pittsburgh: University of Pittsburgh Press, 1973.

**Vroom, V. H., & Yetton, P. W.** *Leadership and decision-making.* New York: Wiley, 1974.

**Vrooman, T. H.** The perceptions and expectations of superintendents and their high school principals with regard to leadership style and delegated formal task-performance. *Dissertation Abstr. Internat.*, 1971, *31*, 6326–6327.

**Waaler, R.** *Management development: a Norwegian experiment.* Boston: Harvard University, Graduate School of Business Administration, 1962.

**Waddell, H. L.** How to make your workers want to become foremen. In *Practical approaches to supervisory and executive development.* New York: American Management Association, 1952.

**Wager, L. W.** Leadership style, hierarchical influence, and supervisory role obligations. *Admin., sci. Quar.*, 1965, *9*, 391–420.

**Wager, L. W.** The expansion of organizational authority and conditions affecting its denial. *Sociometry*, 1971, *34*, 91–113.

**Wagstaff, L. H.** The relationship between administrative systems and interpersonal needs of teachers. Doctoral dissertation, University of Oklahoma, Norman, 1970.

**Wainer, H. A., & Rubin, I. M.** Motivation of research and development entrepreneurs: determinants of company success. *J. appl. Psychol.*, 1969, *53*, 178–184.

**Waite, R. G. L.** *The psychopathic God: Adolf Hitler.* New York: Basic Books, 1977.

**Walberg, H. J.** Varieties of adolescent creativity and the high school environment. *Exceptional Children*, 1971, *38*, 111–116.

**Wald, R. M., & Doty, R. A.** The top executive—a firsthand profile. *Harvard bus. Rev.*, 1954, *32*, 45–54.

**Walker, C. R.** The problems of the repetitive job. *Harvard bus. Rev.*, 1950, *28*, 54–58.

**Walker, C. R.** *Modern technology and civilization.* New York: McGraw-Hill, 1962.

**Walker, C. R., & Guest, R. H.** *The man on the assembly line.* Cambridge, Mass.: Harvard University Press, 1952.

**Walker, C. R., Guest, R. H., & Turner, A. N.** *The foreman on the assembly line.* Cambridge, Mass.: Harvard University Press, 1956.

**Walker, K. F.** Executives' and union leaders' perceptions of each other's attitudes to industrial relations (the influence of stereotypes). *Hum. Relat.*, 1962, *15*, 183–196.

**Walker, K.** Workers' participation in management—problems, practice and prospects. *Bull. internat. inst. labor Studies*, 1974, *12*, 3–35.

**Walker, T. G.** Leader selection and behavior in small political groups. *Sm. grp. Behav.*, 1976, *7*, 363–368.

**Wall, C. C.** Perceived leader behavior of the elementary school principal as related to educational goal attainment. Doctoral dissertation, University of California, Los Angeles, 1970.

**Wall, J. A., Jr.** Effects of success and opposing representatives' bargaining orientation on intergroup bargaining. *J. pers. soc. Psychol.*, 1976, *33*, 55–61.

**Wallace, R. L.** A comparative study of attitude scores of managers toward employees and toward selected leadership policies in groups of firms which have either discontinued or retained cost reduction sharing plans. *Dissertation Abstr. Internat.*, 1972, *32*, 7359–7360.

**Wallace, S. R.** Some problems associated with management criteria in industry. *Psychonomic Monog. Suppl.* 1971, *4*, 236–237.

**Wallace, W. L., & Gallagher, J. V.** *Activities and behaviors of production supervisors.* New York: Psychological Corporation, 1952.

**Wallach, M. A., Kogan, N., & Bem, D. J.** Group influence on individual risk taking. *J. abnorm. soc. Psychol.*, 1962, *65*, 75–86.

**Wallach, M. A., Kogan, N., & Bem, D. J.** Diffusion of responsibility and level of risk taking in groups. *J. abnorm. soc. Psychol.*, 1964, *68*, 263–274.

**Wallach, M. A., Kogan, N., & Burt, R.** Are risk takers more persuasive than conservatives in group decisions? *J. exp. soc. Psychol.*, 1968, *4*, 76–89.

**Wallin, P.** Cultural contradictions and sex roles: a repeat study. *Amer. sociol. Rev.*, 1950, *15*, 288–293.

**Walster, E., Aronson, E., & Abrahams, D.** On increasing the persuasiveness of a low prestige communicator. *J. exp. soc. Psychol.*, 1966, *2*, 235–342.

**Walter, B.** Internal control relations in administrative hierarchies. *Admin. sci. Quar.*, 1966, *11*, 179–206.

**Walter, N.** A study of the effects of conflicting suggestions upon judgment in the autokinetic situation. Unpublished ms., undated.

**Walton, R. E., & McKersie, R. B.** *A behavioral theory of labor negotiations: an analysis of a social interaction system.* New York: McGraw-Hill, 1965.

**Walton, R. E., & McKersie, R. B.** Behavioral dilemmas in mixed motive decision-making. *Behav. Sci.*, 1966, *11*, 370–384.

**Walton, S. D.** *American business and its environment.* New York: Macmillan, 1966.

**Wanous, J. P.** Effects of a realistic job preview on job acceptance, job attitudes, and job survival. *J. appl. Psychol.*, 1973, *58*, 327–332.

**Warbusse, J. P.** *Cooperative democracy.* New York: Macmillan, 1923.

**Ward, C. D.** Seating arrangement and leadership emergence in small discussion groups. *J. soc. Psychol.*, 1968, *74*, 83–90.

**Ward, J. M.** Normative determinants of leadership. *Dissertation abstr. Internat.*, 1977, *37*, 4710.

**Ward, L. B.** The ethnics of executive selection. *Harvard bus. Rev.*, 1965, *43*, 6–28.

**Ward, L. B., & Athos, A. G.** *Student expectations of corporate life.* Boston: Harvard Business School, Division of Research, 1972.

**Wardlow, M. E., & Greene, J. E.** An exploratory sociometric study of peer status among adolescent girls. *Sociometry*, 1952, *15*, 311–318.

**Warner, M. LaV.** Influence of mental level in the formation of boys' gangs. *J. appl. Psychol.*, 1923, *7*, 224–236.

**Warner, W. K., & Hilander, J. S.** The relationship between size of organization and membership participation. *Rural Sociol.*, 1964, *29*, 30–39.

**Warner, W. L., & Abegglen, J. C.** *Occupational mobility in American business and industry, 1928–1952.* Minneapolis: University of Minnesota Press, 1955.

**Warner, W. L., & Martin, N. H.** *Industrial man.* New York: Harper, 1959.

**Warner, W. L., Meeker, M., & Eells, K.** *Social class in America.* Chicago: Science Research Associates, 1949.

**Warr, P. B., & Routledge, T.** An opinion scale for the study of managers' job satisfaction. *Occup. Psychol.*, 1969, *43*, 95–109.

**Warren, J. M., & Maroney, R. J.** Competitive social interaction between monkeys. In R. B. Zajonc (Ed.), *Animal social psychology.* New York: Wiley, 1969.

**Warren, N. D.** Job simplification versus job enlargement. *J. indus. Engineering*, 1958, *9*, 435–439.

**Warriner, C. K.** Leadership in the small group. *Amer. J. Sociol.*, 1955, *60*, 361–369.

**Warwick, D. P.** *The public bureaucracy: politics, personality, and organization in the U.S. State Department.* Cambridge: Harvard University Press, 1975.

**Washburne, N. F.** Rational and interaction decision-making roles in task-oriented groups.

Akron, Ohio: Akron University, Technical Report, 1967.

**Wasserman, P.** *Measurement and evaluation of organizational performance: an annotated bibliography.* Ithaca, N.Y.: Cornell University, Graduate School of Business & Public Administration, 1959.

**Wasserman, P, & Silander, F. S.** Decision-making: an annotated bibliography. Ithaca, N.Y.: Cornell University, Graduate School of Business & Public Administration, 1958.

**Waters, T. J., & Daugherty, R. A.** Student leadership, mathematics aptitude, and college major. *Psychol. Rep.,* 1970, *27,* 406.

**Watson, D.** Reinforcement theory of personality and social system: dominance and position in a group power structure. *J. pers. soc. Psychol.,* 1971, *20,* 180–185.

**Watson, D., & Bromberg, B.** Power communication and position satisfaction in task-oriented groups. *J. pers. soc. Psychol.,* 1965, *2,* 859–864.

**Watson, D. L.** Effects of certain social power structures on communication in task-oriented groups. *Sociometry,* 1965, *28,* 322–336.

**Watson, G. B.** *Civilian morale.* New York: Houghton Mifflin, 1942.

**Watson, J., & Williams, J.** Relationship between managerial values and managerial success of black and white managers. *J. appl. Psychol.,* 1977, *62,* 203–207.

**Watson, J. G., & Barone, S.** The self-concept, personal values, and motivational orientations of black and white managers. *Acad. Mgmt. J.,* 1976, *19,* 36–48.

**Watson, O. M., & Graves, T. D.** Quantitative research in proxemic behavior. *Amer. Anthrop.,* 1966, *68,* 971–985.

**Wearing, A., & Bishop, D.** Leader and member attitudes toward co-workers, intergroup competition, and the effectiveness and adjustment of military squads. Urbana: University of Illinois, Group Effectiveness Laboratory, Technical Report No. 21, 1967.

**Wearing, A. J., & Bishop, D. W.** The Fiedler contingency model and the functioning of military squads. *Acad. Mgmt. J.,* 1974, *17,* 450–459.

**Weaver, C. H.** The quantification of the frame of reference in labor-management communication. *J. appl. Psychol.,* 1958, *42,* 1–9.

**Webb, U.** Character and intelligence. *Brit. J. psychol. Monogr.,* 1915, No. 20.

**Weber, M.** The sociology of charismatic authority. In H. H. Mills & C. W. Mills (Eds. and Trans.), *From Max Weber: essays in sociology.* New York: Oxford University Press, 1946.

**Weber, M.** *The theory of social and economic organization.* New York: Oxford University Press, 1947.

**Weber, M.** *The theory of social and economic organization,* T. Parsons (Ed.). New York: Free Press, 1957.

**Wedel, C. C.** *A study of measurement in group dynamics laboratories. Doctoral dissertation, George Washington University, Washington, D.C., 1957.*

**Weed, S. E., Mitchell, T. R., & Moffitt, W.** Leadership style, subordinate personality and task type as predictors of performance and satisfaction with supervision. *J. appl. Psychol.,* 1976, *61,* 58–66.

**Wehman, R., Goldstein, M. A., & Williams, J. R.** Effects of different leadership styles on individual risk-taking in groups. *Hum. Relat.,* 1977, *30,* 249–259.

**Weick, K. E.** Identification and enhancement of managerial effectiveness: V. The social psychology of managerial effectiveness. Greensboro, N.C.: Richardson Foundation, 1966 (mimeo).

**Weick, K. E.** *The social psychology of organizing.* Reading, Mass.: Addison-Wesley, 1969.

**Weinberg, C.** Institutional differences in factors associated with student leadership. *Sociol. soc. Res.,* 1965, *49,* 425–436.

**Weiner, N.** *Cybernetics,* 2nd ed. Cambridge, Mass.: M.I.T. Press, 1961.

**Weisman, C. S., Morlock, L. L., Sack, D. G., & Levine, D. M.** Sex differences in response to a blocked career pathway among unaccepted medical school applicants. *Sociol. work. Occup.*, 1976, *3*, 187–208.

**Weiss, D. S., Dawis, R. V., England, G. W., & Lofquist, L. H.** *The measurement of vocational needs.* Minneapolis: University of Minnesota, Studies in Vocational Rehabilitation, 1964.

**Weiss, H. M.** Subordinate imitation of supervisor behavior: the role of modeling in organizational socialization. *Org. behav. hum. Perform.*, 1977, *19*, 89–105.

**Weiss, R. S.** *Processes of organization.* Ann Arbor: University of Michigan, Survey Research Center, 1956.

**Weiss, W.** The relationship between judgments of a communicator's position and extent of opinion change. *J. abnorm. soc. Psychol.*, 1958, *56*, 380–384.

**Weiss, W., & Fine, B. J.** The effect of induced aggressiveness on opinion change. Boston: Boston University, Technical Report No. 2, undated.

**Weissenberg, P.** A comparison of the life goals of Austrian, German-Swiss, and West German (FRG) managers. *Economies et Societes*, 1979, *13*, 683–693.

**Weissenberg, P., & Gruenfeld, L. W.** Relationships among leadership dimensions and cognitive style. *J. appl. Psychol.*, 1966, *50*, 392–395.

**Weissenberg, P., & Kavanagh, M. J.** The independence of Initiating Structure and Consideration: a review of the literature. *Personnel Psychol.*, 1972, *25*, 119–130.

**Weitz, J.** Job expectancy and survival. *J. appl. Psychol.*, 1956, *40*, 245–247.

**Weitz, J., & Nuckols, R. C.** A validation of "How Supervise?" *J. appl. Psychol.*, 1953, *37*, 7–8.

**Wells, L. M.** The limits of authority: Barnard revisited. *Publ. admin. Rev.*, 1963, *23*, 161–166.

**Wendt, H. W., & Light, P. C.** Measuring "greatness" in American presidents: model case for international research on political leadership? *Eur. J. soc. Psychol.*, 1976, *6*, 105–109.

**Werdelin, I.** Teacher ratings, peer ratings, and self ratings of behavior in school. *Educ. psychol. Interactions*, 1966, No. 11.

**Werner, D. S.** Personality, environment, and decision making. Ann Arbor, Mich.: University Microfilm No. 12, 1955, 247.

**Werner, L.** MBA: the fantasy and the reality. *Working Woman*, December 1979, 37.

**Wernimont, P. F.** What supervisors and subordinates expect of each other. *Personnel J.*, 1971, *50*, 204–208.

**Weschler, D.** *Weschler adult intelligence scale: manual.* New York: The Psychological Corporation, 1955.

**Weschler, I. R., Kahane, M., & Tannenbaum, R.** Job satisfaction, productivity, and morale: a case study. *Occup. Psychol.*, 1952, *26*, 1–14.

**Weschler, I. R., & Reisel, J.** *Inside a sensitivity training group.* Los Angeles: University of California, Institute of Industrial Relations, 1959.

**Weschler, I. R., & Schein, E. H. (Eds.),** *Issues in training.* Washington, D.C.: NTL-NEA, 1962.

**Weschler, I. R., & Shepard, C.** Organizational structure, sociometric choice, and communication effectiveness: a pilot study. *Amer. Psychologist*, 1954, *9*, 492–493.

**West, N.** *Leadership with a feminine cast.* San Francisco: R & E Research Associates, 1978.

**Westburgh, E. M.** A point of view: studies in leadership. *J. abnorm. soc. Psychol.*, 1931, *25*, 418–423.

**Westerlund, G.** *Behavior in a work situation with functional supervision and with group leaders.* Stockholm: Nordisk Rotogravyr, 1952a.

**Westerlund, G.** *Group leadership: a field experiment.* Stockholm: Nordisk Rotogravyr, 1952b.

**Wetzel, W. A.** Characteristics of pupil leaders. *School Rev.*, 1932, *40*, 532–534.

**Wexley, K. N., & Hunt, P. J.** Male and female leaders: comparison of performance and behavior patterns. *Psychol. Rep.*, 1974, *35*, 867–872.

**Wexley, K. N., & Jaffee, C. L.** Comparison of two feedback techniques for improving the human relations skills of leaders. *Exp. publ. System, Amer. Psychol. Assn.*, 1969, No. 039.

**Wexley, K. N., & Nemeroff, W. F.** Effectiveness of positive reinforcement and goal setting as methods of management development. *J. appl. Psychol.*, 1975, *60*, 446–450.

**Wheatley, B. C.** The effects of four styles of leadership upon anxiety in small groups. *Dissertation Abstr.*, 1967, *27*, 3533–3534.

**Wheatley, B. C.** Leadership and anxiety: implications for employer/employee small group meetings. *Personnel J.*, 1972, *51*, 17–21.

**Wheatley, D.** A study of the management systems of the junior colleges of the State of Texas. Doctoral dissertation, University of Houston, Houston, 1972.

**Wheelan, S. A.** Sex differences in the functioning of small groups. *Dissertation Abstr. Internat.*, 1975, *35*, 4712–4713.

**Wheeler, D., & Jordan, H.** Change of individual opinion to accord with group opinion. *J. abnorm. soc. Psychol.*, 1929, *24*, 203–206.

**Wheeler, L.** Information seeking as a power strategy. *J. soc. Psychol.*, 1964, *62*, 125–130.

**Wheeler, L.** *Interpersonal influence.* Boston: Allyn & Bacon, 1970.

**Wheeler, L., Smith, S., & Murphy, D. B.** Behavioral contagion. *Psychol. Rep.*, 1964, *15*, 159–173.

**Wherry, R. J.** Factor analysis of Officer Qualifications Form QCL-2B. Columbus: Ohio State University Research Foundation, 1950 (mimeo).

**Wherry, R. J.** Hierarchical factor solutions without rotation. *Psychometrika*, 1959, *24*, 45–51.

**Wherry, R. J., & Fryer, D. H.** Buddy ratings—popularity contest or leadership criteria? *Personnel Psychol.*, 1949, *2*, 147–159.

**Wherry, R. J., & Olivero, J.** (**Eds.**), *The Ohio State University computer programs for psychology.* Columbus: Ohio State University, Department of Psychology, 1971.

**Wherry, R. J., Stander, N. E., & Hopkins, J. J.** Behavior trait ratings by peers and references. USAF WADC Tech. Rep., 1959, No. 59–360.

**Whisler, T. L., & Harper, S. F.** *Performance appraisal: research and practice.* New York: Holt, Rinehart & Winston, 1962.

**White, H. C.** How purchasing managers view leadership. *J. Purch.*, 1971a, *7*, 5–18.

**White, H. C.** Leadership: some behaviors and attitudes of hospital employees. *Hosp. Progr.*, 1971b, *52*(10), 46–50; *52*(11), 41–45.

**White, H. C.** Some perceived behavior and attitudes of hospital employees under effective and ineffective supervision. *J. nurs. Admin.*, 1971c, *1*, 49–54.

**White, H. C.** Perceptions of leadership styles by nurses in supervisory positions. *J. nurs. Admin.*, 1971d, *1*, 44–51.

**White, H. C.** Identifying the true leader in industrial management. *Indus. Mgmt.*, 1972a, *14*, 1–7.

**White, H. C.** Perceptions of leadership by managers in a federal agency. *Person. admin. pub. personnel Rev.*, 1972b, *1*, 51–56.

**White, J. C.** Attitude differences in identification with management. *Personnel J.*, 1964, *43*, 602–603.

**White, J. D.** Autocratic and democratic leadership and their respective groups' power, hierarchies, and morale. *Dissertation Abstr.*, 1963, *24*, 602.

**White, J. E.** Theory and method for research in community leadership. *Amer. sociol. Rev.*, 1950, *15*, 50–60.

**White, M. C., DeSanctis, G. & Crino, M. D.** Achievement, self confidence, personality traits and leadership ability: a review of the literature on sex differences. *Psychol. Rep.,* 1981, *48,* 547–569.

**White, R. K., & Lippitt, R.** *Autocracy and democracy: an experimental inquiry.* New York: Harper, 1960.

**Whitehill, A. M.** Cultural values and employee attitudes: United States and Japan. *J. appl. Psychol.,* 1964, *48,* 69–72.

**Whitehill, A. M., & Takezawa, S.** *Cultural values in management-worker relations.* Chapel Hill: University of North Carolina, School of Business Administration, 1961.

**Whitehill, A. M., & Takezawa, S.** *The other worker.* Honolulu: East-West Center Press, 1968.

**Whitehill, M.** *Centralized versus decentralized decision-making in collective bargaining: effects on substantive contract language.* Iowa City: University of Iowa, Center for Labor & Management, 1968.

**Whitelock, D.** *The beginnings of English society.* London: Penguin, 1950.

**Whiteman, M.** The performance of schizophrenics on social concepts. *J. abnorm. soc. Psychol.,* 1954, *49,* 266–271.

**Whiteman, M., & Deutsch, M.** Some effects of social class and race on children's language and intellectual abilities. In M. Deutsch, I. Katz, & A. Jensen (Eds.), *Social class, race, and psychological development.* New York: Holt, Rinehart & Winston, 1968.

**Whyte, W. F.** *Street corner society: the social structure of an Italian slum.* Chicago: University of Chicago Press, 1943.

**Whyte, W. F.** The social structure of the restaurant. *Amer. J. Sociol.,* 1949, *54,* 302–310.

**Whyte, W. F.** Small groups and large organizations. In J. H. Rohrer & M. Sherif (Eds.), *Social psychology at the crossroads.* New York: Harper, 1951.

**Whyte, W. F.** *Leadership and group participation—an analysis of the discussion group.* Ithaca, N.Y.: Cornell University, New York State School of Industrial & Labor Relations, 1953.

**Whyte, W. F.** *Money and motivation: an analysis of incentives in industry.* New York: Harper, 1955.

**Whyte, W. F.** *Men at work.* Homewood, Ill.: Dorsey, 1961.

**Whyte, W. F.** Culture, industrial relations and economic development: the case of Peru. *Indus. labor relat. Rev.,* 1963, *16,* 583–593.

**Whyte, W. F., & Gardner, B. B.** Human elements in supervision. *Appl. Anthrop.,* 1945, *4,* 7.

**Whyte, W. H.** *The organization man.* New York: Simon & Schuster, 1956.

**Wicker, A. W.** Size of church membership and members' support of church behavior settings. *J. pers. soc. Psychol.,* 1969, *3,* 278–288.

**Wickert, F.** *Psychological research on problems of redistribution.* AAF Aviat. Psychol. Program Research Report No. 14. Washington, D.C.: U.S. Government Printing Office, 1947.

**Wickert, F. R.** Turnover and employees' feelings of ego-involvement in the day-to-day operations of a company. *Personnel Psychol.,* 1951, *4,* 185–197.

**Widgery, R. N., & Tubbs, S. L.** Using feedback of diagnostic information as an organizational development strategy. *Proceedings of the International Communication Association,* 1975.

**Wiener, W.** Selected perceptions and compatibilities of personnel in innovative and non-innovative schools. Doctoral dissertation, Syracuse University, Syracuse, N.Y., 1972.

**Wiggam, A. E.** The biology of leadership. In H. C. Metcalf (Ed.), *Business leadership.* New York: Pitman, 1931.

**Wikstrom, W. S.** *Developing better managers: an eight-nation study.* New York: National Industrial Conference Board, 1961.

**Wikstrom, W. S.** *Managing at the foreman's level.* New York: National Industrial Conference Board, 1967.

**Wilcox, D. S., & Burke, R. J.** Characteristics of effective employee performance review and development interviews. *Personnel Psychol.*, 1969, *22*, 291–305.

**Wildavsky, A.** *Leadership in a small town.* Totowa, N.J.: Bedminster Press, 1964.

**Wile, D. B., Bron, G. D., & Pollack, H. B.** The group therapy questionnaire: an instrument for study of leadership in small groups. *Psychol. Rep.*, 1970, *27*, 263–273.

**Wilemon, D. L., & Cicero, J. P.** The project manager—anomalies and ambiguities. *Acad. Mgmt. J.*, 1970, *13*, 269–282.

**Wilensky, H. W.** Human relations in the workplace. In C. Arensberg (Ed.), *Research in industrial human relations.* New York: Harper, 1957.

**Wilkins, E. H.** On the distribution of extracurricular activities. *School Society,* 1940, *51*, 651–656.

**Wilkins, E. J., & DeCharms, R.** Authoritarianism and response to power cues. *J. Pers.*, 1962, *30*, 439–457.

**Wilkinson, R.** *Gentlemanly power.* London: Oxford University Press, 1964.

**Willerman, B.** Organizational involvement as reflected in type of member complaint: an indirect method of measurement. Minneapolis: University of Minnesota, Technical Report No. 4, 1954.

**Willerman, B., & Swanson, L.** An ecological determinant of differential amounts of sociometric choices within college sororities. *Sociometry,* 1952, *15*, 326–329.

**Willerman, B., & Swanson, L.** Group practice in voluntary organizations: a study of college sororities. *Hum. Relat.*, 1953, *6*, 57–77.

**Williams, C. H.** Employing the black administrator. *Pub. personnel Mgmt.*, 1975, *4*, 76–83.

**Williams, E.** An analysis of selected work duties and performances of the more effective versus the less effective manager. Doctoral dissertation, Ohio State University, Columbus, 1968.

**Williams, F. J., & Harrell, T. W.** Predicting success in business. *J. Psychol.*, 1964, *48*, 164–167.

**Williams, J. L.** Personal space and its relation to extroversion-introversion. Edmonton: University of Alberta, Master's thesis, 1963.

**Williams, J. L.** Group geography and the assumption of leadership. *Dissertation Abstr. Internat.*, 1969, *30*, 1642.

**Williams, L. K., Whyte, W. F., & Green, C. S.** Do cultural differences affect workers' attitudes? *Indus. Relat.*, 1966, *5*, 105–117.

**Williams, S. B., & Leavitt, H. J.** Group opinion as a predictor of military leadership. *J. consult. Psychol.*, 1947a, *11*, 283–291.

**Williams, S. B., & Leavitt, H. J.** Methods of selecting Marine Corps officers. In G. A. Kelly (Ed.), *New methods in applied psychology.* College Park: University of Maryland, 1947b.

**Williams, V.** Leadership types, role differentiation, and system problems. *Soc. Forces,* 1965, *43*, 380–389.

**Williamson, E. G.** The group origins of student leaders. *Educ. psychol. Measmt.*, 1948, *8*, 603–612.

**Willis, F. N.** Initial speaking distance as a function of the speakers' relationship. *Psychonomic Sci.*, 1966, *5*, 221–222.

**Willits, R. D.** Company performance and interpersonal relations. *Indus. mgmt. Rev.*, 1967, *8*, 91–107.

**Willmorth, N. E., Taylor, E. L., Lindelien, W. B., & Ruch, F. L.** A factor analysis of rating scale variables used as criteria of military leadership. *USAF Personnel Train. Res. Cent. res. Rep.*, 1957, No. 57–154.

**Willower, D. J.** Leadership styles and leaders' perceptions of subordinates. *J. educ. Sociol.*, 1960, *34*, 58–64.

**Wilpert, B.** Research on industrial democracy: the German case. *Indus. Relat. J.*, 1975, *6*, 53–64.

**Wilson, A. T. M.** How to appraise. *Manag. Today,* December 1972, 99–100, 104–108.

**Wilson, R. C., Beem, H. P., & Comrey, A. L.** Factors influencing organizational effectiveness. III. A survey of skilled tradesmen. *Personnel Psychol.*, 1953, *6*, 313–325.

**Wilson, R. C., High, W. S., & Comrey, A. L.** An iterative analysis of supervisory and group dimensions. *J. appl. Psychol.*, 1955, *39*, 85–91.

**Wilson, S. R.** Leadership, participation, and self-orientation in observed and nonobserved groups. *J. appl. Psychol.*, 1971, *55*, 433–438.

**Wilson, T. P.** Patterns of management and adaptations to organizational roles—a study of prison inmates. *Amer. J. Sociol.*, 1968, *74*, 146–157.

**Wilson, W. K.** The challenge of leadership. *J. Coast Artillery*, 1938, *81*, 363–366.

**Winder, A. E.** White attitudes toward Negro–white interaction in an area of changing racial composition. *Amer. Psycholist*, 1952, *7*, 330–331.

**Winder, C. L., & Wiggins, J. S.** Social reputation and social behavior: a further validation of the Peer Nomination Inventory. *J. abnorm. soc. Psychol.*, 1964, *68*, 681–684.

**Winn, A.** Social change in industry: from insight to implementation. *J. appl. behav. Sci.*, 1966, *2*, 170–184.

**Winkler-Hermaden, V.** *Zur Psychologie des Zugenführers.* Jena: Fisher, 1927.

**Winston, S.** Studies in Negro leadership: age and occupational distribution of 1,608 Negro leaders. *Amer. J. Sociol.*, 1932, *37*, 595–602.

**Winter, D. G.** *Navy leadership and management competencies: convergence among tests, interviews and performance ratings.* Boston: McBer & Co., 1978.

**Winter, D. G.** *An introduction to LMET theory and research.* Boston: McBer & Co., 1979.

**Wirdenius, H.** *Supervisors at work.* Stockholm: Swedish Council for Personnel Administration, 1958.

**Wischmeier, R. R.** Group-centered and leader-centered leadership: an experimental study. *Speech Monogr.*, 1955, *22*, 43–48.

**Wispé, L. G.** A sociometric analysis of conflicting role-expectancies. *Amer. J. Sociol.*, 1955, *61*, 134–137.

**Wispé, L. G.** The success attitude: an analysis of the relationship between individual needs and social role-expectancies. *J. soc. Psychol.*, 1957, *46*, 119–124.

**Wispé, L. G., & Lloyd, K. E.** Some situational and psychological determinants of the desire for structured interpersonal relations. *J. abnorm. soc. Psychol.*, 1955, *51*, 57–60.

**Wispé, L. G., & Thayer, P. W.** Role ambiguity and anxiety in an occupational group. *J. soc. Psychol.*, 1957, *46*, 41–48.

**Wittenberg, R. M.** Reaching the individual through the group. *Pastoral Psychol.*, 1951, *2*, 41–47.

**Wittig, M. A.** Sex differences in intellectual functioning: how much of a difference do genes make? *Sex Roles*, 1976, *2*, 63–74.

**Wittreich, W.** Managerial motivation development: business managers. In J. B. Miner (Ed.), *Motivation to manage.* Atlanta: Organizational Measurement Systems Press, 1977.

**Wofford, J. C.** Behavior styles and performance effectiveness. *Personnel Psychol.*, 1967, *20*, 461–495.

**Wofford, J. C.** Factor analysis of managerial behavior variables. *J. appl. Psychol.*, 1970, *54*, 169–173.

**Wofford, J. C.** Managerial behavior, situational factors, and productivity and morale. *Admin. sci. Quar.*, 1971, *16*, 10–17.

**Wolberg, A. R.** Selecting potential group leaders for training in group techniques. *Transnational*

*Mental health Newsletter,* 1977, *19,* 7–8.

**Wolf, W. B.** Precepts for managers—interviews with Chester I. Barnard. *California Mgmt. Rev.,* 1963, *6,* 89–94.

**Wolin, B. R., & Terebinski, S. J.** Leadership in small groups: a mathematical approach. *J. exp. Psychol.,* 1965, *69,* 126–134.

**Wollowick, H. B., & McNamara, W. J.** Relationship of the components of an assessment center to management success. *J. appl. Psychol.,* 1969, *5,* 348–352.

**Wolman, B.** Leadership and group dynamics. *J. soc. Psychol.,* 1956, *43,* 11–25.

**Wolman, B. (Ed.),** *The psychoanalytic interpretation of history.* New York: Basic Books, 1971.

**Wolozin, H.** Teaching personnel administration by role playing. *Personnel J.,* 1948, *27,* 107–109.

**Women's Bureau, Employment Standards Administration, U.S. Department of Labor.** *The myth and the reality.* Washington, D.C.: U.S. Government Printing Office, 1974.

**Women's Bureau, Employment Standards Administration, U.S. Department of Labor.** *Women workers today.* Washington, D.C.: U.S. Government Printing Office, 1975.

**Wood, J. T.** Leading in purposive discussions: a study of adaptive behavior. *Commun. Monogr.,* 1977, *44,* 152–165.

**Wood, M. M.** What does it take for a woman to make it in management? *Personnel J.,* 1975, *54,* 38–41.

**Wood, M. M.** Women in management: how is it working out? *Adv. Mgmt. J.,* 1976, *41,* 22–30.

**Wood, M. M., & Greenfeld, S. T.** Women managers and fear of success: a study in the field. *Sex Roles,* 1976, *2,* 375–387.

**Wood, M. T.** Effects of decision processes and task situations on influence perceptions. *Org. behav. hum. Perform.,* 1972, *7,* 417–427.

**Wood, M. T.** Power relationships and group decision making in organizations. *Psychol. Bull.,* 1973, *79,* 280–293.

**Wood, M. T., & Sobel, R. S.** Effects of similarity of leadership style at two levels of management on the job satisfaction of the first level manager. *Personnel Psychol.,* 1970, *23,* 577–590.

**Woods, F. A.** *The influence of monarchs.* New York: Macmillan, 1913.

**Woodward, J.** *Management and technology.* London: Her Majesty's Stationery Office, 1958.

**Woodward, J.** *Industrial organization: theory and practice.* Oxford: Oxford University Press, 1965.

**Woodworth, D. G., & MacKinnon, D. W.** The use of trait ratings in an assessment of 100 air force captains. USAF WADA tech. Note., 1958, No. 58–64.

**Woodworth, R. S.** The Woodworth personal data sheet. In S. I. Franz (Ed.), *Handbook of mental examination methods.* New York: Macmillan, 1920.

**Worchel, P.** Status restoration and the reduction of hostility. *J. abnorm. soc. Psychol.,* 1961, *63,* 443–445.

**Worden, P. E.** The impact of two experimental time-limited leadership training programs on youth. *Dissertation Abstr. Internat.,* 1976, *36,* 5067.

**Worthy, J. C.** Organizational structure and employee morale. *Amer. sociol. Rev.,* 1950, *15,* 169–179.

**Worthy, M. M., Wright, J. M., & Shaw, M. E.** Effects of varying degrees of legitimacy in the attribution of responsibility for negative events. *Psychonomic Sci.,* 1964, *1,* 169–170.

**Wray, D. E.** Marginal men of industry: the foremen. *Amer. J. Sociol.,* 1949, *54,* 298–301.

**Wright, D. G.** Anxiety in aerial combat. *Res. pub. assoc. nerv. ment. Dis.,* 1946, *25,* 116–124.

**Wright, D. W.** A comparative study of two leadership styles in goal-bound group discussions. *Dissertation Abstr. Internat.,* 1972, *32,* 7121.

**Wright, M. E.** The influence of frustration upon social relations of young children. *Charact.*

*Person.*, 1943, *12*, 111–122.

**Wrong, D. H.** Some problems in defining social power. *Amer. J. Sociol.*, 1968, *73*, 673–681.

**Wurster, C. R., & Bass, B. M.** Situational tests: IV. Validity of leaderless group discussions among strangers. *Educ. psychol. Measmt.*, 1953, *13*, 122–132.

**Wurster, C. R., Bass, B. M., & Alcock, W.** A test of the proposition: we want to be esteemed most by those we esteem most highly. *J. abnorm. soc. Psychol.*, 1961, *63*, 650–653.

**Wyatt, S., & Langdon, J. N.** *Fatigue and boredom in repetitive work.* London: Industrial Health Research Board, 1937.

**Wyndham, A. J., & White, E.** Joint consultation: case study no. 3. *Personnel pract. Bull.*, 1952, *8*, 3–13.

**Wyndham, C. H., & Cooke, H. M.** The influence of the quality of supervision on the production of men engaged on moderately hard physical work. *Ergonomics*, 1964, *7*, 139–149.

**Yeager, T. C.** An analysis of certain traits of selected high school seniors interested in teaching. Teachers College Contribution Education, 1935, No. 660.

**Yerby, J.** Attitude, task, and sex composition as variables affecting female leadership in small problem-solving groups. *Speech Monogr.*, 1975, *42*, 160–168.

**Yntema, D. B., & Torgerson, W. S.** Man-machine cooperation in decisions requiring common sense. *IRE Trans. hum. fact. Electronic.*, 1961, *2*, 20–26.

**Yoga, M.** Patterns of supervisory authority. *J. Indian acad. appl. Psychol.*, 1964, *1*, 44–48.

**York, M. W.** Reinforcement of leadership in small groups. *Dissertation Abstr. Internat.*, 1969, *30*, 1643.

**Yukl, G. A.** Leader personality and situational variables as co-determinants of leader behavior. *Dissertation Abstr.*, 1968, *29*, 406.

**Yukl, G. A.** A situation description questionnaire for leaders. *Educ. psychol. Measmt.*, 1969, *29*, 515–518.

**Yukl, G. A.** Leader LPC scores: attitude dimensions and behavioral correlates. *J. soc. Psychol.*, 1970, *80*, 207–212.

**Yukl, G. A.** Toward a behavioral theory of leadership. *Org. behav. hum. Perform.*, 1971, *6*, 414–440.

**Yunker, G. W., & Hunt, J. B.** An empirical comparison of the Michigan four-factor and Ohio State LBDQ leadership scales. *Org. behav. hum. Perform.*, 1976, *17*, 45–65.

**Yura, H.** *Nursing leadership: theory and process.* New York: Appleton-Century-Crofts, 1976.

**Yuzuk, R. P.** The assessment of employee morale: a comparison of two measures. Doctoral dissertation, Ohio State University, Columbus, 1959.

**Yuzuk, R. P.** *The assessment of employee morale.* Columbus: Ohio State University, Bureau of Business Research, 1961.

**Zagona, S. V., Willis, J. E., & MacKinnon, W. J.** Group effectiveness in creative problem-solving tasks: an examination of relevant variables. *J. Psychol.*, 1966, *62*, 111–137.

**Zagona, S. V., & Zurcher, L. A.** Participation, interaction, and role behavior in groups selected from the extremes of the open-closed cognitive continuum. *J. Psychol.*, 1964, *58*, 255–264.

**Zais, M. M.** The impact of intelligence and experience on the performance of army line and staff officers. Seattle: University of Washington, Master's thesis, 1979.

**Zajonc, R. B.** The effects of feedback and probability of group success on individual and group performance. *Hum. Relat.*, 1962, *15*, 149–163.

**Zajonc, R. B.** *Animal social psychology: a reader of experimental studies.* New York: Wiley, 1969.

**Zajonc, R. B., & Wolfe, D. M.** Cognitive consequences of a person's position in a formal organization. *Hum. Relat.*, 1966, *19*, 139–150.

**Zald, M. N.** Decentralization—myth vs. reality. *Personnel*, 1964, *41*, 19–26.

**Zald, M. N.** Urban differentiation, characteristics of boards of directors, and organizational effectiveness. *Amer. J. Sociol.*, 1967, *73*, 261–272.

**Zaleznik, A.** *Foreman training in a growing enterprise.* Boston: Harvard University, Graduate School of Business Administration, 1951.

**Zaleznik, A.** *Worker satisfaction and development.* Boston: Harvard University, Graduate School of Business Administration, 1956.

**Zaleznik, A.** Interpersonal relations in organizations. In J. G. March (Ed.), *Handbook of organizations.* Chicago: Rand McNally, 1965.

**Zaleznik, A.** *Human dilemmas of leadership.* New York: Harper & Row, 1966.

**Zaleznik, A.** Charismatic and consensus leaders: a psychological comparison. *Bull. Menninger Clinic*, 1974, *38*, 222–238.

**Zaleznik, A., Christensen, C. R., & Roethlisberger, F. J.** *The motivation, productivity, and satisfaction of workers.* Boston: Harvard University, Graduate School of Business Administration, 1958.

**Zaleznik, A., Dalton, G. W., & Barnes, L. B.** *Orientation and conflict in career.* Boston: Harvard University, Graduate School of Business Administration, 1970.

**Zaleznik, A., & Moment, D.** *The dynamics of interpersonal behavior.* New York: Wiley, 1964.

**Zammuto, R. F., London, M., & Rowland, K. M.** Effects of sex on commitment and conflict resolution. *J. appl. Psychol.*, 1979, *64*, 227–231.

**Zand, D. E.** *Collateral organization.* Unpublished mimeograph presented at a meeting of the NTL Organizational Development Network, 1971.

**Zander, A.** Role playing: a technique for training the necessarily dominating leader. *Sociatry*, 1947, *1*, 225–235.

**Zander, A.** The problem of resistance in creating social change. *Proceedings of the American Society of Public Administration*, 1949.

**Zander, A.** Resistance to change—its analysis and prevention. *Advanced Mgmt.*, 1950, *15*, 9–11.

**Zander, A.** The effects of prestige on the behavior of group members: an audience demonstration. *Amer. Mgmt. Assn., Personnel Ser.*, 1953, No. 155.

**Zander, A.** Group aspirations. In D. Cartwright & A. Zander (Eds.), *Group dynamics: research and theory*, 3rd ed. New York: Harper & Row, 1968.

**Zander, A.** *Motives and goals in groups.* New York: Academic Press, 1971.

**Zander, A., & Cohen, A. R.** Attributed social power and group acceptance: a classroom experimental demonstration. *J. abnorm. soc. Psychol.*, 1955, *51*, 490–492.

**Zander, A., Cohen, A. R., & Stotland, E.** *Role relations in the mental health professions.* Ann Arbor: University of Michigan, Institute for Social Research, 1957.

**Zander, A., & Curtis, T.** Effects of social power on aspiration setting and striving. *J. abnorm. soc. Psychol.*, 1962, *64*, 63–74.

**Zander, A., & Curtis, T.** Social support and rejection of organizational standards. *J. educ. Psychol.*, 1965, *56*, 87–95.

**Zander, A., & Forward, J.** Position in group, achievement motivation, and group aspirations. *J. pers. soc. Psychol.*, 1968, *8*, 282–288.

**Zander, A., & Gyr, J.** Changing attitudes toward a merit rating system. *Personnel Psychol.*, 1955, *8*, 429–448.

**Zander, A., & Havelin, A.** Social comparison and interpersonal attraction. *Hum. Relat.*, 1960, *13*, 21–32.

**Zander, A., & Medow, H.** Individual and group levels of aspiration. *Hum. Relat.*, 1963, *16*, 89–105.

**Zander, A., & Medow, H.** Strength of group and desire for attainable group aspirations. *J. Pers.*, 1965, *33*, 122–139.

**Zander, A., Medow, H., & Dustin, D.** Social influences on group aspirations. In A. Zander & H. Medow (Eds.), *Group aspirations and group coping behavior.* Ann Arbor: University of Michigan, Institute for Social Research, 1964.

**Zander, A., Medow, H., & Efron, R.** Observers' expectations as determinants of group aspirations. *Hum. Relat.,* 1965, *18,* 273–287.

**Zander, A., & Wolfe, D.** Administrative rewards and coordination among committee members. *Admin. sci. Quar.,* 1964, *9,* 50–69.

**Zavala, A.** Determining the hierarchical structure of a multidimensional body of information. *Percept. mot. Skills,* 1971, *32,* 735–746.

**Zdep, S. M.** Reinforcement of leadership behavior in specially constructed groups. *Dissertation Abstr.,* 1968, *29,* 1599.

**Zdep, S. M.** Intra group reinforcement and its effects on leadership behavior. *Org. behav. hum. Perform.,* 1969, *4,* 284–298.

**Zdep, S. M., & Oakes, W. F.** Reinforcement of leadership behavior in group discussion. *J. exp. soc. Psychol.,* 1967, *3,* 310–320.

**Zeira, Y.** Overlooked personnel problems of multinational corporations. *Columbia J. world Bus.,* 1975, *10,* 96–103.

**Zeleny, L. D.** Characteristics of group leaders. *Sociol. soc. Res.,* 1939, *24,* 140–149.

**Zeleny, L. D.** Objective selection of group leaders. *Sociol. soc. Res.,* 1940a, *24,* 326–336.

**Zeleny, L. D.** Experimental appraisal of a group learning plan. *J. educ. Res.,* 1940b, *34,* 37–42.

**Zeleny, L. D.** Experiments in leadership training. *J. educ. Sociol.,* 1941, *14,* 310–313.

**Zeleny, L. D.** Selection of compatible flying partners. *Amer. J. Sociol.,* 1946/1947, *52,* 424–431.

**Zeleny, L. D.** Adaptation of research findings in social leadership to college classroom procedures. *Sociometry,* 1950, *8,* 314–328.

**Zelko, H., & Dance, F. E. X.** *Business and professional speech communication.* New York: Holt, Rinehart & Winston, 1965.

**Zenger, J. H.** Third generation manager training. *MSU Bus. Topics,* 1974, *21,* 23–28.

**Zentner, H.** Morale: certain theoretical implications of data in the American soldier. *Amer. sociol. Rev.,* 1951, *16,* 297–307.

**Zigon, F. J., & Cannon, J. R.** Processes and outcomes of group discussions as related to leader behaviors. *J. educ. Res.,* 1974, *67,* 199–201.

**Zilboorg, G.** Authority and leadership. *Bull. World Fed. ment. Health,* 1950, *2,* 13–17.

**Ziller, R. C.** Four techniques of decision making under uncertainty. *Amer. Psychologist,* 1954, *9,* 498.

**Ziller, R. C.** Scales of judgment: a determinant of the accuracy of group decisions. *Hum. Relat.,* 1955, *8,* 153–164.

**Ziller, R. C.** Four techniques of group decision making under uncertainty. *J. appl. Psychol.,* 1957, *41,* 384–388.

**Ziller, R. C.** Leader acceptance of responsibility for group action under conditions of uncertainty and risk. *J. Psychol.,* 1959, *47,* 57–66.

**Ziller, R. C.** The newcomer's acceptance in open and closed groups. *Personnel Admin.,* 1962, *25,* 24–31.

**Ziller, R. C.** Leader assumed dissimilarity as a measure of prejudicial cognitive style. *J. appl. Psychol.,* 1963, *47,* 339–342.

**Ziller, R. C.** Individuation and socialization: a theory of assimilation in large organizations. *Hum. Relat.,* 1964, *17,* 341–360.

**Ziller, R. C.** The leader's perception of the marginal member. *Personnel Admin.,* 1965a, *28,* 6–11.

**Ziller, R. C.** Toward a theory of open and closed groups. *Psychol. Bull.,* 1965b, *64,* 164–182.

**Ziller, R. C., Behringer, R. D., & Jansen, M. J.** The newcomer in open and closed groups. *J. appl. Psychol.*, 1961, *45*, 55–58.

**Ziller, R. C., Stark, B. J., & Pruden, H. O.** Marginality and integrative management positions. *Acad. Mgmt. J.*, 1969, *4*, 487–495.

**Zillig, M.** Führer in der Schulklasse. (Classroom leaders). *Indust. Psychotechn.*, 1933, *10*, 177–182.

**Zimet, C. N., & Fine, H. J.** Personality changes with a group therapeutic experience in a human relations seminar. *J. abnorm. soc. Psychol.*, 1955, *51*, 68–73.

**Zink, H.** *City bosses in the United States: a study of twenty municipal bosses.* Durham, N.C.: Duke University Press, 1930.

**Zoll, A. A.** *Dynamic management education,* 2nd ed. Reading, Mass.: Addison-Wesley, 1969.

**Zollschan, G. K., & Hirsch, W.** *Explorations in social change.* Boston: Houghton Mifflin, 1964.

**Zuberbier, L. W.** Fostering a greater balance of participation in small leaderless discussion groups. *Dissertation Internat.*, 1971, *32*, 3430–3431.

**Zuckerman, M., & Wheeler, L.** To dispel fantasies about the fantasy-based measure of fear of success. *Psychol. Bull.*, 1975, *82*, 932–946.

**Zurcher, L. A.** Particularism and organizational position: a cross-cultural analysis. *J. appl. Psychol.*, 1968, *52*, 139–144.

**Zurcher, L. A., Meadow, A., & Zurcher, S. L.** Value orientation, role conflict, and alienation from work: a cross-cultural study. *Amer. sociol. Rev.*, 1965, *30*, 539–548.

**Zweig, J. P.** The relationships among performance, partisanship in labor–management issues, and leadership style of first line supervisors. *Dissertation Abstr.*, 1966, *26*, 4801.

# AUTHOR INDEX

# SUBJECT INDEX